Property of
David C. Piatt

BEACON DICTIONARY OF THEOLOGY

BEACON DICTIONARY OF THEOLOGY

RICHARD S. TAYLOR, Editor

Associate Editors

J. Kenneth Grider & Willard H. Taylor

BEACON HILL PRESS OF KANSAS CITY
KANSAS CITY, MISSOURI

ISBN: 0-8341-0811-9

Printed in the
United States of America

Preface

One sign of an aroused interest in family or personal health is the presence in the home of a layman's medical dictionary or encyclopedia. In most homes such a volume is referred to frequently, with great interest and concern.

It is equally true that a person or household awakened intellectually and spiritually will desire to have handy a means of becoming informed concerning their faith, both in its major outlines and in its more intricate details. The desire to possess a dictionary of theology is therefore as natural and logical as the desire to have a medical guide. But the importance of such a reference work is as much greater than the medical guide as spiritual health is greater than physical health.

The ground covered in the following 954 articles is as comprehensive as would be covered by a standard systematic theology. The difference is that the subject matter is divided up into small units and arranged alphabetically, for easy reference. One can thus pursue one's particular interest of the moment, or seek out the answer to some puzzling question, without having to wade through scores of pages.

By following the cross-references at the end of the article, the student can pursue his special area of interest as far as he desires. In the process his theological horizons will be pushed farther and farther back, and he will discover the excitement of the intellectual chase—a chase of infinitely greater consequence and more lasting benefit than could ever accrue from pursuing the fox or the possum. Many an enthusiastic hunter thinks nothing of scrambling through brush all night, spurred on by the baying of his possum hounds. It is to be hoped that many a budding intellectual, or just plain honest Christian with an aroused thirst for knowledge, will follow his own inner inquiring "hounds," poring through this dictionary. At least if it is in the house, or on the student's or pastor's desk, as a readily available tool, it may even come second to the Bible itself for frequency of handling.

This volume has been designed for the busy pastor, evangelist, missionary, student, teacher, doctor, and lawyer, as well as for the alert homemaker and farmer or shopkeeper who desires to acquire a better understanding of God and His redemption. The use of foreign words has been restrained, and those used are transliterated into English spelling. Some abbreviation has been used, but the key is found in the front of the book. Under the heading "For Further Reading," reference items have usually been reduced to last name of author and a minimal title.

It must be admitted that the desired simplicity and clarity will not be found in all the articles equally. But if the reader encounters more verbal fog than he can comfortably handle, he should glance at the cross-references and proceed to a related article. Perhaps by following through in this way the fog will be dispelled. In the process he will gradually find himself becoming more and more at home in these strange "lands," and in time will be a truly knowledgeable Christian. And really, he owes this much to his Lord.

Readers with some degree of expertise in these matters will note that this dictionary represents a very broad definition of *theology.* As a consequence, many topics are discussed which might be expected to be found in other kinds of dictionaries. The gamut covers such areas as philosophy, psychology, history, practics, and devotion. A sincere attempt has been made to relate every topic to the basic concerns of theology and the Bible.

This dictionary is unabashedly evangelical and just as unabashedly Wesleyan. Some immensely valuable help has been given by scholars who are not themselves identified with the Wesleyan-Arminian school of interpretation. We are grateful to them. This is possible because among evangelicals the basic points of agreement are very wide indeed. However, it is the conviction of the editors and publishers that a scholarly dictionary frankly committed to a Wesleyan understanding of salvation has been long overdue.

These 954 articles do not reflect total unanimity of opinion, either among the contributors themselves or between them and the editors. There are areas of tolerable variation in viewpoint. But every effort has been sought to avoid a muffled or uncertain trumpet in respect to sin, salvation, holiness, and eternal destiny. Certainly it does not need to be stated that equal care has been taken to preserve utmost fidelity to the historic doctrines of the faith respecting the Trinity, Christ Jesus our Lord, the authority of the Bible, the atoning death of Christ, and His bodily resurrection.

May God whet our intellectual and spiritual appetites, quicken our understanding, and mercifully bestow His blessing upon the efforts of the 157 contributors of this volume, to the edification of all and the misdirection of none.

RICHARD S. TAYLOR, *Editor*

Associate Editors

J. KENNETH GRIDER
WILLARD H. TAYLOR*

---

*The untimely death of Willard H. Taylor, just as this volume was in the final stages of completion, was a great loss to the project. He assisted as consulting editor only about 31 months, during which time his counsel was of inestimable value. He lived long enough to write some of the major articles, but was to have written more—articles for which he had made partial preparation but in the providence of God had to leave to others. In many important and subtle ways the impress of his great mind, wide learning, mature experience, and intensely devoted heart is on this volume. It is stronger because he was on the team.

R. S. T.

List of Contributors

Abraham, William J., M.Div., D.Phil.
Associate Professor of Theology, Seattle Pacific University

Adams, J. Wesley, M.Div., M.A., Ph.D.
Associate Professor of New Testament Studies, Mid-America Nazarene College

Agnew, Milton S., B.D.
Salvation Army Officer (Col.); Retired

Aikens, Alden, M.Div., Th.M., Ph.D. cand.
Pastor, Church of the Nazarene

Airhart, Arnold E., B.D., D.D.
Professor of Theology, Nazarene Bible College

Amaya, Ismael E., Ph.D.
Professor of Religion, Point Loma College

Arnett, William M., Ph.D.
Frank Paul Morris Professor of Christian Doctrine, Asbury Theological Seminary

Baldeo, Isaac, M.R.E., M.Div., D.Min.
Pastor/Counselor

Bassett, Paul M., B.D., Ph.D.
Professor of the History of Christianity, Nazarene Theological Seminary

Beals, Ivan A., M.A., D.Min.
Office Editor, *Herald of Holiness*

Benner, Forest T., B.D., Th.M., Ph.D.
Professor of Religion, Mount Vernon Nazarene College

Berg, Daniel N., B.D., Ph.D.
Associate Professor of Theology and Ministry, Seattle Pacific University

Blaney, Harvey J. S., M.Div., S.T.M., Th.D.
Professor Emeritus of Religion, Eastern Nazarene College

Bloesch, Donald G., B.D., Ph.D.
Professor of Theology, University of Dubuque Theological Seminary

Bonner, Norman N., Ed.D.
Professor of Missions/Christian Education, Bartlesville Wesleyan College

Boring, Glenn R., M.Div.
Pastor, Evangelical Church of North America

Bouck, Louis A., M.A.
Radio Bible Teacher, Kentucky Mountain Holiness Association

Box, Maureen H., M.R.E.
Director of Christian Education

Branson, Robert D., Ph.D.
Associate Professor of Biblical Studies, Warner Southern College

Brower, Kent, M.A., Ph.D.
Associate Professor of Religion, Canadian Nazarene College

Brown, Allan P., Ph.D.
Chairman, Division of Bible, Hobe Sound Bible College

Brunk, George R., III, B.D., Th.D.
Dean and Associate Professor of New Testament, Eastern Mennonite Seminary

Butler, D. Martin, M.A., M.Div., D.Min.
Administrative Assistant to the President, Nazarene Theological Seminary

Caldwell, Wayne E., B.D., Th.M., Th.D.
Professor of Theology and English New Testament, Marion College

Carter, Charles W., M.A., Th.M., D.D.
Scholar-in-Residence, Marion College

Carver, Frank G., Ph.D.
Professor of Biblical Theology and Greek, Chairman of the Department of Philosophy and Religion, Point Loma College

Cauthron, Hal A., M.A., M.Div., Ph.D.
Associate Professor of New Testament, Trevecca Nazarene College

Chambers, Leon, B.D., M.A., Ed.D., D.D.
Visiting Lecturer in Pastoral Ministries, Wesley Biblical Seminary

Childers, Charles L., M.A., M.Div., Ph.D.
Professor Emeritus, Trevecca Nazarene College

Clapp, Philip S., M.A., Ph.D.
Professor of New Testament Greek, Retired, Western Evangelical Seminary

Cockerill, Gareth Lee, Th.D.
Assistant Professor, Wesley Biblical Seminary

Coker, William B., Ph.D.
Dean of Academic Affairs, Asbury College

Cowles, C. S., M.Div., S.T.D.
Professor of Biblical Literature, Northwest Nazarene College

Cox, Leo G., Ph.D.
Professor of Religion, Bartlesville Wesleyan College

Cubie, David L., B.D., Ph.D.
Chairman of the Division of Religion and Philosophy, Mount Vernon Nazarene College

Dayton, Wilber T., M.A., Th.D.
Professor of Biblical Literature and Historical Theology, Wesley Biblical Seminary

Deasley, Alex R. G., M.A., Ph.D.
Associate Professor of New Testament, Nazarene Theological Seminary

DeLong, Russell V., Ph.D.
Author, Evangelist, Educator; Deceased

Demaray, Donald E., B.D., Ph.D., Litt.D.
Granger E. and Anna A. Fisher Professor of Preaching, Asbury Theological Seminary

Dieter, Melvin Easterday, Ph.D.
Professor of Church History and Historical Theology, Asbury Theological Seminary

Duewel, Wesley L., M.Ed., Ed.D.
President, OMS International

Dunning, H. Ray, M.A., Ph.D.
Chairman, Department of Religion and Philosophy; Professor of Theology, Trevecca Nazarene College

Dunnington, Don W., D.Min.
Associate Professor of Practical Theology, Trevecca Nazarene College

Earle, Ralph, M.A., Th.D.
Emeritus Professor of New Testament, Nazarene Theological Seminary

Failing, George E., M.A., Litt.D.
General Editor, *The Wesleyan Methodist*

Fairbanks, LeBron, B.D., M.A., M.Th., D.Min.
Academic Dean, European Nazarene Bible College

Findlay, Thomas, B.D.
Lecturer in Biblical Studies, European Nazarene Bible College

Fine, Larry, M.A., M.Div., D.Min.
Professor of Religion, Mid-America Nazarene College

Finley, Harvey E., B.D., Ph.D.
Professor of Old Testament, Nazarene Theological Seminary

Ford, Jack, Ph.D.
Former President, British Isles Nazarene College; Deceased

French, G. R., M.Div.
Pastor, Chairman of Ministerial Division, Hobe Sound Bible College

Fuhrman, Eldon R., B.D., M.A., Ph.D.
President, Wesley Biblical Seminary

Galloway, Chester O., B.D., M.R.E., M.Ed., Ph.D.
Dean of Faculty and Professor of Christian Education, Nazarene Theological Seminary

Goldsmith, Myron D., B.D., Ph.D.
Professor of Religion, George Fox College

Gray, C. Paul, Ph.D.
Professor of Old Testament and Church History, Bethany Nazarene College

Greathouse, William M., M.A., D.D.
General Superintendent, Church of the Nazarene

Grider, J. Kenneth, B.D., M.Div., M.A., Ph.D.
Professor of Theology, Nazarene Theological Seminary

Gunter, W. Stephen, Drs. Theol.
Chairman, Division of Philosophy and Religion, Bethany Nazarene College

Haines, Lee M., Th.M., D.Min.
General Secretary of Education and the Ministry, The Wesleyan Church

Hall, Bert H., Th.D., D.D.
Professor of Philosophy and Religion, Azusa Pacific University

Hamilton, James E., M.Div., Ph.D.
Professor of Philosophy, Asbury College

Haney, M. Estes, M.A., D.D.
Administrative Assistant, Graduate Department of Education, Point Loma College, Pasadena Campus

Hardesty, Nancy A., Ph.D.
Writer and Church Historian, Atlanta

Harper, A. F., M.A., Ph.D., D.D.
Emeritus Professor, Nazarene Theological Seminary

Harris, Maxie, III, M.Div.
Instructor in Theology and Science, European Nazarene Bible College

Harris, Merne A., Ph.D.
President, Vennard College

Hendrick, Kenneth E., M.Div., Th.M., D.Min.
Associate Professor of Biblical Literature, Olivet Nazarene College

Hightower, Neil E., B.D., D.D.
President, Canadian Nazarene College

Howard, Richard E., M.Th., D.D.
Evangelist

Hynson, Leon O., M.Div., Th.M., Ph.D.
President and Professor of Historical Theology, Evangelical School of Theology

Jennings, Otho, M.A., M.Div., Ed.D., LL.D.
Emeritus Professor of Sociology, Olivet Nazarene College

Joy, Donald M., Ph.D.
Professor of Human Development and Christian Education, Asbury Theological Seminary

Kauffman, Alvin Harold, Ph.D.
Professor of Philosophy and Chairman of the Division of Philosophy and Religion, Eastern Nazarene College

Keefer, Luke L., Jr., Ph.D.
Assistant Professor of Bible and Religion, Messiah College

Killen, R. Allan, B.D., Th.M., D.Th.
Emeritus Professor of Contemporary Theology, Reformed Theological Seminary

Kinlaw, Dennis F., Ph.D.
Professor of Biblical Theology, Asbury Theological Seminary

Knight, John A., B.D., M.A., Ph.D.
President, Bethany Nazarene College

Knox, Lloyd H., D.D.
Retired General Publisher, Free Methodist Church of N.A.

Koteskey, Ronald L., Ph.D.
Professor of Psychology, Asbury College

Kuhn, Harold B., S.T.M., Ph.D., D.D.
Professor of Philosophy of Religion, Asbury Theological Seminary

Ladd, George Eldon, Th.B., B.D., Ph.D.
Professor Emeritus of New Testament Theology and Exegesis, Fuller Theological Seminary

Lawhead, Alvin S., Ph.D.
Associate Professor of Old Testament, Nazarene Theological Seminary

Layman, Fred D., B.D., Th.M., Ph.D.
Butler-Valade Professor of Biblical Theology, Asbury Theological Seminary

Lindsey, Leroy E., B.D., Th.M.
Academic Dean and Professor of Pastoral Studies, Vennard College; Retired

Livingston, George Herbert, Ph.D.
Professor of Old Testament and Chairman of the Division of Biblical Studies, Asbury Theological Seminary

Lovell, O. D., B.D., M.A., M.Ed.
Professor, Circleville Bible College

Lown, John S., M.A., Ph.D.
Professor of Philosophy and Religion, Point Loma College

Luik, John C., D.Phil.
Professor of Philosophy and Religion, Canadian Nazarene College and University of Manitoba

Lyons, George, M.Div., Ph.D.
Assistant Professor of Biblical Literature, Olivet Nazarene College

McCant, Jerry W., M.Div., Ph.D.
Associate Professor of Religion, Point Loma College

McCown, Wayne G., B.D., M.A., Th.M., Th.D.
Dean and Professor of Biblical Studies, Western Evangelical Seminary

McCumber, W. E., M.A., D.D.
Editor, *Herald of Holiness*

McGonigle, Herbert, B.D., M.A.
Lecturer in Old Testament and Church History, British Isles Nazarene College

Mattke, Robert A., B.D., M.A.
Professor of Bible and Theology, Houghton College

Mavis, W. Curry, M.A., M.Th., Ph.D., D.D.
Professor Emeritus, Asbury Theological Seminary

Mayfield, Joseph H., M.A., D.D.
Faculty Emeritus, Northwest Nazarene College

Merritt, John G., M.Div., M.A.T.S., A.M.
Instructor, The Salvation Army School for Officers' Training

Metz, Donald S., B.D., M.A., D.R.E., Ph.D.
Executive Vice-President and Academic Dean, Mid-America Nazarene College

Mitchell, T. Crichton, D.D.
Professor of Church History, Preaching, and Wesley Studies, Nazarene Bible College

Mulholland, M. Robert, Jr., Th.D.
Assistant Professor of New Testament Interpretation, Asbury Theological Seminary

Nielson, John B., B.D., M.A.
Editorial Director of Adult Ministries, Church of the Nazarene

Noble, T. A., B.D., M.A.
Dean, British Isles Nazarene College

Ockenga, Harold J., Ph.D., D.D., LL.D., Litt.D.
President Emeritus, Gordon-Conwell Theological Seminary

Oke, Norman R., B.D., D.D.
Professor, Nazarene Bible College; Retired

Orjala, Paul R., B.D., M.A., Ph.D.
Professor of Missions, Nazarene Theological Seminary

Parker, J. Fred, B.D., Th.M., Litt.D.
Book Editor, Nazarene Publishing House; Retired

Parrott, Leslie, M.A., Ph.D.
President, Olivet Nazarene College

Peisker, Armor D., M.A.
Executive Editor of Curriculum, Wesleyan Church; Retired

Perkins, Floyd J., B.D., M.A., Ph.D.
Professor, Nazarene Bible College

Peterman, Donald R., M.A., D.Min.
Pastor, Church of the Nazarene

Porter, James L., M.Se., M.Div., Ph.D.
Professor of Christian Education, Wesley Biblical Seminary

Price, Ross E., Ph.D., D.D.
Former Dean of Graduate Studies in Religion and Professor, Pasadena College; Retired

Prince, Herbert L., M.Div., M.A., Ph.D. cand.
Associate Professor of Philosophy and Theology, Point Loma College

Purkiser, W. T., M.A., Ph.D.
Professor Emeritus of Biblical Theology, Point Loma College; Former Editor of *Herald of Holiness*

Rae, Hugh, M.A.
Principal, British Isles Nazarene College

Raser, Harold E., M.A., M.Div.
Assistant Professor of the History of Christianity, Nazarene Theological Seminary

Reams, Max W., Ph.D.
Professor of Geology and Chairman of Division of Natural Science, Olivet Nazarene College

Reed, Gerard, Ph.D.
Professor of History and Philosophy, Mid-America Nazarene College

Reed, Oscar F., M.Th., Ph.D.
Professor of Preaching, Nazarene Theological Seminary

Ridgway, James M., D.D.A., M.A., M.Div., Ph.D.
Principal, Kingsley College, Australia

Riggle, Mary Lou, M.S., M.Div.
Academic Dean and Professor of Theology, Nazarene Theological Institute, Guatemala

Riley, John E., M.A., D.D.
President Emeritus, Northwest Nazarene College

Roberts, Arthur O., B.D., Ph.D.
Professor of Philosophy and Religion, George Fox College

Robertson, James E., Ed.M., A.M., Ph.D.
Retired

Rose, Delbert R., M.A., Ph.D.
Dean-Registrar and Professor of English Bible, Wesley Biblical Seminary

Rothwell, Mel-Thomas, A.M., Ph.D.
Professor Emeritus of Philosophy, Bethany Nazarene College; Deceased

Sack, Nobel V., S.T.B., Th.D.
Chairman, Department of Christian History and Thought, Western Evangelical Seminary

Sanner, A. Elwood, M.A., D.D.
Chairman, Division of Philosophy and Religion, Northwest Nazarene College

Sawyer, Robert L., Sr., B.D., Th.M., Th.D.
Professor of Biblical Languages and Literature; Chairman, Division of Religion and Philosophy, Mid-America Nazarene College

Sayes, J. Ottis, B.D., D.R.E.
Chairman, Division of Religion and Philosophy, Olivet Nazarene College

Schrag, Martin H., Th.M., Ph.D.
Professor of History of Christianity, Messiah College

Smith, Charles Wilson, M.Div.
Pastor, Church of the Nazarene

Smith, Timothy L., M.A., Ph.D., Litt.D.
Professor of Education and History, The Johns Hopkins University

Staples, Rob L., M.A., Th.D.
Professor of Theology, Nazarene Theological Seminary

Strait, C. Neil, B.D.
District Superintendent, Church of the Nazarene

Strickler, Dwight J., M.S., D.Sc.
Professor of Biological Science, Emeritus, Olivet Nazarene College

Taylor, Mendell L., Ph.D.
Professor Emeritus of Church History, Nazarene Theological Seminary

Taylor, Richard S., M.A., Th.D.
Professor Emeritus of Theology and Missions, Nazarene Theological Seminary

Taylor, Willard H., M.A., Ph.D.
Dean, Professor of New Testament Theology, Nazarene Theological Seminary; Deceased

Thompson, R. Duane, M.A., Ph.D.
Chairman, Division of Religion and Philosophy; Chairman, Division of Graduate Studies; Professor of Philosophy, Marion College

Thompson, W. Ralph, M.A., Th.D.
Professor Emeritus, Spring Arbor College

Truesdale, Albert L., Jr., Ph.D.
Assistant Professor of Philosophy of Religion and Christian Ethics, Nazarene Theological Seminary

Turner, George Allen, S.T.M., Ph.D., Litt.D.
Professor of Biblical Literature, Emeritus, Asbury Theological Seminary

Varughese, Alexander, M.A., M.Div., M.Phil., Ph.D. cand.
Assistant Professor in Religion, Eastern Nazarene College

Wall, Robert W., Th.M., Th.D.
Associate Professor of Biblical Studies and Ethics, Seattle Pacific University

Weigelt, Morris, A., B.D., Th.M., Ph.D.
Professor of New Testament, Nazarene Theological Seminary

Wetmore, Gordon, B.D.
Pastor, Church of the Nazarene

Wilcox, Leslie D., M.A., D.D.
Professor of Greek and Theology, God's Bible School; Retired

Wilson, Ronald E., M.Div., D.Min.
Pastoral Ministries, Vennard College

Winget, Wilfred L., B.D., Ph.D.
Professor of Philosophy and Religion, Spring Arbor College; Deceased

Wood, Laurence W., Ph.D.
Associate Professor of Systematic Theology, Asbury Theological Seminary

Young, Fred E., B.D., Ph.D.
Dean and Professor of Old Testament, Central Baptist Seminary

Young, Samuel, M.A., D.D.
General Superintendent Emeritus, Church of the Nazarene

Abbreviations

ARNDT, GINGRICH—W. F. Arndt and F. W. Gingrich, *A Greek-English Lexicon of the New Testament*

ASV—*American Standard Version of the Bible*

BAKER'S DCE—Carl F. H. Henry, ed., *Baker's Dictionary of Christian Ethics*

BAKER'S DT—Everett F. Harrison, ed., *Baker's Dictionary of Theology*

BBC—Albert F. Harper, ed., *Beacon Bible Commentary*

BBE—*Beacon Bible Expositions*

CC—Adam Clarke, *Clarke's Commentary*

DCT—Alan Richardson, ed., *A Dictionary of Christian Theology*

EBC—*Expositor's Bible Commentary*

EGT—*The Expositor's Greek Testament*

ER—Vergilius Ferm, ed., *An Encyclopedia of Religion*

ERE—Hastings' *Encyclopedia of Religion and Ethics*

GMS—Purkiser, Taylor, and Taylor, *God, Man, and Salvation*

HBD—*Harper's Bible Dictionary*

HDB—Hastings' *Dictionary of the Bible*

HDCG—Hastings' *Dictionary of Christ and the Gospels*

HDNT—Hastings' *Dictionary of the New Testament*

IDB—George Buttrick, ed., *Interpreter's Dictionary of the Bible*

ISBE—James Orr, ed., *International Standard Bible Encyclopedia*

KITTELL—G. Kittel, ed., *Theological Dictionary of the New Testament*

KJV—*King James Version of the Bible*

MOFFATT—*The Bible: A New Translation*, by James A. R. Moffatt

NASB—*New American Standard Bible*

NBD—*The New Bible Dictionary*

NBV—*Modern Language Bible, New Berkeley Version in Modern English*

NEB—*New English Bible*

NIDB—*The New International Dictionary of the Bible*

NIDCC—*New International Dictionary of the Christian Church*

NIDNTT—T. Colin Brown, ed., *The New International Dictionary of New Testament Theology*

NIV—*The Holy Bible, New International Version*

NKJB—*New King James Bible*

ODCC—*Oxford Dictionary of the Christian Church*

PHILLIPS—*New Testament in Modern English*

RSV—*Revised Standard Version of the Bible*

THAYER—Joseph Henry Thayer, *Greek-English Lexicon of the New Testament*

TLB—*The Living Bible*

TNTC—*Tyndale New Testament Commentaries*

TWNT—*Theological Wordbook of the New Testament*

VINE, ED—W. E. Vine, *Expository Dictionary of New Testament Words*

WBC—Charles W. Carter, ed., *Wesleyan Bible Commentary*

WESLEY, NOTES—*Explanatory Notes upon the New Testament*

WESLEY, WORKS—*The Works of John Wesley*, 14 vols.

WEYMOUTH—*Weymouth's New Testament in Modern English*

WILEY, CT—H. Orton Wiley, *Christian Theology*, 3 vols.

WILLIAMS' NTLP—Charles B. Williams, *New Testament in the Language of the People*

WMNT—Ralph Earle, *Word Meanings in the New Testament*

WTJ—*Wesleyan Theological Journal*

ZPBD—Merrill C. Tenney, ed., *Zondervan Pictorial Bible Dictionary*

ZPEB—Merrill C. Tenney, ed., *Zondervan Pictorial Encyclopedia of the Bible*

Subject List

Abba (See Lord's Prayer)
Abide, Abiding
Ability
Abomination of Desolation
Abortion
Abraham
Absolute (See Attributes, Divine)
Absolution
Absolutism
Abstinence (See Fasting)
Acceptance
Accountability
Acquired Depravity
Adam
Adamic Sin (See Original Sin)
Adoption
Adoptionism
Adoration (See Worship)
Adultery
Adventism
Adversary (See Satan)
Advocate
Aesthetics
Affections
Agapē
Age, Ages
Agnosticism
Alexandrian School
Allegorical Interpretation
Allegory
Alpha and Omega
Altar
Ambassador
Amillennialism
Anabaptists (See Rebaptism)
Analogy
Analyticism (See Positivism)
Anathema
Angel
Anger
Anglo-Catholicism
Anglo-Israelism
Annihilationism
Anointing
Anthropology (See Man)
Anthropomorphism
Antichrist (See Man of Sin)
Antilegomena
Antinomianism
Antioch, School of
Antitype
Anxiety
Apocalyptic, Apocalypse
Apocrypha
Apollinarianism
Apologetics
Apostasy
Apostle
Apostles' Creed
Apostolic Constitutions and Canons
Apostolic Decrees
Apostolic Fathers
Apostolic Succession
Arianism
Ark of the Covenant
Armageddon
Arminianism
Articles of Faith (See Dogma)
Ascension, The
Asceticism
Assumption of Mary (See Mother of God)
Assurance (See Witness of the Spirit)
Astrology
Athanasian Creed
Atheism
Atonement
Atonement, Theories of (See Governmental Theory, Moral Influence Theory, Mystical Theory, Penal Satisfaction Theory)
Attributes, Divine
Augsburg Confession
Augustinianism
Authentic Existence
Authenticity
Authority
Avarice (See Covetousness, Seven Deadly Sins)
Awakening
Awe (See Reverence)
Axiology

Baalism
Babylon
Backsliding
Baptism
Baptism for the Dead
Baptism with the Holy Spirit
Baptismal Regeneration
Baptists
Beatitudes
Beauty
Beelzebub (See Satan)
Beginning
Begotten (See Only Begotten)
Being
Belief
Believer (See Christian)
Benediction
Benevolence
Betrayal
Bible
Bible, Inspiration of (See Inspiration of the Bible)
Bible: The Two Testaments
Biblical Authority
Biblical Criticism, Lower (See Textual Criticism)
Biblical Inerrancy
Biblical Realism
Biblical Theology
Biblicism
Binding and Loosing
Birth of Christ (See Virgin Birth)
Birth of the Spirit (See New Birth)
Bishop
Bitterness (See Hardness of Heart)
Blame, Blameless
Blasphemy
Bless, Blessed, Blessing
Blood
Body
Body Life
Body of Christ
Boldness
Bondage
Breaking of Bread (See Love Feast)
Bride, Bridegroom
British-Israelism (See Anglo-Israelism)
Brotherhood
Brotherly Love
Buddhism
Burnt Offering

Cabala (See Kabbala)
Call, Called, Calling
Calvinism
Canon
Canon Law
Canonization
Canons of Dort
Capital Punishment
Cardinal Virtues (See Seven Cardinal Virtues)
Carnal Christians
Carnal Mind
Carnality and Humanity
Casuistry
Catastrophism
Catechism
Catholic
Catholicism

Catholicism, Greek
(See Eastern Orthodoxy)
Catholicism, Roman
Cause and Effect
Celibacy
Ceremonial Purification
(See Purification, Ceremonial)
Chain of Command
Chance
Character
Charismata (See Gifts)
Charity (See Love)
Chasten, Chastise
Chastity
Checks to Antinomianism
Cherub, Cherubim (See Angel)
Child, Children
Chiliasm (See Millennium)
Christ
Christ in You
Christian
Christian Education
Christian Ethics
Christian Holiness
(See Holiness)
Christian Humanism
Christian Perfection
Christian Socialism
Christian Warfare
(See Spiritual Warfare)
Christian Year
Christianity
Christlikeness
Christocentrism
Christology
Chronos
Church
Church Councils
Church Government
Church Growth
Church Music
Church Rules (See Canon Law)
Circumcision
Citizenship
City
Civil Disobedience
Civil Religion
Civil Rights
Clean, Unclean
Cleansing
Clergy
Collection (See Tithe)
Comfort
Comforter, The
Command, Commandment
Commission, Great
(See Great Commission)
Common, Community
Common Grace
Communicate, Communication
Communion, Holy
(See Holy Communion)
Communism (See Marxism)
Comparative Religion
Compassion
Complementarianism
Conceptualism
Conciliarism
Concupiscence
Condemn, Condemnation
(See Judge, Judgment)
Conditional Immortality
Confession, Confessional
Confession of Faith
Confession of Sins
Confidence (See Self-Image)
Confirmation
Conformity
Congregationalism
(See Church Government)
Conscience
Consecrate, Consecration
Consolation (See Comfort)
Consubstantiation
Contentment
Contingent
Contrition (See Penitence)
Conversion
Convict, Conviction
Corban
Cornerstone
Corruption (See Original Sin)
Cosmology
Councils (See Church Councils)
Counseling
(See Pastoral Counseling,
Rogerian Counseling)
Counteraction
Courage
(See Seven Cardinal Virtues)
Covenant (See New Covenant)
Covenant Theology
Covenanters
Covetousness
Creation
Creationism
Credentials of Scripture
Credulity (See Superstition)
Creed, Creeds
Crisis
Crisis Theology
(See Neoorthodoxy)
Criticism, NT
Criticism, OT
Cross
Cross-bearing
Crown
Crucifixion
Cults
Culture
Culture, Personal
Cup
Curse
Custom, Customs

Darkness
Darwinism
Davidic Promises
(See Promises, Davidic)
Day of Atonement
Day of the Lord
Days of Creation
Deacon
Dead Sea Scrolls
Death
Death of Christ
Death of God Doctrine
Death to Self
Decalogue
Decision
Decrees (See Divine Decrees)
Deism
Deity of Christ (See Christ)
Deliverer (See Redeemer)
Deluge (See Flood)
Demiurge
Demons, Demon Possession
Demythologization
Denomination
Deontology (See Duty)
Depotentiation Theories
(See Kenosis)
Depravity (See Total Depravity)
Deprivation
Descent into Hell
Desire
Despair
Destiny, Eternal
Determinism
Development, Theories of
Devil (See Satan)
Devote, Devotion
Dialectic
Diaspora (See Dispersion)
Dichotomy
Dictation Theory
(See Inspiration of the Bible)
Didache
Discernment

Labor
Laity
Lamb, Sacrificial
Lamb of God
Language, Theological
(See Theological Language)
Lasciviousness
Last Days, The
Latitudinarianism
Law
Law and Grace
Law of Liberty
Lay Baptism
Laying On of Hands
Leaven
Legal Sin, Ethical Sin
Legalism
Leisure
Lent
Liability to Sin
Liberalism
Liberation Theology
Liberty (See Freedom)
License
Lie, Liars
Life
Life-style
Light
Likeness (See Divine Image)
Limbo
Limited Atonement
(See Atonement)
Liturgy, Liturgics
Logos
Long-suffering
Lord
Lord's Day
Lord's Prayer
Lord's Supper
(See Holy Communion)
Lost, Lost Soul
Love
Love and Law
Love Feast
Lust (See Desire)
Lutheranism

Macedonianism
Magic (See Sorcery)
Majesty
Mammon
Man
Man of Sin
Manhood of Christ
(See Humanity of Christ)
Manichaeism
Marcionism
Mariolatry
Marriage
Martyr, Martyrdom
Marxism
Mass
Materialism
Maturity
Means of Grace
Mediation, Mediator
Meditation
Meekness
Melchizedek
Memorial Theory
(See Holy Communion)
Mercy
Mercy Seat
Merit (See Work, Works)
Messiah
Metaphysics
Metempsychosis
(See Reincarnation)
Methodism
Might (See Power)
Millennium
Mind
Mind of Christ
Minister, Ministry
Miracle
Mission, Missions, Missiology
Mission of Christ
Mistakes
Modalism (See Sabellianism)
Moderation (See Temperance)
Modern Realism
Modernism (See Liberalism)
Monarchianism
Monasticism
Monergism
Money
Monism
Monophysitism
Monotheism
Monothelitism
Montanism
Moral Attributes of God
Moral Influence Theory of the Atonement
Morality
Mortal, Mortality
Mortify, Mortification
Mosaic Law
Moses
Mother of God
Motif Research
Motives
Murder
Mystery, Mysteries
Mystical Theory of the Atonement
Mysticism
Myth

Nation
Natural Law
Natural Man, The
Natural Revelation
(See Revelation, Natural)
Natural Theology
Nature
Nazarene
Necromancy (See Sorcery)
Neighbor
Neoevangelicalism
Neoorthodoxy
Neo-Pentecostalism
Neoplatonism
Neo-Thomism
Nestorianism
New Being
New Birth
New Commandment
New Covenant
New Heavens and New Earth
New Hermeneutic
New Morality
New Testament (See Bible: The Two Testaments)
Nicene Creed
Nominalism
(See Realism and Nominalism)
Non-Christian Religions
Nonconformity
Nondirective Counseling
(See Rogerian Counseling)
Numinous, The
Nurture (See Discipling)

Obedience
Obedience of Christ
Objectivity
Oblation (See Offer, Offering)
Occult, Occultism
Offer, Offering
Offices, Ecclesiastical
Offices of Christ
(See Estates of Christ)
Old Man
Old Testament (See Bible: The Two Testaments)
Omnipotence
Omnipresence
Omniscience
(See Attributes, Divine)
Oneness (See Unity)

Only Begotten
Ontological Argument
Ontology
Ordain, Ordination
Ordinances
Ordination of Women
Original Righteousness (See Divine Image)
Original Sin
Orthodoxy
Overseer (See Bishop)

Pacifism
Paganism
Pain (See Suffer, Suffering)
Panentheism
Pantheism
Papacy (See Catholicism, Roman)
Papal Infallibility
Parables
Paraclete
Paradise
Paradox
Pardon (See Forgiveness)
Parents and Children
Parousia
Paschal Controversy
Passion of Christ (See Death of Christ)
Passover
Pastor
Pastoral Counseling
Pastoral Theology (See Practical Theology)
Patripassianism (See Monarchianism)
Peace
Pelagianism
Penal Satisfaction Theory of the Atonement
Penance
Penitence
Pentateuch
Pentecost
Pentecostalism
Perdition, Son of Perdition
Perfect, Perfection
Perfect Love
Perfectionism
Perish (See Lost, Lost Soul)
Permissive Will (See Providence)
Permissiveness
Perpetual Virginity
Persecution (See Tribulation)
Perseverance
Person, Personality
Personalism
Personality of God
Personality of the Holy Spirit
Pharisaism
Pharisees
Philanthropy (See Liberality)
Philia (See Brotherly Love)
Philosophy
Pietism
Pietism, English Evangelical
Piety
Pigeon (See Dove)
Pilgrim
Pity, Pitiful (See Compassion)
Platonism
Pleasure
Plenary
Pluralism
Polygamy
Polytheism
Pope (See Catholicism, Roman)
Positional Holiness
Positivism
Postmillennialism
Poverty
Power
Powers (See Principalities and Powers)
Practical Theology
Pragmatism
Praise
Prayer
Prayers for the Dead
Preaching
Predestination
Preeminence
Preexistence of Christ
Preexistence of Souls
Prejudice
Premillennialism
Presbyter (See Elder)
Presence, Divine
Presumption
Prevenient Grace
Pride
Priest, Priesthood
Priesthood of Believers
Primal History
Primitive Holiness (See Divine Image)
Principalities and Powers
Principles
Priority (See Values)
Priscillianism
Probabilism
Probation
Process Theology
Procession of the Spirit
Profane, Profanity
Progressive Revelation
Progressive Sanctification
Promise
Promises, Davidic
Property Rights
Prophet, Prophecy
Propitiation
Propositional Theology
Proselyte
Proselytism
Protestantism
Providence
Prudence
Pseudepigrapha
Pseudo-Isadorian Decretals (See False Decretals)
Psychoanalysis
Psychology
Psychology of Religion
Psychotherapy
Public Prayer
Punishment
Purgatory
Purification, Ceremonial
Purification from Sin (See Heart Purity)
Puritan, Puritanism
Purity and Maturity

Quietism

Rabbinic Theology
Racial Sin (See Original Sin)
Racism
Ransom
Rapture
Rationalism
Rationality
Real Presence
Realism
Realism and Nominalism
Realism in Theology
Reality Therapy
Realized Eschatology
Reason
Rebaptism
Receiving the Holy Spirit
Reconciliation
Redeemer, Redemption
Reformation (See Protestant Reformation)
Regeneration
Reincarnation
Rejoice (See Joy)

Suppression
Supralapsarianism (See Infralapsarianism)
Surrender
Swedenborgianism
Symbolic Eschatology (See Eschatology)
Symbolics (See Creed, Creeds)
Symbolism
Syncretism
Synergism
Systematic Theology

Tabernacle (See Temple)
Talmud
Targum
Teach, Teaching, Teacher
Teleological Eschatology (See Eschatology)
Teleology (See Theistic Proofs)
Temperance
Temple
Temptation
Temptation of Christ
Ten Commandments (See Decalogue)
Testimony, Witness
Textual Criticism
Thanksgiving (See Praise)
Theism
Theistic Evolution
Theistic Proofs
Theocracy
Theodicy (See Evil)
Theological Language
Theological Methodology (See Systematic Theology)
Theology
Theology, Natural (See Natural Theology)
Theology of Missions (See Mission, Missions, Missiology)
Theophany
Theosophy
Theothanatology (See Death of God Doctrine)
Thomism
Thought (See Reason)
Time
Tithe, The
Tolerance
Tongues, Gift of
Torah (See Mosaic Law)
Total Depravity
Tractarianism
Tradition
Traducianism
Transactional Analysis
Transcendence
Transcendental Meditation
Transfiguration
Transgression (See Sin)
Transignification
Transmigration of Souls (See Reincarnation)
Transubstantiation
Tribulation
Trichotomy
Trinity, The Holy
Tritheism (See Trinity)
Trust (See Faith)
Truth
Type, Typology

Ultimate Concern
Unbelief
Unblamable (See Blame, Blameless)
Unconditional Election (See Election)
Unction (See Anointing)
Understanding (See Wisdom)
Unification Church
Union with God (See Mysticism)
Unitarianism
Unity
Universalism
Universals
Unlimited Atonement (See Atonement)
Unpardonable Sin
Unrighteousness (See Iniquity)
Upright, Uprightness (See Right, Righteousness)

Values
Values Clarification
Veil
Vengeance (See Revenge)
Verbal Inspiration (See Inspiration of the Bible)
Vicarious
Vice
Victory, Victorious Living
Virgin Birth
Virtue
Vision
Vocation
Voluntarism (See Intellectualism)
Vows

Walk (See Life-style)
War
Warfare, Spiritual (See Spiritual Warfare)
Water
Wealth (See Money)
Wedding Garment
Wesleyan Synthesis
Wesleyanism
Whitsunday (See Christian Year)
Whole, Wholeness
Wholly Other
Wicked, Wickedness (See Sin)
Will (See Freedom)
Will of God (See Guide, Guidance; Providence)
Wine (See Temperance)
Wisdom
Witchcraft (See Sorcery)
Witness (See Testimony)
Witness of the Spirit
Woman
Women, Ordination of (See Ordination of Women)
Women's Liberation
Word of God
Work, Works
Work Ethic (See Labor)
World, Worldliness
World View (See Cosmology)
Worship
Wrath
Write, Writing, Written

Yahweh (See Jehovah)
Yoke

Zeal
Zealots
Zionism
Zoroastrianism

BEACON DICTIONARY OF THEOLOGY

A

ABBA. See LORD'S PRAYER.

ABIDE, ABIDING. To abide is to remain or to endure. God abides (Ps. 9:7; Dan. 6:26), in contrast to what is earthly and human (Isa. 40:6-8). Therefore, His *word* endures and prevails (1 Pet. 1:23-25), and His *purpose* stands undefeated (Isa. 14:27; Rom. 9:11).

The primary Greek word for abide is *menō.* It occurs 112 times in the NT, 66 in Johannine literature, 40 of these in his Gospel. John 15:1-17, where *menō* is found 11 times, is a key passage for understanding the concept.

The Christian life is essentially *union with Christ:* "Abide in me, and I in you" (v. 4). The *condition* for abiding is obedience: His "words" abide in the believer, who keeps His "commandments" and thus abides in His love (vv. 7-10; 1 John 2:17). The *consequence* of abiding is continued fruit bearing (v. 5), and this fruit is unselfish, sacrificial love (vv. 10-13). When we abide in Christ and His words abide in us, answered prayer is assured (v. 7).

Abiding in Christ is not automatic or unconditional, as His imperatives ("Abide in me . . . abide in my love") indicate. It calls for resolute decision. The *alternative* to abiding is separation and destruction (v. 6).

The believer is promised an abiding place *(monē)* in the Father's house (John 14:2) for eternity. Meanwhile, Father and Son have an abiding place in the believer's heart (14:23) through the abiding Holy Spirit (14:16-17). The Spirit abiding in us is the assurance that we abide in God (1 John 4:13).

Believers abide in *light* (1 John 2:10), *love* (4:16), *life* (3:14-15) and *truth* (2 John 9). Unbelievers, in sharp contrast, abide in *darkness* (John 12:46), in *death* (1 John 3:14), and under God's *wrath* (John 3:36).

Abiding salvation is grounded upon the abiding priesthood of Jesus Christ as Sacrifice and Intercessor (Heb. 7:23-25).

See ETERNAL SECURITY, PERSEVERANCE, OBEDIENCE.

For Further Reading: Kittel, 4:574-88; Westcott, *The Gospel According to St. John;* Morris, *The Gospel According to John.*

W. E. MCCUMBER

ABILITY. This term, as used in the Bible, has reference to the idea of strength or capacity to perform in material, mental, or moral realms (cf. Dan. 1:4; Matt. 25:15; 1 Pet. 4:11). Theologically, ability has reference to the question of the extent to which man can respond to divine revelation and to what degree he is responsible for the decisions he makes.

In the main, three answers have been given. First, some contend that unregenerate man's fallenness is so total as to make him incapable of any initiation or response whatsoever, except as God is pleased to impart a measure of power to him on a highly selective basis. Hence the explanation for some being saved and others lost reverts to the eternal decree.

A second answer, in marked contrast to the first, is to affirm native ability to such an extent that little or no damage occurred to anyone except Adam. Hence man retains his full power of self-determination and is capable of negotiating his own destiny with little more than instructional and inspirational help from outside sources.

A third answer is to affirm that notwithstanding the tragedy of the Fall and man's consequent moral impotence, there is given to all men as a gift of grace sufficient strength and illumination to make them fully dependent upon God's grace on the one hand and fully responsible for its use on the other. Thus it is of grace that man can respond to grace, for grace includes God's power acting *in* man as well as *for* him. Man's accountability is based upon the grace-given ability to respond as God would have him to (cf. Josh. 24:15; Phil. 2:12-13; Luke 13:1-5; Acts 5:31-32; Rev. 9:20; 16:9, 11). Such is the teaching of the Bible generally as well as in explicit statement.

See SIN, RESPONSIBILITY, SYNERGISM, MONERGISM, PREVENIENT GRACE.

For Further Reading: Wiley, *CT,* 2:356-57; Hills, *Fundamental Christian Theology,* 1:356-75, 2:144-51.

ELDON R. FUHRMAN

ABOMINATION OF DESOLATION. This phrase is first found in Dan. 11:31 and 12:11, the latter being translated in the RSV by "the abomination that makes desolate." This certainly refers to the abominable act of Antiochus Epiphanes, king of

Syria, who in 168 B.C. built a pagan altar on the site of the great altar in Jerusalem and offered heathen sacrifices on it.

In the NT the phrase occurs in Matt. 24:15 and Mark 13:14, where it seems to have a double meaning. Luke 21:20 renders it "when you see Jerusalem surrounded by armies." Therefore, the nearer meaning of the phrase is seen in the conquest of Jerusalem by Rome in A.D. 68-70. However, most scholars see a secondary meaning in the phrase, referring it to Antichrist, who will demand universal worship of man and thus profane the temple of God. 2 Thess. 2:4 describes him as one who "opposes and exalts himself against every so-called god or object of worship, so that he takes his seat in the temple of God, proclaiming himself to be God" (RSV). However these words may be interpreted, they mean that Antichrist tries to displace God in favor of himself.

See JERUSALEM, MAN OF SIN, TEMPLE, TRIBULATION.

For Further Reading: Biederwolf, *The Millennium Bible.* GEORGE ELDON LADD

ABORTION. This term is usually used to mean the intended termination of a woman's pregnancy. Most at issue in the question of the morality of abortion is when human life begins. If a fetus is not an individual human being when it is aborted, to force it to exit the womb before the time when it can live outside the mother is not as serious a matter as if it is already in fact a human being. The proabortion advocates tend to suggest that it is not a human being. Often they have said that it is simply "tissue" of the mother's body.

Numerous factors argue for the fetus' being a human individual from conception onwards. Nothing that is obvious happens between conception and birth that is an originatively new step-up in the fetus' life. It used to be thought by many that the time of the so-called quickening is the time when the soul joins the fetus, making it a human person. Yet it is not now believed by knowledgeable persons that the quickening is anything more than the first time the mother is aware of the fetus' movements. The chromosomes are present at conception, the later changes being only more or less quantitative, not qualitative. Not even at birth is there any special step-up qualitatively. At that time, respiration and nutrition occur by direct contact with the environment, but that is not a material qualitative change in the fetus. It is now known that the baby's circulation is an independent one during almost the whole of the pregnancy—and does not start when the umbilical cord is cut. One reason why the new specialty of fetology is being replaced by the still newer specialty of perinatology, which cares for its patients from conception to about a year after birth, is because the birth does not change the fetus very much—except to make it more accessible.

Scripture seems to teach that the unborn fetus is an individual person. Isaiah says, "The Lord called me from the womb" (49:1, RSV). Paul says that God "set me apart before I was born, and had called me through his grace" (Gal. 1:15, RSV). John the Baptist was "filled with the Holy Spirit, even from his mother's womb" (Luke 1:15, RSV). And a psalm writer called himself a "me," a self, when referring to the time of his conception, as he wrote that "in sin did my mother conceive me" (Ps. 51:5, RSV). Also, in Ps. 139:13 we read, "Thou didst knit me together in my mother's womb" (RSV). And in Jeremiah, Yahweh says to the prophet, "'Before I formed you in the womb I knew you, and before you were born I consecrated you; I appointed you a prophet to the nations'" (1:5, RSV).

Another significant factor in the question of abortion is that of whose rights are to take precedence. Since the right in question, to the fetus, is the right to life itself, its right to live should take precedence over the mother's various less-basic rights. Yet most Protestants concede the legitimacy of abortion in those rare instances when the pregnancy clearly jeopardizes the life of the mother. In contrast Roman Catholic law forbids abortion under any circumstances.

See FAMILY, CHRISTIAN ETHICS, MURDER.

For Further Reading: Lester, "The Abortion Dilemma," *Review and Expositor* (Spring, 1971); Hilgers and Moren, eds., *Abortion and Social Justice;* Bonhoeffer, *Ethics,* ed. E. Bethage. J. KENNETH GRIDER

ABRAHAM. Abraham, who lived about 2000 B.C., was the father of the people of Israel, which in time became a political order. Called by God to leave idolatrous Ur of the Chaldees and journey to a land which God promised him, he was to become the father of a people through which the knowledge of the true God would be preserved. In a covenantal relationship, God promised him in Genesis—chapters 12; 13; and 15—that through his seed all nations of the earth should be blessed. This promise was fulfilled when God sent, through Abraham's descendants, two outstanding blessings to humanity: God's personal Revelation, the Messiah; and God's written Revelation, the Bible. Abraham believed God's promise, and the Scripture declares his faith was accounted to him for righteousness (15:6).

This OT background becomes the foundation on which certain vital NT doctrines are built. The great truth at the heart of the gospel is justification by faith. In Romans 4, when Paul shows how a guilty world can be reconciled through the death of God's Son, Paul cites Abraham's faith, describes it, and concludes that one is justified by faith (5:1). This subject is treated again in Galatians 3, where the idea that the deeds of the law could justify is countered by the fact that the promise to Abraham antedated the law and represents God's true way of justifying men in all ages.

This doctrine of justification by faith came into collision with the belief that physical lineage from Abraham ensured acceptance with God. John the Baptist refuted this idea in Luke 3:8, and Jesus pointed out in John 8 that mere claim of Abraham as ancestor should be matched by deeds that would correspond to those of Abraham. Paul goes so far as to say in Rom. 9:6 that "they are not all Israel, which are of Israel."

Another theological truth founded on the life of Abraham is the obedience of faith. The doctrine of justification by faith has been misapplied to teach the antinomian doctrine that men may be justified while continuing in disobedience. The Bible refutes this error by declaring that true faith produces obedience. The passage in Jas. 2:21-23, which some have taken to contradict Paul in Romans 4, insists that the faith that Abraham had was more than nominal, but was practical in producing obedience to God. This obedience of faith is presented in Hebrews 11, where Abraham is listed among the heroes of faith, and again the stress is on the fact that obedience in Abraham's life demonstrated that he possessed an operative faith.

See JUSTIFICATION, OBEDIENCE, ANTINOMIANISM, IMPUTED RIGHTEOUSNESS.

For Further Reading: Greathouse, *BBE*, 6:69-86; Clark H. Pinnock, *Truth on Fire: The Message of Galatians*, 37-49; Thomas, *Genesis: A Devotional Commentary*, 217-22; Wiley, *The Epistle to the Hebrews*, 366-69.

LESLIE D. WILCOX

ABSOLUTE. See ATTRIBUTES (DIVINE).

ABSOLUTION. This is a term which denotes release from obligations, penalties, or consequences attached to motives and actions. It declares that censures are removed.

According to the Roman Catholic view, absolution means that sin and/or punishment due to sin is remitted. The power to do this absolving of sin is peculiarly vested in the Roman Catholic priesthood. It is not only declaratory; it is judicial and effective. It was received from Christ and continues to be valid in the history and life of the church as given to the priesthood. For the valid execution of this sacrament, contrition, confession, and satisfaction are required of the penitent before the act of absolution can be pronounced by the priest. It is understood that the confession of sin is to be humble, sincere, and entire.

Charismatic prayer for the healing of the whole person in connection with the act of absolution is a recent development. Six steps are usually followed in the execution of this sacrament. They are: (1) the priest receiving the penitent; (2) the reading of an appropriate passage of Scripture; (3) the penitent's confession of sin; (4) the penitent's prayer of confession of sin in his own words; (5) the prayer of absolution by the priest; (6) the expression of praise to God for sins forgiven.

Protestant theology rejects the concept that the minister has the power to absolve a person from the guilt and consequences of sin, either in a declaratory or a judicial way. It does not even teach the absolution concept in any formal sense. Instead, it teaches and even emphasizes something much less formal and priestly: forgiveness, simply. For this forgiveness, the penitent can go directly into the presence of Christ, repent of his sins, accept forgiveness by faith, and receive the assurance of that forgiveness. Authority for the information about forgiveness is in Scripture.

See CONFESSION OF SINS, CATHOLICISM (ROMAN), REPENTANCE, JUSTIFICATION.

For Further Reading: Dyer, *The American Catholic Catechism;* Hodge, *Systematic Theology,* Vol. 3.

NOBEL V. SACK

ABSOLUTISM. The term *absolute* or *objective* as employed in the phrase *ethical absolute* or *ethical objectivism* is much like the term *ethical relativism* or *ethical subjectivism,* in that it is frequently employed in contexts in which its meaning is unclear. Most theologians and philosophers, however, would accept that when one speaks of ethical absolutes or objective moral values, one is asserting that certain values such as (but not limited to) goodness, beauty, and right are true and commendable as defined irrespective of personal, cultural, or temporal considerations. This theory is to be contrasted to ethical relativism or ethical subjectivism, which holds that there are no values which are true and commendable apart from personal, cultural, or temporal considerations.

One of the most characteristic aspects of Christian ethical teaching has been its commitment to ethical absolutism. According to this theory, God has declared certain actions to be right and certain actions to be wrong, and that it is impossible for two people, one of whom claims that certain action is right and the other that the action is wrong, both to be correct.

Within this absolutist framework, Christian ethicists have taken at least two distinct positions on why certain values are absolute. One school has argued that the fact that God commands us to do X makes X a moral absolute. Another school has suggested that the intrinsic rightness of X is what leads God to enjoin it as a value. Both of these views can be objected to, the first on the grounds that God could command a certain action X which might be *prima facie* wrong, and the second on the grounds that God would appear to be determined by an independent moral order. This suggests that perhaps it should be maintained that X is good and X is commanded by God are one and the same thing.

As to the question of *which* values are absolutes, again one finds in the history of Christian ethical thinking at least two decidedly different theories, each of which has various formulations. On one hand there are the views known variously as antinomianism, nominalism, contextualism, or situationalism, which hold that there is but one ethical absolute, generally described as some form of Jesus' summary of the law of love. On the other hand there are the views of those who might be described as Christian deontologists or Christian formalists, who argue that there are ethical absolutes additional to and independent of the law of love.

See ETHICAL RELATIVISM, ETHICS, INTELLECTUALISM, AUTHORITY, DUTY.

For Further Reading: Lehmann, *Ethics in a Christian Context;* Ramsey, *Basic Christian Ethics;* Thomas, *Christian Ethics and Moral Philosophy.* JOHN C. LUIK

ABSTINENCE. See FASTING.

ACCEPTANCE. The family of English words which derive from "accept" translates a large slice of Hebrew and Greek words. Because of this plurality, it is difficult for the Bible student to settle upon one central meaning which in turn gathers all the different nuances and contexts together. There are, however, three critical senses to consider in understanding in a general way how Scripture defines "accept."

First, there is the *relational* sense. Whether one accepts by taking or by receiving something from someone else, the assumption or sense of such a transaction is that *two* parties are involved. What is exchanged between the two parties can be tangible (i.e., an acceptable prayer or behavior, monies, gifts) or intangible (i.e., an acceptable or accepting attitude); yet, the critical observation in every context is that a relationship is being established or recognized in such acceptance.

Second, in most cases, Scripture speaks of God-human relationships; it is acceptance which has a *covenantal* sense. In the OT, acceptance as covenantal is often scored cultically. An offering is said to be accepted *(rasa)* by God when it conforms to a certain pattern of worship as established in the covenant between Yahweh and Israel. So not to submit the covenant to an external form only, the OT is very careful to establish certain internal requirements as well (such as faith or obedience, or a repentant attitude). Thus, an acceptable offering was one which met both religious and spiritual conditions.

Yet, the OT story of the covenant between Yahweh and Israel (especially in the prophetic books) stresses the grace and faithfulness of God, who accepts Israel or who will accept Israel at some future point in spite of her disobedience. Such acceptance of Israel would presuppose a purpose to cleanse her from her disobedience (e.g., Ezek. 36:25-27).

God's loyal commitment for His people which assures an ongoing acceptance of them is fully interpreted by the incarnation of His Son, Jesus Christ. Thus, acceptance has, in the third place, a *messianic* sense. This is true especially in the NT, where the story of God's acceptance of the whole world is told by His Messiah who has come to earth in the "acceptable year of the Lord" (Luke 4:19; 2 Cor. 6:2). Further, anyone who accepts God's salvation as worked out through Jesus finds life (Eph. 1:6).

See NEW COVENANT, JUSTIFICATION, REPROBATION.

For Further Reading: Purkiser, ed., *Exploring Our Christian Faith,* 290-301; *GMS,* 336 ff, 390, 403-7, 421-32. ROBERT W. WALL

ACCOUNTABILITY. Accountability implies sufficient knowledge of duty and freedom of action to justify being called to account, or being held responsible. Implied also is a reasonable level of both native intelligence and current sanity. A moron or insane person cannot be held accountable for his actions. Small children have not reached the age of accountability, hence are not subject to judgment as are those who have.

The Bible universally presents man as a being who in his normal state is responsible to God, and who therefore will be held accountable by God for the way he lives, and punished or rewarded accordingly (Matt. 12:36-37; Luke 16:2 ff; 2 Cor. 5:10; 1 Pet. 4:5).

A further refinement is that accountability extends only to the measure of light and opportunity one has (Luke 12:47-48). However, one may properly be held accountable for knowledge which could and should have been acquired but was missed through carelessness or deliberate blindness (Matt. 11:16-24; 23:37-38). Obviously persons in Western nations, where Bibles are readily available and churches abound, bear a greater relative accountability for religious ignorance than do those completely without access either to the Bible or to the spoken gospel. The accountability of the latter will necessarily be limited to the light of conscience (Rom. 2:14-16).

Theologically, the pervasive assumption of human accountability found in the Scriptures implies a true freedom, or free moral agency. This, in turn, argues for a divine sovereignty which decrees this freedom and adjusts to it, and likewise for a sufficient degree of prevenient grace to counteract the paralyzing effects of the Fall. Otherwise, free moral agency would be a theoretical but not a practical reality. If God's relation to man is completely and monergistically deterministic, accountability is impossible in any truly moral or meaningful sense.

See FREEDOM, DETERMINISM, PREVENIENT GRACE, DIVINE SOVEREIGNTY, MONERGISM.

For Further Reading: Curtis, *The Christian Faith,* 117-41, 464-69; Purkiser, ed., *Exploring Our Christian Faith,* 212-22; *GMS,* 410-38. RICHARD S. TAYLOR

ACQUIRED DEPRAVITY. Acquired depravity refers to the pollution resulting from one's own choice and acts of sin (cf. Rom. 3:23). Defilement and guilt increase as long as one commits sin. Thus, an unconverted person at age 40 is more depraved than he was at 20, and more sinful at 20 than he was at 10.

R. T. Williams lists "spiritual death," "transgression, or sins committed," and "acquired pollution" as necessitating "regeneration (conversion, or the new birth)." "Thus regeneration has cleansing, not from the moral corruption inherited through the fall, but cleansing from the moral pollution acquired by his [one's] own acts of disobedience" (*Sanctification,* pp. 12, 14).

The new birth delivers one not only from sin in act but also this acquired sin in condition. Besides pardon, men need "washing and cleansing from this acquired pollution resulting from their sins" (C. W. Ruth, *Entire Sanctification,* p. 36). This "washing of regeneration" is a work of the Spirit (cf. Heb. 9:14; 1 John 1:9).

Wesleyanism holds therefore that sanctification begins with regeneration, but limits this "initial sanctification" to "cleansing from the pollution of guilt and acquired depravity" attached to sinful acts (cf. Wiley, *CT,* 2:423, 476). The corruption of actual sins must first be cleansed before the state of inherited depravity is cleansed in entire sanctification (Wiley, *CT,* 2:480-81).

See SANCTIFICATION, INITIAL SANCTIFICATION, ORIGINAL SIN.

For Further Reading: Taylor, *A Right Conception of Sin;* Corlett, *The Meaning of Holiness;* Williams, *Sanctification.* IVAN A. BEALS

ADAM. In its more general usage, the Hebrew word *adham* occurs approximately 560 times in the OT, and most frequently means "man" or "mankind" (e.g., Gen. 1:26-27). As a proper name, however, in the opening chapters of the Book of Genesis, Adam is the first man and "son of God" (Luke 3:38), the crown and climax of God's creation. The name which God gave him (Gen. 5:2) is akin to the Hebrew word for ground or earth, *adamah,* thereby denoting the earthly element in man, or physical life he shares in common with animals. Man was formed by the Creator out of the dust of the ground, and through divine inbreathing he became a living soul (2:7). Created in God's image (1:26-27) and endowed with superior qualities, Adam was given dominion over all other creatures. And for a helper and companion, God gave him Eve, who became his wife, "the mother of all living" (3:20).

Although created perfectly by God and placed on probation in an ideal situation in the Garden of Eden, Adam had the power of choice, was temptable, and liable to sin. From that lofty estate he fell through the temptation of Satan, thereby bringing a curse upon himself and his posterity (Rom. 5:12).

Adam was not only an individual; he was also a racial being. As an individual, he was responsible for his own transgression. As a racial being, his fall implicated the human family. In that sense, we are bound to Adam by birth (Gen. 5:3; Ps. 51:5; Eph. 2:3).

Before Adam and Eve were banished from the garden, God graciously gave them a "lamp of promise," thus revealing that a Deliverer would eventually come who would crush the serpent's (i.e., Satan's) head (Gen. 3:15). Expelled from Eden, Adam's life was reduced to toil, sorrow, and pain. The enormity of his fall became more fully apparent when his firstborn son, Cain, murdered his brother, Abel (4:8). Other sons and daughters were undoubtedly born in the first home, though only the name of Seth is given (v. 25). Adam lived to the age of 930 years (5:5).

The full significance of the fall of Adam is unfolded in the NT, particularly in the writings of the apostle Paul. Romans 5 and 1 Corinthians 15 are especially illuminating, where Paul, by a series of contrasts, sets forth the tragedy which the human race has sustained through the first Adam, and the gracious benefits which have been made possible through Jesus Christ, the God-man, whom he calls the "last Adam" (1 Cor. 15:45). Paul accepts without question the fact that Adam was a historical personality, and that the account in Genesis was a record of facts, though couched in rich symbolism. In Rom. 5:12-21 he recognizes Adam as the head of the race, whose disobedience introduced sin and death into the human family, and, at the same time, points to Christ as the Head of a new race and the Source of righteousness and salvation. The loss that accrues through Adam is more than matched by the gain through Christ (Rom. 5:20).

In 1 Cor. 15:22 the contrast between Adam and Christ relates to death and life: "For as in Adam all die, even so in Christ shall all be made alive." Our Lord assures us that the hour will come when they who are in their graves shall hear His voice and all will rise, whether to life or condemnation (John 5:28-29). In 1 Cor. 15:45 Paul declares that "the first man Adam was made a living soul; the last Adam was made a quickening [life-giving] spirit." The first part of the verse is obviously a reference to Gen. 2:7, while the latter part of the verse concerning the "last Adam" calls attention to Christ's redemptive ministry in making men spiritually alive (Eph. 2:1), as well as His power to resurrect all men hereafter.

The historical approach here presented is in contrast to the interpretation of many contemporary theologians. They have been strongly influenced by Soren Kierkegaard who regarded the account of the Fall as myth (*The Concept of Dread,* p. 42). Reinhold Niebuhr viewed Adam symbolically (*The Nature and Destiny of Man,* 2:77-78). "Adam" is "Everyman" (J. S. Whale, *Christian Doctrine,* p. 52; Alan Richardson, ed., *A Theological Word Book of the Bible,* pp. 14-15). For Karl Barth the entire account is a saga, and thus Adam is the name of the transgressor "which God gives to world-history as a whole" (*Church Dogmatics,* 4:1, 508). Generally, these views reject the biblical doctrine of inherited depravity, thus precluding the gracious provision of God's sanctifying work in the heart as a full remedy for racial corruption.

See FALL, MAN, HUMAN NATURE.

For Further Reading: Pearce, *Who Was Adam?* Scroggs, *The Last Adam;* Barth, *Christ and Adam;* Wiley, *CT,* 2:7-140.

WILLIAM M. ARNETT

ADAMIC SIN. See ORIGINAL SIN.

ADOPTION. This is one of the concomitants of the first work of grace. It refers to God's welcome of the converted person into His family as one of His children. This occurs at the same time as justification, regeneration, and initial sanctification, though logically it follows other aspects of conversion. It is the consequence of getting right with God. The Holy Spirit, as the "Spirit of adoption," bears witness to our acceptance by God as His children. This inner assurance puts within us the cry "Abba, Father," which is the spontaneous recognition by children of their father (Rom. 8:15-17; Gal. 4:6-7). It is on the basis of adoption that we become "joint-heirs with Christ" of all the treasures, resources, and privileges of God's kingdom.

See NEW BIRTH, JUSTIFICATION.

J. KENNETH GRIDER

ADOPTIONISM. Adoptionism is a type of Christological thought which arose in Spain in the seventh and eighth centuries. Its first proponent was Elipandus of Toledo, although its most vigorous champion was Felix of Urgel. The theory distinguished between a "natural" and an "adoptive" sonship, the former predicated of the deity and the latter of the humanity of Christ. Christ was held to be naturally and properly the Son of God only in respect to His divinity, but in respect to His humanity He was Son of God only by adoption and grace. This view was condemned by the Synod of Frankfort in A.D. 794 and by the Synod of Rome in A.D. 799.

Although the term *adoptionism* itself usually refers to this Spanish heresy, the theory has antecedents in earlier Christologies such as Ebionism, Dynamic Monarchianism, and Nestorianism. The latter, by making a strict separation between the divine and human natures of Christ, is especially anticipatory of the views of Elipandus and Felix. Adoptionistic tendencies characterized the entire "Antiochene school" of theology.

The strength of adoptionism, and of Antiochene Christology in general, lies in its grasp of the real humanity of Christ as over against the Alexandrian theology in which Christ's humanity tends to be truncated. Its weakness is that if God had to wait until a man proved good enough to be adopted as His Son, Christian faith would have to abandon its central affirmation that God *sent* His Son to redeem the world. Belief in the divine initiative in salvation and in the prevenience of grace would thus be impoverished.

See ANTIOCH (SCHOOL OF), CHRISTOLOGY, HYPOSTATIC UNION, MONARCHIANISM, NESTORIANISM.

For Further Reading: Gonzalez, *A History of Christian Thought,* 1:253-58, 2:105-10; Kelly, *Early Christian Doctrines,* 115-19, 138-40, 301-17; Pelikan, *The Christian Tradition,* 1:175-76. ROB L. STAPLES

ADORATION. See WORSHIP.

ADULTERY. This is a term used in the Bible to designate the act of voluntary cohabitation with a person other than one's legal spouse. It differs from fornication inasmuch as adultery implies marriage, whereas fornication is a term applicable to any kind of sexual irregularity whether married or not.

In the Bible adultery is treated as a heinous sin. Not only is it explicitly prohibited in the Ten Commandments, but under Mosaic law adulterous parties were both to be put to death. The gravity of the sin is in its betrayal of trust, its violation and destruction of the most sacred human relationship, and its disruptive effects on the home and society in general.

The Bible also speaks of spiritual adultery, as constituting the unfaithfulness of Israel or the Church, or an individual Christian, in his sacred relationship to God. Spiritual adultery occurs when one relates more loyally to the world than to God.

While the gospel offers forgiveness for either physical or spiritual adultery, rather than demanding the death penalty, it in no degree minimizes its gravity. Moreover, Jesus refused to allow guilt for adultery to be confined to the overt act, but attached it to the intent of the heart. According to the NT standards of pure motivation, persons could be adulterous in God's sight even when the outward act was avoided. This must not be interpreted, however, as a condemnation for every thought which is sexual in nature or every experience of involuntary temptation. It is an expression of the moral principle that God weighs character by secret decisions and intentions, rather than by behavior alone.

See FAMILY, DECALOGUE, SEX (SEXUALITY).

For Further Reading: Wiley, *CT,* 3:79-94; *Baker's DCE.* RICHARD S. TAYLOR

ADVENTISM. Adventism is the belief in the imminent and literal return of Jesus Christ to the earth. The English word *Advent* is derived from the Latin *adventus,* which means "arrival" or "coming." The NT equivalent of the word *Advent* is the term *parousia* (Gr., "coming" or "presence"). A significant facet of the second coming of Christ included in Adventism is the inauguration of a new age when the wicked will be overcome and the kingdom of the saints will be established on earth for 1,000 years.

In a generic sense millenarianism (Latin *mille,* "thousand"), chiliasm (Gr. *chilioi,* "thousand"), and apocalypticism are related to Adventism. The belief in a coming age of divine rule has its historical roots in late pre-Christian Judaism and early Christianity. Parts of the books of Daniel and Ezekiel are Jewish canonical literary examples of the apocalyptic genré. Several apocalyptic books teach millenarian and Adventist tenets (e.g., 2 Esdras 7:50; 14:5; 1 Enoch 93:1-19; 91:12-17; 2 Enoch 33:1-2; 2 Baruch 44:11; 48:50; Testament of Issachar 6:1; and Testament of Judah 25:3).

Historically, Adventism has had prominent proponents in early Christianity, including Polycarp, Ignatius, Papias, Hermas, and Justin Martyr. Montanus prophesied (between A.D. 150 and 175) that a new age would begin with the descent of a heavenly Jerusalem near Pepuza in Phrygia. Tertullian espoused one form of Montanism in the early third century A.D.

Reaction against Montanism squelched Adventist interests for nearly a thousand years until Joachim of Fiore, a priest (c. 1132-1202), began to write about a new age of the Spirit which was to commence in c. 1260. The Taborites in the 15th century and certain Anabaptists during the Reformation period promoted Adventism. The term has a particular historical connection with the Adventist groups which arose as the result of the preaching of William Miller, a Baptist cleric born in 1782, in Massachusetts.

Miller began preaching in 1818 that the second coming of Christ would occur in 1843-44. He based his pronouncements upon a somewhat literal interpretation of portions of Daniel 9—10 and Rev. 20:1-10. America was experiencing the Second Great Awakening which heightened interest in Miller's prophecy. Great expectation was followed by great disillusionment when the proclaimed dates passed with no return of Christ.

Ellen Harmon, a Methodist teenager, was one of the followers of Miller who was not disillusioned. She had a vision which aided her in reinterpreting Miller's schedule for the Second Coming. Ellen married Elder White and became the guiding voice in the development of the

Seventh-Day Adventist church, the largest of several Adventist groups which remain active.

Although most of the doctrines of the Seventh-Day Adventist church are generally orthodox, they hold to at least three doctrines which set them apart from orthodoxy. They believe in the "doctrine of the sanctuary" as a special and final ministry of Christ in the holy of holies in the "heavenly" sanctuary; in the observance of the seventh day to keep the commandments of God; in the "spirit of prophecy" (Rev. 19:10) which pertains to special latter-day messages. Ellen White was accepted as the latter-day possessor of the "spirit of prophecy."

See APOCALYPTIC (APOCALYPSE), SECOND COMING OF CHRIST, JUDGE (JUDGMENT), MILLENNIUM.

For Further Reading: Martin, *The Kingdom of the Cults,* 360-423; Russell, *The Method and Message of Jewish Apocalyptic,* 263-303; *GMS,* 642-48; Wiley, *CT,* 3:243-319; Meagher, "Adventism," *Encyclopedic Dictionary of Religion,* 55-56.

KENNETH E. HENDRICK

ADVERSARY. See SATAN.

ADVOCATE. Only in 1 John 2:1 is the Greek word *paraklētos* translated "advocate" in the KJV and the RSV. In John's Gospel (14:16, 26; 15:26; and 16:7) the words "Counselor" or "Comforter" are used to identify the Holy Spirit as the One who is called to stand alongside of the accused.

The word "advocate" in John's First Epistle uniquely refers to Jesus Christ, the first Comforter. It was the prayer of Jesus Christ which was answered by the Father on the Day of Pentecost by the sending of another Comforter in the person of the Holy Spirit (John 14:16).

The setting for this exceptional use of the word "advocate" is a court of law where the condemned is not forsaken but lovingly represented by the only One who can stand between the sinner and a just God. This Advocate does not plead the case but points to His own blood as an acceptable substitute for penalty.

It should not be overlooked that in this setting, sin is not an inevitability in the life of the Christian, but rather it is an ever-present possibility. If sin should be committed, the Advocate becomes the assurance of fresh forgiveness and continued acceptance with the Father. The mediation is not a vindication (as if the Christian were falsely accused and needed to be exonerated) but an ever-available basis for forgiveness, based on the once-for-all atonement of Calvary.

See PROPITIATION, ATONEMENT, MEDIATION (MEDIATOR).

For Further Reading: Kittel, 5:800-14; Westcott, *Gospel According to St. John,* 2:188-91.

ROBERT A. MATTKE

AESTHETICS. Aesthetics is a branch of philosophy which investigates the meaning and forms of beauty. It is sometimes described as a normative science like ethics and logic since it deals with the field of values. It studies the nature of aesthetic pleasure, the objective and/or subjective character of beauty, even the very nature of beauty itself. Included in this field are music, poetry, drama, literature, painting, and sculpture. It also includes the field of natural beauty like the waving fields of grain, the setting sun, the gorgeous leaves of autumn, and the human face and form. It is also a study of the mind and emotions in relation to the sense of beauty.

History. The great art periods of history were in ancient Greece and the medieval and Renaissance periods in Europe. The older theories of beauty were metaphysical and religious. Both religion and national feeling inspired the work of the Greek masters. Plato believed beauty to be a reality in itself, a kind of eternal and unchanging essence or form. Plotinus, the Neoplatonist, believed beauty to be the pure effulgence of the divine reason. Ruskin believed that beauty in objects is found in certain qualities such as unity, repose, symmetry, purity, and moderation, which typify divine attributes.

The modern theories of beauty are psychological in contrast to the earlier ones. Immanuel Kant represents the beginning of the modern scientific and psychological study of aesthetic theory. For him beauty was a quality of objects, not a merely subjective taste. Today, the nature of beauty is much in question. People vary so widely in the area of artistic appreciation that many thinkers who would insist upon the existence of norms in ethics and religion, are inclined to be quite subjective in the field of aesthetic appreciation.

Theories. (1) The ancient Greeks, especially Plato, thought of art and the art object as an imperfect attempt and result to portray the universal. (2) Those who are involved in the creation of beautiful objects, to them art is pleasure, and pleasure is its proper function. (3) Related to pleasure, art can be seen as an escape from life. It can be a form of relaxation in which man uses his creative imagination to pursue the arts. (4) Psychologists interpret art as empathy, in which people experience to a lesser degree what they would experience if they were participating in a situation or performing the actions which the work of art depicts. (5) Art is also a means of communication. Leo Tolstoy says, "By art man transmits his feelings." (6) According to the Italian philosopher B. Croce, art is intuition that is expressed; it reveals preference and sense of values. (7) For John Dewey art is experience. Art reflects experience, like the grace of a baseball player. Art is a judgment on the quality of life and a means of promoting its development.

For the Christian the field of aesthetics says something basic about the nature of the universe and its Creator. Warren C. Young expresses it succinctly: "If man is to receive aesthetic satisfaction, this must be the kind of universe which works with his efforts. The interrelation of man and nature reflected in aesthetic experience is an additional argument for the existence of a Supreme Being." This Supreme Being is revealed in the Bible. The Psalmist in Ps. 96:5-6 testifies that "the LORD made the heavens. Splendor and majesty are before Him, strength and beauty are in His sanctuary" (NASB). To understand, experience, and appreciate the world of the aesthetic in its fullness, one needs to research the One who is the Source of all beauty, and to enter into a relationship with Jesus Christ, who is altogether lovely.

See AXIOLOGY, BEAUTY, VALUES, CHRISTIAN ETHICS.

For Further Reading: Wiley, *CT,* 2:51-61; Titus, *Living Issues in Philosophy,* 5th ed., 380-97; Taylor, *A Return to Christian Culture.*

NOBEL V. SACK

AFFECTIONS. Affections are one's emotional attachments; in a popular usage, one's "loves." To possess an affection for or toward a person or thing is to be *affected,* i.e., moved by that object.

Pathos and *pathēma* are in the NT "inordinate affection," i.e., irregular and uncontrolled emotional attachments and desires (translated "passion" in recent versions, Rom. 1:26; Gal. 5:24; Col. 3:5; 1 Thess. 4:5). Approved affections are represented by *splanchna,* lit. "the bowels." By the Greeks the bowels were regarded as "the seat of the more violent passions, by the Hebrews the seat of the tender affections" (Vine); hence in the NT the word is rendered "affection" in such passages as 2 Cor. 6:12; 7:15; Phil. 1:8 (NASB); a "heart of compassion" in Col. 3:12 (NASB).

While not an exact translation, perhaps, of *phroneite* (Col. 3:2), the KJV admirably expresses the sense: *"Set your affection* on things above"; for the Bible holds us accountable for the quality and direction of our affections. They are to be controlled by the will and directed, first to God, then toward persons and things in a holy and lawful way. Straying affections may very probably be the most common cause of backsliding. Loving people with deep and tender attachment is not in itself to be feared, as long as such affection is disciplined by a primary passion to please God. Christians are to be "devoted to one another in brotherly love" (Rom. 12:10, NASB).

See LOVE, DISCIPLINE, VALUES.

For Further Reading: Vine, *Dictionary;* Wesley, *A Plain Account of Christian Perfection.*

RICHARD S. TAYLOR

AGAPĒ. Deriving from the verb *agapaō,* this is the most significant biblical term for love. Found almost exclusively in the LXX and the NT (of its three supposed occurrences in prebiblical Greek, two are now read otherwise and the third is doubtful), *agapē* has become the word which expresses most accurately the Christian meaning of love.

The three key verbs for love in prebiblical Greek are *eran, philein,* and *agapan. Eran* (n. *eros*) describes the passionate love which desires the other for itself, in order to experience personal fulfillment. *Philein* (n. *philia*) usually denotes the love of gods for men or friends for friends. In *agapan* is found little of the passion of *eran* or the warmth of *philein. Agapan* means "to prefer," "to esteem one person (or thing) more highly than another."

The specific meaning of *agapan* now becomes apparent. *Eran* expresses a general love seeking satisfaction where it can; *agapan* means to love another by choice. *Eran* speaks of a love determined by its object; *agapan* denotes the free and decisive act of the subject. So, *eran* is more emotional while *agapan* is carefully volitional.

Probably because of its orgiastic associations *eran/eros* does not occur in the NT. However, *philein* is found in 25 references, sometimes synonymous with *agapan* (e.g., John 16:27; 1 Cor. 16:22; Rev. 3:19) but usually in its etymological sense (e.g., John 11:3, 36; 20:2; 21:17 [3]; trans. "kiss" in Matt. 26:48; Mark 14:44). *Agapan,* however, occurs 140 times, and *agapē* 85.

The volitional meaning of *agapan/agapē* is everywhere apparent in the NT. *Agapē* may be good or evil, depending on whether one "prefers" God or the world (cf. Matt. 22:37 with 1 John 2:15; 2 Tim. 4:10; and see John 3:19).

In the Great Commandment Jesus uses *agapēseis,* "thou shalt love," and declares our obligation to love God with our whole being. The same word is used to affirm our obligation toward our neighbor. To love God is to assign supreme value to Him, i.e., to worship Him alone. To love neighbor as oneself is to prefer his highest good as one should seek his own true welfare. In Matt. 5:43-48 (cf. Luke 6:32-36) *agapē* is love of enemy on the pattern of God's own inclusive love (cf. 1 John 4:10-11).

The Cross is the supreme expression of the divine *agapē* (Rom. 5:8-10). This is the love of God which is not "caused" by anything attractive or worthy in man but, originating in God's own being, is directed toward the unlovable and unworthy. *Agapē* does not seek but creates goodness. God, who loves us, does not seek anything for himself (cf. 1 Cor. 13:5); all He desires is to benefit us. And the benefit He wishes to impart is not some "thing" but His very Self. By His Spirit He pours His *agapē* into the believer (Rom. 5:5). Imparted to us by the new birth (1 John 4:7), *agapē* is "perfected" in us when, by God's sanctifying grace, it reaches its intended goal of becoming fully regnant within us so that of us it may be said, "As he is, so are we in this world" (vv. 17-18; cf. Rom. 12:9-21; 1 Corinthians 13). *Agapē* is both God's gift (Rom. 5:5) and His command (13:8-10).

Agapē was also a term used for a solemn meal held in the Early Church in connection with the Lord's Supper. It probably began with the separation from the original eucharistic meal of everything except the two acts connected with the bread and the cup instituted by Jesus. The practice of the *Agapē* varied from place to place, and was largely extinct by the seventh century in the Western church.

See AFFECTIONS, GREAT COMMANDMENTS, BROTHERLY LOVE, DEVOTE (DEVOTION).

For Further Reading: Kittel, 1:20-55; Moulton and Milligan, *The Vocabulary of the Greek New Testament;* Nygren, *Agape and Eros* (2 vols.); Williams, *The Spirit and Forms of Love;* Furnish, *The Love Command of the New Testament;* Wynkoop, *A Theology of Love.*

WILLIAM M. GREATHOUSE

AGE, AGES. The concept of age can be associated with the years of a person's life, indicating how old he or she may be. Old age was respected in the OT (Lev. 19:32; Deut. 32:7) and also in NT times (1 Tim. 5:1-2). Thus honor and the blessing of God were associated with old age (Prov. 16:31).

The term "age" was also loosely used of a long span of time, whether in the past, or the future. Even the eternity of God could be expressed in the phrase *Rock of Ages* ("Rock eternal," [Isa. 26:4, NIV]). The KJV margin of Ps. 145:13 states that the Lord's kingdom is "a kingdom of all ages," meaning it has no beginning or end.

In the OT, KJV has other translations for the Hebrew word behind "ages," such as "everlasting" and "ancient." The Hebrew word is *olam* or *olamim* (plural). Its basic meaning is unlimited time; or, a future without an end. The word designates both God's covenant and promises as everlasting. The same is true of the Messianic King and His kingdom (Ps. 45:6; 89:35-37; 110:4). It is part of the title "Everlasting Father" (Isa. 9:6, NIV). The Hebrew word is also employed in NIV to describe existence after death in such phrases as "eternal home" (Eccles. 12:5) and "everlasting life . . . everlasting contempt" (Dan. 12:2).

In the NT, the concept of eschatological time is found in the phrase "in the coming ages" (Eph. 2:7, NIV), when the full riches of salvation will be revealed. This idea of a future without an end is also found in the phrase "for ever and ever" (3:21, NIV). These phrases rest in the Greek word *aiōn,* which has the meaning of indefinite past time and indefinite future time. It is often translated with futuristic words like "everlasting," "eternal," "eternity," "forever," etc. See passages such as 1 Tim. 1:17; Eph. 3:11; 1 Pet. 1:25; Heb. 5:6.

See ETERNITY, TIME.

For Further Reading: *ERE; IDB,* 2:135-410.

GEORGE HERBERT LIVINGSTON

AGNOSTICISM. This is the doctrine that man cannot have any certainty about God's existence or the supernatural generally, since such knowledge is by nature beyond the limits of human reason. Agnosticism is a type of skepticism. The skeptic is concerned with showing that human reason is restricted to function within set boundaries. These boundaries limit the types of knowledge which are available to the mind. While the skeptic has doubts about the availability of human knowledge in general, the agnostic confines his doubts to the areas of theology and metaphysics.

In the Greek language agnosticism means "unknown" or "without knowledge." The term was first used in the 19th century by Thomas Huxley. Annoyed by the dogmatic assertions of the church which he felt were unsupported, Huxley reacted by refusing to commit himself on theological issues.

For all practical purposes the agnostic is one who claims to be ignorant of the answers to life's ultimate questions. He refuses to take responsibility for this ignorance because the fault, he believes, lies not in himself but in the subject matter. The Christian response is that the agnostic is responsible, since he has kept the blind drawn on the sunlight of revelation. The Holy Spirit will bring assurance to a willing mind (John 7:17).

See EPISTEMOLOGY, KNOWLEDGE, FAITH, THEISTIC PROOFS.

For Further Reading: Schaff, ed., *Encyclopedia of Religious Knowledge,* 1:36-38; Muggeridge, *Albion Agnostics;* "Man's Relationship with His Creator," *Vital Speeches,* Oct. 30, 1975.

ROBERT A. MATTKE

ALEXANDRIAN SCHOOL. The name may apply to either the Christian catechetical school which originated with Pantaenus (c. 180) in Alexandria, Egypt, or to a school of Christian thought developed there by such famous teachers as Clement (150-216) and Origen (185-254). The school finally closed because of local theological controversies at the close of the fourth century, but the influence of its teachers on all subsequent Christianity has been unceasing.

The greatest significance of this school lay in bringing Greek philosophy, particularly Platonism and Stoicism, to the service of Christian theology, creating what is commonly known as Christian Platonism. The impact of this union upon Christianity as a whole is inestimable. Its mystical theology set the permanent patterns of Eastern Orthodox thought; through Gregory of Nyssa and the Cappadocian Fathers this interpretation of Christianity in Neoplatonic categories passed into the mainstream of the church's life. By the end of the eighth century speculative Alexandrian theology had overcome the opposition of the more historically oriented school at Antioch. Through the growing influence of the teaching of Augustine, the mystical theology of Alexandria soon became dominant in the Western church as well.

Largely rejected by the Reformers, Alexandrian theology nevertheless has left its impact upon Protestantism. In England it became the theological base for the Cambridge Platonism of the 17th century. Its emphases upon (1) all truth being God's truth wherever it may be found; (2) the permeation of all creation with the active presence of the Logos, who is leading all persons to the truth; and (3) wholehearted love of God as the goal and sum of Christian perfection, contributed to the central Wesleyan doctrines of prevenient grace and perfect love. Wesley's *Christian Library* drew heavily upon Macarius, the Greek fathers, and the Cambridge Platonists.

The Alexandrian School will always be a source of controversy in Christian theology, not only because of its use of speculative allegory in interpreting Scripture, but because its union of Greek and biblical thought in the service of Christian theology continually raises two radically contradictory responses. The abiding issue is: Was Greek thought radically altered by being Christianized, or, Was Christian teaching radically altered by being Hellenized?

See ANTIOCH (SCHOOL OF), ALLEGORICAL INTERPRETATION, PLATONISM.

For Further Reading: Biggs, *The Christian Platonists of Alexandria;* Oulton and Chadwick, *Alexandrian Christianity;* Sellers, *Two Ancient Theologies.*

MELVIN EASTERDAY DIETER

ALLEGORICAL INTERPRETATION. This is a method of interpreting the Bible which is based on the assumption that the narratives of Scripture are divinely designed to represent hidden spiritual truths, and that the task of the interpreter is to get behind the literal sense to the intended allegorical meaning. The method was used by Philo of Alexandria, later adopted by Origen and the Alexandrian School. Augustine also was prone to allegorical interpretation. For example, he allegorized the parable of the Good Samaritan by forcing a correspondence between each detail of the parable and the gospel plan of salvation.

There is little allegorical interpretation, as such, in Scripture. One instance is Paul's reference to the "allegory" of Hagar and Sarah as representing two covenants, one of bondage and one of freedom (Gal. 4:21-25). A different type of allegory is found in Eccles. 12:1-7; John 10:1-16; and Eph. 6:1-17.

A parable differs from an allegory, inasmuch as a parable is a true-to-life illustration, or extended metaphor, which is designed primarily to teach one truth. The allegory, in contrast, is an illustration so designed that each detail represents a corresponding spiritual meaning. Often modern Christians mistakenly attempt to treat parables as allegories.

Allegorical interpretation, in which one finds hidden meanings in casual details of events and personages, leads to uncontrolled speculation, resulting in a bewildering variety of theories and fancies.

Although the lessons which can be drawn from historical narratives and events may be apt, and may be edifying, they are not to be understood as a discovery of the true meaning or interpretation of the passage itself. Seeing events as illustrative of truth, and making practical applications to everyday life, is not the same as seeing events as representing a divinely written code language.

Doctrines may therefore be supported and illustrated by allegorical application but not established or grounded on such, excepting in those few cases where we have clear NT support for such procedure.

See ALLEGORY, HERMENEUTICS.

For Further Reading: *Baker's Dictionary of Practical Theology,* ed. Turnbull, 99-147; Taylor, *Preaching Holiness Today,* 99-106.

MILTON S. AGNEW

ALLEGORY. Greek *allos,* "other," and *agoreuō,* "to speak in a place of assembly" (*agora,* the marketplace). The term has come to mean a veiled presentation in a figurative story of a meaning metaphorically implied but not expressly stated. It may be called a prolonged metaphor, such as *Pilgrim's Progress.* Allegory produces a dual interest—in the story and in the ideas or truths being conveyed. The incidents may be historical or fictitious. An allegory always veils its true meaning (its underlying or allegorical sense) by leaving that to be deduced from the story it tells. There may be more than one allegorical meaning.

See ALLEGORICAL INTERPRETATION.

MILTON S. AGNEW

ALPHA AND OMEGA. These two terms are the names of the first and last letters of the Greek alphabet. The compound expression is of great theological significance because in the NT it is used as a title for God and also for Christ.

All three of its occurrences are in the Book of Revelation (1:8; 21:6; 22:13). Neither term is found elsewhere in the NT. (The KJV has the expression in Rev. 1:11, but it is not in the best Greek text.) It is generally held that God is the Speaker in 1:8 and 21:6. Without question Christ applies this title to himself in 22:13. This is one of John's strong affirmations of the full deity of Jesus.

The meaning of the title—literally, "the Alpha and the Omega"—is given in 21:6 as "the Beginning and the End" and in 22:13 as also "the First and the Last" (NIV). Not only is God the Beginning and End of all things, but Christ, as Creator and Redeemer, is in a unique way the Beginning and End of all history. The main thrust of the title is on the eternity of God and of Christ. Swete says: "The phrase is seen to express not eternity only, but infinitude, the boundless life which embraces all while it transcends all" (*Apocalypse of St. John,* 11).

See CHRIST.

For Further Reading: *Baker's DT,* 37-38; *ZPEB,* 1:111.

RALPH EARLE

ALTAR. An altar is a structure or place where religious rites are performed and offerings are made to God.

In the OT, the Hebrew word for altar is "slaughter," usually signifying an elevated structure where sacrifices were made. However, incense was burned on the altar of incense (Exod. 30:1-7). An altar could be made from a mound of earth (20:24), an unhewn stone (v. 25), or bronze (2 Kings 16:15). A large rock became the central place of sacrifice on Mount Moriah (2 Sam. 24:15-25) and can now be seen in Jerusalem under the Moslem prayer place, the Dome of the Rock.

The altar reminded Israel that "without shedding of blood is no remission" of sin (Heb. 9:22).

In the NT, *thusiastērion,* place of sacrifice, refers either to the Temple altar or a pagan altar until Heb. 13:10, when the concept is spiritualized. The Christian's altar is the place where the soul meets God on the basis of faith in Christ's atoning sacrifice. The believer thus erects his own altar in his heart. He may also think of it as a place where he meets God.

However, when the church reverted to a Judaistic type of formalism, the visible altar in the church again became the center of worship. So it is today not only in Roman Catholicism but in so-called high Protestant churches.

In revivalistic circles another type of altar has come into vogue, a kneeling rail or bench to which penitents or other distressed persons are invited to come for prayer. With some denominations this kind of an altar has virtually become a hallmark. Whether it is a crude bench or one of finished craftsmanship, it becomes a place to meet God, to pray, to receive members, to baptize, to give marriage vows, and to make commitments of life to God.

The term *family altar* applies to the practice of worshipping God as a family, usually in a semistructured setting and routine.

See PRAYER, WORSHIP, ATONEMENT.

For Further Reading: *IDB,* 1:96-100; Child and Colles, *Christian Symbols;* Stafford, *Christian Symbolism in the Evangelical Church;* Oke, *We Have an Altar.*

J. OTTIS SAYES

AMBASSADOR. An ambassador is an official representative sent by or to a sovereign power. By regulations adopted at the Congresses of Vienna and Aix-la-Chapelle and accepted by all nations, diplomatic agents are divided into four classes, the highest of which is ambassador (see Webster's *New International Dictionary*).

In the OT ambassadors were distinguished

messengers, but something less than absolute representatives entitled to the same honors as their sovereigns. The word "ambassador" is the rendering of three different Hebrew words, *mal'ak,* messenger, *sir,* envoy, *melis,* interpreter (2 Chron. 35:21; Josh. 9:4; 2 Chron. 32:31).

Evangelical interest in the word centers around the NT usage where it is rendered from the Greek words *presbeuō* (2 Cor. 5:20; Eph. 6:20) and *presbeia* (Luke 14:32). As used by Paul, "ambassador" gives to every Christian witness the dignity of being a representative of the King of Kings.

Careful interpretation of the Scriptures seems to lend authority to the scriptural believer who proclaims the "Thus saith the Lord," but to remind him of his creatureliness, thus restraining him from claiming excessive honors or "diplomatic immunity." He is a "voice," a messenger.

See EVANGELIST, APOSTLE, GREAT COMMISSION, TESTIMONY.

For Further Reading: *Baker's DT;* Fallows, Zenos, Willett, *Bible Encyclopedia;* Purkiser, *The NT Image of the Ministry,* 41 ff.

JOHN E. RILEY

AMILLENNIALISM. This view finds traditional premillennialism impossible and therefore interprets the 1,000-year reign of Christ with His saints (Rev. 20:4) spiritually, not literally. This interpretation usually takes one of two forms: Those who come to life again may refer to those who have been martyred by the Beast, the Antichrist. Contrary to appearances when they were martyred, they really were not dead. Rather, they lived with Christ in heaven throughout the Church age.

The other interpretation is that the "millennial" passage refers to the Church. It is to be understood in light of such passages as Eph. 2:1-6: "And you he made alive, when you were dead through [your] trespasses and sins . . . even when we were dead through our trespasses [he] made us alive together with Christ (by grace you have been saved), and raised us up with him" (RSV). The binding of Satan has an analogy at Matt. 12:26-29, where Jesus speaks of a binding of Satan He has accomplished.

The main reason for interpreting Revelation 20 in an amillennial manner is that this is the only passage in the NT that speaks of such an event.

Two things must be admitted. First, usually the NT sees the resurrection of redemption occurring at the second coming of Christ; and second, a premillennial interpretation is also beset by some theological difficulties. Two other points could be emphasized: Those who hold the amillennial interpretation do so because they are convinced that the NT demands it. However, those who reject the amillennial interpretation argue that if the phrase about coming to life in verse 5 refers to eschatological resurrection, which is generally admitted, then the same word in verse 4 must refer to the same kind of event, viz., bodily resurrection, with the 1,000 years intervening.

See MILLENNIUM, PREMILLENNIALISM, POSTMILLENNIALISM, RESURRECTION OF THE BODY.

For Further Reading: Ludwigson, *A Survey of Bible Prophecy;* Ladd, *Crucial Questions About the Kingdom of God;* Hughes, *A New Heaven and a New Earth.*

GEORGE ELDON LADD

ANABAPTISTS. See REBAPTISM.

ANALOGY. Analogy exists when a term applied to one thing is directed to another in a related, though not identical, thus analogical, sense. For instance, creation reflects the Creator. If parallels can be drawn, analogies exist to some extent.

As Thielicke suggests, there is scant, if any, relation between a man and a star, with only slight similarity between man and dog; but through Christian truth there is an encounter that concerns man's existence, that touches his personal identity, and thus applies to him unconditionally. On that account vital major analogical relevance is presupposed.

Harvey notes that analogy answers two vital theological questions: (1) How can one make significant statements about the infinite in concepts that are derived from the finite? (2) How can one draw inferences about the nature of the Creator from the created, and thus provide the basis for natural theology that requires no special appeal to revelation? Roman Catholic use of analogy of being, *analogia entis,* was rigorously attacked by Barth, who argued that when theologians embrace it, they create an intolerable division between all general knowledge of God and knowledge of His action as revealed in Jesus Christ.

See NATURAL THEOLOGY, ANTHROPOMORPHISM.

For Further Reading: Gundry, *Tensions in Contemporary Theology;* Harvey, *A Handbook of Theological Terms;* Thielicke, *The Evangelical Faith.*

MEL-THOMAS ROTHWELL

ANALYTICISM. See POSITIVISM.

ANATHEMA. A thing or person which is under the ban, forbidden, untouchable, polluted, accursed. Some interpret the word to mean "the object of a curse"—that which has been found as taking an unworthy place and, hence, has been cursed or ruled forbidden. The word occurs in 1 Cor. 16:22—"If any one has no love for the Lord, let him be accursed [anathema]" (RSV). Anathema thus signifies a thing or person devoted to destruction. The Jews, in pronouncing any man anathema, were pronouncing a curse upon him.

Another strong use of "anathema" is in Gal. 1:8-9. Here Paul uses the term in reference to anyone, even though an angel, who would dare dilute or distort the gospel. Such is termed "anathema" or accursed.

But to pronounce such a curse on Jesus would be impossible, if the Holy Spirit is in charge (1 Cor. 12:3).

Paul's desire to see his fellow Jews saved was so intense that he went so far as to be willing to be "anathema" himself, if such personal loss would bring about their faith (Rom. 9:3).

These NT renderings would imply the category of the finally lost. At the judgment, those accursed will be banished.

If Paul's imprecations seem unchristian, it should be remembered that the Holy Spirit was prompting him to remind the church (and us) of what was already a solemn, inherent fact. Deuteronomoy was God's proffer to the Israelites of either blessing or cursing—the option was theirs. In the NT we learn that this option hangs not now on the Mosaic Law but on one's attitude toward Jesus Christ.

See UNBELIEF, APOSTASY, ETERNAL PUNISHMENT.

For Further Reading: *BBC,* 8:483; 9:30; Wesley, *Explanatory Notes upon the NT,* ad loc.

C. NEIL STRAIT

ANGEL. The term "angel" is derived from the Greek word *angelos.* The English word denotes a supernatural being; the Greek word, like its Hebrew counterpart, may additionally mean any kind of messenger.

In the Old Testament. Two distinguishable uses are found. First, there is the "angel of the Lord" who comes to give help or guidance to the individual or nation in need and who is usually recognized as one in whom God himself is present and is treated accordingly (Gen. 16:13; 22:15-16; 31:11-13). Second, there are heavenly beings who are sharply distinguished from God (Gen. 28:12-13; 32:1-2). These are variously called "sons of God" (Job 1:6), "the host of heaven" (1 Kings 22:19)—and are regarded as divine servants or attendants (Isa. 6:2).

Between the Testaments. Already in the OT the doctrine of angels was developing. In the Book of Daniel they are presented as intermediaries between God and men (4:13, 17; 7:10); as rulers and guardians (10:13, 21); and they are individualized by being given personal names (8:16; 10:13). This tendency was greatly increased during the period between the Testaments in the belief that this was the fulfilment of OT teaching. In the Apocrypha and Pseudepigrapha angels are arranged in hierarchies; while in the Dead Sea Scrolls they are ranged on opposing sides, light and darkness, each side under a leading angel or prince. In all of this, however, there is no suggestion that the angels are divine or independent. Always they are seen as subordinate to Yahweh, representing His presence and power; and even though on occasion they are pictured as presenting men's prayers to God (Enoch 99:3), it is not as intercessors so much as conveyors of men's petitions.

In the New Testament. The Greek word *angelos* is used approximately 175 times in the NT, only 6 of which refer to human messengers. The remainder, referring to supernatural beings, are concentrated in the Synoptic Gospels (51), the Acts of the Apostles (21), and the Book of Revelation (67), with the balance chiefly in the Pauline Epistles. However, Paul uses other terms to refer to evil angels (e.g., "principalities and powers") which increase the incidence considerably. In general, the NT writers take over the views of the OT and of Judaism on the subject; angels are mentioned in a purely incidental way; there is no direct teaching about them.

Aside from Paul the NT teaching is that in nature, angels are part of God's invisible creation, though capable of visiblity when occasion requires (Acts 10:3; 12:15). They are possessed of free will (2 Pet. 2:4; Jude 6) and knowledge, though of a limited variety (Mark 13:32). Little stress is laid on their individuality, however. Only two are named: Gabriel (Luke 1:19) and Michael (Jude 9). Their qualities of power (Rev. 10:1) and glory (Luke 2:9; 24:4) are stressed more than their personality; and in some contexts there seems to be an intent to reduce the estimation of them as much as possible (Heb. 1:14). Not only is there no suggestion of equality between the angels and Jesus (v. 4); it is repeatedly insisted that the saints themselves are greater (2:16; Rev. 19:10; 22:8-9).

In function, apart from their engagement in the ceaseless praise of God, angels are the media of God's service of men. Accordingly, all creatures and even created things have their angels (Matt. 18:10; Acts 12:15; Rev. 7:1; 9:15; 14:18) through whom God is able to effect His purposes (Matt. 26:53). Their chief role, however, is in furthering the work of redemption, and the vast majority of NT references to angels indicate their role in the three great events of redemptive history: the Incarnation (1:20; 2:13; Luke 1:11, 19, 26, etc.); the Death and Resurrection (24:4, 23; Acts 1:10); and the Consummation (Rev. 8:2, etc.).

Paul's basic conception of angels does not differ from that of the rest of the NT. The distinctiveness of his teaching lies more in emphasis, triggered no doubt by the situation he confronted. In response to the Gnostic worship of angels, Paul stressed the uniqueness of Christ and His Lordship over all angelic beings (Eph. 1:20-21; Phil. 2:9-10; Col. 1:15-16; 2:18-19). But inasmuch as such angelic beings were rivalling Christ, they constituted the real enemy in the spiritual realm which lay behind the visible order (Gal. 1:8; Eph. 6:12). Paul's tendency is to depreciate angelology, not because angels are unreal but because the best of them are vastly inferior to Christ and the worst of them have been defeated by Him (Col. 2:15).

Theological Evaluation. In Scripture, angels are expressive of God's active care for His creation, while their evil counterparts are concerned to subvert His loving purposes. The rationalistic mind has consistently scouted such conceptions. However, both the scale and significance of the biblical evidence make it difficult to dissent from the conclusion of J. S. Stewart that "here we are dealing, not with some unessential apocalyptic scaffolding, but with the very substance of the faith" (*Scottish Journal of Theology* 4 [1951]:300). Brunner argues persuasively that "the truth of Christ, the Victor, implies negatively, the presupposition that there is a supra-human power of darkness" (*The Christian Doctrine of Creation and Redemption,* 2:134). The spiritual world is no less real than the visible, both underlying it and at times overflowing on to it like a subterranean sea so that in important respects it is the world of true reality.

See SATAN, DEMIURGE, GNOSTICISM, DEMONS (DEMON POSSESSION).

For Further Reading: Bietenhard and Budd, "Angel," *NIDNTT;* Schlier, *The Relevance of the New Testament,* 172-92; Stewart, *The Scottish Journal of Theology,* 4:292-301; Brunner, *The Christian Doctrine of Creation and Redemption,* 2:133-47. ALEX R. G. DEASLEY

ANGER. We must deal with two manifestations of anger both in the NT and the OT, the anger of God and the anger of man. The anger of God is always righteous and is ethically motivated. It is the other side of holiness, love, and His justice, so that it is always against sin, and eventually the sinner, if he remains unrepentant. Repentance and petition can stay or reverse the anger of God which is like a consuming fire, and ultimately hell is the result for the unrepentant.

Human anger, on the other hand, is often vicious and self-defensive. The Scriptures remind us that human anger may be righteous or unrighteous. For this reason the Bible gives us about three or four different admonitions to deal with the emotion.

First, we are admonished by the writer of Proverbs (6:34; 15:1; 16:14) not to incite others to anger.

Second, we are not to yield to unholy anger (Ps. 37:7-9; Prov. 14:29; 15:18; 16:32; 19:19; 21:14; 27:4) because as Jesus reminds us, it is the root of murder (Matt. 5:22), it does not produce righteousness (Jas. 1:19-20), and it must be controlled by those in authority (1 Tim. 2:8; Titus 1:7).

Third, it is an essential element of the man of God, whether he be a prophet of the OT or a minister of the NT. Man must be capable of a great love and/or a great anger. He must not only love God with all his soul, mind, and strength, but he must hate sin. Hate and anger are inseparable, as Jesus points out. Therefore it is imperative that we hate sin and love the sinner. God is the consuming Fire to settle the destinies of the sinner (Heb. 4:1-6; 12:18-29).

The fourth admonition is related to the third in that as we are re-created in the image of God, we are to be angry and sin not, and not let "the sun go down" on our anger (Eph. 4:26; Matt. 5:2).

See HATE (HATRED), PERFECT LOVE.

For Further Reading: *Baker's DCE;* Snaith, *A Theological Word Book of the Bible.*

ROBERT L. SAWYER, SR.

ANGLO-CATHOLICISM. The term Anglo-Catholicism denotes the loosely defined conviction of a large and influential minority of adherents to the Anglican tradition (Church of England, Protestant Episcopal church, etc.) that an authentically Christian church bears two marks: a line of specially ordained leaders, normally called bishops, which reaches back to the apostles in unbroken succession; and fidelity to the doctrinal and liturgical tradition of that succession.

Some Anglo-Catholics demand quite explicit and detailed conformity to the pre-Reformation tradition, insisting on the sacramental character of such acts as confession, confirmation, and ordination, in addition to the two sacraments accepted by Protestantism (baptism and the Lord's

Supper). They also claim an authority for the church and for tradition close to that claimed for Scripture, and give to worship, public and private, a priority coordinate with that of formal doctrinal statement.

"Anglo" refers to roots in the Church of England and is meant to distinguish this form of "catholicism" from Roman Catholicism. It rejects absolute papal authority and is not unanimous on such matters as purgatory, the invocation of saints, and the number and nature of the sacraments. It is not doctrinally anchored to the principle of justification by grace alone through faith, though many Anglo-Catholics believe thus. "Catholic" conveys the conviction that there is but one true church across the world and across time. With this conviction, many Anglo-Catholics do accept the pope as the first bishop among equals.

Always of influence within Anglicanism since the 1530s, Anglo-Catholicism's heyday was in the 19th century under the leadership of the Oxford Movement. Principal advocates have been Thomas Bilson (16th century), Lancelot Andrewes, and William Laud (17th century), William Law (until toward the end of his life, 18th century), and R. H. Froude, John Keble, and E. B. Pusey (19th century).

See CATHOLICISM (ROMAN), PROTESTANTISM.

For Further Reading: Hurst, *History of the Christian Church*, vol. 2. PAUL M. BASSETT

ANGLO-ISRAELISM. This teaching is concerned primarily with the identity of the Anglo-Saxon and Celtic peoples. These are found in Britain, Western Europe, the United States, and the Anglo areas of the British Commonwealth, i.e., Canada, Australia, and New Zealand. Anglo-Israelism claims that these peoples are the lineal descendants of the house of Israel, the 10 tribes of the Northern Kingdom, and are therefore the heirs of the OT promises concerning their expansion, prosperity, and divine protection (e.g., Isa. 27:6; 49:3, 6; 54:17; Jer. 51:20). "British Israelism," as this theory is frequently called, is neither a religious sect nor a political organization but regards itself as a fellowship of all those who embrace what it terms the "national message," viz., the Anglo-Israel identification.

Traces of this teaching are found in various Christian writers since the Reformation, but the more standard expositions are John Wilson's *Our Israelitish Origin* (London, 1840) and Edward Hine's *Identification of the British Nation with Lost Israel* (London, 1871). Currently there are affiliated Anglo-Israel federations in many parts of the world. The main organizational and publishing body is the British Israel World Federation with headquarters in London. This body is responsible for the most influential British-Israel periodical, the monthly, *The National Message.*

Following the fall of Samaria in 722-21 B.C., the 10 tribes, i.e., Israel as distinct from the Southern Kingdom of Judah, were taken captive to Assyria (2 Kings 17:5-18). From that time, the OT is silent about those exiled Israelites, but Anglo-Israelism claims that during the subsequent dissolution of the Assyrian Empire, they fled from Assyria and settled in areas south and east of the Black Sea. Centuries later they trekked through Asia Minor and finally into Europe and the British Isles in particular. These Jutes, Vikings, Angles, Normans, and Saxons, known collectively as Anglo-Saxons, are said to have been distinguished by their enterprise, expansion, and colonization. In the 17th and 18th centuries many of them migrated to populate North America, southern Africa, Australia, New Zealand, etc. Anglo-Israelism claims that this alleged continuing identification and worldwide influence is a fulfillment of the divine promises made to Abraham (Gen. 13:14-16; 17:19-21; 22:15-18) and particularly the promises renewed to Jacob (i.e., Israel, Gen. 35:11-12). Outside Scripture, British Israelism claims corroborating evidence in heraldry, archaeological discoveries, history, philology, and ethnology.

Most reputable Bible scholars view Anglo-Israelism as a fabric of fancy and speculation. The thesis depends not only on a literal, and very nationalistic, interpretation of the many promises made to Israel in the OT, but proof positive of the ethnic connections back to those people. In the light, however, of how the NT reinterprets many of these OT prophecies, it is equally acceptable to see all these promises spiritually fulfilled in the worldwide fellowship of Christ's Church (see, e.g., Acts 15:13-18; Rom. 9:24-26; Heb. 8:8-13). Also, whether or not these Anglo-Israel claims can be substantiated, salvation is only by personal faith in Christ and not on any grounds of alleged Israelite identification or privileged ancestry (Matt. 3:8-9; Rom. 9:6-9; Gal. 3:6-9).

See ISRAEL, PROMISES (DAVIDIC), CHURCH, KINGDOM OF GOD, RESTORATION OF ISRAEL.

For Further Reading: Berry, *British-Israelism: The Problem of the Lost Tribes.* HERBERT MCGONIGLE

ANNIHILATIONISM. This doctrine comes from the term *nihil,* which means "nothing," hence the doctrine that after death man ceases to exist and is "like the beasts that perish" (Ps. 49:12). This was the teaching of the ancient Sadducees, who denied the survival of the soul after death and appealed to the OT. Several biblical texts seem to support their position. When the Psalmist is facing death, he prays for a prolongation of his life with the plea, "Shall the dust praise thee?" (30:9; cf. 6:5). The voice of the cynic appears also in the Preacher, "For the fate of the sons of men and the fate of beasts is the same" (Eccles. 3:19, RSV).

The prevailing mood of the writers of the OT could infer that the soul survives in sheol in a semiconscious state, not unlike animals in hibernation. Even when it may assume (as in the Book of Kings) that no *future* rewards and punishments are to be expected, the writers come short of annihilationism. This view of extreme cynicism is attributed to the ungodly who not only deny a future life but even deny God's existence (Ps. 53:1; cf. 63:9-10).

Modern advocates of this doctrine, such as the Adventists, argue that it is a much more merciful doctrine than that of everlasting punishment for the impenitent; it is better that sinners be simply deprived of eternal life—that is punishment enough. However, it is contrary to many passages in the Scriptures, especially in the NT, which teach that all souls will survive the body either in everlasting bliss or torment. Jesus, specifically and emphatically, warned against eternal punishment (Matt. 5:29-30; 13:42, 50; 22:13; 25:30, 41, 46; Luke 16:19-31). And He refuted the Sadducees by declaring that they misinterpreted their Scriptures on the subject (Matt. 22:29-32).

See IMMORTALITY, CONDITIONAL IMMORTALITY, HELL.

For Further Reading: Smith, *The Bible Doctrine of the Hereafter;* Bultmann, *Thanatos* (Death); Kittel, 3:7-25; Stendahl, ed., *Immortality and Resurrection.*

GEORGE ALLEN TURNER

ANOINTING. Anointing, literally, is applying oil (or fat or grease) to a person or object. Persons have long been anointed to give relief from the sun (Ps. 104:15) or for cosmetic and medical purposes. In hot climates, oils and ointments were applied generously to the body after bathing. Herodotus reports that the Scythians never bathed but plastered their bodies with a sweet-smelling substance of thick consistency. Ancient Egyptians considered ointments a necessity. Workers have been known to strike because of lack of food and ointments. In many parts of the world today oils, ointments, and salves are used as cure-alls.

The ceremonial and metaphorical uses of *mashach* (in the OT) and of *chriō* (in the NT) are of special importance. From the Hebrew word comes *Messiah* and from the Greek word comes *Christ.* Oil is a symbol of the Holy Spirit. And Jesus is the Messiah or Christ—the Anointed One. In revealed religion, God uses anointing as the symbol of His relation to His people.

In the OT, kings and priests were inducted into office by the rite of pouring oil on their heads. The anointing was by a divine representative (as Samuel anointing Saul and David). While the connotations of magic are absent in the Scriptures, there is a definite implication of authority and of a power beyond the natural reach of mortal man. Emphasis was on both responsibility and enablement. When "God's anointed" (king) governed God's people, God was exercising His own Kingship through His anointed one. Likewise, the priest was representing man before God in the power of God in the divinely ordained way.

Prophets also are referred to as anointed, though specific ceremonial incidents are lacking. Possibly the references are metaphorical, as in Isa. 61:1. In any case, the essence of prophecy is to "speak from God" in the power of God.

Jesus, the Anointed One (Messiah, Christ), encompasses all three functions. He is Prophet, Priest, and King—in the ultimate sense. Since He is the "brightness of his [God's] glory, and the express image of his person" (Heb. 1:3), it pleased God to anoint Him "with the oil of gladness above [His] fellows" (v. 9). As the supreme Prophet, He "speaketh the words of God" because "God giveth not the Spirit by measure unto him" (John 3:34). He is a "priest for ever after the order of Melchisedec" (Heb. 7:17). And He is King of Kings and Lord of Lords (Rev. 19:16). The Anointed One is the fulfillment of the types and shadows in revealed religion. What oil only symbolizes, He manifests in himself. In Him dwells "all the fulness of the Godhead bodily" (Col. 2:9).

Anointing or unction is also for Christians. With the "unction from the Holy One" we have valid knowledge in the things of God (1 John 2:20). As the oil was poured out of old upon selected individuals, the Holy Spirit is poured out upon us (Acts 2:17). As Jesus was anointed to preach the gospel (Luke 4:18), we are established, anointed, and sealed to live and speak for Him (2 Cor. 1:21-22). Anointing, or unction, is a spiritual enablement. However, the symbolism continues in anointing the sick (Jas. 5:14). And at least one church (Mar Thoma, in India) pours oil into the waters of baptism.

See EMBLEMS OF THE HOLY SPIRIT, HOLY SPIRIT, POWER.

For Further Reading: Helmbold, "Anoint, Anointed," *ZPEB*, 1:170-72; Huey, Jr., "Ointment," *ZPEB*, 5:515-18; Wiley, *CT*, 2:324-25; Kittel, 9:493-580.

WILBER T. DAYTON

ANTHROPOLOGY. See MAN.

ANTHROPOMORPHISM. This is ascribing to God human characteristics. The word comes from the Greek *anthrōpos* for "man" and *morphos* for "form." Philosophical and theological problems arise whenever God in either His essence or action is described. His form of existence is different from that of man; and besides that, any attempt to describe Him is also an attempt to define, and thus to limit.

The transcendent God who is not only distinct but separate from creation poses little problem. When, however, God acts in His creation He is immanent. How is that action to be described in the language of man without speaking of God in human form?

This problem did not disturb the Hebrews as much as it did the Greeks. The OT describes God as "walking," "being angry," "smelling," "repenting"; ascribes to Him "arms," "feet," "eyes," "ears," "hands"; depicts Him as a woman screaming in childbirth, a beast tearing its prey, a moth eating a garment. There is, however, some sensitivity to the problem reflected in the later writings, but too much should not be made of this, because even the prophets use graphic anthropomorphical language.

Anthropomorphisms in the OT are not indications of primitive religious thought but are graphic portrayals of a living God. He is preeminently the Living One, the Source of life. The portrayal of God in dramatic imagery points to One who is suprahuman.

In the NT, God's essential spirituality is recognized (John 4:24), and thus, generally, He is not described in such vivid anthropomorphic terms as in the Old. However, the Incarnation, the ultimate anthropomorphism, speaks of both God's immanence and His livingness. God the Son, himself fully divine, literally and fully became man to live, die, and be raised from the dead to provide for our redemption.

See GOD, REVELATION (SPECIAL).

For Further Reading: Eichrodt, *Theology of the Old Testament;* Jacob, *Theology of the Old Testament.*

ROBERT D. BRANSON

ANTICHRIST. See MAN OF SIN.

ANTILEGOMENA. Origen (third century A.D.) called books not universally accepted in the NT canon *antilegomena* (spoken against) to distinguish them from *homologoumena* (on which all agree). Eusebius (fourth century A.D.) also used the term but referred to the antilegomena as "known to the majority." Both accepted most or all of the books of the present canon. The distinction seemed to be within the canon as opposed to apocryphal (hidden) or spurious.

Especially in Alexandria, certain popular books were used as if they were Scripture. These were weeded out of the canon by questions of authorship, apostolic authority, destination, and local reference. Similar questions were applied to certain less-known or less widely used books as Hebrews, James, 2 Peter, 2 and 3 John, and Jude. Origen included these and four noncanonical books in the antilegomena, as spoken against only in the sense of questioning their place in the canon. Ridderbos remarks that the early differences were more of usage than of principle (*The Authority of the New Testament Scriptures,* 48). No real conflicts are reported. Appreciable differences in practice were few and temporary.

See CANON, INSPIRATION (OF THE SCRIPTURES), APOCRYPHA, BIBLE.

For Further Reading: Ridderbos, *The Authority of the New Testament Scriptures,* 42-51; Harris, *Inspiration and Canonicity of the Bible;* Thiessen, *Introduction to the New Testament.*

WILBER T. DAYTON

ANTINOMIANISM. The word *antinomian* is a compound of two Greek words, *anti* (against) and *nomos* (law). The term identifies those who reject moral law as binding, in terms of conduct, for Christians. This stance has had adherents since the beginning of the Christian era. Exegetically, the belief overemphasizes and therefore misinterprets Paul's teaching that "Christ is the end of the law for righteousness to every one that believeth" (Rom. 10:4), forgetting that the same author in the same Epistle asked, "Do we then make void the law through faith? God forbid: yea, we establish the law" (3:31).

Theologically, antinomianism positions *law* and *grace* in an antithetical relationship, insisting that in choosing the latter, one has no further commitment to the former. Thus the ethical implications of "faith which worketh by love" (Gal. 5:6) are lessened, if not altogether destroyed, as a result of a serious misuse of the familiar term *free grace.*

Historically, outbreaks of antinomianism have appeared sporadically throughout Christendom since NT times. Sometimes political and social aspirations have combined with religious concerns to make it an enemy to be opposed by military might as well as disputational rhetoric.

Three features provide the structural framework for all varieties of antinomian teaching: (1) the "aristocratic democracy of the elect" who, claiming the moral law is abolished in Christ, are "free" in matters of church doctrine, polity, and practice; (2) a contempt for all "unregenerated" values and standards, of which moral law is a supreme example; (3) the all-sufficiency of a divine afflatus for any purpose whatsoever. Thus the need to read NT Epistles such as James is virtually abolished. These three matters produce, and are the product of, an acute individualism, an extreme libertinism, and a perfectionism where intention and fulfillment coincide.

Evangelical Christendom has rebutted antinomianism lengthily. At the center of the reply is this: That faith in Christ which is imputed for righteousness is not only the *condition* of salvation but also the *motivation* for Christian conduct in terms of a life clearly described by Christ in the Sermon on the Mount. Thus the logical thrust of justification is to lead to sanctification of heart and life.

See LAW, LAW AND GRACE, FREEDOM, CHRISTIAN ETHICS, HOLINESS.

For Further Reading: Fletcher, *Checks to Antinomianism;* Gataker, *Antinomianism Discovered and Confuted;* Huehns, *Antinomianism in English History.*

ELDON R. FUHRMAN

ANTIOCH, SCHOOL OF. Antioch, in NW Syria, was one of the three greatest cities of the Greco-Roman world. Many were converted here (Acts 11:21), and this is where the disciples were first called Christians (v. 26). In this church, the School of Antioch had its roots.

The common doctrinal characteristics of the Antiochene theologians were developed through the influence of their famous teachers. The originator of their distinctive emphasis was Diodore (d. 394), who later became bishop of Tarsus. He was instructor of John Chrysostom, the great preacher, and Theodore of Mopsuestia (d. 428), the greatest Bible commentator of antiquity. Antiochene theology was scholarly and critical, attaching great importance to the grammatical sense of Scripture and to the humanity and historical character of Jesus (F. J. Foakes-Jackson, *The History of the Christian Church,* 457). Antiochene theology was never fully developed. One of the more radical pupils of the school was Nestorius.

A unique relationship developed between the School of Antioch and the School of Alexandria. Sometimes their theology was complementary, other times in opposition. The School of Alexandria was more Platonic, mystical, and fond of allegorizing the Scripture, looking for a hidden meaning in the text. The School of Antioch tended to be Aristotelian, historical, and more literal. They were critical in their approach to Scripture, holding some parts to be of more doctrinal and spiritual value than others. Their method of exegesis was to find the sense intended by the inspired writer (F. L. Cross, ed., *ODCC,* 63). Theodore of Mopsuestia sought to curb the tendency of the Alexandrians to read the OT and the NT as "words of Christ" in the same sense of the term. One was not to read Scripture "without reference to the occasion and historical connection of the passage" (J. Pelikan, *The Christian Tradition,* 1:243).

The Antiochenes generally emphasized the humanity of Jesus over His divinity. They believed that the Logos, through taking the form of a servant (Phil. 2:5 ff), has himself become man for man's salvation. Also, that this salvation could not have been secured had not the Man Jesus been constant in His obedience to God's will (R. V. Sellers, *Two Ancient Christologies,* 143). These humanists emphasized the moral achievements of Christ in soteriology, and that man can freely choose to be in union with Him.

See ALEXANDRIAN SCHOOL, HERMENEUTICS, ALLEGORICAL INTERPRETATION, NESTORIANISM.

For Further Reading: *NIDCC,* 49; *Baker's DT,* 49 ff; Wiles, *The Christian Fathers,* 72 ff.

CHARLES WILSON SMITH

ANTITYPE. Antitype refers to the NT truth that is prefigured by an OT type. The antitype is the great NT reality that is foreshadowed by the OT picture (type). Thus the antitype is the culmination or fulfillment of the type.

Types served the purpose of preparing for the acceptance of NT truth. When John the Baptist presented Jesus as "the Lamb of God, which taketh away the sin of the world" (John 1:29), he was moving his hearers from the OT picture or type of the sacrifice of a lamb for atonement to the reality or antitype of the Son of God offering himself as the perfect atonement for sin.

By recognizing the correspondence between the antitype and the type, NT realities can be illustrated by the use of OT types. Laurence Wood shows that the Resurrection-Pentecost events of salvation history (the antitype) are illustrated by the Exodus-Conquest events in the history of the children of Israel (the type). Thus, the Promised

Land motif is an object lesson or picture of the "promise of the Father" (Acts 1:4; cf. Luke 24:49).

The recognition of the correspondence between the antitype and the type also underscores the continuity between the Old and New Testaments. That this continuity is real is borne out when Jesus, speaking to the two disciples on the road to Emmaus, "expounded unto them in all the scriptures the things concerning himself" (Luke 24:27). Christ is the primary antitype. In addition to the sacrificial lamb, He is variously prefigured by Adam, the ark of Noah, Isaac, Jonah, Melchizedek, the priesthood, etc.

See TYPE (TYPOLOGY), BIBLE (THE TWO TESTAMENTS), HERMENEUTICS.

For Further Reading: *ISBE,* 5:3029; Wood, *Pentecostal Grace,* 1-95.

GLENN R. BORING

ANXIETY. Theologically, this has to do most especially with Reinhold Niebuhr's understanding as expressed in his Gifford Lectures, published as *The Nature and Destiny of Man.* Niebuhr says that anxiety arises in us because we see that we are both unlimited, with vast possibilities, and limited, unable to accomplish our potential. He says anxiety is desirable; that we should not try to resolve it, but that we should live with it. If we try to resolve it by asserting the limited side of our nature, we enter into sinfulness. Alcoholism is a result of trying to resolve our anxiety by asserting that limited side of our nature. If, instead, we try to resolve our anxiety by disregarding our limitations and asserting our possibilities, we enter into sinful pride—which last would be Pharisaism, the ultimate sin (since we do not think we need any redemption when we actually do).

Other theories of anxiety, more psychological, also have theological dimensions, because anxiety in any form reduces spiritual victory and ability to cope with life. In fact, anxiety is such a pervasive malady of contemporary society that major attention to it has been given by all schools of psychiatry and psychology. Unfortunately, too many panaceas have missed the primary cause, which is guilt; or else all guilt has been dissolved by denying its reality—thus compounding anxieties manyfold in the long run.

See CARNALITY AND HUMANITY, GROW (GROWTH), VICTORY, FRUIT OF THE SPIRIT, GUILT, MATURITY, PEACE.

For Further Reading: Barkman, *Man in Conflict;* Mavis, *The Psychology of Christian Experience.*

J. KENNETH GRIDER

APOCALYPTIC, APOCALYPSE. The title *apocalyptic* is applied to a type of largely Jewish literature dating for the most part between 170 B.C. and A.D. 135. The period began with the Maccabean rebellion and climaxed in the Bar Kokhba revolt at the end. It was an era of upheaval and recurring crises, a situation reflected in one after another of the apocalyptic books. The apocalyptic message was directed to a people in trouble, a people who could not otherwise understand the working of God in the midst of persecution and overwhelming evil. In such circumstances the apocalyptists attempted to rationalize and justify the ways of God with man and thereby to instill courage and confidence in God's people.

The term *apocalyptic* is derived from the Greek noun *apokalupsis,* which means a "disclosure" or "revelation." The NT Book of Revelation generally fits the apocalyptic literary style and is the first known book to be designated as an *apokalupsis* (Rev. 1:1). Another common title for the book therefore is The Apocalypse.

The nearest OT parent of apocalyptic was the Book of Daniel, which furnished many of the themes and a good deal of the symbolism for the later literature. But the historical roots of apocalyptic may be traced back to other OT books, particularly to Isaiah 56—66, several passages in Ezekiel, and to Zechariah 9—14.

The most obviously apocalyptic books from the period 170 B.C. to A.D. 135 are *1 Enoch, 4 Ezra,* and *2 Baruch.* The latter two books are of special interest because they were probably written during the same generation as Revelation, and they reflect numerous parallels with this last book of the NT. But in addition to these three books, several other writings which originated at this time contain apocalyptic passages and elements. These include *Jubilees, Sibylline Oracles* (especially Books 3, 4, 5), the *Testaments of the Twelve Patriarchs* (especially the Testament of Levi), *Psalms of Solomon* (especially Psalms 17-18), the *Assumption of Moses,* the *Apocalypse of Moses* (especially chap. 29), the *Apocalypse of Abraham* (especially chaps. 9—32) the *Testament of Abraham,* and *2 Enoch.*

The apocalyptic books were chiefly concerned to reveal what had previously been hidden, particularly secrets about the heavenly world and the time of the end of the present world. These secrets were allegedly given in ancient times to OT worthies, but their content was sealed until the time of the end (cf. Dan. 12:9), to be disclosed to the last generation of the faithful.

Throughout apocalyptic, eschatology determines everything that is said. The apocalyptist possessed a strong consciousness of living at the end of the old age, just prior to the dawn of the new age. He expected the OT eschatological events to occur imminently. He was pessimistic about any good coming from the present age, which he regarded as totally dominated by Satan and evil powers and abandoned by God. His hope was in the imminent kingdom of God which would break in violently from beyond history.

See REVELATION (BOOK OF), HERMENEUTICS, ESCHATOLOGY, PROPHET (PROPHECY).

For Further Reading: Hanson, *The Dawn of Apocalyptic;* Morris, *Apocalyptic;* Rowley, *The Relevance of Apocalyptic;* Russell, *The Method and Message of Jewish Apocalyptic.*

FRED D. LAYMAN

APOCRYPHA. The term Apocrypha (from *apokryphos,* "hidden") designates a collection of documents which at times has been included with the Christian Scriptures. These writings originated in a time of religious and political ferment in the life of Judaism, mainly from the two centuries preceding and the century following the birth of Christ. They constitute only a small portion of the surviving literary production from that period. To this time also belong the Pseudepigrapha and the Dead Sea Scrolls.

The books of the Apocrypha are normally listed as:

1 Esdras
2 Esdras
Tobit
Judith
The Additions to Esther
The Wisdom of Solomon
Ecclesiasticus, or the Wisdom of Jesus the Son of Sirach
Baruch
The Letter of Jeremiah
Additions to the Book of Daniel
- *a.* The Prayer of Azariah and the Song of the Three Young Men
- *b.* Susanna
- *c.* Bel and the Dragon

The Prayer of Manasseh
1 Maccabees
2 Maccabees

These writings were preserved because of the importance inscribed to them by various segments of the Jewish and Christian communities. Although never a part of the Hebrew canon, they were included in the Greek OT or Septuagint which, along with the NT, became the Bible of the Early Church. When the Latin Bible or Vulgate appeared, the Apocrypha was included. As a result these writings functioned as a part of the Church's Scripture until the Protestant Reformation.

With the Reformation there was a gradual change. Although often printing the Apocrypha as part of its Bible, Protestantism did not consider it as authoritative as the Hebrew canon and the NT writings. The Roman Catholic church, in reaction to the Reformers, soon declared it to be canonical and of equal value for doctrine with the OT and NT. The Apocrypha remains an integral part of Catholic versions of the Bible. Martin Luther included the Apocrypha in his first complete Bible translation in 1634 with the heading, "Apocrypha, that is books which are not held to be equal to Holy Scripture and yet are profitable and good to read." Subsequent to the Reformation these books were sometimes excluded but more often included in the printed editions of the Bible. They were not, however, ever accorded the status of canonical Scripture. The first edition of the King James Bible of 1611 printed the Apocrypha as a separate work and inserted it between the Testaments.

The books of the Apocrypha are of lasting value for our knowledge of the historical and religious situations from which they arose. They are a significant record of men in conflict over political, moral, and spiritual values. As such their message transcends their own times.

See ANTILEGOMENA, CANON, BIBLICAL AUTHORITY, INSPIRATION OF THE BIBLE.

For Further Reading: Metzger, ed., *The Oxford Annotated Apocrypha, Revised Standard Version;* Charles, ed., *The Apocrypha and Pseudepigrapha in English, with Introductions and Critical and Explanatory Notes to the Several Books,* vol. 1; Metzger, *An Introduction to the Apocrypha;* Eissfeldt, *The Old Testament: An Introduction,* 574-602; Pfeiffer, *History of New Testament Times, with an Introduction to the Apocrypha,* 233-524.

FRANK G. CARVER

APOLLINARIANISM. Apollinarius, bishop of Laodicea (d. 390), was the first theologian known to grapple with the question of how the divine and human natures could unite in Christ. A convinced believer in realistic redemption, he insisted that the union and fusion of the two natures was absolutely essential to salvation. While accepting with Athanasius the full deity of Christ, he considered the Arians were right in objecting to the current doctrine that it predicated of Christ two personalities, saying: "If perfect God were joined to perfect man, there would be two—one, Son of God by nature, one by adoption."

Applying the logic that two perfect entities cannot become one, he insisted that if Christ possessed a rational human soul He could not be God incarnate but only a God-inspired man. Furthermore, how can we ascribe freedom of will to the Man Jesus without making Him mutable and liable to sin? For these reasons he felt obliged to deny the completeness of Christ's humanity.

At first he taught that the Logos had taken merely a human body. Later, however, he developed a view, based on a trichotomous psychology, that Christ's body *(sōma)* and soul *(psychē)* were human, but that the place of the human spirit *(pneuma)* was assumed by the Logos. Thus the mutable human spirit in Christ was replaced by the immutable Divine Word. The Logos and abridged human nature were fused in "a single nature," "a single essence." Instead of two natures, which imply two self-determining subjects, there is but one incarnate nature of God the Word.

Mackintosh levels three criticisms at this view. (1) Christ's humanity is a partial and mutilated personality. The part left out is that which alone is capable of God, and the remaining humanity is simply that of the beasts. (2) Since sin is primarily an affair of human willfulness, Christ failed to take possession of the focal point of human life and need and therefore left our situation unredeemed. "That which is unassumed is unhealed" (Gregory Nazianzen). (3) Employing physical and metaphysical rather than ethical categories, Apollinarius defined God and man as absolute contraries which render the theanthropic union impossible. "The sublime thought that Christ is perfect in His humanity just because of the personal indwelling of God, and thereby becomes the Head of a new redeemed race, has completely fallen out of sight."

Apollinarianism was condemned by the Second Ecumenical Council, held in Constantinople, in 381.

See CHRIST, CHRISTOLOGY, HYPOSTATIC UNION, ADOPTIONISM.

For Further Reading: Wiley, *CT,* 2:158-59; McGiffert, *A History of Christian Thought,* 1:277-82; Berkouwer, *The Person of Christ,* 64-66; Mackintosh, *The Person of Jesus Christ,* 196-201. WILLIAM M. GREATHOUSE

APOLOGETICS. Apologetics (Gr. *apologētikos*) is the science which presents the proofs and fundamentals of things or systems. The root meaning of the verb *to apologize* (Gr. *apologeisthai*) is "to answer," "to account for," "to defend," or "to justify." An apology (Gr. *apologia*) is a verbal or written discourse in defense or praise of persons or things. Christian apologetics refers properly not to a science, but to the art of defending or explaining the Christian faith to the nonbeliever. Since through the centuries nonbelievers have been of many different sorts, Christian apologetics has assumed a diversity of postures and has used a diversity of methods. In this sense the Judeo-Christian tradition has a rich apologetic history that goes back to its very beginning.

The OT, for instance, is not merely a recital of past events, but rather a theologically interpreted account of Yahweh's activity in history in relation to His chosen people Israel. We see, therefore, in the broadest sense of the term, an "accounting for" God's actions, or an apologetic concern.

Likewise, the very structure of the NT may be considered to be apologetic in the sense that the thinking and the witnessing of the holy writers are directed to religious persuasion, i.e., to give a convincing account of God's activity in Christ. The best examples of this are the Gospel of Mark, and Peter's and Paul's speeches in the Book of Acts.

The most outstanding apologies in favor of Christianity, however, come from the second and third centuries, when some of the earliest Christian apologists (Justin Martyr, Origen, Tertullian) defended the Christian faith from the threats of heresies and the hostility from the Roman Empire during those critical centuries when Christianity was struggling for survival.

During the Reformation, apologetics was represented by the great Reformers (Luther, Calvin, Zwingli), who defended among other things the principle of *sola Scriptura,* in opposition to the traditional position of the Roman Catholic church which endorsed both Scripture and tradition as sources of authority. During the post-Reformation period apologetics was directed to the defense of the supernatural and the historical reliability of Scripture against those who denied the supernatural and held that both the Bible and tradition were unreliable sources of historical truth. Towards the end of the 19th century, Christian apologetics centered about the historical reliability of the Gospels, especially their testimony to the resurrection and divinity of Christ. Modern apologetics is directed toward the issue of the relevance of the gospel to the "here and now" temporal existence of man. The best-known apologist in the 20th century was C. S. Lewis, the Oxford don.

See THEISTIC PROOFS, THEOLOGICAL LANGUAGE, COMPARATIVE RELIGION, CREDENTIALS OF SCRIPTURE.

For Further Reading: Rogers, *The Case for Christianity: An Outline of Popular Apologetics;* Sweet, *The Verification of Christianity: Introductory Studies in Christian Apologetics.* ISMAEL E. AMAYA

APOSTASY. The Greek word *apostasia* appears twice in the NT (Acts 21:21; 2 Thess. 2:3). In English versions it is usually translated "falling away," a term descriptive of what will happen when the man of sin, or the Antichrist, is revealed. It expresses the idea of abandonment of the faith, an unbelief which jettisons hope and is in fact a capitulation to the false beliefs of heretics.

But apostasy is not just a thing of the future. There is an obvious awareness of this danger in the early literature of the Jews. Note the warnings and prohibitions in the laws of Moses (Exod. 20:3-23; Deut. 6:14; 11:16). When the 12 tribes took possession of the land in the days of Joshua, caution was exercised with regard to the danger of apostasy (Josh. 22:21-29). Jude reviews the period of Israel's history following the Red Sea deliverance and states that apostasy did in fact take place (Jude 5-7). Furthermore, it is stated that not only are men capable of apostasy but also angels.

In classical Greek the term signifies a defection or revolt from a military commander. Following in its wake came shame, disgrace, infamy, and reproach or censure. The victim was thus labelled a deserter.

When the history of the Early Church is examined, it is apparent that in many instances the persecutions produced a harvest of apostasy. Against this backdrop the martyrdoms stand in marked contrast. The developing heresies also produced their share of turncoats. Paul warns the Thessalonians with regard to this possibility (2 Thess. 2:2-3).

Apostasy needs to be differentiated from what might be described as falling into error. Ignorance may result in error (Acts 19:1-6), or a Christian may suddenly discover that he has been ensnared by Satan (2 Tim. 2:25-26). Merrill F. Unger defines apostasy "as the act of a professed Christian, who knowingly and deliberately rejects revealed truth regarding the deity of Christ ([1] John 4:1-3) and redemption through his atoning sacrifice (Phil. 3:18; II Pet. 2:1)." Heb. 6:4-6 is a sobering delineation of apostasy.

The *ISBE* lists the following causes and examples of apostasy: "Causes of: persecution (Mt. 24:9-10); false teachers (Mt. 24:11); temptation (Lk. 8:13); worldliness (2 Tim. 4:4); defective knowledge of Christ (1 Jn. 2:19); moral lapse (Heb. 6:4-6); forsaking worship and spiritiual living (10:25-31); unbelief (3:12). Biblical examples: Saul (1 Sam. 15:11); Amaziah (2 Ch. 25:14-27); many disciples (Jn. 6:66); Hymenaeus and Alexander (1 Tim. 1:19-20); Demas (2 Tim. 4:10). For further illustration see Deut. 13:13; Zeph. 1:4-6; Gal. 5:4; 2 Pet. 2:20-21" (1:202).

See BACKSLIDING, PERSEVERANCE, ETERNAL SECURITY.

For Further Reading: Kittel, 1:512-13; *ISBE*, 1:202; *Unger's Bible Dictionary*, 72. ROBERT A. MATTKE

APOSTLE. This word is a transliteration of the Greek *apostolos*, which means "sent one." The Greek root is *stel* which means literally "to set in order" or "to equip." In classical Greek usage *stel* was a noun denoting "naval expedition" or "bill of lading." The eventual controlling idea, expressed in *apostolos*, was that of equipping or commissioning. Thus, the noun came to mean "delegate," "ambassador," "messenger," or "missionary." The NT employs apostle in this sense.

The 12 disciples, who were chosen by Christ and who accompanied Him throughout His ministry, became known as apostles. Generally, to speak of "the apostles" is to refer to this particular group of men. The Synoptic Gospels and the Book of Acts follow this practice, with the exception of a reference to Paul and Barnabas as apostles (Acts 14:14). In the rest of the NT the title is used of a larger group of Christian leaders. In Romans, Paul claims this title for himself (1:1) and for Andronicus and Junias (16:7). He also speaks of James, the Lord's brother, as an apostle (Gal. 1:19; cf. Epaphroditus in the Greek text of Phil. 2:25). The author of Hebrews uses the title for Christ (3:1). The general impression is that the Church, following the time of Paul, restricted the use of this word to the Twelve and Paul.

Paul's statement that the Church is "built upon the foundation of the apostles and prophets" (Eph. 2:20; 3:5) implies that the apostles were a group of persons with special roles in the founding and administering of the Church in its primitive period. This thesis finds support in the qualifications set down by the pre-Pentecostal community of followers for the selection of a replacement for Judas (Acts 1:15-26). The person must have been with Jesus throughout His ministry and must have witnessed His resurrection. Matthias therefore took on the "apostleship from which Judas turned aside" (v. 25, NASB, RSV).

Moreover, the apostles went on special evangelistic missions to other geographical areas (Acts 8:14-25; 9:32; 10:1-48; Gal. 2:11-14). It appears that the essential activity of the apostles was to proclaim the Word (Acts 1:7-8; 20:24; Rom. 11:13; 2 Cor. 6:3 ff). The task of these persons was a unique, first-century task, which included not only a firsthand witness to Christ but also guidance to the growing Church in matters of theology and the development of leadership.

The apostolate was a creation of the risen Lord. Its function was to proclaim the Good

News under the anointing of the Spirit. A strong missionary concern characterized its ministry.

See APOSTOLIC SUCCESSION, CLERGY.

For Further Reading: Munck, "Paul, the Apostles, and the Twelve," *Studia Theologia* 3 (1949); Rengstorf, "Apostello," Kittel, vol. 1; Schmithals, *The Office of the Apostle in the Early Church.* WILLARD H. TAYLOR

APOSTLES' CREED. This is a direct descendant of the *Rituale Romanum,* the "Old Roman Creed" current among Christians at Rome from about A.D. 150. The original form of words was used chiefly as a Trinitarian baptismal confession of faith (cf. Matt. 28:19). It was apparently framed in opposition to Marcion for the purpose of guarding candidates for church membership against his errors. Phrases were added through the centuries, but in substance the present creed is virtually identical with the *Rituale Romanum.*

In protecting the faith from the Marcionite heresy, the Church appealed to the apostolic witness. The Trinitarian framework is filled in with key historical and theological affirmations which reveal the creed's biblical roots. Both in content and phraseology the creed is strikingly similar to that of the NT witness to the faith of the earliest Church. Christianity began with certain indubitable historical events which occurred "under Pontius Pilate." But the history enshrined is *interpreted* history, and the symbol is a confession of *faith* in Jesus Christ, who He was and what God was doing "for us men and our salvation" through Him. The creed is the faith of the *Church* and not of the individual as such. *Credo* ("I believe") is the believer's personal signature to the apostolic witness.

Rooted as it is in the biblical revelation and formulated originally as the "Old Roman Creed," the *Textus Receptus* dates from the eighth century. Recognized later by the churches of the Reformation, the Apostles' Creed became the fundamental confession of the common Christian faith. The following analysis is intended to show more definitely the various ages when the present clauses were added and to suggest in general the meaning which has attached to the various statements.

"I believe in God the Father Almighty" is ancient. "Almighty" is more accurately "all-controlling."

"Creator of heaven and earth" was not in the *Rituale Romanum* but is found from the earliest times in the Eastern creeds. It appeared first in the Western creed about A.D. 375.

"And in Jesus Christ his Son our Lord" is ancient. "Jesus" means "Savior" and is the name of the Man, while "Christ" means "anointed" and is representative of God. "Our Lord" designates Him as the Object of our faith and obedience.

"Who was [conceived] of the Holy Spirit, born of the virgin Mary, [suffered] under Pontius Pilate, was crucified, [dead], and buried" is ancient.

"Descended into hell *[infernos]*" is from the late fourth century but without any controversial animus. It is generally understood to mean that our Lord descended into the realm of the dead, preached to them, and led away to Paradise those who would follow Him. "Hell" here certainly does not signify *gehenna* but *hadēs,* the place of departed spirits (see Acts 2:27).

"The third day He arose again from the dead, ascended to heaven, where he sits at the right hand of [God] the Father [Almighty]" is ancient. It signifies that the glorified Jesus now lives with God in glory.

"[From thence] He shall come again to judge the living and the dead" is ancient.

"I believe in the Holy [Catholic] Church." *Catholicam* (late fourth or fifth century) at first meant universal as opposed to local, but from the third century the universal Church as opposed to the schismatic or heretical.

"The communion of saints" is contemporary with *catholicam* and signifies the unity of the life of all the Church, living and dead.

"The forgiveness of sins, the resurrection of the flesh" is ancient. "The body will be raised—the same body by personal continuity, but in a very different condition—a spiritual body" (Wiley).

"And in the life everlasting" is late fourth century.

See CREED (CREEDS), MARCIONISM, ORTHODOXY.

For Further Reading: Wiley, *CT,* 1:40-42; McGiffert, *A History of Christian Thought,* 1:156-65; Barr, *From the Apostles' Faith to the Apostles' Creed;* Barclay, *The Apostles' Creed for Everyman.*

WILLIAM M. GREATHOUSE

APOSTOLIC CONSTITUTIONS AND CANONS. A fourth-century collection of decisions made by earlier councils and leaders concerning Christian faith and church order. Its sources are the now lost *Didascalia Apostolorum,* a Greek manual on church order from early third-century Syria; the *Didache,* a Greek church order from the early second century; Hipollytus of Rome's *Concerning Spiritual Gifts* (now lost) and *Apostolic Tradition* from the early third century. Its familiarity with the worship patterns of Antioch (Syria) and its internal references and sources seem to place its origins in Syria about 380. The language with which it talks about Christ indicates that its compiler was not a strictly orthodox Christian but a moderate Arian (the difference then was not as clear as it later became) who nonetheless had no concern in this document to evangelize for or against any particular Christian positions.

Although its original title was "The Ordinances of the Holy Apostles Through Clement," there seems never to have been any inclination to accept the work as being authentically apostolic in origin. In the West, where the Roman church predominated, only the first 50 Apostolic Canons, which are found in VIII 47, were generally accepted as binding. The rest of the work, including the other 35 canons, varied in authority according to time and place. The canons themselves were taken from the *Constitutions* and the canons of councils at Antioch (341) and Laodicea (363). The last of the canons lists the biblical books accepted as canonical in the church of the 380s. It excludes Revelation but includes the Apostolic *Constitutions* and the two letters traditionally called the Epistles of Clement to the Corinthians.

The *Constitutions* is not an orderly book, but there is some coherence to each of its eight books (we would call them chapters). Book I is for the laity and is especially concerned to warn them about the kinds of association with pagans that would destroy their ethical sensitivities. Book II is for the clergy and presents the qualities of character, the prerogatives, and the duties belonging to each of the orders of clergy: bishops, presybters, and deacons. It also treats the question of penitential discipline. Book III considers widows and their special office in the church. A consideration of their limitations carries the author-compiler to a concern for the duties of deacons. And he also puts a small treatise on baptism in this book. Book IV talks about the Christian's concern for charitable works, especially for such persons as orphans. Book V moves from a discussion of the Christian's responsibility toward those suffering persecution to discussions of martyrdom and idolatry. Book VI offers a history of earlier schisms and heresies.

From the perspective of influence in the later church, Books VII and VIII are most important. Book VII, which has 49 chapters, is a manual on church order. Chapters 1—32, which are based on the *Didache*, talk of baptism and the Lord's Supper and of such practices as fasting; 33—38 is a collection of prayers of Jewish origin; 39—45 present the rites of baptism and a prototype of confirmation as they were practiced in Antioch; 46—49 are also liturgical materials. Book VIII, in 47 chapters, interweaves several concerns, including several liturgies and a section on the duties of various persons (16—46). The so-called Liturgy of St. Clement, for the consecration of a bishop, is especially valuable as it contains a complete Eucharistic service. It is in chaper 47 that one finds the Apostolic Canons as has been mentioned.

The Apostolic *Constitutions* and Canons were exceptionally important in the early and medieval church as guides to understanding the nature of the church and its worship.

See APOSTOLIC FATHERS.

For Further Reading: Witteick, *A History of Christian Thought*, 44-56; Westcott, *A General Survey of the History of the Canon of the New Testament.*

PAUL M. BASSETT

APOSTOLIC DECREES. Apostolic refers to something traceable to the apostles. Decrees are resolutions proposed by the apostles at the Council of Jerusalem about A.D. 50 (Acts 15).

The Jerusalem Council convened to decide a critical issue that had arisen in connection with the spread of the gospel to the Gentiles and which threatened to divide the Early Church. The issue was: Shall Gentiles who convert to the Christian faith be *required* to accept the ritual for Gentile proselytes to the Jewish faith, especially circumcision? After debating pro and con, the council decided with Paul that salvation was by faith, not by works of the law such as circumcision.

Having settled this crucial theological issue, however, there remained a practical issue of table fellowship between Jewish and Gentile believers. It was difficult for a first-century Jew, even a Christian Jew, to eat at the same table with a Gentile, even a Christian Gentile. This difficulty was compounded if the Gentiles ate food which was abhorred by Jews. The council recommended, therefore, that Gentile Christians abstain from food and practices obnoxious to the Jews (Acts 15:20, 29).

There were four apostolic decrees according to the ancient Alexandrian text. The Gentiles were asked to abstain from (1) things associated with idols; (2) fornication; (3) what is strangled; and (4) blood. The later Western text omits "what is strangled" and regards the prohibitions as referring to the three cardinal sins: (1) idolatry; (2) fornication; and (3) murder. The Alexandrian text commands the strongest evidence and is preferred by most translations (cf. Acts 15:20).

See CIRCUMCISION, JUDAISTIC CONTROVERSY, FREEDOM, LAW AND GRACE.

For Further Reading: Bruce, *The Acts of the Apostles: The Greek Text;* Bruce, *The Book of Acts, The New International Commentary on the New Testament;* Mounce, "Apostolic Decree," *Baker's DT,* 59-60.

J. WESLEY ADAMS

APOSTOLIC FATHERS. The title Apostolic Fathers is given to a group of second-generation Christian writers who are believed to be (and in many cases were) immediate followers of the original 12 apostles and whose theology is in harmony with those original apostles. The adjective "apostolic" is applied therefore, either to the fact that they were disciples of the apostles, or that their theology is orthodox.

Strictly speaking, the name can be given to only three (or perhaps four) personalities in the Early Church: Ignatius (c. A.D. 35-107), bishop of the church in Antioch in Syria, and author of six letters to churches in Asia Minor and one to Polycarp, bishop of Smyrna; Polycarp himself (c. A.D. 69-155), bishop of Smyrna and author of an epistle to the church at Philippi; and Clement, bishop of Rome (flourished around A.D. 95), who wrote a letter to the church at Corinth in the name of the Roman community. There are also fragments of the writings of Papias, bishop of Hierapolis, extant, but they do not give us a great deal of information regarding the personality of their author.

Other writings which are included among the Apostolic Fathers while, in many cases bearing the names of well-known personalities in the Church, are, in fact, anonymous. These writings are: the epistle of Barnabas; the "second" epistle of Clement; the Teaching of the Twelve Apostles (known as the *Didache*); the Shepherd of Hermas; and the epistle of Diognetus. All of these writings are dated between the end of the first and the beginning of the second centuries A.D. and are extremely important sources of information on the expansion and inner development of Christianity in the period immediately prior to the earliest Christian historians and apologists.

In four areas the writings of the Apostolic Fathers are of particular value for the student of Christian origins:

1. In the first place they give crucial information on the status of the writings which were later collected to form the NT. They are the only link we possess between the autographs and the church's canon. Rarely do the Fathers quote the NT as such; but their allusions are a tantalizing challenge to the scholar in reconstructing the way to the canon of the NT, and demonstrate that the idea, if not the fact, of a canon was already in existence.

2. The second area of importance is the development of the idea of the Christian ministry and church government. This is particularly true of the epistles of Ignatius with their strong promotion of the office of the bishop. We must be careful, however, not to seek in Ignatius early evidence for the later episcopal system. For Ignatius, the bishop has an exclusively local function and is therefore equivalent to a modern pastor. (Interestingly, in his epistle to the Romans he makes no mention of a bishop there!) There is not the slightest hint of a bishop standing in succession to an apostle, nor are there any sacerdotal functions associated with the office.

3. The fathers are also a valuable source of information on the developing liturgical practice of the Church. In the *Didache,* for example, information is given of the practice of baptism ("In running water . . . and if you are not able to baptize in cold water, then in warm" [*Did.* 7.2]) and of celebrating the Lord's Supper ('Let no one eat or drink of this eucharistic thanksgiving except those who have been baptized" [*Did.* 9.5]).

4. Finally, the fathers are a valuable source for the study of the Christian understanding of the OT. The writer of the epistle of Barnabas has left us with one of the most valuable examples of a thoroughgoing Christian typological understanding of the OT. The OT is ransacked for "types" of events of the Christian era, and the claim is made that this Christianized reinterpretation is nothing less than the divine intention in the OT record. His interpretations are at once a fascinating and fantastic insight into the Christian use of the OT.

See APOSTOLIC SUCCESSION, CANON, ANTIOCH (SCHOOL OF), ALLEGORICAL INTERPRETATION.

For Further Reading: Lightfoot and Harmer, *The Apostolic Fathers.*

THOMAS FINDLAY

APOSTOLIC SUCCESSION. Apostolic Succession is the dogma of the Catholic church by which it teaches that the mission and the sacred power to teach and rule that Christ conferred to His apostles are perpetuated in the church's college of bishops. Although the Catholic church recognizes the uniquenes of the role that the apostles had as eyewitnesses, and of having been personally chosen and sent by Christ to proclaim the kingdom of God and lay the foundation of the church, it believes that the apostles had successors in their pastoral mission, to whom their unique authority as overseers was transmitted.

This doctrine has ecclesiastical but not scriptural authority. Nowhere in the NT are found any words of Christ or the apostles teaching the doctrine of apostolic succession.

There is no clear evidence of the early development of the tradition of apostolic succession. It was not until the fifth century that historians began to trace a chain of Roman popes back to Peter. From this time on, the church claimed its bishops as the successors of the apostles. It was on the basis of this tradition that the Councils of Trent, Vatican I, and Vatican II declared the bishops to have by divine right special apostolic authority. Vatican II further explained that it is the episcopal college that succeeds to the apostolic college; individual bishops, therefore, share in the apostolic succession by their membership in the episcopal body.

Protestants have had no problem in accepting the perpetuity of the apostolic office. In every generation God has raised up ministers and messengers who fulfilled the Great Commission in the apostolic spirit and in the power of the Holy Spirit, but not pretending to the special authority invested in the original Twelve. What Protestantism rejects is the doctrine which invalidates the ordination of men whose ordination is not by hands authorized by bishops in an approved Roman line of succession, as if the stream of power and authority flowed through this narrow stream and no other.

See CHURCH GOVERNMENT, APOSTLE, CLERGY, ORDAIN (ORDINATION).

For Further Reading: Brown, *Apostolical Succession in the Light of History and Fact;* Enrardt, *The Apostolic Succession in the First Two Centuries of the Church;* Ralston, *Elements of Divinity,* 866-71. ISMAEL E. AMAYA

ARIANISM. This is the anti-Trinitarianism of Arius, which held that Christ was not eternal; that He was made "out of nothing"; that His substance or nature was not the same as that of the Father, but quite different, a lower kind of nature—neither divine nor human, but a third kind, in between deity and humanity.

Arius, a presbyter at Alexandria, conflicted with his bishop in about A.D. 318 over this kind of teaching, and the first Ecumenical Council was convened in A.D. 325 at Nicea to discuss the matter. Bishops numbering 318, from both the East and the West, came together, and Emperor Constantine presided. They voted overwhelmingly against the Arian view—there being only about 20 bishops in all who were either Arian (saying Christ's nature was *unlike* that of the Father), or in agreement with Eusebius, who said Christ's nature was *like* that of the Father *(homoiousios).*

Since the view voted as orthodox, that Christ's nature was the same as that of the Father, *homoousios* (without the *i*), Historian Gibbon later made light of the matter by saying that it was a huge squabble merely over a diphthong. Yet most historians of doctrine would agree that it was indeed a gravely significant issue. Not only was it significant because the orthodox teaching came to be that Christ was fully divine instead of less than divine, but because, of all the Christological heresies, Arianism came to be believed the most widely and the most persistently in the West. Sometimes, during the 50 years after Nicea, it was Athanasius who was sent into exile, while Arianism was given status. And still later, many peoples, especially among the barbarians who helped to make up the Roman Empire, were Arian. Besides, it has been revived in modern times in Socinianism and Unitarianism.

See UNITARIANISM, SOCINIANISM, ATHANASIAN CREED, CHRISTOLOGY, HYPOSTASIS.

For Further Reading: Athanasius, "Discourse I Against the Arians," *A Library of Fathers of the Catholic Church,* vol. 18; Leith, *Creeds of the Churches;* MacGregor, *The Nicene Creed;* Orr, *The Progress of Dogma.*
J. KENNETH GRIDER

ARK OF THE COVENANT. The central object of the Tabernacle was the ark of the covenant, sometimes referred to as the "ark of the testimony," "ark of God," and "ark of the Lord." The phrase "ark of the covenant" implies two theological truths relating to law and grace. Law may be seen in the contents of the chest, while grace can be seen in its lid called the "mercy seat," a pure gold cover (Exod. 25:17) surrounded by two antithetically-placed cherubim with outspread wings. These heavenly figures were not detached but were sculptured into the pure gold mercy seat itself.

As is usually the case in biblical presentations, God gave Moses very specific instructions as to how to construct the ark with a somewhat limited explanation as to its purpose. At a later date when the ark was pressed into the religious service of the nation, its purpose would become clear (Num. 10:33-36). The Bible's minimal use of explanation and maximal use of affirmation (and command) is in deference to man's freedom to choose. True choice implies man's ability to make decisions while not fully understanding why. Were it not for this specific biblical procedure, decision making would require very little faith.

God's precise instruction was to make a rectangular box of acacia wood measuring 2½ by 1½ by 1½ cubits (i.e., 3¾ by 2¼ by 2¼ feet), covered both inside and outside with gold, to be carried (when the camp moved) on poles inserted in rings located at the four lower corners. Bezaleel made the ark at Sinai according to God's exact instruction to Moses. Upon completion it became the receptacle for the two tablets of the Decalogue (Exod. 25:16, 21; 40:20; Deut. 10:1-5): and Heb. 9:4-5 indicates that it contained also the golden pot of manna (Exod. 16:33-34), and Aaron's rod which budded (Num. 17:10). Its especially designated place was in the holy of holies.

When the moment arrived for the congregation to leave Sinai, the ark of the covenant "went before them" (Num. 10:33). It played a significant role at the crossing of the Jordan (Joshua 3—4) and the fall of Jericho (chap. 6); but it was to be carried into battle only with God's specific command. Years later when it was carried into battle against the Philistines without God's orders (1 Sam. 4:3-4), tragedy occurred and the ark was captured. The ark was permanently deposited at Shiloh by Joshua and still resided there at the close of the period of the judges (1 Sam. 1:9; 3:3).

It was God's obvious intention that the ark should symbolize His very presence in the midst of Israel. The people readily grasped this meaning from their early experience at Sinai and never deviated from it. Although many times they fell into idolatry, the ark was never idolized. The Decalogue gave them guidance for the development of interpersonal, divine-personal, and social relationships as they evolved into a unified nation. It taught them that without law there can be neither personal nor interpersonal stability. Aaron's rod was a constant reminder that God demands accountability to His elected leadership and to himself. The golden pot of manna perpetuated the concept that God is the Provider of human necessities. The mercy seat with its heavenly representations helped them never to forget that mercy and forgiveness are not earthborn but heaven-sent.

In NT concepts, according to the writer to the Hebrews (6:18-20; 8:1-2; 9:8-12, 23-26), the ark of the covenant, together wtih its contents and mercy seat, prefigured the work of Christ on the Cross where He brought man to God, and God to man (the mercy seat). Power dispensed at Pentecost makes possible through the Spirit the achievement of the ethical standards of the Decalogue (Rom. 8:1-4); and in the figurative language of Revelation (2:17) the manna represents special strength made available to Christians during times of great distress.

See TYPE (TYPOLOGY), TEMPLE, MOSAIC LAW, PENTATEUCH, MERCY SEAT, PROPITIATION, COVENANT, DECALOGUE, HOLY OF HOLIES.

For Further Reading: *IDB*, 222-26; *NBD*, 82; Livingston, *The Pentateuch in Its Cultural Environment*, 153-62; Talbot, *Christ in the Tabernacle*, 224-57; Wood, *Pentecostal Grace*. FLOYD J. PERKINS

ARMAGEDDON. This word occurs only once in the Bible, in Rev. 16:16, and literally means the "Mount of Megiddo." Megiddo is a promontory on the south side of the plain of Jezreel, and an ancient military stronghold (Josh. 12:21; 17:11; Judg. 1:27; 5:19; 2 Kings 23:29; etc.). In the Revelation (16:16), Armageddon represents the last great battle between Christ and the Antichrist. From this biblical background, the word has become a very familiar term designating the final holocaust resulting from the struggle between good and evil.

The basic theme of the Revelation is the struggle between Christ and Antichrist. Chapter 12 pictures the struggle which is being waged behind the scenes of history. A great red dragon appears, so huge that when he wagged his tail, he swept a third of the stars from heaven. His opponent is a heavenly woman clothed with the sun, with the moon under her feet. (She is the symbolic representation in Gal. 4:26 of the heavenly Jerusalem, our mother.) The nations of men line up on either side—on the one side the Church, symbolically portrayed as Israel, sealed by God that they may be delivered from His wrath which He is about to pour out (Rev. 7:9); and on the other the pagan nations of the earth who follow and worship the Antichrist, and who are sealed with his seal (13:16 ff). Armageddon is the last great battle on the day of God the Almighty (16:14). The battle itself is not described. Christ's victory is portrayed in chapter 19, where He is pictured riding a white battle horse, with His garments stained in blood. He is accompanied by the armies of heaven who are also garbed in white, but who do not participate in the battle. The carnage wrought by Christ's victory is described in vivid terms of a battlefield covered by corpses (19:18), which many feel will be literally fulfilled. And Christ then consummates His victory by destroying first the Antichrist, then Satan himself.

See TRIBULATION.

For Further Reading: Biederwolf, *The Millennium Bible*, 662. GEORGE ELDON LADD

ARMINIANISM. This refers to the kind of Protestant theology taught by James Arminius (c. 1560-1609), and by others who have agreed with him in basic ways. It stresses human freedom, but not in a Pelagian sense. It teaches predestination, but not of the unconditional sort. It emphasizes God's grace, but opposes the view that grace is irresistible. It emphasizes our being spiritually secure in Christ, but it opposes eternal security in favor of the view that believers will lose their regeneration if they cease to be believers and wilfully disobey God.

James Arminius, the ablest exponent of this kind of teaching in his time, opposed the Calvinism of his day which emphasized God's absolute sovereignty. Arminius' teacher at Calvin's school at Geneva, Calvin's son-in-law, Theodore Beza, was a supralapsarian. That is, Beza believed that even Adam's first and racially crucial sin was not free, but was unconditionally determined by God. In fact, he believed that the first decree of God, before the decree to create man, was the decree to predestinate some individuals to be saved and other individuals to be damned. Francis Gomarus, Arminius' colleague on the faculty of the University of Leiden, was also a supralapsarian. Augustine and Luther had only been sublapsarians—teaching that Adam's first sin was done freely, but that after that time, that is, after the Fall, the eternal destiny of every other person was decreed by God. And it cannot be definitely determined whether or not John Calvin himself was sublapsarian or supralapsarian.

Arminius, however, opposed both of those unconditional predestination views, giving 20 arguments against them in his *Declaration of Sentiments*—delivered by him before the governmental authorities at The Hague in 1608. He said that all 20 arguments boil down to this: that they make God the author of sin.

In that treatise, Arminius presents his own understanding of what he calls the divine decrees. He says that (1) the first decree was to send Christ to redeem sinful people; (2) the second decree was to receive into favor the ones who would repent and believe; (3) the third decree was to grant prevenient grace to help people to repent and believe; and (4) the fourth decree was to save and damn individuals according to His foreknowledge of the way in which they would freely respond to or reject the offer of grace through Christ.

It is important to note that Arminius, therefore, did believe that some individuals are predestinated to be damned, before they are ever born—but that this is based solely on God's foreknowledge of the way individuals will freely decide, about Christ, in their lifetime. Some Arminian evangelicals, today, disagree with Arminius as to this fourth decree. They say that God does not foreknow free acts—because that would prevent their being free. The "regular" Arminians, however, understand that God does foreknow free acts. They quote, in support, e.g., where Paul says, "Whom He foreknew, He also predestined to become conformed to the image of His Son" (Rom. 8:29, NASB). They also wonder how biblical prophecy could otherwise be fulfilled—such as that in Zechariah about Jesus' betrayal, and what would be done with the 30 pieces of silver. Surely Jesus' enemies, Judas and the ones who later received the silver, were not setting out to fulfill biblical prophecy.

One matter pointed out in *Grace Unlimited*, edited by Clark Pinnock, is that the predestination, in Scripture, is never to heaven or to hell. Pinnock writes, "There is no predestination to salvation or to damnation in the Bible. There is only a predestination for those who are already children of God with respect to certain privileges out ahead of them" (18).

Something else pointed out in this symposium, written largely by scholars who have been widely associated with the Calvinistic position, is that classical Calvinism twists the meaning of numerous Scripture passages in order to teach that Christ died only to save some—the elect. Donald M. Lake, a professor at Wheaton College, in his chapter on "He Died for All," writes, "*It is a fact that these redemptive events in the life of Jesus provided a salvation so extensive, so broad as to potentially include the whole of humanity past, present and future!*" (31). He shows that while Christ had said, "'I, when I am lifted up from the earth, will draw all men to myself'" (John 12:32, RSV), John Calvin had commented, "When He says *all* it must be referred to the children of God, who are His flock" (*Calvin's New Testament Commentaries: St. John Part Two*, 11-21, and *I John*, 43). Lake comments, "The critical judgment remains: has Calvin been consistent with the text and its obvious meaning? Personally, I cannot help but give a negative answer to this question" (ibid., 37). According to classical Calvinism, the atonement of Christ was only efficacious for the ones God had previously predestinated to be saved. Its adherents, e.g., John Owen, have usually understood that the passages which say that Christ died for all (e.g., 2 Cor. 5:15), mean "all of the elect." Arminianism has always taught an unlimited atonement: that anyone at all who repents and believes may be saved through Christ's atonement.

After 42 followers of Arminius drew up a document called the *Remonstrance* in 1610, which outlined their differences with the Calvinists, it was responded to by the Calvinists, and the controversy became a serious matter in the United Netherlands. Prince Maurice, who favored Calvinism, arranged for a national synod to meet at Dort; and that synod, with its official Calvinist delegates, drew up the Canons of Dort, a most official Calvinistic creed.

Arminianism was outlawed in the United Netherlands until 1623; but it never did die out in that country. Later it spread to England where it was basically espoused by John Wesley (1703-91) and the Methodists—Methodism being sometimes called "Arminianism on fire." It was through Methodism—and the Holiness movement generally—that Arminianism has been widely disseminated in America.

See CANONS OF DORT, CALVINISM, PREDESTINATION, FOREKNOWLEDGE, INFRALAPSARIANISM, WESLEYANISM.

For Further Reading: Arminius, *The Writings of James Arminius,* trans. Nichols and Bagnall; Bangs, *Arminius: A Study of the Dutch Reformation;* McCulloh, ed., *Man's Faith and Freedom.*

J. KENNETH GRIDER

ASCENSION, THE. The English term Ascension as used in Christian theology renders a variety of Greek words meaning "to go up" or "take up," and refers to the departure of Jesus for the heavenly sphere at the close of His historical ministry. The idea, though not frequent in the NT, has wide bearings for Christian theology.

The Ascension as an Event. As to the *fact* of the Ascension this is described only in Luke 24:51 and Acts 1:9-11; though it is presupposed more often (John 20:17; Acts 1:2; Eph. 4:8-10; 1 Tim. 3:16). The clue to the *meaning* of the Ascension-event lies in what it evidently signified to those who had known Jesus both during His historical ministry and in the period following His resurrection. What was needed by the disciples to whom the resurrected Jesus manifested himself was an indication that such appearances were not to continue indefinitely but rather were terminated. This indication the Ascension conveyed. Such an understanding explains both the relatedness and the distinctness of the Resurrection and the Ascension.

Theological Implications. Jesus' departure into the eternal world, of which the Ascension is the symbol, is linked with at least five aspects of His work for men.

1. His ascension to the Father is the sign of the completion of His redemptive mission on earth. As such it is directly related to His session at God's right hand, in which He takes the role of the enthroned, victorious King (Heb. 1:3; 10:12-14), whose final triumph over all His foes is thereby assured (Eph. 1:20; Phil. 2:9-11; 1 Pet. 3:22).

2. Christ is enthroned not merely as King but as Priest-King (Heb. 10:11), in virtue of which office He exercises a continuous ministry of intercession on behalf of men: not as pleading for boons which He may be refused but rather those to which He has already received title by His victorious death (Rom. 8:34; Heb. 7:25; 9:24; 1 John 2:1-2).

3. The Ascension is likewise connected with Christ's work as Forerunner (John 14:3; Heb. 6:20). His entry into heaven is the guarantee of our own, demonstrating that transformed manhood in the form of the spiritualized body can inhabit the eternal sphere (Eph. 2:6).

4. The Ascension is also the precondition of the giving of the Spirit, whose task is to continue on earth the work formerly effected by the historical Jesus (John 14:16-18; 15:26-27; 16:13-14; Acts 2:32-33).

5. Finally the Ascension is the occasion for the angelic assurance of Christ's second coming, in the words "this Jesus, who has been taken up from you into heaven, will come in just the same way as you have watched Him go into heaven" (Acts 1:11, NASB). That the apostolic community did not interpret this as a prediction of Pentecost, or suppose that the outpouring of the Spirit was the second coming of Christ, is clear from Acts 2:33; 3:19-21; 7:55; et al.

We may say therefore that the entire mission and work of the Church in proclamation and accomplishment alike are dependent on the ascended Christ.

See ESTATES OF CHRIST, SECOND COMING OF CHRIST.

For Further Reading: Bernard, "Assumption and Ascension," *ERE,* 2:151 ff; Ramsey, "Ascension," Richardson, ed., *A Theological Word Book of the Bible,* 22 ff; Wright, "Ascension," *NBD,* 14; Lewis, *Miracles,* chap. 16.

ALEX R. G. DEASLEY

ASCETICISM. This is an expression of religion characterized by a disregard of the physical or natural side of existence and a preoccupation with the development of one's own spiritual condition. It is a rigorous commitment to a life apart from the "evils" of normal living. Individuals from many religious orientations have turned to asceticism in their attempt to obtain salvation.

The intent is to become disengaged from sin and united with the ultimate spirit so as to live a holy life. Methods of doing so include fasting, prayer, poverty, celibacy, withdrawal from society, contemplation, and self-mortification.

In the early days of the Christian Church the belief that Christ's return was imminent and that the world was soon to come to an end fostered asceticism. Thus, concern with the temporal world was not expedient. Because persecutions grew intense in the second and third centuries, believers were consoled by the idea that Christ would especially crown the sufferers of this world. Thus, it was a natural step to believe that voluntary suffering would lead to God's special favor.

Probably the greatest factor in the rise of asceticism in the Early Church was the confusion of Gnostic dualism with biblical teachings. The Gnostics emphasized that the body is evil while the spirit is good. Thus, the body was to be flagellated in order to cultivate the spirit. This emphasis soon led to the monastic movement with its attempt to withdraw from the world in order to concentrate on holy practices.

Sacrifice, self-denial, and separation from the world should be the legitimate concerns of biblical Christians. To avoid extremes, the Scriptures will have to be studied carefully in order to discover the healthy balance between the body and the spirit, the spiritual and the secular, and separation from the world and penetration into the world.

See DISCIPLINE, BODY, GNOSTICISM, CELIBACY, TEMPERANCE.

For Further Reading: Turner, *The Vision Which Transforms,* 90, 166-67, 275; Flew, *The Idea of Perfection in Christian Theology,* 340; Kirk, *The Vision of God.*

ROBERT A. MATTKE

ASSUMPTION OF MARY. See MOTHER OF GOD.

ASSURANCE. See WITNESS OF THE SPIRIT.

ASTROLOGY. Astrology is the study of the supposed influence of stars upon human fortunes—the belief that heavenly bodies foretell or reflect the destinies of individuals and nations. Widely practiced in the ancient world, and eventually suppressed by the impact of Christianity, astrology experienced revival in the West in the 13th century, becoming powerful again in the 16th century. With the growth of the scientific temper in the 18th century it again went into the shadows. The religious indifference and skepticism of our times has produced a renewal of interest in astrology.

The word *horoscope* (Greek, *hōra,* time; *scopein,* to look) refers to the study of the position of the stars at the time of one's birth in order to foretell one's destiny. Horoscopy is the major aim of astrology. The few passages in the OT that mention astrologers refer to Babylonian practice. Isaiah in his lamentation over Babylon scornfully repudiates it: "Thou art wearied in the multitude of thy counsels. Let now the astrologers, the stargazers, the monthly prognosticators, stand up, and save thee from these things that shall come upon thee" (Isa. 47:13). Jeremiah warns the house of Israel: "Thus saith the Lord, Learn not the way of the heathen, and be not dismayed at the signs of heaven; for the heathen are dismayed at them" (Jer. 10:2).

See CULTS.

For Further Reading: *IDB,* 1:304; *ODCC,* 100.

JAMES D. ROBERTSON

ATHANASIAN CREED. This, along with the Apostles' and Nicene creeds, is one of the three most important of the ancient formulas of the Christian faith. No one knows who wrote it, or just when it was composed. Its wording shows that it would have had to be written some time after the Council of Chalcedon in A.D. 451. The first mention of it is at a synod held some time between 659 and 670. It could not have been written by Athanasius, who died in 373. Indeed, it was no doubt written in the West, in Latin. It was only named for the great fourth-century defender of orthodoxy, Athanasius. In content it defines the orthodox doctrine of the Trinity—guarding against tritheism—and also the orthodox doctrine of Christ.

See CREED (CREEDS), TRINITY (HOLY), CHRISTOLOGY, APOSTLES' CREED, NICENE CREED.

For Further Reading: Schaff, *Creeds of Christendom,* 2:66-71; Heick, *A History of Christian Thought,* 1:154-69.

J. KENNETH GRIDER

ATHEISM. The term derives from the Greek negative particle *a,* which means "no" or "not," and *theos,* meaning "god." Thus, dogmatically considered, atheism means "God is not," or "There is no God"—a total denial of the existence of God. In this sense atheism must be distinguished from *agnosticism, infidelity,* and *skepticism.* Atheism is a self-contradiction in that its attempted denial of God's existence rests upon the prior assumption of His existence.

The Bible takes little note of atheism *per se.* The Hebrews never argued the existence of God; they simply testified to His activities.

Paul's nearest approach to acknowledging

atheism is his statement that before conversion the Gentiles were "godless in the world" (*atheoi en tō kosmō:* Eph. 2:12), and that confirmed pagans "did not see fit to acknowledge God any longer" (Rom. 1:28, NASB). However, in neither case is God's existence actually denied. In the first they were simply ignorant of the true God, whereas in the second they had put out of mind the God they knew to exist (vv. 19-21). The Psalmist declared, "The fool has said in his heart, 'There is no God'" (Ps. 53:1, NASB). Jean-Paul Sartre seemed to recognize this folly when he said, "If there is no God, then I am God," obviously a yet greater folly.

An atheist would be a person or universe without invisible or metaphysical support. Without a personal, intelligent God there is no way to account for the ultimate origin, existence, or destiny of man or the universe.

In the 1960s a modern form of atheism came to full flower in the "God Is Dead" movement, coupled with a thoroughgoing ethical relativism, sponsored by such thinkers as Thomas Altizer and William Hamilton. However, this movement hardly outlasted the decade.

Practical atheism is a mode of life quite unrelated to belief in God. It divorces belief from action and lives as though God did not exist. Of practical atheism there is much in the world, sometimes even among Christians. Whatever form atheism may take, and there are many, it destroys faith in the very basis of all human relations and removes any foundation from religious and social ethics, and thus reduces human life and the universe to utter meaninglessness.

See THEISM, AGNOSTICISM, SKEPTICISM, UNBELIEF, SECULARISM, APOLOGETICS, THEISTIC PROOFS.

For Further Reading: *ISBE,* 1:318-19; *Baker's DT,* 70-71; K. Hamilton, *What's New in Religion?*

CHARLES W. CARTER

ATONEMENT. This word does not appear in the Greek NT, but it does appear in the Hebrew OT. There, its literal meaning is "to cover." The word refers to our sins being "covered" or "covered over."

Calvinists tend to interpret the word to mean that our sins are still there, but are hidden from view by the blood of Christ—so that the holy God excuses us of them when Christ's righteousness is imputed to us.

Arminians, who believe in actual, imparted righteousness, understand that the believer's sins are covered in the way that a wound is covered when new flesh heals it (see Ps. 32:1-2).

Christians in general understand that it is Christ's death on the Cross (and His resurrection) which provides an atonement for our disobedience. Yet the precise way in which Christ's crucifixion is efficacious is conceived differently by various groups of Christians.

Some Calvinists teach the *limited* Atonement theory. That is, that the saving benefit of Christ's atonement is limited to the ones God the Father had previously elected to salvation (and heaven). Arminians teach the *unlimited* Atonement theory—that the benefit it provides for extends to the entire human race. Naturally, the Arminians understand that the salvation the Atonement provides is conditional—it awaits our repentance and faith before the salvation it provides is realized. Many Calvinists teach that its benefit is unconditional—that is, that the elect, for whom it was accomplished, cannot finally resist saving grace, but will indeed be saved eternally.

All the groupings of Christians more or less believe in the *ransom* theory of the Atonement, since the NT (in Mark 10:45; 1 Tim. 2:6) states that Christ died to ransom us. Yet there is much difference among Christians as to Atonement theories per se.

The *moral influence* theory, pretty much originating with Peter Abelard (1079-1142), suits modernism in theology. It overstresses God's love and denies man's utter sinfulness. Christ's death does not need to satisfy anything in God's nature to make it possible for Him to forgive man. Christ's death helps us to see that God loves us. Thus we call it a subjective theory of the Atonement—nothing objective for man being accomplished by it, but only something within man.

Anselm (1033-1109) taught the *satisfaction* theory of the Atonement, which view peculiarly suits Roman Catholicism. This is an objective theory, for something is accomplished in God's nature—objective of man—by Christ's death. Specifically the Atonement made it possible for God to forgive man and still maintain His own honor—so important in those feudal times. According to Anselm's *Why the God-Man,* man, a sort of serf, got into debt to God by sinning; and Christ, who, as sinless, did not need to suffer physical death, nonetheless died, and therefore did a most meritorious act. He paid man's debt by dying, since He was man; and since He was divine, He paid an infinite debt. God received the payment, forgives us, and maintains His honor. This theory suits the vast merit system of Roman Catholic theology. It precludes actual forgiveness, however, as Arminians view the matter; for, if a payment of a debt is received, how can the debt then be forgiven?

The penal *(punishment) satisfaction* theory of the Calvinists says that the claims of God against the elect were satisfied by Christ's death being a vicarious punishment. The emphasis here is not on debt (Anselm) but justice. Sin must be punished. In Christ's death the sins of the elect were punished in full, and justice can make no further claim against the elect. Although the KJV does not use the specific word that Christ was "punished" for us, the view suits the unconditional and the limited Atonement understandings taught by Calvinism. Besides its not being scriptural, the view, like the satisfaction theory, precludes forgiveness—for, surely, God cannot accept Christ's punishment as what satisfies His justice, and still really forgive man. If the sin has already been fully punished, it cannot now be forgiven.

The *governmental* theory is the one which peculiarly suits Arminianism. According to this theory, Christ suffered, as Scripture so often says, in man's behalf, more precisely, as a provisional substitute for penalty. And He suffered for all men, not for a limited number. Because of Christ's suffering, God can forgive those who repent and believe—and still maintain His governmental control.

However, not all Arminians are willing to rest their doctrine of Atonement entirely on the governmental theory. This would be true of Watson, Pope, Summers, Tigert, and Wiley—to name but a few. According to H. Orton Wiley, the Atonement is not only grounded in governmental necessity but in the divine holiness and in the appeal of divine love. Thus the propitiatory idea and the moral influence idea also represent facets of truth which are indispensable to a full-orbed doctrine of the Atonement. In fact, Wiley says that the "idea of propitiation is the dominant note in the Wesleyan type of Arminian theology" (*CT,* 2:284).

Furthermore, Wiley stresses what he calls the "vital principle" of the Atonement. The Atonement, he says, is "God's method of becoming immanent in a sinful race" (*CT,* 2:276). Among other things this includes that restoration of the Spirit as indwelling Sanctifier which the death and resurrection of Christ made possible. The Logos who became Man, and who represented the race on the Cross in atonement, is now available to the believer in a personal, vital, inner relationship.

See CROSS, ESTATES OF CHRIST, RANSOM, FORGIVENESS, EXPIATION, PROPITIATION, GOVERNMENTAL THEORY, PENAL SATISFACTION THEORY, MORAL INFLUENCE THEORY, MYSTICAL THEORY.

For Further Reading: Galloway, *The Cosmic Christ;* Hodgson, *The Doctrine of the Atonement;* Miley, *The Atonement in Christ;* Wiley, *CT,* 2:270-95.

J. KENNETH GRIDER

ATTRIBUTES, DIVINE. The divine attributes may be defined as the perfections of God which are revealed in Scripture, exercised in God's redemptive relationship to man, and demonstrated in His various works. The divine perfections, called attributes, provide essential descriptions of what God *is* and how God *acts.* These divine perfections are *not* traits, qualities, or characteristics in the sense that God *has* them. They are essential expressions of what God *is.* Nor are the attributes specific qualities which man assigns to God in order to understand Him. The attributes are objective and real. The names designating the attributes are ways of describing God as He *is,* according to revelation.

God thus does not possess the quality of love. God *is* love. When God loves, He is not manifesting a particular quality of His nature. When God loves, He expresses His essential Being. Again, when God is said to be holy, this reference is to His essential Being, not to a characteristic of His nature.

Current Approaches. Many theologians of the mid or late 20th century tend to reject the use of the word *attribute.* One reason given is that the traditional use of the word at times seemed to reduce God to the sum total of all His qualities, or attributes. Another reason directed against the traditional use of *attributes* was that such terms as *omniscience, omnipresence,* and *omnipotence* do not appear in biblical terminology. The claim is made that, instead of abstract terms expressing Greek thought, the Scriptures use descriptive terms of God in action.

It is true that the Bible uses action words to describe God. But the Scriptures also employ imperative words to describe God's nature and His sovereign relationship to man, such as Lev. 19:2: "Ye shall be holy: for I the Lord your God am holy." And on occasion the Scriptures do use abstract terms in reference to God. For instance, Moses requests that he be allowed to see God's glory (Exod. 33:18). Also, the Psalmist writes that "the Lord is a great God, and a great King above all gods" (Ps. 95:3). Isaiah's lofty vision of God included the joyful exclamation of the seraphim: "Holy, holy, holy, is the Lord of hosts: the whole earth is full of his glory" (Isa. 6:3).

For all practical purposes, then, it appears

sound to use any terms available in referring to God, as long as the terms convey accurately the revelation of God in Scripture. For example, one may use the phrase "God is everywhere," or he may say that God is omnipresent. Both the phrase "God is everywhere" and the word *omnipresence* mean that there are no limits to His presence—that God is free from the restraints of space.

Revelation the Source of Knowledge. The mystery of God eliminates all knowledge of God except when He makes himself known by revelation. As Emil Brunner points out, God is not an object which man can manipulate by his own reasoning (*The Christian Doctrine of God,* 14). Except when He chooses to reveal himself, God is a mystery dwelling in the depths of inaccessible light. And even when He reveals himself, "the believer will not even be able fully to understand all that God has revealed concerning His attributes" (Fred H. Klooster in *Basic Christian Doctrines,* 22). Finite man can never fully understand the infinite God.

But man must state some sweeping and final affirmations about God's essential being, or the whole idea of God becomes merely formal, theoretical, and sterile. The modern mind, with its bent toward secularism, seems unable or unwilling to present or to accept any ultimates about God. This confusion about the nature of God has minimized the influence of the redemptive message. As Carl Henry writes: "The modern inability to speak literally of God's essential being, the contentment with merely relational reflection, . . . augur but further religious decline for the Western world" (*Christian Faith and Modern Theology,* 92).

Taking our directives from Scripture, the discussion below deals with specific attributes of God.

Classification of the Attributes. The divine attributes may be arranged under two headings: (1) the absolute or incommunicable attributes; (2) the moral or communicable attributes.

1. *The absolute or incommunicable attributes.* The term *absolute* is derived from the Latin *absolutus,* a compound of *ab* (from) and *solvere* (to loosen). *Absolute* means free as to condition, or free from limitation or restraint. The absolute attributes are reserved for God alone. Neither God's general creation, the universe, nor God's special creation, man, shares these divine perfections. The absolute attributes are infinity, self-existence, eternality, immutability, immensity (omnipresence), perfect knowledge (omniscience), perfect power (omnipotence), and spirituality.

The term *infinite* refers to that perfection of God by which He is free from all limitations. God is in no way limited by the created world, by time-space relationships. God's perfection is His infiniteness. The only limitations of God are self-imposed or inherent in His nature. God cannot lie, sin, change, or deny himself (Num. 23:19; 1 Sam. 15:29; 2 Tim. 2:13; Heb. 6:18; Jas. 1:13, 17).

By *self-existence* (or self-sufficiency, independence, or aseity of God) is meant that God has no origin, that He is uncreated, that He depends on nothing. This self-existence of God finds expression in the name Jehovah. God is the great I AM (Exod. 3:14). John states that God is self-caused: "For as the Father hath life in himself . . ." (John 5:26). The fact that God is independent of all things and that all things exist only through Him is found in Ps. 94:8 ff, in Isa. 40:18 ff, and Acts 17:25. See also Rom. 11:33-34; Eph. 1:5; Rev. 4:11.

The *eternality* of God is His timelessness. He exists outside the categories of time or space. Moses paid his tribute by singing: "Before the mountains were brought forth, or ever thou hadst formed the earth and the world, even from everlasting to everlasting, thou art God" (Ps. 90:2; cf. Gen. 21:33; Isa. 57:15; 1 Tim. 1:17).

Immutability refers to the unchanging nature of God. A perfect being cannot increase or decrease in any respect. God does not change in regard to His being, in relation to His decrees, or in respect to His works. The prophet Malachi states it precisely: "For I am the Lord, I change not" (Mal. 3:6). See also Exod. 3:14; Ps. 102:26-28; Isa. 41:4; Heb. 1:11-12; 6:17; Jas. 1:17. In God, as absolute perfection, neither improvement nor deterioration are possible.

When God is stated to be superior to space, or transcendent over space, or unlimited by space, this perfection is called *immensity.* When God is said to be present everywhere in creation, this perfection is named *omnipresence.* Though God remains distinct from creation and may not be identified with the world, yet He is present in every part of His creation. The omnipresence of God is a basic teaching of the Bible. Heaven and earth cannot contain Him (1 Kings 8:27; Isa. 66:1; Acts 7:48-49); yet He occupies both at the same time and is a God who is always present (Ps. 139:7-10; Jer. 23:23-24; Acts 17:27-28).

God's perfect knowledge is called *omniscience.* God knows all that is knowable. His knowledge is inclusive and comprehensive. He knows himself and all that comes from Him. He knows all things as they actually come to pass, past, present, and future. He knows all relations and relationships. He knows what is actual and what is possible. The omniscience of God is a distinct revelation in Scripture. God's knowledge is perfect (Job 37:16); He knows the inner heart of man (1 Sam. 16:7; 1 Chron. 28:9; Ps. 139:14; Jer. 17:10). God sees the ways of men (Deut. 2:7; Job 23:10; 24:23; Ps. 1:6; Ps. 37:18). God also knows about contingent events (1 Sam. 23:10-12; 2 Kings 13:19; Ps. 81:14-15; Isa. 42:9; Ezek. 3:6; Matt. 11:21).

Omnipotence, or God's perfect power, means that by the exercise of His will He can realize whatever is present in His will. The idea of God's omnipotence finds expression in the name *El-Shaddai.* The Bible is emphatic in speaking of the Lord God Almighty (Job 9:12; Ps. 115:3; Jer. 32:17; Matt. 19:26; Luke 1:37; Rom. 1:20; Eph. 1:19); God reveals His power in creation (Isa. 44:24; Rom. 4:17); in works of providence (Heb. 1:3), and in the redemption of sinners (Rom. 1:16; 1 Cor. 1:24). God's absolute power, however, may never be divorced from His perfections.

The Bible does not contain a definition of God. The nearest approach to anything like a definition is found in the word of Christ to the Samaritan woman, "God is a Spirit" (John 4:24). "By teaching the spirituality of God theology stresses the fact that God has a substantial Being all His own and distinct from the world, and that this substantial Being is immaterial, invisible, and without composition or extension" (Erickson, ed., *The Living God,* 347 f). By accepting the *spirituality* of God it is affirmed that He has none of the properties belonging to matter, and that He cannot be discerned by the bodily senses. Paul speaks of Him as "the King eternal, immortal, invisible" (1 Tim. 1:17).

2. *The moral or communicable attributes.* Among the divine perfections which God may impart, to a degree, are holiness, truth, righteousness, justice, love, grace, goodness, and faithfulness. We can briefly discuss only some.

In the OT the word "holiness" carried three meanings—*brilliance* (glory), *separation,* and *purity* (Exod. 29:43; Lev. 10:3; Isa. 6:3; 10:17; 1 Kings 8:10-11; Exod. 13:2; 28:41; Isa. 40:25; Ezek. 43:7-9). While holiness is in one sense the unique and exclusive perfection of God, it is capable, under divinely appointed conditions, of being imparted to persons, places, and things. Wiley writes that "the love of God is in fact the desire to impart holiness and this desire is satisfied only when the beings whom it seeks are rendered holy" (Wiley and Culbertson, *Introduction to Christian Theology,* 107). In essence, God's love is His unceasing and benevolent desire to share all of His perfections, to the extent possible, with man.

Truth as an attribute of God means that God can never be capricious, whimsical, indulgent, or misleading. Any act or any word of revelation by God must be an expression of holy love. Truth as a perfection of God indicates that God's analysis of man is based on His perfect knowledge of what man is and what man can be.

God is true and faithful, in that He always acts in harmony with His nature. His purposes never waver, and His promises are never annulled. Paul wrote to the wavering Corinthians that "God is faithful" (1 Cor. 10:13).

Righteousness is the conformity of God to the moral and spiritual law which He has revealed. To put it another way, righteousness is the consistent and unvarying expression of God's nature in complete harmony with His holiness. To Brunner the righteousness of God means "the constancy of God's will in view of His Purpose and Plan for Israel" (*The Christian Doctrine of God,* 275). Thus righteousness "is simply the Holiness of God as it is expressed when confronted with the created world" (ibid., 278). To Barth the righteousness of God means that in founding and maintaining fellowship with His creation God "wills and expresses and establishes what corresponds to His own worth" (*Church Dogmatics,* 2:377).

The Psalmist sang of the righteousness of God (Ps. 19:9). Isaiah longed for a time when God's righteousness would be supreme (Isa. 11:5). Paul wrote that righteousness was the glory of the gospel (Rom. 1:17). At the end of the Bible angels testify to God's righteousness: "Thou art righteous, O Lord, which art, and wast, and shalt be" (Rev. 16:5).

See GOD, INFINITE, IMMUTABILITY, OMNIPOTENCE, SPIRIT, HOLINESS, LOVE, RIGHTEOUSNESS, JUSTICE, GRACE, GOOD (THE GOOD, GOODNESS), FAITHFUL (FAITHFULNESS), CONTINGENT.

For Further Reading: Wiley, *CT,* 1:320-93; Berkhof, *Systematic Theology,* 52-81; Brunner, *The Christian Doctrine of God;* Henry, ed., *Christian Faith and Modern Theology,* 67-93; Erickson, ed., *The Living God: Readings in Christian Theology;* Barth, *Church Dogmatics: The Doctrine of God.*

DONALD S. METZ

AUGSBURG CONFESSION. A declaration of Lutheran belief, composed in 1530 by Philip Melanchthon with the approval of Luther. Melanchthon's own revision, in 1540, attempted to encourage ecumenical discussion by softening some anti-Calvinistic and anti-Roman statements. The 1530 edition has been taken historically as the more adequate and is called the *invariata.* The normative interpretation of the *Confession* is the *Apology,* also written by Melanchthon in 1530.

Originally, the *Confession,* signed by seven of the electors (political rulers) of Germany and also for the cities of Nuremberg and Reutlingen, was presented in the Diet (parliament) held by the Holy Roman Emperor Charles V, in Augsburg in 1530. The electors hoped to present Lutheranism favorably before the emperor, a sincere Catholic, and so aid in settling Reformation-born religious and political issues. The Catholic-dominated Diet declared the *Confession* refuted by its own *Confutation.* Also refuted were confessions by South German Lutherans (Tripolitana) and Ulrich Zwingli *(Ratio fidei).* Neither of these was allowed to come directly to the Diet, however.

Attempts at compromise at Augsburg failed. The Protestants (who called themselves Evangelicals) were ordered to recant within a year or face armed suppression. The Protestant-Roman Catholic division dates from this Diet. The *Confession* quickly became the Lutherans' principal doctrinal authority, though its original purpose was lost.

The *Confession* has two major parts: 21 articles stating positive Lutheran doctrine and 7 articles outlining abuses within Roman Catholicism that Lutheranism has corrected. The spirit of the *Confession* is irenic and conservative. It cites the church fathers, canon law, and other traditionally accepted authorities in addition to Scripture. The Lutherans sought to demonstrate their faithfulness to historic orthodoxy (there was no hint of the later position that the abuses within Catholicism really arose from its very nature), and their positive declarations were as broadly and traditionally stated as possible.

The principal corrected abuses were: withholding the cup from lay persons, priestly celibacy, believing that the Mass is a sacrifice and a meritorious work, believing that only sins specifically confessed to the priest can be absolved, giving traditions the force of divine commandments, believing that the monastic life is a meritorious good work and the truly perfect and biblical Christian way, believing in supererogatory good works of monks and other saints and that they may be applied to others, and so establishing episcopal authority that it is believed that a bishop may rightfully act even in contradiction to the gospel. The Epilogue hints at even more abuses corrected by Lutheranism, but these gave sufficient clue to the principles of assessment.

Serious theological controversies within Lutheranism after Luther's death (1546), and conflict with and about the Calvinists, Zwinglians, and Anabaptists threatened to sunder and destroy Lutheranism. In response, the contending parties formulated the *Book of Concord* (1580) as the basis of doctrinal agreement. It contains both the *Augsburg Confession* (1530) and the *Apology,* along with the Apostles', Nicene, and Athanasian creeds, the *Smalcald Articles,* Luther's two *Catechisms,* and the *Formula of Concord.*

See PROTESTANTISM, LUTHERANISM.

For Further Reading: Schaff, *Creeds of Christendom,* 3:3-180; Heick, *A History of Christian Thought,* 1:404-17.

PAUL M. BASSETT

AUGUSTINIANISM. The theological and philosophical thought of Augustine, bishop of Hippo (354-430), has shaped the assumptions of Western Christianity down to the present day.

Augustine's Teachings. Augustine's thought was deeply colored by Neoplatonism, especially his doctrine of man and his theory of knowledge. Man was a body-soul dualism. The rational soul (i.e., the mind) perceived the eternal realities or "Forms" (Plato) by illumination from God and so was able to think rationally about objects in the physical, temporal world. Only by this knowledge of the Absolute could men make judgments about the relative.

Only the Christian with faith in the teachings of the Church and the Bible, however, truly knows God as the Holy Trinity. Augustine's doctrine of God emphasizes the unity and equality of the three Persons, as is seen in his chosen model for the Trinity—memory, understanding, and will in the mind of man. Augustine also taught the double procession of the Spirit from the Father and the Son *(filioque).* This became the major theological division between the Western (Latin) church and the Greek East.

Against the Pelagians, Augustine insisted that salvation is by grace, not by merit. Evil is not an eternal principle equal to Good, as the Manichaeans said, but, as Neoplatonism taught, the negation of Good. Adam had free will, but his descendants, inheriting his original sin, were free only to choose evil. God's grace works irresistibly in the elect (those predestinated to salvation) till they "freely" choose the good and thus receive salvation. Those not predestinated are damned because of their own sinfulness.

The sacraments, by which this grace is infused into man, could be valid among schismatics, but were only celebrated properly in the one Catholic church whose bishops stood in succession to the apostles. Not all the visible church belonged to the invisible Church (the elect).

In his philosophy of history, Augustine saw two cities engaged in struggle since the Fall—the City of God (now represented by the Church) and the earthly city, human society apart from God.

Later Augustinianism. Augustine's teachings were mediated to the Middle Ages in a coarser, more superstitious form by Gregory the Great (pope, 590-604) who did, however, moderate Augustine's doctrine of predestination. Western Christianity became quite Augustinian. In the 13th century, Alexander of Hales, Bonaventure, and Duns Scotus (all Franciscans) defended the Platonist tradition of Augustinianism against the reawakened interest in Aristotle; but Thomas Aquinas, the great Dominican theologian, produced a massive synthesis of Aristotelianism and Christian doctrine which became the dominant form of medieval Catholicism.

The Reformation, begun by the Franciscan Martin Luther (d. 1546), can be seen as a revival of Augustinianism in some respects. The Reformers professed to follow much of Augustine's doctrine (notably Calvin on predestination), but not his Neoplatonist philosophy. The distinction is not so easily made, however, and much Western Christianity is still pervaded by Augustinian concepts and assumptions. These include the concepts of eternity as timelessness, of man as a mind-body dualism, of grace as an impersonal influence, and of the "spiritual" as esoteric and other-worldly.

See PELAGIANISM, CALVINISM, WESLEYANISM, ARMINIANISM, PROTESTANTISM.

For Further Reading: Heick, *A History of Christian Thought,* 1:130-42, 196-206; Chadwick, *The Early Church,* 216-36.

T. A. NOBLE

AUTHENTIC EXISTENCE. This is a term introduced by the existentialist philosopher Martin Heidegger and later taken over by Jean-Paul Sartre. It should be paired with its correlative term, *inauthentic existence,* and relates to the existentialist stress upon individuality and self-determination. Existence is authentic to the extent that the individual has taken possession of himself and determined his own life-style. Inauthentic existence, on the other hand, is molded by external influences whether these be circumstances, moral codes, or political or ecclesiastical authorities.

Heidegger felt that in the everyday routines of life, one may, and he thought usually does, become absorbed in the world. He tends to become part of the system, to be caught up in the processes which man himself has originated, and to become just another part of the machinery, an "organization man." This is an ironical destiny, yet it is one that has overtaken millions of people in industrial societies. This reflects one of the reasons for the existentialist reaction to the technological age which stifles individuality. In inauthentic existence the individual turns the "self" into an object among other objects and thus in Heidegger's special sense, ceases to "exist." One who lives authentically refuses to be dehumanized by becoming subservient to a system of things; or in Sartre's version, refuses to play roles that do not truly express himself. Authentic existence in relation to others involves a concern for the other which helps him to freedom and to his own unique possibilities for selfhood.

From the Christian perspective, authentic existence would be better expressed by the theistic existentialist, Soren Kierkegaard. For S. K., man is created in the image of God, and thus his *essential* nature entails his relation to God. His *existential* predicament is that he is in a state of alienation from God, producing anxiety, and this would be inauthentic existence. Authenticity, in this context, would occur when man exists in right relationship to his Creator. It would not result in the kind of individualistic existence outlined by Sartre and others but rather in dependence on, radical faith in, and obedience to God.

See EXISTENTIAL (EXISTENTIALISM).

For Further Reading: Blackham, *Six Existentialist Thinkers;* Heinemann, *Existentialism and the Modern Predicament.*

H. RAY DUNNING

AUTHENTICITY. This term derives from the Greek *authentein,* to have authority or dominion over someone. The Greek term *authentia* came to mean the authority or author of a book. In the juridical sense, authenticity means that a book is authoritative; that is, its claims can be trusted. In this sense, authenticity is a term used in discussion of sacred writings, particularly the Old and New Testaments.

Apparently, Tertullian (*De prascr, haer.,* 16) was the first to use this word with regard to the sacred books. Authenticity became a category for denoting books accepted as fully inspired in opposition to apocryphal writings. Books that were said to be authentic were accorded infallible authority. Canonical books were treated as authentic documents of divine revelation.

Many would grant authenticity in the full sense only to the autographs (i.e., the original documents as written or dictated by the author). In the absence of autographs, copies are said to be authentic when they faithfully reproduce the autographs. Translations may be judged authentic by competent authority, which, in the case, e.g., of Roman Catholicism, is the church. The Latin Vulgate was declared authentic by the Council of Trent because the church had used it for many centuries.

Biblical criticism in the modern period has popularized the term authenticity. A book is deemed authentic if it really originated with the author and time attributed to the work. Thus, Romans is considered an authentic Pauline Epistle, while Hebrews is not.

In its adjectival form, authenticity has become an important philosophical and theological word. Martin Heidegger coined the expressions "authentic existence" and "inauthentic existence." Among existentialists such as Rudolf Bultmann and Paul Tillich this has gained wide usage. Christian existentialists equate "inauthentic existence" with sin, and "authentic existence" is understood as the life of faith in Jesus Christ. Non-Christian philosophers have a more humanistic understanding of "authentic existence" as self-actualization, while "inauthentic existence" is the failure to realize one's potential.

See AUTHENTIC EXISTENCE, EXISTENTIAL (EXISTENTIALISM), CRITICISM (NT), CRITICISM (OT), TEXTUAL CRITICISM.

For Further Reading: Macquarrie, *Twentieth Century Religious Thought;* Tillich, *The Courage to Be;* Heidegger, *Being and Time;* Kümmel, *Introduction to the New Testament.* JERRY W. MCCANT

AUTHORITY. God is the ultimate, final Authority. He is the Author with a capital *A,* the Creator, the First Cause, the Beginning and End of All. Every lesser authority is derived from Him, however it is used, whether for good or ill. By this voluntary delegation of lesser authorities, God has chosen in His wisdom to limit himself. In a sense there is no power but of God.

Authority is as complex and varied as life itself. There is legal authority, derived from the will of the people, or from some official figure or constituted body. There is physical authority derived from brute strength, great numbers, or force of arms. There is intellectual authority derived from learning and/or rational superiority. There is social and economic authority derived from emotional charm and talent. There is moral authority derived from character and commitment. There is ecclesiastical authority derived from the Scripture and the Church. And, along with other forms of authority, there may be in certain persons or in certain groups a blending of different kinds of authentic power and influence.

Right living is to be found in the healthy balance between the basic factors—one's own individuality and self-determination; a positive relationship with other persons and groups; and the overarching will of God.

In writing on the sources of authority, Purkiser, Taylor, and Taylor *(GMS)* point out the four divinely appointed mediums of guidance under the sovereignty of God: the Bible, Jesus, the Holy Spirit, and the Church. They go on to say, "The three sources of authority for the Early Church merge into one for us: the New Testament." To restate this, the written Word, the Bible, inspired by the Holy Spirit, brings to us by faith the Living Word, Jesus Christ. And to move a step further, the Bible is best understood and lived out within the fellowship of Christian believers, illuminated by the Holy Spirit.

As Roger Nicole says, the evangelical Christian seeks to avoid on the one hand "the views which pay homage to ecclesiastical tradition as coordinate with Scripture, and on the other hand the views which locate God's voice in some element of human nature whether conscience (moralism), emotions (romanticism), or mind (rationalism)."

Our authority is Jesus Christ, the Living Word, as revealed in the written Word and illuminated by the Holy Spirit.

See DIVINE SOVEREIGNTY, OBEDIENCE, BIBLICAL AUTHORITY.

For Further Reading: Taylor, *Biblical Authority and Christian Faith.* JOHN E. RILEY

AVARICE. See COVETOUSNESS, SEVEN DEADLY SINS.

AWAKENING. In the NT, sleep is occasionally used as a figure or image of death (Matt. 9:24; John 11:11; 1 Thess. 4:14). There is a consistent follow-through in the use of the image when a subsequent awakening comes to pass as a result of the resurrection power of Jesus Christ.

This same metaphor is also used to illustrate spiritual death. The "sleep" spoken of in Rom. 13:11; 1 Cor. 15:34; Eph. 5:14; and 1 Thess. 5:6 is of this kind. It should be noted that this sleep is not that essential rest required to maintain good health but rather a careless insensibility that should provoke alarm as in the case of the foolish virgins (Matt. 25:1-13). Wesley called this kind of sleep a "stupid insensibility" (NT *Notes,* Eph. 5:14). Spiritual laziness, self-indulgence, and irresponsibility produce this kind of lethargy.

The exhortation to "awaken" is the call of God to all who are spiritually dead or asleep. It is the individual's responsibility to awaken and consequently Jesus Christ will "give thee light" (Eph. 5:14), righteousness (1 Cor. 15:34), and salvation (Rom. 13:11; 1 Thess. 5:9).

To be thus awakened is to experience a quickening (Eph. 2:1, 5) or a reviving. And this experience is not limited to the individual but can also be shared corporately.

See CONVICT (CONVICTION), REVIVAL.

For Further Reading: Kittel, 2:333-39; Orr, *The Light of the Nations;* Smith, *Revivalism and Social Reform.*

ROBERT A. MATTKE

AWE. See REVERENCE.

AXIOLOGY. Axiology is the theory and study of value and disvalue; it is an investigation of the nature, types, and metaphysical status of value. The word is a compound of two Greek words, *Axios* (worth), and *logos* (reason, meaning).

In modern philosophy the word *axiology* has generally been replaced by the phrase *value theory.*

Axiology (or the theory of value) has (1) a *wider* and (2) a more *narrow* meaning. In its wider use, it means the general theory of all prescriptive predicates about what ought or ought not to be valued, and it includes the disciplines of moral theory, psychology, the social sciences, and the humanities. In its more narrow sense, "value" is limited to moral theory, in which case axiology is a part of the field of ethics.

Axiology has its roots in the pre-Socratics who asked the question of the "really real"; what is the foundation of all other values, what is it that persists in the midst of change? Axiology is developed in Plato's theory of the *Forms* or *Ideas* which are the metaphysical archetypes of all values. In the *Dialogues,* he discusses the meaning of the right, obligation, beauty, virtue, moral judgment, aesthetic value, and truth. How are all these related? Plato believed that all questions about value belong to the same family and that they finally cohere in the *good,* the crowning and unitive form.

For Aristotle axiology is a constant topic of interest. It receives treatment in the *Organon, Ethics, Poetics,* and the *Metaphysics.* For him the highest value is the ultimate final cause, God. For Thomas Aquinas also, the *summum bonum* (the highest good or value) is God, who is the sole Ground for all other values.

The belief that questions about the good, the right, the beautiful, etc., could be answered through metaphysics was not seriously questioned until Kant's *Critique of Pure Reason.* According to Kant, the inherent epistemological limitations associated with the categories, and the two forms of knowing (space and time) make such knowledge unobtainable through speculative reason. The second and third *Critiques,* as well as the *Groundwork of the Metaphysics of Morals* which led to the second *Critique,* sought to establish another basis for value.

Hegel restored the metaphysical basis of axiology (value as the expression and self-realization of Absolute Spirit). But this restoration collapsed under the criticism of such people as Bauer, Feuerbach, and Marx.

In the 19th century Plato's idea that questions of value belong to one family was reborn. According to this position, questions about the good, the right, obligation, virtue, aesthetic and moral judgment, the beautiful, and truth are better dealt with when systematically thought of as components of a general theory of value and valuation that includes economics, ethics, aesthetics, jurisprudence, education, and perhaps even logic and epistemology. The idea of a general theory of value was very popular early in this century on the Continent, in Latin America, and in the U.S. (e.g., Ralph Barton Perry, John Dewey, and Paul Taylor).

Value theory holds a very important place in the process metaphysics of Alfred North Whitehead and Charles Hartshorne. For both, God is the Comprehensive Valuer who offers to the world *ideal aims,* the fulfillment of which satisfies value.

Ralph Barton Perry and Paul Taylor, who understand axiology in its *wider* sense, distinguish eight "realms of value": morality, the arts, science, religion, economics, politics, law, and custom (or etiquette).

Several meanings or forms of "value" or "the valuable" can be distinguished: (1) *extrinsic* or instrumental value, i.e., valued as a means to something else that is believed to be desirable or good; (2) *intrinsic* or inherent value or goodness, i.e., that which is judged good or valuable as an end in itself; (3) *contributory* value, i.e., value that contributes to a whole value of which it is a part (a violin contributes to an orchestra); (4) *moral* value, i.e., the sort of value or goodness that belongs to a virtuous person, or to a morally approved trait of character. (Some philosophers make an even sharper distinction between utilitarian and extrinsic or instrumental value, and between inherent or intrinsic value. But these distinctions seem to be forced.)

A distinction is also made between *normative* and *nonnormative* values. For those who believe that this is a proper distinction, some values are held to be normative, i.e., binding on everyone. Values that are judged normative are independent of the valuer's preferences. They *ought* to be valued; hence they are judged to be religiously or morally compelling. By contrast nonnormative values do arise from preference, e.g., when a person prefers one form of art over another. In this case it is, or should be, understood that the value is not generally binding; it carries no religious or moral authority.

Partly through the influence of language analysis philosophers, there is significant disagreement over whether values are *cognitive* or *noncognitive* in nature. Those who hold the first view believe that some values are *normative,* that they *ought* to be adhered to because they express ontological realities whose authority is independent of human preference, i.e., they have a purely objective basis. Such values denote a real property that transcends the desires and estimates of the valuing subject. Some phenomenologists, for instance, say that our experience of "normative values" is actually an experience of objective ethical essences that are *recognized* or *discovered* and that do not depend simply on one's choice of them.

Noncognitivists such as A. J. Ayer and Bertrand Russell deny the objectivity of values. They insist that all values are expressions of societal or individual preference. They express no absolutes, but are wholly expressions of attitudes, desires, and emotions. Accordingly, values are not *prescriptive,* i.e., they cannot tell us what people *ought* to value, but *descriptive,* i.e., they simply indicate what people in various times and under various circumstances *choose* to value. The philosopher's task is not to tell people what to value, but to examine the meaning of value language. What are we doing when we say that something is valuable? How do communities employ this language?

For some only one thing is valuable. For Aristotle this is *Eudaemonia* (excellent activity); for Augustine and Aquinas it is communion with God; for F. H. Bradley it is self-realization; for Neitzsche it is power. Other philosophers are more pluralistic; they hold that a number of things are good or good-making in themselves. These thinkers include Plato, G. E. Moore, W. D. Ross, Max Scheler, Nicolai Hartmann, and Ralph Barton Perry. Their list of "the valuable" include two or more of the following: pleasure, knowledge, aesthetic experience, beauty, truth, virtue, harmony, love, friendship, justice, freedom, and self-expression.

For some recent Protestant theologians, such as Bonhoeffer, Brunner, and Barth, the *good* is what God wills, vis., His word of creation, redemption, and fulfillment, spoken preeminently through the incarnation of God in Christ and His sanctification of human life in the world.

See VALUES, VALUES CLARIFICATION, ABSOLUTES, DUTY, BEAUTY.

For Further Reading: Ramsey, *Basic Christian Ethics;* Fronddizi, *What Is Value?*

ALBERT L. TRUESDALE, JR.

B

BAALISM. The greatest challenge to the religion of Israel from the time of Moses to the destruction of Jerusalem came from Baalism. While not a unified system of religion, Baalism, in its variegated expressions, was always a nature religion. The forces of nature, personified as gods, were worshipped through ritual dramas designed to manipulate those forces for the benefit of the worshipper.

The term "Baal" signifies an owner or lord. It is translated by a wide range of terms, including "master" (Isa. 1:3), "owner" (Exod. 21:28), "husband" (Prov. 31:11), and "man" (Gen. 20:3). Any deity called Baal, such as Baal-peor (Num. 25:3) or Baal-berith (Judg. 8:33), was thought of as a lord. The term was used early to refer to Yahweh. During the period of the prophets, when Yahwism came into sharp conflict with Baalism, it was dropped.

The most prominent deity in the Palestinian area was the rain god, Baal Hadad. The Syrian kings were named after him, Ben-hadad, "son of

Hadad" (1 Kings 15:18). Rainfall, which is essential to sustain life in this semiarid region, was thought of as the act of Hadad fertilizing the earth with his semen.

Worship included the ritual reenactment of the fertilization process. Periodically, the king played the part of Baal, and the high priestess, that of earth. By sympathetic magic it was believed that the gods could be induced to provide the necessary fertility for both crops and cattle.

Baalism thus conflicted with Yahwism in that it (1) conceived of deity as part of the forces of nature, (2) believed that deity could be controlled by magic, (3) encouraged sexual promiscuity, and (4) ascribed the reproductive forces of nature to deities other than the one who had delivered Israel from Egypt.

See IDOLATRY.

For Further Reading: Gray, *The Canaanites;* Habel, *Yahweh Vs. Baal: A Conflict of Religious Cultures.*

ROBERT D. BRANSON

BABYLON. An ancient city located on the Euphrates in Mesopotamia, now in modern Iraq, Babylon was founded by the Sumerians sometime during or before the third millennium B.C. It first came to prominence under the rule of Hammurabi (1792-50 B.C.) who extended his rule over southern Mesopotamia. Its most notable period of dominance came under the Chaldean rulers of the Neo-Babylonian Empire (626-539 B.C.). When Cyrus conquered the city in 539, he established Persion control which was maintained until Alexander the Great overthrew that empire (333-23 B.C.). Under the Persians, Babylon began a decline from which it never really recovered. The Parthians took the city in the second century B.C. and defended it a number of times against the Romans. When Emperor Julian took and destroyed the city in A.D. 363, it was not rebuilt.

Nebuchadnezzar, the most famous Chaldean ruler, besieged Jerusalem in 597 B.C. and deported its prominent citizens. Eleven years later he put down another revolt, destroying the city with its Temple and deporting its population.

The destruction of Jerusalem and the subsequent Exile had profound theological effects on the people. Exile meant living in an unclean land and being ruled by people who rejected the Lord as their God. The corruption, luxury, power, and immorality of the city typified all that God opposed. Babylon became symbolic both of existence alienated from God and of the powers of wickedness opposed to God.

In 1 Pet. 5:13, Babylon is interpreted by Catholics (and others) as being used metaphorically for Rome. In the Revelation, Babylon represents those forces of evil ranged against God and His people. As the city in which every type of wickedness exists, it stands in opposition to the city of God, Jerusalem.

See CITY, REVELATION (BOOK OF).

For Further Reading: Larue, *Babylon and the Bible;* Roux, *Ancient Iraq;* Saggs, *The Greatness That Was Babylon.*

ROBERT D. BRANSON

BACKSLIDING. Backsliding is a term occurring only in the OT (see Jer. 2:19; 3:5 ff; 5:6; 8:5; 14:7; Hos. 11:7; 14:4), where it means "to rebel against God" in favor of other gods and idols. Similar ideas are expressed in Hos. 4:16-17, "to become rebellious"; in Jer. 3:14, 22, to become apostate; and in Prov. 14:14, to "turn back."

The term is not used in the NT, but the danger of reversion to the old life by those who begin the Christian life is affirmed (Mark 4:16 ff; Luke 9:62; Gal. 5:1-5; 1 Tim. 5:15; 2 Tim. 4:10; Heb. 2:1-4; 10:38; Rev. 2:4 ff).

Backsliding refers to any degree of loss of commitment, fervor, spiritual priorities or testimony, with apostasy as a final consequence if uncorrected. Viewed as a process, backsliding begins with neglect of the means of grace or light, and leads to sin, broken fellowship with God, a defiled conscience, spiritual indifference and hardness of heart, unbelief, and apostasy.

It may be viewed as grieving, quenching, or resisting the Holy Spirit, and may extend to even "blasphemy against the Holy Spirit."

Arminian teaching is that backsliding may reach a point where a Christian becomes unrepentant and by turning his back on Christ does "despite unto the Spirit of grace," is no longer covered by Christ's sacrifice for sins (Heb. 10:26 ff), and has, therefore, fallen from grace and would be eternally lost if he were to die in such a state. Such can happen under the permissive will of God while probation continues.

Calvinistic teaching is that positional imputation and predestination to salvation secures even the backslider, though some affirm rather that if a person does not "endure to the end" (Matt. 24:13), it is evidence that the person was never truly saved.

Scripture holds out the offer of forgiveness and restoration to the backslider.

See APOSTASY, ETERNAL SECURITY, RESTORATIONISM.

For Further Reading: Shank, *Life in the Son;* Clarke, *Christian Theology.*

JAMES M. RIDGWAY

BAPTISM. This, with the Lord's Supper, is one of the two Christian sacraments believed in and practiced by almost all Protestants, the Quakers and the Salvation Army being perhaps the only significant exceptions. As a sacrament, baptism is both a sign and a seal of saving grace. As a sign, says Wiley, baptism symbolizes both regeneration and the baptism with the Holy Spirit (*CT,* 3:176). As a seal, it has both divine and human aspects. "On God's part, the seal is the visible assurance of faithfulness to His covenant—a perpetual ceremony to which His people may ever appeal." On man's part, "the seal is that by which he binds himself as a party to the covenant, and pledges himself to faithfulness in all things; and it is also the sign of a completed transaction—the ratification of a final agreement" (Wiley).

Some people have supposed that baptism is not very important, in part because the apostle Paul said to the divided church at Corinth, "Christ did not send me to baptize, but to preach the gospel" (1 Cor. 1:17, NASB). But the context of this shows that he had not baptized very many people lest those baptized by him would form a clique. He says, "I thank God that I baptized none of you except Crispus and Gaius, that no man should say you were baptized in my name" (vv. 14-15, NASB).

Baptism's importance is signified in part by Jesus' being baptized and by His including it in what we call the Great Commission (Matt. 28:19-20). Also, John the Baptist baptized many; and "Jesus was making and baptizing more disciples than John (although Jesus himself was not baptizing, but His disciples were)" (John 4:1-2, NASB). Besides, according to Acts, whenever people were converted to Christ, they were baptized in or with water (see Acts 2; 8—11; etc.).

The mode of baptism was not made altogether clear in Scripture. Sprinkling is only possibly alluded to when it was asked, "What did you go into the wilderness to look at? A reed shaken by the wind?" (Matt. 11:7, NASB). Perhaps John the Baptist was dipping a long reed into the Jordan and sprinkling water upon the believers. Immersion might be implied by the "buried with him by baptism" reference in Rom. 6:4. Pouring might be suggested because twice in Acts 2 (vv. 17-18), reference is made to the prophecy in Joel 2:28 about the Spirit being poured out; and surely Pentecost fulfilled that prophecy, as well as those in Matt. 3:11-12 and Acts 1:4-5.

See INFANT BAPTISM, BAPTISMAL REGENERATION, SACRAMENTS, SACRAMENTS (QUAKER AND SALVATION ARMY VIEWS), SACRAMENTARIANISM.

For Further Reading: Cullmann, *Baptism in the New Testament;* Wiley, *CT,* 3:155-89; *GMS,* 586-91

J. KENNETH GRIDER

BAPTISM FOR THE DEAD. Paul made a curious reference to baptism, and we can only conjecture about what he meant by it. He said, "Now if there is no resurrection, what will those do who are baptized for the dead?" (1 Cor. 15:29, NIV). Adam Clarke considered it one of the most difficult-to-interpret passages in all of Scripture.

Numerous possible meanings have been given by commentators, most of which are not deserving of mention here. Some are a little more deserving, but are still not apt interpretations. One of them is that it refers to baptisms of Christian believers "for the dead," meaning, to take the place, in the church, that is left vacant when Christians die. The main problem with this interpretation is that it would not apply to Paul's argument: it would not be an argument for the resurrection of the body, but for the need of new Christians taking the place, in service, of Christians who die.

The passage probably refers to a practice which Paul did not believe in, but which his readers would have known about, of the living being baptized on behalf of the dead—as is now practiced in Mormonism. He is saying that if the dead do not rise, why do people who are not even Christian evidently believe that they do, and show such by being baptized for them? This would suit the argument, and it would interpret a difficult passage consistently with the plain passages (in which baptism is only entered into by the living). This meaning might also be suggested by the switch Paul seems to be making, from non-Christians to themselves, by saying, in the very next words, "And as for us, why do we endanger ourselves every hour?" (1 Cor. 15:30, NIV).

See BAPTISM, BAPTISMAL REGENERATION.

For Further Reading: *BBC,* 8:465; *WBC,* 5:232.

J. KENNETH GRIDER

BAPTISM WITH THE HOLY SPIRIT. "You shall be baptized with the Holy Spirit not many days from now" (Acts 1:5, NASB). This promise-command is Christ's last word to His disciples, and it consummates His redemptive ministry. Seven passages in the NT refer to being baptized with the Holy Spirit (Matt. 3:11; Mark 1:18; Luke 3:16; John 1:33; Acts 1:5; 11:16; 1 Cor. 12:13). However, this doctrine is implicit throughout the NT.

Baptism with the Holy Spirit is distinctive of the NT and does not occur in the OT per se, although it is anticipated there (see Joel 2:28-32; 3:1-2; Isa. 32:15; 44:3; Ezek. 39:29). The NT clearly distinguishes between water baptism and baptism with the Holy Spirit. John the Baptist specifies the distinction between his preparatory water baptism and Christ's subsequent baptism with the Holy Spirit and fire for power and purity (Matt. 3:11-12).

In Christ's fulfillment of "all righteousness" (v. 15), John notes that Christ's symbolic water baptism preceded His Spirit enduement (vv. 13-17). John then links Christ's own Spirit enduement with His mission to baptize His followers with the Holy Spirit (John 1:33), which was not to be accomplished until the Pentecostal effusion (Luke 24:49; John 7:38-39; Acts 1:5; 2:1-4).

All of the promises concerning baptism in the Spirit find their fulfillment in the Pentecostal effusion but never before. When Jesus "breathed on them [His disciples], and said to them, 'Receive the Holy Spirit'" (John 20:22, NASB), He was acting symbolically and in anticipation, according to some scholars. However, Wesley understood it to be an "earnest of Pentecost" *(Notes).*

It is noteworthy that Christ claimed these disciples as His own before their baptism with the Spirit at Pentecost (John 17:6-18). He endued them with authority and power and commissioned them to preach, heal the sick, raise the dead, and cast out demons long before their Pentecostal experience (Matt. 10:1-16; 28:18-20). This would appear absurd had they not been truly converted. But again He verified their spiritual citizenship in God's kingdom (Luke 10:20) long before their Pentecost baptism. And moreover they were communicant members of His Church (Matt. 26:26-29), and they waited expectantly for the promised baptism with the Spirit (Acts 1:13-14; 2:1).

The baptism with the Spirit fulfills the predictive promises of the OT prophets (Joel 2:28-32; cf. 3:1-2; Isa. 32:15; 44:3; Ezek. 39:29); of John the Baptist (Matt. 3:11); of God the Father (Luke 24:49; Acts 1:4-5; 2:33); of Christ himself (John 7:38-39; 14:16-17, 26; 15:26; 16:7; Acts 1:8); and of the apostles (Acts 2:38-39).

The disciples' experience of the baptism with the Holy Spirit is recorded in Acts 2:1-4 and reflects the following four main aspects: *power* for holy living and effective service; *purity* or sanctification, symbolized by "tongues as fire" (cf. Matt. 3:11; Acts 10:44-47; 11:5-17; 15:8-9); full *possession* of their beings as "they were all filled with the Holy Spirit"; and *proclamation* or witness for Christ as they "began to speak . . . as the Spirit was giving them utterance" (NASB). Thus converted and baptized with the Holy Spirit, these servants of Christ were to inundate the Roman Empire with the message of full salvation from all sin.

See HOLY SPIRIT, ENTIRE SANCTIFICATION, PENTECOST, ANOINTING, DISPENSATION OF THE SPIRIT.

For Further Reading: Carter, *The Person and Ministry of the Holy Spirit,* 89-247; Agnew, *The Holy Spirit: Friend and Counselor;* Chadwick, *The Way to Pentecost;* Wood, *Pentecostal Grace.*

CHARLES W. CARTER

BAPTISMAL REGENERATION. This doctrine holds that the sacrament of water baptism, if administered by prescribed persons according to the prescribed form, communicates to the baptized the blessings and the benefits of the new birth. An extreme position is that without such water baptism regeneration and hence eternal salvation are impossible.

The NT does connect regeneration with water, as in John 3:5; Acts 22:16; Titus 3:5. However, careful exegesis does not justify understanding these passages to teach that water is the actual means by which people are regenerated.

The best-known passage is John 3:5, "Unless one is born of water and the Spirit, he cannot enter into the kingdom of God" (NASB). If the water here refers to the rite of baptism, then indeed we have strong support for the idea of baptismal regeneration, since Jesus clearly makes water an equally indispensable condition for entering into the kingdom of God. However, John Calvin took the position that water here is a metaphor and that there is no more need to interpret it literally than to demand literal fire in our understanding of Matt. 3:11.

If water is to be understood metaphorically, what does it represent? Some have seen it as "a symbol of the old order of the Law with its ritual of baptisms, purifications, and cleansings" *(BBC).* Therefore, Jesus is saying to Nicodemus, in effect "Begin where you are, but fulfilment, life, . . . will come only with birth from above, the birth of the Spirit!" *(BBC).* Still others understand the phrase "of water" to refer to the water of natural physical birth, and they point to Isa. 48:1 as suggesting this. Another understanding of the word "water" as a metaphor is to see it as representing the Word in its rejuvenating, regenerating, and cleansing power so that the two agencies in our new birth are the Word and the Spirit (John 15:3; Eph. 5:26, NASB). This view is to be preferred.

In Acts 22:16 the real meaning seems to be, "Be baptized in water and thereby assert to all that your sins have been washed away." Speaking of this passage, A. T. Robertson says: "It is possible, as in 2:38, to take these words as teaching baptismal remission or salvation by means of baptism, but to do so is in my opinion a complete subversion of Paul's vivid and picturesque language. As in Rom. 6:4-6 where baptism is the picture of death, burial and resurrection, so here baptism pictures the change that had already taken place when Paul surrendered to Jesus on the way (v. 10)" *(Word Pictures).*

Titus 3:5 speaks of "the washing of regeneration and renewing by the Holy Spirit" (NASB). Gould comments: "Baptism is not to be understood as the actual means by which men are saved, but rather is to be regarded, here at least, as symbolical of the experience of death to sin and spiritual resurrection in newness of life" *(BBC).*

Theologically, the concept of baptismal regeneration is totally antithetical to the spiritual emphasis of the NT. The gospel order is not the perpetuation but the termination of the religious mechanics by which spiritual privileges are dependent upon prescribed times, places, and external rites. This basic and pervasive NT principle is expressed by Paul: "Neither is circumcision anything, nor uncircumcision, but a new creation" (Gal. 6:15, NASB).

See SACRAMENTS, BAPTISM, SACRAMENTARIANISM.

For Further Reading: Hills, *Fundamental Christian Theology,* 2:282-325; Wiley, *CT,* 3:161-71.

ARMOR D. PEISKER

BAPTISTS. The Baptist movement originated in England and Holland, and is closely related to the Anabaptists and Mennonites of the Reformation period.

The movement began as a protest against infant baptism. The Anabaptists rebaptized adults who had been baptized as infants. Before 1640 immersion was not an issue, but became a custom and belief by 1644.

Although there are at least 27 Baptist denominations (or sects), there are common beliefs and principles among them:

(1) Church membership is restricted to baptized (immersed) believers; (2) the local church is autonomous (independent); and (3) church and state should be completely separate. They hold in common with evangelical churches the inspiration and trustworthiness of the Bible, the Lordship of Jesus, the freedom of the individual to come to Christ, and salvation by faith.

The Baptists vary in their understanding of atonement and salvation. Some (Freewill Baptists) accept a universal atonement and freedom of a person to choose, while others (Primitive Baptists) believe strongly in predestination. Most Baptists, however, hold a moderate Calvinism. This is salvation by faith, and freedom to choose. Often they teach the security of the believer as fixed, and that sinning does not separate from God. Complete freedom from sinfulness is usually denied.

See CHURCH, CHURCH GOVERNMENT, REBAPTISM, BAPTISM.

For Further Reading: *Baker's DT,* 89-91; Hardon, *The Protestant Churches of America,* 19-43; Henry, ed., *Christian Faith and Modern Theology,* 375-86.

LEO G. COX

BEATITUDES. Beatitude, from the Latin *beatitudo,* means "blessedness" or "happiness." The beatitude is a literary form used in the Bible, especially in the NT in the sayings of Jesus Christ. It begins by pronouncing someone "blessed" or "happy" (Gr. *makarios*). It then states the reason for his happiness.

The two large collections of Beatitudes in the NT are the ones which Jesus used to introduce the Sermon on the Mount (Matt. 5:3-12; Luke 6:20-26). When we compare the two collections as recorded by Matthew and Luke, we are impressed by the resemblances and the differences between them. In Matthew we find nine Beatitudes, while in Luke we find four (6:20-23), followed by four woes (6:24-26). While Matthew emphasizes the moral and eschatological viewpoint, Luke emphasizes more the present and social aspects.

The Beautitudes should not be interpreted as portraying separate types of Christian character, but rather as a list of qualities and experiences which are typical of the ideal character of the Christian as conceived by Jesus Christ, and as exemplified in His own life and person.

Following the literary structure described above, each one of the Beatitudes associates a blessing with a promise. This promise sometimes has an immediate realization, and sometimes a future and even an eschatological fulfillment. The declaration of the blessedness is based not only on the possession of the quality or experience, but rather on the present or future reward.

The term *beatitude* is not only used in the Bible as an abstract term denoting blessedness, but also in a secondary, concrete sense of a particular declaration of blessedness. In the OT we find examples of this kind of beatitude in the Wisdom Literature, particularly in the Psalms (1:1; 32:1; 41:1; 65:4; 106:3), and in Proverbs (3:13; 8:32, 34; 20:7; 28:14). Although the nearness of God is the source of such happiness, the rewards are usually in terms of a full life on earth. In the NT Jesus on several occasions used the term in this sense (Matt. 11:6; 13:16; 16:17; 24:46; John 13:17; 20:29).

See HAPPINESS, HOLINESS, WHOLE (WHOLENESS), HOPE.

For Further Reading: Barclay, *The Beatitudes and the Lord's Prayer for Everyman;* Pink, *An Exposition on the Sermon on the Mount,* 15-42. ISMAEL E. AMAYA

BEAUTY. For the Greeks, beauty came to embody what was of highest value. Beauty was not simply an abstraction or an incidental pleasure, but the real value of life by which the various goods were judged. The meaning broadened to include the intellectual and moral life as well. The aesthetic, moral, and metaphysical aspects of beauty could not be separated.

Socrates knew that the beauty of outward form and the goodness of inner form did not necessarily appear together. He insisted that for the concept to be true it must characterize the inner life of man as well.

Plato distinguished between relative or instrumental beauty, and intrinsic or absolute beauty. Beauty includes all aspects of the Greek aesthetic consciousness. The lover of beauty is classified with the lover of truth. He is a philosopher.

According to Aristotle, the main characteristics of beauty are: "order, symmetry, and definite limitation." Virtues are beautiful and are worthy of praise.

Generally, after Plato the whole question of aesthetics revolved around the question of beauty. In the history of philosophy efforts to specify a set of conditions by which intrinsic beauty could be recognized have been disappointing. In the 16th and 17th centuries conditions for recognizing beauty were detailed and formalized. But a rebellion against the stated criteria soon followed.

In the 18th century a number of thinkers turned from primary examination of the beautiful as such to the subject who recognizes beauty. They began by examining the experiences of the percipient to determine the conditions under which beauty and art are appreciated. Francis Hutchison (1725) maintained that the beautiful is that which excites or raises the idea of beauty in us. Later, Kant raised an obvious question about this estimate of beauty: If the aesthetic judgment arises from subjective feeling and predicates nothing inherently true about the object, how can the "beautiful" claim to be more than an autobiographical report? Or, how can an aesthetic judgment claim to be universally binding if beauty is not a property of that which is judged to be beautiful?

In sharp contrast to such thinkers as Socrates, Plato, Aristotle, Cicero, and Plotinus, the Bible does not attempt to define beauty (Gr. *to kalon*). There is in the Bible no articulated aesthetic doctrine as such. Rather, the Bible describes that which is beautiful. Here there is no sharp distinction between the aesthetically beautiful and the ethical. A rich and diverse vocabulary is used to speak of beauty.

In the OT numerous Hebrew words, translatable by "fair," "honor," "glory," "delightful," "lovely," "handsome," "splendor," and "grace" are used to speak of that which is beautiful. In the NT several Greek terms bear the meaning of "beautiful," "charming," "attractive," "handsome," "fine appearance," and "honor."

In the Bible, nature is judged to be beautiful (good). Genesis and the Psalms express repeated wonder over the beauty of God's handiwork in nature (Psalms 8; 19:1-6; 29; 65:9-13; 104; 147:8-18). Hebrew appreciation for the beauty of nature is made possible in part because of the belief that the world is the direct creation of the God of the Covenant.

The Bible lavishly describes the beauty of Palestine and Jerusalem, the Jewish nation and the Temple (Jer. 3:19; Ps. 48:1; Lam. 2:15; Ezra 7:27). People such as Sarah, Rebekah, Rachel, and Esther are described as beautiful. The same is true of Joseph, Moses, David, Absalom, Jonathan, and Daniel. According to Isa. 33:17, the Messiah will be beautiful.

God himself is described as being beautiful. His beauty passes before Moses (Exod. 33:19). He is the God of *glory* (16:7, 10; 24:16-17; Lev. 9:6, 23; Deut. 5:24; Josh. 7:19). He is a beautiful emblem of regal power and dignity for His people (Isa. 28:5).

In the NT the word *kalon* (noun; *kalos,* adjective) is used to speak of the beautiful and the good. It denotes that which is of good quality or disposition. Jesus describes fertile and rich soil as beautiful (Matt. 13:8, 23). It can also mean that which is useful and profitable (Luke 14:34). *Kalon* is also used to describe what is excellent, choice, select, goodly (Matt. 7:17, 19), pleasant, and delightful (17:4). In the NT beauty also has a clear association with what is morally excellent, worthy, upright, and virtuous (John 10:11, 14; 1 Tim. 4:6). Good deeds and rectitude (Matt. 5:16; Rom. 7:18, 21), as well as the fulfillment of one's duty may also be spoken of as beautiful.

See AESTHETICS, VALUES, AXIOLOGY.

For Further Reading: Dean, *Coming to a Theology of Beauty;* Pelikan, *Fools for Christ: Essays on the True, the Good, and the Beautiful;* Santayana, *The Sense of Beauty.*

ALBERT L. TRUESDALE, JR.

BEELZEBUB. See SATAN.

BEGINNING. *In the beginning God.* These opening words of Gen. 1:1 are compressed into two words in Hebrew: *"bereshith . . . Elohim."* They express two profound foundational truths of the Christian faith. First, *bereshith* is used absolutely and refers to the beginning before which there was nothing which is now part of the material universe. This excludes the Aristotelian idea of a universe that was "ungenerated and indestructible," having an infinite past and an infinite future. The biblical revelation affirms that the world had a beginning, in due course will have an ending, and God is responsible for both.

Second, the Hebrew name for God, *Elohim,* is plural in form but takes the singular verb. This is regarded by some as a rudimentary allusion to the triunity of God. In the very least it is a "plural of majesty" which sums up in the Creator God all the divine powers and attributes. In Gen. 1:1 God is self-existent, the First Cause of all that is, an eternal Being who existed before the beginning.

Theocentric Character of Creation. The material universe is distinctly God's work, not an independent process of nature. Some 50 times in Genesis 1—2 God is the subject of verbs showing what He did as Creator: "God created," "God said," "God called," "the Lord God made," "the Lord God formed," etc. This theocentric character of creation is repeatedly emphasized in both the OT and NT.

Creatio ex Nihilo. This classical formula of theology means "creation out of nothing." "In the beginning God created the heaven and the earth," not out of preexistent matter, but out of nothing. Many theologians argue that this is religious or symbolic language, not a factual statement about the world's origin. Some change the meaning of Gen. 1:1 by translating it as a dependent or temporal clause: "In the beginning when God created the heavens and the earth, when the earth was waste and desolate, . . . then God said . . ." The NEB is one of several modern translations that take this approach. This rendering alters "in the beginning" to mean some indefinite point when God and matter coexisted and God began to form matter into the present universe. This translation discounts *creatio ex nihilo,* sets up a dualism making matter coexistent with God, and conforms the Genesis account to the Babylonian Epic of Creation. Although the above translation is technically possible, the construction is contrary to the simple grammatical construction found elsewhere in the chapter and the normal simplicity of Hebrew sentences generally. (For a definitive study of the issue, see E. J. Young.)

See CREATION, GOD, THEISM, COSMOLOGY.

For Further Reading: Keil and Delitzsch, *Commentary on the Old Testament,* 1:37-48; Lehman, *Biblical Theology: Old Testament,* 42-52; Morrow, "In the Beginning: God and Science," *Time,* 113 (Feb. 5, 1979), 149-50; Schaeffer, *Genesis in Space and Time,* 13-31; Young, *Studies in Genesis One,* 1-14. J. WESLEY ADAMS

BEGOTTEN. See ONLY BEGOTTEN.

BEING. The term "being" is a participle used to translate the Greek abstract noun *ousia* which is related to the verb "to be." While not entirely accurate as a translation, "being" traditionally denotes the substance, essence, or nature of some entity, or signifies some general property common to all that is. *Ousia* is not a NT term. However, medieval thinkers often cited Exod. 3:14 ("I AM WHO I AM") to identify God with Being itself.

Plato first discussed being in a systematic manner, contrasting the world of change with the unchanging being of metaphysical forms. Since then the meaning of being has played an important part in Western thought. Those inclined towards metaphysics view being as the object of their inquiry (idealism, process philosophy); those opposed to metaphysics consider being as the most empty of all general concepts (positivism, analytical philosophy). In recent thought continental philosophers reject being as some underlying substance of "stuff" by relating being to human existence (Marxism, existentialism).

In Christian theology being primarily appears in three contexts. First, being expresses the underlying unity wherein all three Persons of the Godhead are One. This is the sense in which classical theology speaks of God as absolute. Or ancient creedal statements mention the "same substance" *(homoousios)* with respect to the Father and Son in Trinitarian discussion. Second, Roman Catholic theology distinguishes between the substance and accidents of the Eucharistic elements. The substance of the bread and wine is transubstantiated into the very body and blood of Christ, while the elemental accidents (taste, color) remain the same. Third, Paul Tillich and John Macquarrie suggest that being be understood as that which empowers us to be and that God be identified with Being as such. However, critics charge that this departs from the traditional emphasis on God as *a* being.

See METAPHYSICS, GOD, NATURE, HUMAN NATURE.

For Further Reading: Wiley, *CT,* 1:249-54; Tillich, *Systematic Theology,* 1:163-204, 235-41; Macquarrie, *Principles of Christian Theology,* 107-22; Stead, *Divine Substance.*

HERBERT L. PRINCE

BELIEF. A belief is a specific conviction of truth. The plural, "beliefs," refers to the set of doctrines to which one commits himself. The term is not necessarily religious. One may have political, philosophical, or scientific beliefs, or beliefs in a variety of other categories. In the religious sphere one's beliefs are one's intellectual understandings and convictions about God and religious matters.

By and large it may be said that belief is the cognitive side of faith—the content side—which may fall short of Christian faith, for it may stop with the assent of the mind. Many have subscribed to a creed or to a religious philosophy or way of life who have never personally put their trust in a living Christ.

Yet sometimes the NT uses "the faith" as equivalent to the particular body of teachings marking the boundaries of that which is authentically Christian in distinction from that which is still pagan (e.g., Acts 6:7; 13:8; 14:22; Rom. 1:5; Gal. 1:23; Jude 3).

See FAITH, FIDELITY, OBEDIENCE.

For Further Reading: Purkiser, ed., *Exploring Our Christian Faith* (1960), 26-38.

RICHARD S. TAYLOR

BELIEVER. See CHRISTIAN.

BENEDICTION. The words "benediction" and "blessing" are closely related in the Scriptures. The former, when used in the active voice, normally refers to God blessing things, as in Gen. 22:17-18. Thus God blesses men. In time the human response to God's blessings naturally became associated with worship and with meals. A part of the Talmud consists of "blessings" in the form of prayers to be used before the eating of meals, or the reading of the Law. The practice is a humble acknowledgment of dependence on God's goodness for physical and spiritual food and strength.

A benediction may be a prayer for God's blessing, or an acknowledgment of its having been received. The "blessing" of the bread and cup during the Last Supper (Matt. 26:26-27; 1 Cor. 10:16) is the most important and far-reaching now in use. The Christian appellation *Eucharist* for the Lord's Supper indicates the believer's acceptance of God's greatest Benediction on mankind, and the believer's gratitude for it.

A benediction may also be a form of good words spoken on God's behalf, to a congregation of His people, by His representative. In this sense the words and the spokesman's gestures are closely related (2 Chron. 30:26-27; Neh. 9:5; Ps. 134:2; 1 Tim. 2:8). There are many such benedictions or blessings in Scripture, the most familiar being found in Num. 6:24-26; 2 Cor. 13:14; Heb. 13:20-21; Phil. 4:7; Eph. 1:3 ff; Rev. 1:4 ff. Many other scriptures may readily be used as blessings or benedictions. Perhaps we can grasp a little more of the meaning of the words if we remember that they sometimes stand in contrast with the curse (Gen. 27:12; Deut. 11:26-28; 23:5; etc.). Also, Paul sometimes links material and spiritual blessing (cf. Rom. 15:29; 2 Cor. 9:5; Heb. 6:6-7; 12:17).

See CURSE, PRAYER, PRAISE, WORSHIP.

For Further Reading: Blackwood, *The Fine Art of Public Worship;* Pugsley, *A Preacher's Prayer Book.*

T. CRICHTON MITCHELL

BENEVOLENCE. Benevolence was a common word in the *koinē* Greek (the language of the people or "common" Greek). Having a variety of uses, it generally means goodwill, affection, and favor. When used as a verb it means "to be well disposed," friendly, attached, or "to meet halfway" in general dealings between men. In Matt. 5:25 (NIV), the direction given to the debtor is, "Settle matters quickly with your adversary." The Greek *(eunoōn)* carries the meaning of the urgency of removing the wrongs men do one another. Because of impending judgment, the wrongdoer must repent quickly and show good will to the other.

Early Greek writers list benevolence *(eunoia)* among the qualities of the wise and of a good ruler. In Jewish and Christian usage, it also means affection and love between relatives; and love between husband and wife (even being used for sexual union, as in 1 Cor. 7:3, KJV).

Benevolence, as a civic virtue, implies devotion, fidelity, goodwill, loyalty, and willingness. As a duty of Christian slaves (*employees* in modern society), it requires service with "good will" (Eph. 6:7). This is a readiness and zeal with a religious basis. For the church, a NT example is Paul's love offering for the poor and needy Jerusalem saints (1 Cor. 16:1-3).

See CHARITY, LOVE, AGAPĒ.

For Further Reading: Arndt, Gingrich, 323; Kittel, 4:972 ff; Wiley, *CT,* 3:76-79.

CHARLES WILSON SMITH

BETRAYAL. In Scripture "betrayal" refers to the manner in which Jesus was delivered into the hands of the ecclesiastical and the civil authorities for trial and death. Judas Iscariot is the primary figure in this foul deed, according to each of the four Gospel writers (Matthew 26; Mark 14; Luke 22; John 13). Hence, the name Judas has become a byword for one who will falsely betray another for personal gain.

The impetus for the betrayal was satanic (John 13:2); however, there was something in the character of Judas which made him susceptible to such a suggestion (12:4-6). Characteristically, betrayal involves treachery, as seen in Judas' kiss.

That the betrayal of Jesus was a violation of trust is further illustrated by the giving of the "sop" (John 13:26-27). In conformity to oriental custom, Jesus, as the Host at the feast, dipped a small piece of bread in the gravy from the roast lamb, probably gathering some crumbs of roast with the bread. This was placed by Jesus in the mouth of Judas, signifying first, that the recipient was an honored guest and that, second, the host was now obligated to protect, with his life if necessary, the recipient.

Few sins are more despicable or inexcusable than the violation of trust. This could have been an element in the primal sin of the universe, when (according to the traditional view) an archangel became Satan the Adversary. Jesus spoke of Satan as the father of lying (John 8:44).

See FAITHFULNESS, INFIDELITY, TRUST.

For Further Reading: Turner, Martey, *The Gospel of John,* 271 ff.

LEROY E. LINDSEY

BIBLE. The Holy Bible is the sacred book of Christians, and its first major division is also the sacred book of the Jews. Throughout Christendom it is commonly referred to as the Word of God, and by evangelicals believed to be the final and sufficient authority in all matters pertaining to doctrine and Christian life.

The English word *Bible* is derived from the Greek word *biblion,* meaning "a written volume, roll, or little book" (cf. Luke 4:17, 20; Rev. 10:9). *Biblion* is derived from the Greek word *biblios,* a word for the pith of the papyrus plant which, when processed, became paper (*papyri* in Latin). The plural of *biblion* is *biblia.* Thus books written on paper were called *biblia.* How a plural word derived a singular meaning is not clear. Possibly the neuter plural word *biblia* was assumed to be a femine singular (spelled the same). At any rate the word *Book* (Bible) came to be applied to the entire collection of Christian sacred writings. That was fitting because of the unity of the Scriptures.

The Bible is composed of the OT ("the old covenant") and the NT ("the new covenant"). The OT is the body of Scriptures adopted by Judaism centuries before Christ's birth, but made official by the Council of Jamnia in A.D. 90. While other religious works had been produced by the Jews, the 39 books of the OT are the only books which they considered to be inspired. Inspiration itself seems to have been determined by the standing of the person or persons who wrote the books. The writings of prophets (as Moses, Samuel, Jeremiah, etc.) and of others who, although not prophets, possessed the prophetic gift (as David, Solomon, etc.) were believed to be inspired. Other writings, though having religious value, found no place among their Scriptures. In general, the Christian church accepted the judgment of Judaism in this matter, though apocryphal (uncanonical) books sometimes have been bound separately in their versions. Only the Roman branch of Christianity has pronounced the Apocrypha inspired (Council of Trent, 1545-63).

There was a time of disagreement in the Early Church over which books should comprise the NT. The present 27 books were suggested first by Athanasius (A.D. 315). Again inspiration was the chief determinant. Books were considered to be inspired if they were written by an apostle (as Peter, Paul, etc.) or by one who worked closely with, and under the influence of, an apostle (as Mark or Luke). Besides apostolicity, the tests of spirituality, agreement with unquestioned books in doctrine and morality, and the usefulness of the books also were applied.

The original languages of the Bible were Hebrew and a few Aramaic passages for the OT, and Greek for the NT.

Christians generally divide the literature of the OT into the Pentateuch (Genesis through Deuteronomy), the Historical Books (Joshua through Esther), the Poetical and/or Wisdom Literature (Job through Song of Solomon), and the Prophets. The Prophets extend from Isaiah through Malachi and are subdivided into Major Prophets (Isaiah through Daniel) and Minor Prophets (Hosea through Malachi). Jews divide their Scriptures into the Law, the Prophets, and the Writings. The Law *(Torah)* contains the books traditionally attributed to Moses (Genesis through Deuteronomy). The Prophets *(Nabim)* are subdivided into Former and Latter Prophets. The Former Prophets include Joshua, Judges-Ruth, and Samuel and Kings each as one book. The Latter Prophets are Isaiah, Jeremiah-Lamentations, Ezekiel, and the Twelve (Hosea through Malachi). Other books are listed as Writings *(Kethubim),* sometimes called "The Psalms" (cf. Luke 24:44) after the most prominent book of that division.

Christians divide the NT into the Gospels (Matthew through John), the Historical Book (Acts), the Epistles, and the Apocalypse (Revelation). The Epistles are subdivided into the Pauline Epistles (Romans through Philemon) and the General Epistles (roughly James through Jude). Disagreement over who wrote the Epistle to the Hebrews has continued since the second century A.D.

Originally the Bible was not divided into chapters and verses. The words of the OT text were not separated from each other in the earliest manuscripts, neither did they contain vowel letters. Jewish scholars called Masoretes added vowel points after A.D. 600. Stephen Langton (d. 1228) probably was the first to divide the Bible into chapters. Robert Stephens divided the NT into verses about A.D. 1551.

The overall theme of the Bible is the redemption of man. The OT reveals the need for redemption and God's preparatory stages in its unfolding. The NT presents Christ as God's means of redemption, and more fully displays its nature, both in time and eternity. If read aright, the Bible always leads to Christ. An epitome of the progressive revelation found in the Bible is Heb. 1:1-4.

Disciplines closely related to the Bible are: apologetics, the defense of the Bible's authority; biblical criticism, which inquires into the origin, character, and purposes of the several books (higher criticism), and which seeks to bring the text to the highest possible level of accuracy (lower criticism); biblical theology, which discovers the doctrines of the Bible; and hermeneutics, the science of biblical interpretation.

See BIBLICAL AUTHORITY, BIBLICAL INERRANCY, BIBLICAL REALISM, INSPIRATION, HERMENEUTICS, APOCRYPHA, CANON, BIBLE: THE TWO TESTAMENTS.

For Further Reading: Demaray, *Bible Study Source Book; ZPBD; Eerdman's Handbook to the Bible;* Wakefield, *A Complete System of Christian Theology,* 51-123.

W. RALPH THOMPSON

BIBLE, INSPIRATION OF. See INSPIRATION OF THE BIBLE.

BIBLE: THE TWO TESTAMENTS. The relation between the Old and New Testaments has posed a problem at various periods in the history of the church. Marcion's rejection of the OT as witnessing to an inferior god, and the widespread disuse of the OT in the modern church, are but two illustrations of the phenomenon. These examples embody two aspects of the problem. Marcion's discarding of the OT was based on *theological* grounds; current attention focuses on the *hermeneutical* issues: the difficulty of justifying the way in which the NT uses the OT, which in turn raises questions as to how the OT may be validly used today.

Ultimately, the two questions are one, especially when the term *hermeneutic* is used in a normative (rather than a merely descriptive) sense. If it can be shown that the OT is *related* to the NT by a valid hermeneutic, then it follows that the OT is theologically *relevant* to the NT and thereby to the Christian Church. Comprehensive treatment here is impossible. What will be attempted is an account of representative features of the hermeneutic of each Testament followed by an analysis of the principles upon which both Testaments are linked.

Characteristics of the Hermeneutic of the Old Testament

Before taking up the question of the relationship between the OT and the NT, it is worth inquiring as to the nature of the interpretative process within the OT itself. Three features figure prominently.

1. *Promise and Fulfillment.* This motif, which is sometimes advanced as being characteristic of the relationship between the Testaments, functions significantly within the OT. Several aspects of its use are worth noting.

a. There are specific promises which find specific fulfillment. Moses' word promises deliverance from Egypt when such an event seems utterly improbable (Exod. 3:10-12, 15-17; 4:29-31); and the promise is fulfilled in the Exodus and the eventual occupation of the land of Canaan. Isaiah promises deliverance from Sennacherib (Isa. 37:21 ff; cf. 30:15), and his prophecy is vindicated (37:36).

b. Other promises are more far-reaching in their scope and therefore more complex in their fulfillment. So much is this so that in many cases the form of the fulfillment could not be deduced from the terms of the promise. The covenant promise is a good example (Gen. 12:3). The original covenant had to do with *land* (13:14-17; 15:12-21). The Sinai covenant, though linked with the patriarchs (Exod. 3:6, 15-16) and related ultimately to land (vv. 8, 17), was concerned in its immediate form with *law* (24:3, 7-8), indispensably necessary for ordering the life of a larger community than that with which the Abrahamic covenant was made. The Davidic covenant differed yet again as being concerned with *dynasty* (2 Sam. 7:12-17); nonetheless, it was related to the earlier events at Sinai (vv. 22 ff), and had as its object the permanence of the people in the land (vv. 10 f, 23 f). What this amounts to is that the fulfillment of the promise is transmuted on account of the contingent events of Israel's history.

c. Amid the fulfillment there remains an element of incompleteness. Thus Jeremiah speaks of a new covenant which will supersede the old in the act of fulfilling it (Jer. 31:31-34). Cullmann's generalization is sound: "Many fulfillments are also the promises of another fulfillment. Fulfillment within the biblical framework is never complete" (*Salvation in History,* 124).

2. *Salvation History.* In the OT, salvation is realized within history and therefore has a history. The covenants alluded to in illustration of promise and fulfillment are regularly formulated in association with the recital of God's mighty acts (Exod. 20:2; 2 Sam. 7:8-9, 23 f). The significant feature is that, in this developing process, there takes place the amalgamation of a *constant,* the divine plan, with a *contingency,* the unfolding events unforeseen by this plan, especially those which are in opposition to it. This means that the new saving events require to be placed in connection with the old, necessitating a reinterpretation of them. That is, in the course of salvation history the divine plan is clarified, modified, and transformed.

3. *Typology.* While commonly regarded as a means of relating the Testaments, typological interpretation is part of the hermeneutical process within the OT. The concept originates within prophetic eschatology whereby present events are interpreted in terms of past events. The prime example is the Exodus which is viewed as the prefigurement of God's later deliverances of His people (cf. Isa. 43:14-21; 48:20 f; 51:9-11). A related example is the new covenant (Jer. 31:31-34; Isa. 43:16-21). Implicit in such typological exegesis, as L. Goppelt points out (art. "types," *TDNT* 8:254), is that the divine plan reaches its goal in spite of judgment; but also, that the renewal does not simply correspond to what went before: it transcends it. The new covenant is not a repromulgation of the old, but an advance upon it.

The importance of the foregoing features within the OT is that they demonstrate the presence there of hermeneutical dynamism. The fulfillment is not bound by the literal terms of the promise or the type but spills over beyond these, to the extent that the fulfillment could not be deduced from the terms of the promise or the type. There may be correspondence of substance between the two, but not correspondence of form. The importance of these observations regarding OT hermeneutics is that the NT is often criticized for handling the OT *in the very way in which the OT interprets itself.*

Characteristics of the Hermeneutic of the New Testament

Whereas the field of investigation for OT hermeneutic is the OT's interpretation of itself, the field of investigation for NT hermeneutic is the NT's interpretation of the OT. The OT was the Bible of the primitive Church, and among the conspicuous features of the latter's interpretation of the former were the following.

1. *Christocentricity.* The fundamental feature of the NT reading of the OT is that the OT speaks of Christ and finds its fulfillment in Him. According to the Synoptics, this view goes back to Jesus himself. It is made comprehensively by the risen Christ with specific reference to His death (Luke 24:26 f, 44-47). A similar approach is evident during His ministry, again with particular reference to His death (Mark 9:12; 14:49; Matt. 26:54-56), though not exclusively thereto (Luke 4:21). Nowhere is the point affirmed more strongly than in the Gospel of John (5:39, 46; 13:18). If this is so, then Jesus' followers learned from Him well as is shown in the Gospels by Matthew's fulfillment formulae (1:18; 2:15, 17; etc.), as well as in the Epistles where OT passages which, in their original, historical sense do not refer to Jesus, are taken in fact to do so (Gal. 3:16; cf. 1 Cor. 9:8-12; etc.). To echo Cullmann's image: The light of Christ is reflected back upon the OT, which is now illuminated by the later event (*Christ and Time,* 90 f).

2. *Typology.* If Christocentricity is a hermeneutical perspective, typology is the hermeneutical method by which that perspective is applied. E. Earle Ellis describes typology in the NT as "not so much a system of interpretation as a 'spiritual perspective' from which the early Christian community viewed itself" (in I. Howard Marshall: *NT Interpretation,* 210 ff). This "spiritual perspective" rests upon three assumptions. *(a)* The essential unity in all ages of man's need, and the similar unity in all ages of God's redemption. *(b)* The distinction between type and antitype, the latter going beyond the former and fulfilling it. *(c)* The historical character of Scripture out of whose literal (as opposed to allegorical) sense the meaning of the text arises (Ellis, op. cit., 212). In the NT the three main areas of the OT which are treated typologically are the Covenant, Creation, and Judgment.

3. *Creative Exegesis.* The hermeneutical dynamism observed in OT is present also in NT in various forms in which the interpretation spills over beyond the terms of the text. For example, the application to Jesus of the words "He shall be called a Nazarene" (Matt. 2:23) is most probably to be understood as a wordplay on the words "Nazirite" (drawn from Judg. 16:17) and "Nazarene" (inhabitant of Nazareth). For a full statement see R. N. Longenecker: *Biblical Exegesis in the Apostolic Period,* 145 ff). Again, Paul's interpretation of Deut. 30:12 in Rom. 10:6-8 as a reference to Jesus (a conclusion to which no amount of historical exegesis could ever lead) is based on the principle that the entire OT speaks of Christ.

Hermeneutical Principles Underlying the Unity of the Testaments

The question remains as to the validity of the kind of interpretation noted above in both Testaments, and as depending thereon the role of the OT as a Christian book. Three features have a bearing upon this issue.

1. *Dynamic Interpretation.* Reference has been made above to what was called the hermeneutical dynamism of the OT and creative exegesis in the NT. What this means in practice is that, not only is Scripture used to interpret events, but events are used to interpret Scripture. Just as the adult "comes out of the child," but in a developmental way, by the addition of and interaction with new factors and forces; so the meaning of the OT comes out of it only in the light of the long history of Israel culminating in Christ. But such a meaning is accessible only to faith. Historical exegesis alone cannot prove that Jesus is the true Servant of the Lord; and historical exegesis cannot be allowed the last word in interpreting the OT. There is a supraliteral or spiritual dimension which is inaccessible to the historical method, the adjudication of which lies at the level of faith. Longenecker says, with reference to the apostolic authors: "Accepting the Messiahship and Lordship of Jesus, and believing that in His teaching and person was expressed the fullness of revelation, they took a prophetic stance upon a revelatory basis and treated the OT more charismatically than scholastically" (op. cit., 212).

2. *Objective Coherence.* Taken by itself, dynamic interpretation might seem to open the door to unbridled exegetical subjectivism. The impression is frequently given that this is largely what is found in the NT—OT passages being torn out of context and forced by exegetical acrobatics to say what was desired. Against this may be set the judgment of F. F. Bruce who, comparing the use of the OT at Qumran with that in the NT, says: "In great areas of OT interpretation there is a coherence we do not find in Qumran exegesis. Atomizing exegesis like that of the Qumran texts is present in the NT too, but the distinctive feature of the NT use of the Old is the contextual exegesis that so often lies behind the citation of individual texts" (*Tradition and Interpretation,* 413). If, as many say the apostolic authors believed, Jesus is the true Israel, then the door is opened at once to finding Christ in the OT in a spiritual yet thoroughly objective way. The extent to which this was done has been shown by (among others) C. H. Dodd, who concludes his study thus:

> In general, then, the writers of the NT, in making use of passages from the OT, remain true to the main intention of their writers . . . the main line of interpretation of the OT exemplifed in the New is not only consistent and intelligent in itself, but also founded upon a genuinely historical understanding of the process of the religious—I should prefer to say the prophetic—history of Israel as a whole (*According to the Scriptures,* 130, 133).

3. *The Distinction Between the Interpretative and the Illustrative in Intrabiblical Interpretation.* It remains the case, however, that in some instances (such as, noted earlier, Paul's use of Deut. 30:12 in Rom. 10:6-8 or Matthew's of Judg. 16:17 in Matt. 2:23) the NT interpretation has little more than a verbal basis. Here it is important to distinguish between the *illustrative* use of the OT and the *interpretative* use. Paul did not come to believe that Jesus was the Christ because of a rabbinic interpretation of Deut. 30:12; he came to believe because, by faith and spiritual insight based on prophetic exegesis of the OT, he recognized in Christ the true Servant and People of God. The rabbinical exegetical techniques in which he had been trained enabled him to illustrate this in a variety of ways, but these did not constitute the interpretative foundation. The same distinction is expressed by C. F. D. Moule as between the "vehicular" and "relational" uses of Scripture (*The Origin of Christology,* 132); and by R. N. Longenecker as between the "descriptive" and the "normative" (op cit., 214-20).

Conclusion. On such a basis as the foregoing, it is possible both to perceive and affirm the theological unity of the Testaments as bearing witness to the single yet developing saving activity of God, gradually unfolded in the OT and fully disclosed in the New.

See BIBLE, HERMENEUTICS, INSPIRATION OF THE BIBLE, PROGRESSIVE REVELATION, BIBLICAL INERRANCY.

For Further Reading: Bruce, *The NT Development of OT Themes;* Dodd, *According to the Scriptures;* Ellis,

"How the NT Uses the Old" in Marshall, ed., *New Testament Interpretation: Essays on Principles and Methods;* Hasel, *OT Theology: Basic Issues in the Current Debate,* chap. 5; idem., *NT Theology: Basic Issues in the Current Debate,* chap. 4; Longenecker; *Biblical Exegesis in the Apostolic Period* (esp. chap. 8); Moule, *The Origin of Christology,* chap. 5; Westermann, ed., *Essays on OT Hermeneutics.* ALEX R. G. DEASLEY

BIBLICAL AUTHORITY. The authority of the Bible is more than the relatively superior authority of eyewitnesses or primary documents. Its nature is rather determined by the nature of the Bible as God's Word; therefore the authority is divine. Divine authority is predicated on divine inspiration; any other basis is quicksand.

Since the authority is divine, it is both final and timeless. It is final in the sense that on matters of revelation it is the last court of appeal. The Bible takes precedence over tradition, creeds, churches, philosophy, psychology, and even systematic theology. This authority is timeless in the sense that changing cultures or circumstances do not abridge it; it is as binding in the 20th century as in the 1st. The authority is inherent and unchanging, therefore not subject to the fluid tides of human thought.

This authority is limited to the Bible itself; it does not extend to its interpreters or to particular theological opinions. These lesser authorities are relative because they do not possess the same kind or degree of inspiration which God invested in the Holy Scriptures.

Furthermore, biblical authority is in each part only as it is properly related to the whole. Some parts of the Bible, when isolated from the whole, may carry no divine authority at all, then or now, as for instance, words of Satan or foolish or evil men.

Or, the authority of parts in isolation from the whole may be obsolete; the parts were relevant to a particular time and place, and no longer are binding, e.g., the requirement to attend the annual feasts at the Tabernacle or Jerusalem.

The locus of biblical authority keeps step with the unfolding stages of progressive revelation. In that locus, and surrounding it, are some strands of truth which are cumulative, gathering power and radiance until they shine in the effulgence of Christ's glory. The NT gathers up these strands into itself and transmutes them into gospel. Though ancient, going back to Moses, David, or the prophets, they are never outmoded. Even so, the authority of their OT strands is in the light that Christ shines upon them.

Equally, there are other strands in the OT which are finished, because fulfilled, to be quietly laid aside as a spent garment. To distinguish old wine which has become new from old wineskins which are to be discarded, is a primary task of biblical interpretation. Only as this is properly done will our understanding of biblical authority be truly biblical.

Furthermore, the authority of the Bible is relevant to matters about which it claims authority. This means that its authority is absolute in two basic areas: what we are to believe (of a religious nature), and how we are to live. More specifically, it is authoritative in its teachings about God, man, sin, God's plan of redemption of Christ, God's provision and will for man now, and God's program for the future. Hence culture, morals, social relationships and institutions—including the Church, the family, and the state—as well as the substance of doctrine (truth), all come within the province of biblical authority. The finally authoritative answers to such questions as, What is man? Why is he here? or What is his destiny? are to be found only in the Scriptures. Science offers additional information, e.g., man's chemistry and anatomy; but only the Bible can inform man about himself at deeper levels.

Biblical authority, moreover, is not only dynamic, in governing those who read it, but academic, in assuring its own internal integrity. That is, events which the Bible narrates as plainly historical are to be accepted as historical. Yet because the Bible contains literary forms of story, parable, and drama, aimed to teach spiritual truths rather than record actual happenings, careful discrimination is needed.

This caution notwithstanding, the Genesis account of origins should be accepted as authoritative. There are in the narrative chronological gaps, no doubt, and certainly the material is highly selective; moreover, there are some events which bear symbolic and typological meanings imbedded in their historicity. Nevertheless, the sober teaching is that the human race began with a primal pair in a God-prepared garden, living with a challenging assignment and under an imposed law; that they disobeyed, thereby plunging themselves and their posterity into an incredible morass of sin and depravity, and thereby precipitating all the complex actions of the Triune God which we call Redemption. This is history, the truthfulness of which provides the spine and continuity of everything which follows, from Genesis to Revelation: and this history we are to believe. It is a teaching guaranteed by biblical authority.

It is sometimes said that the Bible is culturally conditioned. This is true in the sense that many of its timeless teachings are expressed in thought forms which belong to the cultural setting of the writing. Matters purely cultural, therefore local, should not be credited with universal authority; yet the disentanglement of the timeless from the temporary, and the universal from the local, is very subtle, and requires great skill and honesty. For example, the rules for the care of widows laid down in 1 Tim. 5:1-16 have within them principles as authoritative for the 20th-century Church as for the 1st-century Church; but the principles are imbedded in some details which must be regarded with great flexibility, for a cultural situation is reflected which does not prevail now. For instance, it would surely be an example of wooden literalism to insist on the exact age of 60 as the age of Church responsibility in all countries and in all centuries.

While apostolic regulations for the administration of the Church in that culture were inspired, and still authoritative in principle, they were not in the same category as the Decalogue or the Sermon on the Mount. Perhaps the difference may be somewhat similar to the federal Constitution, applicable to a nation, versus county or city ordinances, applicable to the local situation, and readily subject to change.

See BIBLE, INSPIRATION OF THE BIBLE, PROPOSITIONAL REVELATION, PROPOSITIONAL THEOLOGY, PROGRESSIVE REVELATION, BIBLE: THE TWO TESTAMENTS, BIBLICAL INERRANCY, CANON.

For Further Reading: Taylor, *Biblical Authority and Christian Faith;* Pinnock, *Biblical Revelation;* Ridderbos, *Studies in Scripture and Its Authority.*

RICHARD S. TAYLOR

BIBLICAL CRITICISM, LOWER. See TEXTUAL CRITICISM.

BIBLICAL INERRANCY. In recent years *inerrancy* has come to replace *infallibility* by those who wish to place emphasis on a "high view" of biblical authority. Obviously the term *inerrancy* means "without error," as its synonym *infallible* means "without fault." Both mean "without mistake." The insistence on *inerrancy* is based upon the conviction that to admit the presence of mistakes in Holy Scripture carries with it a diminution of biblical authority. The argument runs: God is true and since the Bible comes from the God of truth, it contains nothing untrue. This follows a deductive pattern of thought: Given the premise (inerrant Source), the consequence is logical (inerrant Product).

No one disputes the fact that our extant copies of Scripture contain errors, but most if not all of these are attributable to the human errors inevitable in transmission and translation. Thus advocates of inerrancy limit their claim to the "autographs." By "autographs" is meant the original documents direct from the hands of the canonical writers: prophets, apostles, lawgivers, wise men. Unfortunately none of the "autographs" are extant; they are not available for our inspection. Therefore to attribute to them inerrancy is to project from extant documents the prototypes to which extant scriptures are believed to bear witness.

It is thus apparent that "inerrancy of the autographs" must remain to a large extent a matter of faith rather than something demonstrable. Many who affirm inerrancy admit that such things as genealogies and the dates of the kings may have been copied from written documents which were not wholly free from errors of detail which the divinely inspired author-editor was not led to correct.

Some evangelicals would limit the concept of inerrancy to matters of "faith and practice." This implies that in the areas of scientific and historical detail, inerrancy is not needed; but in matters pertaining to salvation, freedom from error is required and is demonstrable in the canonical Scriptures.

Does the Bible claim for itself inerrancy? One may answer yes with certain qualifications. Scriptures do not pretend to present technically scientific data. Instead allusions are often made to the cosmos in pictorial terms (as today when we speak of seeing the sun "rise" in the east). Yet the Bible's basic cosmogony cannot be detached from its theology.

Jesus emphasized the importance of Scriptures and their fulfillment (Luke 24:44). The NT writers refer constantly to the Scriptures as being fulfilled in the new covenant. They had no hesitancy in attributing to the OT full and complete veracity. In spite of the difficulties encountered in an affirmation of inerrancy, the alternative—to conclude that the Bible contains statements contrary to fact—seriously undermines its claim to faith and obedience. A widely accepted formula comes from the Lausanne Conference, which includes the statement: "without error in all that it affirms." The student today can scarcely make a more responsible statement of inerrancy.

See INSPIRATION OF THE BIBLE, BIBLICAL AUTHORITY, BIBLE: THE TWO TESTAMENTS.

For Further Reading: Beegle, *The Inspiration of Scripture;* Lindsell, *The Battle for the Bible;* Taylor, *Biblical Authority and Christian Faith.*

GEORGE ALLEN TURNER

BIBLICAL REALISM. The term is largely alien to continental theologians although such men as Oscar Cullmann and Otto Piper are correctly identified with it. The main body of British and Scottish scholars are comfortable with this approach, especially such men as C. H. Dodd and James Denney.

Standing somewhere between radical liberalism and conservative orthodoxy, the biblical realists seek to discover the essence of early Christian faith and apply it to contemporary life. The biblical realists accept the NT as, essentially, records of that which the Early Church believed and for which they died. Pressing through to the essence of the gospel, these men seek to apply these truths to 20th-century situations. Biblical realists neither depreciate the methods and conclusions of historical criticism nor the truth of divine inspiration in their insistence that the content of the message is far more important than the matters of authorship, chronology, or the exact wording in which the message was couched. Convinced that the task of the Church is to announce rather than to adjust the message to its generation, biblical realists concern themselves with the essence of the biblical message.

See HERMENEUTICS, PROPOSITIONAL THEOLOGY.

For Further Reading: Ramm, *A Handbook of Contemporary Theology,* 22-23; Henry, *Baker's Dictionary of Christian Ethics,* 403.

FOREST T. BENNER

BIBLICAL THEOLOGY. Amid competing definitions, biblical theology may be said to be that branch of theological study in which the affirmations and implications of the self-revelation of God recorded in Scripture are given coherent conceptual expression. This assumes that the Christian Scriptures are bound together by a certain community of themes, concerns, and categories such as can find expression in a recognizable conceptual unity. Even where individual theologies are discerned (e.g., the theology of Paul or John), it is assumed that these can be subsumed in some fundamental sense under a single umbrella. Indeed, if this be denied, biblical theology would seem to be impossible in any meaningful sense. A further assumption is that in an important sense biblical theology is normative for the Christian faith. The way in which it is so has been variously defined, but that it enters indispensably into the formation and formulation of the Christian faith is beyond question. We may say therefore that biblical theology is the middle term between the record of revelation in Scripture on the one hand and systematic theology on the other.

History. Biblical theology as a distinct discipline developed as a reaction against systematized formulations of the Christian faith which were felt to impose on Scripture an alien and lifeless rigidity. Of critical importance was the contribution of Johann Philipp Gabler who, in a lecture delivered in 1787, distinguished the *historical* aspect of biblical theology (i.e., what the biblical writers *thought*) from the *normative* (i.e., what the Bible as a whole *teaches*). The effect of this distinction was threefold. *First,* biblical religion as man's faith-response to God's self-revelation was distinguished from biblical theology understood as a correct conceptual expression of the same. *Second,* the historical conditioning implicit in the progressiveness of God's self-revelation raised the possibility, not only of theological diversity among the biblical witnesses, but also of distance between their mind and that of readers in later centuries. *Third,* a clear distinction was made between biblical theology on the one hand and systematic theology on the other, the former being viewed as an indispensable, though not the sole, component in the latter.

It exaggerates little to say that the history of biblical theology since Gabler has consisted of a wrestling—with varying degrees of success—with these three problems. A conspicuous historical expression of the discipline in the mid-20th century is what came to be known as the biblical theology movement which exercised great influence, especially in the English-speaking world. Overemphasis on the differences between Greek and Hebrew modes of thought; on word studies; on the inseparability of theological concern from the practice of biblical study, and other matters have brought it under heavy criticism. It is important to note, however, that the weaknesses of the biblical theology movement are not endemic in the discipline of biblical theology, and the disclosure of the one does not necessarily involve the demolition of the other.

Problems of Method

1. The validity of the descriptive method. Biblical theology presupposes the possibility of reconstructing the thought of the biblical writers: to echo a much-used phrase, "what they meant." Some have distinguished sharply between what Scripture *meant* and what it *means,* arguing that the former is a strictly historical or descriptive task, while the latter is a theological enterprise. Others have replied that, since the biblical authors were themselves writing from the standpoint of faith, the perspective of faith is necessary for determining what they meant.

Thus clinical detachment is impossible. The affirmation of the one does not necessarily require the denial of the other. Any interpreter of the past must and can place himself (at least tentatively) in the frame of reference of that which he wishes to interpret; historical judgment consists in the readiness to test the data within any competing frames of reference which are available. The faith-approach may thus prove to be the truly descriptive approach.

2. The problem of the center. With material so diverse as that contained within each Testament (not to mention both together), a major challenge with which biblical theologians have wrestled is that of establishing the unifying concept or approach around which biblical theology is found to cohere. Little unanimity has been achieved. Among the suggestions made are: the kingdom of God, the covenant, communion with God, Christ, God's saving work in history, etc. If it is appropriate to look for a single, unifying center, then it would seem necessarily to have to be broadly conceived, embracing both God's saving activity and man's response thereto.

See BIBLE, BIBLE: THE TWO TESTAMENTS, SYSTEMATIC THEOLOGY, PROGRESSIVE REVELATION, CANON.

For Further Reading: Hasel, *Old Testament Theology: Basic Issues in the Current Debate;* idem., *New Testament Theology: Basic Issues in the Current Debate;* Childs, *Biblical Theology in Crisis;* Taylor, "Biblical Theology," *ZPEB;* Smart, *The Past, Present, and Future of Biblical Theology;* Boers, *What Is New Testament Theology?*

ALEX R. G. DEASLEY

BIBLICISM. This refers to certain extreme views of Scripture and of its function as the principal Source for Christian doctrine and practice. To say that one has no creed except the Bible is a form of biblicism. It implies that the Bible does not need to be interpreted, that it does not have any problem passages, and that one aspect of its teaching is as important as any other aspect.

A biblicist is likely to deny any real human element in the writing of Scripture—in which the writers' own personalities and circumstances colored what was written.

A biblicist is likely to tend toward bibliolatry, and to use the Bible superstitiously, as in bibliomancy (e.g., opening the Bible at random for guidance).

See BIBLE.

For Further Reading: Berkouwer, *Holy Scripture;* Brunner, *The Word of God and Modern Man;* Lindsell, *The Battle for the Bible; The Bible in the Balance;* Young, *Thy Word Is Truth.*

J. KENNETH GRIDER

BINDING AND LOOSING. "Bind" *(deō)* and "loose" *(luō)* are common words for tie, attach, fasten, join, or otherwise restrict or restrain—and the opposite. The rabbis used these words of judicial decisions in binding duties and forgiving sins. And Jesus used them in Matt. 16:19; 18:18; and John 20:23. When the Roman church was trying to establish its primacy, these verses were claimed to authenticate sacerdotalism—the idea that Jesus authorized Peter and his successors to make binding demands and to forgive sins. Such claims are without historical or scriptural validity. There is no instance in the NT of anyone's having practiced sacerdotalism, nor is there record from the first two centuries of the Christian era of anyone's using these verses to support the system. Nor does any Greek-writing Ante-Nicene father cite these passages to support such a doctrine.

The judicial function of Peter or the disciples did not lie in a personal authority distinct from the gospel. Peter was a little stone *(petros).* Jesus himself is the living Rock *(petra)*—Matt. 16:18; 1 Pet. 2:8. The authority is in the Word of God proclaimed. It binds and looses.

The perfect and future perfect tenses in all three verses indicate a caution as well as a commission in the gospel proclamation. These terms, properly interpreted, affirm that God has already bound or loosed by the gospel. The perfect tense in John indicates the present abiding result of completed action. The future perfect tense in Matthew indicates the future abiding results of the then-completed act. "Whose soever sins ye remit, they are [already in a state of having been] remitted," etc. The keys are the gospel and only the gospel.

See ABSOLUTION, PRIEST, PRIESTHOOD OF BELIEVERS.

For Further Reading: Mantey, "The Mistranslation of the Perfect Tense in John 20:23, Mt. 16:19 and Mt. 18:18," *Journal of Biblical Literature,* 58 (1939), 243-49; Dayton, "John 20:23; Matthew 16:19 and 18:18 in the Light of the Greek Perfect Tenses," *The Asbury Seminarian,* 2, 2 (1947), 74-89; Keylock, "Binding and Loosing," *ZPEB,* 1:611-12; Meding, Muller, "Bind," *NIDNTT,* 1:171-72.

WILBER T. DAYTON

BIRTH OF CHRIST. See VIRGIN BIRTH.

BIRTH OF THE SPIRIT. See NEW BIRTH.

BISHOP. The term "bishop" is derived from the Saxon *biscop* used to translate the Greek word, *episcopos,* meaning "overseer" (e.g., Acts 20:28). From NT days it was used as the title of an office in the Christian ministry. In the Septuagint it indicated a holder of public office, civil or religious.

In the classical usage it specified the commissioners or inspectors sent by the national government to its subject states.

When the organization of the Christian churches in the Gentile cities involved the assignment of the work of pastoral superintendence to a distinct class of the ministry, this title of bishop was at once convenient and familiar and was therefore adopted as readily as the word "elder" (*presbyteros,* presbyter) had been in the mother church at Jerusalem.

Such men were originally appointed by the apostles to superintend the spiritual, secular, and organizational arrangements of the local churches (Acts 14:23; 11:30; 2 Tim. 2:2). They also are said to *preside* (*proistasthai,* 1 Thess. 5:12; 1 Tim. 5:17) but never to *rule (archein)* over the churches. In the Epistle to the Hebrews (13:7, 17, 24) they are named *hēgoumenoi,* "leading men" (cf. Acts 15:22), and in Ephesians (4:11) they are designated under the figurative term *poimenas,* "shepherds."

Their function was to teach the church sound doctrine, the true interpretation of the Scriptures, and administer the sacraments, while exercising both pastoral care and church discipline. These functions are also ascribed to elders *(presbyteroi)* in NT times. Nowhere are the two named together as being orders distinct from each other, as is the case with "bishops" and "deacons." The elders discharged the functions which are essentially *episcopal,* namely, pastoral superintendence.

Men who were chosen to such an office were to be of a blameless life and reputation, both within and outside the church. They were to possess a fitness for teaching, a hospitable temperament, and a suitable marriage relationship. They must show an ability to govern their own household, manifest self-control, and must not be a recent or unproven convert (1 Tim. 3:1-7; Titus 1:5-9).

Later in the history of the church the bishops became overseers of more than one church, having responsible care for the churches of a larger area in at least an advisory capacity to their various pastors and congregations.

See CLERGY, CHURCH GOVERNMENT, ELDER.

For Further Reading: Morris, "Bishop," *Baker's DT;* Carpenter, "Minister, Ministry," *Theological Word Book of the Bible,* ed. Richardson.

ROSS E. PRICE

BITTERNESS. See HARDNESS OF HEART.

BLAME, BLAMELESS. Our concept of sin determines our concept of blame, either blameworthiness or blamelessness. Because wilfulness is a necessary element of guilt-incurring sin, no blame attaches to involuntary transgression. The words are of great importance to our ideas, not only of sin and guilt, but also innocence, perfection, integrity, and performance.

In the consideration of "blame" and "blameless" such related factors as foreknowledge and forethought, ignorance and forgetfulness, culpability and responsibility, would all demand attention. The ethical concept of sin postulates a proper and clear distinction between sin wilfully committed and errors springing from human infirmity, or lack of knowledge. Hence it is entirely scriptural to describe Christians living obediently and with pure intention of pleasing the Lord as "blameless but not faultless."

Due to the Fall we shall never in this life be free from the infirmities of human nature. Grace can make us clean and well-pleasing to God (Phil. 4:18; Heb. 13:21), but does not make us infallible. We may become "completely His" (2 Chron. 16:9, NASB), "guiltless" (Job 9:20-21, NASB), "innocent" (Gen. 44:10, NASB, cf. KJV), "blameless and harmless" (Phil. 2:15), and be kept "blameless" until the day of Christ (1 Cor. 1:8; 2 Pet. 3:14).

Blamelessness therefore is a matter of the heart, according to the measure of our knowledge of the Lord's expectation of us. Hence Asa was "blameless" (2 Chron. 15:17, NASB) and "completely His" (16:9, NASB). Many persons are described as "blameless" according to their light (Job 1:1; 9:20-21; Gen. 6:9; 17:1; Luke 1:6; 1 Cor. 1:8). Sometimes the emphasis is "completeness," at other times "integrity" or "perfectness." "Blameless" can mean "above reproach" (1 Tim. 3:2; 5:7; Titus 1:7, all NASB).

It is noteworthy that the idea is related to the unblemished sacrifices presented in OT worship, and is applied to the life of the believer as being pleasing and acceptable to God, especially in relation to the *Parousia* (1 Cor. 1:8; Col. 1:22).

Blame is also apportioned to responsibility (Gen. 43:9); or related to bringing holy things into discredit (2 Cor. 6:3; 8:20); it may be a synonym for "condemned" (Gal. 2:11).

See SIN, MISTAKES, GUILT, RESPONSIBILITY.

For Further Reading: *NIDNTT;* Chapman, *The Terminology of Holiness;* Taylor, *A Right Conception of Sin.*

T. CRICHTON MITCHELL

BLASPHEMY. The English word "blasphemy" is transliterated from the Greek word *blasphēmia,* which means slander, reviling, railing, language of reproach against God and man (Matt. 27:39;

Mark 14:64; Eph. 4:31). It is to speak of God or divine things impiously or irreverently (Mark 3:29; Rev. 16:9, 11, 21).

In modern English the term is used only in reference to God. But in the NT blasphemy is reproachful or slanderous speech against either God or man (e.g., "evil spoken of"—Rom. 14:16). It is included in lists of sins of the most heinous type (Mark 7:21-22). Its intentional aim is to harm another person's good name or reputation, as in the case of the apostle Paul (1 Cor. 4:13; 10:30). In reference to God the word takes on more serious meaning, including deprecations in His name (Ps. 74:10-18; Isa. 52:5, Rev. 16:9).

Under Mosaic law blasphemy against God was punishable by death by stoning (Lev. 24:11-16). Naboth and Stephen suffered this fate though falsely accused (1 Kings 21:9-13; Acts 6:11; 7:58). Our Lord was charged with blasphemy on three counts at His trial. His words about the temple of His body were maliciously misinterpreted (Mark 14:58). He was scorned and railed against when He claimed messianic powers (Matt. 26:63-66).

Under NT grace, all manner of blasphemies against God the Father, His Son, and man may be forgiven, upon sincere repentance, said Jesus. But blasphemy against the Holy Spirit is "an eternal sin" (NIV) and has no forgiveness whatsoever (Mark 3:28-29). This sin should not be confused with the "sin unto death" (1 John 5:16) nor the sin of apostasy (Heb. 6:4-6; 10:26-30). Jesus limits the unpardonable sin to the intention of attributing the work of the Holy Spirit done in Christ to the power of Satan.

See PROFANITY, SPEECH, UNPARDONABLE SIN.

For Further Reading: Vine, *ED;* Wesley, *Works,* 5:210; 6:52 ff.

JOHN B. NIELSON

BLESS, BLESSED, BLESSING. Those words primarily derive from *baruk* in Hebrew and *eudokia* in Greek. In some instances the word means to enrich, prosper, protect, multiply, and obviously has temporal overtones (Gen. 12:2-3; 22:17; Deut. 28:3). The blessing was sometimes a hereditary benefit (Gen. 27:30), and sometimes was given because of obedience and faithfulness (1 Sam. 2:20; Luke 24:50).

In other cases to bless meant to praise, to thank, and/or to congratulate (Judg. 5:2; 2 Sam. 14:22; Ps. 72:15; 103:1). A blessing is sometimes a benediction (Num. 6:22-27; Deut. 23:5; Luke 24:50-51; Rev. 1:3). Again, to be blessed is to be happy, to be joyful, to be fulfilled (Ps. 128:1-4; John 13:17; Titus 2:13; Jas. 5:11).

To bless often is to invoke God's blessings upon, as Jesus blessed the loaves and fish before distributing them (Mark 6:41) and as He blessed the bread before the two disciples in Emmaus (Luke 24:30), who may have recalled the original blessing prior to feeding the 5,000. And this blessing we are to invoke before the distribution of the elements in the Lord's Supper (1 Cor. 10:16).

More importantly, and often in the NT, the word *eudokia* is associated with grace, the gift of God's redemptive love. This seems to be forecast in Prov. 10:22: "The blessing of the Lord, it maketh rich, and he addeth no sorrow with it." To "bless" others would mean to manifest God's grace toward them (Luke 6:28). There is no doubt of the blessing of grace when the Greek verb is first used in Acts 3:26: "Unto you first God, having raised up his Son Jesus, sent him to bless you, in turning away every one of you from his iniquities." Then comes Paul's hope of the ministry of God's grace: "I am sure that, when I come unto you, I shall come in the fulness of the blessing of the gospel of Christ" (Rom. 15:29). Paul certainly refers to the supreme blessing of God's grace in Gal. 3:14 and in Eph. 1:3.

Another Greek word translated "blessed" is *makarios,* which though sometimes meaning happy or favored (as in Luke 1:45), more often signifies divine approval. One thinks particularly of the Beatitudes (Matt. 5:3-12), which register more of divine sanction and promise than of happiness. The ultimate approval of God and the ultimate happiness of the creature is stated in Rev. 20:6: "Blessed and holy is he that hath part in the first resurrection."

In the NT two related Greek words are translated "blessed." One, *eulogēmenos,* always applied to the creature as blessed by God. The other, *eulogētos,* invariably is applied to God himself. It is interesting to note that both these words are applied to Christ, since He unites two natures in one Person (cf. the Greek of John 12:13 with Rom. 9:5).

See HAPPINESS, GRACE, BENEDICTION.

For Further Reading: "Blessing," *Dictionary of Biblical Theology,* rev.; "Blessedness," *The New Schaff-Herzog Encyclopedia of Religious Knowledge.*

GEORGE E. FAILING

BLOOD. This is a key word in understanding the redemptive message of the Bible. Its meaning is essential to an understanding of the OT sacrifices. More significantly, the word "blood" carries a primary theme in understanding the work of Christ. Vincent Taylor has pointed out that the blood of Christ is mentioned in the writings of the NT nearly three times as often as the cross of

Christ, and five times as frequently as the death of Christ (*The Atonement in NT Teaching,* 177). Obviously a careful interpretation cannot be avoided if we would have any semblance of NT Christianity. As interpreted by contemporary writers, the term carries two meanings.

The Blood as Life. With reference to the blood of the sacrifices of the OT and to the blood of Christ in the NT, some scholars state that by "blood" *life* is meant rather than death. Among such writers are G. Milligan, B. F. Westcott, Vincent Taylor, Lindsay Dewar, and C. H. Dodd. The following statements from Vincent Taylor represent the thought of the authors just mentioned. In commenting on the teaching of Paul and his use of the term "blood" with reference to the death of Christ, Taylor writes: "To explain the allusions to 'blood' as synonyms for death is mistaken" (op. cit., 63). In commenting on the Epistle to the Hebrews, he expresses a similar idea: "It will be found, I think, that when he uses the term 'blood' his main emphasis is upon the idea of life freely surrendered, applied, and dedicated to the recovery of man" (op. cit., 123). Wesleyan writers, and evangelicals generally, find it difficult to accept this concept of life as being the primary meaning of "blood."

The Blood as Death. From a biblical perspective the emphasis is on death, not life. As J. A. Robinson writes: "To the Jewish mind, 'blood' was not merely—nor even chiefly—the life-current flowing in the veins of the living: it was especially the life poured out in death; and yet more particularly in its religious aspect it was the symbol of sacrificial death" (*St. Paul's Epistle to the Ephesians,* 29). Johannes Behm also supports this view: "The interest of the New Testament is not in the material blood of Christ, but in His shed blood as the life violently taken from Him. Like the cross . . . the 'blood of Christ' is simply another and even more graphic phrase for the death of Christ in its soteriological significance" (Kittel, 1:174). James Denney, in his classic work, *The Death of Christ,* comments on Heb. 9:12-28: "There is the same sacrificial conception in all the references in the epistle to the blood of Christ. He entered into the most holy place with . . . His own blood (9:12). The blood of Christ shall purge your conscience from dead works (9:14). We have boldness to enter into the holiest in the blood of Jesus (10:19). His blood is the blood of the covenant with which we are sanctified. . . . In all these ways the death of Christ is defined as a sacrificial death" (215). Wesleyan scholars have followed the second meaning of "blood," that it means death, or life poured out.

In summary it can be said that while the Hebrew word *dam* (blood), used 362 times in the OT, carries various meanings, its most common use, says Leon Morris, is to denote "death by violence" (*The Apostolic Preaching of the Cross,* 13). The institution of the Passover, the ceremonial law and the sacrificial system, and the prophetic concept of suffering and death all stand for life laid down or taken in death.

In the NT the Greek word *aima* (blood) is also most frequently used to refer to violent death, or life given or laid down for others. The great NT themes of *propitiation* (Rom. 3:25), *justification* (5:9), *redemption* (Eph. 1:7; 1 Pet. 1:18-19; Rev. 5:9), *reconciliation* (Eph. 2:13; Col. 1:19-20), *cleansing* (Heb. 9:11-14), *sanctification* (1 John 1:7; Eph. 5:25-26), *victorious living* (Rev. 12:11), are all directly bound to the shedding of blood, sacrifice, and death.

The valid conclusion is that the phrase "blood of Christ" is, like the word "cross," a specific expression for the sacrificial and redemptive death of Christ.

See CROSS, CRUCIFIXION, ATONEMENT, SACRIFICE.

For Further Reading: Stibbs, *The Meaning of the Word "Blood" in Scripture;* Denney, *The Death of Christ;* Morris, *The Apostolic Preaching of the Cross; GMS,* 400 ff.

DONALD S. METZ

BODY. For the key NT word *sōma,* body, there is, strictly, no Hebrew equivalent. The OT knows no word for "body." In the LXX *sōma* translates no less than 11 Hebrew words, for which none is a true equivalent. The most important term it represents, the only one with theological significance, is *basar.* Yet *basar* is essentially not *sōma* but *sarx,* flesh, man in his weakness and mortality.

The Platonic idea of man as an immortal soul slipped into an oppressing bodily envelope is found in neither the OT nor the NT. Throughout Scripture man is a body-soul unit. In his body man has his true existence, and in his body he will ultimately come to heaven or hell (Matt. 10:28). Disembodied spiritual existence is not a biblical goal; man's hope is not a Platonic immortality but a resurrection of the body.

It is in Paul's Epistles that the theological significance of the body is developed. Life after death continues for the believer as conscious existence with Christ (2 Cor. 5:6-8; Phil. 1:23; cf. Luke 23:43), but the Christian's final expectation is the resurrection (1 Cor. 15:50-58). The present body is the "outer" man and is mortal (2 Cor. 4:16; Rom. 8:10); but the Christian knows by faith that he is destined to be clothed in the resurrection with a new "building" or "house" which is not earthly but which comes from God (2 Cor. 5:1-10). Then the body of our humiliation will be made like Jesus' body of glory (Phil. 3:21; Rom. 8:11). The bodily redemption promised is not redemption *from* but *of* the body (v. 23).

The NT knows no identification of man's body with sin. While our bodies with their desires are one source of temptation (Jas. 1:14) and may lead to sin (Rom. 6:12) and must therefore be kept in subjection (1 Cor. 9:25-27; Rom. 8:13), they may be set free from sin (6:6-7), yielded to God (v. 13; 12:1), and sanctified (1 Thess. 5:23), so that in them we may glorify God (1 Cor. 6:19-20).

See FLESH, SOUL SLEEP, INTERMEDIATE STATE, IMMORTALITY, RESURRECTION OF THE BODY, MAN.

For Further Reading: Kittel, 7:1024-66; Robinson, *The Body;* Robinson, *The Christian Doctrine of Man.*

WILLIAM M. GREATHOUSE

BODY LIFE. This term denotes among evangelicals an emphasis which has as its objective the reversal of the trend toward depersonalization in the church. The basis for this emphasis is a literal interpretation of Paul's concept of the church as a living organism. With this is the corollary claim that the modern church, functioning as a body, should enjoy the whole range of the gifts of the Spirit (1 Corinthians 12—14). Only thus does Christ become actually the living Head.

All persons and all functions of the church are believed to be integral and indispensable parts of the whole. Therefore the "supreme task of every Christian's life is to discover his gift and put it to work. . . . If anyone does not do this the whole body will suffer" (Ray C. Stedman, *Body Life,* p. 131). It takes the whole church, he adds, to do the work of the church.

As an attempt to be faithful to the apostle's doctrine of the Church, the "Body Life" movement has much to commend it. However, Paul equally insisted on authoritative leadership and ordained, well-organized functionaries. Also the contemporary movement is in danger of overemphasizing the gifts of the Spirit to the neglect of the fruit (or graces). Gifts without fruit tend to divide; the smooth interfunctioning of the gifts can only be assured by the fruit as enumerated in Gal. 5:22-23.

See CHURCH, GIFTS OF THE SPIRIT, FRUIT OF THE SPIRIT, KOINONIA, BODY OF CHRIST.

For Further Reading: Stedman, *Body Life;* Palms, *Decision* magazine, May 1975, 8 ff; Richards, *A Theology of Christian Education,* 244-83.

FOREST T. BENNER

BODY OF CHRIST. This phrase in the Greek NT *(to sōma tou Christou)* is used to indicate the whole community of Christians which constitutes the extension of our Lord's earthly incarnation. It connotes the many-faceted relations between Jesus as Lord of all those who belong to Him—their relation to Him as members, and their relations to one another in Him. The term is symbolic of the mutuality and solidarity of all who are born into His life and governed by Him as their ever living Head. Christ is embodied in His Church. This analogy may be taken too literally, but it cannot be taken too seriously. (It is taken too literally when it becomes definitive of Christ's resurrection.)

Within the solidarity of the members of His Body there is no distinction of race, sex, learning, or social status. As the new people of God there is a mutual helpfulness, wherein each member, each joint and ligament, makes its contribution to the growth of the whole toward the fullness of the measure of the stature of Christ. Within the one Body, the Spirit apportions His gifts to each member in such a fashion as enables each to be nourished by the whole and the whole by each of its interdependent parts (Rom. 12:4-6; 1 Cor. 12:7-12).

Christ is a "one" who includes within His resurrection Body "the many" as a corporate personality. Therefore, believers are exhorted to present their *bodies* as a living sacrifice, holy and acceptable to God (Rom. 12:1), for it is not right to take the Body of Christ and join it to a harlot (1 Cor. 6:15). The Church may then become the means of Christ's work in the world. It is His hands, His feet, His tongue, and His voice. In His resurrection life in this age He still needs a pure, clean body as His instrument to gospelize a lost world. The vibrant personalities of redeemed and sanctified human servants of God make a powerful impact upon the imaginations and minds of men. Every type of person, and every gift man has, can find its place in the total work of God. He who turns to God can remain no longer neutral. The Church must ever be that fellowship wherein people find God's righteous will and His outreaching grace.

See CHURCH, BODY LIFE, RESURRECTION OF CHRIST.

For Further Reading: Davidson, *The Bible Speaks,* 228-33; Wiley, *CT,* 3:108-10.

ROSS E. PRICE

BOLDNESS. In its biblical context, boldness is the confident and courageous assumption of privileges provided by grace. "Let us then with confidence draw near to the throne of grace" (Heb. 4:16, RSV). Wiley explains it as "saying all." That is, to come boldly is to come at the invitation of God—with confidence in the request—then, saying all you wish, ask with confidence for what you need.

A biblical boldness exercises the claims and privileges of faith, implying a trust in the object of one's faith (cf. Eph. 3:12; Heb. 10:19; 1 John 4:17). Such boldness/confidence is to be distinguished from a brash, cocky, self-confident, egotistical attitude.

The exercise of a spiritual privilege implies that the believer is putting his will (and his faith) into action, and such an exercise is a bold move. For it means that man is speaking to God or using a privilege from God. Such a dialogue between God and man can only be interpreted as boldness, for man has no human right to do such. All privileges are initiated by God.

Boldness before men (e.g., Peter and John, Acts 4:13) is not humanistic courage but a gift of the Holy Spirit (Matt. 10:19-20). Its source is God, not man. The context of the boldness of the apostles was the fact that they had been with Jesus.

But Jesus is also the basis for boldness in our approach to God (1 Tim. 2:5). Through Him we claim positively the privileges of the covenant.

See PRAYER, FAITH, INTERCESSION, ADVOCATE.

For Further Reading: Wiley, *The Epistle to the Hebrews,* 166-69.

C. NEIL STRAIT

BONDAGE. Bondage is unwilling and unhappy servitude. The fundamental bondage experienced by fallen human beings is slavery to sin. "Every one who commits sin," Jesus said, "is a slave to sin" (John 8:34, RSV; cf. 2 Pet. 2:19). Sin brings one under its power and reduces its victim to abject helplessness by the tyranny of its guilt, the irresistibility of its pull, and the grip of its habit.

Because of sin, law becomes a form of bondage (Gal. 4:24-25; 5:1; cf. Acts 15:10). The physical bondage of disease and weakness also is a consequence of sin (Rom. 8:18-23). Outside of Christ, people are in bondage to fear (v. 15; Heb. 2:14-15). A form of sin's power is bondage to appetites and vices. Historically, bondage has been not only an internal problem but sociological as well, for men have been in bondage to other men, either through ownership, as in outright slavery, or through economic oppression.

However, not all bond service is bondage. The bonds of matrimony need not be miserable servitude. Paul delighted to call himself a slave of Jesus Christ (Rom. 1:1; et al.). His ear was pierced with the mark of eternal fealty (Exod. 21:1-6; Deut. 15:17). It is love which prevents bonds from being bondage, and turns them instead into perfect freedom.

See SERVANT, SERVICE, SLAVE (SLAVERY), FREEDOM.

RICHARD S. TAYLOR

BREAKING OF BREAD. See LOVE FEAST.

BRIDE, BRIDEGROOM. Biblical writers use the metaphor "bride" (*nymphē,* young wife, bride) and "bridegroom" (*nymphios,* young husband, bridegroom) for Israel and God in the OT and for the Church and Jesus Christ in the NT. In Hosea, God is the divine Husband and Israel His unfaithful wife (chaps. 1—3). The metaphor is also found in Isa. 54:5-7; 61:10; 62:5; Jer. 2:2; 3:8. Psalm 45 and the Song of Songs express the love of God the divine Husband for His bride Israel. Israel thus understood the ratification of the covenant at Sinai as the marriage of Yahweh (Israel's God) with Israel and the covenant feast as the marriage feast (Exod. 24:3-11). Along this line, Isaiah introduces the thought of an eschatological feast on Mount Zion which brings the nations into fellowship with God (Isa. 25:6), an event which the NT writers describe as the Messianic wedding feast (Rev. 19:7-9).

It is clear that the early Christian community and Jesus himself made the identification between the Messiah and the Bridegroom. Jesus' statement to John's disciples describes himself as the Bridegroom (Mark 2:19). In the parable of the marriage of the king's son, Christ takes the place of the heavenly Bridegroom (Matt. 22:1-14). The same identification is also found in the parable of the 10 virgins (25:1-13). In his testimony to Jesus, John the Baptist identifies Jesus as the Bridegroom and himself the friend of the Bridegroom (John 3:29).

The metaphor of bride as the Church is fully developed in the letters of Paul. In 2 Cor. 11:2 he compares the church at Corinth with a bride and Christ with the Bridegroom and himself with the person who will present the bride to the Bridegroom. A further development of this metaphor appears in Eph. 5:22-32. The marriage bond between Christ the Bridegroom and His Bride the Church is set in analogy to the divinely ordained union between Adam and Eve (cf. Gen. 2:24). As in the parables of Jesus, the actual marriage is to be a future event in which the bride will be presented "holy and without blemish" (Eph. 5:27).

This eschatological union will be the occasion for the marriage supper of the Lamb (Rev. 19:7-9). The announcement in v. 7 indicates that the time for this union has come and that the preparation of the bride is complete. The Marriage will be followed by the Marriage Supper (v. 9). While the metaphor of the Bride is used for the Church prepared for this union, individual members of this community are invited to attend the Marriage Supper. John's visions conclude with the invitation "come," the longing of the Bride for her union with the Bridegroom as well as an invitation to those who are not yet a part of her to drink the water of life (Rev. 22:17).

See SECOND COMING, CHURCH.

For Further Reading: Best, *One Body in Christ,* 169-83; Ladd, *A Commentary on the Revelation of John,* 246-50.

ALEXANDER VARUGHESE

BRITISH-ISRAELISM. See ANGLO-ISRAELISM.

BROTHERHOOD. In its general sense this term indicates the social bond which people enjoy under some common head. In the theological sense it indicates unity and kinship under the Fatherhood of God. While this brotherhood includes all mankind under the generic fatherhood of God (Acts 17:28), the bond of creation has been disrupted by sin. Jesus frankly told the rebellious unbelievers of His day, "Ye are of your father the devil" (John 8:44).

Christian brotherhood, *adelphotēs,* comes as we acknowledge the Lordship of Christ (1 Pet. 2:17; 5:9). The same thought is carried out under the slightly different Greek word *adelphoi,* "brethren," indicating the fellowship of the family of God (Matt. 28:10; John 20:17; Acts 9:29-30). That "brothers" includes women is repeatedly obvious, e.g., Matt. 23:8; Acts 1:16; Rom. 1:13; 1 Thess. 1:4; Rev. 19:10. Indeed, Paul would say that this brotherhood is inclusive of all sex, nationality, social or material status (Gal. 3:28).

Among others, the chief admonitions to this spiritual fellowship is "Love the brotherhood" (1 Pet. 2:17); "Love the brethren" (1 John 3:14); and love them sacrificially: "Hereby perceive we the love of God, because he laid down his life for us: and we ought to lay down our lives for the brethren" (v. 16).

See LOVE, AGAPĒ, KOINONIA, BROTHERLY LOVE.

For Further Reading: Agnew, *Transformed Christians,* 84; Vine, *ED,* 154; *ISBE,* 1:525.

MILTON S. AGNEW

BROTHERLY LOVE. The English term, brotherly love, is bound up in the name of a city in Lydia called Philadelphia (Rev. 1:11; 3:7), and a city in the United States as often referred to as the City of Brotherly Love; from *phileō,* to love; and *adelphos,* brother. The compound word is found six times: Rom. 12:10; 1 Thess. 4:9; Heb. 13:1; 1 Pet. 1:22; 3:8; 2 Pet. 1:7.

The word *philos* is one of a family of Greek words. *Eros,* lust, usually illicit love, is not found in the Bible. *Storgē,* indicating family or natural affection, is used only in a compound form. With the negative prefix *a, astorgoi,* it is found in Rom. 1:31, "without natural affection." Curiosly it is used in Rom. 12:10 in a compound with *philos* to define an aspect of brotherly love. "Be kindly affectioned *[philo-storgoi]* one to another with brotherly love *[philadelphia];* in honour preferring one another." *Agapē,* scarcely found in the early extrabiblical papyri or the inscriptions, became the word usually used to designate Christian love (the word does not always mean Christian or divine love, however).

Philos identifies a wholesome, natural affection between friends. Combined with *adelphos,* as *phil-adelphia,* it represents warm Christian fellowship. Its practice is encouraged (Heb. 13:1). It is to be associated with the verb *agapaō* (1 Pet. 1:22). In 2 Pet. 1:7, translated as "brotherly kindness," it is to be added to godliness and then, in turn, perfected by *agapē,* "charity," "that ye shall neither be barren nor unfruitful in the knowledge of our Lord Jesus Christ" (v. 8; cf. 1 Thess. 4:9).

See LOVE, AGAPĒ, PERFECT LOVE, KOINONIA.

For Further Reading: *WBC* on Rom. 12:10; Heb. 13:1; 1 Pet. 1:22; Wuest, *Treasures from the Greek New Testament,* 57.

MILTON S. AGNEW

BUDDHISM. An offshoot of Brahminism, Buddhism originated in India six centuries before the Christian era. Presumably, its founder was Siddhartha, who is better known as Sakyamouni. Also, he is known by the title of Buddha (English, "The Enlightened") which he assumed, and from which his followers are called Buddhists. Gautama Buddha supposedly was born about 563 B.C. into a very wealthy family. At the age of 29, according to the traditions, he renounced home, wealth, power, a young wife, and an only child. Allegedly he became an extreme ascetic and attached himself to Brahman teachers. However, there is an unresolved debate whether there ever was such a person as Buddha.

Basic to Buddhistic philosophy is the assumption of a casual nexus in nature and in man, of which the law of karma is but a specific application. Also, it assumes the impermanence of things and the illusory notion of substance and soul. In ethics, Buddhism assumes the universality of suffering and the belief in a remedy for the problem of evil.

The multifarious forms which the teachings of Gautama Buddha produced center around the Four Noble Truths and the Eightfold Path. Neither devotion to the world nor asceticism saves a man, but only a complete detachment. There are four great truths concerning suffering: (1) Life is full of pain and unfilled desire; (2) This pain is caused by craving of some kind, either for things of this world or for happiness in a future life; (3) This craving can be extinguished; (4) The way this is done is by means of the Eightfold Path. The Eightfold Path includes: Right Views, Right Desires (resolves), Right Speech, Right Conduct, Right Livelihood, Right Effort, Right Mindfulness, and Right Rapture (concentration).

One is not asked to renounce love in Buddhism, but one is asked to renounce love for self. Such self-renunciation is the goal of the noble Eightfold Path. At the end of the path one finds Nirvana, and it can be attained even in this life. Scholars are not certain of the meaning of the term *Nirvana;* some believe it means annihilation, while others think it means absorption into Buddha. It is certain that this end is to be attained by the extinction of the self.

In Buddhism a man must save himself; no gods and no rituals will help him. There is no god in Buddhism, but there is a kind of worship of Buddha, for which temples are erected. Each person may become a Buddha, an "Enlightened One." Buddhism has always had the remarkable power of assimilating into itself some of the features of other religions; Buddhists will also claim to be adherents of other religions, and they do not see any contradiction in this. The number of Buddhists is estimated to be from 200 to 400 million. It is known as a missionary religion.

See HINDUISM, COMPARATIVE RELIGION, NON-CHRISTIAN RELIGIONS, CHRISTIANITY.

For Further Reading: Perry, *The Gospel in Dispute,* 175-225; Parrinder, *A Dictionary of Non-Christian Religions;* Ferm, *A History of Philosophical Systems.*

JERRY W. MCCANT

BURNT OFFERING. The burnt offering was one of four sacrifices described in Leviticus in which the blood of the sacrificial victim was shed (1:2-17; 6:1-6). The distinguishing feature of the burnt offering was that, after the blood had been taken and sprinkled on the sides of the altar, the rest of the sacrifice was burned on the altar without any part being returned to the offerer or to the priest (except the skin, 7:8). The victim was usually an unblemished male taken from the cattle or the sheep (1:2). A turtledove or a pigeon could be offered, however (v. 14), a provision probably intended for the poor (cf. 5:7; 12:8).

The blood sacrifices in the OT included the ideas of atonement and presentation of a gift to God. But these two ideas were not equally balanced in the various sacrifices. Although atonement was involved in the burnt offering (Lev. 1:4), the element of presentation of a gift as an act of divine worship had special prominence. As an act of worship it expressed praise, thanksgiving, and rejoicing on the part of God's people (Gen. 8:20; 1 Sam. 6:13 ff; 1 Chron. 23:30 ff; 2 Chron. 29:25-30). It implied the complete consecration of the offerer to God (v. 31). The offering served to maintain and renew the existing bond of fellowship between God and His people.

Christians express the meaning inherent in the burnt offering when they present themselves in worship to God, and as a definite and complete sacrifice according to Rom. 12:1.

Also, they glorify God by their sacrifices of praise and faithful service (Heb. 13:15 f). These offerings are acceptable (Lev. 1:3 ff) because of the atonement of Christ, "a fragrant offering and sacrifice to God" (Eph. 5:2, RSV).

See CONSECRATION, LAMB (SACRIFICIAL).

For Further Reading: Cave, *The Scriptural Doctrine of Sacrifice;* Ringgren, *Sacrifice in the Bible;* De Vaux, *Studies in Old Testament Sacrifice.*

FRED D. LAYMAN

C

CABALA. See KABBALA.

CALL, CALLED, CALLING. Of all the various uses of the idea or word "call" in the Bible, the most significant is the divine invitation to sinners to accept the redeeming grace of God in the gift of His Son (John 3:16-17; Matt. 11:28; Luke 14:16-17; Rev. 22:17; cf. Isa. 55:1). This call is universal in its scope through the gracious influence of the Holy Spirit in the sense of awakening (a phase of prevenient grace) (John 1:9; 6:44; Rom. 1:19; 2:15; cf. Acts 14:17). It is more direct or immediate through the Word of God and/or preaching of the gospel (Rom. 10:17; Matt. 28:19-20).

Broadly speaking, there is a twofold call relating to full salvation in Jesus Christ because of the twofold nature of sin, i.e., sin inherited and sins committed. It issues first in a call to repentance (Matt. 9:13; Luke 5:32), and secondly, in a call to holiness, addressed to believers (Rom. 12:1-2; 1 Thess. 4:7-8; 1 Pet. 1:15-16).

The call to salvation in Christ can be accepted or rejected, and those who accept are *the called,* or elect. Hence the Church is the *ecclesia,* or "called-out ones." The apostle Paul speaks of "the called of Jesus Christ" (Rom. 1:6; cf. 1 Cor. 1:24). The divine call, described as "upward" and "heavenly," to freedom and happiness (1 Cor. 7:22; Gal. 5:13; Phil. 3:14; Heb. 3:1; 1 Pet. 5:10) includes ethical standards relating to a manner of life or life-style, demanding a worthy walk (1 Thess. 2:12; Eph. 4:1), in holiness (1 Thess. 4:7; 1 Pet. 1:15; Heb. 12:14), with patience, even in suffering (1 Pet. 2:20-21), and in peace (1 Cor. 7:15; Col. 3:15).

The word "call" also relates to the *vocation* or calling of individuals (e.g., Abraham, Gen. 12:1; Moses, Exod. 3:10; Isaiah, Isa. 6:8; Paul, Acts 26:16); as such it may pertain to some special office or function, such as judge (Judg. 3:9-10), prophet (Isa. 6:8; 8:11), missionary (Acts 13:2; 16:10), apostleship (Rom. 1:1), and craftsman, like Bezaleel (Exod. 31:2). Israel was called as a nation to be God's chosen people through whom the Savior came (Isa. 41:8-9; cf. Deut. 7:6-8).

For Calvinists, "effectual calling" pertains only to the elect, who, by divine decree, are predestinated to salvation. This view, however, fails to give due regard to the many "whosoever wills" in the NT regarding salvation (e.g., John 3:14-16; Acts 2:21; 10:43; Rom. 10:12-13; 1 Tim. 2:3-4; Rev. 22:17).

Regarding prayer, in Gen. 4:26 we are told that men began "to call upon the name of the Lord" (cf. Ps. 105:1; Zeph. 3:9). In the NT "call" is used to show that men were accustomed to invoke God in prayer (Acts 7:59; Rom. 10:12; 1 Cor. 1:2).

See EFFECTUAL CALLING, ELECT, VOCATION.

For Further Reading: Wiley, *CT,* 2:334-44; Calvin, *Institutes of the Christian Religion,* ed. Allen, 2:217-41; Kittel, 3:487-500.

WILLIAM M. ARNETT

CALVINISM. This is one of the three major theology systems of Protestantism, the other two being Lutheranism and Wesleyan-Arminianism. It takes its name from its primary systematizer, John Calvin (1509-64) of Geneva. His thought was expounded in his epochal three-volume *Institutes of the Christian Religion,* published in its final form in A.D. 1559 (the last of several revisions and expansions of the original one-volume treatise published when Calvin was 27 years of age). Supportive were Calvin's *Commentaries* on the Bible, and lesser works.

As a system Calvinism has been articulated in such creeds as the Canons of the Synod of Dort (The Netherlands, A.D. 1619) and The Westminster Confession (England, A.D. 1647). Most Presbyterian, Reformed churches, and Baptists would classify themselves as Calvinists, though in many groups the adherence is very partial—a fact which has given rise to such loose distinctions as hyper-, moderate-, and mild-Calvinism (which last is actually about 80 percent Arminian). Other divisions have been Old School and New School Calvinism.

As a pure system Calvinism is logically coherent, consisting of five major interdependent and interlocking doctrinal positions. For both understanding and memory, students have sometimes resorted to the acronym TULIP, which stands for Total depravity, Unconditional election, Limited atonement, Irresistible grace, and Perseverance (eternal security). While these constitute the "bones" of the entire system of thought, they are not always handled in this order. The Canons of Dort, for instance, begin with Predestination. Historically, however, the doctrine of depravity proved to be the springboard in Augustine's mind for the doctrine of predestination. Moreover the TULIP order was the order of the *Remonstrance* document presented in 1610 to the political authorities at The Hague by the 42 Remonstrant signers, led by John Uitembogaert.

The first tenet, Total depravity, does not mean that humans are as evil as they can be, but that they are depraved in every faculty and facet of their being. This depravity is the result of complete alienation from God due to Adam's sin, and constitutes a complete moral inability. Man in this state is unable to live a truly meritorious life, or do one effective thing toward turning to God or acquiring personal salvation.

The second tenet—Unconditional election—concerns the basis of God's redemptive plan, in the face of this abject helplessness of man. Salvation must be totally the work of God, not only in initiation and prosecution but in final consummation. This stress on the divine will implies that if God does not save all men, it can only be because He does not choose to do so. Instantly we have on our hands some idea of election and predestination—that God has foreordained in advance those who will be saved.

This develops in different directions. Some declare a "double predestination," meaning that the damned are predestined to be lost as surely as the saved are predestined to be rescued (e.g., Canons of Dort). In contrast the advocates of "single predestination" declare that only the "elect" are predestined by a divine decision or decree, the others simply being allowed to suffer the fate inherently their just desert—a desert not only attached to their personal sins but their "real" participation in Adam's first sin.

Another difference is indicated by the terms supralapsarianism and infralapsarianism. The first means that the election of individuals was determined in the divine mind before the Fall—indeed, that the Fall was included in the divine decree. The second term represents the belief that it was after the Fall, and was God's response to it. Supralapsarianism can scarcely escape the criticism that it makes God "the author of sin" (as James Arminius said in his *Declaration of Sentiments* of 1608).

Having once declared a doctrine of predestination, the remaining tenets of Calvinism follow naturally. The third therefore concerns the Atonement: that Christ atoned only for the sins of those predestined to be saved. This is called Limited atonement. Congenial to this is that theory of the Atonement which sees it as an objective transaction, consisting of a full satisfaction of the claims of God's holiness and justice, in the form of a full payment of the exact penalty. The elect, therefore, are necessarily freed. Calvin thus speaks not of Christ *providing* (i.e., making possible) salvation for us, but that "salvation was obtained" (*Institutes,* 2:77).

The fourth tenet is called Irresistible grace (or effectual calling). This relates to God's mode of bringing about the salvation of the elect. The gospel call is impressed on the hearts of elect sinners by the Holy Spirit in such a manner as to assure their faith and repentance. Others may be moved by the gospel also, but their response will fall short of saving faith because they are left without the crucial aid of the Spirit—which Calvin calls "the secret efficacy of the Spirit" (ibid., 2:86).

The fifth letter of TULIP stands for Perseverance, meaning that since God has decreed the salvation of the elect, it is impossible for them to be lost, for that would be a failure of the divine will. Therefore the assurance of final salvation is inseverable from the initial infusion of saving grace. God undertakes full responsibility for preserving the "saints" in a state of sonship.

Calvinists divide into different camps respecting sin in the Christian after conversion. While assuming that a person in this life could never be free from sin, or perfect, John Calvin made no allowance for willful sinning, but insisted that the desire and endeavor to live a holy life was endemic to regeneration and a prime evidence of being among the elect. Other views have not been so guarded, some even veering into virtual antinomianism.

Today the usual Calvinistic stance is that sin breaks one's fellowship with God, and may even jeopardize one's rewards, but has no bearing on final destiny. That destiny is unchangeably settled. Some go so far as to declare that a backslider is still saved even if he dies in his backslidden state; others would say that such terminal backsliding only proved that the person was never truly born again in the first place.

The single most distinguishing mark of Calvinism is its emphasis on divine decrees. The world, including men, is governed not merely by the power of God but by His decrees (Calvin, 1:236). "That men do nothing save at the secret instigation of God, and do not discuss and deliberate on anything but what he has previously decreed with himself and brings to pass by his secret direction, is proved by numberless clear passages of scripture" (1:268). Thus God's providence is not viewed as flexible response but advance determination, and divine sovereignty is not seen as absolute authority primarily but as absolute efficiency. The divine will cannot be thwarted.

This system is believed to magnify God. Only by exalting God as the Source and Cause of all things can all ground for human pride be removed.

Yet throughout Calvin's *Institutes* he struggles with the implications of such one-sided monergism. Many words are used in seeking to protect the honor of God from the stigma of arbitrary selectivity in saving people. All sorts of hedging and qualifying are engaged in, seeking to prove that while God alone is responsible for good deeds, for faith, and for final salvation, the sinner alone is responsible for his sins and his final lostness.

In the Calvinistic system the will is central not only in God as the Source but in man, as the soteriological pivot. While in Arminianism the will is *enabled* by grace, in Calvinism it is essentially and supernaturally *altered* by grace. Calvin says: "The Lord both corrects, or rather destroys, our depraved will, and also substitutes a good will from himself" (*Institutes,* 1:346; cf. 350, 389, et al.). This is the first action of God upon the elect in the sequence of saving grace. From this alteration of the will flow faith, and *then* repentance (which Calvin defines as regeneration—cf. ibid., 2:159). A turned will thus moves *freely* in the direction of righteousness. But the sinner is powerless to effect the turning himself or even to aid it.

The tension between the absolute exercise of sovereignty and human freedom, together with any rational philosophy of moral responsibility, has been felt by each generation of Calvinistic thinkers. Jonathan Edwards, America's greatest Calvinistic theologian, struggled with the problem in his remarkable essay on *Freedom of the Will.* In this effort he sought to preserve both predestination and human freedom by the ingenious utilization of the concept of motives. While the will is free, and not coerced, the human psychology is such that the will always chooses the strongest motive—or responds to the strongest reason for action. And motives are determined not from within, but from without—by divine providence; and thus God retains full suzerainty.

Following Edwards, the modifying process of Samuel Hopkins, Timothy Dwight, and Nathanael Taylor resulted in what is called the New England Theology, a move away from hyper-Calvinism's extreme view of moral inability toward the granting of a larger role to human freedom and responsibility. The greatest revivalist of this era, Charles G. Finney, a New School Presbyterian (later a Congregationalist), was a sworn foe of moral inability.

Calvin's conception of justification by faith alone was similar to both Luther's and Wesley's in the sense that it was viewed as the hinge of evangelical soteriology. However, with Calvin, faith was not a gift in the sense of an enablement, but a direct creation, an infusion. The elect person was given faith; from then on he possessed faith, which meant that from then on he remained justified.

Calvin along with Wesley and Luther affirmed initial sanctification as a universal concomitant of justifying faith. He said that "holiness of life, real holiness, as it is called, is inseparable from the free imputation of righteousness" (ibid., 2:151). But it is the free and unconditional justification which is determinative of eternal life, and in no sense the success or failure of sanctification. The deficiency in sanctification can never be fatal, for it is more than compensated by the imputed obedience of Christ. As Christ's death is imputed for justification, so His obedience is imputed for sanctification, so that God sees us as perfect and complete in Him (cf. ibid., 2:216, et al.).

In all fairness it must be said that Calvin's deficient concept of the possibilities of sanctifying grace in this life stemmed in large part from his faulty doctrine of sin. "Nothing can be accepted that is not in every respect entire and absolute, and tainted by no impurity; such indeed as never has been, and never will be, found in man" (ibid., 2:334).

In evaluating Calvinism, only certain very brief observations can be made, though at the risk of seeming superficial. Calvinism's hold on much of the evangelical world can be accounted for, in part, by the fact that the Bible contains much apparent support for the system. It is only as careful students such as James Arminius, John Wesley, John Fletcher, and hundreds of others, have taken a second look, and turned Calvin's textual stones over, that they have become convinced that the net teaching of the Bible respecting the relation of a sovereign God to His human creatures, and respecting the conditions and processes of salvation, move in a different direction.

The appeal of Calvinism also lies in its absolutism. It is a comforting teaching for those who have reason to believe they are among the elect.

To feel that personal security is settled, by God himself, takes from one's shoulders an immense load of responsibility. Wesleyans and others who disagree, however, insist that their sense of security is as satisfying, but on a sounder foundation: It rests in the assurance that as long as one *wants* to be kept, the love of God is faithful and the power of the Spirit adequate. But it sees neither moral nor scriptural ground for presuming that security is unrelated to continued trust and willing obedience.

Calvinism can be faulted for its inadequate conception of the present possibilities of grace for both inner and outer holiness. Strange grace, that can overwhelm the will in conversion but cannot energize it against sin! It would be better to redefine sin than to retain a definition which puts a limit on Christ's power to save, which makes Him a Savior in sin rather than from it, and which contradicts the many promises in the Bible for thorough cleansing. Calvinism fails utterly to see entire sanctification in this life as either possible or necessary.

Furthermore, Calvinism's absolute divine sovereignty, expressed in the form of inviolable decrees, does not really honor God but shamefully dishonors Him. For one thing, a redemption that can be accomplished only by commandeering the human will must be branded as a colossal failure. This is a salvation which depends on arbitrary power, not on the winsomeness of love. A human will taken over by an irresistable divine energy must of necessity be acknowledged for what it is—a violated will. Such a person is not free, even though he may have the illusion of freedom.

But the most terrible stigma on the Creator is the implication of selective predestination, entirely on the basis of God's own pleasure, without regard to foresight of human response, with the balance of mankind left to rot eternally in their inherited corruption. The God who can save whom He will could save all if He willed. The God who can save all but chooses not to, cannot escape responsibility for their lostness, by His default. This seems to thoughtful persons to be a travesty on any doctrine of divine love, which no amount of adroit dodging can evade.

See ARMINIANISM, AUGUSTINIANISM, MONERGISM, SYNERGISM, DIVINE DECREES, FREEDOM, INFRALAPSARIANISM, ATONEMENT, CANONS OF DORT.

For Further Reading: Wesley, *Works,* 7:373 ff; 10:358-63; Calvin, *Institutes of the Christian Religion;* Wiley, *CT,* 2:334-439; Wynkoop, *Foundations of Wesleyan-Arminian Theology;* Kantzer and Gundry, eds., *Perspectives on Evangelical Theology,* 81-104; Purkiser, *Conflicting Concepts of Holiness;* Taylor, *A Right Conception of Sin; GMS,* 410-38.

RICHARD S. TAYLOR

CANON. The Hebrew word *qaneh,* "cane" or "reed," underlies both its Greek and English derivatives *canon.* In Greek it came to denote a yardstick but also acquired the secondary sense of a "list" or "index," probably from the marks it bore as a measuring rod. In either sense it was related easily to Holy Scripture, first as referring to the official list of books which comprise the Scripture, and then as constituting the rule for measuring belief.

Presuppositions. Much confusion is created in the interpretation of the evidence of the formation of the canon by the failure to understand clearly the assumptions on which the concept of canonicity is based. Two are of particular significance.

1. Canonicity does not impart authority but derives from it. That is to say, it is books already regarded as authoritative which are incorporated into the canon, not their incorporation into the canon which confers authority upon them. This means that it is of prime importance to determine the ground on which such authority rested.

2. The kernel of canonical authority is revelation. The unspoken premise of a canon regarded as the measure of truth can scarcely be other. Now if it be conceded that God has revealed himself in the Jewish and Christian covenants of which we have knowledge through their literary records, there follows almost irresistibly not merely the idea of an authoritative canon, but also the providential care which is necessary for its formation and preservation. This principle rules out suggestions that the canon is a purely fortuitous creation, and that accidents in transmission might well have given it a shape other than it has.

The Canon of the OT. The threefold division of the Hebrew Bible into the Law, the Prophets, and the Writings may well reflect the stages in which the OT canon developed, though there is no direct evidence of this. If this is so, the Law will have been regarded as divine from its earliest beginnings down through any editions and recensions it may have undergone. Much of the Prophetic division was in existence by the fall of Jerusalem in 587 B.C. apart from the postexilic sections of the Latter Prophets. The Writings are later still, though they contain much earlier material. What may be said with certainty is that well before the NT era, the OT canon was fixed in the form in which we now know it, i.e., that which it holds in the Hebrew Canon. The author of Ecclesiasticus, writing about 132 B.C., speaks in the Prologue of his work of the things that have been "delivered to us by the law and the prophets and by the others that have followed in their steps."

This canon was evidently accepted by Jesus. In Luke 24:44 His reference to all that was written about himself "in the Law of Moses, and in the prophets, and the psalms" (the last-mentioned standing as representative of the Writings) appears to bear this meaning. Each division apparently contained everything now found in its Hebrew counterpart. (This would appear to hold for the Writings as well as the Law and the Prophets. Luke 11:51 is clearly intended to be a comprehensive statement covering all the acts of violence mentioned in Scripture from first to last. If the Zechariah in question is the one mentioned in 2 Chron. 24:20-21—the book which stood last in the Writings in the Hebrew Bible—then evidently the Writings was at that time constituted as it is now in the Jewish Canon.)

As noted above, books were admitted into the canon on the basis of their previously acknowledged authority which rested on their acceptance as inspired revelation. This character derived ultimately from their origin in prophecy. Since the prophet was immediately inspired to utter the divine word, the same quality attached to his written utterances (see Isa. 8:16; Jer. 36:1 ff). It cannot be shown that every OT book is of prophetic authorship. However, although the principle cannot be applied materially, it can be applied at least formally in the sense that much of the OT is of prophetic authorship and that which is not (e.g., the Wisdom Literature) is inspired response to the prophetic message.

Two difficulties alleged against the above reconstruction may be referred to.

1. *The Alexandrian Canon.* The suggestion is frequently made that the inclusion of the Apocrypha in LXX points to the existence of an Alexandrian Canon which was distinct from the Palestinian Jewish Canon. Against this should be placed the fact that even Jewish writers who used the LXX do not seem to have regarded the Apocrypha as inspired. Philo quotes only the OT as authoritative; while Josephus, who used the Apocrypha, distinguished them from the "divine" books since they were written after the gift of prophecy had ceased (*Against Apion* 1. 8). This accords with the understanding of the Prologue to Ecclesiasticus suggested above. The Apocrypha appears first to have been canonized by Greek-speaking Christians rather than Greek-speaking Jews (Bruce, *The Books and the Parchments,* 164).

2. *The Council of Jamnia,* A.D. 90. Also alleged against the final definition of the canon by the time of Ben Sira (132 B.C.) are the discussions of the rabbis at Jamnia. It is true that they debated the inclusion of canonical recognition to such of the Writings as Proverbs, Ecclesiastes, and the Song of Solomon, eventually deciding in the affirmative. It is also true that they debated the inclusion of other works such as Ecclesiasticus, and decided negatively. However, this does not necessarily reflect uncertainty regarding the limits of the canon. G. F. Moore points out that the canonicity of Ezekiel was also debated (*Judaism,* 1:235-47), though its inspiration had been unchallenged for centuries. This, together with the general obscurity of the proceedings at Jamnia, raises the question as to whether it was a "council" in an official sense at all, or whether it was little more than a sequence—though not unimportant—of rabbinic debates (Childs, *Introduction to the OT as Scripture,* 66).

The Canon of the NT

1. *History.* The Early Church had a canon from the very first: the OT Scriptures and the tradition of the works and teaching of Jesus. To begin with, the latter existed only in oral form, and the history of the NT canon is the history of the reduction of that tradition as well as its apostolic interpretation to writing and its acceptance by the universal Church. That process may be summarized in these stages.

The Gospels and the Epistles were gradually collected and used as Scripture, a process which was accomplished substantially by the third quarter of the second century. It is impossible to pinpoint these events with absolute precision. The collection of Paul's Epistles may have been effected as early as A.D. 100. Both 1 Clement and 2 Pet. 3:15 f attest that Paul's letters were regarded as having authority for the Church at large, the prerequisite of canonization. As to the Gospels: the high value placed on the spoken tradition of the teaching of Jesus probably militated against their early collection; but any such inhibitions had been overcome by 170 as the appearance of Tatian's *Diatessaron* indicates. But 20 years before this, Justin referred to the "memoirs of the apostles" and the "writings of the prophets" (= the OT) in the same breath, saying that both were read on Sunday in worship and introducing both with the authoritative phrase "it is written" (*First Apology,* 67. 3).

This means that by the middle of the second century the canon of the four Gospels was now completed, and the Pauline Epistles held equal standing. Such a conclusion excludes the often-suggested theory that the heretic Marcion, who flourished about this time, was the first to construct a NT canon which consisted of Luke's Gospel and 10 of the Epistles of Paul. (Marcion's detestation of everything that savored of Judaism caused him to discard the entire OT and the rest of the New.) More probably Marcion's efforts constituted a response to an existing (if not finally defined) Christian canon, even if his work prompted the orthodox Church to define its canon more precisely.

The next stage, which may be defined roughly as extending from 180 to 250, was marked by two characteristics. On the one hand, the use of the four Gospels and the Pauline Epistles observed in an earlier stage was continued in the writings of Irenaeus, Tertullian, and Clement of Alexandria. Not only so, but additional Epistles were grouped around the Pauline core so that in the Muratorian Canon, generally held to reflect the canon recognized in Rome about 200, all the books finally included in the canon are present except for Hebrews, James, 1 and 2 Peter, and 2 or 3 John. It is this that has led to the widely accepted conclusion, in spite of some varied phenomena, that by the end of the second century agreement regarding the canon was substantially complete.

From the mid-third to the mid-fourth century the pattern just noted of movement towards consensus together with a degree of variation continued. Eusebius of Caesarea, writing early in the fourth century, divided the books of the canon into two groups: the *Homologoumena* (those which were universally accepted); and the *Antilegomena* (those which were subject to some degree of question). This latter category he subdivided into "disputed" and "spurious." 1 Peter and 1 John were homologoumena; James, 2 Peter, 2 and 3 John, and Jude were "disputed," the struggle arising largely from a varying evaluation of these books in the Eastern and Western areas of the Church. The same was true of Hebrews and the Apocalypse.

The most important stage was that from 350 to the beginning of the 5th century, since it was then that agreement was fully and finally achieved. The immediate impulses toward exact definition consisted of the decisions of bishops and the decrees of councils and synods. No small part of the difficulty lay in the reaching of agreement between East and West, a problem which was solved largely through the work of "bridge personalities." Thus the 39th Festal Letter of Athanasius, dated 367, defines the canon as we have it today including the Apocalypse, which had long been suspect in the East; a significant influence in this regard may well have been Athanasius' long exile from Alexandria in the West at Constantinople. Conversely, the promulgation of the same canon by the Second Council of Carthage in 397 owed much to the influence of Jerome (as well as Augustine), who had migrated from the West to the East, where the Epistle to the Hebrews was widely regarded as Pauline. It took a long time for the canon thus defined to percolate down to the grass roots of the Church, but any subsequent discussion took place against this baseline.

2. *Principles.* As with the OT, books were admitted into the NT canon on the basis of their previously recognized authority. In the case of the NT that authority derived from the relationship of the written works to the spoken words of Jesus which, as indicated above, constituted the earliest Christian canon together with the OT. It followed naturally that those who were best in position both to report and interpret the teaching of Jesus were those who had known Him and been commissioned by Him. Inevitably, therefore, apostolicity came to be applied as a prime criterion of canonicity. This principle, however, was not applied rigidly since Mark and Luke—to mention no others—were not apostles in the narrowest sense, even though they were the associates of apostles. This shows that in reality the line lay farther back: namely, in consonance with the apostolic faith. Wherever that faith was expounded in such a manner as to evince the presence of authoritative, prophetic revelation, there was inspired Scripture. In short, the ultimate criterion for canonicity in the OT is not dissimilar from that in the NT. Whatever contribution was made by church fathers or church synods was but the recognition of this authority, not its impartation.

3. *Problems.* Perhaps the major difficulty felt with regard to the shaping of the canon is the circuitousness of the process by which this was achieved. Why did it take so long? Why were some books now included, now excluded? Why were church fathers, and especially the Eastern and Western areas of the Church, at odds on this issue for so long? The assumption underlying this difficulty is that canonical authority must be immediately evident and therefore instantly and universally accepted. If it has been soundly argued above, however, that the touchstone of canonicity is prophetic revelation in consonance with the apostolic faith, then it is easier to see how differences of opinion might arise which could be settled only by studied reflection, not by

the mechanical application of any literary litmus test.

It is sometimes objected, also, that other books, contemporary with or later than the NT period, might profitably have been added to the canon. This overlooks two factors: first, the uniqueness of the canonical books as the deposit of the Incarnation which, as its witnesses, are incapable of replacement; and second, the difficulty of finding a page outside of the NT canon which stands on a level with the material contained in it. No doubt there is a degree of subjectivity in such a statement; but Kurt Aland's judgment would command widespread assent: "Not a single writing preserved to us could properly be added" (*The Problem of the NT Canon,* 24).

Conclusion. It may be freely admitted that there is no logical or historical argument that can prove with mathematical conclusiveness that the Jewish-Christian canon is divinely authorized and complete. Such a claim could not be made for the Christian faith itself. But that is not the question. The question is whether, having come to faith in Christ through Scripture as the written Word of God, the Christian believer can perceive with a faith that is not stretched to the breaking point "the singular care and providence of God" in the preservation and selection of these and only these documents. Ultimately, this is a judgment of faith. It is not a groundless faith, however, but one which rests upon the coherence of the scriptural canon in its witness to God's saving activity as well as upon the inward attestation of this truth by the divine Spirit to the individual Christian and the believing community. In the light of the evidence surveyed above, it seems that the answer to this question must necessarily be in the positive.

See BIBLE, INSPIRATION (OF THE BIBLE), BIBLICAL AUTHORITY.

For Further Reading: Bruce: *The Books and the Parchments,* chap. 8; Bruce, "New Light on the Origins of the Canon," Longenecker and Tenney, *New Dimensions in NT Study,* 3-18; Harris, *The Inspiration and Canonicity of Scripture;* Aland, *The Problem of the NT Canon;* Von Campenhausen, *The Formation of the Christian Bible;* Westcott, *A General Survey of the History of the Canon of the New Testament.*

ALEX R. G. DEASLEY

CANON LAW. This refers to the rules or standards of action for individuals and institutions in Roman Catholicism, Eastern Orthodoxy, and Anglicanism. From ancient times to now, in both Eastern and Western Catholicism, these rules for Christian behavior have gradually been developed, often through the decisions of general councils of the church. These rules are so numerous and so diverse that many churchmen specialize in the knowledge of their history and their significance.

While the term *canon law* is not common among Protestants, many denominations nevertheless have their church rules, which serve the same function. These are both ethical and ecclesiastical, the first being rules for the conduct of the members, and the second being regulations and laws governing church business. Ethical rules may be understood as guidelines only, in which case church members tend to relate themselves to them as mere advice. They are thus pedagogical in nature rather than prescriptive and mandatory. In some denominations, the ethical rules are stated conditions of membership, and their infraction subjects one to disciplinary action. The general attitude of a denomination to the question of rules will depend in part on (1) the depth and precision of its commitment to a spelled-out life-style, and on (2) its conviction that its witness before the world, its duty to its members, and its integrity as a body, depend on careful conformity to the declared standards.

See CHURCH, LAW AND GRACE, FREEDOM.

For Further Reading: *GMS,* 545-47.

J. KENNETH GRIDER

CANONIZATION. Canonization is an act by which the pope decrees that a person, a member of the Catholic church and already having been cited as a venerable person and declared blessed, be included in the book of saints. The act of canonization is based on ecclesiastical, but not scriptural, authority.

This practice started very early as respect paid to persons who had been good and pious, especially those who had suffered martyrdom during the persecutions of the first two centuries. These martyrs were believed to be perfect. This fact induced believers to invoke their intercession before God. The remembrance of the martyrs took the form of true veneration. The date, place of martyrdom, and the burial place were held sacred, and eventually their anniversaries were entered into the calendar. At the beginning of the fourth century, this veneration, which until then had been reserved only for martyrs, was extended to those who, still alive, had defended the Christian faith and suffered for it, and to those who had lived an exemplary Christian life, or excelled in the Christian doctrine or apostolic faith.

During the first 3 centuries the popular fame of the person or the *vox populi* was the only criterion to determine the holiness of a person. But between the 6th and 10th centuries the number of deceased who received the cult of the saints increased so rapidly, and legendary accounts and abuses were so many, that the intervention of ecclesiastical authority, represented by the bishop, was introduced as a regulatory measure.

The first papal canonization on record was that of St. Udalricus in A.D. 973. The pope's action consisted of simply giving his consent for the canonization. But as time went by, papal canonization developed a more definite structure. Eventually the Code of Canon Law became effective on May 9, 1918. The process to become a saint is: (1) to be cited as a venerable person; (2) to be declared a blessed person; (3) two documented miracles performed in the name of the person; and (4) canonization.

The NT teaching is that all Christians are to be saints, in the sense of inward and outward holiness. Canonization implies a standard reached by only a few. Furthermore, it fosters a superstitious veneration of the "saints," including prayers to them.

See SAINT (SAINTLINESS), HOLINESS.

ISMAEL E. AMAYA

CANONS OF DORT. This refers to the third of the three official confessions of the Reformed denominations (and Calvinism generally), the other two being the Heidelberg Catechism and the Belgic Confession. While the two earlier confessions treat Christian doctrine in a general way, the Canons of Dort (1619) treat only the differences between the Calvinists and the Arminians.

In Holland, where the break-off from Roman Catholicism had occurred in 1560, the Protestants became divided into two groups. There were the Calvinists, who agreed with Theodore Beza, John Calvin's son-in-law who taught at Calvin's school in Geneva; and also with Francis Gomarus, who taught at the University of Leiden in Holland. Beza and Gomarus were supralapsarians, teaching that long before Adam's fall, before Creation itself, God had unconditionally predestinated some individuals to eternal bliss and the others to eternal torment.

James Arminius (c. 1558-1609), who had studied under Beza, and who later taught at Leiden with Gomarus, came to teach only a predestination that was conditioned on whether or not people freely repent and believe. There was a third significant view, sublapsarianism, which was not quite as extreme as supralapsarianism. It was—and is—the view that Adam's fall was freely willed; but that, after that, every other individual's eternal destiny was unconditionally determined by God.

Prince Maurice, the Calvinistic head of state in Holland, called a synod to meet at Dort to decide this predestination issue; he stacked things on the side of Calvinism since, of the 42 delegates, all except 3 were Calvinists, and the 3 Arminians could not act as delegates because they were not willing to take a certain required "Calvinistic" oath.

Beginning in November of 1618, and finishing five months later, the Synod of Dort made sublapsarian predestination official and outlawed Arminianism—disallowing the Arminians from having public services, and banishing from the country all their ministers (this, from 1619 to 1623).

See CALVINISM, ARMINIANISM, INFRALAPSARIANISM.

For Further Reading: Bangs, *Arminius: A Study in the Dutch Reformation;* McCulloh, *Man's Faith and Freedom.*

J. KENNETH GRIDER

CAPITAL PUNISHMENT. This is punishment by death. At some times, e.g., 18th-century England, scores of crimes (even stealing food) were punished by hanging. In the United States and most Western nations where capital punishment has not been abolished, only such crimes as first-degree murder and treason qualify for capital punishment.

Though capital punishment has long been used and justified, it has also been vigorously disputed. Largely on humanitarian grounds it has been abolished in a number of European countries.

Some Christians strongly support capital punishment for capital crimes. The primary reason is that wantonly destroying a human life *deserves* the death penalty. Only in this way can the sanctity of human life be affirmed. Secondary reasons include the possible deterrence value, the removal from society of habitual criminals, and the financial relief to society.

These thinkers interpret the "sword" of Rom. 13:4 to imply a literal meaning as well as figurative—as Paul's readers would undoubtedly understand. The sword-wielding state is "the minister of God." This would seem to be a clear statement that the power of life and death, which in the absolute sense belongs to God only, has to a degree been deputized by God to the state.

Other leaders in Christendom, such as Karl Barth and Chuck Colson, oppose the death penalty. The claim is made that the judicial system mainly executes the poor and nonwhite; that mistakes have been made and innocent people executed; and that no data show any correlation between capital punishment and capital crimes. Rehabilitation for the killer is always possible. Vengeance, not justice, they argue, motivates executions. For these leaders, God alone has the right to take life and has not delegated that right to man.

See MURDER, PUNISHMENT, REVENGE, RETRIBUTION (RETRIBUTIVE JUSTICE), SOCIAL ETHICS, STATE (THE).

For Further Reading: Colson, *Life Sentence;* Lewis, *God in the Dock,* 287-300; Geisler, *Ethics: Alternatives and Issues,* 240-49.

GERARD REED

CARDINAL VIRTUES. See SEVEN CARDINAL VIRTUES.

CARNAL CHRISTIANS. "Carnal Christians" involves a contradiction. Christians serve Christ. Carnal persons serve self. Divided loyalty is an unstable and untenable position (Matt. 6:24). It is deadly (Rom. 8:6). But, in some measure, for a time, "babes in Christ" do exist in this perilous condition. Paul addresses "brethren" who are "carnal" (1 Cor. 3:1-4).

The Corinthian "babes" are born indeed. But, being victims of arrested development, they are problems to themselves and to others (cf. Heb. 5:12-14). They are "called to be saints" and are, to some degree, "sanctified" (1 Cor. 1:2). But they are not established (v. 8). They are not "spiritual" (3:1). Fruit is lacking. They are "carnal" *(sarkinos),* overcome by selfish interests (vv. 1-3). They walk as men—not after the Spirit, at least not consistently.

Such people are in danger of apostasy and perdition (Heb. 6:7-8). The doublemindedness (Jas. 4:8) cannot continue indefinitely. The balance tips. Christ becomes Lord of all or He ceases to be Lord at all. It is not enough to "call upon the name of the Lord" (1 Cor. 1:2) if one yields to the carnal pull of envy, strife, and factions.

There is a remedy. Entire sanctification is an act of God in which by faith the believer is cleansed from all sin and filled with the Holy Spirit (1 Thess. 5:23-24; 1 John 1:7; Acts 2:4). Belonging wholly to God, he is enabled to live in the Spirit, to walk after the Spirit (Gal. 5:25; Rom. 8:4), and to bear the fruit of the Spirit (Gal. 5:22-23).

See CARNALITY AND HUMANITY, DOUBLE-MINDEDNESS, CARNAL MIND.

For Further Reading: Wesley, *Sermon* on "Sin in Believers"; Taylor, *A Right Conception of Sin,* 102-20; Geiger, comp., *The Word and the Doctrine,* 89-138.

WILBER T. DAYTON

CARNAL MIND. The carnal mind is a mind-set toward the flesh. As such, it is the opposite of the mind of Christ. Though restrained and counteracted, it is a mind-set of the believer as well as the worldling, until cleansed by the baptism with the Holy Spirit. Until this cleansing, the believer struggles with conflicting sets of psychic complexes within himself, the new life in Christ and the old life of self.

The term *the carnal mind* is a translation of *to phronēma tēs sarkos,* used three times in Rom. 8:6-7. The phrase in v. 7 is translated "carnal mind" by KJV, NIV; "the mind set on the flesh" by NASB (cf. RSV); "worldly-mindedness" by NBV, and "carnal attitude" by Phillips.

"Attitude" does not do justice to the depth and strength of *phronēma* (as also in Phil. 2:5). According to Godet, the term includes both "thinking and willing." Denney understands "mind" to be "their moral interest, their thought and study" (quoted by Earle, *WMNT,* 3:145). Vincent says that to "mind" (as a verb) is to *"direct the mind to something,* and so *to seek or strive for" (Word Studies in the New Testament,* 3:90; cf. Matt. 16:23; Phil. 3:19; Col. 3:2).

The carnal mind then is a mind-set or striving for the values represented by *sarx,* "flesh." This is the world of self, including both appetites and aspirations. It is the opposite of spiritual-mindedness, or the mind set on the values of the Spirit. To be carnally minded (totally) is to be spiritually dead; to be spiritually minded is to be alive and inwardly whole and at rest.

The destructiveness of the carnal mind is explained by its essential hostility toward God ("enmity," Rom. 8:7). The hostility toward God is the consequence, or inevitable obverse, of the carnal mind's attachment to self. For God is the supreme threat to the autonomy of self; therefore the carnal mind spontaneously resents and resists God. As a principle or disposition of self-willfulness, it "does not submit to God's law, nor can it do so" (v. 7, NIV). If the *phronēma* submitted to God, it would cease to be carnal.

Telltale marks of the carnal mind therefore include any form or degree of opposition to God's rule, whether mediated by law in the Bible, by the Spirit in personal demands and claims, or by divinely appointed deputies, such as parents or the church. The deputies may have to be resisted when they themselves violate the rule of God; but this is different from that dispositional set against external authority, per se, which is the very essence of the carnal mind.

The carnal mind is not an entity in the sense of a thing in itself, which can exist in abstraction from personality. Yet it is an entity in the sense of a subsistent (rather than existent) entity, somewhat like love, reason, and beauty. It is a psychic organism of traits which impacts the whole of life with its influence, and which is predictable in its attributes or manifestations. Paul spoke of the "law of sin" and the "sin that dwelleth in me" as an "it," yet obviously he was not intending to imply a physical substance. As a subsistent entity it is a more pervasive nature than an opinion, belief, prejudice, or attitude—though it tends to impregnate all of these with its own character.

The NT concept of carnality is not to be confused with sexuality. Within divine law sex itself is not "carnal" in the sense of being sinful (Heb. 13:4), and a person is not "carnal" simply because he has a strong sexual nature. On the other hand, a person with little interest in sex may be carnally minded; for *sarkos* can take many forms (Gal. 5:19-21).

Neither should carnality be confused with material things. Paul refers to wages and material goods as "carnal things" without thereby implying that they are sinful or illegitimate (Rom. 15:27; 1 Cor. 9:11). They are the fleshly and earthly side of life (innocent in themselves) in contrast to the spiritual and heavenly.

The discussion in Romans treats carnal-mindedness and spiritual-mindedness as mutually exclusive absolutes. It is in 1 Corinthians that we discover the possibility of a mixed state. Here Paul pits the spiritual person over against the natural man (*psuchikos,* or "soulish"), then designates the Corinthians as being neither natural (they are "babes in Christ") nor "spiritual"; rather, they are "carnal" (*sarkinos* [UBS text], "fleshy" or "fleshly," Thayer). In Corinthians *phronēma,* "mind," is not used but its sense is implied. These unspiritual babes in Christ were still plagued by a mind-set which savored more of the world than of Christ. As evidence Paul pinpoints their cliquishness and party spirit, and more especially their jealousy and quarreling.

That it is possible for true believers to still be infected by a carnal spirit, or carnal-mindedness, is seen not only throughout the Corinthian letters, but also in a study of the disciples before Pentecost, supplemented by other major NT portions, particularly Hebrews and James. While regeneration brought spiritual life and radical changes, the change was not yet complete. There still remained a cluster of unchristlike traits gathered around an inner core, as yet uncleansed, of proneness to self-sovereignty.

The problem in postulating the presence of the carnal mind in believers is in supposing that a regenerate heart, reconciled to God, can still be in a state of enmity toward God. This, of course, is contradictory and not implied. Though present, the carnal mind is no longer dominant; it is suppressed and denied. The Christian opposes the movements of carnal feelings and attitudes which he occasionally feels within. However, even while loving God, he becomes aware that the old hostility is latent, ready to rise in outbursts of resentment—even against God—when self is thwarted. It is this self-discovery which humbles Christians and enables them to see the awful nature of their remaining corruption and their desperate need for total cleansing from it.

See CLEANSING, ERADICATION, CARNALITY AND HUMANITY, ENTIRE SANCTIFICATION, OLD MAN.

For Further Reading: *CC,* 6:202; Wiley, *CT,* 2:473 ff; Geiger, *The Word and the Doctrine,* 127-36; Taylor, *Holiness the Finished Foundation* (unabridged), 28-46; Purkiser, *Sanctification and Its Synonyms,* 49-62; *WMNT,* 3:111-47.

RICHARD S. TAYLOR

CARNALITY AND HUMANITY. This has to do with what is carnal, and what is simply human, in our conduct. It is an issue particularly in the holiness movement, which teaches that carnality is original sin, and that it is expelled or cleansed or eradicated at the time of one's entire sanctification—but that one is of course still in his humanity. In this movement, much debating has occurred on what is carnal and what is human—and therefore, on what we can and cannot expect to be cleansed from at the time of our entire sanctification.

Some have taught that such aberrations as impatience, psychological hostilities, and prejudices are instances of carnality; and that we can expect to be delivered from all such when we receive entire sanctification. Others view such matters as stemming from our humanity, and as needing to be worked through, by God's help, in growth in the holiness life. Impatience might stem from a given kind of temperament, and it is felt that our temperament is not basically changed when we are sanctified wholly.

Also, it is felt that psychological hostilities, such as an aversion to an authority figure, arises in us environmentally through, say, poor upbringing—and that we might not necessarily be delivered from them at the time of our entire sanctification. The same is so, it is felt, regarding prejudices, such as a racial bias. Since the apostle Peter was still prejudiced against Gentiles well after Pentecost, the time of his entire sanctification (see Acts 2:4; 15:8-9; 10—11), it is understood that we might have racial and other prejudices after our entire sanctification. In this case, we can hope to correct them through growth in grace.

While many earlier holiness leaders, such as J. A. Wood and J. O. McClurkan, taught the more extreme view of the extirpation of such aberrations at the time of our entire sanctification, present holiness theologians tend to understand that they are to be corrected through Christian growth. This, because it is the Adamic sin that we are born with that is expelled at entire sanctification; and these other aberrations develop during our lifetime.

See CARNAL NATURE, PURITY AND MATURITY, INFIRMITIES, RACISM, DEVELOPMENT (THEORIES OF).

For Further Reading: Baldwin, *Holiness and the Human Element;* Chambers, *Holiness and Human Nature;* Grider, *Entire Sanctification,* 105-13; Taylor, *Life in the Spirit,* 149-68.

J. KENNETH GRIDER

CASUISTRY. Casuistry is defined as the art of applying general moral principles to particular cases—applied morality. It is not to be confused with law itself but is the attempt to determine in advance how the law is to be applied to specific possible situations.

While morality has tended to move between the extremes of an outwardly legalistic position, on the one hand, and a more inwardly dispositional position on the other, each has tended to develop a casuistry of its own. The legalists rely on logic, while the dispositionalists depend on such inner faculties as conscience, common sense, or sentiment. The former group is the older of the two and is the one to whom the term is often exclusively reserved.

Casuistry often involves elaborate rules which specify the expected action and the appropriate penalties for noncompliance. The rabbinic teachings of Judaism and later the *Penitential Books* of Roman Catholicism were examples of casuistry against which the Reformation found itself in violent disagreement. The Roman Catholic was motivated by fear of losing his soul if he thought for himself. The Protestant was certain that he would lose it if he left his thinking to another.

At its best, casuistry is both necessary and inescapable. Yet because it tends toward rigid and often petty legalism, the term has come to have a largely negative connotation.

See LAW, LEGALISM, CHRISTIAN ETHICS, ETHICAL RELATIVISM, RELATIVISM.

For Further Reading: *Encyclopaedia Britannica;* Ford and Kelly, S.J., *Contemporary Moral Theology,* vol. 1 (1960).

ALVIN HAROLD KAUFFMAN

CATASTROPHISM. This is the theory that the earth has been affected by one or more cataclysmic events which have modified rocks, landscape, and life. Catastrophism was developed to relate the natural world to the Genesis account of Creation. There are five stages in the historical development of the theory of catastrophism:

1. During the 16th, 17th, and 18th centuries many fossils were found, leading to the belief that the Flood was the source of sediments which buried animals and plants.

2. In the early 19th century, George Cuvier proposed a series of catastrophic floods which affected parts of the earth. These floods were later followed by the Great Deluge. The modification was made to explain geological data which presented serious challenges to the earlier explanation of a single flood.

3. Louis Agassiz, attempting to retain special creation and also to answer the naturalists' criticism of Cuvier's theory, assumed a series of special creations, punctuated by successive catastrophes. This seemed to better fit the observations of geologists.

4. In the latter part of the 19th and early 20th centuries, catastrophism was essentially replaced by theories Christians had developed to relate not only geology but also Darwin's natural selection to Christian theology.

5. In the 1920s, a revival of a form of catastrophism began, known as flood geology. Repudiating Cuvier and Agassiz, George Price and others sought to overturn more than a century of geologic work and to return to a simple theory of catastrophism. This activity diminished by the middle of the 20th century. In the 1960s several fundamentalist organizations emerged in response to an interest in teaching flood geology and special creation in the public schools.

Christians should carefully weigh the arguments of the proponents of catastrophism. Many attempts have been made to relate the Genesis creation account to the natural world. Many Christians are comfortable with the uniformitarian approach advocated by James Hutton, which sees the earth developing over millions of years by processes similar to those we see at work today. Evangelical biblical scholars are divided over questions relating to catastrophism, uniformitarianism, theistic evolution, progressive creation, fiat creation, etc. Easy correlations between the observations of science and simple interpretations of the Scriptures may lead to serious problems. Scientists have a way of unearthing new data which forces a revision of comprehensive theories. The problem is acute when a Christian rests his faith on a particular theory and then has the theory and his faith knocked down because a new fossil or fact is discovered. The better approach is to keep one's faith solidly anchored in God as Creator and not to place too much confidence in any particular theory which correlates science and theology.

See EVOLUTION, THEISTIC EVOLUTION, CREATION, CREATIONISM, DAYS OF CREATION, DARWINISM.

For Further Reading: Bube, ed., *The Encounter Between Christianity and Science,* 135-70; Ramm, *The Christian View of Science and Scripture,* 171-249; Whitcomb, Jr., and Morris, *The Genesis Flood;* Wonderly, *God's Time-Records in Ancient Sediments.*

MAX W. REAMS

CATECHISM. A catechism summarizes the principal doctrines of the Christian faith, commonly in question and answer form, and is used for the instruction especially of children. It grew out of the instruction used by the Early Church to lead converts to a desired level of understanding and conduct before baptism. After the nominal conversion of the pagan world, instruction was reoriented to leading children to a personal understanding of and commitment to the faith. The Reformers developed catechisms for this purpose, beginning with the Smaller and Larger Catechisms published by Martin Luther (1529). The use of such books spread throughout Protestantism and was later taken up by Roman Catholics and the Eastern Orthodox.

See CREED, DOCTRINE, TEACH, DISCIPLING.

For Further Reading: *NIDNTT,* 199-201; *ERE,* 3:251-56; Schaff, *The Creeds of Christendom.*

LEE M. HAINES

CATHOLIC. The word *catholic* derives from the Greek term *katholikos,* which means universal. In historical as well as linguistic usage, the term sustains a richer significance than it has in its common use, reflecting what is universally shared by all Christians, in grace, sacraments, and practices.

Popularly, the term *catholic* directs attention to the Church of Rome. The word is also used of the Christians of Eastern Orthodoxy. However, the Christians everywhere recognize a deep bond of fellowship among God's people—something transdenominational. Consequently, true catholicity transcends all ecclesiastical bounds to embrace believers in a bona fide universal union and allegiance. Jesus prayed, "Holy Father, keep them in Thy name, the name which Thou hast given Me, that they may be one, even as We are" (John 17:11, NASB).

See CHURCH, BODY OF CHRIST, KOINONIA, CATHOLICISM, APOSTLES' CREED.

For Further Reading: *NIDCC.*

MEL-THOMAS ROTHWELL

CATHOLICISM. An averment by Etienne Gilson, eminent Catholic scholar, suggests the prime meaning of *catholicism*—"In the conviction that there is nothing in the world above universal truth lies the very root of intellectual and social liberty" (*The Wisdom of Catholicism,* 983). However, from that valid, high-minded viewpoint two spheres of catholicism have evolved. First, a politico-religious order with the See of Rome as its center, and, second, a focus of power and worship at Constantinople known as the Eastern Orthodox church. The East axis accepts the hierarchy, apostolic succession, the episcopate, and the priesthood, but it rules our infallibility of the pope.

Polycarp, martyred bishop of Smyrna about A.D. 156, called believers the "holy catholic church." However, in the popular mind catholicism is predominantly associated with the Rome axis. After the Reformation in the 16th century, a crucially developed Protestant theology, with less ritual, forced a congealing of the beliefs and practices focused in Rome, from which the Protestant branch separated. The Rome-dominated division appropriated the title *Catholic* and became a closed socio-political-religious state, a stronghold and citadel of authority and tradition.

Protestantism extended its openness to cover eventually a highly diverse world fellowship, including all Christians of like precious faith. Councils at Nicaea and Chalcedon had proposed to speak under the guidance of the Holy Spirit as to creed and power. Are these rules and standards to be received as church absolutes or as logical propositions, open to debate and subject to change? The Roman See avowed the absolute position, but Protestantism defended a broad stance of faith as an attitude rather than a creed or belief. Beliefs can be limited and compressed in group forms, but faith is representative of believing Christians everywhere regardless of classification or group persuasion. Faith, therefore, stands fair to be the only possible universal posture. A revival of the spiritual reality of true *catholicism* integral to all true Christians has developed in Protestantism, especially, in the past three decades. Also, the Roman church has been in the birth pangs of its own Reformation, a mark of which has been a more conciliatory attitude toward non-Catholics, which in effect is a greater catholicity of spirit.

See CATHOLIC, CATHOLICISM (ROMAN), CHURCH, EASTERN ORTHODOXY.

For Further Reading: Pegis, *The Wisdom of Catholicism;* Dye, *Religions of the World;* Wiley, *CT,* 3:111-16.

MEL-THOMAS ROTHWELL

CATHOLICISM, GREEK. See EASTERN ORTHODOXY.

CATHOLICISM, ROMAN. While the word *catholic* means "general" or "universal," the words *Roman Catholicism* refer to the body of Christendom ruled from Rome by the pope, and the teachings, organization, and practices of this body.

Roman Catholicism, through medieval times, consisted of the Western, usually Latin-speaking Christians who accepted the authority of the bishop of Rome, the pope—in distinction from the Eastern, Greek-speaking Christians whose main center was Constantinople; and whose patriarch, after A.D. 1054 (or somewhat thereafter), was their main authority.

It was from Roman Catholicism that Protestantism stemmed out, in the 16th century—led by Martin Luther (1483-1546) and others.

Many important Christian beliefs are held in common by both Roman Catholicism and Protestantism: e.g., the doctrines of the Trinity, the Incarnation, the virgin birth of Christ, Christ's resurrection, miracles, providence, and heaven and hell.

Yet the differences are considerable, and they relate to a number of significant matters.

1. Roman Catholicism teaches that, besides the 66 books of Scripture viewed as canonical by Protestantism generally, there are 14 intertestamental apocryphal books which were made canonical by the Council of Trent just after Luther's death. Furthermore, it teaches that, besides Scripture, church tradition (e.g., ecumenical and other councils) is authoritative; indeed, it is more authoritative, even, than Scripture. This is in part, for Catholics, because the church decided upon the canon.

2. Roman Catholicism also teaches that good works are meritorious, whereas Protestantism teaches that we are justified by faith alone and not by works—although, of course, it emphasizes the importance of good works after salvation.

3. Another important difference is in the fact that Roman Catholicism teaches the doctrine of purgatory, as a temporal place where fire will punish those who do not go into eternal hell—for their venial (less grave) sins; and for the temporal aspect of the punishment accruing to them for their mortal sins (sins that, if not remedied at all, would occasion a person's eternal punishment in hell).

4. Still another difference has to do with the sacrament of Holy Communion. Roman Catholicism teaches as required dogma that, in this sacrament, the substance of the bread and wine (but not their appearance) becomes transformed into the actual body and blood of Christ—whereas most Protestants teach that the elements are only symbolical of Christ's body and blood, and that Christ is spiritually (and not literally) present.

5. And while both Roman Catholicism and Protestantism (generally) teach the virgin birth of Christ, Roman Catholicism teaches (as dogma, since 1854) that Mary herself, when she was conceived in her mother's womb, by normal marital relations, was conceived in such a way that, miraculously, original sin was not passed on to her. Protestants also teach (since Scripture makes it clear, e.g., in 2 Cor. 5:21) that Christ was entirely sinless—but on different bases: some, because He did not have a human father, and others of us, because He was a new Adam, a new representative for the race, and did not get represented by the first Adam (so, was not born with original sin).

6. Roman Catholicism has taught since 1870 that the teachings of the pope, when speaking *ex cathedra* (in his most official office, as bishop), are infallible. Protestantism (of the evangelical sort) teaches only the infallibility of the inspired Scriptures.

7. Roman Catholicism has a lower view of human sexuality, expressed in marriage, than Protestantism has; so that its priests, monks, and nuns are not permitted to marry, whereas, for Protestants, sexuality expressed in marriage is entirely consistent with the most devoted kind of Christian life.

8. Whereas Protestants direct prayers only to a member of the Trinity, and usually to God the Father, Roman Catholics often pray directly to certain deceased persons—especially to the Virgin Mary.

9. Roman Catholicism usually teaches that, besides heaven and hell as eternal states, there is another such state, *limbo,* where unbaptized infants go, due to the guilt of Adamic sin; while Calvinistic Protestants are supposed to teach that unelected babies go into hell due to the guilt of Adamic sin. Arminian evangelicals, however, teach that all babies, if they die, will go into eternal heaven, because the guilt of Adamic sin has been cleansed in everyone through the death of Christ, and because the depravity is cleansed, in these cases, by an imputation to the infants, of the cleansing benefits of Christ's atonement.

See CATHOLICISM, CHURCH, SACRAMENTS, PURGATORY, JUSTIFICATION.

For Further Reading: Boettner, *Roman Catholicism.*

J. KENNETH GRIDER

CAUSE AND EFFECT. The principle of causality states that every event is determined by a cause, and every event results in a corresponding effect.

Science. Aristotle viewed all science as the search for cause/effect explanations. The concept of efficient causation prevails today. Although the universality of causation is occasionally debated, for example in physics the Heisenberg Principle, yet science works from the premise that all events can be explained by cause-effect relations capable of formulation in laws. This principle prevails in all branches of science—natural, social, and behavioral.

Philosophy and Theology. The causation principle has definite ramifications for philosophy and theology. First, one may argue rationally for the existence of a Creator-God based on efficient causation. Known as the "cosmological argument," the reasoning is that nothing in the material universe is eternal. Furthermore, material existence cannot be the cause of itself since that would require it to exist before itself, which is impossible. Nor can there be an infinite regression of causes. Ultimately there must be a First Cause which is itself uncaused and therefore eternal, i.e., God.

Second, there is the question whether or not the causality principle excludes the possibility of human freedom. The dilemma is: If every event is determined by antecedent cause(s), then are human choices predetermined or even excluded? If God really exists, then there is a spiritual as well as physical order. Trueblood argues that if humankind is capable of responding to both orders at once, then "the mystery of freedom is partly dispelled" (Elton B. Trueblood, *Philosophy of Religion,* 286).

Third, there is the related issue of moral responsibility. If our actions are determined by antecedent causes, are we morally responsible for our actions? We are responsible if we possess intellectual, spiritual, and moral capacities which through prevenient grace enable us to respond positively to alternative moral choices based on God's revealed will. Although cause and effect law operates continually, we are not locked exclusively into one causal order. The possibility of right choice makes us morally responsible for our actions and their influence.

See FREEDOM, DETERMINISM, RESPONSIBILITY.

For Further Reading: Mead, *Types and Problems of Philosophy,* 304-24, 378; Taylor, "Causation," *The Encyclopedia of Philosophy,* 2:56-66; Trueblood, *Philosophy of Religion,* 92-93, 277-88.

J. WESLEY ADAMS

CELIBACY. Celibacy refers to abstinence from marriage. Usually the term is applied to certain clerical groups. Although celibacy is found among some sects in nearly any religion, with Christianity it is usually associated with the Roman Catholic church. Celibacy is considered necessary in order to dedicate one's life totally to God's service. During the first three centuries of the church married men were accepted into the clergy, but many practiced celibacy as a matter of choice. By the 12th century all major clerics were required to be celibate. Reformers, such as Martin Luther and John Calvin, denied the necessity of celibacy for the clergy.

Those who support celibacy point out that Jesus was not married and emphasize passages in Matthew 19 and 1 Corinthians 7. Jesus said that some people do not marry for the sake of the kingdom of heaven, but that not everyone can accept this way of life (Matt. 19:10-12). Paul noted that unmarried people concern themselves with the Lord's work, trying to please the Lord, but married people concern themselves with worldly matters, trying to please their spouses (1 Cor. 7:32-34).

On the other hand, Philip, Peter, and other apostles were married (Acts 21:9; Matt. 8:14; 1 Cor. 9:5). Furthermore, in two of his Epistles the apostle Paul specified that an appointed clergyman must be "the husband of one wife" (1 Tim. 3:2; Titus 1:6). That is, the clergy in biblical times were not required to be celibate.

Since the requirement that all clergy be celibate is obviously of ecclesiastical, rather than biblical origin, clergy outside the Roman church do not feel bound by it. Celibacy continues to be a topic of debate even in the Roman Catholic church. The Bible presents celibacy as an option to marriage, so celibacy should be based on personal choice, regarded as neither better nor worse than marriage.

See MARRIAGE, CATHOLICISM (ROMAN).

For Further Reading: "Celibacy," in the *New Catholic Encyclopedia,* 3:366-74; Lea, *The History of Sacerdotal Celibacy in the Christian Church;* Raguin, *Celibacy for Our Times.*

RONALD L. KOTESKEY

CEREMONIAL PURIFICATION. See PURIFICATION, CEREMONIAL.

CHAIN OF COMMAND. Of recent usage, this term reflects the conviction that Scripture teaches a hierarchy of authority in which every person is assigned his or her place by divine will. Thus a chain of command is found linking all classes of persons by a progression of headship and submission. A clear picture of the lines of authority governing social relationships emerges. Each individual is in the chain of command in four spheres—family, government, church, business. A biblical basis for this view is found in the lists of household duties such as Eph. 5:21 ff and passages like Romans 13 and Heb. 13:17 (with many parallels in OT and NT).

Submission and obedience are the key concepts. In point of fact, these significant words do call the believer to a respect for structures of authority willed by God for the good of His creatures. They call into judgment the individualism of Western society which isolates the person from community support and guidance.

The school of thought which promotes the chain of command does not, however, do justice to the whole of biblical teaching. The tension between the Church as the redeemed community and society as the fallen world is missed. A prophetic voice of the Church is unlikely in the implied monolithic, Constantinian view of society. Moreover, the idea of mutual submission which pervades the NT passages in question is overlooked. This equality-in-submission among believers conditions the specific forms of submission (cf. Eph. 5:21-22). Lastly, any chain of command will be destructive of human worth without a balancing emphasis on a "channel of love"—divine and human; no chain of command with its one-to-one vertical relationships is full community without the "bond of love" that links persons in horizontal relationships.

See AUTHORITY, INSTITUTIONS OF CHRISTIANITY, FAMILY.

For Further Reading: Bockelman, *Gothard: The Man and His Ministry;* Gothard, *Institute in Basic Youth Conflicts: Research in Principles of Life;* Jewett, *Man as Male and Female;* Yoder, *The Politics of Jesus,* 163-214.

GEORGE R. BRUNK III

CHANCE. The *Oxford English Dictionary* defines chance as "absence of design or assignable cause, fortuity; often itself spoken of as the cause or determiner of events, which appear to happen without the intervention of law, ordinary causation, or providence." The implications of this concept have exercised the philosophers (determinism vs. nondeterminism) and the theologians (sovereignty, free will, responsibility).

The idea that everything occurs by mere chance is not held by many thinking persons. Such a concept would exclude all purpose and, hence, meaning. The determinist has no use for the word, while the nondeterminist may use it in some limited way to explain the unpredictable aspect of reality. Pure chance undermines the possibility of science and would offer no basis for responsible freedom. Many would agree that "chance seems to be only a term, by which we express our ignorance of the cause of any thing" (Wollaston).

In the Christian world view involving a creating, ruling God, the idea of chance is incompatible. The confession that "in everything God works for good with those who love him" (Rom. 8:28, RSV) excludes pure chance. Nothing is merely accidental or capricious. Although Christians differ regarding the manner of God's control in history (His sovereignty) and its relation to human freedom or the power of evil, all can agree thet the divine will is active in everything, that divine power undergirds all.

The Scriptures show God at work in and through all events, accomplishing His purposes. This does not answer the question as to how particular events such as natural disasters are to be explained. Yet the Bible does not appeal to chance to explain these incongruities in God's creation. It is evil's entrance into the world (and God's reaction) that determines, in part, the course of history (Genesis 3; Rom. 8:20). History is a stage where the drama of the encounter of divine, human, and demonic wills is played out. Therefore ultimately nothing, not even the acts of nature, take place in the absence of all purpose.

See PROVIDENCE, DETERMINISM, DIVINE SOVEREIGNTY.

For Further Reading: *The Encyclopedia of Philosophy,* 2:73 ff; Forster and Marston, *God's Strategy in Human History;* Pinnock, ed., *Grace Unlimited.*

GEORGE R. BRUNK III

CHARACTER. Among the many possible meanings of this word, that which is theologically significant is the meaning of personal moral quality. To say that Barnabas was "a good man" (Acts 11:24) is to say that he was a man of good character—true, pure, stable, and reliable. He was a man of integrity.

But conversely, men may have an evil character, as did Herod. Also, character may be weak or strong, whether good or evil. The strong character normally has qualities of forcefulness and leadership. The weak character is constantly being reshaped by the latest environment.

Within limits, non-Christian persons can develop strong moral character, in the sense of being honest and trustworthy. Without their knowledge they are being aided by the prevenient grace of God. They may also be the product of a Christian background. Moreover, high intelligence will perceive the superior happiness and well-being accruing to basic decency and honorableness. Yet such good character is not holy. Self-righteousness always falls short of the glory of God (Rom. 3:23). Paul saw the futility, in the final scale of things, of such sub-Christian goodness (Phil. 3:6-9).

When forgiven and cleansed, Christians have essentially good character as a true quality of heart. But they are still responsible for applying themselves to those disciplines which will make their good character strong (Eph. 4:12-16; 6:10).

See RIGHT (RIGHTEOUSNESS), HOLINESS, GROW (GROWTH), DISCIPLINE. RICHARD S. TAYLOR

CHARISMATA. See GIFTS.

CHARITY. See LOVE.

CHASTEN, CHASTISE. The NT *paideuein* (noun *paideia*) which means "to instruct, to train, to inculcate or to draw out mentally and physically" is used in the Septuagint to translate Hebrew *yasar* (substantive *musar*). Those OT terms are most often rendered "chasten" or "chastise." Typically, one may learn in the school of chastisement through habitual evaluation and "reflection," the instruction that comes "in the night" (Ps. 16:7). Or, as in childhood, one learns at the side of his father: "As a man disciplines his son, so the Lord your God disciplines you" (Deut. 8:5, NIV).

So, chastening is discipline and instruction of the sort that is lovingly provided by the benevolent parent. Chastening has as its objective the welfare of the person being disciplined; it in no sense is to expiate the guilt of the son or to ventilate the wrath of the father (Prov. 19:18). The biblical concept of chastening/discipline thus is no harbor for child abusers. The destruction of self-worth which accompanies child abuse and child neglect cannot be justified on any biblical injunction to "chastise" the child. To be sure, no discipline is pleasant at the time, no occasion to say, "Praise the Lord, anyway" (Heb. 12:11).

The ultimate purposes of God's discipline are that we may "share in his holiness" (Heb. 12:10, NIV). Discipline in these senses is never offered by God to the heathen or unregenerate person or nation; *paideuein* is exclusively the discipline of absolute affection and is thoroughly laced with verbal and nonverbal affection and unconditional love.

See PUNISHMENT, DISCIPLINE, FAMILY, FATHERS.

DONALD M. JOY

CHASTITY. The Greek word translated "chaste" or "pure" is *hagnos,* from a family of terms denoting the sacred or holy. Traditionally, chastity has been defined as abstinence from sexual misconduct. The biblical meaning goes beyond this to include purity in the whole life, not only moral but spiritual.

Spiritual chastity preserves the honor of the church. In 2 Cor. 11:2 Paul reminds the church that it has been betrothed to Christ as "a chaste virgin." He warns that "another gospel" proclaiming "another Jesus" will corrupt the purity of the church. Here chastity involves a single-minded devotion to Jesus Christ.

Chastity also protects the reputation of the gospel. In Titus 2:5 chastity is enjoined upon "the young women," along with other ethical norms, in order that "the word of God be not blasphemed." Chastity relates to sex life in this passage but is not restricted to this area. Bound up with the character of believers is the credibility of the Word. Christian women, should they yield to impurity, would cause the gospel to be "maligned" or "discredited" by non-Christians.

Similarly, chastity safeguards the integrity of the ministry. Timothy is charged, "Keep yourself pure" (1 Tim. 5:22, NIV, RSV). The context is a warning against the hasty ordination to sacred office of unexamined men. Ordination vouchsafes character, and to ordain a wicked man is to partake of his sins.

While *hagnos* occurs sparingly, the whole tenor of Scripture makes moral purity imperative.

See HOLINESS, PURITY, MORALITY.

For Further Reading: *ZPEB,* 1:784; *EBC,* 10:384-86; 11:380-82, 435-37. W. E. MCCUMBER

CHECKS TO ANTINOMIANISM. The *Checks to Antinomianism* comprise a series of five small books written by John Fletcher during the years 1771-73 to answer charges concerning his own theological position and to put into clear perspective the Wesleyan doctrine of sanctification.

"Fletcher was one of the few parish clergy who understood Wesley and his work. . . . In theology he upheld the Arminian against the Calvinist position, but always with courtesy and fairness" (*Britannica,* 9:373).

"Fletcher was a mediating theologian who sought a middle way between theological extremes in accordance with his understanding of Scripture. This characteristic makes him significant for the problem . . . namely, the doctrinal difficulty and necessity of holding in complementarity crisis and progress, holiness and hope, discipleship and grace" (Knight, *The Holiness Pilgrimage,* 64).

Antinomianism can and does take two extremes which Fletcher attempted to guard against. The first is the devout Christian who declares that because salvation is dependent solely upon the grace of God, the life lived does not necessarily need to conform to the level of grace professed. This position has often been described as a "sinning religion." In contrast, Fletcher and Wesley insisted that a life of holiness would flow out of the grace received in the heart.

The other extreme is the humanistic expression of antipathy to all law—anything that interferes with personal freedom. This spirit is prevalent today just as it was in the days of the judges when "every man did that which was right in his own eyes" (Judg. 21:25).

See ANTINOMIANISM, IMPUTED RIGHTEOUSNESS, IMPARTED RIGHTEOUSNESS.

For Further Reading: Knight, *The Holiness Pilgrimage;* Smith, "How John Fletcher Became the Theologian of Wesleyan Perfectionism," *WTJ,* Spring, 1980.

LEROY E. LINDSEY

CHERUB, CHERUBIM. See ANGEL.

CHILD, CHILDREN. In the Bible children are considered a gift from God (Gen. 4:1). In older Hebrew and Eastern societies, the birth of a son was considered most important. Inheritance and birthright blessings were bestowed upon the firstborn son (Gen. 27:4, 27, 32).

In the OT, bearing children was considered a sign of favor and respect (Gen. 16:4; 29:32; 30:1).

The naming of a child was extremely important, for it marked some aspect of God's relation to the father, or the family or nation (Gen. 4:1; Isa. 8:1; Matt. 1:21).

Children were to be trained and taught (Deut. 6:1-9; Ps. 78:1-8). Failure at this task resulted in a generation which did not know the Lord (Judg. 2:10). However, many were true to the responsibilities, and Paul recognizes the value of faithful teachers in the life of Timothy (2 Tim. 3:15).

Throughout Proverbs and Ecclesiastes, "My son" is a prominent form of address. This is a common pattern by other writers (2 Tim. 1:2; Matt. 9:2; Mark 2:5).

Jesus valued children (Mark 9:36; Matt. 19:14). He illustrated the ideal childhood in His own life in subjection to His parents' control (Luke 2:51-52). Jesus also manifested tenderness of affection for children (Matt. 19:14; Mark 10:14; Luke 18:16) and recognized that they had a place in His kingdom. "Becoming as a little child" Jesus asserts is a fundamental condition to receive the kingdom of God. He hallowed the role of a child by adopting His own place in saying My "Father" when He referred to God (Luke 10:21-22; John 14:2; 15:1, 8).

Those who follow peacekeeping and the way of the Lord have been called the children of God (Matt. 5:9). Furthermore, the Holy Spirit witnesses to our adoption as sons in the experience of the new birth (Rom. 8:16).

One can also be a child of hell (Matt. 23:15). The difference between children of God and the children of the devil is that children of God do not sin, but practice righteousness and love one another (1 John 3:10).

Paul indicates there is a childish state or condition which must be left when one matures (1 Cor. 13:11).

See ADOPTION, NEW BIRTH, REGENERATION, FAMILY.

For Further Reading: *IDB,* 1:558-59; *New Catholic Encyclopedia,* 3:569-71; *HBD,* 98; *ZPEB,* 1:793-94.

J. OTTIS SAYES

CHILIASM. See MILLENNIUM.

CHRIST. This is a transliteration of the Greek *Christos* which means "the Anointed," the verb form of which is *chriō* ("I anoint"). "Christ" is one of the many titles by which our Savior was known in the Scriptures. *Ho Christos* ("the anointed") was used in the OT as an epithet for "the king," the anointing being the outward sign of his official appointment to kingship (1 Sam. 10:1; 12:3; 15:1; 26:11; Ps. 89:20). It was also used of prophets and priests in the OT. "The Messiah" is the Aramaic equivalent of "Christ" (John 1:41). In the NT the epithet "Christ" became the recognized title by His disciples, which was usually conjoined with "Jesus" for "the Messiah." Eventually "Christ" became the proper name for the "Son of God" (Souter, *Pocket Lexicon,* 284 ff).

Christ in the NT

In the NT the title *Christ* occurs a total of 569 times (most frequently by Paul). Jesus' frequent use of "Son of man," designating himself, was apparently designed to hide His true Messianic identity from the masses, and thus evade suspicion of political aspirations on their part, while conveying His Messiahship to His disciples. Among the many Messianic titles attributed to Christ in the NT are Servant, Lord, High Priest, Son of God, the Word, Prophet, Savior, the Righteous One, the Holy One, King, and Judge.

Christ a Member of the Divine Trinity. If Christ is the highest expression of God's redemptive plan and provision for man (John 3:16; 1 John 4:9-10), then God is by His very nature love (vv. 8, 16). However, love is a relationship, and thus the eternal existence of the God of love demands an eternal love relationship.

Although he was a Jewish religious philosopher, Martin Buber clearly saw the necessity of such a logical conclusion for *personal self-identity* expressed in the "I-Thou" relationship (cf. Carter, *The Person and Ministry of the Holy Spirit,* 28-29).

Christ the Incarnate Son of God. Of supreme importance is Christ's unique divine incarnation by means of the Virgin Birth and His consequent divine-human nature. He was perfect God and perfect Man united in one Person. To relinquish faith in these essential aspects of the Christ is to cancel His entire redemptive mission and ministry.

Christ the Divine Prophet, Priest, and King (or Lord). The person and inseparable redemptive accomplishments of Christ may be best understood in relation to His threefold office of Prophet, Priest, and King (or Lord). With greater or lesser clarity and emphasis, Christian theologians of practically all schools have recognized this threefold office of Christ since Eusebius (A.D. 260-340?), which had been taken for granted by the NT writers. These characteristics are implicit and explicit in both Testaments. All other characteristics and redemptive activities of Christ are included in one or another of these three offices.

Christ the Divine Prophet. While Christ bore certain resemblances to the OT prophets (Deut. 18:15; Acts 3:22), His was a unique prophetic character and ministry. They bore the message of God to men, but Christ, as God, was in himself both the Message and the Messenger of God (John 1:1; Heb. 1:1-3). Christ was in himself the very righteous character of God. They were fallible men called of God for specific temporary missions. Christ was promised and sent of God as His unique redemptive Messenger to all men under all circumstances for all time (Isa. 9:6-7). They were God's messengers *concerning salvation.* Christ was in His own person God's *salvation Message.* In His omniscience Christ's prophetic ministry included both the divine revelation of truth for man's salvation, and predictions of events yet future in God's redemptive plan—thus forthtelling *and foretelling,* both *proclamation* and *prophecy.* Whereas other prophets were fallible, Christ was the infallible truth of God in His own person (John 14:6). Christ bore a divine self-consciousness of the fulfillment of His redemptive prophetic mission (Luke 4:14-22). This was manifest in His manner, His message, and the resultant fruit of His redemptive ministry (Isa. 61:1-3).

Christ the Divine Priest. Between the prophetic and priestly offices of Christ there exists a close interrelation. As Prophet He spoke of what He would accomplish as Priest, and as Priest He fulfilled redemptively what He promised as Prophet. As Prophet He represented God's redemptive provisions for man; but as Priest He represented man's saving needs before God. As Priest He was appointed to deal with God in behalf of men. In their fallen state men could not reconcile themselves to God, and God could not at will reconcile men to himself. Thus it required one who represented both God and man to effect this reconciliation (2 Cor. 5:18-19). As the unique divine Prophet and Priest, Christ *only* and *alone* could bridge the gulf between fallen and sinful man and the holy God. Christ as the divine Priest fulfilled a twofold mission. First, He offered to God an atoning sacrifice sufficient for the salvation of all repentant believing sinners (Isa. 53:10-11; Heb. 2:17). But as Priest He was both the One who offered the sacrifice to God as a sufficient atonement for sins, and He was also in His own person the sacrifice which He offered to God on the Cross (Heb. 9:26, 28). Christ's self-offering as portrayed in His parable of the good shepherd admirably summarizes His divine priestly ministry in behalf of man's salvation as *voluntary, vicarious,* and *victorious* (John 10:7-18).

Christ the Divine King (or Lord). While there are shades of differences in the titles and functions of Christ as King and Lord, in essence they equally represent His universal divine sovereignty. One has well said that

> the promise of the Messianic Kingdom is clear in the Davidic covenant, in the expectation of the prophets, in the ejaculation of Nathaniel, in the care with which our Lord guarded Himself from the impetuous crowd, and in the ironic superscription on the cross. He was thought of as a king, declared a King, and expected to return in regal power and splendor (Samuel J. Mikolaski, *Basic Christian Doctrines,* 150).

It was not until after His resurrection that Christ openly declared His divine sovereignty over the entire universe when He said, "All authority *[exousia]* has been given to Me in heaven and on earth" (Matt. 28:18, NASB). Thus through His resurrection victory Christ rose to universal Lordship over all creation for all eternity. That Christ is Lord over all became the burden of the Early Church's witness to the entire world of mankind. In the Book of Acts alone the Lordship of Christ is declared no less than 110 times. And finally, Christ declared His Lordship over man's last and greatest enemies, *death* and *hades* (Rev. 1:17-18; cf. Heb. 10:13).

See ESTATES OF CHRIST, INCARNATION, MESSIAH.

For Further Reading: Jukes, *The Names of God in Holy Scripture;* Vincent, *Word Studies in the New Testament,* 1:10-11; Henry, ed., *Basic Christian Doctrines,* 145-51; Kittel, 9:527-80. CHARLES W. CARTER

CHRIST IN YOU. It is "Christ in you," Paul writes (Col. 1:27), which is "the hope of glory" (cf. Rom. 8:10; Gal. 2:20; Eph. 3:17). Whereas the phrase "in Christ" is far more frequent, we are reminded that the relationship conveyed by "in Christ" is dependent on the presence, power, and control of Christ in us. One term speaks of position and privilege, while the counterpart, "Christ in us," speaks of power and validity. It is through Christ in us that we can do "all things" (Phil. 4:13). Christ's reign within must ever be seen not only as the counterpart of but the essential condition for being in Christ.

The references to the indwelling of Christ are few, doubtless because the ministry of inwardness is ascribed primarily to the Holy Spirit (e.g., Rom. 8:11; 1 Cor. 3:16; 2 Cor. 1:22; Eph. 3:16; 5:18). Christ indwells us in the person of the Holy Spirit, as He promised (John 14—16). Nowhere is this vanguard role of the Spirit in effecting our salvation, in relation to the Father and the Son, more precisely stated than in Eph. 2:21-22: "In him [Christ] the whole building is joined together and rises to become a holy temple in the Lord. And in him [Christ] you too are being built together to become a dwelling in which God lives by his Spirit" (NIV).

See IN CHRIST.

For Further Reading: *GMS,* 452 ff; *WMNT,* 4:280. RICHARD S. TAYLOR

CHRISTIAN. This familiar name may have arisen from the common Latin practice of identifying followers of sages and political leaders by adding the ending *iani* to the name of the leader. For example, some religious leaders in Judea who supported the political policies of the ruling family, were called *Herodianoi* (Mark 12:13). Probably no more specific identification of the Christians prevailed in the early years of the movement than that they were "disciples of Jesus of Nazareth" or, as Acts states, followers of "the Way" (Acts 9:2; 19:9, RSV).

The title "Christian" occurs only three times in the NT (Acts 11:26; 26:28; 1 Pet. 4:16, RSV). The first instance reads: "The disciples were called Christians first in Antioch" (in Syria). Herod Agrippa II employs the title in his response to Paul's testimony (Acts 26:28). And in the third usage the apostle Peter, in a passage dealing with the proper response to persecution, writes: "Yet if one suffers as a Christian, let him not be ashamed, but under that name let him glorify God."

Was this a self-chosen name by the Christians in Antioch? Essentially, two views prevail. (1) E. J. Bickerman translates *chrēmatisai* in Acts 11:26 not as "were called" but "styled themselves," thereby recommending the idea that the Antiochene Church created the name. (2) On the other hand, it is the opinion of other scholars that "Christian" had a pagan origin, that is to say, it was given to the followers of Christ in derision. Willingale notes, in support, that elsewhere the name is so employed by non-Christians, i.e., Agrippa and Tacitus (*Ann.* 15. 44). Also, the reference in 1 Pet. 4:16 may not have been used by the writer in a felicitous sense but simply as a recognition of the fact that being a disciple of Christ carried the possibility of persecution from those who express their hatred by use of the name. One should not overread these fragmentary statements, however. It might well be that in the first purely Gentile church in Antioch, where separation from the Jewish community perhaps came more rapidly than in other cities, a name for the sect was needed and was developed most naturally in the manner suggested above in item (1). The love of the Christian converts for Christ would certainly incline them to use His name for their identification. As the Jews wished to be called "the Sons of Torah," so the Christians would be inclined to accept the public reference to them as *Christianoi,* disciples or followers of Christ.

The distinctive element in this new religion was that it was centered in the Person, Christ, and this fact would suggest the type of name by which the disciples were finally identified. By the second century the name "Christian" was firmly established and was being used by Ignatius, the bishop of Antioch, and even by Pliny, the pagan Roman governor, in other areas of the Mediterranean world.

"Christian" carries several shades of meaning: (1) fervent commitment to Christ as Savior and Lord; (2) formal identification with the Christian Church; (3) acceptance of the general religious principles of the Christian community. To be "Christian" includes a faith relationship to Christ as Lord and a continuing identification with the Church, the common Body of Christ.

See CHRISTIANITY, DISCIPLE.

For Further Reading: Bickerman, *Harvard Theological Review,* 42 (1949), 109 ff; "Christian," *IDB,* A-D; "Christian," *ISBE,* rev. ed., vol. 1. WILLARD H. TAYLOR

CHRISTIAN EDUCATION. Christian education is the activity of the church in fulfilling the teaching function of the Great Commission. Its task is the transmission and inculcation of the teachings of Jesus, and, by extension, the apostolic interpretation of His person and saving work. Lawrence C. Little defines it as "the process through which the church seeks to enable persons to understand, accept, and exemplify the Christian faith and way of life" (*Foundations for a Philosophy of Christian Education,* 193).

During the 19th century, with its crosscurrents of science, theology, and the humanities, Horace Bushnell, sometimes called "The Father of Christian Education," initiated humanistic concepts by opening basic theological questions as to how man, as a product of the physical world, is related to God, its Creator. He perceived the growth and development of man from natural being to spiritual being as accomplished through personal nurture within the Christian community and an unfolding consciousness of relation to God. This concept tended to obviate the necessity of a crisis experience of conversion. Most writers during the past 50 years in the field of liberal Christian education have been Pelagian in their view of human nature, discounting the biblical concept of original sin and man's inability to do good aside from saving grace (Rom. 1:18 ff; 3:10-18, 21).

A century of scientific and philosophic ferment has subjected almost every inherited concept and assumed value to scrutiny and challenge. During much of the century, evangelical Christians have been in search for a biblical philosophy of education. For several decades prior to 1940, students of religious education were indoctrinated with a theological liberalism that had a philosophic rather than a biblical basis. The influence of John Dewey and progressive education impacted on Christian education. Educators such as George A. Coe and Harrison Elliott devoted their energies to the support of religious education within the context of theological liberalism. Sanner and Harper state, "As a proponent of the liberalist viewpoint, Harrison Elliott had raised the question in 1940, 'Can religious education be Christian?' and had replied in the affirmative" (*Exploring Christian Education,* 95).

A call for reexamination of liberal Christian nurture was made in 1948 by H. Shelton Smith in *Faith and Nurture.* He held that Christian nurture should find its basis in the biblical and historical roots of the Christian Church rather than in secular positions. Sanner and Harper conclude: "The watershed issue, separating the discredited liberal *religious* education from the emerging *Christian* education was, and continues to be, the extent to which the biblical, historical, and theological roots of the Christian faith are allowed to nourish the educational ministry of the church" (95 ff).

Secular philosophical theories have seriously impacted on Christian education during the past century. Some of these are: (1) Naturalism, which finds the ultimate explanation of reality, knowledge, and value in the material world; (2) Idealism, which finds these explanations in mind, or ideas; (3) Personalism, which holds that ultimate reality and ultimate values must be personal to be real; (4) Pragmatism, an empirical viewpoint that holds that the way to test truth of ideas is to see how they work out in practical experiences; and (5) Existentialism, which places importance on the present, "the existential moment." By contrast, education which is truly Christian bases its philosophy of life in the biblical interpretation of the universe and an adequate understanding of the nature of God, the world, man, sin, and salvation.

Christian education, in contrast with secular education, is basically spiritual. Within evangelical Christianity the understanding of Christian education has too often been equated simply with organization and methodology, rather than with an intellectual and spiritual integration of the total ministry of the church. Christian education may be guided in the right direction by seeking to devote itself to the total task of the Christian movement in the world, based on a deepening understanding of spiritual communication and the radical nature of the Christian faith.

In seeking to establish a set of objectives within a Wesleyan frame of reference, Sanner and Harper define Christian education as

> one of the essential ministries of the church *(ecclesia),* by means of which the fellowship *(koinonia)* of believers seeks: (1) to prepare all learners to receive the power of the gospel in conversion and entire sanctification; (2) to inspire and lead them to experience personal growth in the Christian graces and in the knowledge of the truth as it is in Jesus; and (3) to assist them in preparing for and finding a place of productive service in the Body of Christ and in the world outside the Church (19).

See TEACH (TEACHING, TEACHER), DISCIPLING, DEVELOPMENT.

For Further Reading: Byrne, *A Christian Approach to Education;* Eavey, *History of Christian Education;* LeBar, *Education That Is Christian;* Little, *Foundations for a Philosophy of Christian Education;* Rood, *Understanding Christian Education;* Sanner and Harper, *Exploring Christian Education.* NORMAN N. BONNER

CHRISTIAN ETHICS. This is a specialized branch of general ethics and shares with it the major concern of determining what is good and right. It may be divided into two major aspects, the exegetical and the philosophical, the division not being entirely precise, since there are areas of overlap between the two. The former of these concerns itself in a major way with the ethical content of biblical revelation; the latter, while usually not neglecting the written revelation, calls upon the more speculative resources which philosophical endeavor provides.

With reference to content, Christian ethics is frequently divided into two phases, Christian Personal Ethics and Christian Social Ethics. The first of these is usually adopted as a point of departure for ethical study and will so be used here. In both cases the major concern is, not human morality in general, but the content of ethical truth in Christianity, both historic and contemporary. The sources for Christian ethics are the following: the two Testaments, taken especially in relation to the total revelation of Christianity's redemptive message; the historic development of ethical thought, beginning with apostolic times, continuing in the cumulative ethical insights of the Fathers and of the medieval thinkers; and finally, the funded ethical wisdom of the Christian Church since the Protestant Reformation.

Christian ethics assumes that there is a valid and binding relationship between God and men, and usually accords this precedence over the relationships of persons to others persons. In practice, as well as from the biblical perspective, the two are hemispheres of one sphere. Both Testaments assume that there are overarching principles which govern men and women in the entire grid of their interpersonal behavior, including their attitudes and behavior toward God himself.

The Bible as a whole abounds in statements detailing the obligations of the creature to the Creator, and assumes rather than argues the validity of His requirements. The formulation of God's ethical demands upon human beings found a special focus in the giving of the Law at Sinai. The Decalogue (Exod. 20:3-17) was bestowed in close and intimate relation to the miracle of the Exodus, and assumes a relation of covenant between Jehovah and the Israelitish people. And as distinguished from the ceremonial and strictly political legislation of the Pentateuch, the Ten Commandments represent basic moral legislation.

It follows that the requirements of the Decalogue devolved in a special manner upon the Jewish people, but their underlying premise is that God is holy and righteous, and as Creator He has a right to lay His demands upon all persons everywhere. The fact that the mandates of the Ten Words are found, at least in part, in the codes of nations and people outside the Jewish tradition suggests that their content commends itself to the sensitive moral dispositions of persons outside the Judeo-Christian tradition. This suggests that they are of universal application, so that God implicitly demands of the pagan world the same type of ethical behavior that He explicitly requires of His chosen People.

Christian ethics assumes the validity of the Decalogue, this assumption being inferred both from the holiness of God, and as well from the intimate connections between Judaism and the Christian evangel. We are persuaded that the NT writers were supernaturally guided in reaching the conclusion that the Ten Commandments are binding upon the Christian person. The underlying elements of covenant were thus brought to bear upon the Christian life. Chief among these were: that God's demands were right and just; that God is everywhere seeking a response from His creatures; that Jesus Christ came to fulfill the law, not by merely keeping it himself, but by revealing the love which must underlie behavior which is truly ethical, and by providing the dynamic by which the Christian person can live ethically.

Our Lord's statements both *simplify* the requirements of the Decalogue (by reducing all the commandments to two, namely total love to God and sacrificial love for the neighbor) and *internalize* many of its requirements. This latter tendency appears most evidently in the Sermon on the Mount, in which the locus of visible sins was placed within the realm of the intention of the inner life.

See ETHICS, DECALOGUE, MORALITY, RIGHTEOUSNESS.

For Further Reading: Monroe, *An Introduction to Christian Ethics;* "Ethical Relativism," "Interpersonal Relations," "New Testament Ethics," and "Personal Ethics," *Baker's DCE;* Henry, *Christian Personal Ethics;* "Ethics," "Ethics of Jesus," *ZPEB.* HAROLD B. KUHN

CHRISTIAN HOLINESS. See HOLINESS.

CHRISTIAN HUMANISM. Christian humanism attempts to bridge the gap between Christ and human culture. This view can be called "humanism" because of its positive approach to man and his culture, including academics, aesthetics, and human relationships. It is "Christian" in that all is brought under the Lordship of Jesus Christ.

Appreciation of the arts and sciences is appreciation of God's handiwork in creation, whether the artist or scientist is pagan or Christian. To the Christian, all truth is God's truth, regardless of its source. Even unregenerate minds provide insight into truth which reveals God's glory. Divine revelation can be understood only within the context of human culture. Therefore, the Christian must understand human culture in order to make sense of God's truth. Such scriptures as Exod. 31:2-5; Psalms 14, 139; 1 Corinthians 13; Phil. 4:8; Col. 2:3; and Jas. 1:17 are used to emphasize the importance of human culture.

Erasmus of Rotterdam, Thomas More, John Henry Newman, and Thomas Aquinas represent a broad form of Christian humanism which drew upon classical Greek learning in their interpretation of Christianity. Philipp Melanchthon, John Calvin, Abraham Kuyper, C. S. Lewis, and H. Richard Niebuhr represent a humanism closer to the Reformed tradition. Christian humanism differs from secular humanism in that it subordinates the human to Christ.

Many evangelicals are suspicious of human reason and culture. Martin Luther saw Christ and human culture as a paradox. According to this view, the Fall left man so deeply affected that his thinking and his work are contaminated with pride and rebellion. The pagan mind, lacking biblical revelation, has little to offer Christianity. The unregenerate world is dominated by "the prince of the power of the air" who rules the children of disobedience. The world is far gone and ripe for destruction, and the Christian's duty is not to preserve or enrich it, but to call the Church out of the world to establish a redeemed society with a distinctly Christian culture.

Study of God's handiwork through science does not pose so serious a problem for those who hold this view as does the study of the arts, "the handiwork of man." Scriptures cited in support of this view are Lev. 20:22-26; Deut. 6:3-15; 2 Cor. 6:14-18; 1 John 2:15-17.

See HUMANISM, CULTURE, LIFE, SEPARATION, WORLD (WORLDLINESS).

For Further Reading: Blamires, *The Christian Mind;* Kilby, *Christianity and Aesthetics;* LaHaye, *The Battle for the Mind;* Mollenkott, *Adamant and Stone Chips;* Niebuhr, *Christ and Culture;* Ramm, *The Christian College in the Twentieth Century;* Taylor, *A Return to Christian Culture.*

G. R. FRENCH

CHRISTIAN PERFECTION. Christian perfection is full salvation from sin and the completeness of the Christian life. It refers to the perfect act of God in entire sanctification by which the heart is cleansed from all sin and to the life of perfect (or unmixed) love of those who live and walk in the Spirit.

There are mainly two words in the NT that are rendered "perfect" in English. The less common one is *artios* (15 times as *katartizō,* or variant), which refers to complete equipment for effective function (cf. 2 Tim. 3:17). These abilities and skills for service do not immediately and necessarily follow the fullness of grace and love. The more common word for "perfect" is *teleios,* which indicates the completeness and fullness of the moral nature as renewed in the image of God (Matt. 5:48). This perfection is not so much a human achievement or skill as it is a work of God's grace in the human heart. It has to do with motive and attitude. Its expression is love.

Christian perfection is not absolute perfection. Only God is absolute, unrelated, and underived in His perfection. It is not the perfection of angels. Man was not created for that order of beings. It is not the perfection of Adam as originally created. There are permanent consequences of the Fall. It is not humanly achieved freedom from fault or weakness. It is evangelical perfection, disclosed by the gospel that promises full salvation through Jesus Christ by the Holy Spirit.

Christian perfection must be distinguished from philosophic perfectionism. NT writers know nothing of an absolute perfection—a point beyond which there can be no further development (Wynkoop, *A Theology of Love,* 273 ff). But there is a completeness of Christian commitment and love that is unmixed and without exception. Neither moral nor civil law allows voluntary deviation. One murder proves a person a murderer. One robbery classifies one as a thief. One sin can make a sinner. But Christian perfection is a pure heart, dedicated to God.

There is a perfection of maturity; this takes time. There is a perfection of youth; this requires strength. There is a perfection of childhood, dependent on relationship (1 John 2:12-14). From the standpoint of completeness, Christian perfection is a fullness of love—not of years or skills. It is, then, compatible with various stages of development. In the common use of the term, there can be a perfect baby as well as a perfect adult. Each is suited to his purpose or place in life. That is the essence of perfection. One can be what God intended a Christian to be—loving God and man fully.

Christian perfection is purity of heart. It is not necessarily maturity. It is a term of quality, not of quantity. It admits of growth and increase. Indeed, the fruits of holiness grow best in a heart that is pure and free. It is sin, not purity, that prevents progress, growth, fruit, and maturity. There is no perfection, in this life at least, that does not admit of and demand improvement. The pure in heart see God (Matt. 5:8). As they continue to see, they continue to be transformed into the image of the One they see (2 Cor. 3:18). This program of perpetual improvement is the hallmark of true children of God, culminating in "resurrection perfection" (1 John 3:1-3). The act of God by which one is made pure is instantaneous (Acts 15:8-9). The grace of God and the human response by which one becomes mature is gradual and progressive.

Christian perfection is equated with perfect love. To the question "What is Christian perfection?" John Wesley answered, "The loving God with all the heart, mind, soul, and strength" (*Works,* 11:394). This, in essence, is holy living, "as he which hath called you is holy" (1 Pet. 1:15). As Wesley says, "Not that they have already attained all that they shall attain, either are already in this sense perfect. But they daily 'go on from strength to strength; beholding' now, 'as in a glass, the glory of the Lord, they are changed into the same image from glory to glory, by the Spirit of the Lord'" (ibid., 379).

To avoid misunderstanding and false hopes, Wesley explained carefully what Christian perfection is not. He summarizes from his sermon on "Christian Perfection" as follows:

> They are not perfect in knowledge. They are not free from ignorance, no, nor from mistake. We are no more to expect any living man to be infallible, than to be omniscient. They are not free from infirmities, such as weakness or slowness of understanding, irregular quickness or heaviness of imagination . . . impropriety of language, ungracefulness of pronunciation, to which one might add a thousand nameless defects, either in conversation or behavior. From such infirmities as these none are perfectly freed till their spirits return to God; neither can we expect till then to be wholly freed from temptation; for "the servant is not above his master" (ibid., 374).

See HOLINESS, PERFECT LOVE, ENTIRE SANCTIFICATION, HEART PURITY.

For Further Reading: Wesley, *A Plain Account of Christian Perfection;* Wesley, *Sermon* on "Christian Perfection," *Works,* 6:1; Wiley, *CT,* 2:440-516; Turner, *The Vision Which Transforms,* 129-60; Cox, *John Wesley's Concept of Perfection,* 68-137; Wynkoop, *A Theology of Love,* 268-301; Taylor, *Life in the Spirit,* 11-28, 56-90.

WILBER T. DAYTON

CHRISTIAN SOCIALISM. Socialism as generally understood means the national ownership and control of the means of economic production. This includes capital, land, and all other property which should be administered by government for the common good of all. It is basically a political term applied to economics. As such there can be no such thing as Christian socialism in the present world order. This is true simply because all men are born in sin, totally depraved, and government is composed of men. Just as man acts naturally out of selfish interests, so governments act out of selfish interests.

The experience of the Christians of Jerusalem, as recorded in Acts 4:32—5:4, is sometimes cited as an example of Christian socialism; but a close look at the passage will show two important aspects: (1) the actions were motivated by love one for another, and (2) the actions were entirely voluntary, not compulsory. Even after their property was sold, it was entirely up to them to contribute or not contribute the sum to the common fund (5:4). This was cooperation but not socialism.

Such experiences as working together, sharing goods and services, helping the needy from a common fund or source, do not constitute socialism. These activities should be based on the plain teachings of the NT, both in the Sermon on the Mount and elsewhere, which show clearly that Christians should have love and concern for the needs of others, both to fellow believers and unbelievers.

Although it is impossible to have a free society in a completely socialistic framework, and although Christian socialism in the correct sense is an impossibility, there are several ways in which Christian cooperative action for the common good may be compared to and somewhat resemble socialism. For example, there are cases where misfortune afflicts a Christian to the extent he could not survive without the support of other Christians. A second comparative aspect is the fact that the Christian community should and often does make provision to care for its needy. Pension funds, retirement and nursing homes, orphanages, parochial schools, camps, and many other enterprises are examples of provisions which many individuals could not provide alone. This is Christian collective cooperation, but hardly socialism.

See STATE, INSTITUTIONS OF CHRISTIANITY.

For Further Reading: *Baker's DCE,* 637-43.

OTHO JENNINGS

CHRISTIAN WARFARE. See SPIRITUAL WARFARE.

CHRISTIAN YEAR. The Christian year is the framework within which, by means of special seasons and days, the Church as the family of God remembers, reiterates, and reappropriates the major events of its faith and history, somewhat as families celebrate wedding anniversaries or birthdays.

Every day of the year is dedicated to God by the Christian; however, from the beginning God himself regarded some days as special. In Creation it was the seventh day; in the deliverance of His people it was the Day of Atonement. There was Passover Day, the Day of the Firstfruits, etc. The writer of the apocryphal Ecclesiasticus wrote of the days: "In much knowledge the Lord hath divided them and made their ways diverse. Some of them hath he blessed and exalted, and some of them hath he sanctified, and set near himself" (33:7-12). Compare the Hebrew Year in Leviticus 23.

The Christian Year enables us to keep the spiritual and secular more properly related without allowing the latter to swallow up the former.

In the beginning the main celebration of the Church was Easter—a comprehensive celebration of the death, resurrection, and exaltation of Jesus, all on a single day. Thereafter, a spirit of joy pervaded Christian life and worship for the period covering Pentecost, 50 days after the Passover. Leading up to Easter, "discipling" classes were held to prepare new Christians for baptism.

But there were other days observed by non-Christians and Christians alike: e.g., the followers of Mithras held as sacred "the Day of the Sun" and also December 25 as "natalie solis invicti" which became sacred to the Church as Christmas Day, but not until c. 350 because of its pagan association.

The following have come to be widely recognized as the main special days in the Christian calendar: Epiphany, Ash Wednesday, First Sunday in Lent, Palm Sunday, Good Friday, Easter Sunday, Ascension Day, Pentecost (Whitsunday), Trinity Sunday, First Sunday in Advent, Christmas. In addition numerous denominational, national, and quasi-religious days have been added, such as Mother's Day, Father's Day, Thanksgiving Day, Memorial Day, Laymen's Sunday, etc. Andrew W. Blackwood warns of the danger of the Church becoming dominated by a proliferation of special days. Yet the utilization of the basic traditional seasons can provide incalculable aid in religious education. Care must be taken to prevent these occasions from degenerating into mere traditions, which often lose sight of the true spiritual meaning.

See WORSHIP, CHURCH.

For Further Reading: Blackwood, *The Fine Art of Worship; Planning a Year's Pulpit Work.*

T. CRICHTON MITCHELL

CHRISTIANITY. The term "Christianity" has several definitions and referents, not all of them consistent with one another. Here, Christianity will be described from two points of view: the theological and the cultural-sociological, with a passing reference to the historical.

Theologically, Christianity shows its roots in Judaism by its confession that there is but one God, and that He is the Creator of all things, creating out of nothing. So He is the presupposition of all else. Both religions hold that the human being is a special creation of this God, not simply another aspect of material creation but a person given stewardship over it. Both also believe that God has established a personal relationship between himself and the human as the norm. Both religions hold that morality, as it may be defined by this God, is the fundamental concern in this relationship and that it should be fundamental to the relationships between humans, and between humans and material creation as well. Both religions hold that the norm is more often disregarded than regarded by humans and that therefore humanity must repent. Both hold that God forgives, not because of some necessity, but out of His grace. Both religions believe that this God has revealed himself to humanity, especially through certain writers whom He has inspired and whose writings have been collected in the OT. These writings contain history, law, poetry, wisdom, prediction, and moral-spiritual evaluations, all of it intended to establish and maintain an appropriate relationship between God and humanity. Both religions hold that the OT is authoritative for faith and practice, but the "how" and "why" of that authority are debated.

More specifically, Christianity may be defined as that religion whose keystone is the belief that the God described in the OT has revealed himself in Jesus of Nazareth, who is the only true Savior of man, effectually of all who believe in Him for redemption from their sinfulness.

It is universally affirmed by all types of Christians that Jesus of Nazareth is a genuinely historical figure, a unique person who inhabited the time and space that we experience. It is agreed that He died at the hands of the Roman government on instigation of some of the religious leaders among the Jews about the year A.D. 30, just outside the wall of Jerusalem. Obviously He was fully human in His physical characteristics, but the nature of that humanity, and just what it means to say that He was also divine, and the relationship between these two natures, human and divine, are points perpetually debated. However, the mainstream of Christianity has insisted that He is both fully human and fully divine. The debates have circled around the meaning of "fully."

Christians agree that humankind in its fallen state is sinful, though definitions of sin vary widely, sometimes contradicting one another. All believe that the principal concern of Jesus was to remedy that sinfulness, though again definitions of how and why the remedy are many and sometimes contradictory.

Going beyond the sacred book of the Jews, Christians recognize the 27 books called the New Testament as authoritative for faith and practice, though the "how" and "why" are contested. In the NT, Christians believe they have the God-inspired perspective on the person and work of Jesus and also faithful guidance for living as Christians. There they believe they learn that Jesus' suffering and death were in vicarious atonement for their sins; that He was raised from among the dead by God himself to show that our sin is conquered (as is death); that He is coming again to judge living and dead and to take those who believe in Him to be with himself forever; that He has established the Church as His agent to proclaim what He has done and will do, and to make it possible for Him to do it; and that He has sent the Holy Spirit to work in and through the Church as Convincer, Corrector, Comforter, and Sanctifier.

It is agreed among Christians that the ethic of Christianity is generated by love—God's love at work in human beings. The Holy Spirit is especially at work in this generating.

The eschatological element in Christianity is very pervasive and fundamental. There is a paradoxical tension between its celebration of earthly creation and its assurance that the earthly is temporary, that its purpose is probationary and preparatory, and that while the kingdom of God is manifest now among Christians its "center of gravity" is in heaven. The chief concern of Christianity is the redemption of a lost race, and the eternal destiny of persons. Its *eschatos* includes not reincarnation or Nirvana, but a real heaven and a real hell.

Christianity as a historical phenomenon is difficult to define. At present, there are four major divisions that have roots in the time of Jesus and His apostles: Eastern Orthodoxy, Roman Catholicism, Protestantism, and Anglicanism. There are numbers of groups, some authentically Christian, some marginally related, some clearly spurious, that either do not want to be or cannot be placed in one of the four large categories.

Having viewed Christianity from an abstract, theological vantage point and noted in passing its great historical expressions, it remains to note something of its cultural-sociological manifestation. The most common designation of this phenomenon is "Christian civilization."

Obviously, the term is very problematic. Nonetheless, it does point to a highly significant collection of attitudes and behaviors which has shaped much of the contemporary world, either directly or in reaction.

First, one may note the presence, where Christianity has been strong, of a positive regard for this world. It is looked upon as real, not illusory; as of essentially positive value, not as negative or neutral. However, it has not been viewed as an end in itself, but as an arena, a locus, in which eternal issues are determined.

Second, there has usually been an insistence upon the special value of the human being in relation to the value of all else. The human being has been seen as essentially different from nature and its processes, though not separate from them nor immune to them.

Third, value has usually been expressed in moral categories, as opposed to physical, material, intellectual, or pragmatic categories. Even the course of physical nature has been assumed to have some moral significance.

Fourth, morality has been defined in terms of a personal Being external to any particular human being or human society. Value has been thought to have been the subject of revelation, not of human invention, and certainly not of natural necessity.

Fifth, the passage of time, with its coming to be and passing away of things, of people, of ideas, has been assumed to be real and linear. History is not believed to repeat itself, though there may arise future situations analogous to situations already experienced. This, in turn, has given rise to the notion of progress—that is, the notion that history is headed somewhere. Generally, that "somewhere" has been thought to be better than the here-and-now.

Sixth, where Christianity has seen to the permeation of its message, there has been an assumption that individuals and societies need law, if not to bring in a better future, at least to restrain humankind from self-destruction in the present. It has also been understood that while humankind must take moral responsibility for itself and develop its own law, the essentials of that law have been revealed by Deity, and it has been understood that human law is basically an explication of divine revelation. This has generally meant that no one in the society has been assumed to be above the law, but it has also meant that the law was viewed as "made for man, and not man for the [law]." That is to say, it has generally been accepted that law is to be suited to particular human circumstances.

None of these characteristics has ever been practiced by the society at large in an entirely Christian manner. Each of them has been open to abuse, and each of them has been transformed from time to time into a completely secular mode. Nonetheless, they do seem to be uniquely Christian in their inspiration and in their original expressions. Thus, it seems appropriate to refer to them as the characteristics of "Christian civilization."

Christianity, therefore, must be defined in terms of its historical roots, its normative teachings, its institutional expressions, and its sociological and ethical principles as they affect society.

See EASTERN ORTHODOXY, CATHOLICISM (ROMAN), PROTESTANTISM, ANGLO-CATHOLICISM, NON-CHRISTIAN RELIGIONS, RELIGION (RELIGIOUS), BIBLE, CHRIST.

For Further Reading: Perry, *The Gospel in Dispute;* Curtis, *The Christian Faith;* Hamilton, *What's New in Religion?* Smith, *Therefore Stand;* Stewart, *A Man in Christ.*

PAUL M. BASSETT

CHRISTLIKENESS. Christlikeness refers to a state or quality of being like Christ. Such phrases as "mind of Christ" (Phil. 2:1-5; 1 Cor. 2:16), "love of Christ" (2 Cor. 5:14; Eph. 3:19), and "crucified with Christ" (Gal. 2:20; 5:2) direct one's attention toward a biblical concept of Christlikeness.

These phrases call to mind such characteristics as meekness, obedience, and submission. In the minds of some, meekness may revive the words "Jesus meek and mild," popularized a few years ago by some writers, which made Jesus a rather frail caricature of what He truly was. Meekness as seen in the life of Christ was an expression of self-control. He did what duty demanded even though He had within His power the ability to avoid suffering. At His arrest when one of His companions drew a sword in an effort to protect Him, Jesus commanded, "Put your sword back," and then declared that should He call upon His Father, He would "at once" dispense to the Lord Jesus "more than twelve legions of angels" (Matt. 26:52-53, NIV). This type of meekness is restrained, controlled, and demanding. It is meekness with a purpose.

Closely associated with meekness are obedience and submission. Obedience characterized the life of our Lord from the earliest account of an interpersonal relationship. When but a youth, 12 years of age, after He had lingered behind in the Temple and His parents had returned for Him, He "went down to Nazareth with them and was obedient to them" (Luke 2:51, NIV).

It is impressive that some of the mystics who spent a lifetime endeavoring to imitate Christ placed obedience and submission at the top of the list for Christlikeness (Kempis, *The Imitation of Christ,* bk. 3, chap. 13). In the Lord's Garden experience, as His earthly ministry was terminating, He demonstrated again these leading characteristics of His life—meekness, obedience, and submission—as He prayed, "Father, if you are willing, take this cup from me; yet not my will, but yours be done" (Luke 22:42, NIV).

Another phrase, "The mind of Christ," deserves some comment. When Paul professes to "have the mind of Christ" (1 Cor. 2:16) he probably means he understands the thought and intention of Christ, therefore is qualified to instruct the Corinthians. But when he exhorts the Philippian believers to possess the mind of Christ, he uses a different word, *phroneō,* "to be minded," a word more germane to our subject. To be likeminded with Christ is to follow Him in the surrender of our rights, becoming an obedient servant "even unto death" for the sake of a lost race (Phil. 2:5-8).

It is a simple transition to move from a consideration of the "mind of Christ" to the "love of Christ." Paul speaks to the Ephesians of being "rooted and grounded" in love (3:17) and of knowing "the love of Christ, which passeth knowledge" (3:19). Love does not eliminate knowledge, but goes beyond the learning process. Christlikeness requires the use of one's mental faculties, but love relates more to the emotions. How does a Christlike person react under stress? Such stresses as those caused by rejection, when one's motives are of the highest and purest order; suffering without mitigation over extended periods of time; and ridicule that appears to be unrelenting, may be common to some lives. Peter makes it clear that patience in unjust suffering is the highest level of Christlikeness (1 Pet. 2:19-24; 4:12-16).

Although sometimes overlooked, mature Christlikeness is not only a gift of the Spirit in inner sanctification, but a learning process produced through a study of God's Word, through a more perfect understanding of the teachings of Christ, through the discipline of suffering, and through the modeling of brethren in the Lord who have achieved a measure of Christlikeness in their Christian living.

See SPIRITUALITY, CHRISTIAN, DISCIPLESHIP, MIND OF CHRIST.

For Further Reading: Bonhoeffer, *Ethics*, 188-213; *Baker's DT*, 114-15; Henry, *Christian Personal Ethics*, 398-418; Jones, *Christian Maturity*, 147-58; Kempis, *The Imitation of Christ*, bk. 3, chaps. 55—56; Lewis, *Mere Christianity*, 64-129; Murray, *Be Perfect*.

FLOYD J. PERKINS

CHRISTOCENTRISM. This has to do with the constructing of the various aspects of one's theology with special regard to how they relate to Christ, so that Christ is at the center of one's theology. Whereas Augustine's theology is usually regarded as theocentric; and whereas modernistic theologies are usually regarded as anthropocentric, Christocentric theologies are those of such theologians as Martin Luther (1483-1546), Karl Barth (1886-1968), and Dietrich Bonhoeffer (1906-45).

See THEOLOGY, SYSTEMATIC THEOLOGY.

J. KENNETH GRIDER

CHRISTOLOGY. Christology is the doctrine or teaching of the Christian Church concerning the nature of Jesus, the Messiah of Israel and the Son of God. Mark combined these titles into one phrase, "Jesus Christ, the Son of God" (Mark 1:1). Christology attempts to answer the question, "What think ye of Christ? whose son is he?" (Matt. 22:42).

Christians believe that Jesus Christ is both human and divine, that He unites these two distinct natures in one Person, and that this union is permanent and eternal. The implications of this affirmation include: (1) that in Jesus we have a full and final revelation of God; and (2) that in Him redemption from all sin is possible and available.

Christology may be approached either from the standpoint of the Synpotic Gospels (Matthew, Mark, and Luke), or from the standpoint of the Gospel of John and the Epistles. The one is inductive (from "below"), the other deductive (from "above").

The 12 disciples knew Jesus first as Teacher or Rabbi (Mark 1:22), and only later as Messiah (8:29), Lord (12:35-37), and Son of God (15:39; John 20:28). The young Church, however, soon found it necessary to proceed in the opposite direction as well. Thus it was that John began his Gospel: "In the beginning was the Word, and the Word was with God, and the Word was God. . . . And the Word was made flesh, and dwelt among us" (1:1, 14; cf. Rom. 1:1-4; Gal. 4:4; Heb. 1:1).

Survey of basic issues. Central to Christology is the doctrine of the Incarnation, that God became man, and that thus in a unique sense, "God was in Christ, reconciling the world unto himself" (2 Cor. 5:19).

Questions inevitably arise: (1) When and how did the Incarnation take place? (2) In the Incarnation did the Eternal Son (John 3:16-17) unite with an existent being or with generic human nature? (3) What is the relationship of Jesus to the Triune God? (4) Was Jesus truly and fully human?

Development of the doctrinal idea. The classic creedal statement of Christology emerged out of an atmosphere of ferment and conflict. J. L. Neve's summary of the first four ecumenical councils is helpful: Christ is *divine*, vs. Arius (Nicea, A.D. 325); Christ is *human*, vs. Apollinaris (Constantinople, A.D. 381); Christ is *one in Person*, vs. Nestorius (Ephesus, A.D. 431); Christ is *two in nature*, vs. Eutyches (Chalcedon, A.D. 451).

The Nicene and Chalcedonian creeds have stood the test of time. Such creeds are evidence of stability amidst centuries of change. Their function is to exclude extreme or erroneous positions and to describe a Christian consensus.

Numerous attempts have been made, especially in the modern and contemporary periods, to displace these creeds. Such efforts have been largely unsuccessful. It is true that these creeds should be translated into relevant terms. However, the NT teaches that Christ was truly human and truly divine, that He was one Person, the Eternal Son, and that His divine and human natures will remain real and distinct forever.

The biblical position affirms the identity of Jesus with God and with man. This suggests that true understanding of Christology is not possible without reference to the doctrine of the Trinity. In the richness of His being, God is triune in essence, revealed as Father, Son, and Holy Spirit.

In the Incarnation, it was the Son—not the Father nor the Spirit—who assumed human nature in the womb of the Virgin Mary. This union was accomplished by the Holy Spirit. "And the angel said to her, The Holy Spirit will come upon you, and the power of the Most High will overshadow you; therefore the child to be born will be called holy, the Son of God'" (Luke 1:35, RSV).

In that moment of conception a unique Person began to be: Jesus of Nazareth, the Son of God and the Son of Man. "The union of the divine and human natures in Christ is a personal one—that is, the union lies in their abiding possession of a common Ego or inner Self, that of the eternal Logos" (Wiley, *CT,* 2:180).

The Scriptures make it clear that Jesus lived a fully human life, even as He understood that He and the Father were one (John 10:30). "And Jesus increased in wisdom and stature, and in favour with God and man" (Luke 2:52). He was tempted just as we are (Heb. 4:15); He learned discipline and obedience through suffering (5:7-8); He struggled in agony with the Father's will (Luke 22:39-46). Nevertheless, through all these experiences, Jesus knew that He was the Father's unique Son (Mark 1:11; 9:7) and would soon resume His place with the Father (John 17:5). The form of His consciousness was human, its content divine (William Temple).

See CHRIST, HYPOSTATIC UNION.

For Further Reading: Bruce, "The Person of Christ: Incarnation and Virgin Birth," *Basic Christian Doctrines,* 124-30; Green, *The Truth of God Incarnate;* Horton, *Christian Theology: An Ecumenical Approach,* 173-77; Kung, *On Being a Christian,* 119-65; Neve, *A History of Christian Thought,* 1:125-36; *GMS,* 303-65; Wiley, *CT,* 2:143-86.

A. ELWOOD SANNER

CHRONOS. This is one of the most common Greek words for "time" in the NT. The other word is *kairos.* Actually it is the second of these that has special theological significance.

Chronos, from which we get *chronology,* is used for "time in the sense of duration," while *kairos* signifies "time in the sense of a fixed and definite period" (Abbott-Smith, *Manual Greek Lexicon of the New Testament,* 226). In modern Greek, *kairos* means "weather," while *chronos* means "year." The former is often correctly translated "season" or "appointed time" in modern versions. "It is significant of the NT emphasis that *kairos* occurs more frequently (86 times) than *chronos* (53 times). In the Scriptures time is thought of in its redemptive and often eschatological significance" *(WMNT).* Trench writes: "*Chronos* is time contemplated simply as such; the succession of moments. . . . *Kairos* . . . is time as it brings forth its several births" (*Synonyms of the New Testament,* 210).

See TIME, AGE.

For Further Reading: *WMNT,* 3:238-39; Trench, *Synonyms of the New Testament,* 210-12.

RALPH EARLE

CHURCH. That division of theology which deals with the Church is called *ecclesiology.* The term "church" in the NT is from the Greek *ekklēsia,* meaning "called out." The word is translated "church" in 112 of its 115 instances in the NT, the exceptions being Acts 21:32, 38, 41—the account of the assembly of irate tradesmen called by Demetrius in Ephesus (an example of the word's classical usage). With these exceptions (plus Acts 7:38 and Heb. 2:12), *ekklēsia* is reserved exclusively in the NT for the followers of the Lord Jesus Christ, viewed collectively, either as a local body of believers or the aggregate of believers everywhere.

While the English word "church" etymologically signifies a building, called the house of God, no such sense is attached to *ekklēsia* in the NT. In the four instances where *oikos,* "house," refers to the Church (1 Tim. 3:15; Heb. 3:2; 1 Pet. 2:5; 4:17) the usage is metaphorical, meaning the household or family of God.

According to the Gospels Jesus spoke directly of the church on only two occasions. In Matt. 18:15-17 Jesus says that if an offending brother refuses to get the offense straightened out on a one-to-one basis, it should be taken to a small committee; but if he refuses to hear the small committee, the offended person should "tell it to the church; and if he refuses to listen even to the church, let him be to you as a Gentile and a tax-gatherer" (NASB). Jesus is clearly referring to a local body of believers who constitute the people of God, with internal disciplinary power. The disciples would understand Jesus to be saying that the corporate authority of the synagogue, with which they were familiar, was to inhere in the Christian church. The church therefore is more than a worshipping community; it is a governing body. Christians are not to be a law to themselves, but to be subject to one another, and this not simply on a one-to-one basis but as one in relation to an organized, structured community. This power of the church to discipline is affirmed also by Paul, in his specific applications of it (1 Cor. 5:1—6:5; et al.).

The other occasion occurred earlier, while Jesus and His disciples were in Caesarea Philippi: "And I also say to you that you are Peter, and upon this rock I will build my church; and the gates of Hades shall not overpower it" (Matt. 16:18, NASB). The play on words here between *Petros,* a stone, designating Peter, and *petra,* a large rock, bedrock, suggests that Jesus will build His Church on a foundation much more stable than Peter as a person, indeed on nothing less than the great truth of Peter's confession, "Thou art the Christ, the Son of the living God" (v. 16, NASB). And so it is that the Church's very existence is tied to the person and deity of Christ.

But other aspects of a biblical doctrine of the Church are here also. Jesus not only indicates that He is himself the Foundation of the Church, but that His resurrection will be the sufficient guarantee of its perpetuity and indestructibility. This is the probable meaning of "the gates of Hades [death] shall not overpower it." A. T. Robertson says: "Christ's church will prevail and survive because He will burst the gates of Hades and come forth conqueror" (*Word Pictures*, 1:133).

Obviously also Jesus is referring to the Church in its generic or universal sense, not simply as a local group. In this universal or general sense He portrays the Church as a building—"I will build my church." The foundation has already been declared. The materials will be the apostolate, their teaching, and those receiving the teaching as believers (Matt. 28:19-20; Acts 2:41-46; 1 Cor. 12:28; 15:1-9; Eph. 4:11-13; 2 Tim. 2:2; et al.). As a building its creation is a process—"I will build." And as a building it has walls—boundaries, definitions, and limitations.

Both Paul and Peter pursue the metaphor of the Church as a building (1 Cor. 3:9-17; 1 Pet. 2:5-8).

While Jesus uses the term *ekklēsia* only these two times (as found in the Gospels), He implies the Church in His use of *poimnē* (or *poimnion*) a "flock" (Matt. 26:31; Luke 12:32; John 10:16; cf. Acts 20:28-29; 1 Pet. 5:2-3). Schmidt believes that the "flock" of 1 Cor. 9:7 "is rightly equated" with the *ekklēsia;* and he sees a significant parallel between the "my sheep" of John 21:16 f and the "my church" of Matt. 16:18 (Kittel, 3:520). At any rate, this term casts the concept of the church in a more tender and intimate light, as the place not only of discipline but of personal care and security.

If direct references to the church are sparse in the Gospels, church consciousness dominates the Acts and the Epistles. The overwhelming emphasis is on the church as a local body of disciples. This is shown by the frequent plural, "churches," and such expressions as "the church that is in their house" (1 Cor. 16:19) and "the church of God which is at Corinth" (2 Cor. 1:2). The church is never thought of as simply a numerical aggregate of isolated believers, but as of a close-knit community which meets for worship and shares common bonds of spiritual life, suffering, commitment, belief, and service. Each local group is *the* church in that place, coequal with all other churches.

It is primarily in Ephesians and Colossians that the concept of the Church as the mystical Body of Christ is unfolded. The "body-life" metaphor is already in Romans 12 and 1 Corinthians 12, used to illustrate the variety of functions in the work of God, and to inculcate a proper evaluation of gifts. In these earlier Epistles the Spirit's ministry in the Church is explained. But in the Ephesians and Colossians Christ himself is seen as the Head of the Church; His headship illuminates the divine nature of the Church.

Christ is the *Head* in the sense of being the ground of the Church's very existence, the source of the Church's life, and the Ruler of the Church—"the church is subject unto Christ" (Eph. 5:24). The Church is also the object of Christ's atoning death: as the Father gave His Son for the world (John 3:16), so Christ gave himself for the Church, "that He might sanctify her, having cleansed her by the washing of water by the word" (v. 25, NASB).

Three brief words from Scripture shed light on the constitution of the church. Jesus said: "For where two or three have gathered together in My name, there I am in their midst" (Matt. 18:20, NASB). While this is not said in verbal reference to the church, its relevance can hardly be missed. The church could be defined, in simplest terms, as a gathering in the name of Christ with Christ in the midst. This does not imply, of course, that believers are the church only when together, and not the church when dispersed in their daily employments (cf. Acts 8:1). But the primary implication must not be missed—that any religious group not meeting from time to time in the name of Jesus, with Him in their midst, is not the church.

The second illuminating passage is Acts 2:47. After describing the unity, cohesion, and fellowship of the Early Church, Luke says: "And the Lord was adding to their number day by day those who were being saved" (NASB). The Lord himself was gathering into the body those being saved. Salvation is personal, subjective, and highly individual; being in the church is corporate. Two things are to be noted: Only the "saved" can belong to the church, and their being brought into the church—their bonding—is the Lord's action. The relation of this to the sacrament of baptism cannot be discussed in this article.

The third text is 1 Cor. 12:13: "For by one Spirit we were all baptized into one body, whether Jews or Greeks, whether slaves or free, and we were all made to drink of one Spirit" (NASB). The great divergence of opinion about this statement suggests the need for avoiding undue dogmatism. However, it seems to this writer that this is saying exactly what the Acts passage said, with more precision. The Lord who adds to the Church is the Holy Spirit, who alone can baptize (or induct) into the Body as a spiritual organism. That this is a reference to water baptism is not at all certain, since the baptizing could be as spiritual and metaphorical as the drinking "of one Spirit." But even if the sacrament is intended, it is still true that apart from the Spirit's action, people are joiners but not members; members perhaps of an earthly organization but not of the true Church. The essential note here is that the Holy Spirit, in His sovereign presence and regenerating power, constitutes in himself the life of the Church, without which it is but a wax museum.

Traditionally theologians have ascribed to the church certain qualities or notes. The church may be said to be both *visible* and *invisible;* i.e., as an institution it is seen of men, yet only God knows in any congregation who is in the mystical Body of Christ through regeneration. Further, the church is *local* and *universal;* i.e., it is a definite group of believers meeting in one place, yet it also is the totality of all believers everywhere in every generation. (The expression "holy catholic Church," as found in the Apostles' Creed, has no reference to the church of Rome, but to this universality.) Again, the church is characterized by both *unity* and *diversity.* Its unity is in its "one body and one Spirit, . . . one Lord, one faith, one baptism, one God and Father of all" (Eph. 4:4-6, NASB). Every Christian has a mystical oneness with every other Christian (but a oneness which will only be experienced at its deepest level through sanctification—John 17:17-23). Notwithstanding this unity, great local differences have always been present.

The Church is also both *holy* and *sinful.* As the Body of Christ it is holy; as local groups of struggling Christians, many of whom are "yet carnal," it often betrays sinful weaknesses dishonoring to Christ (e.g., the Corinthian church). Christ is continuously in the process of sanctifying the Church (Eph. 5:27, NASB)—but that can only be done by sanctifying one person at a time.

The Church is also both *impregnable* and *vulnerable.* While "the gates of Hades" cannot prevail against the Church, it can be contaminated and compromised from within—by sin, by false doctrine, by worldly alliances. Hence the deadly serious warning: "If any man destroys the temple of God, God will destroy him" (1 Cor. 3:17, NASB), or, as A. T. Robertson puts it, "The church-wrecker God will wreck" (*Word Pictures,* 4:99; cf. Revelation 2—3).

It is the vulnerability of the church which led to the Protestant Reformation and the subsequent rise of various denominations. Insofar as a denomination represents an honest attempt to emulate the NT Church in its purity, its existence should be viewed as a sign of vigor as much as a sign of illness. While an unfortunate necessity, such groupings are not essentially sinful. Sectarianism can be properly charged only when (1) there is significant doctrinal defection from historic orthodoxy, and/or (2) an exclusiveness which brands all others as unsaved, together with a refusal to cooperate or fellowship with others.

There are intricate questions concerning the relation of the church to Israel, to the Kingdom, to a possible Millennium, and to the world (including the state), which cannot be discussed here. There is also the thorny and perennial question of the church and Apostolic Succession. In addition the acute issue for some (especially where there is a state church) is whether the inclusive concept of the church, with every baptized infant being registered as a member, is not a travesty on any authentic NT viewpoint.

The Church then is a divine institution, founded by Christ and composed of true believers. It is the community of redemption, constituting a new and unique race, united by the Spirit in the blood-ties of Calvary. Its internal function is to be a matrix of worship, nurture, fellowship, and service. Its external mission is to represent God in Christ to the whole world, through holiness of life and the proclamation of the gospel to every creature.

The Church must be in the world but not of it. Ethically it should constitute a community apart, yet socially a community involved and concerned.

The distinction between the Church Universal and the churches severally could hardly be articulated better than in the following sentences: "The Church of God is composed of all spiritually regenerate persons, whose names are written in heaven. The churches severally are to be composed of such regenerate persons as by providential permission, and by the leadings of the Holy Spirit, become associated together for holy fellowship and ministries" (*Manual,* Church of the Nazarene).

See SACRAMENTS, CHURCH GOVERNMENT, CHURCH GROWTH, GREAT COMMISSION, CANON LAW, BODY OF CHRIST, DENOMINATION.

For Further Reading: *GMS,* 560-611; Wiley, *CT,* 3:103-42; Kuen, *I Will Build My Church;* Allis, *Prophecy and the Church;* Bright, *The Kingdom of God,* 215-74; Kittel, 3:501-36; Robertson, *Word Pictures in the NT,* 1:130-34.

RICHARD S. TAYLOR

CHURCH COUNCILS. Great doctrinal controversies developed early in the church, giving rise to ecumenical (general) councils called to settle those controversies. The Council of Nicea (A.D. 325) affirmed that the Son had always existed and is of the same essence as the Father. The Council of Constantinople (A.D. 381) reaffirmed the Nicene Creed. At Toledo (A.D. 589) *filioque* ("and the Son") was added to the doctrine of the Holy Spirit, declaring that the Holy Spirit proceeds from the Father "and the Son." The Council of Ephesus (A.D. 431) condemned Nestorianism, which denied the true humanity of Jesus Christ. The Council of Chalcedon (A.D. 451) affirmed the twofold nature of Christ, human and divine. Ecumenical councils held in A.D. 553 and 680 concluded that Jesus possessed both a human and a divine will. In the Second Nicean Council (A.D. 787) iconoclasts (image breakers) were condemned.

In the Reformation Period the Western church subdivided into Roman Catholics and Protestants. The latter, hoping to reform the church, had rejected tradition and refused to place the authority of the church above that of the Scriptures. Justification by faith and the priesthood of every believer were made central doctrines. The "confessions" which various Protestant groups formulated were creedal in nature.

The Roman Catholic church drew up pronouncements against Reformation theology (in the Council of Trent, A.D. 1545-63). Later it declared the Immaculate Conception of Mary (A.D. 1854) and Papal Infallibility (A.D. 1870). More recently (A.D. 1950) the Assumption of Mary (her physical resurrection and ascension to heaven) was affirmed. In the Second Vatican Council (A.D. 1962-65), Roman Catholicism took measures to heal some of the rift between herself and other Christians.

See CREED (CREEDS), HISTORICAL THEOLOGY, CHRISTOLOGY, HYPOSTATIC UNION.

For Further Reading: Briggs, *Theological Symbols;* Brown, *Christian Theology in Outline;* Fuhrmann, *An Introduction to the Great Creeds of the Church;* Harnack, *History of Dogma,* vols. 1—7, trans. Neil Buchanan.

W. RALPH THOMPSON

CHURCH GOVERNMENT. The government of the Church includes both divine and human control. Paul says, "Christ is the head of the church" (Eph. 5:23). The word "church" *(ekklēsia)* refers to a homogeneous assembly or congregation, not to a disorganized mob. The designation "body of Christ" (1 Cor. 12:27; Eph. 4:12) implies unity. The members are dependent on each other, and each is related to the Head of the Church, the Lord Jesus Christ.

Christ did not organize the Church in the sense of practical, minute details. Instead, He brought into existence a new spiritual community which He commissioned to carry on in His absence. The true Church "was not organized, but born (Heb. 12:23), that is, the new birth is the first condition in the founding of this Church. The second is the baptism of the Spirit (1 Cor. 12:13)" (Henry Clarence Thiessen, *Lectures in Systematic Theology,* 414). Thus the Church is an institution of the redeemed, a blessed society, engaging in certain practices and believing certain doctrines.

Organization and government are necessary, however. Believers must organize in local bodies in order to engage in physical achievements, social accomplishments, and spiritual advance. The Church must have system and structure if it is to fulfill the Great Commission efficiently.

In seeking biblical guidelines, leadership should avoid two errors. One is the claim that even matters of detail are legislated, and that therefore no rule, however insignificant, should be adopted unless it is clearly taught in the NT. Others are of the opinion that no system of church government has been prescribed in Scripture, and the Church is given complete freedom. The proper position is found between these two extremes.

Church government in the NT pertains primarily to local congregations, under the general supervision of the apostles. An example of the decision-making process, in the larger body, is seen in the Jerusalem conference (Acts 15; cf. 6:1-6).

Other God-ordained leaders were prophets, evangelists, pastors, and teachers (Eph. 4:11). What ecclesiastical powers or governmental responsibilities these persons had is not clear. In the discussion of gifts (1 Corinthians 12) and functions (Rom. 12:4-8) the implication is strong that organization should be designed to implement these basic body principles.

As the Church expanded, a rather standardized ecclesiastical structure took shape. Elders were ordained in every congregation (Acts

14:23); and subordinate to them, in charge of benevolence, was the diaconate. Our best source of information concerning duties and qualifications of both groups are the letters to Timothy and Titus. It would appear that the elders served as pastors and administrators; some more particularly were charged with teaching and preaching (1 Tim. 5:17). Titus and Timothy, judging by Paul's instructions to them, represented an intermediate authority, between the local body and the apostolate—similar to modern district superintendents.

Organization was sufficient to safeguard doctrinal standards (Acts 2:42; Eph. 2:20; 2 Tim. 2:2); devotional practices (Acts 4:32-37; 1 Cor. 14:26-38); practical duties (Acts 6:3; 1 Cor. 6:1-6); discipline of members (Acts 18:17; Rom. 16:17; 1 Cor. 5:9 ff); and day of meeting (Acts 20:7; 1 Cor. 16:2). In these passages we have indications of planned and orderly procedure.

See CHURCH, WORSHIP.

For Further Reading: *ISBE,* 1:653; Thiessen, *Lectures in Systematic Theology,* 403-21; *ZPEB,* 1:857-62.

O. D. LOVELL

CHURCH GROWTH. As a technical term, church growth is the discipline in missiology which studies the multiplication of the qualitative growth of the Church. It addresses itself to the strategic issue of how to win the most people to Christ in the most direct way in the shortest time possible with the highest quality of result in faithfulness to God, in individuals' lives, and in the corporate life of the Church and its ministry in the world.

Though there are earlier studies of church growth, modern church growth theory dates from 1955 when Donald A. McGavran published *The Bridges of God* and initiated the structural framework which characterizes the church growth movement. His definitive statement is found in the 1980 revision of *Understanding Church Growth,* which has an extensive bibliography. Though general church growth theory grew out of Third World mission research, it has now been contextualized for American church growth (by such as C. Peter Wagner) and applied to such issues as church planting and the communication of the gospel.

Major emphases of church growth theory. (1) Commitment to church growth is faithfulness to God, who is not willing that any should perish (2 Pet. 3:9). Jesus said, "I will build my church" (Matt. 16:18); and we must endeavor to be the ones He can use to do it. (2) Added to the base of biblical and theological input is the conviction that research disclosing how churches do in fact grow can lead to the discovery of growth factors that are unique to a given situation or transferable to other situations. (3) God's spiritual gifts to members of the Body of Christ are what help His Church to grow. The discovery, development, and deployment of these gifts is therefore a high priority for the program of the church. This view is rooted in the doctrine of the universal priesthood of believers. (4) Evangelism, whether personal or public, is to be understood in terms of making disciples (cf. Matt. 28:19) who are incorporated into the church as responsible witnessing members.

(5) Evangelism flows through the internal communication networks of societies and subcultures but crosses linguistic or cultural borders with difficulty. People most easily become Christians among people like themselves. This is the homogeneous unit principle. (6) However, faithfulness to the mission of God to reach all people can permit no selective evangelism or segregation of God's people. It requires that means be discovered and multiplied which will facilitate the cross-cultural communication of the gospel and the planting of churches in every segment of every society. (7) Another of McGavran's most important contributions is the concept of receptivity. At any given time, one group or individual may be responsive to the gospel, while another group or individual may be resistant. The church's responsibility to the resistant is to create readiness for receiving the gospel, while its responsibility to the responsive is to maximize the opportunity for harvesting through adequate evangelism.

The critique of church growth. (1) Some object to the statistical emphasis as dehumanizing or success-oriented. While some promoters may use it this way, this is very far from the church growth emphasis on discipling of individuals and on the use of statistics so that none may be lost through oversight or neglect. (2) The church growth priority for evangelism as contrasted with social concern and social justice is attacked by others who reject the idea of priorities in mission and ministry. It should be noted that his is not a temporal priority but a value priority (Mark 8:34-37), which is seriously neglected by many churches with universalistic tendencies. McGavran staunchly espouses holistic ministry and advocacy of social justice. (3) The most severe criticism is directed toward the homogeneous unit principle, as divisive when the church should be reconciling and segregationist when it should be integrating. This critique ignores Mc-

Gavran's own words as to how the homogeneous principle should be applied and his prior commitment to the mission of God to reach all people and unite them in His love.

See CHURCH, EVANGELISM, GREAT COMMISSION.

For Further Reading: McGavran, *Understanding Church Growth*, rev. ed.; Orjala, *Get Ready to Grow;* Wagner, *Your Church Can Grow.* PAUL R. ORJALA

CHURCH MUSIC. Church music includes hymnology and hymnody. The first is a branch of theology consisting of the study of the place and principles of singing as a biblical part of worship. The second term refers to the actual treasury of songs and hymns which a church possesses and uses. But *church music,* as the broader term, includes also instrumentation, organization, administration, and direction. Highly complex questions arise concerning the direction and training of choirs and ensembles, suitable types of music, the tension between church music as a form of worship and as an evangelistic tool, and the proper subordination of church music to pastoral leadership.

As for importance of singing in the house of God, the Reformers early made this a prominent emphasis. Martin Luther said: "Faith is a living, daring confidence in God's grace, so sure and so certain that a man would stake his life on it a thousand times." Luther not only knew the meaning of faith, he also knew the way to inculcate faith in the hearts and minds of the people. He placed in their hands a Bible in their own language and on their lips hymns with great theological force which the people could sing from their hearts. Luther undertook the composition of the German songs "that the Word of God might be preserved among them, if by nothing else but by singing."

John Wesley also understood the importance of church music. In his introduction to a hymnbook he wrote, "Considering the various hymnbooks which my brother and I have published in these forty years last past . . . it may be doubted whether any religious community in the world has a greater variety of them." He further said, "In these hymns there is no doggerel . . . no words without meaning."

John Wesley not only wrote songs himself but edited all that were published by Charles and himself. These singing preachers taught their people what to sing and then wrote out detailed instructions on how to sing in church. Any revival of the spirit of early Methodism will be a revival of singing. The early holiness people laid a deep foundation of doctrine in their hymns and embodied saving truth in almost every verse.

In an introduction to an early hymnbook J. B. Chapman wrote, "If one is forced to choose between the privilege of preaching what the people are to believe or teaching them the songs they will sing, he might do wisely to choose the latter."

Although the technical definition of a hymn is somewhat flexible, a hymn may be considered to be a song addressed to God. This may be a prayer, an expression of praise, or a poem of adoration.

The gospel song is almost always a testimony. This type of song is addressed to the people and is usually a report of the writer concerning his or her own spiritual experience. Such songs are popular in evangelical churches and compose a large portion of the hymnody.

A gospel chorus is a gospel song without stanzas. The chorus may be a definite testimony or in its poorer form may be nothing more than words with religious overtones set to a rhythmic tune.

Today church music has become a professional field of ministry. Highly organized music programs, including choirs, ensembles, even instrumentalists, are designed both to add enrichment to the public service and appeal to outsiders. Without careful guidance this movement may in the long run prove debilitating, by doctrinal thinness, and by shifting the emphasis from congregational participation in the freedom of the Spirit to the performance of professionals.

See HYMNOLOGY, WORSHIP.

For Further Reading: McCutzhan, *Our Hymnody;* Bailey, *The Gospel in Hymns;* Hildebrandt, ed., *Wesley Hymnbook.* LESLIE PARROTT

CHURCH RULES. See CANON LAW.

CIRCUMCISION. This primarily is the Jewish rite of incising the foreskin (prepuce) of the male genital, usually in the eighth day after birth, signifying the covenant relation between God and His people.

Various theories of the extrabiblical origin of circumcision have been advanced, including the "hygienic," "tribal initiation," celebration of "coming of age," a "sacrificial offering," and "a sacramental operation, or shedding of blood to validate a covenant" (*ISBE,* 1:657). Circumcision is widely practiced among many different people besides the Jews, and is extended to females among certain primitives.

In the OT circumcision was not only a religious significance, but crucially so. When God made His perpetual covenant with Abraham and his posterity, He imposed the rite of circumcision as the inviolable sign of belonging (Gen. 17:9-14; cf. Exod. 4:24 ff; Josh. 5:2-12). Very early it came to be seen as a type and promise of internal spiritual and moral transformation wrought by God (Deut. 10:12-21; 30:6; cf. Isa. 52:1; Ezek. 44:7, 9).

In the NT circumcision as a rite is displaced by the revelation in Christ of its personal, spiritual meaning and reality. Paul disdainfully applies the name "concision" (Greek *katatomē*, "to cut up, mutilate") to the Judaizers who insisted on physical circumcision for salvation (Phil. 3:2-3), and even wished upon them excommunication (Gal. 5:10-12; 2:3-5; cf. Deut. 23:1). In fact Paul equates physical circumcision with uncircumcision in relation to personal salvation, and he regards neither as having any saving value.

Positively considered, circumcision is regarded by Paul as the seal of Abraham's saving faith, since it followed his faith, rather than being the means of that faith, much as baptism relates to regeneration (Rom. 4:9-13). Thus circumcision is not a condition of saving faith (Gal. 5:6).

One of the severest threats to the unity of the Early Church arose over the question of circumcision in relation to salvation and church membership. That question was finally settled at the Jerusalem Council (c. A.D. 48/49). There it was declared a nonrequirement for Gentile salvation or church membership (Acts 15).

Wesley remarks on Paul's argument concerning circumcision in Col. 2:8-15 that "it is evident the apostle thus far speaks, not of justification, but of sanctification only" *(Explanatory Notes upon the NT)*. Thus the spiritual significance of circumcision in the Bible is the purification or sanctification of the heart by the cleansing power of the Holy Spirit (2 Thess. 2:13).

See CLEANSING, HEART PURITY, JUDAISTIC CONTROVERSY.

For Further Reading: *IDB*, 1:629-31; *ZPEB*, 1:866-68.

CHARLES W. CARTER

CITIZENSHIP. Citizenship involves participation in the life of the state by one who belongs, i.e., is a citizen, on the basis of birth or constitutional process (naturalization).

In the NT citizenship is discussed by the use of three words derived from *polis* (city): *politeia* (Eph. 2:12; Acts 22:28), meaning a citizen or a commonwealth; *politeuma* (Phil. 3:20), which is translated as citizenship or homeland; and *sunpolitēs* (Eph. 2:19), meaning fellow citizen. Paul's use of the concept possesses political, soteriological, and eschatological connotations. The first of these is shown where Paul affirms his Roman citizenship (Acts 22:28). In the second, the Gentiles are declared to have been strangers from the commonwealth of Israel, but in Christ to be citizens of the household of faith (Eph. 2:19). The eschatological sense is evidenced in Paul's description of heaven as the Christian's homeland (Phil. 3:20).

The classic passage setting forth the responsibilities of the Christian citizen in political society is Romans 13. To some, Paul's words seem to give a virtual blank check to the exercise of political authority. The Christian is to obey or else respond passively to civil injustice. Is this Paul's concern?

The passage (13:1-7) refers to the normal regulatory functions of the state by which the good are benefited and the evil punished. No intimation is given that the state may become demonic in its activity. To understand Paul's intention we should note his teaching concerning the duty of Christian love, a powerful theme in the context (12:19-21; 13:8-10). What does love require? In general, good citizenship is an expression of Christian concern for the neighbor (13:8-10). Further, love evokes an attitude of support for the political order since God has ordered it. The state is arranged as a part of God's order. The powers "are subordinate to, or orderly disposed under, God." So Wesley interprets v. 1. Recognition of the relationship of the political order to divine order both supports and qualifies Christian obedience. When a conflict arises between God's will and state expectation, the higher command takes precedence. The appeal to Christian conscience (v. 5) enlarges the qualification.

Citizenship in NT teachings about salvation centers around Christ's reconciling work. In describing citizenship in the Christian community, Paul makes use of theological themes relating both to the process of becoming, and enjoying the rights of, a citizen. The doctrines of the Fall, the reconciling death of Jesus Christ, and the creation of the new man and the new community are discussed (Eph. 2:11-22). Everyone has participated in the Fall—in pride and self-trust—and has become a stranger to God. When Adam and Eve sinned, they were driven from home. In Jesus Christ citizenship is restored. Jesus reconciles the alien world to God, bringing believers into the new community. Thus Paul writes: "You are no longer foreigners and aliens, but fellow citizens with God's people and members of God's household" (v. 19, NIV).

The eschatological significance of citizenship is expressed in Paul's joyous declaration: "But our citizenship is in heaven. And we eagerly await a Savior from there, the Lord Jesus Christ, who . . . will transform our lowly bodies so that they will be like his glorious body" (Phil. 3:20-21, NIV).

The closest relationship exists between our citizenship in the Church of Jesus Christ and in the heavenly commonwealth. The grace of our Lord Jesus Christ has made our membership in His Church the foretaste and pledge of the heavenly Kingdom. We are not yet aware of the "things God has prepared for those who love him" (1 Cor. 2:9), but we savor them through hope and love. Christian hope draws the promise of things to come into our human experiences. Thus the new heaven and earth draw ever nearer. Heavenly citizenship gives us the freedom to be totally concerned with our earthly home and to be unafraid of its idolatries as we seek its healing.

See STATE (THE), CHAIN OF COMMAND, AUTHORITY, CONSCIENCE, CIVIL RIGHTS, CIVIL RELIGION, CIVIL DISOBEDIENCE, PILGRIM, HEAVEN, KINGDOM OF GOD.

For Further Reading: *BMS,* 538 ff; Wiley, *CT,* 3:96 ff; Purkiser, ed., *Exploring Our Christian Faith,* 519-37.

LEON O. HYNSON

CITY. The time when men began to live together in groups larger than families for the purposes of mutual defense and trade remains shrouded in the mist of prehistoric times. The two oldest walled cities yet discovered are OT Jericho and Jarmo in Syria (c. 7000 B.C.).

There was no sharp division in biblical times between urban and agricultural societies, the former being based on the latter. The city represented the place of physical security, political power, and economic control. Its fortification provided for defense and its larger population for both military resources and accumulation of wealth.

Biblically, the city originated with Cain who dwelt east of Eden in the land of Nod (Gen. 4:16-17). Having left the presence of God, Cain sought security by building a city, thus the city originated as an expression of man's rebellion against God. Separated from God spiritually, man still seeks to master his own destiny by controlling the forces which affect his existence. The city becomes man's greatest achievement wherein he gains control over those forces, including his physical environment.

It is the city, however, that controls man, not he it. Its spirit is destructive, ever alluring individuals with the promise of security, but enslaving them in an existence alienated from God. Justice, the basis of an equitable society, does not exist, for the rights of the individual become subservient to the survival of a society in rebellion against God.

The primary biblical symbol of the city of man is Babylon, whereas opposed to it is the city of God, Jerusalem. The true "city of God" remains an apocalyptic hope. Those who wait for it have been reconciled to God and live now as its citizens. Thus they participate in both the city of man and of God. Whereas a temporal city, through repentance, may become an expression of the city of God, as did Nineveh (Jonah 3:6 ff), wherever man's existence is grounded in rebellion, injustice and alienation characterize his society.

See HUMANISM, COMMUNITY, BABYLON, JERUSALEM, CITIZENSHIP.

For Further Reading: Augustine, *The City of God;* Ellul, *The Meaning of the City.*

ROBERT D. BRANSON

CIVIL DISOBEDIENCE. Civil disobedience is the refusal to observe the command of a civil authority out of conviction that this violates a higher principle of right or justice. It is based on the underlying conviction that the social order (government) is not an end in itself and that its demands may deviate from a higher standard. For a Christian that higher standard would be the will of God.

The earliest Christians expressed a form of civil disobedience when they chose "to obey God rather than men" (Acts 5:29). But the idea is rooted deeply in the entire biblical story. God was the King over Israel, and when the earthly rulers did not follow the divine will, God's spokesmen, the prophets, did not hesitate to rebuke them (1 Sam. 15:16 ff; 2 Sam. 12:1 ff) and counsel the people to obey God (1 Kings 18). Daniel was a true son of Israel and model for the Christian when he, with his friends, refused to obey Nebuchadnezzar's demands.

For the Christian the right and obligation to disobey is not based on selfish interest or human preference but on what is considered to be the claims of God. In Romans 13 Paul exhorts the believer to recognize the state as an authority over him (also 1 Pet. 2:13, 17). Therefore disobedience is permitted only when the authorities do not represent the good desired by God (Rom. 13:3-4).

There is difference of opinion among Christians regarding the areas of legitimate disobedience. These areas will correspond to those aspects of belief which a given Christian or church considers to be essential for doing the will of God. From the earliest times believers have openly defied attempts to stop gatherings for worship and acts of witness. Some groups have also refused obedience in such areas as the swearing of oaths, military service, and payment of taxes for government activities considered unjust or morally wrong.

The dual call of Scripture to honor human authorities and yet to disobey wrong demands means the Christian must attempt to display respect and not rebelliousness in the situation of protest and noncompliance.

See CITIZENSHIP, STATE (THE), CIVIL RELIGION, CIVIL RIGHTS.

For Further Reading: Wenger, *Introduction to Theology,* 316-25; Cullmann, *The State in the New Testament;* Wiley, *CT,* 3:98-100; Kaufman, *What Belongs to Caesar?*

GEORGE R. BRUNK III

CIVIL RELIGION. Civil religion is a rather recent term to describe an old fact of human existence. As the words suggest, it is the merging of religious beliefs and practices with the civil order that molds a society. The values that characterize society are the values of the religious system held by the same people. According to Will Herberg, civil religion is an amalgam (mixture) of values and ideals from various sources, welded together with patriotism in the national consciousness to form a society's religious foundation (see Smart, 15).

The term was originated by Robert Bellah to designate the religious convictions agreeable to the mass of Americans. According to Bellah such a common religion is essential to a stable, strong society. The product has been characterized as "a nation with the soul of a church."

From the Christian viewpoint the concept of civil religion arouses conflicting feelings. From the time of Christianity's emergence as the major religion of Western civilization, the values of society and church have intermingled and blended. For some this was a triumph, but for others this mixture has been a disastrous fall. The rise of conviction in the separation of church and state since the Reformation reflects a critical stance toward making the Christian faith into a civil religion. The OT skepticism of kingship (1 Sam. 8:4-9), the critical freedom of the prophets, and Jesus' creation of a new people of faith, all point in this direction.

In practice, however, American Protestantism has defended and promoted a civil religious order that reflects Christian values. By dividing the sphere of influence of the church and state, the conflict of faith and patriotism disappears. All too easily God and country are peaceful partners. The Christian defends the church and his society as if of equal importance.

The Bible reflects the tension in Romans 13 where the state is God's agent for *good* but the Christian is called to *love* (13:8) and *peace* (12:18). The Christian will support and promote righteous standards for general society, but the NT concept of the Kingdom and the Church forbids us to put a "Christianized" society on the level of the redeemed people of God, the Church.

See CITIZENSHIP, STATE (THE), CHURCH, KINGDOM OF GOD, CIVIL DISOBEDIENCE.

For Further Reading: Smart, *The Cultural Subversion of the Biblical Faith;* Niebuhr, *The Kingdom of God in America;* Herberg, *Protestant-Catholic-Jew;* Bellah and McLoughlin, eds., *Religion in America;* Cutler, ed., *The Religious Situation;* Verduin, *The Anatomy of a Hybrid.*

GEORGE R. BRUNK III

CIVIL RIGHTS. As generally understood, civil rights includes the right of every person to participate in government, but does not mean that every person is qualified to do so. It also means the right to protection from attack on personal liberty—such as freedom to live, travel, or possess property—either by government agents or other persons. In courts of law it means the guarantee to defendants of a fair trial, and protection against discrimination on account of race, religion, or national origin.

The term is often used interchangeably with the term *civil liberties.* Sometimes the latter expression is used to refer to the personal rights of individuals, while the main term has in recent years come to refer more and more to the rights of minority groups. Such a distinction, however, is hardly justifiable from the standpoint of Christian ethics.

The whole issue is one of human relationships, whether it is a matter of person-to-person, of group-to-group, or of group-to-person. Reinhold Niebuhr claims that it may be possible, though it is never easy, to guarantee just relationships between individuals within a group purely by moral or rational pressures. But in intergroup relations this is practically impossible. In such cases relations between groups must therefore be largely political rather than ethical.

As viewed by our American Founding Fathers, these rights are natural, that is, that all men are endowed by their Creator with certain inalienable rights which government has no right to confer or prevent. The first 10 amendments to the Constitution, commonly referred to as the Bill of Rights, spells out the position of the government in keeping with the concepts of the

Founding Fathers. The violation of any of these rights therefore becomes a violation of the Constitution and entitles the injured party or parties to the resources of the federal courts.

Prior to the Fall man was in complete harmony with the natural world in which God had placed him. Because of sin man found the world of nature under a curse and found himself depraved and out of complete harmony both with his fellowmen and with his environment. As a result those "inalienable rights" were no longer guaranteed naturally. Man found himself in conflict with his Creator, his fellowmen, and his earthly environment. The purpose of the Atonement was to redeem man from sin so that he might live in harmony with God, his fellowmen, and his temporal home in this life and finally be restored to complete harmony in the perfected kingdom of God hereafter.

See CITIZENSHIP, CIVIL DISOBEDIENCE, COMMUNITY, SIN, REDEMPTION.

For Further Reading: *Baker's DCE*, 105 ff; "Rights of Man," *Encyclopedia of Theology*, Karl Rahner, ed., 1473-76.

OTHO JENNINGS

CLEAN, UNCLEAN. In Israel "clean" and "unclean" meant holy and unholy (Lev. 20:25). That was clean (holy) which God had chosen for himself, whether persons, places, animals, or objects. The unclean (unholy) was that which violated this relationship or was excluded from it. Thus ritual and moral cleanness were linked, and rites of purification involved sacrifices for sin.

Cleansing agents included *fire* (Num. 31:22-23; Mal. 3:3); *water* (Num. 8:7; Ezek. 16:4); *blood* (Lev. 12:6-7; 14:25; 16:19); and *ashes* (Num. 19:17). Signs and symbols, these possessed no inherent or magical cleansing power. Only God could cleanse, and restore the relationship broken by sin (Job 14:4; Ps. 51:10). Atonement effected cleansing and preserved Israel before God (Lev. 16:30). God rejected ritual purity divorced from moral purity (Ps. 24:3-5; 51:6, 16-19; Isa. 1:10-20).

Moral and ethical purity are emphatic in the NT. Jesus condemned mere outward cleanness (Matt. 23:25-26); located defilement's source in man's heart (Mark 7:18-23); and declared the pure in heart blessed (Matt. 5:8). He demonstrated power to cleanse by healing lepers (8:2-3) and pardoning sinners (Mark 2:5-12; Luke 7:36-50)—implicit claims to Deity.

This authority anticipated His death as an atonement. Prophets spoke of a man who would be an atoning sacrifice, and of a cleansing from inward defilement (Isaiah 53; Ezek. 36:25-27). Jesus is that Sacrifice, whose blood actualizes what animal offerings only symbolized (Heb. 9:11-15). Christ's death becomes the ground of *regeneration* and *sanctification*, by which believers are cleansed from sin and enabled to serve God (Titus 3:5; 1 John 1:7; Heb. 13:12, 20-21).

Though God atones and cleanses, man is summoned to repent, trust, and obey—to cleanse himself by responding to God's cleansing provision in Christ (Isa. 1:16; Jas. 4:8; 2 Cor. 7:1).

Because cleansing is the ultimate expression of grace, its refusal is the ultimate expression of sin, inviting terrible judgment (Ezek. 24:13; Heb. 10:26-31).

See HEART, HEART PURITY, ORIGINAL SIN, EXPIATION, HOLINESS, RIGHTEOUSNESS, PURIFICATION (CEREMONIAL), CLEANSING, PURITY AND MATURITY.

For Further Reading: Kittel, 3:413-31; *A Companion to the Bible*, 59-63; *ZPEB*, 1:884-87.

W. E. MCCUMBER

CLEANSING. Three kinds of cleansing are to be found in the Scriptures: physical, ceremonial, and moral.

Jesus referred to the *first* when He instructed, "Wash thy face" (Matt. 6:17) as a preparation for fasting. Peter insisted that baptism had a deeper significance than simply washing dirt off (1 Pet. 3:21). Yet physical cleanliness was very important in the life of the Jewish people. It was easy for them to suppose that they were clean because their bodies were; but Jesus rebuked this illusion by insisting that cleansing the hands did nothing for the heart (Matt. 15:1-20). In this discourse Jesus was teaching that the deeper defilement—man's real problem—was not dirt on the body but sin in the heart.

Ceremonial uncleanness and ceremonial cleanness were very prominent in the Mosaic system. A typical example was the contamination accruing to the person eating an animal which had died of itself. "He shall both wash his clothes, and bathe himself in water" (Lev. 17:15) in order to be free from his uncleanness by nightfall; if he did not bathe—or ceremonially cleanse himself—his contamination remained.

That which defines either defilement or cleansing as *ceremonial* is (1) both the defilement and the cleansing are symbolic rather than moral, and (2) the cleansing depends on the exact performance of a prescribed ritual, or ceremony. God saw the pedagogical value of such ceremonies as a means of inculcating (1) the concepts of clean and unclean; (2) a sense of responsibility before God in observing the required rituals; and, by transfer, only (3) to come to see the seriousness of the reality symbolized—the real uncleanness of sin and the need of a real cleansing from it.

The tendency of the Hebrews, however (as has been the tendency of all ceremonialists of whatever religion), was to be content with the ceremony or to suppose that the punctilious observance of the niceties of the ceremony was in itself sufficiently virtuous to constitute an acceptable substitute for inner change. This leads to the blight and barrenness of a ceremonial religion.

The peril of ceremonialism was seen at the very threshold of the Christian era by John the Baptist, who refused to baptize as a mere form. There was no automatic guarantee of true forgiveness simply by receiving or being in the water. Therefore he insisted on repentance, even *evidences* of repentance (Luke 3:8-14), without which the ceremony would be valueless. The history of Christianity would be brighter if the Church had maintained John's insight. Ceremonialism has symbolic and pedagogical value, but no saving power.

Moral cleansing is the reality which ceremonial cleansing only pictures. It is a real purging of the heart from sin, a purging made possible by the blood of Christ and actual by faith.

The crucial theological issue is whether the cleansing provided in the Christian scheme of redemption is expiatory only, or also a purging, or removal, of the evil propensity itself. There is a feeling of cleanness and of newness in the assurance of forgiveness. Pollution in the sense of defilement, guilt, and condemnation is gone. Is this, however, merely a feeling of cleansing resulting from an objective, or forensic, transaction, or is it also a subjective cleansing, or purification, at the level of character—a substantive change in the inner being?

Undoubtedly the provision of the Cross is for a thorough heart cleansing. That cleansing of *acquired* depravity is a concomitant of the first work of grace is implied by Paul's description of the Corinthians: "And such were some of you: but ye are washed, but ye are sanctified, but ye are justified in the name of the Lord Jesus, and by the Spirit of our God" (1 Cor. 6:11). That kind of cleansing which is ascribed to the immediate agency of the Holy Spirit is a subjective, or inner, cleansing.

But cleansing from inbred sinfulness is a boon of grace also. This can be seen, for one thing, in the figure of fire, in contrast to water. Forgiveness is the cleansing for which water is a fitting type (Matt. 3:11; John 3:5; Acts 22:16; Eph. 5:26, NASB; Titus 3:5). Fire, however, is the official insignia of Pentecost—"He Himself will baptize you with the Holy Spirit and fire" (Matt. 3:11, NASB). On the Day of Pentecost fire, not water, was one of the inaugural signs. Fire is a deeper cleansing agent than water, reaching the inner recesses of the heart. And according to Peter, this is exactly what Pentecost did (Acts 15:9), thus fulfilling the promise of Malachi: "And He will sit as a smelter and purifier of silver, and He will purify the sons of Levi and refine them like gold and silver, so that they may present to the Lord offerings in righteousness" (Mal. 3:3, NASB).

The fullness of that cleansing possible can be seen also in a study of *katharizō*, a verb found 30 times in the NT, and variously translated "make clean," "cleanse," "purify," and "purge." Only once is its use clearly ceremonial (Heb. 9:23). Once it is used in a ceremonial metaphor but with a moral intent—"Cleanse your hands, ye sinners" (Jas. 4:8). Twelve instances refer to the healing of lepers, obviously a substantive cleansing of a physical disease. The rest relate to the cleansing of man from sin.

In some cases the cleansing is primarily expiatory, i.e., the cleansing of guilt (Acts 10:15; Eph. 5:26, NASB; Heb. 9:14, 22; possibly 1 John 1:7). But in other cases the cleansing of the sinful nature is clearly in view (1 John 1:9; Acts 15:9; Titus 2:14).

Twice we are told to cleanse ourselves. For the sinner to "cleanse his hands," he would have to put away his evil deeds and bring his guilty hands to the Cross. This (again) is the expiatory level. But believers are to cleanse themselves of "all defilement of flesh and spirit, perfecting holiness in the fear of God" (2 Cor. 7:1, NASB). We cleanse ourselves by confession, repudiation, and appropriation. That which we confess is the inner defilement which we find, that which we repudiate is every alliance which fosters the defilement, and that which we appropriate is the covering of the Blood and the sanctifying office of the Holy Spirit (2 Thess. 2:13).

Since the depraved and fallen heart of man, Jesus said, is the source of all inward and outward sin (Mark 7:21-22), a purified heart would have to be much more than a forgiven heart. It could be nothing less than a heart healed of its corruption, so that it ceased to be a fountain of "evil thoughts, adulteries, fornications, murders, thefts," but instead was the throne of the Spirit and the fountain of piety and holiness.

Speaking psychologically, this cleansing is the correction of the excessive egoism of the self. It is the purging of the sin which can be spelled with a capital I—*sIn.* The self is subdued and chastened, and subordinate to divine rule. The abnormal warfare is over between self-will and God's will.

The psychological questions sometimes raised concern the extensiveness of the cleansing of memory, of the subconscious, and of personality flaws and mental complexes. These questions relate to the distinction between carnality and humanity. The purifying of the heart is from sin, and God designs that it should be entire. But "heart" is the moral seat of life—the hidden springs. The heart is not the total person, only the quality center. Much in the area of the subconscious and of mental aberrations cannot be said to be the condition of the heart, in God's sight; hence is not the objective of the cleansing in the sanctifying work of the Spirit.

See CARNAL MIND, CARNALITY AND HUMANITY, ACQUIRED DEPRAVITY, HEART PURITY, CLEAN (UNCLEAN), PURITY AND MATURITY, ERADICATION.

For Further Reading: Wiley, *CT,* 3:442-48, 454-63, 487-96; Taylor, *Holiness the Finished Foundation,* 82-102.

RICHARD S. TAYLOR

CLERGY. The clergy consists of those persons who have been set apart—usually by ordination —for special religious services. The term *clergy* is derived from the Greek *kleras* which often means "lot" or "chosen by lot."

The concept of special persons in the Church to carry on distinctive functions is generally traced to Jesus who chose and set apart 12 apostles whom He trained for their work. Furthermore, the Apostolic Church set apart 7 men to carry on appointed tasks (Acts 6:3). Later persons were set apart as bishops and deacons (1 Tim. 3:1-13). All of the NT ministers were recognized for the work they performed; they were not primarily office bearers.

Persons today are called to the ministry by an inner and God-given sense that they *ought* to be full-time workers for God. Their subjective sense of oughtness is normally confirmed by the congregations to which they belong and/or by delegates of a conference or a synodical meeting.

The term *clergy* has traditionally embraced bishops, priests, presbyters or elders, and deacons, though some churches in the Reformed tradition have lay deacons. There have been times when the minor orders of ministry and even members of religious orders were considered clergy.

Many clergymen today are pastors of local churches or parishes, and they must carry on a threefold work that consists of (1) preaching, teaching, and public worship; (2) pastoral care through a personal ministry to members; and (3) administration of the affairs of the congregation. These functions differ greatly, and they demand broad training and experience.

See MINISTER (MINISTRY), CHURCH GOVERNMENT, ELDER, DISCIPLING.

For Further Reading: Lightfoot, *The Christian Ministry;* Gore, *Ministry of the Christian Church;* Lindsay, *The Church and the Ministry in the Early Centuries;* Purkiser, *The NT Image of the Ministry.*

W. CURRY MAVIS

COLLECTION. See TITHE.

COMFORT. The Greek word *paraklēsis* is rendered "consolation" and "encouragement." 2 Cor. 1:4 uses the word *parakaleō* which means "to call to one's side so as to derive strength and support." In John 14:16 and 16:7, *paraklētos* is used, meaning one who stands with an individual, such as an attorney, and pleads his case; one who gives strength through affirmation, who consoles in the midst of pressure and challenge, and who supports with presence and advice.

The English word is from the Latin *confortis,* which means "brave together." Comfort, then, is that emotional support we derive from the knowledge that another is sharing our load with us. This sense of reassurance is intensified when the other is God.

Comfort in its NT setting, therefore, for the believer, is that consolation, sense of rest, encouragement, strength, and hope which one receives from knowing that God is in charge. It is the strength which comes from knowing that behind events is a God who can take life's worst and turn it into something meaningful (Rom. 8:28); that God can somehow nurture life through its hard, broken moments, encouraging the heart in the process, giving strength, and infusing grace. This is consolation indeed in life's most desperate hours.

See COMFORTER, COMPASSION, PARACLETE.

For Further Reading: *CC,* 6:314; Robertson, *Word Pictures,* 4:208 ff; Lloyd-Jones, *Studies in the Sermon on the Mount,* vol. 1.

C. NEIL STRAIT

COMFORTER, THE. Jesus is the only Person in Scripture who speaks of the Holy Spirit as a "Comforter." The Greek word *paraklētos,* translated "Comforter" in the KJV, occurs five times in the NT: four times referring to the Holy Spirit (John 14:16, 28; 15:26; 16:7), and once in reference to Christ (1 John 2:1). *Paraklētos* is a compound noun derived from *para,* "by the side of," and *kaleō,* "to call," and has the root meaning of "someone called to one's side." There are several suggestions for the best English equivalent for this Greek word: "Comforter" (KJV), "Counselor" (RSV, NIV), "Advocate" (NEB), and "Helper" (NASB).

Jesus' statements concerning the "Comforter" explain (1) who He is, (2) how He is to come, and (3) what His work will be.

First, Jesus identifies the Comforter as the Holy Spirit (John 14:26) and explains that He is the Spirit of Truth (v. 17; 15:26; 16:13). The Comforter is not a power; He is a person with power. He is to be "another" (of the same type as Jesus himself) "Comforter" (14:16).

His coming into the lives of the believers is equivalent to Christ's personal presence; He is the successor of Jesus' person. The believer is not the initiator or the cause of the Holy Spirit's coming; He is sent to the aid of the believer by the Father as the result of Jesus' prayers (John 14:16, 26; 15:25; 16:7). He could not come as "Comforter" until Christ left the earth (16:7). The world (unsaved people) cannot receive the Comforter because it (they) "seeth him not, neither knoweth him" (14:17). His place of abode is with the believer (v. 17), and that forever (v. 16).

The primary work of the Comforter is to exalt Christ (16:14). He does not speak from himself (v. 13), but communicates only the truth He has received about Christ (15:26; 16:14). This communication involves both bringing back to mind what Jesus had personally said to the disciples (14:26) and revealing truth about things to come (16:13). He thus functions as both a Reminder and as a Teacher. Jesus promises His disciples that the Comforter will guide them into all truth (v. 13). This latter promise is passed on to all believers (1 John 2:20, 27).

The Comforter also has a work in reference to the unsaved world. As such He is a convictor. He convinces and convicts "the world of sin, and of righteousness, and of judgment" (John 16:8). How He does this is not clear. Many commentators believe that He does this by His work and influence in and through the lives of the believers; however, He undoubtedly impresses directly the mind and conscience of sinners.

See HOLY SPIRIT, PARACLETE.

For Further Reading: Braumann, "Advocate, Paraclete, Helper," *NIDNTT,* 1:88-91; Morris, *The Gospel According to John,* 662-66; Carter, *The Person and Ministry of the Holy Spirit,* 126-43; Ladd, *A Theology of the New Testament,* 286-97.

ALLAN P. BROWN

COMMAND, COMMANDMENT. The concept of commandment appears almost immediately in the relationship between God and man. As a free moral agent, man had the privilege and the responsibility of choice. In order to guide man in the proper use of this power, God said to him, "Thou shalt not" (Gen. 2:17). This is known as "The law of positive command." This law is the basis of the relations between God and man from that time onward. God commanded simple obedience. In the final analysis, this is what God has expected from His creation in every generation.

The right to command is based on God's revelation of himself as the infinite, holy Creator of the universe and all that is in it. Man as the lower, created being is thereby subject to the authority imposed upon him. Law is nonrestrictive in that its authority extends over all within its prescribed sphere, not just the obedient (Rom. 13:3).

When Moses wrote the Ten Commandments (Exodus 20), the basic relationship between God and man was not changed. Again, God was asking for obedience. The primary differences were two: First, the law was now written so that it could be read again and again. The Israelites were without excuse. Second, through the commandments God pointed out areas of life to be guarded in conformity to the known will of God—both religious and social. In brief, all of life is under the watchful care of an almighty, ever-present God. The ceremonial law which follows in the Book of Leviticus is the practical outworking of the inner relationship between God and man.

It was this inner relationship that was so important in the ministry of the prophets in their day (e.g., see Mic. 6:7-8) and for Christ in His day (Matt. 23:1-39). The relationship of Christ to the law or commandments is summarized in His own words, "I am not come to destroy, but to fulfil" (5:17).

The basic demand for simple obedience has not been changed. The ministry of the Word of God has been directly toward the goal of man's acceptance of and submission to the divine directive. Ultimately all of mankind will be held accountable for obedience to the revealed will of God (Rom. 1:14-25).

In recent years, beginning with German higher criticism about 1850, there has been an effort on the part of liberal theology and liberal scholasticism to discount the idea of a written revelation from God to man. It is held that OT concepts of law and authority are vestiges of an archaic past and should not be considered authoritative for today. According to this view, God reveals himself in a new way to each generation and to each individual. Obedience, then, is not to a written standard but to an intrinsic personal "revelation."

The NT presents no conflict between the commandments and the gospel of love. The gospel, instead of repudiating the law, anticipates obedience to all the commands of God as an expression of love toward God and man.

See OBEDIENCE, LAW AND GRACE.

For Further Reading: *Baker's DCE.*

LEROY E. LINDSEY

COMMISSION, GREAT. See GREAT COMMISSION.

COMMON, COMMUNITY. These words have an apparent relationship in English usage. The terms *mutual, joint, together,* or *group* suggest a concept similar to common and community. In the biblical languages, however, the word "common" may have two quite different connotations. It may mean that which is mutually shared or that which is profane.

"Common" in the OT may refer to a group sharing in a single (Heb. *ehad,* one) purse, as in Prov. 1:14. Or it may refer to that which is "common" (Heb. *chol*) bread, presumably to be used by the masses as opposed to holy bread (1 Sam. 21:4, RSV), which is for divine use exclusively. The Hebrew term *(chol)* may be translated "profane" in the OT, especially in Ezekiel (cf., e.g., RSV of 7:21; 20:21-22, 24), or it may mean that which is polluted or sexually defiled (Gen. 49:4, RSV).

"Common" in the NT is also used in two significant ways. It is used primarily to indicate that which is public, shared by the group or universal (Gr. *koinos*). Examples of this usage are the common faith (Jude 3) and common possessions (Acts 2:44; 4:32). This meaning is contrasted with that which is peculiar, unique, individual, not shared with many (also Gr. *koinos*).

Two meanings provide the tension from which develops the understanding that common is merely ordinary or lacks honor and esteem. Peter abhorred the thought of eating meat that was common or unclean (Acts 10:14-15). The Pharisees considered themselves religiously superior to the common people (Heb. *am ha eretz,* people of the land). Holiness and separateness from the larger community of humanity were in some ways equated. Identification with society in general jeopardized one's holiness. There is a concern that by being common one is profaned.

The term *community* may refer to a geographical neighborhood or any homogeneous group of people united by a common bond. The concept is expressed in the NT by "church" *(ekklēsia),* "city" *(polis),* and "synagogue" *(synagōgē). Koinonia,* "fellowship," conveys a sense of community. Two meanings merge—that which is shared and that which is peculiar. A community has that in it which is common to all in the community at the same time it has that which distinguishes it from other communities. The church community is that "communion of the saints" or separated people who celebrate their union in the sacrament of the Lord's Supper as Communion.

See KOINONIA, CHURCH, FELLOWSHIP, LOVE, SECULARISM.

For Further Reading: Gager, *Kingdom and Community;* "KOINOS," Kittel, 3:789-809; "Common," *IDB,* 1:663; *NIDNTT,* 1:635-39; "Koinonia," *NIDNTT,* 1:639-44; *GMS,* 594; "Common, Commonly," Vine, *ED,* 1:212.

KENNETH E. HENDRICK

COMMON GRACE. Common grace is a Calvinistic term referring to the grace God gives universally for the purpose of preserving the human race from total putrefaction and self-destruction. It accounts for whatever benevolence and nobility there is in the unregenerate world. It is not designed to lead to salvation, thus is sharply distinguished from the Calvinistic idea of efficacious grace, which has personal salvation as its certain objective. The Wesleyan doctrine of prevenient grace differs in that (1) universal or common grace has as its objective not only the preservation of civilization but personal salvation, and (2) it is efficacious only in those who respond to it and cooperate with it.

See PREVENIENT GRACE.

For Further Reading: Wiley, *CE,* 2:344-57.

ELDON R. FUHRMAN

COMMUNICATE, COMMUNICATION. A sharing either by giving (Gal. 2:2) or receiving (Phil. 4:14) or by interchange (alluded to in v. 15). The medium is usually conversation, and a bridge of mutual understanding and empathy is essential to make it effective. Various Greek words are translated "communicate" in the KJV, principally *dialaleō* from which comes the English *dialogue* (Luke 6:11; 22:4—"discussed," NIV), and *homileō,* which simply means "to speak with" (Acts 24:26). The verbal aspect also comes through in such phrases as "filthy communication" (Col. 3:8—"filthy language," NIV; "foul talk," RSV).

The more inclusive word related to communication, however, is *koinonia,* which is used of the fellowship and sharing characteristic of the Early Church. It is variously rendered "communion," "fellowship," "contribution," "distribution," etc. (e.g., Rom. 12:13). This puts the emphasis on nonverbal communication and includes both the sharing of goods and of spiritual blessings. It is also part of almsgiving which implies that communication is not always a two-way street. Illustrative of the latter is the offering to the Jerusalem church from the Gentile Christians (Rom. 15:26; 2 Cor. 8:4; 9:13).

In Paul's instruction to Timothy to urge the wealthy to be "willing to communicate" (1 Tim. 6:18) he uses a cognate of *koinonia* which is more accurately translated "to be generous," or as the NIV has it, "willing to share." The same root word occurs in Rom. 12:13, "Distributing to the necessity of saints" (KJV), which in newer translations conveys the idea of sharing with those in need.

It is in this spirit of sharing that bridges of communication with others are built and thus avenues of witnessing opened up. "Ye shall be witnesses unto me" (Acts 1:8)—communicators of the faith.

See SPEECH, KOINONIA, STEWARDSHIP, GOOD WORKS.

For Further Reading: *HDB,* 1:460; *Baker's Dictionary of Practical Theology,* 330-63; *ISBE,* 2:688 ff.

J. FRED PARKER

COMMUNION, HOLY. See HOLY COMMUNION.

COMMUNISM. See MARXISM.

COMPARATIVE RELIGION. This is a designation for the comparative analysis of religious experience used especially in the late 19th and much of the present century. It was developed in a liberal philosophical context which muted the distinctive differences of the religions of man. The "History of Religion" school, which included such thinkers as Ernst Troeltsch and Hermann Gunkel, stressed the common elements in the religions rather than their uniqueness. It sought to explain Christianity in purely historical terms or in terms of historical contexts. By this methodology, Christianity was judged to be dependent upon various religious and cultural influences drawn from Judaism, Zoroastrianism, the "mystery religions," and other Near Eastern philosophies. The Johannine emphasis on light and darkness, for example, was believed to be adapted from Zoroastrian theology. The method could be described as religious syncretism.

Max Muller's extensive labors in comparative religion concentrated upon the scriptures of world faiths and resulted in publication of his edited works, *Sacred Books of the East,* a 51-volume series. Parallel studies of religion in primitive cultures were carried on by anthropologists using the comparative approach.

The expansion of the discipline gradually led to a change in nomenclature, with emphasis being placed more upon the "history of religions" and less upon "comparative religion." Joachim Wach used the latter term in his 1958 title, but the former gradually gained ascendancy. Primary figures in this progression were Mircea Eliade and Wilfred Cantwell Smith. The older syncretism continued to influence studies of religion, but new approaches appeared. Comparative religion was usually characterized by judgments of value, just as theological statements are evaluative. The historian of religion believed his approach to be more objective, but this was not always true. Indeed, Arnold Toynbee's *Historian's Approach to Religion* was laden with subjective value statements. The scientific analysis of religion as carried on by the phenomenologists of religion developed to a fine art the study of "the phenomena" while working with many of the egregious errors of the comparativists. Nevertheless, the process of selecting and arranging the various "structures" of the religions (by taking similar ideas or categories in religion, e.g., mother figures like Eve, Mary, Sarah, Ashtoreth, etc., and showing the similarity of their roles in their particular religious setting) involved judgments of value if nothing more than placing them all on the same level of significance.

Much analysis of the religions was theological in method. Toynbee's assessment belongs to this category of study, although he failed to recognize it. He was also reductionistic, seeking for the common elements in the various "higher religions." More starkly theological (more properly Christological) was the work of Karl Barth, Hendrik Kraemer, and Edmund Perry. Following Barth's lead, the latter scholars viewed religion as sinful humanity's attempt to transcend its estrangement from God by autonomous effort. Even Christianity could become a religion, an idolatrous substitute for the living God revealed in Jesus Christ.

Generally, the history of religions movement today involves scholarly studies in the various world religions. In many Western universities, we perceive a diminished interest in the Judeo-Christian heritage and a heavy concentration upon Eastern religions, especially Hinduism, Buddhism, and Islam.

See RELIGION, SYNCRETISM, CHRISTIANITY, NON-CHRISTIAN RELIGIONS.

For Further Reading: Smith, *The Faiths of Other Men;* Perry, *The Gospel in Dispute.* LEON O. HYNSON

COMPASSION. It is not adequate to view compassion as a superficial psychological phenomenon equivalent to feeling sorry for someone. When Jesus looked on His followers with compassion (Matt. 15:32; 20:34; Mark 8:2; 9:22; Luke 7:13; 10:33), He was looking on in love. Thus compassion is love's emotional response to actual distress or some impending calamity in the life of another.

In reference to animals or to human frailty, compassion may take the form of pity. The parable of the unmerciful servant is an excellent illustration: "Shouldest not thou also have had compassion on thy fellowservant, even as I had pity on thee?" (Matt. 18:33). When the believer has compassion on or pities someone, he not only sympathizes, he empathizes.

The implications of the above are important when we move from the human to the divine-human realm. The compassion of God is a result of the infinite greatness of His love. Seeing the misery of creation, the Creator sympathized, pitied, and conspicuously displayed His empathy in the gift of His Son (John 3:16). Jesus is the Creator's embodiment of compassion, and by His life that embodiment teaches His followers that the Christian way of life is one of compassion.

See MERCY, LOVE, AGAPĒ, GOOD WORKS, BENEVOLENCE.

For Further Reading: *Baker's DT,* 132 ff; "Pity," *HDB,* 774.

W. STEPHEN GUNTER

COMPLEMENTARIANISM. It was John Fletcher who introduced the idea of complementarianism to the Wesleyan movement of the 18th century. This was the methodology he used as an apologist in the Antinomian Controversy of 1770-76. It has been variously described as the *via media* or the "middle way." The word *dialectical* is used of this view in more technical circles.

This method of doing theology was found to be particularly helpful in reconciling religious truths which from certain perspectives appear to be cast in opposite molds. Examples of such truths are as follows: law and gospel, faith and works, doctrine and morality, rationalism and mysticism, Christianity and culture, Arminianism and Calvinism.

Rigid adherence to the particulars of one emphasis to the exclusion of equal attention to a complementary or corresponding truth was a dangerous procedure in Fletcher's estimation. To pit one truth against another was to do damage to both. The seeming contradictions were never considered by Fletcher to be irreconcilable.

His position was that one truth complemented the other. He spoke of the "harmonious opposition of the Scriptures" and the "golden mean." The *Checks to Antinomianism* which he wrote in the course of the controversy display the kind of balance which his complementarianism produced. In the words of Charles L. Feinberg, Fletcher found the "key to true theology."

See DIALECTIC, CHECKS TO ANTINOMIANISM, WESLEYAN SYNTHESIS.

For Further Reading: Knight, "John Fletcher's Influence on the Development of Wesleyan Theology in America," *WTJ,* 13:13-33; Mattke, "John Fletcher's Methodology in the Antinomian Controversy of 1770-76," *WTJ,* 3:38-47; Stott, *Balanced Christianity,* 7-10.

ROBERT A. MATTKE

CONCEPTUALISM. Conceptualism is the philosophical theory that general ideas separated from particular objects exist in the mind. It is close to realism but differs from it by insisting that general ideas are mind-dependent; it is contrasted with nominalism which denies that general ideas exist independently of particulars. None of these positions is directly related to theological issues. Historically conceptualism was used to buttress a certain view of the Church, especially in the Middle Ages. Against nominalists who tended to see the Church as the totality of believers from whom the hierarchy receives its authority, it saw the Church as a celestial reality that is not dependent on men for its authority. The connection between the philosophical theory and the theological inference is precarious, to say the least. So-called nominalists like William of Ockham were in fact realistic conceptualists and yet were excommunicated. Theologians simply tended to use the philosophical theory at this point as a cipher for theological convictions that had other sources and warrants.

In modern times conceptualism has fallen on very hard times. The question to which it is an answer is still discussed; philosophers still want to know how general words have meaning. But conceptualism presupposes that they have meaning only because they must refer to or name some entity. This theory of meaning has been abandoned. Words have many functions rather than simply a naming function. General words, on this alternative view, are logical constructions generated by the actual or possible occasions of their employment. To have a concept of a "man" or a "cat" is to be able, say, to distinguish a man or a cat from other entities. Because of this change in theory of meaning, conceptualism is now of historical interest only, both theologically and philosophically.

See REALISM AND NOMINALISM.

For Further Reading: Geach, *Mental Acts;* Woozley, "Universals," *Encyclopedia of Philosophy,* ed. Edwards, 8:194-206; Gonzalez, *A History of Christian Thought,* 2:66-68, 316-21.

WILLIAM J. ABRAHAM

CONCILIARISM. This term refers to a movement within the Roman Catholic church which espoused the theory that a general council constitutes the highest authority in the church, the pope himself being subject to its decrees. The chief proponent of such teaching was Marcilius of Padua (c. 1275-1342). The movement became most prominent in response to the crisis of authority created by the claims and counterclaims of popes and antipopes which arose out of the Great Schism of the late 14th century. In an effort to restore the unity of the church the General Council of Pisa (1409) elected a third pope. The resulting confusion was not resolved until the succeeding General Council of Constance (1414-18) deposed all papal claimants and elected a new pope, Martin V. The General Council also subordinated papal authority to the will of the council by requiring certain promises for church reform from Martin V before his election.

Such actions subsequently constituted the basis for all conciliar movements within the church. The successes of the early 15th-century conciliarists in restoring the unity of the church nevertheless proved to be the downfall of the principle itself. The new pope, with the support of the Curia who had always rejected the movement's claims, quickly reasserted papal authority. From the 15th century onward, the papacy has retained firm control over all subsequent church councils.

Some effort was made at Vatican II to broaden the exercise of authority in the Roman Catholic church through greater emphasis upon the principle of collegiality shared by the bishops; however, nothing substantive resulted. The pope continues to legitimize legislation of the general councils by reserving to himself alone the final approval of all their decrees and disciplinary canons.

See CATHOLICISM (ROMAN).

For Further Reading: Tierney, *Foundations of the Conciliar Theory;* Küng, *Structures of the Church.*

MELVIN EASTERDAY DIETER

CONCUPISCENCE. The term means "illicit desire" but especially "sexual lust." Augustine introduced the teaching that sinful concupiscence was the penal consequence of the Fall, prior to which the sex act was purely volitional and devoid of passion. Concupiscence thus understood is now constituent to humanity and will be healed only by the resurrection. Individually each member of the fallen race must contend with concupiscence until he lays aside "this body of sin and death." Augustine interpreted the conflict of Romans 7 in the light of this doctrine, as "the quarrel between will and lust," and therefore denied the possibility of entire sanctification in this life (retracting his earlier advocacy of the possibility of perfection of believers). Even the apostles experienced this conflict until death; the only exceptions Augustine allowed were Jesus and His mother Mary.

Both Calvin and Luther subscribed to the Augustinian doctrine of concupiscence and denied the possibility of true sanctification specifically on the basis of this view.

The fundamental error of the doctrine is the notion that the Fall resulted in a *metaphysical* change in human nature which can be reversed only by glorification. Wesley returned to a pre-Augustinian understanding of original sin and is free from the taint of this doctrine.

See SIN, ORIGINAL SIN, MARRIAGE, SEX (SEXUALITY), DESIRE.

For Further Reading: Augustine, *City of God,* 14:16-28; Calvin, *Institutes of the Christian Religion,* bk. 3, chap. 3, secs. 10-14; Kerr, *A Compend of Luther's Theology,* 69, 81, 83, 86, 114, 133.

WILLIAM M. GREATHOUSE

CONDEMN, CONDEMNATION. See JUDGE, JUDGMENT.

CONDITIONAL IMMORTALITY. Although this view of immortality varies in some aspects, it basically claims that man was created mortal, and that immortality is a gift which God confers upon believers, while annihilation, or cessation of being, will be the lot of the wicked. Among Christian writers this teaching was first advanced by the African apologist, Arnobius, at the beginning of the fourth century, but was condemned at the Lateran Council in 1513. Present-day advocates of this teaching include Seventh-Day Adventists and Jehovah's Witnesses. They contend that the Bible does not say that man is inherently immortal, but that innate immortality is ascribed only to Deity, citing 1 Tim. 6:16, "who only hath immortality." Accordingly, the unsavory elements in the doctrine of eternal punishment are avoided, and universalism, the doctrine of the ultimate reconciliation of all men to God, is also denied. It is their contention that eternal damnation cannot be harmonized with the redemptive love of God, while universalism is inconsistent with the freedom of man to reject divine love.

It is impossible to reconcile this view with the clear teaching of Jesus Christ as found in Matt. 25:46; Mark 3:29; Luke 16:19-26; and John 3:36, and in other passages such as Isa. 66:24; Acts 1:25; and Rev. 20:10. Furthermore, annihilation does not allow for degrees in punishment as Jesus taught in Luke 12:47-48, nor can it be regarded as a proper punishment for sin.

See IMMORTALITY, ETERNAL PUNISHMENT, ETERNAL LIFE.

For Further Reading: Buis, *The Doctrine of Eternal Punishment,* 123-26; Boettner, *Immortality,* 117-24; *ERE,* 3:822-25; Wiley, *CT,* 3:360 ff.

WILLIAM M. ARNETT

CONFESSION, CONFESSIONAL. The word "confess" *(homologeō)* has the basic idea of "agree" and is the common word for making a legal contract. The concept broadens to "promise," "assure," "admit," "confess," "declare publicly," "acknowledge," and "praise." Etymologically, it means "to say the same thing as." Jesus is revealed as the Christ, the Son of God, and the Lord. To confess Him is to profess Him by saying the same thing as God has said and by acting consistently with the words. To deny Caesar (as Lord) and to confess Jesus (as Lord) was the formula that led to martyrdom in the Early Church.

Early Christian literature used the noun and verb to indicate the content of the confession more than the act of confessing. Thus arose the early confessions, from which were developed the creeds. "In the early church the content of the gospel was understood to be Jesus Christ himself, and the verb has as its direct object Christ, Jesus, Jesus and the resurrection, or Son of God" (Neufeld, *The Earliest Christian Confessions,* 21). The earliest confessions (among Jewish believers), as seen in the Gospels, were "Jesus is the Christ [or Messiah]" and "Jesus is the Son of God." Later, as the gospel spread throughout the Roman world, the third Christian confession emerged as an explicit affirmation of universal sovereignty in the profession "Jesus is Lord."

The term *confessional* is sometimes used of a church or institution which teaches that the profession of certain basic dogmas is (1) essential to salvation, or (2) at least required for membership in that group. *Confessional* also may refer to the place where confession of sins is made to a priest.

See CONFESSION OF FAITH, TESTIMONY, CREED, REPENTANCE, RESTITUTION, CONFESSION OF SINS.

For Further Reading: Neufeld, *The Earliest Christian Confessions;* Grounds, "Confession," *ZPEB,* 1:937-39; Michel, *"homologeō,"* Kittel, 5:199-220.

WILBER T. DAYTON

CONFESSION OF FAITH. The object of confession in the Bible is basically twofold: confession of sin and confession of faith. Confession of sin marks the beginning of a new life of faith. Confession of faith involves public avowal and loyalty to God and to the Word of Truth through which God is revealed.

In the OT the believer's confession usually focused on trust in and praise to God for His redeeming love and acts on behalf of Israel or his own life. In the NT the believer's confession of faith centers in Jesus Christ. The believer confesses Jesus to be the Messiah (John 9:22, 38), the Son of God (1 John 4:15), that He came in the flesh (v. 2), that He is Lord, evidenced by His resurrection/ascension (Acts 2:31-36; Rom. 10:9; Phil. 2:11).

Confession of Christ is linked closely to confession of sin. To confess Christ is to confess that we are sinners, that He "died for our sins" (1 Cor. 15:3), and that we trust Him for forgiveness and cleansing (1 John 1:4—2:2).

Also, to confess Christ is to openly acknowledge Him before men (Luke 12:8; 1 Tim. 6:12). Confession in this sense always accompanied baptism in the Early Church. Although it be costly or risky, public confession of faith was and is essential. Unless we confess Christ before men, He will not acknowledge us before the Father (Matt. 10:32-33). Confessing Christ is the opposite of denying Him.

The believer's confession of faith is made possible by the Holy Spirit's enablement (1 Cor. 12:3; 1 John 4:2-4; John 15:26). It involves not just verbal avowal of faith in Christ, but also visible obedience to Christ in one's whole life. When total obedience is absent and one settles simply for understanding of and knowledge about salvation, "it is equivalent to denial, which Jesus will 'confess', when he says in judgment, 'I never knew you'" (Matt. 7:23) (D. Fürst).

See CONFESSION, TESTIMONY, CHRISTIAN, DISCIPLE, DISCIPLESHIP.

For Further Reading: Fürst, "Confess," *NIDNTT,* 1:344-48; Quanbeck, "Confession," *IDB,* 1:667-68; Stauffer, *Theology of the New Testament,* 235-53; Michel, *"homologeō,"* Kittel, 5:199-220. J. WESLEY ADAMS

CONFESSION OF SINS. Confession of sins is the acknowledgment of one's guilt to God. A person cannot turn to God without first turning from sin. Confession says, in effect, "I am wrong, I have sinned, I want You to forgive me." The Psalmist expressed the spirit of the penitent: "I acknowledged my sin unto thee, and mine iniquity have I not hid. I said, I will confess my transgressions unto the Lord; and thou forgavest the iniquity of my sin" (Ps. 32:5; cf. Prov. 28:13).

In the Early Church confession of sins was often public confession to the whole congregation. Chrysostom, by the end of the fourth century, indicated the need for confession before baptism or Communion. Gradually, however, private confession grew as a practice with the development of monasticism. Confession of sins to a priest was a medieval development made obligatory for the laity at the Fourth Lateran Council in 1215. It was not enforced until the 16th century when confessional stalls were introduced into the church.

Biblical evidence suggests, however, that confession of sins is primarily before God (Ps. 51:3-4; Rom. 14:10-12). Confession is made because we acknowledge the sovereignty of God in our lives (3:19). When confronted with the revealed character and will of God, we admit our unworthiness and sinfulness in confession to a holy God (cf. 1 Kings 8:33-34). Confession of sins to God should be as specific as possible; yet recalling every sin ever committed is neither possible nor necessary (cf. Luke 18:13). We are assured of God's forgiveness when confession of sins is made (1 John 1:9).

The sovereign God to whom confession of sins is made is the God to be worshipped and served. The acknowledgment that the sovereign God has accepted our confession and granted pardon moves quickly to praise and thanksgiving. The same Hebrew word which is translated "confession" in Josh. 7:19 and in Ezra 10:11 is translated "praise" in Ps. 42:4, and "thanksgiving" in Ps. 100:4.

There may be occasion for a general confession of the church to God either collectively or by a representative of the people (Ezra 9:6 ff). It may be necessary for individuals to confess their sins against God in the presence of the church (Matt. 18:17; Acts 19:18; Jas. 5:16). The public confession of sins is important when the church has been involved and its integrity and witness have been compromised. Such confession is implied in 2 Cor. 2:5-7 and Gal. 6:1. Great care, however, must be exercised in the specificity of public confessions lest it degenerate into a form of exhibitionism and become an occasion of embarrassment and reproach to others. In Jas. 5:16 confession is mutual among church members. There is no suggestion of private confession of sins to a pastor or group of church leaders, though this may at times be helpful. Sin against a brother calls for confession to be made to the offended person.

See CONFESSOR, ABSOLUTION, REPENTANCE, CONFESSION OF FAITH.

For Further Reading: *Baker's DCE,* 123.

LEBRON FAIRBANKS

CONFIRMATION. The rite of confirmation has been an established practice in the history of the church from very early times. In the Catholic tradition it comes after the rite of baptism. In the earlier centuries it was performed immediately following baptism, as it is still done in the Eastern Orthodox church. However, in the Western church it was postponed in the case of baptized infants until their childhood years. In the Catholic and Anglican traditions only the bishop confirms baptized believers by the laying on of hands.

The basis for confirmation is not explicit, but the biblical practice of laying on of hands of baptized believers in Acts 8 and 19 is appealed to as the first instance of confirmation. In Protestant churches where infant baptism is practiced, the rite of confirmation serves more of a practical function of permitting older children who have received catechism to take Christian vows for themselves which had been made for them by their parents who had them baptized as infants.

The Catholic and Anglican traditions, along with Eastern Orthodoxy, give confirmation a theological prominence which is highly significant for the Wesleyan tradition. In Catholic theology, baptism has to do with inauguration into the church, whereas confirmation relates to the Pentecostal outpouring of the Holy Spirit, who empowers the individual believer to live the Christian life. Hence there are two sacraments of initiation into the church, not just one. Without experiencing both baptism and confirmation, one has not been duly initiated into the Christian life, for they "belong together in the single Christian initiation"; and although they are "extended in time," they are "ultimately one" (Rahner, *Foundations of Christian Faith,* 416). Catholic scholars cite as exegetical support for the subsequent rite of confirmation the very same passages in Acts (8:14-17; 19:1-7) that Wesleyan exegetes cite for their distinction between the birth of the Spirit and the fullness of the Spirit.

William J. O'Shea points out that baptism and confirmation are not in opposition to each other. Rather, confirmation "completes, brings to full development, what is already there" in baptism.

In this respect, "there are Scripture texts which refer verbally to baptism, but the fullness of what is connoted there is attained only through confirmation." An example of this is "the Pentecost-event itself, because Pentecost was at once the baptism and the confirmation of the infant church" (*Sacraments of Initiation,* 62). Consequently, there is no competition between the importance of baptism and confirmation. It is clear that the Catholic doctrine of confirmation, like the Wesleyan doctrine of entire sanctification, is supposed to signify the perfection of sanctifying grace begun in conversion whereby "the believer's being as a Christian is completed" since "he is clothed with the fullness of the Spirit after the likeness of Christ" (O'Shea).

It is also clear that for the Catholic doctrine of confirmation, like the Wesleyan doctrine of entire sanctification, there is "prescribed" a time lapse between "these two separate, yet related, anointings" (ibid., 63). The definitive nature of this subsequent work of grace is such that it cannot be repeated for any baptized believer because it has to do with the perfection of character, and if one's character is perfected in confirmation, there can be no need for further confirmation. Hence confirmation, like entire sanctification, is a second definite work of grace in the life of the Christian believer, though the Wesleyan doctrine of entire sanctification does not absolutize the concepts of crisis and subsequency.

Another significant comparison between Catholic theology of confirmation and the Wesleyan doctrine of entire sanctification is that it is the Pentecostal gift of the Spirit which effects "Christlikeness" in the life of the baptized believer. Baptism with water signifies that one has become an "adopted son of God," whereas confirmation signifies that the baptized believer has received the fullness of the Spirit of Pentecost (ibid., 63).

John Fletcher, the first Methodist systematic theologian and John Wesley's personally designated successor as leader of the Methodist movement, defended Wesley's doctrine of Christian perfection by appealing directly to the Anglican rite of confirmation (which was essentially the same as the Catholic doctrine). Among the Methodists, Fletcher was the first to make explicit the connection between Christian perfection and the fullness of the Spirit. Fletcher referred to the rite of confirmation as substantiating Wesley's view of the doctrine of entire sanctification. The Samaritans' experience (Acts 8) and the Ephesians' experience (Acts 19) of the Spirit are used by Fletcher as examples of entire sanctification. However, instead of arguing for these biblical passages as supporting the rite of confirmation, Fletcher (and Wesley) refers to these as sanctifying experiences. It can thus be said that the genius of John Wesley and John Fletcher was not that they created a doctrine of entire sanctification, but that they gave it a more evangelical rather than a high sacramentarian interpretation. For all practical purposes Wesley ignored the rite of confirmation in his writings, probably because he wanted to get away from a purely formalistic understanding of grace. Wesley's stress was upon an "experimental religion"—that is, a religion of the heart.

See BAPTISM WITH THE SPIRIT, ENTIRE SANCTIFICATION, SACRAMENTARIANISM.

For Further Reading: Wood, *Pentecostal Grace,* 240-57; O'Shea, *Sacraments of Initiation;* Rahner, *A New Baptism in the Spirit; Confirmation Today.*

LAURENCE W. WOOD

CONFORMITY. Conformity refers to the voluntary acceptance of and adherence to a given set of standards, values, expectations, and practices. The question of conformity thus becomes what Lord Morley called "a question of boundaries." This may at times create an apparent conflict of duties.

There is *civic conformity,* or the behavior expected of the citizen by the state. An unquestioning obedience by the Christian does not appear to be the teaching of the NT; a humble dissent leading to nonconformity is present there despite the norm of obedience to authorities. Peter, who urges conformity to Caesar even when that Caesar is Nero (1 Pet. 2:17), himself refused to conform to the expectation of the Jerusalem rulers (Acts 4:17-19). Obedience to God must come first.

Yet the norm is clear. Jude, v. 8, prophesies eternal fire for those who "reject authority" (NIV), or, "speak evil of dignities" (KJV). Paul unqualifiedly counsels conformity to the "powers that be" (Rom. 13:1-7; cf. Titus 3:1).

There is *religious conformity* expected by some sections of the Christian church. When the choice lies between conformity and excommunication, as with Roman Catholics, there is likely to be at least an external conformity. On the other hand, reformers are usually nonconformists in some point or degree: Luther and Melanchthon in the 16th century, and Hans Küng and Schillerbeex in the 20th, are notable examples. *Nonconformist* indeed is a historic term for those persons who, although members of the Anglican community, nevertheless refused to accept certain laws and procedures of ritual. However, there is little basis for such nonconformity today, since church membership is itself an option, and there is no necessity of remaining in a church with which there is serious disagreement. Commitment to a church should be marked by a reasonable degree of conformity. Otherwise the integrity of both church and member is compromised, and the influence of the church undermined.

There is *spiritual conformity* which Paul presents as the goal of redemption—conformity "to the image of his Son"; that having borne the likeness of the first Adam, believers shall also bear the likeness of the last Adam (1 Cor. 15:49; Rom. 8:29). That *full* conformity to the image of Christ lies in the future (1 John 3:2); but there is to be growth in Christlikeness through the gracious aid of "the Spirit of Christ" (Rom. 8:9, 11). Christians are not to choose to be conformed to the society in which they live (12:2; cf. Phillips). They are to allow the Holy Spirit to remold their lives from within by His transforming power; only thus will Christ be formed in them (Gal. 4:19). Full conformity to Christ can come about only by continuing in the way of Christ (Phil. 3:10-14). Grace delivers us from the corruption that is in the world, and gives us "his very great and precious promises, so that through them [we] may participate in the divine nature" (2 Pet. 1:4, NIV).

See OBEDIENCE, CHRISTIAN ETHICS, FELLOWSHIP, KOINONIA, WORLD, CONSCIENCE.

For Further Reading: *GMS,* 527-47; Thielicke, *Theological Ethics.* T. CRICHTON MITCHELL

CONGREGATIONALISM. See CHURCH GOVERNMENT.

CONSCIENCE. The OT provides no word for conscience. The NT word *suneidēsis,* translated "conscience," refers to the moral instinct in man (Rom. 2:15; 9:1; 13:5; 1 Pet. 3:21). The conscience is the aspect of the human psyche reflecting God's moral image by which man monitors right and wrong. The NT word is used for self-awareness in both the moral and nonmoral sense. It is by the conscience that we become conscious of right and wrong in ourselves.

Each man's conscience has a code or standards of obligation, and a signalling or monitoring capacity. The signalling function is brought out by such scriptures as Rom. 2:15, where conscience is described as either accusing or excusing.

First Peter 3:16 refers to an affirming conscience—"a good conscience." We may have a conscience "void of offence" (Acts 24:16), where it "bears witness" to one's integrity (Rom. 9:1; cf. 2 Cor. 1:12; 1 Tim. 1:5, 19; 3:9; Heb. 13:18; 1 Pet. 3:16, 21). A "seared" conscience (1 Tim. 4:2), hardened as a result of maintained and wilful disobedience, ceases to signal effectively. A "quickened" conscience has its signalling function sharpened in regard to God's will. The misinformed, oppressive, and legalistic conscience is described as "weak" (Rom. 14:2, 20; 1 Cor. 8:7-12).

Paul identified one element of the conscience code as the universal intuitive awareness of obligation to honor God (Rom. 1:19, 21; 2:15). References to the "heart" and "understanding" of unregenerate man being "darkened" (1:21; Eph. 4:18) are descriptions of the faulty conscience code.

Sinful acts—violations of the conscience code —"defile" the conscience (Titus 1:15) and bring a sense of condemnation (Rom. 8:1).

Christian conversion brings a purging and cleansing of the conscience (Heb. 9:14; 10:22), removing the sense of offense and changing the conscience signal from condemnation to approval (Rom. 5:1). This is one of the unique and precious accompaniments of saving faith.

The development of the conscience code is influenced by environment, relationships, and obedience (Heb. 5:14). Hence the code content of conscience is different for every person. Each, however, is obligated to walk in the light of his conscience code, and will be judged according to that light (Rom. 2:12, 15; 14:2, 5, 14, 22; 1 John 1:7). A disparity between knowledge and truth exists in all. Enlightenment of the conscience is by obedience to Scripture and the illumination of the Holy Spirit (2 Tim. 3:16; 1 Cor. 2:10).

The psychological study of conscience has shown that it may be subject to maladjustive distortions, unconscious motivations, neurotic guilt, and impairment of the signalling function. There is also interest in the study of the normal stages of development of conscience from the self-preservation interest through the rule-oriented stage to a principle-based code. Mental and emotional illnesses are closely related to conscience problems. The cure for a troubled conscience is in the cleansing of real guilt and the rejection of neurotic guilt, leading to healing.

See CONFORMITY, GROWTH, HOLINESS, RIGHTEOUSNESS, DEVELOPMENT (THEORIES OF).

For Further Reading: Wiley, *CT,* 1:30 ff; Purkiser, *Exploring Our Christian Faith* (1960), 480 ff; Kittel, 7:902-7.

JAMES M. RIDGWAY

CONSECRATE, CONSECRATION. These English words have been used to translate several Hebrew and Greek words, such as *charam, nazar, qadash, male yad; egkainizō, teleioō, hagiadzō,* to name the most important. The primary meaning of these terms is "to separate" someone (or something) from that which is common, ordinary, and unclean, and devote him (or it) to the exclusive use of Deity. And whatever is so devoted has about it a certain quality of holiness because of its relation to Deity.

In the OT. The verb form "to consecrate" is used frequently in the OT for the induction of a person into sacred office, e.g., a priest, prophet, king, etc., but it is also used of things, times, and places. The Temple is said to be consecrated, likewise, its furniture, vessels, and offerings. The Sabbath Day, the various Hebrew festivals, and the Year of Jubilee were sacred times. The noun form "consecration" indicates the act by which a person or thing was set apart for sacred use.

Charam means "to devote" something to Deity usually for destruction—a city (Josh. 6:17-19) or a people (1 Sam. 15:3). The person or group that sought to divert the "devoted" thing to some other use was accursed. *Nazar* is a verb form meaning "to separate," while the noun form means "separation" (see Nazarite). *Qadash* means "to set apart" or "to be set apart" as in Exod. 30:30 where Aaron and his sons are "separated" from the rest of the people to fill the priest's office. This term also carried with it the idea of cleanliness and holiness.

Male yad is the most characteristic expression for consecration in the OT, and the literal meaning is "to fill the hand." Although its origin is obscure, its meaning apparently developed from the ordination ceremony of the priest: "filling the hand" of the candidate for the priesthood was the unmistakable token that he was a priest (Exod. 29:9). To be a priest one must have something in his hand to offer to God. The noun form *milluim* refers to "the setting in office" of the priest, i.e., the installation, and it is also used for what "fills the hand," the installation offering, or sacrifice (Lev. 8:28, 31-36; Exod. 29:22, 26-27, 31).

In the NT. The words "consecrate" and "consecration" do not appear as often in the NT as in the OT. The Greek words that are translated "consecrated" in KJV are (1) *egkainizō,* which means to "dedicate" or "make new," as found in Heb. 10:20, where Christ is said to have "consecrated" for us (or opened to us) the new and living way; and (2) the word *teleioō* in Heb. 7:28 is used to speak of Christ's eternal "consecration" to that High Priesthood which is so much better than that of Aaron.

The RSV translators have chosen to use the term "consecrate" for the Greek word *hagiadzō* in a number of passages (John 10:36; 17:19; 1 Cor. 7:14; 1 Tim. 4:5; 2 Tim. 2:21). Certainly the idea of consecration is implied by *hagiadzō,* and in some contexts "consecration" may be the more appropriate translation. The same is true of its counterpart in the OT, *qadash.* Two other words which express the idea of consecration are significant. One of the meanings of the verb *aphoridzō* is "to separate," and in passages like Acts 13:2; Rom. 1:1; Gal. 1:5 it has the theological significance of "consecrate." The same is true of *paristanō* in passages like Rom. 6:13, 19; 12:1 where the idea of "present" also has the thrust of "consecrate."

Church usage. The idea appears often in the theology and praxis of the church. It appears in the rite of confirmation, in the dedication of church buildings, and especially in the ordination of the clergy. These functions are always accompanied with deep solemnity and reverence, and the person or object is thought to be "set apart" for a holy purpose. Some ministers call upon their parishioners to consecrate, or reconsecrate, themselves to serve God more faithfully in their daily living.

In the Wesleyan-Arminian wing of Protestantism consecration is commonly thought to be a prerequisite to the experience of entire sanctification. When a Christian brings the new life that he has received through the regenerating power of the Holy Spirit and consecrates it to God (Rom. 6:13, 19; 12:1), the Lord responds by cleansing the heart of inbred sin and filling it with perfect love. It is man's responsibility to consecrate himself (and this is all he can do), while it is God's responsibility and pleasure to sanctify the heart of His obedient child. In this view, consecration and sanctification, while related, are not identical. In John 17 the translation (RSV) of *hagiadzō* by "sanctify" in verse 17 and "consecrate" in verse 19 is a recognition of the distinction between *hagiadzō* as something which God does to and in the subject and something which the subject himself does.

See SURRENDER, ENTIRE SANCTIFICATION, HOLINESS, ORDAIN (ORDINATION).

For Further Reading: Kittel, 5:454, 839; Pope, *A Compendium of Christian Theology,* 3:31 ff, 224 ff; Wiley, *CT,* 2:467; *ZPEB,* 1:951.

C. PAUL GRAY

CONSOLATION. See COMFORT.

CONSUBSTANTIATION. This is the view that, in the Lord's Supper, Christ is literally in, with, and under the elements. Although the word was not invented until shortly after Luther's time, it describes the view which the great Reformer taught.

Like the transubstantiation theory of the Roman Catholic church, it is a view of Christ's being literally—and not just spiritually—present in the Communion bread and wine. According to this view, Christ's words, "This is my body" (1 Cor. 11:24), should be interpreted in a most literal sense. Luther even said that we actually and literally chew Christ when we eat the Communion bread.

Besides the view's being based on a literal interpretation of Christ's "This is my body," it is based also on a view of the ancient Augustine and others that Christ's body was ubiquitous during the enfleshment years: i.e., that it was everywhere, as well as localized.

Luther's view on the Supper was not accepted by Protestantism generally—which has thought of Christ's presence in the bread and wine as a spiritual accompaniment. Actually, Luther's friend and associate in the Reformation, Karlstadt, because of Luther's similarity to the Roman church at this point, quite frustrated Luther by calling him "Antichrist's [i.e., the pope's] younger friend." Karlstadt pointed out that in the NT Greek the word "this" in "This is my body" is neuter in gender and therefore agrees with "body" and not with "bread." Thus, Karlstadt taught, Christ was not saying that the bread was Christ's body, but was simply calling attention to the fact that His real body was soon going to be given for an atonement on the Cross.

Karlstadt also pointed out that when Paul said that we Christians are to receive the Lord's Supper "till he come" (1 Cor. 11:26), the implication is that Christ is not already present in any literal sense.

Karlstadt's kind of understanding of the Lord's Supper was more or less the view accepted generally in Protestantism. Indeed, Luther's consubstantiation is not even accepted today in any general way in Lutheranism itself.

See REAL PRESENCE, TRANSUBSTANTIATION, HOLY COMMUNION.

For Further Reading: Smith, *History of Theophany;* Baillie, *Theology of the Sacraments;* Smith, *The Sacramental Society.*

J. KENNETH GRIDER

CONTENTMENT. A state of being satisfied with one's lot in life, or being willing to accept conditions as they are. The commonly used Greek word is *autarkia,* which basically means "sufficiency," as in 2 Cor. 9:8. It is a state of mind in which there is a freedom from care because of acquiescence to the status quo. But it must not be confused with either lethargy or stoicism. "It does not exclude aspiration and a concern for improvement" (H. Stob, *ZPEB*). A person can be goal oriented and still be contented provided his ambitions are not self-centered.

To reach the goal of contentment, Buddhism urges the suppression of all desire, while Stoicism extols resignation to what is perceived to be unalterable fact. But both approaches are pessimistic in nature, whereas the Christian concept of contentment rests in an inner trust that a loving God is concerned about His children and seeks their highest good. It is a rest that comes from commitment to God based on the assurance that "no good thing will he withhold from them that walk uprightly" (Ps. 84:11).

Negative, self-centered attitudes such as envy and jealousy are the antitheses of contentment. The warnings in Scripture against covetousness are meant to affirm the true bases of inner peace. As J. C. Lambert puts it: "Contentment is not found in measuring ourselves with others."

OT references are somewhat oblique, such as the implications of the 10th commandment and advice found in the Book of Proverbs. The NT treats the subject more directly. Jesus attacked the tendency to greed and covetousness, and also warned against unwarranted anxiety, emphasizing the care of the Father God and the importance of establishing proper priorities in life (e.g., Matt. 6:25-34). Paul by word and example extolled the virtue of contentment, capsulized in his famous statement, "I have learned in whatsoever state I am, therewith to be content" (Phil. 4:11), and in his declaration that "all things work together for good to them that love God" (Rom. 8:28).

See PEACE, GROWTH, VICTORY (VICTORIOUS LIVING), MIND OF CHRIST, SPIRITUALITY, HAPPINESS, COVETOUSNESS.

For Further Reading: *ZPEB,* 1:953; *HDB,* 1:476-77; *IDB,* 1:677-78.

J. FRED PARKER

CONTINGENT. That which is contingent is undetermined in advance. In this sense most financial budgets include what is called a Contingent Fund, providing for possible but uncertain expenditures. Personal plans may be said to be contingent in that they hinge on future events or factors as yet unknown. Theologically, events, including final salvation, are called contingent to the extent that they are not predetermined by God but dependent on human decisions, decisions as yet unmade and unknown. The theological problem consists in the difficulty of harmonizing God's foreknowledge (including prophecy) with pure contingency.

Some theologians maintain that events which are truly contingent are by definition unknowable in advance, not only to man but to God. To foreknow unknowable events is contradictory. This limitation God accepted, along with other self-limitations in the exercise of His sovereignty, when He created man as a free being. "If God knows now every choice any man will ever make, then every choice is already determined and freedom is an illusion," says L. Harold DeWolf (*A Theology of the Living Church,* 109). If God, he says, "has put a check on His power to give man freedom of will, then He must have limited somewhat His knowledge of the future" (ibid.).

At the opposite pole of theological thought is pure determinism, of which Calvinism is the prime example. This position frankly rules out true contingency, subjecting all events to the sovereign will of God. Thus foreknowledge and foreordination are inseparable correlates. But Macquarrie is correct in labeling this simple fatalism. Calvinism, he says, "in an attempt to uphold God's glory and sovereignty," in fact debases the relation of God and man "to that subpersonal level where man is little more than a puppet and God too has been degraded to the one who pulls the strings" (*Principles of Christian Theology,* 224).

Generally Wesleyan theologians have avoided either horn of the dilemma by affirming both foreknowledge and contingency, on the grounds that to foreknow an event is not to cause it. Contingency in moral actions, says Richard Watson, is "their *freedom,* and is opposed, not to *certainty,* but to necessity" (quoted by Ralston, *Elements of Divinity,* 25). Ralston argues that Judas could have acted loyally instead of treacherously, in which case God's foreknowledge would have foreseen the faithfulness just as in the real event the unfaithfulness was foreseen. He argues: "The error of the necessitarians on this subject is, they put the effect for the cause, and the cause for the effect. They make the foreknowledge *the cause of the event,* whereas the event is *the cause of the foreknowledge.* No event ever took place because God foreknew it; on the contrary, the taking place of the event is the cause of his having foreknown it" (184).

Undoubtedly some events are fully predetermined by God as well as foreknown, as for instance the delivering of Jesus to be crucified (Acts 2:23). But the individual moral decisions involving this person and that person in the action were all made in freedom and could all have been different. Furthermore, though Christ died for all, and the salvation of all is God's will, the ultimate destiny of any one person is contingent on his own response to the gospel.

See DIVINE SOVEREIGNTY, DETERMINISM, FOREKNOWLEDGE, PREDESTINATION, MONERGISM, SYNERGISM, CALVINISM, ARMINIANISM.

For Further Reading: Wiley, *CT,* 2:343-57; Ralston, *Elements of Divinity,* 24-25, 184-85; Macquarrie, *Principles of Christian Theology,* 224-25; DeWolf, *A Theology of the Living Church,* 108-9. RICHARD S. TAYLOR

CONTRITION. See PENITENCE.

CONVERSION. As it is most often used in common religious speech, "conversion" is a general term used to indicate the initial crisis of salvation, and in this sense it includes the works designated by the terms "justification," "regeneration," and "adoption." "Conversion," as thus used, has the advantage of simplicity and inclusiveness.

In the Scriptures the term "conversion" is less general and somewhat varied in its meaning. The Greek word *epistrephō* (the verb form) means basically "to turn" or "return" (more specifically it can mean "to turn around," "to turn back," or "to turn to" or "toward"). In its religious and metaphorical sense, it means to turn *from* sin and *to* God.

The act of repentance is included in the biblical meaning of conversion (as in Acts 9:37). Also, human responsibility is clearly implied in such passages as Acts 3:19 ("Repent ye therefore, and be converted"; cf. Matt. 18:3; Luke 22:32).

But the term is also used in the NT to indicate the converting work of the evangelist. Paul's task is "to *turn* them from darkness to light, and from the power of Satan unto God" (Acts 26:18). And James applies the term to the personal evangelism of one who "converts" a backslider. He says, "Brethren, if any of you do err from the truth, and one convert him; let him know, that he which converteth the sinner from the error of his way shall save a soul from death, and shall hide a multitude of sins" (Jas. 5:19-20).

See REPENTANCE, FAITH, FIRST WORK OF GRACE.

For Further Reading: Wiley, *CT,* 2:376 ff; Purkiser, ed., *Exploring Our Christian Faith,* 287-88; *ISBE,* 2:706 ff; Wiley and Culbertson, *Introduction to Christian Theology,* 273-74. CHARLES L. CHILDERS

CONVICT, CONVICTION. "Conviction is that operation of the Spirit which produces within men, a sense of guilt and condemnation because of sin" (Wiley, *CT,* 2:342). The verb "convict" indicates the divine act, and the noun "conviction" specifies the work produced by this act. The basic Greek word used in the original language of the NT is *elegchō* (verb form), which can be translated "to put to proof," "to test," "to convict," "to reprove," etc. The exact meaning in a particular passage depends in part upon the context.

That conviction is the work of the Holy Spirit is clearly indicated in John 16:8—"And when he is come, he will reprove [convict] the world of sin, and of righteousness, and of judgment." This convicting work of the Spirit goes far beyond a merely intellectual convincing; it is a moral demonstration. It produces in men a sense of personal guilt and a realization that punishment would be just.

But this conviction produces hope rather than despair, for there is an accompanying offer of divine forgiveness and salvation. Thus it combines *uncompromising* condemnation of personal sin with a gracious call to repentance and an offer of salvation to those who repent. The many divine invitations to repentance and salvation found throughout the Bible make it clear that God's purpose for conviction for sin is pardon, release, restoration. The prodigal son is an excellent example.

The Holy Spirit is the divine Agent in conviction, but He makes use of the human conscience, which is an ally of the Holy Spirit in men's hearts. In John 8:9 we read of the Jewish leaders who brought the adulterous woman to Jesus: "They which heard it [Jesus' word], being convicted by their own conscience, went out one by one."

The Spirit also uses intermediate means, such as the Scriptures, songs, testimony, tracts, books, a holy life, victory in suffering. The cardinal means ordained by God is preaching (1 Cor. 1:17-24; 2:1-4; cf. Acts 24:24-25).

See AWAKENING, REPENTANCE.

For Further Reading: Wiley, *CT,* 2:342-43; *ISBE,* 2:707 ff; *BBC,* Eph. 5:11-13.

CHARLES L. CHILDERS

CORBAN. This Hebrew word meaning "gift" occurs only once in the NT (Mark 7:11), where a son is pictured as saying to his father or mother: "Whatever help you might otherwise have received from me is Corban," and then the NIV has in parentheses: "that is, a gift devoted to God." Jesus condemned this misuse of sacred vows. In God's sight human need gets highest priority. "The reprehensible practice arose of children's giving no aid to parents needing their support, on the pretense that the money or service which would otherwise have been available for the parents had been dedicated to God and that it would be sacrilege to divert it from this sacred purpose" (*Westminster Dictionary of the Bible,* 115).

See PHARISAISM, LEGALISM.

RALPH EARLE

CORNERSTONE. In Eph. 2:20 and 1 Pet. 2:6 Christ is described as the "chief corner stone." This is all one word in Greek, *akrogōniaios.* It is compounded of *akros,* "top" or "extremity," and *gōnia,* "an angle." Abbott-Smith defines it as the "corner foundation stone" (*Manual Greek Lexicon of the New Testament,* 18).

But Joachim Jeremias says that it means "the 'final stone' in a building, probably set over the gate." He goes on to say: "Christ is the cornerstone who binds the whole building together and completes it" (Kittel, 1:792).

But why not both? Christ is both the Cornerstone *and* the Capstone of His Church.

See CHRIST, FOUNDATION.

For Further Reading: Selwyn, *First Epistle of Peter,* 163; Ellis, *Paul's Use of the Old Testament,* 87-92.

RALPH EARLE

CORRUPTION. See ORIGINAL SIN.

COSMOLOGY. *Cosmology* is that branch of metaphysics which treats the character of the universe as an orderly system or cosmos—as distinguished from ontology, which deals with the ultimate nature of the real. As a division of theology it considers the world (everything extrinsic to God, i.e., the universe) as having been created by God. *Cosmogony* is a particular explanation or system, as the Mosaic Cosmogony, found in the Bible.

The act of creation is beyond the experience of man and therefore must be learned by revelation or else discerned from projecting backward the present processes of nature. The latter option presupposes what is called uniformitarianism. However, uniformitarianism is modified by cataclysms which interrupt the process, such as the Flood. There is widespread evidence of the Flood, a catastrophe which could have altered developmental processes and laid down sediments of rock and sand which recorded life at an earlier age. Working on a uniformitarian hypothesis, however, man must elect between projecting present processes backward or accepting revelation by which he learns of heaven and hell, of the divine nature, and of the creation of physical nature.

One must believe in God or endow nature and matter with the properties which he affirms of God. A theist believes that God created the universe. The naturalist believes that matter accounts for the universe. The Bible is theistic. It begins with God as Creator, Sustainer, and Judge.

The Hebrew belief is that by fiat creation the universe came into being, without the need of antecedent material (Heb. 11:3). This took six days (Exod. 20:11). These days are variously interpreted as ages, or periods, or 24-hour days. Certainly, the method of the development was used in describing the creation: first, the earth before the light, the light before the firmament, and the firmament before the dry land. Also, there was the order of beings: plants, fish and birds, cattle and man. Each event was described as a period. A succession of events involves a succession of periods. The period assigned to each individual act is a day. The idea of time elapsing between the completion of one act and the undertaking of another act is present.

Scripture uses the terminology known to man in referring to the natural creation. No other terminology could have been understood; yet it does not teach that the world was flat, that the heavens stood on pillars, or that the sun rose and set. These figures of speech are still used.

See CREATION, CREATIONISM, DAYS OF CREATION, MATTER (MATERIALISM), CATASTROPHISM, EVOLUTION, FLOOD.

For Further Reading: Wiley, *CT,* 1:441-68; Berkhof, *Systematic Theology,* 126-40.

HAROLD J. OCKENGA

COUNCILS. See CHURCH COUNCILS.

COUNSELING. See PASTORAL COUNSELING, ROGERIAN COUNSELING.

COUNTERACTION. This refers to an explanation of the victorious Christian life preferred by those of a Keswickian persuasion. Based on the belief that inbred sin is a force for evil inherent in human nature, it describes victory in terms of the Holy Spirit's counteractive power in the life of the person abiding in Christ, rendering sin at best inoperative, not extinguished.

The view is an alternative to the other view commonly held by some with a Calvinistic orientation that the motions of inbred sin can only be "suppressed" in the Christian. As descriptions of the victorious life, both positions deny the posibility of a radical or actual death, destruction, cleansing, or freeing from inbred sin in this life.

Scriptures most frequently used to teach this aspect of the victorious Christian life are: Rom. 8:2; 5:17; Phil. 4:13; Gal. 5:16 ff. The "law of the Spirit of life in Christ Jesus" makes free from "the law of sin and death." To make free is interpreted to mean "overcomes." "The law of sin is seen to be relentlessly working in our members and is counteracted by the law of the Spirit which persistently operates to abrogate its power over the will" (Barabas). The victory is by walking in the Spirit, being led by the Spirit—by taking sides with the Spirit.

Wesleyan theology recognizes counteraction as the mode of victorious living for the Christian prior to entire sanctification. The counteraction of the impulses of the inborn sinful tendency and other desires of human nature is by the indwelling Holy Spirit as the believer relies upon Him. Following the point of entire sanctification (1 Thess. 5:23; 2 Cor. 7:1) in one's spiritual pilgrimage, the counteracting action of the Holy Spirit is understood to be directed toward those continuing impulses which derive from human nature rather than the carnal nature.

Wesleyan theology can accept counteraction as a lifelong phenomenon of Christian experience as it applies to the impulses of the human nature, but affirms the teaching of Scripture that the pollution of inbred sin may be entirely cleansed (1 John 1:7), thus freeing from the contaminating influence of this sinful disposition. The consequence is a state affected and maintained by the fullness of the Holy Spirit, not so much by counteraction as by a purging displacement.

See ERADICATION, CLEANSING, HEART PURITY, HOLINESS.

For Further Reading: Barabas, *So Great Salvation,* 71 ff, 80 ff, 94 ff; Purkiser, *Conflicting Concepts of Holiness.*

JAMES M. RIDGWAY

COURAGE. See SEVEN CARDINAL VIRTUES.

COVENANT. See NEW COVENANT.

COVENANT THEOLOGY. Covenant theology, also referred to as "federal theology," is based on the concept that God has entered into a pact with man in which certain forms of belief and behavior are incorrect, even damnable. God has made specific promises to man; but they are conditioned upon man's obedience to His laws, which can be discerned in Scripture.

Basically there are two covenants: (1) a covenant of works between God and Adam as the representative of God and mankind in which God promised eternal life on condition of obedience; and (2) a subsequent covenant of grace between God and His elect, whereby Christ redeems them.

The concept of the covenant developed originally in Zwingli (that is, he is the first during the Reformation) and those who succeeded him. As early as 1527 the idea of the covenant was used in biblical theology in Zurich by Oecolampadius (1482-1531), the German Protestant Reformer.

The modern context of covenant theology can be traced to the Civil War period in Great Britain, 1640-50. The Scottish church had succeeded in breaking away from the Roman Catholic church in 1560 and moved in the direction of a Presbyterian form of church government. The movement toward Presbyterianism separated Scotland ecclesiastically from England, for under King James I and his successor, Charles, the Church of England remained staunchly Episcopal in form of government.

When an effort was made by the Anglicans to bring Scotland into conformity by preparing a prayer book for Scotland, a book even more Roman Catholic in some ways than the English *Prayer Book,* Scottish nationalism and Presbyterianism were permanently welded into a united front, reflected in the Covenant of 1638. Practically all of Scotland signed the Covenant. The Scottish General Assembly voted for the abolition of episcopacy as well as the *Prayer Book,* and in 1639 war between England and Scotland broke out. The war between the two countries developed into a Civil War by 1642—the king and Anglicanism on one side, and Parliament and Puritanism (both Presbyterians and Independents) on the other.

To strengthen its position, Parliament tried to enlist the support of the Scots by having the Westminster Assembly draw up the Solemn League and Covenant in 1643. This declares that they have entered into a "mutual and solemn league and covenant" for the extirpation of popery, prelacy [that is, church government by archbishops, bishops, their chancellors and commissaries, deans, archdeacons, and all other ecclesiastical officers depending on that hierarchy], superstition, heresy, schism, profaneness, and whatsoever shall be found to be contrary to sound doctrine and the power of godliness."

Since many of the clergy who signed the document were Puritans, covenant theology has since been most often associated with Puritan-Reformed theology. Its fullest expression was the theology of Johannes Cocceius (1603-1669), German Calvinist professor of theology at Franeker and Leiden, the Netherlands, who held that God and man entered into a covenant of works before the fall of Adam, followed by a covenant of grace which Christ fulfilled. The specific theological emphases are reflective of Puritanism, the description of sin as man's own act and responsibility, and a strict observance of the Sabbath.

See NEW COVENANT, COVENANTERS, FEDERAL THEOLOGY.

For Further Reading: Latourette, *A History of Christianity,* 814; Moorman, *A History of the Church in England,* 221-42; Walker, *A History of the Christian Church,* 402-14. JOHN A. KNIGHT

COVENANTERS. Covenanters were Scottish Presbyterians who risked their lives and fortunes upon the subscription of a National Covenant in Greyfriars churchyard, Edinburgh, in February, 1638. At issue was the attempt of Charles I of England, inspired by Archbishop William Laud, to impose uniformity of worship and church government upon the Scots. Laud was already suspect in Calvinistic Scotland for his Arminian sympathies. The prescription of a prayer book and liturgy, essentially that of the Church of England, added the further suspicion of "prelacy."

In the National Covenant the Scots avowed their loyalty to the king. But they also pledged themselves to resist any religious innovation not first approved by the free assemblies of the Scottish church. A period of government persecution ensued in which many Covenanters were taken prisoner and even executed. The zeal of the Covenanters, however, triumphed in the Bishop's Wars of 1639 and 1640 and doubtless contributed to the English Civil War.

See NEW COVENANT, COVENANT THEOLOGY.

For Further Reading: Douglas, *Light in the North: The Story of the Scottish Covenanters.* DANIEL N. BERG

COVETOUSNESS. This is inordinate desire for what we do not have. It may be a wicked desire for that which already belongs to another, in which case the 10th commandment of the Decalogue is violated. Or it may simply be a feverish desire to possess not necessarily that which is the neighbor's but that which is like it. Covetousness in this case is sister to envy. Paul calls it idolatry (Col. 3:5), because by putting things ahead of God it puts them in the place of God.

The 10th commandment word used in Deut. 5:21 is *avah,* "to desire for oneself," while in Exod. 20:17 it is *chamad,* "to desire." Paul uses *epithumeō,* "to fix the mind on," as the Greek equivalent for the tenth commandment, "Thou shalt not covet." This sin he sees as being so deeply rooted in fallen human nature that it becomes the cause of his spiritual death when he reaches the age of accountability (Rom. 7:5-11). Proneness to covet can compete with proneness to pride and self-willfulness as the epitome of original sin.

The most frequent word for covetousness is *pleonexia,* "the wish to have more." The covetous spirit is never satisfied. Even more graphic is Paul in 1 Tim. 6:10 when, describing those who covet riches, he aptly uses the word *oregomai,* "to extend the arms." Here is the grasping and reaching (often overreaching) of greed.

Covetousness is always listed in the Bible among the more heinous sins (Mark 7:22; Rom. 1:29; 1 Cor. 5:11; 6:10; Eph. 5:3; Col. 3:5). This sin becomes avarice and miserliness when it becomes fixated on money. It then may prompt not only hoarding but stealing, as in the case of Achan (Josh. 7:21). Or it may prompt murder, as in the case of Ahab and Naboth (1 Kings 21).

Covetousness is no respecter of classes; it infects the poor as well as the rich. And it takes many forms: It may be lust for position and power as well as for possessions. It is a deceitful sin, as it may masquerade as prudence, and hide in the heart, destroying the soul, behind a facade of respectability, even religion.

Yet not all desire to possess is covetousness. Certain basic, natural desires belong to our common humanity. These desires become inordinate —and soon sinful—when they are centered in self, when they are imperious and feverish, and when they tend to push aside the obstacles of divine law and the rights of others.

Only entire sanctification is the adequate cure for the disease of covetousness. In the complete consecration to God which this experience requires, and in its cleansing of the heart and enthronement of love, all desires become chastened, disciplined, and subject to the will of God. Sanctified Christians will remain so only as long as they keep their desires "on the altar" and continually submitted to the Holy Spirit for His evaluation and direction. No matter what the nature of a desire is, when it is allowed to become feverish and get out of hand until we suppose we can no longer be happy without its satisfaction, we have become reinfected with the sin of covetousness. No wonder Jesus said, "Take heed, and beware of covetousness" (Luke 12:15). No peril is more subtle or more treacherous for the Christian.

See SEVEN DEADLY SINS, CARNALITY, SIN, CONTENTMENT.

For Further Reading: *GMS,* 270 ff, 293-95; Vine, *ED,* 1:252 ff; Denny, *Tables of Stone for Modern Living,* 107-20.

RICHARD S. TAYLOR

CREATION. Among the great affirmations of the Christian faith is the declaration that "God the Father Almighty" is "maker of heaven and earth."

Creation deals with origins—the origin of matter, energy, stars, planets, plants, animals, man, and all things that existed or exist. Creation may be defined as the free act of God by which He brought into existence the universe and all that it contains, without the use of preexistent materials—*creatio ex nihilo.*

The Ground of Creation. Creation was, and is, the free act of God. The world, including man, was not created to meet a need or a deficiency in God, for divine nature has no inherent needs. Thus the question of *theodicy,* or why did God create, must remain forever in the ultimate mystery of God. Creation was the result of a voluntary decision of God's sovereign will, and it stands as a demonstration of God's power and an expression of His glory.

As created, the world has a distinct and separate existence. The world should not be regarded as part of God or as God himself (pantheism). Yet the world is absolutely dependent on God and must be upheld from moment to moment by His almighty power.

The Agent of Creation. The Triune God was, and is, involved in creation. The first chapter of Genesis (v. 2) states that the Spirit of God moved upon the waters beneath the primeval mass. The Book of Job declares that man was made by the Spirit of God (33:4; cf. Ps. 33:6; Isa. 40:12).

In Ephesians Paul explicitly declares that God "created all things" (3:9). He also refers to general creation when he writes: "For it is the God who said, 'Let light shine out of darkness'" (2 Cor. 4:6, RSV). Other Pauline declarations which affirm a God-centered view of creation are Rom. 4:17; 11:36; and 1 Cor. 11:12.

Christ, as the Word, assumes the leadership in creation in the NT. John's Gospel presents the essence of NT teachings: "All things were made by him; and without him was not any thing made that was made" (1:3). Paul joins John with this grand affirmation: "For in him all things were created . . .. all things were created through him and for him" (Col. 1:16, RSV). Paul also states that Christ's role in creation includes sustaining it as well as creating it, for "in him all things hold together" (v. 17, RSV). Christ is Lord and Creator (cf. Heb. 1:1-3).

The Time of Creation. In speaking of the time of

creation the Bible employs a very simple statement: "In the beginning God created the heaven and the earth" (Gen. 1:1). Here is the beginning of all temporal things, and even of time itself. "The world was created *with* time rather than *in* time. Back of the beginning mentioned in Gen. 1:1 lies a beginningless eternity" (L. Berkhof, *Manual,* 96).

The Manner of Creation. First it must be stressed that creation was by the simple command or word (fiat) of God. God said, "Let there be . . . and there was" (Gen. 1:3, 6, 9, et al.).

The Hebrew word "create" *(bara)* is used only a limited number of times (55) in Scripture. The overwhelming meaning attached to the word is to create. The word always refers to God as Subject. This is particularly true of the specific form used in Gen. 1:1, 21, 27, and 5:1-2.

The first use is where God created out of nothing (Gen. 1:1); the second use is the point at which God created conscious life (v. 21); and the third point is the climax of God creating man (v. 27).

The Scriptures do not attempt to describe in detail the "how" of creation. Multiple mysteries surround the history of the earth and the human race. But, as Harold Kuhn observes: "At the core of the doctrine of creation stands the mighty assertion that the universe is the product of the release of creative energies of an infinitely free and completely holy God, utterly self-sufficient in His being and infinite in His ability to perform that which His heart of love dictates" (in *The Living God,* ed. Erickson, 484). And finally, all creation moves to a redemptive climax in Jesus Christ.

See CREATIONISM, EVOLUTION, NATURALISM, THEISTIC EVOLUTION, COSMOLOGY, DAYS OF CREATION.

For Further Reading: Berkhof, *Manual of Christian Doctrine,* 96; Wiley, *CT,* 1:441-72; Erickson, ed., *The Living God: Readings in Christian Theology,* 484.

DONALD S. METZ

CREATIONISM. Creationism carries two meanings in current thought. One use of the term refers to *scientific creationism*—the assumption of an initial special creation out of nothing. The second use of creationism relates to the origin of the human soul—*theological creationism.*

Scientific creationism represents the belief in an eternal Creator who created all things *ex nihilo.* This belief also involves catastrophic intervention in the normal processes of nature on at least one occasion in history subsequent to the primeval creation. Opposed to scientific creationism stands *scientific evolution,* the idea of the uniform operation of all natural laws and processes from the beginning. This theory, called *evolutionary uniformitarianism,* assumes the natural development of all things due to the innate processes and qualities of eternal matter.

Theological creationism maintains that God directly creates each human soul, while the body is propagated by the parents. Wiley states that "Creationism as a theory seems to be closely connected with the attempts to emphasize the importance of the individual as over against an emphasis upon racial continuity and solidarity" (*CT,* 2:27). According to creationism, the soul is created pure and free from sin. The soul, however, becomes sinful by its essential relationship to the complex of sin which burdens every member of the human race.

Those who support creationism base their biblical support on Eccles. 12:7; Isa. 42:5; Zech. 12:1; Heb. 12:9; and Num. 16:22. The claim is also made that creationism makes the sinlessness of Christ more natural and logical. In the history of the church the theory of theological creationism has been adopted or favored by the schoolmen of the Middle Ages, by the Roman Catholic church, and by the Reformed church. Individuals who supported this position are Jerome, Pelagius, Cyril of Alexandria, Theodoret, Ambrose, Hilarius, and Hieronymus.

Opposed to creationism is the doctrine of traducianism, which holds that the soul of each individual is propagated along with the body by natural generation.

See CREATION, DAYS OF CREATION, SOUL, TRADUCIANISM.

For Further Reading: Morris, *Creation: Acts, Facts, Impacts;* Harris, *Man—God's Eternal Creation,* 25-71; Smith, *Man's Origin, Man's Destiny;* Wiley, *CT,* 2:9-28.

DONALD S. METZ

CREDENTIALS OF SCRIPTURE. The Bible claims to be: (1) a divinely inspired record of God's self-disclosure to and through men in history; (2) an accurate and trustworthy disclosure of God's nature, God's ways, and God's redemptive plan culminating and centering in the person of His Son Jesus Christ, and (3) infallible truth and divine authority which men are called to hear and heed. Credentials by definition derive from evidence which shows a right to authority.

Literary Credentials. The term Bible, from the Greek *ta biblia,* means "the books." The Bible comprises 66 books, composed over 15 or more centuries, by 40 or more writers, and in three languages. In spite of differences in time, culture, education, language, and human authors, there is a remarkable unity in the Bible's totality. As an orchestra where multiple diversity of musicians and instruments blend together in harmonious symphony, so the Bible's coherence testifies to a divinely directed symphony of redemptive truth.

Also, there is the Bible's universal and contemporary appeal. Although a book of antiquity, it is never antiquated. It surpasses in interest and value "all the ancient and modern classics combined" (Philip Schaff, *History of the Christian Church,* 1:572). This phenomenon confirms in its own way the Bible's unique character.

Historical Credentials. First, the matter of preservation is significant. Although the original copies of Scripture are not extant (undoubtedly providentially), over 5,000 ancient handwritten manuscripts of whole or parts of the NT alone have been recovered, some as old as A.D. second century. The miracle of preservation is seen in that 10 or 15 manuscripts are a good number for an ancient classic. We are assured a high degree of certainty about the original text from these manuscripts, with the Bible's message preserved 100 percent intact.

Second, the Bible's phenomenal record of translation into other languages is unparalleled. The Bible's first translation was the Septuagint, two centuries or more before Christ. Since that time, the Bible has been translated into virtually every written language of modern times (1,685 translations as of 1980), as well as pioneering efforts to reduce many unwritten languages to writing.

Third, the Bible's historical influence justifies its claim to divine origin. No other book has attracted so much attention, been so minutely studied, had so much written about it, been so keenly assailed, inspired so many noble thoughts and deeds, or transformed so many lives. The magnitude of the Bible's influence is incalculable. "To tell all the Bible has been or done for the world would be to rewrite in large part the history of modern civilization" (*ISBE,* 1:468).

Finally, archaeology continues to unearth ancient artifacts which confirm or support the Bible's historical credibility. The 1975 discovery of the Ebla Tablets in Syria is a recent example.

Supernatural Credentials. Since supernaturalism transcends the natural order, it cannot be tested by the scientific method. Many scholars, therefore, view the suggestion of supernatural credentials as circular reasoning. If divine revelation is necessarily supernatural, however, it follows that the occasions of God's intervention in history are supernatural in character. Miracles, prophecy, and the incarnation of Christ are three examples. The biblical concept of miracle is an intervention by God in the established course of nature as part of His outworking of redemption. The incarnation of Christ is the supreme miracle. Prophecy is the intervention of God in the realm of knowledge. Miracles, prophecy, and the incarnation of Christ are all demonstrative and supernatural manifestations of God in history which convey truth and certitude. Even the capstone of the Incarnation miracle, Jesus' resurrection, was accompanied "by many convincing proofs" (Acts 1:3, NASB). God's supernatural acts are one with the written Word and attest its true character.

The Witness of the Spirit. To the self-attestation of the Bible and the weight of combined evidence, we must add the inward testimony of the Holy Spirit. Wiley states: "The strongest evidence for the authority of the Scriptures is to be found in the fact that the Spirit of Inspiration, to whom we are indebted for the authorship of the Bible, is Himself the Divine Witness to its genuineness and authenticity" (Wiley, *CT,* 1:206). Ultimately, only the faculty of faith through the witness of the Spirit can fully discern God's Word for what it is—infallible truth and divine authority (see 1 Cor. 2:14, NASB).

See MIRACLES, BIBLE.

For Further Reading: Bruce, *The New Testament Documents: Are They Reliable?;* Henry, ed., *Revelation and the Bible;* Wiley, *CT,* 1:147-66, 177-82, 205-14; Taylor, *Biblical Authority and Christian Faith.*

J. WESLEY ADAMS

CREDULITY. See SUPERSTITION.

CREED, CREEDS. A creed is "a brief authoritative doctrinal formula" confessed within the Christian church. The term is from the Latin *credo,* "I believe." Other synonymous terms are "Symbol" (Council of Trent), "Confession" (Westminster Confession), "Articles of Religion" (The 39 Articles), and "Articles of Faith" (*Manual,* Church of the Nazarene). A creed is an affirmation with others in the fellowship of the church, for, like the Scriptures, a creed is not of "private interpretation" (2 Pet. 1:20), but rather affirms those truths which, from the perspective of its composers, ought to be held universally in the church and which are judged essential for redemption and sanctification. A creed may also condemn those errors deemed destructive to faith. Thus the Nicene Creed (A.D. 325) affirmed the deity of Christ and anathematized the Arians who taught that Christ, though preexistent, was created and was not from all eternity.

Although some creeds are conciliatory in nature (e.g., "The Definition of Chalcedon," A.D. 451), others have been devisive in intent, seeking to exclude all who did not hold to a narrowly defined theology (e.g., "The Anathemas of the Second Council of Constantinople," A.D. 553). This pattern of defining and excluding continued through the Reformation. The tendency of modern creeds is merely to affirm those doctrines judged as essential without denouncing those Christians who do not affirm them.

The Apostles' Creed, the one most universally held, is also the oldest. Legend ascribed this to a special outpouring on the apostles 10 days after Pentecost. Contemporary scholarship traces its origin to Rome at the end of the second century. Its oldest extant version is the "Creed of Hippolytus" (c. A.D. 215). Its present form dates from A.D. 700.

Creeds have their origin in creedlike formulas in the Scriptures. An OT confession begins, "We were Pharaoh's slaves in Egypt; and the Lord brought us out of Egypt with a mighty hand" (cf. Deut. 6:21-25; 26:5-10, RSV). Paul's confession in 1 Cor. 15:3-8 is a creedal affirmation of his identification with the Church: "For I delivered to you as of first importance what I also received, that Christ died for our sins in accordance with the scriptures, that he was buried, that he was raised on the third day in accordance with the scriptures" (RSV).

The early Christian affirmed his faith in God the Creator, in his resurrected Lord, and in the Holy Spirit by repeated affirmation of the creed. Affirmation by repetition was part of the Church's heritage from the OT: the Israelite was commanded to make a "response before the Lord your God" by reciting God's mighty deeds (Deut. 26:5). In the NT, the principle of repetition is expressed in Paul's account of the Lord's Supper: "'Do this in remembrance of me.' . . . For as often as you eat this bread and drink the cup, you proclaim the Lord's death until he comes" (cf. 1 Cor. 11:23-26, RSV). Similarly, through its creeds, the ongoing Church affirms its trust in God, identifies with its past, proclaims its present unity in its Lord, and seeks to serve and prepare the future Church.

The Church has used the Trinitarian form of the Apostles' Creed for pastoral preaching and for systematic exposition of the gospel. This practice is rooted in the Bible where two standard confessions serve as outlines for preaching. The old covenant affirmation of (1) God's call to Abraham, Isaac, and Jacob; (2) the deliverance from Egypt; (3) the gift of the Law; (4) the gift of the land; and (5) the gift of promise of a righteous King served as a sermonic outline even into NT times (Deut. 6:5-11; Neh. 9:7-37; Psalms 78; 105—6; Acts 7; 13:17-25). The new covenant affirmed Jesus' Davidic lineage; His life, death, and resurrection; and His exaltation as Messiah, Lord, and Son of God (Acts 13:17-25; Rom. 1:3-6). Using these as outlines, the prophets and apostles proclaimed judgment, deliverance, repentance, and sanctification. The Apostles' Creed was used as a lesson outline in the instruction of new Christians and was the framework for the teachings of Justin Martyr, Irenaeus, Tertullian, Clement, Origen, and Augustine, the theologians of the Early Church.

See APOSTLES' CREED, CATECHISM.

For Further Reading: Leith, *Creeds of the Churches;* Wiley, *CT,* 1:28-30, 39-48; Barclay, *The Apostles' Creed for Every Man,* 9-20; Schaff, *Creeds of Christendom,* vol. 3; Karl Barth, *Credo.*

DAVID L. CUBIE

CRISIS. The term *crisis* as used herein refers to a critical turning point in one's religious life. Negatively, a crisis of conviction and confrontation with God may issue in a decisive rejection of God's claims. Positively, it is in a crisis of repentance and faith that the new birth occurs. Similarly, entire sanctification is a crisis experience. Such crises initiate new and advanced states of grace.

The crucial nature of sanctification is seen in the terms used in the presentation and consideration of it. The verb "sanctify" means to separate, cleanse, purify, consecrate. These words imply clean-cut, decisive actions, not imperceptible gradualism. Often "sanctify" appears in the punctiliar (and completed) aorist tense (e.g., John 17:17; 1 Thess. 5:23).

The following verbs in Acts all appear in the aorist tense, and they all have reference to the coming of the Holy Spirit. The words are "filled" (2:4), "fell" (10:44), "came" (19:6). It is acknowledged that in Acts 8:17, the verb "received" is in the imperfect tense; and in Eph. 5:18, the verb "filled" is in the present tense. However, both are in the plural. Daniel Steele writes, "We have looked in vain to find one of these verbs in the imperfect tense when individuals are spoken of" (*Milestone Papers,* 72). The same may be said of the present.

The word "baptize" (Acts 1:5) refers to an event. "Crucifixion" as a means of death may be sudden or slow, but it is always certain and indicates an event (Rom. 6:6). The terms "root out," "kill," and "destroy" add weight to the position. "When now we summarize all these words, we gain an almost irresistible impression of climax, epoch, or crisis: . . . All of these terms describe actions which most naturally take place at a definite time and place, and which do not admit of degrees" (Purkiser, ed., *Exploring Our Christian Faith,* 359-60).

See SECOND WORK OF GRACE, ENTIRE SANCTIFICATION.

For Further Reading: Geiger, *Further Insights into Holiness,* 123-38; Purkiser, ed., *Exploring Our Christian Faith,* 350-64; Steele, *Milestone Papers,* 41-46.

O. D. LOVELL

CRISIS THEOLOGY. See NEOORTHODOXY.

CRITICISM, NT. New Testament criticism is forming judgments about historical, literary, textual, or philological questions on the basis of the available data. The science neither requires nor excludes faith in God and in the supernatural character of the Word of God. Those who insist that the Bible is solely the word of man tend to sit in judgment on the veracity and authenticity of the documents. Those who accept the Bible as the Word of God submit to its authority and use criticism to understand better how the Word came and what it means.

The historical-critical approach offends many conservatives because of the dominance of the Age of Reason influence in the development of the science over the past two centuries. Assuming that the supernatural and the miraculous are mythical and have no part in historical research, the rationalists found little historical evidence for a true Word of God. "Rationalism set man firmly on the throne and all else, revelation included, was expected to bow to him" (Guthrie, *Biblical Criticism, Historical, Literary, and Textual,* 86). Werner Kümmel systematically illustrates the assumption that a comprehensive historical consideration of the NT could only come to those who are free from all dogmatic bias (*The New Testament: The History of the Investigation of Its Problems,* 51).

Some reject historical criticism as unnecessary and destructive. Others wisely insist on subjecting their judgments to all the data, including the supernatural. Richard S. Taylor makes a distinction between the so-called historical-critical, as popularly treated, and the historico-grammatical, which accepts the Scriptures as true and unique (*Biblical Authority and Christian Faith,* 70).

Source criticism attempts to discover the data available to the writers of the NT documents. Literary and historical studies create and illustrate a variety of hypotheses. Many theories are at conscious variance with the traditional understanding of Scripture and the testimony of church fathers.

Form criticism attempts to identify sources by studying the form of the fragments of Gospel data and reconstructing documents that may have been available to the compilers of the Gospels. Many are convinced of the so-called priority of Mark, Matthew's and Luke's use of "Q," and the creative genius of the Early Church in the production of the Gospels. Other scholars find these "assured results" inconclusive. It is objected that the gospel produced the Early Church —not vice versa. The late dates of the Gospels are inconclusive. Apostles and/or their associates could have been alive to write the documents. The Holy Spirit could have brought to their remembrance the data from their Lord. Granting the miraculous and the prophetic, the Gospels could be faithful reports of proper witnesses, as in the traditional scriptural view.

Redaction criticism attempts to answer the questions that baffled form criticism (Simon Kistemaker, *The Gospels in Current Study,* 50). The emphasis moved from fragments of form to the aims and purposes of the individual Evangelists. The possibility reappears of a man with a message and a method. Those who deny the supernatural must settle for brilliant human authors of the NT books. Christian believers may identify the writers as faithful witnesses speaking from Jesus Christ through the inspiration of the Holy Spirit.

Textual criticism compares the thousands of manuscripts of NT documents to identify and eliminate copyist errors in the Greek text. While the task is not completed, we do have God's Word in a form that is reliable and remarkably faithful to the documents as they must have come from God and His servants.

See BIBLICAL CRITICISM, EXEGESIS, TEXTUAL CRITICISM, CRITICISM (OT).

For Further Reading: Harrison, Waltke, Guthrie, Fee, *Biblical Criticism: Historical, Literary, and Textual,* 85-155; Kistemaker, *The Gospels in Current Study,* 21-129; Taylor, *Biblical Authority and Christian Faith,* 69-83; Ladd, *The New Testament and Criticism;* Guthrie, *New Testament Introduction,* 121-236, 643-84; Kümmel, *The New Testament: The History of the Investigation of Its Problems,* 15-120.

WILBER T. DAYTON

CRITICISM, OT. Biblical criticism in general is the scholarly study of the Bible and does not necessarily involve the negative connotation of "criticism."

"Lower" criticism is concerned with textual readings and seeks to recover the originals as exactly as possible by careful comparison of manuscript copies and versions.

"Higher" criticism is concerned with matters of authorship, integrity, and reliability of the biblical materials.

Old Testament lower criticism has been radically affected by the discovery of the Dead Sea Scrolls in 1947 ff at Wadi Qumran on the northwest shore of the Dead Sea. The scrolls date from around 200 B.C. and include about 100 OT manuscripts representing all OT books except Esther. The discovery provided biblical manuscripts over 1,000 years nearer the autographs than any previously known, and has had the overall effect of strengthening confidence in the essential accuracy of the so-called Massoretic or standard Hebrew text of the OT.

Old Testament higher criticism is divided roughly into two approaches:

1. Scholarship based largely on naturalistic presuppositions. OT religion is conceived as subject to development on evolutionary principles, and OT documents are evaluated as secular documents would be. Such criticism in the modern period may be said to have begun with Baruch Spinoza (1632-77), known as "the father of higher criticism." H. B. Witter in 1711 and Jean Astruc in 1753 began the documentary analysis of the Pentateuch, based in part on the use of different divine names.

The documentary hypothesis developed in the 19th century in association with the work of Hupfeld, K. H. Graf, and Julius Wellhausen, and resulted in the analysis of the Pentateuch into four or more documents usually labelled J (Jahwistic), E (Elohistic), D (Deuteronomic), and P (Priestly).

Early in the 20th century, Hermann Gunkel and a group of German scholars pioneered a type of "form criticism" which seeks to understand the OT in terms of the oral tradition underlying it, its relationships with the literature of other ancient religions, and a study of the literary forms employed.

2. Another approach to OT higher criticism is the reverent, scholarly study of these materials which gives credence to the element of divine inspiration and the supernaturalistic aspect of biblical faith (2 Tim. 3:15-17; 2 Pet. 1:21).

Conservative OT scholars have been open to positive values that have come from the work of those with whose basic positions they did not agree, but have insisted that criticism itself must submit to the examination of its presuppositions. The current search for a biblical theology has, on balance, done more to justify the conservative than the liberal attitude.

See CRITICISM (NT), BIBLICAL CRITICISM, TEXTUAL CRITICISM, DEAD SEA SCROLLS.

For Further Reading: DeVries, "Biblical Criticism," *IDB,* 1:407-18; Kraeling, *The Old Testament Since the Reformation;* Orr, "Criticism of the Bible," *ISBE,* 2:748-53; Terrien, "History of the Interpretation of the Bible, Modern Period," *Interpreter's Bible,* 1:127-41.

W. T. PURKISER

CROSS. Very early the Cross became the predominant symbol of Christianity. It was *the* mark of Christianity's identity. It is difficult today to appreciate how miraculous was the transformation in people's thinking about the Cross. Once a symbol of shame and ignominy, the Cross became the impetus to adoration and worship. This diabolical and ugly instrument of torturous execution was glorified as the altar where a holy God and sinful man could meet.

What made this Cross so different? Concisely stated: Jesus was Victor and not victim! He went to the Cross voluntarily, deliberately—and consciously. Christ not only set His face like a flint to go to Jerusalem, but even more, to the Cross (Phil. 2:5-11). He knew that the end of His mission was a cross, and He freely spoke of it to His disciples. Yet, He was no martyr who simply died—even willingly—for a noble cause. He died there for a lost race. As this was increasingly realized through the ministry of the Holy Spirit, the Cross was transformed into the cherished symbol of the Church.

When we attempt to explain the meaning of that vicarious Cross-death, we discover the inadequacy of our understanding. It is clear that in the Cross there is in some sense an atonement for man's sin. It must be more than what is popularly called "at-one-ment" with God. Technical theories of the Atonement have made their appearance in the Church from the time of the Apostolic Fathers to our 20th century. None of them totally satisfies the mind *and heart.* Metaphors, such as "ransom," "redeem," "sacrifice," "expiation," "propitiation," "satisfaction," and "substitution" have limitations often reflecting the immediate culture in which they were born. What speaks to people in one day often fails to bridge the culture gap of a later age.

One thing would seem of primary importance: the meaning of the Cross to the Early Church. That meaning must be ascertained before one can adequately relate the Cross and its atonement to our day. Without fear or apology, the first preachers of the Cross accepted and even proclaimed its scandal! "For the word of the Cross is to those who are perishing foolishness, but to us who are being saved it is the power of God" (1 Cor. 1:18, NASB). It is increasingly popular to view the Cross today as *simply* the supreme expression of God's love (cf. John 3:16)—but it is more, far more!

Mahatma Gandhi described the dynamic of his nonviolence as "love force." History eloquently witnesses to that force. The power of love, in the Cross, destroys the barrier that man's sin has erected—isolating him from God. In the simplest terms, the Cross is seen—in the NT—as the only basis of man's acceptance with God (*Newness of Life,* 77). Then, in union with God, man discovers the supernatural dynamic for victorious living in three dimensions: internal, with oneself; horizontal, with others; vertical, with God.

See CRUCIFIXION, ATONEMENT, BLOOD, DEATH OF CHRIST.

For Further Reading: Barclay, *The Mind of Jesus;* Howard, *Newness of Life,* chap. 8; Morris, *The Apostolic Preaching of the Cross; Glory in the Cross;* Moule, *The Sacrifice of Christ.* RICHARD E. HOWARD

CROSS-BEARING. This term is significant in the NT and in theology because of the obvious relationship it has to the Cross upon which Jesus was crucified. Crucifixion was a horribly painful and slow death. It was not a capital punishment technique of the Jews, but the Romans made widespread use of this form of execution.

Jesus said, "Whosoever doth not bear his cross, and come after me, cannot be my disciple" (Luke 14:27). This must be understood metaphorically. He could hardly have meant that one must bear the entire cross, especially when the upright stake was rather permanently set in the ground at crucifixion sites. The horizontal piece of the cross could be carried by the victim. However, this is not the thought in Luke 9:23, where disciples are challenged to "take up [their] cross daily." The intent is certainly expressed figuratively.

There are five references to cross-bearing in the Synoptic Gospels. The term *airō* (Greek: to lift, carry, take up, or take away) is used in three instances (Matt. 16:24; Mark 8:34; Luke 9:23). The word *bastazō* (Greek: carry, bear) is used in Luke 14:27, and *lambanō* (Greek: take up, carry, take along) is used in Matt. 10:38. The sayings in Matt. 10:38 and Luke 14:27 came in a series of statements describing the conditions of discipleship. As Jesus the Master died on a cross, so His disciples must live sacrificial lives. His disciples take up their own crosses. The Cross is the ensign of Christian discipleship.

The majority of the Synoptic Gospel references to cross-bearing are placed after Peter's confession and the first suggestion of the passion. Cross-bearing is inescapably linked to suffering for the disciples. Bonhoeffer said it most succinctly, "When Christ calls a man, He bids him come and die."

Cross-bearing proves to be the singular way to triumph over suffering. Through Christ's suffering the whole universe will be restored and enhanced. The pathway to blessing is the way of suffering for the one who suffers and for others who benefit from the life of the sufferer.

The true disciple of Christ does not seek to suffer, but suffering should be no surprise to one who follows Jesus. The Christian will not avoid suffering when it is encountered along the path of obedience to the will of God and identification with his Lord. The consecration of a true disciple includes suffering and death when faithful service demands it.

See CROSS, CRUCIFIXION, OBEDIENCE, DISCIPLESHIP, IN CHRIST.

For Further Reading: Bonhoeffer, *The Cost of Discipleship,* 70-77; Morris, *The Cross in the New Testament,* 25-26; Schwiezer, *The Good News According to Mark,* 174-80; Weber, *The Cross.*

KENNETH E. HENDRICK

CROWN. Crowns of kings and priests symbolized honor and authority. The Hebrew term for "crown" in Exod. 29:6; 2 Kings 11:12; and other passages, means "dedicated" or "consecrated," for the office had sacred character. Leadership over people was stewardship under God. Crowns were inscribed "Holy to the Lord," and crowning was accompanied by anointing, indicating God's Spirit as the Source of the wearer's right to exercise authority.

"Crown" is used metaphorically in the OT. Examples: Man is crowned with glory and honor by the Creator (Ps. 8:5); the harvest is God's crown upon the year (65:11); the hoary head is a crown of glory (Prov. 16:31); and a noble wife is her husband's crown (12:4).

Most NT references to crowns employ the Greek word *stephanos* symbolically. Willing athletes were crowned with perishable wreaths, but Christians who persevere will receive an incorruptible, unfading crown (1 Cor. 9:24-25; 1 Pet. 5:4).

The crown rewards victory over sin, and fidelity in service. The "crown of righteousness" (2 Tim. 4:8) means a crown appropriate to a righteous person—to the eternal righteousness he will enjoy. The "crown of life" (Jas. 1:12; Rev.

2:10) is associated with endurance of trials even unto death. The Chief Shepherd rewards faithful undershepherds with the "crown of glory" (1 Pet. 5:2-5).

These crowns await Christ's coming. Similarly, Paul's converts are his crown, for their appearance in glory with Christ will be his reward (1 Thess. 2:19; Phil. 4:1).

The royal crown *(diadēma)* appears in Revelation, worn by evil rulers (12:3; 13:1) and by Christ, who defeats and destroys them (19:12).

One tragic crown is mentioned, the "crown of thorns" forced upon Jesus' head (Matt. 27:29) to intensify His suffering. It became a symbol of quenchless, atoning love. His the crown of thorns, ours the crown of glory. Such is the grace of God!

See MAJESTY, REWARDS, ETERNAL LIFE.

For Further Reading: *IDB*, 1:745-46; Kittel, 7:615-36.

W. E. MCCUMBER

CRUCIFIXION. In both its verb and noun forms this term occurs over 50 times in the NT, thus indicating something of its importance in Christian history and theology.

Crucifixion, as a form of capital punishment, goes as far back as the Assyrian Empire, when victims were impaled upon stakes or posts and left to die. By the Persians and Seleucids the stake became a cross. It is believed the Romans borrowed it from the Carthaginians and made it their favorite method of torture for slaves and criminals. It was not used on Roman citizens because it was too cruel and shameful. Julius Caesar crucified the pirates who had captured him. Crassus crucified 6,000 rebellious slaves and left them to rot along the Appian Way south of Rome. Augustus claimed to have crucified 30,000 fugitive slaves. Two thousand followers of Judas of Galilee were captured and crucified by the Roman general Varus.

Recent excavations near Jerusalem by archaeologists of Israel have recovered the bones of one crucified early in the first Christian century, the only such victim thus far recovered. In this case the feet were fastened by one large spike driven through both ankles into a piece of wood.

The *Tau* cross was common and consisted of an upright with a beam on the top at right angles. Sometimes the upright portion extended above the crossbeam and was used to support a sign indicating the identity of the victim and his crime. The hands were fastened by cords or nails driven through the wrist (to prevent pulling loose); the feet were secured in a similar fashion. The victim was left to die of thirst and starvation—usually in 40 hours or more. Pilate marveled that Jesus died the same day of His crucifixion (Mark 15:44). The breaking of the legs was the means used to hasten death (John 19:31-33) because it prevented the victim's rising in order to breathe. If supported only by the arms, death by asphyxiation would come quickly. It was the most shameful and cruel way of dealing with offenders; shameful for Jews because it implied a curse (Deut. 21:23; Gal. 3:13). It was also considered disgraceful by the Romans and used only for the worst offenses. By the time of the Emperor Constantine (called a Christian by many), it was abolished because it was then considered disdainful to Christianity.

Theologically, the Crucifixion focused on Jesus' vicarious or substitutionary death for mankind, and the Cross became the revered and widely used symbol of the faith. Its use spread to the West, where gradually it emphasized the sufferings of Christ and popularized the crucifix as the object of devotion.

The Cross, in addition to the Eucharist, focused attention increasingly on Jesus' death and its ghastly and revolting mode. Increasingly the Cross lost its shameful connotation, and "the old rugged Cross," instead of being "the emblem of suffering and shame," occasioned many to sing "In the cross of Christ I glory." Recent church history has followed this development. As the NT insists, the most distinctive element in Christian theology is Jesus' death and resurrection. The Cross is involved in discipleship. Paul could write, "I am crucified with Christ" (Gal. 2:20). Yet he always balanced the death of Christ with the resurrection of Christ; the negative and positive were kept in equipoise.

See CROSS, BLOOD OF CHRIST, CHRIST, ATONEMENT.

For Further Reading: Holzmeister, *Crux Domini;* Goguel, *The Life of Jesus;* Morris, *The Cross in the New Testament;* N. Hass, "Anthropological Observations on the Skeletal Remains from Giv'at ha Mivtar," *Israel Exploration Journal* 20:51-59.

GEORGE ALLEN TURNER

CULTS. Traditionally the word *cult (cultus)* has been a neutral term meaning simply the sum of liturgical forms and manifestations of a religious movement. The cult of Christianity, for example, is characterized by the singing of hymns, preaching, the saying of prayers, the building of churches, etc.

More recently the term has taken on a pejorative connotation suggesting exclusiveness, disaffection with established religious values and practices, and heterodoxy, if not heresy. Thus the term is now used more popularly for religious movements which are strongly sectarian and also distinctive for their conspicuous devotion to a particular doctrinal position or leader. Such devotion is usually defended on the grounds that the doctrine or leader expresses a rediscovery or a reemphasizing of fundamental religious truth which, according to the cult, establishment religion has suppressed. Typically, therefore, the cult assumes an adversary position with broader religious sentiments.

Anthony A. Hoekema *(The Four Major Cults)*, following the German author Kurt Hutten, distinguishes five major characteristics of the cult: (1) an extrascriptural source of authority—"a Bible in the left hand"; (2) the denial of justification by grace alone; (3) the devaluation of Christ; (4) the group as the exclusive community of the saved; and (5) the group's central role in eschatology.

Hoekema's characteristics apply when the movement being described purports to share certain Judeo-Christian presuppositions (for example, the authority of Scripture). The gain in strength of Eastern religions which do not share these presuppositions requires that the characteristics of the cult be redefined, since in popular usage these religions too are sometimes designated as cults. The hallmark of the cult, whether or not it shares any Judeo-Christian presuppositions, is absolutism. The absolutism of the cult demands extraordinary commitment from its members. In return it provides a strong sense of community (belonging) and an uncritical assurance of authority in matters of doctrine and conduct.

Attempts to explain the emergence and strength of cults on sociological grounds have had mixed success. Nevertheless certain constants can be demonstrated. Cults seem to be the issue of periods of social instability. Their origins are more often urban than rural. And they often function in contention with secular values and authorities. Also, many evangelicals believe the mushrooming popularity of cults is a sign of the end times (cf., e.g., 1 Tim. 4:1-3).

The approach of the Christian to a member of a cult must be replete with understanding. The cult is attractive because of its absolutism. No major question of life and faith is allowed to remain unanswered. To challenge any answer, however questionable it may be, is to challenge the absolute wisdom and authority of the cult and thus to challenge the entire world view and life-style of its members.

The consistent theological flaw of the cultic mentality from the perspective of the Judeo-Christian tradition is the tendency to promise knowledge *about* God in place of the knowledge *of* God. Thus the cult protects its position as the only and essential intermediary and dispensary of theological truth, without being able to bring its members into that saving, life-changing personal relationship with the crucified and resurrected Christ, which is the hallmark of authentic Christianity.

See HERESY, CREED (CREEDS), CHRIST, CHURCH, SALVATION.

For Further Reading: Hoekema, *The Four Major Cults;* Starkes, *Confronting Popular Cults.*

DANIEL N. BERG

CULTURE. *Culture* is the summary term for a whole way of life, material, intellectual, and spiritual. Originally culture was simply a biological term signifying the care and tending of natural growth. The appropriateness of the term to the development of human powers was obvious, and the educated or sophisticated person came to be called the "cultured" person. During the 19th century, culture was applied as a social term encompassing the material, intellectual, and spiritual values which served to distinguish societies from each other.

The evolution of the usage of culture has created a significant change. The simple amorality of culture used biologically was swallowed up in the sociological use of the term. Culture, in this latter usage, denotes a repository of values (including moral, religious, and political values).

Thus where two cultures differ, the differences are not infrequently substantial and significant. A biblical example is the conflict of Hebrew and Hellenistic values in the intertestamental and NT periods. Cultural conflict is inherent in a missionary religion. Its manifestation is a challenge of authority. In particular, universal applicability is denied certain cherished absolutes of either culture. What had been perceived as absolute is made to appear in more tentative light.

Although the Christian experience of cultural conflict is very old, the attempt to deal with it has only recently received a systematic analysis. Cultural monism represents one attempt, cultural pluralism another, and cultural relativism still another.

Cultural monism cannot, perhaps because it will not, identify as culturally conditioned and, at best, fortuitous, certain elements in its expression of Christian faith. The immediate culture becomes identical with Christian faith, and the spread of the gospel implies a corresponding spread of the culture.

Cultural pluralism attempts to distinguish essentially Christian elements from culturally conditioned elements in the expression of Christian faith. It tolerates differences so long as the essential elements of Christian faith remain intact. Any challenges are directed not against whole cultures but against elements of the culture which are perceived to be clearly anti-Christian.

Cultural relativism is the most tolerant of cultural variation. Culture itself is conceived to be the absolute. The legitimacy of the Christian faith is determined by the ability of the faith to maintain and enhance the authentic values of a culture.

See CHRISTIAN LIFE, LIFE-STYLE, ANTHROPOLOGY, MISSIONS.

For Further Reading: Franco, *The Challenge of the Other Americans;* Williams, *Culture and Society, 1950-1970;* Niebuhr, *Christ and Culture;* Taylor, *A Return to Christian Culture.* DANIEL N. BERG

CULTURE, PERSONAL. As used in this article, the term means a high level of personal development, including the acquisition of manners, tastes, skills, and personal bearing, which are in conformity to the highest standards of the society in which one lives. Culture thus includes the aesthetic, social, vocational, and communicative facets of life. A cultured person has a reasonable mastery of his language, a trained mind and trained hands, and an above average perception of beauty and excellence. He is a gentleman, and she is a lady, both in heart and manner. A cultured person is productive, not parasitical; is disciplined, not flabby; is socially sensitive, not callous; and is refined and gentle, not loud, crude, or boorish.

Christian culture is culture which is judged by Christ and conformed to Christ. Christ judges culture through the Scriptures as illuminated by the Spirit. Much in our respective societal cultures can be sanctified; in fact, the Christian *should* conform. As John Wesley pointed out, there is no virtue in being different to the point of singularity, just for the sake of being different, when no ethical issue is involved. Yet much is pagan, completely incompatible with Christian holiness; therefore the Word commands, "Be not conformed to this world" (Rom. 12:2; cf. Phillips). Christians must be honest in seeking intelligently to discern what Christ can use. Moreover, even within the framework of the legitimate, it is the duty of the Christian to distinguish between "good, better, best," and seek that which excels (Phil. 1:11).

To conform culture to Christ is to make sure that it is Christlike in its inner holiness, redemptive in its motivation, and loving in its relationships. Since culture includes one's total life-style, it is obvious that it should honor Christ, not dishonor Him. Becoming cultured, therefore, is an expression of devotion and also a matter of stewardship. Poor culture is poor stewardship, as truly as mismanagement of money or time.

See CULTURE, GROWTH, CHARACTER, WITNESS, RESPECT.

For Further Reading: Niebuhr, *Christ and Culture;* Taylor, *A Return to Christian Culture.*

RICHARD S. TAYLOR

CUP. The "cup," in biblical metaphor, connotes a vessel containing either salvation or judgment. The Psalmist rejoiced as his "cup of blessing" overflowed (Ps. 23:5). "I will lift up the cup of salvation and call on the name of the Lord" (116:13, RSV). Paul, in like manner, exclaimed, "The cup of blessing . . . is it not a participation in the blood of Christ?" (1 Cor. 10:16, RSV). The "cup" therefore is linked with the "fruit of the vine" in the Lord's Supper or Eucharist. Jesus is quoted as saying, "This cup is the new covenant in my blood" (11:25, RSV; cf. Luke 22:20).

The "cup" may also designate judgment. In the language of the Apocalypse, worshippers of "the beast" will drink the wine of God's wrath, "poured unmixed into the cup of his anger" (Rev. 14:10, RSV; cf. 16:19). In Gethsemane Jesus prayed, "My Father . . . let this cup pass from me" (Matt. 26:39, RSV). Here the "cup" from which Jesus shrank has the connotation of judgment against sin.

This usage has its roots in OT imagery. "In the hand of the Lord there is a cup, with foaming wine, well mixed; and he will pour a draught from it, and all the wicked of the earth shall drain it down to the dregs" (Ps. 75:8, RSV). The same metaphor is repeatedly used by the prophets to symbolize God's wrath. The Lord is pictured as compelling the nations to get drunk, vomit, and stagger in disgrace (Isa. 51:17, 22; Jer. 25:15-28; 49:12; 51:7; Ezek. 23:31-33; Hab. 2:15-16; Zech. 12:2). Judgment is likened to a drunken stupor.

See HOLY COMMUNION, SUFFER (SUFFERING), JUDGMENT, GETHSEMANE.

For Further Reading: Leenhardt, *Le Sacrement de la Sainte Cene,* 43-45; Cranfield, *Expository Times,* 59 (1947-48), 137 ff. GEORGE ALLEN TURNER

CURSE. The main biblical vocabulary of curse consists of three Hebrew synonyms and the Greek words *katara* and *anathema.* In Scripture a curse is "a directly expressed or indicated utterance which in virtue of a supernatural nexus of operation brings harm by its very expression to the one against whom it is directed" (Friedrich Büchsel). Two kinds of curses may be distinguished in Scripture: (1) the curse initiated by God, and (2) the curse initiated by man.

The Divine Curse. The first divine curse occurred at the Fall when God pronounced curses on the serpent, the woman, and the man (Gen. 3:14-19). As on this occasion, God's curse is always a judicial action—i.e., an expression of divine judgment related to the consequences of sin or disobedience. God's ultimate curse is stated in Gen. 2:17 and affects all of Adam's descendants. The covenant curses and blessings were designed to protect the covenantal agreement between Yahweh and the Hebrew people (Deut. 27:15-26; 28:15-36).

The Horizontal Curse. On the horizontal plane, man may curse another man. In the OT, curses were employed against such persons as murderers (Gen. 4:11-12; 49:6-7; 2 Sam. 3:29), sexual offenders (Gen. 9:25-27; 49:4), and enemies who might inflict harm in the future (2 Sam. 18:32; Job 27:7; Dan. 4:16) or had already inflicted hurt (Ps. 35:4-8; 40:15-16; 109:6-15, 17-19, 29; Jer. 11:20; 12:3; 17:18). Curses were effective only when the word was backed by the power of the soul; otherwise they were "only empty words" (2 Kings 18:20, NASB). The horizontal curse served "to castigate and chastise, to protect, and to punish" (S. Gevirtz). When the human curse is directed against God, it is blasphemy (Job 1:5, 11; 2:5, 9).

New Testament Emphasis. In keeping with the spirit of the new age, the human curse is rare in the NT. Since God forbids men to initiate divine judgment, Christians are forbidden to curse others (Rom. 12:14, 19; cf. Matt. 5:44; Luke 6:28; Jas. 3:9-10).

Furthermore, the curse—like most NT topics—has a definite Christological significance under the new covenant. Inasmuch as the curse of the law affects all who do not abide in the commandments of the law (Gal. 3:10), there is none righteous (Rom. 3:9-10, 19-20). Consequently, the whole of sinful humanity is subjected to the law's curse—i.e., God's wrath and judgment. Christ, in His substitutionary death on the Cross, bore the curse for us and thereby redeems us from the curse of the law (Gal. 3:13). Now instead of the curse, there is the blessing of Abraham, sonship, and eternal life through faith in Christ. For the one who rejects Christ, however, there remains the curse, judgment, and eternal damnation.

See JUDGE, JUDGMENT, PUNISHMENT, ANGER, REVENGE.

For Further Reading: Büchsel, Kittel, 1:448-51; Gevirtz, *IDB,* 1:749-50; Mundle, *NIDNTT,* 1:413-18; Payne, *The Theology of the Older Testament,* 201-3, 218-21.

J. WESLEY ADAMS

CUSTOM, CUSTOMS. The word *custom* refers to behavior patterns handed down by tradition and accepted by a whole society or by a particular class. Custom accepted and practiced over a long period of time may come to have the force of law as in English common law. Further, some customs may have the psychological force of moral law in a particular society, while others may be accepted as contributing to social cohesion but be considered morally indifferent. The apostle Paul was willing to conform to some customs for the sake of social harmony (Acts 21:21-26; Rom. 14:13-21; 1 Cor. 9:19-23), while rejecting others as incompatible with his new life in Christ (Rom. 12:2). William M. Greathouse points out that the consecrated, sanctified believer rejects the customs and behavior patterns of the age and by a divine transformation is guided by a "fresh and independent insight into moral realities" (*BBC,* 8:239-40).

Cyprian, bishop of Carthage, in the third century exhorted Christians not to be guided by custom but by truth contained in evangelical and apostolical tradition written in the Gospels and Epistles (esp. 74).

Luther rejected much of ecclesiastical custom as not conforming to the one true gospel faith and doctrine found in Holy Scripture (*A Compend of Luther's Theology,* 133). This leaves open the question whether it is enough for custom not to be against Scripture or whether it must be positively deduced from Scripture.

See NONCONFORMITY, CULTURE, SEPARATION, WORLDLINESS.

For Further Reading: *ERE,* 4:374-77; *New Catholic Encyclopedia,* 4:551-53; *BBC,* 8:239-40.

M. ESTES HANEY

D

DARKNESS. The Genesis account of creation sets forth a clear distinction between light and darkness. Darkness which once covered over the primeval waters continues to exist as a constituent part of the cosmos apart from light, God's first act of creation (Gen. 1:2-3). OT writers frequently equate darkness with wickedness, evil, and death (Job 23:17; Jer. 13:16; Deut. 28:29). In contrast to light which leads man to the knowledge of God and to a blessed life, darkness in human life is referred to as a wilful lack of knowledge of God's will and therefore the source of sinful actions (Job 24:13-17; Ps. 82:5; Isa. 29:15).

This OT theme receives a further development in the NT, particularly in the Johannine literature. Darkness is clearly equated with evil and therefore described as a natural condition of the world. Moreover, the world itself is darkness, and Jesus came into the world to give light to those who walk in darkness (John 8:12; cf. Isa. 9:2). Darkness is also the natural condition of the human heart (John 3:19; see also Matt. 6:23; Eph. 5:8-14).

The apostle Paul expounds this theme and argues that a conversion experience brings a person from darkness to light, an event analogous to God's creation of light out of darkness (2 Cor. 4:3-6; Acts 26:23). God's creative work in the life of a believer also includes deliverance from the dominion of darkness (Col. 1:13). Therefore it is possible to address the believers as "the saints in light" (v. 12), "sons of light" (1 Thess. 5:5), and "the light of the world" (Matt. 5:14). Yet there remains the possibility for a believer to return to darkness by his own sinful actions (2 Cor. 6:14; 1 John 1:6).

In the NT the term "darkness" also receives eschatological application. Those who continue to dwell under the dominion of darkness are destined for the underworld of gloom and eternal darkness (Matt. 8:12; 2 Pet. 2:17; Jude 6).

See LIGHT, EVIL, HELL.

For Further Reading: Kittel, 7:423-45; Westcott, *The Epistles of St. John,* 14-17.

ALEXANDER VARUGHESE

DARWINISM. This refers to the naturalistic evolution theory taught by Charles Darwin in his 1859 publication, *The Origin of Species.* It theorizes that all biological organisms have originated from some form of unicellular life which happened to begin to exist; and that a process of natural selection, in which the fittest members of each species tend to survive and to reproduce their kind, has resulted in all the species that did exist and all the present ones.

Darwin taught that animal life tends to reproduce itself according to the geometric ratio (2, 4, 16), whereas plant life, that which animal life so much needs for its survival, tends to reproduce itself only according to the arithmetic ratio (2, 4, 6, 8). Consequently, organisms tend to come into conflict with each other in order to obtain food supply. In this conflict, the weaker ones die and the fittest ones tend to survive and reproduce themselves.

The theory still enjoys at least a general kind of acceptance in the field of science; but evangelical Christianity has not accepted the view, teaching, instead, that God created each species—or, at least, each of the "kinds," of Genesis 1—2, which a few evangelicals think might mean families instead of species.

See EVOLUTION, THEISTIC EVOLUTION, NATURALISM, CREATION, CREATIONISM.

For Further Reading: Clark, *Darwin: Before and After;* Hoover, *Fallacies of Evolution.*

J. KENNETH GRIDER

DAVIDIC PROMISES. See PROMISES, DAVIDIC.

DAY OF ATONEMENT. The Day of Atonement, now known as Yom Kippur, was an annual festival in ancient Israel. It was held on the 10th day of the seventh month or Tishri (September-October). As described in Leviticus 16 (cf. 23:27-32 and Num. 29:7-11), it was the one day in the year when the high priest entered the holy of holies to atone for the sins of all Israel (v. 34).

It was a day of fasting and repentance, 24 hours in which no work was to be done (v. 29). At an assembly in the Tabernacle (later the Temple) special sacrifices were offered to make atonement for the priesthood (vv. 6, 11), the sanctuary (vv. 16, 18), and the people (vv. 30, 33).

In the first ceremony of the day's ritual the high priest sacrificed a bull for his own sinfulness and for that of the priesthood (v. 6). He then entered behind the veil of the holy of holies with a censer of incense (v. 13) and again with the blood to sprinkle it on the mercy seat (v. 14). In a second ceremony he sacrificed the goat which was "for the LORD" (v. 8) for the sins of the people, sprinkling its blood on the mercy seat (v. 15). Both rites served also for the cleansing of the sanctuary (vv. 16-19).

The high priest now took the second of the two goats which had been set before "the LORD" (vv. 7-10) and confessed over it the iniquities of the people. The goat was then sent away into the wilderness, carrying the sins of Israel (vv. 20-22; cf. 14:7, 51-53).

The entire OT sacrificial system as climaxed in the Day of Atonement furnishes a background for understanding the significance of the atoning death of Christ as presented in the NT. The letter to the Hebrews makes specific reference to the Day of Atonement as fulfilled and transcended in the self-offering of Jesus (9:7-15).

See SACRIFICE, ATONEMENT, SIN OFFERING.

For Further Reading: *Wycliffe Bible Encyclopedia,* 1:604 ff; *IDB,* 1:313-16; *The Broadman Bible Commentary,* 2:43-47; *The Jewish Encyclopedia,* 3:284-89; Bruce, *The Epistle to the Hebrews,* 181-224; Kaufmann, *The Religion of Israel,* 302-9.

FRANK G. CARVER

DAY OF THE LORD. The ancient Canaanites saw in the rhythm of the natural world, the ebb and flow of the tides and the recurring of the seasons, a human odyssey in a changeless recurrence of nature. The day that was important in their natural theology was New Year's Day. This day ushered in the new cycle in the eternal, changeless natural order. The day became a religious day, filled with worship and ritual. Moses and the prophets saw in the mighty acts of God a Lord of history, whose disciplining purpose was not mere repetition but the coming of God's kingdom over all the world. The day that was important to Israel's religious leaders was the one that would consummate time and history and so justify God's ways and will in the linear view of time.

Amos was the first of the prophets to refer to the Day of the Lord (Amos 5:18-20). Israel saw in this day the sovereignty of God over all the world and the glorification of Israel; therefore they eagerly awaited the day. Amos corrects their view and sees the day as a time of judgment upon a rebellious Israel whose power, wealth, and inordinate ambition made the nation self-deifying.

Joel 1:15; 2:1, 11, 31; 3:14-18 states that no such day had yet occurred in history. He saw in the locust plague and the ensuing drought previews of the Day of the Lord.

Zephaniah extends the Day of the Lord to cosmic proportions and sees both the historical and the apocalyptic aspects of that day.

The NT writers picked up the idea of the day and see in it the Day of Christ and speak of the Last Judgment and the glorious triumph of the kingdom of God.

See SECOND COMING OF CHRIST, LAST DAYS, JUDGE (JUDGMENT).

For Further Reading: Ludwigson, *A Survey of Bible Prophecy;* Biederwolf, *The Millennium Bible.*

FRED E. YOUNG

DAYS OF CREATION. In the Bible, "day" commonly means a time period of 24 hours, i.e., a solar day. It also suggests an epoch or an extended period of time like "day of trouble" (Ps. 20:1), a time of judgment and revelation (Matt. 10:15). The people of God are described as "children of the day" (1 Thess. 5:5), meaning that their lives reflect God's light. One of the most significant biblical phrases is the "day of the Lord" (v. 2; 2 Pet. 3:10), which has reference to a time of visitation from God.

The days of creation are first of all to be considered as historical, not mythical times. The Genesis record details the events of these days as within the context of the divine order which we call "natural." The order of God in creation is a progressive movement from the basic stuff of creation to the perfection of creation, beginning with the provision of light which is essential to photosynthesis. God created material space for physical life and movement, including both sea and dry land. Then God provided vegetable life which could not grow without light and water. The sun and the moon may be more specialized forms of light. Animal life is sustained by vegetable life. And, finally, when everything is congenial and ready for man, he is created. The seventh day is the day which crowns the whole creative epoch. God's creative work is complete, and the "theater of the divine glory" is set for the drama of human history. The thrust of these creative days is decisively oriented toward the human story. These are clearly not mythical nor ahistorical days.

Some of the interest in the "days of creation" centers upon the length of time intended by "day." Citing the Genesis record, "the evening and the morning were the first day," some interpret this literally as a 24-hour day. Others believe that "day" means an extended period of time. The Hebrew word *yom* is found some 1,480 times in the OT. It is translated "day," "time," "age," "forever," and "life." Wiley suggests that the word "day" refers to day-periods of indefinite duration. This could mean either solar days or extended periods of time. This position is more congenial to some form of theistic evolution, while the literal interpretation is more in accord with *fiat* creation. If the key accent of Genesis 1 is the glory of God and the divine origin of creation, then either interpretation is worthy. That appears to be the decisive point on which the analysis should turn.

See CREATION, EVOLUTION, THEISTIC EVOLUTION, CREATIONISM.

For Further Reading: Wiley, *CT,* 1:454-55; Berkhof, *Systematic Theology,* 152-55. LEON O. HYNSON

DEACON. The Greek word *diakonos* means "minister" or "servant." In its generic sense it applies to all ministers of the gospel as servants of God. More technically it refers to an order of church officers (Phil. 1:1; 1 Tim. 3:8), usually designated the *diaconate,* and subordinate to bishop-presbyters. The office had precedent in synagogue officers who collected and distributed alms. The NT diaconate is traditionally thought to have originated with the choosing of the seven to serve tables, recorded in Acts 6:1-6 (*New Schaff-Herzog Encyclopedia of Religious Knowledge,* 3:370).

After the direct apostolic supervision of the church ended, the permanent order of the ministry consisted of the *pastorate* and the *diaconate.* The pastorate had oversight of spiritual matters, the diaconate of temporal affairs (Wiley, *CT,* 3:132). Deacons were closely associated with and subordinate to presbyter-bishops and charged with ministering to the poor and the sick. Gradually comfort and instruction became a part of their ministry.

The postapostolic diaconate became a third order of the ministry below presbyters or priests and bishops. The deacon assisted the bishop and the presbyter in administering the sacraments and conducting public worship and largely lost the function of ministering to the poor.

In Lutheran churches deacons hold full orders and are distinguished by function only. In Reformed and Presbyterian churches their function is conducting the material affairs of the church, while in Baptist and Congregational churches they are assigned more spiritual functions (*ODCC,* 380).

See ELDER, CHURCH GOVERNMENT, MINISTER (MINISTRY).

For Further Reading: Schaff, *History of the Christian Church,* 1:499-501; Wiley, *CT,* 3:129-35.

M. ESTES HANEY

DEAD SEA SCROLLS. The Dead Sea Scrolls refer to the over 500 Hebrew, Greek, and Aramaic manuscripts discovered beginning in 1947 west of the Dead Sea. Among these manuscripts, dating from the period 200 B.C. to A.D. 100, are some complete copies and fragments of (1) OT books; (2) works from the Apocrypha and Pseudepigrapha; and (3) documents relating to the life of the Qumran sect.

The bulk of the manuscripts were preserved by the people who lived at the monastery at Qumran, possibly Essenes. They lived a strictly disciplined communal life, believing that they were living in the last days before the coming of the Messiah and the final battle with the wicked.

The importance of the Dead Sea Scrolls lies (1) in the discovery of written records, formerly scarce, from biblical times in Palestine, and (2) in the recovery of Hebrew manuscripts of OT books a full 1,000 years earlier than previously possessed. A complete scroll of Isaiah was among them. The Scrolls contribute greatly to OT textual criticism and to the understanding of NT backgrounds. They also tend to confirm the essential accuracy of our present text.

See TEXTUAL CRITICISM.

For Further Reading: Vermes, "The Dead Sea Scrolls in English," *Wycliffe Bible Encyclopedia,* 1:434-42; Burrows, *The Dead Sea Scrolls; More Light on the Dead Sea Scrolls;* LaSor, *Amazing Dead Sea Scrolls;* Yadin, *The Message of the Scrolls.* FRANK G. CARVER

DEATH. Death is the antonym of life, whether this be physical or spiritual. Physical death is the separation of the spirit or soul from the body. Spiritual death is the separation of the spirit or soul from God. Physical death is made obvious by every cemetery and every obituary column. Spiritual death is understood only by revelation, as expressed in the inspired Word of God. Its definition is not carried in the dictionary nor in the encyclopedia. It is denied by the unbeliever and ignored by the world. Yet its importance is eternal.

Death, both physical and spiritual, came upon the earth at the Fall (Gen. 2:17; Rom. 5:12-17; 1 Cor. 15:21-22). Physical death actually came upon Adam himself some years later, as recorded in

Gen. 5:4-5, although it had come upon mankind at an earlier date, at the murder of Abel (4:8).

Spiritual death for Adam and Eve occurred immediately and was indicated, by type, when God drove them out of the garden and from His immediate presence (3:23-24; cf. Isa. 59:1-2). Since man alone was created in the image and likeness of God (Gen. 1:26-27), since man alone became a living soul, created for immortality (2:7), man alone of all God's creatures can die spiritually.

Throughout the OT physical death is routinely reported, and "long [physical] life" is declared to be the reward of the righteous (Ps. 91:16). Spiritual death is not in the OT so clearly defined. Apart from the aforementioned statement from Isa. 59:1-2, probably Dan. 12:2 is the one OT reference declaring the eternal consequence of spiritual rebellion, implying spiritual death.

The Synoptic Gospels say little about spiritual death, as such. John records our Lord on several occasions on the subject, however. John 5:24, for example, declares that, upon hearing and believing, one passes "from death unto life." Jesus elaborates further on this to Martha: "He who believes in Me shall live [spiritually] even if he dies [physically], and everyone who lives and believes in Me shall never die [spiritually]" (11:25-26, NASB). See also John 6:50; 8:44, 51-52; 10:10.

Other NT writers also declared themselves on the matter of spiritual death. Paul speaks of it in Rom. 5:12; 6:23; 1 Cor. 15:21; and, in Eph. 2:1-9, includes himself: ". . . Even when we were [spiritually] dead in sins, [God] hath quickened us [to spiritual life] together with Christ." Also see Jas. 5:19-20; 2 Pet. 3:9; 1 John 5:11-12.

Although physical death descends upon the unbeliever as the original penalty of sin, to all who are united to Christ it loses its aspect of penalty and becomes a means of discipline and of entrance into the eternal presence of their God. With Paul they can say, "O death, where is thy sting?" (1 Cor. 15:55); with the Psalmist, "Precious in the sight of the Lord is the death of his saints" (Ps. 116:15; cf. Rom. 8:10; 14:7-8). During physical life those in spiritual death are offered the opportunity of "hearing" and "believing," and thereby passing "from death unto life." But, at physical death, the door of opportunity is closed and they face, in God's chosen day, "the resurrection of damnation" (John 5:24-25, 29). Eternal death, also known as "the second death" (Rev. 20:6, 14), is spiritual death persisted in until the opportunity for repentance is lost at physical death.

See ETERNAL LIFE, ETERNAL PUNISHMENT.

For Further Reading: *GMS*, 137-44, 281 ff, 665; Bavinck, "Death," *ISBE*, 811 ff; Wiley, Culbertson, *Introduction to Christian Theology*, 405 ff; Wiley, *CT*, 2:91-95; 3:212-14; Salvation Army *Handbook of Doctrine*, 87.

MILTON S. AGNEW

DEATH OF CHRIST. The death of Christ is at the heart of the NT message. Both the fact and the meaning are central in the attention of the NT writers. But the death is never treated apart from the eternal purpose of God and its outcome in resurrection triumph and salvation for mankind.

The fact is made unmistakably clear. All four Gospels elaborate the event. The horrible Cross, the pierced side, the anointed body, the sealed tomb, and the observations of innumerable witnesses—all confirm the fact and circumstances of His death. Even Bultmann calls the death of Jesus a historic *(geschichtlich)* fact originating in the historical *(historisch)* event which is the crucifixion of Jesus. Jesus truly died.

But it was a planned death, not by enemies but by God himself and by Jesus. He came to die (Phil. 2:5-8; John 10:11, 15; 12:32). On at least three specific occasions in the last year of His earthly ministry, Jesus announced both His death and resurrection (Mark 8:31; 9:31; 10:33-34). At the Arrest, Trial, and Crucifixion, Jesus was the composed Person who was most in charge (see esp. John 18:1-13).

More was involved in laying down His life for the sheep than the death pangs when He "gave up the ghost." Human sin and need spoiled heaven for the Son of God. He chose to come and die for our redemption (Phil. 2:5-8). Then there was the suffering of rejection which dogged His life and ministry. Moreover, He suffered the direct assaults of Satan in temptation. And sin-bearing shadowed His earthly life as well as His death. It was in the Garden that He sweat blood, not on the ugly Cross. It was all with loving purpose—for us and our salvation. As He took on man's lot and died, so He shares with us the triumphant resurrection and heavenly life.

See ATONEMENT, CROSS, BLOOD.

For Further Reading: Jewett, "Death of Christ," *ZPEB*, 2:72-77; Schmithals, "Death, Kill," *NIDNTT*, 1:429-41; Vollmer, *The Modern Student's Life of Christ*, 211-67; Denney, *The Death of Christ*. WILBER T. DAYTON

DEATH OF GOD DOCTRINE. This refers to a strange understanding, made newsworthy in the middle 1960s by such theologians as Thomas J. J. Altizer and William Hamilton. It is not at all easy to understand what these theothanatologists were saying. Altizer seemed to be saying that God died when Christ died on the Cross.

Frederick Nietzsche (1844-1900) had declared, "God is dead." And Ludwig Feuerbach (1804-72) had announced similar impudence.

Shortly after the newspapers began to carry headlines about the death-of-God teaching, Altizer and Hamilton and others were hoping to start a learned society and a magazine through which the view would be promulgated. In 1971, the writer attended one of their "Radical Caucus" sessions, in conjunction with a large gathering of professors. In a small circle, they took up such matters as how not to commit suicide; how to get your children, now, to disbelieve; and whether there are still any satisfactions in life, and joys.

Soon the movement sustained a well-deserved virtual demise.

Powerful commentary on it was made on a wall in a New York City subway. Someone had written, "God Is Dead. Nietzsche." And some wag had written underneath it, "Nietzsche Is Dead. God."

See GOD, ATTRIBUTES (DIVINE).

For Further Reading: Altizer, *The Gospel of Christian Atheism;* Hamilton, *The Death of God;* Vahanian, *The Death of God.*

J. KENNETH GRIDER

DEATH TO SELF. *Death to self* is an expression used in Christian circles to refer to full consecration to Christ. It involves the renunciation of personal ambitions and selfish interests such as self-love, self-pleasing, and self-sufficiency.

Deeper life teaching makes death to self a postconversion experience. Keswickians make it the point at which a "definite decision for holiness" is made. It is portrayed as a transaction involving the yielding of self to God—a dethronement of self, and the other side of dedication to God.

The term is variously described as an inner crucifixion; a cutting off from self-infatuation; a disownment of self; the dethronement and denial of self, self-righteousness, self-esteem, self-vindication, self-glory, and self-pity. Keswickian teaching characterizes it as a point of surrender, leading into the surrendered or exchanged life. It leads to the "crucified life."

The teaching is based on such Scripture passages as Gal. 2:20; 5:24; Luke 14:26; 2 Cor. 5:15; 1 Pet. 4:2; Rom. 12:1; 8:13; 6:11, 13.

Wesleyans see death to self as accomplished not by consecration alone but by entire sanctification—God's answer to man's response of faith. The promised "rest" of Heb. 4:9-11 results in "ceasing from one's own works"—the crucified life of Gal. 2:20.

In using the expression *death to self,* distinction must be made between the intrinsically normal selfhood needs, such as the need for appreciation, security, fulfilment, etc., and the demands of the carnal mind, or selfish nature. The latter needs to be crucified, the former to be fulfilled. Death to selfishness is portrayed in Scripture as the way to such fulfilment. See, e.g., Luke 14:26 and Matt.. 11:29 f.

See CONSECRATE (CONSECRATION), CARNAL CHRISTIANS, HEART PURITY, ENTIRE SANCTIFICATION, SECOND WORK OF GRACE, KESWICK (KESWICKIANISM).

For Further Reading: Barabas, *So Great Salvation,* 111 ff, 125 ff; Maxwell, *Born Crucified,* 57 ff.

JAMES M. RIDGWAY

DECALOGUE. *Decalogue* is a term meaning "ten words" as used in Exod. 34:28 and Deut. 4:13; 10:4. The "words" themselves are found in Exod. 20:2-17 and Deut. 5:6-22.

In the NT references are made to the Decalogue by using "commandments" (Matt. 19:17; Eph. 6:2; et al.). Today we commonly speak of the Ten Commandments.

The "ten words" were given under the most awe-inspiring circumstances from the top of the mountain of Sinai, 50 days after Israel was delivered from Egyptian bondage by Jehovah. The giving of the Decalogue stands out in bold relief as the most memorable day in all of Israel's history. It is one of the bases for the national Feast of Pentecost.

The Decalogue provides the religious and moral underpinning of both Judaism and Christianity. It inculcates two basic principles: reverence for God and respect for man. The two can never be separated. The majesty of God and the rights of human personality are alike preserved.

Thus God gave fallen man a twofold, objective moral norm. The first four commandments comprise a vertical, religious moral norm, while the last six afford fallen man a horizontal, social moral norm.

As a standard of conduct the Decalogue has never been abrogated or superseded. It is still binding upon Christians. Love to God and love to neighbor are the summaries of Christ for the first four and the last six commandments, respectively.

Many controversies surrounding the commandments began with the Reformation. A distinction between a permanent and a transitory element in the law of the Sabbath was found, not only by Luther and Melanchthon, but by Calvin and other theologians of the Reformed church.

The Reformers were unanimous in their observation that the Lord's Day and the Sabbath Day were not the same day, and they were equally unanimous that the fourth commandment was abrogated for the Christian.

The binding obligation was that all men have one day in seven to rest their bodies and their souls. Thus, early Christians used the Lord's Day for rest, study, prayer, fellowship, praise, and to strengthen the moral fiber of life.

By the beginning of the second century the Lord's Day, the first day of the week, had completely superseded and replaced the Jewish Sabbath.

The first day of the week celebrates the resurrection of Christ, while to this day for the Jews, the seventh day Sabbath commemorates the creation of the earth.

See COMMAND (COMMANDMENTS), LAW, LAW AND GRACE, ANTINOMIANISM, AGAPĒ.

For Further Reading: Beebe, *The Old Testament,* 99-100; Wiley, Culbertson, *Introduction to Christian Theology,* 341, 382; Sampey, "Ten Commandments," *ISBE,* 5:2944; Carter, "The Biblical Morality, Its Continuing Validity," *WTJ,* 2:36. WAYNE E. CALDWELL

DECISION. Decision lies at the very center of personhood, for the human power of freedom enables persons to decide upon their actions and goals.

Determinists reject the view that human actions can occur apart from general causal forces such as nature or God. According to determinism, human beings have no power in themselves to originate or resist action. Even when and if the term *decision* is used, such a theory rejects any notion of freedom: All actions are caused, but some are overtly compelled while others are supposedly free.

According to those who believe in human freedom, a person's freedom is the basis of the moral and religious life. Decision may be a choice from among presented alternatives (Wm. James); it may negate the given in favor of something radically new (Sartre); or by an original decision, one's life can issue forth into that habitual action and character in which pursuit of the good becomes second nature (Merleau-Ponty).

Although man's freedom is finite, his desire for the thrust toward infinity sometimes gives his decisions the character of an irrational voluntarism with strong potentials of violence. Man must recognize his limitations and make his decisions in thoughtful relation to God and others.

"Decision for Christ" is an expression used by contemporary Christians for the new birth. This kind of decision emphasizes the element of freedom in responding to Christ; for if Christ died for all, then the appropriate response of the individual is required in order to make salvation actual. Some do not appreciate the expression, however, because, they say, it smacks of superficiality; it encourages quantity without quality, and thus it reflects little of the genuine trauma connected with the new birth. The expression may even promote the idea of a humanistic mind-change without a divine transformation.

Certain biblical passages indicate the central character of decision in relation to salvation (cf. exhortations in the form of "let us" in the Book of Hebrews; encouragements in Colossians; appeal in Rom. 12:1-2). Decision is thus integral to and at the heart of salvation; but decision is always within the divine context and grounded in God's enabling.

See DETERMINISM, FREEDOM, RESPONSIBILITY, MORALITY, PREDESTINATION.

For Further Reading: James, *The Dilemma of Determinism; Sacramentum Mundi,* 2:62-64; Titus, *Living Issues in Philosophy.* R. DUANE THOMPSON

DECREES. See DIVINE DECREES.

DEISM. Deism is the name applied to a particular philosophy or theory concerning the nature of God, which arose during the Enlightenment or so-called Age of Reason. In the flush of scientific discovery and revolt against medieval superstitious ideas, reason was regarded as sufficient to answer all the problems of life. When applied to God, this meant that human reason was able to apprehend all that needed to be known about God. Thus it rejected any need for a divine revelation and all idea of the miraculous. This opinion is represented by Voltaire and Thomas Paine.

The result was the idea of a God totally apart from the universe. It has been called the "absentee landlord" view (see Dagobert D. Runes, ed., *Dictionary of Philosophy,* 75). Bruce describes deism as a teaching of a transcendent Deity "banished to the outside of the world" (quoted by Wiley, *CT,* 1:281). Some of its advocates proceeded from deism to ideas of pantheism or outright atheism.

Wiley points out that a similar idea about God was current among the Epicureans with whom Paul had to deal, as in Acts 17 (*CT,* 1:256).

See THEISM, ATHEISM, PANTHEISM.

For Further Reading: Purkiser, ed., *Exploring Our Christian Faith,* 42; *DCT,* 89 ff; Wiley, *CT,* 1:223, 280-81.
LESLIE D. WILCOX

DEITY OF CHRIST. See CHRIST.

DELIVERER. See REDEEMER.

DELUGE. See FLOOD.

DEMIURGE. The term *(demiurgos)* is frequently found in classical Greek literature as a designation for "one who works for the people," "handicraftsman," "the artisan class," etc. In Plato's *Timaeus, demiurgos* is the craftsman or the artificer who created the visible world. Gnosticism, the Valentinians in particular, attributed this designation to an inferior deity who is responsible for the fashioning of the universe. In Plato, the Demiurge is conscious of his creative task and of his creation. Contrary to this, the Valentinians taught that the Demiurge fashioned the universe in "ignorance" and "conceit" (H. Jonas, *The Gnostic Religion,* 191).

The biblical doctrine of creation does not include the concept of an inferior deity involved in the creation of the universe. The Septuagint consciously omits the use of the word in reference to the creative work of God. The NT writers, while speaking of God as the sole Creator of the universe, also present a Christological view of creation (John 1:3; Col. 1:16; 1 Cor. 8:6; Rom. 11:36). In these passages Christ, the Son of God, is explicitly referred to as the Mediator or Agent through whom God accomplished His creation of the universe.

See GNOSTICISM, CREATION, CHRIST.

For Further Reading: Jonas, *The Gnostic Religion,* 174-94; *GMS,* 226-30. ALEXANDER VARUGHESE

DEMONS, DEMON POSSESSION. The few references to demons in the OT are generally ambiguous. There are no provisions for casting out demons in OT rituals.

References to demons *(daimonia)* and evil spirits *(pneumata akatharta)* in the NT are largely confined to the Synoptic Gospels, which in many cases attribute illness to demon possession (cf. Matt. 17:14-18). The outstanding case of possession and deliverance is that of the Gadarene demoniac(s) (Matt. 8:28-34; Mark 5:1-20; Luke 8:26-33).

The Gospel of John mentions demons only twice, when the people accuse Jesus of being demon possessed (8:48; 10:19). The Acts associates illness with possession of evil spirits (5:16; 8:7), although a cause and effect relationship is not necessarily implied. In the case of the girl at Philippi (16:18) the spirit which Paul cast out is called neither a demon nor an unclean spirit, but a spirit of divination or prophecy. As in the Synoptics, many healings are recorded with no mention of demon influence.

As in John, there are no cases of demon possession in the Epistles. Demons are mentioned in 1 Cor. 10:21; 1 Tim. 4:1; and Jas. 2:19. There is no consistent pattern of demon possession or deliverance in the NT, nor is there any suggestion as to the nature or character of demons or evil spirits, except that they are evil and the emissaries of Satan or Beelzebub (Mark 3:22-26). The differences between the NT narratives and those of pagan cults are far greater than any possible similarities which might be found.

The literature on this subject is a mixture of fact and fiction, magic and superstition, with few if any clear distinctions between demons, evil spirits, devils, witches, the occult, and psychosomatic experiences. That there is a personal devil having "angels" (Rev. 12:9) which affect men and society there can be no doubt. And that the human mind can become deranged beyond our ability to understand is also evident.

Undoubtedly there exists the possibility of relationships between human beings and demonic forces, a spiritual relationship that amounts to domination. This should be thought of in terms of control or obsession rather than possession in the materialistic sense. (Actually the term is used to denote occupation and not possession as usually understood.) We must not allow our concept of demonic forces greater range of activity and influence in the propagation of evil than we allow angelic forces in the dissemination of good.

Demon possession, like other forms of sin, must include the element of consent, if not choice, except in cases of insanity or mental irresponsibility. The idea that a Christian may be demon possessed is a contradiction in terms and strongly suggests a denial of the efficacy of redeeming grace and the power of the Holy Spirit.

See EXORCISM, SATAN, POWERS, EVIL, DARKNESS.

For Further Reading: Kittel, 2:1864; *ISBE,* 2:1915; *The New Schaff-Herzog Encyclopedia of Religious Knowledge,* 3:1909; Unger, *Demons in the World Today;* Vine, "Demon," *ED.* HARVEY J. S. BLANEY

DEMYTHOLOGIZATION. In his 1941 article "New Testament and Mythology," Rudolph Bultmann defines *myth* as the prescientific depiction of transcendent reality in this-worldly, objective terms. For him "the conception of the world as being structured in three stories, heaven, earth, and hell; the conception of the intervention of supernatural powers in the course of events; and the conception of miracles" (*Jesus Christ and Mythology,* 15) are all mythological. The earliest Christians used mythological expressions in formulating their Christology and eschatology.

Bultmann does not seek to eliminate myth, rather to interpret it, for he insists that all mythology expresses a truth, although in an obsolete way. The truth contained in the NT is that of the saving *kerygma* of Christ, i.e., the announcement that God has come to man through Christ in grace to accomplish a radical change in his existence. Bultmann's existential interpretation presupposes that the mythologies have their point in the specific self-understanding of man: what is being said about man's existence before God, about his self-understanding in the midst of this world and history.

Bultmann can be criticized from the standpoints (1) of his view of myth in the NT, calling myth what should be identified as history, and (2) of interpretative presuppositions, exchanging the old myth for a new philosophical one of existentialism. Yet the problem of interpretation remains in the hermeneutical enterprise.

See MYTH, HERMENEUTICS, BIBLICAL INERRANCY, INSPIRATION OF THE BIBLE.

For Further Reading: Hordern, *New Directions in Theology Today,* Introduction, 1:23 ff; Bultmann, *Jesus Christ and Mythology;* Johnson, *The Origins of Demythologizing.*
FRANK G. CARVER

DENOMINATION. This is the term most often used for the various organized divisions of Christianity and especially of Protestantism. *Webster's New Collegiate Dictionary* (1976) defines the term, in its religious context, as "a religious organization uniting in a single legal and administrative body a number of local congregations." Such a body, or denomination, may be large or very small.

There is some confusion in general usage between *denomination* and *sect.* There are two distinctions between these two terms. First, scholars usually use the word *denomination* to designate organizations with a historical and/or a doctrinal connection to the original church, while the term *sect* is used to designate groups which are radically divergent from the orthodox church and which have no distinct historical relation to traditional Christianity. A second distinction is that sect is more frequently used with a negative connotation (as a term of reproach) than is denomination.

While denominationalism grew out of the Protestant Reformation, the term *denomination* was not commonly used until the 18th century. Denominationalism reached its peak in the 19th century when marked independence and hostility became the rule. In the 20th century the mood has changed to cooperation and to moves toward unity.

A climate of religious freedom combined with strong doctrinal, liturgical, and organizational homogeneity for effective ministry and growth, justifies denominationalism in principle. While the Bible rebukes divisions which are carnal in origin and nature (1 Cor. 3:1-11), there is much implied support for organized movements which grow out of an honest desire to preserve and propagate a pure gospel (Gal. 1:6-8; 2 Tim. 4:1-5).

See CHURCH, CULT, SECT, DIVISION, SCHISM.

For Further Reading: Newman, *Manual of Church History,* 2:419-21; Brauer, ed., *The Westminster Dictionary of Church History,* 622-23; Mead, *Handbook of Denominations in the U.S.* CHARLES L. CHILDERS

DEONTOLOGY. See DUTY.

DEPOTENTIATION THEORIES. See KENOSIS.

DEPRAVITY. See TOTAL DEPRAVITY.

DEPRIVATION. This has to do with mankind's being deprived of certain ministries of the Holy Spirit, due to Adam's racially significant disobedience to God. It denotes something only negative, a lack—and not what is itself a positive detriment. But this lack, this deprivation, results in what is positive: depravity, an inclination to acts of sin which characterizes the whole human race, until it is cleansed away by the baptism with the Holy Spirit.

See TOTAL DEPRAVITY, ORIGINAL SIN, PREVENIENT GRACE. J. KENNETH GRIDER

DESCENT INTO HELL. In the misnamed Apostles' Creed (it comes from the middle of the second century, not from the apostles), we find the statement that Christ "descended into hell." This theological statement is based on Eph. 4:9: "Now that he ascended, what is it but that he also descended first into the lower parts of the earth?" (cf. Acts 2:27). The last words of this verse were interpreted by Tertullian, Irenaeus, and Jerome as meaning Hades. Some modern commentators have adopted this.

At this point it should be noted that the English form of the Apostles' Creed is a mistranslation. The original form (about A.D. 150) did not have *Gehenna,* "hell," but *Hades,* the place of departed spirits. So Chrysostom and other Greek fathers interpreted "the lower parts of the earth" as meaning death.

Some interpreters understand the "descent into hell" to refer to 1 Pet. 3:19—"By which [by the Spirit] also he went and preached unto the spirits in prison."

But plain logic points in still another direction. The ascent was clearly to heaven, 40 days after Christ's resurrection. The descent would therefore be to earth, in the Incarnation. T. K. Abbott wisely says that "it seems preferable to take 'the lower parts of the earth' as = 'this lower earth.'"

See ESTATES OF CHRIST, APOSTLES' CREED, ASCENSION, HADES.

For Further Reading: *BBC,* 9:207; 10:290-91; *WBC,* 5:409; 6:267 ff.

RALPH EARLE

DESIRE. Desire itself *(epithumia)* is morally neutral. Jesus "earnestly desired" to eat the Passover with the Twelve in Jerusalem (Luke 22:15; cf. Phil. 1:23; 1 Thess. 2:17).

To "desire" is more than to contemplate or to wish for. *Epithumia* denotes firm resolve and the gathering of literal physical energy to drive for the accomplishment of the vision held in mind. In the later NT the word is used exclusively as synonymous with evil (Jas. 1:14-15; 2 Tim. 2:22; Titus 2:12).

First-century rabbis taught that evil desire and evil action were both condemned. "The eye and the heart are the two brokers of sin," they taught. But their teaching was less sweeping than Jesus' in Matt. 5:28, where "lust" is made the equivalent of "adultery" already committed in the heart.

Part of the curse affecting the woman was said to be that in spite of her greatly multiplied pain in childbearing, and her bringing forth her children in pain, "yet your desire shall be for your husband" (Gen. 3:16, NASB). This persistent bonding of two who become "one flesh" survived even the Fall. So whether desire leads to intimacy or to exploitation (1 John 2:16) becomes the real question; and the answer to that arises from whether self (lust) or God (affirmation) rules the heart.

See SEVEN DEADLY SINS, TEMPERANCE, SELF-CONTROL, HEART PURITY, MOTIVES.

For Further Reading: Vine, *ED.*

DONALD M. JOY

DESPAIR. Despair is basically a lack of hope in relation to some good which one desires. Religious despair may bring one to the point of denial of God's mercy, love, and goodness.

Catholic theology looks upon despair as the root of all sin, thus requiring repentance and forgiveness in order to be overcome. And since resistance to God and grace is a form of despair, despair is further related to the sin against the Holy Spirit.

Nihilism, with its denial of reality, meaning, and values, is one of modern man's chief struggles; and it corresponds to despair. Man is threatened by death, condemnation (damnation), and meaninglessness (Tillich), and Maslow suggests that the "ultimate disease of our time is valuelessness." In relation to all of these there may be despair, taking on the particular hue of the specific threat. Contemporary existential philosophy regards the conquest of despair as one of its chief concerns.

To presume to have or be something which one is not is to be at the opposite pole from despair. Thinking of oneself soberly, with divinely touched understanding and poise, would be to steer a course between the twin dangers of despair and presumption. Each pole may tend to perpetuate itself or to provoke its opposite; i.e., despair may create a real "slough of despond"; or since one can scarcely live in such a dismal world, despair may call forth presumption.

Faith, hope, and courage are biblical qualities which are available to those who seek them. The Bible is replete with examples of persons who were brought to the brink of despair (Job, Jeremiah, and other heroes of faith found in Hebrews 11), but who were able to find in God sufficient resources to triumph.

See HOPE, FAITH, DOUBT, UNBELIEF.

For Further Reading: Vine, *ED; Baker's DCE; Sacramentum Mundi,* 2:69-70.

R. DUANE THOMPSON

DESTINY, ETERNAL. The Bible teaches that man's earthly, temporal destiny is probationary and preparatory. The true or ultimate destiny, for which preparation is being made now, is beyond death. This ultimate destiny is predesigned but not predetermined. God's design for man, or his "chief end," is "to glorify God, and to enjoy Him forever" (Westminster Shorter Catechism). However, sin thwarts this design in those who die impenitent. The sinner's destiny is not the happiness of heaven but the misery of hell. It is apparent that in the final analysis each individual is responsible for his own destiny (Rom. 2:1-11).

The fact that man's true destiny was beyond the grave was not always clear. In the days of antiquity Job raised his memorable question, "If a man die, shall he live again?" (14:14). It was only in part that he answered his own question with the resounding "I know that my redeemer liveth" (cf. 19:25-27). Further enlightenment in the OT on the subject is scattered and incomplete. In the 18th century before Christ Abraham bravely made his way up the mountain to offer his son Isaac in obedience to God's command (Genesis 22). The writer of Hebrews observes that, even at that early point in history, Abraham, by faith, accounted that "God was able to raise him up, even from the dead; from whence also he received him in a figure" (Heb. 11:17-19).

About 800 years later, in David's time, there came further glimpses of the glory, and of man's accountability in death (Ps. 17:15; 49:15; 73:24-26; 116:15; Eccles. 12:7). Isaiah caught fleeting views of the overthrow of death (25:8; 26:19). It was left to Daniel, however, to give a remarkable summation, mentioning for the first and only time in the OT the eternal quality of life and its alternative (12:2).

The revelation of the full status of man's eternal destiny was established only by Jesus, to be restated and enlarged upon by the writers of the NT.

Jesus spoke of a prepared place for believers (John 14:2; 2 Cor. 5:1 ff), a place where He and His Father will be (John 14:2-3; Eph. 6:9; Col. 4:1; 1 Pet. 3:22; Rev. 7:15), the eternal home of God's children (Matt. 5:12; 6:20; Heb. 11:10); He spoke of a "kingdom prepared for you from the foundation of the world" (Matt. 25:34; Acts 14:22; Jas. 2:4), a place of glory (John 17:24; Rom. 8:18; Jude 24; Rev. 21:11).

Men will be fulfilling the purpose for which they were created as they "serve him day and night in his temple" (Rev. 7:15; Heb. 12:28). Heaven will be a place of growth and progress. By the parables of the talents (Matt. 25:14-30) and the pounds (Luke 19:11-27) Jesus taught that the faithful servant is to be given opportunity to direct to greater tasks the increased powers he has developed by work well done here on earth.

See HEAVEN, HELL, IMMORTALITY, RESURRECTION.

For Further Reading: *GMS,* 136-44, 661-65; "Punishment," *ISBE;* Wiley, Culbertson, *Introduction to Christian Theology,* 335-49, 440-44; Wiley, *CT,* 3:356-86; The Salvation Army *Handbook of Doctrine,* 174-79; Agnew, *Manual of Salvationism,* 47-50.

MILTON S. AGNEW

DETERMINISM. Determinism is the view that every event must be what it is without any other alternatives, because the conditions for its occurrence not only precede its appearance but are inviolably causal in nature.

From a Christian perspective God is the primary Cause of all things as their Creator. But man as a secondary cause either has or does not have some initiating powers. If he has such powers, to any extent, he is to that extent free. If man does not have such powers in any sense, then he is determined.

Some determinisms distinguish between a "free" and a "coerced" cause. If someone robs a bank on his own or in cooperation with someone else, then though his nature may not have permitted him to do otherwise, he is free even though his action is caused. On the other hand, if a bystander is forced by a robber to drive a getaway car, he is not free, he is coerced.

The difference between soft and hard determinism is that soft determinism holds that some acts are free (note preceding paragraph) while hard determinism calls no acts free. But both determinisms regard all acts as produced by forces which permit no alternatives. Hard determinism may become fatalism by the addition of the psychological and emotional element of inability to change things.

With respect to salvation, determinism promotes the view of total depravity with human ability reduced to nothing. Thus man cannot respond to God except as God produces the response in him. *Sola fide* (by faith alone) and *sola gratia* (by grace alone) can be understood either as absolute determinism or as placing the initiative on God's part without eliminating human capacity to cooperate and respond.

The Christian view of the Creator God does place all things in a position of dependency upon God. The real issue is whether the relationship is one of total control, or whether grace has provided a degree of independent action on man's part.

Moral issues are raised, because human freedom is tied in with the very possibility of moral decision, and upon this the very nature of personhood depends. Thus no more critical question can be raised than that of freedom or determinism. The fact that God holds man accountable for his actions (from Genesis to Revelation) implies some measure of real freedom and contingency.

See CONTINGENT, FREEDOM, MORALITY, PREDESTINATION, MONERGISM, SYNERGISM.

For Further Reading: James, *The Dilemma of Determinism;* Luther, *The Bondage of the Will; NIDNTT,* 294-95.

R. DUANE THOMPSON

DEVELOPMENT, THEORIES OF. Biblical evidences and understanding of the human species are classically developmental. Jesus of Nazareth, in whom God incarnates His presence and action in the world, passes through conception, birth, and puberty; enters adult status at age 12; and announces His own vocation at 30—suggesting that physical, moral, and spiritual maturity take time. Paul explicitly speaks of the shift from childhood to maturity: "When I was a child, I talked like a child, I thought like a child, I reasoned like a child. When I became a man, I put childish ways behind me" (1 Cor. 13:11, NIV).

In spite of the clear biblical evidences urging us to respect developmental differences between adults and children, until recent times the Western world has regarded children as miniature adults. It has remained for the 19th and 20th centuries to begin to probe the actual sequences and characteristics of human development. Today three major theoretical bases are available from which to begin the trek toward understanding. They are, in order of their appearance, (1) psychodynamic theory; (2) behavior/learning theory, and (3) cognitive/constructionist theory.

Sigmund Freud (1905) is regarded as the father of psychodynamic approaches to human development. He worked largely with pathological adult women, and theoreticians since Freud have tended to work largely with adults in institutional or clinical/psychiatric settings. Psychodynamic theory has contributed to our understanding of conscience (the superego) and of the self (ego). The theory regards growth as the passage from one "conflict" arena to another. These have been reconstructed to include "complexes" through which boys and girls pass; the obscenity of the Oedipal and Electra complexes may tell us more about the psychologists and their adult patients than they do about children. Particularly helpful are the psychodynamic contributions of Erik Erikson who traces the "eight stages or crises of human development," each with a positive and a negative option for resolution. R. J. Havighurst elaborates a life span of "developmental tasks." The other developmental theories are indebted to the work of Freud for isolating research areas and for early definitions of problems.

Behavior/learning theory moves on the assumption that all learning is acquired; nothing is innate. All children are born as a blank slate. Only behavior can be observed; hence inner attributes such as love or personality are only important as certain behaviors may be labeled "loving" or "gracious." Ivan Pavlov's animal studies in Russia (1927) gave us "classical conditioning" formulas, but it was B. F. Skinner who developed the model called "operant conditioning." "Behavior modification" is a "learning" application of conditioning. "Brainwashing," as in Korean prisoner of war camps, was an application of conditioning to control behavior. Conditioning ahd behavior modification application tend to work well with animals and young children, less well with reflective adults (not all American prisoners of war "learned" in the brainwashing experience). The theory makes extensive use of animals in research and theorizing; yet humans are capable of going far beyond animals in learning tasks.

Cognitive/constructionist theory is rooted in the work of Jean Piaget (1932) whose imagination was triggered by the wrong answers children gave on a new intelligence test at the Binet Institute in Paris. He went to children playing marbles on the street to begin unfolding his genetic epistemology—the science which now helps us understand "how we know what we know." Piaget concludes that the neurological possibilities of the human brain, combined with sensory processors such as sight, hearing, smelling, tasting, and touching, permit the child to receive or *assimilate* data which is then processed in the brain within the developmental/experiential limits of current structures—ways of organizing data received. As experience overloads the cognitive *structure,* the structure explodes and reorganizes—called *accommodation.* Thus a person is constantly growing as new experiences are transformed into new structures.

Jerome Bruner traces the young child's ways of knowing from "enactive representation" in which gesture is speech, through "iconic representation" in which images substitute for speech, finally to "symbolic representation" which is speech itself. Noam Chomsky, in studying the transformational nature of language, concludes that every child is born with a "predisposition to speak." He holds that children's speech cannot be accounted for simply by attributing it to modeling parent speech (psychodynamic) nor by attributing it to rewards/punishments (behavior/learning). The human brain, Chomsky holds, is predisposed to discover and follow rules of grammar and language. If a child grew up without hearing speech, it would invent language all over again. The biblical idea of a speaking God who creates humans in the image of that speaking God and finally discloses himself through the Word made flesh and announced by the voice of one crying in the wilderness suggests the close affinity between language development, the apprehension of true meanings, and the arrival at our true destiny as humans.

In all developmental theories there is a common thesis: Human development is strongly cumulative, but it is not continuous. All past experience is present with us; but we may also arrest, stop, and stagnate. Paul, the track star racing toward the crown of life (Phil. 3:14; 1 Cor. 9:24), also offers the golden formula for moral and spiritual transformation: "We all, with unveiled face, beholding the glory of the Lord [that is, looking into the face of Jesus], are being changed into his likeness from one degree of glory to another; for this comes from the Lord who is the Spirit" (2 Cor. 3:18, RSV).

All of us who work with people use a basic "theory of development," whether we know it or not. If we regard people as incapable of change and use pity, we are essentially influenced by psychodynamic views. If we regard people as manipulable—using prizes, praise, or gimmicks—we are reflecting behavior/learning beliefs about learning and change. If we regard persons as freely choosing beings able to construct positively and to follow hope and vision, we are awakened more to cognitive/constructionist ideas. But the theories themselves have developed across most of a century; the latest theory is enriched by the earlier research and theory of psychoanalysis and behaviorism.

See GROW (GROWTH), FREEDOM, PERSON (PERSONALITY), TEACH (TEACHING, TEACHER).

For Further Reading: Chomsky, *Language and Mind*, enlarged ed.; Erikson, *Childhood and Society*; Joy, "Human Development and Christian Holiness," *The Asbury Seminarian*, Apr., 1976; Piaget, *The Moral Judgment of the Child*.

DONALD M. JOY

DEVIL. See SATAN.

DEVOTE, DEVOTION. Basic and central to Christian holiness is devotedness and devotion. The heart of the matter is the matter of the heart. Objectively, to "devote" is to give voluntarily to the Lord, no strings attached, as in Mic. 4:13, e.g., where the prophet calls for the "devoting" to God of the spoils of victory. Contrast this with Josh. 6:18 ff where Achan's tragedy was rooted in his unwillingness to recognize the curse hanging over the "things devoted to destruction." Compare also how the faithful ministers of God share in the blessings of true devotion (Ezek. 44:15-16, 29). The modern expression "devotedly giving of our means" indicates that the love of the heart discerns and gives the things that are the Lord's. A "devout" person is a person devoted to God (Luke 2:25; Acts 22:12).

In the NT "devotion" is the undying love of the Christian for the Lord Jesus Christ (Eph. 5:24), absorbing every rightful lesser love. It is indicated in the giving over to Christ of all life and possessions in order to follow Him and share His life, whatever the consequence (Matt. 10:38; 16:23; cf. Ruth 3:10; Jer. 2:5).

The only real defense of the holy life against the evil cunning of the adversary is an ever deepening and intensifying devotion for Christ (2 Cor. 11:3). The citadel of the soul is strongly fortified only when devotion to Christ is complete. This was the citadel surrendered by our first parents. The apostle John capsulizes the principle in 1 John 3:19-20.

Devotion, however, requires "devotions." We must feed the fires of devotion, remembering that the "world" is anything, however seemingly "bad" or "good," that cools our devotion for Christ. Devotion may be cultivated and fed by listening to His Spirit as we read His Book; by holding conversations—not monologues—with Him in prayer; by doing what and as He says; by loving those whom He loves and those who love Him.

There are programs of "devotions," but devotion is not a program; it is the core condition of the holy heart. Our prayer should always be:

More love to Thee, O Christ,
More love to Thee!

See PRAYER, CONSECRATION, HOLINESS.

For Further Reading: Christensen, *The Inward Pilgrimage;* Murray, *With Christ in the School of Prayer;* Clark, *A Testament of Devotion;* Chambers, *My Utmost for His Highest.*

T. CRICHTON MITCHELL

DIALECTIC. Originally "conversation," dialectic has had a variety of meanings throughout history: art of discourse by question and answer (Socrates); pattern of logical reasoning (Aristotle); pairing of contrasting opinions by authorities, followed by a reconciling view (medieval theology); dynamic process of universal reality through thesis, antithesis, and synthesis, evident in history (Hegelian idealism, Marxian materialism).

Influenced by the Reformation and particularly Kierkegaard's revolt against idealism, neoorthodox "dialectical theologians" (Barth, Brunner, Niebuhr, et al.) stressed the complexities and apparent opposites or paradoxes of human existence under God. Finitude and infinity, time and eternity, culture and the kingdom of God, natural reason and divine revelation—such discontinuities between humanity and God cannot be dissolved by rational coherence, but only held together in God-given faith. The radical tension between divine judgment on human sinfulness and grace which alone can redeem is manifest to faith in the supreme paradox of the Incarnation—"not a logical contradiction" but an event which "transcends all human expectations and possibilities" (Tillich, *Systematic Theology,* 1:57).

Theology that is dialectical is never final or fixed. It acknowledges human limits before the mystery of God and the ambiguities and polarities of life (2 Cor. 4:7-12; 6:3-10), yet calls for faithfulness to Christ that makes these tensions creative.

See NEOORTHODOXY, MARXIANISM, PHILOSOPHY, REASON.

For Further Reading: Macquarrie, *Principles of Christian Theology,* 2nd ed., 38, 147-48; Moltmann, *The Church in the Power of the Spirit,* 20-24, 282-88; Niebuhr, *The Nature and Destiny of Man,* vol. 1 and 2:204.

WILFRED L. WINGET

DIASPORA. See DISPERSION.

DICHOTOMY. This term is from the Greek *dichotomein,* "to cut in half." In anthropology it is the doctrine that human nature is twofold in essence, spiritual and material, or soul/spirit and body. It thus differs from trichotomy, the view that spirit, soul, and body are three distinct constituent elements of human nature. Spirit and soul are seen as different aspects of man's immaterial self, spirit being the Godward capacity or nature, while soul is the selfward and manward life. Dichotomists therefore grant a *functional* trichotomy even though insisting on an *essential* dichotomy.

Of recent years there has been a tendency in some circles to minimize if not repudiate the implicit dualism in dichotomy, in favor of a holistic view of man. This emphasizes body-mind as a unity. While this may be a wholesome corrective to an extreme Platonism which postulates the body as evil, to be shed as soon as possible, and the spirit preexistent, entirely distinct, and inherently incompatible with the body, the reaction, if pushed to its own extreme, contains error as equally unbiblical. It implies natural mortality of the total person, with no form or degree of extended survival after death excepting on the basis of redemption in Christ.

See TRICHOTOMY, MAN, IMMORTALITY, CONDITIONAL IMMORTALITY, DUALISM, SOUL, SOUL SLEEP.

For Further Reading: Purkiser, *Exploring Our Christian Faith,* 209-11; *GMS,* 262-63.

RICHARD S. TAYLOR

DICTATION THEORY. See INSPIRATION OF THE BIBLE.

DIDACHE. *Didache* is the process of teaching or instruction and also that which is taught (the doctrine). Both a body of knowledge and a way of life are to be interpreted, absorbed, and learned. Matters requiring knowledge, as *catechism,* are often described by *katēcheō.* Discipline or training, relating to character and conduct, corresponds to *paideia,* from which *pedagogy* is derived. "Discipling" (from *mathēteuō*) emphasizes making the learners to be like the teacher (Matt. 10:25). As *kerygma* is the specific proclamation of God's saving purpose and acts, so *didache* is the broader teaching and doctrine.

When the expression "the teacher" *(ho didaskalos)* is used without qualification, it refers to the one Teacher whose word is authoritative and complete, Jesus Christ. The *didache,* then, refers to His teaching. This body of knowledge and this way of life were handed down as a tradition *(paradōsis)* by the oral teaching of the apostles and then in the Scriptures.

Didache is also the name of a document in subapostolic literature that purports to be a summary of the teachings of Jesus through the apostles. It was not written by the apostles.

See DOCTRINE, CHRISTIAN EDUCATION.

For Further Reading: Ridderbos, *The Authority of the New Testament Scriptures,* 72-80; Wegenast and Fürst, "Teach, Instruct, Tradition, Education, Discipline," *NIDNTT,* 3:759-81.

WILBER T. DAYTON

DISCERNMENT. This is the ability to distinguish reality from appearances and truth from falsehood. Such insight is needed in respect to persons, doctrines, impressions, and specific situations.

Discernment is one of the special gifts of the Spirit (1 Cor. 12:10). The province of this gift is primarily that of discernings "of spirits." The "spirits" here may refer to different moods or atmospheres, or to supernatural influences, perhaps both. Atmosphere or impression may come from evil spirits, even when persons involved may ascribe the various psychic or spiritual movements to the Holy Spirit. Or the human spirit may be the sole, or at least primary, agency. The gift of discernment enables its possessor to sense what the truth is behind the vocal claims and psychic phenomena.

The classic biblical example of this gift being demonstrated is Peter's perception of the ruse of

Ananias and Sapphira (Acts 5:1-6). It is possible that Peter did not always have this dramatic power of "seeing through" people—which raises the question whether anyone can properly claim the gift as a permanent and infallible possession. To publicly claim such a gift advertises oneself as being privy to divine secrets and comes perilously close to setting oneself up as clairvoyant. The much-vaunted claims of so-called seers or psychics is at base a claim to a special power of discernment.

Especially to be suspect are persons who in the name of a "gift of discernment" presume to tell other people what they should do, such as whom they should marry, when they should move, what should be their vocation, and such matters.

It is more likely that the gift of discernment is given by the Spirit as needed, to the persons whom He has made responsible—as in the case of Peter.

Yet while false claims are to be avoided in respect to a "gift," the ability to discern, as a matter of good judgment and common sense, on the basis of biblical principles and mature experience, is of inestimable value. Without it we will be gullible and forever taken in by charlatans or by Satan posing as an "angel of light" (2 Cor. 11:14). John's admonition to "test the spirits to see whether they are from God" (1 John 4:1, NIV) suggests not direct intuition or revelation but the intelligent application of definite criteria.

The prayerful exercise of common sense, through knowledge of the Bible, understanding of people, and sensitivity to the Holy Spirit are the components of that kind of discernment which every Christian should prayerfully strive to acquire.

But not only should "spirits" be discerned. "What is best" should also be discerned (Phil. 1:10, NIV)—things that matter or that make a difference. These are cultural and methodological matters. Those who cannot distinguish between what is important and what is not, what is essential and what should belong to personal opinion, will tend to become preoccupied with minor matters and proliferate needless divisions among God's people.

See DISCRIMINATION, CULTURE, DOCTRINE, GUIDANCE, GIFTS OF THE SPIRIT.

For Further Reading: Knapp, *Impressions.*

RICHARD S. TAYLOR

DISCIPLE. The general meaning of the word in the Greek means "pupil" or "learner." A disciple is an understudy or apprentice to a teacher. Moses had disciples (John 9:28) as well as John the Baptist (Mark 2:18) and even the Pharisees (Matt. 22:16). A disciple is one who accepts the views of his teacher and is an adherent, both in belief and practice (*ISBE,* 2:851).

In the NT, the word "disciple" has both a special and general meaning. The special group of 12 apostles were called Christ's disciples (Matt. 10:1; 11:1). These were the ones closest to Him and were given a special mission (Acts 1:15-22).

However, the name "disciple" is most commonly given to all Christ's followers. The term appears only in the Gospels and Acts and refers to those adhering to Christ's teachings. They were first called Christians at Antioch (Acts 11:26). Clearly they were the believers; they were learners in Christ's school (Matt. 11:28-30); they were to make disciples of others (Matt. 28:19); and their lives were to be sacrifices (Luke 14:26).

A disciple of Jesus is one who "believes His doctrines, rests upon His sacrifice, imbibes His spirit, and imitates His example" (*ISBE,* 2:851-52).

See DISCIPLESHIP, DISCIPLING, CHRISTIAN, CROSS-BEARING.

For Further Reading: *ZPBD,* 217; *Baker's DT,* 166-67; *Unger's Bible Dictionary,* 265.

LEO G. COX

DISCIPLESHIP. The Christian concept of discipleship is distinctive, first of all, because of its personal emphasis. Who Jesus is and what He did overshadows what He taught. His entire teaching ministry led up to the question "Who do you say that I am?" (Mark 8:29, NASB). The authority of His teaching derived from the fact that He was Christ the Savior, the Son of God. If He had not risen from the dead, there would be no point in preserving His teaching. But as the living Lord He invites people to be His disciples (Matt. 11:28-30; Mark 1:17), and they must individually decide their commitment to Him (John 6:60-71). He communicates things to them as His friends (15:14-15) which the world cannot receive (14:15-24). This intimate relationship is reflected in the fact that Jesus calls His disciples His brothers and sisters (Matt. 12:49-50). Apart from this personal aspect Christianity would be another philosophic tradition like the ancient Greek schools or another legalistic religion like Rabbinic Judaism.

Second, because Jesus is Lord of God's kingdom which has come to men, He is to be obeyed absolutely. Loyalty to Him supersedes ties to self-interests (Luke 14:33), family (v. 26), social custom (9:59-60), and worldly authorities (Acts 5:29). The disciple of Jesus is to obey all His commandments (Matt. 28:20; John 8:31). One must take up his cross and follow Jesus in suffering (Matt. 10:38-39) and in serving (John 20:21). Realizing that the disciple is not above his Master (Matt. 10:24-25), he will follow His example in lowly service to his brethren (John 13) and in nonretaliatory love when wronged (Luke 6:27-30; 1 Pet. 2:21-23). Like his Master, the disciple seeks to be holy (1 Pet. 1:15-16) and perfect in love (Matt. 5:45).

Jesus summed up the essence of Christian discipleship in Matt. 28:19-20. One first becomes a disciple (through a personal commitment to Jesus) and then is instructed to keep all Christ's commandments (absolute obedience). Both the sequence and the balance are essential if one would avoid legalism on the one hand or cheap grace on the other.

See CONVERSION, OBEDIENCE, CROSS-BEARING, DIDACHE, DISCIPLING, PIETISM.

For Further Reading: Hershberger, *The Recovery of the Anabaptist Vision,* 29-54; Bonhoeffer, *The Cost of Discipleship;* Kittel, 4:390-461. LUKE L. KEEFER, JR.

DISCIPLINE. Discipline is the regulation of life by principle and rule. Regulation by rule is imposed discipline, while regulation by principle is self-discipline. Self-discipline may include rules too, but they will be self-imposed. Regulation by principle is the higher level (if the principles are Christian).

Some imagine that the acquisition of self-discipline should free one from any subordination to rule. But that is impossible in any civilized society. Traffic rules, licensing laws, property restrictions, and hundreds of other laws which one takes for granted all constitute imposed regulation. One's maturity is measured by one's capacity to live within this system cheerfully and without losing a sense of essential freedom.

The possession of a high level of self-discipline is not in itself an evidence of saving grace. The principles which govern one's life may be thoroughly selfish and mercenary. An intense desire to gain a certain position may become the principle governing the whole of one's activities. Any dominating ideal, commitment, moral standard, or personal ambition may constitute a "principle" generating self-discipline. But clearly, principles may be low and unworthy as well as high and lofty. And even the more lofty principles may be forms of self-righteousness, commendable in themselves, perhaps, but not expressions of discipleship.

But while discipline may not prove discipleship, discipleship demands discipline. Without discipline discipleship dissolves. Discipleship increases rather than diminishes the imposed forms of discipline. For the supreme subordination is to Christ: "Take my yoke upon you." The disciple says good-by to autonomy forever.

Subordination to Christ is proven by subordination to the Church, His Body. Christ clearly in the NT, by personal word and by His Spirit, delegated authority to the Church to direct and restrict believers who expected to maintain fellowship in the Body.

The familiar Methodist *Discipline* exemplifies this principle. This represents the regulations under and within which Methodists govern themselves. Corporately it is self-government. As it affects the individual, it is imposed government. Every branch of the Christian Church from the apostles until now has had some such disciplinary structure, in some cases simple and in others elaborate, perhaps even oppressive. But the right of the Church to exercise discipline over its members is without question a biblical right. To profess subordination to Christ and practice insubordination to the Church is a form of self-delusion; for it is Christ through the Spirit who commands, "Obey them that have the rule over you" (Heb. 13:17; cf. Phil. 2:12; 2 Thess. 3:14). (The relationship of a believer to an apostate or heretical church is a totally different matter.)

The acceptance of the imposed disciplines, both of society and the Church, is a great aid in achieving self-discipline. Here too the true point of beginning for the Christian is to be found in the words of Jesus: "If any man will come after me, let him deny himself, and take up his cross, and follow me" (Matt. 16:24). Christian self-discipline demands self-denial. This is first and foremost the denial of self's rule. There must be nothing less than the dethronement of self, then it can become self-denial as a pattern of life in the sense of self-control. This includes the control of moods, affections, appetites, expenditures, time, tongue, not for the glory of self but the honor of Christ. At this level discipline is the governor which keeps the wheels of life from flying apart. Whether it is the works of a watch or a human personality, balance and control will increase both durability and efficiency. And a self-controlled person is easier to live with and work with, for there is less friction, vibration, and noise.

See DISCIPLESHIP, DISCIPLING, OBEDIENCE, GROW (GROWTH), SPIRITUALITY, LEISURE.

For Further Reading: Gardner, *Personal Religious Disciplines;* Cattell, *The Spirit of Holiness;* Shoemaker, *Ex-*

traordinary Living for Ordinary Men, 31-48; Taylor, *The Disciplined Life.* RICHARD S. TAYLOR

DISCIPLING. In its simplest definition, discipling is making disciples. However, the wording of the Great Commission seems to imply an extended obligation. For not only is the original imperative "make disciples" modified by "going" and "baptizing," but by "teaching them to observe all things whatsoever I have commanded you" (Matt. 28:19-20). It would seem clear, therefore, that discipling includes more than making converts.

This understanding has been the springboard for a relatively new but burgeoning movement called "discipling." This has become the technical term for a special form of teaching activity within the local church. The "discipler," generally the pastor or other qualified person, gathers around him a group of "disciples" whom he instructs at a deeper level and a more rapid, concentrated pace than the regular ministries of the church provide.

Methods, and even philosophies, greatly vary. A typical program is the use of a syllabus by a small, committed group in two-hour sessions each week for a year. Elton Trueblood's Yokefellow program envisions a five-year reading course under competent guidance in Bible, theology, church history, and related areas. Simpler plans call for shorter periods; some plans are much less structured. Some pastors focus on one-to-one (or two or three) relationships.

With some disciplers the task is seen to be the reproduction of the leader, with the idea that these in turn reproduce themselves, in a geometric progression and expansion of disciples and disciplers, until virtually the entire church has been not only discipled but become a body of disciplers.

The discipling approach is seen by its advocates as the quickest and most effective way to develop an efficient, spiritually mature, and soul-winning church. Undoubtedly it has great potential for the accomplishing of such a worthy objective. When properly managed, it has already revitalized many churches and opened to many pastors an exciting and much-needed new form of ministry.

Observers of the movement see possible perils which could counteract effectiveness. One is the additional load placed on the already hard-pressed laymen, resulting in further fragmentation of families, and further fatigue and frustration, which could prove counterproductive, if not disastrous. Furthermore, a pouring of pastoral and lay time and energies into discipling could also weaken the structure of the church as a whole, since many of the most willing disciples are the very ones most needed to hold office in the church schools, on the board, and elsewhere. Some pastors believe that better nurturing can be achieved by strengthening the agencies already in place, primarily the pulpit ministry and Christian education entities.

Perhaps also the supposed biblical base needs more careful examination. For one thing, it is unrealistic to try to pattern after the Jesus-Disciples model. No modern pastor has the authority or wisdom of Jesus; nor can he expect 12 or so people to leave their vocations, even their homes, to virtually live with him for three years. Even a very modest facsimile can result in damaging family disruption. This smacks more of some modern cults than of a soundly biblical church.

Lurking in the background, in some cases, is the disavowal of the distinction between clergy and laity, a disavowal widely popularized in recent times. Implicit is the understanding of Eph. 4:12 which interprets the ministries for which the saints are to be equipped to be those of the apostles, evangelists, prophets, and pastors and teachers (v. 11). This cannot possibly be the apostle's meaning. God has called these persons to these special vocations in the Church; they in turn are not authorized to "play God" and presume to reproduce themselves. Rather the equipping of laymen is for the ministries which belong universally to the Christian life—prayer, witnessing, stewardship, churchmanship, holy living. The erasing of a distinction between clergy and laity cannot be soundly supported biblically.

What could safely be acknowledged as proper goals of a discipling program? Perhaps five can be listed. (1) The program should aim at achieving a thorough grounding in Christian theology and biblical knowledge. This cognitive content should never be pushed into a corner by fellowship and inspiration, or an emphasis on personal support and affirmation. (2) There should be the aim of achieving Christian stability: commitment, devotional depth, and disciplined patterns of living. Knowledge must be supplied with self-control (2 Pet. 1:6). (3) Discipling provides a means of helping a Christian discover his "gifts" and to come to an understanding of God's will for him. (4) Discipling should result in a deeper, more all-absorbing concern for people—especially the lost—and increased skill *(a)* in interpersonal relationships and *(b)* in influencing the unconverted Christward. (5) Discipling should lead to or build upon a crisis experience of entire sanctification and should never be permitted to be a substitute.

See DISCIPLE, DISCIPLESHIP, DISCIPLINE, KOINONIA, CHURCH MEMBERSHIP, GROW (GROWTH), PIETISM.

For Further Reading: *Baker's Dictionary of Practical Theology,* 414-42; Eims, *The Lost Art of Disciple Making;* Kuhn, *The Dynamics of Disciple Building.*

RICHARD S. TAYLOR

DISCRIMINATION. This is a derivative of the Latin term *discriminare,* "to separate," and is related to the Greek *krisis* (verb, *krinō;* noun, *krisis;* adj., *kritikos*), from which we get such words as *critical.* In both Latin and Greek, it originally meant "to separate, to sunder." *Discriminare* means to have the rational power to distinguish between objects, real or logical. Also, it has the sense of distinguishing between moral right and wrong. In Aristotelianism, there is a function of internal senses by which men and higher animals distinguish the good from the bad in their sensory experiences.

Since the simple *krinein* means to "sunder," *diakrinein* is a stronger form of the same word (Latin, *discerno*). The NT emphasis is on making a distinction between persons (Acts 15:9; 11:12; 1 Cor. 4:7). It is used in the sense of judging between two in 1 Cor. 6:5. Matt. 16:3 uses this word to mean "assess."

In its noun form *(diakrisis),* it has several meanings: "separation," "distinction," "strife," "appraisal," and "exposition." Most often it means "differentiation" in the NT. At 1 Cor. 12:10, it is the differentiation of the prophets, while Heb. 5:14 is the differentiation between good and evil. To discern or differentiate between the spirits of the prophets is a gift of the Spirit (1 Cor. 12:10). Discernment or discrimination is an ability which the Holy Spirit gives to certain Christians so that they may discern between those speaking by the Spirit of God and those who speak by false spirits.

Discrimination is a term which has fallen into disrepute because of the negative connotations it has acquired. It has come to mean acting against someone on the basis of prejudice or bias. Originally its meaning was just the opposite: the ability to judge correctly. The ability to discriminate between good and evil is necessary to any kind of Christian ethic. One must be able to think and act discriminately if he is to have sound moral judgments. To think "critically" *(krinein),* to make judgments, and to discriminate is a sign of moral, emotional, and intellectual maturity. Without such ability one is like a ship without a rudder. Therefore, when used in the right sense, discrimination is positive rather than negative.

See DISCERNMENT, JUDGE (JUDGMENT).

For Further Reading: *ZPBD;* Bourke, *Dictionary of Philosophy;* Kittel, 3:921-54; Arndt, Gingrich.

JERRY W. MCCANT

DISPENSATION. The term is derived from the Latin *dispenso* (to weigh out, to administer as a steward) which translates the Greek *oikonomia,* rule of the house.

In Luke 16:2 ff *oikonomia* means the office of household management. It is rendered "stewardship" in KJV and NASB, and "management" in NIV. Paul's usage of the term has two chief meanings: first, the apostolic ministry to which he has been entrusted (1 Cor. 9:17); and second, the "plan of salvation" which God has undertaken to administer in the fullness of time (Eph. 1:10; cf. 3:9). Sometimes it is unclear which of these meanings is primary; the two are closely entertwined in the Prison Epistles (cf. Col. 1:25; Eph. 3:2).

Theological usage follows the second of Paul's meanings, in which dispensation refers to God's redemptive purpose and His method of executing it, e.g., "the Mosaic dispensation" (the old covenant) and "the Christian dispensation" (the new covenant). Sometimes these are improperly contrasted as the "dispensation of law" and the "dispensation of grace." However, God's purpose is from beginning to end one of grace. But this one gracious purpose has been revealed in, and administered through, two dispensations, the old and the new.

In Roman Catholic theology, dispensation refers to the official relaxation of canon law in particular and unusual instances.

In modern times, some evangelicals have claimed to find many dispensations in the Bible and have developed this into a hermeneutical principle. The Wesleyan-Arminian tradition generally rejects this hermeneutic.

See DISPENSATIONALISM, COVENANT THEOLOGY, PENTECOST.

For Further Reading: Kittel, 5:151 ff; *Baker's DT,* 167-68; *DCT,* 97.

ROB L. STAPLES

DISPENSATION OF THE SPIRIT. The outpouring of the Holy Spirit at Pentecost was the fulfilment of Joel's prophecy concerning the *end* of days (Acts 2:16 ff). In a distinctive manner the coming of the Spirit was an eschatological occurrence. It signified that the coming kingdom of God had already begun. The dispensation of the Spirit is unique to this period of time known as the last days, a period of time extending from Pentecost until the second coming of Christ.

Simultaneous with this dispensation of the Spirit is thus the establishment of the coming kingdom of God. This Kingdom began with the reign of the exalted Christ through the outpouring of the Spirit in the hearts of believers and will be consummated at the second coming of the exalted Lord at the final end. Luke related the coming kingdom of God with the Pentecostal gift of the Spirit (Acts 1:3).

This Kingdom had its preparation in the Promised Land motif. God entered into covenant with Abraham, promising to give His descendants the land of Canaan where they might worship Him with their whole heart. Hence Canaan was the sanctuary of Yahweh, His abode on earth (Exod. 15:17). Living in Canaan was conditioned upon an exclusive worship of God, i.e., a perfect love for God expressing itself in personal obedience and Temple observance. Failure to keep this command of perfect love resulted in captivity. From the beginning Moses had made it clear that the only basis for remaining in the Promised Land (Deut. 6:1-2) was a perfect love and exclusive worship of Yahweh (vv. 4-5). Because they failed to love Yahweh perfectly, they yielded to idolatry, and Yahweh "scattered them among the nations" (Ezek. 36:19, RSV). This punishment of exile from the Promised Land and the ensuing captivity was not the last word for Israel. Out of an act of sheer grace Yahweh freely chose to restore and renew the ancient promise which had been made with Abraham.

This hope of a new covenant and a restored kingdom became the theme of the prophets of the Exile. It is significant that Ezekiel equates the restoration of the Promised Land with the promised gift of the Spirit: "And I will put my Spirit within you, and you shall live, and I will place you in your own land" (37:14, RSV). What this restoration of the kingdom in the Promised Land further suggested was the sanctification of Israel and the perfecting of their love for Yahweh (Deut. 30:5-6, 16; Ezek. 37:28). Even before Israel had originally possessed the Promised Land, Moses had forseen that Israel would be removed because the people would fail to love God perfectly (Deut. 29:25 ff). He also saw that Israel would be regathered to the Promised Land where they would remain forever because "the Lord your God will circumcise your heart and the heart of your offspring, so that you will love the Lord your God with all your heart and with all your soul" (30:6).

Likewise the prophets interpreted their captivity as a punishment for failure to love God perfectly, but they also perceived the inability of Israel to measure up to Yahweh's requirement within the context of the ancient covenant. Yehezkel Kaufmann has shown in this regard that the prophets had come to see that "experience teaches that mankind as now constituted cannot keep God's covenant, hence a new mankind must be created whose heart God has refashioned" (*The Religion of Israel,* 426). Kaufmann has shown that the essence of this new covenant is a perfect love for God who "will purify them with pure waters, plant in them his spirit, and give them a 'heart of flesh' so that they will obey him forever" (475).

Luke's writings in particular show that the Pentecostal event fulfills this eschatological hope of the kingdom restored in the Promised Land. However, he shows that Jesus' understanding of the restored kingdom was radically different from the popular notion. The true Kingdom which was brought about by the Pentecostal event means that the exalted Christ reigns in the life of believers through the indwelling Spirit. In this respect, it is of symbolic significance that "the promise of the Father" which brought about the inauguration of this spiritual Kingdom occurred in Jerusalem, the capital city of the Promised Land (Acts 1:3-4).

Jesus' commission to His followers had stipulated that their proclamation should begin at Jerusalem and then extend to the ends of the earth (Luke 24:47). The power with which they were to conquer the world for the sake of God's kingdom was the power derived from "the promise of my Father" (v. 49; Acts 1:8). This is why the disciples were to wait in Jerusalem until the Pentecostal gift of the Holy Spirit had come to dwell within them. Only then could it be truly said that the Kingdom had come and the Temple fully restored to its former glory. For the Church as the Body of Christ is the temple of the Holy Spirit and the earthly center of the kingdom of Christ whose Spirit infills believers.

The primary meaning of the dispensation of the Spirit is that the righteousness of the Kingdom has become a reality. This means that the disciples and all believers may experience the personal, sanctifying grace through the infilling of the Holy Spirit (Luke 3:16; Acts 15:8-9). This means they are empowered to conquer the world because the Kingdom has been established in their hearts. Wesley's equation of the imagery of the promised rest of Canaan land with perfect love is appropriate. His hymns often allude to the imagery of Canaan land as descriptive of

Christian perfection. The following two verses cited in his *Plain Account of Christian Perfection* link the language of Pentecost, perfect love, and the Promised Land:

Choose from the world, if now I stand,
Adorn'd with righteousness divine;
If, brought into the promised land,
I justly call the Savior mine;
Thy sanctifying Spirit pour,
To quench my thirst, and wash me clean;
Now, Savior, let the gracious shower
Descend, and make me pure from sin.
Oh that I now, from sin released,
Thy word might to the utmost prove,
Enter into Thy promised rest,
The Canaan of Thy perfect love.

There is a historical distinction between the sending of the Son and the sending of the Spirit, but it can also be implied that there is in the life of the believer an experiential distinction between receiving the Son and receiving the fullness of the Pentecostal Spirit (cf. Gal. 4:4-7). Jesus' disciples were genuinely converted (Luke 10:20) before their subsequent experience with the Pentecostal Spirit. To be sure, the Spirit was with them before Pentecost, but He did not dwell in them (John 14:17). Hence in their case their experience of the Son and the Spirit were historically distinct. It is also significant that Jesus said that only those who were already believers could receive the Spirit (ibid.). Yet there is a sense in which one could be "born of the Spirit" even before Pentecost (3:5), though after Pentecost one could receive the gift of the indwelling Spirit in His fullness (14:15-20; cf. Acts 2:4). If one accepts at face value the accounts in Acts 8:14-17 and 19:1-7, the Samaritans and the Ephesians illustrate the possibility that one may have faith in Christ without having received the fullness of the Pentecostal Spirit.

See BAPTISM WITH THE SPIRIT, RECEIVING THE SPIRIT, PENTECOST, FILLED WITH THE SPIRIT.

For Further Reading: Wood, *Pentecostal Grace;* Thomas, *The Holy Spirit of God,* 185-89; Steele, *The Gospel of the Comforter;* Bultmann, *Theology of the New Testament,* 155; Hoffman, *The Holy Spirit,* 35-51; Carter, *The Person and Ministry of the Holy Spirit,* 221-59; *GMS,* 484-91, 619-23.

LAURENCE W. WOOD

DISPENSATIONALISM. This is a term referring to a type of interpretation of the Scripture which for all practical purposes originated early in the 19th century among a group of people who are known as Plymouth Brethren. Their most dominant leader and most original thinker was John Nelson Darby, whose teaching was marked by antagonism toward the organized church. The tenets of Darby and his peers have been popularized and proliferated through the notes of the Scofield Bible, edited by Cyrus Ingerson Scofield (1843-1921).

The distinguishing feature of dispensational teaching is the idea that the Bible portrays seven dispensations, a dispensation being incorrectly defined as a span of time marked by a different method of divine dealing with man, and all except the last ending in failure. The present dispensation is the Church age, which will culminate in judgment. This related to Darby's original disparagement of the organized church.

Dispensationalism's most popular ideas relate to its eschatological teachings. Building upon a Calvinistic view of covenant as unconditional, it is deeply interested in national Israel and in particular in her relation to the land of Palestine, which dispensationalists insist will be possessed in the end time for the establishment of an earthly, Jewish kingdom in fulfillment of God's promise to David.

The kingdom of heaven they say refers to the earthly, nationalistic rule which Jesus offered to the Jews but which they rejected. Thus God's program for Israel had to be postponed until later, and as an interim arrangement the Church age was ushered in. A further implication of this is the dispensationalist teaching of a secret Rapture of the Church to remove the Church from the earth so God can resume His original plan of establishing a Jewish earthly kingdom.

See DISPENSATION, CHURCH, RAPTURE, TRIBULATION, MILLENNIUM, ISRAEL, DISPENSATION OF THE SPIRIT.

For Further Reading: Ladd, *The Blessed Hope;* Bass, *Backgrounds to Dispensationalism;* Kraus, *Dispensationalism in America.*

H. RAY DUNNING

DISPERSION. This term (Greek, *diaspora*) refers to the movement of the Israelites and Judeans out of Palestine into foreign lands. It began with the Assyrian (722 B.C.) and Babylonian (597 B.C.) deportations. While these were enforced military actions, other dispersions were voluntary and took the Jews to Egypt, Asia Minor, Italy, and Greece. According to the Jewish philosopher Philo, there were at least 1 million Jews in Alexandria during his time. Acts 2:5 states that nearly every nation under heaven was represented among the worshippers at the Feast of Pentecost. In his First Epistle, Peter writes to the exiles of the Dispersion in Pontus, Galatia, Cappadocia, Asia, and Bithynia (1 Pet. 1:1), and James speaks of the 12 tribes of the Dispersion (1:1). Whether these references are to Jews or Christian Jews need not be debated here; suffice it to say, the

Dispersion was a widespread phenomenon of the first century B.C. and the first century A.D.

In the Roman Empire the Jewish religion was considered a *religio licita* (permitted religion), and thus the Jews lived in comparative peace. Contact was maintained with the homeland. The Temple tax was faithfully paid, and advice on ethical matters was sought from the Palestinian rabbis. The Torah was diligently studied in the synagogues, and its exhortations were assiduously followed in daily life.

However, Diaspora Judaism faced some opposition from the general populace because of its exclusiveness, evidenced in its denunciation of the Gentile idolatry and in its insistence on living strictly by the OT laws. When Christianity's missionary thrust was felt in the known world, Judaism's missionary interest, such as it was, diminished and virtually disappeared. All in all, the Jews of the Dispersion kept their identity religiously and culturally but not without significant intrusion by the cultures in which it existed.

In recent centuries, the Jews of the Reformed tradition have been much less exclusive and have moved freely into other ethnic groups even to the extent of marriage. The Holocaust on the continent of Europe during the Second World War era and the return of thousands of Jews to Israel have brought this term *dispersion* into prominence again in our time.

See JUDAISM, ISRAEL.

For Further Reading: Pfeiffer, *History of New Testament Times;* Tenney, *New Testament Times.*

WILLARD H. TAYLOR

DIVINATION. See SORCERY.

DIVINE ATTRIBUTES. See ATTRIBUTES, DIVINE.

DIVINE DECREES. By this term is meant God's will and purpose for His creation, especially in relation to the salvation of mankind. Strictly speaking, there is but one divine decree that comprehends all God's purposes, what Paul calls "the counsel of his will" (Eph. 1:11). The Greek term translated "counsel" is *boulē,* meaning "intention," "purpose," "resolve," and it embraces the totality of God's will, as the whole verse says: "According to the purpose of him who *accomplishes all things* according to the counsel of his will" (RSV, emphasis added). Christian theology does speak of the divine "decrees," but this is merely the language of accommodation, human understanding being unable to fully grasp the purposes of God.

Christian thought is historically divided into two schools, Calvinism and Arminianism. Calvinism, named after the teaching of the Genevan reformer John Calvin (1509-64), has built its entire system on an understanding of the divine decrees as absolute, eternal, and immutable, and as including, in advance, the final destiny of every descendant of Adam. This has resulted in the famous "Five Points" of Calvinism: (1) Unconditional election; (2) Limited atonement; (3) Natural inability, sometimes termed, after Augustine, "Total depravity" (i.e., man is so totally corrupt and dead in sin that, apart from grace, which is given only to the elect, he cannot will or do any spiritual good); (4) Irresistible grace; (5) Final perseverance, or "eternal security."

Arminianism, named after the Dutch theologian James Arminius (1560-1609), reacted strongly against what it saw as the unscriptural assumptions of Calvinism's Five Points. Historic Arminianism was modified in certain respects by the warm evangelicalism of John Wesley's teaching. What follows is a Wesleyan-Arminian understanding of the divine decrees.

All God's knowledge is immediate, simultaneous, and complete. To speak, therefore, of foreordained decrees is a misnomer, for, as John Wesley argued: "There is no foreknowledge, no more than afterknowledge, with God, but all things are known to Him as present from eternity to eternity" (*Explanatory Notes upon the NT* on 1 Pet. 1:2). Man was created free, and his subsequent fall was divinely permitted but not ordained. All God's purposes for man flow from His holiness and love, consequently He sent His Son that whoever believes in Him should be saved (John 3:16; 1 John 4:14). God's saving purpose extends to all men; He "desires all men to be saved and to come to the knowledge of the truth" (1 Tim. 2:4, RSV). Christ's sacrificial death is potentially efficacious for all men (Rom. 5:6-8; 1 Tim. 2:6; 1 John 2:2); it cancels the guilt of Adam's transgression (Rom. 5:18) and actively saves all who, through grace, consciously repent and believe on Christ. It also atones for all who die in infancy and for those who are mentally retarded. Salvation is wholly dependent on grace, for man is naturally dead in trespasses and sins (Eph. 2:1) until, through the gracious bestowment of prevenient grace, he is awakened by the Spirit to the sense of sin, his need of redemption, and thus enabled to cooperate with the Spirit in coming to Christ. Wesleyan-Arminianism further asserts that the "counsel of his will" makes provision for the believer in Christ to progress in holiness and righteousness and thus persevere through grace.

See CALVINISM, ARMINIANISM, PREDESTINATION, FOREKNOWLEDGE, CONTINGENT, ELECT (ELECTION), DIVINE SOVEREIGNTY.

For Further Reading: Berkhof, *Systematic Theology;* Calvin, *Institutes of the Christian Religion;* Arminius, *The Works of Arminius;* Pope, *A Compendium of Christian Theology;* Watson, *Theological Institutes;* Dayton, "A Wesleyan Note on Election," *Perspectives on Evangelical Theology,* Kantzer and Gundry, eds., 95-104; *GMS,* 424-38.

HERBERT MCGONIGLE

DIVINE ESSENCE. See ATTRIBUTES, DIVINE.

DIVINE HEALING. See HEAL, HEALING.

DIVINE IMAGE. The Scriptures inform us of the fact that man was created in the image of God *(imago Dei),* as a rational moral being (Gen. 1:26-27).

> Man's personality, linking him to what is above, separating him from what is beneath, constitutes him a being apart—a rational, self-conscious, self-determining creature, intended by his Creator for fellowship with Himself. . . . Knowledge, righteousness and holiness may fitly be considered elements in the character of man as originally designed by God. Likeness to God therefore is man's privilege above all created beings (J. I. Marais, *ISBE,* 1:146).

Man is a being that gathers up the meaning of all animal life as he rises into the dignity of personality. And rise he can, and must, to the realms of existence in peculiarity as an isolated individual with power of self-decision. As a self-directed being, man makes moral distinctions, senses moral obligation, and seeks some justifiable moral settlement. He is an animal, not only with a *reason* (cf. Aristotle's definition of man: "A rational, featherless biped"), but a *conscience.* And "conscience is that somewhat or someone within us that pronounces as to the rightness or the wrongness of our choice of motives" (Carlyle stated it thus, and Bresee and Wiley both championed the statement). Man does make choice of motives. The motive does not seize the man, but man seizes the motive. He is free to choose and use his motives. "Personal freedom . . . is the power to use uncoerced any motive given in self-consciousness" (Curtis, *Christian Faith,* 45). Man feels responsibly free.

So the taproot of man's moral concern is his intuitive sense of belonging to a supernatural Overlord. Man feels himself under authority and knows his supreme moral action is obedience.

Hence, only one motive is capable of organizing man into a whole person, and that one motive is holy love. Thus man seeks a *master motive* that he may be knit up into one coherent whole. Moral fear must be changed into moral love, and the moral law must become a personal friend to man. It is in the perfect love of the perfect God that man discovers the flower and perfection of true religion. Here his manhood rests in God, and the human person has deliberately chosen his everlasting home, where his heart rejoices in the supreme joy of self-consciously choosing to live *forever in God.* This is the religion of love, consummated by absolute personal unification with God. "For God created man to be immortal and made him to be an image of His own eternity" (Wisdom of Solomon, 2:23).

Theologians usually make a distinction between the *natural* and the *essential* image of God in man (his personality, his original constitution, that which makes him man), and the *moral* or *incidental* image (that original holiness and moral likeness to God which must remain dependent upon the use which man makes of the powers with which he was endowed at creation). And theologians usually argue that the first cannot be, and has not been, lost in the fall of man into sin; but that the second, or incidental, image and likeness to God was lost. The deepest fact of the essential image is man's likeness to God as a finite spirit. Man's cognitive powers (for knowledge) belong there also. And since man is spirit, an eternal existence of some character and state belongs there too—not the deathlessness of the body, but the nonextinction of man's being. Thus the soul may continue its existence forever, either in a state of sin and rebellion against reality, or in a state of love and commitment to that which is righteous and good.

What man lost in the Fall through the misuse of his God-given freedom was the original holiness and moral character, the blessed quality of his personality, which he enjoyed before "he made his wife, the serpent, and his own belly, his false trinity, under the fatal tree" (John Fletcher). Here was the wicked, wilful, self-surrender of man to enslavement by sin (Genesis 3). Thus to create a free moral agent cost God both a heartbreak and a cross. "The prophecy of the Serpent is the great deception" (Nicolai Hartmann). For sin does not open man's eyes, and to this day man lacks true knowledge of good and evil, and is plagued by a false sense of values.

The ruin was great, but the remedy is adequate (Gen. 3:15). And since man did not lose the natural image, and since the "free gift of God" passed back upon all men (Rom. 5:15-16, 18), mankind still retains its possibility for redemption, which fact gives value to the life even of the unregenerate. Man's lost spontaneity for holiness and God's gift of the Holy Spirit may be restored to him in regeneration and sanctification. Man was created internally harmonious with the possibilities of sinless development, which only his free act has annulled. It is only by God's enabling grace that any man returns in repentance to its renewment. Man's depravation comes by reason of his deprivation of the positive, personal, indwelling presence of the Holy Spirit, but God's free grace goes deeper than the stain of sin has gone. Man in likeness of God is still the promise of redemption through the *One Man* who never lost that image, for He only can baptize us with the Holy Spirit.

See ANTHROPOLOGY, HUMAN NATURE, REDEMPTION, SANCTIFICATION.

For Further Reading: Carl F. H. Henry, "Man," *Baker's DT;* Wiley, *CT,* 2:7-50. ROSS E. PRICE

DIVINE PRESENCE. See PRESENCE, DIVINE.

DIVINE SOVEREIGNTY. This concept is twofold. First, it may be seen as the divine *right* to rule totally; second, it may be extended to include God's *exercise* of this right. As to the first aspect, there is no debate. Difference of opinion (mainly between Calvinists and Arminians) arises in respect to the second aspect. Calvinists assume no limitation in God's active rule, in the sense that there can be no defeat to His will. Arminians postulate a self-limitation in God's exercise of His sovereignty, sufficient to allow for real free agency. They point to the biblical acknowledgment that some men will be lost in spite of the equally positive declaration that God wills the salvation of all (Ezek. 18:23, 32; John 3:16; 1 Tim. 2:4; 2 Pet. 3:9).

Yet the general concept of divine sovereignty is basic to any truly biblical theism (Ps. 115:3). First, it is essential to monotheism. God is not only divine; He is the only deity. God definitely reminded Moses, "Thou shalt have no other gods before me" (Exod. 20:3). God being the one and only God, He alone is responsible for the determination of the ends and purposes of the universe and all the creatures in it.

Second, the concept of divine sovereignty is vital in that God is clearly the Creator of the universe. No creative power could ever be finally successful unless that power also had a sense of final control over the destiny of its creation. It would be unthinkable to consider God as utterly adequate as Creator, and yet deny to Him ability to be sovereign over that creation.

In the third place, the biblical concept of God as Father requires the presupposition that His careful supervision over the affairs of mankind must be maintained with a fatherly purpose in mind.

But it must also be affirmed that it is no abrogation of divine sovereignty, even in accordance with His Fatherhood, for God to permit human beings to make their own choices relative to their final destiny. The term self-limitation has often been used to describe this extremely vital, yet amazing factor of divine sovereignty. This does not state that God would not be *able* to predetermine every decision of the human will, if He so chose. But it does affirm that God has given to men the power of determining their individual spiritual destiny. Thus, when God made man in His own image, He bestowed on man the capacity to make moral decisions which would be ultimate and final.

This is not a limitation of God's sovereignty intrinsically, since it is not an *imposed* limitation but established by God's own sovereign will. God could cancel out the gift of partial sovereignty to man, at any time, if He so desired.

Some aspects of divine sovereignty are still absolute with reference to man. God absolutely decrees that no man can be saved except through faith in His Son, Jesus Christ. Furthermore, the final destiny of the physical universe, "the new heavens and the new earth," is also God's sole prerogative.

See FREEDOM, FREE AGENCY, MONERGISM, SYNERGISM, PROVIDENCE, OMNIPOTENCE, DIVINE IMAGE.

For Further Reading: "God," *Baker's DT;* "Sovereignty," *ERE; GMS,* 116-19; Hills, *Fundamental Christian Theology.* NORMAN R. OKE

DIVINITY OF CHRIST. See CHRIST.

DIVISION. There is a *necessary* division of people. In the OT, Israel was "singled . . . out from all the nations of the world" (1 Kings 8:53, NIV). By God's choice they became His covenant people. In the NT, the Son of Man will gather all the nations at the Judgment, and "he will separate the people . . . as a shepherd separates the sheep from the goats" (Matt. 25:32, NIV). The basic and necessary division is between believers and nonbelievers.

A division from sin is mandatory. Believers are to be separate from sin and "come out from them and . . . touch no unclean thing" (2 Cor. 6:17, NIV).

A division in Christian service is essential. God sets apart believers for different ministries, service, and types of witness (Acts 13:2; Rom. 1:1; Gal. 1:15). In the parable of the prodigal son, the father divided his property (Luke 15:12), and division meant "to apportion" or "to distribute." The same word is used in 1 Cor. 12:4. Here it refers to the allotment of "different" spiritual gifts and implies the great variety and diversity of the gifts given by God for the purpose of carrying out His will.

But there is a *carnal* division which is to be deplored. This is shown in a disregard for Christian charity and love in the church. Schism often results from carnal division. A separation develops in the Body of Christ, not necessarily from heresy or because of a rejection of orthodox doctrine, but because of factious dissension and disagreements over nonessentials. A division hurts the witness and internal functioning of a church. The division may take the form of dissension on objectives, methods, and purpose; undermining leadership; and a lack of the necessary love for reaching out to nonbelievers. Jesus prayed that believers be one (John 17:11). Paul admonished us to "keep the unity of the Spirit through the bond of peace" (Eph. 4:3, NIV). The early Christians were "one in heart and mind" (Acts 4:32, NIV). The church should have a spirit of understanding, unity, love, and cooperation.

Carnal division is included in the list of the "works of the flesh" (Gal. 5:19). These are really the acts of the sinful nature as opposed to the "fruit of the Spirit" (vv. 22-23). The carnal mind (Rom. 6:6-7) is self-centered and only interested in having its own way. In Jude 19 is an example of apostates dividing the church.

Not all useless and hurtful division is necessarily carnal. Divisions may occur due to sincere but misguided rigidity. Sometimes there is a failure to distinguish between matters which are truly basic and those which only seem to be. The best-known example of division due to differences of honest judgment is the separation of Paul and Barnabas over Mark (Acts 15:39-40).

See SCHISM, UNITY.

For Further Reading: Wilbur E. Nelson, *Believe and Behave.*

CHARLES WILSON SMITH

DIVORCE. Divorce, the legal ending of a marriage, is recognized in the Bible record as early as Lev. 21:7. In the OT divorce was permitted. The law provided that a man might divorce his wife if she displeased him through any "indecency" (Deut. 24:1-4). The provision stated also that if a divorced wife married another man, she could never again become the wife of her first husband.

The word "indecency" is not defined. The Hebrew term indicates "nudity" and implies some sex defect. It could not, however, have been adultery (Lev. 20:10; Deut. 22:22-27), or suspected but unproved adultery (Num. 5:11-31). Mosaic law cited the practice of divorce in numerous situations (Lev. 21:7, 14; 22:13; Num. 30:9; Deut. 22:13-29; Ezek. 44:22). But Malachi points out God's displeasure toward the practice (Mal. 2:14-16).

Jesus repealed the allowance of Deut. 24:1-2, indicating that such a provision was sufferance, not approval (Matt. 19:3-9); and that the only reason for which a man might divorce his wife was marital unfaithfulness on her part (Matt. 5:31-32; 19:3-10). "Marital unfaithfulness," according to the Greek word, can include any kind of sexual immorality: adultery, incest, or other deviant sex practice. Mark 10:2-12 implies that a woman, if she be the innocent party, may for the same cause also rightfully divorce her husband.

Jesus' attitude toward remarriage of a divorced person is variously interpreted. This arises because of the apparent difference between the record in Matt. 19:9 and in Mark 10:11-12 and Luke 16:18. The first passage seems to allow remarriage for the innocent party, while the latter two passages mention no such allowance.

The teachings of these passages do not, however, necessarily differ. The three agree that Jesus abrogated the Mosaic permission. Mark and Luke focus attention on that one fact, while Matthew points out that Jesus also made two other provisions: that a spouse may divorce a mate only for marital unfaithfulness and, that having done so, may remarry.

The apostle Paul also taught about divorce. From 1 Cor. 7:10-15 we gather that a Christian spouse is not to divorce an unbelieving companion simply because of his unbelief, but if the unbelieving spouse willfully deserts the Christian partner, the believer is free from the marriage bond. It seems consistent with Jesus' teaching to say that if the desertion is final, as when the unbeliever disappears or is known to have remarried, the believer is free to marry in that he/she was wantonly deserted, which is tantamount to infidelity.

See FAMILY, MARRIAGE.

For Further Reading: Wiley, *CT,* 3:79-92; *GMS,* 555 ff.

ARMOR D. PEISKER

DOCETISM. In the dynamic tension between Jesus' humanity and divinity, Docetism, the earliest Christian heresy, erred on the side of Jesus' divinity. This belief held that Christ did not come in the flesh, and presupposed a radical dualism between spirit and matter, divine and human, in which the two cannot be conjoined. Docetism had two ways of understanding Christ's presence: (1) the "humanity" of Jesus was only an "appearance" (Greek *dokeō*, from which the term Docetic comes), a phantasm of some sort which *seemed* to be human flesh; (2) the divine, spiritual Christ came "into" or "upon" Jesus of Nazareth (usually associated with His baptism) and departed prior to the Crucifixion. This heresy, first encountered in 1 John 4:2-3 (cf. 2:22) and 2 John 7, and strongly contested in the writings of the Apostolic Fathers (cf. Ignatius to Ephesus [7:2; 18:2], Tralles [9-10], Smyrna [1-7]; Polycarp to Philippi [7:1]), became one of the features of the Christian Gnostic heresies of the second century. Both Docetism and Gnosticism stressed Jesus' divinity at the expense of His humanity.

See HUMANITY OF CHRIST, GNOSTICISM.

M. ROBERT MULHOLLAND, JR.

DOCTRINE. The word "doctrine" derives from the Latin *doctrina,* meaning "teaching" or "instruction." As used by teachers, it refers to the authoritative tenets accepted by a particular body of believers or adherents.

The OT employs the Hebrew *leqah,* meaning literally "what is received," to express the idea of doctrine (cf. Deut. 32:2; Job 11:4; Prov. 4:2; Isa. 29:24). In the developed OT thought, "doctrine" is associated with Torah, the teaching of Moses as found in the Pentateuch.

In the NT *didachē* is the principal word carrying the concept of doctrine. It denotes both the act of teaching and the substance of teaching. It is employed with respect to the general teachings of Jesus (cf. Matt. 7:28; John 7:16-17; etc.). According to the Book of Acts, new converts after Pentecost gave themselves to the teaching (*didachē,* "doctrine," KJV) of the apostles (Acts 2:42, RSV). The apostle Paul gives thanks to God that the Romans were "obedient from the heart to the standard of teaching" ("doctrine," KJV) to which they were committed (6:17, RSV).

Another NT word, sometimes translated "doctrine" or "teaching," is *didaskalia.* The instruction of the Pharisees is so called (Matt. 15:9; Mark 7:7). In the later Pauline writings (Ephesians; Colossians; the Pastorals) this Greek term is more frequently used. *Didaskalia* in the Pastorals suggests a fairly fixed body of orthodox thought.

Careful reading of both Testaments leads to the conclusion that a doctrinalizing process was operative both among the Jews and the Christians. It is not without significance, in this regard, that Paul includes teachers in his lists of needed personnel in the Church (cf. Rom. 12:7; 1 Cor. 12:28-29; Eph. 4:11).

The salient features of doctrine are the following: (1) the natural urge of the believing community to give the fullest expression to its faith; (2) special revelation as its basis; (3) the status of dogma when recognized by the entire Church as necessary, and when incorporated in her creeds. Any systematic theologizing in the Church must be sensitive both to doctrinal development and Church commitment.

See DOGMA (DOGMATICS), TEACH (TEACHING, TEACHER), DIDACHE.

For Further Reading: Orr, *The Progress of Doctrine,* 11-14.

WILLARD H. TAYLOR

DOGMA, DOGMATICS. This term is a transliteration of a Greek word and in the Greek literally means "decision," "command," "decree," or "ordinance." In popular usage today, *dogma* denotes a fixed principle or strong opinion which governs a wide range of a person's thought. In ecclesiastical usage it refers to an official teaching of a Christian community, the denial of which might constitute a person a heretic. Acts 16:4 is the only passage in the NT in which the word is employed somewhat in this more technical sense, though the reference involves matters more ethical than doctrinal in nature.

Generally two elements are required to make a teaching a dogma: (1) it must be considered revealed truth; (2) it must be contained in Scripture and/or tradition (as may be the case in Catholicism).

When the Christian Church had moved beyond the early period of proclamation of her faith and had begun to incorporate believers from many walks of life, it became necessary for her to define more precisely what she had been preaching. Her theological affirmations needed to be stated in dogmas. The Apostolic Fathers began to use the word *dogma* to denote the generally agreed-upon teachings. Ignatius and Origen in particular employed the word in this manner.

Orthodox Christians and many Anglican Christians accept as dogma the doctrinal decisions of the seven ecumenical councils. The Roman Catholics include as dogma the decisions of the ancient and modern councils plus the *ex cathedra* declarations of the pope. In Protestantism, dogma has not taken, for the most part, an ecumenical, hardened form, and considerable freedom has been permitted in the doctrinal development of the varied affirmations of the faith. However, some segments of Protestantism hold their doctrines to be so sacrosanct and unalterable that they may properly be designated as dogmas.

Dogmatics is the "systematic reflection on everything necessary and helpful, in method or content, for the understanding of dogma" (K. Rahner). As a theological discipline, dogmatics is "the scientific test to which the Christian Church puts herself regarding the language about God which is peculiar to her" (K. Barth). Dogmatics begin with the biblical affirmations or themes and with the church's preaching, and moves through the church's authoritative statements across the centuries. Thus, it is a task peculiarly responsible to the church. It includes, also, a speculative dimension which arises out of the dogmatist's own life, ethos, and previous instruction.

See DOCTRINE, CREED (CREEDS), SYMBOLICS, CHURCH COUNCILS, CONFESSION OF FAITH, EX CATHEDRA.

For Further Reading: "Dogma, dogmatizō," *TWNT,* 2:230-32; Barth, *Church Dogmatics: The Doctrine of the Word of God,* 1:1-47; Harnack, *History of Dogma,* 1:1-40; Pelikan, "Dogma," *A Handbook of Christian Theology;* "Dogma," *Sacramentum Mundi,* 2:95-111.

WILLARD H. TAYLOR

DOMINION. This is the possession of authority, power, control, or jurisdiction, whether exercised or not. In the OT, the English "dominion" translates several Hebrew words. The most frequent is some form of *mashal* which suggests the notion of rule or reign. The term is used to identify the sovereign position of the Messiah figure (Zech. 9:10), the enduring and encompassing realm of God's kingdom (Ps. 145:13), and the rightful place of prominence of Jerusalem among the nations of the world (Mic. 4:8).

The exercise of strong control and subjugation is the connotation of "dominion" when it translates *yad,* "hand" (Jer. 34:1, NASB). Similar force is conveyed by the use of *radah* ("tread down, rule"), for military dominion over an enemy (Num. 24:19). *Radah* is the term used in the Genesis creation account to indicate mankind's God-given "dominion," i.e., the authority and power to exercise dominance over the other living creatures on the earth (Gen. 1:26). This is not license to devastate creation but a mandate to master nature.

The Hebrew *sholtan,* "rule" or "dominion," found a dozen times in the Book of Daniel, signifies a specific political power structure. Ultimate rule over all other lesser domains will be given to the holy ones who constitute the kingdom of the "Highest One" (Dan. 7:27, NASB).

In the NT the English word "dominion" occurs infrequently (once in the Gospels). Two Greek words, *kurieuein,* "to be master or lord," and *kratos,* "power," "strength," "might," convey the idea of "dominion." The lordship humans exercise over other humans (Matt. 20:25), and the oppressive power of law (Rom. 7:1), sin (6:14), and death (v. 19), are instances in which the verb "to exercise dominion" (Greek, *kurieuein*) is used. Supreme power is attributed to God by the word "dominion" (Greek, *kratos*) in six NT doxologies (1 Pet. 4:11; 5:11; 1 Tim. 6:16; Jude 25; Rev. 1:6; 5:13, NASB). Nowhere in the NT does *kratos* describe the power or position a human possesses. In a single instance the term is used to refer to a power denied to the devil (Heb. 2:14).

In their awareness of the varieties of dominion, authority, mastery, control, capability, or lordship, the biblical writers clearly reserve ultimate power exclusively for God and recognize all other power as derived power and subject to permission. All dominions are within His domain.

See CREATION, MAN, GOD, ATTRIBUTES (DIVINE), ECOLOGY.

For Further Reading: *HDNT,* 489 ff; Schnackenburg, *God's Rule and Kingdom,* 14 ff; Liddell and Scott, *A Greek-English Lexicon,* "Kratos," 992-93.

KENNETH E. HENDRICK

DOUBLE PREDESTINATION. According to this doctrine, God has predetermined not only the salvation of the elect but the damnation of the nonelect. The classical expression of double predestination is in the words of Calvin: "Predestination we call the eternal decree of God, by which he has determined in himself, what he would have to become of every individual of mankind. For they are not all created with a similar destiny; but eternal life is foreordained for some, and eternal damnation for others. Every man, therefore, being created for one or the other of these ends, is, we say, predestined either to life or to death" (*Institutes,* 3. 21. 5). According to this view, divine grace operates arbitrarily, selectively, and monergistically.

In a radical restatement of this doctrine, Karl Barth contends that Jesus Christ is the Elect Man and that all mankind is elected in Him collectively, and not as separate individuals. Christ has taken election and reprobation unto himself for the entire race. Some critics see in Barth's view an implicit universalism.

See PREDESTINATION, INFRALAPSARIANISM, UNIVERSALISM, DETERMINISM.

For Further Reading: Calvin, *Institutes of the Christian Religion,* 3. 21; Barth, *Church Dogmatics* 2, no. 2, chap. 7.

WILLIAM M. ARNETT

DOUBLE-MINDEDNESS. See CARNAL MIND.

DOUBT. In its broadest scope, doubt means suspension of judgment. It is the method employed in any quest for truth when the conclusion has not yet been arrived at. But doubt can become agnosticism if the mind is unable to embrace hope or truth in its search. Skepticism is a further hardening of the categories into the position that not only does one not know (agnosticism), but one cannot know the truth.

Thomas, as the doubting disciple, is often thought of as having a scientific bent of mind, for he demanded evidence or proof of Christ's resurrection (John 20:24-29). But that he was able to accept the proof given is commendable. God does not arbitrarily demand "blind obedience," but He does expect response to adequate evidence. And the Christian basically regards the agnostic as one who refuses to believe reasonable evidence—not as one who rejects or doubts the ridiculous. Nor can the Christian accept some form of credulity or easy believism, which is the opposite of doubting.

Faith is the cure of doubt. While many may "not enter in because of unbelief" (Heb. 3:19), to those who believe is given "power to become the sons of God" (John 1:12).

See FAITH, UNBELIEF, SKEPTICISM.

For Further Reading: *Dictionary of Moral Theology,* 432; Hastings' *Encyclopaedia of Religious Knowledge,* 4:862-65.

R. DUANE THOMPSON

DOVE. The word is the same in Hebrew for both dove and pigeon. This common bird of Bible lands is often used in Scripture as an illustration due to its familiar characteristics, such as its mournful voice (Nah. 2:7), homing instinct (Isa. 60:8), harmless disposition (Matt. 10:16), and false sense of security in danger (Hos. 7:11). The very word became a term of endearment (Song of Sol. 2:14).

More important is the OT use of the bird as a sacrifice which the poor could offer in place of a lamb (Lev. 5:7). This shows that God's great atoning sacrifice was for all classes.

The dove is also prominent to typifying the Holy Spirit at the baptism of Jesus (Luke 3:22). At this event the threefold personality of the Trinity is clearly disclosed. The emblem of the dove to typify the Holy Spirit demonstrates His own nature of love, and His descent upon Christ fulfills the prophecy of the Spirit's anointing upon our Lord (4:18), and symbolizes the purity and meekness which mark the character and disposition of the Messiah.

See EMBLEMS OF THE HOLY SPIRIT.

For Further Reading: Earle, "Luke," *WBC,* 4:223; Morgan, *Crises of the Christ,* 121; Wiley, *CT,* 2:332.

LESLIE D. WILCOX

DREAMS. The Hebrew word for "dream," *chalom,* is used 33 times in Genesis and 29 times in other places in the OT. Daniel uses *chelem* 22 times. The Greek word for "dreams," *onar,* is used 6 times in Matthew. Acts 2:17 uses *enupnion:* "that which happens in sleep," a dream.

There seem to be three sources of dreams, and their influence is felt in at least three areas of man's experience in life. The three originating sources are (1) natural (Eccles. 5:3); (2) divine (Gen. 28:12); and (3) evil (Deut. 13:1-2; Jer. 23:32).

The significance of dreams is felt in these areas: (1) the intellectual; (2) ethical; (3) spiritual.

Most agree that the mind and emotions are very active while the body is asleep. Many problems are solved and great poetic and musical works are conceived during sleep while the recipient is dreaming. Some believe that dreams reflect the true character or desires of the person; others deny this.

The spiritual nature of dreams is reflected in the fact that God has used them in direct and special communication between himself and man.

The visions of the prophets should be differentiated from dreams per se. The former may be given during either waking or sleeping times.

Obviously God warned people by dreams (Gen. 20:3; 31:24; Job 4:12-21); gave special orders concerning His will (Gen. 28:12; 31:10-13; 1 Sam. 28:6; 1 Kings 3:5; Matt. 1:20) for the present and the future (Daniel).

Most dreams needed interpretation, and some men possessed this gift from God (Gen. 40:5; Dan. 2:1-9; Deut. 2:27). But the Preacher reminded the OT believer as well as us not to put too much reliance in dreams (Eccles. 5:7). The interpretation must not be contradictory to the Law (Deut. 13:1; Jer. 27:9).

The Gentile nations—Babylonia, Greece, Rome, Egypt—all placed heavy emphasis on dreams and the temple as the proper place to receive them *(HBD).* It is not surprising that the OT gives more examples of God revealing himself to Gentiles in this manner than to the Hebrews. The visions of the prophets were a more direct means of God's revelation to the chosen people.

It is important to notice that dreams were more apparent at the beginning of OT and NT times than in the later portions of these periods.

The Scriptures are for guidance and direction, and there is little need for special dreams or visions for the NT believer today.

See REVELATION (SPECIAL), SORCERY.

For Further Reading: *HBD; HDB; ZPBD.*

ROBERT L. SAWYER, SR.

DRUNKENNESS. Drunkenness has been a severe problem since antiquity. The evil of intoxication is condemned in the Bible. It is clearly listed as a vice (Rom. 13:13; Gal. 5:21; 1 Cor. 5:11; 6:10). Immoderation is an evil of the night (1 Thess. 5:7) and will leave one unprepared for the coming of the Kingdom (Luke 21:34). Christians must resist strongly even a suspicion of drunkenness (Acts 2:15) because of its association with pagan cults (H. Preisker, *methē,* Kittel, 4:548). In Communion (1 Cor. 11:21), drunkenness and the new way of Christian living are not compatible. Clearly, drunkenness is a characteristic of pagans (1 Pet. 4:3). Christians are admonished, instead, to be filled with the Spirit (Eph. 5:18).

Wine and strong drink appear together often, referring to intoxicants in general (Isa. 5:11). Wisdom literature reads, "Wine is a mocker, strong drink a brawler" (Prov. 20:1, NASB). Jesus gives no ethical or religious judgment to the drinking of wine (John 2:10), but abstinence seems to be a higher ethic than so-called temperance. Nazarites vowed to refrain (Num. 6:3); Daniel and his friends chose to stop (Dan. 1:8-16); and priests while on duty in the sanctuary were required to abstain (Lev. 10:9). Paul's charge to Timothy is to "be sober in all things" (2 Tim. 4:5, NASB) so he can keep clarity of mind. Total refraining from intoxicants is implied in Matt. 16:24 ff. The thoughtful Christian is asked to abstain from wine if it will cause his weaker brother to fall back into sinful ways (Rom. 14:13-21; 1 Cor. 8:8-13).

In ancient times the poor could not afford to drink to excess. The cheapening of alcoholic drinks and the complicated fast pace of modern living have made drunkenness a greater social problem (S. Barabas, *ZPBD,* 229).

See DISCIPLINE, INFLUENCE, WORKS OF THE FLESH, TEMPERANCE.

For Further Reading: Arndt, Gingrich, 540; *NIDNTT,* 1:513 ff; Kittel, 4:545, 936 ff; Nelson, *Believe and Behave.*

CHARLES WILSON SMITH

DUALISM. Dualism is the theory which, in contrast to monism, argues that reality is composed of exactly two substances which are equally primordial, mutually opposed, and irreducibly different. These two substances are variously designated, e.g., as spirit and matter, mind and matter, mind and body, good and evil, God and Satan, etc.

There have been many forms of dualism, such as Zoroastrianism and Manichaeism in Persia, Taoism in China, much of Greek thought, and the Gnosticism of the early Christian era.

Probably the most influential form of dualism in modern Western thought is the Cartesian bifurcation of reality into mental substance and material substance, or mind and matter. For Descartes, mind is immaterial, conscious, and characterized by thinking. Matter is characterized by extension. Man's body is part of the world of matter and is subject to its laws. Mind, on the other hand, cannot be destroyed except by God, who is the only nondependent substance.

Faith in the one God who is Creator and Lord rules out any absolute dualism in the OT. Nevertheless Israel's faith refused all easy attempts to reconcile the unfathomable contrast between sin and forgiveness, misery and salvation. This realism is continued in the NT where Christian existence is expressed dialectically; by Paul, as the antithesis between law and gospel, works and faith, flesh and spirit, the inner and the outer man; and by John, as the opposition between light and darkness, life and death, truth and the lie. But these practical biblical descriptions do not constitute an ultimate dualism, since God is Lord of all nature and all history.

Dualistic systems often seem to give a plausible account of what is so obvious in the world around us, the presence of both good and evil, order and disorder. "Dualism requires one to shut one's eyes to neither side of the picture" (MacGregor, *Introduction to Religious Philosophy,* 71). Thus its appeal is understandable. It *describes* very well the universe as we ordinarily experience it. But as an *explanation* of ultimate reality it falls short. It is in fact simply a refined form of polytheism.

See REALISM, METAPHYSICS, MONISM, BODY, MIND, MAN, SOUL, DIVINE IMAGE.

For Further Reading: MacGregor, *Introduction to Religious Philosophy,* 70-72; Shaffer, "Mind-Body Problem," *The Encyclopedia of Philosophy,* 5:336-46; Simons, "Dualism," *Encyclopedia of Theology,* 370-74.

ROB L. STAPLES

DUTY. In ethics or moral philosophy, duty is an obligation perceived to be inherent in the situation or relationship. In philosophy this perception may be *deontic* or *axiological.* The deontologist stresses the intuitive insight into the duty of the moment without regard to consequences or analysis in terms of objective values. The axiologist emphasizes the necessity of determining duty by a system of values, including the consideration of consequences.

According to Immanuel Kant, the foremost exponent of deontological ethics, there is only one entity which can be called "good" without qualification (i.e., without reference to something else) and that is the "good will." The good will, for Kant, is the will which chooses in accordance with duty for duty's sake alone, i.e., with no thought whatever for the consequences of obeying one's duty—such as, for example, one's own self-interest, the rationally coordinated interests of the majority of people, or the sanctions of social or legal conventions.

Duty, for Kant, finds expression in the categorical imperative, the three forms of which can be simplied as follows: (1) never make an exception of yourself (universability of moral principles); (2) always treat persons (including oneself) as ends and never as means only (or merely as a tool or an object of manipulation); (3) always organize society so as to promote the maximum of personal freedom within the boundaries of moral law and mutual respect (moral autonomy).

The application of duty in this fashion in concrete situations of life has been criticized by some as unable to resolve conflicting duties—for example, one's duty to tell the truth (to a Nazi soldier) and one's duty to save a life (if you are hiding a wanted Jewish person in your home). Other criticisms question where the "goodness" to which Kant refers is the same as the "rightness" which the consequentialists hold that our action should bring about.

The Bible recognizes the role of duty in the daily life of the child of God. In fact the Law in the OT imposed by its very presence the duty of every Jew to obey it (2 Chron. 8:14 ff; Ezra 3:4). It may be said that the ethic of the OT has a strong deontic emphasis, i.e., a bias toward the keeping of the law, sometimes without regard to the motive (1 Chron. 13:9).

In the NT we find an important distinction made by Jesus between the ceremonial law and the moral law. It was necessary to make this distinction because the Pharisees had overlooked the weightier moral law in their selfish desire to manipulate the ceremonial law for their own interest. Jesus said that our duty to God and to our fellowman is completely embraced in *sacrificial love* (John 13:34; 15:12-17). The writers of the NT were convinced that if we *love* God supremely, we would have no undue concern about obeying God as we should (e.g., Rom. 13:10). Such a Christian view of duty will aid in providing the solution to conflict of either a purely philosophical approach or a legalistic approach. Such a view will go a long way to resolving the problems which arise when two duties seem to conflict (see above). The Christian who faces such a dilemma, after assuring himself that he truly desires God's will at this point in his life more than anything else, should seek direction prayerfully from God's Word and from more experienced Christians until he is illumined. Only under such guidance can one ascertain what one's loving duty is.

The courage to do one's duty lovingly and sacrificially irrespective of pleasure or pain is derived only from the grace of God. Moralists who rely only on the intellectual approach to their duty tend also to rely on their own strength to perform it. The result at worst may fall short of the mark; at best such "duty-bound" conduct is cold and formal. Only that motivation which is supplemented by divine grace (in Wesley's terms "perfect love") is sufficient to result in the actual performance of one's loving duty toward God, toward one's neighbor, and even toward oneself.

Christian theology therefore is both deontic and axiological. Holiness of heart enables one to fulfill Kant's categorical imperative, for only a sanctified will is a will strong enough to implement itself to conduct as a "good will" should. Holiness of heart will also help the soul searching for his duty amid conflicting duties, to discover "his duty in that situation" through the help of the Holy Spirit, amidst prayerful study of the Scriptures and prayerful counsel. The respect which Kant teaches one should have for all persons is much easier to show when one is filled with divine love. Such motivation is not based upon rewards—such as to escape hell or gain heaven, or even to have done one's duty—but rather it is based upon our love of God which for Christ's sake has been shed abroad in our hearts. God, therefore, is our supreme Reality and our final Authority.

See OBEDIENCE, VALUES, ETHICS, CHRISTIAN ETHICS.

For Further Reading: Purkiser, ed., *Exploring Our Christian Faith,* 489 ff; Wiley, *CT,* 3:36-79; *Baker's DCE,* 194 ff; Facione, et al., *Values and Society;* Hospers, *Human Conduct* (shorter ed.)

ALVIN HAROLD KAUFFMAN

DYOTHELITISM. See MONOTHELITISM.

E

EARNEST. This word occurs three times in the KJV. In 2 Cor. 1:22 we read that God has "given the earnest of the Spirit in our hearts." In 5:5 we find a very similar statement: "God, who also hath given unto us the earnest of the Spirit." In Eph. 1:14 we find that the promised Holy Spirit "is the earnest of our inheritance until the redemption of the purchased possession."

The Greek word is *arrabōn.* Arndt and Gingrich say that it was a technical legal term, meaning "first instalment, deposit, down payment, pledge" (p. 109). In Kittel, Johannes Behm writes: "The Spirit whom God has given them is for Christians the guarantee of their full future possession of salvation" (1:475). That is, the Holy Spirit is the down payment on our heavenly inheritance, the guarantee that we will receive the full inheritance in due time. As such, it is a foretaste of what heaven will be like. The conscious presence of the Holy Spirit in our hearts is "a little bit of heaven in which to go to heaven."

Moulton and Milligan write: "The above vernacular usage (found in the papyri of that period) confirms the NT sense of an 'earnest,' or a part payment given in advance of what will be bestowed fully afterwards" (*Vocabulary of the Greek Testament,* p. 79). But they also note that in modern Greek, *arrabōna* is used for the engagement ring. When we say a full, final "yes" to the will of God, to belong to Him forever, He fills us with His Holy Spirit, sealing our betrothal to Christ.

The NIV brings out the force of *arrabōn* by translating it in 2 Corinthians as "a deposit, guaranteeing what is to come." In Eph. 1:14 it is "a deposit guaranteeing." RALPH EARLE

EASTER. See HOLY WEEK.

EASTERN ORTHODOXY. This refers to that large branch of Christendom which, long before the Reformation, gradually separated itself from the Christianity that obtained in the Western European countries. It has had Constantinople (the modern Istanbul) as its main see, whereas the West has maintained its main center of control in Rome—and has thereby come to be called Roman Catholicism.

Several factors figured in the break-off of the East from the West. One matter was a difference of view about when Easter should be celebrated. A much more important matter was the East's contention that the Holy Spirit has proceeded eternally only from God the Father; whereas, in the West (Roman Catholic; and later, Protestantism in general) it has been understood that He has proceeded eternally from both the Father and the Son. In the East, they feel that it suggests a higher status for the Holy Spirit if He has proceeded only from the Father, and not from the Son as well.

Differences from Roman Catholicism today include the fact that, in Eastern Orthodoxy, infants are given Communion, and most priests may marry.

Although Eastern Orthodox theologians teach that theirs is the only true church, unlike Roman Catholicism, many of their national branches (at least 16) are officially members of the World Council of Churches.

For many centuries, Eastern Orthodoxy received little attention from the Catholic and Protestant West. But in our century, the West has become much more conscious of Eastern Orthodoxy and much more appreciative of the richness of its traditions.

See CATHOLICISM, CATHOLICISM (ROMAN).

For Further Reading: Bulgakov, *The Orthodox Church* and *The Wisdom of God;* Pelikan, *The Christian Tradition;* Constantelos, *The Greek Orthodox Church;* Zankov, *The Eastern Orthodox Church.* J. KENNETH GRIDER

ECCLESIA, ECCLESIOLOGY. See CHURCH.

ECCLESIASTICAL OFFICES. See OFFICES, ECCLESIASTICAL.

ECOLOGY. A century ago Ernst Haeckel coined the word *ecology,* conjoining two Greek words: *oikos* (house) and *logy* (word, reason), i.e., an awareness of our Mother Earth's household. As the word is used, it further implies a moral attitude, a reverence or respect for, as well as a theoretical knowledge of, the whole of creation.

Ecology encompasses and ties together virtually everything: in biology it emphasizes the harmonious interaction of organisms and their environment; in sociology it relates human societies to natural resources; in ethics it assesses our moral responsibility for the world around us; in theology it suggests stewardship of God's creation.

Our "environmental crisis" reveals our lack of ecological wisdom. We human beings have failed to appreciate the intricate balance of nature. Consequently we have abused and destroyed enormous parts of a finely tuned planet Earth. Though noted ecologists warn we are destroying the very foundation of life itself, few folks seriously heed them. In order to raise our standard of living, to boost the nation's GNP, to stockpile genocidal weapons, human beings have willfully assaulted earth, air, and water.

Taking a long look into the future, probably few issues should concern us more than ecology. Overpopulation and overconsumption of energy and resources threaten to literally destroy the earth. Unless radical changes take place, people will face truly unsolvable problems within a century. By the year 2000, some scholars argue, crises will rage around the world as ecosystems collapse.

Given this situation, Christians must hear the Word of the Lord. For "all things were made by" the Word (John 1:3), and "in him all things hold together" (Col. 1:17, RSV). The very word of God indwells and enstructures every creature, so David declared: "the earth is the Lord's, and the fulness thereof" (Ps. 24:1). Whatever God made should be used but not abused, for all God made is good in His sight (cf. Genesis 1). Whenever the land and its creatures are selfishly exploited for pleasure-seeking or empire-building ends, God's will is thwarted.

In a thoroughly biblical sense, environmental abuse is sinful. We call those who destroy a building *vandals* and hold them guilty of wronging the building's owner. How much worse are those who willfully plunder the planet and ravage the forests and foul the air God made?

Our approach to the environment reveals much of our attitude toward God. Whereas idolaters seek to impose their will on creation, servants of God seek to live humbly with the world given them. God's people are called to be stewards of God's gifts, including the world of nature. Christians who sense their bodies are a temple of the Holy Spirit need to further sense how God cares for all He created. As His people, our task in the world is to faithfully reverence and preserve all God is and does and makes.

See STEWARDSHIP, CREATION.

For Further Reading: Berry, *The Unsettling of America;* Commoner, *The Closing Circle;* Schaeffer, *Pollution and the Death of Man;* Wilkinson, ed., *Earthkeeping: Christian Stewardship of Natural Resources.* GERARD REED

ECONOMIC TRINITY. The *economic Trinity* is a theological concept which describes the *revelation* of the Trinity in the divine economy *(oikonomia)* or work of salvation. *Oikonomia,* which originally referred to the management of a household, here defines *economic Trinity* in contrast to *essential Trinity.* The latter describes God as He is intrinsically or in essence, without reference to His relation to the order of creation. As Thielicke writes: "The so-called essential Trinity means that God's trinity is grounded in God himself and is thus independent of the relation of our consciousness" (*The Evangelical Faith,* 176 ff). Another way to express this is to say that God is eternally triune and would be truine even if He had never made himself known to His creation.

In Pauline theology may be recognized the primary lines of the economic Trinity. Father, Son, and Holy Spirit are distinguished by their differing functions or operations in salvation, i.e., the Father elects, the Son redeems, the Spirit seals (Eph. 1:3-14). This economic or operational doctrine of the Trinity was the primary concern of the Puritan John Owen and prominent in John Wesley's theology.

Care must be exercised to avoid any suggestion that God, in reaching out to humanity in Christ and in the Holy Spirit, communicates the mere notion or appearance of Trinity. This would approximate the error of the modalists, who suggested that God puts on a different mask to appear as Son or as Spirit. The mission of the Son or the Spirit to the world must not be confused with the Gnostic conception of emanations from God that are only pale reflections of Deity.

God communicates himself *as* Trinity because He *is* Trinity. The economic Trinity is the essential Trinity communicated to humanity, or else it is not Trinity at all.

H. E. W. Turner treats the concept of economic Trinity as heretical (*DCT,* 104). By his definition, it means that in the self-communication of God through the Son and Spirit, the latter do not sustain full coinherence to the Godhead. If the conception of God's triunity is forgotten (as in a unitarianism of the "Second Person") in the zeal to magnify His operation in creation and redemption, then the danger of monism is great.

When it is recognized that God communicates himself in Son and Spirit (see John 15:26 on the Son's procession, or mission, other words for communication), and that this in no sense is a changing of His essential triunity, then Turner's concerns seem obviated.

Karl Rahner interprets and updates the economic concept by speaking of "three distinct ways of being there (in the economy of salvation)" and restates the essential concept as "three different ways of subsistence (immanently [by which Catholic theologians mean 'essential']), for the one God" (*Sacramentum Mundi,* 6:302).

The Trinity is the fundamental mystery of Christian faith. Without God's self-communication (revelation) it could never be remotely conceived. Yet this revelation must be accommodated to human limitations. "God's absolute self-communication to the world, as a mystery that has approached us, is in its ultimate originality called Father; as itself a principle acting in history, Son; as a gift bestowed on us and accepted, Holy Ghost" (Rahner). This revelation is God's self-communication, not something of creation.

Wiley distinguishes the essential relations of God (within the Trinity) which are eternal, from the economic relations which are "to some temporal and external effect," i.e., creation, salvation (*CT,* 2:421 ff). He points out the value of the term *economical Trinity,* when one keeps both *essential* and *economic* in careful balance.

See TRINITY, GOD, CHRISTOLOGY, ESSENTIAL TRINITY.

For Further Reading: Thielicke, *The Evangelical Faith,* 2:176 ff; Wiley, *CT,* 1:422 ff.

LEON O. HYNSON

ECUMENICAL, ECUMENISM. These terms denote the beliefs, principles, or practices of those who desire and work for worldwide unity and cooperation among all Christian churches. The adjective *ecumenical* is used to identify the movement which seeks to promote worldwide church unity and cooperation.

These terms come from the Greek word *oikoumenē,* which originally meant "the whole inhabited world." The term *ecumenical* was adopted by the ancient church to designate general councils which formulated general or ecumenical creeds. The Roman Catholic church acknowledges 20 church councils as ecumenical, but the non-Roman communions acknowledge as ecumenical only those 7 general councils ending with the Second Council of Nicaea in A.D. 787.

Though this use of these terms goes back to the early centuries of the history of the church, the movement which seeks to foster church unity and which is called the ecumenical movement is quite recent. Some events which helped to bring this movement into being are the Interdenominational Missionary Conference in New York City in 1900, which took the name Ecumenical Missionary Conference; the World Missionary Conference in Edinburgh in 1910; and the founding of the World Council of Churches in 1948, which has devoted a major part of its interests to the ecumenical movement.

C. Stanley Lowell (*The Ecumenical Mirage,* 11-12) points out that there are two facets of ecumenism: "One refers to cooperation or to a feeling of cooperativeness among the churches. The other aspect of ecumenism is a drive for Christian unity which envisages bringing all churches . . . under one ecclesiastical tent." The first of these aspects is the goal of a sizable part of the Christian world, but a much smaller number is willing to go on to the second.

See CHURCH, DENOMINATION.

For Further Reading: Goodall, *The Ecumenical Movement;* Lowell, *The Ecumenical Mirage.*

CHARLES L. CHILDERS

EDIFICATION. The Greek word *oikodomē,* used frequently in the Synoptic Gospels, means literally "to build or construct." Paul speaks of the Church as "built upon the foundation of the apostles and prophets" (Eph. 2:20). He often uses the word to mean "edify" in the sense of strengthening, unifying, making for peace, "Let all things be done unto edifying" (1 Cor. 14:26). "Wherefore comfort yourselves together, and edify one another, even as also ye do" (1 Thess. 5:11). Edification is the test of a healthy church (Acts 9:31). Edification also is the touchstone of what is allowable and appropriate in corporate worship (1 Cor. 14:5, 12, 26, 31-33).

Believers are built-up, growing together, strengthened by one another into a "holy temple in the Lord" (Eph. 2:21). In achieving this goal, great stress is placed on the ministry of the Word (Acts 20:32). Also the Christian must maintain a growing, consistent love relationship with his fellow Christians. No one has a right to exercise a gift to secure human approbation or for other selfish gain. The Church is a partnership with God and our fellow believers. "Let us therefore follow after the things which make for peace, and things wherewith one may edify another" (Rom. 14:19). "We do more for truth by edification than by wrangling. It is better to pray for the erring than to confute them" (François Fénelon).

See WORSHIP, FELLOWSHIP, GIFTS OF THE SPIRIT.

For Further Reading: *IDB,* 2:24; *Wycliffe Bible Encyclopedia,* 490.
JAMES D. ROBERTSON

EFFECTUAL CALLING. God's call to salvation is extended through the gospel and the agency of the Holy Spirit. Two major positions are taken concerning the nature of this call.

The term *effectual calling,* as used by those who believe in particular predestination, indicates that the call operates effectually unto salvation for all to whom it comes, without regard to any "works" of their own. *The Westminster Shorter Catechism,* a basic authority for Calvinistic theology, states, "Effectual calling is the work of God's Spirit, whereby, convincing us of our sin and misery, enlightening our minds in the knowledge of Christ, and renewing our wills; He doth persuade and enable us to embrace Jesus Christ, freely offered to us in the gospel."

Effectual calling is one of the five major points of Calvinism. Sometimes the term *Irresistible grace* is used instead (Wiley, *CT,* 2:351, fn.). Either term means that all who are "called" (by the Spirit) will infallibly be saved. Rom. 8:29-30 is adduced in support of this view. But this passage is a series of statements, enumerating God's provisions for those mentioned in the opening statement, "Whom he did foreknow." J. Agar Beet explains this passage: "It might be thought that what God ordained must in every case be realized. But God has thought fit that the accomplishment of His own purposes shall depend upon man's faith" (*Commentary on St. Paul's Epistle to the Romans,* 248).

The Wesleyan position holds that passages like this must be interpreted in the light of other scriptures which plainly state that the gospel is for "whosoever" and that fulfillment of its benefits is dependent upon man's response. The total teaching of the Bible is that the gospel call is an open call, an unrestricted call, and an enabling call to those who respond favorably.

See CALVINISM, ARMINIANISM, MONERGISM, SYNERGISM, FREE WILL.

For Further Reading: Dayton, "Romans," *WBC,* 5:58; Purkiser, *Exploring Our Christian Faith,* 270-78; *GMS,* 428; Wiley, *CT,* 2:340-44, 351-53.
LESLIE D. WILCOX

ELDER. The Greek word for "elder" is *presbyteros,* which has been taken over into English as "presbyter." It occurs 66 times in the NT and is translated "elder" in all but 2 places (in KJV). Twenty-six times in the Gospels (13 in Matthew alone) it is used for the "elders" of the Jews, that is, members of the Sanhedrin. This continues for the first 4 times in Acts (4:5, 8, 23; 6:12). But in the rest of Acts it refers (11 times) to the elders of the church and only 3 times to Jewish elders.

The first of these occurrences is found in Acts 11:30, referring to the elders of the church at Jerusalem. Especially significant is the next use of the term, in 14:23. On Paul's first missionary journey he and Barnabas "ordained," or "appointed" (NIV), elders in every church they had founded in the province of Galatia. This was the earliest form of church organization: a group of elders to supervise each local congregation. This followed somewhat the Jewish pattern.

In 1 Tim. 5:17 Paul speaks of "the elders that rule well." And in verse 18 he warns against accepting any accusation against an elder unless it is backed by two or three witnesses.

Titus 1:5-9 is especially significant. Verses 5-7 definitely suggest that "elder" and "bishop" ("overseer," NIV) refer to the same office. Even Bishop Lightfoot of the Church of England supported this interpretation.

See BISHOP, CLERGY, CHURCH GOVERNMENT.

For Further Reading: Lightfoot, *Saint Paul's Epistle to the Philippians,* 95-99; Wallace, "Elder," *Baker's DT,* 178-79.
RALPH EARLE

ELECT, ELECTION. The term "elect" may be either a verb, noun, or adjective. As a verb it specifies the act of choosing from among a number of possibilities for any function or use. As a noun it may identify the object of this action or choice. And as an adjective it would indicate a person chosen for an office but not yet installed, such as the president-*elect.* The theological *verb* would indicate the act of Deity in selecting for special service, or choosing to salvation. Theologically the *noun* would specify those who have been thus chosen by God, with the more frequent idea of those chosen for salvation and special grace. When the apostle Peter wrote to the "elect who are sojourners of the Dispersion" (1 Pet. 1:1, ASV) in the five provinces of Asia Minor, he was using the term as a noun (*eklektois,* dative plural). Similarly when he refers to them as "an elect race" (2:9, ASV), he also uses the term as a noun. In our English language the term is synonymous with *choose* as a verb, or *chosen* as a noun. The elect are objects of the action of God and members of the resultant state or status.

Both Peter and Paul (1 Pet. 1:1; 2 Thess. 2:13; Eph. 1:4) indicate that those who may be considered the elect of God are such as have come by way of sanctification, belief of the truth, and sprinkling of the blood of Christ (cf. Heb. 10:22). They indicate that the election of God is to the end that one might be holy and undeserving of censure before Him in love. It was God's decision, before He ever laid the foundation of the cosmos, that His elect should incarnate such characteristics (Eph. 1:4; note here the use of the verb *exelexato,* "elected," aorist middle indicative, third person singular, of *eklegō,* "to choose out for one's self"). Hence the elect are those whom God has "elected," and the basis for this divine choice is in the moral character which they have been enabled, through God's transforming grace, to embody and experience.

In summary, then, we may note that God's election is that of a *class* of persons exhibiting a certain *type of character,* and not merely an arbitrary, precreation decision, that certain ones shall be saved and all others be damned. Whether, therefore, one stands among God's elect is an *elective* decision, God having elected all who will acclaim Jesus Christ as Lord of all the kingdoms of their life, and having reprobated all Christ-rejectors to eternal death.

See PREDESTINATION, FOREKNOWLEDGE, CALL.

For Further Reading: Dunelm, "Elect," *ISBE,* 925; Wiley, *CT,* 2:335-40; Wynkoop, *Foundations of Wesleyan-Arminian Theology,* chap. 2.

ROSS E. PRICE

ELIJAH. The prophet Elijah (1 Kings 17:1—2 Kings 2:11) makes his first appearance during a critical time in the history of Israel when faith in the God of Israel was threatened by King Ahab's decision to erect an altar for the Canaanite god Baal in Samaria (1 Kings 16:31-33). He makes a prediction concerning a drought and indicates to the king that he is a true prophet who stands before God to receive His word in order to communicate it to the people. His subsequent encounters with the followers of Baal religion reveal that he was also a fierce advocate of the Sinai covenant.

Elijah's return is mentioned in the prophecies of Malachi. He predicts that a messenger would appear to prepare the way before the Lord (3:1), and that Elijah would come before the Day of the Lord to turn the hearts of the fathers together with their children to God (4:5-6). Malachi's prophecy receives its first direct reference in Luke's account of the birth story of John the Baptist. The angel announces to Zechariah, "He [John] will go before him [the Lord] in the spirit and power of Elijah" (Luke 1:16-17, RSV). However, John said an emphatic "I am not" when the question "Are you Elijah?" was asked to him by the priests and Levites (John 1:19-23). Jesus on the other hand declared that John fulfilled the prophecy of Malachi (Matt. 11:7-15; cf. 17:12; Mark 9:12). His sayings concerning John reveal Jesus' own conviction that the task of the prophet to come has already been fulfilled by the Baptist.

The Gospels record that at the Mount of Transfiguration Moses and Elijah appeared to Jesus and talked with Him (Matt. 17:1-8; cf. Mark 9:2-8; Luke 7:28-36). Both Moses and Elijah had played significant roles in the history of Israel. Moses the lawgiver led Israel to their first redemption from slavery in Egypt. Elijah was the first great prophet who attempted to emancipate the nation from their bondage to Baal and to restore true worship in Israel. Thus the appearance of these two men with Jesus confirms His statement, "Think not that I have come to abolish the law and the prophets; I have come not to abolish them but to fulfill them" (Matt. 5:17, RSV).

See JOHN THE BAPTIST, PROPHET (PROPHECY).

For Further Reading: Edersheim, *The Life and Times of Jesus the Messiah* 2:706-9; Wiener, *The Prophet Elijah in the Development of Judaism,* 1-17, 141-51.

ALEXANDER VARUGHESE

ELOHIM. *Elohim* is the Hebrew word generally used for "gods." Plural in form, it is often a plural of majesty and translated as a singular, "God." Other Hebrew terms for Deity, such as Yahweh and Adonai, are usually translated as "Jehovah" and "Lord," respectively. Each of these terms implies specific connotations about what God is like.

Occurring some 2,550 times in the OT, Elohim refers in its broadest sense to God as absolute, unqualified, unlimited energy. Scripture begins with the affirmation, "In the beginning *Elohim* created the heaven and the earth" (Gen. 1:1). Obviously only a God with such power could perform such a feat. This power also pertains to God's relationship with His creation. Elohim commands (Gen. 3:3); He blesses (9:1); He enters into covenant (vv. 16-17); He destroys (19:29); He leads (Exod. 13:17); He saves (20:2). This God of power is not a being who created only to leave creation at the mercy of a naturalistic system. His power is so unlimited in scope that He providentially superintends and enters into relationship with His creation.

See GOD, OMNIPOTENCE, DIVINE SOVEREIGNTY, PROVIDENCE.

For Further Reading: "God, Names of," *IDB; GMS,* 53, 134, 342; Stone, *Names of God in the OT.*

W. STEPHEN GUNTER

EMANATION. See GNOSTICISM.

EMBLEMS OF THE HOLY SPIRIT. An emblem is a visible representation or sign of a greater reality.

It may be a badge which identifies the wearer with some entity.

Fire is an emblem which suggests judgment, i.e., testing, purging, and cleansing. It is used with reference to the Spirit's baptism (Luke 3:16); the coming of the Spirit at Pentecost (Acts 1:5; 2:3-4); the nature of the Spirit ("Quench not the Spirit," 1 Thess. 5:19). At Pentecost tongues "like as of fire" sat on the disciples of Jesus, suggesting their preparation for bearing the gospel to the ends of the earth.

A second emblem is the dove. In the baptism of Jesus, the Spirit descended "like" a dove lighting upon Him (Matt. 3:16). Matthew does not say that the Spirit descended clothed in the form of a dove, but Luke stresses the Spirit's coming "in bodily form, as a dove" (Luke 3:22, RSV). In the Scripture the dove represents peace. The confirmation of God's favor is suggested in the baptismal story.

Paul describes the sealing of the Holy Spirit unto the day of redemption (Eph. 1:14), a work of the Spirit suggesting being marked and owned by the Spirit. Thus the symbolism of the dove and the seal are close.

The seal conveys a larger meaning than approval or mark of ownership. It suggests the guardianship of the Spirit and forms the heart of a biblical theology of Christian perseverance. When Paul says we are sealed by the Holy Spirit, he teaches the supervisory care of the Spirit. No one need fall from God's love since the Spirit of God is present. Everything that the Father and the Son have done for us is being effected by the Spirit.

In legal terms the seal indicates a finished transaction; that everything contained on the document sealed is complete and accurate. Scripture suggests that the Spirit's seal is God's affirmation of this grace bestowed upon us, i.e., the Spirit confirms that we are genuine.

Oil is a familiar emblem of the Spirit. Associated immediately with the anointing for the sick, for the ministry, and for the injured (as seen in the parable of the Good Samaritan), oil commonly represents the Spirit's work in preparation for service. Peter states that God anointed Jesus of Nazareth "with the Holy Spirit and with power" (Acts 10:38, RSV). Earlier Jesus had seized the words of Isaiah: "The Spirit of the Lord is upon me, because he has anointed me" (Luke 4:18-19, RSV). The prophet Zechariah's vision of olive trees pouring their oil into the bowl of the candlestick is an allusion to the power of the Holy Spirit (Zech. 4:1-14).

The coming of the Spirit is promised by God as a "pouring out" (Joel 2:28-29), a probable allusion to the anointing oil.

A fourth emblem is wind. First employed in Gen. 1:2, the word *ruach* is translated both "wind" and "spirit." The metaphor "wind" is descriptive of the sovereign movement of the Holy Spirit. In speaking of the new birth to Nicodemus, Jesus indicated that the wind blows where it will. This was seen to be a reference to the Spirit's work of regeneration (John 3:8). The wind of the Spirit is suggestive of His creative work. Further, the wind's free flow is the basis for describing the "surprises of the Spirit."

The earnest, enduement or clothing, and rivers are other emblems of the Spirit. As earnest, He is recognized as the down payment or pledge for the future glory (Eph. 1:14). The "earnest" is an archaic word but familiar in the KJV. Luke employs enduement (or being clothed) by the Spirit to describe the Christian's environment of power. The Spirit encompasses as a garment is placed on a person, conveying power *(dunamis)* (Luke 24:49; Acts 1:8). Finally, the presence of the Spirit becomes a river of living water flowing out of the believer (John 7:37-39). The true ecstatic (*ekstasis* = outreaching) character of the Spirit is manifested in His influence in the world, not simply in private spiritual satisfaction.

See HOLY SPIRIT, TYPE, TYPOLOGY, EARNEST, SEALING OF THE SPIRIT.

For Further Reading: Marsh, *Emblems of the Holy Spirit;* James, *I Believe in the Holy Ghost,* 79-96.

LEON O. HYNSON

EMOTION, EMOTIONALISM. The word *emotion* derives from the Latin verb *emovere,* to move out, and refers to one of the three basic elements of human life, i.e., thinking, feeling, willing. These elements are functions of the self or ego and indispensable to life and being. "To experience emotion is to become aware of larger than usual differences in the continuous changes in feeling which are experienced by all normal healthy people in the waking state" (*Baker's DCE,* 203).

Emotion is often pictured as the driving force in life, as it were, as wind in the sails; while thought is the nautical calculations, and volition the hand on the wheel or rudder. Each function or area of expression is inextricably related to the other so that either normalcy or even ideal living will include them all in balanced interplay.

This means then that one of the essential factors in religion is emotion, expressed as a sense of awe, dependence, adoration, or reverence before the Divine Presence, or as a sense of meaning, purpose, and value in life. The daily and momentary peace, the comfort in sorrow, the glory of life's mountaintop experiences, and all other genuine religious emotions both derive from and contribute to the intellectual content and the ethical demands of the Christian faith.

The history of Christianity reveals an ever changing pattern of emphasis upon doctrine, religious emotion, and ethics. When emotion has been overemphasized, it has often been accompanied by intense physiological phenomena, and by compulsive action in which rational control and ethical discipline are diminished.

Emotionalism is defined by Webster as "cultivation of an emotional state of mind; tendency to regard things emotionally." Thus, on the opposite end of the spectrum from the intellectual or legalist who would deny religious emotion, the emotionalist would fan the flames of feeling until the structures of thought and moral action are weakened or destroyed.

See JOY, BLESS (BLESSED, BLESSING), HAPPINESS, FAITH, REASON.

For Further Reading: *Baker's DCE,* 203; *King's Introduction to Religion,* 68, 264, 272, 306-10; Rahner and Vargrimler, *Theological Dictionary,* 146.

JOHN E. RILEY

ENCOUNTER. A term variously used to oppose the Socratic notion of the truth about man, the natural theology of medieval times, and the use of science to authenticate religion in 19th-century liberalism. The concept of encounter is the epitome of neoorthodox theology. Encounter emphasizes revealed truth, not truth that man can discover. According to Emil Brunner, "Truth as encounter is a concept of truth unknown to philosophy and science" (*Truth as Encounter,* 7).

In a rudimentary form, Pascal used the concept of encounter in *Pensées.* Pascal believed that man could know God only as he is confronted by Jesus Christ. Proofs for God's existence and natural theology have no significance in comparison to encounter. His oft-quoted phrase sums this up: that God is not the God of the philosopher but "the God of Abraham, Isaac, and Jacob." Similarly, Martin Buber in his *I and Thou* has used language which might be construed as "encounter" language when he emphasizes the personal nature of one's relation to God. According to him, "All real living is meeting (encounter, *begegnung*)" (11).

Socrates believed that the philosopher must not teach the truth about man. This truth, even if latent, is already in every man. The philosopher has the humble task of a midwife, by bringing the truth to light. Opposing Socrates, Kierkegaard, in his *Philosophical Fragments,* argued that the truth about man cannot be discovered by us because it is not in us and we are not in it. Truth comes from outside of man and outside the world. It comes in as a unique event in time, a historical moment. This event is the incarnation of the divine word in Jesus Christ and can only be perceived by an act of faith.

From an existentialist perspective, Rudolf Bultmann has made use of the concept of encounter. In this way he places great emphasis on preaching and faith. We know very little of the biography of the historical Jesus, but we know His teaching. When the words of Jesus are proclaimed, Jesus encounters the hearer. One cannot hear the gospel preached and avoid an encounter with Jesus. Similarly Karl Barth spoke of revelation as encounter, coming from outside of man, and not to be discovered by man. "Biblical knowledge is always based on an encounter of man with God" (*Church Dogmatics,* 2. 1. 23). In this encounter, God exercises His Lordship over man; He is acknowledged as sovereign Lord.

Emil Brunner has made the most of this concept. He believes that in the NT, faith is the relation between two persons; man obediently trusts God and God stoops to meet him. "Here revelation is truth as encounter and faith is knowledge as encounter" (*Revelation and Reason,* 9). Encounter takes place in the sermon or the sacrament. "The truth about man is founded in the divine humanity of Christ, which we apprehend in faith in Christ, the Word of God. This is truth as encounter" (*Truth as Encounter,* 21). Truth as encounter is in conflict with the naturalistic idea of truth, the doctrine of evolution, and in conflict with idealism. Brunner believes that both Barth's extreme objectivism and Bultmann's extreme subjectivism bypass truth as encounter.

See EXPERIENCE, TRUTH, NEOORTHODOXY, EXISTENTIAL (EXISTENTIALISM).

For Further Reading: Brunner, *Truth as Encounter; Revelation and Reason;* Barth, *Church Dogmatics,* vols. 1, 2; Bultmann, *Jesus and the Word.*

JERRY W. MCCANT

ENTIRE SANCTIFICATION. Throughout its history, the Christian Church has taught a doctrine of sanctification. Since the Reformation the Calvinists and Lutherans have stressed growth and development. Some expect completeness "at and in the article of death." On two things virtually all agree. Sanctification is necessary, and it is not complete at conversion. For a time, Zinzendorf and the Moravians took exception to the latter point but then yielded the issue (Wesley, *Works,* 5:145).

Entire sanctification is conceived as a radical act of God through the Holy Spirit, cleansing the deep springs of inherited sinfulness from the heart. From the positive side, it is being filled with the Holy Spirit for life and service (Acts 1:8; 2:4). Each such experience is a true baptism with the Spirit. It is the distinctive emphasis of the Wesleyan movement that this crisis experience is not only possible but is the proper norm for the Christian life.

More is involved than the human act of pledging, dedication, or consecration. Though the deepest factor is relationship with God, man is not able to sanctify himself. Jesus was. Because He was utterly sinless, He could devote himself completely to God and to man's redemption (John 17:19). But in man's sanctification God is the Actor; man is the object (John 17:17; 1 Thess. 5:23). The verb "sanctify," as the verb "convert," is generally in the passive voice. Only God can purge sin from the human heart, restore the moral image of God, and produce the communion with God that is reserved for the pure in heart. And only as inbred sin (inherited depravity) is destroyed can the human personality be set free to mind the things of God (Rom. 6:6, 22; 8:1-5).

Some are confused in their doctrine of sin. The depravity, sin, or carnal mind must not be viewed as a separate and independent substance or entity. Sin does not exist apart from persons. Separate the two and sin no longer exists. The "carnal mind" (Rom. 8:7) is a mindedness, attitude, or preoccupation. They that are renewed after the pattern of the Spirit no longer set their minds on the carnal, self-centered, and selfishly human. They that are dead to sin are fully alive to God (Rom. 6:11). It is a matter of the heart, the center of the personality, the controls. Nothing material is removed. But the person is set free to serve God with perfect love.

Entire sanctification does not deliver from all the consequences of the Fall. Bodies still die. Impaired humanity still suffers frustrations. Temptations continue to be felt. Time, effort, and patience are still required to develop the skills of Christian living. New light demands fresh improvements. But we are committed in our hearts to the will of God and to the guidance of the Holy Spirit. God's complaint is not against our limited ability but only against our reluctance. He gives more grace.

Entire sanctification does not end growth. It promotes it. Indeed, the overall work of sanctification that began at conversion is made full and entire by a definite act of God (1 Thess. 5:23). Though still finite and fallible, we are cleansed from all sin, the main hindrance to growth and development. And we are filled with righteousness (Matt. 5:6) and with the Holy Spirit (Acts 2:4). Some call the growth of the entirely sanctified a progressive sanctification. It is safer to use the scriptural terms of growth (2 Pet. 3:18), change (2 Cor. 3:18), transformation (Rom. 12:2), and the like. The aorist and perfect tenses are generally used in the Greek references to sanctification to indicate a definite, explicit act of God or to stress the abiding result of a completed act. It is an initiation into an abundant and growing fullness of life.

The time to experience entire sanctification is soon after conversion. This is the burden of the Epistles to the Romans and the Thessalonians, the churches which were deprived of extended early apostolic visits. Within months of the remarkable conversions in Thessalonica, Paul referred to the "lack" in their faith (1 Thess. 3:10), described that lack (vv. 12-13), and identified the need as a sanctification (4:1—5:22), issuing in victorious Christian living. He prayed for their entire sanctification and assured them of God's answer (5:23-24). Likewise, the burden of Romans is a gift *(charisma)* to establish them (1:11). The pinnacle and goal of the plan of salvation is the normal life of full sanctification (chapter 8). And early experience is the open door to growth and security.

Faith is the one immediate and necessary condition for receiving entire sanctification. We are sanctified by faith (Acts 26:18). But faith has its conditions. One cannot fully believe until he has fully consecrated. Faith demands this obedience. The Holy Spirit is given to those who obey (5:32).

See CONSECRATION, SECOND WORK OF GRACE, PERFECT LOVE, CARNAL MIND, ERADICATION, CLEANSING.

For Further Reading: Wiley, *CT,* 2:440-96; Taylor, *Life in the Spirit,* 91-107; *A Right Conception of Sin,* 102-20; Rose, *Vital Holiness,* 219-35; Metz, *Studies in Biblical Holiness,* 11-46; Grider, *Entire Sanctification: The Distinctive Doctrine of Wesleyanism;* Wood, *Pentecostal Grace.*

WILBER T. DAYTON

ENVY. According to Theodore M. Bernstein, *envy* "means discontented longing for someone else's advantages" (*The Careful Writer,* 167). It leads to resentment and hate, even murder; therefore in the Bible it is always seen as a serious sin.

In the OT, envy can be included in the prohibition of covetousness in the tenth commandment (Exod. 20:17). Aristotle said envy grows naturally in relationships between equals. It also grows between brothers (Cain and Abel, Jacob and Esau, Joseph and his brothers, and the prodigal son and the elder brother) over a parental blessing. King Saul "eyed David" (1 Sam. 18:7-9) and envied him.

In the NT, those who envy will not "inherit the kingdom of God" because envy is one of the "works of the flesh." These works are opposed to the "fruit of the Spirit" and to living "in the Spirit" (Gal. 5:19-26). Envy marks out those whom God has given up to a "depraved mind" (Rom. 1:28, NIV). It is a feature of life before conversion which is done away through Christ (Titus 3:3). Envy is to be "put away" by those who "grow up in [their] salvation" (1 Pet. 2:1-2, RSV, NIV). There also is a warning against becoming the kind of unsound teacher who "has an unhealthy interest in controversies and arguments that result in envy" (1 Tim. 6:4, NIV).

The evil depths to which envy can go is shown in the trial of Jesus, where Pilate knew "it was out of envy that they had handed Jesus over to him" (Matt. 27:18, NIV) to be crucified. One theologian even concludes that envy and jealous strife among Christians helped bring martyrdom to their opponents in the church (Oscar Cullmann, *Peter,* 104-9).

One possible positive example of envy is a verse that is difficult to translate (Jas. 4:5). This verse either means God's Spirit is jealous (i.e., "zealous") for our friendship, or it refers to the human spirit that "turns towards envious desires" (Jas. 4:5, NEB). This latter understanding of envy is the usual evil sense. Envy was the motivation for preaching the gospel in Phil. 1:15. The result was good, but the desire to preach Christ came out of "selfish ambition" to "stir up trouble" for Paul (v. 17, NIV).

See JEALOUSY, CARNAL MIND, COVETOUSNESS.

For Further Reading: Fairlie, *The Seven Deadly Sins Today,* 61-83; May, *A Catalogue of Sins,* 76-79.

CHARLES WILSON SMITH

EPISCOPACY. This term is usually taken to mean the government of the church by bishops. However, this definition reflects a long development in Christian thought which cannot be traced back to the NT. Episcopacy should be seen as a generic term for the oversight or supervision of the church.

OT and NT terminology clearly support the generic use of the term to cover various forms of government or oversight or supervision within Israel and the church. The term can be used in the sense of a particular office and was so used both within Scripture (Num. 4:15; Acts 1:20) and outside Scripture. But this is derivative, and within this usage bishops were for the most part synonymous with presbyters, whose duties are set forth in 1 Timothy and Titus and resemble that of the average parish minister of today. It is anachronistic to see contemporary bishops as even a faint copy of the bishops referred to in the NT. Wesley clearly understood this and relied on it for warrant in his own ordinations for the work in America.

It was in postapostolic times that episcopacy was narrowed to mean the particular form of church government presently advocated by Roman Catholics, Eastern Orthodox Christians, and many Anglicans. This is unfortunate because it hinders the perception that a conference, as much as a bench of bishops, can exercise episcopacy. Worse still, it has made it virtually impossible to have any mutual recognition of ministries within the various segments of the church.

See CHURCH GOVERNMENT, CLERGY, ELDER.

For Further Reading: Lightfoot, "The Christian Ministry," Diss. 1, commentary on *Philippians;* Barrett, *Signs of an Apostle;* Hanson, *Christian Priesthood Examined.*

WILLIAM J. ABRAHAM

EPISTEMOLOGY. This term is composed of the Greek *epistēmē,* "knowledge," and *logos,* "a study or rationale"; thus, an inquiry about the nature, sources, possibilities, and limitations of knowledge. Loosely, a "theory of knowledge."

The pre-Socratic philosophers did not give any fundamental attention to the problem of knowledge. It was only through the Sophists (fifth century B.C.) that doubts began to be raised about the knowledge of reality.

As human practice and institutions came under scrutiny, philosophy began to ask if we had any knowledge of nature as it really is. This general skepticism led to the beginning of epistemology as it is generally known—that is, the attempt to justify the claim that knowledge is possible and to evaluate the parts played by the senses and reason in the acquisition of knowledge.

Credit must be given to Plato, however, who began to ask the essential questions about the problem of knowledge: What is knowledge? Where do we find knowledge? How much of what we think we know is really knowledge? Are we to approach knowledge empirically (through the senses)? Can reason be a reliable guide to knowledge? Can belief be cognitive? Et cetera.

It is customary to date the beginning of modern epistemology through John Locke's *Essay Concerning Human Understanding,* published in 1690. Locke felt that an examination of the limits of knowledge was important to an understanding of reality. Locke's modest inquiry has affected all the subsequent history of philosophy.

The great names that have influenced the development of contemporary theory include: the differing forms of realism in Augustine and Aquinas; the conceptualism of Abelard; the nominalism of Ockham; the continental rationalism of Descartes, Spinoza, and Leibnitz; the empiricism of Locke, Berkeley and Hume; the superlative thought of Kant (*Critique of Pure Reason,* etc.); the post-Kantian idealism of Fichte, Hegel, Bradley, and Schopenhauer; the later 19th-century leaders such as Brentano, Meinong, Husseril, and Bergson; the practical philosophy of James, Pierce, and Dewey; and 20th-century realism including Perry, Russell, and the "very different" Whitehead whose thought resulted in process theology.

Contemporary movements include the logical positivism of the Vienna Circle which has had so much influence on current epistemological and metaphysical theory; the later "ordinary-language philosophy" of Ludwig Wittgenstein; and the significant implications of phenomenalism for metaphysics and theology. Much time and investigation is currently being given to religious language and the problem of religious knowledge.

See KNOWLEDGE, RELIGIOUS KNOWLEDGE, PHILOSOPHY, REALISM, SCOTTISH REALISM, MODERN REALISM.

For Further Reading: Barrett, *A Christian Perspective of Knowing;* Titus, *Living Issues in Philosophy,* 23-108; Ayer, *The Foundations of Empirical Knowledge;* Stace, *The Theory of Knowledge and Existence;* Berkeley, *Of the Principles of Human Knowledge.*

OSCAR F. REED

ERADICATION. *Eradication* is a term used by certain Wesleyan theologians to describe the radical destruction of inbred sin by divine grace. The term has been employed in opposition to the teaching that sin is suppressed, repressed, or counteracted, but not destroyed. According to suppressionists, sin exists until death but can be effectively rendered inoperative by the power of the indwelling Holy Spirit. Eradicationists insist that Greek verbs and verb forms employed in the NT point to the removal of sin, not to its repression. The issue focuses upon the degree of deliverance from inward sin possible in this life by the redeeming grace of God.

Two criticisms have been persistently leveled against the term among Wesleyans: (1) *eradication* is not a biblical word; (2) it lends itself too easily to the mistaken notion that sin is a substance, some *thing* that can be removed from the soul as a rotten tooth is extracted from the jaw.

Defenders of the term reply that many nonbiblical words are regularly employed to express biblical concepts, a chief example being *Trinity,* and that employment of physical language to express and discuss metaphysical subjects is not only common but inescapable.

No one preferred to stick to actual terms employed by Scripture more than Wesley, as the most casual reading of his works makes evident, Nevertheless, he was embroiled in controversy throughout his ministry because he insisted upon a radical deliverance from sin. In his day the issue was extinction vs. suspension, terms only slightly removed from eradication and suppression. Wesley said, "I use the word 'destroyed' because St. Paul does; 'suspended' I cannot find in my Bible."

The wisdom of using any particular terminology must be decided by each individual thinker, writer, or preacher. The concept discussed, however, is more than semantic. The destruction of inbred sin, the radical purification of the inner life, remains a distinguishing tenet of the modern holiness movement.

See CLEANSING, HEART PURITY, CARNAL MIND, CARNAL CHRISTIANS.

For Further Reading: White, *Eradication;* Gould, *The Whole Counsel of God,* 39-58; Wiley, *CT,* 2:440-517.

W. E. MCCUMBER

EROS. See LOVE.

ERROR. An error is a mistake or failure due to incomplete information, forgetfulness, or faulty judgment. These errors do not necessarily arise from antagonism of the will toward God. Since man is finite, his knowledge and information are limited. Since he is also living under the curse, which brought mortality and its accompanying physical and mental weaknesses, man's memory and judgment are affected. Thus, errors are due either to man's finite character, or to disabilities arising from consequences of the Fall as they touch man's mind and body. They are not sinful acts since they involve no purpose to rebel against God. Consequently writers of the holiness tradition ever since Wesley have ascribed such errors to infirmities, and usually discuss them under that head, as in the first three readings suggested below. Such errors do not separate the soul from God, although they often bring disappointment or embarrassment. The child of God will do his best under grace to overcome such disabilities as much as possible.

The word *error* also denotes a wrong and unscriptural system of doctrine or teaching. This may arise from overemphasis, or from neglect of some phase of truth, or from outright denial of some truth. It always arises whenever men substitute their ideas for the revealed truth of God. Whatever its source, any system of error is dangerous in leading men away from the truth and usually leads men to deviation in practice and finally to outright wickedness. Hence the Bible frequently warns us against deception.

See MISTAKE, INFIRMITY, SIN (LEGAL), HERESY.

For Further Reading: Chadwick, *The Call to Christian Perfection,* 56-58; Wesley, *Works,* 6:2-5, 412-13; Wiley, *CT,* 2:498; Breese, *Know the Marks of the Cults.*

LESLIE D. WILCOX

ESCHATOLOGY. The word *eschatology* is derived from two Greek words, *eschatos,* meaning "last" or "last things," and *logos,* meaning in this instance "knowledge." Eschatology has thus traditionally referred to the biblical teachings concerning events which will occur at the end of world history.

In classical systematic theology the discussion of echatology has commonly been carried out under two subheadings: Individual Eschatology and General Eschatology. Individual eschatology treats the scriptural teachings regarding the character of life after death, considering the nature and place of the existence of the soul between death and the final resurrection, and such matters.

General eschatology discusses the final events which are to transpire at the end of human history. Themes commonly treated under this heading include the great apostasy and the Antichrist, the second coming of Christ, the resurrection, the millennial Kingdom, the final Judgment, and the age to come.

The modern discussion of biblical eschatology no longer limits the term exclusively to future events at the end of world history. Scholars note that the OT prophets sometimes spoke of the Day of the Lord—an eschatological *terminus technicus*—as drawing near or impinging upon events in their own times. The NT writers speak even more clearly of the *eschaton*—the last times—and specific eschatological events as already inaugurated in the first century, in connection with the Christ event.

The boundaries within which biblical eschatology has been interpreted in this century were established by Albert Schweitzer and C. H. Dodd. The older liberal interpretation had dismissed the eschatological content of the Bible as an expression of the mythological outlook of the ancient world. Adolf von Harnack referred to it as the disposable "husk" which surrounded the "kernel" of universal ethical truth in the Scriptures.

Albert Schweitzer is widely credited with reestablishing the determinative eschatological basis of NT theology, even though it is generally agreed that he overstated the issue. According to Schweitzer, Jesus was an apocalyptic figure who anticipated the end of the present world and the arrival of the eschatological kingdom of God in the near future. This expectation conditioned all His preaching and the understanding of His mission. Following Jesus' death, this same hope continued in the earliest Church. In fact, however, both Jesus and the Early Church were mistaken, as subsequent history made clear, declared Schweitzer.

C. H. Dodd agreed with Schweitzer that the message of Jesus centered in eschatology, but he insisted that the portrait of Jesus sketched by Schweitzer precluded any basis for Christian faith in such a deluded apocalyptist. Dodd's own study of the NT evidence led him to conclusions quite different from those of Schweitzer. Dodd contended that for Jesus the eschatological Kingdom was not a future entity but rather had its absolute arrival in His own person and mission. All that the prophets had hoped for in the eschatological age was realized in the Christ event and is experienced by Christians as they are related to Christ by the Spirit. This was the essence of the teaching of Jesus and was at the heart of early Christian proclamation. Dodd recognized that there were passages in the NT which spoke of eschatological events in the future, but he neutralized these by designating them as poetic expressions or by rejecting them as corruptions of the primitive *kērygma* by a later generation which had lost touch with the message of Jesus.

The work of Schweitzer and Dodd made clear that the NT contains two kinds of statements about the eschaton. One collection of sayings speaks of the inauguration of eschatological events in connection with the mission of Jesus. The coming of the Messiah, the operation of the Kingdom in power, the outpouring of the Holy Spirit, the gift of salvation—these are all eschatological events in the estimate of OT and Jewish eschatology. That claim is made for them by the writers of the NT also.

But the NT likewise speaks of eschatological

events which were not yet realized and which await a future fulfillment. The old age and the fallen sinful order have not been terminated, death has not been destroyed, the Messiah is to appear again, the resurrection and the final Judgment are yet to occur, the new heavens and the new earth are matters of hope.

Schweitzer and Dodd treated these sayings in an antithetical manner, gravitating to one group and minimizing or rejecting the validity of the second group. More recently NT scholars—most notably Oscar Cullmann and Werner Kümmel—have attempted to interpret the two sets of sayings in a dialectical way, speaking of the tension which exists between the "already" and the "not yet" in NT theology. According to this view, the Christ event signified the inauguration of eschatological events and realities, but the full realization of the eschaton lies in the future. However, the future will only bring to completion that which was begun in the mission of Jesus. This latter interpretation seems to reflect the NT teachings most accurately.

All of the interpretations above assume that NT eschatology is a statement of beliefs about events which will occur—or which have occurred—in history. For Rudolf Bultmann, however, this represents a mythological world view which is meaningless to modern man. Such statements have to be demythologized and reinterpreted with the aid of existentialist philosophy in order to have contemporary significance.

From this perspective Bultmann concluded that the eschatological content of the NT describes human existence before God, encountered by God in judgment and with the offer of salvation. In this manner biblical eschatology is removed from the objective sphere of world history and is made to apply to the subjective history of the individual.

See REALIZED ESCHATOLOGY, LAST DAYS, APOCALYPTIC, TRIBULATION, MILLENNIUM, PREMILLENNIALISM, AMILLENNIALISM, SECOND COMING OF CHRIST.

For Further Reading: Bultmann, *Jesus and the Word;* Cullmann, *Salvation in History,* 166-291; Dodd, *The Parables of the Kingdom;* Ladd, *The Presence of the Future;* Kümmel, *Promise and Fulfilment;* Schweitzer, *The Quest of the Historical Jesus,* 223-403; Wiley, *CT,* 3:355-93.

FRED D. LAYMAN

ESSENES. The Essenes were a Jewish religious sect that flourished in the first century B.C. and until A.D. 135. Josephus and Philo estimated their number at around 4,000. They lived in colonies scattered throughout Palestine. Their chief employment was literary, especially that of copying the Scriptures. They supported themselves by agriculture, eking out a living usually from unfriendly soil. Novitiates gave their property to the sect, which lived communistically. Certain scholars have tried unsuccessfully to associate John the Baptist and even Jesus with this sect.

The Essenes had no dealings with the Temple priesthood, whom they considered to be corrupt. They observed strictly the law of the Sabbath, and took no oath except that of loyalty to the sect. Rules were many. Infractions of rules were punished severely.

Though female skeletons have been found in their cemeteries, most Essene groups were male and celibate. Membership was retained through the adoption of children and by making adult proselytes.

The people of the Dead Sea Scrolls (at Qumran) are believed to have been Essenes.

The Essenes expected a teacher of righteousness to appear who would lead the righteous ("the Sons of Light") in overthrowing their enemies ("the Sons of Darkness") and establishing the Messianic Kingdom.

See DEAD SEA SCROLLS.

For Further Reading: Josephus, *War* 2. 8. 2 ff; *Antiquities,* 18. 1-5; Gaster, *The Dead Sea Scrolls in English Translation;* Harrison, "Essenes," *ZPEB,* vol. 2; LaSor, *Amazing Dead Sea Scrolls and the Christian Faith.*

W. RALPH THOMPSON

ESSENTIAL TRINITY. This term is the counterpart of the term *economic Trinity.* Whereas this latter term refers to the respective roles or offices of the Persons in the Godhead in effecting man's redemption, the term *essential Trinity* is a reminder that the threeness of God is not a temporary accommodation to the requirements of redemption, but is eternal, because such threeness belongs to the very nature of God. God would be Three-in-One even if there had been no creation and no redemption. To affirm the economic Trinity without also affirming the essential Trinity is to open the door to some form of modalism.

There is only one God (Deut. 6:4; Isa. 43:10-11; 1 Tim. 2:5; Gal. 3:20). Yet three Persons are mentioned in the NT who are each called God. In 2 Pet. 1:17 there is a person called the "Father," who is identified as God. Another person is also mentioned, distinct from the Father, who is called the "Son," and in verse 16 is identified as Jesus Christ. Now according to Exod. 34:14 and Matt. 4:10, one is absolutely forbidden to worship anyone besides God; yet in Heb. 1:2-6 God commands the angels to worship Jesus Christ, and we know that Jesus Christ accepted worship from Thomas (John 20:28). Furthermore, the

Jewish leaders clearly understood Jesus to teach that He was just as much God as was God the Father (John 5:18; 8:51-59).

In addition to this, Acts 5:3 teaches that there is a person called the Holy Spirit. That He is a person is established by the fact that Ananias lied to Him. The succeeding verse reveals that the Holy Spirit is God. This scriptural data forces one to conclude that there is only *one* God, but there are three distinct Persons who are called God. Therefore it would be wrong to say that the names Father, Son, and Holy Ghost are simply three ways in which the one God-Person manifests himself (Sabellianism). It would also be wrong to say that the three Persons of the one God are three parts of the whole, sharing divine perfections among themselves. Each is equally possessed of all. These three Persons are the one God.

Thus all three Persons of the Godhead are eternal because the one God is eternal (Ps. 90:2; 102:24-27). And since the one God is unchangeable (Mal. 3:6), He has always existed as Father, Son, and Holy Spirit. In this sense the threeness is an eternal and essential aspect of the Godhead.

See TRINITY (THE HOLY), ECONOMIC TRINITY, SABELLIANISM.

For Further Reading: Carter, *The Person and Ministry of the Holy Spirit;* Wiley, *CT,* 1:426-32; Wood, *The Secret of the Universe.*

ALLAN P. BROWN

ESTATES OF CHRIST. The estates (or states) of Christ are two: humiliation and exaltation. Humiliation describes the descent of Christ in the Incarnation, His self-emptying (the *kenōsis*), His servant role, and His death on the Cross. The exaltation concerns the stages of ascent, particularly the Resurrection, the Ascension, and the Session. These followed the descent into hell.

The state of humiliation includes several specific stages or steps, most clearly described in the famous kenosis passage (Phil. 2:5-8). Christ's humiliation includes self-renunciation and relinquishing His full divine prerogatives.

Was the kenosis a separation by the Son from the divine attributes or simply from the use of these attributes? Were the attributes concealed in the kenosis? The incarnate Logos did not cease to be God; hence, it must be argued that He was not severed from the attributes of Deity. The kryptists (a word meaning "to conceal") believed the attributes were not displayed until Christ's glorification.

That the kenosis meant renouncing the use of these attributes appears to be a contradiction of the miracles and power of Jesus on earth, a point against the kryptists, too. Another suggestion is offered. The kenosis was the Son's yielding of His autonomy as God (albeit an autonomy within the *perichoresis*) and taking on the state of subjection and dependence. In any event His self-renunciation of equality with God and assumption of the form of man was followed by His glorification.

The estate of exaltation begins with the descent into hell. Based upon Ps. 16:10, quoted by Peter in Acts 2:27, 31, and 1 Pet. 3:19-20, the descent seems to describe Jesus' proclamation of His Lordship over both life and death. Some construe the descent as describing the terrible intensity of Jesus' suffering on the Cross, but this makes "preaching unto the spirits" meaningless.

The Resurrection followed the entombment. It was Christ's victory over the power of death to which He had become obedient (Phil. 2:8). The Resurrection confirmed the validity of His atoning death.

The Ascension marks a new stage in Christ's resumption of His place with God and His mediation for us. Having become man, the Son bears that humanity to glory where He intercedes for us. Further, the Ascension establishes the divine condition for the coming of the Spirit (John 16:7). Finally, the Session describes the Son at the Father's right hand. Mark connects Ascension and Session (16:19), thus linking Christ's priestly and royal offices.

See CHRIST, KENOSIS.

For Further Reading: Wiley, *CT,* 2:187-210.

LEON O. HYNSON

ETERNAL GENERATION. This construct, which Olin A. Curtis called "one of the most fruitful conceptions in all Christian thinking" (*The Christian Faith,* 228), was used by theologians in the third and fourth centuries (most notably Origen and Athanasius) to combine two ideas deemed necessary in rightly describing the inter-Trinitarian relation between the Father and the Son.

It was necessary to say that the Son was *generated,* or "begotten," in order (1) to counteract the idea that the Son was a mere "emanation"; (2) to show a distinction between the Persons of the Godhead, and thus guard against the heresy of modalism; and (3) to show that the Son was not a creature, as the Arians maintained, but was rather of the very essence of God.

Likewise it was necessary to say that this generation is *eternal* in order to show that the Father was never without His Son. Hence the Son exists eternally alongside the Father, His generation being an eternal process. Contrary to Arianism, there was never "a time when the Son was not." Since God is eternal, and since the Son shares the divine essence, the Son exists from all eternity.

See CHRIST, TRINITY (THE HOLY), ETERNALLY BEGOTTEN.

For Further Reading: Danielou, *Gospel Message and Hellenistic Culture,* 345-86; Gonzales, *A History of Christian Thought,* 1:191-233, 299-310; Grillmeier, *Christ in Christian Tradition,* 1:133-326; Kelly, *Early Christian Doctrines,* 126-36, 226-47. ROB L. STAPLES

ETERNAL LIFE. Eternal life has ever been one of man's deepest concerns. Job voiced this universal quest in one of his darkest moments thus: "If a man dies, will he live again?" (Job 14:14, NASB; cf. Mark 10:17; Luke 10:25). Pascal observed: "The immortality of the soul is a thing so important that only those who have lost all feeling can rest indifferent to it."

The clearest biblical statement on eternal life is the declaration of Christ in His high-priestly prayer: "This is life eternal, that they might know thee, the only true God, and Jesus Christ whom thou hast sent" (John 17:3, NASB). The *meaning* of eternal life focuses upon three words in this statement: "life" *(zōē)*, "eternal" *(aiōnios)*, and "know" *(ginōskō)*.

While *zōē* is sometimes used in the NT to express man's natural life, it is the one word used for God's own life. The Greek word *bios* seems never to be used in this sense in the NT, but rather expresses natural, temporal life, whether of men or other creatures. While *zōē* is sometimes used in the latter sense, when it is qualified by the Greek adjective *aiōnios* ("eternal, or unending"), it signifies a quality of life that endures, and not simply quantitative or temporal life.

Eternal or everlasting life, as applied to man, is mainly a NT concept (especially favored by John and Paul), although it is implicit in the OT (see Job 19:25-27). It was Christ "who abolished death, and brought life *[zōēn]* and immortality to light through the gospel" (2 Tim. 1:10, NASB; cf. 2 Cor. 5:1-5).

Technically "eternal life" characterizes God only. However, Jesus said, "I *give* eternal life to them" (John 10:28; cf. 17:2). Thus *zōē* signifies a quality of life which is *eternal as God's life,* but "everlasting" as received and experienced by believing man. With God eternal life has neither beginning nor end, whereas with man it has a beginning in his salvation experience, but no end. God's eternal life was implanted in man at his creation (Gen. 2:7), but was forfeited in the tragedy of the Fall. It was subsequently provisionally restored to man through Christ's redemptive accomplishments. It is now freely offered by Christ to all who will receive it (Rev. 22:17; John 1:4).

Eternal life comes to men through *experiential knowledge* of God which is expressed by Christ in the verb "know" *(ginōskō)* which signifies an intimate personal knowledge of God (John 10:38; 14:7-8; 5:20; cf. Hos. 6:3). To know Jesus Christ is to know the "true God." The two are inseparable (John 14:7-11). Eternal life is both present and future; both *now* and *eschatological* through the resurrection of the whole person. The possession of eternal life is inseparable from being vitally in Christ. It cannot survive an apostasizing from Christ (John 15:6; Col. 1:21-23).

See ETERNAL SECURITY, APOSTASY, BACKSLIDING, FAITH, REGENERATION, ETERNITY.

For Further Reading: Kittel, 2:832-72; *ISBE,* 3:1458-61; *ZPEB,* 3:927-32. CHARLES W. CARTER

ETERNAL PUNISHMENT. To punish is to cause pain, loss, or discomfort to a person for some offence. Eternal punishment as a biblical and theological term refers to the endless punishment which falls upon those persons who reject God's love revealed in Jesus Christ.

The NT Greek word usually translated "eternal" is *aiōnios* (literally, "an age" or "agelong"). It indicates infinity of time, endless duration. Eternal punishment, then, is not simply agelong, after which it ceases, but is unceasing, everlasting. The same word is used to indicate the life the believer receives from God through faith in and obedience to the resurrected Christ—eternal life (Matt. 25:46). "The Greek language possesses no more emphatic terms with which to express the idea of endless duration" (A. A. Hodge).

Jesus on numerous occasions affirmed the reality of eternal punishment. Records of His teaching in this regard are found in Matt. 18:8; 25:41-46; Mark 3:29; Luke 3:17; John 5:28-29. Peter also wrote of eternal punishment (2 Pet. 2:9-10). Paul warns that God "will punish those who . . . do not obey the gospel . . . They will be punished with everlasting destruction and shut out from the presence of the Lord" (2 Thess. 1:8-9, NIV).

Shut out, banished from the presence of God is, indeed, the basic meaning of eternal punishment (Matt. 25:41). It comes through persistent rejection of God and His will as revealed in Jesus Christ. Continued rejection forges the chains of sin ever more strongly in this life as persons misuse their freedom to choose. Alienation from God and loneliness result. Remorse and inner turmoil follow. We cannot suppose that the Judge of all the earth will remit these penalties beyond death if persons continue persistently in their sins, refusing to recognize His claims upon their lives. "Sin must be purged or the sinner both banished and punished" (cf. Mark 9:49; Matt. 3:12; Heb. 10:26-31; 12:29).

Eternal punishment is not vindictive. God forces no one to love and serve Him; but when a person refuses His invitation and disregards His laws, he must bear the penalty. Such impenitents condemn themselves (John 12:47-50).

The NT frequently uses symbolic terms in referring to realities beyond the grave. This is necessary, for we can understand concepts only as they are expressed in terms of our earthly vocabulary. God must speak our language until we can understand His. So it is that the place of eternal punishment, so different from anything we are familiar with in this world, is described by comparing it with things within our knowledge. It is referred to as a place of fire. Jesus referred to it as "everlasting fire" (Matt. 18:8; 25:41), as "unquenchable fire" (Luke 3:17), as a "furnace of fire" (Matt. 13:42). John called it the "lake of fire" and the "second death" (Rev. 20:14-15; 21:8). It is said to be a place of "darkness" (Matt. 8:12; 2 Pet. 2:4; Jude 13), a place of "torment" (Luke 16:23, 28; Rev. 14:10-11).

The fact that this is considered by some as symbolic language does not suggest that the suffering depicted is unreal. The symbols convey ideas of reality strictly conformable to truth.

See HELL, ETERNAL LIFE, FREEDOM.

For Further Reading: Hills, *Fundamental Christian Theology*, 2:415-31; Wiley, *CT*, 3:356-75; *GMS*, 662-68.

ARMOR D. PEISKER

ETERNAL SECURITY. More traditionally known as "perseverance of the saints," eternal security was formerly derived from John Calvin's doctrine of unconditional predestination—"The eternal decree of God by which He hath determined in himself what He would have to become of every individual of mankind" (Calvin, *Institutes*, 3. 21. 5). If salvation is by God's decree, then the elect will be saved no matter what they do or fail to do.

More recently, the unconditional security of believers (also known as "once in grace, always in grace") has been inferred from selected passages of Scripture such as John 10:27-29; Rom. 8:35-39; Phil. 1:6; and 1 Pet. 1:5. It is claimed that once a person becomes a child of God by acceptance of Christ in faith, he can never be lost. Should a believer backslide, he will either be brought back before death or, in some teachings, be finally saved in spite of continued sinning to the end of his earthly life.

Although reputable teachers of eternal security make every attempt to avoid antinomianism, the conclusion that former believers will be saved even if they die in a backslidden and sinful state is drawn by some and is popularly assumed.

Eternal security views faith as a single act of acceptance or believing which is forever efficacious. The NT places its stress on evangelical faith as a present-tense, ongoing attitude of trustful obedience (John 3:36, NASB; Jas. 2:14-26).

Even the positive texts alleged in support of eternal security are less specific than supposed. Jesus affirmed that His sheep would never perish and no man would pluck them out of His Father's hand; in the same passage He stated, "They follow me," a phrase which by no means could describe a backslider (John 10:27-29).

Rom. 8:35-39 says that no earthly or demonic force or "any other creature" shall be able to separate us from the Father's love. It pointedly makes no mention of personal sin which, while not a "thing," does separate man from God (Isa. 59:1-2).

Phil. 1:6 presupposes the normality of Christian obedience and continued trust; and 1 Pet. 1:5 identifies continuing faith as essential to final salvation.

The data in Scripture on the other side of the question are extensive and conclusive: Ezek. 18:24; Matt. 18:21-35; Luke 8:13; 12:42-47; John 15:2, 6; Acts 1:25; Rom. 11:20-22; 1 Cor. 8:10-11; 9:27; 10:12; Gal. 5:1, 4; Eph. 5:5-7; 1 Tim. 4:1; Heb. 6:4-6; 10:26-29; Jas. 1:14-16; 2 Pet. 2:18-22; 1 John 2:4; 3:8-9; 2 John 8-9; Jude 4-6; Rev. 3:11; 21:8; 22:19 show that the practice of sin and sonship to God are totally incompatible, and apostasy is possible although not normal or expected in Christian experience.

The positive values of a biblical doctrine of Christian security must not be discounted. All obedient followers of the Lord Jesus Christ are secure in the Father's keeping. While regeneration does not cancel the God-given human power of choice, it does guarantee abundant grace and both possibility and probability of final salvation.

See BACKSLIDING, PERSEVERANCE, IMPUTED RIGHTEOUSNESS, CALVINISM.

For Further Reading: Purkiser, *Security: The False and*

the True; Shank, *Life in the Son;* Steele, "The Present Tenses of the Blessed Life" in *Milestone Papers.*

W. T. PURKISER

ETERNALLY BEGOTTEN. This phrase is used to indicate the relationship that exists between the First and Second Persons of the Trinity. More particularly, it specifies the relationship of the Son by the fact that He is eternally generated, and not created in time, but begotten before all time. It is the contention that the generation of the Son of God is in eternity, and not a temporal emanation. Moreover, it is used by those who contend that there never was a time when the Son did not exist as Son to the Father in the being of the Trinity. It further denotes that the *per seity* of the Second Person of the Godhead is derived from the *aseity* of the First Person. There never was a time when the Father existed without the Son, and there never was a time subsequent to the being of the Father that the Son was begotten (much less created, or otherwise brought into being).

When the Psalmist declares (Ps. 2:7) "Thou art my Son, this day have I begotten thee," he is teaching the eternal generation of this Second Trinitarian Person. The phrase "this day" denotes the universal present, the everlasting *now* which is put for eternity (cf. W. G. T. Shedd, *Dogmatic Theology,* 1:326). And when the Gospel of John (1:18; cf. 3:16, 18; 1 John 4:9) refers to Jesus as the "only begotten God" *(monogenēs theos)* (NASB), it teaches the unique and solitary nature of His Sonship and eternal Deity. When, in Heb. 1:6, the writer speaks of God bringing "the first-begotten *[prōtotokon]* into the world," he is indicating a unique, metaphysical relationship of essence that constitutes Christ's prehistorical existence with the Father—an existence which excludes all becoming. The same truth is taught by Paul in Col. 1:15 as he speaks of the Son as begotten before all creation. It is the apostle's contention that Christ is prior to all things (*ta panta,* the created universe) "for by him were all things created" (v. 16).

The phrase therefore indicates the preexistence of Christ and the metaphysical union of essence between Christ and God the Father, and it speaks of a Sonship that reaches back into eternity and depends upon this original relationship of identity of essence. Christ has a pretemporal existence in a continuous and abiding union with the Father. Hence He could declare that "before Abraham was born, I AM" (John 8:58, NASB). Furthermore, He can pray, "And now, glorify Thou Me together with Thyself, Father, with the glory which I ever had with Thee before the world was" (17:5, NASB). Jesus possessed the consciousness of having personally existed previous to His life on earth in an essential life fellowship with God, to which He knew that He should return after His work here on earth was finished. "This sonship is something super-terrestrial and eternal" (G. B. Stevens, *Johannine Theology,* 126).

See ARIANISM, CHRIST, TRINITY (THE HOLY), UNITARIANISM, ETERNAL GENERATION, FIRSTBORN.

For Further Reading: Pope, *The Person of Christ; Shedd, Dogmatic Theology,* 1, chap. 4; Stevens, *The Johannine Theology,* chap. 5; Wiley, *CT,* 1:432-36.

ROSS E. PRICE

ETERNITY. The OT has little concept of chronological time, more often making reference to events, seasons, or divine appointments either natural or miraculous. Life is not just prolonged existence, i.e., so many days and months and years; it is comprised of the long list of experiences in the lives of men and nations ordained by God. The cause and effect relationship between events is largely absent. The sands of the hourglass are fused with the great expanse of God's activity. The prophets spoke of the "day of the Lord" with eschatological and messianic connotations. To biblical writers time is essentially theological rather than chronological.

Following this line of thought, the NT uses the Greek *kairos.* The coming of Christ was the great *kairos.* "The time *[kairos]* has come . . . The kingdom of God is near. Repent and believe the good news!" (Mark 1:15, NIV). The life of Jesus is more than a birthday to be celebrated, followed by 30 or more years before He was crucified. It would be missing the mark to measure that life in years or judge it by its length. It was the great "Christ event" of God's ceaseless activity in His quest for man's salvation.

The NT uses still another term, *aiōn. Kairos* time gives promise of *aiōn* time, an age to come above and independent of *chronos* time and the consummation of the *kairos* time of Christ. This is the chief word for the concept of eternity. Eternal life is experienced by all who believe in Jesus Christ; they are already living in the *aiōn,* that unbroken age which is to come but which through Christ is already present. The adjective *aidois,* "everlasting," is used only twice in the NT.

Eternity, then, is what may be called the mode or manner of God's existence and self-revealing activity in history. It is infinity, immutability, timelessness—mysterious, inscrutable, sublime. It has to do with righteousness and holiness and love, with good rather than with evil. It is related essentially to God rather than to man, to the spiritual rather than to the physical, to quality rather than to quantity. Eternity is a revelation of God, active in history and giving the promise of life in a new dimension.

In this context, eternal punishment (which is another subject) must be seen as part of God's redemptive activity, the purging of His creation which was mutilated by the fall of man.

The promises of *kairos* time are fulfilled in the *aiōn* when God's enemies will be put under His feet, when the Son himself will be made subject to Him that put everything under Him, "that God may be all in all" (1 Cor. 15:26-28). This is eternity which can only be known or experienced as it is revealed in the sovereign power of God. In Christ can be seen the true nature of both time and eternity. "This is life eternal, that they might know thee the only true God, and Jesus Christ, whom thou hast sent" (John 17:3).

See CHRONOS, ETERNAL LIFE, ETERNAL PUNISHMENT.

For Further Reading: Richardson, *A Theological Word Book of the Bible;* Gilkey, *Naming the Whirlwind;* Quick, *Doctrines of the Creed.* HARVEY J. S. BLANEY

ETHICAL RELATIVISM. This is the position in ethical theory that right and wrong are purely relative to human factors, rather than determined by divine revelation or any form of moral absolutes. In so-called situation ethics, as popularized by Joseph Fletcher and others, the human factor is the concrete situation which alone can provide the basis for making the ethical judgment pertinent to it. Rules are not sufficiently flexible to anticipate all the unique complexities of a given set of circumstances, therefore rules are unable to specify in advance what will be the right thing. Some situationists do acknowledge one universal law, viz., love, so that the ethical obligation is to exercise judgment in determining what is the most loving thing to do.

While the concrete situation is the locus of attention with the situationists, the human factor most determinative for the anthropologist and most sociologists has been the standards of the community. Accordingly "the sense of duty is purely relative to the customs of society in which it occurs, so that the proper form of ethics is simply a description of mores in different societies" (L. Harold DeWolf, *Responsible Freedom,* 26). Rather than such ethical relativism being solely private—relative only to one's personal opinion—it is standardized in the sense that it carries the sanctions of that particular society. As a part of a particular society, a man *ought* to be faithful to its mores. Theoretically, this leads to a solidarity of moral action which the usual understanding of moral relativism does not hold. In this respect it is an improvement over the extreme individualism of situationism, and certainly superior to the exaggerated freedom of antinomianism.

However, neither personal judgment in the situation nor the customs and mores of a society can be trustworthy guides for determining right and wrong. This is precluded by human sinfulness which is swayed more by passion than principle, by the limitations of personal judgment, and by the pagan and demonic elements in non-Christian cultures. The Christian builds on the practical necessity and the historical factuality of divine revelation, in which God has given to man His moral law, and made available both the Bible and the Holy Spirit for the understanding and application of this law. The law is absolute in at least two respects: (1) its principles are timeless, universal, and unchangeable; (2) it carries the supreme authority of God himself, therefore is not optional, and cannot be superceded by the vagaries of social custom.

Therefore, while there is some truth in ethical relativism, viz., that some secondary details are relative to times, situations, and cultures, as a basis for ethical theory it alone is not adequate.

See ETHICS, CHRISTIAN ETHICS, MORALITY, SIN, REVELATION (SPECIAL), ANTINOMIANISM.

For Further Reading: DeWolf, *Responsible Freedom;* Strauss, *Baker's DCE,* 219; Fletcher, *Situation Ethics: The New Morality;* Brunner, *The Divine Imperative;* Thielicke, *Theological Ethics,* vol. 1. OSCAR F. REED

ETHICAL SIN. See LEGAL SIN.

ETHICS. The Greek *ēthos* is found only once in the NT (1 Cor. 15:33), and then it is in a current proverb. Originally, the word meant "dwelling" or "stall." To this word, the Latin *mos* was given, from which *morality* is derived.

There is a real distinction, however, between ethics and morality. The original sense of "stability" or "stall" suggests that ethics deals with the stability and security which is necessary if one is to act at all. "It was really the primary office of custom to do in the human area what the stall did for animals: to provide security and stability" (Paul Lehmann, *Ethics in a Christian Context,* 23-25). Ethics, then, is concerned with what holds human society together. In the developing discipline, ethics deals with reflection upon the principles that govern behavior, while morality deals with the behavior according to approved standards.

Natural law or philosophical ethics is usually divided into three categories.

1. *Normative ethics* deals with what is right and wrong, good or bad, virtuous or evil in accordance with standards. In this area, ethics is concerned with establishing norms by which moral action can be evaluated. While it draws information from many descriptive sciences, its primary focus is on what *ought to be* followed by what persons *ought to do.*

Normative ethics can be divided into *utilitarian* and *formalistic.* The utilitarian approach is best represented by John Stuart Mill, who argued that the right act is that act which brings the greatest happiness to the greatest number. Formalism searches for those constituent elements of our moral world which actually exist among people.

The dialogue between utilitarianism and formalism is particularly crucial today in medical ethics. With the increasing application of "utilitarian cost benefit analyses to social policy," the physician is confronted with decisions which from the standpoint of utility may be normatively justifiable (utilitarian). On the other hand, his obligation to each patient may lead him to life-saving procedures regardless of utility (formalistic) (Dyck, *On Human Care,* 14-21).

2. *Metaethics* deals analytically with the kind of language that ethics works with. Metaethics is theoretical and critical. The discipline is not as remote as one might think. If a medical authority takes the position that professional judgments are not moral judgments, the ethicist is obligated to analyze whether the judgment is moral or nonmoral. Practical ethical judgments are statements about actions, such as "This is right (or wrong). Metaethical judgments define and appraise the standards, rules and principles that justify those practical decisions" (Dyck).

3. *Moral policy* is the design that ethicists use to make descriptive and critical analyses of what to do in specific situations. Whether the issue relates to a nation's decision in war and peace, responsibility to a civil code, or medical decisions, the perplexities encountered demand decisions which are moral in content. *Moral policy* can provide descriptive and critical analyses of the sources of agreement and disagreement. But it can also make judgments which in light of the known (descriptive) can control historical events and human destiny. The hostage issue with Iran was filled with moral judgments coming from such *moral policy.* Empirical definitions, affirmations of loyalty, the range of human freedom, and the interests of the nation all entered the picture.

See CHRISTIAN ETHICS, MORALITY, CASUISTRY, ETHICAL RELATIVISM.

For Further Reading: Bonhoeffer, *Ethics;* Titus and Keeton, *Ethics for Today;* Lehmann, *Ethics in a Christian Context;* Freedman, "A Meta-Ethic for Professional Morality," *Ethics* 1978, 8 ff; Dyck, *On Human Care;* DeWolf, *Responsible Freedom.* OSCAR F. REED

EUCHARIST. The Greek term *eucharistia* means "thanksgiving as an act of worship." Eucharist is a traditional name for the sacrament more commonly known as Communion, Lord's Supper, Agapē, and Mass (R.C.). The Early Church seems to have observed the "breaking of bread" at every service (Acts 2:42). Historically the Roman Catholic church has taught that the bread and wine become the body and blood of Christ. Martin Luther taught that Christ's body and blood coexist with the bread and wine. Zwingli believed that the Eucharist was only a symbolic commemoration of Christ's death. Christians today hold to one of these three or some variations of them. The Eucharist is one of the two Protestant sacraments along with water baptism.

The Eucharist is a celebration of Christ's atoning sacrifice, and its repetition serves to keep us aware of the enduring nature of the work of Christ, so that we can say, "He is born, He is crucified, He is resurrected." Whatever one's theology of this sacrament, Christ's presence is a mystery of faith—and who would dare to say that He is not present at His own table? The bread and wine are symbolic, not only of His "body broken and blood poured out," but also of the Bread of Life that nourishes and the Blood that cleanses. The implications of the various periods of the Christian calendar, such as Advent, Christmas, Lent, Good Friday, Easter, and Pentecost, find expression in the celebration of the Eucharist. Its observance is our dedicated, thankful, expectant response to the salvation wrought by Christ's atoning sacrifice. It is also our acceptance by faith of God's grace for pardon and purity, fellowship and service.

See SACRAMENTS, COMMUNION (HOLY).

For Further Reading: Battenson, ed., *The Early Church Fathers;* Richardson, ed., *A Theological Word Book of the Bible.* HARVEY J. S. BLANEY

EUTHANASIA. The term is derived from the Greek *eu,* "well," and *thanatos,* "death," and so means easy or painless death. In contemporary usage it refers to the practice of "mercy killing," the painless putting to death of persons suffering from incurable and extremely painful disease. It is also used for the painless putting to death of the socially unfit, such as the feebleminded and deformed.

Euthanasia is sometimes considered as being either passive or active. Passive euthanasia would be simply deliberate failure to use the means available to prolong life. (Most authorities deny this meaning to the concept.) Active euthanasia is the positive and intended use of means to end life painlessly.

Euthanasia is also classified as either voluntary or compulsory. Voluntary euthanasia presupposes the rational request for and consent of the person to be killed, whereas compulsory euthanasia presupposes neither request nor consent of the person to be killed.

Those who advocate the practice of euthanasia tend to do so on the utilitarian ground of the good of society. Nineteenth-century utilitarians held euthanasia to be a sensible means of disposing of persons who are a burden or embarrassment to society. The Nazis even included those who are economically, politically, or racially an embarrassment.

Those who oppose euthanasia base their argument on the dignity of the individual and the sacredness of human life. The Christian church, both Catholic and Protestant, has consistently condemned euthanasia. Its position is that life is the gift of God and only God has the right to terminate it. The right of life is natural and inalienable and is a part of man's stewardship responsibility. "Mercy killing" assumes the right of others to make decisions for which they have insufficient knowledge. Human motives are too complex, and euthanasia offers the possibility for concealment of selfish and criminal motives. It also fails to understand the Christian concept of suffering as having positive and redemptive value, both for the sufferer and those around him.

Theologians such as Karl Barth, Dietrich Bonhoeffer, and Emil Brunner have condemned euthanasia as being a usurpation of God's sovereign right over life and death (John Dedek, *Human Life: Some Moral Issues,* 122-23).

See LIFE, MURDER, ABORTION, SUFFER (SUFFERING).

For Further Reading: Dedek, *Human Life: Some Moral Issues;* Heifetz, *The Right to Die,* 99-117; Koop, *The Right to Live, The Right to Die,* 85-117.

M. ESTES HANEY

EUTYCHIANISM. In the fifth century the church was formulating a doctrinal statement concerning the relationship of the human and the divine in Christ. Monophysites (Gr. *one nature*) affirmed a belief that Christ had only one nature. Eutyches, a monk from Constantinople (d. 454), gave his name to the doctrine which affirmed that after the Incarnation, Christ's nature was only divine, not human. Eutychianism now includes modifications of the original doctrine.

The Council of Chalcedon (451) adopted the statement of the oneness of Person without denying either the complete divine nature or the complete human nature of the incarnate Christ.

See APOLLINARIANISM, CHRISTOLOGY, HYPOSTATIC UNION, CHRIST.

For Further Reading: Latourette, *A History of Christianity,* 164-72; Wiley, *CT,* 2:160-84.

RICHARD S. TAYLOR

EVANGELICAL. This adjective derives from the Greek noun *euangelion,* translated "gospel" or "good news" (often transliterated "evangel"). That which is evangelical therefore relates to the gospel, the message of salvation of the Christian faith. Paul wrote: "For I am not ashamed of the gospel: it is the power of God for salvation to every one who has faith, to the Jew first and also to the Greek" (Rom. 1:16, RSV). The evangel is synonymous with *kerygma,* "preaching." Evangelical also connotes the spirit of zeal and earnestness with which the message of salvation is witnessed to or proclaimed.

Evangelical and *evangelicalism* were not widely used in the history of the church until the time of the Reformation, during which period they took on a somewhat pejorative meaning. Luther's insistence that the light of the gospel of justification by faith had been "hidden under a bushel of ecclesiastical authority, tradition, and liturgy" led Erasmus, Thomas More, and Johannes Eck to employ the term *evangelicals* derisively to refer to the Lutherans. Luther reacted negatively to being so named because he believed evangelical could be used for all Christians who accepted the gospel of free grace. Eventually, following the Peace of Westphalia in 1648, with its recognition of the Reformed churches as evangelical; with the publication of the *Corpus Evangelicorum* in 1653; and with the union of Lutheran and Reformed churches in Germany in 1817, evangelical came to be used of all Protestants. The Methodist revival under Wesley in England was characterized as an evangelical revival.

The term was given more specific content when the Evangelical Alliance was formed in London in 1846. The Alliance adopted a set of nine doctrines as representative of the meaning of evangelical: (1) the inspiration of the Bible; (2) the Trinity; (3) the depravity of man; (4) the mediation of the divine Christ; (5) justification by faith; (6) conversion and sanctification by the Holy Spirit; (7) the return of Christ and judgment; (8) the ministry of the Word; (9) the sacraments of baptism and the Lord's Supper.

Since that time the word *evangelical,* both in Europe and America, has taken on broader and narrower definitions. The term is often used to refer to neoorthodoxy on one end of the spectrum and to fundamentalism on the other end. Broadness and narrowness are determined mainly by the theological stance of the definer. The hallmarks of evangelicalism, as delineated by Donald Bloesch, are 10 in number: (1) the sovereignty of God; (2) the divine authority of Scripture; (3) total depravity; (4) the substitutionary Atonement; (5) salvation by grace; (6) by faith alone; (7) primacy of proclamation; (8) scriptural holiness; (9) the Church's spiritual mission; (10) the personal return of Christ.

See ORTHODOXY, FUNDAMENTALISM, CHRISTIANITY, EVANGELISM, NEOEVANGELICALISM.

For Further Reading: Bloesch, *The Evangelical Renaissance;* Quebedeaux, *The Young Evangelicals;* Ramm, *The Evangelical Heritage;* Wells and Woodbridge, eds., *The Evangelicals.* WILLARD H. TAYLOR

EVANGELISM. Evangelism is that activity of Christians by which they seek to make known the gospel and persuade people to believe in Christ the Lord. This activity may be private and personal or public, involving an evangelistic type of preaching and methods of inducing immediate response. Generally evangelism is seen as a primary responsibility of the Church, to be engaged in continuously and by some degree of system and organization. A popular method in the 19th and 20th centuries has been the planned revival campaign. However, of more recent years greater stress has been placed on training laymen to evangelize by means of everyday vocation and personal witnessing.

Everything the church does which aims at conversions is a form of evangelism. Even the Sunday School, while primarily an educating and nurturing agency, has been widely effective as a tool of outreach and evangelism. All other auxiliaries and activities should also be geared to evangelism, and evaluated in terms of their evangelism potential.

While missions and evangelism are generally disconnected in the local church, they are essentially the same. In the broader sense, missions constitute a subdivision of evangelism, i.e., evangelism carried out by missionaries serving elsewhere, whereas evangelism as popularly conceived is soul-winning activity locally.

Evangelism has the word *angel* at the heart of it, and an angel is always thought of as a messenger of the Lord. All Christians are to be involved in evangelism, since all are to be witnesses or messengers of the Lord. Anyone who is truly Christian will be involved in sharing with someone else what the Lord has done for him. No one is to be a spectator, but all are to be participators in circulating the good news of Christ's redeeming love.

The pulpit type of evangelism places the emphasis on congregational participation in spiritual activities which generates an atmosphere in which the unsaved have a confrontation with the Holy Spirit. In such a setting the worshippers are blended into a spirit of collective obedience that makes it normal for individuals to be obedient to the Lord. This is often referred to as "mass evangelism," though the term is of doubtful accuracy, since the ultimate decisions are personal and individual. Evangelism is not crowd psychology or mob hysteria.

Personal evangelism involves one-to-one, person-to-person contacts for the Lord. Every Christian will have a means to make a living, but he will also have a meaning for living, and the latter is related to his concern about winning another to the Lord. Total mobilization of the laity for winning men to Christ is the greatest challenge confronting the Church world today. Only as Christians turn the casual contacts that come on the job, in the office, and in the neighborhood into occasions for witnessing will the Church have an impact on contemporary society.

Theologically, evangelism is the Church's primary task, as it is a fulfillment of the Great Commission (Matt. 28:19-20). It presupposes the lostness of men, their universal salvability in Christ, and the faithfulness of the Holy Spirit in working through witnessing and preaching to bring about awakening and conversion. Evangelism is in one sense a human work, involving intentional activity, and requiring training, skill, planning, strategy, and generally some degree of organization. Yet the Church's efforts, while they may *win* adherents, will fail in bringing about NT conversion unless guided by the Spirit and endued with His power.

See SOUL WINNING, EVANGELIST, MISSION (MISSIONS, MISSIOLOGY).

For Further Reading: Turnbull, ed., *Baker's Dictionary of Practical Theology,* 148-92; Taylor, *Exploring Evangelism.* MENDELL L. TAYLOR

EVANGELIST. The evangelist *(euangelistēs)* is a messenger or proclaimer of good news. The "good news" (gospel, *euangelion*) is clearly delineated in the NT (1 Cor. 15:1-5; 1 Tim. 1:15; 2 Tim. 1:8-11). All Christians are evangelists, since regeneration creates a spontaneous impulse to share the Good News (Acts 8:1-4). However, it is evident from Eph. 4:11 that some are called "evangelists" in a specialized and official sense. This function and office is one of God's gifts to the Church for its equipping; therefore the Church suffers when and if this particular form of ministry is depreciated. The implication of Ephesians is that not only are evangelists called to spend their time in taking the gospel to those who have not yet heard, but they must have a function in teaching evangelizing to the Church.

Only Philip is called "the evangelist" (Acts 21:8); yet he was elected to "serve tables" and was ordained as a deacon (Acts 6:1-6). But that he was first of all an evangelist at heart was demonstrated in the first persecution, when his elective position was dissolved and he went to Samaria. Apparently thereafter the Church recognized that God through providence and inner urge had promoted him. Since there is no hint of a subsequent special ordination, we may conclude that the evangelist represents a function and at times an office but not necessarily an *order* of ministry. Not only the apostles but ordained deacons and ordained elders could serve as evangelists.

While some are called to specialize as evangelists, and the office is distinct from the "pastors and teachers" (Eph. 4:11), we are not to conclude that nonspecialists may remain aloof from evangelizing activities and interests. Timothy was primarily a pastor-administrator, yet he is commanded to "do the work of an evangelist" (2 Tim. 4:5). Only thus could he "fulfill" his ministry (NASB). The "work" of an evangelist would be repeated proclamation of the essential message and a systematic seeking out of those who had not yet heard or at least were not yet won.

See EVANGELISM, SOUL WINNING, MISSION (MISSIONS, MISSIOLOGY), CLERGY.

For Further Reading: *Baker's Dictionary of Practical Theology*, 148-89; Purkiser, *The New Testament Image of the Ministry*, 79-84.

RICHARD S. TAYLOR

EVE. The name, mentioned only twice in the OT (Gen. 3:20; 4:1), is given by Adam to his female companion and wife in the Garden of Eden. He first calls her "Woman" (*ishah*, 2:23). The significance of the name *ishah* is highlighted in the Samaritan Pentateuch and LXX rendering "out of her man," which contrasts the woman with the beasts which are taken "out of the ground" (v. 19). The name Eve is first applied at the mention of childbearing in the curse of 3:14-19.

The significance of the name is explained in the text as denoting that the woman is "the mother of all living" (v. 20). Yet in the biblical account it is not clear whether she is yet a mother at all. And even when she becomes a mother, she is not literally "mother of all living" (for example, of animals).

The problem is that though the name appears to be related to the Hebrew verb meaning "to be," its form is not Hebrew. Thus alternate explanations have been offered as to the origin of the name. For example, the suggestion has been made that the name is actually built upon a Semitic root translated "clan." Thus Eve is understood to mean "mother of every human clan."

Another approach has been to relate the name Eve to the Aramaic word for serpent and suggest that Eve is so named because she had done the serpent's work in tempting Adam. Neither explanation adduces any better evidence for itself than the simple biblical explanation that the name Eve appears to be related to the Hebrew verb "to be," and thus Eve is "the mother of all living."

The creation of Eve is justified in Genesis 2 as God's provision for a man in his lonely solitude (v. 18). The solitude was not alleviated by the presence of the beasts. But the woman is immediately recognized as "bone of my bones, and flesh of my flesh" (v. 23). This unity of flesh is symbolized and sealed in the singular commitments of marriage (v. 24) which include the separation from family and bearing of children. Thus the origin of human sexuality is assigned to the commonality shared by man and woman rather than to the reflection of some erotic nature in the creating Deity. This point heightens the contrast between the worship of the Israelites and the worship of their Canaanite neighbors who understood the nature and function of their deities in chiefly sexual terms.

New Testament references to Eve occur in 2 Cor. 11:3 and 1 Tim. 2:13. In both passages the susceptibility of Eve to the solicitations of the tempter is the important element. In the Timothy passage it is used to support an understanding of the subordination of women to men in the Church assumed from the account in Genesis 3 in which Eve sinned first, then Adam. In Corinthians it serves as a warning by example of how easily one may be led astray.

Eve was the mother of Cain, Abel, and Seth.

She was also the mother of numerous unnamed children.

See WOMAN, SEX (SEXUALITY), FAMILY, PARENTS AND CHILDREN.

For Further Reading: Von Rad, *Old Testament Theology,* 1:149; Thielicke, *How the World Began.*

DANIEL N. BERG

EVENT. *Event* is important for Christian theology in discussions regarding revelation. Before critical study of the Bible no questions were raised about the character of the biblical events, and little particular value was placed on event as part of revelation. Emphasis was on the concepts of Scripture as the source for doctrine and theology. Liberalism bypassed the historical character of the record in favor of universal truths of religious and ethical value. Yet the outlook of the 19th and 20th centuries has made history and, hence, *event* important. Both orthodox and modernist thinkers have taken the historical character of the Bible seriously but disagree on its implications.

The question of events points to the larger issue of the relation of history, eternity, and time. Where does revelation occur on the line that connects the eternal acts of God and the temporal events of history? Some emphasize the suprahistorical character of revelation (and its eventness) in order to preserve the otherness of God and the uniqueness of the gospel. The event of revelation is located variously in "great acts of God" in the past or existential encounters, eschatological events, or language events in the present. Others accent the historical character of revelation (and events) in order to guarantee its verifiability and relevance. The inability to hold these concerns together is present where the supernatural and natural are seen as incompatible. Evangelical theology has sought to avoid this dilemma by accepting the biblical view of miracle and of creation as the point of contact between God the Creator and His world.

Event is significant for revelation in several ways. First, event points to the external, objective dimension of the divine work in the world. Thus the Resurrection is not just an idea but an event that affects the real world (1 Cor. 15:3-19). Second, and as a consequence, event secures the exclusiveness of Christianity inasmuch as God has acted for the world's salvation in special, once-for-all events, e.g., the Exodus and the death and resurrection of Jesus.

For biblical faith, event and word must be seen as complementary aspects of revelation—God speaks and acts. The divine word causes events; the divine word through a prophet interprets or foretells events.

See HEILSGESCHICHTE, HISTORICAL JESUS (THE), HISTORICISM, REVELATION (SPECIAL).

For Further Reading: Brown, *History, Criticism, and Faith;* Henry, *God, Revelation, and Authority,* 2:247-334; *IDB,* supp. vol., 746 ff; Ramm, *Special Revelation and the Word of God.*

GEORGE R. BRUNK III

EVIL. As the opposite of good, evil is any quality, condition, or event which is inherently negative and destructive. The pain and unhappiness which result from evil are generally viewed as evils in themselves, but their evil quality is reflective and sometimes more apparent than real.

The Bible commonly uses "evil" as a synonym for sin, as "the fear of the Lord is to hate evil" (Prov. 8:13). There follows a listing of some evils: "pride, and arrogancy, and the evil way, and the froward mouth." From these personal evils of spirit and conduct grow all the social evils which plague men.

Far less serious are the nonmoral forms of evil such as disease, accident, natural calamities, and death. These evils are nonmoral in the sense that they do not imply immediate culpability in the one who experiences them. It is not a sin to be ill or to die, when such is not self-induced.

Nonmoral evil is relative and temporary. Indeed it is often difficult to distinguish between real evil and that which merely seems to be. If God "causes all things to work together for good" in the life of a trusting believer (Rom 8:28, NASB), do the "evil" things remain evil, or are they transmuted by God's grace into good? Chastening also seems like evil ("grievous," Heb. 12:11) when being experienced, but with sons of God the evil is only apparent; it is really a blessing in disguise. We must conclude that unpleasant events and experiences will fall into their final category only when viewed from the vantage point not only of God but of eternity.

The presence of evil in the world has long been a knotty problem to philosophy and theology. Particularly crucial is what some have called "surd" evil—that for which there is no compensating benefit or rationale, such as useless pain in children or the tooth and claw of nature. In some minds this problem has been so acute that they have despaired of reconciling absolute omnipotence in God with infinite goodness. To resolve the difficulty, they have postulated a "finite God," i.e., that surd evil reflects the limitations in God himself, against which He is struggling (Edgar S. Brightman). This of course is the self-made dilemma of rationalism which (1) rejects the biblical answer; (2) overevaluates pain in terms of this life; and (3) presumes that man is capable of determining what is and is not surd evil, or even proving that there is such a thing.

The Bible traces the presence of evil in the universe to the fall of Satan, and the presence of evil on earth to the fall of man. In both cases nonmoral evil is the consequence of moral evil. Christians are divided as to the extent this statement should include violence in nature such as windstorms and earthquakes. Are these irregularities which would not have been known in the world if man had not sinned?

It seems certain at least that pain and hardship are decreed by God to be not only a consequence of sin but in some cases a direct judgment on sin. In this sense God does "create" evil as well as good (Isa. 45:7). The hold of sin is such that without evil in the natural order sufficient to prevent complacency, the possibility of winning man back to God would be small if not nil. Evil becomes an instrument of the Spirit in fostering that sense of dependence so basic to religion.

Furthermore the Bible casts the light of redemption and eternity upon the apparent evils of life. In this light believers know no surd evils; they are surd solely for the unbeliever. The Christian perceives that the only absolute evil is unforgiven sin, since such evil alone is eternal and irremediable in its consequences.

That branch of theology which seeks to justify God in permitting evil in the world is called *theodicy.*

See SUFFER (SUFFERING), GOD, ATTRIBUTES (DIVINE), MORAL ATTRIBUTES OF GOD, PROVIDENCE.

For Further Reading: Henry, *Answers for the Now Generation,* 39 ff; Harvey, *A Handbook of Theological Terms,* 236 ff; Purkiser, ed., *Exploring Our Christian Faith,* 153-63.

RICHARD S. TAYLOR

EVOLUTION. This is the theory that biological organisms that used to exist, and that presently exist, evolved through long processes. Naturalistic evolution, often also known as Darwinism, is the view that the evolvement of organisms took place because, in the conflict over food, the fittest ones tended to survive and to reproduce themselves.

Theistic evolution is the view that God created the first form of life and other special step-ups in the complexity and fitness of organisms. Especially, according to theistic evolution, God stepped in with His creative genius to make the rational animal, man.

Creationists usually understand that God created each species—although some of them understand that He created outright only the different families. Importantly, they understand that Genesis 1—2 teach creationism instead of evolution. Also, they find that, while new varieties occur, it is problematic whether anyone has ever started a new species. Exceedingly good individuals of a given species can be developed, but not new species. Indeed, many of them understand that, when natural processes are left to themselves, what you have is devolvement, instead of evolvement. They also question whether characteristics which an organism acquires during its lifetime can be passed on—especially if it means a step up to a new species. And, of course, they know that in those cases where members of two species can breed and have offspring, they find that the offspring (e.g., the mule) cannot reproduce.

Only a relatively few Christians today believe in Archbishop Ussher's chronology, which got into many KJV Bibles, according to which creation occurred in 4004 B.C. But as to the length or nature of the creation "days" evangelicals are divided. Some are firm in postulating a relatively recent creation and believing that the creative fiats were circumscribed within 24-hour solar days. Others would agree with H. Orton Wiley, who said that each of the days was no doubt a geological age of indefinite duration. Wiley wrote, "The best Hebrew exegesis has never regarded the days of Genesis as solar days, but as day-periods of indefinite duration" (*CT,* 1:456). The Hebrew word for day, *yom,* is often elsewhere translated "age" in KJV. When the six days are viewed as ages, every actual discovery of science is in accord with the Genesis account. Such a view allows for all the "hard and fast" finds of paleontology—e.g., all the forms of fossil remains known to us. It also allows for whatever has been learned in such other biology subsciences as taxonomy, serology, embryology, morphology, eugenics, and the geographic distribution of species.

See DARWINISM, CREATION, CREATIONISM, DAYS OF CREATION, MAN, THEISTIC EVOLUTION.

For Further Reading: *Symposium on Creation,* vols. 1-6; Hoover, *Fallacies of Evolution.*

J. KENNETH GRIDER

EX CATHEDRA. In present-day church usage, *ex cathedra* refers to the Roman Catholic pope issuing an infallible statement. *Ex* means "out of" or "from." The Latin, *cathedra,* from the Greek, *kathedra,* originally designated a chair or a seat. Thus the literal meaning of the term, *ex cathedra,* is "from the chair." In ancient Roman times the chair referred to the seat from which officials presided at meetings. With the rise of the office of the bishop in the early Christian centuries, *cathedra* was the name given to the chair from which the bishop carried on his work. The chair came to symbolize the authority of the bishop, and thus any communication made from the chair carried the authority of the office.

The supreme authority of the pope has long been an article of Roman Catholic faith. Such power is symbolized by his throne. This authority was fully formalized at the First Vatican Council, 1870. At that conclave, it was affirmed that when the pope, as the successor of Peter, issues a statement from his throne *(ex cathedra)* regarding faith and morals, and speaks as the supreme pastor under the guidance of the Holy Spirit, his pronouncements have the infallible authority of divinely revealed truth.

See CATHOLICISM (ROMAN), KEYS OF THE KINGDOM.

For Further Reading: *The New Catholic Encyclopedia,* 5:699; Hughes, ed., *The Encyclopedia of Christianity,* 4:138.

MARTIN H. SCHRAG

EXALTATION OF CHRIST. The exaltation of Christ is a theological phrase which refers to one of the two estates of Christ, the other being His humiliation. The exaltation includes in its scope successive stages in the redemptive work of Christ, variously identified as the *descensus ad infernus* (descent into Hades), His resurrection, ascension, session at the right hand of God, together with His second coming in the Rapture, the Revelation, and the final consummation in judgment.

Arminians in general hold that the exaltation of Christ begins following the words of Christ from the Cross, "It is finished," although there is some favor for the view that Christ's exaltation begins with His resurrection and victory over death and the grave. It is not a point of great theological tension.

The exaltation of Christ must be studied and understood in the light of His humiliation and the great kenosis passage of Phil. 2:5-11, with 2 Cor. 8:9 being its best commentary (Carl F. H. Henry, *Basic Christian Doctrines,* 131-37).

The exaltation implies the restoration of the divine person of the Son, together with His assumed human nature, to His pristine place and condition of glory at the right hand of the Father (John 17:4-5; Acts 2:33-36; Heb. 1:3, 13; 8:1; 10:12-13; 12:2). The purposes of the exaltation include (1) the restoration of Christ to His rightful place and condition of glory and majesty; (2) His enablement to intercede for mankind; (3) His reinvestment with omnipresence according to His divine person and His glorified human nature; and (4) His empowerment to pour out the Holy Spirit on His Church from the plentitude of His glorified personality (J. A. Huffman, *A Comprehensive System of Christian Doctrine,* 104).

Thus, by virtue of His death and resurrection, Christ has been exalted to a place of sovereignty over all men, both living and dead (Rom. 14:9). Further, God will restore a fallen universe in the person of His incarnate Son. In brief, the elevation of Christ to the loftiest height above all other gods and lords, real and imagined, is a rank or status of absolute sovereign Lord in God's redemptive purpose that He had not previously enjoyed (George Eldon Ladd, *A Theology of the New Testament,* 415-19).

See CHRIST, ESTATES OF CHRIST, HUMILIATION OF CHRIST.

For Further Reading: Curtis, *The Christian Faith,* 237-47; Forell, *The Protestant Faith,* 184-88; Henry, *Basic Christian Doctrines,* 145-51; Wiley, *CT,* 2:187-216.

WAYNE E. CALDWELL

EXAMPLE. The attempt to pattern after the example for human life given in the life and teachings of Jesus Christ has prompted such guidebooks as *Imitation of Christ* (Thomas a Kempis). *Imitatio Christi* as an ethical ideal, however, has been understood in different ways, depending upon the particular perspective of the period of tradition within which it has been viewed.

For the apostle Paul, the example of Jesus is presented not so much as something to be copied as something which the Holy Spirit molds into the character and life of the Christian.

During the patristic period the imitation of Christ certainly was reflected in the strong tendency toward martyrdom, celibacy, and virginity. The later movement toward monasticism may be seen as an attempt to identify with the poverty of Jesus. The Lutheran attitude toward this ideal reflected its generally negative view of what it considered to be a concealed doctrine of works.

Early 20th-century social gospel thinkers stressed the example of Jesus as that which we should emulate by our concern for the needy and the oppressed. However, later in the century, when it became clear that the "historical Jesus" was not going to be found, the views of Kierkegaard, which stressed personal self-giving, found root, and the radical commitment to which Bonhoeffer calls Christianity is strongly reminiscent of Pauline teaching.

Present-day psychology has recognized the

role of imitation in personality formation. Moral development, according to Kohlberg, involves a process of moving from egoistic beginnings to the levels of personal value and universal principles—a movement which allows creative expression of individuality but also may have a generic likeness to a personality ideal—that of Jesus Christ.

See CHRISTLIKENESS, KENOSIS.

For Further Reading: Macquarrie, ed., *Dictionary of Christian Ethics;* Kierkegaard, *Journals,* ed. and trans. A. Dru; Bonhoeffer, *Ethics.*

ALVIN HAROLD KAUFFMAN

EXCOMMUNICATION. The word is from the Latin and literally means "out of communion." Excommunication is the severest form of discipline in the church and entails exclusion from the fellowship, rights, and benefits of membership in the Christian society. Biblical basis for excommunication is found in 1 Cor. 5:3-5 and 9-13, where Paul urges the Corinthian congregation to "put away from yourselves" the offending member (cf. Ezra 10:8; Matt. 18:15-18).

The official position of the Roman Catholic church is that the "power of the keys" (Matt. 18:18) embraces the power not only to remit sin but coercive and penal power necessary to carry out the mission of the church. Excommunication's chief purpose is not punishment but the correction of the offender. The offender does not thereby cease to be a Christian, since the benefits of baptism are considered inalienable (*The New Catholic Encyclopedia Dictionary,* 353).

Roman Catholic sacramentalism makes excommunication a very serious matter, since the central thrust of excommunication is denial of the sacraments. For Protestantism the effect of excommunication is confined largely to exclusion from office and fellowship in the Christian congregation, because of its doctrines of justification by faith alone and the universal priesthood of believers. Greater emphasis is put on the redemptive and healing aspects of excommunication (Tillich, *Systematic Theology,* 3:179-80). In most Protestant churches excommunication can be applied only after a trial by one's peers and with the right of appeal to a higher court (*Cyclopaedia of Methodism,* 351).

See CHURCH, CHURCH GOVERNMENT, DISCIPLINE.

For Further Reading: Tillich, *Systematic Theology,* 3:179-81; *The New Catholic Encyclopedia,* 5:704-7; Wiley, *CT,* 3:136 ff.

M. ESTES HANEY

EXEGESIS. *Exegesis* is from the Greek *exēgēsis,* meaning "narration" or "interpretation." The verb form occurs in Luke 24:35; John 1:18; Acts 10:8; 15:12, 14; and 21:19. Exegesis refers to the process by which the text of Scripture is interpreted, and as such is both a science and an art. Two questions are basic: (1) what the text meant in its original historical and literary setting, and (2) what it means for the contemporary reader in terms of its subject matter. The latter question is best answered through the former. The principles by which exegesis is done are traditionally called *hermeneutics.*

Exegesis utilizes all the methods of biblical criticism: textual, philological, literary, form, tradition, redaction, and historical. Textual criticism seeks to establish the original wording of the biblical text. Philological study deals with the intended meaning of its vocabulary and syntax. Literary criticism studies the compositional, poetic, and rhetorical devices the author used to structure and embellish his thought. Form criticism identifies and classifies according to form units of originally oral material, relates them to their setting in the life of the community, and defines their function. Tradition criticism explores the oral and written stages the material has undergone in reaching its final form. Redaction criticism studies the special interests of the final composer of a literary work as revealed in the selection, grouping, arrangement, and modification of the material which has gone into his work. Historical criticism is concerned with the historical situation from which the document comes, investigating the author, the audience, and the conditions and flow of the cultural and historical context, and how the document reflects and relates to the historical situation. These methods overlap and their sequence varies with the nature of the material and the particular function of the exegetical task.

This describes the scientific side of exegesis, without intending to ignore the divine side. As the Holy Spirit was active in the formation of the Scriptures, so must He guide and aid the interpreter in understanding its meaning for contemporary faith and life. It is this primacy of the Holy Spirit which is unique to the Bible, and forbids approaching it solely as any other book. Either extreme must be avoided: a reliance on the Spirit which discounts scientific method, and equally a reliance on method unaccompanied by an adequate openness to the Spirit of Revelation.

See BIBLE, INSPIRATION OF THE BIBLE, HERMENEUTICS.

For Further Reading: Soulen, *Handbook of Biblical Criticism,* 57-60; Ladd, *The New Testament and Criticism;*

Kaiser and Kümmel, *Exegetical Method: A Student's Handbook;* Ramm, *Protestant Biblical Interpretation.*

FRANK G. CARVER

EXHORTATION. The English word *exhortation* is from the Latin word *hortari,* meaning "encouragement," with the intensifying prefix *ex.* Thus it means "encouragement" or "earnest admonishment." It is one of several words of related meaning in the English Bible used to translate the Greek word *paraklēsis.*

In the NT the phrase "word of exhortation" apparently has the technical meaning of an exposition of the Scriptures. The writer of the Epistle to the Hebrews calls his work "the word of exhortation" (13:22); and when Paul is invited to preach in the Jewish synagogue at Antioch in Pisidia, he is asked if he has "any word of exhortation for the people" (Acts 13:15). This designation seems also to be implied in 1 Pet. 5:12. In all of these passages the "encouragement" is related to the scriptural exegesis; and this, for Paul at least, is one of the main functions of Holy Scripture, reflecting in this aspect the character of their Divine Author (Rom. 15:4-5). Exhortation, therefore, or encouragement which results from it, does not originate in or from the individual who is exhorting, but rather from God whom the individual preacher represents (2 Cor. 5:20). Little wonder then that for Paul exhortation is a gift of divine grace (Rom. 12:8). When admonishment or exhortation is given, it is usually preceded by an appeal to its divine origin, and is thus distinguished from mere human moral or ethical advice (see Rom. 12:1; 2 Cor. 10:1; Eph. 4:1; 1 Thess. 4:1; 2 Thess. 3:12).

In the NT, therefore, exhortations, warnings, and admonishings are regularly preceded by a theological exposition which is presented as the basis for the exhortation. This in turn is presented as the practical expression of God's saving act in Christ as foretold in the Holy Scriptures. When addressed to the ungodly, it is normally a call to repentance. When the believer is the object, it is usually a word of divine encouragement in a difficult situation.

See PROPHET (PROPHECY), PREACHING, TEACH (TEACHING, TEACHER).

THOMAS FINDLAY

EXISTENTIAL, EXISTENTIALISM. Existentialism holds essentially that existence is primary to essence, the general and universal features of anything. Existence refers rather to the concrete, individual, human posture distinguished by action. Its provocative effect in philosophy, the dregs of dread and the drag of sterile nothingness, was offset for some, especially in religion, in that existentialism sustained the identity of the self. Though otherwise deeply disjointed, existentialism is loosely united universally by four prime categories: *Humanism,* that human beings are the only actual existents (Socrates); *Infinitism,* that man is finite but is confronted incessantly by infinity in conscious experience (Plato); *Tragedy,* that cares of life and fear of death beset man with tragic adversity (Pascal); and *Pessimism,* that nothingness surrounds the whole, making escape futile (new existentialism).

Kierkegaard, Pascal, and Jaspers integrated religion into their philosophy of existence. Bergson, Dostoevski, and Husserl treated metaphysics meaningfully though they were not religiously contained. But Nietzsche, Heidegger, and Sartre rejected religion forthrightly, holding that God and all metaphysical paraphernalia are only inauthentic objective trappings, an exercise in abstractionism.

Theologians shifted to meet the challenge of the philosophy of existence. Barth, Bultmann, Brunner, Tillich, Niebuhr, and others proposed theological adjustments. No two agreed precisely, but each brought superb method and style to the intellectual struggle. Working accord focused on the self, which they argued is a "unity of radical freedom and limitedness, and faith is the acceptance of this paradoxical unity. But faith is not the possession of a creed or a doctrine, nor is it belief. It is, rather, the decision to be oneself as *this* PERSON in *this* situation. . . . Existential theologians try to interpret Scripture in this manner, to show that in and under the mythological concepts and ideas is an understanding of human life that is a viable possibility for modern man" (Harvey, 93 f).

A critique of the neoorthodox response to existentialism should include the reminder that the objective of theology is not to find a "viable possibility for modern man" but to understand and proclaim the doctrines of the Bible, whether acceptable or not. Furthermore, while faith is more than belief, it cannot exist apart from belief. And there is no virtue in the decision to be oneself in this situation if the decision is merely the confirmation of a rebellious, unredeemed, and unchanged self.

See BEING, NATURE, PROPOSITIONAL THEOLOGY, MAN, PHILOSOPHY, METAPHYSICS.

For Further Reading: Peterfreund, *Contemporary Philosophy and Its Origins;* Jones, *Kant to Wittgenstein and Sartre;* Macquarrie, *Principles of Christian Theology;* Harvey, *A Handbook of Theological Terms.*

MEL-THOMAS ROTHWELL

EXODUS. This term *(exodon)* means "a going out," "a way out," or "departure." It also is the name of the second book of the OT. There are but three references to this term in the NT: twice in relation to death (Luke 9:30-31; 2 Pet. 1:15), and once in reference to Israel's deliverance, under Moses' leadership, from over 400 years of Egyptian bondage (Heb. 11:22). However, the importance of the Exodus in OT history is assumed throughout the NT.

Exodus signifies a victorious deliverance and symbolizes redemption. Exodus is the principal motif of the OT, and its recurrent theme as it rises to its grand climax in the *exodon* of Christ, which is discussed with Moses and Elijah on the Mount of Transfiguration, and witnessed by Peter, John, and James.

It is significant that Moses, who led the Exodus from Egypt, and who represented the law, and Elijah, representing the prophets, should have appeared in the glory of their translation victory to witness the culmination of the Exodus in Christ's victorious death and resurrection, prefigured in His transfiguration. Thus heaven, represented by Moses and Elijah, and earth, represented by Peter, John, and James, witnessed Christ's redemptive *exodon* accomplished for both himself and all mankind. It is further significant that His death and resurrection victory, or *exodon,* was something He would himself "accomplish," and not something that would happen to Him as death does to others (Luke 23:46).

As Israel's Exodus from Egypt was accompanied by many miracles which authenticated God's intervention in their deliverance, so Christ's culmination of the Exodus at His victorious death and resurrection, prefigured in His transfiguration, was authenticated by God's miraculous interventions. Thus the redemptive Exodus begun under the leadership of Moses was completed in the *exodon* of Christ.

See ELIJAH, REST (REST OF FAITH), REDEEMER (REDEMPTION).

For Further Reading: MacRae, "Exodus," *ZPEB,* 2:428-50; *ISBE,* 2:1052-67; Wood, *Pentecostal Grace.*

CHARLES W. CARTER

EXORCISM. This is the use of a formula of incantation and prayers for the purpose of expelling evil spirits or devils. In the strict sense of the term, there is no exorcism in the NT. The method used by Jesus was authoritative, not ritualistic; the giving of a command, not the casting of a spell. And when He gave His disciples power over sickness and demons in His name, it was His power, the power of God, not His name that effected the cure. In no instance was the name of Jesus used as a magic weapon against evil.

Exorcism as incantation arose in the Early Church from the practice of Jesus and His disciples of healing by the laying on of hands and prayer. This included the casting out of unclean spirits. In time the formula came to be used to drive out Satan from catechumens coming from heathenism, for Satan dwelt among the heathen. Soon it became united with the baptismal ritual, and this finally led to fantastic magical rites. These grew up, as it were, with the Catholic church. Martin Luther did not reject the practice, but in time the Lutheran church questioned its value, abbreviated it, and finally did away with it entirely by the close of the 18th century.

The Roman Catholic church has continued to practice exorcism but provides strict rules for its regulation. The Greek Orthodox church continues to include exorcism in the rite of baptism to expel every kind of evil by the use of a series of prayers. Some churches require a reputable psychiatric examination as the first step in suspected cases of demon possession.

The term *exorcism* is an unfortunate one, for as here defined it is alien to the true spirit of evangelical Christianity, unless it also acknowledges, in relation to the cure sought, the exercise of faith in the atoning death of Jesus Christ and the power of the Holy Spirit for deliverance from all sin.

See DEMONS (DEMON POSSESSION), SATAN, PRAYER, FASTING.

For Further Reading: Nauman, ed., *Exorcism Through the Ages;* Newport, *Demons, Demons, Demons;* Koch, *Christian Counseling and Occultism.*

HARVEY J. S. BLANEY

EXPEDIENCY. The word is sometimes used to mean haste or dispatch; however, its most common use is to describe the nature of any means taken to achieve a desired end that gives more attention to personal advantage than to possible moral implications of the action. In this sense, that which is expedient is characterized by a concern for what is opportune, is governed by self-interest, and usually implies what is immediately advantageous without regard for ethics or concern with consistent principles. A less derogatory implication of the term occurs when it indicates an improvised or temporary solution to a problem taken out of necessity, or to any morally neutral means of achieving a particular end.

It is possible for expediency to be indifferent to moral or ethical principles, to be opposed to them, or, in some instances, to be identical with them. Moral sensitivity informed by Christian values enables a person to detect whether or not there is conflict between that which is expedient and that which is morally and ethically right.

The term "expedient," as it appears in the Bible, literally means "to bring together" (Acts 19:19); however, it is more frequently translated to indicate "advantage" or "benefit." Jesus told His disciples, "It is to your advantage that I go away, for if I do not go away, the Counselor will not come" (John 16:7, RSV).

Paul's teaching is that though things may be lawful, they are not necessarily expedient, i.e., advantageous to the kingdom of God. And Christians should go beyond the question of legality to the question of what is helpful and wise (1 Cor. 6:12; 10:23). For other examples of the use of this term in the NT see Matt. 5:29-30; John 11:50; 2 Cor. 8:10; 12:1. Its NT use is, for the most part, morally neutral; it is not used to indicate that which is profitable, convenient, or advantageous as opposed to that which is strictly right.

The possible exception is Caiaphas' statement to the Jews with regard to Jesus that illustrates the important relationship between expediency and one's value system: "It is expedient for you that one man should die for the people, and that the whole nation should not perish" (John 11:50, RSV; cf. 18:14). From the perspective of the high priest it seemed right that Jesus die rather than create a political problem with Rome for the Jewish nation. From a Christian perspective, however, the expediency advocated by Caiaphas was wrong, for it was at the expense of justice. Ironically, in speaking of one who "should die for the people," he spoke of a greater expediency that he did not understand.

See RIGHT (RIGHTEOUSNESS), MOTIVES, INTEGRITY.

DON W. DUNNINGTON

EXPERIENCE. Experience consists of events and influences in which a person has been involved. Religious experience differs from ordinary experience in terms of its source and the interpretation one is persuaded to place upon it. It finds its source in the various types of relationships with the supernatural and is associated with ultimate reality and values. In the Bible, experience is expressed in terms of discovery and knowledge and the testing of something.

It is customary in some circles to speak of Christian experience when referring to initial conversion, when a person by faith accepts Jesus Christ as Lord and Savior. However, the concept must be broadened to encompass one's total understanding of and relationship with God and the Church. God has been revealed as Trinity—a triunity, a Three in One—and we know Him as such through experience, personal and corporate.

God can be known only by experiencing Him. Israel knew God by a sense of the Divine Presence in the great events of her corporate existence. From Abraham to Moses, to the Red Sea and Sinai, across the Jordan and into the Promised Land, Israel saw God at work and realized herself to be His chosen people. This did not come by sovereign announcement only but by the experience of entering into a covenant relationship with Jehovah. Israel experienced election to a unique relationship with her God.

God made himself one with mankind in the person of Jesus Christ, thereby dispelling all doubt of the reality of His relationship with His people. And now since Pentecost God has been present in the life of the new Israel, the Church, so that all who will accept the new covenant may know Him in personal experience.

Christian experience is knowing God through the presence and power of the Holy Spirit. Because this closest of all relationships to Deity is so personal, it elevates one to the highest potential of his own personality. The experience of the Holy Spirit is the *sine qua non* of man's knowledge of God.

While Christian experience is intensely personal and individual between a person and his God, it should be observed that it is usually dependent upon the corporate experience of the church, the *koinonia.* It is this corporate fellowship which provides both the incentive for sharing and the norm for the interpretation of private experience. Unguided and unexamined personal experience can easily degenerate into arrogant fanaticism.

Christian experience is comprised of both knowledge and faith. One needs to know something before he can have faith in anything, even though it be only by intuition. At the same time, faith as trust is basic to all knowledge. The apostle Paul speaks of a faith that leads to faith (Rom. 1:17). Faith is walking in light, not stepping into the darkness. And experience is confirmed by the witness of the Holy Spirit. This is what brings balance and stability, confirming believers as children of God.

See WITNESS OF THE SPIRIT, KOINONIA, FAITH.

For Further Reading: Robinson, *Christian Experience of the Holy Spirit;* Mackintosh, *The Christian Experience of Forgiveness;* Moberly, *Atonement and Personality;* Taylor, *Biblical Authority and Christian Faith.*

HARVEY J. S. BLANEY

EXPIATION. Expiation describes the process and/or means of our at-one-ment with God. Thus, it embraces several concepts/realities: (1) sin as an offense to a holy God; (2) His consequent wrath; (3) an atoning sacrifice; (4) God's forgiveness and pardon; and (5) restoration to fellowship.

An admittedly obscure, technical term, "expiation" (which never occurs in the KJV) has partially replaced, in some more recent Bible translations such as the RSV, an even bigger word, "propitiation." Leon Morris argues that we need both to explain the biblical concept of atonement. Propitiation answers to the righteous anger of the Holy One and His judgment against sin. Punishment can be stayed only if the requirements of God's justice are satisfied by the death of another, in the sinner's place. Expiation points us to God's provision for our forgiveness, and our restoration to divine favor.

The root meaning of the Hebrew word for atonement *(kaphar)* is debated: Some maintain it means "to cover"; others, "to blot out" or "to wipe out." R. Abba (*IDB,* 2:200) concludes: "It is probable that both meanings are present. . . . Common to both is the idea of annulling or obliterating sin." The Greek (the NT follows the LXX at this point) uses a word *(hilaskesthai)* related to mercy. Thus in Luke 18:13, it means "be merciful to" and expresses a penitent's humble plea to Almighty God. In response, once a sinner, he is declared "justified" (rather than the self-righteous Pharisee).

The OT stresses the substitutionary character of the sacrifices by which expiation for sin is made. By the blood of the sin, trespass, guilt, and burnt offerings, atonement was made daily for the guilt of Israel. Once a year, a "great day of expiations" was observed (see Leviticus 16). On this occasion, the priests made atonement for the sins of the people (vv. 30, 33), but also for the Tabernacle, altar, and holy place (because defiled by sinful men).

The NT highlights God's gracious mercy in providing for our atonement. He gave His own Son, to die in our stead: "God was in Christ, reconciling the world unto himself" (2 Cor. 5:19). Four texts speak of this accomplished mission as our expiation. Rom. 3:25 describes the Cross as our mercy seat, the place where God made manifest His forgiving grace. First John 2:2 and 4:10 point to Christ as the "expiation for our sins" (RSV), i.e., our "sin offering." Heb. 2:17 pronounces the work of our High Priest, "to make expiation for the sins of the people," as perfect and complete (a sacrifice offered once for all). Thus Jesus Christ fulfills the OT conception of atonement. He is our Expiation.

See ATONEMENT, PROPITIATION, SACRIFICE.

For Further Reading: Morris, *The Apostolic Preaching of the Cross,* 125-85; Abba, "Expiation," *IDB,* 2:200-201.

WAYNE G. MCCOWN

F

FAILURE. Failure is coming short or lacking in attainment of some desired end, action, or result. In a biblical context, failure is of two kinds: the shortcoming resulting from sinful moral disability; and the shortcoming that is the result of involuntary human weakness or infirmity.

Sinful failure is vividly described by Paul in Rom. 7:14-25. Speaking, in all probability, of his awakened but unregenerate state, the apostle mourns his inability both to do the good he desires and to avoid the evil he rejects.

Some measure of this disability remains with the unsanctified believer. To the extent any person attempts to achieve desired freedom from sin (Rom. 6:18, 22) in his own strength apart from the dynamic of the Holy Spirit (8:2-4), to that extent there is an echo of the failure of 7:14-25 in his experience.

A second source and corresponding kind of failure is in the area of human shortcoming and weakness, both physical and psychological. The NT unfailingly condemns sinful or moral failure, but speaks of an area of human failure in which the Spirit helps (Rom. 8:26) and Christ sympathizes (Heb. 4:15).

Christians must maintain a fine balance in the area of human failures between unwarranted condemnation for the unavoidable, and a too-easy acceptance of what may be improved in their life-styles.

See FAULTS (FAULTLESS), BACKSLIDING, LIABILITY TO SIN.

For Further Reading: Baldwin, *Holiness and the Human Element;* Chambers and Chambers, *Holiness and Human Nature;* Corlett, *Holiness in Practical Living;* Smith, "Failures," in *The Christian's Secret of a Happy Life.*

W. T. PURKISER

FAITH. Faith is that voluntary assent that man gives to the revelation of God and the self-committal or trust of the entire man to the control of such truth.

The Hebrew word *aman* means "to be firm, steadfast, and trustworthy." The essential ideas are faithfulness and truthfulness. The concept is that of holding firm in a time of testing because of confidence in God's rewards. In this sense God is the faithful and unchanging One, loyal to His promises and covenant. In return man must be obedient, steadfast, and trustfully relying on God's promises.

The NT word for faith is *pistis,* meaning "a firm belief, persuasion, or conviction based on hearing." In a majority of cases in the teaching of Jesus and the apostles the words "reliance" and "trust" can be used as a synonym for faith. The NT concept of faith includes the following: the intellectual assent to revealed truth, acting upon its requirements, and confidence in the Person of the revelation.

First, then, faith involves the intellectual elements of apprehension and conviction of the truth (Rom. 10:11). But in addition: Where there is faith, there will be a willingness to act on this truth. Noah, "warned of God of things not seen as yet, moved with fear, prepared an ark" (Heb. 11:7). James clearly states the connection between believing and acting: "Even so faith, if it hath not works, is dead, being alone" (2:17). Faith in the sense of intellectual assent to truth is possessed by devils. It is not true faith, for they do not act on the knowledge (cf. Matt. 8:29).

There are degrees in the content of faith. One man knows more truth and, therefore, believes more than another. A little faith, well cultivated, may be the seed of great faith. One person may be walking in the light but be less informed concerning things spiritual than another. Such are not to be despised. "Him that is weak in the faith receive ye, but not to doubtful disputations" (Rom. 14:1). This person has faith. There is the disposition to accept truth. This faith will grow as the knowledge of God and experience in His fellowship advances.

Christian maturity is a factor in the experience and realization of the truth and thus in the degrees of faith. In this sense the degree of faith is not a condition of nor dependent upon our will. Degrees of faith are seen in the difference between the well-established Christian who is not easily overcome by temptation to unbelief and another who lacks such maturity. This is seen in the case of Abraham: "He staggered not at the promise of God through unbelief; but was strong in faith, giving glory to God" (Rom. 4:20).

The disciples needed time to be equal to a hard case of demon possession. They had cast out some demons, but later they failed. When they asked Jesus why, He answered, "Because of your unbelief" (Matt. 17:20). The more a man exercises faith in his walk with Christ, the more he is able to believe. As one matures in his experience with God, the time will come when he, as Abraham, is not staggered by the promises of God.

Strong faith makes it possible for the believer to face the future with the calm confidence that comes from absolute assurance. "Faith is the substance [confidence or assurance] of things hoped for, the evidence [proof, conviction, title-deed] of things not seen" (Heb. 11:1).

Faith, then, is that belief which a soul has in the infinite wisdom, power, and goodness of God. Being quickened by the Spirit, he is able to believe, claim, and experience the promises of God.

See BELIEF, FIDELITY, OBEDIENCE.

For Further Reading: Sheldon, *Christian Doctrine,* 438-40; Westcott, *The Epistle to the Hebrews,* 349-52; Wiley, *Epistle to the Hebrews,* 352-60.

LEON CHAMBERS

FAITH HEALING. This term is generally intended to designate a healing which occurs as the result of faith rather than purely medical agencies. It is popular among those who claim the gift of healing, i.e., the "faith healers."

The Bible mentions several incidents where healings were attributed to faith. Jesus said to the woman who touched His garment, "Daughter, your faith has made you well" (Mark 5:34, RSV). In John 4:50, we see a healing which is the result of another's faith, rather than the faith of the one being healed.

Faith healing, in and of itself, is not an infallible evidence of either the power or endorsement of God. Faith may be misplaced, yet work. In this case the healing is either satanic or psychological. When the illness is psychosomatic, faith can be a releasing mechanism. Christian

Science and other cults can cite cases of seemingly authentic faith healing.

True *divine* faith healing, wherever it occurs, will be consistent with the character of God. God will always act in consistency with His holiness, wisdom, and knowledge. Hence, legitimate faith must be confidence not only in the power of God but trust in the wisdom and benevolent sovereignty of God, who will always do what is best for the person. Thus, if healing does not occur, faith is not negated, for it is founded on something deeper than experiencing a miracle.

Much of modern "faith healing" is grounded in the "courtesy" of God—a God whom the healers see as One who responds invariably to the call of a petitioner, especially to the call of a person with "much faith." Such a belief puts God at the disposal of our petitions and our faith. It creates an "errand boy" God. Much of modern "faith healing" dialogue reveals this kind of demanding mentality.

All boons of redemption derive from the Atonement. But the redemption of our body to full health and perfection is not designed for this life, but will be subsequent (Rom. 8:23; 1 Cor. 15:44; 2 Cor. 4:10; 12:7-10; Phil. 3:21). Healing in this life, therefore, is a special mercy of God, subject to His sovereignty, as a small foretaste of the future. It is not a "right" which believers may uniformly claim, with that confidence which is properly theirs in appropriating salvation from sin.

See HEAL (HEALING), WHOLE (WHOLENESS), FAITH, GIFTS OF THE SPIRIT, MIRACLE.

For Further Reading: Purkiser, *Beliefs That Matter Most,* 83-86; Barkman, *Man in Conflict,* 133-52; McMillen, *None of These Diseases;* Boggs, *Faith Healing and the Christian Faith;* Wilcox, *God's Healing Touch.*

C. NEIL STRAIT

FAITHFUL, FAITHFULNESS. See INTEGRITY.

FALL, THE. Although a theological rather than a biblical term, the fall of man from holiness into sinfulness and from communion with God to estrangement from Him is well attested in Scripture. Created in the moral likeness of God (Gen. 1:26-27; 9:6), Adam and Eve were placed in the Garden of Eden, given dominion over all creation, and commanded to multiply and fill the earth (1:26-31). In this state of paradisical innocence, man was holy, i.e., in full communion with God and desirous only of doing His will. All his aspirations were towards God, and the loving, harmonious relationship between Adam and Eve was a reflection of their perfect relationship with God.

The Genesis account of Adam and Eve in paradise must be interpreted as historically factual—not mythical, idealistic, or even symbolical. Three arguments support the literal interpretation. (1) It is presented in Genesis as part of a historical chronicle; of Adam, Seth, Enoch, Noah, etc. (2) It is clear that Jesus read it as history. His argument with the Pharisees on the indissolubility of the marriage relationship (Matt. 19:3-6) depends for its pertinency on the Adam-Eve union that was divinely blessed (Gen. 2:21-25). (3) Paul's argument for the universality of sin is based unequivocally on the Genesis record: "Sin came into the world through one man" (Rom. 5:12 ff, RSV).

Not only was Adam's paradisical existence such that with our many limitations we can now barely conceive it, but also only the briefest details are recorded in Scripture. The fact of probation, however, is very clear. Adam and Eve were permitted freedom of action and initiative with but one restriction—they were forbidden access to "the tree of the knowledge of good and evil" (Gen. 2:17). A loving God unquestionably revealed to them all the implications of this prohibition, although only the negative command and the threat of death are recorded in Genesis.

The temptation to disobey God came from without, from "the serpent" (Gen. 3:1), an incarnation of Satan, as Paul argues in 2 Cor. 11:3, 14. The tempter's attack was threefold: on the physical senses ("the tree was good for food"), on aesthetic appreciation ("a delight to the eyes"), and on intellectual stimulus ("to be desired to make one wise," Gen. 3:6, RSV).

But the temptation was not irresistible. Free moral choice implies the possibility of temptation but not the inevitability of transgression. Adam and Eve chose to disobey God and transgress His clear command. Their sin was, first, doubt ("Did God say . . . ?"), then disbelief ("You will not die"), and, finally, disobedience ("She . . . and he ate," vv. 1, 4, 6, RSV).

The fall of man was an epoch, a turning point in the history of the race, a catastrophe so far-reaching that its consequences have affected the entire creation without exception. The whole of biblical revelation is predicated on the reality of the tragedy of Eden, and any attempt to assess the Fall must be determined solely by the biblical witness; though the history of man affords innumerable sad illustrations of what John Milton called

Man's first disobedience and the fruit
Of that forbidden tree whose mortal taste
Brought death into the world and all our woe.
(*Paradise Lost,* book 1)

The consequences of the Fall were immediate and long-term, personal and racial, spiritual and physical, human and cosmic. Man's moral conscience was disturbed by his sense of guilt and degradation, and shame and fear drove Adam and Eve to hide from the presence of God. They were then driven from Eden, the earth was cursed because of sin, and man was sentenced to unending toil, pain, and sorrow with the forces of nature, the powers of evil, and the weakness of mortal flesh. "In the day that you eat . . . you shall die" (Gen. 2:17, RSV) had been the solemn Edenic interdict, and Paul concludes: "Sin came into the world through one man and death through sin" (Rom. 5:12, RSV).

The Fall brought death. Adam lost the indwelling Holy Spirit, was excluded from "the tree of life," and his body became mortal and heir to pain, disease, and eventual dissolution. Separated from God, with moral rebellion in their hearts, Adam and Eve fell from a sinless fellowship that provided for endless progress in glory to an alienation that brought internal depravity, external conflict, and ultimately, apart from grace, eternal exclusion from the Creator's presence. Death—physical, spiritual, and eternal—is the consequence of the Fall, as Rom. 5:12-21; 1 Cor. 15:21-22; etc. make very plain. To what precise extent the Fall brought death and the curse to the whole creation, Scripture does not assert; but a cosmic consequence is implied when Rom. 8:19-23 speaks of creation "groaning in travail" until the consummation of the ages.

Orthodox Christian theology has always recognized the fundamental importance of the doctrine of the Fall, but its various schools have not spoken unanimously on how the Fall constituted the race sinful and corrupt. In Adam "all men sinned" (Rom. 5:12, RSV). The whole race was represented in Adam the head, and from him all men share, through genetic reproduction, a "fallen" nature, i.e., they are physically mortal, morally vitiated, and prone to pride, indulgence, and self-gratification. The Fall has rendered the whole race guilty, not by a legal imputation of Adam's guilt, but, as Adam fathered a son "in his own likeness" (Gen. 5:3), so sinful man reproduces his own kind. The divine image in man is marred and defaced, and fallen human nature, lacking the indwelling Spirit, is prone to evil and susceptible to temptation.

Though the whole race is guilty and under condemnation, yet the gracious covenant of grace, provided by God in Eden (Gen. 3:15), prevents the sentence from immediate and irrevocable execution. While the Fall, in and through the first Adam, made the whole race corrupt and culpable before God, grace, mediated by the Last Adam, constitutes men accountable only for their own cherished and unconfessed sin.

See ADAM, PROBATION, TEMPTATION, ORIGINAL SIN, FREEDOM, PREVENIENT GRACE, CURSE, DEATH.

For Further Reading: Moxon, *The Doctrine of Sin;* Pope, *A Compendium of Christian Theology,* 2:15-19; Wiley, *CT,* 2:62-65; *GMS,* 79-87, 296-302.

HERBERT MCGONIGLE

FALSE CHRISTS. Jesus warns against false Christs in the Olivet Discourse (Matt. 24:5, 24, and parallels). Their appearance will constitute one of the signs of the end of the age. Each will attempt to authenticate himself as the Messiah by using signs and wonders, and will succeed in leading many astray.

History has noted several who have claimed to be Christ. Gamaliel noted two, "claiming to be somebody," Theudas and Judas of Galilee (Acts 5:34-37, NASB). Luke said that Simon, the magician in Samaria, was called "the Great Power of God" (Acts 8:10, NASB). Josephus, the historian, mentioned one who was a pretender. Joachim Camerarius told of a man named Manes who called himself Christ and who even called 12 disciples to follow him.

False Christs are not to be confused with the Antichrist, though the Antichrist could rise from among the false Christs. Also, the false prophets referred to in Matthew 24 and Mark 13 are not the same as the false Christs.

See MAN OF SIN, TRIBULATION.

For Further Reading: Robertson, *Word Pictures in the NT,* 1:188-92.

JAMES L. PORTER

FALSE DECRETALS. Decretals are papal pronouncements on points of church law. During the Middle Ages several collections of decretals were made, among which was one by Isidore, archbishop of Seville. About the 9th century certain documents were inserted in this collection and accepted as genuine until scholars in the 16th century demonstrated their falsity. Due to such origin they are called "false decretals," "forged decretals," or "Pseudo-Isidorian decretals."

Some of these documents purported to be written by popes from as early as Clement I. One document, known as the "Donation of Constantine," claimed to be a gift of the western Roman Empire to the pope, made when Constantine moved his capital from Rome to Constantinople (A.D. 330).

The general tenor of these decretals was to

augment the authority of the pope, especially in temporal affairs. Papal advisers used them to urge Gregory IV to claim increased authority. Their greatest use was made by Nicholas I to justify claims to papal supremacy over all secular authority.

For Further Reading: Cannon, *History of Christianity in the Middle Ages,* 95-96; Douglas, ed., *NIDCC,* 289, 308, 368; Newman, *A Manual of Church History,* 1:487, 498.

LESLIE D. WILCOX

FAMILY. The term "family" expresses the idea that man is not made to dwell alone (Gen. 2:18) but in love, fellowship, and covenant responsibility. In the Scriptures man is always in family, i.e., always in covenant relationship with others, whether this be the extension of Jacob's family into tribes and nations or the Church, God's new covenant family.

Among the Israelites a family is a covenant concept binding all together, blood relatives, slaves, concubines, hired servants (Gen. 17:23, 27; 46:5-7, 26; Acts 10:24, 44-48; 16:15, 33), and relatives through marriage (Gen. 34:8-12). Kings, chiefs, and elders are covenant fathers, agents of God's blessings (Num. 7:2; 13:3; 17:3; 1 Sam. 24:11; 2 Kings 5:13; 6:21; 13:14) and shepherds who care for God's people (Ezekiel 34; John 10:1-18). Similarly in the Church, bishops, elders, and deacons are overseers of the flock of God (Acts 20:28; John 21:15-19; 1 Tim. 3:2-5, 8-12).

The individual's needs are met through family affection, provision, and discipline. Lack of family affection is a perversion (Rom. 1:31) and is abnormal (Isa. 49:15). All members of the family, including servants, are given clear commands regarding mutual care, support, love, honor, kindness, and obedience (Eph. 5:21—6:9; Col. 3:18—4:1).

The ideal father is to be "temperate, sensible, dignified, hospitable, an apt teacher, no drunkard, not violent but gentle, not quarrelsome, and no lover of money. He must manage his own household well, keeping his children submissive and respectful in every way" (1 Tim. 3:2-5, RSV, also 8-12). Similarly, the ideal woman is to provide, nurture, and rule (Prov. 31:10-31; 1 Tim. 5:10, 14). All are in some way to be submissive to one another (Eph. 5:21—6:9, et al.) and equal (Gal. 3:23—4:7; Philem. 16).

This covenant community is religious as well as social. God's covenant laws and promises are to be taught to one's children (Deut. 11:18-19). Worship and sacrifice are performed as a family (1 Sam. 1:3-4; 20:29), assembled tribe (Josh. 24:1; 1 Sam. 7:1-9), or nation (1 Kings 8:62-64). In the NT, families respond to the gospel and are baptized (Acts 10:24, 44-48; 16:15, 33; 17:5-9). Covenant promises are for the family; the promised Spirit is "for you and your children" (2:39, NASB); the Gentile is grafted into Abraham's family (Rom. 11:17-24); "brought near by the blood of Christ" (Eph. 2:11-14, NASB). Paul claimed his "advantage" that as a Jew he was an heir to God's promises (Rom. 3:1; 9:5; 11:28; Eph. 2:12). This advantage Paul applies to the family of believers, all of whom are under the sanctifying influences of the new covenant (1 Cor. 7:12-16).

The terms "family," "children," "son," "daughter," and "wife" are used to describe the relationship between God and His people, both Israel and the Church. Even angels are called sons of God (Job. 1:6). God himself can be known as Kinsman (Heb. *gaal* = redeemer and kinsman; see Roland de Vaux, *Ancient Israel,* 1:10-12, 21-22) and Father to Israel (Isa. 54:5; 63:16). In the NT, the Christian is taught to pray, "Our Father" (Matt. 6:9) and "Abba, Father" (Rom. 8:15; Gal. 4:6). God is the Father *(patēr)* from whom "his whole family *[patria]* in heaven and on earth derives its name" (Eph. 3:15, NIV). As Father, God provides (Psalm 23; Ezekiel 34; Matt. 5:43-48; Jas. 1:17) and disciplines (Prov. 3:11-12; Heb. 12:5-6). God's covenant care includes both "overflowing wrath" and "everlasting love" (Isa. 54:7-8, 10; Heb. 12:10; 1 Cor. 5:5). Obedience is the condition of maintaining the Father-child relationship (John 1:12; 14:21). Nevertheless, God as my Kinsman is my Redeemer. God is likened to the father (Heb. 12:10), mother (Isa. 49:15), and kinsman (63:15-16) who always disciplines us for our good, never forgets us, and always acknowledges and redeems us.

Paul and John both address the Christians as "dear children" or "little children" (1 Cor. 4:14 f; 1 John 2:1; 3:18; 4:4). Christians are mothers, fathers, brothers, and sisters (1 Tim. 5:1-2; Jas. 2:15; et al.) to each other. Christ is our Brother (Rom. 8:29; Heb. 2:11, 17). The Christian is adopted (Rom. 8:15), an heir with Christ (v. 17; Eph. 2:12), and a member of the household of God (v. 19).

See CHILD (CHILDREN), PARENTS AND CHILDREN, FATHERS, KOINONIA, FATHERHOOD OF GOD, MARRIAGE.

For Further Reading: Riley, *This Holy Estate; GMS,* 94, 115, 547-59; de Vaux, *Ancient Israel,* 1:10-12, 19-61; David, "Marriage: III. Family," *Sacramentum Mundi: An Encyclopedia of Theology,* 3:412-17.

DAVID L. CUBIE

FANATICISM. Fanaticism may be seen in various areas of life. A religious fanatic is a person utterly convinced that God or a god has directly grasped his spirit and mind. He rejects reason and mistakes personal emotion for the direct control of the Holy Spirit.

In a more general sense fanaticism may refer to persons obsessed by one idea, whether that idea appears to others to be good or evil. A person may be a sports fanatic, a nuclear disarmament fanatic, a political or religious fanatic.

John Fletcher wrote, "Fanaticism is the child of false zeal and of superstition, the father of intolerance and of persecution; it is therefore very different from piety, though some persons are pleased to confound them" (*Works,* 7:353). In earlier generations it was defined as "enthusiasm."

Fletcher goes on to contrast the two different characters of a presumptuous fanatic and an enlightened Christian in such terms as follows: "The one extinguishes the torch of reason, the other entertains a just respect for reason. . . . The one destroys the clear sense of Scripture language: the other refers everything to the law and the testimony. The former flatters that while the means may be neglected the end may be obtained, presuming that God will illuminate him in a miraculous manner, without the help of prayer, study, meditation, sermons, or sacraments; the latter unpresumingly expects the succours of grace in a constant use of appointed means" (*Works,* 9:36).

The fanatic imagines himself free to behave without reference or obedience to authority, whereas the wise Christian acknowledges, respects, and is ready to account for his faith and conduct with meekness.

The fanatic pays little regard to graciousness and charity; the true Christian is motivated by brotherly love. The former seeks spectacular gifts, the latter seeks those gifts that will assist him to serve God and men.

Agitation of his animal spirit is by the fanatic taken to indicate the inspiration of the Holy Spirit; by the biblically enlightened Christian as those manifestations that make the gospel contemptible in the eyes of those people who are always ready and eager to treat devotion as fanaticism.

Fanaticism is life governed by mere impressions; it is the unteachable life, considering itself enlightened by the Holy Spirit far beyond the enlightenment afforded to others. It may be caused directly by devils or evil spirits (1 Tim. 4:1), an ignorance of scriptural teaching having stripped the soul of its defences against presumption, pride, and lovelessness.

Fanaticism threatens the zealous life and seldom endangers the heart that is cool towards Christ; formalism knows no fanaticism. Fanaticism may be light and heat without grace or love; the heart under the control of the imagination, and the understanding dominated by the emotions, a fire that heats but does not purify or refine. Fanaticism is the caricature of holiness: it is painted fire.

See ZEAL, GUIDE (GUIDANCE), REASON.

For Further Reading: Fletcher, *Works,* 7:32-41; Wesley, Sermon, "The Nature of Enthusiasm," *Works,* 5:467 ff; Smith, *Religious Fanaticism,* 155; Sargent, *The Battle for the Mind.* T. CRICHTON MITCHELL

FASTING. Scriptural fasting *(nēsteia)* is a spiritual discipline or religious exercise generally associated with prayer and involving voluntary abstinence from certain foods. The term can be used in the general sense of self-denial from normal or enjoyed activities to permit more prayer, e.g., fasting from sleep, recreation, or normal work routine.

Its purpose is to set oneself apart for communion with God, and more earnest seeking of God. It complements and strengthens desire, whole-souled intercession or petition, and faith.

Biblical fasting dates back to Moses and is repeatedly mentioned. The Day of Atonement involved 24 hours of fasting (Lev. 23:32). After the Exile four other annual fasts were observed (Zech. 8:19). Jesus fasted during the wilderness temptation (Matt. 4:2), and while He did not specifically command fasting, He clearly expected His followers to fast and gave guidelines (6:16-18; 9:15).

Scriptural fasting includes: (1) Self-humbling, mourning for sin, repentance, and seeking God's forgiveness (Samuel and Israel—1 Sam. 7:5-6; Ahab—1 Kings 21:27); (2) Vicarious repentance for one's nation or people (Moses—Deut. 9:9); (3) Humbly seeking God's mercy, help, or guidance (Joshua—Josh. 7:6-7; Israel—Judg. 20:26; David—2 Sam. 12:16; Ps. 35:13; Jehoshaphat—2 Chron. 20:3; Esther—Esther 4:16; Nineveh—Jonah 3:5; Ezra—Ezra 8:21); (4) Invoking God's blessing and aid on a new spiritual venture (Acts 13:3) or on the consecration of new church leaders (14:23); (5) Prolonged and/or secret communion with God (Moses—Exod. 34:28; Jesus—Matt. 4:2); (6) As a disciplined devotional habit (Cornelius—Acts 10:30); (7) As part of a deep intercessory life and ministry (Anna—Luke 2:37); and (8) As a manifestation of sorrow (1 Sam. 31:13; 2 Sam. 1:12).

Scripture and church history illustrate the dangers and possible abuses of religious fasting: It can (1) become an end in itself (Zech. 7:5); (2) be relied on as a means of earning God's favor (Isa. 58:3; Luke 18:12); (3) be a substitute for repentance and doing God's will (Jer. 14:11-12); (4) be a parade of religiosity (Matt. 6:16).

There is need for evangelicals today to restore fasting to its scriptural role.

See PRAYER, TEMPERANCE, DISCIPLINE, INTERCESSION.

For Further Reading: *Baker's DCE,* 244 ff.

WESLEY L. DUEWEL

FATALISM. Fatalism is the doctrine that all events are determined in advance. It is thus another name for determinism. "Fate" is believed to be so inexorable and unavoidable that neither gods nor men can cause any change. Fatalism presupposes impersonal and unknown forces, although men who do not believe in divine providence usually tend to personify fate.

This doctrine has no place in Christianity, for it is a denial of (1) a supreme, personal, and rational God who is Creator, Preserver, Redeemer, and Judge; (2) an eternal plan of God for the universe and man; (3) the personal action of God in providence and history; (4) man as created in the image of God as a rational free moral agent responsible to God; (5) salvation by grace through faith, and (6) choices in this life leading to eternal blessedness or punishment.

To follow fatalism to its ultimate logical conclusion (which obviously fatalists do not do) is to deny a rational basis for human society, government, law and justice, education, science, industry, or religion. It is destructive of human dignity, personal motivation, human initiative, and belief in the meaning of life. Fatalistic teaching is found in varying degree in some oriental religions.

See DETERMINISM, CHANCE, CAUSE AND EFFECT, FREEDOM, PROVIDENCE, ACCOUNTABILITY.

For Further Reading: *Baker's DT,* 215.

WESLEY L. DUEWEL

FATHERHOOD OF GOD. The liberal understanding is that God is the father of everyone. Along with "the brotherhood of man," the "Fatherhood of God" is one of the two basic tenets in the liberal creed. The evangelical understanding is that God is not the Father of everyone, but only of those who are responsive to Him. While Paul recognizes God's Fatherhood of all by creation (Acts 17:28-29), this does not imply a personal, spiritual relationship, which can be brought about only by regeneration and adoption (John 1:12-13; 3:3-5; 8:44; Rom. 8:14-16; Gal. 4:6).

In the OT, God's Fatherhood of Israel is often implied—by Israel's being called His child. We read, e.g., "'When Israel was a child, I loved him, and out of Egypt I called my son'" (Hos. 11:1, NIV). And in Isa. 1:2 we read, "'I reared children and brought them up, but they have rebelled against me'" (NIV). And Jer. 31:20 asks, "'Is not Ephraim [the Northern Kingdom] my dear son, the child in whom I delight?'" (NIV).

It is interesting, however, that, in all the prayer intimacies of the Psalms, God is not addressed as "Father" in that literature. God's Fatherhood is implied there, and in such passages as those quoted above. But He is not addressed in that way in the OT, except perhaps in Jer. 3:4 where we read, "'Have you not just called to me: "My Father, my friend from my youth . . . ?"'" (NIV).

In the NT, however, this is an oft-used way of addressing God. Jesus often spoke of God as His Father; and He wanted the disciples to glorify the "Father" (Matt. 5:16). He also wanted them to pray for their persecutors "that you may be sons of your Father" (v. 45, NIV). Paul referred to God as Father in the opening of all his Epistles.

Hence God's Fatherhood expresses a special kind of relationship which He has in the OT with Israel and in the NT with redeemed persons. Terry says, "The highest and most endearing concept of God, whether in the OT or in the New, or among the nations anywhere, is that of Father" (*Biblical Dogmatics,* 549).

See GOD, ADOPTION, REDEEMER (REDEMPTION).

For Further Reading: Lockyer, *All the Doctrines of the Bible,* 199-203.

J. KENNETH GRIDER

FATHERS. The idea of "father" is rooted in the natural reproductive relationship which emerges between an infant and the male parent. Adam is the first father, but Abraham becomes the tribal father to the emerging nation. Thus the idea is enlarged to multigenerational dimensions; Abraham is to be a "father of many nations" (Gen. 17:4), but still in a reproductive sense. To pass on the faith from father to son was the mandate of the Shema (Deuteronomy 6), and in a tribal sense one generation is obligated not to hide the true faith from their fathers' sons—in some leapfrogging sense all sons yet to be born are the sons of the fathers (Ps. 78:1-8).

The "fatherless" were the special concern of ancient Israel, more than 40 times cited as the object of true justice or as the lost estate. A tribal people found ways of incorporating the fatherless into economic and emotional resources, thus preventing the destructive and erosive effects which modern society endures at the hands of deformed fatherless delinquents (see Heatherington). The extreme concern for fatherless children first sounded in Exod. 22:22, 24; Deut. 10:18; and Ps. 82:3 is nailed down as the acid test of the quality of faith in the Early Church—the essence of pure religion is concern for fatherless and widows (Jas. 1:27).

"Father" relationships, however, do not require the reproductive or even the long-range genetic connection. Paul saw himself as surrogate father of Timothy, fulfilling the father formation responsibilities to the younger man (1 Tim. 1:2; 2 Tim. 1:2). Joseph, bound to Mary, and a "just man," determined to divorce her instead of turning her over for a public stoning for her prenuptial pregnancy. But God had a better idea which Joseph quickly accepted—instead of getting rid of Mary and her Baby, he acted to marry the Baby's mother. Then, he named the Baby, giving both legality to the birth and establishing Jesus in Joseph's lineage—all of this without sexual access to Mary.

We know little of Joseph as a father from explicit records. But we know a great deal of him by looking at the Boy he reared. The young Man was well formed in His identity; He was absolutely safe around women; He was not swept along by peer influence and the spirit of the age—all signs of health not usually present in father-deprived boys. What is more, Joseph's Boy gave God a new name. The Holy One of Israel, Yahweh, Adonai, the Lord, became at last "Our Father," even "Abba" or "Daddy Father." There is little question where Jesus learned the meaning of that name.

See FAMILY, PARENTS AND CHILDREN, FATHERHOOD OF GOD.

For Further Reading: Barclay, *Train Up a Child;* Joy, *Toward Freedom and Responsibility; A Parent's Guide to Faith Formation;* Heatherington, et al., "The Effects of Father Absence," *Young Children* (March, 1971), 233-42.

DONALD M. JOY

FAULTS, FAULTLESS. The word "fault" is defined as "neglect of duty or propriety, resulting from inattention or lack of prudence rather than from design to injure or offend, but liable to censure or objection." It is also whatever "impairs excellence," and hence is a "defect" or "blemish" *(New Standard Dictionary).* Faultless would be freedom from any fault or blemish.

While a sanctified person can possess a pure heart (Matt. 5:8), he will still be limited by a weak and infirm body. These infirmities cause mistakes in word, thought, and deed. Though these are objectionable and need confession, they cannot be sin in the strict moral meaning. They still need the Atonement but are not inconsistent with the sanctified life.

These faults can show up in "temperament," "emotional immaturity," "cultural variations," and "infirmities" (Taylor, *Life in the Spirit,* 153-60). Wesley called these faults "sins of infirmity" and "sins of ignorance," but always distinguished them from "sins properly so-called" (Cox, *John Wesley's Concept of Perfection,* 168-88).

Someday the Christian will be presented "faultless" before God (Jude 24). Until that day he will be beset with faults and failures which often embarrass him.

See SIN, INFIRMITIES, MISTAKES, FAILURE.

For Further Reading: Geiger, ed., *Insights into Holiness,* 145-72; Geiger, ed., *Further Insights into Holiness,* 179-212; Geiger, ed., *The Word and the Doctrine,* 293-316; Purkiser, ed., *Exploring Our Christian Faith,* 376-80.

LEO G. COX

FEAR. This word is found 514 times in the KJV. Its sheer frequency reflects the faithfulness of the Scriptures to the emotions of humanity in confronting the dangers and uncertainties of life. The emotion of fear ranges all the way from stark terror to a calm attitude of awe and reverence. A pervasive teaching is that the "fear of the Lord is the beginning of wisdom" (Prov. 1:7, et al.). This is not only awe and reverence but fidelity. It thus differs from the awe without love exhibited by the imported inhabitants of Samaria who feared not the Lord until He sent lions among them; after that they "feared the Lord, and served their own gods" (2 Kings 17:33). People can fear God in the sense of an enemy instead of reverencing Him as a benevolent but just Sovereign.

The saying "There is nothing to fear but fear" is a superficial philosophy of life. There are real perils both in life and in death, and fearing them is an intelligent reaction. Some degree of fear is necessary to prompt carefulness and prudence. Accident, pain, and bereavement are some of the experiences which may properly be feared; but even more fundamentally persons should fear sin and its consequences, both temporal and eternal.

Christians are not to be condemned for experiencing some constitutional fear, such as fear of tornados, or high places, or high speeds. Yet faith in God is the best antidote to fear. It is the knowledge that in life's perils we are not alone, nor are we the victims of chance. God will either protect and deliver us or enable us, and He will ultimately translate us into His very presence.

The relation of fear to love can be confusing, in

view of John's statement: "There is no fear in love; but perfect love casteth out fear: because fear hath torment. He that feareth is not made perfect in love" (1 John 4:18). The context shows that it is fear and love in relation to God and His judgment which is primarily in view here. Those who love God perfectly are not afraid of God in the sense of terror, for they have no need to so fear. The dread and fear of the judgment—or that kind of fear which has spiritual "torment"—is the consequence of an uneasiness in one's relationship to God. Something is not quite right, so naturally there is no "boldness" in contemplating death and the future. But a child with a clear conscience, who loves its father and is sure of its father's love, welcomes the father's arrival with joy and laughter, and utterly without dread.

However, this verse is not to be made so universal and absolute as to make perfect love for God the total expulsion of occasional struggles with natural fears in relation to men and the vicissitudes of life. The conquest of natural fears belongs to the sphere of growth in grace.

See FAITH, PERFECT LOVE.

For Further Reading: Wise, *Psychiatry and the Bible,* 33-65.

RICHARD S. TAYLOR

FEASTS, JEWISH. In the broadest sense "feast" may refer to any set time of communal observance in Israel's history. Even though the Day of Atonement is actually a day of fasting, it is referred to by the same Hebrew phrase which in Leviticus 23 is used for festive celebrations. The most important distinction among the various feasts, however, was the differentiation between those that were canonical, provided for in the Law, and those that rested simply on custom. The major canonical feasts were the Sabbath, the Feast of Booths, the Feast of Weeks, and the Passover. The latter three were annual and were called Pilgrim Feasts, because all able-bodied men were required to attend.

The observance of the Sabbath was probably originally attached to the lunar cycle, but its structure in the OT is the dedication of one day in seven to God. It is a commemoration of creation (Exod. 20:8-11), a reminder of release from captivity (Deut. 5:12-15), and a sign of Israel's holy relationship to their God who graciously entered into covenant with them. The Temple sacrifices were doubled to distinguish the Sabbath from an ordinary day.

The Feast of Booths, or Tabernacles, is last of Israel's three great annual festivals. The end of the harvest year is the occasion for recalling the wilderness pilgrimage and renewing the people's commitment to their covenant (cf. Lev. 23:33-44). The term "booths" is apparently related to the agricultural practice of building a booth over the olive orchards in September to protect them until harvest.

The Feast of Weeks is chronologically the second of the three annual festivals. It is also known as the Feast of Harvest, and among Greek-speaking Jews the feast was called Pentecost (lit., "the 50th" day), having reference to the seven-week period following the Passover. Thus the word "weeks" came into use, for from the waving of the barley sheaf "the day after the [Paschal] Sabbath" were to be counted seven weeks (Lev. 23:5-17). This entire period had a special sanctity both in its relation to the Passover and in recognition that God is the Source of rain and agricultural fertility (Exod. 23:16; Lev. 23:17; Jer. 5:24).

The Passover, Feast of Unleavened Bread, is the first annual feast, held in the spring to commemorate the deliverance from Egypt. The term "Passover" is used both of the feast as a whole (Exod. 12:48) and of the sacrifice itself (vv. 11, 27; Deut. 16:2). It was first celebrated during bondage and is related in the narrative of the slaying of the firstborn of the Egyptians and the departure of the Israelites out of Egypt (cf. Exod. 12:1—13:16). Whereas the Passover commemorates the slaying of the firstborn, Unleavened Bread emphasizes the Exodus itself (12:17).

Of the noncanonical celebrations, the Feast of Dedication (Hanukkah), also known as the Feast of Lights, is most well known. Hanukkah is an eight-day festival to commemorate the victories of Judas Maccabeus against the Syrian forces in the face of insurmountable odds. The Syrian king, Antiochus Epiphanes, had commanded Jewish sacrifices and offerings to cease. A shrine to Zeus was erected on the altar, and 10 days later (Dec. 25, 168 B.C.) a swine was sacrificed in the Temple while soldiers committed unclean acts in the sacred enclosure. This "abomination of desolation" led to the Maccabean Revolt (168-42 B.C.), and Hanukkah is the feast in celebration of victory over the Syrians. Only three years after the abomination, the smoke of sacrifice rose to Jehovah from a newly constructed altar in a recleansed Temple.

See LORD'S DAY, JUDAISM, PASSOVER, PENTECOST.

For Further Reading: *Encyclopedia Judaica;* Trapp, *Judaism: Life and Development.*

W. STEPHEN GUNTER

FEDERAL THEOLOGY. Federal theology holds that redemptive history revolves around one single covenant covering the entire stretch of history from beginning to end. While the idea was presented as early as the sixth century by Pope Gregory I (540-604), the doctrine became prominent in the early Reformation. Reformed theologians like Andreas Musculus (1514-81) and Stephanus Kis (1505-72) extended the covenant to the whole nation.

In Holland the outlines of federal theology had been formed by the activities of Hyperius, Olevian, and Bullinger.

One of the strongest advocates of federal theology was Johannes Cocceius (1603-69), a Dutch theologian. The central idea in his biblical theology was the covenant of God. The relation between God and man is represented as a covenant existing first as a divine order, then as a compact between God and man. Cocceius taught that God initiated two covenants, a covenant of works and a covenant of grace. The covenant of works ended when Adam sinned. The broken covenant with Adam after the Fall was replaced immediately by the better covenant of grace. On this basis both Old and New Testaments testify to one single covenant of grace mediated by Jesus Christ. Because the covenant of grace applies to the whole of humanity, the covenants with Noah, Abraham, and Israel were only a renewal of God's covenant with Adam after the Fall.

A chief exponent of federal theology in the United States was Charles Hodge (1797-1878) of Princeton. According to Hodge's approach, God entered into a covenant with Adam as the head and representative of the entire race. As a result, every promise to Adam, and any threat of punishment, has a direct bearing upon the whole race. The plan of salvation is conceived as the history of a covenant relationship. Hodge distinguished between a covenant of grace and a covenant of redemption. The covenant of grace is extended to all people. The covenant of redemption is limited to the Father and the Son. Grace becomes efficacious only in the elect who are given to the Son by the Father.

A contemporary approach to the covenant relationship is found in these words: "God's covenant extends over history from beginning to end. Those before Christ, those under law, those after Christ, are all under the same grace of God" (Jakob Jocz). The covenant thus covers the totality of history. "The ingathering of the nations under the reign of God is the ultimate expression of covenantal grace," says Jocz. In some current thinking, the concept of one overarching covenant eliminates the idea of a sequence of redemptive dispensations.

See COVENANT THEOLOGY, DISPENSATION, DISPENSATIONALISM, PREVENIENT GRACE.

For Further Reading: Hodge, *Systematic Theology,* 2:323-24; Jocz, *The Covenant: A Theology of Human Destiny,* 284.

DONALD S. METZ

FEELING. See EMOTION.

FEET WASHING. This is a religious ceremony, practiced by some groups, in which believers wash one another's feet as an expression of love, humility, and service.

Originally, feet washing was an act of oriental courtesy, expressed toward a guest in one's home. The act was usually performed by a slave, or if necessary, by the host himself (Gen. 18:4; 19:2; 24:32; 43:24). Later it symbolized an act of humility and servitude (1 Sam. 25:41); also contrition (Luke 7:36-50).

The classic NT example is Jesus washing the disciples' feet in the Upper Room just prior to His crucifixion (John 13:1-17). He did it to break their spirit of pride, jealousy, and quarrelsomeness. Then He challenged them: "You call me Teacher and Lord; and you are right; for so I am. If I then, the Lord and the Teacher, washed your feet, you also ought to wash one another's feet" (vv. 13-14, NASB).

Since NT times it has been a matter of controversy whether Jesus meant that feet washing should be literally observed as a part of Christian worship. The postapostolic Church felt it was mandatory. Augustine (354-430) states that it was observed on Maundy Thursday. Bernard of Clairvaux (1091-1153) understood it to be a sacrament. Yet the Christian church generally did not accept it as a sacrament, even though it was practiced by certain segments and leaders in the church. Since the Protestant Reformation some Protestant groups have reinstated it. Among them are branches of the Mennonites, the Church of the Brethren, and the Brethren in Christ. Whether observed literally, liturgically, sacramentally, or figuratively, feet washing calls the Christian to a life and attitude of humility and service. Most Christians do not believe Jesus was intending, in the Upper Room, to establish a liturgical rite.

See HUMILITY, SERVICE, SACRAMENTS.

For Further Reading: *BBC,* 7:156; *WBC,* 4:436 ff.

NOBEL V. SACK

FELLOWSHIP. The concept of "fellowship" stems from a root idea of sharing or participating together in some common event or agreement. The secular Greek world used *koinōnia* both for friendship between man and man and in the sacred understanding of union with their gods. The OT uses the idea of the relationship of man to man, but never of man to God. Man always understands himself to be a servant and not a colleague of God. Even Abraham, the "Friend of God" (Jas. 2:23), and Moses, whom the Lord knew "face to face" (Deut. 34:10), were servants who were subordinate and obedient (Num. 12:7-8). While they enjoyed a kind of fellowship, it was not the fellowship of equals.

The NT uses the idea in similar patterns (e.g., Matt. 23:30; Acts 2:42). Jesus calls His disciples friends, subject to their obedience (John 15:14). Thus fellowship with Christ depends on the subordination of discipleship. While a degree of fellowship with one's fellows is possible even when moral likeness is lacking, the moral factor is all-important in the divine dimension. Sin destroys one's fellowship with God (Amos 3:3).

Nowhere is this moral demand more sharply drawn than in Paul's discussion of the Lord's Supper. Paul argues that participation and fellowship at the Lord's table excludes participation at the table of demons (1 Cor. 10:16-21). The sacred rite signifies the close inner union with Christ. In a similar manner Paul declares the impossibility of maintaining fellowship with Christ while entering into partnership *(metochē)* with unbelievers (2 Cor. 6:14-18; cf. Eph. 5:11).

Paul also frequently speaks of fellowship in suffering (e.g., Phil. 3:10), and fellowship in the glory of Christ (Rom. 8:17). In 1 Cor. 1:9 Paul speaks of the fellowship of the Son in designating the Body of Christ. Fellowship with Christ then marks the fellowship with other Christians in a special way.

John also declares that fellowship with God is morally conditioned (1 John 1:3-6), and that even the maintenance of fellowship with other Christians is dependent on walking in the light (v. 7). It is evident that fellowship finds its model and meaning in Christ and is dependent on a right relationship with Him.

The benediction of 2 Cor. 13:14 adds the significant concept of the fellowship with the Holy Spirit. It is through the Spirit that fellowship with the Father and the Son is possible. But it is also the "unity of the Spirit" which bonds Christians together in a fellowship that is holy, beautiful, and satisfying.

See KOINONIA, LOVE, AGAPĒ.

For Further Reading: Hauck, "Koinonia," Kittel.

MORRIS A. WEIGELT

FESTIVALS. See FEASTS.

FIDEISM. This term refers to that view in the field of religious epistemology which states that truth in religion rests on faith, not on reason or written propositions. Even though the term is new, the concept is not. All people in their processes of thinking, selecting data, and drawing conclusions are guided by a set or sets of presuppositions or assumptions. However, a fideist is one who places faith above reason, and in some cases this faith is contrary to reason. He places his faith in faith.

The emphasis on faith as the supreme anchor for religious truth is found in the writings of modern and contemporary religious philosophers such as Blaise Pascal (1623-62), Soren Kierkegaard (1813-55), and Karl Barth (1886-1968). Each felt it necessary to combat the rationalism in religious philosophy of their day. Pascal countered Cartesian philosophy; Kierkegaard, Hegelianism; and Barth, the optimistic liberal rationalism of the Jesus of History movement. Pascal and Kierkegaard both held that one does not know God through reason, but through the heart, by personal faith. Pascal summarized his position in his famous quotation, "The heart has its reasons which reason knows nothing of." For Kierkegaard, "reality is not found in the objective world of universal reason, but in the subjective realm of individual choice" (Geisler, *Christian Apologetics,* 50). Religious truth is personal and subjective, which involves the commitment of the whole person to Jesus Christ. For Barth God is the "wholly other" who reveals himself to man only through direct revelation. When one responds by faith to God's revelation of himself, and there is encounter and communion between God and man, God creates the conditions for it by His Holy Spirit.

Even though fideism provides important insights into the problem of religious knowledge, with its emphasis on the personal and subjective in religious experience, it has one basic weakness. It cannot, by its method, test the truth claims of its position. Faith in a religious system is not sufficient to test its truth claims. There must be some objective standard by which conflicting religious systems can be judged to be either true or false. Fideism has failed "to distinguish between the order of knowing and the order of being" (Geisler, 61). In concentrating on the subjective and the existential, and ignoring the need of the propositional, it has no foundation upon which to prove its system to be right. It then leaves the field of philosophy and becomes a study in psychology. The evangelical Christian, even though he emphasizes the experiential nature of the Christian faith, does not sacrifice the propositional. He believes the Bible to be the Word of God—a statement of faith—but opens the way for that position to be tested as to its truth claims.

See FAITH, TRUTH, PROPOSITIONAL THEOLOGY.

For Further Reading: Schaeffer, *Escape from Reason*, and *The God Who Is There*; DeWolf, *The Religious Revolt Against Reason*.

NOBEL V. SACK

FIDELITY. The Greek word *pistos* is translated "faithful" 52 times in the NT. Whereas its sister word, *pistis*, is generally translated "faith," it also frequently carries the meaning of faithfulness. Paul's heroic testimony, "I have kept the faith" (2 Tim. 4:7), could be interpreted to mean (1) the faith of God (doctrine); (2) faith in God (trust); or (3) faith with God (fidelity). The word is used with all three meanings; and all three could be equally applicable to Paul. Only once is *pistis* translated "fidelity" (Titus 2:10), though in many other cases such a translation would be apt.

If there is a difference between fidelity and integrity, it would be the accent of outwardness over against the accent of inwardness. Integrity is faithfulness within and to oneself. It is loyalty to one's own convictions, standards, and commitments. Fidelity is faithfulness to persons and causes. "It is required in stewards," writes Paul, "that a man be found faithful" (1 Cor. 4:2). There is in fidelity a stubborn adhesiveness, an enduring dependability, which makes it one of the most precious of virtues.

See INTEGRITY.

For Further Reading: Vine, *ED*, 2:71 ff.

RICHARD S. TAYLOR

FIG TREE. This tree was valued in Palestine both for fruit and shade, so that the expression "to sit under one's own fig tree" was proverbial for peace and security (1 Kings 4:25; Mic. 4:4). The destruction or barrenness of the fig tree indicated calamity (Hos. 2:12; Hab. 3:17). At three points in the Gospels the fig tree is used to illustrate specific truths.

Luke 13 tells the parable of the barren fig tree. This is usually interpreted as a warning to Israel. This view seems the more likely since the chapter closes with Jesus' lament over Jerusalem. The parable also applies to a fruitless life.

The cursing of the fig tree in Matthew 21 and Mark 11 has also been interpreted as an indictment of Israel. Since the miracle was apparently not done publicly, this seems doubtful. Jesus' only explanation of the event was to teach a lesson in faith.

The parable of the budding fig tree in the Olivet Discourse (Matthew 24 and parallel passages) makes a comparison between signs of approaching spring and signs of the coming of Christ. Some have thought the fig tree symbolizes the restoration of Israel, but Jesus' comparison is with "these things," which refers to certain events named in the preceding verses, and makes no mention of Israel.

See SIGN, PARABLES, FAITH.

For Further Reading: *BBC*, 6:536; Whedon, *Commentary on the New Testament*, 1:250, 2:135.

LESLIE D. WILCOX

FILIOQUE. See PROCESSION OF THE SPIRIT.

FILLED WITH THE SPIRIT. This expression must be considered and understood in the light of the context where it appears in Scripture. Therefore, definition is difficult; it does not always have the same meaning.

There are numerous examples of people being filled with the Spirit (used in place of "Ghost" in article). John the Baptist was filled from birth (Luke 1:15). We are informed that Elisabeth and Zacharias, John's parents, were filled with the Holy Spirit (vv. 41, 67). We note that Bezaleel, much earlier, was filled with the Spirit of God (Exod. 31:3; 35:31).

There are many references to people being filled with the Spirit in the Acts. These refer to the disciples (2:4), to Peter (4:8), to those engaged in prayer (v. 31), to Paul (9:17; 13:9), and to the disciples (v. 52).

There are also a number of other similar expressions used in connection with the Holy Spirit. A much-discussed one is "*baptized* with the Holy Spirit" (Acts 1:5; 11:16). The converts at Samaria "*received* the Holy Spirit" (8:17). At the house of Cornelius we note that "the Holy Spirit *fell* on all them which heard the word . . . [and that they had] *received* the Holy Spirit" (10:44-47). We read that at Ephesus "the Holy Spirit *came* on them" (19:6, emphases added).

The above expressions call for explanation. The terms "baptized [and] filled with the Spirit" may refer to the same event and have the same meaning. In Acts 1:5 and 2:4 this is the case. However, these two terms do not always have the same meaning. We read about fullnesses of the Holy Spirit prior to the Day of Pentecost, but these might not have been baptisms with the Holy Spirit as such, for He was not yet "given" (John 7:37-39).

Following the Holy Spirit's descent on the Day of Pentecost, there seem to have been subsequent infillings with the Holy Spirit upon the same people who had received the "filling" earlier in the Upper Room (Acts 4:8, 31). "However," as Delbert Rose says, "what occurred within Peter's heart in Acts 2:4 was not identical with what took place in Acts 4:8 and 31. In the Upper Room, Peter's heart was cleansed as well as his life empowered for service, whereas in Acts 4:8 and 31 a 'fresh influx of power' entered the already cleansed heart of the Apostle" (*WTJ*, 1974, 9).

See HOLY SPIRIT, BAPTISM WITH THE HOLY SPIRIT, ENTIRE SANCTIFICATION.

For Further Reading: Steele, *A Defense of Christian Perfection*, 108-11; Rose, *WTJ* (1974), 5-14; Mattke, *WTJ* (1970), 22-32; GMS, 494-97. O. D. LOVELL

FINAL PERSEVERANCE. See PERSEVERANCE.

FIRE. See EMBLEMS OF THE HOLY SPIRIT.

FIRST WORK OF GRACE. This is a term used only by those Christians who believe in a special second work of grace. This particularly includes the Wesleyan-holiness groups, who teach that entire sanctification is a second definite work of grace received sometime subsequent to the first work of grace. It also includes the Pentecostal groups, who believe that the baptism in the Holy Spirit is received subsequent to conversion—and who say that at that time the believer speaks in tongues. The Roman Catholics teach something very much like a second work of grace in their sacrament of Confirmation—in which a baptized believer "receives the Holy Spirit." They therefore imply a first work of grace received when one is baptized either as an infant or as a believer.

But the phrase "first work of grace" is most naturally used by the Wesleyan-holiness groups. To them it is another name for conversion. This first work consists of several experiences which happen at the same time, but that have about them a logical sequence.

1. First is *justification.* This is the action of God, as a judge, in absolving the repentant sinner from the guilt that has accrued to him, for his acts of sin (Rom. 5:1).

2. The second concomitant of the first work of grace is *regeneration.* This is the inward change from being spiritually dead to being made spiritually alive. It is also called the new birth, or being born again (John 3:5-8).

3. Something else which occurs at the time of the first work of grace is *initial sanctification*—although not everyone would distinguish this from regeneration. This is a cleansing from the inclination to acts of sin which has built up in us due to our sin acts. If there was not a cleansing from this propensity, from a depravity which we acquire due to our sin acts, we would not be able to live out the justified life once we are forgiven; we would likely go right back to the sins we had been committing. Scriptural support for this aspect of the first work of grace is in Paul's mention of the washing, or the cleansing, that accompanies our regeneration (1 Cor. 6:11; Titus 3:5; and Eph. 5:25-27 in a version other than the KJV).

4. *Reconciliation* also occurs at the time of this first work of grace. Once we are forgiven and regenerated, we are reconciled to God (2 Cor. 5:18). That the holy God becomes reconciled to us at this time is implied when the NT states that Christ's death propitiated, assuaged, or softened God's holy wrath (e.g., Rom. 3:23-26).

5. The last concomitant of the first work of grace is *adoption.* Logically (but not chronologically) following our forgiveness, regeneration, initial sanctification, and reconciliation, God adopts us into His family as His children (John 1:12; 1 John 3:1; Rom. 8:15-16).

See CONVERSION, JUSTIFICATION, REGENERATION.

For Further Reading: Grider, *Entire Sanctification;* Jessop, *Foundations of Doctrine;* Winchester and Price, *Crisis Experience in the Greek New Testament;* Purkiser, ed., *Exploring Our Christian Faith,* 287-304; *GMS,* 436-61. J. KENNETH GRIDER

FIRSTBORN. This refers to the first of human or animal offspring (Luke 2:7). The term acquired deeper connotations through the OT period until, in the NT, it came to be used almost exclusively of Jesus (except Heb. 11:28 = Exod. 12:12-30; and Heb. 12:23 [see below]) to describe: His precreation existence and role as the Image of God (Col. 1:15), and His resurrection as the beginning of a redeemed order of being conformed to that Image (Rom. 8:29; Col. 1:18; Rev. 1:5).

As a consequence of the Exodus, both human and animal firstborn were sanctified to the Lord (Num. 8:17, et al.). While the firstborn of animals were sacrificed, the firstborn of the Hebrews were replaced by the Levites (3:40-41; 8:14-19), who were sanctified to God as ministers to the priests instead of the firstborn. This may explain the puzzling use of "firstborn" in Heb. 12:23. Just as the Levites became the sanctified ministers of the Aaronic priest in place of the firstborn, so Christians now become sanctified (10:10) servants of Jesus, the Great High Priest (4:14, et al.) who has replaced the Aaronic priesthood (7:11).

Just as the Levites were sprinkled and washed, had atonement made for them by Aaron, and entered into the tent of meeting (Num. 8:7, 21-22), so Christians are sprinkled and washed, have been atoned for by Jesus, and enter the sanctuary (Heb. 10:19-22). Thus Heb. 12:23 may be portraying Christians as the new Levites (firstborn) under Jesus the Great High Priest.

The OT firstborn had special rights of inheritance (Deut. 21:15-17), blessing (Gen. 27:19-35), privilege (43:33), succession (2 Chron. 21:3), and line of family descent through them (many OT references). "Firstborn" came to represent an object of special favor, attention, and love (Zech. 12:10), and thus a term for God's special relationship with Israel (Exod. 4:22; Jer. 31:9) and the Davidic king (Ps. 89:27).

Rabbinic exegesis of that verse equated "firstborn" with the Messiah and may provide the context for NT application of the term to Jesus.

While the unique use of "firstborn" as a title of Jesus in Heb. 1:6 may derive from Jewish Messianic expectations, it must be seen in conjunction with verses 2-3 which set forth the deeper connotations of Jesus as firstborn found in the other NT passages.

Jesus is firstborn as the Image of God (Col. 1:15; Heb. 1:3), to which God purposed humanity to be conformed (Rom. 8:29). As the Image of God (the very essence of God's being) Jesus is firstborn of all creation in that the whole created order has its origin and existence in Him (Col. 1:15-17; Heb. 1:2-3). But Jesus is also firstborn of the New Creation in that He is firstborn from the dead (Col. 1:18; Rev. 1:5; [Rom. 8:29?]), the Source for the restoration of the image of God in fallen humanity (Rom. 8:29), through His atoning death (Col. 1:20; Heb. 1:3; Rev. 1:5) and regenerating resurrection. Thus Jesus as "firstborn" is the Origin (Col. 1:18) of the New Creation, the Head of the Church (ibid.), the Firstborn of many children (Rom. 8:29), and the Victor over the powers of the fallen order (Rev. 1:5; Heb. 1:3).

See CHRIST, ETERNALLY BEGOTTEN.

For Further Reading: Kooy, "First-born," *IDB*, 2:270-72; Milgrom, "First-born," *IDB*, supp., 337-38; Michaelis, "Prōtotokos," Kittel, 6:871-81; Bartels, "prōtotokos," *NIDNTT*, 1:667-69.

M. ROBERT MULHOLLAND, JR.

FLESH. This is the usual translation of the Greek *sarx*, found at least 150 times in the NT. Seven distinct usages have been identified by Lambert (*HDNT*, 3:411 ff). In general the term refers to the natural life of man in its earthly and therefore temporary context. That it does not necessarily imply sinfulness is shown by such passages as: "And the Word was made flesh, and dwelt among us" (John 1:14), and "[Jesus] was made of the seed of David according to the flesh" (Rom. 1:3).

Even Paul uses the term with considerable flexibility, as two examples are sufficient to illustrate: After testifying to being "crucified with Christ," he explains, "The life which I now live in the flesh I live by the faith of the Son of God" (Gal. 2:20). Here the term would almost be equivalent to *sōma*, "body," but with special emphasis on his present life on earth. Clearly the "crucified life" can be lived while yet in the flesh; and equally clearly, the selfish ego which is crucified is not to be confused with the earthly humanness of our nature.

A second example of Paul's usage is 2 Cor. 10:2-4. He rejects the insinuation of some in the Corinthian church that he walks "according to the flesh." Then he adds: "For though we walk in the flesh, we do not war after the flesh." He lives among them as a man, with all of a man's weaknesses and earthly limitations. It is not a sin so to live, nor is living "in the flesh" (in this sense) living in sin. Yet sin would soon enter if he attempted to fight a spiritual warfare with merely human or fleshly resources. Paul admits therefore to living (walking) "in" the flesh, but denies walking "according to the flesh." This is what people do who rely on "the arm of flesh" rather than on God, and who operate within a wordly-minded, humanistic frame.

Theological problems arise when Paul uses *sarx* to designate not just human nature in its earthiness but in its sinfulness—as man without grace. This is the usage in Romans 7—8 and Galatians 5. Whereas he pleased God even though "in the flesh" in Gal. 2:20 and 2 Cor. 10:2-4, now in Rom. 8:8 he says, "So then they that are in the flesh cannot please God." Obviously the term now means something different from what it meant in the other passages. It stands for the natural man in control—for self-centeredness and for sensual propensities. This "flesh" is antithetical to the "mind" in Rom. 7:25 and contrary to the Spirit (or "spirit") in Galatians 5. It is human nature under the dominion of the inherited sin principle.

Where it can be certain that Paul is thus using *sarx*, the translation "sinful nature" in NIV may be appropriate. But following this translation slavishly can lead to absurd results, as when NIV translates 1 Cor. 5:5, "Hand this man over to Satan, so that the sinful nature may be destroyed and his spirit saved on the day of the Lord." If by "sinful nature" is meant original sin or the carnal mind, then we are astounded at the prospect of Satan doing what some say the grace of God cannot do—destroy it. But if, as is Paul's obvious intention, the flesh to be destroyed is the bodily life, then to call this "sinful nature" is to betray an inexcusable theological bias, viz., that the body is sinful, and hence the only deliverance from sin is in death.

If we preserve biblical distinctions, we will say that flesh in one sense will characterize us until death, but that flesh in another sense may be crucified now—put to death. The first sense is that of our natural life on earth, both bodily and mental, with all the weaknesses and propensities incident to this contextual situation. The second sense is that of a psychic entity which is "enmity against God" (Rom. 8:7), and which tends to the "works of the flesh," but which "they that are Christ's have crucified" (Gal. 5:17-24).

See CARNAL MIND, CARNAL CHRISTIANS, CARNALITY AND HUMANITY, SIN, ORIGINAL SIN.

For Further Reading: *GMS,* 257, 287-89; *WMNT,* 129-47; *HDNT,* 411 ff. RICHARD S. TAYLOR

FLOOD, THE. This refers to the biblical account of the destruction of the ancient world due to the prevailing wickedness of the day. This event, recorded in Genesis 6—9, takes place at a critical juncture in human history, for after describing the state of continual evil in the heart of man, the Bible states that "the Lord was sorry that He had made man on the earth" (6:6, NASB). The Flood is important in the history of revelation because it indicates how God deals with the problem of human sin—bringing judgment upon unrepentant evildoers and providing divine deliverance for righteous Noah. Herein then are two important theological emphases to be noted.

First is the divine judgment for sin. The context of Genesis 6 graphically illustrates the moral condition of mankind which brought about the necessity of judgment. Elsewhere in Scripture reference is made to the time of Noah as symbolic of great wickedness and resulting judgment. In Isa. 54:9 God refers to the Babylonian captivity as being "like the days of Noah to Me" (NASB); and in the NT Jesus compares the moral climate of the time of His return to that of Noah's age (Matt. 24:37-39; Luke 17:26-27).

The second important theological emphasis in the story of the Flood is the gracious deliverance provided by God for righteous Noah. Amid the moral decadence of his day Noah is "a righteous man, blameless in his time; Noah walked with God" (Gen. 6:9, NASB). God's justness and mercy are manifested in that He gives clear direction to insure the deliverance of Noah and his family.

In connection with Noah there is the occurrence of two important words for the first time in Scripture: (1) "Grace" or "favor" in Gen. 6:8, "But Noah found favor in the eyes of the Lord" (NASB); (2) "covenant" in verse 18, "But I will establish My covenant with you" (NASB). Both of these terms, so characteristic of biblical redemption, are initially expressed in the deliverance of Noah.

See NEW COVENANT, JUDGE (JUDGMENT), CATASTROPHISM, SIN.

For Further Reading: Richardson, ed., *A Theological Word Book of the Bible,* 159; von Rad, *Old Testament Theology,* 1:154-57. ALVIN S. LAWHEAD

FOOL, FOOLISHNESS, FOLLY. These terms denote unwise conduct, careless judgment, witlessness, not necessarily implying lack of intellect. "A fool is not one who is deficient in the power of logical thought, but one who lacks the natural discernment and tact required for success in life" (*HDB,* 43). A man may be a fool who is careless, thoughtless, or just indifferent, but he may also be so because he ignores God and scoffs at religion and the instruction of others. It can imply a practical atheism as in Ps. 14:1 and 53:1.

In the KJV one or the other of these words occurs some 60 times, almost all in the OT and two-thirds of these in the Wisdom Literature. The Hebrew word *kesil* is most commonly used (particularly in Proverbs) and refers to one lacking in judgment, a stupid person (e.g., Prov. 10:1, 18, 23; 13:19) but the stronger word *holelot,* found more often in Ecclesiastes, is translated "madness" (e.g., 1:17; 2:12; 7:25; 9:3; 10:13). The ethical implications are included in the word *nebal* or *nebalah* meaning "contemptible" or "shamelessly immoral," as in Gen. 34:7; Deut. 32:21; 2 Sam. 3:33; Job 2:10; Isa. 32:5-6.

The common root word used in the NT for fool or foolishness is *mōros.* Although it implies a moral content, it more generally means merely thoughtless or imprudent behavior such as that of the man who built his house on the sand (Matt. 7:26), the foolish virgins (25:2), etc. It is considered by some to be a transliteration of the Hebrew *moreh,* which is broad in meaning and at worst describes a perverse person or a rebel (Num. 20:10). The word *aphrōn* (commonly used for "fool" in LXX) has the moral overtones of impiety and unbelief, but the folly is of the heart, not the result of mental weakness.

See SIN, ATHEISM, WISDOM, ACCOUNTABILITY, VALUES.

For Further Reading: *HDCG,* 1:604-5; *HDB,* 2:43-44; *ZPEB,* 2:581. J. FRED PARKER

FOOT WASHING. See FEET WASHING.

FOREKNOWLEDGE. Foreknowledge has as its frame of reference God's omniscience. It is the precipitate awareness of an all-knowing Mind. God knows because He is everywhere, but He does not act necessarily because He knows, else we face sheer determinism and its end, natural mechanism. Knowledge may activate, but not because of the necessity of its nature. The knower may act, that is freedom; that the knower must act countermands freedom for purposeless fixation. God is both omniscient and free. "Foreknowledge is one aspect of omniscience; it is implied in God's warnings, promises and predictions. . . . God's foreknowledge involves His elective grace, but this does not preclude human will" (Vine, *ED,* 2:189).

Foreknowledge and predestination are not synonymous terms; knowledge, "fore" or otherwise, does not require a willed act to be, but predestination cannot obtain apart from an act of will. Since, according to the Arminian interpretation of Scripture, predestination is based on foreknowledge, the two terms obviously relate; yet they are discrete. The temporal forms of past, present, and future in respect to foreknowledge are not essential modes of reality or aspects of omniscience, but they are conveniences for rational human thought. "God cannot be grasped in the categories which we use in our knowledge of secular realities," says Thielicke (*The Evangelical Faith,* 366).

How God knows antecedently cannot be gauged by human comprehension; God is not a big man, nor in fact is He a big God, either: He is God! That God knows the past and present fully is a judgment at least tolerated by most theists; His knowledge of the future, however, is questioned by many. Yet a God thus limited is something less than God, prompting the complaint, "Your god is too small."

Foreknowledge refers to God's antecedent knowledge of persons, how they respond to His provision for salvation. He predestines those whom He foreknows "to be conformed to the image of His Son" (*Elect in the Son,* 206).

The strongest evidence for and demonstration of God's foreknowledge is fulfilled prophecy. To be able to predict events not possibly within the range of human foresight is explainable only on the ground of a divine knowing incomprehensible to man.

The most difficult theological problem in the doctrine of foreknowledge is in knowing how to relate God's foreknowledge to contingency.

See ATTRIBUTES (DIVINE), CONTINGENT, PROPHET (PROPHECY), DETERMINISM, PREDESTINATION, ELECT (ELECTION).

For Further Reading: *GMS,* 152, 424-38; Shank, *Elect in the Son;* Dayton, "A Wesleyan Note on Election," *Perspectives on Evangelical Theology,* 95-104; Wiley, *CT,* 1:356-61. MEL-THOMAS ROTHWELL

FOREORDINATION. See PREDESTINATION.

FORERUNNER. The OT proposes in various places the notion of the one who is to prepare the way of the Messiah (Isa. 40:3-11; Mal. 3:1). In at least one context, this forerunner is specifically viewed as Elijah (Mal. 4:5-6). In the Gospels, this role is attributed to John the Baptist, principally by Jesus (Matt. 11:10 and Luke 7:27; cf. Matt. 17:10-13 and Mark 9:11-13; 1:2-8; Luke 1:17). John himself denies any claim to the Elijah title but does accept the role of the forerunner (John 1:19-23). Some of the contemporaries of Jesus attempted to attribute the Elijah title to Him (Mark 6:15 and Luke 9:8; cf. Matt. 16:14; Mark 8:28; Luke 9:19). The literal term "forerunner" is applied to Jesus in only one place (Heb. 6:20), where it pictures Him as the One who has preceded us into the very presence of God in heaven.

See JOHN THE BAPTIST, ELIJAH.

For Further Reading: Ladd, *A Theology of the New Testament,* 34-44; Robinson, *Twelve New Testament Studies,* 28-52. HAL A. CAUTHRON

FORGIVENESS. In their awesome picture of the holiness of God set over against the sinfulness of His fallen human creatures, the Hebrew and Christian Scriptures steadfastly refuse to make God the author of evil. He is the Creator only of what is good, including the freedom of human beings to choose holiness (out of thankfulness for His divine goodness) or, alternatively, to choose sin and death.

Amidst this somber setting springs up, in biblical testimony, the fountain of God's forgiveness. It began at Eden, in the Father's confrontation with the willful determination of our first parents to know both good and evil. Amidst the curses pronounced in that moment shined a promise: The Seed of the woman would bruise the serpent's head. Thereafter, God's mercy offered forgiveness to sinful Noah, frightened

Abraham, thieving Jacob, Joseph's spiteful brothers, and to Moses, adopted son of Pharaoh and the first Jewish terrorist. Little wonder that when Moses found the children of Israel making a golden calf to worship while he was receiving the covenant of law at Sinai, he understood at once that a direct appeal to Yahweh, to "forgive their sin," and if not, to blot him out of the book of life, would be successful (Exod. 32:32).

The vision Moses had of a forgiving God has been central in Hebrew and Christian faith ever since. Yahweh himself confirmed it. He passed before Moses, whom He had hidden in the cleft of the rock, proclaiming, "The Lord, the Lord God, merciful and gracious, longsuffering, and abundant in goodness and truth, keeping mercy for thousands, forgiving iniquity and transgression and sin," even though He visited "the iniquity of the fathers upon the children, and upon the children's children, unto the third and to the fourth generation" (Exod. 34:6-7).

Always thereafter, when Jews came face-to-face with God, whether in their ancient feasts, in their sacrifices at the Temple in Jerusalem, or in the meetings of their congregations in the lands of their exile, the confession of their sins and the assurance of God's readiness to forgive them was central in their worship. "Their heart was not right with him," they sang in the psalm we call the 78th; "but he, being full of compassion, forgave their iniquity" (vv. 37, 38). In another they asked the question, "If thou, Lord, shouldest mark iniquities, O Lord, who shall stand?" And they answered it with a testimony straight out of Moses: "But there is forgiveness with thee, that thou mayest be feared" (130:3-4). The young Daniel, in exile, grasped by the spirit of prophecy, put it simply: "To the Lord our God belong mercies and forgivenesses, though we have rebelled against him" (Dan. 9:9).

What made Jesus of Nazareth recognizable to faithful Jews as the promised Messiah was His consummate embodiment of this image of a forgiving Yahweh. "Behold the Lamb of God," John the Baptist cried the day after Jesus' baptism, "which taketh away the sin of the world" (John 1:29). When at the Last Supper Jesus passed the cup, saying, "This is my blood of the new [covenant], which is shed for many for the remission [that is, the taking away] of sins" (Matt. 26:28); when He prayed at the Cross, "Father, forgive them; for they know not what they do" (Luke 23:34); and when He opened the understanding of His disciples to what was "written in the law of Moses, and in the prophets, and in the psalms," concerning Him, namely, "that repentance and remission of sins should be preached in his name among all nations" (24:44-47), first-century Jews recognized Him, as we do, to be the godlike Christ. The love incarnate in Him was meant also to remind both Jews and Gentiles that Yahweh was a Christlike God.

Totally absent in every case of divine forgiveness recorded in Hebrew and Christian Scriptures is the custom, nearly universal in other world religions, of bargaining for divine favor. Making a deal, setting a price on reconciliation between man and God, has no place in biblical faith. God himself provided the basis of forgiveness in the vicarious death of His Son. Although keeping covenant with God or renewing broken covenants brought economic and psychic advantages, the preoccupation of Hebrew priests and prophets was with the moral and ethical relationship of the people with the One who had called them to righteousness. In the face of their manifold sins, the only hope for reconciliation the patriarchs ever saw, from Abel to Abraham, rested on divine goodness, God's grace.

The biblical picture, therefore, is first of a God who makes and keeps His promises to be *faithful,* even when those in covenant with Him have broken theirs. Though He stands in judgment of all sin, His love is longsuffering and kind. Hosea declared this in his beautiful image of God the Father, remembering in His wrath that he had taught faithless Ephraim his first steps and held him as a babe against His cheek. Out of that faithfulness, Hosea, Jeremiah, Isaiah, and Ezekiel saw, God was forging a new covenant of forgiveness, in which His law would be written in our hearts and we would be able to keep His statutes.

From goodness and grace comes also, in biblical faith, a second characteristic of divine forgiveness, *power.* Very early in Jesus' ministry, the Gospel of Mark tells us, four people carried a man ill of the palsy into the presence of the Lord and heard the Master say, "Son, thy sins be forgiven thee." When some of those present questioned this as near blasphemy, Jesus told the sick man to take up his bed and walk, which he promptly did. The Lord then explained that He wanted His hearers to "know that the Son of man hath power on earth to forgive sins" (Mark 2:3-10). Both the words and the event point to the root meaning of the word "forgive": "to take away." That meaning survives in medical as well as theological usage in the connotation of the English word "remission." Jesus sent His followers to proclaim good news: that the divine forgiveness, executed in the life-giving power and presence of the Holy Spirit, constituted in fact deliverance—freedom from both the psychic burden of guilt and the moral burden of bondage to the habits of evil that imprison and corrupt human life.

John and Charles Wesley and the young George Whitefield were precisely correct in their understanding of Scripture on this point: The grace which by faith brought justification, that is, forgiveness, brought in that same moment a rich measure of sanctification, breaking the power as well as cleansing away the guilt of sin. Here lies the biblical basis of the theology of liberation. Jesus himself had announced to the synagogue at Nazareth that the Spirit of the Lord was upon Him, to preach release to the captives, and to proclaim the year of jubilee (Luke 4:18).

Little wonder that Peter should have declared to the multitude at Pentecost the good news that they could every one "repent, and be baptized . . . in the name of Jesus Christ for the remission of sins" and "receive the gift of the Holy [Spirit]" (Acts 2:38), or that the apostle Paul should have written to the Ephesians of the abounding riches of the grace that comes through faith in Christ, and the "exceeding greatness of his power to usward who believe" (1:19). They had received the forgiveness of their sins and become "his workmanship, created in Christ Jesus unto good works" (2:10).

At no point in either Old or New Testament teaching, however, is the promise of forgiveness offered apart from the recognition by both the divine and human partners in the covenant of grace of the "exceeding sinfulness" of our sin. The modern impulse, recently reinforced by counseling psychology, to shun the awakening of feelings of guilt, has no standing in biblical religion. There, publicans who beat their breasts go down to their houses justified. Godly sorrow becomes a healing gift of grace. And if the seekers are reticent to confess the evil, the word of the Lord, speaking through priests and prophets, apostles and pastors, prods them on. The bleak judgments of the prophet Hosea that "there is no truth, nor mercy, nor knowledge of God in the land" (4:1) lie back of the Father's plaintive cry in 11:8: "How shall I give thee up, Ephraim? how shall I deliver thee, Israel?"

Here lies the difference between modern sentimentality and biblical mercy. The former, masquerading as forgiveness, passes off deep wrongs as matters of no consequence. "Oh, forget it," we say jauntily, "it was nothing." Biblical forgiveness in fact is demeaned by such denials of the consequences of our rebellion against God or violations of the principle of ethical love in our relations with one another. Christians can afford to face guilt directly, and they encourage others to do so, in the confidence that the healing forgiveness of the eternal God, attested at Calvary, offers a judgment that is "true and righteous [right making] altogether" (Ps. 19:9). "Godly sorrow" (2 Cor. 7:10), which the NT defines as the basis of true repentance, flows from that recognition of both the depth of our guilt and the power of saving grace.

All this points up one further characteristic of the Christian doctrine of forgiveness, namely, that it takes place amidst the making of a covenant of mutual commitment between God and His children. The story of Zaccheus in the Gospel of Luke illustrates the point clearly. A tax collector whose obvious success made other Jews despise him, Zaccheus sought to see Jesus and welcomed Him as a guest. Then, inspired by Christ's acceptance, he gave half his goods to the poor and pledged to restore fourfold all the taxes he had wrongly collected. Jesus responded, "This day is salvation come to this house . . . For the Son of man is come to seek and to save that which was lost" (Luke 19:9-10).

The doctrine of God's gracious forgiveness, like all the other doctrines of grace, is grounded not only in the divine initiative, but in God's expectation of our active and persisting response to His love.

See JUSTIFICATION, MERCY, ATONEMENT, REPENTANCE, CONFESSION OF SINS, RESTITUTION.

For Further Reading: *GMS,* 380-405, 441-43, 454-57.

TIMOTHY L. SMITH

FORM CRITICISM. Form criticism (Ger. *Formgeschichte,* form history) is concerned with the history of the oral tradition behind the documents of the Bible. It arose in part as a corrective to source criticism, which is limited to the study of the written text. The study of the background of the biblical material is not new, but it was introduced as a recognized discipline at the close of the last century by the German scholar Herman Gunkel in his work on Genesis and Psalms. It was made popular in NT studies a quarter of a century later by Martin Dibelius. Its most influential advocate has been Rudolf Bultmann, who has worked in this area chiefly with the Gospels.

The forms of oral tradition are found within the written Gospels and may be classified as stories about Jesus, sayings of Jesus, parables, and miracle stories. Bultmann claims that these arose in the contexts of Jewish apocalypticism and Hellenistic Gnosticism, both of which employed the unscientific concepts of a three-storied universe

—heaven, earth, and hell—and the ability of celestial spirits to associate with humans. The Gospel writers were editors more than historians and therefore unreliable in terms of the original forms of the material. What they set down represents the life setting of the Church rather than that of Jesus and the disciples. This is supported by the "alterations" made to Mark's Gospel by Matthew and Luke.

There are several serious criticisms of this method. First, it minimizes the value of any eyewitness accounts by those who followed Christ. It also ignores the uniqueness of Christ and His claim to be the Savior of the world. It also disregards the special character of the NT Church. The claim of both Jesus and the Gospel writers that the Holy Spirit was their great moving Force is denied as unhistorical, which means that it cannot be proven scientifically. The Virgin Birth and the Resurrection are also said to be unhistorical. As a consequence it is impossible to write an accurate life of Christ.

Form criticism has had value in opening up some doors into the 20 or 30 years between the death of Christ and the writing of the first Gospel. But it has been too ambitious, judging historical data by modern standards of philosophy to the point of cancelling its value. This is professedly done in the interest of discovering the unadulterated *kerygma* or message. Actually, the attempt to modernize the gospel message has been a liability. There is peril in trying to modernize Jesus, even though our aim may be to make Him meaningful to the present age. Not the discipline per se but the excesses of its philosophical presuppositions and professed expertise should be labeled objectionable.

See EXEGESIS, INSPIRATION OF THE BIBLE, BIBLICAL INERRANCY, BIBLICAL REALISM, CRITICISM (OT, NT), HISTORICAL JESUS (THE).

For Further Reading: Guthrie, *New Testament Introduction,* "Gospels and Acts"; Bultmann and Knudsin, *Form Criticism;* Martin, *New Testament Foundations,* vol. 1; Ladd, *The New Testament and Criticism;* Anderson, *Jesus and Christian Origins.* HARVEY J. S. BLANEY

FORMALISM. In music and art, formalism is the preeminence of formal rules regulating form and style over content, especially over novelty. In ethics, formalism is the belief that conduct should be determined by formal principles (e.g., Kant's "categorical imperative") rather than by considerations of utility, pleasure, or consequence. In religion, formalism is an excessive emphasis on liturgy, which is permitted to become performance without feeling or moral validity. It thus tends to become form without life, outward appearance devoid of inward substance.

Formalism in *creed* is barren orthodoxy. The "pattern of sound teaching" is preserved without faith and love (2 Tim. 1:13, NIV). Truth is proclaimed from the lips, but not believed in the heart or practiced in the life (Isa. 29:13; Jas. 2:18-19).

Formalism in *worship* is empty ritual. Ceremony is valued for itself and divorced from the reality it symbolizes. Sacrament is viewed as magic. A "form of godliness" is displayed, but its power is denied (2 Tim. 3:5).

Formalism becomes *hypocrisy,* the substitution of appearance for reality, and a cloak for sin. Against this evil the prophets thundered (Isa. 1:10-20; Jer. 6:19-21; Amos 5:18-27), as did our Lord (Matt. 15:1-14; 23:13-28).

Formalism, as hypocrisy, becomes defensive and justifies the persecution of those who oppose and denounce it (Matt. 23:29-35; John 16:1-3). This has been the consistent history of Christendom. The greatest hindrance to the gospel is often not a blatant atheism but an apostate theism.

Formalism is a constant temptation. Churches may have "a reputation of being alive" while they are actually dead. The only remedy is to awaken and repent (Rev. 3:1-3, NIV).

See ETHICS, VALUES, AESTHETICS, WORSHIP.

For Further Reading: Scott, *The Relevance of the Prophets,* 180-203; Earle, "Matthew," *WBC.*

W. E. MCCUMBER

FORNICATION. In the Scripture, "fornication" describes three levels of sexual activity between persons of the opposite sex. It is used to denote sexual relationships between unmarried persons of the opposite sex in its narrowest and most general usage (1 Cor. 6:9). In a broader sense, it relates to cohabitation of a person of either sex with a married person of the opposite sex (Matt. 5:32). It thus becomes equivalent to adultery. In its broadest usage, "fornication" may refer to immoral conduct in general (1 Cor. 5:1).

In a spiritual sense, "fornication" is used to describe unfaithfulness in one's relationship to God. The OT refers to Israel as the beloved of God; espoused to Him; married to Him. The unfaithful spiritual wife is in danger of being cast out just as the unfaithful marriage partner could, justifiably, be divorced. (See Hosea for an amplification of this position.)

The use of "fornication" to describe a spiritual relationship marked by unfaithfulness is appropriate because of the tendency, or penchant, on the part of the Hebrew people to adopt heathen idol worship and customs which were, frequently, fertility cults involving sexual promiscuity as a part of worship.

The NT supports the OT in its claim for moral purity before marriage as well as under the marriage contract. The spiritual relationship to Christ is described as a marriage between Christ and His Church (Eph. 5:25-27). This relationship demands fidelity to Him as an essential part of the faith covenant.

Modern-day humanism, with its emphasis upon freedom in all areas of life, is promoting the view that sexual intercourse prior to marriage is not only permissible but desirable. Consequently, the stigma of shame and sin is being removed from all such activity. However, the position of Scripture cannot be ignored. As in all areas of life, no one can sin without opening himself to the consequences of that sin.

See ADULTERY, PURITY AND MATURITY, INTEGRITY, IDOL (IDOLATRY), WORLD (WORLDLINESS), MARRIAGE.

For Further Reading: *ERE.* LEROY E. LINDSEY

FOUNDATION. "Foundation," the base or that part of an object on which other parts rest for support, is in the English OT frequently translated from some form of the Hebrew *yasad.* In the NT two Greek terms are so translated: *katabolē* and *themelios.*

Foundation is used with reference to buildings such as a house (Job 4:19) or the Temple (1 Kings 5:17). *Themelios* is used in describing the foundations of God's eternal city (Heb. 11:10; Rev. 21:14).

The term is also used to indicate the beginning of something: the founding of Egypt (Exod. 9:18), the founding of the earth (Job 38:4). On numerous occasions in the NT *katabolē* is used with reference to the beginning of the earth (Eph. 1:4).

The apostle Paul used *themelios* in significant figures of speech. In Rom. 15:20 he expresses his purpose not to build on someone else's foundation. In 1 Cor. 3:10 he speaks of the results of his work as a foundation upon which others may build. Verses 11 and 12 of the same passage says that Christ Jesus is the Foundation upon which all gospel workers must build. Eph. 2:20 indicates that the Word of God as declared by the apostles and prophets is the Foundation for faith. Paul also declares that by living worthily, believers lay up treasure as a foundation for everlasting life (1 Tim. 6:18-19). He assures believers that they can depend upon the foundational fact that they are known of God (2 Tim. 2:19). The writer of Hebrews, using the same term, refers to repentance as the foundation of Christian experience (Heb. 6:1).

Besides referring to such biblical concepts, theologians use some form of "foundation" in various other ways. For example, they speak of foundational facts, studies, beliefs, and scriptures when speaking of those essential to understanding, explaining, and accepting Christianity.

See FUNDAMENTALISM, TRUTH, SUBSTANCE (SUBSTANTIVE).

For Further Reading: Richardson, ed., *A Theological Word Book of the Bible,* 204; *Baker's DT,* 229.

ARMOR D. PEISKER

FREE AGENCY. See FREEDOM.

FREE GIFT. The term has its origin in Rom. 5:15-18 where it appears five times (RSV). It is one of the NT terms for salvation which comes through Christ's atonement. "The free gift . . . brings justification" (v. 16, RSV).

No man merits this salvation. It is of grace, a gift from God. This "grace is the spontaneous, unmerited manifestation of divine love upon which rests the redemption of the sinner" (*Encyclopedia of Religious Knowledge,* 5:41). "God was in Christ, reconciling the world unto himself" (2 Cor. 5:19). Arminian-Wesleyan theology yields no ground in asserting the initiative and sovereignty of God in man's redemption. Salvation is God's gift of grace, freely offered to all. "One man's act of righteousness leads to acquittal and life for all men" (Rom. 5:18, RSV).

But the Bible teaches that redemption comes only to those who accept God's terms of faith and repentance. "Believe on the Lord Jesus Christ, and thou shalt be saved" (Acts 16:31). "Repent ye therefore, and be converted, that your sins may be blotted out" (3:19). Our Lord himself teaches, "The kingdom of God is at hand: repent ye, and believe the gospel" (Mark 1:15). To those who think there is some other way to God's grace of salvation, Jesus declares, "Except ye repent, ye shall all likewise perish" (Luke 13:3, 5).

Repentance for sin and faith for salvation are thus required of men, but they are not the works of man apart from the enabling grace of God. The Bible affirms, "Every good gift and every perfect gift is from above, and cometh down from the Father" (Jas. 1:17). Wesley writes: "All our works, thou, O God, hast wrought in us." And again, "Were they ever so many, or holy, they are not [our] own, but God's" (*Works,* 5:7).

The biblical view of God's free gift to responsible men is accurately described by Paul: *"By grace* are ye saved *through faith;* and that not of yourselves: it is the gift of God: not of works, lest any man should boast" (Eph. 2:8-9).

See SALVATION, FREEDOM, SYNERGISM.

For Further Reading: Schaff-Herzog, *Encyclopedia of Religious Knowledge,* 5:41-42; Wesley, *Works,* 5:7-16; 7:373-86; Wiley, *CT,* 2:352-57. A. F. HARPER

FREE WILL. See FREEDOM.

FREEDOM. The extremely broad concept signified in Scripture by the essentially synonymous English terms "freedom" and "liberty" comprehends numerous Hebrew and Greek words and their cognates, deriving from various spheres of life and conveying many nuances including liberation, emancipation, release, frankness, leisure, right, remission, redemption, forgiveness, deliverance, etc. (The basic terms are Heb. *deror* and Gr. *eleutheria.*) Never far in the background of discussions of freedom in the biblical world was the ever-present antithesis, the socio-politico-economic institution of slavery. The related verb (Gr. *eleutheroō*) means "to set free" (not to be free) and involves negatively: release from bonds, subjection, determinism, or involuntary servitude; and positively: independence of choice or action. Scripture employs freedom in its ordinary secular usages as well as in an extended theological metaphor for salvation.

In Israel as throughout the ancient Near East, liberation was conceived as a change of masters. In the crucial Exodus event, Israel was freed from Egyptian bondage under the harsh taskmaster Pharaoh by the benevolent initiative of Yahweh, to whom it was subsequently bound in covenant as "a people for his own possession" (Deut. 7:6, RSV; cf. Exod. 20:2). Reminded of his solidarity with the slave (Deut. 15:12-18), the free Israelite was instructed to extend equal rights to his slaves (5:14-15; cf. Job 31:13-15), to sympathize with the runaway slave rather than his master (Deut. 23:15-16), and generally to view all lack of liberty as something provisional (cf. Leviticus 25, especially v. 10: "Proclaim liberty throughout the land," RSV). The glad tidings of the Servant of Yahweh proclaimed liberty to the captives (Isa. 61:1 ff; cf. Luke 4:16-21).

Greek and Roman views of freedom have profoundly influenced Western civilization. Whereas the Hebrews considered freedom as a gift of God, the Greeks regarded every man as free by nature. Freedom included the possibility of the citizen's participation in politics (free speech) and the opportunity to live as he wished. Slavery of any kind was considered debasing and contemptible. Later philosophers internalized and individualized the Greek nation to identify freedom as self-sufficiency and ascetic withdrawal from the world that came increasingly to be perceived as oppressive and imprisoning. The Romans understood freedom as civic rights under law and therefore renounced the irresponsible individualism as libertinism and anarchism.

The NT is aware of the secular origins of the contrast between slave and free. All such social, economic, political, and racial distinctions are implicitly repudiated by the principle of coequal unity in Christ (Gal. 3:28; Col. 3:11; Philem. 15-20). Early Christians followed Jesus in rejecting the zealot path of political revolution, violence, and force to achieve worldly freedom (1 Cor. 7:21-23; Rom. 13:1-7; 1 Pet. 2:13-25) and yet made the Church the realm and advocate of freedom in the world. Christian freedom, salvation in Christ, may be experienced in an unchanged world.

Uniformly God, Father, Son, or Spirit, is the Author of Christian freedom (John 8:32, 36; Rom. 6:18, 22; 8:15, 21; 2 Cor. 3:17-18; Jas. 1:25; 2:12), achieved through the free self-sacrifice of Christ (Gal. 3:13-14; 4:28-31; Rom. 4:24-26; 8:1-4, 14, 21; cf. Phil. 2:5-11; 2 Cor. 8:9; Rom. 15:7-13). The entire B.C. world is regarded as basically unfree (cf. Gal. 3:23—4:11; Rom. 3:9; 5:12-21; 6:20; 8:1-8). God alone is absolutely free, but His is not an arbitrary sovereignty exercised without respect to human choice (Romans 9—11 is an extended argument in defense of divine freedom in the face of its apparent denial in the unbelief of Israel, an argument which takes human freedom for granted [cf. Rom. 8:5-8; Eph. 2:1-10]). Human freedom of choice, although limited, is yet real. Biblical imperatives presuppose that man is in some measure free to choose between real moral alternatives and consequently responsible for his conduct and accountable to God. (The substance of Rom. 1:18—3:20 is that all men are *responsible* sinners.)

Paul presents the most coherent interpretation of Christian freedom. Outside the sphere of Christ's rule all men are under the *dominion of sin* (Romans 6, especially vv. 17-18, 22; 8:2; cf. John 8:34-36); *law,* i.e., legalism (Rom. 7:1-6, 25; Gal. 3:23; 4:4-5; 5:2-6; Col. 2:20-23); *Satan* and the cosmic powers of this world (Gal. 4:3, 8-9; Eph. 1:15-23; 6:10-17; Col. 1:15-20; 2:18, 20; cf. John 15:19; 17:14-18; 1 John 5:4); *death* (Rom. 5:17, 21; 6:20-23; 7:5; 1 Cor. 15:56; cf. Heb. 2:15); *base passions* (Rom. 13:11-14; 16:18; Phil. 3:18-19; Titus 3:3); and/or in the grip of some other form of slavery. Freedom from these powers liberates the Christian from the inevitability of their compulsion and claim.

But Christian freedom is primarily freedom from the compulsive power of sin (John 8:34; Rom. 6:5-23), man's obsessive illusion that he can secure life and freedom by his own power. "That which the Greeks regarded as the highest form of freedom . . . becomes in the NT the source of man's most abject bondage" (R. Tvente, "slave," *NIDNTT,* 3:597). Real freedom opens the possibility of a new kind of slavery after the pattern of the Liberator (cf. Matt. 20:26-28; John 13:12-17; Phil. 2:5-16; Rom. 6:22; 15:1-3), a service to the Lord (Rom. 12:11; 14:18; Col. 3:24) and one another (Gal. 5:13; 1 Cor. 9:19; 2 Cor. 4:5; Phil. 2:22) in the bond of peace and love (Eph. 4:3; Col. 3:14).

Christian freedom is a process arising from radical changes in value structure and behavior patterns (Gal. 5:1, 13, 19-23; 2 Cor. 5:14-21) which transforms the whole person (Romans 5—8; 12:1-2; 2 Cor. 3:17-18) and inspires hope (Rom. 8:18-30; the Greek *parrhēsia* in the various NT contexts may be translated as either "freedom" or "hope"). It begins in baptism (Rom. 6:3-11; Gal. 3:27-28; Col. 2:11-15), which establishes the believer in the community of the free, the Body of Christ (Gal. 4:21-31; Rom. 8:21; Eph. 1:15-22; Col. 1:13-23). But it is not guaranteed by formal membership in the church, for although it is a gift of grace, it must be voluntarily preserved (Gal. 4:9, 21; 5:1, 13; Eph. 6:10-17). Freedom may be forfeited as easily in license as in legalism (1 Cor. 6:12-20; 9:1, 12, 15, 19; 10:23—11:1; Gal. 5:1-26; Col. 2:16-23). The Christian's theoretical freedom is voluntarily restricted in practice by expediency and the desire to edify (cf. 1 Cor. 4:14—11:1; especially 6:12; 9:1, 12, 15, 19-23; 10:23-24; Rom. 14:1—15:13).

Genuine human freedom has been effectively denied by a number of ideologies, both ancient and modern, e.g., astrological fatalism of the Hellenistic age, hyper-Calvinistic double predestination, modern behavioristic determinism. In every expression, whether the determining force be called Nature or God, it has borne the fruit of moral irresponsibility and license, the same abuses as unrestrained freedom. In contrast stands the paradox of Christian freedom, well described by Luther: "A Christian is a perfectly free lord of all, subject to none. A Christian is a perfectly dutiful servant of all, subject to all."

See LICENSE, BONDAGE, PREDESTINATION, FATALISM, DETERMINISM, FREEDOM OF SPEECH, CONTINGENT.

For Further Reading: Betz, *Paul's Concept of Freedom;* Blunck, "Freedom," *NIDNTT,* 1:715-21; MacGregor, "Freedom and Necessity," *He Who Lets Us Be,* 111-28; Mundle, Schneider, and Brown, "Redemption, Loose, Ransom, Deliverance, Release, Salvation, Savior," *NIDNTT,* 3:177-223; *GMS,* 116-19, 265; Wiley, *CT,* 1:239; 2:130-31, 134, 356; 3:74-75.

GEORGE LYONS

FREEDOM OF SPEECH. Freedom of speech is a particularly modern concept usually regarded as the bequest of the Enlightenment. Its roots are much older, surely fixed in the convictions of the prophets and apostles that they were called to freely speak God's Word. It was developed in the Christian humanism of Erasmus and his contemporaries, and in the forerunners of the Reformation like Wyclif, Tyndale, and Huss. Their quest for freedom of expression was contrary to the interests of a totalitarian church. Subsequently, Luther stressed the concept of private judgment, emphasizing the responsibility of every individual before God. While free speech was not explicit in this concept, it was a natural and logical consequence of the doctrine. The logic was developed by men like Castellio, who led the way toward religious toleration.

Vital support for free expression was given by Jeremy Taylor's *Liberty of Prophesying.* The Enlightenment of the 17th and 18th centuries gave impetus to free speech by appealing to the doctrine of natural right. William Blackstone, John Locke, and Richard Price espoused this position and the great leader of Methodism, Wesley, declared his fervent commitment to civil and religious liberties rooted in natural right. Nevertheless, freedom of expression had not arrived even in relatively liberal England. A common distinction was made between right to personal, private belief and the right to freely express that faith. The latter was denied. In America the Bill of Rights asserted freedom of speech as an irrevocable benefit. Freedom of speech may be seen as the enduring contribution of religious men in search of an unconstrained witness to their faith.

Any commentary on freedom of speech must address the issue of the lawless and socially irresponsible expression of any freedom. No person has the freedom to cry "Fire!" in a crowded theater if there is no fire. Freedom of speech requires responsibility and the appropriate time and place for sharing one's opinions. Yet, neither president nor pope have the unqualified right to silence dissenting voices. In time of war there must be a "clear and present danger" before free speech may be curtailed. Refusal by religious leaders to permit free and frank discussion about the issues of the faith prevent an adequate exploration of the margins of the faith, depriving the people of God of the truths which Scripture expounds. Sensitive as the issue is, the right of free expression must be seen as one of the great benefits of civil and ecclesiastical society. Scarcely any peril is as serious as the deliberate, coercive restraint of free speech. In the end, to deny it may be far more damaging to any society than the evils which sometimes flow from an extreme form of free expression.

See FREEDOM, ACCOUNTABILITY, CIVIL RIGHTS.

For Further Reading: DeWolf, *Responsible Freedom.*

LEON O. HYNSON

FRIENDSHIP. Friendship is a largely ignored theme in the modern world's discussion of love. To many, friendship does not even rate as a form of love. Martin Marty suggests, however (Marty, *Friendship*), that friendship and love are related and have family resemblances. C. S. Lewis points out in *The Four Loves* that the value of friendship is enhanced because it is the least instinctive of the loves—it is neither biologically necessary nor imperative for the life of the community.

There are at least three basic elements in friendship. *First,* there is the element of choice. While we have no choice in the selection of our parents or our siblings, friendships cannot be forced upon us. Friendships are freely chosen.

A *second* basic element in friendship is that of sharing. Friendships begin with a shared hobby or interest, a shared appreciation of a particular author or composer, a shared fondness for a certain type of food or style of art, or even shared dislikes.

The *third* element of friendship, that of separation, logically follows from the first two. On the basis of that which they share, those who are friends have freely chosen to draw apart from the crowd of companions.

Friendships, as such, are amoral. They can be experienced by saint and sinner alike, and they can be either ennobling or degrading. Jesus said, "I have called you friends" (John 15:15); and James reminds us that Abraham was called "the Friend of God" (Jas. 2:23); but James also warns that "friendship with the world is hostility toward God" (4:4, NASB). Not only does this warning spell out the danger of friendship with the wrong object, but when taken with John's statement that "if any one loves the world, the love of the Father is not in him" (1 John 2:15, NASB), it demonstrates the close relationship between friendship and love.

See LOVE, KOINONIA, GREAT COMMANDMENTS.

For Further Reading: Lewis, *The Four Loves,* 87-127; Marty, *Friendship.*

GLENN R. BORING

FRUIT OF THE SPIRIT. Bible scholars are generally agreed that the fruit of the Spirit differs from the gifts of the Spirit. This distinction seems clear in the NT. The Spirit bestows His gifts severally according to His sovereignty, for usefulness in the church. The fruit of the Spirit expresses growing Christlikeness of character and is the product of the Spirit's indwelling. No one gift is God's will for all believers, but every manifestation of fruit is God's will for all.

The most familiar passage is Gal. 5:22-23: "The fruit of the Spirit is love, joy, peace, patience, kindness, goodness, faithfulness, gentleness, and self-control. Against such things there is no law" (NIV). Here the fruit of the Spirit is set against the background of the evil works of the flesh (vv. 15-21).

Love, joy, and peace, as the first triad, are concerned primarily with the state of the believer's relationship to the Spirit. Patience, kindness, and goodness describe the Spirit's outworking through the believer in his relation to others. Faithfulness, gentleness, and self-control, the third triad, indicate the influence of the Spirit upon the character of the believer. No amount of culture, education, or effort on man's part that is not motivated by God's Spirit can produce the fruit of Christian character. Character is what one is. Christian character is what a person can acquire through the growth and development of the fruit of the Spirit.

See GRACE, GIFTS OF THE SPIRIT, GROW (GROWTH), HOLINESS, LOVE, HOLY SPIRIT.

For Further Reading: Carter, *The Person and Ministry of the Holy Spirit;* Barclay, *The Promise of the Spirit;* Arthur, *The Tongue of Fire.*

LESLIE PARROTT

FRUIT OF THE VINE. The most familiar use of this expression in Scripture is no doubt the words of Jesus at the Last Supper (Mark 14:25; cf. Matt. 26:29; Luke 22:18). The phrase is a metonym for wine, which was itself a metaphor of His fellowship with them in His heavenly kingdom. The sacrament points forward ("till he come," 1 Cor. 11:26), as well as back to Calvary. Indirectly the phrase "fruit of the vine" could be linked to Jesus' discourse on the Vine and the branches in John 15:1-8. There will be no drinking of the "fruit of the vine" with Christ then if there is no abiding and fruitbearing now.

On the other hand, Jesus' statement reminds one of the symbolism of the new wine of the Kingdom which bursts the old wineskins of Judaism (Mark 2:22; cf. Matt. 9:17; Luke 5:37-38). And the miracle at the wedding in Cana includes the symbolism of the superior, abundant wine that has been reserved until the later moment (John 2:1-11). Jesus also likens the consummation of the Kingdom to a great eschatological meal (Matt. 8:11; 22:1-14).

See HOLY COMMUNION, FRUIT OF THE SPIRIT.

HAL A. CAUTHRON

FULFILL, FULFILLMENT. These words suggest three ideas: fullness, achievement, and/or perfection. To fulfill is to "fill-full," to complete, to accomplish. A word, a command, a promise—each is incomplete until it is fulfilled.

God's commands were fulfilled. For example, on the first day God said, "Let there be light," and there was light. And so the creation story progresses. God commands, and the work is done.

God also promises. He promised (predicted) judgment if His explicit command was disobeyed (Gen. 2:17). The later record proves that in fact man did die to innocence, to holiness, to fellowship with God. But after the Fall, God promised a Savior (or so the word is commonly taken): "her seed . . . shall bruise thy head" (3:15). And Paul specifically refers that "seed" to the promised Savior (Gal. 3:16).

God promised Abraham that in him all nations of the earth would be blessed. No one can read the history of economics, of medicine, of law, or of philosophy, without realizing that the fulfillment has far exceeded the numerical potential of Abraham's seed.

God also promised that "in the fullness of time" He would send forth His Son, made of a woman, made under the Law, born of a virgin and born in Bethlehem, and the promises were fulfilled. He also promised that His Son would be denied, abused, crucified; all that was fulfilled to the letter—so literally, in fact, that on the Cross in the final hours, not one bone of Christ was broken.

God promised the resurrection of His Son. All those promises were fulfilled, as Peter so eloquently testified at the Jerusalem Pentecost: "It was not possible that he should be holden of" death (Acts 2:24).

After His resurrection Christ pledged to "send the promise of my Father upon you" (Luke 24:49). The promise was kept (Acts 1:8; 2:4). And He promised that the gates of hell would never prevail against the Church. As the Church has trusted her living Lord through the centuries, it has prevailed.

God has promised the restoration of Israel to their own land; He has promised "the restitution of all things." Some of these promises have been and are being fulfilled; some seem to be definitely future.

The last book of the Bible, the Revelation, not only promises the fulfillment of God's unbreakable Word; the text often describes just how that fulfillment will be accomplished. Though we cannot, with mathematical certainty, outline the exact events of fulfillment, we Christians are fully persuaded that what God has promised He is fully able—and utterly dependable—to perform.

The final chapters of the Revelation describe the final fulfillments of all God's promises, to the ungodly and to the godly. And if we believe Genesis 1, we shall certainly believe Revelation 21—22.

See PERFECT (PERFECTION), PROMISE, MORAL ATTRIBUTES OF GOD, PROPHET (PROPHECY), HOPE.

For Further Reading: *Baker's DT,* 231; "Promise and Fulfillment," *DCT,* 277.

GEORGE E. FAILING

FULL SALVATION. This is one of the many synonyms of the Wesleyan doctrine of entire sanctification. It is more widely used among the holiness people of Britain (where the hymn "Full Salvation" is often sung) than among those in the U.S.A. Its infrequent use in the U.S.A. is due, in part, to the fact that the word "full" in "full gospel" very often denotes tongues-speaking. Yet "full salvation" is an altogether proper term for denoting the second work of grace. The word "salvation" is used here not in the sense of conversion, but in the sense of redemption broadly conceived— as it is sometimes used in Scripture (e.g., Matt. 10:22). The word "full" in this phrase denotes especially that God does not grant us simply a partial redemption, in which our acts of sin are forgiven, but in which we struggle throughout life with our original sin. It denotes a redemption that is full, or complete, because original sin, in a second work of grace, can be cleansed away.

See SECOND WORK OF GRACE, ENTIRE SANCTIFICATION, ORIGINAL SIN, CLEANSING, HOLINESS.

J. KENNETH GRIDER

FULLNESS. See FILLED WITH THE SPIRIT.

FUNDAMENTALISM. The name *fundamentalist* or *fundamentalism* is for some a badge of honor and for others describes an obscurantist approach to Christian thought (it is also used to describe a Muslim whose views are restrictively orthodox).

While the concept of the "fundamentals" is much older than its use in the late 19th and early 20th centuries (it was used by Wesley to describe "essential" doctrines such as the new birth), it received its present meaning through the "fundamentalist-modernist" controversy of the present century.

Fundamentalism emerged in response to the liberal reinterpretation of orthodox Christian teachings that the faith might be reconciled to the new currents of thought—science, psychology, philosophy, e.g., as taught by Darwin, Freud, or Lotze. Emphasizing a lofty optimism regarding man, liberal theology denied the traditional doctrine of original sin. Building on Darwin's dogma of evolution, liberals accented human progress. Freud's concept of the sexual drive as the key determinant to human behavior was reductionist, proposing a conception of man as product of psychosexual forces rather than a creation *imago Dei.*

In response to liberal views, conservative Christian teachers stressed certain fundamentals which must be preserved and defended, particularly the virgin birth of Christ, the substitutionary Atonement, inspired Scripture, physical resurrection, and the physical second coming of Christ. These doctrines were emphasized at Niagara Bible Conference in 1895. In 1909 Lyman and Milton Stewart funded the publication of 12 paperbound books, *The Fundamentals,* and circulated 3 million copies. James Orr and W. H. Griffith Thomas were prominent authors in the series.

An important analysis of fundamentalism (by Ernest Sandeen) traces it to British premillennial eschatology which was pessimistic about social amelioration. Dwight L. Moody was influenced by the Plymouth Brethren in his "lifeboat evangelism." He asserted that the world was like a sinking ship and that he must do all he could to save as many as possible. Clarence Larkin and C. I. Scofield popularized this eschatology in dispensational charts and in an annotated version of the Bible, the *Scofield Reference Bible.* The fundamentalists established Bible institutes and seminaries to counter the growing influence of liberalism, especially since the liberals had gained control of most seminaries.

If fundamentalism is identified by its commitment to certain key doctrines, it is also characterized by a distinctive mood. Committed to defense of the faith, and employing a scholarly apologetic, especially at Westminster Seminary in Philadelphia, it created a thoroughly rational approach to theology and biblical hermeneutics in some circles. Cornelius Van Til was the guiding spirit of this methodology. J. Gresham Machen (who rejected the appellation of fundamentalist) was one of the movement's greatest scholars.

A more militant mood was manifest in some of the movement's spokesmen. Sharply critical and sometimes uncharitable, they resorted to *ad hominem* arguments which played into the hands of their opponents. George Dollar's contemporary study of fundamentalism describes the mood of sharp, bitter criticism toward any deviations from the separatist mentality of some fundamentalists.

In the maturation of fundamentalism may be perceived the progress toward the theological conservatism expressed in the evangelical/neo-evangelical movement which seeks to develop an evangelical ecumenism (N.A.E.), greater openness in biblical hermeneutics, and a significant social ethics which addresses the ills of the world —poverty, overpopulation, hunger, and political processes.

See EVANGELICAL, LIBERALISM.

For Further Reading: Dollar, *A History of Fundamentalism in America;* Sandeen, *The Roots of Fundamentalism: British and American Roots 1800-1930.*

LEON O. HYNSON

FUTURE PROBATION. The word *probation* derives from the Latin *probare,* "to try, examine, prove." It means an act, process, or period of testing. It is commonly used in many areas of life, including the legal and academic. In theological terms it is a state or period in which man has an opportunity to demonstrate his obedience or non-obedience to God, and thereby qualify for a happier state or disqualify himself.

The supreme significance of probation in the Christian faith can hardly be overemphasized. "The starry heavens above and the moral law within" remind us that this life is the anteroom of eternity and is the arena of choice and testing for our unending destiny. "For we must all appear before the judgment seat of Christ; that every one may receive the things done in his body, according to that he hath done, whether it be good or bad" (2 Cor. 5:10).

The term *future probation* refers to the possible freedom of choice for salvation sometime after death; very rarely it may be used in reference to salvation choice for those who remain on earth after "the Rapture of the saints" at the time of Christ's second coming.

Historic Protestant Christianity has been virtually unanimous in renouncing future probation as being completely unscriptural. The verdict of the Bible is that death constitutes a closed door (Luke 13:25; cf. Rom. 2:2-11; 2 Thess. 1:5-9; Heb. 9:27; 10:26-31; 1 Pet. 4:17-18; 2 Pet. 3:7-14; Rev. 20:11-15; 21:7-8, 27; 22:11, 14-15, et al.).

See PROBATION, ETERNAL PUNISHMENT.

For Future Reading: Wiley, *CT*, 3:236 ff.

JOHN E. RILEY

G

GEHENNA. This Greek word for "hell" is found seven times in Matthew, three times in Mark, and once each in Luke and James. Aside from the passage in Jas. 3:6, this word is found only on the lips of Jesus. The term literally means "Valley of Hinnom."

Abbott-Smith puts the matter succinctly: "Gehenna, a valley W and S of Jerusalem, which as the site of fire-worship from the time of Ahaz, was desecrated by Josiah and became a dumpingplace for the offal of the city. Later, the name was used as a symbol of the place of future punishment, as in NT" (*Manual Greek Lexicon of the New Testament,* 89).

The most striking passage, paralleled partly in Matt. 5:29-30, is Mark 9:43, 45, 47. Here Jesus said that if one's hand, foot, or eye causes one to sin, that precious part of the body had better be destroyed than for one "to be cast into hell, into the fire that never shall be quenched." And then He gives the added description: "Where their worm dieth not, and the fire is not quenched" (vv. 44, 46, 48). This is "everlasting punishment" (Matt. 25:46).

See HADES, HELL, ETERNAL PUNISHMENT.

For Further Reading: Hills, *Fundamental Christian Theology,* 2:415-31; Wiley, *CT,* 3:356-75.

RALPH EARLE

GENERAL REVELATION. See REVELATION, NATURAL.

GENERATION. Jesus' use of *genea,* "generation," in Matt. 24:34 (cf. par. Mark 13:30; Luke 21:32) has often been cited by liberals as proof of Jesus' own fallibility. The statement is: "Truly, I say to you, this generation will not pass away till all these things take place" (RSV). Error, however, may be predicated only on the assumption that Jesus intended by "generation" a span of time of approximately 40 years. What is overlooked is that this meaning of *genea* is a derived and secondary meaning, the primary meaning being "family, descent . . . a clan, then race, kind" (Arndt and Gingrich). Vine believes this was Jesus' intended meaning in Matt. 17:17; Mark 9:19; Luke 9:41; 16:8 (cf. Acts 2:40).

Even though Adam Clarke believed that much of what Jesus predicted did come to pass within that current age, he says of the word "generation": *"This race;* i.e., the Jews, shall not cease from being a *distinct people,* till all the counsels of God relative to them and the Gentiles be fulfilled" *(Commentary).*

The charge of error in Jesus thus falls to the ground when the word "generation" is examined more accurately.

In systematic theology the term "generation" (from *gennēsis*) is a highly important technical term pertaining to the Trinity, specifically the relation of the Son to the Father.

See ESCHATOLOGY, LAST DAYS (THE), ETERNAL GENERATION, ETERNALLY BEGOTTEN.

For Further Reading: Vine, *ED,* 1:42; *Baker's DT,* 235.

RICHARD S. TAYLOR

GENETICISM. This is the view that original sin, in the sense of moral depravity, is transmitted from Adam to his posterity by natural generation. If the view is combined with creationism (that bodies physically conceived become persons by the incarnation of a soul or spirit especially but separately created by God), the resulting implication is that depravity is entirely a physical condition. In other words, sinfulness is in the body. If the spirit becomes sinful, it will be as a result of contamination by the body. On the other hand, if geneticism is combined with traducianism (that the soul as well as the body is propagated by the parents), the way is left open to see original sin as spiritual propensity, not primarily bodily; but a propensity nevertheless which affects and permeates the whole person.

Wesleyan-Arminianism and Augustinianism presuppose geneticism. Wiley says: "Arminianism has made much of this genetic law in its explanation of native depravity" (*CT,* 2:118).

Geneticism is usually discussed in connection

with the so-called Realistic Mode and Representative Mode. These also are theories which seek to account for the transmission of original sin. The relation of geneticism to these theories is intricate and complex, and as a result there is often misunderstanding. Some suppose that if one is a realist or federalist (representative theory adherent), he cannot be a geneticist. This is an error. Wesley was a geneticist, but also a federalist. The simplest way to explain this is to point out that geneticism relates primarily to the transmission of depraved nature itself, whereas realism and federalism are diverse ways of explaining the transmission of guilt from Adam to his descendents. No matter what one's theory is concerning whether or not guilt is attached to original sin, he may still be a geneticist. A geneticist is simply one who believes that each generation inherits a sinful bias from the previous generation, and so on back to Adam.

Yet the question of guilt cannot lightly be dismissed. The close relationship is expressed by Wiley: "Hereditary depravity then, is only the law of natural heredity, but that law operating under the penal consequences of Adam's sin" (*CT,* 2:125). While many Arminians reject outright any notion of guilt being attached to original sin, such rejection is not strictly Wesleyan. Wesley believed that inbred sin carried with it legal liability for Adam's sin, exposing even the infant to condemnation; but that such liability was universally cancelled in the prevenient grace which was an unconditional benefit of the Atonement.

See ORIGINAL SIN, PREVENIENT GRACE, ATONEMENT, REALISM IN THEOLOGY, REPRESENTATIVE THEORY, FALL (THE), GUILT.

For Further Reading: Wiley, *CT,* 2:107-28; *GMS,* 286-89, 296-302. RICHARD S. TAYLOR

GENTLENESS. "Gentleness," commonly thought of as being synonymous with kindness and mildness, appears only twice in the OT, and then in identical clauses: 2 Sam. 22:36; Ps. 18:35. The NBV marginal note at the Psalms passage indicating the meaning of the Hebrew *anah* to be "condescension" and the NIV translation of it as to "stoop down" suggest that the Almighty is not only gentle and kind, but that He willingly condescends to meet the need of the individual person (cf. Ps. 130:3).

In the NT, "gentleness," referring to a quality of Christ's character, appears in 2 Cor. 10:1 (KJV, NEB, RSV, NIV), a translation of the Greek noun *epieikeia.* The noun occurs only once more in the NT, Acts 24:4, where it is translated "clemency" (KJV), "kindness" (RSV), and "indulgence" (NEB).

This same term had wide usage in the ethical Greek writings of the NT times and before. In such literature it was used to describe the person who, aware that on occasion a thing may be legal but at the same time morally wrong, was willing to forego his legal rights rather than to be involved in wrong.

The adjective *epieikēs* is used five times in the NT. In Phil. 4:5 Phillips translates it "gentleness." It is also rendered "moderation" (KJV) and "forbearance" (RSV). In 1 Tim. 3:3 it is rendered "patient" (KJV), "gentle" (RSV), "forbearing" (NEB). In Titus 3:2; Jas. 3:17; and in 1 Pet. 2:18, it appears as "gentle" (KJV) and as "considerate" (NEB, NIV).

In Gal. 5:22 (KJV) "gentleness" appears as a translation of *chrēstotēs;* but that term is more generally translated "kindness." In Eph. 4:2 *prautēs* is translated "gentle" in the NIV and "gentleness" in the NASB and the NBV. According to Hodge, this term refers to a disposition of mind which "enables us to bear without irritation or resentment the faults and injuries of others."

Gentleness, always intent on doing what is right, signifies mercy, kindness, forbearance, and condescension.

See CHRISTLIKENESS, FRUIT OF THE SPIRIT, MEEKNESS.

For Further Reading: Barclay, *New Testament Words,* 94-96; *Baker's DT,* 235-36. ARMOR D. PEISKER

GENUINENESS OF SCRIPTURE. This has to do with whether a book of Scripture was indeed written by the person which the book itself mentions as the author. Evangelicals (conservatives) are so respecting of Scripture that, if a book of the Bible, in its early manuscript form, gives a certain person as its author, that person is understood to have indeed written it—although it would be allowed that later editors might well have emended the manuscript in places.

Nonconservatives, not respecting Scripture in this way, often question a book's genuineness. This has occurred, widely, among nonevangelicals, in the case of the Pastoral Epistles. But, since they all three state that Paul wrote them, evangelicals in general accept the fact that he did.

Since the Book of Hebrews does not state who wrote it, evangelicals are divided over the matter of who did. Paul's name got associated with it in certain early KJV Bibles; but that statement of authorship was an addition not contained in the manuscripts we have of Hebrews.

See BIBLE, CRITICISM (OT, NT).

J. KENNETH GRIDER

GETHSEMANE. Gethsemane was the site where Jesus regularly prayed (Luke 21:37; John 18:2) and retreated on the night of His betrayal. Though only named in Matt. 26:36 and Mark 14:32, yet Luke 22:39-40 and John 18:1-2 refer to the same site. John alone calls it "garden," leading to the designation "Garden of Gethsemane." The precise location cannot be identified conclusively.

Without doubt the evangelists believe that Jesus was confronted with a real choice in Gethsemane. From His baptism and culminating in Gethsemane, Jesus faced the temptation to abandon His God-appointed and self-chosen role as Suffering Messiah in exchange for another, less arduous path to glory. Once Jesus had reconfirmed His acceptance of the Father's will in Gethsemane, He went to His death without a murmur. But the choice was real. To suggest that Jesus could not have done otherwise is to make Gethsemane into a meaningless charade. Neither the Gospels nor Heb. 5:7-8 will allow such an interpretation.

The precise nature of the "cup" has attracted many suggestions. A once popular and recently revived view (cf. Hewitt, *Hebrews,* 97 ff) is that Jesus feared He would die in Gethsemane and thus prayed for strength to reach Calvary. Clearly at variance with Heb. 5:7-8, only a forced reading of the Gospels can support this view which appears to spring from a too mechanical view of the Atonement on the one hand and a reverent but misguided attempt to safeguard the divinity of Jesus on the other.

Another interpretation is that Jesus shrank from the prospect of breaking His hitherto unbroken filial fellowship with the Father—which He knew His sin-bearing would cause. Partially based upon Mark 15:34 and Matt. 27:46, this view takes seriously the horror of sin and its awful consequence: separation from God. But attractive though this view may be from a doctrinal perspective, it alone cannot do justice to the text.

Recent biblical studies have shown the strength of the apparently obvious meaning of the text, namely, that Jesus shrank from the prospect of death. The profound influence of the OT suffering figures in the Psalms and Prophets upon both Jesus and the evangelists provides the background for understanding the meaning of the cup. In the Psalms, the righteous sufferer cries to God for deliverance, and Jesus, as the righteous Sufferer par excellence, seeks deliverance from death. This, coupled with His role as Suffering Messiah largely based upon the Isaianic servant, means that though Jesus shrank from death, "he recognized the path of the Father's will and followed it to the end" (Bruce, *Hebrews,* 102). Jesus placed His confidence in His Father, and He became obedient unto death (Phil. 2:8).

For us, the significance of Gethsemane lies in our assurance that Jesus endured the utmost temptation to abandon the Father's will, that He paid the ultimate cost for following it, and that God vindicated Him. Thus, we too have hope as we follow Jesus.

See CUP, HUMANITY OF CHRIST, HUMILIATION OF CHRIST, OBEDIENCE OF CHRIST.

For Further Reading: Bruce, *Epistle to the Hebrews, NICNT;* Clark, "Gethsemane," *IDB;* Hewitt, "Epistle to the Hebrews," *TNTC;* DeYoung, "Gethsemane," *ZPEB.*

KENT BROWER

GIFTS OF THE SPIRIT. *Charismata* (grace gifts) are to be distinguished from *tēn dōrean tou hagiou pneumatos* ("the gift of the Holy Spirit," Acts 2:38; 10:45). The Holy Spirit is God's gift (John 14:15-17) to His believing people, and in turn the Spirit becomes the Giver of various *charismata*—from *charis,* "grace," and *charisma,* "a gift of grace."

Paul (16 times) and Peter (once, 1 Pet. 4:10) are the only biblical writers to use the terms *charisma* (sing.)/*charismata* (pl.). Peter uses *charisma* to describe capacities to be used in service *(diakonia)* and communication *(lalein).* Paul lists 22 abilities, capacities, benefits, or graces divinely imparted as *charismata.*

Paul uses *charisma/charismata* eight times to indicate general bestowals as varied as the benefit of his own ministry (Rom. 1:11), justification (5:15-16), eternal life (6:23), manifestations of God's elective mercy (11:29), a particular station or condition of life (1 Cor. 7:7), answered prayer (2 Cor. 1:11), and ability for ministry (1 Tim. 4:14; 2 Tim. 1:6).

However, Paul's most distinctive use of the precise word *charismata* is found in Rom. 12:6 and 1 Cor. 12:4, 9, 28, 30-31 where he names capacities or abilities for carrying on the work of the Church. H. Orton Wiley defines them as "the divinely ordained means and powers with which Christ endows His Church in order to enable it to properly perform its task on earth. . . . [They are] supernatural endowments for service . . . determined by the character of the ministry to be fulfilled" (*CT,* 2:317-18).

Paul gives two lists of *charismata* (Rom. 12:6-8; 1 Cor. 12:7-11) with only prophecy common to both, and so different in range and tone as to hint that no complete catalog is intended. Prophecy is defined in 1 Cor. 14:3 as speaking to others for "strengthening, encouragement and comfort" (NIV). It is listed first in Romans 12, and throughout 1 Corinthians 14 it is valued above unfamiliar languages.

The Romans list deals with gifts that are essential to the everyday life of the normal Christian community:

1. Prophecy, *prophēteia,* from *pro,* "forth," and *phēmi,* "speak"—more in the basic biblical sense of "forth-telling" the Word of God ("thus saith the Lord") than in the more limited current sense of "foretelling."

2. Serving, *diakonia* (as in 1 Pet. 4:11 also), with usual reference to ministering to physical needs (Acts 6:1-2).

3. Teaching, *didaskōn,* instructing and grounding others in the truth.

4. Encouraging, *paraklēsis,* lit., "going to another's help" in whatever way that help might be needed.

5. Contributing to the needs of others, *metadidōmi,* lit., "to give a part, to share."

6. Leadership, *proïstēmi,* "ruling or taking the lead."

7. Compassion, *eleeō,* showing mercy.

The Corinthians list deals with gifts that are more exceptional, less universal, possibly transitory (1 Cor. 13:8-9), reflecting in part the unusual conditions in the church at Corinth:

1. Ability to speak with wisdom, *logos sophias*—understanding and applying revealed truth (cf. Jas. 3:17).

2. Ability to speak with knowledge, *logos gnōseōs*—to grasp and communicate spiritual truth.

3. Faith, *pistis,* "as a mustard seed" (Matt. 17:20), to claim and receive extraordinary answers to prayer.

4. Gifts of healings, *charismata iamatōn* (both plural, as also in v. 30)—not a generalized gift for healing all who come, but specific gifts for specific instances of healing as in Jas. 5:14-15.

5. Miraculous powers, *energēmata dunameōn*—producing results not fully accounted for by natural agencies.

6. Prophecy (as above).

7. Ability to distinguish between spirits, *diakriseis pneumatōn*—discriminating between true and false impressions or leadings (1 John 4:1).

8. Different kinds of languages, *genē glōssōn,* and

9. The interpretation of languages, *hermēneia glōssōn.* As also in 1 Corinthians 14, the modern "charismatic" movement understands this as relating to glossolalia (languages the speakers do not understand) or "unknown tongues" (influenced by the KJV addition of "unknown" to the Greek of 1 Cor. 14:2, 4, 14, 19, 27). However, since this passage was written nine years before Acts 2, it is more likely that Acts 2:4-11 better describes the authentic NT gift of languages, while 1 Corinthians 14 deals with problems arising from the introduction of ordinary but unfamiliar human languages into the public worship of the church.

First Cor. 12:28 adds two *charismata* not previously mentioned:

1. Ability to help others, *antilēmpsis*—help, support, rendering assistance, closely paralleling *diakonia* and *paraklēsis* in the Romans list.

2. Administrative ability, *kubernēsis*—used of piloting a ship, to guide—related to *proïstēmi* in the Romans list.

Paul cites four principles governing the distribution of gifts: (1) Value and profit for the Church as the Body of Christ (1 Cor. 12:7; 14:6, 19); (2) The sovereign will of the Spirit (Rom. 12:6; 1 Cor. 12:11-18, 28-30); (3) The unity of the Church with varied functions in one Body (vv. 14-27); (4) The subordination of gifts to graces, especially love (12:31—13:13).

See HOLY SPIRIT, FRUIT OF THE SPIRIT, KOINONIA, BODY LIFE.

For Further Reading: Wiley, *CT,* 2:317-21; Purkiser, *The Gifts of the Spirit;* Koenig, *Charismata: God's Gifts for God's People;* McRae, *The Dynamics of Spiritual Gifts;* Wagner, *Your Spiritual Gifts Can Help Your Church Grow;* Kildahl, *The Psychology of Speaking in Tongues;* Samarin, *Tongues of Men and Angels: The Religious Language of Pentecostalism;* Synan, *The Holiness-Pentecostal Movement in the United States.*

W. T. PURKISER

GLORIFICATION. See RESURRECTION OF THE BODY.

GLORY. The OT term most commonly translated "glory" is *kabod,* meaning "weight, importance, radiance." It frequently refers to things which display human glory. For example, there are: man's riches (Ps. 49:16), his good reputation (Job 29:20), and his spiritual status (Ps. 8:5). Generally, however, it designates God's presence and power (Deut. 5:24).

Sometimes, it is a synonym for *godesh,* "holiness," in that the latter often denotes "radiance." Since God has designed through Christ to transmit His own holiness to those who trust and obey Him, every believer should be reflecting in his person and life something of the divine radiance or glory (2 Cor. 3:18; Col. 3:10). That glory should also be seen in the church, the body of believers, as it meets in corporate worship, for it is to reflect and promote the glory of Christ (2 Cor. 8:23).

In both Testaments the glory of God is an expression of God's inherent majesty which is to be recognized and acclaimed by His people (Exod. 33:18; Rom. 1:23). The NT Greek term for "glory" *(doxa)* occurs many times, carrying much the same general meanings as the OT *kabod.* Paul uses it often in his Epistles. For him glory was something that rightly belonged to God, even though he did use it to express the illumination which comes to human relationships through Christ (Eph. 3:16).

In the KJV there is "vain glory" (Gal. 5:26) and "vainglory" (Phil. 2:3). In current parlance these terms are perhaps better rendered "conceit" or "boastful" and "selfish or empty ambition." See NASB and NIV.

See HOLINESS, MAJESTY, ATTRIBUTES (DIVINE).

For Further Reading: Turner, *The Vision Which Transforms,* 15-17; *IDB,* 2:401-3. ARMOR D. PEISKER

GNOSTICISM. Gnosticism was a dualistic, hydra-headed heresy which penetrated the church in the first and second centuries. According to Qualben the movement was Jewish in origin, with roots in Philo of Alexandria. Other authorities trace it to India and the East. As its name suggests (*gnōsis,* knowledge), Gnosticism stressed esoteric knowledge as the key to salvation. It thus became a religious philosophy which corrupted the gospel of salvation by simple faith in Christ the Redeemer.

Incipient in form soon after Paul established churches in Asia Minor, Macedonia, and Achaia (e.g., the "Colossian Heresy," Col. 1:12-20, 23, 28; 2:8, 11, 16, 18-19; 3:11), Gnosticism was subtle, speculative, and elaborate in its many forms and milieus. Among its many deviations was the denial of Christ's incarnation. Jesus was only quasi-human, not genuinely "bone of our bone" and "flesh of our flesh." But Gnosticism also rejected the true deity of Christ. It maintained that the heavenly Christ who appeared among men was an emanation from the one true God. The notion that Christ belonged among the hierarchy of angels is denounced by Paul in Col. 2:16-19.

In the Gnostic system the entire number of intermediary beings emanating from God and linking Him to this world were called the *plērōma.* Paul countered this idea by stating that Christ was the "*plērōma* of the Godhead" who suffered in the flesh to reconcile us to the Father (Col. 2:8-10).

Near the close of the first century, Cerinthus, the first known Gnostic by name, taught at Ephesus that the heavenly Christ descended upon the human Jesus at His baptism, remained upon Him during His earthly life, and ascended at Jesus' death back to the spiritual world. In effect this made Jesus and Christ two different persons. The apostle John wrote against such ideas in his First Epistle.

The Gnostics made it necessary for the Church to present a Christian view of God and the world, and it was quick and decisive in its condemnation of those who deny either the humanity or the deity of Christ. On the positive side, Gnosticism gave indirectly a powerful impetus to the shaping of the NT canon and the earliest creeds of the Church, because the Church in opposing the heresy was compelled to define Christian truth.

Gnosticism was also heretical in its doctrine of sin. Matter was essentially evil; only pure spirit was sinless. This partially explains the Gnostic hostility to a true incarnation: A Savior in a material body would necessarily be sinful. The body thus was inherently sinful, while the spirit could never be contaminated. Hence a moral dichotomy was created in which a religious person could maintain his holiness while grovelling in fleshly indulgence. This encouraged libertinism, since what the body did was of no ultimate moral consequence. On the other hand, in some Gnostics the positing of sin in the body drove them to excessive asceticism and masochism.

Gnosticism has frequently appeared in the church through its history. The teaching was revived in the 3rd century and again in the Paulician heresy of the 12th century. Traces may be seen in the 19th and 20th centuries in any system which refuses to accept the personal, Triune God of orthodox Christianity, or which denies the Virgin Birth, an objective Atonement, the resurrection of Christ, or which denies the possibility of cleansing from sin while in the body.

In the late 1940s were found, in a cemetery in Upper Egypt, 43 different Gnostic writings in the Coptic language. The Egyptian government was not altogether cooperative with scholars; but finally, by the early 1970s, all these writings got translated and commented upon. These are the only extant writings of the Gnostics. Until the present time, we had to depend almost entirely upon the attacks upon the Gnostics by the Fathers (e.g., Irenaeus' *Against Heresies*) to learn what Gnosticism was like. With these many Gnostic writings in hand (*The Gospel of Thomas; The Gospel of Truth,* etc.) we can see that the Fathers were generally correct in the way they described Gnosticism.

See DOCETISM, HERESY, KNOWLEDGE.

For Further Reading: Gundry, *A Survey of the New Testament*, 37, 57, 307-10, 323, 358-59; Purkiser, ed., *Exploring Our Christian Faith*, 172-73; Rutherford, "Gnosticism," *ISBE*, 2:1240-48; Qualben, *A History of the Christian Church*, 74-79. WAYNE E. CALDWELL

GOD. The concept of God is one of the crucial elements in any theological system. All else is colored by that definition. The word *theology* in basic derivation means a study of God. The Bible is, in fact, a continuous unfolding of the implications of the concept of God.

The opening words of the Bible are: "In the beginning God . . ." The biblical doctrine of God begins with an understanding of God as Creator. The opening pages portray God as the Initiator and Source of all things. His creative activity rules out many other approaches to basic definition. That God is a Person who knows, feels, and acts, is everywhere assumed in the Scriptures.

The biblical doctrine, however, does not reflect a God who has abandoned His creation upon its completion; any concept of Deism is ruled out. He is Sustainer and Guide of the whole process from creation to consummation. Paul writes, "Of him, and through him, and to him, are all things" (Rom. 11:36).

The God of the Bible is also revealed to man as the God and Lord of history. Again and again the biblical writers acknowledge the sovereignty and Lordship of God over all of the nations of the world. The basic faith that God would work together the exigencies of history and accomplish His goals through a Messiah is a profound expression of the Lordship of God over nations.

God's sovereignty is exercised in the election of Israel to special covenantal relationships. Israel understood God in redemptive terms. His covenant love led Him to intervene for His people to redeem and restore and guide them. Again and again He is called the Redeemer of Israel.

Israel also understood the essential holiness of the nature of God. The requirements of God's holiness formed the basis for the whole sacrificial system of the people of Israel. This system reflected a basic understanding of God's transcendence, unapproachableness, and utter purity. He is frequently called "The Holy One of Israel."

The justice of God and the wrath of God are closely related. The sovereign God of history is not a vindictive tyrant, but One whose reliability and fidelity are unquestioned. Even His love flows from His justice and righteousness. Mercy and grace are dependable precisely because He is just and holy.

The NT is harmonious with the OT in its understanding of God. The primary difference is the definitive revelation of the essential nature of God made visible in Christ. Paul affirms that "in Him all the fulness of Deity dwells in bodily form" (Col. 2:9, NASB), and the writer to the Hebrews maintains that Christ "bears the very stamp of his nature" (Heb. 1:3, RSV). The exclusive nature of God, expressed under the terms of sovereignty in the OT, is in the NT revealed in the exclusive nature of the salvation available through Christ.

The redemptive nature of God is underlined by the Cross and the Resurrection. He is the Father-King, who seeks relationship with His created beings through the atonement of Calvary (cf. 2 Cor. 5:19).

The Gospels reveal the sovereignty of God through the understanding of the kingdom of God. The Kingdom inaugurated in the person and work of Christ is moving toward the final consummation designed by God. The obedient and responsive citizens who have found salvation through Christ will share in the final victory.

The history of Israel and the faith expressed in the Early Church underlines repeatedly the understanding of God's eternality and complete sovereignty. Revelation, the last book of the NT, reaffirms in vivid language the faith that God will accomplish His purpose despite all opposition. Paul's delineation of life after death guaranteed in the power of God operating through the resurrection of Christ is an expression of the same faith.

It cannot be overstated that the concept of God is the crucial element in any theological system. Yet when all material about God is gathered, there is still an element of mystery that is unfathomable. The revelation of God to Moses through the title "I AM THAT I AM" (Exod. 3:14) expresses this combination of revelation and mystery.

See THEISM, DEISM, PANTHEISM, ATTRIBUTES (DIVINE), PERSONALITY OF GOD, MORAL ATTRIBUTES OF GOD, TRINITY (THE HOLY), GOD AS SUBJECT.

For Further Reading: Wiley, *CT*, 1:217-440; Gilkey, *Naming the Whirlwind: The Renewal of God Language;* Brunner, *The Christian Doctrine of God;* Kittel, 3:65-120. MORRIS A. WEIGELT

GOD AS SUBJECT. God as Subject refers to what may be understood about the subjective or psychological aspect of the Divine Being—or to what kinds of inner processes or characteristics may be asserted to belong to God. In some circles the term is used to emphasize the hiddenness of God—that He cannot properly be an object of man's inquiry (as in natural or philosophical theology), but can be known only as He the Subject reveals himself, and becomes a datum of consciousness in man's own subjectivity. This was the sense of God as Subject implicit in Pascal and explicit in Kierkegaard, Brunner, and Barth.

Traditionally, however, theologians have approached God's subjectivity objectively, i.e., by reason and Scripture. Thomas Aquinas held that we can know *that* God is and *that* He is His own essence but that we cannot know *what* His essence is. Thomas went on to assert that God is not body, not material, not compound; that He is perfect, good, intelligent; that He knows things other than himself, including other things that exist; that He is volitional and Creator; and that He is providential.

Much earlier, Augustine of Hippo had held that God is both *ultimate reality* (an idea he derived from his earlier philosophical education) and a *personality* in contact with human beings (which he derived from his study of earlier Christian writings and from his own conversion experience). Thus God is an "infinite personality." Despite the fact that this concept is very difficult for us to grasp—we have no experience of infinity on the one hand, and personality seems so anthropomorphic on the other—the orthodox church has followed what Augustine taught as the implied teaching of the Scripture.

Wiley speaks of the personality of God as possessing "self-consciousness" without "sentiency" or "development"; He is ever self-conscious, self-contemplating, self-knowing, and self-communing. In reply to those who contend that personality implies finiteness, Wiley, quoting Lotze, says that finiteness, although implying a limitation of personality, is not an essential quality of personality. Nor is God's personality limited by a created world of existence apart from himself. Since God created the world and gave it the position which it holds, any limitation which it may provide would be at most a self-limitation.

With respect to the distinction of powers within the Godhead, Wiley admits that personal powers may correspond to certain objective distinctions in God, but it is His whole being that knows and feels and wills, and this in such a manner that their exercise does not break the absolute unity of His being.

See GOD, REVELATION (NATURAL, SPECIAL), NATURAL THEOLOGY, NEOORTHODOXY, EXISTENTIAL (EXISTENTIALISM).

For Further Reading: Ramm, *A Handbook of Contemporary Theology*, 54; Brown, *Subject and Object in Modern Theology;* Wiley, *CT,* 1:290-99.

ALVIN HAROLD KAUFFMAN

GODLINESS. The Greek NT word for "godliness," *eusebeia,* is a noun not found in the OT, but which appears 15 times in the NT—all in the Pastoral Epistles except one (Acts 3:12).

Basically, godliness means "godlikeness," or "toward God," and goes beyond what constitutes formal religion or even Christian morality. Godliness derives from a vital union with the righteous God himself through the indwelling presence and enabling of the Holy Spirit in the Christian's life. Godliness implies a right attitude toward both God and man, with commensurate Christian conduct. In Acts 3:12 *eusebeia* is usually translated "piety," though the KJV renders it "holiness." The meaning is approximately the same. The objective *eusebēs* is ascribed to Cornelius in Acts 10:2, which answers well to the use of *eusebeia* in the NT, and incidentally speaks favorably for Cornelius' prior conversion experience. The Greek term *theosebeia,* "God-righteousness," occurs but once in the NT (1 Tim. 2:10), and forms the basis of the meaning of human godliness, or "righteousness like God" (cf. Matt. 5:48). This is the believer's righteousness relative to God's absolute righteousness.

Godliness is the aim of prayer for and thanksgiving for political rulers (1 Tim. 2:2); it is the revealed mystery of God in the person and redemptive work of Jesus Christ (3:16); and it is enjoined for the accomplishment of a disciplined life here and now, and the attainment of eternal life hereafter (4:7-8). True godliness is the Christian's greatest security against a professed but false godliness motivated by selfishness that leads to doctrinal and practical corruption of the Christian faith and life (6:3, 5-6, 11).

Paul is God's designated apostle for the instruction in godliness of the elect (Titus 1:1). God's power is granted through a true knowledge of himself for everything necessary to a life of godliness (2 Pet. 1:3), while self-control and perseverance lead to godliness (v. 6); and godliness is productive of brotherly kindness and Christian love (v. 7). Finally, holy conduct and godliness are the Christian's security in the final events of biblical eschatology.

See CHRISTLIKENESS, HOLINESS, PIETY.

For Further Reading: *ISBE,* 2:1270; *IDB,* I-J:436; *Baker's DT,* 248; *ZPEB*, 2:767.

CHARLES W. CARTER

GODS. See POLYTHEISM.

GOOD, THE GOOD, GOODNESS. When we say that something is good, we usually mean it is pleasing, satisfying, healthful, or conducive to happiness. Thus in calling anything good, we are making an assertion about its value to some conscious being. The concept belongs to the field of ethics.

Whenever we speak of "good" or "goodness," we need to make clear the sense in which we use the terms. *Cruden's Concordance* lists 14 different ways that *good* is used in the Bible. The following are illustrative: *(a)* that which is honest and morally right, "Depart from evil, and do good" (Ps. 34:14); *(b)* that which is according to the Creator's plan, "God saw every thing that he had made, and, behold, it was very good" (Gen. 1:31); *(c)* that which is right and commendable, "The woman . . . hath wrought a good work upon me" (Matt. 26:10); *(d)* that which is lawful to be used, "Every creature of God is good" (1 Tim. 4:4); *(e)* all that comes from God, "Every good gift and every perfect gift is from above, and cometh down from the Father" (Jas. 1:17).

For the humanist these values come from man's own estimates. Something is good if I like it, or if most human beings like it. Christian theology would not stop here. For a Christian, goodness is determined by standards which God has established and made known to us.

Christian theology holds that the goodness that God requires of me, made possible through grace, brings happiness to me. Aristotle taught that happiness was "activity in accordance with human nature." In contrast, Christian faith asserts that happiness is activity in accordance with *God's good plan for human nature,* as redeemed through Christ.

Here is the difference between a purely subjective criterion and an objective standard. The Christian believes that following God's plan brings life's greatest happiness—usually now, and certainly in the long run. But even if I doubt this truth, God's will is still good. Goodness thus becomes not just what I want but *what I ought to want.* The good has objective character. It is praiseworthy and valuable because it conforms to the will of God that is built into the moral order of the universe.

Ethicists often speak of intrinsic good and instrumental good. An intrinsic value is something that is good for its own sake, e.g., honesty or health. An instrumental value is good because it enables me to gain some other good, e.g., I value money because it enables me to purchase food and shelter. Jesus recognized this difference between instrumental, earthly values and intrinsic, eternal good when He counselled, "Lay not up for yourselves treasures upon earth . . . but lay up for yourselves treasures in heaven, where neither moth nor rust doth corrupt" (Matt. 6:19-20).

See ETHICS, ETHICAL RELATIVISM, CHRISTIAN ETHICS, HUMANISM, VALUES, EVIL, AXIOLOGY.

For Further Reading: *ISBE,* 2:1277-79; *Encyclopedia of Philosophy,* 3-4:367-70. A. F. HARPER

GOOD WORKS. Biblically, good works are deeds of religious devotion, benevolence, and practical righteousness which are approved by God. That such works are mandatory is clearly taught by both Jesus and Paul (Matt. 5:16; 25:35 ff; Titus 3:8). And James declares that without visiting the fatherless and widows in their affliction there is no "pure religion" (Jas. 1:27).

Yet Jesus and the apostles equally repudiate good works as a means of earning or meriting salvation (Luke 18:9 ff). "Not of works," writes Paul, "lest any man should boast" (Eph. 2:9). He follows at once, however, with the declaration: "created in Christ Jesus unto good works." The NT teaching is, not *by* good works are we saved, but *to* good works.

Furthermore, works which relate to repentance are seen, while not as a basis of merit, nevertheless as necessary for the demonstration of sincerity (Luke 3:8-14; 2 Cor. 7:10-11). In this sense they may be said to be conditional to salvation without identifying them as a meritorious means to salvation.

It was at this point that Wesley differed sharply with the Moravians when, in developing their "stillness" theology, they denigrated the importance of any works whatsoever as aids to the full assurance of faith, even Communion and reading the Bible. Rather, taught Wesley, good works should be practiced until faith is perfected, then continued as the outflowing of faith.

Such works, says Wiley, "are pleasing to God, (1) because they are performed according to His will; (2) because they are wrought through the assistance of divine grace, and (3) because they are done for the glory of God" (Wiley, *CT,* 2:374).

The Scriptures perceive good works as springing from divine love implanted in the believer's soul and as the outworking of that love in service to God and man. Works therefore are an evidence of heart purity (Titus 2:14) and are to be a criterion both in rewards and final judgment (1 Cor. 3:14; Rev. 20:12 ff; 22:12).

See FAITH, WORK (WORKS).

For Further Reading: *The Works of John Fletcher,* 1:53-55, 185, et al.; Manschreck, *A History of Christianity in the World,* 294; Ragsdale, *The Theology of John Wesley.* RICHARD S. TAYLOR

GOSPEL. The word "gospel" (Gr. *euangelion*) is somewhat enigmatic. Literally, of course, it means "Good News." Yet its use among early Christian evangelists is so diverse, so multifaceted, that one has difficulty describing all that the Good News is. Perhaps the word "gospel" served a more *symbolic* function for the early Christians who used it: the "gospel" embraced the whole Christian message—in all its many written and preached forms—of what God did for the world through His Son, Jesus from Nazareth.

It seems reasonable to suggest that "gospel" was selected for its symbolic task because of what it had come to mean in later Hellenistic Greek and in the Greek OT *(Septuagint)* which informed early Christianity. *Euangelion* had come to be attached to various announcements of victory or of success. A "gospel" was the public notification that someone had won a battle or had fulfilled that which had previously been hoped for. Indeed, this meaning lies behind two very important passages in Isaiah which the Church had associated with her Lord Jesus. In Isa. 40:9 and 52:7 (cf. Acts 10:36; Rom. 10:15; 2 Cor. 5:20; Eph. 2:17; 6:15), the prophet promises that *God's Messiah would come and announce God's victory over His foes and so His people's liberation from them.* This Messianic announcement of God's victory is called by Isaiah, "gospel." Unquestionably, the early Christians read these Isaianic passages in light of what Jesus had done: Jesus was for them the fulfillment and embodiment of Isaiah's promised "gospel."

Thus, the gospel is first of all the good news of *victory.* The gospel announces that sin has been defeated, that death has been conquered, and that the rulers of the world which oppose God's purposes for the world are on the run.

The gospel is the good news of *God* (1 Thess. 2:2, 8-9; Rom. 1:16-17). It is God who is victorious over His foes, and that news is good not only because God is good but because God intends that His victory over sin, death, and the evil powers will usher in His kingdom where all that is good can be found.

The gospel is the good news of *Jesus Christ* (Mark 1:1, 14; 2 Cor. 4:4; 9:13; 10:14). As God's Messiah, Jesus came into the world to announce God's victory. Through His dying and rising, He not only testified to God's love and concern for the world (John 3:16), but He effected the reconciliation of the world to God (2 Cor. 5:11-21). Further, it is through Jesus' obedient death and His exalted resurrection that God actually defeats His foes and establishes His kingdom on earth. In all of its rich diversity, therefore, the Christian gospel proclaims Jesus as Lord as its unifying theme because it is Jesus who has revealed God's gospel to humankind.

The gospel is good news for the *whole world.* The public who hears the Messiah's announcement of God's victory is the whole world. Indeed, God's victory is *for* the world, because it is through faith in the gospel that the world enters into the eternal goodness of God's kingdom (Mark 1:15). Certainly, the world can freely reject the gospel (1 Peter 4:17); however, to do so is to miss out on all that God desires for the world and promises the world in Christ. To reject the gospel is to miss out on immortality (2 Tim. 1:10), peace (Eph. 6:15), and life itself (John 2—6).

The gospel is good news for the *Church.* The heart of the Church's task in the world is to proclaim the gospel to others (Rom. 15:29; 1 Cor. 9:14-18; 2 Cor. 10:14; 11:7; Gal. 2:2), and she is to risk everything in serving her God in that way so that the gospel can break into the lost world with transforming power (Heb. 4:2).

See EVANGELISM, CHURCH, KERYGMA, MISSION (MISSIONS, MISSIOLOGY).

For Further Reading: Barclay, *New Testament Words,* 101-6; Dodd, *The Apostolic Preaching and Its Developments;* Dunn, *Unity and Diversity in the New Testament,* 11-32; Kittel, 2:721-36; Morris, *The Apostolic Preaching of the Cross.* ROBERT W. WALL

GOVERNMENTAL THEORY OF THE ATONEMENT. This is the theory of the Atonement that has long been associated with Arminianism. It is the view that Christ's death on the Cross made it possible for God the Father to forgive those who repent and believe, and still maintain His governmental control over us creatures. According to this view, if God were simply to forgive us, without Christ's death, we would not understand that our sin was very serious. Thus we would likely go back to sin, not breaking with it.

If, however, we see that the Father could offer the forgiveness only because of Christ's crucifixion, we will see the seriousness of sin and will more likely break with it. Thus God would be able to justify us and still remain just (Rom. 3:23-26). That is, He would be able to justify us and still maintain His governmental control over us—without having anarchy on His hands, that is.

The initial seeds of this Atonement theory are in the teachings of James Arminius (c. 1560-1609), yet it was one of his students, Hugo Grotius, a lawyer, who first developed it formally.

John Miley, late 19th century, in his *The Atone-*

ment in Christ, gave the theory its fullest elucidation. According to Miley, and to Arminians generally, several things obtain regarding the Atonement.

For one thing, it is *unlimited:* it is not limited to persons God had previously elected to be saved, but is accomplished for everyone. Such phrases as "he died for all" (2 Cor. 5:15) means "all," literally, and not, as in Calvinism, "all of the elect." It is also *vicarious:* Christ died *for* us (Isaiah 53). Further, it is *substitutionary:* Christ died in our stead (2 Cor. 5:21). It emphasizes such matters as God's love (John 3:16).

Importantly, according to this theory, Christ did not pay the penalty for our sins; instead, He suffered for us. Scripture never says that Christ was punished for us, or paid the penalty, as Calvinists teach. Instead, Scripture teaches, often, that Christ suffered for us (Luke 24:46; Heb. 2:18; 1 Pet. 2:21; 3:18; 4:1). His death was of such a nature that a holy God could accept it as a *substitute* for penalty. Its merits as a substitute could provide a moral basis for forgiveness without compromising either God's holiness or the integrity of moral government, including the morality of the terms of forgiveness, viz., repentance, faith, and obedience.

Scripture teaches in this way for several reasons. (1) Since Christ had not sinned, He was not guilty; so when He died on the Cross, He suffered, instead of being punished. (2) Also, had He been punished, God the Father could not have still forgiven us who believe—He would have had what His justice demanded, and could not have also forgiven us. (3) Further, if Christ had died for all, and if, for all, He had taken the punishment, there would have been no punishment in hell for anyone. We Arminians believe that what He did could not have been to pay the penalty. Calvinists can teach this (although Scripture does not), since they say He died only for the elect, and that it will be applied to the elect unconditionally.

See ATONEMENT, LAMB OF GOD, ARMINIANISM, DEATH OF CHRIST, HIGH PRIESTHOOD OF CHRIST, SATISFACTION, MORAL INFLUENCE THEORY OF THE ATONEMENT, MYSTICAL THEORY OF THE ATONEMENT, PENAL SATISFACTION THEORY OF THE ATONEMENT.

For Further Reading: Miley, *The Atonement in Christ;* Wiley, *CT,* 2:217-300. J. KENNETH GRIDER

GRACE. In the Christian sense, grace is God's spontaneous, though unmerited, love for sinful man, supremely revealed in the life, death, and resurrection of Jesus Christ. Grace is a foundational element of the gospel.

Although most often connected to the NT, especially Paul, the OT is not without a similar concept. One OT word for grace, *chen,* is most often used in the sense of undeserved favor: "If I have found grace in thy sight, shew me now thy way, that I may know thee, [to the end] that I may find grace in thy sight" (Exod. 33:13). This important OT concept has often been hidden by an undue legalistic interpretation. When we read the prophets, we encounter the zenith of Israel's monotheism, with a corresponding emphasis on the great truth that God is the One who, by His grace, enables His people to respond to Him, and He in turn blesses the faithful. Perhaps the most profound and extended passages which build on a true OT concept of grace are Ezekiel 36 and Isaiah 49—51; 54.

The above are anticipations of the full NT usage of the term "grace," especially as developed by the apostle Paul. We do not know for certain that it was the apostle who first developed the peculiar meaning of the Greek *charis* beyond its secular reference to "charm" or "attractiveness," but it is certain that he, by his Epistles, made a special place for "grace" in the theological vocabulary of the Early Church. That the special Christian use of the term is predominantly Pauline may be seen in its total absence in Matthew, Mark, 1 John, 3 John, and Jude. In all the non-Pauline books the word appears only 51 times. Twice as many occurrences, 101, are found in the Pauline corpus as in the rest of the NT.

It is not totally accurate to say that grace is the undeserved favor of God toward sinful man, especially if this be interpreted statically. God's grace is dynamic. It is God's love in action empowering those whom God regards with favor. Even so, it is clear that grace excludes every pretense of merit on the part of the recipient; any legal conception of religion is excluded. Grace is God's free, unmerited, and nonlegal way of dealing with sinful man.

The essence of the doctrine of grace is that although man deserves God's being against him, He is for him. In a very specific and concrete way God is for us. In the person of Jesus Christ, God has effectively acted. Through Him rebellious man experiences the undeserved love of God and enters into a relationship with Him. For this reason the NT almost invariably connects the word "grace" with Christ, either explicitly or by implication. The life, suffering, death, and resurrection of Jesus reflect the action of God's grace in history to redeem mankind.

See GOSPEL, AGAPÊ, MERCY, REDEEMER (REDEMPTION), MEANS OF GRACE.

For Further Reading: *IDB,* 2:463-68; *HDB,* 345-46; *GMS,* 410-13. W. STEPHEN GUNTER

GRATITUDE. See PRAISE.

GRAVE. See HADES.

GREAT COMMANDMENTS. Found in Matt. 22:36-39; Mark 12:29-31; and Luke 10:27-28, the Great Commandments occur in three forms. Though very similar, they contain some significant differences.

(1) Mark and Luke have a fourfold description of man, though ordered differently, adding "strength" to Matthew's trilogy of heart, soul, and mind, probably on the basis of the LXX of Deut. 6:5. Attempts at determining the original form on the lips of Jesus have met with limited success. (2) In Matthew and Mark, Jesus speaks in response to a question from a scribe, while Jesus' questioner recites the commands in Luke. (3) The context in Matthew and Mark is a controversy with Jewish religious leaders, while Luke's context includes the parable of the Good Samaritan told as a response to the scribe's attempt at self-justification. Whether Luke is reporting a separate incident or using his own, divergent source here is a moot point. (4) In Matthew, the scribe is clearly hostile and does not commend Jesus, while in Mark he expresses grudging admiration for Jesus' perceptiveness. (5) Especially in Matthew and less distinctly in Mark, a distinction is made between the first and second commandments while in Luke, they are combined into one. (6) Mark alone includes the *Shema* (Deut. 6:4).

But these differences ought not to obscure the clear intention of Jesus: Total love of God shown in love of neighbor is the foundation of the Christian's response to God. Without these two facets of love, Christianity does not exist.

The discussion of which was the greatest commandment was not among the rabbis, nor was the general combination of these two precepts totally foreign to Judaism. Their combination, though not explicitly made, lies behind the clear call for justice by the prophets (cf., e.g., Mic. 6:5) and permeates the whole covenant scheme instituted by Yahweh as the rule of all relationships in Israel. Both Philo and *The Testament of the Twelve Patriarchs* contain similar sentiments, although the latter may have come under Christian influence. What is new is the decisive manner in which Jesus cuts through the legal morass and penetrates to the very heart of the Deuteronomic belief. If Judaism wished to find a commandment which could sum up the whole system of law and which would inevitably happen if the law were followed, Jesus took the opposite track of pointing to the Great Commandments as the very basis of the whole covenant relationship of which the law was merely an expression. "For Judaism, good conduct is a part of religion; for Jesus, it is a product of religion" (Manson, *The Teaching of Jesus,* 305).

The first commandment, taken from Deut. 6:5, demands total and undivided loyalty to God. Heart, soul, mind, and strength are not constituent elements of human nature, but four dimensions of function or activity (cf. Wiley, *CT,* 3:52). Together they leave no room for doubt that God demands nothing less than absolute and complete devotedness. By citing Deut. 6:5, Jesus shows the essential continuity between the old covenant community and the basis of the new.

The second commandment, found in Lev. 19:18, also formed part of Jewish piety, but Jesus deliberately broadens the definition of neighbor well beyond the common point of view, though the same breadth of understanding is also seen in rare instances in ancient Judaism.

The link Jesus makes between the two commandments is as close as possible. Though love of God is not love of neighbor, Jesus implies what other NT writers make explicit: Loving one's neighbor is an inseparable corollary of loving God (1 John 4:20 f). "Love to man is dependent upon love to God and love to God is proved by love to man" (Cranfield, *A Theological Word Book of the Bible,* 135). All moral demands are fulfilled by love of neighbor, according to Paul (Rom. 13:8; Gal. 5:22; 6:2; Col. 3:14); and, according to John, love is the sign of the new community (John 13:35).

But while love is commanded, its practice is wholly dependent upon God's love to us and His work in us. Its presence and practice in our lives is not an ability we cultivate and thereby earn merit. Rather, it is the gift of God, demonstrated in the life and death of His Son and spread abroad in our hearts by the Holy Spirit (Rom. 5:5, 8; 15:30). Clearly, the commands are not enforceable but can only be obeyed by one who has an inward transformation which manifests itself in outward behavior (cf. Manson, 305). This wholeness of response to God and its expression in love to our fellowman lies at the very heart of Christian holiness. "Faith working by love is the length and breadth and depth and height of Christian perfection" (Wesley, *Works,* 14:321).

See LOVE, AGAPĒ, HOLINESS, LOVE AND LAW.

For Further Reading: Cranfield, "Love," *A Theological*

Word Book of the Bible, 131-36; Johnston, "Love in the New Testament," *IDB,* 3:168-78; Wiley, *CT,* 3:37-64.

KENT BROWER

GREAT COMMISSION. The Great Commission is found in some form in all of the Gospels and in Acts: Matt. 28:18-20; Mark 16:15-18; Luke 24:46-49; John 20:21-22; Acts 1:8. Two different accounts of this command of our Lord to the apostles supplement each other to give a brief summary of elements that are involved in the mission to which Christ has called the Church.

The resources of the mandate are the unimpeachable authority of Christ and the inexhaustible power of the Holy Spirit. Christ was sent into the world by the authority of His Father, and He sends us into the world by His own authority (John 20:21), which is cosmic in extent —over heaven and earth (Matt. 28:18)—and over all powers (Mark 16:17-18). This authority is accompanied by the enabling power of the Holy Spirit for the task of mission (Acts 1:8), which came to the disciples historically first at Pentecost, but which was and must be repeated successively, in every generation, for the full empowerment of believers for mission.

The privileges embodied in the Commission are the unmerited representation of Christ as God's ambassadors (2 Cor. 5:20) and the undaunted witness to Christ as God's way of salvation. Each Gospel indicates that we are chosen to be sent and have the consequent responsibility to go. The role of witness is explicitly mentioned in Luke and Acts as empowered by the Spirit, and the medium of preaching is indicated by Mark and Luke. The content of the message to be shared is identified as the gospel (Good News) by Mark but further specified by Luke as including repentance and forgiveness of sins.

The purpose of the mission is the uncompromising goal of making disciples, which results in the unveiling of the mystery of the constituting of the Church. Jesus said little about His Church other than that He would build it (Matt. 16:18), yet here in this command He indicates that evangelism by the Church ("make disciples") is to be accompanied by incorporation into the Church (by baptism as the rite of initiation) and followed by discipling in the Church ("teaching them") (Matt. 28:19-20). The Great Commission does not make sense unless it is assumed that the Church is God's primary agent of mission.

The extent of the task is indicated by the unlimited assignment made glorious by the unending presence of Jesus himself. The universal intent of the gospel is to be matched by the pursuit of the mission of making disciples in "all the nations" (Matthew; Luke), "all the world" (Mark), and "to the remotest part of the earth" (Acts, all NASB). How long is the task to continue? "To the end of the age" (Matthew, NASB), but never without the divine presence of Jesus himself mediated to us by His Holy Spirit. Acts 1:8 forms the outline for the whole Book of Acts in the account of how the Early Church fulfilled the Great Commission in its day. The Reformers mistakenly believed that the Great Commission was addressed only to the apostles and was fulfilled by them, making it no longer relevant for the Church in their day. It was not until the churches rediscovered the Great Commission as a contemporary mandate that the modern missionary movement developed in the 18th and 19th centuries.

See MISSION (MISSIONS, MISSIOLOGY), EVANGELISM, DISCIPLING, HEATHEN (FATE OF), CHURCH.

For Further Reading: Barth, "An Exegetical Study of Matthew 28:16-20," in Anderson, ed., *The Theology of the Christian Mission;* Boer, *Pentecost and Missions;* Warren, *I Believe in the Great Commission.*

PAUL R. ORJALA

GREEK ORTHODOX. See EASTERN ORTHODOXY.

GROTIAN THEORY. See GOVERNMENTAL THEORY OF THE ATONEMENT.

GROW, GROWTH. To grow is to spring up and develop to maturity. The concept comes from the biological world, where plants and animals, once very small, gradually enlarge until they are full grown.

The essential elements are (1) a small beginning, often only microscopic, (2) enlargement through assimilation of nourishment from outside the organism, (3) increments of change so small that growth is almost imperceptible, (4) progressive enlargement until maturity is reached.

Several Hebrew words translated "grow" mean to "spring up," "grow up," or "go out." The Greek *auxanō* means "to increase," "grow up." Theology, however, is chiefly concerned with the use of the word to describe personal development and spiritual maturing.

Luke recognizes growth of body, person, and spirit when he writes: "Jesus increased in wisdom and stature, and in favour with God and man" (2:52). Paul knew that such growth normally brings changes for the better: "When I was a child, I spake as a child . . . but when I became a man, I put away childish things" (1 Cor. 13:11).

In spiritual growth Jesus implied immaturity at the beginning when He said, "Except a man be born again, he cannot see the kingdom of God" (John 3:3). And Peter exhorts Christians to "grow in grace, and in the knowledge of our Lord and Saviour Jesus Christ" (2 Pet. 3:18).

The facts of growth undergird the importance of Christian education. In children, the church deals with mental and emotional immaturity; for children there must be nurture and time to grow. Even adult new Christians are often almost completely ignorant of biblical doctrine and practice. Such persons must be helped to "grow . . . in the knowledge of our Lord and Saviour." This growth occurs from assimilating new spiritual understandings. Then, based upon a continuing commitment to translate Christ's truth into a way of life, one makes gradual changes in his lifestyle. Here is the educational and biblical process of "precept upon precept; line upon line . . . here a little, and there a little" (Isa. 28:10).

Spiritual growth, like biological development, requires nourishment from the outside. But because each person largely determines the conditions of his own spiritual growth, each must take initiative in reaching out for sustenance. Peter exhorts, "As newborn babes, desire the sincere milk of the word, that ye may grow thereby" (1 Pet. 2:2).

Organic growth stops at some size predetermined by the Creator, but personal growth continues as long as the spirit seeks nourishment from divine resources. Ideally growth in spirit continues until we "become full-grown in the Lord—yes, to the point of being filled full with Christ" (Eph. 4:13, TLB).

Because growth depends also on favorable environment, Paul reminds us that the church includes God's husbandmen (cf. 2 Tim. 2:6). They are charged with setting up conditions and incentives conducive to spiritual nurture and growth. Christian teachers are called to explain biblical truth and to urge personal choices based on the new understandings.

The Bible also teaches that God's whole kingdom grows. Jesus says, "The kingdom of God [is] as if a man should cast seed into the ground; . . . and the seed should spring and grow up, . . . first the blade, then the ear, after that the full corn in the ear" (Mark 4:26-28).

All who understand God's plan for growth are content to keep working at the causes—and to let God give the increase (cf. 1 Cor. 3:6).

See DISCIPLING, PROGRESSIVE SANCTIFICATION, MEANS OF GRACE, LEISURE.

For Further Reading: Kennedy, *The Westminster Dictionary of Christian Education*, 298-300; *ERE*, 6:445-50.

A. F. HARPER

GUIDE, GUIDANCE. The Hebrew word *nachah* is a primary word that means "to lead, to guide." It is used frequently with reference to divine guidance. The Greek noun *hodēgos* means "leader, guide"; the verb, *hodēgeō*, to lead.

Being guided by God is a major emphasis of the OT. Repeatedly divine guidance is seen hovering over God's people: "Thou in thy mercy hast led forth the people . . . thou hast guided them" (Exod. 15:13). David was confident of God's guidance and by faith yielded himself to divine providence although he did not see or understand the mystery of the divine plan (Ps. 31:3). There is compassion in the guidance given: "I will lead him also, and restore comforts unto him" (Isa. 57:18). Typically the guidance of the OT was by dreams, by voice, or by test.

In the NT guidance is primarily by the indwelling Spirit. John teaches that knowledge of the truth is dependent upon guidance: "Howbeit when he, the Spirit of truth, is come, he will guide you into all truth" (John 16:13). This was a promise that the Holy Spirit would guide the unfinished education of the disciples. This same guidance is promised to all the sons of God: "For as many as are led by the Spirit of God, they are the sons of God" (Rom. 8:14).

Guidance may be positive or negative. While Paul was forbidden to preach in Phrygia and Galatia (Acts 16:6-7), he was later positively guided to Macedonia (vv. 9-11).

Guidance is promised to those who by consecration are willing to be led (Ps. 25:9; 37:5). The destiny of the Christian will be accomplished if he confidently trusts all to God.

The leading of the Spirit requires that the believer be Spirit-filled: "For it is God which worketh in you both to will and to do of his good pleasure" (Phil. 2:13). The major concern of the Christian is not performing a certain task or living at a specific location, but being fully consecrated (Rom. 12:1-2), thus permitting the Spirit to work His will within. The guiding role of the Spirit is based upon His intimate knowledge of the will of the Father (Rom. 8:26-27). God will make His will known sufficiently for the believer to be able to act in obedience.

The more mature a Christian, the better he understands the intimate and personal guidance of the Spirit. The immature Christian lives in the now and demands immediate satisfaction. The mature disciple can wait and deny himself in the present for clear guidance in the future. The mature are not led away by imagination, sudden impulses, or strong impressions.

The Bible is consistent in its recognition of the need for divine guidance. While Jeremiah saw man's lack of knowledge as the basis of the need for guidance (Jer. 10:23), the Psalmist saw the lack of rest and peace (Ps. 23:2); Isaiah saw the lack of foresight (Isa. 42:16); and John saw lack of knowledge of the truth (John 16:13).

The Spirit does guide through inner impression or revelation, but always in harmony with the Scriptures and with providence. If in accord with the Scriptures the impression will also be in accord with righteousness. There is also in true guidance an inner reasonableness. The criteria of Scripture, providence, rightness, and reason enable us to judge whether our impression is truly of the Spirit.

See COMFORTER (THE), PROVIDENCE, REASON.

For Further Reading: Metz, *Studies in Biblical Holiness,* 186-87; Rose, *Vital Holiness,* 190-93; Taylor, *Life in the Spirit,* 125-48. LEON CHAMBERS

GUILT. Guilt is blameworthiness for having committed a moral offence. It implies responsibility for sin and liability to judgment. In adjective form ("guilty") it translates *asham* 17 times in the KJV OT; and in the NT *hupodikos* ("under judgment"), Rom. 3:19; *enochos* ("subject to punishment"), 1 Cor. 11:27; Jas. 2:10; etc.; and *opheilō* ("owe, be indebted"), Matt. 23:18.

Guilt is correlative to righteousness and holiness. Where the prevailing idea of righteousness is ceremonial (as in Leviticus 4—5), guilt may be incurred for unwitting defilement. But where the prevailing idea of righteousness and holiness is moral, as in the later OT and throughout the NT, guilt implies personal and conscious responsibility that can only be put away by God's gracious act of justification (Rom. 5:1, 8-10; cf. 1 John 1:9-10).

Guilt attaches to "sins of omission" as well as positive acts of rebellion against God (John 3:17-21; Jas. 4:13-17)—and chiefly to "unbelief," the failure or refusal to accept the gospel offer of grace in obedient faith (John 3:18; 16:9).

Theologians have long discussed whether or not "original guilt" comes upon the individual as a consequence of Adam's sin. Reformed (Calvinistic) theologians generally affirm that all are guilty in Adam of the original transgression and some could thus speak of "infants a span long" burning "in hell" because of their "guilt in Adam." Most Arminians affirm original sin as the consequence of Adam's transgression but deny personal responsibility (guilt) as a result of that sin until it is confirmed by the individual's own sinful choices.

Guilt is universal upon all who have come to the age of moral choice (Rom. 3:23; 1 John 1:10). It cannot be expunged by works of righteousness (Titus 3:5-7) or by obedience to the law in the present and future (Rom. 3:10-20) but only "by his grace as a gift, through the redemption which is in Christ Jesus, whom God put forward as an expiation by his blood, to be received by faith" (Rom. 3:24-25, RSV).

A recognition of guilt leading to repentance and confession is the work of the Holy Spirit as an act of God's prevenient grace, the grace that comes to us before we come to Christ (John 16:7-11).

The remedy for guilt therefore is justification as set forth in Paul's sustained argument in Rom. 1:18—5:11. Justification places the believer before God absolved of moral responsibility for his guilty past "as if he had never sinned," although in remembered gratitude for grace conferred (1 Tim. 1:15-16).

See JUSTIFICATION, FORGIVENESS, ACCOUNTABILITY, ORIGINAL SIN, FALL (THE), GENETICISM.

For Further Reading: Rall, "Guilt," "Guilty," *ISBE,* 2:1309-10; Taylor, *Forgiveness and Reconciliation;* Wiley, *CT,* 2:82-95, 125-28. W. T. PURKISER

H

HADES. The term *Hades,* a transliteration of the Greek *hadēs,* is often mistranslated "hell." The word itself means "the unseen," a technical Greek religious term used to designate the world of those who have departed this life. Hades is the equivalent of the Hebrew term *sheol* in the OT. Both terms refer to the intermediate abode of the departed dead, both righteous and unrighteous.

The term *hadēs* occurs 11 times in the NT (Matt. 11:23; 16:18; Luke 10:15; 16:23; Acts 2:27,

31; 1 Cor. 15:55; Rev. 1:18; 6:8; 20:13-14). In each case, except 1 Cor. 15:55, where the more critical editions substitute *thanatos,* "death," the word *hadēs* is translated "hell" in the KJV. Wuest points out that the Greek word should probably be transliterated, that is, the English word Hades be used in the above cases except Rev. 1:18 and Matt. 16:18, where the translation should be "the unseen" (Wuest, *Word Studies,* 3:46 ff).

Thus the English word "hell" derives from three Greek words, *gehenna, hadēs,* and *tartarus.* To understand the term Hades, one should understand the other two terms.

See HELL, INTERMEDIATE STATE, GEHENNA.

For Further Reading: *GMS,* 662-65; Wiley, *CT,* 3:224-42, 363-75.

NORMAN N. BONNER

HAGIOGRAPHA. This Greek word, meaning "sacred writings," refers to the third division of the Hebrew OT known as *kethubhim.* It is comprised of a miscellaneous collection of books which were separately canonized, unlike the other two divisions, namely, the Law and the Prophets. These two sections achieved canonization corporately. In the Hebrew text of the OT, the hagiographa are grouped together as follows: (1) poetical books—Psalms, Proverbs, Job; (2) the five scrolls—Song of Solomon, Ruth, Lamentations, Ecclesiastes, Esther; (3) history—Ezra, Nehemiah, 1 and 2 Chronicles; (4) a book of prophecy—Daniel. A different order is found in the English text because it follows the Greek text of the OT (LXX).

The tripartite division of the OT (cf. Luke 24:44) had been established by the middle of the second century B.C., as suggested by the prologue of Ecclesiasticus (written about 130 B.C.), which reads, "the law, the prophets, and the other books of our fathers." Josephus, writing about the end of the first century A.D., acknowledges this division of the books (*Contra Apionem,* 1, 38-41).

These writings contain some very old material, as in the case of Psalms and Proverbs in particular. They are valuable because they give some insight into the process of canonization of the entire OT, even though settled conclusions can hardly be expected in this area of study.

See BIBLE, APOCRYPHA, PSEUDEPIGRAPHA.

For Further Reading: Pfeiffer, *Introduction to the Old Testament,* 61-65; "Hagiographa," *The Jewish Encyclopedia;* "Canon of Scripture," *Sacramentum Mundi.*

WILLARD H. TAYLOR

HALFWAY COVENANT. Historically, the Halfway Covenant refers to that compromise effort in Puritan New England to incorporate unregenerate children of believers into the life of the church. The problem which evoked the covenant is as old as the Church (see Jesus' parable on the tares). The first generation of believers in New England were a "sifted" people, having demonstrated the vigor of their Christian faith in their emigration to America. There they formed "gathered" churches whose regenerate members controlled the life of church and community.

With the passing of the first generation and the decline of the initial spiritual fervor, the communities became embroiled in disputes over church membership and the baptism of children. Second-generation children had been baptized as infants but did not possess awareness of saving grace. These persons were not permitted to be full communicant members of the church, and they could not present their children for baptism.

In 1662 the Massachusetts Synod declared that baptism constituted church membership and granted the privilege to its recipients to have their own children brought within the "external covenant" through baptism. Full communicant membership was reserved for those attesting to regeneration. This Halfway Covenant was an accommodation to the changing perceptions of society. The consequence of this covenant was the gradual weakening of the church's spirituality. Later, Solomon Stoddard proposed that the Lord's Supper was a "converting ordinance" open to professing, if unconverted, Christians.

The larger issues of the covenant are amplified by Ernest Troeltsch's distinction between "sect" type and "church" type. A "sect," said Troeltsch, is by definition exclusive, insisting on clear evidence of conversion, while a "church" is inclusive, stressing a broad basis for membership. The "sect" emphasizes an identifiable crisis of regeneration, while the "church" focuses more on a process abetted by instruction and nurture. Although arbitrary distinctions, they point up recurrent tendencies in Protestantism. In the final analysis, attention must be given to the doctrine of the Church (ecclesiology). Evangelicals insist that the Church is the company of the faithful, i.e., those who possess saving faith.

See CHURCH, DENOMINATION.

For Further Reading: Sweet, *The Story of Religion in America;* Walker, *History of the Congregationalists;* Ahlstrom, *A Religious History of the American People.*

LEON O. HYNSON

HAMARTIOLOGY. See SIN.

HAPPINESS. For the Christian faith, probably the best definition of happiness is found in the Beatitudes of Jesus in the Sermon on the Mount (Matt. 5:1-12). Here Jesus calls the poor in spirit, the mourners, the meek, the merciful, the poor in heart, etc., "blessed" (*makarioi,* or happy). This happiness is not dependent on outward circumstances or the satisfaction of sensual appetites. It results from one's knowledge that he or she has been filled with God's righteousness (Matt. 5:6); has obtained God's mercy (v. 7); and can because of a pure heart see the God who is himself pure (v. 8). God calls them His children and they therefore know His peace (v. 9).

Before and after Christ, theologians and philosophers have reflected on the meaning of happiness. Aristotle (384-22 B.C.) spoke of a state of settled happiness or well-being, *eudaemonia.* The happiness of man, according to Aristotle, is to achieve the goal of that activity which is the function of man as such, "activity of soul according to virtue, and if there are several virtues, according to the best and most complete. And in a complete life." Thomas Aquinas (1225-74), the most important theologian of the Middle Ages, spoke of *beatitudo,* which involves a state of well-being brought about by the perfection of an individual's potentiality. John Wesley often used the word *happiness* as a synonym for true blessedness which is not a temporary, superficial pleasantness, but a settled, unshakable awareness of God's presence and favor.

Although external well-being is not entirely excluded, Christian happiness or blessedness consists in the confidence of reconciliation with God through Christ our Lord, by grace through faith (Rom. 4:6-9). It issues from the fundamental reality of God's redeeming love expressed in Christ, and consequently is a happiness from which nothing can separate us (8:35-39).

Therefore, for the Christian the word *happiness* refers to a much deeper and more constant reality than do such words as *pleasant, enjoying oneself,* or *pleased.* These refer primarily to moods that are highly contingent and to influences over which one may not have control.

Happiness is not the primary goal or end of the Christian's life, but the result or fruit of having first sought the kingdom of God and His righteousness. He is not happy who hungers and thirsts for happiness, but he who hungers and thirsts for righteousness and justice. He who follows Christ in the way of the Cross will not always make choices that, from the world's point of view, promote happiness; but, if he or she is striving to accomplish God's will, then happiness or blessedness may be expected now and in the world to come. The expectation and hope of eternal life is, in fact, a prominent source of happiness in the Scriptures. Even Jesus himself "for the joy set before Him endured the cross" (Heb. 12:2, NASB).

See PEACE, VALUES, JOY, HOLINESS.

For Further Reading: "Beatitude," *HDNT.*

ALBERT L. TRUESDALE, JR.

HARDNESS OF HEART. Hardness of heart is a spiritual density and obduracy toward God and truth, and also an unfeeling callousness toward persons, which is the cumulative effect of resisting light.

The fact that the Scriptures sometimes ascribe hardness of heart to God becomes an acute theological problem (Exod. 7:13; John 12:40; Rom. 9:18), in view of the counterbalancing fact that the Scriptures also hold man accountable for his hardheartedness and everywhere warn him against it (Deut. 15:7; Ps. 95:8; Prov. 29:1; Mark 3:5; Rom. 2:5, et al.). Paul cites Pharaoh as the prime example of God's hardening; but a careful study shows that in this case we also find pointers to the resolution of the paradox. For the Scriptures equally describe Pharaoh's hardness as self-chosen (Exod. 8:15; 9:7). God does not create evil character, but He respects the direction of one's choices, and intensifies the sharpness of the issues by engineering the circumstances which compel open decision and commitment. He thus may be said to be indirectly effecting the hardening, in order that the moral lines be drawn tight, and God's moral objectives be clear. God may therefore accelerate the hardness of sinners by surrounding them with inescapable demands for decision and action, thus bringing into bold relief the hardness which hitherto may have lain dormant.

Self-hardening against truth is fatal (Prov. 29:1; Rom. 2:5). It is a special peril of sinners being awakened by the Holy Spirit. This is exemplified by the Jews in Ephesus. When exposed to the gospel, it is impossible to remain neutral; there will be either yielding or resistance. The statement "But when some were becoming hardened and disobedient" (Acts 19:9, NASB) implies an inward, cumulative process of choosing. Inward resistance became hardness, hardness issued in disobedience and open, increasingly confirmed opposition. There comes a moment of "no return" in the process, when the soul is set in the concrete of its own mixing, and future change is unlikely if not impossible.

But the reversion to hardness is equally a peril

of Christians. It is to God's people that the warning is sounded: "Harden not your heart, as in the day of provocation" (Ps. 95:8). The writer to the Hebrew believers seizes upon this warning and applies it to them with telling effect (Hebrews 3—4). He urges mutual support and encouragement "lest any one of you be hardened through the deceitfulness of sin" (3:13). Sin, in its very nature, so allures that it blinds the spiritual eyes to its consequences, thus making the heart presumptuous, stubborn, and insensitive to peril.

The presence of the Greek article *tēs,* "the" sin, could be a reference to the carnal mind yet remaining in these Hebrew believers (cf. 12:1). The entire Epistle bears witness to the tendency of unsanctified believers to drift into spiritual hardness. This tendency is even more graphically seen in the disciples before Pentecost. The overwhelming impact of the miraculous feeding of the 5,000 was soon dissipated, "for their heart was hardened" (Mark 6:52), so that they were as astonished at Christ walking on the water as if they had never seen a miracle before. A mark of this endemic proneness to hardness is spiritual dullness—"for they understood not" ("had not gained any insight," NASB). Another mark is a short memory (Mark 8:17-21). When there is hardness, truth does not penetrate, and the same lessons must be "learned" repeatedly.

Hardness of heart toward truth always becomes hardness of heart toward people. This too the disciples manifested toward each other before being cleansed by the baptism with the Holy Spirit. Later one of them could write: "But whoever has the world's goods, and beholds his brother in need and closes his heart against him, how does the love of God abide in him?" (1 John 3:17, NASB).

The most devastating havoc of hardheartedness is in the home. It was because of their hardness of heart, Jesus said, that Moses permitted a certificate of divorce (Matt. 19:8). Nothing could expose more openly and glaringly the callous cruelty of hardheartedness than such a concession. The implication is that their hearts were so stony and unfeeling that a legal divorce was a lesser evil than the cruelty or even death which the wife might otherwise be forced to suffer. Herein do we see the absolute depths of human depravity and selfishness. The feelings of tenderness and care which properly belong to true manliness and humanity are destroyed.

The havoc of sin in hardening the hearts of people makes Ezek. 36:26 the very kernel of the gospel: "Moreover I will give you a new heart and put a new spirit within you; and I will remove the heart of stone."

See SIN, ORIGINAL SIN, CARNAL MIND.

For Further Reading: Wesley, "On Conscience," *Works,* 7:186 ff; "The Deceitfulness of Man's Heart," *Works,* 7:335 ff; cf. *Works,* 8:137 ff. RICHARD S. TAYLOR

HARE KRISHNA. The International Society of Krishna Consciousness (IKSON), known by the chant "Hare Krishna," was founded by A. C. (Abhay Charen De) Bhaktivedanta Swami Prabhupada in 1965 at age 70, fulfilling the commission which he received from his spiritual master in 1935, to spread Krishna consciousness to the world. He began his work among the "flower children" of New York and Los Angeles, then reacting against materialism. Unlike Transcendental Meditation, he called them to a purged life-style excluding meat, fish, eggs, intoxicants, drugs, illicit sex, gambling, and, where possible, mechanization.

The Krishna Consciousness movement is a division of Vishnuite Hinduism, which occurred when Caitanya, a 16th-century devotee, proclaimed that Krishna, a ruler of 3000 B.C., formerly thought to be a manifestation of Vishnu, was the uncreated supreme transcendental personality of Godhead and that the great gods Brahma, Shiva, and Vishnu were manifestations of Krishna. In contrast with Vedantic Hinduism and Buddhism, where salvation is escape to nothingness, Caitanya taught that salvation is the ecstatic union of each soul, which is always feminine, in loving embrace with Krishna, the heavenly spouse. Krishna, as the transcendental lover, is pictured as having lived in playful sexual union with not only his wives, but all women, married or unmarried, including the 108 Gopis or milkmaids. Ecstasy, expressed by crying, singing, and dancing, is induced by chanting, "Hare Krishna." All activity occurs in strict regimentation toward Krishna consciousness. As in other religions where religious ecstasy is induced through sexual symbols, love for one's spouse rivals love for Krishna. Thus, sexual union is limited to once a month within strict Krishna consciousness.

See CULTS, OCCULT (OCCULTISM), NON-CHRISTIAN RELIGIONS.

For Further Reading: Boa, *Cults, World Religions, and You,* 178-87; Ellwood, *Religious and Spiritual Groups in America,* 239-45; Means, *The Mystical Maze,* 146-58; Zaehner, *Hinduism,* 144-46. DAVID L. CUBIE

HATE, HATRED. To hate is to have a strong aversion, springing up from a sense of fear, anger, or duty, attended by ill will.

Hatred is used of God hating evil (Prov. 6:16), and of the wicked hating the light (John 3:20). When directed toward persons, hatred is a fruit of the flesh (Gal. 5:20).

God is declared to hate all sinful thoughts and deeds—a holy feeling known also by all righteous persons. The Hebrews used love to express strong affection, and hate *(miseō)* to express a lesser affection (cf. Rom. 9:13). Jesus said, "If any man come to me, and hate not his father, and mother, . . . yea, and his own life also, he cannot be my disciple" (Luke 14:26). Thus, a follower of Christ is to hate his own life, or be willing to lay it down for Jesus' sake. He is to hate father and mother not in the sense of ill will (which is forbidden), but in the sense of depriving them of first place.

Jesus promised that the world would hate the believer because it hated Him and because believers are separated from the world (John 15:18-20). Hate, especially that of one's brother, is an attribute of darkness (1 John 2:9-11). "He that [hateth] his brother whom he hath seen, cannot love God whom he hath not seen" (4:20, ASV).

In the NT the overcoming of hatred is brought about by God's love, revealed in Jesus Christ. The infinite love of God exhibited in Jesus Christ conquers the emotion of hatred. Hatred is the basis for evil deeds and all wickedness, and is the mark of the world. God's love for the world is displayed by the Church in its evangelistic passion and social responsibility.

Christian ethics is the exact opposite of heathen ethics. Christians are to love their enemies, that is, to do good to them that persecute them and use them despitefully (Matt. 5:43-45). Love is the permeating principle of Christian ethics.

See LOVE, ANGER, MALICE, SEVEN DEADLY SINS.

For Further Reading: Vine, *ED,* 2:198.

HAROLD J. OCKENGA

HEAD, HEADSHIP. The physical relationship of head and body makes the head a natural symbol of command, leadership, or direction. From this natural metaphor, the word has assumed a derived meaning in expressions like "headman of a tribe," "head of a company," etc. Consequently, the word has several applications in the Bible.

Christ is the Head of creation, for He is called the Head of all principality and power (Col. 2:10). To Him every knee shall bow (Phil. 2:10), and eventually all things shall be brought together in Him (Eph. 1:10).

He is the Head of the Church. In 1 Cor. 12:12-27 and Eph. 4:15-16 the symbol of head and body shows the interdependence of members of the Body (Church) and the dependence of all upon the Head (Christ).

The word "head" also applies in the social order. Christ is the Head of the man, and the man is the head of the wife. This order is based on the order of creation (1 Cor. 11:3, 8). However, the headship of the man is not to be a despotic, harsh, or unnatural rule. Eph. 5:22-33 expands the subject by likening the relationship of husband and wife to that of Christ and the Church, and Christ's love is the pattern for the husband's love.

The word "head" is used in a theological sense to denote the relationship of Adam to the human race. Although the word is not so used in Scripture, Rom. 5:19 and 1 Cor. 15:22 assert the fact that through Adam sin and death came upon all men. No attempt is made to explain the method, but the emphasis is that Christ has made full provision to undo all which man inherits from Adam. Many attempts have been made to explain the fact of the racial inheritance of sin and death. For this purpose, terms such as *federal head* or *federal headship* have been used. Wiley discusses various theories advanced regarding this subject.

See CHAIN OF COMMAND, MARRIAGE, BODY LIFE, CHURCH GOVERNMENT.

For Further Reading: Bruce, *Epistle to the Ephesians,* 114-20; Metz, "I Corinthians," *BBC,* 8:414-16; Wiley, *CT,* 2:96-137.

LESLIE D. WILCOX

HEAL, HEALING. To make whole or well; to restore to health, more specifically by miraculous, divine intervention. In the metaphorical sense, as is often its use in the OT, it has to do with the restoration of the soul to spiritual health (Ps. 41:4) or the repair of damage caused by sin (Jer. 30:17). The Hebrew word *shalem,* meaning "healthy" or "whole," is a cognate of *shalom,* meaning "peace." The most frequent word used in the NT for "heal" is *therapeuō,* from which comes the English word *therapy.* Luke, himself a physician, seems to prefer the word *iaomai,* which has the added dimension of spiritual healing.

The fact that medical science was not highly developed in biblical times would make divine healing particularly significant. At any rate, Jesus exercised His power in this way rather freely. Kelsey states that 41 instances of physical and mental healing are recorded in the Gospels. The miracles Jesus performed were motivated by compassion and were often spontaneous in nature. But they were not without "sign" value—

i.e., they were confirmation of His deity—a factor which John's Gospel emphasizes. He often performed His miracles by the spoken word, but He also on occasion used supplementary means such as laying His hands on the sufferer, making clay to anoint a blind man's eyes, etc. Some cures were accomplished when He was not even present (e.g., the nobleman's son). Furthermore, the healing was frequently conditioned on the faith of the recipient (Matt. 9:29; Mark 10:52; Luke 17:19), though not always.

Jesus' ministry was to the whole man, and rarely did He heal the body without dealing with the sins of the individual. Indeed in some cases the latter came first (Matt. 9:2-7). This does not imply that sickness is necessarily the result of sin or that sickness is a form of divine punishment. It could be one of God's ways to develop such virtues as patience and courage (cf. 2 Cor. 12:9).

Jesus' instructions to the Twelve and to the Seventy when they were sent out included healing, and, according to Acts, miracles of healing were a part of the experience of the Early Church. It was subsequently practiced among the early fathers (Justin, Irenaeus, Tertullian, Origen) but only rarely thereafter until more recent times. Paul lists healing among the gifts of the Spirit and practiced it himself on behalf of others. Some have noted that Luke travelled with him on much of his journeys, presumably to help relieve his own physical problems (perhaps his "thorn in the flesh," from which Paul three times asked God for deliverance, 2 Cor. 12:8-9).

This "gift of healing" has been exploited by some so-called faith healers in recent years to the disillusionment of many. Their claim is that "healing is in the Atonement," basing this on Isa. 53:5 ("with his stripes we are healed") and 1 Pet. 2:24, and that physical sickness is an oppression of Satan. The claim is a tenuous one at best and on the basis of the best exegesis untenable. The unfortunate use of psychological gimmickry to accomplish "miracles" has clouded the genuine manifestation of God's healing power. There is ample evidence that miracles of healing do take place today and that in response to faith there can be divine intervention.

See FAITH HEALING, MIRACLE, GIFTS OF THE SPIRIT.

For Further Reading: Torrey, *Divine Healing,* 6-13; Kelsey, *Healing and Christianity; ISBE,* 2:1349-50; *HDNT,* "Cures," 1:402-4; *IDB,* 2:541-48; Wilcox, *God's Healing Touch.*

J. FRED PARKER

HEAR, HEARKEN. See OBEDIENCE.

HEART. The *heart* (Heb., *lev;* Gr., *kardia*) is "the seat of physical, spiritual and mental life" (Arndt, Gingrich). References to the bodily organ as the center and source of physical life are rare and need no explanation. The same may be said of figurative allusion to the center or interior of a material substance. The usual scriptural reference is to "the whole inner life with its thinking, feeling and volition" (ibid.).

The heart, in Scripture, is not an isolated element of personality along with other elements. It embraces the whole inner man, including motives, feelings, affections, desires, the will, the aims, the principles, the thoughts, and the intellect (Girdlestone, 65). As such, it came to stand for the man himself (Deut. 7:17; Isa. 14:13). The reference is not to a physical organ as the seat of intelligence or personality as the Mesopotamian concept of liver, the Egyptian idea of heart, the Eastern Mediterranean reins or kidneys, or the Western concept of head. Whatever the relation to the body or to any of its parts, the heart is personal and spiritual—the center of moral and intellectual consciousness and decision. It is the "control room" of the soul, by which one functions as a self-conscious and self-determining being.

Moral quality, then, relates primarily to the heart. The pure are pure in heart (Matt. 5:8). The Holy Spirit purifies the heart (Acts 15:9). The state of the heart determines whether one is good or evil. Out of the heart are the issues of life (Prov. 4:23). Likewise, one can be wise-hearted (Exod. 31:6). Or the fool can deny God in his heart (Ps. 14:1). With the heart man believes (Rom. 10:10) and loves (Mark 12:30). And it is in the heart that Christ dwells (Eph. 3:17).

See MAN, HUMAN NATURE, CHARACTER, HEART PURITY.

For Further Reading: Arndt, Gingrich; Girdlestone, *Synonyms of the Old Testament;* Marais, "Heart," *ISBE,* 2:1350 ff.

WILBER T. DAYTON

HEART PURITY. If power for service is the distinctive deeper life accent of the Keswick movement, if enjoying the gifts of the Spirit is the central emphasis in the Pentecostal/charismatic movement, heart purity remains the particular thrust of the Wesleyan movement. It is unfair to exclude any one of these three emphases from any movement, but it may be realistic to recognize the primary thrust of each. In passing, it is interesting to note that some of the Methodist movement retains the emphasis on sanctification/inward purity so often emphasized in Roman Catholic devotional writings.

Early biblical injunctions regarding purity concerned ceremonial purity (though the ceremonial easily illustrated the intended purpose of the admonition or prohibition). In meats, there were the clean and the unclean. Garments were to be woven of one fabric, so it would be pure wool or pure linen. Fire expressed purity. "Whiter than snow" described an experience of purity. Sexual acts (and even desires) were pure or impure. So the ceremonial led into the ethical, and the ethical into the moral and spiritual.

No theological emphasis, if it is biblical, can ignore the commands of "clean hands, and a pure heart" (Ps. 24:4; cf. 51:10; Jas. 4:8). Relegating as secondary the cleansing of the outside, Jesus commanded, "Cleanse first that which is within the cup and platter" (Matt. 23:26).

Christians at Pentecost and in Cornelius' house experienced a purifying of the heart by faith (Acts 15:8-9). It is not expressly stated that they prayed for heart purity, but God often bestows the gifts we need most rather than those we seek most. Jesus pronounced a peculiar blessing upon the pure in heart: "They shall see God" (Matt. 5:8). They both recognize and enjoy God more as their hearts are cleansed (see also Titus 2:13-14). It is strongly implied that this inward cleansing, though begun in a crisis Isaiah-type experience ("I am a man of unclean lips . . . thy sin [is] purged" [Isa. 6:5-7]), is a continuing process. Christians are exposed to defilement by "fleshly lusts, which war against the soul" (1 Pet. 2:11). They are encouraged to believe that by walking in the light, i.e., in obedient fellowship with God, they may enjoy continuous cleansing from all sin (1 John 1:7).

Any attempt to define heart purity in its full NT meaning must include freedom from double-mindedness (Jas. 4:8), and certainly also a cleansing of the heart as a source of "evil thoughts" and such other actual sins (Mark 7:21-22). By implication a pure heart is cleansed not only of a sense of guilt, but of filthiness and self-sovereignty, and is therefore undivided in its allegiance to God (Ps. 86:11). The concept of heart purity can hardly be separated from the idea of a radically altered and corrected moral nature.

Purity is not a negative but a positive virtue; it is not mere absence of impurity. Impurity really defiles; purity really sanctifies.

While no denomination or movement has a monopoly on this emphasis of heart holiness (it was biblical before it became theological), recent serious books and articles from those outside the Wesleyan holiness movement are calling strongly and clearly to renewed emphasis on a holy heart and a holy life.

See ENTIRE SANCTIFICATION, PERFECT LOVE, ERADICATION.

For Further Reading: *"Kadapos,"* Kittel; "Purity," *NBD*; *"Kadapos," Synonyms of the New Testament,* by Archbishop Trench.

GEORGE E. FAILING

HEATHEN, FATE OF. Respecting the eternal destiny of heathen who have not heard the gospel of Christ, Abraham's question suggests one confident answer: "Shall not the Judge of all the earth do right?" (Gen. 18:25).

Several issues are raised. First, is any person saved apart from Christ's redemptive work on Calvary? Second, does any person's salvation depend entirely on hearing and believing the record of Jesus' life and words? And thirdly, how do some theologians speak to this matter?

In answer to the first question it must be affirmed that Jesus Christ is the only Savior of men. Not one person can enter heaven except by "the blood of the Lamb" (Rev. 12:11). No one is saved either by cultural religion or by self-generated goodness. Only the Second Adam can undo the damage and ruin brought upon all men by the first Adam's sin.

The interpretation of Acts 4:12 is often questioned. To affirm that there is "none other name under heaven" is to affirm that there is no Savior except Jesus Christ. However, to imply that only men who hear that name and know His story (as told in the four Gospels) can be saved, is to affirm something else. John Wesley, in his sermon "On Faith," pitied the heathen for "the narrowness of their faith. And their not believing the whole truth is not owing to want of sincerity, but merely to want of light" (*Works,* 7:197). And in his comments on Acts 10:34-35 in *Explanatory Notes upon the NT,* Wesley believed that Cornelius was accepted "through Christ, though he knows him not. He is in the favor of God, whether enjoying his written word and ordinances or not."

The noted Baptist theologian A. H. Strong, whose *Systematic Theology* is still in print, believed that "no human soul is eternally condemned solely for this sin of nature, but that, on the other hand, all who have not consciously and willfully transgressed are made partakers of Christ's salvation" (*Theology,* 664). Strong also expressed the hope "that even among the heathen there may be some, like Socrates, who, under the guidance of the Holy Spirit working through the truth of nature and conscience, have found the way of life and salvation" (843).

Richard S. Taylor, in his chapter "A Theology of Missions" in the volume *Ministering to the Millions,* writes, "No man can possibly be finally lost entirely as a result of what someone else does or does not do. Every man will be judged according to what *he* does in the body, not what someone else does (II Cor. 5:10; Ezek. 18:19-21). This means that the lostness of the heathen is not due simply and exclusively to their ignorance of the gospel, but due to their willful failure to walk in the light they have. They will be judged by that light, not ours (Rom. 2:4-16) . . . Since we believe that the mercy of God, through the atoning work of Christ, provides for the salvation of infants, and also regenerate believers who have not yet received light on entire sanctification, it is not unreasonable to grant the same mercy to the repentant heathen."

Wesley, Strong, and Taylor suggest scriptures which encourage us to believe that God's initiatives in salvation are not restricted to what Christians do in missionary labors.

See GREAT COMMISSION, EVANGELISM, MISSION (MISSIONS, MISSIOLOGY).

For Further Reading: Taylor, "A Theology of Missions," *Ministering to the Millions;* Anderson, ed., *The Theology of the Christian Mission;* Stewart, *Thine Is the Kingdom;* Wesley, *Works,* 7:353, 506; 8:337; *CC,* Acts 10:35.

GEORGE E. FAILING

HEAVEN. "Heaven" in contemporary language refers to the eternal abode of God. In contrast, the OT term *shamayim* and the NT term *ouranos* express a wide variety of concepts. They may refer to the physical universe which is created (Gen. 1:1) and will be destroyed (Joel 3:16; Matt. 24:25 ff) to be recreated with the earth into the "new heaven" and the "new earth" (Isa. 65:17; 66:22; 2 Pet. 3:13; Rev. 21:1). They may also refer to the spiritual creation, the realm inhabited by principalities and powers (Eph. 3:10) which, though nonphysical, is also subject to change and to reconquest by Christ who must reign "until he has put all his enemies under his feet" (1 Cor. 15:25, RSV).

As the eternal abode of God, heaven is transcendent and changeless. God dwells there and Christ is "exalted" above the heavens (Ps. 57:5; Heb. 7:26). The Christian, though a created son, is also to inherit a kingdom which cannot be shaken (Heb. 12:28), where he is to live in an imperishable body (1 Cor. 15:42), "a house not made with hands, eternal in the heavens" (2 Cor. 5:1, RSV). As the eternal abode of God (Matt. 5:18), heaven is no more describable by spatial language than eternity is by the language of time. For example, the "heaven and the highest heaven cannot contain" God (1 Kings 8:27; 2 Chron. 6:18, RSV); "The kingdom of God is within you" (Luke 17:21); "The dwelling of God is with man" (Rev. 21:3, RSV) and "with him who is of a contrite and humble spirit" (Isa. 57:15, RSV). Christ fills all things (Eph. 4:10) and God is near at hand (Rom. 10:6-8). Even as God is omnipresent, so heaven in this sense is everywhere God is.

The Scriptures also describe heaven as the source of everything in this world that is authentic, good, changeless, and subject to God's will. The authenticity of John's baptism is tested by its origin: "Whence was it? From heaven or from men?" (Matt. 21:25, RSV). Jesus and His work are from "heaven" and "above" (John 3:13, 31, 35). Accordingly "every good gift and every perfect gift is from above" (Jas. 1:17; see Matt. 19:17) and the kingdom of heaven on earth is identified as God's will being done "in earth, as it is in heaven" (Matt. 6:10).

As the Christian's hope and eternal home, heaven is both a place and the perfect experience of God's presence. The place Jesus prepares for us is an abode (*monē,* John 14:2, 23), and His presence is an abiding (*menō,* vv. 10, 17, 25; 15:4-10). As the place prepared for those who love God, heaven's quality exceeds the language of wealth, of gold and jasper (Rev. 21:18); it is "what no eye has seen, nor ear heard" (1 Cor. 2:9, RSV; cf. Isa. 64:4). It is a place of holiness (Isa. 35:8; Rev. 22:3), of love (1 Cor. 13:13; Eph. 3:19), of rest (Heb. 4:9), of joy (12:2; Luke 15:7), of knowledge (1 Cor. 13:12), and of perfect service and sonship (Rev. 22:3; Rom. 8:17). Nothing that is unclean or that destroys can dwell there (Rev. 21:8, 27). There, every tear shall be wiped away and there shall be no death, no mourning, nor pain, for everything will become new (vv. 4-5).

See ETERNAL LIFE, RESURRECTION OF THE BODY.

For Further Reading: *IDB,* E-J:551-52; *GMS,* 668-75; *ISBE,* 2:1352-54; Wiley, *CT,* 3:375-93.

DAVID L. CUBIE

HEILSGESCHICHTE. This term, literally meaning "holy history," identifies a movement in biblical and systematic theology which understands that the divine provision for salvation relates uniquely to history, especially the events of biblical history. Thus, this German term is frequently translated "history of salvation" or "history of redemption." While the word has been used by others in biblical interpretation (Bengel and the dispensationalists), it has been particularly identified with J. Christian K. von Hofmann, a Lutheran theologian, who insisted that interpreters of the Bible must take the events of biblical history seriously in dealing with matters of revelation and salvation. In his principal writing, *Der Schriftbeweis,* he asserted that the Bible was not to be treated basically as a textbook in theology, morals, or philosophy of religion, but as the story of God's redeeming acts in particular historical events. The entire Bible is an account of God's saving action in behalf of sinful mankind. Together, then, the Old and New Testaments constitute this salvation history. Out of this seminal idea of von Hofmann developed what has become known as *Die Heilsgeschichtlich Schule,* the holy history or salvation history school.

The central theses of this theological movement, as now conceived generally, are:

1. God, taking the initiative, has revealed himself in saving ways in particular events in history. These events are recorded in the Bible and relate to the history of Israel, to Christ, and to His Church. Theology, therefore, is interwoven with this history. The "mighty events," that is, the events which carry the heaviest weight of revelation, are the calling of Abraham, the Exodus from Egypt, the Exile, and the incarnation, death, and resurrection of Christ. From the Christian viewpoint the "mightiest event" is the incarnation of Christ and all that ensues from it.

2. These revelatory events are real historical happenings and are part of the larger stream of human history. God, however, has chosen to reveal himself and His saving purposes through these events.

3. Salvation is not reserved for those who happen to be in this line of history; the salvation of the whole of human history relates to this one particular line of history.

4. Time, in contradistinction to the Greek cyclical view, is linear. History is moving to a consummation, to a final day. Salvation history declares that at some future moment God will bring His redeeming work to a conclusion. Already the power of the future age is being realized through Christ, but the day of fulfillment is yet to come. The Jew still looks for the day of fulfillment in the coming of the Messiah, but the Christian has already gained assurance of final salvation because the Messiah has already appeared. A tension exists nevertheless between the "already fulfilled" and the "not yet consummated" dimensions of the salvation God has provided.

The major criticism of *Heilsgeschichte* relate to its concepts of revelation in history and time. Serious questions have also been raised as to the relationship between the saving events and the record of these events in the Bible.

See HISTORICAL JESUS (THE), DEMYTHOLOGIZATION, BIBLE.

For Further Reading: Cullmann, *Christ and Time; Salvation in History;* Barr, *The Semantics of Biblical Language;* Kümmel, *The New Testament: The History of the Investigation of Its Problems;* Ladd, "The Saving Acts of God," *Christianity Today,* 18 (1961); Rust, *The Christian Understanding of History.* WILLARD H. TAYLOR

HEIR. Israel's patriarchal society involved a great variety of legal language directing and controlling the process of inheritance. Rich theological connotations grew out of reflection upon Israel's relationship with the God of the covenant. The NT carries these ideas still further in describing the decisive work of God in Christ.

Both the OT and the NT use the normal meaning of the terms in discussion of legal transfer of property from one generation to another. Jesus, for example, is asked to arbitrate in a dispute over an inheritance (Luke 12:13).

The first stage in theologizing begins with the affirmation that Canaan is Israel's inheritance (Deut. 4:21; Josh. 1:6; etc.). The second stage is the recognition that Israel as a people is God's inheritance (Exod. 19:5; Deut. 7:6). The failures of Israel as a nation led to the spiritualizing of the symbolism of inheritance. The prophets and the wisdom writers use such terminology regularly.

The NT speaks of inheriting eternal life (Matt. 19:29) and the Kingdom (25:34). In the parable of the wicked tenants, Jesus is understood to be the Heir and the kingdom of God is the vineyard (21:38-43). Paul considers those in Christ as heirs of Abraham (Gal. 3:29) and fellow-heirs with Christ (Rom. 8:17). In Ephesians Paul understands the Holy Spirit to be the guarantee of the inheritance in the future Kingdom (1:13-14). Hebrews speaks of the death of Christ as the enactment of the will or covenant of God (9:16-17).

It is clear that inheritance has moved from specifically legal and earthly language to powerful spiritual and heavenly language. The major focus of the theologizing revolves about the concept of God as it is definitively expressed in the Christ event.

See CHILD (CHILDREN), ADOPTION, INHERITANCE.

For Further Reading: Foerster, "Klēronomia," Kittel, 3:758 ff; Hammer, "A Comparison of Klēronomia in Paul and Ephesians," *Journal of Biblical Literature,* 79:267-72. MORRIS A. WEIGELT

HELL. This term refers to eternal punishment. To the Hebrew mind the idea of extinction was unacceptable. The dead continue to exist in an underworld of shadow and silence. The word used in the OT was *sheol,* which had as its equivalent in the NT the word *hadēs.*

Sheol was divided into two areas: paradise, the meeting place of the righteous dead, and gehenna, reserved for the wicked. While the Greek word *hadēs* is often translated by the English word "hell," it is *gehenna* which is employed in association with the punishment element. According to Matt. 10:28, while the souls of the wicked go to *hadēs* after death, both soul and body are cast into *gehenna* after the resurrection and final Judgment.

The historical background to the Hebrew usage of the word *gehenna* is in relation to the "valley of Hinnom," near Jerusalem. Here child sacrifice had been offered to Moloch, a cult god, by Ahaz (2 Chron. 28:3) and by Manasseh (33:6). It was reputed to have become the city's refuse dump, where fire continually burned and so was seen as a type for the idea of punishment, relating to fire (as developed later). In late Jewish literature, e.g., Enoch 27:2, Gehenna became the popular name for the place of future punishment.

While the doctrine of hell has its sources in Hebrew and Greek thought, it was the early Christian centuries which gave the doctrine shape. Of the many ideas expounded, the main view maintained is that which denotes separation from God. Wiley says that "those who reject Christ and the salvation offered through Him shall die in their sins and be separated from God forever."

In the development of the doctrine in the Church, the term *hadēs* came to be closely associated with the thought of punishment. The NT illustration of the rich man and Lazarus is often used to illustrate the teaching on future rewards and punishment. Lazarus is depicted as being in "Abraham's bosom," sometimes likened to Eden, while the rich man was also dead, but he is found in torment.

Whatever the nature of future punishment, it seems difficult to avoid the severity of Jesus' words against unrepented sin. No amount of sentiment can take from the implication of these words. Mark 9:43 speaks of "unquenchable fire," while Matt. 18:8 uses the phrase "eternal fire" (both RSV). To treat these as purely symbolic is not a liberty we dare assume.

The NT does not answer many of the questions which arise to our minds, but there is no doubt left as to the seriousness of sin and its consequences. Hell at least is a negation of the real values of life as related to personal moral integrity.

See ETERNAL PUNISHMENT, RETRIBUTION (RETRIBUTIVE JUSTICE), SOWING AND REAPING, JUDGE (JUDGMENT), HADES, GEHENNA.

For Further Reading: Richardson, ed., *A Theological Word Book of the Bible;* Wiley, *CT,* 3:356-75; Rowell, *Hell and the Victorians.*

HUGH RAE

HELLENISM. Hellenism is the term for the culture arising in Hellas or Greece. It refers to the original culture, called Hellenic, and its development after Alexander the Great into a form including other cultural accretions and known as Hellenistic.

Hellenism is one of the most powerful factors in Western civilization. Contained in it are the grand epics of Homer; the beginnings of philosophy along with its profound development in Socrates, Plato, and Aristotle; the production of drama, architectural splendor, and other artistic achievements; as well as the military, political, and cultural accomplishments of Alexander; and indeed the extraordinary Greek language.

The so-called intertestamental period provides the historical development of the Hebrew encounter with Greek military forces as well as Greek modes of thought and practice. And it was during this period that the Greek language became so widespread that even the OT was translated into Greek in Alexandria (the Septuagint, or LXX). The extra books (i.e., the Apocrypha, not found in the Hebrew Scriptures) which were in this translation were widely used in the NT Church and were accepted as canonical in the 16th century by the Roman Catholic church. The Wisdom of Solomon in the Apocrypha is called the crowning work of Hellenistic-Hebrew synthesis, and Philo Judaeus (c. 20 B.C.—A.D. 50) of Alexandria is an important example of Hellenistic-Hebrew synthesis.

Christian theology derives much of its methodology from Greek principles of thought: Christian mysticism has a neo-Platonic base; Thomism is profoundly Aristotelian; *Logos* has Greek roots; and Christian views of God derive from Plato and Aristotle.

Logic, systematic thinking, and rationality have been carefully examined and developed by the Greek mind as interpretations of human nature and the world.

The Western world cannot comprehend its own unfolding without some very careful elucidation of the role of Hellenism in that process.

See JUDAISM, HEILSGESCHICHTE, HISTORICAL THEOLOGY, PHILOSOPHY, PLATONISM, THOMISM.

For Further Reading: *Sacramentum Mundi,* 3:10-16; *NIDCC,* 430-31. R. DUANE THOMPSON

HERESY. Heresy has come to mean deviation from belief and worship commonly accepted by the Christian Church.

The Greek word for heresy, *hairesis,* is used more broadly. It means a chosen course of thought or action, and refers to sects within Judaism (Acts 5:17; 24:5; 26:5) and factions within the Church (Gal. 5:20; 1 Cor. 11:19). The strong rebuke of these factions implies a unity of faith and practice which ought to be safeguarded and preserved among Christians.

Concern for unity led to the traditional understanding of heresy as serious and rebellious departure from established doctrine. It begins to emerge in the NT, especially in the Pastoral Epistles, with their injunctions to teach sound doctrine and oppose false teaching (1 Tim. 1:3-11; 4:1-16; 2 Tim. 1:13-14; 4:1-5; Titus 1:9—2:1), and in 2 Peter 2, where "false teachers" and "destructive heresies" (RSV) are vehemently exposed.

Heresy implies orthodoxy, an objective standard of doctrine and life against which aberrant opinions may be measured. Heresy required the formulation of approved creeds, summaries of the Church's understanding of its faith. As early as the NT period "the faith" and "the truth" as a body of normative teaching appears (1 Tim. 1:15; 2:4-6; 2 Tim. 1:14; Titus 3:4-8). Creedal fragments preserved in Scripture, however, were insufficient, and the great creeds of the fourth and fifth centuries became standards of orthodoxy. These identified and suppressed the most virulent heresies, those which falsified the trinity of the Godhead and the full humanity and/or deity of Jesus Christ.

When church and state are united, heresy is often legally punished. This occasioned sad chapters of brutal persecution in church history. Torture and execution of heretics created sympathy for heretical opinion. Arrogant orthodoxy proved its own worst enemy.

Heresy is too serious to be carelessly charged against anyone. It must refer to centuries-abiding essentials of Christian belief and practice, not to denominational variants of this continuing core of apostolic traditions.

See ORTHODOXY, DOGMA (DOGMATICS), CREED (CREEDS), GNOSTICISM.

For Further Reading: *HDNT,* 246; Kittel, 1:180-85; Kelly, *Early Christian Creeds.* W. E. MCCUMBER

HERMENEUTICS. This is the science of interpretation, especially of the Scriptures. It is that branch of theology that deals with the principles of biblical exegesis, understood as seeking and setting forth the original meanings of the biblical text.

The term is derived from a NT word, *hermēneuō* ("explain, interpret, or translate"); from which comes *hermēneia* ("interpretation, explanation"). Devout biblical interpretation seeks to discover meanings, not to decide them. To suggest meanings foreign to the original intent is *eisegesis* ("reading into") rather than *exegesis* ("reading out of").

Principles of hermeneutics may be suggested as follows:

1. Recognition that the Bible is God's Word in a totally unique and authoritative way. It is divinely and fully inspired, and while subject to grammatico-historical understanding, is to be approached with reverent amenability to its teaching.

2. Attention to literary form. Literary genre is a frame of reference logically prior to the words themselves. The Bible embraces many literary forms—poetry, proverbial wisdom, history, chronicle, sermon, oracle, parable, allegory, apocalyptic, Epistle—each of which must be interpreted in a manner proper to itself.

3. Awareness of Hebraisms in both OT and NT. Although written in Greek, the NT is basically a Hebraic writing, and its characteristic thought forms are those of the OT.

Examples of such Hebraisms are the use of "hate" for a lesser degree of love (Luke 14:26) and the statement of comparisons in absolute terms (John 6:27, which does not forbid working for a living; and 1 Tim. 5:23, which does not forbid drinking water).

Colloquialisms are used and must be understood as such. "Three days and three nights" (Matt. 12:40) does not mean 72 hours but "a very short time," as is seen in the fact that all four Gospels declare the crucifixion and burial of Jesus to have occurred on "the preparation" (the normal Greek term for Friday) and the Resurrection on the morning of the first day of the week (Sunday, Mark 16:9); and the NT declares 16 times that the Resurrection took place on "the third day."

Hebrew writers frequently employ what is called "the prophetic present" or "prophetic perfect," in which future events that are seen as certain are spoken of as already occurring (Isa. 9:6, the birth of Messiah, 700 years in the future, spoken of as accomplished; Rom. 8:30, future glorification described in the present tense).

4. Special attention must be given to the key

words in any passage under consideration. Individual words are the ultimate units of meaning. Meanings of words are determined in two ways: by lexicon or dictionary definition; and even more significantly, by their usage in any piece of writing. Hence the observation of A. B. Davidson that the concordance is often more important than the lexicon in determining the meanings of words.

5. Key words must be related to the content of the passage as a whole in its context. The principle rule of exegesis is "context." Context is of two kinds: literary and historical. Literary context is the paragraph, the chapter, the book, the Testament, and ultimately the whole of Scripture. The part must be interpreted in light of the whole.

Historical context is what the words would have meant to the persons by whom they were originally written, as far as it is possible for us to find out. The literal meaning (as versus any allegorizing) is what the sentences signify in a normal, customary sense in their historical context.

6. Interpretation in the light of progressive revelation. Especially must the exegete be careful about reading back into the OT the religious experiences and ethics of the NT. *Where* a statement appears in Scripture determines its theological weight and to some extent its very meaning. "Sanctify" does not mean in Josh. 3:5 what it does in John 17:17. Eccles. 3:19 cannot be taken to cancel the meaning of 2 Cor. 5:1-8 and Phil. 1:21-24 as to the state of the Christian soul between death and the resurrection.

There is unity in Scripture, but the core of that unity is Christ. The whole of Scripture interprets the parts of Scripture, and no part may be interpreted in such fashion as to distort the whole. The circularity implied here is overcome by application to the generalizations of a sound biblical theology, which is the theological exegesis of the Bible.

See BIBLE, EXEGESIS, BIBLICAL THEOLOGY, BIBLICAL REALISM, CRITICISM (OT, NT), TEXTUAL CRITICISM, PROGRESSIVE REVELATION, BIBLICAL AUTHORITY.

For Further Reading: Farrar, *History of Interpretation;* Gilbert, *Interpretation of the Bible;* Grant, *The Bible in the Church;* Kuitert, *Do You Understand What You Read?* Ramm, et al., "Hermeneutics," *Baker's Dictionary of Practical Theology,* 99-147; Taylor, *Biblical Authority and Christian Faith.*

W. T. PURKISER

HETERODOXY. See ORTHODOXY.

HIERARCHICALISM. Hierarchicalism is one way the problem of authority is resolved, especially as authority is defined for either a religious cultus or an ethical system. For a religious cultus, the problem of authority is often resolved by structuring a vertical ranking or grading of its communicants according to the nature or amount of responsibility the cultus assigns to each. In an ethical system, rules are sometimes arranged in a pyramid so that when two or more rules of that system conflict in a certain moral dilemma, the one designated by that system as having greater value operates over the rule having lesser value.

There are two fundamental constraints found in most hierarchical structures of authority. First, the ranking or grading of rules or of communicants in a very real sense depends upon the *historical situation* in which the religion or ethical system operates. While there remains an absolute ordering of rules or communicants which operates in any situation, there is a certain dialectic or dynamic in how that ordering actually works itself out in reality. For instance, a conflict of wills between a person and his boss might be resolved by obeying the will of the boss as one having the greater authority in this case. However, let's say a conflict breaks out between the will of the boss and some higher authority (e.g., God); in this case, it is the will of the boss which is disregarded. This same principle applies to the cultus as well. Certainly in the Pauline material, the hierarchy of the Church is ordered by "gift" or by "call," and both of these categories arise out of and are related to churches with specific (i.e., historical) needs for those "gifts" or "callings."

Second, the ranking of members ought never be enforced in a degrading manner. Members of an ethical system (rules) or a religious body (communicants) are ranked according to *function* and not inherent worth. In a hierarchical system of ethics, for instance, the question is never whether the lesser rules have lesser morality or lead to a lesser moral existence; indeed, every rule has moral content (deontology) or can lead when obeyed to a moral existence (teleology). In a religious organization, every communicant, whether priest or parishioner, has equal worth before God and should also before humankind. A Christian hierarchicalism maintains that it is Scripture's stress that the people of God are likened as a Church to the very structure of the Triune Deity: like the Godhead, the people of God are one in substance, and like the Godhead, the people of God are different in function.

See CHRISTIAN ETHICS, AUTHORITY, CHAIN OF COMMAND, CHURCH GOVERNMENT, DUTY, THEISTIC PROOFS.

For Further Reading: Geisler, *Ethics: Alternatives and Issues.*

ROBERT W. WALL

HIGH PRIEST. Once the priesthood is established in Israel, one from among them is to be "chief among his brethren" (Lev. 21:10, RSV), serving as the high priest. Aaron, brother of Moses, is set aside for this office (Exodus 28—29), to be succeeded by his son Eleazar and his descendants. (For a time some of the later high priests are descended from Ithamar, another of Aaron's sons, but the office is returned to the line of Eleazar in Zadok during Solomon's reign.)

During Israel's national existence (until 587 B.C.) the high priest is an important spiritual figure. Following the Babylonian exile, secular responsibilities are added to the office of high priest. We see the high priest Joshua placed on the same level with the Davidic governor Zerubbabel, but with the disappearance of Davidic rulers the high priest becomes head of the Jewish state. Under the Hasmoneans (c. 164 B.C.) eight high priests took the title of king. Following Roman conquest (64 B.C.) and Herodian rule, the office became a tool of the administrators.

The religious importance of the high priest is reflected in the biblical instructions given for his consecration which lasted for seven days. This consecration included (1) purification, with washing and special sacrifices; (2) special clothing signifying his office, and (3) anointing with oil. The high priest was to be scrupulous in observing ceremonial purity; any sin he committed was especially grave and required a special sin offering (Lev. 4:3-12).

The authority of the high priest was supreme in spiritual matters. His functions included offering sacrifices, intercession, and giving the Torah, all on the common basis that he was an intermediary between God and man. His most important function occurred on the Day of Atonement when he alone entered into the holy of holies to make atonement (Leviticus 16). Significantly, he must atone for his own sin before acting on behalf of Israel (Heb. 5:3).

In the NT Christ is the perfect High Priest of the new covenant, fulfilling everything represented in the high priest of Judaism. The Epistle to the Hebrews presents Christ in this fashion, one with the Father through eternal Sonship (chap. 1), yet by His incarnation perfectly identified with man (2:14-18; 4:15; 5:1-10). Thus He is the perfect Mediator who once and for all offers himself as atonement for sin (9:11-28; 10:11-18) and opens a new and living way into the very presence of God (10:19-25).

Christ is also unique as High Priest. His death was not that of a mere mortal, but that of a priest offering himself as a sacrifice for man's sin. Being sinless, He did not need to offer sacrifice for himself, and it is His own blood which He offers in God's presence, not that of animals. Moreover, the order of His priesthood is not after Aaron, but Melchizedek, who was without predecessor or successor. Finally, Christ continues forever an effective ministry of intercession from His seat at the right hand of the Father.

See MOSAIC LAW, PENTATEUCH, PRIEST (PRIESTHOOD), CHRIST, MELCHIZEDEK, MEDIATION (MEDIATOR), PRIESTHOOD OF BELIEVERS, DAY OF ATONEMENT.

For Further Reading: *IDB*, 3:876-91; *NBD*, 1028-34; de Vaux, *Ancient Israel*, 2:397-403.

ALVIN S. LAWHEAD

HIGH PRIESTHOOD OF CHRIST. "High Priest" (Gr. *archiereus*) is the title ascribed to Jesus Christ at least 12 times in the NT, notably in Hebrews (2:17; 3:1; 4:14-15; 5:5, 10; 6:20; 7:26; 8:1, 3; 9:11; 10:21). In numerous other instances the term is implied both in Hebrews and in other NT passages, such as in Christ's High-Priestly prayer (John 17) and in His cleansing of the Temple (2:13-17). That His was a royal office is indicated by reference to Melchizedek, who was king of righteousness and peace and a priest of God Most High (Heb. 5:6; 7:12; Ps. 110:4; Gen. 14:18). Christ's High Priesthood is the central theme of the Hebrew Epistle.

In His incarnation, Christ united divinity with humanity in order to become the instrument of God's saving efficacy to lost men, and to become man's High-Priestly Representative before the Father. Christ's High Priesthood involved intercession for himself (John 17:1-5), for His disciples (vv. 6-19, 22-26), and for the unconverted (vv. 20-21). He exercised His High-Priestly ministry by offering himself to God on the altar of His cross where He "made purification of sins" (Heb. 1:3, NASB). Having accomplished this redemptive act, Christ "sat down at the right hand of the Majesty on High" (ibid.), having removed the veil between the holy place and the holy of holies, thus providing permanent access to the immediate presence of God, both for himself and all who accept His Saviorhood (Matt. 27:51; Heb. 6:20; 9:3; 10:19-20).

Since Christ suffered all our human weaknesses and temptations in His humanity, He sympathizes with our cause as He represents us before the Father (Heb. 4:15). The expression "sat down at the right hand of the Majesty on high" denotes Christ's redemptive accomplishment which looks back to His final word on the Cross, "It is finished" (John 19:30). Wesley says, "The priests stood while they ministered: *sitting,* therefore, denotes the consummation of His sacrifice" (*Notes,* 811).

The virtue of Christ's High-Priestly atonement is both retroactive and prospective for man's salvation. "His high priesthood is perfect and permanent, as compared with the temporary and imperfect Aaronic system, and is typified by Melchizedek (Heb. 5:6, 10; 6:13—7:17)" (S. E. Johnson, *IDB,* A-D, 568).

See CHRIST, ESTATES OF CHRIST, CHRISTOLOGY.

For Further Reading: Davidson, *The Epistle to the Hebrews,* "Extended Notes on the Priesthood of Christ," 146-54; Carter, "Hebrews," *WBC,* vol. 6; Thomas, *Let Us Go On,* chaps. 2; 10; 14—16; 18.

CHARLES W. CARTER

HIGHER CRITICISM. See CRITICISM (NT, OT).

HIGHER LIFE. The *higher life* is a term commonly used by non-Wesleyan adherents of the holiness movement to describe the quality of Christian life experienced by those who have been filled with the Holy Spirit in a moment of faith and commitment subsequent to their justification and regeneration.

William E. Boardman, author of *The Higher Christian Life* (1858), one of the first leaders in this movement, was directly influenced by the American Wesleyan holiness teaching on entire sanctification; however, Boardman, like others who followed him, consciously sought to make his newfound experience more theologically winsome to his non-Methodist public by using new terminology for it.

This "higher life" teaching spread the Wesleyan teaching of two stages in the believer's restoration to fullest relationship with God to every major Protestant tradition. Robert Pearsall Smith and Hannah Whitall Smith, along with William E. Boardman, Asa Mahan, and sympathetic English Methodists, introduced the message to a broad spectrum of English and Continental evangelicals after 1873. The famous Keswick Convention was born out of this coalition, creating a bridge for the message to pervade Anglican evangelicalism. The Keswick holiness tradition continues to be influential in the evangelical tradition around the world.

This "fullness of the Spirit" as a distinct experience essential to effective Christian living was preached to the larger evangelical public by such influential leaders as Dwight Moody, Reuben Torrey, Arthur Pierson, and others. Such leaders, along with espousal by such influential fundamentalist voices as the *Sunday School Times* and the publications of Moody Bible Institute, assured that all American evangelicalism—Calvinistic and Wesleyan—was infused with a "second blessing" emphasis on holiness.

See HOLINESS MOVEMENT, KESWICK (KESWICKIANISM), WESLEYANISM.

For Further Reading: Marsden, *Fundamentalism and American Culture;* Warfield, *Perfectionism;* Dieter, *The Holiness Revival of the Nineteenth Century.*

MELVIN EASTERDAY DIETER

HINDUISM. See NON-CHRISTIAN RELIGIONS.

HISTORICAL JESUS, THE. The historical Jesus is the Jesus who really lived, distinct from the myths and legends about Him. The NT reports the Christ event in terms of this Jesus. In Him the divine and the supernatural, as well as the human, are "historical actuality."

The term, however, came into common use in a context of doubt. With the shift from Reformation faith to Renaissance rationalism and naturalism in much of historical criticism, human reason discounted the divine and supernatural as myth. Negative criticism has concluded (with Bultmann and others) that the real Jesus has been obscured by Christian faith. Since the only significant documents were written by people of faith, they were suspected of enthusiastic imagination. Though Bultmann considered the search for the historical Jesus hopeless, he tried by form criticism *(formgeschichte)* to peel away layers of tradition from the Gospels to come nearer to the real Jesus. Disappointed by his negative results, some of his disciples have made "new quests."

The assumption that the supernatural is mythical has, for many, robbed the reported data of historical actuality. Interacting with this approach was the tendency to date the Gospels too late for any witnesses that had been acquainted with Jesus in the flesh. On this theory, the Gospels came not from Jesus through the apostles but from the creative faith and preaching of the Early Church. Though the supposed time gap between Gospel events and Gospel records has shrunk and the credibility of the evangelists has risen, negative criticism is still extant.

History is defined as "events in time and space with social significance" (E. E. Cairns, "History," *ZPEB,* 3:162). The Christ event, then, is of supreme significance. As "absolute history," it did indeed occur only once and so cannot be studied statistically by scientific analysis (ibid.). Again, the four Gospels were never intended as full biographies or complete histories. But they do contain the essential facts in a clear and reliable manner for the countless useful volumes on the life and ministry of Jesus. And the whole NT interprets His significance in history. This is in perfect accord with the early use of the German word for history *(geschichte)*.

See DEMYTHOLOGIZATION, BIBLE, BIBLICAL INERRANCY, CRITICISM (NT), FORM CRITICISM.

For Further Reading: Marshall, *I Believe in the Historical Jesus;* Cairns, "History," *ZPEB,* 3:162 ff; Simon Kistemaker, *The Gospels in Current Study,* 63-77.

WILBER T. DAYTON

HISTORICAL THEOLOGY. This is a study of Christian theology as it has been taught in all the centuries of our era. Taking the writings of individual theologians, and considering the creeds and confessions of the church, along with the movements that have arisen, and whatever else might relate importantly to Christian beliefs, historical theology studies them all for the light they throw upon what our teachings and our emphases and our gravitating interests ought to be in the time when it is ours to serve Christ.

Such a study will help us to avoid repeating the doctrinal errors that have arisen at earlier times. It will help us, also, to conserve the important doctrinal emphases of our own kind of Christian tradition. Study of the errors and the near errors, also, helps us to refine aspects of Christian doctrine in ways that are more biblical and more practically useful than otherwise our theology would be. It helps us, further, to know what is the historical background of various groupings of Christians that we might associate with in local communities.

See BIBLICAL THEOLOGY, SYSTEMATIC THEOLOGY.

J. KENNETH GRIDER

HISTORICISM. Historicism is the view that all of reality can be explained by reference to historical development. In this broad sense it is compatible with views which see history as under a controlling Providence, or as manifesting certain identifiable laws in some meaningful pattern. However, the concept generally assumes a radical relativism with respect to history. In this view history is the manifestation of the unique, the individual, the ever-changing, without reference to any pattern, underlying structure, or meaning. The concept of *eternal truth* is obviously negated by such an outlook. Values, truth, and falsity are seen as altogether relative to the particular historical moment in which they are formulated. Arising out of the Enlightenment and attaining forceful expression in the 19th century, this form of historicism underlaid the work of a generation of historians who sought to gather only the concrete historical "facts" with no attempt at historical theory or evaluation.

Historicism in the broad sense therefore may be biblical and Christian, since the biblical revelation is uniquely an historical revelation, including the very incarnation of God in concrete time and existence. The narrower, thoroughly relativistic expression of historicism is, however, incompatible with biblical affirmations of God's sovereignty over, and redemptive purposes in, history.

See PROVIDENCE, PROPHET (PROPHECY), TIME, ESCHATOLOGY, HEILSGESCHICHTE, PRIMAL HISTORY.

For Further Reading: D'Arcy, *The Meaning and Matter of History;* Lee and Beck, "The Meaning of Historicism," *American Historical Review,* 59 (1953-54): 568-77; Maier, "Historicism," *Sacramentum Mundi,* 3:29-31; Harvey, *A Handbook of Theological Terms,* 119; Ramm, *A Handbook of Contemporary Theology,* 59.

HAROLD E. RASER

HISTORY OF RELIGION. See COMPARATIVE RELIGION.

HISTORY, PRIMAL. See PRIMAL HISTORY.

HOLINESS. When God began to reveal himself to Israel, one of His problems was language. Man's speech was as fallen as man himself. To reveal himself, God had to redeem man's words. Nowhere is that story more obvious than in the development of a biblical vocabulary for holiness.

Every culture differentiates the sacred from the secular and has terminology to make that distinction. Canaan already had such terms when Israel adopted its language. The problem was that what was holy to the Canaanite was abominable to Jehovah. In Canaan the temple prostitute was a holy woman and the homosexual priest was a holy man (cf. Gen. 38:21-23; Deut. 23:17-18). The result of this is that the adjective "holy" is not found in the English translation of the Book of Genesis. The words for the holy had to be filled with new content before they were usable. That process begins in Exod. 3:5 and continues throughout the Pentateuch. Only Jehovah and that which is associated with Him is to merit that description.

The writers of the NT had a similar problem. Five terms were available: *hieros, hosios, semnos, hagios, hagnos.* All, though, had associations with the pagan gods, their temples, or their services. The writers of the Septuagint, in seeking an equivalent for the OT *kadosh,* chose *hagios.* This was the least used of the five terms in Greek literature. It never occurs in Homer, Hesiod, or the Tragedians. It is not used in the Greek literature in reference to gods or man. It was the least familiar and the least corrupted. This term was related in the Septuagint to Jehovah and used to describe His essential nature. The writers of the NT take this term as the primary NT word for "holy." From it a family of terms developed which do not occur in classical Greek. Thus the unique character of the holiness of Jehovah found vocabulary to express itself.

The above illustrates the thrust of this article. Our understanding of God's holiness must not be determined by our language and concepts. He alone is holy in himself. All holiness finds its origin in Him. He must determine the content of the words that uniquely describe Him.

The process of defining *kadosh* and *hagios* begins with Exod. 3:5. The ground on which Moses stands is holy because Jehovah is there. Holiness is inseparably related to His presence. After this many things and persons are called holy in the OT. The land, Jerusalem, the Temple site, the Temple itself, its precincts, the vessels used in its service, the persons who minister there, and the sacrifices that are properly devoted to Jehovah are all called holy.

Such holiness comes only by association with the presence of Jehovah and is an imparted holiness. Where He is, His presence sanctifies or judges. Without His presence, all is profane. Where His presence is welcomed, His holiness is imparted. Where His presence is rejected, His holiness inexorably brings judgment. Certain phrases found especially in Leviticus as sanctions to the law are used synonymously and interchangeably and express this identification of Jehovah and sanctification. "I am Jehovah," "I am holy," "I am Jehovah who sanctifies you," "I am Jehovah your God, who sets you apart" (cf. Lev. 19:1, 4, 10, 12; 20:7, 24, 26; 21:8, 12, 15, 23, et al.; free translation).

Holiness is not to be treated as simply another of the attributes of God. If thought of as an attribute, it must be seen as the attribute of attributes, the essence of God's character which determines the nature of His attributes. It is the outshining of the goodness of the Living God.

God's holiness speaks of His difference from His creatures in terms of His transcendence, majesty, moral and ethical perfection, and sovereign love. When confronted by God's holiness, man is smitten by a consciousness of his creatureliness and of his sin. His proper response is awe, reverence, fear, and guilt (cf. Exod. 20:18-19; Isa. 6:5-7; Luke 5:8; Rev. 1:17). For man this divine holiness is both attractive and repelling (cf. Ps. 96:9; 99:1-3, 9; et al.). To the man who will not be separated from his sin, it is destruction (Exodus 32 and Num. 11:1-3).

The holiness of God is always moral and ethical. It is always related to God's love. The Decalogue is an expression of this, given to a people whom God has lovingly redeemed (Exod. 20:2). He seeks them for His own, but the same holy love that seeks and redeems demands that they be like Him. Fellowship with the Holy One must and can only be on the basis of holiness. Thus His love and His wrath are never to be separated. Both are inevitable expressions of His holiness.

It is His holiness that in love necessitated the Cross. It is His holiness that likewise necessitates the ultimate separation of the holy and the unholy (Rev. 22:11, 15). A holy God must either save or judge. Man, a moral being, must in his freedom determine which it will be.

The purpose then of the Incarnation and the Atonement must be seen in these terms. Hebrews makes it clear that Jesus suffered without the city, rejected by sinful man, so that unholy men could be made holy and could live in an eternal fellowship with a holy God (12:2; 13:12). This makes the word in 12:14, which affirms the necessity of holiness for ultimate salvation, comprehensible and establishes the prayer of Paul in 1 Thess. 5:23 for entire sanctification as an appropriate prayer for all who would be saved.

A significant change occurs in the use of the term "holy" in the NT. Whereas the thrust of the OT is to establish the holiness of Jehovah, the NT speaks relatively little of this. It is assumed. Now the emphasis is upon Jesus being "the Holy One" (Mark 1:24; Luke 4:34; Acts 3:14; cf. John 6:69) and upon the holiness of the Spirit (the ever-present adjective "holy"). The Trinitarian implications of this are obvious. But the NT from Acts on uses the plural adjective *hagioi* consistently for the believers who made up the Early Church. Thus the term primarily reserved for Jehovah in the OT has now become clear enough and stable enough in meaning that it can be used of the Christian believer. As such it speaks of God's will for every believer (1 Thess. 4:3-7), God's provision for every believer (Col. 1:22), and God's requirement for every believer (Rev. 22:11). The God who is holy love has now provided through the atonement of the Holy One, Jesus, and through the sanctifying work of the Spirit, the possibility of likeness unto Him who alone is holy in himself.

See SANCTIFICATION, CONSECRATE (CONSECRATION), ENTIRE SANCTIFICATION, HEART PURITY, ATTRIBUTES (DIVINE), SINNING RELIGION, WESLEYAN SYNTHESIS, RELATIONAL THEOLOGY.

For Further Reading: Cremer, *Lexicon;* Kittel, 1:88-115; Brunner, *The Christian Doctrine of God,* 157-74.

DENNIS F. KINLAW

HOLINESS MOVEMENT, THE. A term currently used to identify those individuals, denominations, and other religious institutions in the Wesleyan tradition which emphasize a second, distinct experience of evangelical faith subsequent to regeneration by which the Christian believer is filled with the Holy Spirit and entirely sanctified. This modern movement evolved out of the mainstream of a revival of Christian holiness which originated in America in the late 1830s in both Calvinistic and Methodist churches. Both the early Methodist revival, under the leadership of laypersons Walter and Phoebe Palmer, and the early Oberlin revival, under the leadership of Charles Finney and Asa Mahan, represented a concern for a quality of Christian life more stable and deep than that which had commonly issued from the Second Great Awakening, which had swept through the churches in the first three decades of the century.

The spiritual force of the movement was expressed by utilizing the dynamic directness of American revivalistic methods to call the churches to the higher Christian life which John Wesley and his Methodists had contended was both biblically commanded and experientially confirmed. Such intense promotion of "second blessing holiness" produced a distinctively American pattern of Wesleyan holiness teaching. Nevertheless, the movement has consistently contended for its loyalty to Wesley against those who see in its history varying doctrinal emphases from those of the founder of Methodism himself.

By mid-century, the movement had rallied support from such diverse advocates as: Congregationalist T. C. Upham, professor of moral theology at Bowdoin College; Presbyterian W. E. Boardman, author of *The Higher Christian Life* (1859); Baptist A. B. Earle, well-known deeper-life evangelist; and British Methodist William Arthur, author of the influential work of the new age of the Spirit, *The Tongue of Fire.*

The establishment of the National Campmeeting Association for the Promotion of Holiness at Vineland, N.J., in 1867, marked a new phase in the movement's development. John Inskip and the other Methodist ministers of the NCAPH assumed a leadership role in the revival which they maintained for a quarter of a century. By 1875, holiness adherents had come very close to their goal of reforming Methodism under a holiness church pattern. At the same time, large national camp meetings and the numerous state and local associations extended Wesleyan doctrines into most evangelical denominations. There were converts among Quakers, Mennonites, Presbyterians, Baptists, and Episcopalians.

Through the lay evangelism of Quakers Robert Pearsall and Hannah Whitall Smith (author of *The Christian's Secret of a Happy Life,* 1870), the evangelical communities of Britain and the Continent were indelibly imprinted with the "higher Christian life" message. The British Keswick Convention, a Calvinistic holiness movement, largely among evangelical Anglicans; the German Heiligungsbewegung, a holiness movement mostly among Lutheran and Reformed Pietistic groups; and the more Methodist-oriented English holiness denominations, among them the Salvation Army, resulted from this European phase of the revival. Through such missionary leaders as Methodist Bishop William Taylor and Hudson Taylor, the revival touched all the major mission fields of the world.

By the end of the 19th century the success of the movement, both within the established churches and among unchurched people, led to growing pressures for the organization of distinctively holiness churches. In spite of efforts among leaders to discourage such separatist tendencies, many of the adherents left or were forced out of the established churches. A large number of Methodists and lesser numbers from many other evangelical churches joined nonchurched holiness converts to form what now are known as "the holiness churches." New denominations such as the Church of the Nazarene, the Pilgrim Holiness church, and the Church of God (Anderson, Ind.), took their place as American churches alongside of the Wesleyan Methodist and Free Methodist churches, two older holiness groups who had separated from Methodism in 1843 and 1860 respectively. From its earliest introduction into America, the Salvation Army also closely identified with the movement. Many Christian and Missionary Alliance churches were born out of the same milieu. Other than the Church of God (Anderson) and the Christian and Missionary Alliance, all the above churches (some through subsequent mergers) became members of the Christian Holiness Association (successor to the National Holiness Association).

Numerous holiness adherents, particularly in Methodism, did not leave the larger churches but maintained continuing loyalties to the movement through independent agencies such as NHA camp meetings. These people have provided the traditional supporting constituency for such institutions as Asbury College, Asbury Theological Seminary, Taylor University, Vennard College, Western Evangelical Seminary, and such missionary societies as the OMS International and the World Gospel Mission. Worldwide membership in holiness bodies approximates 1.75 million, with over 1 million of these in the United States and Canada. More than 50 educational institutions are maintained. More than 1,000 camp meetings are still held annually. By their denial of the sign of glossolalia, these bodies distinguish themselves from Pentecostal churches, many of whom also were born out of the 19th-century holiness revival and may even maintain Wesleyan perfectionism.

Since the end of World War II, there have been a series of small defections from each of the major holiness churches. In the main these represented expressions of discontent in conservative sectors of the holiness denominations as increased growth and a more favorable response to contemporary culture brought changes in traditional holiness life-styles. Many of these new holiness bodies gather together under the aegis of the International Holiness Convention, a more conservative counterpart of the Christian Holiness Association.

See WESLEYANISM, PENTECOSTALISM, KESWICK (KESWICKIANISM), HOLINESS.

For Further Reading: Dayton, *Discovering an Evangelical Heritage;* Dieter, *The Holiness Revival of the Nineteenth Century;* Jones, *A Guide to the Study of the Holiness Movement; Perfectionist Persuasion;* Rose, *A Theology of Christian Experience;* Smith, *Revivalism and Social Reform;* denominational histories, e.g., Smith, *Called unto Holiness* (Church of the Nazarene).

MELVIN EASTERDAY DIETER

HOLY COMMUNION. This term is used interchangeably with the Lord's Supper and the Eucharist. *Communion* is from the Greek word *koinōnia,* which means "sharing," "fellowship," "communion," "partnership," *"participation,"* the latter being the nearest equivalent in English. The other term *eucharist* means "giving of thanks," and stresses the note of "celebration" so favored in contemporary Christian circles. Both terms are rooted in Pauline usage and in that of the Gospels. As reported in the Synoptic Gospels, it was at the last Passover meal with His disciples that Jesus invested the bread and wine with emblematic meaning respecting His body and His blood. The Fourth Gospel does not say that this occurred at the time He washed the feet of His disciples, but in the discussion at Capernaum (John 6:25-65) Jesus asked His audience to recognize that His body and blood typified divine life that He alone could impart.

What in NT times served as a "memorial" of His death (1 Cor. 11:26), and a foretaste of "the marriage supper of the Lamb" (cf. Matt. 26:29; Luke 22:18; Rev. 19:9), came, in the course of Christian history, to be construed as the "Mass," the partaking of which resulted in the "infusion" of divine grace. In Roman Catholicism the Mass is perceived as a sacrifice each time it is enacted, rather than as an expression of gratitude for the one sacrifice once offered for sin by our High Priest himself (Heb. 9:26).

The words "This is my body" and "This is my blood" have led Roman Catholics to believe that modern bread and wine, duly consecrated, miraculously become, in their substance, the actual body and blood of Jesus. This is called transubstantiation. Luther, concerned to be literal but less dogmatic, insisted on the actual presence of Christ in, with, and under the elements. This is called consubstantiation. Calvinists and Arminians think of the Supper as a memorial and emphasize Christ's spiritual presence, ask communicants to come forward to receive Holy Communion from the celebrant. Evangelicals in that tradition (Methodists and those influenced by them) came to link renewal at Holy Communion with an "altar service" at which penitents publicly confess spiritual needs and seek direct divine intervention.

Central in all observances is the blood of Christ representing His life surrendered in death. The "blood" of Communion signifies that "Christ, our paschal lamb, has been sacrified" for us (1 Cor. 5:7, RSV).

This sacrament, with few exceptions, is celebrated by Christians of all nations and languages, under all sorts of conditions. It is an act by which we affirm our faith in Christ.

See CONSUBSTANTIATION, TRANSUBSTANTIATION, SACRAMENTS, HOLY WEEK, EUCHARIST.

For Further Reading: Higgins, *The Lord's Supper in the NT;* Jeremias, *The Eucharistic Words of Jesus;* Lietzmann, *Mass and Lord's Supper;* Barclay, *The Lord's Supper.*

GEORGE ALLEN TURNER

HOLY OF HOLIES. When the Hebrew Tabernacle's floor plan and specifications were given to Moses (Exodus 25—27; 30—31; 35—40), it was stipulated that at the center of the layout was to be the sanctuary of Yahweh. This holy of holies was to be known as the dwelling place of God where He would meet with His people and commune with them (Exod. 25:22).

This innermost sanctuary was separated from the holy place by a curtain which also served as its only access. The dimensions of the holy of holies made it cubed shaped (10 cubits or 15 feet in the Tabernacle and 20 cubits or 30 feet in the Temple).

In the Tabernacle and in the first Temple the principal furnishing was the ark of the covenant (Exod. 25:16) over which was positioned the mercy seat (v. 21). Two cherubim replicas watched over the ark, one being stationed at either end (v. 20). The ark was commonly called "the ark of the testimony" (vv. 21-22), since it contained the Decalogue (Deut. 10:5), Aaron's rod (Heb. 9:4), and a portion of manna (Exod. 16:32-34). These significant objects gave testimony to Yahweh's steadfast love for His people.

Aaron, the first of the high priests, entered the holy of holies only once a year on the great Day of Atonement (Leviticus 16). Completely clothed in white linen, he passed beyond the curtain into this most sacred of sanctuaries. In his hands he carried an offering bowl containing the blood of the atonement which he was to sprinkle with his finger upon the mercy seat. Surrounding him was a cloud of incense that arose from the censer. At this point in history this was Yahweh's designated procedure in providing an atonement for the sins of His people.

Before the first Temple was destroyed in 586 B.C., it had been ransacked on several occasions. Sometime during this tumultuous period the ark passed from the scene of history. The holy of holies in the second Temple (commonly called Zerubbabel's Temple) was evidently devoid of furnishings. This was also true of Herod's Temple (Zerubbabel's Temple rebuilt). Could it be that this Temple which stood in the days of Jesus Christ had an unoccupied holy of holies in order that Jesus, himself, might possess it?

The holy of holies is not mentioned in the NT until the time of Christ's death. Then the Synoptics report the rending of the curtain when Christ died, signifying that the way into the holiest of all was now open (cf. Heb. 10:19 ff). It is Jesus Christ who fulfills all the Tabernacle symbolism. He is our Sanctuary, our High Priest, our Altar, and our everlasting Sacrifice.

See TEMPLE, SACRIFICE, MOSAIC LAW, ATONEMENT, TYPE (TYPOLOGY), HIGH PRIESTHOOD OF CHRIST.

For Further Reading: Kiene, *The Tabernacle of God in the Wilderness of Sinai,* 133-53; Strong, *The Tabernacle of Israel in the Desert.* ROBERT A. MATTKE

HOLY SPIRIT. The Holy Spirit, the Third Person of the Trinity, is the Executor of the Godhead through whom all that God does in the world is done. He is God in action, especially, although not exclusively, in carrying to fulfillment His redemptive purpose. The name is not descriptive, inasmuch as the Holy Spirit is not spirit in some sense other than the Father and Son are spirit. Thus, He has been termed God the Servant or the Helper, a concept in keeping with Jesus' teaching concerning Him as the Paraclete.

The Holy Spirit mediates to men the glorified Christ, continues Christ's work in the world, creates and vitalizes the Church, administers salvation, intercedes for men, and inspires, preserves (within the canon), and illuminates the Scriptures. He is God-close-at-hand, God universally present (Ps. 139:7). By the Spirit as well as the Son we have access to God (Eph. 2:18), and He is the essence of all God's good gifts to us (Luke 11:13).

Without the Spirit the Christian faith would be mere historicism without credentials, and Christian worship would be no better than ceremonialism or magic. The Spirit makes Christianity morally pungent, personally real, and gives it life-changing power. Even so, His work is not limited to salvation or the Church. Wherever in creation God is at work in providential control or care, in conscience or moral concerns, wherever there are works of mercy, the discovery or exploration of truth and beauty, there the Spirit is in action (Acts 17:28; Rom. 2:15; 9:1; 13:4).

The distinctive and full revelation of the Holy Spirit as a person is found in the NT where the term is used 93 times. In comparison, "Holy Spirit" occurs only 3 times in the OT (Ps. 51:11; Isa. 63:10-11), although other names for Him occur.

The OT emphasis is practical, expressing activity without definition of being. The biblical words for Spirit (Heb. *ruach,* Gr. *pneuma*) can be translated "breath," "wind," "storm," as well as "life" or "vitality." *Ruach* signifies not quiet breath but strong, even violent motion. The Spirit of the Lord is the mysterious, irresistible *power* of God, the mode of His activity, God's dynamic *presence* in creation, and also the animating *principle* in man. Even so, man is not represented as His mere instrument, but as a voluntary servant or co-worker with the Spirit.

Although a moral significance is not absent in the ministry of the Spirit in the OT, it is, in the main, the enduement of chosen persons here and there with special spiritual, intellectual, and physical gifts, usually for leadership. This was signified by the anointing of kings with oil. Joseph is given wisdom (Gen. 41:38), and Bezalel artistry and craftsmanship (Exod. 31:3). The Spirit "came upon" or "clothed," sometimes "rushed upon," certain leaders, gifting them for various exploits (Judg. 3:10; 6:34; 11:29; 13:25; 14:6; 1 Sam. 11:6; 16:13, NASB marg.). From Saul the Spirit also "departed" (v. 14) because of disobedience.

The primary OT revelation of the Spirit presents Him as the Inspirer of the prophets, through whom God spoke. Micah is "filled" with the Spirit of the Lord to make known God's will (3:8, cf. Ezek. 11:5 and Zech. 7:12). The ideal fulfillment of this ministry is to come in the future in the Messiah (Isa. 11:1-2, 42, the first of the "Servant Songs"; and chap. 61).

With Isaiah, the peculiar work of the Spirit, which is to sanctify, comes more distinctly into view. The outpoured Spirit will work righteousness, justice, and confidence (32:15-17). The Spirit represents God's personal, redemptive presence (63:10-14).

In the prophets a future "age of the Spirit" is forseen when not to the few, but to all the people, the Spirit will be given (Isa. 32:15; 44:3; 59:21; Ezek. 36:27; Joel 2:28-29; Zech. 12:10). Such a grand design had been envisioned by Moses (Num. 11:29). In the fullness of time John the Baptist announced that the age of the Spirit was at hand, to be inaugurated by Jesus Christ (Matt. 3:11; John 1:32-34).

In the NT the Holy Spirit is revealed first in a twofold relationship with Jesus Christ. On the one hand, especially in the Synoptics, the Spirit is the energizing and controlling principle of Jesus' life and ministry. Jesus is the Bearer of the Spirit. On the other hand Jesus is the Giver or Sender of the Holy Spirit to the Church (Luke 24:49; John 15:26; 16:7).

In the first relationship Jesus is conceived by the Spirit, anointed with the Spirit at His baptism, and throughout His ministry inspired, empowered, and given authority by the Spirit (Mark 1:12; Matt. 12:28; Luke 10:21). The Spirit enabled His vicarious death (Heb. 9:14) and was the ground of His resurrection (Rom. 8:11). The completeness and permanence of Jesus' relationship with the Spirit is stressed by John (cf. John 1:33; 3:34). Jesus himself announced that in Him the promise of the Spirit was fulfilled (Luke 4:17-21; cf. Matt. 12:18). Thus, in Jesus' humanity, by His union with the Father through the Spirit, there is revealed that perfect fellowship between God and man which is at the heart of redemption.

In the second aspect of His relationship with the Spirit, Jesus, now glorified and exalted to the right hand of the Father, pours out on His disciples the gift of the Holy Spirit at Pentecost, a gift which awaited the completion of His redemptive work (John 7:39). Jesus is the One who baptizes with the Holy Spirit (cf. Acts 11:15-17). In Jesus Christ, the "last Adam" (1 Cor. 15:45), is demonstrated the goal and purpose of the Spirit's work upon mankind. Thus, from, and because of, the One in whom the promise is realized, the Spirit's blessings are graciously extended to the many whom He represents (John 16:7; Acts 2:33; cf. Rom. 5:5, 15-19). The gift is now the privilege of all "in Christ." In believers, the special work of the Spirit is their renewal in the image of Christ (2 Cor. 3:17-18). An intimate relationship with God through the Spirit has been opened wide. This event (Pentecost) is the vitalization of the Church as an organic union of believers, and as the Body of Christ with Christ as the Head.

Furthermore, the NT interrelates the work of the Spirit with that of the glorified Christ. To be "in Christ" has the same import as to be "in the Spirit." John represents the receiving of the Spirit as being the impartation of the very life of Christ (20:22). In Revelation 2 and 3 the words of the glorified Christ are "what the Spirit is saying to the churches" (TLB). The Spirit is "the Spirit of Christ" (Rom. 8:9-11; cf. Eph. 3:16). The ministry of the Spirit is Christocentric (1 John 3:24). As the Son makes known the Father, so it is the Spirit's work to reveal the Son (John 16:13-14).

The Spirit at work in believers is seen also by Paul as the "pledge," a "firstfruits," or kind of first instalment of the completion of redemption at the resurrection of the body (Rom. 8:23; 2 Cor. 1:22; 5:5; Eph. 1:13-14).

The Spirit is the mode in which Christ exercises His Headship over the Church. More than resident, the Spirit is President (Acts 15:28). The Church derives its missionary impetus, equipment, authority, and ability for mission from the empowering Spirit (Acts 1:4-8; Gal. 3:5; Phil. 1:19). The Spirit administers necessary gifts (the charismata) for service to each member of the Church, in proper proportion, and according to His choice (1 Cor. 12:4-31). The Body of Christ is strengthened, guided, and filled with joy by the Spirit (Acts 9:31; 13:2-4, 52). The Spirit preserves the Church's unity (Eph. 4:3), creates and hallows its fellowship (2 Cor. 13:14), and makes real its worship (Phil. 3:3). The Church's ministry, sacraments, preaching, teaching, and evangelism are made effective by the Spirit (Acts 1:8; 1 Pet. 1:12; Rev. 22:17). The Church is God's household, building, and dwelling place through the Spirit (Eph. 2:18-22).

The ministry of the Spirit of Truth within the Church of Jesus Christ as the Conservator and Guarantor of orthodoxy deserves a special word. The Spirit witnesses inwardly to the truth. The Protestant doctrine is technically known as the *testimonium Spiritus Sancti.* The Spirit's subjective, dynamic, and unhindered work in believers (vital Christian experience) is the only final safeguard against the encroachment of false authorities such as tradition (churchly authority) or biblicism (a merely intellectual and legal use of Scripture). The *testimonium Spiritus Sancti* reconciles reason and revelation, and points to Christ the Eternal Word, who is Lord of both Scripture and inward experience (1 Cor. 2:10-12, 14; 2 Cor. 3:6, 14-17; cf. Luke 24:27, 32).

Protestants generally have placed more stress on the Spirit's individual rather than corporate ministry. The revelation of God to the soul is the Spirit's work (1 Cor. 12:13; 1 John 4:2). The Spirit convicts sinners, leads to repentance, points to Christ as the Object of faith, is the Source of the believer's new life through regeneration (John 3:5; Titus 3:5), and adopts the believer into God's family (Rom. 8:14-16). The particular work of the Spirit in the believer is sanctification (1 Cor. 6:11; 1 Thess. 4:3-8; 1 Pet. 1:2). He delivers from sin (Rom. 8:2) and gives liberty (2 Cor. 3:17). The NT norm (not special privilege) for believers is to be "filled with the Spirit," and this becomes the hallmark and secret of their ministries (Acts 4:8, 31).

The Spirit brings inward certainty and assurance of right relationship with God (Rom. 8:16). He seals, that is, signifies God's ownership and protection of those who belong to Him (2 Cor. 1:22; Eph. 1:13; 4:30). The Spirit works for inward righteousness (Rom. 14:17) and produces spiritual fruit as the normal result of His unhindered ministry in believers: love, joy, peace, patience, kindness, goodness, faithfulness, gentleness, self-control (Gal. 5:22-23). He helps in our infirmities and in prayer (Rom. 8:26; Jude 20), supplies courage (Acts 4:31) and strength in testing (Eph. 3:16), and makes spiritual discipline effective (Rom. 8:13).

Christians are to "walk in the Spirit" (Gal. 5:16), a carefully maintained relationship. The Spirit's work is noncoercive, moral, and personal. He never suppresses or overwhelms true selfhood, but rather liberates and enriches the human self. Believers are not to grieve the Spirit (Eph. 4:30) or dampen His work (1 Thess. 5:19). Each is a temple to be "indwelt" by the Spirit (Rom. 8:9; 1 Cor. 6:19), that is, the Spirit wishes to take up permanent residence.

See TRINITY (THE HOLY), ECONOMIC TRINITY, PERSONALITY OF THE HOLY SPIRIT, WITNESS OF THE SPIRIT, BAPTISM WITH THE HOLY SPIRIT, SINS AGAINST THE SPIRIT, DISPENSATION OF THE SPIRIT, GUIDE (GUIDANCE), EMBLEMS OF THE HOLY SPIRIT, NEW BIRTH, PROCESSION OF THE SPIRIT, FRUIT OF THE SPIRIT.

For Further Reading: Barclay, *The Promise of the Spirit;* Berkhof, *The Doctrine of the Holy Spirit;* Carter, *The Person and Ministry of the Holy Spirit.*

ARNOLD E. AIRHART

HOLY WEEK. This is the week in the Christian year which begins with Palm Sunday, the day of celebration of the triumphal entry of our Lord into Jerusalem for the last time (Mark 11:1-10; parallel passages) and ends with Easter Sunday, the celebration of His resurrection (Matt. 28:1-10; parallel passages). According to the Gospel records several memorable events happened during this week, including the cleansing of the Temple, the Last Supper, the Gethsemane prayer time, the arrest and trial, and finally the Crucifixion. Across the centuries the church developed ceremonies by which to remember these significant events.

Maundy Thursday is the traditional day of observance of the Last Supper, but it also includes the rite of foot washing (John 13:1-20). The term "maundy" is probably taken from the Latin *mandatum,* referring to the new commandment of the Lord as recorded in verse 34. In the Catholic tradition this day became a special day of penitence.

The name "Good Friday" for the day of remembrance of the crucifixion of the Lord in all likelihood arose out of the realization of the manifold salvific blessings which the Lord's death released to believers.

Resurrection Sunday was originally called *Pascha* on account of its association with the Jewish Passover. Very early in the Christian community Christ was proclaimed "the true Paschal Lamb" and "the first fruits of the resurrection" (cf. 1 Cor. 5:7; 15:23). Centuries later, the name "Easter" came to be used to identify this special day. According to Bede, "Easter" was taken from "Eastre," a Teutonic goddess, whose festival was observed in the spring of the year, at the time of the vernal equinox. To Christians, the spiritual meanings of Easter are dominant; however, some of the new-life concepts associated with the thought of springtime have been introduced into the Easter celebrations. As in the case of Christmas, the Easter feast appears to have superseded an old pagan festival.

Easter has been recognized as the oldest and most important feast of the Christian Church because of the authentication of the Lord's life and death which the miracle of the Resurrection provided. In many segments of the Church Easter is preceded by the 40 days of Lenten preparation.

See PASCHAL CONTROVERSY, LENT, DEATH OF CHRIST, CHRISTIAN YEAR.

For Further Reading: "Easter," *HBD;* Finegan, *Handbook of Biblical Chronology;* "Easter," "Maundy Thursday," "Good Friday," "Holy Saturday," *ODCC.*

WILLARD H. TAYLOR

HOMOLOGOUMENA. See ANTILEGOMENA.

HONESTY. "Honesty" is the sense of the Greek word *kalos,* which means, first, "beautiful" as to outward form of persons and things. Sometimes in Greek it was added to names to indicate admiration or respect; e.g., "My good Henry." The word indicates excellence of quality—as genuine silver. In the moral sense it indicates noble, honorable, good, excellent character; hence, moral beauty, virtue, or honor. Of women *kalos* meant "chaste" in King James's day.

Kalos must be differentiated from *agathos,* which also means "good" but in a general sense, carrying the notions of serviceability, capability; brave, valiant; e.g., a good soldier, a good horse, but not necessarily morally so.

"An *honest* . . . heart" (Luke 8:15) is like the "good" earth, eminently suitable for received seed to grow to full maturity. Honest ("noble," NIV) hearts hear the Word, keep it, and bring forth fruit (see John 1:47).

In Rom. 12:17 *kalos* is "honest" (KJV); "honorable" (ASV); "right" (NIV, NASB); "noble" (RSV). In 2 Cor. 8:21 we have "honest things" (KJV); "things honorable" (ASV, RSV, NASB); and "what is right" (NIV). And 2 Cor. 13:7 exhorts, "Do that which is honest" (KJV); "honorable" (ASV); and "right" (NIV, RSV, NASB). In Heb. 13:18 the NIV reads, "A clear conscience." In 1 Pet. 2:12 *kalos* is rendered "seemly" (ASV); "excellent behavior" (NASB); "good conduct" (RSV); and "good lives" (NIV).

Synonyms for *kalos* are:

1. *Semnos*—honest, majestic, august, holy, honorable, reputable, worthy of reverence. In 1 Tim. 2:2 it is rendered "holiness" (NIV); "dignity" (NASB); hence, excellent moral quality, "honesty" (KJV) (see Phil. 4:8).

2. *Euschēmonōs,* "honestly" in 1 Thess. 4:12 (KJV), equals "becomingly" (ASV); "win the *respect*" (NIV, RSV); "behave properly" (NASB). See Rom. 13:13 which defines the term negatively.

3. *Marturoumenos,* translated "honest report" (Acts 6:3), is derived from one word meaning simply "witness" (martyr); hence, testimony, evidence, proof, attestation; as an "honest," reliable reporter or witness. The NIV omits the word "honest," reading simply, "choose."

"Honesty" denotes the quality of excellence of moral living, of honorable reputation, of genuine and godly character.

See CHARACTER, TRUTH, INTEGRITY THERAPY.

For Further Reading: *ISBE;* Trench, "The Sower," *Notes on the Parables of Our Lord; HDNT.*

JOHN B. NIELSON

HONOR. In English usage *honor* denotes esteem, respect, and reverence. In subtle ways, it suggests excellence of character and personal integrity. In biblical usage honor carries the additional idea of glory and majesty because the term is used primarily with reference to God. God is holy and for that reason He possesses a certain glory and is worthy of honor (cf. 1 Tim. 1:17; 6:16; Rev. 4:9; 7:12). God is also the Source of all blessings including the blessings of honor (2 Pet. 1:17; Rev. 4:11). By the gift of himself in death, Christ has been "crowned with glory and honour" (Heb. 2:9). These concepts, of course, root in the OT's reverence for Deity.

Honor is a gift of God, a grace bestowed on man. A person whose life has been transformed by faith in Christ and who now partakes of the divine life, receives God's love and respect in the same way that a child receives his father's love and respect. This special relationship is the basis of an honorable life-style for the believer. Also in the whole of his life the Christian honors Christ in the body (Phil. 1:20) and gives God the glory or honor due Him (Acts 12:23).

See GLORY, RESPECT, INTEGRITY.

For Further Reading: "Honor," *IDB,* E-J.

WILLARD H. TAYLOR

HOPE. In the context of biblical theology, hope is the expectation that *all* God's promises to us and for us will (soon) be realized. It is trusting—and waiting—on God.

Of course, hope may be based on ephemeral things instead of God. The Scriptures judge such secular hopes, despite their personal intensity, as ultimately futile. The hope of the godless (i.e., "fool") will come to nothing (Prov. 11:7). It has no basis, no substance, no reality.

It is faith which gives "substance" to hope (Heb. 11:1); and hope must have such a basis or foundation. And where does faith find its stability and strength? In God's faithfulness. So Abraham grew strong in faith, "being fully assured that what He had promised, He was able also to perform" (Rom. 4:20-21, NASB). So, too, Sarah experienced a quickening of ability, "since she considered Him faithful who had promised" (Heb. 11:11, NASB).

The OT describes God as the "hope of Israel" (Jer. 14:8; 17:13). He is the Author and Source of hope, its sustaining power and object. The horizon of hope in the OT stretches far into the future. It embraces the coming of Messiah and God's eternal kingdom, the realization of a new covenant with provision for forgiveness and inward holiness, and the conversion of the Gentiles.

All that has become a reality in Jesus Christ, our glorious hope (cf. Col. 1:27; 1 Tim. 1:1). The Christian's hope is now centered on Him. His resurrection is a "surety" to us of eternal life, His ascension an "anchor" to the storm-tossed soul (Heb. 6:18-19). Once, being without God, we had no hope—like the rest of mankind (Eph. 2:12). But now, in Christ Jesus, we have been "born again to a living hope" (1 Pet. 1:3, NASB). Thus, we await the consummation of God's promises with trust, eagerness, and patience.

See FAITH, PERSEVERANCE, DESPAIR.

For Further Reading: *IDB,* 2:640-43; *NIDNTT,* 238-46; Moule, *The Meaning of Hope.*

WAYNE G. MCCOWN

HUMAN NATURE. Man as a racial being partakes of a basic ontic essence that is manifested in his actions and decisions. Surely enough, man is a *homo faber,* he makes tools, he uses language, and creates cultures. But also back of each of his decisions lies a nature that manifests itself in action. Existentialism's basic position that "existence is prior to essence" rules out any ontological self for the individual and any racial continuity for human nature, thus making man the builder of his own basic nature and an *activity* rather than an *agent.* But man (like his God and Creator) has his *existence* as a consequence of his *essence.* God is *ens a se* and man is *ens per se.* Moreover, an entity whose existence does not follow from its essence can never be eternal. "God himself eternally and necessarily establishes His own existence in conformity with His essence" (Max Scheler, *On the Eternal in Man,* 226).

Likewise man behaves according to his basic essence. For the *being* and *thusness* of man are self-evidently independent of the here and now existence of any individual or his acts. Man cannot escape his humanity. The race is under the law of solidarity and is bound up in a common life. The instant God created the first pair He created the human nature in and with them. "Men, as *persons* are separate and distinct from each other, and must ever be; but each is possessed of a common human nature and together they form a living organism which as such, constitutes the human race" (Wiley, *CT,* 2:25). We must never lose sight of two basic facts—man's personal responsibility and his racial solidarity.

See MAN, DIVINE IMAGE, NATURE, SELF, PERSON (PERSONALITY), SOUL.

For Further Reading: Wiley, *CT,* 2:7-50; Scheler, *On the Eternal in Man;* Pittenger, *The Christian Understanding of Human Nature.*

ROSS E. PRICE

HUMANISM. "Broadly this term suggests any attitude which tends to exalt the human element or stress the importance of human interests as opposed to the supernatural, divine element—or as opposed to the grosser animal element" (Thrall and Hibbard, *Handbook of Literature,* 226). The term implies devotion to the concerns of mankind. It stresses the adequacy and perfectibility of man, and the importance of the present life in contrast to life after death. The term comes from Latin *humanitas* (the human race).

Humanism as a doctrine was born in the Renaissance in Italy in the 14th century and spread in the next two centuries to northern Europe and England. The man who is generally regarded as the first great humanist was Petrarch (in Italy). The most noted humanist was Erasmus, who was born in Holland in 1469, but who lived also in England, France, and Germany and became a "citizen of the world."

In its beginnings humanism was a reaction against the extreme "otherworldliness" (asceticism) of the Middle Ages which downgraded man and made the physical and material worlds mortal foes of the spiritual and heavenly worlds. In "the battle between the body and the soul," it was not possible for both to triumph. But humanism was also a reaction against scholastic theology with its tendency toward deductive and intensely dogmatic reasoning. Over against the asceticism and scholastic dogmatism of the medieval church, the Renaissance humanists set up the newly rediscovered classics of ancient Greece and Rome, in which man was magnified, often to a point where the distinction between gods and men was all but obliterated.

Through such men as Erasmus, humanism had many of the same goals as did Luther and the other leaders of the Reformation—purging the church of its grosser evils, etc. Erasmus, who gave to the church and the world his edited text of the Greek NT, could well be called the father of textual criticism of the NT. But at the other extreme from Erasmus were humanists who were anti-Christian and antireligious.

This antireligious bias was present in Renaissance humanism only among the extremists, the majority of humanists expressing respect and devotion to the Bible and to Christ. But what was originally the attitude of a small minority has since become a dominant tenet of the movement, and this was predictable: the seed of antireligion was present at the beginning. The glorification of man and the proclamation of his sufficiency would lead eventually to the eclipsing of God. A fully sufficient man would see little need of God.

It is at this point that humanism is most unchristian, for though the Bible exalts man to a plane "a little lower than the angels" (Ps. 8:5), it most clearly pictures him as desperately in need of a Savior.

See CHRISTIAN HUMANISM, CREATION, MAN.

For Further Reading: *ERE,* 6:830 ff; *DCT,* 161-62; Shaw, *Concise Dictionary of Literary Terms,* 135-36; Thrall and Hibbard, *Handbook of Literature,* 226-27.

CHARLES L. CHILDERS

HUMANITY OF CHRIST. The humanity of Christ has two foci: His humanity in relation to God and His humanity in relation to human beings. These foci are conjoined in His physical existence in human flesh.

From Jesus' conception until now, Christendom has struggled with the mystery of Jesus' humanity and deity: How could Jesus have been both fully human and fully God? The danger of any answer is to stress one aspect of Jesus' nature over the other. Yet Jesus' humanity must always be viewed against the background of His deity, for it was out of His deity that Jesus took on humanity (John 1:1-4, 14; Rom. 8:3; Phil. 2:6-8; Col. 2:9). His humanity, like ours, has its origin of meaning, purpose, and value in God.

That Jesus was truly human, with a body like ours, is abundantly clear from Scripture (John 1:30; Acts 2:22; 17:31; Rom. 5:15; 9:5; 1 Cor. 15:21; Gal. 4:4; 1 Tim. 2:5; Heb. 2:14-18; et al.), as well as from the biblical witness to such human experiences as birth (Matt. 1:25), growth (Luke 2:40, 52), hunger (Matt. 21:18; Luke 4:2), thirst (John 4:7; 19:28), weariness (Mark 4:38; John 4:6), temptation (Matt. 4:1; Heb. 2:18; 4:15), grief (Luke 19:41; John 11:35), limited knowledge (Mark 13:32), anxiety (14:33-36), suffering (15:16-34), death (v. 37), etc.

Yet Jesus' humanity is also consistently qualified by the biblical writers: His conception is unique (Matt. 1:18, 20, 25; Luke 1:34-35); His earthly ministry has a heavenly context (Mark 1:11; 9:7); He came "in a likeness of sinful flesh" (Rom. 8:3); He "took the form of a servant, becoming in a likeness of men, and being found in appearance as a man" (Phil. 2:7-8); and He was "tempted in all things as *we are, yet* without sin" (Heb. 4:15, author's free translations).

These biblical emphases, along with the qualifications of Jesus' humanity, provide the key to understanding. Phil. 2:7 states, "Jesus took the form of a servant," which entailed "becoming in a likeness of men." This suggests that to be "man" is to be a servant—to be a being which is completely determined by the will of another. This is made clear in Phil. 2:8 where Jesus, having placed himself in this role in relationship to God ("being found in appearance as a man"), "became obedient unto death." Thus Jesus' humanity is the complete actualization of God's intended role for man—a being completely yielded and obedient to the will of God.

The crucial point is that in His humanity Jesus had complete free will. He did not succumb to the temptation "to be equal with God" (Phil. 2:6; cf. Gen. 3:5—at its core, temptation is the lure to substitute our will for God's, i.e., to be God), even though He was tempted with this at all points as we are. (Jesus' temptation was deeper, since for Him it was a live option to be God, whereas for us it is only servants "playing" master.) Thus Jesus was *fully* human, but not *fallen* (necessitating the biblical qualifications of His humanity).

As fully human, Jesus is: (1) the Mediator (1 Tim. 2:5) through whom God addresses fallen humanity (John 1:18; 14:9; Heb. 1:2; et al.) and fallen humanity approaches God (John 14:6); (2) the Redeemer (Rom. 5:15-19) in whom are met God's judgment and humanity's condition (8:3); God's grace and humanity's sin (5:21); God' love and humanity's rebellion (v. 8); (3) the New Humanity (cf. Rom. 13:14; Gal. 3:27; Eph. 4:24) in whom believers find a new order of being (2 Cor. 5:17; Col. 3:10) and into whose likeness they are being transformed by the sanctifying work of the Holy Spirit (2 Cor. 3:17-18; Eph. 4:13, 15, 24).

See DOCETISM, CHRIST, CHRISTOLOGY, HYPOSTATIC UNION, MEDIATION (MEDIATOR).

For Further Reading: McDonald, *Jesus—Human, Divine:* Baillie, *God Was in Christ;* Hendry, "Christology," *DCT,* 51-64; Johnson, "Christ," *IDB,* 1:563-71; "Divinity of Christ," ibid., 858-59; "Humanity of Christ," ibid., 2:658-59; Blackman, "Incarnation," ibid., 691-97.

M. ROBERT MULHOLLAND, JR.

HUMILIATION OF CHRIST. The humiliation of Christ was twofold. First was His self-emptying by which He divested himself of His glory and of the full use of the attributes of Deity that He might become man (Phil. 2:5-11). Much of the second area of Christ's humiliation relates to the negative reception which He and His message were given by many of His contemporaries. This area of humiliation includes: (1) those sufferings which were physical, and (2) His mental and spiritual anguish.

Jesus endured many types of physical indignity at the hands of His enemies during His trial and crucifixion (Matthew 26—27; Mark 14—15; Luke 22—23; John 18—19).

To grasp His mental and spiritual suffering, one must know the mind of Deity. One must experience the sensitivity of Him who is perfectly holy. That which would merely cause discomfort to the sin-jaded souls of ordinary men would cause excruciating pain to the God-man. For the higher the order of being, the greater the capacity for suffering, and the keener the hurt of humiliation.

He who is the Truth knew the hurt of having His motives impugned. He knew the pain of men's deliberate refusal to believe the truth which He so clearly manifested. He whose great compassion made Him rejoice to make lepers well and restore wholeness to the maimed, the halt, and the blind, had His own visage "marred more than any man" (Isa. 52:14). He who gave His life that men might not have to die heard the clamor of the mob for His own blood.

But His deepest humiliation was imposed upon Him by the Father himself. He who knew no sin was made to become sin for us (2 Cor. 5:21). His pure soul was contaminated with the sins of the whole world. And He who forever had enjoyed perfect fellowship with the Father suddenly was forsaken by God in His earthly darkest hour.

So He in whom was life (John 1:4), He who was the Fountain of all being, submitted himself to death. The Eternal Son died, was buried, and descended into the place of departed spirits. He drank the dregs of humiliation to the full.

See KENOSIS, EXALTATION OF CHRIST, CHRIST.

For Further Reading: Berkhof, *Systematic Theology*, 327-29; Strong, *Systematic Theology*, 701-6; Thiessen, *Introductory Lectures in Systematic Theology;* Wiley and Culbertson, *Introduction to Christian Theology*, 207-9.

W. RALPH THOMPSON

HUMILITY. In the KJV the word "humility" occurs only three times in the OT (Prov. 15:33; 18:12; 22:4) and four times in the NT (Acts 20:19; Col. 2:18, 23; 1 Pet. 5:5). And the two Colossian references are to false humility.

But a good case could be made for the assertion that the virtue most emphasized by Jesus was humility. He said, "Learn of me; for I am meek and lowly in heart" (Matt. 11:29). This was His implied condition for finding rest of soul. In the history of Christendom humility has been almost universally recognized as a hallmark quality of true Christlikeness.

The importance of humility to the Early Church appears dramatically when we study the Greek word usually translated "humility," *tapeinophrosynē*, literally, "lowliness of mind." This is the way it is translated in Phil. 2:3: "in lowliness of mind let each esteem other better than themselves."

On this passage J. B. Lightfoot writes: "Though a common word in the New Testament, *tapeinophrosynē* seems not to occur earlier." He adds: "In heathen writers *tapeinos* has almost always a bad meaning, 'grovelling,' 'abject.'" He concludes: "It was one great result of the life of Christ (on which St. Paul dwells here) to raise 'humility' to its proper level" (*St. Paul's Epistle to the Philippians*, 109).

See MEEKNESS, CHRISTLIKENESS, MIND OF CHRIST.

For Further Reading: Marchant, "Humility," *Baker's DT*, 274; Grounds, "Humility," *ZPEB*, 3:222-24.

RALPH EARLE

HYPOCRISY. One of the most despised words and one of the worst epithets is "hypocrite." Originally, it was applied to the stage actor who put on a false face, adopted an artificial voice, and pretended to be another person. It has come to mean pretending to be better than one is, or to profess to feel or think other than one really feels or thinks.

Despite some OT examples of cultural behavior which seem less than honest to us, the Bible is thorough in its condemnation of dishonest pretense. Jesus was especially sharp in His judgment against hypocrites. Vine points out that *hupokritēs* as found in the Synoptic Gospels is used only by the Lord himself, 15 times in Matthew, and elsewhere, Mark 7:6; Luke 6:42; 11:44; 12:56; 13:15.

The Scripture is clear in its indication that the "pretense face" of hypocrisy is not only dishonest. It also tends to breed, under its cover, all kinds of unhealthy, sinful, and destructive moral vices. Furthermore, all of the efforts of the hypocrite are in vain, for the Lord sees and knows the innermost heart and will one day expose it in judgment.

A world-famous actor said of himself, "I am nothing, unless I am playing the part of another person." A critic, speaking of him, asserted, "You can never find him. You probe for him, and all you find is the characters he has played."

With the guidance of the Holy Scriptures and the illumination of the Holy Spirit, the Christian believer must first find out who he really is and then must walk the path between the vain world of show and pretense and the troubled neuroticism of constant self-doubt. Might it not be quite as dishonest to appear to be less good than to be better than one is?

See HONESTY, SELF-IMAGE, SINCERITY.

For Further Reading: *HDNT,* 1:765.

JOHN E. RILEY

HYPOSTASIS. The Greek word *hypostasis* may be translated by the words "nature," "substance," or "essence." It describes those characteristics which make something *what* it is, or its essence, as distinct from its existence, or *that* it is.

A way to understand the concept is by distinguishing between "appearance" and "reality." *Hypostasis* (from the Greek word *hyphistasthai*—to stand under) describes that which stands under the appearance, i.e., the reality. In Heb. 1:3 it is declared that Christ is the image of the Father's hypostasis *(hupostaseōs).* In other words, Christ clearly shares in the divine substance. The Greek words in Heb. 1:3 state that Christ is the *"charaktēr* of his *hypostasis." Charaktēr* here means that Jesus "bears the very stamp of his nature" (RSV). The substance of God is not an appearance but is really in Christ. This is what Jesus was teaching when He declared: "He who has seen me has seen the Father" (John 14:9, RSV).

In Christian theology the path to full clarification of *hypostasis* is quite ambiguous. The Chalcedonian Creed described the Trinity by the terms "one essence *[ousia]* in three hypostases *[hypostaseis]."* In the Nicene Creed (A.D. 325) these two terms were used synonymously, meaning "being" or "nature." The work of the Cappadocian Fathers was important in giving the two terms somewhat distinct meanings. With Basil of Caesarea *ousia* indicates the universal and *hypostasis* the particular. "One essence in three hypostases" when translated into Latin becomes "one substance in three Persons." It is legitimate to translate *hypostasis* into "persons," but it does not simplify the formula. The formula conveys first the unity of the Godhead. The *ousia* is identical in each Person, e.g., the goodness of the Son and Spirit is the same as the Father's. When the Father acts, the Son and Spirit are acting jointly. But, second, the formula suggests a distinction, using the term "Persons." In this distinction between the persons the Cappadocians and Chalcedon are biblically sound. It remains necessary to recognize that the distinction does not mean separateness, but the diversity which is in the essential Deity. The "hypostatic union" means that Jesus Christ may be really united to flesh while remaining equal with God.

See CHRIST, CHRISTOLOGY, TRINITY (THE HOLY), HYPOSTATIC UNION.

For Further Reading: Hardy, ed., *Christology of the Later Fathers.*

LEON O. HYNSON

HYPOSTATIC UNION. This is a Christological term which refers to the union of the divine and human natures in Christ. The Greek term *hypostasis,* from which we derive the word *hypostatic,* basically means "substantial nature," "essence," or "actual being." Orthodox Christianity has consistently maintained that Jesus was theanthropic, "very God and very man." Although there has been divergence of opinion on how to express this belief, there are certain foundational elements which are crucial. First, the NT language which stresses at one time His humanity (Rom. 1:3; Heb. 5:1-10; John 14:28) and at other times His deity (Rom. 1:3; Heb. 1:1-4; John 10:30) does not lead to the conclusion of a double personality. Second, care must be taken not to absorb the human nature into the divine, nor to reduce divinity to humanity. Either of these sacrifices the genius of the inspired biblical writers who juxtaposed theanthropic assertions, thus keeping human and divine in a constructive tension. In contrast to orthodox Christianity, liberal theologians have usually asserted that the union of God and man was a moral union of two wills, not an actual union of being.

See CHRISTOLOGY, HYPOSTASIS, CHRIST.

W. STEPHEN GUNTER

I

ICON, ICONOCLASM. One of the great controversies in the history of the Christian church occurred in the seventh and eight centuries and centered on the use of religious images and pictures (icons) in worship, religious art, and in the appointments of churches. Those who opposed the use of icons were called iconoclasts (derived from the two Greek words, *icon* and *klastein,* which means "to break"). The controversy was most heated in the Byzantine Empire and the Eastern church.

In A.D. 717 Leo III (ruled to A.D. 740) came to power as emperor and restored to considerable strength the crumbling Byzantine Empire (Eastern Empire). As part of his restoration program Leo promoted an iconoclastic policy by banning the veneration of religious pictures. But protest against the use of icons in worship did not begin with Leo. The see of Constantinople (the ecclesiastical center of the Eastern church) was in constant contact with Moslems, Jews, and Monophysites. All of these, for differing purposes, were opposed to the use of icons. They exterted considerable influence in the Eastern Empire.

The iconoclastic efforts of Leo would help to unite many important elements of the citizenry under his rule. He also wished to make himself master of the church and to destroy the power of the monks who were the champions of the icons. In 725 Leo forbade the use of icons in worship, and the result was a religious revolt led by the monks and the common people. They resisted in defense of the freedom of the church and the veneration of images. The decree was enforced by Leo's use of the army.

It is also probable that Leo and at least some of his iconoclastic successors to the throne were motivated by theological considerations. The use of icons had hinted of idolatry to many sensitive Christians from the earliest days of the Church.

John of Damascus, one of the great theologians of the Eastern church, was a champion of those who resisted the iconoclastic movement. In his *Exposition of the Orthodox Faith,* he argues that since the invisible and formless God took visible form in the true man Jesus Christ, the use of images is not only permissible but also a great help, especially to illiterate Christians for whom the written word was not an aid in worship.

After more than 100 years of controversy and political intrigue, icons were finally restored in A.D. 842 under a woman regent, Theodora. The Eastern church still celebrates that restoration as the Feast of Orthodoxy.

See WORSHIP, IDOL (IDOLATRY), MARIOLATRY.

For Further Reading: Qualben, *A History of the Christian Church,* 152 f, 258 f; Heick, *A History of Christian Thought,* 2:247 ff. ALBERT L. TRUESDALE, JR.

IDEALISM. See REALISM.

IDOL, IDOLATRY. The English word "idol" is a transliteration of *eidōlon,* the Greek term for "image." Specifically, it denotes the image of a god which is an object of worship. Also the term may refer to any material symbol of the supernatural which is worshipped.

Idolatry refers to idol or image worship. Wiley defines it as "the paying of divine honors to idols, images, or other created objects, but may consist, also, in excessive admiration, veneration or love for any person or thing" (Wiley, *CT,* 3:39).

In the OT the term may signify the worship of foreign false gods, whether by means of images or otherwise. However, such gods were generally represented by concrete images. Idolatry in the OT also may refer to the use of symbols in the worship of Yahweh, Israel's true God.

All such practices were specifically forbidden in the Decalogue (Exod. 20:3-5); and the numerous Hebrew words appearing in the OT translated "idol" in English all express either the falseness (*eleel,* Lev. 19:4; Ps. 96:5), the emptiness and vanity (*hebel,* Jer. 2:5, NIV; cf. KJV) of idolatry; or they show the shame (*bosheth,* Jer. 11:13), the contempt (*ghillovleem,* Ezek. 30:13), the terror and dread (*mipletseth,* 1 Kings 15:13) godly men felt toward it.

In the NT idolatry is further used figuratively to indicate too great obsession with any object less than God. In this connection Rom. 1:25 points out God's displeasure in the preoccupation with the material benefits of creation while failing to give due consideration to the nature and will of the Creator. Covetousness or greed, the undue setting of the heart upon earthly things instead of God, is said to be idolatry (Matt. 6:24; Eph. 5:5; Col. 3:5). Gluttony, the inordinate care of the appetite, is put in the same category (Phil. 3:19). So it is that in the NT the OT concept of idolatry is widened to include anything which tends to dethrone God from the human heart.

See WORSHIP, DECALOGUE, ICON (ICONOCLASM), COVETOUSNESS, IMAGE.

For Further Reading: Clarke, *Christian Theology,* 210; Fallows, ed., *The Popular and Critical Bible Encyclopaedia,* 2:847-50; *IDB,* 2:673-78; Wiley, *CT,* 3:39.

ARMOR D. PEISKER

IGNORANCE. Theologically this term has had a lengthy history. Thomas developed an extensive system of levels of ignorance. The purpose, of course, was to determine which kinds of ignorance were culpable and which were innocent. The elaborate Catholic system allows for five classes of ignorance with several subclasses within each.

The issue hinges upon the activity of the will in the thought and activity process. If a person does not know God's direction on a certain issue and has not purposefully propagated his lack of knowledge through neglect or refusal to listen, that ignorance is innocent (Luke 12:48; John 9:41; 1 Tim. 1:13-14). If the person has been exposed to knowledge of the issue, however, and fails to recognize it because it would interfere with his thoughts or plans, he is responsible for his ignorance (John 9:41). The practice of refusing God's instruction is referred to often in Scripture as hardening the heart.

It is of serious concern to note that the fuller the revelation denied, the greater the guilt and punishment (Matt. 10:15; 11:20-24). Thankfully, however, it is God who determines the culpability of our ignorance rather than man.

See ACCOUNTABILITY, LIGHT, KNOWLEDGE, OBEDIENCE, CARNAL MIND.

For Further Reading: Aquinas, *Summa Theologica,* 17:31, 33; *New Catholic Encyclopedia,* 1967 ed.

D. MARTIN BUTLER

ILLUSIONISM. Illusionism is an evaluation of theism which asserts that the reality of God as claimed by theists is an illusion. According to this position, the true locus of "God's existence" is in the human mind and in its religious imagination. Hence, there is no objective reality to God. What is taken to be His objective reality is but an image that man, the true creator of God, projects and solidifies in ritual and doctrine. To this projection is attributed powers far superior to anything man is willing to claim for himself. The result of this illusion is that "God" becomes the "creator."

This evaluation of theism is generally common to most forms of 19th- and 20th-century atheism. The first systematic statement of illusionism was made by Ludwig Feuerbach (1804-72), German philosopher of religion and theologian, and lecturer at the University of Heidelberg. He was a student of Hegel, but he went beyond Hegel by denying the reality of God.

Philosophies of religion similar to Feuerbach's may be found in Karl Marx (1818-83); Emile Durkheim (1858-1917), the pioneer sociologist; Sigmund Freud (1856-1939); Friedrich Nietzsche (1844-1900), who believed that "the death of the idea of God" was the most profound and fundamental truth about the modern world; and numerous present-day humanists such as Julian Huxley, Kai Nielson, and Paul Kurtz. Although there are significant differences among these thinkers, there is common agreement among them that there is no corresponding reality to the theist's language about the reality of God.

A. C. Knudson (1873-1953), a Christian theologian and philosopher of religion, discusses and critiques illusionism in *Present Tendencies in Religious Thought* and *The Doctrine of God.* In the latter volume he lists three types of illusionism: psychological, sociological, and intellectualistic. In addition to Feuerbach, he names as representatives of the first type the Greek philosopher Lucretius (95-55 B.C.), who thought the basis of religion to be fear, and Freud, who viewed religion in part as the result of a distorted sexuality. Karl Marx is named as the primary sociological illusionist. Auguste Comte (1798-1857) represents the third type. He viewed man's intellectual development as beginning with theology, growing up through metaphysics, and finally maturing in positivism, where God is no longer needed for human self-understanding.

Karl Barth's theology was in many respects an attack on illusionism and on all forms of theology in which God seems to be but an exaggerated reflection of man, where thinking about God is governed by thought about man. The place to begin a critique of Feuerbach and all forms of illusionism, Barth said, is to realize that Feuerbach has accurately, even if unwittingly, described the fruit of man's efforts to grasp God through his own religious efforts or imaginations. Religion, as man's own creation, is an attempt to shape God in man's own image, and is the cardinal evidence of the Fall.

The gods produced by religion are in fact illusions, products of man's alienation from the God of whom the Bible speaks, who alone is the Holy One. He alone is Sovereign Creator, Redeemer, and Lord of history. Knowledge of Him comes through His saving acts and His self-disclosure in Jesus. This knowledge refutes man's idolatrous projections and confirms that God cannot simply be explained by man's own ideas, as the illusionists claim.

The God of the Bible is the Wholly Other God. Before Him we would all pass away were it not for His creative love for us.

Justification by grace through faith means the end of idolatry, the absolute end to god-making, and the reign of the free, eternal, and gracious God who became incarnate in Jesus of Nazareth. This God is certainly not of man's own making, as Isaiah and Jeremiah's scorn for idolatry clearly shows (Isaiah 40; Jeremiah 10).

See GOD, THEISM, THEISTIC PROOFS, REVELATION (SPECIAL).

For Further Reading: Knudson, *The Doctrine of God;* Miller, *Karl Barth,* 49-94.

ALBERT L. TRUESDALE, JR.

IMAGE. The word "image"—commonly understood to mean a likeness of one person or thing to another, or a reflection or representation of such—appears numerous times in the Bible. In the OT it is the English translation of a dozen or so Hebrew terms. Most of them refer to material representations of something, usually an idol.

Tselem is used when referring to personal likenesses. Examples are in Gen. 1:26-27; 5:3. The NT Greek word translated "image" (except in Heb. 1:3) is *eikōn.*

"God created man in his own image" (Gen. 1:27) is particularly significant. The divine image in man is not physical, for God is a Spirit without physical form. But that very spiritual nature He has shared with man. Indeed, spirituality is one aspect of the divine image which theologians have chosen to consider under the heading of the natural image of God. It is that quality which makes man unique among and superior to all other earthly creatures, giving him capacity to commune with and fellowship with his Creator.

Other elements of the natural image of God are immortality and intelligence. As a spiritual being, man is immortal. An ancient Jewish scholar stated it: "God created man to be immortal . . . an image of His own eternity" (Wisdom, 2:23). Man's intellectual powers, reflecting the Creator's, enable him to know, to reason, to imagine, to remember, to judge, and to will (Col. 3:10).

The natural image of God—referring actually to the elements of human personality and selfhood—is the basis whereby man may bear the moral image of God. Man was created upright (Eccles. 7:29). It is true that through his disobedience man lost that original holiness; but with the power to choose, he may accept the divine provision of God in Christ and be restored. Therefore, the apostle Paul could declare that believers may "be conformed to the image of his Son" (Rom. 8:29; cf. Eph. 4:24). And God further intends that those who have thus come to bear His moral image should grow and mature, ever coming to bear more of His likeness "till we all come . . . unto the measure of the stature of the fulness of Christ" (Eph. 4:13).

Today the term is popularly used in reference to one's reputation or name: how one is perceived by others. To have a "good image" is to be well thought of. This contemporary concern can lead to mere window dressing. But it can also prompt Christians to be aware of the impression their appearance and conduct will have on others (Prov. 22:1; Acts 6:3).

See MIND OF CHRIST, CHRISTLIKENESS, IMITATION OF CHRIST, DIVINE IMAGE, MAN.

For Further Reading: Blackman, *A Theological Word Book of the Bible,* 110-11; Purkiser, ed., *Exploring Our Christian Faith,* 212-15.

ARMOR D. PEISKER

IMAGINATION. Imagination means "creative ability: ability to confront and deal with a problem; resourcefulness" (Webster). Imagination is also said to be "the reorganization of past experiences into novel combinations." Man puts old elements into new formations and thus creates new concepts. This capacity is part of the image of God in man.

In imagination the mind passes through four overlapping stages: (1) *Preparation:* thought on the subject—usually prolonged; (2) *Incubation:* the materials lie back in the mind; (3) *Illumination:* the creative idea suddenly emerges; (4) *Verification:* the idea is given tangible form, e.g., in a poem, a sermon, a Kingdom plan.

A second meaning, obsolete today, occurs frequently in the Bible. Imagination is "a plotting or scheming, especially of evil" (Webster). "They . . . have not obeyed my voice . . . but have walked after the imagination of their own heart" (Jer. 9:13-14). Even in these contexts the term is often morally neutral. The prophet must qualify the word to express his meaning, as in "the imagination of their *evil heart*" (3:17; 11:8; et al., italics added).

In the NT Paul describes men who "became

vain in their imaginations, and their foolish heart was darkened" (Rom. 1:21). The natural image of God was corrupted by the carnal spirit and by evil acts.

But depraved imagination can be transformed when yielded to God. "Present all your faculties to Him . . . be transformed by the entire renewal of your minds" (Rom. 12:1-2, Weymouth). When the cleansed, creative imagination reflects on things of God, innovative progress comes to the kingdom of God. "Whatever is true . . . whatever is just . . . whatever is gracious . . . think about these things" (Phil. 4:8, RSV).

See MIND, MAN, DIVINE IMAGE.

For Further Reading: *Encyclopedia Americana*, 4:706-7; *Baker's DT*, 278-79. A. F. HARPER

IMAGO DEI. See DIVINE IMAGE.

IMITATION OF CHRIST. The concept of the imitation of Christ has had a significant impact on the development of Christian mysticism, monasticism, Christian ethics, and Christian spirituality in general. Because of the varying interpretations of the phrase it is impossible to say definitely what the imitation of Christ has meant in the history of the church without examining its theological and practical development in a variety of historical contexts.

The notion that the essence of Christianity is to be found in the imitation of Christ has a solid basis in the Gospels, particularly in such passages as Mark 8:31-38 and Luke 9:23-27, 57-62, where Jesus indicates that His disciples should follow His own example of cross-bearing. In the Early Church, such summonses were perceived as a literal call to martyrdom.

The Gospels, however, are not the only biblical source of the *imitatio Christi* ideal. Paul, in 1 Corinthians 13 and 2 Cor. 13:3, 5 suggests that the following of Jesus by His disciples is not so much a literal imitation of the historical Jesus but the operation of the Holy Spirit in bringing Christians into conformity with the total self-abandonment and other-love of Jesus.

The Middle Ages, with its twin emphases on mysticism and monasticism, conceived of the imitation of Christ, for the most part, as a literal reproduction of the life of the historical Jesus. This can be seen most clearly in the works of Bernard of Clairvaux, Francis of Assisi, and the liturgy of the Mass with its enactment of the "stations of the Lord's life." This emphasis on literalness, however, is not to be found in the greatest medieval if not the greatest work of all time on *imitatio Christi*, Thomas a Kempis' *The Imitation of Christ*. While Thomas is certainly mystical in his understanding of following Christ, he is also profoundly biblical in his portrayal of Christian imitation as requiring the personal discipline and self-resignation of redemptive servanthood in conjunction with God and for man (e.g., chap. 12).

Since the Reformation there has been a substantial degree of reinterpretation of the idea of *imitatio Christi*. Luther, for instance, though greatly admiring the works of many of the medieval mystics, gradually became convinced that the believer's attempt to literally replicate the conditions of life of the historical Jesus perverted the doctrine of grace and established a doctrine of works which led to the belief that man through his own efforts could follow Christ. Luther thus preferred to talk about conformity to the image of Christ rather than the imitation of Christ.

The concept of a literal emulation of the historical Jesus has encountered a further difficulty in the development of 20th-century biblical studies. Many NT scholars have been convinced that it is impossible to recover a sufficiently accurate and detailed picture of the historical Jesus to make an exact *imitatio Christi* possible. However, we know, from the Gospel record, enough about Jesus' life to understand what is intended by His call to discipleship. Jesus calls His disciples to follow Him in cross-bearing servanthood in perfect love (Matt. 5:48). His teaching and Paul's understanding of the work of the Holy Spirit seem to provide a model of *imitatio Christi* which suggests that imitation of Christ is essentially a discipleship brought about both through the disciple's *willing* acceptance of the demands of following Christ and the Holy Spirit's *enabling* grace which allows the disciple to approximate the full measure of Christlikeness. Christlikeness in this sense is thus a perfect love toward God and man dependent upon both the disciple's continual willing and God's constant working.

See DISCIPLESHIP, CROSS-BEARING, IMAGE.

For Further Reading: Kempis, *The Imitation of Christ*; Kierkegaard, *Training in Christianity*; Luther, *Commentary on Galatians*; Tinsley, *The Imitation of God in Christ*. JOHN C. LUIK

IMMACULATE CONCEPTION. This doctrine of the Roman Catholic church as defined by Pope Pius IX in the papal bull *Ineffabilis Deus* (Dec. 8, 1854) holds that the Virgin Mary was preserved immaculate, free from all stain of original sin in the first instant of her conception by a singular grace and privilege of Almighty God (cf. Denzinger, *The Sources of Catholic Dogma,* 413). The official definition declared by Pius IX was the final result of a long history of debate within the Roman church to establish a uniform doctrine of Mary's holiness.

Belief in the original sinlessness of Mary lacks biblical support. First, Scripture makes no explicit or implicit reference to Mary's conception. Second, although Mary is described as a devout person who had found favor with God, the degree of grace or holiness bestowed upon her is not given in the Gospels (Luke 1:28-30). Finally, a belief in the immaculate conception of Mary naturally excludes her from the redemptive work of Christ who came to save all men (1 Tim. 2:4; 4:10). Furthermore, she humbly joined those who tarried for the baptism with the Holy Spirit, thus acknowledging her need and her subjection to the command of her Son (Acts 1:14).

See MARIOLATRY, MOTHER OF GOD, VIRGIN BIRTH.

For Further Reading: Denzinger, *The Sources of Catholic Dogma,* 413; O'Connor, *New Catholic Encyclopedia,* 7:378-82. ALEXANDER VARUGHESE

IMMANENCE. Where deism teaches that "God stepped out of this universe once he created it" (Willis, *Western Civilization,* 546), immanence affirms the fact that God is present in all creation. Although a wholesome corrective against one error, immanence can lead to others.

For example, to believe that God is in all is to come very close to pantheism, for if one accepts the fact that God is present in nature, it becomes difficult to separate Him from that nature.

Another possible error stemming from too great a stress on immanence is polytheism. In this view, the awesome manifestations of the natural world are deified. In this setting God retains no unique identity; and if He is worshipped at all, it is as one of many gods.

It is a comfort to believe that God is present in all of His creation in a unique and personal way. It is His uniqueness which elicits our worship, and His personality which gives credence to His promises of grace, guidance, and general care. Above all, it is the sureness of His holiness which establishes Him as the Moral Arbiter of the world. Because He is holy, He can expect us to be holy. And that is the strongest representation of immanence: God present in the lives of His people.

See TRANSCENDENCE, DEISM, PANTHEISM, OMNIPRESENCE, ATTRIBUTES (DIVINE).

For Further Reading: Shedd, *Dogmatic Theology;* Wiley, *CT,* vol. 1; Willis, *Western Civilization, an Urban Perspective.* MERNE A. HARRIS

IMMANUEL. This name occurs three times in the Bible (Isa. 7:14; 8:8; Matt. 1:23). The Hebrew and Greek words mean "God is with us." There are strong theological overtones in this name, pointing to Divinity ("God") and the Incarnation ("with us").

The word first appears in a very precise historical setting (Isa. 7:1—8:15). The year is 735 B.C., and the kings of Syria and Ephraim have formed an alliance as the first step towards a confederacy into which they wish to draw Judah as a means of defense against Assyrian aggression. Ahaz, king of Judah, resists the idea; and consequently, the two kings seek to overthrow him.

In the midst of this crisis Isaiah encourages Ahaz to ask of the Lord a sign, which he refuses to do. In spite of the king's refusal, God insists on giving a sign according to the following terms: a young unmarried female—an *almah*—is to give birth to a son who is to be called Immanuel (Isa. 7:14).

Since the 19th century this sign has created some serious exegetical problems. When it comes to the fulfillment of this prophecy in Ahaz's time, no abundance of specific evidence is to be found in the biblical record. This vagueness appears to be out of character when the precision with which the prophecy was given is considered. Ahaz's unbelief, however, may be a critical factor.

For this reason the traditional interpretation of the sign is that it was Messianic in nature and could only be applied to Jesus Christ. Matt. 1:23 substantiates this view. (A delayed fulfillment is also described in Mic. 5:2-3.)

There is something singular about the virgin birth of Jesus Christ, and the miraculous dimension is so transcendent that a precursor in Ahaz's time would only make the problem more acute. This element of transcendence causes us to note that Jesus Christ did not come out of history but rather He came into history from above.

This fact introduces us to the essential meaning of the name Immanuel. Harold Lindsell writes, "By the light of nature we see God above us. By the light of the law we see God against us. By the light of the Gospel we see Jesus as Immanuel who is God with us" (*Christianity Today,* 22 [Dec. 9, 1977]: 25).

See CHRIST, INCARNATION, VIRGIN BIRTH, PROPHET (PROPHECY).

For Further Reading: Heb. 4:14—5:10; J. D. Douglas, *NBD,* 556-57; J. Gresham Machen, *The Virgin Birth of Christ,* 287-93. ROBERT A. MATTKE

IMMERSION. The term *immersion* relates to one of the three modes of water baptism (presumably

Christian), which are: immersion, effusion, and sprinkling. The mode of immersion signifies a total submersion in water.

It has often been argued that the Greek term for baptism, *baptidzō,* intrinsically denotes immersion. Of course there are many and varied authorities, but one which is widely recognized as reliable on most questions gives the root meaning of *baptidzō* in Christian usage as: "dip, immerse, dip oneself, wash." In other Greek literature its meaning is given as: "plunge, sink, drench, overwhelm" (cf. Arndt and Gingrich).

The observation that baptism by pouring was allowed in cases of necessity in the apostolic age would strongly indicate that the normal mode was immersion (cf. *Didache* 7; Ignatius' *Letter to Smyrnaeans* 8:2). Thus, although other modes than immersion were practiced in the Early Church when considered necessary, the evidence indicates that immersion was the usual method. This is particularly so when the symbolic significance of the sacrament is considered (cf. Rom. 6:3 ff; Gal. 3:27; Col. 3:9; see Beasley-Murray, *Baptism in the NT,* 262). On the other hand, when baptism has typological significance (cf. 1 Cor. 10:2) or even relates to martyrdom (cf. Mark 10:38), the meaning of immersion is not so evident.

It must be recognized, however, that insistence on the *theological significance* of immersion, to the exclusion of any other mode, is a relatively modern development. Even among those of the Baptist persuasion the all-essential issue principally concerns infant baptism. In 17th-century England this was the issue over which the Separatists (Baptists) broke with the Nonconformist communion. It was not until later that the exclusive mode of immersion was adopted (cf. W. S. Hudson, *Religion in America,* 43). When Adoniram Judson was converted to Baptist doctrine, while studying his Greek Testament on the long trip to Burma, the fundamental question was infant baptism and not immersion.

When one remembers that Luther, Calvin, Wesley, and a great host of other post-Reformation leaders accepted and practiced a mode of baptism other than immersion, there is hardly a sound basis for theological dogmatism to the contrary.

See BAPTISM.

For Further Reading: Wiley, *CT,* 3:176-82; *GMS,* 590.

RICHARD E. HOWARD

IMMORTALITY. The word literally means "deathlessness" (from the Greek, *thanatos,* "death," transformed into *athanatos,* "deathless," by the addition of the Greek *alpha* privative, from which comes *athanasia,* "immortality"). The latter is used concerning the nature of God in 1 Tim. 6:16, "who only hath immortality," in that God alone inherently possesses it and thus is the Source of all life. It appears also in 1 Cor. 15:53-54, relating to the glorified body of the believer. In 1 Tim. 1:17 it means "incorruptible," and in Rom. 2:7 and 2 Tim. 1:10 it signifies "incorruption." As generally used, immortality means the unending, conscious existence of man after his earthly life is terminated.

There are strong intimations of life beyond the grave in the OT, particularly in the Psalms and in Job. The Psalmist anticipates life hereafter, for example, in Ps. 17:15 and 23:6. He struggles with the problem of the disparity of rewards of the wicked and the righteous in this life in Psalms 49 and 73, and expresses the hope of the righteous in Ps. 49:15 and 73:24-26. Job asks a universal and perennial question in 14:14, "If a man die, shall he live again?" and answers it with his greatest affirmation of faith in 19:25-27. The doctrine of a future life is also plainly asserted elsewhere in the OT, such as in Isa. 26:19 and in Dan. 12:2-3.

It is in the NT, however, that the full glow of life hereafter is given. The apostle Paul asserts that Jesus Christ "hath abolished death, and hath brought life and immortality to light through the gospel" (2 Tim. 1:10). Our Lord's own triumph over death and the grave "has broken the power of death" (NEB), stripped it of any terror, and has brought into full view of faith both life and immortality. The apostle is not inferring that the doctrine of immortality was previously unknown, but is declaring that "the gospel pours light upon and discloses the author, origin, and true nature of life and immortality to our view" (Whedon, *Commentary on the NT,* 4:445).

Our Savior repeatedly mentioned existence beyond earthly life, not only for the righteous, but also for the wicked: e.g., Matt. 5:12, 22; 8:11-12; 10:28; 25:31-46; Mark 9:43; Luke 16:19-31; 18:29-30; 23:43; John 3:16; 5:24-29; 6:47-58; 11:25; 14:1-3; et al.

The Christian message offers hope for the total person. Though physical death and dissolution ensue, through resurrection man will be reembodied at a loftier, glorified level, and will live forever in Christ's presence (1 Cor. 15:53-54; 1 Thess. 4:16-17). Such a glorious future has been assured to believers through the mighty power of God over death, "which he wrought in Christ, when he raised him from the dead" (Eph. 1:20).

See MAN, CONDITIONAL IMMORTALITY, SPIRIT, ETERNAL LIFE, SOUL, INTERMEDIATE STATE.

For Further Reading: Boettner, *Immortality;* Cullmann, *Immortality of the Soul or Resurrection of the Dead? GMS,* 80-81, 138-44, 649-52; Wiley, *CT,* 2:34-37; 3:215-24; Rawlings, *Beyond Death's Door.*

WILLIAM M. ARNETT

IMMUTABILITY. Changelessness, or immutability, in the Scripture is frequently attributed to Deity in contrast to the changeableness of humankind. God is seen as changeless as the mountains and the heavenly bodies. Man, by contrast, is compared to grass (Ps. 90:2-6), to chaff (1:4), to a morning cloud, to dew (Hos. 6:4), and to smoke (Prov. 10:26). Even the earth and the heavens will change "like a garment," but God remains unchanged (Heb. 1:8, 10-12). Writers of the Bible find relief as they reflect that while mankind is vacillating and unreliable, God, by contrast, is unchanging and, therefore, trustworthy.

Linked to this characteristic of the divine nature is the concept of the absolute in the realm of ethics. Since God is unchanging, His law is likewise unchanging; it is not subject to man's vacillation or alteration. God's "throne" or realm is immutable. Because of God's constancy His dealings with mankind remain fixed and dependable. Because of the "unchangeableness of his promise" (author's tr.) the believer now has hope (Heb. 6:17-19).

Modern "process theologians," like the ancient philosopher Heraclitus (fl. 500 B.C.), stress the mutability of things divine, preferring the dynamic to the static. Similarly, "situation ethics" eschews an absolute system of values and prefers instead to see ethics as related to the immediate environment rather than to unchanging absolutes. While divine revelation is seen in the NT to be progressive (cf. Heb. 1:1-2), the essentials are changeless as the cosmos (Matt. 5:17-18).

The biblical world (and ours) is one in which God's will and ways are not capricious and unpredictable. In such a world man would be irresponsible. Instead man exists in a universe in which moral values do not change; God's will is known and His actions are consistent. Therefore, man is responsible for his conduct because God is revealed as consistent, equitable, immutable, and hence credible (Rom. 1:17-20).

However, the biblical concept of immutability does not include what has often been ascribed to it, viz., total passivity in every sense. God has feelings and responses toward man and His universe, and both acts and reacts in a dynamic way (cf. Rom. 11:20-23).

See GOD, ATTRIBUTES (DIVINE), MORAL ATTRIBUTES OF GOD, PROCESS THEOLOGY, ABSOLUTISM, NEW MORALITY.

For Further Reading: Kantzer, Gundry, eds., *Perspectives on Evangelical Theology,* 15:42; Wiley, *CT,* 1:332 ff, 340-42.

GEORGE ALLEN TURNER

IMPANATION. The term literally means "embodied in bread." It is one of the theories of explanation regarding the presence of Christ in the Lord's Supper. Berengarius of Tours (d. 1086) is credited with its development. He disagreed with the traditional view of the church of his day. That view, called transubstantiation, suggested that the substance of the bread and wine actually became the body and blood of Christ at the moment of consecration. Berengarius argued, however, that the Lord became united with the elements without any substantial change occurring in them. The body of Christ is present in the Eucharist, but only in power rather than in essence.

The theory predated the Lutheran position of consubstantiation and is considered to be quite similar to it. The majority of Protestant Christianity sets all of these theories aside in favor of considering the elements as signs and seals of Christ's presence.

See CONSUBSTANTIATION, HOLY COMMUNION.

D. MARTIN BUTLER

IMPARTED RIGHTEOUSNESS. This has to do with God's not only declaring us to be righteous, as a judicial act in which He absolves us of the guilt of our acts of sins, but with His actually making us righteous. God, who surely would not declare a fiction, declares us to be righteous because He actually makes us so. The term is somewhat similar in meaning to that of regeneration, because it has to do with what God does within us, subjectively, in distinction from what He does for us.

Righteousness is also sometimes imputed to us—in which case we are reckoned as righteous when we are not. An instance of this is when God imputes righteousness to us, through the atonement of Christ, when we unknowingly transgress what His will for us is.

One of the most significant biblical supports for the understanding that God actually imparts righteousness to us is in Rom. 8:3-4, where we read, "And so he condemned sin in sinful man, in order that the righteous requirements of the law might be fully met in us, who do not live according to the sinful nature but according to the Spirit" (NIV). Here, we are not righteous merely in a "declared" sense or in an "imputed" sense. We ourselves are actually made righteous by God's grace. It is not that Christ fulfills God's expectations, and that, because we are Christ's, we are reckoned as righteous when we are not actually so. Paul here says that, by grace, God's just expectations are fulfilled "in us"—and not simply and solely in Christ.

See IMPUTED RIGHTEOUSNESS, REPENTANCE, REGENERATION, CLEANSING, RIGHT (RIGHTEOUSNESS).

For Further Reading: Purkiser, ed., *Exploring Our Christian Faith,* 311 ff; Wiley, *CT,* 2:385-401; Taylor, *A Right Conception of Sin.* J. KENNETH GRIDER

IMPECCABILITY OF CHRIST. See SINLESSNESS OF CHRIST.

IMPENITENCE. To be impenitent is to be obdurate in one's sin, in full awareness and hence full responsibility. An "impenitent heart" is linked with "hardness" in Rom. 2:5. There may be some measure of remorse and what Paul calls "the sorrow of the world" (2 Cor. 7:10), yet a refusal to abandon sin and turn wholly to God in humility, confession, and brokenness. An impenitent person knows he has done wrong but is not profoundly sorry for the wrong, only annoyed by its consequences. Impenitence is thus thoroughly ethical and not to be confused with the moral blindness of true ignorance. The lost are those who die in final impenitence.

See IGNORANCE, PENITENCE, REPENTANCE.

RICHARD S. TAYLOR

IMPUTED RIGHTEOUSNESS. In theology "imputed righteousness" is inextricably bound up with the doctrine of justification. The doctrine represents the efforts of the theologians to relate the work of Christ (His obedience to the Father, His suffering and death) to the justification of believers.

The word "impute" is derived from the Greek word *logidzomai,* which means "to reckon or account." A man's sin or a man's righteousness is imputed to him when he personally commits the sinful or righteous acts (cf. Wiley, *CT,* 2:396).

The older theologians were agreed that there is a doctrine of imputation in the Scripture, and the phraseology they used was quite similar. However, their interpretations differed rather widely. This is especially true of Calvin and Arminius. Calvin's idea of imputation seems to be that the righteousness of Christ is accounted or imputed to us as if it were our own, and is beneficial only for the elect. Arminius insisted that Christ's righteousness is bestowed on all who believe—faith is imputed to them for righteousness.

The hyper-Calvinists pushed Calvin's position to its logical conclusion and fell into error. These antinomians claimed that "Christ's righteousness is substituted for theirs in such a way as to render them as legally righteous as if they had themselves rendered perfect obedience to the law of God" (Wiley, *CT,* 2:396). This turns out to be righteousness by proxy. John Wesley strongly rejected this theory of imputation: "What we are afraid of is this;—lest any should use this phrase, 'The righteousness of Christ is imputed to me,' as a cover for his unrighteousness. We have known this done a thousand times. A man has been reproved, suppose for drunkenness: 'O,' says he, 'I pretend to no righteousness of *my own;* Christ is *my righteousness'"* (*Works,* 5:244). Wiley says, "The Antinomianism that would lead a soul to a reliance upon the imputed righteousness of Christ without the concomitant inward impartation of righteousness by the Spirit, is a dangerous perversion of the truth" (*CT,* 2:399).

There is therefore a proper doctrine of imputation, and there is an improper doctrine of imputation. Wesley stated unequivocally: "To all believers the righteousness of Christ is imputed; to unbelievers it is not." Someone asked Wesley, When is it imputed? He replied, "When they believe: In that very hour the righteousness of Christ is theirs. It is imputed to everyone that believes, as soon as he believes: faith and the righteousness of Christ are inseparable" (*Works,* 5:237). From this we see that the Wesleyan-Arminian position is that the believer's faith is imputed to him for righteousness. This is fully supported by Scripture: "Abraham believed God, and it was counted unto him for righteousness" (Rom. 4:3; cf. 5, 9, 22-24). Even here we must not err by identifying faith with righteousness. "All believers are forgiven and accepted, not for the sake of anything in them, or of anything that ever was, or can be done by them, but wholly and solely for the sake of what Christ has done and suffered for them" (Wesley, *Works,* 5:239).

See JUSTIFICATION, IMPARTED RIGHTEOUSNESS.

For Further Reading: "Righteousness," *NIDNTT;* Wesley, *Works,* 5—Sermons "Justification" and "The Lord Our Righteousness"; Wiley, *CT,* 2:394-401.

C. PAUL GRAY

IN ADAM. The term "in Adam" is a technical concept for the solidarity of humanity with Adam and his sin, as recorded in Gen. 3:1-24. Although "the Adam-typology . . . plays a considerable part in Paul's thinking, and . . . is present to his mind when he is writing passages in which the name of Adam is not mentioned" (Alan Richardson, *An Introduction to the Theology* *of the New Testament,* 245), the term only appears explicitly in Rom. 5:12-21 and 1 Cor. 15:22, where it is always used in a consistently antithetical relationship with the redemptive solidaric term "in Christ" (John Murray, *The Epistle to the Romans,* 1:179).

The solidarity to which both terms refer is ethical (as in Arminianism) rather than realistic or imputational (as in some forms of Calvinism). This fact is embedded in Rom. 5:12-21, a passage which occupies a transitional and pivotal position in Paul's discussion in 5:1—8:17 of the meaning, place, and appropriation of holiness in the total process of salvation.

The ethical quality of "in Adam" is discerned by discovering in what sense "many [were] made sinners . . . by one man's disobedience" (Rom. 5:19, RSV). The answer emerges by noting that the interpretive summary of 5:12—which introduces the problem that "all men sinned . . . through one man"—is verse 18 (Murray, ibid.). Gen. 2:16-17 states that condemnation would come to Adam *personally* for *his* transgression. In the same ethical vein, Paul reveals that condemnation comes to all men as a result of *their actual sin:* "One man's trespass *led* to condemnation for all men" (Rom. 5:18, RSV). With "led" as the pivotal word, it becomes evident that Adam's sin, as a universally inherited proclivity to sin, *leads* to condemnation for all men. When this proclivity is yielded to or obeyed, the result is actual sin which brings condemnation.

In light of this, the solidaric emphasis of "in Adam" as ethical requires an effect that is potential rather than automatically actual. This is substantiated by noting the clearly ethical focus of the antithetical solidaric term, "in Christ," for the relation which lost humanity may sustain to Christ is the interpretive key for understanding the relation humanity outside of Christ sustains to Adam. Consequently, if we remember that the seeming justification of all in Christ is potential and only becomes actual when appropriated in an ethical act (Rom. 5:15-18), the complete antithetical construction of 5:12-21 leads to this conclusion: The apparent condemnation of all in Adam because of his disobedience is really potential, only becoming actual when consented to volitionally by an act of sin.

The contextual relation of "in Adam" to holiness in Romans emerges in the rephrasing of the term in the concept of the "old man" in 6:6 (KJV). By this lexical interlocking, the antithetical structure between Adam and Christ in 5:12-21 and the ethical relationship men sustain to either one becomes the pattern for interpreting the meaning and appropriation of holiness in 6:1-14.

See ORIGINAL SIN, PREVENIENT GRACE, IN CHRIST, OLD MAN.

For Further Reading: Howard, *Newness of Life,* 37-44, 61-65, 84-87; Jeremias, "Adam," in Kittel, 1:141-43; Richardson, ed., "Adam, Man," *A Theological Word Book of the Bible,* 14-15; *NIDNTT,* 1:84-87; Wiley, *CT,* 2:108, 125 ff, 133-37.

JOHN G. MERRITT

IN CHRIST. The term "in Christ" and its spectrum of equivalents is an expression which occurs at least 164 times in the NT. There has been a growing consensus among many scholars that the centrality of the frequent occurrence of this term in the structure of his Epistles points to union with Christ as the heart of Paul's theology (see James S. Stewart, *A Man in Christ,* 7:150-52; Nielson, *In Christ,* 48-50). As perhaps the core concept of Paul's message, the expression "in Christ" may be summarized under at least four rubrics:

First, "in Christ" is a *comprehensive* term: it embraces and undergirds such significant biblical themes as justification, reconciliation, sanctification, the Church (cf. Lightfoot, *Sermons in St. Paul's,* 227; Plummer, *Second Corinthians,* 69).

Second, "in Christ" is a *mystical* term. Because the concept is relational—union with Christ—it places the central, historically rooted biblical themes in the arena of Spirit-attested human experience. This warmth which radiates from "in Christ" derives from the mysticism that inheres in the concept. However, this is not a union in which the human is absorbed in and obliterated by the divine; it is a redemptive permeation of the human personality by the divine through the indwelling presence of Christ (see Nielson, ibid., 18; Stewart, ibid., 160-73).

Third, "in Christ" is an ethically *solidaric* concept. The solidarity expressed by "in Christ" is indicated in Rom. 5:12-21, where it is placed in a consistently antithetical relationship with the contrastive solidaric concept, "in Adam." In its larger context of 5:1—8:17, "in Christ" as a solidaric concept reaches its high point of significance in the experience and life of holiness, in which union with Christ centers in subjective identification with His death and resurrection (6:1-14). This solidarity is ethical in nature and is thus potential rather than automatically causal or actual in effect. This is seen in Paul's apparent assertion in 5:15-16 that Christ's obedience resulted in the justification of *all* men. However, this seeming actuality in 5:16, 18 is observed to be *potential* when seen in the light of the *provisional* nature of justification in 5:15, 17-18.

Thus, for the *potential* to become *actual,* an act of the will must be exercised to appropriate the *provisional* effects of Christ's obedience.

The antithetical structure between Adam and Christ in Rom. 5:12-21 and the relationship men sustain to either one becomes the interpretive key to understanding holiness in 6:1-14: Simply because a person is "in Adam," he does not experience the effects of the inherited sin-principle in terms of guilt (i.e., in the sense of full responsibility and condemnation) until he embraces it by personal transgression. In like manner, simply being "in Christ" does not necessarily mean one has fully received experiential holiness, or entire sanctification, in Him. Thus, what can and should be ours by virtue of being "in Christ" is not actually ours until we make it our own by faith.

Fourth, "in Christ" is an *eschatological* concept. "The very phrase describing the status of the believer, 'in Christ,' is an eschatological term. To be 'in Christ' means to be in the new age and to experience its life and powers. 'If any one is in Christ, he is a new creation; the old has passed away, behold the new has come' (II Cor. 5:17)" (George Eldon Ladd, *A Theology of the New Testament,* 551). By "eschatological" is meant that through the redemptive work of Christ and the coming of the Holy Spirit, the age to come has invaded this present evil age (Ladd, 364-65). It is against this eschatological backdrop that life in the Spirit with its soteric content is to be understood. For those "in Christ," the perfect and consummated liberation of the new age has "in part reached back into the present" (Ladd, 371). As both a solidaric and an eschatological term, "in Christ" in Romans has holiness as its high point. As he reaches the climax of his presentation of holiness in Romans, Paul indicates that part of this "reaching back" into the present embraces the experience and life of holiness (8:1-2).

Since the new age reaches back to those "in Christ," the eschatological concept has ethical overtones because it intersects with the solidaric. Thus the soteric content of the eschatological invasion is not automatically effective; it must be appropriated in an ethical act. Therefore, "in Christ" is a solidaric concept that is eschatologically understood and ethically interpreted.

See IN ADAM, CHRIST IN YOU, REGENERATION.

For Further Reading: Harkness, *Mysticism: Its Meaning and Message,* 15-75; Howard, *Newness of Life,* 67-126; Richardson, *An Introduction to the Theology of the New Testament,* 249-52; Nielson, *In Christ.*

JOHN G. MERRITT

INBRED SIN. See ORIGINAL SIN.

INCARNATION. This refers to the eternal Son of God's being enfleshed as Jesus of Nazareth. It refers to the time when, in man's "finest hour," God the Son became man through the Virgin Mary and lived some 33 years in Palestine. It is the time when God (precisely, through the Son) pitched His tent among us (John 1:14); when Christ counted equality with God not something to be held onto, but humbled himself, wore the form of a servant, and became obedient all the way to death on an ignominious Roman cross (Phil. 2:5-8).

In what C. H. Dodd called the "not-yet" times of the OT, God had spoken to us in diverse ways through prophets, priests, and kings; and in the last time span, the last salvific age, God spoke to us through His only begotten, eternally generated Son (Heb. 1:1 ff; John 1:18).

Incarnation means that God was not content simply to think good thoughts about us, nor to help us while keeping a safe distance from us. It means that God visited us for our salvation—"in our sorry case," as the ancient Athanasius expressed it.

Heretical views regarding the Incarnation have sometimes been advocated. In some of them, Christ's humanity has been overstressed in relation to His deity. Ebionism is one such view.

Others have overstressed Christ's deity. One such, certainly, is Docetism, a Gnostic view that Christ was fully divine (and, many of them said, conceived by a virgin); but that He only appeared to be human. Apollinarianism also overstressed His deity in a sense. In this heresy, Christ was said to be human in body and soul, but not in spirit or ego or person. This aspect of Christ's nature was solely divine—the eternal Logos, a person, having amalgamated himself with humanity from the standpoint of assuming a human body and a human soul. Eutychianism, too, overstressed Christ's deity, with its understanding that Christ's humanity got absorbed into His deity at the time of His baptism.

In still other heresies, the error was of a different nature than in the overstress of either Christ's humanity or His deity. One such was the fourth-century Arian position, which became the most serious of all these threats to what came to be hammered out as the Christian teaching. Arius taught that Christ is neither human nor divine, but a third existent, in between—and that He was the first and highest created being.

Nestorianism had to do with the relation of the two natures (human and divine) to the person.

Nestorius pictured Christ's humanity and deity as so separate that this devout heretic was perceived to be saying that Christ possessed two persons (one, human; and the other, divine).

The orthodox Christology, decided upon at the Council of Chalcedon in 451, is that Christ possessed two natures, a fully human one and a fully divine one, and that He possessed only one person—its dictum being that we should not "confuse" the two natures (making them one) nor divide the person.

See CHRIST, CHRISTOLOGY, HYPOSTASIS, HYPOSTATIC UNION, VIRGIN BIRTH, DOCETISM, APOLLINARIANISM, ARIANISM, NESTORIANISM.

For Further Reading: Baillie, *God Was in Christ.*

J. KENNETH GRIDER

INDULGENCES. In Catholic theology, this is the church's remission or waving of the temporal punishment for sins whose guilt has already been forgiven. Remission is granted out of the treasury of merit of the church created by the holiness of Christ and the saints. Such indulgence may be granted to the living or to the dead who are suffering in purgatory.

This teaching grew out of the penitential discipline of the church in earlier centuries. A distinction was made between the guilt of sin and the temporal punishment required for complete absolution, the former to be forgiven by the work of Christ, the latter to be satisfied by acts of penance in this life and, as the doctrine of purgatory developed historically, in purgatory.

Gradual development of the teaching expanded the theology and practice of indulgence granting to include not only the plenary remission of temporal and purgatorial penalties but of the guilt of sins already or yet to be committed. Souls of persons living holding such plenary indulgences would go straight to heaven upon death, or those in purgatory would immediately be released from further suffering.

The blatant abuse of such liberal indulgence teaching aroused Martin Luther to challenge the authority of the medieval church and papacy. Since the Protestant Reformation, the granting of indulgences within the Roman Catholic church has steadily diminished even though their dogmatic validity was affirmed by the Council of Trent.

See CATHOLICISM (ROMAN), PENANCE, REPENTANCE.

For Further Reading: Greenwood, ed., *A Handbook of the Catholic Faith,* 288-92; Klotsche, *History of Christian Doctrine,* 152-54.

MELVIN EASTERDAY DIETER

INERRANCY. See BIBLICAL INERRANCY.

INFALLIBILITY, BIBLICAL. See BIBLICAL INERRANCY.

INFALLIBILITY, PAPAL. See PAPAL INFALLIBILITY.

INFANT BAPTISM (PRO). Support for baptizing infants is considerable. It is surely implied when entire households are baptized, according to several biblical passages (Lydia's, Acts 16:15; the Philippian jailer's, vv. 33-34; Stephanas', 1 Cor. 1:16). A "household" included any children of servants, as well as those of the household's head. Especially in the case of prime-of-life people such as Lydia and the jailer, in an era when children could not be planned as they can be in our day, it would have been mathematically improbable that in these households there were no children who had not as yet reached the age of accountability. In this connection John Wesley, who believed profoundly in the importance of baptizing infants, said that, although infants are not singled out for specific mention, women are seldom singled out, either (exceptions are in Acts 8:2; 16:15).

H. Orton Wiley, Oscar Cullmann, and many other scholars understand, furthermore, that infant baptism is the NT counterpart of the OT circumcision of male infants. Just as an infant, on the eighth day of his life, was to be circumcised, and thereby brought within God's special covenantal favor, so an infant is to be baptized. In some kinds of covenants, humans needed to enter into individual agreement with God; but in others, God made agreements without regard to human cooperation. In circumcision and infant baptism, the covenant is of this nature—except that, of course, the parents agree, in infant baptism, to rear the child to come to know Christ.

Infant baptism, further, is the sacrament which affirms prevenient grace. In the Arminian-Wesleyan tradition, in which infants have been baptized for centuries, the doctrine of prevenient grace has been emphasized. That is, in this tradition, it has been emphasized that we love God "because he first loved us" (1 John 4:19); that no one comes to the Father except the Spirit first summons him (see John 6:44; Ps. 85:4; Jer. 31:18-19). And to baptize infants affirms this kind of grace.

Evangelicals do not believe that infant baptism obviates the need of the new birth, when the child comes to the age of accountability and senses the awakening of the Spirit to his personal sinning.

Infant baptism is the practice of all but a very small percent of Christendom, and it has been, from the earliest centuries. Only Tertullian, connected with an early offshoot group (the Montanists), oppsed it, among the Greek and Latin fathers. It is taught in the *Didache,* the Early Church "manual" dating to around A.D. 100. Even the fifth-century Pelagius, who denied original sin, taught it. It was taught by Luther, Calvin, Arminius, Wesley, Wiley, etc.

See INFANT BAPTISM (CON), INFANT SALVATION, BAPTISM.

For Further Reading: Bromiley, *Children of Promise: The Care for Baptizing Infants;* Small, *The Biblical Basis for Infant Baptism;* Wall, *The History of Infant Baptism;* Wesley, *Thoughts upon Infant Baptism;* Jeremias, *Infant Baptism in the First Four Centuries.*

J. KENNETH GRIDER

INFANT BAPTISM (CON). The baptism of infants in the Christian Church had its origin, according to its proponents, in the Apostolic Church. It is assumed that the household of Cornelius (Acts 10:44-48) and the jailer at Philippi (16:33-34) included infants. Against this assumption it is noteworthy that those baptized with water in Caesarea were those who previously had been baptized with the Holy Spirit and spoke with tongues, "acclaiming the greatness of God" (10:46). Those on whom the Spirit came were "all who were listening to the message" (v. 44), who in turn were "relatives and close friends" of Cornelius (v. 24, all NEB). Were those who gathered to *listen* to Peter, and who later *acclaimed* the greatness of God, infants as well as those old enough to comprehend the message? It seems unlikely. The Philippian jailer and his household became believers between midnight and dawn; were sleeping infants aroused to participate in the baptism? Again, it seems an unwarranted assumption.

Some go back of the Apostolic Church to the ministry of Jesus who welcomed children to His embrace and declared, "Of such is the kingdom of heaven" (Matt. 19:14). It may be asked, "Does baptism make them such, or are they 'of the Kingdom' without baptism?" The OT is often cited in defense of infant baptism. Since children of Hebrew parents were circumcised, and thus brought into the Abrahamic covenant, and since Christians are the "true Israel," therefore infants, to be made participants in the covenant relation, are to be baptized.

Pauline support is sought: "In him also you were circumcised . . . and you were buried with him in baptism" (Col. 2:11-13, RSV). Here Paul uses circumcision as a metaphor, the "circumcision made without hands" being equated with the removal of sin. Paul would be the last one to insist on circumcision as the condition for being a Christian; his concern was that believers experience "real circumcision . . . a matter of the heart, spiritual and not literal" (Rom. 2:29, RSV). John the Baptist, Jesus, and the apostles emphasized that outward rites are not essential and that parents cannot bring their offspring into a saving relationship to Christ by any outward rite. The NT consistently and emphatically asserts that salvation is a personal matter and cannot be passed from generation to generation as the Jews believed (John 8:39-59).

Infant baptism is properly linked with confirmation, hence the importance of the latter in Catholic churches. Both are widely practiced in state churches of Europe including the Anglican, and thence via the Wesleys to the Methodist churches. Because of the embarrassment of seeing that baptized adults often continue to live in sin, the Anabaptists arose in wake of the Reformation to make baptism available only to believers. Recently in Europe, for the same reason, theologians including Karl Barth have called for believers' baptism rather than the administration of the rite to helpless infants. Many who wish to give baptism its maximum significance are sympathetic to this position and prefer to dedicate their infants while reserving baptism to the time when the candidate becomes a willing participant.

See BAPTISM, INFANT BAPTISM (PRO), SACRAMENTS, BAPTISMAL REGENERATION, REBAPTISM, INFANT SALVATION.

For Further Reading: Aland, *Did the Early Church Baptize Infants?* Schnackenburg, *Baptism in the Thought of Paul;* Cannel, *The Historical Antecedents and Development of John Wesley's Doctrine of Christian Initiation* (Ann Arbor Microfilms, 1965); Fisher, *Christian Initiation: Baptism in the Medieval West;* Cho, *A Study of John Wesley's Doctrine of Baptism in Light of Current Interpretations* (Ann Arbor Microfilms, 1967); Lampe, *The Seal of the Spirit;* Turner, "Infant Baptism in Biblical and Historical Context," *WTJ,* Spring, 1970, 11-21; King, "Infant Baptism in Biblical and Wesleyan Theology," M.Th. thesis, Asbury Theological Seminary (1975).

GEORGE ALLEN TURNER

INFANT COMMUNION. For many centuries, infants and small children received the Lord's Supper. This obtained in both the West and in the East. However, although infants still receive Communion in Eastern Orthodoxy, they do not receive it in Roman Catholicism.

The practice was discontinued in medieval times in Roman Catholicism after it had officially accepted the teaching of transubstantiation—that at the priest's consecration of the elements, their substance becomes the actual body and blood of Christ. The Council of Trent, in one of its sessions in 1562, supported its withholding Communion from children by saying that Communion, for them, is "not a divine command."

Protestantism in general has likewise withheld Communion from infants—except that, if a child accepts Christ at a very early age, he is usually considered to be a proper recipient for the Communion Supper.

See CHILD (CHILDREN), SACRAMENTS.

For Further Reading: Smith, *A Short History of Christian Theophagy,* 83-91; Smith, *A Sacramental Society.*

J. KENNETH GRIDER

INFANT SALVATION. Infant salvation refers to the destiny of those who die in infancy. Wesleyan-Arminians affirm that all infants who die will be saved through Christ's atonement, though they are born in pollution and in some sense bearing legal guilt. Jesus said, "Do not look down on one of these little ones. For I tell you that their angels in heaven always see the face of my Father in heaven" (Matt. 18:10, NIV). In Romans 5, Paul contrasts the consequences of Adam's sin with the benefits of the atonement made by Jesus Christ. Verse 18 declares, "So then as through one transgression there resulted condemnation to all men, even so through one act of righteousness there resulted justification of life to all men" (NASB).

All who fell in Adam are provisionally restored in Christ. His atonement provides salvation for all men—not to justify them immediately and unconditionally, but according to God's plan. Adults are justified by faith when they repent and believe. If an infant dies, the Spirit of God regenerates, justifies, and prepares it for heaven. Infant salvation thus depends on the prevenient grace of God, and not on baptism.

Olin A. Curtis (*The Christian Faith,* 403-4) rejects any concept of "unconditional regeneration." He contends infants are moral persons who reach full personal experience in the "intermediate state," as children do in this life. They come to know and freely accept the Savior as individuals under moral test. In companionship with Him, they achieve the equivalent of Christian perfection.

See PREVENIENT GRACE, ORIGINAL SIN, INFANT BAPTISM (PRO, CON).

For Further Reading: Hills, *Fundamental Christian Theology,* 1:433-38.

IVAN A. BEALS

INFANTICIDE. This has to do with the intended killing of an infant after it has been born. The practice has had a long history in primitive societies, especially in the case of unwanted females and of malformed infants. It is illegal in most societies today. But the permission, as in the U.S.A. (unless states make special prohibitions), of abortions even during the last three months of the gestation period is considered by many to be not entirely different from the permission of infanticide. In fact, when there are late abortions, and the fetus exits the womb alive, it is sometimes at least permitted to die.

See MURDER, ABORTION, CHILD (CHILDREN).

J. KENNETH GRIDER

INFIDELITY. See UNBELIEF.

INFINITE, INFINITY. *Infinite* (Lat. *infinitos*) is defined by Webster as "without limits of any kind." *Infinity* is defined as "unlimited extent of time, space or quantity." Webster quotes Raleigh: "There cannot be more infinities than one; for one of them would limit the other." Since this is true, only God can be said to be infinite. In Christian theology infinity is treated as one of the absolute attributes of God. All created beings, including man, are limited in respect to space, size, origin, power, and mind; hence, finite.

Man finds it impossible to comprehend infinitude even though he may define it. In mathematics, optics, music, logic, metaphysics, or any other discipline he can do no more than point toward what he calls infinity.

One of the problems of theology is that of describing the interrelation between infinity and finiteness. Leighton says: "God cannot be infinite in the sense that he can be anything we can think of . . . He cannot will things that contradict his fundamental purposes and aims . . . the only limitations on his actions are the self limitations involved in his own creative love and providence . . . God must be an unchanging being, the changeless ground of the coherent and intelligible order of change" (*The Field of Philosophy,* 337 ff).

See GOD, ATTRIBUTES (DIVINE), DIVINE SOVEREIGNTY.

For Further Reading: Wiley, *CT,* 3:217 ff.

JOHN E. RILEY

INFIRMITIES. The NT word *astheneia* is translated "weakness," "infirmity," and "sickness." In Rom. 15:1 infirmities refer to errors arising from weakness of mind or judgment.

Scriptures refer to infirmities in a nonjudgmental way and assure us of God's gracious enabling in the face of infirmity (see Rom. 6:19; 8:26; 2 Cor. 12:5, 10; Heb. 4:15).

There is no scriptural warrant for regarding either physical infirmities or mental weaknesses and any of their proper consequences as culpable sins, though they are part of the human condition resulting from the Fall.

Theologically, infirmities may be defined as involuntary faults and weaknesses in mental, emotional, and physical dimensions. They fall short of Adamic and divine perfection in ways other than by wilful transgression. So-called sins of ignorance, for instance, are violations of God's perfect law due to the infirmity of ignorance. While theologians differ in assigning culpability to such violations of perfection, all agree that there is no one so perfect in this life as to be free from these natural imperfections of impaired human finiteness.

Wesleyan theology carefully distinguishes mistakes (involuntary shortcomings) from sins (wilful transgressions); and infirmity from carnality. While the complete remedy of infirmities awaits the resurrection and glorification, redemption from perversity and carnality is possible now. Infirmities require compassion and healing, whereas sin provokes God's displeasure and needs forgiveness and cleansing. Infirmities of various kinds, are, therefore, not inconsistent with entire sanctification, as John Wesley clearly enunciated in his *Plain Account of Christian Perfection*.

Some infirmities—such as deficiencies of knowledge, immaturity, forgetfulness, prejudice, emotional impairment, weaknesses of temperament—are capable of improvement in this life. Others, such as certain birth defects, are not.

A catalogue of infirmities would include such diverse defects as poor judgment, dullness, errors of discernment, faulty reasoning, inferiority complexes, misconceptions, clumsy communication, etc. It is evident that infirmities bring much pain and inconvenience to others. They are, however, quite different in kind to sin, which requires God's forgiveness. An infirmity which is capable of correction may become sin, if, after detecting our fault, we choose to continue in it.

See MISTAKES, LEGAL SIN (ETHICAL SIN), SIN, GROW (GROWTH).

For Further Reading: Baldwin, *Holiness and the Human Element;* Taylor, *A Right Conception of Sin;* Geiger, ed., *Insights into Holiness* and *Further Insights into Holiness.*

JAMES M. RIDGWAY

INFRALAPSARIANISM. Infralapsarianism is one answer to the question in Calvinistic thought of the chronological order of the decrees of God relating to creation and the fall of mankind. That is, it is one possible way of explaining predestination. Formulated in question form, the issue is: "Did God decree to save and damn certain men *before* the act of creation, or did He decree to create men and then *after* the Fall decree their election or reprobation?"

The assertion that God decreed salvation or damnation prior to creation is termed supralapsarianism ("*before* the Fall"). This view holds that before the foundations of the world were laid, God issued His eternal decrees. Thus the fall of Adam becomes a part of God's plan. In a sense, God is responsible for the Fall (*lapsus* means "Fall"), making election necessary. Placement of election subsequent to creation and the Fall is known as infralapsarianism ("*after* the Fall"). According to this position, God issued His decrees of election *after* the Fall, so as to redeem a part of His creation.

The respective positions are of theological consequence only for those subscribing to some type of Reformed or Calvinistic theology. John Calvin found it repugnant to speculate about the thought processes of God, but contrary to his pupil, Theodore Beza, Calvin's theology in his *Institutes of the Christian Religion* (esp. Book 3) is generally infralapsarian.

Wesleyan-Arminian theologians are not confronted with the dilemma within the boundaries of Wesleyan dogmatics. The question does not arise, for the nature of election is defined in different terms. Rather than referring to the election of certain individuals, Wesleyans define election in terms of class, namely believers. The gracious purpose of God is to save mankind, as many as believe. This plan includes provisionally all men and is conditioned solely on faith in Jesus Christ.

See PREDESTINATION, FOREKNOWLEDGE, CALVINISM, ARMINIANISM.

For Further Reading: Toon, *Hyper-Calvinism,* 3-31, 104-19; Wiley, *CT,* 2:334-79; Dayton, "A Wesleyan Note on Election," *Perspectives on Evangelical Theology,* ed. Kantzer and Gundry.

JOHN A. KNIGHT

INHERITANCE. In theology, inheritance refers to the benefits that come to man as a child of God. In the OT the word includes not only "an estate received by a child from its parents, but also to the land received by the children of Israel as a gift from Jehovah" (*ISBE,* 3:1468).

This inheritance was promised to Abram on the basis of obedience: "Go from your country and your kindred and your father's house . . . And I will make of you a great nation" (Gen. 12:1-2, RSV). The inheritance was to be "for ever"

(13:15), yet was contingent upon continued faithfulness to Jehovah.

"The patriarchs and people certainly looked to the possession of the land . . . but the light in which they regarded it, was that of a settled place of abode with God, where he would be fully present, and where they would find repose in his fellowship" (*HDB,* 2:472). In a similar vein David sings, "The Lord is the portion of mine inheritance" (Ps. 16:5).

The NT counterpart is the new covenant given to God's people—"the promise of eternal inheritance" (Heb. 9:15). "God . . . hath in these last days spoken unto us by his Son, whom he hath appointed heir of all things" (1:1-2).

Paul reasons that if we are children of God, we are heirs of the Father. To make that concept fully Christian, he relates it to Christ, the Son and Heir. In Him we become joint-heirs of all the blessings from a Heavenly Father. Here the NT also indicates obedience as the condition for enjoying our inheritance. If we walk with our Lord in His obedience to suffering, we shall "be also glorified together" (Rom. 8:16-17).

In Christ we have "an inheritance incorruptible, and undefiled, and that fadeth not away, reserved in heaven for you, who are kept by the power of God through faith" (1 Pet. 1:4-5).

See HEIR, EARNEST, ETERNAL LIFE.

For Further Reading: Bennett, "Heir," and Martin, "Inheritance," *HDB; Baker's DT,* 266; Easton, "Heir," and Hirsch, "Inheritance," *ISBE.* A. F. HARPER

INHERITED SIN. See ORIGINAL SIN.

INIQUITY. Iniquity describes man's violation of God's character. When a person denies God's holy sovereignty, by whatever attitude or act, he commits iniquity. As first demonstrated by Adam, iniquity primarily consists of disobedience to God (Gen. 2:17; 3:12). This has caused a breach between man and God. And only God can bridge that rift.

The biblical usage of iniquity teaches four key concepts. First, man is personally accountable for iniquity (Num. 5:31). Second, the ensuing punishment is only just (Amos 3:2; Isa. 26:21). Third, man stands helpless when faced with the enormity of his iniquity: "For my iniquities are gone over my head; as a heavy burden they weigh too much for me" (Ps. 38:4, NASB). Finally, the Bible teaches a sole solution. God alone can provide the forgiveness required to cancel man's guilt (Isa. 40:2; Ps. 51:2; Jer. 31:34).

The principal Hebrew (OT) terms translated "iniquity" depict futile deviation from true virtue *(aven, avon).* Comparison of several related terms further clarifies the meaning: sin—failure before a declared standard; rebellion—deliberate revolt; straying—ignorant wandering; godlessness—willful ignorance; guilt—inner conviction of chargeable offense. The Greek (NT) terms for iniquity suggest injustice and unlawful activity *(adikia, anomia).* The following concepts also are related: trespass, or transgression—a specific violation; wickedness—a state of failure; impiety—a blatant offense against God.

Today the concept of iniquity has been severely undermined by vacillating values and humanistic philosophy. Certain theological camps have minimized the extent and influence of man's depravity and sinfulness. A weakened view of iniquity leads at once to a weakened view of the Savior, and a false gospel results.

Iniquity does indeed inflict deep stains. But they are not indelible. The blood of Christ is able to cleanse us (Titus 2:14).

See SIN, DECALOGUE.

For Further Reading: *Unger's Bible Dictionary,* 526; *IDB,* 4:361-76. WAYNE G. McCOWN

INITIAL SANCTIFICATION. In Wesleyan circles, sanctification is described both as initial and as entire, to make clear that sanctification *begins* in regeneration and may be completed in a second work of grace, following regeneration. Thus initial sanctification is cleansing from *acquired* depravity (the guilt and pollution associated with the acts of sin), whereas entire sanctification is cleansing from *inherited* depravity (indwelling or inbred sin). John Wesley developed the doctrinal basis for sanctification, both initial and entire. "When we are born again, then our sanctification, our inward and outward holiness, begins" (*Works,* 6:74).

Initial but incomplete sanctification is implied in such passages as 2 Cor. 7:1 and Eph. 4:13. One of the clearest examples is in 1 Cor. 6:9-11. The Corinthians who were once stained by sin have been "washed . . . sanctified . . . justified." "Here indeed are both real and relative changes" (*GMS,* 458).

See ACQUIRED DEPRAVITY, NEW BIRTH, SANCTIFICATION, ENTIRE SANCTIFICATION, FIRST WORK OF GRACE.

For Further Reading: Harvey, *A Handbook of Theological Terms*, 214 ff; Wiley, *CT*, 2:423 ff, 474-76; Grider, *Entire Sanctification*, 137 ff. A. ELWOOD SANNER

INSPIRATION OF THE BIBLE. The doctrine of biblical inspiration affirms the unique and controlling involvement of the Holy Spirit in the production of the Bible. The activity of the Spirit is such that the Bible can properly be called the Word of God. This inspiration is unique in the sense that, as the term is used theologically, it applies to the Bible in a way and to a degree not true of any other collection of writings. The doctrine is violated when the assumption is made that the inspiration which produced the Bible is no different from the inspiration which prompts great hymns or great sermons.

Jesus and the NT writers saw in the Scriptures an immediate impulse of the Spirit so pervasive that they could ascribe the words to the Holy Spirit as well as to the human authors. In a general way this is implied by the formula, "It is written," used approximately 74 times, always as the final court of appeal (e.g., 1 Pet. 1:16). The Scriptures are not only called "holy" (Rom. 1:2; 2 Tim. 3:15), but universally treated as holy with a deference amounting to complete faith and submission. The belief of Jesus and the apostles that "the scripture cannot be broken" (John 10:35) and that the prophetic elements must be fulfilled (e.g., Mark 14:49; Luke 24:44) are further testimony to the divine origin and hence the inviolable authority of the OT.

But the direct ascribing of the words of the OT to the Holy Spirit, noted above, is unmistakable. Jesus said that David "in the Spirit" called the coming Messiah "Lord" (Matt. 22:43, NASB). Our Lord responded to Satan in the wilderness by quoting Deut. 8:3: "Man shall . . . live . . . on every word that proceeds out of the mouth of God" (Matt. 4:4, NASB). That Jesus equated these words not just with some original oral pronouncement by God but with their preservation in the Bible is clear from "It is written" and subsequent frequent references to the OT.

It is equally clear that Jesus did not confine the Word of God to specific instances of "Thus saith the Lord" which were recorded in the Bible, but to the Scriptures themselves. There is no "God said" prefacing Gen. 2:24—"For this cause a man shall leave his father and his mother, and shall cleave to his wife" (NASB); on the surface this is the writing of Moses. But Jesus ascribed Moses' word here to God: "Haven't you read . . . that . . . the Creator 'made them male and female,' and said, 'For this reason . . . ?'" (Matt. 19:4-5, NIV). Moses was the penman, but the words were God's—hence the authority.

This was Zacharias' understanding too. God's action in raising up Christ was the fulfillment of what "He spoke by the mouth of His holy prophets from of old" (Luke 1:70, NASB). This view of Scripture is echoed by Peter: "Brothers, the Scripture had to be fulfilled which the Holy Spirit spoke long ago through the mouth of David" (Acts 1:16, NIV). If this view of Scripture was overly primitive and simplistic, the Holy Spirit did not correct them! For on the Day of Pentecost Peter speaks in the same manner: "This is what was spoken by the prophet Joel: 'In the last days, God says, . . . '"(Acts 2:16-17, NIV; 28:25). Paul's conception of Scripture was exactly the same: "The gospel he promised beforehand through his prophets in the Holy Scriptures regarding his Son" (Rom. 1:2-3, NIV; cf. Heb. 3:7; 4:3-4; 9:8; 10:15). It is apparent that the Early Church accepted without question the OT Scriptures as literally the Word of God. In its words God is speaking; since this is true, the words are valid for the Church.

The most direct affirmation of an apostolic doctrine of inspiration is in 2 Tim. 3:16—"All Scripture is God-breathed" (NIV). "All Scripture" would to first-century readers mean the canon of the OT, corresponding to the 39 books with which we are familiar. The KJV phrase "given by inspiration of God" is better rendered "God-breathed," since it translates a single word, *theopneustos*: *theo,* "God," and *pneustos,* "breathe" (from *pneō,* "to breathe"). Inspiration is in-breathing. That the Third Person of the Trinity is the active Agent in this inspiring is affirmed by Peter: "For prophecy never had its origin in the will of man, but men spoke from God as they were carried along by the Holy Spirit" (2 Pet. 1:21, NIV). This is the *written* word, not merely the spoken, as the context shows. As Bishop Westcott observes: "The book is thus rightly said to be inspired no less than the Prophet" (quoted by Thomas, *The Holy Spirit of God,* 155).

The Bible does not explain how the Spirit "carried along" the speaking and writing prophets. The Church has almost been unanimous—at least in modern times—in rejecting the theory of dictation, i.e., that the human writers were completely passive instruments. The evidences of very human individuality in style and method, including active research (Luke 1:1-4), are too overwhelming to permit any theory which reduces the writers to mere puppets. They doubtless were aware of divine aid and impulse, and as a consequence often sensed that they were writing beyond their understanding (1 Pet. 1:10-12); yet they were equally aware of intense intellectual activity which resulted in stylistic peculiarities which would have been theirs without inspiration. As Thomas says: "No theory of inspiration can satisfy the conditions which allows the human to exclude the Divine at any point, or the Divine to supersede the human" (ibid., 156).

A so-called dynamic theory has often been understood to imply that the Holy Spirit impressed the mind with thoughts but left writers entirely uninfluenced in their choice of words. In this case we are compelled to speak of inspired men, but can hardly speak of an inspired Bible. If in no sense did the inspiration extend to the words, then it did not reach the concrete volume which we hold in our hands and read. How do we know that the words accurately express the Spirit-given thoughts? Or even perhaps distort them? The *thoughts* died with the writers.

On the other hand the theory of *verbal* inspiration has been often misunderstood to imply simple dictation. But the best adherents of verbal inspiration (e.g., Carl F. H. Henry, Clark Pinnock, R. Laird Harris) unanimously disavow an implied dictation. By verbal inspiration is meant that the influencing and superintending of the Spirit was sufficiently dynamic and dominant to assure that what the Spirit wanted said was said, without distortion or error. The degree of Spirit impression could have ranged all the way from occasional dictation, to heightened insight, to general overruling in the selection of materials.

Stylistic differences, in and of themselves, do not necessarily constitute a stumbling block to belief in verbal inspiration, as long as we steer clear of the idea of dictation. The words are freely chosen by the writer and are peculiar to him; but they express accurately and adequately the truth God intended. To extract this truth, these are the words we must deal with, and no others. If we believe the Holy Spirit led in the writer's free choice of words, then belief in verbal inspiration means that we do not try to correct the words or wish they had been different. To say, for example, "I wish Paul hadn't said that," is to do violence to a proper concept of inspiration.

Wiley defines inspiration as "the actuating energy of the Holy Spirit by which holy men were qualified to receive religious truth and to communicate it to others without error" (*CT,* 1:168). The fact of inspiration is uniform throughout the 66 books; the relative importance of the parts is not uniform, for they differ in level of *revelation.* Wiley sees that inspiration permits degrees of divine activity: *superintendence, elevation,* and *suggestion,* but he refuses to regard them as "degrees of inspiration," since to hold such a view is to "weaken the authority of the Bible as a whole" (ibid., 170). He continues:

> The error springs from a failure to distinguish between revelation as the varying quantity, and inspiration as the constant, the one furnishing the material by "suggestion" when otherwise not available, the other guiding the writer at every point, thus securing at once the infallible truth of his material and its proper selection and distribution. For this reason we conclude that the Scriptures were given by plenary inspiration, embracing throughout the elements of superintendence, elevation and suggestion, in that manner and to that degree that the Bible becomes the infallible Word of God, the authoritative Rule of Faith and Practice in the Church *(ibid.).*

The Church gradually came to perceive in the documents of the NT the same unique inspiration which had been universally ascribed to the OT. The documents themselves are replete with evidences of awareness of divine authority, and 2 Pet. 3:15-18 places Paul's Epistles on a par with "the other Scriptures" (NIV), so divinely authoritative that to distort and twist them is to cause spiritual destruction.

See BIBLE, BIBLICAL AUTHORITY, BIBLICAL INERRANCY, BIBLICAL REALISM, PROPOSITIONAL THEOLOGY.

For Further Reading: Wiley, *CT,* 1:166-84; Thomas, *The Holy Spirit of God*, 147-63; Pache, *The Inspiration and Authority of the Scriptures*; Taylor, *Biblical Authority and Christian Faith*; Henry, *Revelation and the Bible*, 105-52.

RICHARD S. TAYLOR

INSTITUTIONS OF CHRISTIANITY. The institutions of Christianity are the social structures most essential to building the kingdom of God on earth. They are the family, the state, and the church.

The family. The Bible says, "God setteth the solitary in families" (Ps. 68:6). It is His good arrangement for continuing and nurturing the race. For Christ's followers the Bible establishes Christian family standards (Eph. 5:22—6:4). In this family the child first learns the meaning of love, he first hears about God, he learns to cooperate with others and to respect authority. Without Christian family reinforcement, the progress of the Kingdom on earth falters.

The state. This is God's institution to provide social order. The Bible instructs us to give respect and support to every agency that works for order and justice. "Let every person be subject to the governing authorities. For there is no authority except from God, and those that exist have been instituted by God" (Rom. 13:1, RSV; cf. 1 Tim. 2:2). Not all governments are equally good, but even a poor government is better than anarchy. The state that promotes order and equity is given divine approval; it deserves wholehearted Christian support.

The church. Only the church is unique to Christianity. The family and the state are acknowledged by other religions and cultures;

however, it is Christianity, through its Scriptures, which provides adequate information concerning the divine origin even of these institutions. From Scripture we understand their nature and purpose—and what constitutes a Christian attitude and relationship to them.

The church is the organization in which God's people relate to each other. Its roots are found in the OT people of God, but it came into its present form as the Body of Christ (1 Cor. 12:12-30). It is the embodiment and instrument of our Lord who said, "I will build my church" (Matt. 16:18).

The universal Church is composed of all spiritually regenerate persons. The term "church" is also used for a local body of believers. One is included in Christ's Church by becoming a Christian, but he finds adequate fellowship and ministry only as he lives and serves Christ through some local congregation. In the church we identify ourselves with the purposes of Jesus Christ who came "to seek and to save that which was lost" (Luke 19:10). We join in His ministry: "I am come that they might have life, and that they might have it more abundantly" (John 10:10).

These Christian institutions are not only basic to Christianity but also to society and civilization. It is not surprising, therefore, if they should be the objects of satanic attack in every generation, and also the objects of the antiauthoritarian hostility of the carnal heart of man.

Paradoxically the sinfulness of man may take the form, not of opposition to these institutions per se, but of perverting them to selfish ends. Christians must ever be on guard against allowing legitimate and necessary institutions to become masters instead of servants.

See STATE (THE), FAMILY, CHURCH.

For Further Reading: Purkiser, ed., *Exploring Our Christian Faith*, 393-408; Wiley, *CT*, 3:103-37.

A. F. HARPER

INTEGRITY. From the Latin word *integer*, meaning "wholeness," integrity involves moral uprightness and steadfastness, especially as it is revealed in situations that test one's commitments to truth, honesty, purposes, responsibilities, and the fulfilling of trust.

As God's people we have entered into covenant with God in response to His covenant with us. We have confessed our commitment to Jesus Christ as Lord. Integrity is our profession of that commitment in the world, our acting out of our life in God in concrete events.

To live with integrity is to attain a maturity which is a "measure of the stature of the fulness of Christ" (Eph. 4:13). No longer tossed about by human deceptions and illusions, one who is thus mature is marked by settled beliefs, sound moral character, and perfect love, well tested in life's alternating fortunes (cf. Ps. 15:1-5, NASB).

See FAITH, FIDELITY, TRUTH, CHARACTER, HONESTY, LIE (LIARS).

NANCY A. HARDESTY

INTEGRITY THERAPY. This theory reflects a growing dissatisfaction with psychology's failure to recognize and deal with the problem of guilt. Stemming directly from the work of O. Hobart Mowrer, research psychologist and professor at the University of Illinois, and the influence of Anton T. Boisen, teacher and mental hospital chaplain, this approach recognizes that every person has a conscience, the violation of which gives rise to feelings of guilt. Like reality therapy, this technique rejects deterministic theory, holding that each individual is answerable for himself and responsible for making his own decisions.

The theory is reflected in two books by Mowrer, *The Crisis in Psychiatry and Religion* and *The New Group Therapy*. It centers in two major areas: guilt and integrity. Disillusioned by the Freudian approach toward resolving guilt, Mowrer came to see that guilt must be resolved through confession. Integrity therapy is concerned with developing individuals into responsible persons by means of openness, confession, and open action. Each individual is a responsible person with a value system.

Integrity therapy is not really a Christian therapy, although it uses much Christian terminology, such as *guilt, sin, confession,* and *restitution.* The reason that the technique, as represented by Mowrer, is not Christian is that the emphasis is horizontal, not vertical; humanistic, not redemptive. However, John W. Drakeford, in his book *Integrity Therapy,* has placed the theory in a Christian framework. With biblical safeguards, the technique becomes useful to Christian ministers. Drakeford concludes, "Mowrer's theories have been called an 'unfinished symphony' because they leave out the forgiveness which comes from God through Christ. If we are to put this doctrine back into its context, we will have to make the New Testament emphasis on the place of a changed life and behavior pattern in which the individual, experiencing forgiveness through faith, steps up to new heights of behavior and service to his fellowman" (145).

See REALITY THERAPY, ROGERIAN COUNSELING, PASTORAL COUNSELING, GUILT, CONFESSION (CONFESSIONAL).

For Further Reading: Drakeford, *Integrity Therapy;* Hamilton, *The Ministry of Pastoral Counseling;* Mowrer,

The Crisis in Psychiatry and Religion; The New Group Therapy. NORMAN N. BONNER

INTELLECTUALISM. This is the view that, in God, His intellect is supreme, so that it dictates what the will decides. An intellectualist is a person who believes that God's will is subservient to His intellect, so that God always wills to do what His intellect suggests to Him is the proper course of action. Thomas Aquinas (1225-74) was perhaps the most outstanding intellectualist of all the Christian era. In contrast, *voluntarism* is the view that God's will is what is supreme, and not His intellect. Augustine (354-430) was one of the outstanding voluntarists. An intellectualist, then, would say that whatever is right, God wills—whereas a voluntarist would say that whatever God wills is the right thing.

Intellectualism, in the extreme, would result in some form of rationalism, in which God would only be thought of as willing things that are suitable to His intellect and to ours. Voluntarism, in the extreme, has resulted in the doctrine of unconditional predestination—for, in this doctrine, God wills, sovereignly, before individuals are born, what their eternal destiny is to be. And, although this does not seem to our intellects to be fair, it is acceptable because God may will whatever He pleases, whether or not it suits what our intellects suggest to be correct or fair. Probably, on this issue, the correct teaching is somewhere between the extremes of both intellectualism and voluntarism. Arminianism locates somewhere between the two extremes.

See DIVINE SOVEREIGNTY, DIVINE DECREES, ATTRIBUTES (DIVINE), MORAL ATTRIBUTES OF GOD.

J. KENNETH GRIDER

INTENTION. The term *intention* is often used in Roman Catholic theology to designate a priest's purpose in the administration of the sacraments. Right *intention* along with proper *matter* and correct *form* makes a sacrament valid, according to Roman Catholic theologians.

The Council of Trent (1545-63) said, "If any [one] saith, that, in ministers, when they effect and confer the sacraments, there is not required the intention of at least doing what the [Roman Catholic] Church does, let him be anathema" (Canon 11:7). This canon, in effect, declared Protestant sacraments as invalid because Protestant ministers did not intend to fulfill all of the Catholic tenets in that matter.

The doctrine of intention helped to shield the Catholic sacraments from charges of magic by an official acknowledgment that they were invalid if they were administered casually, in a drama or mockery, or by an unbelieving priest who did not intend to do "what the Church does." On the other hand, the doctrine increased the divergence between the Catholic and Protestant views on the sacraments. It strengthened the former's views that validity depends on priests; in the Protestant view validity depends on the faith of recipients.

Today this doctrine is of primary interest to Roman Catholics and Anglo-Catholics.

See SACRAMENTS, SACRAMENTARIANISM.

For Further Reading: *ODCC,* 696-97.

W. CURRY MAVIS

INTERCESSION. Intercession, in both secular and religious thought, implies a mediator, or go-between, who seeks to reconcile the differences between two estranged persons or groups. Intercession is the act of the mediator in seeking to resolve the estrangement. The need for someone to intercede for another may appear on any level of life: political, social, business, marital, etc.; but for the most part it is a vital *religious concept* that reaches far back in Scripture and is most often connected with prayer. Abraham is seen interceding with the Lord for his nephew Lot and the cities of Sodom and Gomorrah in Gen. 18:22 ff. The priest was seen as the intercessor between God and the people of Israel. Moses interceded for Israel in the incident of the golden calf. The prophets of the OT are said to have interceded with God in behalf of the kingdoms of Israel and Judah.

The supreme example of intercession is that of our Lord, who as the merciful and faithful High Priest offered himself without spot to God (Heb. 9:14) in order to make reconciliation for the sins of the people, and thus to become the Mediator of a new covenant (12:24). In doing this, He took upon himself the role of the Suffering Servant and bore "the sin of many, and made intercession for the transgressors" (Isa. 53:12). Paul tells us that because of this, God has highly exalted Him and given Him a name which is above every name (Phil. 2:9).

The resurrected Christ is now seated on the right hand of the Father (Heb. 8:1), and there in His mediatorial office He makes intercession for His followers. The people of God may rest assured that they have an Advocate with the Father, one who is unceasingly concerned about their perseverance and eternal triumph. The fact that He occupies His mediatorial throne also insures the salvation of the penitent suppliant, for "he is able also to save them to the uttermost that come unto God by him, seeing he ever liveth to to make intercession for them" (Heb. 7:25).

Christ is actually continuing in heaven what He started on earth, for in the Gospels we often see Him speaking, acting, and praying on behalf of others. John 17 is a most beautiful example of intercessory prayer, and Christ taught His disciples to follow His example. The NT abounds with instances of the people of God interceding for each other or for unbelievers, so that today intercession is an important element of any well-ordered prayer.

The Holy Spirit is also spoken of as making intercession for the saints according to the will of God (Rom. 8:27).

See INTERCESSION (PROBLEM OF), PRAYER, ADVOCATE.

For Further Reading: Buttrick, *Prayer,* 104-6, 110-12; Pope, *A Compendium of Christian Theology,* 3:236 ff; Wiley, *CT,* 2:214, 299; *ZPEB,* 3:294. C. PAUL GRAY

INTERCESSION, PROBLEM OF. Why intercession is necessary and how it works is a knotty problem. On the human level intercession provides an essential link in communication and sometimes a basis for negotiation. Between God and man the intercessor represents the estranged sinner by proxy, until such time as the sinner pleads for himself. It could be that the goodwill of the intercessor, as a temporary substitute for the sinner, whose own will is still recalcitrant, can provide the holy God with a moral basis for continued divine action on the sinner's behalf. Yet such an arrangement would have to be viewed as a derivative of Christ's once-for-all mediatorial action, as the perfect moral basis for clemency.

The force of any intercession depends on the person of the intercessor. God is pleased to accept the prayers of an Abraham or a Moses who has earned the right to intercede by acquiring a personal relationship with God, and thus an authority, which God honors. By His own obedience and by His vicarious death Christ acquired this intercessory right in perfect measure. Christians who pray for others are entering into that right reflectively.

Yet the idea of intercession must never be construed to be an attempt to wheedle a deserved boon or release from a reluctant deity. This distortion forgets that God as the aggrieved party is the One who himself has provided in His Son the Intercessor. Intercession must therefore be viewed (1) as a one-on-one implementation of the Atonement, and (2) as an appeal to the bridge already established between God's holiness and man's sin. Intercession thus claims in behalf of another the merit of Christ's blood, not for the granting of a deserved blessing but undeserved mercy. Justice would close the door; God is pleased to accept intercession, in Christ's name, as grounds for keeping it open.

See INTERCESSION, PRAYER, MEDIATION (MEDIATOR).

For Further Reading: Hallesby, *Prayer.*

RICHARD S. TAYLOR

INTERMEDIATE STATE. For Christianity the idea of an intermediate state is derived from Jewish thought. Along with many other ancient peoples the Hebrews believed that the soul of man survived the death of the body. But of equal importance to the idea of an intermediate state is the peculiar Hebrew doctrine that for man to be truly man, he cannot be fragmented into body, mind, or soul (spirit). Therefore, the body and the soul of a man cannot forever be separated. These views gave rise to the idea of a resurrection at the end of the age when the soul would be reunited with the body, and thus each man would pass into the "age to come" as an integrated whole. The period between the death of the body and the resurrection has been called by theologians the *intermediate state.* The idea is the product of Scripture and reason.

In the OT, the dwelling place of disembodied spirits is a place called sheol—the nether world—which, at times, seems to be one vast domain, but at other times seems to be divided into two compartments: Paradise, a place of bliss for the righteous; Gehenna (or Hades), a place of torment where dwell the wicked.

During the intertestamental period the idea of an intermediate state continued to develop.

In both the LXX and the NT the Hebrew term *sheol* is translated *hadēs* in the Greek, and becomes "hell" in the KJV. The meaning of Hades in the Greek language originally paralleled that of Sheol, but it has finally come to mean the abode of the wicked dead.

Neither the OT or the NT tells us all that we would like to know about what happens after death, and varying opinions have sprung up concerning the intermediate state of both the righteous and the wicked. Some in the church take the position that the soul sleeps from the time of death to the resurrection. Others insist that if men do not accept Christ in this life, they will have a second chance after death. Still others define the intermediate state as "purgatory."

The traditional Protestant position rejects the idea of soul sleep, the second chance theory, and the Roman Catholic doctrine of purgatory. It does hold, however, that at death the righteous go immediately into the presence of the Lord (2 Cor. 5:8), or Abraham's bosom (Luke 16:23), and that the words of Jesus to the dying thief (23:43) indicate that to be in the presence of the Lord is to be in Paradise. Thus the righteous dead are with Christ and are happy and at rest. Yet Paradise is not the final state of believers, for after the resurrection and the final Judgment (Rev. 20:7-12), the righteous enter into the joys of a new heaven and a new earth (21:1 ff). As to the fate of the wicked, at death they are banished from the presence of the Lord in Hades and are in a state of conscious suffering and unrest. However, Hades is not their final state, for they too will be resurrected (20:12), but only to be consigned to a place of everlasting shame and contempt at the last Judgment (vv. 11-15).

See HADES, PARADISE, SPIRIT, RESURRECTION OF THE BODY, IMMORTALITY.

For Further Reading: Brunner, *Eternal Hope;* Macquarrie, *Principles of Christian Theology;* Pope, *Christian Theology,* vol. 3; Wiley, *CT,* vol. 3. C. PAUL GRAY

INTERPRETATION, BIBLICAL. See HERMENEUTICS.

ISLAM. Islam is the faith of more than 500 million persons in the Middle and Far East. The youngest of the world's major religions, it was founded in A.D. 622 in Arabia by Mohammed. Islam means "submission." A Muslim is one who submits to the word of Allah, the One God.

Mohammed professed to be called by Allah in A.D. 610 to recite the divine message. What he received he wrote in the *Qu'ran* (Koran). Islam believes that the author of the Koran is God. The beautiful Arabic style of the literature, they affirm, could only be from God, not the illiterate prophet. Mohammed began to proclaim his vision, and in A.D. 630 gained control of Mecca, the center of Muslim faith.

Islam has spawned many sectarian groups, but there is a common body of doctrine. The articles of faith are:

1. *Belief in Allah*—He is One, standing alone and self-subsistent. Omniscient and omnipotent, he guides men by his revelation.

2. *Belief in Angels*—The Koran speaks of angels who carry out Allah's commands. The angels support the prophets. Gabriel is the chief angel.

3. *Belief in Prophets*—There are prophets both major and minor. Adam, Noah, Moses, and Jesus are major prophets, but Mohammed is the greatest of the prophets. Prophets are human. They are worthy of respect but not worship.

4. *Belief in Scripture*—Islam calls men to believe in all scripture (Jewish, Christian, and Muslim; there is no reference to Zoroastrian or Hindu Scriptures). The Koran is God's final revelation. Muslims also take tradition *(Hadith)* with great seriousness, but it is not comparable to scripture.

5. *Belief in the Last Day*—It is a day of resurrection and judgment and provides the greatest incentive for the Muslim to perfect himself.

Islam possesses not only articles of faith but a code of law *(Shari'a)* which regulates conduct. These are the "Five Pillars" of Islam:

1. *The worship of God*—The Muslim repeats the confession: "There is no God but Allah, and Mohammed is the prophet of Allah."

2. *Prayer*—Five times a day at specified times following a precise formula; e.g., at dawn he kneels twice, at midday four times.

3. *The fast of Ramadan*—During the ninth month the faithful fast and abstain from sexual relations from dawn to sunset. When one is able to distinguish between a white thread and a black at dawn, it is time for the fast to begin.

4. *Payment of a religious tax*—This is a responsibility of every Muslim. It is used for the benefit of the poor, for education, and even defense.

5. *Pilgrimage*—Once in a lifetime every Muslim is expected to go to Mecca, especially during the sacred month Dhu-al-Hijja. At Mecca all pilgrims are attired with a white seamless robe.

Of the five major sects that have existed within Islam, notice should be given particularly to:

1. *The Sunnis*—These are the traditionalists who follow a moderate rationalism. In interpreting the law of Islam, the community has responsibility. In effect this means the scholars trained in law consider a case and reach a decision or a consensus (the *ijma*).

2. *The Shi'ites*—They rejected the principle of consensus and place the authority for final interpretation in the hands of the *Imam,* the divinely appointed spiritual leader of Muslims, usually descended from Ali, Mohammed's son-in-law. The Shi'ites debate fiercely over the question of descent. Iran is largely Shi'ite and believes that the 12th Imam, Mohammed al-Muntazar, who disappeared in A.D. 878, is the Imam from whom their leadership is descended.

3. *The Sufis*—These are the mystics who developed a monastic life-style and sought union with God. They moved toward pantheism, stretching the limits of Muslim orthodoxy.

See NON-CHRISTIAN RELIGIONS, JUDAISM, CHRISTIANITY.

For Further Reading: Cragg, *The House of Islam;* Parrinder, *A Dictionary of Non-Christian Religions.*

LEON O. HYNSON

ISRAEL. This word has been used as the name of a man, of a people, and of nations.

"Israel" occurs first as the new name of Jacob who persisted one night along the Jabbok until he received a blessing (Gen. 32:22-32, esp. v. 28). This incident and two Bethel experiences (28:10-17; 35:9-15) show that Israel was called by God for the same purpose as Abraham had been. His descendants, "sons of Israel," were to become a company of nations and of kings (35:11; cf. 17:6), the possessors of the land in which Bethel was located (35:12; cf. 17:8 and 28:13), and those through whom blessing (or salvation) would come to the nations of the earth (28:14; cf. 12:3).

"Israel," as a shortened form of "sons of Israel," became the name of a people known from several references outside the Bible but most widely from the many hundreds of OT references. They were the people whom God delivered from Egyptian bondage and with whom He made a covenant at Sinai (Exod. 24:1-8) to be His "own possession," a "kingdom of priests," and a "holy nation" (19:5-6, NASB, RSV; cf. Titus 2:14; 1 Pet. 2:9). This covenant, along with the promise to Abraham and Jacob, was Israel's call to be the witness in the world to God, who loves and delivers enslaved people.

During the reigns of Saul, David, and Solomon (see 1 Samuel 1—1 Kings 10) "Israel" was the name of a nation, applicable in the main to all the tribes under one king. "Israel" was also the name of the Northern Kingdom following the division early in the reign of Rehoboam in contrast to Judah, the Southern Kingdom (1 Kings 12, esp. v. 16; see also 14:19, 29). Israel, the people or the nation which came under scattering judgment, never fully became the means corporately whereby redemption blessing came to the world, for this blessing came individually through Jesus, the Descendant of Israel.

From the time of the Exile onward, "Israel" was replaced by the term "Jew" with little or none of its former national significance. However, it has regained this significance with the establishment of modern Israel in the Holy Land in May, 1948.

A major recent concern in numerous publications has been with modern Israel's biblical or "theological" right exclusively to possess the Holy Land, as well as with any present redemptive role of Israel. Political sympathies and differences in interpreting the Bible will continue to result in disagreement over these questions.

See DISPENSATIONALISM, DISPERSION, JUDAISM, CHURCH, MISSION (MISSIONS, MISSIOLOGY).

For Further Reading: Bright, *A History of Israel,* 105-373; *IDB,* E-J:750-70; *ZPEB,* 335-72.

HARVEY E. FINLEY

I-THOU. "I-Thou" refers to a concept given classical form by the contemporary Jewish philosopher and theologian Martin Buber, in his book, *I and Thou.* "Thou," in Buber's thought, has a special reference to man's relation to God. Here a kind of mystical oneness is found in which the particular things of the world (the It) are not disregarded but are seen in their temporal relation. The contrast between these two ways of thinking are expressed in Buber's own words as follows:

> The world of *It* is set in the context of space and time. The world of *Thou* is not set in the context of either of these. Its context is in the Centre, where the extended lines of relations meet—in the eternal Thou.

Buber does not mean that what happens in this attitude is an experience; nor does he mean that it is a "content" received. Rather man receives a Presence and a power in which something happens, a meaning is assured, a meaning which relates to this life and this world.

The writings of many contemporary theologians, both Catholic and Protestant, reflect Buber's insight. Among Protestants are Emil Brunner, Karl Barth, Reinhold Niebuhr, H. Richard Niebuhr, and Paul Tillich. Catholics include Ferdinand Ebner, Gabriel Marcel, Erich Przywara, and Ernst Michel.

See EXPERIENCE, FELLOWSHIP, PERSONALITY OF GOD.

ALVIN HAROLD KAUFFMAN

J

JEALOUSY. This is a frame of mind which lays claim to undivided devotion, implying no tolerance toward any rivalry. It often involves deep and strong feelings. The word may convey a good or an evil attitude.

God tells His people that they must not worship idols. He gives as the reason, "I, the Lord your God, am a jealous God" (Exod. 20:5, NASB, NIV). God is jealous and accordingly demands what is His due, exclusive allegiance.

Jealousy is a good and wholesome trait when what is demanded is what is due. The Spirit's sanctifying influence generates sensitivity to what is right and good—there will be desire to give and to receive what is morally owed. The cleansed heart will be keenly sensible of the exclusive nature of some relationships. This aspect of the marriage relationship needs constant emphasis. Christian husbands and wives should jealously guard marital fidelity.

Carnal jealousy is indicated when inappropriate demands are made and ill feelings arise because those demands are not met. Jealousy, a neutral impulse, may be set in a wrong direction by a carnal heart, going beyond legitimate demands to seek that which is not proper. That attitude was demonstrated in Joseph's brothers. They were "jealous of him" (Gen. 37:11, RSV). That disposition of mind may also be described as "envy" (as the KJV translates *qana* in that text). Envy properly defines carnal jealousy. While jealousy may at times be righteous, envy never is.

A study of the OT words from which we get "jealous" and "zealous" suggests that those words have some common ground in meaning. Elijah says that he has been "zealous for the Lord" (1 Kings 19:10, NASB, NIV; the KJV and RSV translate *qana* as "jealous"). What is indicated here is deep and strong feeling resulting from sympathetic identification with God's will and purpose. The apostle Paul reflects that attitude where he says, "I am jealous over you with godly jealousy" (2 Cor. 11:2).

See ENVY, CARNAL CHRISTIANS, HARDNESS OF HEART, HATE (HATRED).

For Further Reading: Scharbert, "Jealousy (zeal)," *Encyclopedia of Biblical Theology.* ALDEN AIKENS

JEHOVAH, YAHWEH. Yahweh is the personal name, the covenant name for the God of Israel. He is called by this name more than by all other titles combined. It is a name which not only identifies the Person but also reveals His character.

The sacred name was first written by four consonants, YHWH, technically called the tetragrammaton. Considered to be too sacred to be pronounced at all, in its place was read *Adonai,* "Lord." The combination in writing the consonants YHWH and the vowels *a, o, a* of *Adonai* created the hybrid word Jehovah. This practice dates from the 16th century and thus appears in many English Bible translations. Some translations (e.g., KJV, RSV, NASB, NIV) use capital and small capital letters for the word—LORD—to designate the title.

The Hellenistic Jews, accustomed to using Greek, substituted *Kurios* (Lord) for the title *Adonai.* Hence the title *Kurios* appears 5,321 times in the Septuagint (LXX).

The meaning of the sacred name for the Israelites is clear. For them it meant "He who is" or "He who will be" (Exod. 3:10 ff). "When God himself speaks, He uses the first person, and the name becomes 'I am' or 'I will be.' . . . It is almost equivalent to 'He who has life in Himself' (cf. John 5:26)" (*HDB,* 2:299).

The Israelites perceived in Yahweh a thorough and absolute uniqueness. There is no other like or equal to Him. Hence their unswerving (when faithful to the covenant) monotheism. He alone is God. For them He alone creates, reveals himself, and imposes His will upon man and history. He has the power and authority to dispose over all things. He alone saves and judges. To Him alone belongs the Kingdom, and it is He alone who could and did provide a remnant to assure the fulfilling of His covenant with Abraham.

Yahweh is the One who has revealed himself, not only His name but His personal character, His covenant, through His mighty deeds. Of all His mighty deeds none is greater than His self-revelation through His Son Jesus Christ.

See LORD, NAME, GOD, REVELATION (SPECIAL), THEOPHANY.

For Further Reading: *HDB;* Wiley, *CT,* 1:244-49; *GMS,* 60-63.

JOSEPH H. MAYFIELD

JERUSALEM. Jerusalem became the earthly capital of Israel during the reign of David and continued as such for over 400 years. During that time, the Israelites increasingly regarded Jerusalem as the Holy City, as Mount Zion, the place where God dwelt with His people.

The Temple was built and rebuilt in Jerusalem, and here the Israelites offered sacrifices for their sins, praised God, and prayed. They understood that the Lord, the great King, reigned from Mount Zion (Ps. 48:2-3). Some even believed that the city was immune from destruction, and threatened to stone Jeremiah when he spoke against the city (Jer. 26:6-15). But the Lord did allow the city and its Temple to be torn down, due to the sins of the people. However, the city was not forsaken; it was rebuilt, and an eschatological significance, begun in the kingdom period and the Exile, was attached to it (Ps. 46:4-6; Lam. 2:15; Ezek. 5:5). The Messiah was to reign from Zion, and all nations would come to it to learn truth (Zech. 2:7-13; 3:8-10; 8:20-22; 9:9-11; 14:12-21).

The Messiah did come to Jerusalem, but He was not welcomed by its leaders. The crisis came when Jesus was put to death and arose from the grave outside the city walls. His death and resurrection and the Pentecost event gave the city a greater redemptive importance, an importance that survived its second destruction at the hands of the Romans (A.D. 70).

There was, however, a paradox in this new importance. The earthly city represented sin and slavery, but the new heavenly city represented freedom (Gal. 4:25-26). In the Book of Revelation, we read of a New Jerusalem that comes from God. It has no temple, for God and the Lamb take its place. This is the eternal city, the home of the saints (Revelation 21—22).

See ISRAEL, CHURCH, KINGDOM OF GOD.

For Further Reading: Barclay, *The City of the Great King,* 604-21; "Jerusalem," *Encyclopedia Judaica,* 9:1549-93; Oliphant, *Jerusalem,* 430-521; De Young, *Jerusalem in the New Testament.*

GEORGE HERBERT LIVINGSTON

JESUS. See CHRIST.

JOHN THE BAPTIST. He was the last and greatest of the prophets, an ascetic, and designated by the Holy Spirit as the forerunner of Christ.

After 400 years during which no prophet had spoken to Israel, "The word of God came to John" (Luke 3:2, NIV). As a child of promise he was to be "filled with the Holy Spirit even from birth" (1:15, NIV). This designated him as a prophet who by the Holy Spirit would speak God's message to the people "in the spirit and power of Elijah" (v. 17, NIV). As a prophet he had the distinction of being the consummation of the prophetic order leading to the coming of Jesus Christ. Because of his unique position between the old order and the coming of the Kingdom, Jesus declared him to be the greatest of the prophets while at the same time making it clear that "he who is least in the kingdom of heaven is greater than he" (Matt. 11:11, NIV).

God's word to John was to call people to repentance and to announce the coming One and His kingdom and to give promise of a twofold baptism with the Holy Spirit and fire (Matt. 3:11; Mark 1:8; Luke 3:16; John 1:33). The coming One he designated as the One who "has surpassed me because he was before me" (John 1:30), the One "who will baptize with the Holy Spirit" (v. 33) and "the Lamb of God, who takes away the sin of the world!" (v. 29, all NIV).

John's baptism with water was closely tied to repentance and forgiveness. He came "preaching a baptism of repentance for the forgiveness of sins" (Mark 1:4, NIV). John did not and could not forgive sins. "But John's baptism was the expression of the repentance that results in the forgiveness of sins" (Ladd, *A Theology of the New Testament,* 40).

The message of John centered in repentance—a radical change of mind and heart. Using Isa. 40:3-5 as a text, he warned of "the coming wrath." He called for "fruit in keeping with repentance" and judgment in the figure of ax and fire (Luke 3:3-9, NIV). To inquiring crowds, tax collectors, and soldiers he gave specific instruction of the moral implications of true repentance (vv. 10-14).

John's baptism included Jesus, but for a different reason than any other. Jesus' total identification with man's need included His participation in the symbol of man's need for forgiveness and cleansing, which in the new order would be made possible through the redemptive life, death, and resurrection of Jesus Christ. So John could say to Him, "I need to be baptized by you" (Matt. 3:14, NIV).

See BAPTISM, WATER, FORGIVENESS, CLEANSING, BAPTISM WITH THE HOLY SPIRIT.

For Further Reading: *HDNT,* 1:861 ff; *ISBE,* 3:1708 ff.

JOSEPH H. MAYFIELD

JOY. Joy is an exhilarating emotion of pleasure. It need not be exuberant to be deep and real.

The experience may come with an increase of some good that we desire: wealth or education. It may be found in sensory experiences, in beauty, in mental activity, in moral achievement, and in religious devotion. It may occur with the discovery of a higher value, as when we find that kindness brings more satisfaction than selfishness.

The Bible affirms man's inherent privilege to enjoy nature, music, and social activities. But these natural joys are purified and intensified by a right relationship with God.

The NT recognizes rejoicing as one of God's gifts. Jesus' birth was the source of "great joy" (Luke 2:10). Joy is also one of the fruits of the Spirit (Gal. 5:22). Jesus explained the goal of His ministry: "That my joy might remain in you, and that your joy might be full" (John 15:11).

Joy is deeply linked with the gospel. Liberation from sin, recovery from lostness, and reconciliation with God move the spirit to praise. When life is enriched by God's blessings, we are glad. When we make progress toward goals for the spirit, we rejoice.

The joy of the Christian is sometimes overshadowed by temporal affliction, but never destroyed. When we walk with God, "weeping may endure for a night, but joy cometh in the morning" (Ps. 30:5).

Because joy is an emotion, its intensity varies; at times it may even be temporarily absent (1 Pet. 1:6). But in Christ we have dependable sources of renewal. Paul urges: "Rejoice in the Lord alway: and again I say, Rejoice" (Phil. 4:4). The prophet sings, "God is my salvation; I will trust . . . Therefore with joy shall ye draw water out of the wells of salvation" (Isa. 12:2-3).

See EMOTION (EMOTIONALISM), HAPPINESS, FRUIT OF THE SPIRIT.

For Further Reading: *Baker's DCE,* 356-57; Wiley, *CT,* 3:55-58; Taylor, *Miracle of Joy.*

A. F. HARPER

JUDAISM. Judaism is the complex of Jewish beliefs and customs. It is based upon the teachings of the Torah (Pentateuch) as interpreted continuously by prophets, teachers, and rabbis down to the present time. The term does not appear in most English translations of the Bible. However, it is used in the RSV on two occasions: Gal. 1:13-14; Acts 13:43.

While beliefs and practices have differed considerably among various Jewish sects and parties, Jews have held consistently to the belief in only one God, Yahweh. Indeed, if Judaism can be said to have a creed, it is expressed in Deut. 6:4: "Hear, O Israel: The Lord our God is one Lord." Jews have considered themselves to be God's special people through a covenant relationship with Him.

Jews have accepted the whole OT as authoritative, but the Law of Moses, the Torah, is regarded as God's perfect and final revelation to them. Important, however, is the Talmud which provides commentary and interpretation of the OT. Out of these sources numerous practices have developed quite universally followed by the Jews. They include aversion toward idolatry, an insistence upon moral conduct, the following of certain dietary rules, circumcision, and sabbath-keeping.

Judaism holds that God is related to the world through creation which He has declared to be "very good" (Gen. 1:31). It, therefore, discredits extreme forms of asceticism and teaches rather that man's duty is to live life fully in this world intended for his habitation (Isa. 45:18). Judaism teaches that God is to send to earth a Messiah who will set up the kingdom of God in which the Torah will be perfectly enforced. Judaism says that by creation individuals are endowed with inclinations both toward good and toward evil, but with the capacity to choose which way each will go. Sin, defined as rebellion against God, is considered by Judaism to be common to the race; but through repentance individual sinners may find forgiveness.

Presently Jews are quite generally recognized as either Orthodox, Conservative, or Reformed. Orthodox Jews remain faithful to Talmudic observances, use Hebrew for public prayers, and consider the Messiah to be a real person. Conservative Jews may believe in the essentials of Judaism, but they adapt them to the modern situation. Reformed Jews, while revering their Jewish heritage, do not necessarily hold to the revelational validity of Judaism, give Prophets priority over the Torah, and practice communal good works by social action as a pragmatic Messianism.

There is also a small but growing group of Messianic Jews who accept Christ as the Messiah, consider the NT as a part of God's Word, but retain their Jewish identity, pray in Hebrew, and follow many other Jewish traditions.

See LEGALISM, ISRAEL, DISPENSATIONALISM, JUDAISTIC CONTROVERSY.

For Further Reading: *IDB,* suppl. vol.; Fallon, *Encyclopedic Dictionary of Religion,* vol. 2, Jacob J. Petuckowski, *Encyclopedia International,* vol. 10.

ARMOR D. PEISKER

JUDAISTIC CONTROVERSY. This was the conflict in the Early Church over the question of the relation of Gentile converts to the Mosaic law. While believing Jews, especially Pharisees, accepted Jesus as the promised Messiah, they saw Him as within and as continuing the legal system of Moses. They failed to see that the Mosaic regime was preparatory and prophetic, to be displaced by Christ, not reinforced and augmented. If they had ever heard Jesus' sayings about the peril of patching an old garment with new cloth, or putting new wine in old wineskins (Matt. 9:16-17), they either had forgotten or failed to understand.

These sincere but misguided conservatives are called Judaizers because they supposed that to be saved, Gentiles must become Jews, and that this hinged, not simply on their faith in Christ, but upon their receiving circumcision.

The controversy raged over a period of years. It first came to a head in Antioch, where was thriving the first Gentile Church. Luke explains: "And some men came down from Judea and began teaching the brethren, 'Unless you are circumcised according to the custom of Moses, you cannot be saved'" (Acts 15:1, NASB). The vigorous opposition of Paul and Barnabas precipitated the first general church conference, in Jerusalem, at which Peter sided with Paul, and James, the half brother of Jesus, delivered a decision repudiating the Judaizers and vindicating the freedom party.

But the Judaizers were undeterred in their subversive campaign. Apparently they followed Paul for years, infiltrating the churches and agitating Gentile converts. Their insidious work prompted the writing of Galatians, and to a large extent Romans also. Galatians, says Robertson, is a "flaming torch in the Judaizing controversy. This Epistle was the battle cry of Martin Luther in the Reformation" (*Word Pictures,* 4:273).

Paul especially perceived the radical nature of the issues and the necessity of a no-holds-barred fight. While Peter argued that since God was already saving uncircumcised Gentiles, conformity to Judaism was obviously not necessary, Paul saw that the two systems, Moses and Christ, law and grace, circumcision and experience, ceremonialism and faith, were mutually exclusive, as the ground of salvation. To cling to Moses was to do despite to Christ; hence, "if you receive circumcision, Christ will be of no benefit to you" (Gal. 5:2, NASB). To trust in circumcision is to cling to the shadow and miss what circumcision pointed to—the circumcision of the heart (Rom. 2:25-29; Phil. 3:3; Col. 2:11). The watchword of evangelical religion is Gal. 6:15: "For neither is circumcision anything, nor uncircumcision, but a new creation" (NASB).

Paul's victory against the Judaizers was crucial to the preservation of an authentic Christianity. Today Judaizing tendencies are still with us, but in more subtle forms. The peril of trusting in rites rather than Christ is perennial.

See SACRAMENTARIANISM, CIRCUMCISION, LAW AND GRACE, MOSAIC LAW.

For Further Reading: Ladd, *A Theology of the New Testament,* 354-56; Robertson, *Word Pictures in the NT,* 4:272 ff; *GMS,* 413-17. RICHARD S. TAYLOR

JUDGE, JUDGMENT. God is the Judge of all the earth (Gen 18:25; Heb. 12:23). He alone judges perfectly because He knows perfectly (1 Cor. 4:4-5; Heb. 4:12-13). He judges in *righteousness* (Gen. 18:25; Jer. 11:20; Rev. 16:7) and in *truth* (Rom. 2:2; Rev. 19:2). Human judges are to reflect divine judgment, else they judge falsely (Deut. 1:16-17; Prov. 29:7, 14).

Judgment, in the OT, is the activity of God in preserving His covenant by establishing a right order in society—by delivering His people and punishing His enemies (Deut. 32:36-43; Isa. 30:18-19; Ps. 7:6-11). Human champions raised up to deliver Israel are judges (Judg. 2:16-19), and juridical functions are secondary in their careers. The prophets emphasized the *moral* factor in their preaching of judgment: A disobedient Israel would be punished in the day of Yahweh as surely as the heathen (Amos 5:18-24; Joel 1:13-15). Daniel completes the OT vision of judgment, with the Son of Man reigning in everlasting righteousness and the wicked forever damned (Dan. 7:13; 12:1-3).

In the NT the day of Yahweh becomes "the day of the Lord" (2 Pet. 3:10). Final judgment is committed to Jesus Christ, whose total human experience qualifies Him to judge us all (Acts 17:31; John 5:22). This final judgment has *cosmic* significance, affecting the physical universe as well as its human inhabitants (2 Pet. 3:7-13). All will appear before this final Judge (Rev. 20:12; Rom. 14:10), whose coming in glory will effect the ultimate vindication of His followers and the ultimate destruction of His foes (2 Thess. 1:5-10).

This final acquittal of believers is brought forward into the present age as *justification by faith.* The death of Christ was judgment upon sin and Satan (John 12:31), and His resurrection launched the new age in which forgiveness and eternal life are present possibilities (John 5:24; Rom. 4:24-25). The Cross was a righteous judgment, so that God is "just, and the justifier" of all who trust in Christ (Rom. 3:21-26).

As there is a present justification for believers, so there is a present punishment for sinners. Unbelievers are already *condemned* (John 3:17-21) and the unrighteous already suffer *wrath* (Rom. 1:18-28).

Present judgment does not preclude *future* judgment (John 5:25-29; 2 Cor. 5:10; Heb. 9:26-28), which occurs at "the end of this world" (Matt. 13:40-43).

We are justified by faith, but genuine faith works by love (Gal. 5:6; Jas. 2:14-26). Therefore, judgment is *according to works*—our words and deeds—as these are fruits of faith or unbelief. True faith in Christ evidences itself in obedience to His teachings and emulation of His compassion (Matt. 7:21-27; 12:7; 25:31-46; 2 Cor. 5:10; Rev. 20:12). God mercifully chastens His erring people that they might live holy lives and avoid condemnation (1 Cor. 11:31-32; Heb. 12:5-17). To despise this discipline is to be condemned with the world.

The final judgment is determined irrevocably at death, for then the believer is at peace with Christ (Luke 23:43; 2 Cor. 5:8; Phil. 1:21-23), and the impenitent wicked are in torment in hell (Luke 16:22-24).

As God is Judge of all, we are forbidden to judge one another (Matt. 7:1-2; Rom. 2:1; 14:4, 10). While judgment as *condemnation* is forbidden, judgment as *discrimination* is enjoined (Matt. 7:6, 15-20; Phil. 1:9-10), and the church is responsible for the discipline of its ministers and members (1 Cor. 5:1—6:6; Titus 3:10-11).

See ESCHATOLOGY, JUSTICE, DEATH, PROBATION, DISCRIMINATION, DISCERNMENT, REPROBATION.

For Further Reading: *A Companion to the Bible,* 209-15; *ISBE,* 3:1771-78; Aulen, *The Faith of the Christian Church,* 145-55.

W. E. McCumber

JUST, JUSTIFY. See JUSTIFICATION.

JUSTICE. In its earliest appearance in ethical and legal thought the term *justice* was used as the most adequate term for acceptable and adequate conduct. In attempting to determine and explain the nature of man, the Greek philosopher Plato established four cardinal excellences or virtues: wisdom, courage, self-control (usually translated as temperance), and justice. In spite of Plato's emphasis on human reason and wisdom, justice is particularly important because of its comprehensive character; the excellence of the harmonious functioning of all aspects of human nature is called justice.

The Hebrew Bible is equally emphatic in insisting upon "justice" or "righteousness" (these terms are largely interchangeable in translation; Exod. 23:1-8; Lev. 19:13-15; Deut. 16:18-20; Ps. 82:2-4; Isa. 1:17; 56:1; et al.). By adhering to God's standards of righteousness/justice, a people's character is finally approved or disapproved. Thus the "justification" of a people is determined.

Following Aristotle, classical philosophy tended to make distinctions which gave to justice the more limited character of a particular virtue. And in Christianity love became the dominant motif rather than justice. Christ spoke of divine justice as an impartiality which permitted the divine love to be expressed. And the Incarnation and Cross were/are supreme examples of God's love.

However, justice is still dominant in matters of conduct and salvation. Through Christ, God can be regarded as just even as He justifies the unjust (Rom. 3:26). Love must be paralleled by justice in order to avoid sentimentality, spinelessness, and general emptiness.

In the Middle Ages the cardinal virtues (including justice) were included in a general philosophical/theological system which also comprised love as included among the theological virtues. So important are these concepts both historically and theoretically that Frankena holds that all moral obligation can be basically reduced to justice and benevolence or love.

The call to justice is a call for some standard of rights and/or duties, and it confers a cardinal virtue on those who meet the standard. This standard also requires a fair distribution of honors, wealth, and other goods in accord with some divine or other principle. When just distribution is violated, justice requires the correction of such violation.

Justice thus becomes the acceptance of the dignity of all human beings along with the requirement that that dignity be respected by every other human being.

See JUDGE (JUDGMENT), CIVIL RIGHTS, LAW, LAW AND GRACE, REWARDS.

For Further Reading: *International Encyclopedia of Social Sciences,* 8:341 ff; Tillich, *Love, Power, and Justice; ER,* 409.

R. Duane Thompson

JUSTIFICATION. This concept, though expressed in a limited way in both the OT and the non-Pauline writings of the NT, is essentially Pauline. The substantive "justification" *(dikaiōsis)* occurs only in Rom. 4:25 and 5:18 (see also 5:16), but the verb "to justify" *(dikaioō)* appears 27 times in Paul's Epistles, especially in the passages in which he is opposing the Jewish teaching of achieving righteousness by faithful performance of the duties prescribed by the Mosaic Law. Justification in the Jewish tradition is not a grace per se but a merit of man, "something that God owes to man and to which man, in the strictest sense, has a claim." Also, eschatologically understood, justification as a divine act refers to the final judgment of God on that which a man has achieved ethically in his lifetime (cf. Rom. 2:13; 1 Cor. 4:4).

Paul, on the other hand, gives major attention to man's present existence, though he does not overlook the future meaning of this term. He employs the Greek verb *dikaioō* to carry the basic meaning of his teaching on this point. This predicate derives from the adjective *dikaios,* which means "just" or "righteous." Early Greek writers used this term with reference to persons who faithfully followed *dikē,* that is, custom, rule, or right. In the religious realm, a "righteous" person was the one who regularly performed the duties owed to the gods. In biblical understanding the "righteous" or "just" person is that one who is approved by God or acceptable to God. *Dikaiōsis* (justification) signifies the act in process of completion, and *dikaiōma,* also rendered "justification," signifies the act as already completed. *Dikaiōsunē,* regularly translated "righteousness," is the state or quality of life of one who is justified or declared righteous (Rom. 8:10; 1 Cor. 1:30).

In the history of the church a difference of opinion evolved with respect to the proper translation of *dikaioō,* whether it should be translated "to make righteous" or "to declare righteous." According to some scholars, in its primitive usage the verb carries the former meaning, but in later usage, especially in the LXX, it bears the latter meaning.

When Paul writes in Rom. 5:1 that "we have been justified through faith" (NIV), does he mean, "We have been declared righteous," or "We have been made righteous," or both? Also, when he asserts that the result of the one righteous act of Christ "was justification that brings life for all men" (v. 18, NIV), was he meaning that Christ's obedience provided God the basis for "pronouncing man righteous" or for "making him righteous," or both? Is the act of justification merely forensic or ethical or both? Does it result in imputed righteousness or imparted righteousness? Does God merely view the sinner as righteous through Christ, the sinner having accepted the saving work of Christ by faith, or does He transform the sinner, really making him righteous by His justifying act?

These lines were drawn sharply during the Reformation, particularly because the Reformers felt it necessary to make clear the pervasive nature of sin and to declare that salvation rested upon grace alone. In his earlier teaching, Luther described justification as a "being righteous" and a "becoming righteous." In his later teaching an imputative view prevailed. Calvin wrote: "We simply explain justification to be an acceptance, by which God receives us into His favor and esteems us as righteous persons, and we say it consists in the remission of sins and the imputation of the righteousness of Christ" (*Institutes,* bk. 3, chap. 11). Calvin's followers pressed his thinking on this subject to the point of asserting that the active obedience of Christ is so imputed to the elect as to render them legally as righteous as if they had themselves rendered perfect obedience to the law of God.

In the Tridentine Decrees of A.D. 1547, the Roman church defined its position in opposition to the Reformers. It stated that "justification is not the mere remission of sins, but also the sanctification and renovation of the inward man through the voluntary reception of grace and gifts of grace, whereby an unjust man becomes just, the enemy a friend, so that he may be an heir according to the hope of eternal life." The Holy Spirit imparts to each person a measure of righteousness. A contemporary writer expresses the same view: "Since, for Paul, justification and the reception of righteousness are one and the same thing, it follows that the concept of justification also must have a moral content which can be recognized as an essential component of his idea of righteousness" (Bläser, "Justification," *Sacramentum Mundi,* 3:454).

Wesleyanism, following the thought of Arminianism, sees justification as a forensic or judicial act in which God declares the sinner free from the guilt and penalty of sin, and therefore is righteous, but one must not take this to mean that the sinner is actually made just and righteous. A relative change takes place in justification, that is to say, a new relationship with God is established. Once the sinner was under condemnation; now he is pardoned, his sins are forgiven, and he is accepted by God. Viewed negatively, justification is the forgiving of the sins of the penitent believer, an act of the sovereign grace of God; viewed positively, it is the acceptance of the believer as righteous, a judicial act of remitting the penalty due the sinner. Wesleyans, in taking this position, make a sharp distinction between justification and sanctification. This latter term refers to the inward moral change, or impartation of righteousness, which is concomitant to justification. Justification logically underlies sanctification. In effect, justification takes place in the mind of God and sanctification in the moral nature of man.

1. The *ground* for justification is faith in the redemptive activity of God in Christ. This excludes the view of good works as providing the basis for justification. While the meritorious ground is the Cross, the "conditioning cause" is faith, but as Vincent Taylor observes, it is the interfacing of both the atoning work of Christ and faith that brings one into right relations with God. This means that any righteousness created by the act of justification is real because of the ethical or moral dimension of faith. Moreover, faith is more than trust in God's Word, or assent to theological propositions, but essentially reliance upon God and commitment to Him as the Redeemer. Thus, the righteousness is real and not imagined since one is forgiven and now stands in freedom before God.

2. Justification is not only an act but also a state into which one is brought as a consequence of the divine declaration. This state is maintained by faith and is characterized by righteousness, which is the gift of the new relationship.

The Greek word *logizomai,* meaning "to count, account, or reckon," has spawned the concept of imputed righteousness (cf. Rom. 4:3-5, 9, 22; Gal. 3:6; see also Gen. 15:6). It cannot be taken to mean that one person's acts are accounted as the acts of another. In this context, as Wiley says, "a man's sin or righteousness is imputed to him when he is actually the doer of the sinful or righteous acts. . . . To impute sin or righteousness is to take account of it, either to condemn or acquit, and hence to punish or to exempt from punishment." If through faith a person is accounted righteous, it must be because he is righteous and not because another is righteous.

Calvin taught that imputation in a strict sense means that the obedience of Christ is accepted for us as if it were our own. This is fictional. Wesley, however, taught an accommodated view of imputation which includes the truth of imparted life or righteousness. The righteousness of Christ is imputed to us in its effects, that is, in its merits. We are justified by faith in the merits of Christ. Vincent Taylor writes: "The righteousness springs from faith as it is related to its object; the object gives to it its character as the condition of righteousness."

This is another way of delineating between the objective and subjective aspects of justification. While God's justifying word is objective in that it has been sounded forth in the cross of Christ and is an act of grace on His part toward individual persons, it is also subjective in that it brings about a real change. Jeremias writes: "God's acquittal is not only forensic, it is not an 'as if', not a mere word, but it is God's word that works and creates life. God's word is always an effective word." Justification therefore is both a declaration and a renovation.

3. Justification is an instantaneous act resulting from the immediate response of God to the faith of the sinner in the Lord Jesus Christ.

Justification, therefore, is that gracious and judicial act of God by which He grants the sinner full pardon of all guilt, releases him from the penalty of sins committed, and accepts him as righteous and makes him a new creature with initial righteousness, on the basis of the sinner's trustful and obedient response to the redeeming work of Christ on the Cross.

See NEW BIRTH, FAITH, IMPUTED RIGHTEOUSNESS, IMPARTED RIGHTEOUSNESS, IN CHRIST.

For Further Reading: Brown, *NIDNTT,* 3:352-73; Hill, *Greek Words and Hebrew Meanings;* Jeremias, *The Central Message of the NT,* 51-70; Bläser, "Justification," *Sacramentum Mundi,* 3:449-55; Taylor, *Forgiveness and Reconciliation,* 48-61; Wiley, *CT,* 2:379-401.

WILLARD H. TAYLOR

K

KABBALA. Kabbala or Cabala (lit. "tradition") is a term belonging to Jewish mysticism. It designates its major medieval variety which crystalized in the 13th century. Cabalistic speculation with its mystic symbolism sought to understand the nature of God and how man relates to Him. God's relationship to man was through 10 intermediary emanations *(sefirot).* Along with the Jewish tradition its sources included Neo-Platonism and Gnosticism. The dynamic influence of Kabbala persists in the Hasidic movement in modern Judaism.

See JUDAISM, GNOSTICISM.

For Further Reading: *The Jewish Encyclopedia*, 3:456-79; Sholem, *Major Trends in Jewish Mysticism*, 119-350. FRANK G. CARVER

KAIROS. See CHRONOS.

KENOSIS. The word *kenosis* means "an emptying." It comes from the Greek word *kenoō* ("I empty") and appears in Phil. 2:7 where it is used of Christ's self-humiliation to become man.

While the divine Son might have given up temporarily His function of sustaining and providentially caring for the universe, it is unthinkable to assume that He could have given up any attribute of Deity. Divine attributes belong only to God. To have any of them is to be God, and to be without any of them is to be less than God. Yet by many statements and deeds throughout His ministry Jesus showed himself to be both God and man.

In John 17:5 the Lord reveals that He had emptied himself of His glory (not an attribute) to become man. That was because: (1) otherwise, no earthling could have endured His splendor to come to Him (1 Tim. 6:14-16); (2) with such overwhelming evidence of Deity, the free exercise of volition to choose Him would have been impossible; (3) having such glory, no enemy would have dared resist Him and seek His death; (4) He could not have lived the life common to man nor demonstrate that God supplies grace to meet mankind's common trials; and (5) He could not have died to redeem sinners.

Jesus Christ was not without divine attributes; but He did limit himself in the use of them in order to accomplish His mission. So successful was He in it that many, even of those who had known Him from childhood, thought Him to be a mere man.

Paul spoke of Christ's self-emptying to encourage his readers to imitate their Lord. "Let this mind be in you," he wrote (Phil. 2:5). Paul practiced what he preached (3:4-15).

See CHRIST, CHRISTOLOGY, MIND OF CHRIST, HUMILIATION OF CHRIST.

For Further Reading: Wiley and Culbertson, *Introduction to Christian Theology*, 207-9; Strong, *Systematic Theology*, 701-6. W. RALPH THOMPSON

KERYGMA. *Kērygma* is a Greek word meaning "that which is cried by the herald," "the command," "the communication." In the LXX it is the summons to celebrate the Passover (2 Chron. 30:5) or the message of God to the Ninevites (Jonah 3:2; cf. Matt. 12:41; Luke 11:32). In most NT passages it signifies "the proclamation of the redeeming purpose of God in Christ" (Rom. 16:25; 1 Cor. 1:21; 2:4; 15:14; 2 Tim. 4:17; Titus 1:3).

The herald or crier *(kērux)* was "a public servant of the supreme power" (Cremer, 355). He summoned the assembly *(ekklēsia)*, conveyed messages, etc. In the NT, he is employed by God to proclaim salvation (1 Tim. 2:7; 2 Tim. 1:11) or righteousness (2 Pet. 2:5).

The verb *kērussō* means to proclaim, preach, or discharge a herald's office. It is used 60 times in the NT, once of the public reading of the law of Moses (Acts 15:21) but generally of the declaration of the gospel of Christ. The verb has as its object: gospel *(evangelion)*, gospel of the Kingdom (Matt. 4:23), gospel of God (Mark 1:14), Christ (Acts 8:5), Jesus (9:20), kingdom of God (20:25), Christ crucified (1 Cor. 1:23), or Christ Jesus (2 Cor. 1:19, all NASB). *Kērygma* lays more stress on the publicity of the proclamation. *Gospel* emphasizes the nature of the good news of salvation.

Cremer relates proclamation *(kērygma)* and gospel (*evangelion*, good news) to *akoē*, hearing, and *rhēma*, word (82). The proclaimed gospel is what is heard, what has gone abroad, news, tradition. The *akoē* is the message heard, the communication received. The *rhēma* is the word containing the message. So reference is made to the "word of hearing" (Heb. 4:2, NASB marg.). This "word of hearing" that was received from Paul was indeed the word of God, faithfully proclaimed by the apostle and received by the hearers (1 Thess. 2:13).

There is a difference between the *kērygma* (the gospel proclamation) and *didachē* (teaching, i.e., the doctrinal and practical implications for life situations). The proclaimed gospel of redemption in Christ Jesus is the central core of the *paradosis* —the divinely given tradition or trust handed down from Christ through the apostles and faithful hearers (2 Thess. 2:15; 2 Tim. 2:2). God manifested His saving word through oral and written *kērygma* (Titus 1:3; 1 Cor. 1:21; 2 Thess. 2:15). The *kērygma* produced the Church. The Church did not produce the *kērygma*.

See DIDACHE, GOSPEL, EVANGELISM, PREACHING.

For Further Reading: Cremer, *Biblico-Theological Lexicon of New Testament Greek*; Girdlestone, *Synonyms of the Old Testament*; Ridderbos, *The Authority of the New Testament Scriptures*; Dodd, *The Apostolic Preaching and Its Development*. WILBER T. DAYTON

KESWICK, KESWICKIANISM. This term designates the teaching on the victorious, Spirit-filled life propagated in the main by an annual convention for the promotion of "practical holiness" held at Keswick, England. Keswick teaching, like that of the American holiness movement which originally inspired the convention's beginnings in 1875, emphasizes a "second blessing" or "second crisis" in Christian experience subsequent to justification in which the Holy Spirit completely fills the wholly consecrated Christian. This Spirit baptism enables the believer to live a consistent Christian life.

However, at the point of the nature of the Holy Spirit's operation in the heart in relation to original sin, a continuing tension has existed between Keswick and Wesleyan teachers from the earliest history of the convention. The former have maintained that in the Spirit-filled life, the Holy Spirit counteracts the nature of sin which continues to remain in the heart of the believer; the latter believes that the nature of sin is cleansed from the heart by the Spirit's application of the finished work of Christ.

This point of difference between the two movements arises out of the fact that from the first Keswick Convention the movement was directed largely by evangelical Anglican leaders. Their theology commonly was based on the teachings of John Calvin, who taught that the conflict in the believer between the flesh and the Spirit could not be finally resolved before the point of death. The American holiness movement, following the teachings of John Wesley, believed that the heart could be entirely sanctified and freed from inbred sin by faith in the full redemption wrought by Christ. Both believe that the Spirit-filled life is a life characterized by victory over sin and power for service.

The first Keswick Convention sprang from holiness evangelism in England by Rev. William E. Boardman, Presbyterian author of *The Higher Christian Life* (1859), and Quaker lay evangelists Robert Pearsall Smith and his wife, Hannah Whitall Smith, author of *The Christian's Secret of a Happy Life* (1870). In 1873 to 1875 a series of breakfast meetings was sponsored by Mr. and Mrs. Cowper Temple (later Lord and Lady Mount-Temple), to introduce the American holiness evangelists to their British friends. Subsequently, larger holiness conventions were held in England at Oxford (1874) and Brighton (1875). In these meetings future Keswick leaders such as Revs. Evan Hopkins and T. D. Harford-Battersby, both Anglicans, and Robert Wilson, Quaker, testified to a new intensity of Christian experience. Out of their enthusiasm for their newfound sense of peace and joy, Battersby and Wilson arranged for a convention for the promotion of holiness to be held at the former's vicarage at Keswick in the north of England. The Smiths, who were to be the speakers, did not attend because of personal tragedy in the ministry of Pearsall Smith which threatened the whole revival for a time (see J. C. Pollock, *The Keswick Story,* 34-37).

The success of the first meeting, however, assured its future; it continues to the present. The early patterns of the convention, many of which have become characteristic of Keswick, indicate their American holiness camp meeting lineage. Spontaneity of spirit, a minimum of prearrangement of program, direct appeal to Spirit leadership, extemporaneous addresses—all centered in promoting the victorious life of Christian holiness—were common to both.

By the turn of the century, Keswick speakers and evangelists such as F. B. Meyer, Andrew Murray, Otto Stockmayer, and R. A. Torrey were spreading the Keswick victorious life teaching. A number of small Keswick Conventions were subsequently established and continue to be held annually around the world. As a result, much of Calvinistic evangelicalism in England, Europe, the United States, and Canada continues to be infused with higher-life teaching.

Keswick has often been charged with fostering an inner Christian quietism at the cost of outreach and social concern. Such accusations must be countered by the active inner-city mission movement in Germany led by people committed to Keswick teaching and the widespread foreign mission efforts inspired by such early participants as Hudson Taylor, founder of the China Inland Mission, and Amy Carmichael, founder of Dohnavur Fellowship, India.

See WESLEYANISM, HOLINESS, COUNTERACTION, ERADICATION, HIGHER LIFE, HOLINESS MOVEMENT.

For Further Reading: For the Wesleyan-holiness view of Keswick teaching, see Hills, *Scriptural Holiness and Keswick Teaching Compared* (1910); For Keswick history and teaching, see Barabas, *So Great Salvation* (1957); Pollock, *The Keswick Story* (1964); Sloan, *These Sixty Years* (1935); For the American holiness movement origins of Keswick, see Dieter, "The Holiness Revival in Nineteenth Century Europe," *WTJ,* Spring, 1974, 15-27; and *The Holiness Revival of the Nineteenth Century.*

MELVIN EASTERDAY DIETER

KEYS OF THE KINGDOM. The "keys" of the Kingdom have a twofold significance in the NT. *First,* they symbolize Christ's authority delegated first to Peter (Matt. 16:13-20) and then to the 11 disciples also (John 20:19-23), to open or close the doors of God's spiritual kingdom to the souls of men. "The power of the keys is authority in the dispensing of the word of grace and judgment" (Jeremias, Kittel, 3:752).

Christ's commission to Peter and the Eleven was not without its OT antecedent (Isa. 22:22). As Eliakim was divinely invested with the key of responsible stewardship over the house of David to "open" and "close" its doors, so Peter, as representative of Christ's disciples, was given responsibility for the keys of God's kingdom to "open" or "close" those doors to the souls of men through the *proclamation of* and *witness to,* or *withholding of,* the saving gospel of Jesus Christ (Matt. 28:18-20). Evangelistically this was first to the Jews and then to the Gentiles (Acts 1:8; 2:38-39; 26:16-18; 2 Cor. 5:19-20).

Second, the "keys" signify Christ's delegated authority for ecclesiastical discipline, expressed as "binding" and "loosing" in John 20:19-23, which points back to Matt. 18:15-20. That this disciplinary authority is to be exercised with prayer and under divine approval is evident from the context, which indicates brother-to-brother relationships, and involves the Church, Christ himself, the Holy Spirit, and God the Father in the procedure of judgment (cf. Acts 5:1-11; 8:9-24; 13:8-11; 15:19-29; Gal. 2:11-12; 1 Corinthians 5; 2 Cor. 2:5-11; Titus 3:10-11).

This delegated disciplinary authority is limited to expulsion ("binding") and reinstating ("loosing") of believers for certain doctrinal and moral offenses within the Church. It does not extend to the divine prerogative of forgiveness and condemnation of sin against God. That authority belongs exclusively to Christ (Matt. 9:6). Wesley says: "In the primitive church absolution meant no more than to discharge from church censure" (*Notes,* on Matt. 18:18; so Origen, Tertullian, Cyprian, and Luther).

That the keys of the Kingdom remain ultimately in Christ's possession, and that with them He will finally free men from death through the resurrection, is explicitly declared by Him who unlocked His own tomb and came forth a victor over death and the grave (Rev. 1:18; 3:7; cf. Luke 24:5-7; John 11:25; Acts 2:24; 1 Cor. 15:20).

See KINGDOM OF GOD, CHURCH GOVERNMENT, DISCIPLINE, GREAT COMMISSION.

For Further Reading: *ISBE,* 3:1794-97; Kittel, 3:744-53; Vincent, *Word Studies in the New Testament,* 1:91-98.

CHARLES W. CARTER

KINGDOM OF GOD. To appreciate the significance of this term in its historic biblical and theological usage, an understanding of the correlative "king" motif is essential. The Israelite concept of "king" and its cognates had its linguistic roots in the Syro-Canaanite understanding of the "God most high" as a king *(melek)* accorded unlimited authority. This authority took two forms: one affirmed that "Yahweh is king" (the essential, or ontological mode: cf. Ps. 93:1; Jer. 10:7); the other that "Yahweh has proved to be king" (the existential, or dynamic mode: cf. Ps. 47:8; 97:1). In the cultic setting of Israel the enthronement psalms in particular declared the experience of the present reality of Yahweh's kingship, connecting this theme with His historical acts, such as the Exodus, and future expectation of His eschatological consummation of history (cf. the Messianic theology of Isa. 9:7; 11:1 ff). This stress on covenant kingship in Israel became a primary differentiation of Israel from the divine kingship ideas of their neighbors.

From Israel's initial political stance as a loose confederacy waging holy war, there developed the institution of a monarchy. This was in direct response to the perennial Philistine pressure and at the express command of Yahweh (1 Sam. 9:1—10:16). This predominantly favorable view of the monarchy was vigorously opposed by many in Northern Israel who perceived monarchy as a rejection of theocracy (1 Sam. 8:1-22; 10:17-27). This tension over what was Yahweh's will for His people persisted throughout the monarchic period and beyond, with the "eternal" Davidic kingdom of the South vying for supremacy with the charismatic leadership of the North. The concept of an everlasting Davidic covenant (2 Samuel 7) with the adoption of the king as son of Yahweh (in contrast to other Near Eastern views of the king as divine by nature, e.g., Egypt) led to the enhancement of the eschatological kingship motif, as the reality of *earthly* kingship expectation deteriorated (Isa. 11:1-9; 9:2-7).

Thus, Israel experienced Yahweh's kingship fundamentally in His historical actions toward them, seen in the covenantal provisions and demands of His absolute power and the guidance of His elect people through a tortured history. Despite these sometimes ambivalent historical indicators (e.g., the Exilic period), Israel affirmed that Yahweh was still actively exercising kingship, in a functional and not merely formal sense, and that He would continue to rule variously but emphatically over the whole creation, over Israel and the nations of the world.

This pattern of Yahweh's cosmic, historical, cultic, and eschatological kingship *(malkuth)* was discerned in secular, political kingdoms (Jer.

49:34); in cosmic ideological terms (Ps. 145:11-13); in the eschatological sense of a universal, immanent kingdom (Isa. 24:23; Zech. 14:9); and finally in an apocalyptic mode (Dan. 7:13). The hallmark of this mode was the tension between narrow nationalism and transcending eschatology.

Within later Judaism the national, Messianic eschatology of kingship became prevalent among the masses (cf. *Psalms of Solomon,* the Qumran sectarian War Scroll), and rabbinic thought affirmed the kingship of God in the world by its unswerving loyalty to the one true God and precise observation of His Torah. Whereas in the Qumran literature heaven was a special realm where God's kingship was acknowledged in deed and truth, in rabbinic terms one could take on "the yoke of the kingship of heaven" and thus assist in bringing in the kingdom by penance, study of the Torah, and good deeds.

Alongside these Jewish contributions to the developed concept of kingship which formed the Palestinian religious and social setting of Jesus' ministry was the Graeco-Roman understanding of kingship. Though the king *(basileus)* of Mycenean times was merely a subordinate prince under the divine ruler *(anax)*, by Homer's time the king was generally a hereditary ruler who could trace his power and lineage back to Zeus. Subsequently the term *basileus* was replaced by *tyrannos.* Though initially a neutral concept, *tyrannos* took on a negative connotation in the political upheavals of sixth-century (B.C.) Greece, and *basileus* became the term for a wise, just ruler. Further intimations of divine kingship were infused into the word by the accomplishments of Alexander the Great. The geographical extent of influence and the power of the emperor's office summed up in a kingship terminology reached a climax in the Roman emperor cult begun with Augustus. It was against such a political backcloth of the kingship of Caesar that Christians were challenged to affirm the Kingship of Christ by declaring, "Jesus is Lord."

The kingdom of God motif in the NT affirms the continuity of its OT roots. God alone truly wields Kingship, over against the "kings of the earth" (Matt. 17:25). The positive evaluation of the Davidic monarchy and its Messianic overtones is impressive (2 Samuel 7; Acts 13:22), though the only other king applauded is Melchizedek (Gen. 14:18; Heb. 7:1 ff), the type of Christ, the High Priest, the Son of David.

John the Baptist becomes the turning point of "kingdom" understanding, appearing as he does on the fulcrum of prophetic prediction and eschatological fulfillment (see Luke 7:28), with an appeal for repentance and baptism which can reasonably be explained only from a Messianic, eschatological understanding of the kingdom of God. With his focus on the judgment of God immediately pending, and the advent of a stronger man (Matt. 3:7-10), he invites comparison with Jesus and His message. Indeed, it is suggested (Luke 16:16) that history can be divided into two phases: the Law and the Prophets prior to John, and the presence of the kingdom of God after John (cf. Matt. 11:11 ff and 5:17).

The differences between John and Jesus, however, are crucial. The former threatens judgment, demands repentance and its fruits, promises contingent escape from Messianic judgment, and advises preparation for the future cataclysm. He is the continuation of the prophetic line (cf. Mal. 3:1) and a living symbol of the imminent dawn of salvation. The latter offers himself as the implicit revelation of God's kingdom of love, grace, forgiveness, and salvation, and the eschatological reality of the kingdom of God made present in His own person and claims (cf. Matthew 5—7). In Jesus' gospel of the Kingdom, all previous hopes of salvation find their culmination and fulfillment in the kingdom of God.

This new age of salvation depicts the kingdom of God present as the dynamic of divine activity. It is the sovereign rule of God here and now challenging and demanding our response. It is societal in nature, for the Kingdom is composed of redeemed people who function often under pressure and opposition. It is salvific, in that the summons to repentance is present alongside the offer of mercy in Jesus' words and works (Isa. 52:7; Mark 1:15). It is purely religious in character, a kingdom which transcends nationalistic boundaries (cf. Matt. 4:1-11) in being directed to all mankind. It is the *eschaton* functioning in the present situation, for the primary thrust of Jesus' teaching is not the imperative but the indicative. In Jesus' life and death the present and future kingdom of God stand side by side: in Him who heals miraculously, exorcises demons, and preaches to the poor (Isa. 61:1); in Him who triumphally enters Jerusalem as a new Kingdom bearer and cleanses the Temple for a new reign of God (see Isa. 62:11; Zech. 9:9; John 5:15).

The kingdom of God, therefore, is actually present in Jesus' ministry, portraying a new pattern for living, Christocentrically affirmed, and related to a king who functions as a Father (Matt. 6:9 ff). It is a truly eschatological gospel that Jesus preaches, one of power and authority, which emphasizes constantly the crisic importance and urgency of the present moment *(kairos),* thereby imposing radical demands on His hearers. This kingdom of God springs from divine power and grace in the present because of what the covenant God has accomplished in the past and guarantees to effect in the future (see Luke 12:32; 22:18). The true nature of the world can only be understood in the light of God's kingdom, but the kingdom of God is neither the extension nor the projection of anything in this world. Thus Jesus teaches and preaches in the *parabolic* mode concerning the value of the Kingdom, conditions for membership in it, its productivity and growth, and the final Judgment.

Outside the Synoptics the kingdom of God terminology tends to be replaced by Christological affirmations (cf. Acts 2:36; 8:12; 2 Tim. 4:18). The implicit Christology of the Synoptics is made explicit in the rest of the NT as the kingdom of God present in the person of Jesus now is seen in the person of the risen Lord.

Particularly in Acts God's kingdom is operative in a new way: Jesus as exalted Lord exercises a real rule, indicative of the new age of the Spirit (Acts 2:36; con. 1:6). Where the Kingdom teaching of Paul preserves the "here-not yet" polarity by a Christocentric, ethical motivation, Acts moves towards incorporating God's kingdom into the *ecclēsia* framework of the Early Church. In John's writings the eschatological Kingdom community has become a present fellowship reality, a concept reflected in the General Epistles. By the time of Revelation, of course, the eschatological kingdom of God is identical with the kingdom of Christ (Rev. 11:15), which in turn is equated with the community of saints on earth, where history is merely the battlefield for the ultimate cosmic struggle.

The "here-not yet" teaching of Paul is especially significant. In the Epistles traditionally credited to him, there are 13 references to the Kingdom as such. Three of them assume the kingdom of God to be spiritual in nature and a present reality—e.g., "For the kingdom of God is not food and drink but righteousness and peace and joy in the Holy Spirit" (Rom. 14:17, RSV; cf. 1 Cor. 4:20; Col. 1:13). The balance are either probably or obviously eschatological in orientation; e.g., "Flesh and blood cannot inherit the kingdom of God" (1 Cor. 15:50; cf. 6:9-10; 15:24; Gal. 5:21; Eph. 5:5; Col. 4:11; 1 Thess. 2:12; 2 Thess. 1:5; 2 Tim. 4:1, 18).

The history of theological interpretation of "the kingdom of God" reflects not only the disputes over specific biblical passages (e.g., Matt. 11:12; 13:23; Mark 1:15; 4:11; 10:15; 12:34; Luke 7:28; 17:20), but also the apparent ambivalencies or surface paradoxes in the words of Jesus. Is "building the kingdom" consistent with the "kingdom of God"? Is the Kingdom prophetic or apocalyptic in character? Is it transcendent or immanent?

From the imminent *parousia* teaching of Tertullian, the enthusiasm of Montanism, the spiritualization of Origen and the Eastern wing of Christendom, the reification of the kingdom of God in the West (cf. Charlemagne, the Crusades, the social gospel, Pietism), and the assaults of world conflict, the kingdom of God motif has emerged into the 20th century, where the interpretations of the kingdom of God fall roughly into the following camps: futuristic/apocalyptic/consistent eschatology (see J. Weiss, A. Schweitzer); prophetic eschatology (see W. Rauschenbusch, L. Harold DeWolf); realized eschatology (see C. H. Dodd); proleptic/existential eschatology (see R. Bultmann and demythologization); and dual dimension eschatology —Kingdom both present and future (see G. E. Ladd, Oscar Cullmann, W. Kümmel). Each viewpoint attempts to reconcile the nature of the Kingdom as future, present, or in process of realization, and to do justice to the symbols used while appropriating the message to historical reality. The kingdom of God, however, remains ultimately a mystery still to be revealed.

See CHURCH, ESCHATOLOGY, LAST DAYS (THE), NEW HEAVENS AND NEW EARTH, NEW COVENANT, KINGLY OFFICES OF CHRIST, DISPENSATION OF THE SPIRIT.

For Further Reading: Bright, *The Kingdom of God;* Dodd, *The Parables of the Kingdom;* Harkness, *Understanding the Kingdom of God;* Jeremias, *The Parables of Jesus;* Ladd, *The Presence of the Future;* Lundstrom, *The Kingdom of God in the Teaching of Jesus;* Schnackenburg, *God's Rule and God's Kingdom;* Vos, *The Pauline Eschatology; GMS,* 38-340, 612-23.

JOHN S. LOWN

KINGLY OFFICES OF CHRIST. Christian theologians have for many generations described Christ's work by means of the three offices of Prophet, Priest, and King. He is the One who perfectly combines all three functions (cf. Wiley, *CT,* 2:213-15). That Jesus should have fulfilled a kingly role is only a natural consequence of His identity as the Messiah, God's Anointed One. However, the manner whereby that identity was manifested in His life and work involved a more accurate interpretation of the OT hope than the popular Messianic expectation of first-century Judaism.

That reinterpretation is introduced by the Synoptic Gospels from the very beginning of Jesus' public ministry. The episode of Jesus' baptism by John, and the descent of the Holy Spirit upon Jesus with the accompanying voice from heaven, is Jesus' inauguration into the role of Messiah. Its significance is explained by the words of the heavenly voice. Those words identify Jesus by joining the OT concept of the kingly Messiah with the figure of the Servant of the Lord. The voice from heaven combines words from Ps. 2:7 and Isa. 42:1. This means that the kingly authority of Jesus, His identity as the Anointed One, will be exercised, lived out, as He fulfills the role of the Servant Messiah. Jesus will be the crucified Messiah. That King Jesus reigns from the Cross is accentuated by the Gospel of John. There the hour of Christ's glorification is the moment when He is lifted up on the Cross.

The major theme of Jesus' public ministry was the proclamation that the kingdom of God had come near. But He did more than speak words about the reign of God. He acted in ways which demonstrated to the eyes of faith that the Kingdom was present in His very person. He exercised the kingly authority of God when He healed the sick, cast out demons, forgave sins, and reinterpreted the ethical demand of God (cf. Matt. 11:2-6; Luke 4:16-27).

The ultimate demonstration of Jesus' kingly office was His resurrection. It was because God vindicated Jesus by resurrecting Him that the first disciples were able to confess, "Jesus is Lord" (cf. Acts 2:32-36; Phil. 2:5-11).

See CHRIST, ESTATES OF CHRIST, KINGDOM OF GOD.

For Further Reading: Barclay, *Jesus as They Saw Him,* 38-42, 93-159, 240-44; Bright, *The Kingdom of God,* 187-274; Ladd, *A Theology of the New Testament,* 57-80, 135-58, 237-53, 408-22. HAL A. CAUTHRON

KNOWLEDGE. This area is regarded as so important in philosophy that one of its major branches of study is epistemology or theory of knowledge.

One of man's most important abilities is to be aware, to know, to have knowledge. This grasp of the mind may be almost totally missing, as when there is innocence in the case of the infant or mature person who has the capacity but not yet the experience; or as in the case of ignorance when a person possibly should or could know something but does not. Misinformation is a condition in which something is known, but it is not adequate or is distorted so that there is significant failure to apprehend the situation.

Rising to the level of opinion is progress beyond the preceding stages, because here through a number of ways or through a fairly secure method the person knows something. The level of truth occurs, however, when the method of knowing is fully adequate to the objects being known.

Some of the avenues by which one knows (from philosophic and theological methods) are perception (as in sensory experience), scientific method, custom, tradition, authority, intuition, coherence, and revelation.

While some Christians may occasionally or even frequently speak of the absolute character of their knowledge, others may prefer to speak of assurance. Some stress revelation as found in the Scriptures as the source of sure knowledge. Some believe that the basis of religious knowledge is a reasoned and systematic interpretation of the Bible. For others, the key certainty is a personal assurance of acceptance with God, a knowledge that the God of the Bible is the true God who is the Savior of all mankind and especially of that specific individual. For such persons only the experiential knowledge of the heart is sure, while knowledge of the truth in the form of concepts is relative. The Christian seeks to know truth both propositionally and experientially.

The apostle Paul said, "I know whom I have believed" (2 Tim. 1:12). The person who believes God and His Word is being delivered from the frenetic seeking which fails to turn up genuine knowledge (3:7), for he drinks from a well of truth which deeply satisfies (John 4:7-15).

See EPISTEMOLOGY, WITNESS OF THE SPIRIT.

For Further Reading: *Concise Encyclopedia of Western Philosophy and Philosophers;* Weinberg and Yandell, *Theory of Knowledge;* Barrett, *A Christian Perspective of Knowing.* R. DUANE THOMPSON

KOINONIA. *Koinōnia,* usually translated "fellowship," is the Greek word that identifies the depth fellowship of the NT Christian community. As the fellowship of the Holy Spirit (2 Cor. 13:14), the Church is to be the caring, sharing community.

One aspect of koinonia is that of Christians sharing in their common relationship with God. Being joint partakers of grace (Phil. 1:7) is the result of the vertical koinonia made possible by the work of Christ and the Holy Spirit (John 16:5-15). John Stott summarizes the Christian's mutual participation in God's grace: "Begotten by the will and word of the same Father, redeemed by the blood of the same Son, indwelt by the presence of the same Spirit—that is our koinonia, the common salvation we . . . share" *(One People,* 76).

The vertical koinonia is the basis for the horizontal koinonia experienced among the saints.

Because God loved them, believers are to love; loving one another is to be the trademark of the Church (John 13:35). Christians are to forgive, serve, encourage, instruct, admonish, and weep with one another. Two examples of the new quality of group life are the Jerusalem church in the Book of Acts (John Wesley thought highly of that common life), and the relief offering Paul gathered in his third missionary journey for the saints in Jerusalem. In total, the goal of koinonia is that the Body of Christ might attain "the full measure of perfection found in Christ" (Eph. 4:13, NIV).

A further aspect of koinonia is the common task of sharing the gospel message. Jesus called His disciples to be fishers of men, colaborers in spreading the faith. Paul speaks highly of those who worked with him in proclaiming the Good News. All believers are to work together in the fulfilling of the Great Commission.

See FELLOWSHIP, LOVE, UNITY, BODY LIFE.

For Further Reading: Stott, *One People*, 69-90; Snyder, *The Problem of Wineskins*, 89-150; Bonhoeffer, *Life Together.*
MARTIN H. SCHRAG

L

LABOR. This is the investment of energy and time in productive, purposeful activity. The purpose is the accomplishment of a task or the rendering of a service.

The Genesis record indicates that before the Fall, God instructs, "Have dominion . . . over every living thing" (1:28). Of Adam God says, "I will make an help meet for him" (2:18). Ruling over the world involves labor, and for that Adam receives a helper. After the Fall God declares, "In toil shall you eat of it [the ground] all the days of your life" (3:17, NASB). The Fall is not the occasion of labor but rather the reason for the way in which labor is often performed: "in sorrow" (KJV).

The biblical view is that labor is a part of God's gracious and requisite plan for man. The Psalmist praises God for the fact that man "goes forth to his work" (104:23, NASB). The Lord Jesus is known as "the carpenter" (Mark 6:3). The apostle Paul sees work as an essential element in Christian discipline. The Christian cannot accept the thinking of a society in which there is inordinate concern for ease, pleasure, security; and little or no concern for honest and hard work. Paul writes, "If anyone will not work, neither let him eat" (2 Thess. 3:10, NASB). There is no place in the Christian life-style for drones. However, not all labor is manual; it may equally be mental. It may also be clerical, professional, or in the category of services.

The early Methodists, in both Britain and North America, following the example of John Wesley, were oftentimes occupied with the concerns of the laborer. Their serious interest in this area reflects the view that labor must not be passed over in the total Christian view of stewardship.

The Bible teaches that the exertion of spiritual effort is also labor. Jesus' assignment from the Father is seen as "his work" (John 4:34). The Christian is to appreciate the labor of those who are leaders in the Church (1 Thess. 5:12).

See VOCATION, WORK (WORKS), CHRISTIAN SOCIALISM.

For Further Reading: Hoffner, *Fundamentals of Christian Sociology*, 90-109; Kaiser, *Theology of Work*, 521; Wirt, *The Social Conscience of the Evangelical*, 57-64.
ALDEN AIKENS

LAITY. This term derives from the root word *laos*, the "people," and is virtually synonymous with laymen or laypeople. From some time in the second century the Christian church began to distinguish its general membership from the clergy by the use of this term. In later years it has had a more general usage in distinguishing nonprofessionals from professionals in a number of areas, as, for example, in law and in medicine.

It is probably true that Christendom has swung constantly between the extremes of clericalism on one side and anticlericalism on the other. Certain it is that the Scriptures articulate both the universal priesthood of believers and the special calling of apostles, prophets, evangelists, pastors, and teachers (Eph. 4:7-12).

The distinction between the spiritual privileges, duties, and services of the laity and the clergy are not absolutes. Under certain conditions, any Roman Catholic may offer the sacrament of extreme unction to a dying man. In emergencies there are few things laymen cannot do which clergymen customarily do. And the clergymen must, as did the OT priests, seek forgiveness and grace quite as earnestly as do the laity.

Nevertheless, there are relative distinctions which set the clergy apart. These include the sense of divine call; the recognition of gifts and calling by the church, and even by civil authorities; the advantages of advanced study; the financial support of a congregation; and also special powers officially bestowed on him by his particular church discipline.

Furthermore, the God-called clerics are specifically charged with the responsibility of the "equipping of the saints for the work of service" (Eph. 4:11-12, NASB). Laymen are to be trained in churchmanship, that they may fill their places in the body effectively (Rom. 12:4-8; 1 Cor. 12:14-18). The fact that laymen may be especially Spirit-gifted is the counterpart of their training, not a substitute for it.

The present generation of the Church is vividly conscious of the need for and privilege of lay service in the evangelization of the world.

See GREAT COMMISSION, MINISTER (MINISTRY), EVANGELISM, CLERGY, DISCIPLING.

For Further Reading: *Baker's Dictionary of Practical Theology*, 322-25, 414 ff. JOHN E. RILEY

LAMB, SACRIFICIAL. The lamb, a young male sheep, was the main animal of sacrifice among the Jews. From the time of the Exodus the lamb became the central symbol and dominant sacrifice in religious observances.

Israel's birthday, the Exodus, was marked by the killing of a lamb and using its blood to sprinkle the doorposts to exempt the Hebrews from the angel of death which took the lives of the firstborn of the Egyptians (Exodus 12). The lamb, slaughtered, roasted, and eaten in haste, occupied the center of attention in the observance of the Passover.

Sacrificial regulations for most observances called for the sacrifice of lambs. Lambs were sacrificed for morning and evening burnt offerings (Exod. 29:38-42); on the first day of each (lunar) month (Num. 28:11); for all seven days of the Passover (vv. 16-19); for the Feast of Weeks (vv. 26-27); on the Day of Atonement (29:7-8); for the Feast of Tabernacles (vv. 12-13, all NIV).

In various OT passages the lamb conveyed such ideas as *deliverance* (Exod. 29:38-42); *vicarious suffering* (Lev. 9:3; 23:12); *innocence* (Isa. 53:7); *helplessness* (Ps. 119:176; Hos. 4:16); *gentleness* (Jer. 11:19). The climax of the lamb as a sacrifice in the OT is found in Isaiah 53. "All the qualities of innocence, purity, and meekness, and possibly also a sense of efficaciousness, derived from the actual sacrificial system, are summoned with the deepest poignancy in the figurative use of the lamb as applied to the Suffering Servant" (*IDB*, 3:59).

In the NT the term "lamb" is used only figuratively. The Seventy are sent forth as "lambs in the midst of wolves" (Luke 10:3, RSV). Jesus tells Peter to "feed my lambs" (John 21:15). Most NT references point to the person and work of Jesus Christ (John 1:29, 36: Acts 8:32; 1 Pet. 1:19).

The Early Church community used the innocence and purity of the OT sacrificial lamb in interpreting the life and mission of Jesus Christ.

See SACRIFICE, PASSOVER, ATONEMENT, LAMB OF GOD.

For Further Reading: Nicoll, *The Lamb of God*, 21-36; *ZPEB*, 859-60. DONALD S. METZ

LAMB OF GOD. The introduction of John the Evangelist to Christ took place when John the Baptist said: "Behold the Lamb of God!" (John 1:36). John the Baptist, the son of a priest, knew full well the import of the title "Lamb of God." This spontaneous tribute to Jesus assigns a title to Him which has become woven into the language of redemption and devotion. The title "Lamb of God" carries several meanings.

The Idea of Innocence and Gentleness. The innocence of Christ means that He was absolutely free from any taint of evil. His innocence was not the innocence of ignorance nor the innocence of freedom from temptation. His innocence was the innocence of spiritual struggle and victory. The gentleness of Jesus was the gentleness of one who suffered, not by the constraint of weakness, but by the stronger constraint of love. The innocence and gentleness of Jesus are that of vicarious suffering.

The Paschal Lamb. It was the blood of the Passover lamb which saved the Israelites in Egypt from destruction and death. John pointed to the one true Sacrifice who could deliver from both physical and spiritual death. While in the institution of the Passover the blood of the paschal lamb was not primarily related to redemption from sin, yet the redemptive idea became part of the Jewish tradition. The reference in 1 Pet. 1:19 relates to the paschal lamb rather than to the Lamb of Isa. 53:7.

The Sin Offering. John the Baptist was familiar with Jewish ritual. This ritual required that every morning and every evening a lamb was sacrificed in the Temple for the sins of the people (Exod. 29:38-42). The daily sacrifice was made as long as the Temple stood. The Baptist declared that Jesus was the permanent Sacrifice who would deliver not only Jews but the entire world from sin.

The Suffering Messiah. John's use of the title "Lamb of God" appears as a reference to Isaiah 53 and Jeremiah 11. "Both these great prophets had the vision of one who by His sufferings and His sacrifice, meekly and lovingly borne, would redeem His people" (Barclay, *The Gospel of John,* 1:64). Isaiah's passage is directly applied to Christ in Acts 8:32. Other phrases from the same prophecy (Isaiah 53) are treated as having a Messianic reference in Matt. 8:17; 1 Pet. 2:22; and Heb. 9:28.

Symbol of a Conqueror. During the time between the OT and the NT gigantic struggles were fought to free Israel. During these struggles the lamb, and particularly the horned lamb, became a symbol of a great conqueror. John the Revelator pictured the Lamb as triumphant (Rev. 17:4; 5:13; 7:17).

See SACRIFICE, PASSOVER, ATONEMENT, SIN OFFERING.

For Further Reading: Bernard, *The Gospel According to John,* 1:43-45; Barclay, *The Gospel of John,* 1:63-66; Westcott, *Gospel According to John,* 19-21.

DONALD S. METZ

LANGUAGE, THEOLOGICAL. See THEOLOGICAL LANGUAGE.

LASCIVIOUSNESS. This word is found six times in the NT (KJV), where it translates the Greek word *aselgeia* (Mark 7:22; 2 Cor. 12:21; Gal. 5:19; Eph. 4:19; 1 Pet. 4:3; Jude 4). *Aselgeia* is also translated (KJV) "wantonness" (Rom. 13:13; 2 Pet. 2:18), "filthy" (v. 7), and "pernicious ways" (v. 2).

J. B. Lightfoot says that in the NT the prominent idea of *aselgeia* is "sensuality" (*Epistle of St. Paul to the Galatians,* 210-11). This is rather obvious from its context in most cases. For instance, in Rom. 13:13 it follows a Greek word meaning "sexual immorality" (NIV). In 2 Cor. 12:21 and Gal. 5:19 it follows *porneia,* from which we get *pornography.* In all these cases *aselgeia* may be translated "debauchery" (NIV). This sin marked the pagan society of that day but has no place in the Christian life.

See SIN, SEX (SEXUALITY), FORNICATION, CONCUPISCENCE.

For Further Reading: Kittel, 1:490.

RALPH EARLE

LAST DAYS, THE. This is a Messianic expression denoting the time when God's kingdom is established in the world. "It shall come to pass in the latter days that the mountain of the house of the Lord shall be established as the highest of the mountains, and shall be raised above the hills; and all the nations shall flow to it, and many peoples shall come, and say: 'Come, let us go up to the mountain of the Lord'" (Isa. 2:2-3, RSV). This envisages what we call the end of history which will see the rule of God established in all the earth and the earth transformed by being redeemed from the curse of fallenness.

The phrase is found several times in the NT, but from a very different perspective. Hebrews designates the last days as the days of the Messiah. "In many and various ways God spoke of old to our fathers by the prophets; but in these last days he has spoken to us by a Son, whom he appointed the heir of all things, through whom also he created the world" (Heb. 1:1-2, RSV). Some readers have been offended by the translation of the RSV, "by *a* Son." The simple fact is that the Greek had an idiom which is absent from the NT and cannot be translated. English has both a definite and an indefinite article. Greek has only the definite article. However, its nonuse does not mean one of many, as is suggested; rather, it suggests the quality of that with which it is used. Thus, Heb. 1:1-2 means, God has in these last days spoken to us by one whose nature is that of the Son of God.

The phrase occurs also in the Book of Acts in a Messianic setting. On the Day of Pentecost, Peter quotes at some length from Joel the prophet about the eschatological outpouring of the Holy Spirit. Peter adds this phrase which is not found in Joel, "And in the last days it shall be, God declares, that I will pour out my Spirit upon all flesh" (Acts 2:17, RSV). By placing this event in history, Peter affirms that in some unexpected way, the Messianic age has come into history. The consummation at "the day of the Lord" remains in the future, but in the coming of the Holy Spirit, the new age, the Messianic age, has begun.

A somewhat different form of the expression but the same theology is to be found in 1 Pet. 1:20. "He [Christ] was destined before the foundation of the world but was made manifest at the end [Greek: last] of the times for your sake" (RSV).

However, despite the fact that Messiah has come and we have entered upon the last day, this does not mean that this age will see the complete triumph of Messiah. The last days are the days of

Christ's reign and the outpouring of the Holy Spirit, but evil and wicked men are still to be found. These last days are the days in which God has completed His revelation by no longer speaking in various ways and in many places, but has given His full revelation in His Son, Jesus the Messiah, who in Heb. 1:8 is designated God, who has suffered and died and now is enthroned at the right hand of God where He will reign until all His enemies are subdued.

See ESCHATOLOGY, MILLENNIUM, NEW HEAVENS AND NEW EARTH, PROBATION.

For Further Reading: Ladd, *A Theology of the New Testament; Crucial Questions About the Kingdom of God;* Biederwolf, *The Millennium Bible;* Hughes, *A New Heaven and a New Earth; GMS,* 612-76.

GEORGE ELDON LADD

LATITUDINARIANISM. This is an "attitude of latitude" regarding doctrinal beliefs and political matters. This type of thinking was started by a group of 17th-century English divines who desired to find a common ground between the Anglicans, the Presbyterians, and the Dissenters. They professed to stress life as more important than belief, and attached greater importance to practical piety than they did to forms of reasoning. Because they tried to find a middle ground in doctrinal beliefs, they were often referred to as Indifferents; at other times as Syncretists.

The Latitudinarians kept their creedal statements simple and brief, in order to provide a broad base for cooperation. While this is appealing to the undogmatic temper of mind, it has often degenerated into casual tolerance of fatal error.

See DOGMA (DOGMATICS), BELIEF.

For Further Reading: Qualben, *A History of the Christian Church,* 362; *Baker's DT,* 317; *ER,* 431.

MENDELL L. TAYLOR

LAW. As employed almost 200 times in Scripture, "law" signifies the revealed will of God with respect to human conduct. God has declared to man what is right and wrong. The law spoken of here is a divine standard.

Underlying the biblical notion of law is God's covenant relation with His people. The law revealed in Scripture reflects the character of the God whom we serve. Because the Lord is holy and faithful, His commandments are righteous and true.

The basic OT term is *torah,* which in Hebrew generally signifies guidance or direction. This guidance is the divine teaching as to how the covenant is to be lived. The common Greek word *nomos* is used in the NT primarily in reference to the OT *torah.* Unfortunately, *nomos* is understood legalistically by many people, and the central redemptive purpose of *torah* is missed.

The Ten Commandments given to Moses (Exod. 20:1-17; Deut. 5:1-21) enunciate the broad principles of God's moral law. They specify authoritatively, without qualification, what the covenant conditions are. God's people are called to obedience in accord with these directives.

The NT affirms the continuing validity of the Decalogue. Jesus reiterates its commands, highlighting the primacy of love to God and neighbor (see Mark 12:28-31), and focusing on the spirit of the law as over against merely the letter (see Matt. 5:17-48). Similarly, Paul (Rom. 13:8-10; Gal. 5:13-14) and Jas. (1:25; 2:8, 12).

Nowhere in the NT is there a recognition of the Jewish oral tradition as law. Rather, its rules and regulations are labeled manmade (see Mark 7:6-13).

Moreover, the NT does not require of Christians the observance of the cultic statutes commanded by God in OT times: the regulations governing the sanctuary, offerings, and priesthood; circumcision, feasts and festivals, and other ceremonial laws. These were types and shadows of better things to come (Heb. 10:1); they have been fulfilled in Jesus Christ. He is our Passover Lamb; He is our High Priest; He is the End of the law with respect to righteousness (Rom. 10:4).

Similarly, the social legislation of the OT is not obligatory on Christian society: regulations governing property and slaves, the army and warfare, personal offenses and civil crimes. This legislation was designed for a particular culture at a given period of history. Underlying it, however, are timeless principles applicable to all generations.

But God's moral law is eternal, for it is a reflection of His character. It cannot be changed. Man, in the flesh, cannot fulfill its demands. Thus, the law functions to show up his sinfulness for what it is, disobedience against God (Rom. 7:7, 13). He finds himself condemned as unrighteous, a transgressor of God's law at this point or that (vv. 9-11; Jas. 2:9-11). The answer to his dilemma is Christ. The law is a "tutor" to lead man to Christ, that man might be made righteous through faith in Him (Gal. 3:24). That is the only hope of salvation.

And now, in Christ Jesus, one is freed from the condemnation of the law, but brought under a new law, "the law of the Spirit of life in Christ Jesus" (Rom. 8:1-2). The NT is replete with exhortations, directions, and counsels respecting the conduct of this new life. The Christian endeavors, in the Spirit, to live in a manner that accords with God's will. The goal is conformity to the image of God as reflected in the face of Jesus Christ (Eph. 4:13). The people of God are called to reflect His holiness in their behavior (1 Pet. 1:14-16). Thus they search the law of God to discern more of God's character and His will for their lives (cf. Mark 12:28-34; John 13:34; 15:12; Rom. 13:1-10; 1 Cor. 9:21; Gal. 5:14; 6:2; 1 Tim. 6:11-14; Jas. 2:8; 1 John 3:23).

See LAW AND GRACE, RIGHT (RIGHTEOUSNESS), FREEDOM, OBEDIENCE, BIBLICAL AUTHORITY.

For Further Reading: Kittel, 4:1022-91; *IDB*, 3:77-102.

WAYNE G. MCCOWN

LAW AND GRACE. Rather than being antithetical, the *moral law* (Gr., *nomos*) of the OT, epitomized in the Decalogue, and saving faith through Christ in the NT, are complementary. Christ declared His redemptive mission was to fulfill, or complete, the law (Matt. 5:17-18; cf. 3:15; Rom. 10:4).

For one thing, the Decalogue codifies God's righteousness and will revealed to Moses which was also present to some extent in fallen man's moral constitution, and in objective nature (Rom. 1:18-21; 2:14-15; Psalm 19). Furthermore, the Decalogue was a moral norm for man, the first four commandments to direct his relationship with God, and the last six his relationship with society. Moreover, rather than being an end in itself (which is always legalism), the law was designed as a directive ("a child-conductor," NASB marg.) to bring man to Christ for justification (Gal. 3:23-26). There was no salvation in the law per se, but through faith in the Redeemer to whom it pointed salvation was always available (Heb. 11:13-16).

Christian *grace* (Gr., *charis*) is the freely given, unmerited favor and love of God manifest in His Son for man's salvation (John 3:16). Grace is the heart of the NT and the most distinctive feature of the Christian gospel. The entire message of the Bible is summarized by John thus: "For the law was given through Moses; grace and truth were realized through Jesus Christ" (John 1:17, NASB; cf. v. 14).

Grace is love in action. James designates it the "royal law" (Jas. 2:8). Jesus Christ is God's grace toward undeserving man demonstrated on the Cross (Rom. 8:1-4). Grace transfers the Decalogue from cold, hard tablets of stone to warm, living hearts of flesh throbbing with outflowing love for God and man (Heb. 8:10-13; 10:16-18). Grace reconciles unworthy sinners to God and endows them with life everlasting and the riches of His kingdom (2 Cor. 8:9).

The biblical concept of being "under the law" is a looking to the law as a means of salvation, and being subject to the law as an external control on behavior. The biblical idea of being "under grace" is a view of grace as God's way of salvation, through Christ, and as the secret of inner moral power. Being "under grace" and "not under law" (Rom. 6:14; Gal. 4:21; 5:18; 6:7-8) does not mean that grace cancels law, but that grace, rather than the Mosaic law-system, is the only way the moral claims of the law can be fulfilled (Rom. 8:1-4).

See LAW, DECALOGUE, WORK (WORKS), ANTINOMIANISM, LEGALISM, LOVE AND LAW.

For Further Reading: Davis, "Law," *IDB*, K-Q:77-102; Mitton, "Grace," *IDB*, E-J:463-68; Eaton, "Grace," *ISBE*, 2:1290-92; McCaig and Rule, "Law," *ISBE*, 3:1844-58; Wood, *Pentecostal Grace*. CHARLES W. CARTER

LAW OF LIBERTY. The new freedom which Christ's atonement provides is called by James the "perfect law of liberty" (Jas. 1:25). Paul speaks of it as "the law of the Spirit of life in Christ Jesus" which makes us free from "the law of sin and death" (Rom. 8:2).

Because the guilt of sin has been removed in justification, man is freed from the pangs of conscience for sins committed. Because of the indwelling Holy Spirit, man is also freed from (1) the pull of worldly (unchristian) attractions; (2) the weakness or reluctance one feels when God's will involves that which may be distasteful or possibly repugnant; (3) the tendency to be self-assertive and anxious in matters of secondary importance or in circumstances which try one's patience.

This new law of liberty is an inner law working as the believer's spiritual life unfolds in response to the gentle, persuasive presence of the Holy Spirit. This inner law is to be understood as something neither imposed from without (heteronomy) nor originating from within the self (autonomy). Rather the rule of God's Spirit in a renewed self is the very "key" for which the "lock" was made—the original idea of the Creator for man (theonomy).

The fundamental fact, then, is that the new law of liberty frees man from both outward (worldly) and inward (selfish) compulsion and gives him freedom to develop according to the idea for which he was originally created. The keynote of this development is love, for love is the fulfillment of the law (Rom. 13:8).

See LOVE, FREEDOM, LAW AND GRACE, ANTINOMIANISM.

For Further Reading: Wiley, *CT*, 3:25 ff; Hordern, *A Layman's Guide to Protestant Theology*, 173 ff; Upham, *Principles of the Interior Life.*

ALVIN HAROLD KAUFFMAN

LAY BAPTISM. The Church has been divided over the question of the validity of baptism administered by unordained persons. No clear restrictions are imposed in the NT. Jesus left the rite of baptizing to His disciples, and this before there was any consciousness on their part of special authority. Later, the deacon Philip baptized the Samaritan believers and the Ethiopian official. On the Day of Pentecost the 3,000 converts could have been baptized by many others among the total 120 as well as the Twelve (counting Matthias)—though it can safely be assumed that the baptizing was under the direction of the apostles. In Corinth most of the baptizing was done by Paul's associates (1 Cor. 1:14-17). This slender amount of data would suggest an absence of a view of baptizing which saw it as the sacrosanct preserve of a special ministerial order. Yet, while baptism is not absolutely essential to salvation, its sanctity is such that a denomination which chose to guard the sacrament by definite restrictions and prescribed procedures, in the interests of faith and order, would be in harmony with the apostolic tone of the NT—provided it did not impose ritualistic details as conditions of salvation.

See BAPTISM, BAPTISMAL REGENERATION, SACRAMENTARIANISM.

For Further Reading: *Baker's DT*; Berkhof, *Systematic Theology*, 631.

RICHARD S. TAYLOR

LAYING ON OF HANDS. The practice of laying on of hands, or the imposition of hands, arose about 4,000 years ago, at least, as it was practiced first in families and later in religious bodies. It has had numerous meanings in the course of history, and it remains an important rite in Christianity with distinct purposes.

Jacob placed his hands upon the heads of Joseph's sons so as to convey his blessing to them (Genesis 48). Moses laid his hands on Joshua to commission him to carry on his work and to invest him with some of his God-given authority (Num. 27:18-23). Aaron and his sons laid their hands upon a sacrifice to suggest the peoples' identification with a sacrifice (Exod. 29:10).

The NT suggests further meanings of this practice. Christ used this rite in the performance of some of His miracles (Mark 5:23; 6:5; 7:32). His disciples did likewise after His ascension (Acts 6:6; 9:12, 17; 28:8). Our Lord also used it to convey His blessing on children (Mark 10:13, 16). The Early Church also employed the rite for the reception of the Holy Spirit by those who believed (Acts 8:14 ff; 19:1 ff). It was used, too, for the conferring of an office or assignment in the Church as the apostles laid their hands on the heads of the first deacons (6:6). Prophets and teachers laid their hands on Barnabas and Saul and sent them out to evangelize (13:3). Paul told Timothy that he had received a *charisma* (gift) from God at the time the hands of elders were laid on him (1 Tim. 4:14; 2 Tim. 1:6). The great apostle said the rite should not be used casually, as he told Timothy not to be hasty in the matter of the laying on of hands (1 Tim. 5:22).

The rite is used in contemporary Protestantism primarily in the ordination of ministers, baptism, and praying for the sick.

See ORDAIN (ORDINATION).

For Further Reading: "Laying on of Hands," *New Schaff-Herzog Encyclopedia of Religious Knowledge.*

W. CURRY MAVIS

LEAVEN. Any agent of fermentation added to liquids or dough, leaven receives a religious significance in the OT from the Hebrew Feast of Unleavened Bread. This festival is observed during the seven days following Passover, when only unleavened bread is eaten (Exod. 12:14-20). It was intended as a commemoration of the Israelites' hurried flight from Egypt (vv. 34, 39). Additionally, only the peace offering (Lev. 7:13) and the wave loaves for the Feast of Weeks were to be made of leavened bread (23:17; cf. Exod. 23:18; 34:25; Lev. 2:11).

The NT emphasizes the symbolism of leaven. Jesus uses the imagery of leaven as a positive symbol for the kingdom of God (Matt. 13:33). Negatively, Jesus uses leaven as a symbol of the teaching and the hypocrisy of the Pharisees and others (Matt. 16:6-12; cf. Mark 8:15; Luke 12:1). Paul also speaks of leaven figuratively to describe evil or wickedness (1 Cor. 5:6-8; Gal. 5:9).

HAL A. CAUTHRON

LEGAL SIN, ETHICAL SIN. The first of these terms refers to the broad definition of sin as held by Calvinists, as consisting of any thought, deed, or omission which, whether or not one knows that it falls short, occasions his becoming legally blameworthy—simply because, in any way whatever, it falls short of an absolute standard. In other words, sin is defined solely in relation to law, without taking into account important human factors, such as intelligence and intention.

This way of viewing an act of sin is in contrast to the more precise ethical view as espoused within Wesleyanism. Here, sin as an act, in the sense of sin "properly so called" (Wesley), is an act, thought, or deed in which a person wilfully disobeys a known expectation of God.

Scripture seems, in a few instances, to refer to acts as sins which were not wilfully disobedient. Thus Leviticus 4—5 refers to "sins of ignorance," for which, after a person realized he had committed them, sin offering was to be made for their cleansing. In the NT, the weight is on ethical sin, which is blameworthy in a truly moral sense (cf. John 8:11, 34; 9:41; Rom. 6:1-23; 8:1-4; 14:23; Jas. 4:17; 1 John 3:3-10; 5:18).

While it is very necessary to remember that an absolute law exists, to label every unknown or unintentional infraction as sin, without making any distinction between such infractions and wilful deviations, is to violate the essential sin idea, which is a moral offense against God, an offense which must be condemned because it is culpable. *Morality* loses its proper moral dimension, as do *sin* and *holiness,* if the factors of personal responsibility are eliminated.

This is the reason John Wesley, though he freely conceded that the holiest person was ever in need of the Atonement, refused to call unintentional or unknown errors sins. Mistake, he says, "is not sin, if love is the sole principle of action" (*Plain Account,* 53). They are not "in the Scripture sense, sin" (54). Again, "Such transgressions you may call sins, if you please: I do not." He explained further the danger of failing to discriminate in this, and warned: "Let those who do call them so, beware how they confound these defects with sin, properly so called" (ibid.).

While it is necessary to distinguish between wilful sins and nonwilful sins or mistakes, it should be kept in mind that the nonwilful blunders are often serious in their consequences. Therefore an attitude of humility and dependence on the atoning Blood is always proper, as well as continuous effort to develop ethical awareness and sensitivity.

See SIN, SIMPLICITY OF MORAL ACTION, MORALITY.

For Further Reading: Purkiser, *Conflicting Concepts of Holiness,* 45-62: Taylor, *A Right Conception of Sin; GMS,* 120-26, 268-77.

J. KENNETH GRIDER

LEGALISM. Whereas *legality* is the state or practice of being legal (conforming to law), *legalism* is (1) a dependence on law keeping as the means of salvation, and/or (2) an excessive bondage to the letter of the law which misses its intent and which fails to be motivated by love.

In the Judaism of the postexilic period there was a fanatical observance of both the written law and an added collection of oral traditions. The result was a rigid and external legalism of slavish obedience to commandments, statutes, regulations, rites, and sacrifices.

In the beginning days of the Christian Church, when believers were both Jews and Christians, many continued their former legalism. As the gospel spread to the Gentile world, advocates of legalism, called Judaizers, sought to impose their convictions on the non-Jewish pagan converts. This set the stage for the first doctrinal conflict in the fledgling Church. Although it was *officially* settled at the first Christian council at Jerusalem —with the rejection of legalism—the struggle was continued throughout much of the first century.

With the exception of Jesus, the prime opponent of legalism was the apostle Paul, who had been dramatically delivered from its bondage (cf. Gal. 1:13 ff; Rom. 7:7 ff). He recognized that the observance of the Jewish law—as essential to salvation—was a form of works righteousness that repudiated justification by grace through faith. In his Galatian letter Paul warned that surrender to Jewish legalism was tantamount to the rejection of Christ and His saving cross (Gal. 2:21) and resulted in galling bondage and slavery (4:9; 5:1). Even more significantly, a dependence on the law would make impossible the new life of the Spirit.

The threat of legalism has plagued the Church from the first century to the present. Today the appeal is not to adopt the Jewish law, but to drift into moralism, a "Christian" version of legalism. Law is viewed as the only alternative to a freedom that becomes license. Religion thus becomes *primarily* a matter of following a set of rules and regulations. The believer is entangled in the web of *works* righteousness that very easily becomes a *self-* righteousness. In turn, such self-righteousness often causes one to live by a "legalistic letter" that results in a cutting, critical, and condemning spirit toward other people. This expression of legalism is a tragic contradiction of the love that is the heart of the Christian faith.

The corrective for legalism is not license (Gal. 5:13 ff) but that Spirit-generated love which fulfills the spirit and intent of the law from the heart, in true freedom.

See LAW, LAW AND GRACE, ANTINOMIANISM, LOVE, JUDAISM.

For Further Reading: Fairbairn, *The Revelation of Law in Scripture;* Howard, *Newness of Life;* Barclay, *The Mind of St. Paul.*

RICHARD E. HOWARD

LEISURE. Leisure is free time, time which is not necessary for *existence* (to survive biologically), nor for *subsistence* (to survive economically). Technological advances and labor-saving devices have provided man with more leisure than ever before. The way he uses his leisure is an index of his intelligence, culture, character, and religion. There are four major options in a worthwhile use of leisure time; recreation, improvement, worship, and service.

Recreation. "Your body is a temple of the Holy Spirit," writes Paul. "Honor God with your body" (1 Cor. 6:19-20, NIV). As His stewards, we are charged to take care of His property. Recreation is part of this care. "The tension of both mind and body resulting from the pace and complexity of modern industrial life emphasizes the necessity of periods of rest and relaxation as essential factors in the preservation of the body" (Culbertson, *Introduction to Christian Theology,* 352).

Improvement. The determination of the committed Christian is to be "my utmost for His Highest," says Oswald Chambers. This drive for excellence affects every area of life. Leisure provides time for culture, "the development of the person intellectually, aesthetically, and socially, to the full use of his powers, in compatibility with the recognized standards of excellence of his society" (Taylor, *A Return to Christian Culture,* 16).

Worship and Service. Worship is both adoration and communion with the Lord, and an offering of oneself in service to Him. In private devotions, the child of God is renewed spiritually. In the fellowship of the church, he draws strength from the means of grace and finds avenues of service. He uses his leisure to worship and serve.

Leisure is free time only in the sense that one may choose how it is spent. Man can fritter it away or grasp the opportunities it offers "for learning and freedom, for growth and expression, for rest and restoration, for rediscovering life in its entirety" (Lee, *Religion and Leisure in America,* 35). The Christian is called to faithfulness in his stewardship of this valuable resource (1 Cor. 4:2; Eph. 5:15-16).

See TIME, DISCIPLINE, GROW (GROWTH), STEWARDSHIP.

For Further Reading: Thomas, *Christian Ethics and Moral Philosophy,* 210-16; Taylor, *A Return to Christian Culture,* 15-28, 42-51; Wiley, *CT,* 3:47-64; Lee, *Religion and Leisure in America.* MAUREEN H. BOX

LENT. In the Christian year, Lent is the 40-day period beginning with Ash Wednesday devoted to preparation for the celebration of redemption on Easter Sunday.

That Lent should consist of 40 days seems to have been established by the end of the fourth century and may reflect the time Moses spent on Sinai or the period of Jesus' fasting in the wilderness of temptation. The 40 days might also simply reflect the normal period of preparation for the catechumens who would be baptized at Easter.

Although fasting was practiced in connection with the preparation for Easter, in the Early Church it amounted to only two or three days. From the fourth century to the ninth, fasting was emphasized and its observance rigidly enforced. From the ninth century to the present, Lenten fasting has been deemphasized by the Roman Catholic church so that since 1966 the obligation to fast is restricted to Ash Wednesday and Good Friday.

Fasting has given place to emphasis upon an abstemious life-style through Lent. Celebration is reserved for Easter and is displaced during Lent by abstaining from festivities, by omitting the Alleluia from the Mass, and by devoting more than usual time to religious exercises.

Lenten fasting is encouraged in the Book of Common Prayer. Lent comprises part of the Lutheran year and is observed variously in other Protestant denominations.

The word *lent* is derived from an Anglo-Saxon word for spring *(lencten)* which might have referred to the "lengthen"-ing of the days.

See FASTING, CHRISTIAN YEAR.

For Further Reading: *Baker's Dictionary of Practical Theology,* 364-413. DANIEL N. BERG

LIABILITY TO SIN. The Bible is clear that man's present existence is one of probation, and that he remains liable to sin. "My little children, these things write I unto you, that ye sin not. And if any man sin, we have an advocate with the Father, Jesus Christ the righteous" (1 John 2:1).

People are not liable to sin because they are sinners, but because they are human. Susceptibility to sin is a part of the human predicament; it belongs to the endowment of freedom. It is true that no human is born without the "infection" of sin, but neither is this the basis of one's liability to sin. If it were, then Adam and Eve could not have sinned because they were created pure and perfect, with no natural inclination to sin.

The crux for Wesleyans is whether an entirely sanctified believer is placed beyond the power of sinning. Wesleyans do hold that entire sanctification cleanses the believer's heart from the corruption of inbred sin, whereby he is freed from the bent to sin. However, they do not hold that he is thereby freed from the liability to sin. This susceptibility remains because it is essential to the functioning of free agents in a state of probation. In addition, an entirely sanctified believer must reckon with infirmities of body, mind, and spirit, which increases his liability to falling into sin.

A distinction must be made between sin springing from deliberate purpose, and sin resulting from momentary weakness and unwatchfulness. "In an unguarded moment," Thomas Cook says, "the best Christians may be surprised into some single act of sin; but for this there is merciful provision in our High Priest above" (*New Testament Holiness,* 19).

But liability to sin must never be interpreted as necessity, certainly not as normalcy. "Permanent sonship and continual sinning are contradictions which cannot be combined in the same character. A person can no more remain born of God and continue in sin that he can remain honest and steal, or truthful and tell lies" (Cook, 18).

Wesleyans rejoice that though the liability to sin remains, the Christian need not sin. In the words of Cook: "While *inability* to sin does not belong to Christian experience, *to be able not to sin does*" (16).

Yet if one *is* overtaken in a fault or transgression, one has the sufficient mercy of God for forgiveness and cleansing (1 John 1:9). He also has the resource of a caring body of spiritual persons who, according to Gal. 6:1, have the challenge to exercise the ministry of prayerful restoration.

See SIN, MISTAKES, INFIRMITIES, SINLESS PERFECTION.

For Further Reading: Cook, *New Testament Holiness;* Geiger, ed., *Further Insights into Holiness,* 193 ff; Cox, *John Wesley's Concept of Perfection.*

NEIL E. HIGHTOWER

LIBERALISM. In theology, this is a synonym of modernism. In contrast to conservative, classical Christian teachings, its persuasions are more rational and humanistic than biblical. Emphasizing the function of human reason as what determines the validity of a doctrine, it denies many time-honored Christian teachings that are biblical, but that (in its view) are not scientifically supportable.

Liberalism denies the virgin conception of Christ, His substitutionary atonement, His bodily resurrection, and His second coming. This, in favor of a Jesus who is only human, and not divine. It therefore denies the doctrine of the Trinity. It tends to favor religious education instead of evangelism; spiritual growth instead of conversion. In the doctrine of God, it tends to emphasize His love instead of His holiness; His infinite kindness instead of His judgment.

On Scripture, liberalism tends to view it as not qualitatively different from other early writings, and not as the sole basis for a belief. Instead of emphasizing God's revelation in Scripture and in the Christ of Scripture, it emphasizes God's revelation in nature. It tends to teach that everyone will be saved, instead of the view that the finally impenitent will suffer in eternal hell.

See ORTHODOXY, EVANGELICAL, FUNDAMENTALISM.

For Further Reading: Fletcher, *The Moderns;* Marty and Peerman, eds., *New Theology No. 2; New Theology No. 3.*

J. KENNETH GRIDER

LIBERATION THEOLOGY. The theologies of liberation seek to provide deliverance for oppressed and marginated peoples by changing the structures which deny them the privilege of determining their own destinies. This theological category developed in Latin America in the 1960s and was nourished by the new concern for the problems of underdevelopment that arose out of the Latin American Episcopal Conference held in Medellin, Colombia, in 1968, although Protestant roots may be found in Christian student movements of the post-World War II era and even more remote influences in the French Revolution.

Liberation theology is neither new nor limited to the Latin American context, and it has become a worldwide theme which includes women's liberation and black theologies. It has taken on a reactionary character against traditional theology, and strains of Bonhoeffer, Barth, Moltmann, Pannenberg, and other contemporary European and American theologians are easily recognizable. The Latin American proponents readily admit Marxist influence.

Theology must be done (according to this movement) in the present historical situation, and its initial task is to "awaken the critical consciousness which produces an experience of social discontent." This task is "conscientization," the educational method needed to alert the oppressed to their condition and motivate them to hope for and work toward bringing about a change. Liberation intends to free theology from cultural and philosophical narrowness, often defined as capitalism, individualism, democracy, secularism, and pragmatism.

According to liberation theology, the present historical context can only be understood by utilizing the social sciences, and the most adequate method is the Marxist analysis, which explains the causes of inequality and oppression as well as the necessary steps to correct them.

Theology is not an academic discipline, but rather "praxis," the action which "results from deep motivation," has the goal of bringing about changes, and can be defined as the entire mission of the church. The proper location of theology is "orthopraxis," usually a synonym for "the poor," a designation which may refer to the "weak, destitute, and oppressed," a subhuman condition created by greed and injustice. Simultaneously "the poor" is an attitude of "openness to God, willingness to be used by God, and humility before God." The ambivalent use of terminology may be further illustrated by a definition of salvation which is strangely similar to the last identification of "the poor." "Man is saved if he opens himself to God and to others . . . and this is true for Christians and non-Christians alike" (Gutierrez).

Liberation theology is doctrinally vague. The point of departure is the human condition and not divine revelation. Sin is primarily social and includes all that interferes with liberation. Salvation applies to the whole man and is a kind of universalism. The transcendent God is absent, and the church is not really very important except as a sacrament which symbolizes the reality of the new society.

Liberation theology has developed in nominally Christian situations where true evangelism has never obtained, and where colonization, neocolonialism, and development theologies have been identified with Christendom. Persons who have been educated by Christian institutions and compose the new middle class have often rejected the poor from whose midst they have so recently risen.

At least five factors of the post-1929 period which gave rise to the development of liberation theology are industrialization, the popular social movements, the development of a military class in Latin America, the conservatism and traditionalism of the church, and a theological dualism.

Liberation theology has made some valid contributions to Christian thought. It has served the Church in putting a new and needed emphasis on appropriate Christian social action and recalls to memory the social concerns of John Wesley in 18th-century England and of the early American holiness movement. Salvation can no longer be assumed to be purely individualistic.

Liberation theology is a reminder that Christianity meets the needs of the whole man. The Church is challenged to reevaluate its theology to be assured that it is not abstract, but rooted in concrete human experience. One of the greatest values is the initiation of serious rereading and reflection on the Scriptures as a reaction to liberation theology.

But there are serious deficiencies in liberation theology. The social, political, and economic contexts have been so emphasized that the even deeper problem of personal sin is quickly passed over, if not ignored. If evangelical theology has been remiss in its neglect of earthly matters, then the liberationists have moved to the opposite extreme.

There is a general lack of biblical exegesis. The most serious deficiency is the tendency toward humanism. Man is an unexplained paradox. He is enslaved and exploited, but not to the extent that he cannot free himself from bondage and create a new world with his own hands. While he is dependent and controlled, he is nevertheless able to take control of his problems. The model for the new humanity is Jesus Christ, but little is said about the power of God in Christ to deliver man from his bondage.

See CHRISTIANITY, CHRISTIAN SOCIALISM, HUMANISM, CHRISTIAN HUMANISM, CHRISTIAN ETHICS, SALVATION, WESLEYANISM, MARXISM, WOMEN'S LIBERATION.

For Further Reading: Kuhn, "Liberation Theology; A Semantic Approach," *WTJ*, 15:1 (Spring, 1980), 40; Torres and Fabella, eds., *The Emergent Gospel;* Gutierrez, *A Theology of Liberation;* Anderson and Stransky, eds., *Mission Trends No. 4: Liberation Theologies in North America and Europe;* Miguez-Benino, *Doing Theology in a Revolutionary Situation;* Kantzer and Gundry, eds., *Perspectives on Evangelical Theology,* 117-50.

MARY LOU RIGGLE

LIBERTY. See FREEDOM.

LICENSE. As here understood, license is not a formal permission to do something that is authorized by law, such as a license to marry, to hunt, to practice medicine, etc. Nor does it mean a departure from man-made rules and conventions of a particular society. Rather, it is an "excessive, undisciplined freedom, constituting an abuse of liberty" (*Webster's New World Dictionary,* 1970). It is an assumed right to deviation from basic biblical morality and proprieties.

The word in NT Greek which most closely corresponds to the foregoing definition is *aselgeia*, most often translated "lasciviousness" in the KJV and ASV, as "licentiousness" in the RSV, and as "lewdness" or "debauchery" in the NIV. Other versions characterize such behavior as "indecency, " "sensuality," and "lustfulness." (*Aselgeia* appears in Mark 7:22; Rom. 13:13; 2 Cor. 12:21; Gal. 5:19; Eph. 4:19; 1 Pet. 4:3; 2 Pet. 2:2, 7, 15; and Jude 4. The NIV translates the term as "a license for immorality" in Jude 4.)

Both Jesus and Paul pointed to unregenerate human nature as the basic source of society's licentiousness (Mark 7:20-23; Gal. 5:19-21). And Peter and Jude stressed the shameless conduct of those who wilfully gave themselves over to filthy living (1 Pet. 4:3; 2 Pet. 2:7, 18; Jude 4).

True Christianhood eliminates "debauchery and licentiousness" (Rom. 13:13; 2 Cor. 12:21), and is characterized by loving obedience to God's holy commandments (1 John 1:5-7; 2:3-5; 5:3).

From the early Gnostics to the 20th-century "situationists" the Church has had to resist those movements which have been antinomian in spirit and practice. License is a revolt against both unbiblical legalisms and the disciplined liberties of biblical Christianity.

See FREEDOM, ANTINOMIANISM, LAW AND GRACE, RIGHT (RIGHTEOUSNESS), ETHICAL RELATIVISM, VICE.

For Further Reading: DeWolf, *Responsible Freedom*.

DELBERT R. ROSE

LIE, LIARS. To lie is to practice deceit, falsehood, and treachery. The various biblical words which are used to identify lying signify behaviors or persons which appear to be something that in reality they are not. This is clearly illustrated by such terms as "false brother," "false prophet," "false apostle," "false witness," etc. In the Greek NT these are compound terms, and the first element in each of them is the same root word as the word for lying *(pseudos)*.

The profound seriousness with which the Bible treats falsehood is epitomized in the ninth injunction of the Decalogue: "You shall not bear false witness against your neighbor" (Exod. 20:16, RSV). In biblical terminology, to lie is not merely to practice intellectual dishonesty. It is rather to engage in the distortion of one's own true self, of one's relations with one's fellows, and of one's standing with God. This is expressed by John: "He who says 'I know him' but disobeys his commandments is a liar , and the truth is not in him" (1 John 2:4, RSV); again, "If any one says, 'I love God,' and hates his brother, he is a liar; for he who does not love his brother whom he has seen, cannot love God whom he has not seen" (4:20, RSV). To be a liar is to build for oneself a world which has no basis in reality. The only destiny that is possible for such a world is for it to collapse into the empty void that it in fact is (Rev. 21:8, 27; 22:15).

The inherent evil of lying is clear enough, as is God's condemnation of it. However, in the sphere of moral philosophy there are difficult problems to resolve. Is it lying (in God's sight) to withhold information from those who are not entitled to it? to mislead an enemy in order to save a life? Some would say that any attempt to mislead or deceive is a sin, but that the higher priority of life in the hierarchy of values may justify such a sin. Others would say that sin can never be justified, and that any verbal falsehood demanded by the claims of life cannot properly be called a sin, because its origin is love, not a deceitful heart. In the one case lying is equated with verbal inaccuracy; in the second viewpoint lying involves evil intent, generally for selfish advantage.

See TRUTH, VALUES, INTEGRITY.

For Further Reading: "Lie, Hypocrite," *NIDNTT*, 2:467-74.

HAL A. CAUTHRON

LIFE. The various nuances of the English word "life" allow it to translate a number of words in the original languages of the Bible (e.g., Heb.: *hayyim, ruach, nephesh, basar,* and *yamim;* Gr.: *zōē, bios,* and *psychē).* To generalize, life conveys the positively evaluated idea of animate existence as opposed to the negatively evaluated inert state or death. Animal life refers to moving creatures (cf. Gen. 7:21-23; Acts 17:28); living water is running as opposed to stagnant (cf. Gen. 26:19; John 4:10, 14; 7:38). Despite the obvious differences in emphasis and detail between the two Testaments and among the various biblical witnesses, the Bible presents a holistic view of life which differs markedly from all nonbiblical views.

Old Testament. As applied to man, life refers to the spontaneous activities, experiences, and concrete existence of an individual, not an energizing force within him/her. Life is more than just functioning, existing, or enduring in time; it is well-being. Individual existence is not self-contained but implies coexistence, cooperation, and community. Only apparently spontaneous, life has its origin and sustenance in Yahweh, the Creator (cf. Isa. 40:28-31), the "living God" (frequently in both OT and NT, e.g., Deut. 5:26; Matt. 26:63; cf. Rom. 4:17). Self-actuated and sustaining life (immortality) belongs to Him alone (Exod. 3:13-15; Ps. 90:1-6; cf. 1 Tim. 6:16; John 8:58). He alone is real; the so-called gods are "dead," impotent because nonexistent (e.g., Isa. 44:9-20).

The gift of life imparts to God's creature "man" the possibility of a relationship with the Creator (cf. Gen. 1:26-27; 2:7) and of reproducing human life (cf. 1:28; 9:1). Life is experienced in its fullness only within the worshipping community (Psalm 27) since authentic life is found only in turning to God (e.g., Ps. 63:3; Ezek. 18:32; 33:11; Amos 5:4; Hab. 2:4). It is not intended merely to be enjoyed, but to be actively chosen and pursued (cf. Deut. 30:14, where life refers to successful conquest and possession of the Promised Land) and lived in dependence upon God its Source (8:3). Since life is a divine gift, it has a supreme value, and man is responsible to its Giver for the conduct and disposal of life (cf. Gen. 9:4-7).

There was little thought of life after death during most of the OT period; "immortality" was possible only through the continuation of the nation and/or family. Thus a long and prosperous life blessed with many children was conceived as an obvious evidence of divine favor (cf. e.g., Exod. 20:12; Deut. 5:16; Prov. 3:16; 10:22; Psalms 37:27-29; 127; cf. Jas. 4:13-16). It was only during the Persian and Greco-Roman periods of Israel's history that resurrection faith began to blossom. That there are intimations of a future resurrection in the OT is affirmed by Jesus (Matt. 22:29-32).

New Testament. Hope turned to reality through the death and resurrection of Jesus Christ, "who abolished death and brought life and immortality to light through the gospel" (2 Tim. 1:10, RSV). Throughout the NT it assumes the OT teaching regarding life; its innovation is primarily in clarifying the role of Christ as the Bringer of the new or true life (cf. John 5:26; 11:25; 14:6; 17:3; 1 John 5:20), which is one of several NT modes of referring to salvation. The unregenerate man is dead in sin although physically alive (cf. Luke 15:21-24; Matt. 8:22; Romans 5 and 6; Rev. 3:1); whereas the believer, freed from the oppressive powers of sin, death, and fear, enjoys a new quality of life (cf. Rom. 6:4, 20-23; 8:1-10; John 5:24; 10:10; 1 John 3:14; 4:18; Heb. 2:14-15). Like so-called natural life, this new life is God's gracious gift, but only through the new creation made possible by the reconciling death of Christ (cf. e.g., 2 Cor. 5:14—6:2 and John 6:40, 47).

Salvation life, received by faith (cf. Rom. 1:16-17; 5:6-21; 6:4, 13; 8:6, 10-11), is to be lived *for* the Lord and others (cf. 14:7-9). The life of the Christian is not his/her own, but the life of Christ (cf. 2 Cor. 4:10; Gal. 2:20-21). It is not to be simply preserved but shared in self-giving love (Matt. 10:39; Mark 8:34-35; Rom. 12:1-2; 1 John 4:14-18). Such is not necessarily expressed in the giving of life in martyrdom (1 Cor. 13:3; Phil. 2:17) but in giving of that which constitutes life: time, energy, resources, health, etc. (cf. 1 Thess. 2:7-12; 2 Cor. 2:14-17; 4:7-18; 12:15; Col. 1:24-25).

The new life is lived in an old and dying body (Gal. 2:20-21; Phil. 1:21; 2 Cor. 4:7—5:10) which must be yielded to God for sanctification to "bear fruit" for God in the present, and in the future "reap" eternal life, also God's free gift (Rom. 5:12-21; 6:5-23; 1 Cor. 15:12-58; Phil. 3:7-21). Eternal life is primarily life of the heavenly order, not merely of endless duration. The Christian's resurrection is not a compensation for the miseries of life, but a resumption or continuation of the true eternal life begun already on earth. The Christian lives in the tension of the "already-not yet" characteristic of NT eschatological salvation (cf. Col. 3:1-4), which is both a present reality and a future hope.

See ETERNAL LIFE, SPIRITUALITY, REGENERATION, INTERMEDIATE STATE.

For Further Reading: "Soul," *NIDNTT,* 3:676-89; Kittel, 2:832-75; Howard, *Newness of Life;* "Life," *NIDNTT,* 2:474-84; "Life," *IDB,* 3:124-30; *GMS,* 446-47.

GEORGE LYONS

LIFE-STYLE. The term *life-style* has an innocent sound, as if it meant only our individualistic way of doing things. But suddenly we become aware that the world wants to legitimize such deviant behavior as choosing to live on welfare, or to live together without marriage, or to live with the same sex, by the use of this disarming term. All forms of discernment are loudly shouted down as judgmentalism. Contemporary society is being conditioned to be emotionally neutralized by the innocuous, uncondemning term *life-style.* But evangelicals cannot accept this. They must be prepared to oppose certain life-styles and espouse others; to refuse to endorse an open society; to unhesitatingly evaluate and pass judgment on life-styles, in the light of what it means biblically to be a Christian.

One's life-style cannot be equated with one's Christian experience. Experience is a relationship of heart with God; life-style may point to this relationship, or it may (conceivably) obscure it.

Even heart holiness is not an automatic guarantee of a thoroughly consonant life-style. The saying "Get the heart right and the outward will take care of itself" is only a half-truth.

The translation of sanctifying grace into an appropriate life-style depends, most fundamentally, on the illumination of the Holy Spirit. But the Holy Spirit can be aided or hindered in His tutoring by several secondary factors. Basic intelligence is one. Spiritual depth, governing spiritual sensitivity, is another. Spiritual maturity also is a factor; how far is this Christian up the road? Also, revival will provide an accelerating impulse.

Environment plays a powerful part, since most converts tend to take on the life-style of the religious community to which they belong. Churches (and schools) are pedagogical agents, by example, atmosphere, preaching, instruction, and rules and regulations.

These many strands of influence bear profoundly on the kind of life-style a convert will adopt, how rapidly he or she will adopt it, and how thoroughly. Obviously, therefore, while the Holy Spirit, illuminating the Bible, is primary, the community also has a responsibility of a teaching nature, which it dare not refuse to exercise.

The problem of determining what is a proper holiness life-style is essentially a hermeneutical one. It is necessary, for one thing, to identify the unmistakable biblical standards. But beyond this, it is important to be discerning in applying biblical principles to 20th-century social issues about which the Bible has no explicit word. Tobacco would be a case in point. But the most difficult hermeneutical task is handling wisely the biblical tension between affirmation and denial. The note of affirmation rests on the Creation motif, while the note of denial rests on the Fall. On the one hand this world is a delightful place, and life is rich with pleasures and options—all of which are gifts from the God who pronounced His creation good (Gen. 1:31), and according to the apostle Paul, are to be received with thanksgiving (1 Tim. 4:3-5; 6:17; cf. Jas. 1:17).

Yet struggling with this celebration of life there is in the Bible a somber note of abstention and repudiation. This is seen in the motifs of separation, other-worldliness, and pilgrim mentality, which are unquestionably very pervasive. "Worldliness" is a phenomenon recognized consistently in the Bible and consistently forbidden to God's people. This mood of denial, of disapproval and prohibition, stems from the fact that sin has polluted God's creation. Every good gift has become contaminated and distorted. Many things innocent in themselves have at different times and to different degrees been pronounced off limits because of the world's virtual monopoly.

The history of the Christian Church has been a history of seesawing between these two poles. Space does not permit a tracing of this struggle. But the struggle is still with us, between the humanism spawned by the Renaissance and the puritanism of the Reformation (at least in some of its branches). Richard Niebuhr has delineated very ably the conflict, and its attempted resolutions, in his book *Christ and Culture*.

Much of the time the Church and the world have coexisted quite amicably. The latent hostility of the world has not been aroused because its evils have not been challenged. The Church has adopted the prevailing culture to the extent that the Church and the world have seemed more like brothers than aliens. But something happens when revival sweeps through the Church. Suddenly once again the lines become sharply drawn, and practices which have infiltrated the Church are now rejected, much to the discomfiture and disgust of the unconverted.

Revival always reminds the Church that it must not attempt to remove the tension between affirmation and denial, for the same apostle who says, "All things are yours" (1 Cor. 3:21), and reminds us to enjoy God's gifts with thanksgiving, also affirms the incompatibility of the Church and the world, reiterates the biblical injunction to come out from among them, and exhorts us to cleanse ourselves from all contamination of flesh and spirit, "perfecting holiness in the fear of God" (2 Cor. 7:1).

But while we cannot remove the tension—and dare not blunt the demand for separation—we can transcend the tension at the Cross. For Christ redeemed the natural order as well as the souls of men, and released a grace by which we may live normal lives while yet on earth—lives which are normal because holy. The gifts which have been twisted by sin, such as ownership, beauty, invention, and conjugal love, can be given back to us purified and ennobled—because *we* have been purified.

But this transcending of the tension through redemption presupposes the ongoing control of life by the Cross. This is to say, redemption miscarries without the maintenance of sanctified priorities. The gifts of life are not to be given dominance; that would be a reversion to idolatry, the love of the creature. In practical terms, this means that a holiness life-style will not go overboard in its affirmation of life. Hobbies, recreation, possessions, food, sex (within marriage), sports (within limits), art, music, vacations, education, all may be rejoiced in as good gifts; but all will be disciplined, all will be kept on the altar, none will be allowed to dominate; and all, moreover, will be expendable if more important claims demand.

Holiness by its very nature is the secret of living fully and joyfully, yet equally by its very nature will tend to draw the lines conservatively. In this respect Wesleyans share an affinity with Puritans and Pietists, or any groups which have been born in revival. Several impulses in heart holiness assure such a conservative tendency. One is the capacity for more penetrating ethical perception of potential peril. Another is a supreme devotion to God and His glory, which means a dread of even the appearance of evil which might dishonor Him. Another is a passion for souls which creates a keen awareness of the importance of example and its influence. Another trait endemic to holiness is goodwill—a spirit of cooperation, which is to say, a willingness to conform to the commitments of the group. A final quality is an emancipation from a carnal bondage to human opinion—or the "in" thing.

Paul prayed that the Philippians would have a love that abounded more and more in knowledge and judgment, in order to discern things "that are excellent," or literally, things that *make a difference* (Phil. 1:9-10). Some things make a big difference. Others make a little difference, but not enough to divide over. Still others make no difference at all. The strength of the holiness movement will depend not only on pure motives but enough sound judgment to know which is which. It takes sense as well as piety to know where to draw the line between affirmation and denial. Yet it must be reiterated that spiritual depth will be conducive to greater caution than nominalism, and holiness people will always tend to see evil where carnal Christians see no evil at all.

See HOLINESS, ETHICS, ETHICAL RELATIVISM, HUMANISM, CHRISTIAN HUMANISM, WORLD (WORLDLINESS), IMITATION OF CHRIST, SPIRITUAL WARFARE, SINNING RELIGION.

For Further Reading: Shoemaker, *Extraordinary Living for Ordinary Men;* Lindsell, *The World, the Flesh, and the Devil;* Taylor, *Return to Christian Culture; The Disciplined Life;* Niebuhr, *Christ and Culture.*

RICHARD S. TAYLOR

LIGHT. This is a basic descriptive image of God as revealed in Christ. The scriptural word means brightness either as substance, reflection, or as revelation. God is light (1 John 1:5) who came among us as Jesus Christ (John 1:9); and in Him all men may see light (Ps. 36:9). Christ, as Deity in the flesh, is the embodiment of light.

Creation took place as light was introduced into the world (Gen. 1:3). Being is light. Nonbeing is darkness. The initial dispelling of darkness was prophetic of the continuing drama which looks to the ultimate triumph and destruction of darkness by Christ the Light. The word imagery of light illuminates the old covenant, e.g., the Exodus light (Exod. 13:21), the Tabernacle light (1 Sam. 3:3), the central place of lampstands in Temple worship (2 Chron. 4:7), and the promise of God to illuminate His people (Isa. 60:19-20). Prophetically the Psalmist sought the light of God's face, and Zechariah looked to the day when God's abiding Spirit would dwell as illumination in the cleansed hearts of the redeemed (Zech. 4:6 ff).

The light breaks through in clarity in the person of God the Son (Matt. 5:14-16; John 1:1-18; Heb. 2:6-7). Jesus is the incarnation of God in the present world, and He is announced as the Lamb who is the Light of the new heaven and earth (Rev. 21:22-26).

Light was a religious symbol in ancient nonbiblical traditions, e.g., Babylonian. Some pre-Socratic Greek philosophers expressed light as a presupposition of all understanding. The writings of the Christian saints commonly use the imagery of "radiance" and "light" in their efforts to express a manifestation of God.

Light is a fundamental concept theologically since it is descriptive of the nature of God and is definitive of the mission of Christ. It guides the soul responding to the prevenient and saving grace of God and is part of the new atmosphere in which the regenerate person lives (John 8:12). The soul of man was created to be an earthly lamp of God. It may be proper, therefore, to define light as the spiritual understanding which a person receives as he accepts the revelatory Word of God. His continued acceptance (walking in the light) is his salvation.

Since Christ alone is the Light of life, to be indwelt by Christ is to have light, and not to be indwelt by Christ is to live in darkness (John 1:12; 3:19-21). The unconverted sense spiritual light as blind men sense the light of the sun but do not see. In one respect the fire of hell is the residue of refused light.

The one who receives the gift of life in Christ (1 John 5:12) may live and walk in light (1:7) and be a "child" of light (Luke 16:8) and a bearer of light (Matt. 6:22). The redeemed person begins to take on more of a radiance of His light (Eph. 5:8) and to become light in the world (Phil. 2:15).

See DARKNESS, KNOWLEDGE, REVELATION (NATURAL, SPECIAL).

For Further Reading: Kittel, 9:310-58; Pelican, *The Light of the World;* Robertson, *Light in Darkness.*

GORDON WETMORE

LIKENESS. See DIVINE IMAGE.

LIMBO. In Roman Catholic theology *limbo* (from Latin *limbus,* meaning "border") is the middle ground between hell and heaven. To this place are consigned unbaptized infants and unbaptized but righteous heathen, who do not deserve hell but are not entitled to heaven. Such a doctrine is the logical product of an extreme sacramentarianism, which affirms the absolute necessity of baptism for salvation, combined with an attempt to preserve some semblance of justice in the divine order. Limbo is not marked by unhappiness or pain, but neither is it participation in the glories of redemption. Its nearest non-Christian conception might be the Nirvana of Buddhism. The NT teaches only two possible destinies, not three. There would be no need to invent a third place or destiny if baptism were not invested with such determinative power.

See INFANT SALVATION, SACRAMENTARIANISM.

RICHARD S. TAYLOR

LIMITED ATONEMENT. See ATONEMENT.

LITURGY, LITURGICS. *Liturgics* is the study of the origin, form, and use of liturgies. The term *liturgy* is derived from the Greek *leitourgia,* used in Hellenistic Greek to describe an act of public service, and used in the Septuagint to denote the services of priests and Levites in the Tabernacle and Temple (e.g., Num. 8:22, 25; 18:4; 2 Chron. 8:14). The NT uses the term of Temple services (Luke 1:23; Heb. 9:21), of Christian worship (Acts 13:2), and of works of love and devotion (2 Cor. 9:12; Phil. 2:30). In Patristic writings *liturgy* expresses the whole service of God and is used particularly of the activities of the pastoral office. Later still the meaning of the term became more confined, descriptive of the Eucharist, and most modern writers on liturgies, both Protestant and Roman Catholic, give major attention to the form and significance of the eucharistic rite.

First-century Jewish worship, both in Temple and synagogue (apart from the former's sacrificial ceremonies), consisted chiefly of Scripture reading, prayers, an optional exhortation, psalm singing (often recitation), the antiphonal declaration of the Shema (consisting of Deut. 6:4-9; 11:13-21; and Num. 15:37-41) and the benedictions. The Apostolic Church modelled its worship on the Jewish pattern, and it consisted of praise, prayer, Scripture reading, exposition, and the Lord's Supper (see 1 Tim. 3:16; 2:1-2; 4:13; Rom. 6:3; 1 Cor. 11:20 ff; etc.).

Subapostolic writings such as *First Clement* (A.D. 95), the *Letters of Ignatius* (A.D. 107), and the *Didache* (approx. A.D. 130) all contain liturgical forms and allusions. The *Didache* is basically a manual of liturgical directives. Justin Martyr, writing about A.D. 151, gives the fullest account of contemporary Christian worship: lections, sermon, common prayers, the kiss of peace, praise, prayer, and the Lord's Supper (see *Apology,* chaps. 65—67).

All branches of the Christian Church have had, and have, their own distinguishing liturgical forms, ranging from the ornate ceremonialism of Orthodox, Roman Catholic, and Episcopal churches to the more simple worship patterns of the small groups in evangelical Protestantism. Prominent among those congregations with least liturgical forms are the Quakers and the Salvation Army, neither of which celebrates baptism or the Lord's Supper. (An excellent summary of worship in the Early Church and through the centuries in Catholic, Reformed, and Episcopal churches is found in W. D. Maxwell's *An Outline of Christian Worship*.)

The many liturgical forms found in Christian worship are not only inevitable but desirable, ministering, as they do, to a wide diversity of human feeling, religious aspiration, and temperamental differences. All liturgical acts, whether in words only, or in words and actions (i.e., ceremonial proper), are intended to have a twofold function. Towards God the liturgical act is an expression of the attitude and aspirations of the worshipper; towards man it is an attempt to unite the congregation in and through that particular form of worship.

As far as an ideal liturgical form can be spoken of, it should combine *objectivity*—the contemplation, adoration, and praise of the Holy Trinity; and *subjectivity*—the experience of the grace, forgiveness, and blessing of God mediated by the Holy Spirit. A liturgical form that overstresses the institutional tends to suppress God-given individual expression, while worship that merely gives free rein to individualistic subjectivity tends to eccentricity and an exclusion of institutional devotion. While no one form of liturgical practice will satisfy all worshippers, each form must have both the corporate and the individualistic elements. Ideally, the Spirit should be able to work through the form, not have to go around it. Worship forms should conduct the Spirit's ministrations, not impede them. Yet there is always danger that the best of forms, because of habit and familiarity, can become a sedative instead of a stimulant. Whether a service is formal or informal, it cannot create a spirit of worship when such a spirit is absent from the heart of the worshipper.

See WORSHIP, PUBLIC PRAYER, FORMALISM, SACRAMENTARIANISM, MASS, CHURCH.

For Further Reading: Maxwell, *An Outline of Christian Worship*; Clark, *Liturgy and Worship*; Williamson, *Overseers of the Flock,* 99-112; Stowe, *The Ministry of Shepherding,* 40-56; Jones, *An Historical Approach to Evangelical Worship; Baker's Dictionary of Practical Theology,* 364-92. HERBERT MCGONIGLE

LOGOS. Accommodated from the Greek, *logos* is *word,* not as a grammatical form but as the content or thought conveyed—the living, spoken word (Cremer, 390). It is used both broadly and specifically of what God had to say to man. It is OT revelation, the gospel of Christ, Christ's own words, and the truth about Christ. And it is the Christ himself, the perfect Expression of God.

The NT emphasis on the spoken, written, and living Word is rooted in the OT. The Hebrew *davar,* "speak," refers to the substance of revelation and is translated by *logos* in the Septuagint. The Ten Commandments, then, are the Ten Words. And the "word of the Lord" is God's communication. *Davar (logos)* is quite distinct from words that emphasize form or method of saying. It is even taken as identical with the power of God, as in creation (Ps. 33:6; cf. John 1:3). In a similar way, *wisdom (memra),* especially in Proverbs, is personified and related to God. Inter-Testament Jews carried the idea farther *(Sirach* and *Wisdom of Solomon)*.

Some try to trace the NT *logos* (especially in John 1:1-14) to Philo's attempt to unite Hebrew prophecy and Greek philosophy. Though similarities of terms are seen and though Philo predicates certain attributes of Christ to his *Logos,* the subject is not the same. The Son of God is missing. Philo has no adequate Mediator (Cremer, 395). The *Logos* of John's Gospel and of the NT in general leads to the OT for its source and meaning.

NT usage of *logos* is different from and opposed to the pagan and semipagan concepts. The truth of God corrects the false ideas and half-truths of the philosophers, of the Philonians, of the Gnostics, and of modern unbelief. The *logos* is God's truth proclaimed (Mark 4:14), whether by Jesus himself or by others (Acts 4:4; 1 Thess. 2:13). It is handed down orally and in writing (2 Thess. 2:15). The eternal *Logos* is also a living person, now incarnated (John 1:1-14). The NT gives consistent witness implicitly and explicitly to the *logos* as the spoken, written, and living Word of God.

See CHRIST, BIBLE, REVELATION (SPECIAL), KERYGMA.

For Further Reading: Turner, "Logos," *ZPEB,* 3:953-58; Cremer, "Logos, lego, etc.," *Biblico-Theological Lexicon of New Testament Greek,* 390-96; Girdlestone, "Word, Law, Covenant," *Synonyms of the Old Testament,* 204-14. WILBER T. DAYTON

LONG-SUFFERING. Long-suffering is the demonstration of patience and endurance when one is being provoked or injured.

With Reference to God. In the OT long-suffering literally means slow to anger, a disposition to delay wrath (Exod. 34:6; Num. 14:18; Ps. 86:15). The NT usage also relates long-suffering to wrath (Rom. 2:4-5; 9:22; 1 Pet. 3:20). J. Horst observes that long-suffering does not mean the complete end of God's wrath. "In biblical usage [long-suffering] does not imply renunciation of the grounds of wrath. What it does mean is that alongside this wrath there is a divine restraint which postpones its operation until something takes place in man which justifies the postponement" (Kittel, 4:377). So, in God long-suffering is placing patience or endurance alongside wrath.

In Relation to Man. Paul identifies long-suffering as a Christian character trait by listing it as a fruit of the Spirit (Gal. 5:22). It is further referred to in 2 Cor. 6:6; Eph. 4:2; and 2 Tim. 4:2. In the NT sense, long-suffering literally means "long of mind" or "long of soul," as opposed to shortness of mind or soul. Related to man, long-suffering is patience with others—an even temper under provocation. Yet that which distinguishes it from steely self-control is love. It is patience sustained by compassion and understanding.

See FRUIT OF THE SPIRIT, CHRISTLIKENESS.

For Further Reading: Metz, *Studies in Biblical Holiness,* 191-96; Kittel, 4:377. JAMES L. PORTER

LORD. The title or name is descriptive of one who owns or controls as a master. He is the one in full control, hence a person of high authority, power, and position.

In biblical literature "lord" is a translation of a variety of Hebrew words referring both directly and indirectly to God and Christ. The Hebrew word for God in His essential being is *Elohim.* The word *Yahweh* (Jehovah), designating His relationship to man, is at once grounded in man's experience and God's Lordship, as in "Thus has *Yahweh* spoken."

The Greek *Kurios* is most frequently translated "Lord" but also has other meanings. Many English translations, e.g., KJV, NASB, NIV, RSV, use capital and small capital letters—LORD—for *Kurios* when it is a translation from the Hebrew *Adonia* (which in turn represents *Yahweh*).

In late Judaism the Lord *(Kurios)* was perceived

as the One who could legally dispose. God's Lordship was seen in His creating and sustaining the universe. It was He their Lord who had brought Israel out of Egyptian bondage. Hence He had a legitimate claim on His covenant people. He was for them the One God who had the power, right, and authority to dispose over all things.

In the NT, Lord *(Kurios)* is the name for God in quotations and reminiscences of the OT where the Septuagint is usually followed. The same word, *Kurios*, which is translated "Lord" to refer to God or Christ ("The LORD said unto my Lord" [Luke 20:42]), has also secular meanings variously translated "master," "lord," "owner," and "sir," as a form of polite address.

Jesus addressed God His Father as "Lord of heaven and earth" (Matt. 11:25). Here Jesus recognized His Father as the uncaused divine will while at the same time evincing that His own voluntary subservience to the divine will was in no way either indicative or productive of a lack of willpower.

This attitude of Jesus to His Father gives insight into the early confession where the title and name, Lord, was ascribed to Jesus. According to Paul, "Every tongue should confess that Jesus Christ is Lord" (Phil. 2:11, NASB). His Lordship is the consequence of His humble obedience freely chosen. "He humbled Himself by becoming obedient to the point of death, even death on a cross" (v. 8, NASB).

See JEHOVAH (YAHWEH), CHRIST.

For Further Reading: *GMS*, 328-32; Kittel, 3:1039-95.

JOSEPH H. MAYFIELD

LORD'S DAY. This is Sunday, the first day of the week, the special Christian day of worship.

The term appears in the NT only in Rev. 1:10 where it provides the temporal setting of the revelation given John on Patmos. Despite its appearance in this apocalyptic context, it is doubtful that the "Lord's day" *(Kyriakē hēmera)* refers to the eschatological "Day of the Lord" (always *hē hēmera [tou] Kyriou*). The term in other early Christian literature (e.g., *Didache* 14.1; Ignatius of Antioch's *Letter to the Magnesians* 9.1; Justin Martyr's *First Apology* 67.7; *Epistle of Barnabas* 15.9; and the *Gospel of Peter* 9.35; 12.50) always refers to Sunday (and exceptionally more specifically to Easter Sunday).

The pagan term "Sunday" is certainly of later origin than the Jewish "first day of the week" (Matt. 28:1; Mark 16:2; Luke 24:1; John 20:1, 19; Acts 20:7; 1 Cor. 16:2), and the equivalent "eighth day" (cf. John 20:26 and later Christian usage)—and probably later than the specifically Christian designation, the "Lord's day."

The fact that Christians created a new name for only one day of the week suggests its importance, but not necessarily the significance of the specific designation, "Lord's day." The expression may imply that Sunday (1) as a day belongs to the Lord in some special way; (2) was inaugurated and observed on the Lord's authority; (3) weekly anticipates the eschatological Day of the Lord; or, with greater probability (4) serves as a weekly memorial of Jesus' resurrection; and (5) is the special day on which the "Lord's supper" (*Kyriakon deipnon* [1 Cor. 11:20]) was celebrated.

Scripture nowhere specifically commands the transfer of the day of worship from the Jewish Sabbath to the Lord's day. Nevertheless, probably from the very earliest days of the post-Easter Christian community (cf. references above for "first day") but certainly by no later than A.D. 150 (Justin Martyr's *First Apology* 67), the Lord's day was the chief day of worship,the climactic focal point of which was the Eucharist. Thus the decree of the Roman Emperor Constantine in A.D. 321, making Sunday a public holiday, did not change but merely recognized and officially sanctioned a long-standing Christian customary practice.

See SUNDAY, SABBATARIANISM, LAW, WORSHIP.

For Further Reading: Corlett, *The Christian Sabbath;* Jewett, *The Lord's Day: A Theological Guide to the Christian Day of Worship;* Latourette, *A History of Christianity;* Richardson, "Lord's Day," *IDB*, 3:151-54; Rordorf, *Sunday: The History of the Day of Rest and Worship in the Earliest Centuries of the Christian Church;* Wiley, *CT*, 3:143-50; Beckwith and Scott, *This Is the Day: The Biblical Doctrine of the Christian Sunday in Its Jewish and Early Church Setting.*

GEORGE LYONS

LORD'S PRAYER. The prayer in Matthew 6 and Luke 11 is referred to nowhere in the NT as "The Lord's Prayer," unless one counts the appellation "Abba, Father." The title is most probably a result of Jesus' introductory words, "Pray then like this" (Matt. 6:9, RSV); "When you pray, say" (Luke 11:2, RSV).

In the early centuries of the Church, the Lord's Prayer was a part of the worship service. Cyril tells us that in Jerusalem the prayer was used at the end of the Eucharistic prayers before the Communion. This leads to the conclusion that the privilege of public use of the Lord's Prayer was reserved for the full members of the church. The candidates for believer's baptism learned the Lord's Prayer either shortly before or immediately after baptism. Thereafter they prayed it daily, for it was an integral part of their identification as Christians.

The prayer is composed of an address, six petitions, and a closing doxology. Although it was not unusual for Jewish prayers to be addressed to God as Father, it is remarkable that in the OT God is addressed as Father only 14 times, all of which were very important. Jesus' instructing His disciples to call God "Father" is the more astounding when we examine the word for "Father" in Jesus' spoken language, Aramaic. The Early Church fathers Chrysostom, Theodor, and Theodoret, who came from Antioch and had Aramaic-speaking nurses, tell us that *abba* was the address of the small child to his father. The Talmud confirms it: "The first words for a child when it learns to eat wheat [i.e., when weaned] are: *abba, imma* = dear father, dear mother." *Abba* was an intimate family word, and Jesus gives His disciples a share in this privilege of addressing God as *Abba*. Encompassing the scope of the Good News, Jesus empowers the disciples to speak to their Heavenly Father literally as the small child speaks to his father, in the same confident and childlike manner.

The first three petitions of this prayer (two, in Luke) have a very similar meaning. To hallow God's name, to pray for the Kingdom, and for the doing of God's will, all reflect the living hope of the Church that God as Sovereign will prevail.

In the remaining three petitions, the verbs move from the passive to the active voice. In the context of the eschatological hope expressed in the first three petitions, it is not unlikely that the request for "daily bread" suggested a share in the Messianic banquet. However, a closer, more practical reference is quite probable. The example of the manna in the OT suggests that the bread for the new day would be sufficient for that day only. It is quite possible that this is a reflection of Jesus' concern for the every-day needs of His disciples and means simply "the day's ration."

The fifth petition, a request for forgiveness of debts/sins, is difficult to interpret in the context of the prayer alone. Yet the tenor of the entirety of Jesus' teaching suggests that any person who is not willing to forgive others, is not ready to be forgiven.

Many explanations of the final petition are strained attempts at exonerating God from leading the believer into sinning. The simple truth is that *peirasmos* primarily means a testing, not enticement to sin. The biblical idea is one of putting men to proof, and such trials are to be expected. The meaning is: "Do not allow us to be overcome in our testing."

The final doxology is a liturgical addition which returns to the eschatological theme of the first three petitions, thus rounding out the prayer; but it is not in the oldest Greek NT manuscript.

It would be well for the contemporary Church to recapture the use of this prayer in its liturgical practice, especially the sense of privilege at being allowed to pray, "Our Father."

See PRAYER, FATHERHOOD OF GOD, ADOPTION.

For Further Reading: *IDB*, 3:154-58; "The Lord's Prayer in Modern Research," *Expository Times*, vol. 71, no. 5 (Feb., 1960): 141-46. W. STEPHEN GUNTER

LORD'S SUPPER. See HOLY COMMUNION.

LOST, LOST SOUL. In the present tense a lost soul refers to an unregenerate person who is deprived of the presence of God. In an eternal perspective a lost soul is one who has been judged sinful and sentenced to eternal punishment.

Biblical Terms. Both OT and NT terms, *abad* and *apollumi* (or *apolluō*), literally mean "To destroy, kill, or lose oneself." The implication is strong. Being "lost" is the result of one's own actions. The NT word *apolluō* is the basis for Apollyon (Rev. 9:11, Thayer), a name for Satan, meaning Destroyer. Hence, Satan is the destroyer, and a "lost soul" has taken action to permit himself to be destroyed by Satan. Figuratively, the biblical use of "lost" depicts the struggle between life and death for a soul. The prodigal son (Luke 15:11 ff) and Lazarus in Abraham's bosom (16:19 ff) are examples of the figurative conflict which is related to lostness in the NT.

As Spiritual Death. The lost soul experiences a spiritual death during this life. Spiritual death is a loss of God's presence, the separation of the sinner from God. Spiritual death is caused by the withdrawal of the Holy Spirit, as David indicated by his prayer of repentance, "Do not cast me away from Thy presence, and do not take Thy Holy Spirit from Me" (Ps. 51:11, NASB). The lost soul not only experiences the loss of God in spiritual death, but the lost soul also experiences the loss of the present pleasures of spiritual life: love, joy, and peace.

As Eternal Death. The ultimate experience of the lost soul is eternal death, i.e., to be lost eternally. At the final Judgment the willful separation of spiritual death is pronounced fixed and unalterable. Jesus declared that the lost soul would depart into an everlasting fire which was prepared for the devil and his angels, and that the lost soul would experience this as an eternal punishment (Matt. 25:41, 46).

Universal. The state of being lost is universal: "All we like sheep have gone astray; we have turned every one to his own way; and the Lord hath laid on him the iniquity of us all" (Isa. 53:6). Paul restated the universal lostness of mankind: "They are all gone out of the way, they are together become unprofitable; there is none that doeth good, no, not one" (Rom. 3:12; cf. Ps. 14:3).

Remedy. The Bible also states the remedy for the lost soul. "Whosoever will come after me, let him deny himself, and take up his cross, and follow me. For whosoever will save his life shall lose it; but whosoever shall lose his life for my sake and the gospel's, the same shall save it" (Mark 8:34-35).

See SALVATION, REDEEMER (REDEMPTION), ETERNAL PUNISHMENT, SOUL WINNING, EVANGELISM.

For Further Reading: Anderson, *Our Holy Faith,* 144-78.

JAMES L. PORTER

LOVE. Both Hebrew and Greek have a rich vocabulary regularly translated into English by the word "love." In the OT, these words range from a root primarily denoting passionate love but also family affection and friendship, a root denoting tender mercies, to a root denoting steadfast loyalty. Though not as diverse as the range in classical Greek, the NT usage includes the dominant *agapaō* and its cognates, *phileō* and its cognates, and the rarely used *stergō* and its cognates. Each of these words also has a theological usage. *Eros* never occurs in the NT.

The exceedingly rich theological usage of "love" has its basis in the character of God: according to the Scriptures, God is love (1 John 4:8, 16). Unlike the human expression of love, God's love does not need an object to exist, since it is His very essence. "God is eternally love prior to, and independently of, his love for us" (Cranfield, *A Theological Word Book of the Bible,* 135). This essential character is the only sufficient explanation for God's love to man.

Without doubt, it is God's love for man which is the major theme of the OT and NT alike. His love for Israel is seen in her election, His covenant graciously given to Israel, and His mighty, redeeming acts on her behalf. But His love is supremely demonstrated in the life and death of Jesus. Paul, noting the gracious nature of God's offer of reconciliation to man, writes: "God shows his love for us in that while we were yet sinners Christ died for us" (Rom. 5:8, RSV). On the Cross, the God whose holiness exposes the utter sinfulness and unworthiness of man, from His being of love himself provided all that was necessary to end the alienation and estrangement that man's self-love had caused. Only when one grasps the graciousness of God's love for us can we gain a proper perspective of our love for God and our fellowman.

Man's love for God is a reflection of God's love for us in that the origin is in the response to His love rather than an emanation from our own being. The human condition of sinfulness precludes the possibility of pure love springing from our being, since sin has so infected man that his attitudes and actions are selfish, not loving. Even the highest human love has the character of enlightened self-interest insofar as it is a human motivation. The love which does exist in the world alienated from God is evidence of the prevenient grace of God, even if it is not seen as such by the world. In sum, love is dependent upon God's grace and is impossible apart from it. "We love," says 1 John 4:19, "because he first loved us" (RSV). Consciousness of this utter dependence upon God's grace is the state of the redeemed and becomes more acute as the Christian grows. With the presence of the Holy Spirit, love becomes the basis of the Christian existence. It is this fact which makes obedience to the commands of Jesus into a joyous response to God's love, not an onerous burden.

The inescapable corollary of one's love to God is love for one's neighbor. Jesus and the NT writers alike insist that love for God must find its expression not only in personal piety but in loving action for others (1 John 3:18). "Hate, disobedience, mere profession in words without deeds, pride in one's 'experience', all point to a fundamental hypocrisy" (Johnston, *IDB,* 3:176). True, this love is costly and is often imprudent. It is never to be a thinly disguised self-interest; rather, it is to be "an uncalculating loving kindness" (ibid., 170).

Our love for God and neighbor is the only fitting response to the love of God given to us. But we cannot love in such a fashion without a heart made clean (Mark 7:21), a point with clear ethical overtones. Love, then, is inextricably bound up with Christian holiness, for the truly loving individual is the one who is totally and single-mindedly devoted to the holy God. The loving individual is the one whose highest goal is the complete obedience of the disciple, whose every action springs from the love of God spread abroad in his heart, and whose life is controlled and guided by the Holy Spirit. No wonder Wesley used the biblical phrase "perfect love" so often in describing the holy life.

See AGAPĒ, GREAT COMMANDMENTS, PERFECT LOVE, HEART PURITY, FRUIT OF THE SPIRIT.

For Further Reading: Cranfield, *A Theological Word Book of the Bible;* Johnston, "Love in the NT," *IDB;* Lewis, *The Four Loves;* Wiéner, "Love," *Dictionary of Biblical Theology;* Nygren, *Agape and Eros;* Wesley, *A Plain Account of Christian Perfection.* KENT BROWER

LOVE AND LAW. The summary of Paul's discussion of law and love in Rom. 13:8-10 by "It [Love] is the only law you need" in TLB, not only goes beyond what Paul says, but betrays a grave misunderstanding, which leads straight to situational ethics, if not to antinomianism. What Paul is saying is that love alone can fulfill the moral law from the heart—fulfilling the law's spirit and intention, not just the letter—because it is in the very nature of love to desire to do good and not harm. What Paul is not saying is that therefore all laws are superfluous, since love is wise enough always to infallibly know what will be harmful. This would be a non sequitur. The impulse to seek another's welfare is not in itself knowledge as to what constitutes that welfare, or how it is to be secured. Love does not automatically provide information nor assure sound judgment. The guidance of law is needed to inform the mind in order that love may be directed into modes of self-expression which God has already declared to be proper for the achievement of love's objective. What love will not do—as long as love for persons is governed by love for God—is to despise law or set it aside.

See LAW, LAW AND GRACE, LOVE, NEW MORALITY, ANTINOMIANISM, LAW OF LIBERTY, FREEDOM.

For Further Reading: *GMS,* 532-41; Ladd, *A Theology of the New Testament,* 509 ff. RICHARD S. TAYLOR

LOVE FEAST. The Gospels make reference to Jesus' participation in fellowship at a meal on several occasions. Luke and John especially highlight the theme of table fellowship in their accounts of the appearances of the resurrected Jesus. The memory of such moments was most likely the motivation for the Early Church's practice of regularly sharing a common meal. The desire to celebrate their religious fellowship, and their commitment to care for the poor among them, prompted the Jerusalem Church to eat their meals together (cf. Acts 2:42-47; 4:32-35; 6:1-6). Most probably their common meals included the observance of the Lord's Supper. This latter practice seems to have been carried on in at least one of Paul's Gentile congregations (cf. 1 Cor. 11:17-34). The observance of the love feast was widespread until the time of Augustine. The Eastern Orthodox church persisted in the practice, which was taken up by the Moravians, from whom John Wesley borrowed it for his Methodists.

See CHURCH, KOINONIA, FEET WASHING, EUCHARIST.

For Further Reading: *Baker's DT,* 333-35; *IDB,* 1:53-54; Wesley, *Works,* 8:258-59. HAL A. CAUTHRON

LUST. See DESIRE.

LUTHERANISM. Lutheran was originally a nickname used derisively of the followers of Martin Luther. It later came to distinguish these from Protestants of the Reformed branch which was led by John Calvin, and Protestants of the "radical reformation" or Anabaptists. Lutheran, in time, lost its derisive tone, and Lutheranism became the proper designation for the structural spiritual heritage of Martin Luther.

The doctrinal basis for Lutheranism is broadly the pivotal doctrines of Protestantism: justification by faith, the universal priesthood of believers, and the authority of Scripture. More particularly, Lutherans are informed and influenced in their doctrine by a series of traditional documents. These include Luther's *Longer* and *Short Catechisms,* both produced in 1529; the *Augsburg Confession,* written by Philip Melanchthon (1530-31); *The Schmalkald Articles,* written by Luther for a general council in 1537; and the *Formula of Concord,* published in 1577 in the interests of Lutheran unity.

Lutherans recognize two sacraments. The Lord's Supper involves the "real presence" of Christ but does so without philosophical speculation about a physical change in the bread and wine. The Lord's Supper and baptism are means or channels of grace and thus not just memorials or signs. Baptism is for infants and adults alike and marks the reception of the grace of regeneration through the Holy Spirit.

Worship is liturgical and centers on the altar. Lutherans observe festivals and seasons of the historic church year. In some Lutheran churches certain Catholic forms of worship have been retained but in a simplified form and with an altered understanding of their significance. Medieval traditions of art and beauty were not rejected by Lutheran worshippers as they sometimes were in Reformed Protestantism. In fact, where Luther's influence spread, the place of religious music in worship was firmly established, and European Lutheran churches are often resplendent with works of art.

The local congregation is the basic unit of government in the Lutheran church. While the church rejects the hierarchy of espiscopacy (although bishops are not unknown in European Lutheranism), it also rejects the looseness of denominational bonds as in congregationalism. Congregations unite in synods, territorial districts, or conferences. General unions are national or international and serve either as legislative or consultative bodies.

Lutheranism began with Martin Luther's attempt to reform the Roman Catholic church. Under the political protection of the elector of Saxony, Luther protested against the usurpation of authority over conscience by the hierarchy of the Roman Catholic church. What had begun as an attempt to reform proceeded to become outright rebellion, taking sometimes a secular form as in the Peasant Wars and Peasant Rebellion. From Germany, Lutheranism spread throughout Europe and the Baltic States. Its influence came to be especially strong in Scandinavia.

Lutheranism in America is accounted for chiefly by immigration from Scandinavia and Germany. The first permanent Lutheran residents to arrive in the United States came from Holland and landed on Manhattan Island in 1623. Present membership in Lutheran churches is nearly 12 million in more than 17,000 congregations.

See PROTESTANTISM, CONSUBSTANTIATION, JUSTIFICATION, PRIESTHOOD OF BELIEVERS, BIBLICAL AUTHORITY.

For Further Reading: *Our Church and Others* (Concordia); *The Lutheran Catechism.* DANIEL N. BERG

M

MACEDONIANISM. This is another name for Pneumatomachianism, a fourth-century view that the Holy Spirit is not divine and is not to be worshipped. The Council of Nicea had only declared clearly that Christ is divine, and had only vaguely declared belief in the Holy Spirit. That council's vagueness regarding the Holy Spirit's divinity encouraged the Pneumatomachians to believe they were within orthodoxy by denying the Holy Spirit's divinity. But Basil wrote diplomatically in support of the Holy Spirit's divinity; and the Second Ecumenical Council (Constantinople, 381) declared the Holy Spirit's deity, against the view of the Macedonians.

See HOLY SPIRIT, TRINITY (THE HOLY), CHURCH COUNCILS, CREED (CREEDS). J. KENNETH GRIDER

MAGIC. See SORCERY.

MAJESTY. The term is used in English versions of the Bible to depict the greatness of God in reference to His deity and glory which place Him above any creaturely excellence. Because of His Creatorship, the word also attributes to Him the governance of the entire universe.

The term was used in ancient Rome to signify the highest power and dignity, and was therefore attributed to the whole community of citizens—the *populus* in which Roman sovereignty ultimately resided.

Later the term was used to acknowledge the dignity and greatness of the ruling sovereign of an individual country or state. "Your Majesty" was considered the appropriate salutation for one's king or queen. It expressed the subject's compliment to his ruler.

The earliest use of the term in the English language was to express the greatness and glory of Almighty God. Thus it occurs in the English Bible as a translation for the Hebrew *gaon,* "excellency," and its derivatives (Job 40:10; Ps. 93:1; 96:6; Isa. 2:10, 19, 21; 24:14; 26:10; Ezek. 7:20; and Mic. 5:4).

A second term, *hod* (indicative of grandeur, imposing form and appearance; consequently beauty, comeliness, excellency, glory, and honor), occurs under the concept of God's majesty (cf. 1 Chron. 29:25; Job 37:22). And a third term, *hadar,* (referring to magnificence, grandeur, ornamentation and decoration, adorning in honor), is also translated "majesty" (cf. Ps. 21:5; 29:4; 45:3-4; 96:6; 104:1; 145:12; Dan. 4:30). In a number of instances we have the combination of terms, such as *hod* and *hadar,* to emphasize the exaltation and magnificence of Yahweh (cf. Ps. 21:5; 96:6; et al.).

Majesty was the divine name on the high priest's mitre, according to the apocryphal writer (*Wisdom of Solomon,* 18:24).

In the Greek NT the noun, *megalōsunē,* and the adjective, *megaleiotēs,* are used to express the superhuman glory, splendor, and superbness of both God and Jesus (cf. Heb. 1:3; 8:1; 2 Pet. 1:16; Jude 25). The apostle Peter declared himself to have been an eyewitness of Christ's transfiguration radiance (2 Pet. 1:16-17).

Majesty was expressed in God's action, revealing His royal supremacy and stating His magnificence. Since God is the Source of all majesty, kings and men derive their dignity from God. This appealed to many a sovereign as he espoused the dogma of "the divine right of kings," based on Rom. 13:1-7.

Christ's majesty was manifested in His miracles (Luke 9:43), His transfiguration (2 Pet. 1:16), as He revealed God's majesty (1 Tim. 6:15-16), as He fulfilled man's true dignity (Heb. 2:6-9), as He shared the divine name and throne (Phil. 2:9; Heb. 1:3-4), and in His Messianic Kingship (Rev. 5:6-14; 19:11-16) about to be revealed.

See GOD, ATTRIBUTES (DIVINE).

For Further Reading: Delitzsch, *Commentary on the Psalms;* Thayer; Gesenius, *Hebrew-Chaldee Lexicon.*

ROSS E. PRICE

MAMMON. The word "mammon" is an Aramaic word used exclusively by Jesus Christ in the NT (Matt. 6:24; Luke 16:9, 11, 13). It is evident that the word had a long-established reputation for expressing the evils of money in particular and of temporal wealth in general. Such possessions are spoken of derogatorily because the suggestion is that they were acquired dishonestly.

Jesus was sensitive to man's proclivity to erroneously seek security in accumulating such possessions and thereby become enslaved to them (Matt. 6:21). This was the problem of the unjust steward as described by Jesus to the Pharisees, who were lovers of money (Luke 16:1-14).

The answer Jesus gives to this enslavement is that the righteous must free themselves by an exclusive dependence upon God (v. 13). Human wisdom seeks the best of both worlds; but in the strongest of terms Jesus declares that it is utterly impossible to trust both God and riches. God accepts nothing less than undivided worship, and this requirement is at the heart of the first commandment.

See COVETOUSNESS, MONEY, VALUES, STEWARDSHIP, MOTIVES.

For Further Reading: Kittel, 4:388-90; Vincent, *Word Studies in the New Testament,* 1:394-95; *ISBE,* 3:1972 ff.

ROBERT A. MATTKE

MAN. The technical term for the study of man is *anthropology*. This is a combination of two Greek words, *anthrōpos* and *logos*, meaning *the doctrine of man.* The scientific use of the term covers the problems arising from a study of primitive man, racial distinctions, the geographical distribution of these races, and the factors which enter into man's development of himself in societal groupings. The *theological* use of the term is our interest in this article. We are concerned with man's metaphysical and moral being. Yet the science of anthropology and the theology of man are not absolutely exclusive investigations.

The Scriptures look upon man as the crowning work of God's creation. The Genesis account of the origin of mankind is the Christian believer's authority and source of information. Theories of materialistic origins for mankind, including *epigenesis* and the supposed resultant evolutionary process, are non-Christian, even in the self-contradictory theory of theistic evolution. Genesis 1 gives the basics about man's origin, and Genesis 2 enlarges and elaborates thereon. The two accounts are not contradictory but are complementary.

The account of the origin of this first individual man is a classic statement of Judeo-Christian anthropology (Gen. 2:7): "Then the Lord God formed man [i.e., his flesh, *basar*] of dust from the ground, and breathed into his nostrils the breath *[ruach]* of life [lit., lives, plural]; and man became a living soul [*nephesh,* psychosomatic somewhat]" (NASB). Thus God's fashioning of the empirical man preceded His inbreathing of the ontological self into man, which inbreathing gave to man both his animal and his spiritual life. Man is therefore a combination of both dust and deity, a time-space creature with eternity at the core of him. He is a psychosomatic entity, a combination of mind and matter (*dichotomy* in essence), with the highest functioning of matter evidenced in the brain and nervous system. Mind, involving man's self-consciousness and reasoning functions, also relates him to things spiritual and divine as well as to things material by way of his body. So much for man's essence.

Functionally man is tripartite in his being *(trichotomy),* and is so specified by the apostle Paul as body *(sōma),* soul *(psychē),* and spirit (*pneuma* [1 Thess. 5:23]). Here the body functions earthward and soul-ward, giving man sensation and world-consciousness. The soul functions body-ward and spirit-ward, giving man his self-consciousness. But the spirit functions soul-ward and God-ward, giving man his God-consciousness and also his own self-grasp in personal self-evaluation and self-estimate.

The Hebrew term *ruach* agrees with the Greek *pneuma,* "breath of lives" (both animal and spiritual) and specifies "life bestowed by the Creator." The Hebrew term *nephesh* agrees with the Greek term *psychē* (psychological entity) and specifies "life constituted in the creature." The Hebrew term *basar* (not used in Gen. 2:7) translates "flesh" and agrees with the Greek term *sōma* (body) to indicate man's material essence as composed of "flesh" and "blood" and "bones." Thus man finds himself as a being that is both *noumenal* and *phenomenal,* a combination of both transcendence and immanence, with an *ontological self* as subject, and an *empirical self* as object. The transcendent self knits together in consciousness and memory the totality of its lived-through events and empirical experiences and functions outward and upward toward God and fellowman. The empirical self functions earthward and fields in sensory experience man's contact relationships with his physical environs. So much for man's functions.

Man was created not only as an individual (*ish*—man) but also as a racial being (*adam*—mankind). All the races of mankind have descended from a common parentage (Gen. 3:20; Acts 17:26). Moreover, the primitive state of man was not one of barbarism, but one of maturity and perfection (cf. Wiley, *CT,* 2:21). Adam (the man) walked in fellowship and holy harmony with God and intuitively read off the nature of each animal, so giving each a name appropriate to its characteristics (Gen. 2:19-20; cf. 1:31).

The Genesis account also tells of God's elaboration of the race into two sexes by the creation of Eve from Adam's *side-chamber* (*tsela,* Gen. 2:18, 22, 24), so that mankind includes both as *one flesh*. Thereafter, the basic unit within the race is a community of father-mother-child in societal relationships. So sex is God's invention, for He made mankind both man and woman (the "man with a womb"), both male *(ish)* and female *(ishah);* but since the Fall, nothing about mankind has been more perverted than sex.

See HUMAN NATURE, DIVINE IMAGE, BODY, SOUL, DICHOTOMY, TRICHOTOMY, SEXUALITY.

For Further Reading: Curtis, *The Christian Faith,* 7-93; Laidlaw, *The Bible Doctrine of Man;* Paul Meehl et al., *What Then Is Man?;* Wiley, *CT,* 2:7-50.

ROSS E. PRICE

MAN OF SIN. The "man of sin" is an eschatological figure described by Paul in 2 Thess. 2:1-12. The most obvious source for Paul's thought here is the OT Book of Daniel (chaps. 7—8; 11—12). These and other OT passages gave rise in later Jewish and Christian circles to a belief that the coming of the Messiah would be preceded by a period of religious apostasy and persecution, epitomized in a great world ruler. Jesus appropriated the Dan. 11:31 passage regarding the profanation of the Temple and projected its occurrence into the future, near the end of the present age (Matt. 24:15; Mark 13:14). In the Johannine writings the expectation took the form of a future Antichrist figure (1 John 2:18, 22; 4:3; 2 John 7; Revelation 13).

For Paul the man of sin will be more than a preeminently godless individual; in him humanity in its hostile alienation from God will come to a definitive, eschatological revelation. He will be the final counterpart of Christ. Like Christ, he will have his "revelation" (2 Thess. 2:3, 6, 8) and "parousia" (v. 9). His coming will be marked by all manner of powers, signs, and wonders, by which he will deceive an unbelieving humanity (vv. 9-11). He will proclaim himself to be God and demand the worship of the world (v. 4). He will be the culmination of that satanically inspired hostility to God and to Christ which has been operative throughout history (vv. 7, 9).

See TRIBULATION, RAPTURE, SECOND COMING OF CHRIST.

For Further Reading: Morris, *The First and Second Epistles to the Thessalonians,* 217-36; Ridderbos, *Paul: An Outline of His Theology,* 512-28; Vos, *The Pauline Eschatology,* 94-135.

FRED D. LAYMAN

MANHOOD OF CHRIST. See HUMANITY OF CHRIST.

MANICHAEISM. Manichaeism, also known as the Religion of Light, was once considered a Christian heresy, but significant recent research shows that it should now be regarded as a complex dualistic religion essentially Gnostic in character.

Founded by Manes, Mani, or Manichaeus (c. A.D. 216-76), this religion was based primarily in Babylonia and Persia, but broad missionary activity of Manichaeus and his followers pushed the religion into India, China, Tibet, the Roman Empire, and Egypt. Manichaeism is still alive in small measure in the 20th century both as a result of the conscious efforts of a few disciples and in bits and pieces of views of generally orthodox Christians.

Manichaeism's principal contention is for an ultimate dualism: light vs. darkness; good vs. evil; spiritual world vs. material world. The world itself is the product of a complicated struggle between light and darkness. And while matter per se is evil, certain activities and material entities are more an expression of darkness/evil than others. For example, morality is negatively regarded as abstention from meat, wine, and sexual contact. Luminous foods (melons, fruits) must be distinguished from dark foods (wine, meat). The very purpose of procreation is the enslavement of particles of light (and thus involves the shrouding of light in the darkness of matter).

Ambassadors of light are especially Buddha, Zoroaster, and Jesus. But the final seal of all revelation is Mani.

Those who accept Manichaean dualism will ultimately be liberated into the Kingdom of Light (either immediately if among the elect or through transmigration into an elect). Those who reject this will be reincarnated as beasts and finally end in hell.

During the Middle Ages there was a tendency to apply the term Manichaean to any heresy. Catholics called the Reformers Manichaean after this fashion. This led to studies which exposed the extra-Christian sources of this approach. A whole new era of understanding of Manichaeism has arrived through the great discoveries of texts in the 20th century.

See DUALISM, GNOSTICISM, MEDITATION.

For Further Reading: *Encyclopedia Americana;* Heick, *A History of Christian Thought,* 2:132 ff.

R. DUANE THOMPSON

MARCIONISM. This relates to the teachings of Marcion who, in the middle of the second century of our era, taught a Gnostic-like kind of Christianity which was dualistic, which denigrated the OT, and which preferred the writings of Paul to other writings in what later became Christianity's accepted NT canon. Marcion was excommunicated from the Christian church, and his views did not receive wide acceptance—although Gnosticism as such continued to be a formidable threat in that century.

See GNOSTICISM, DUALISM.

For Further Reading: Heick, *A History of Christian Thought,* 1:76-78.

J. KENNETH GRIDER

MARIOLATRY. Mariolatry is the worship of the Virgin Mary. Through prayer, prostrations, and other forms of veneration honor is ascribed to Mary that ought to be reserved only for God.

Orthodox groups and Roman Catholics have encouraged the adoration of Mary. Centuries of tradition have been formalized into dogma by Roman Catholic popes concerning her place. On December 8, 1854, Pope Pius IX declared that Mary had been preserved from original sin from the earliest moment of her life (immaculate conception). On November 1, 1950, Pope Pius XII gave formal voice to the long-held view that Mary was a virgin throughout her lifetime (perpetual virginity). He also affirmed that she had been received into heaven without having tasted death (bodily assumption). Along with her centuries-old title "Mother of God," Mary was officially declared to be "Mother of the Church" by Pope Paul VI, on November 21, 1964.

Shrines have been built to honor Mary. Matchless paintings and beautifully sculptured madonnas have been created to aid the worshipper in directing his prayers to and through her. She is considered to be a mediator between the penitent and Christ. Songs have been sung, poems have been written, candles have been lit in her honor. Mariolatry goes far beyond the proper biblical appreciation for the lowly "handmaid of the Lord" (Luke 1:38).

See IMMACULATE CONCEPTION, MOTHER OF GOD, IDOL (IDOLATRY).

RONALD E. WILSON

MARRIAGE. Marriage is the institution whereby a man and a woman are joined together in the legal relationship of husband and wife. It was established by God when He created the first human pair (Gen. 2:20-24), and is the foundation on which the family and society are built.

While procreation is a purpose of marriage (Gen. 1:27-28; 9:7), that is but one of its functions. Apart from each other man and woman are incomplete. Marriage gives each a sense of belonging and of fulfilment, and is a citadel of mutual love and concern. But these goals can be reached on the highest level only as the man and woman are united in Christ.

God intended marriage to be a lifelong relationship. Vows and/or agreements made in its inception are done before God and therefore are most sacred (Matt. 19:6). A successful marriage requires a mutual, ongoing attitude of unselfish concern. It must be built on the principles of submission and love stated in Eph. 5:21-22, 28-30. As the couple submits to God, He supplies graces that enrich and cement together the marriage relationship.

The biblical principle of submission of the wife to her husband does not contradict another principle stating the equal dignity of the sexes (Gal. 3:28; 1 Cor. 7:4; 11:11-12). The wife's submission, like the submission of Christ to the Father, of citizens to rulers, and of employees to employers, is functional and does not imply inferiority. Because God ordained a hierarchy of responsibility, He also appointed a hierarchy of authority in keeping with the order in which the human genders were created. The dignity of wives is seen also in the fact that the command to submit is addressed to them personally, not through their husbands (Eph. 5:22).

Marriage is only for this life (Matt. 22:30). But its intimacy, its love, its beauty, its mutual joy and concern make it a fitting symbol of the eternal union between Christ and the Church (Eph. 5:21-32; Rev. 19:7).

See FAMILY, CHILD (CHILDREN), INSTITUTIONS OF CHRISTIANITY, POLYGAMY, SEXUALITY.

For Further Reading: Bailey, *The Mystery of Love and Marriage;* Bowman, *A Christian Interpretation of Marriage;* Granberg, "Marriage," *Baker's DT.*

W. RALPH THOMPSON

MARTYR, MARTYRDOM. One is a martyr who willingly suffers death rather than renounce his religion. The etymology of the word *martyr* ties its meaning and history closely to the Greek word *martus,* meaning witness.

Although the word *martus* does not appear in the Septuagint (LXX), the spirit of the martyr is evident in many parts of the OT from Abel (Gen. 4:10) onward. Judaism held in high esteem those whose suffering and death were within the framework of the Pharisaic ideal of piety. For them suffering and death for the law were considered to be unexcelled works of piety.

In the NT it is Stephen who became known as the first Christian martyr. Paul told it in one simple statement. "When the blood of Stephen thy witness *[martus]* was shed I stood by" (Acts 22:20, NEB). The whole story of Stephen makes it clear that he was not called a witness because he died. Rather he died because he like Abel was a witness, and he engaged in fervent evangelistic activity.

The history of the martyrs in the Christian Church contains some basic elements. There is always evident the conflict with Satan and/or his agents. They all share in the imitation and extension of the sufferings of Christ (cf. Paul, in Rom. 8:17). In some unique if not mysterious way they found His support in the time of persecution and/or death even to the point that they sensed an unusual infilling of power and joy.

These common denominators go back to ideas and ideals set forth in the NT (Matt. 5:11 ff; 10:17 ff; 16:24 ff; Acts 5:41; Rom. 5:3 ff).

To be a valid witness one must stake everything, including his life, on the veracity of the truth he espouses and lives out. Jesus' answer to Pilate's question, "What is truth?" was what He did—the Cross. He had just said, "My task is to bear witness *[martus]* to the truth" (John 18:37, NEB).

See TESTIMONY (WITNESS), CONSECRATE (CONSECRATION).

For Further Reading: Foxe, *Book of Martyrs;* Sangster, *The Pure in Heart,* 62 ff, 107-8.

JOSEPH H. MAYFIELD

MARXISM. Marxism, the ideological basis of Communism, purports to explain everything of importance in history and society. As a social and political movement, it commands the passionate allegiance of millions. As social philosophy, it is also termed *dialectical materialism* and *economic determinism.*

Karl Marx (1818-83), a brilliant, highly educated German radical, produced in 1848, along with Friedrich Engels, the 1,500-word *Communist Manifesto,* which sums up Marxist ideology. Engels, son of a wealthy Englishman, became Marx's lifetime protégé and sponsor. Twice expelled from Germany, Marx lived first in Paris, and from 1849 to his death, in London. His four-volume work, *Das Kapital* (Capital), is the sacred scriptures of Marxism.

Marx borrowed Hegel's dialectical explanation of history, applying it, however, not to spiritual, but to material factors. Thus Marxism is materialistic, deterministic, and atheistic. It is congenial to the theory of evolution applied to cultural matters.

Marx theorized that all cultural change is determined by the mode of economic production. The ultimate social malady is economic. Those who own the means of production (the class called the bourgeoisie) take from those who have only labor to sell (the class called the proletariat) the surplus value of their labor, creating class enmity and struggle. This self-produced dialectic is the inevitable source of new social movements. The state, itself the product of economic forces, must protect the capitalist system, a fact which makes violent revolution necessary. After revolution, the temporary "dictatorship of the proletariat" will yield to "economic democracy," a classless society in which the people control the means of production. The state will "wither away." Religion, which is the "opiate of the people," will be eradicated. The final ideal will be: "From each according to his ability, to each according to his need."

Lenin altered "inevitable progress" to "voluntarism." Under Stalin Communism became infallible state teaching accompanied by secret police and the horror of political purges of all dissident ideas and persons. The inevitability of war became dogma. Various revolutions have produced industrial serfdoms and dictatorships of the Communist Party. The only acknowledged "right" is that which produces desired changes.

There is a popular existential form of Marxism, a philosophy of liberation, based on a theory of human alienation under capitalism, but it is scarcely compatible with the central dogma of Marx.

In spite of the failure of Marxist theories the mythology persists, a tribute to its ambiguous appeal to democratic ideals, and to the proud search for a humanistic salvation.

See CHRISTIAN SOCIALISM, LIBERATION THEOLOGY.

For Further Reading: Shook, in *Dictionary of the History of Ideas;* DeKoster, *Communism and Christian Faith;* Marcuse, *Soviet Marxism: A Critical Analysis;* Solzhenitsyn, *Warning to the West.*

ARNOLD E. AIRHART

MASS. The word *mass* means "sacrifice." In Roman Catholic teaching, the mass is a time when Jesus Christ is resacrificed for the communicant's sins. It is identical to the time when He was sacrificed on the Cross, except that, on Catholic altars, it is an unbloody sacrifice. When Christ is thus resacrificed, Catholics understand this to be a priest's highest office, and the communicant's highest act of worship. They understand that, through the priest, the substance of the bread and wine becomes the actual body and blood of Christ, even though the appearance of the elements does not change

In the early centuries, Origen and others viewed the eucharistic elements as symbols. Others, such as Cyril of Jerusalem, began to teach vaguely that there is some kind of mystical change in the elements. Gradually, the "mystical change" view won out. This, especially in 851 when Paschasius Radbertus wrote a treatise on the Lord's Supper taking the view later called transubstantiation: that the substance of the elements becomes transformed into Christ's body and blood.

As Protestants view the matter, Christ does not need to be resacrificed. Christ is not physically present in the Lord's Supper but is present spiritually. They also understand that the Supper is a sacramental means of grace for the communicant only; not for others, in purgatory, as Catholics teach.

See CATHOLICISM (ROMAN), HOLY COMMUNION.

For Further Reading: Boettner, *Roman Catholicism,* 168 ff; Lebbe, *The Mass;* Sheppard, *The Mass in the West.*

J. KENNETH GRIDER

MATERIALISM. Materialism is one of the oldest attempts to explain systematically the nature of existence. From early Greek philosophers (Thales, Anaximenes, Heraclitus, Democritus) to Thomas Hobbes in the 17th century and Marx in the 19th, materialism has had an appeal. According to this view, all things, including the functioning of the mind and the flow of history, depend upon matter and physical processes. Materialism is not simply the acknowledgment that matter exists, but the doctrine that matter is all there is. Materialism, as such, has no place for God or any kind of transcendent, spiritual, nonmaterial reality. Mind is epiphenomenal.

The strongest argument for metaphysical materialism arises out of the fact that sense-perception is the basis for all knowledge. Nerves, brain, the physical senses—all are material. However, materialism does not adequately explain how new ideas arise out of sense data. Even our perception of matter is incomplete. Recent study of subatomic particles suggests that energy or radiation may come nearer explaining matter. The first act of God in creation ("Let there be light") supports this view (see also Heb. 11:3, NIV).

Moral materialism has been defined by Abraham Kaplan *(In Pursuit of Wisdom)* as "the pursuit of pleasure, power, or profit." Thus persons may be materialists at heart even though they disavow metaphysical materialism. The Pharisees and Sadducees of Jesus' day were theists yet materialistic. It has ever been a problem for man to live for spiritual values in a material world.

Gnosticism viewed all matter as evil and attempted to produce the spiritual man by imparting a special knowledge. Some Gnostics taught that for one who possessed this knowledge, indulgence of the flesh could not affect the spirit. Others emphasized escape from the material world through asceticism.

However, Christianity rejects both views. It distinguishes between *materialism* and *materiality* (the state or quality of being material). Material things are part of God's "good" creation to be received with thanksgiving (Gen. 1:31; 1 Tim. 4:3-4). The body is God's temple and will be resurrected in the last day. What God created, inhabits, redeems, and purposes to resurrect, is not to be despised or misused (1 Cor. 6:18-19; 2 Cor. 6:16; 1 Corinthians 15). The Christian rejoices in material things as gifts from God (2 Cor. 6:10; 1 Tim. 6:19) not as sin, but as responsibility. He is a steward to manage his Master's resources for his Master's pleasure (Matt. 25:14-30).

The Christian is warned of the peril of materialism—of being ruled by lust for the world (Matt. 6:24; 13:22; 1 John 2:15-17). Not setting his heart on riches (Ps. 62:10; 1 Tim. 6:9; Luke 12:16-21), he is to help the needy (vv. 33-34; Acts 20:35; 1

Tim. 6:17-19). Covetousness is sin (Rom. 1:28-29; Eph. 5:5). Moderation, discipline, and freedom from anxiety are the ideal (Matt. 6:24-34; 1 Cor. 7:31; Phil. 4:5-6).

See MONEY, METAPHYSICS, BEING, REALISM, GNOSTICISM, BODY, DUALISM.

For Further Reading: Kaplan, *In Pursuit of Wisdom,* 243; Sider, *Rich Christians in an Age of Hunger: A Biblical Study;* Webber, *Common Roots;* White, *The Golden Cow.*

G. R. FRENCH

MATURITY. The concept of maturity, like the idea of growth, comes from the Latin *maturus,* "ripe." To be biologically mature is to have completed a natural procss of growth and development. All living organisms reach their God-intended maturity unless the process of growth is interrupted and life is altered or destroyed.

A further factor in maturing appears where self-consciousness and purpose enter into the growing process. Human beings are said to be mature when they have attained a reasonable level of stability, wisdom, and competence.

Maturity in a theological sense refers to a high level of spiritual and moral development. The concept is clear in the NT, but the term is seldom used in the KJV; it appears more often in recent English translations.

Natural human maturity comes as a result of two forces, (1) the native, God-given growth patterns of body and mind, and (2) personal study disciplines that improve and expand the mind.

In spiritual growth, however, a third factor comes into play: God gives His Holy Spirit as a purifying, empowering agent. The Holy Spirit is a gift of free grace to all who desire Him: "If ye then, being evil, know how to give good gifts unto your children: how much more shall your heavenly Father give the Holy Spirit to them that ask him?" (Luke 11:13).

When the Spirit comes in His fullness, He purifies our hearts by faith (Acts 15:9). Because He comes in response to faith, and because He is God's gift to us, He brings purity in a moment of time.

"Entire sanctification, as understood by holiness people, does not admit of degrees. It is as perfect and complete in its kind as the work of regeneration and justification is perfect and complete in its kind. This does not mean that there is no growth in grace both before and after sanctification. What it does mean is that sanctification, as an act of God, is instantaneous, and is not produced by growth or self-discipline or progressive control of the carnal nature" (Purkiser, *Conflicting Concepts of Holiness,* 30).

Thus we do not grow *into* holiness, but we do grow *in* holiness after entire sanctification. And we move more rapidly toward mature Christian life because we have been empowered by the Holy Spirit. Such growth and maturity are not accomplished by sheer determination and human effort. We make progress in the things of God when we yield ourselves to Him. Paul writes, "If ye through the Spirit do mortify the deeds of the body, ye shall live" (Rom. 8:13).

But in our movement toward maturity there is also the determined action of a human spirit now completely committed to the whole will of God. The Bible teaches that in addition to being filled with the Holy Spirit (John 16:13), spiritual maturity is achieved by putting away childish attitudes (1 Cor. 13:11); by improved understanding (14:20); by overcoming temptation (1 John 2:14); by partaking of the deeper truths of the gospel (Heb. 5:14); and by striving toward the ideal of Christlikeness (Eph. 4:3).

Christian maturity, then, is completeness in Christ. It is the whole human personality—body, mind, emotions, and will—dedicated to the will of God. But spiritual maturity is also a consequence of this total commitment. Maturity is never fully reached as long as we are still growing—and it is God's plan that we should grow at least as long as we live on this earth. Our goal is complete Christlikeness. While never fully achieved in this life, we are always moving closer to "reaching maturity, reaching the full measure of development which belongs to the fulness of Christ" (Eph. 4:13, Moffatt).

See GROW (GROWTH), PROGRESSIVE SANCTIFICATION, CHRISTIAN PERFECTION, PURITY AND MATURITY.

For Further Reading: Purkiser, *Conflicting Concepts of Holiness,* 29-44; Wiley, *CT,* 3:51-67; *GMS,* 508-26.

A. F. HARPER

MEANS OF GRACE. A broad definition of the *means of grace* is that they are "divinely appointed channels through which the influences of the Holy Spirit are communicated to the souls of men" (Wiley). Such a broad definition would encompass all aspects of Christian life, especially private and corporate worship, including prayer, fellowship, preaching, sacraments, etc.

An examination of how the means of grace have been understood in Christian tradition produces a narrowing of the definition to two main forms: (1) the sacraments and (2) the Word. The place of each as a means of grace is generally established in the Christian world. But a dispute about the primacy of one over the other is a fracture-line in the Protestant/Catholic division.

In Roman Catholic tradition the sacrament takes primacy over the Word as the means of grace. Through the sacrament the virtue of the passion of Christ is mediated to the recipient. A sacrament functions *ex opere operato,* that is, by virtue of a power within the sacrament itself.

The Protestant Reformation insisted upon reversing the primacy of sacrament to Word. Through the hearing of the Word, by the operation of the Holy Spirit, faith is born and thus the benefits of the passion of Christ are mediated. Only inasmuch as a sacrament is joined to the faith of the recipient can it become a means of grace. The Word is primary as the means of grace.

Emphasis upon the Word as the means of grace in Protestantism legitimizes a broader concept of means of grace. The Word is heard in preaching primarily. But it may come to human beings in the home and in the school, through conversation and through literature.

Thus we are led full circle to the broader definition of the means of grace which include prayer, meditation, fellowship, devotional reading, corporate worship, preaching, and the sacraments.

One of the most vigorous accents in the teaching of John Wesley was his insistence on observing all available means of grace. The seeker (for either pardon or perfect love) was instructed to be faithful therein until faith came; those having been justified and sanctified wholly were exhorted to use all regular aids in order to maintain and grow in grace. Wesley refused to be intimidated by those detractors (including the Moravians with their antinomian tendencies) who categorized all such duties as works-righteousness, incompatible with evangelical faith.

See GRACE, WORSHIP, PRAYER, SACRAMENTS, PREACHING.

For Further Reading: Watson, comp., *The Message of the Wesleys,* 157 ff; Wiley, *CT,* 2:460.

DANIEL N. BERG

MEDIATION, MEDIATOR. The infinite distance which separates God and fallen humanity requires mediation if reconciliation is to be realized. Mediation is, theologically defined, the means by which the distance created by sin is bridged, and God and man are reconciled. The heart of the matter is expressed well in 1 Tim. 2:5-6*a:* "For there is one God, and one mediator also between God and men, the man Christ Jesus, who gave Himself as a ransom for all" (NASB).

In the Old Testament. The terms *mediation* and *mediator* do not appear in the OT, but the concepts are worked out in various ways. The principle is embodied in Israel's prophet, priest, and theocratic king. The prophet was God's representative to men; the priest was man's representative to God; and the theocratic king was the anointed representative of Israel's divine Ruler.

Among human mediators in the OT, however, foremost was Moses (cf. Exod. 32:30-32; Num. 12:6-8; Gal. 3:19-20; Heb. 3:2-5), the instrument through whom the covenant was established at Sinai (cf. Exod. 19:3-8; 24:3-8; Acts 7:37-39). Consequently, Jesus, Mediator of the new covenant, is compared and contrasted with Moses.

The supreme eschatological figure of mediator is the Servant of Yahweh who suffers vicariously as an atonement for the people's sins (Isaiah 53). This figure is perfectly fulfilled in the death of Christ.

In the New Testament. The word "mediator," Greek *mesitēs,* occurs six times in the NT (Gal. 3:19-20—of Moses; 1 Tim. 2:5; Heb. 8:6; 9:15; 12:24—of Christ). Oepke questions whether we are justified in regarding Jesus as "the fulfilment of the mediator concept" in view of so few explicit references (Oepke, "mesitēs," Kittel, 4:624). Such skepticism is ill-founded. If the term is rare, the concept is not. All OT figures of mediation intersect in Christ. Only Christ truly brings God and man together. In this sense there is "one mediator" (1 Tim. 2:5). The OT figures were, at best, shadows of the archetypal realities fulfilled in Christ.

The NT presents both the cosmic and redemptive aspects of Christ's mediation. The principal passages bearing on Christ's cosmic mediation are highly significant for Christology (e.g., 1 Cor. 8:6; Col. 1:15-17; Heb. 1:2-3; John 1:1-5). It is the redemptive aspect of Christ's mediation, however, that is most fully presented (e.g., Matt. 11:27-28; 26:26-28; Mark 8:38; 14:22-24; Luke 9:11-27; 22:19-20; John 14:6; Acts 4:12; Eph. 1:10-21; 2:13-18; Col. 1:20; 1 John 2:1-2). The entire Epistle to the Hebrews focuses on Jesus' work as the redemptive Mediator.

Both the Godward and manward sides of Christ's redemptive mediation are emphasized. Since He is the Word become flesh (cf. John 1:14), "the exact representation of His [God's] nature" (Heb. 1:3), Christ is uniquely qualified to represent God to men. Since Jesus can sympathize with our weaknesses, having been tempted as are we, yet without sinning (4:15), He is uniquely qualified to represent men to God. Jesus' death provides the objective ground for our forgiveness and acceptance with God; His resurrection and exaltation provide the basis for His ongoing mediatorial intercession.

See ADVOCATE, PRIEST (PRIESTHOOD), CHRIST, ESTATES OF CHRIST.

For Further Reading: Becker, "mesitēs," *NIDB*, 1:372-76; Blackman, "Mediator, Mediation," *IDB*, 3:320-31; Morris, *The Apostolic Preaching of the Cross;* Murray, "Mediator," *NBD*, 802-4; Oepke, "mesitēs," Kittel, 4:598-624. J. WESLEY ADAMS

MEDITATION. This, generally, is an act in which one thinks carefully in search of or consideration of any truth. Among Christians it is a form of mental prayer or devout reflection involving the memory, the imagination, the emotions, and the intellect, aimed toward spiritual insight and growth. Meditation has always been practiced in the church, and various techniques have been proposed to make it more effective.

As the word *meditation* is used today, it often refers to Transcendental Meditation, a popular movement headed by Maharishi Mahesh Yogi, who left India in 1958 to begin a tour of the West. During a brief training period each meditator is given a secret *mantra* (a Sanskrit word, simply a meaningless sound to the meditator) which is to be repeated during meditation whenever the meditator's mind wanders. The goal of the meditator is unity with the god who is, however, not the personal God of Christianity; and the devotee reaches this by the repetition of his mantra for 20 minutes each morning and evening. He wishes to go beyond all thought to a state of pure awareness. Transcendental Meditation is a version of Hinduism, and advanced meditators find themselves adopting a Hindu philosophy.

Christians are called to a different kind of meditation. They are to meditate on God and His Word day and night so that they will act according to what is in it (Josh. 1:8; Ps. 1:2; 63:6; 119:48). They are also to meditate on God's works (77:12; 143:5). Finally, they are to meditate on true, honest, just, pure, and lovely things which will elevate their thinking (1 Tim. 4:15; Phil. 4:8). Such meditation will be a delight (Ps. 1:2; 104:34). A Christian meditator is *not* to go beyond all thought to lose his individuality in pure being, but to find his identity as a child of God.

See TRANSCENDENTAL MEDITATION, DEVOTE (DEVOTION), PRAYER.

For Further Reading: Haddon and Hamilton, *TM Wants You!* Lewis, *What Everyone Should Know About Transcendental Meditation;* Pipkin, *Christian Meditation.* RONALD L. KOTESKEY

MEEKNESS. Meekness is that poise and selflessness in those who are truly strong which frees them from the compulsion to prove their strength.

Moses, demonstrating massive strength in reserve and unrestricted concern for the people under his care, is an enfleshment of meekness in the OT (Num. 12:3). The perspective which is typified by Moses is in the frame of reference of belief in the God of the covenant who will judge and recompense as well as justify the meek in spirit.

Jesus is the enfleshment of meekness in the NT. He is completely free of motives of self-service. He is confident, sufficient, and thereby free to serve people without using them. He is enough (Matt. 11:29). He is strong enough for any task in the fulfillment of the will of the Father, yet is not compelled to exercise undue force to prove it.

Historically, the concept has been distorted by non-Christian mind-sets which, by their limitations, are incapable of handling strength without subjugating the weak. Consequently, the grand word "meekness" as a Christlike quality (and the eighth of the nine fruits of the Spirit in Gal. 5:22-23), has been changed to denote a weak and passive characteristic.

Meekness resembles humility and gentleness, while it also includes the active qualities of courage and confidence in one's resources. It is the opposite of the pride and self-assertion which results from lack of self-identity as a Christian. It connotes a healing and restorative quality as it deals with other people (Gal. 6:1).

Meekness is in contrast to the characteristics of the carnal nature, since self-centered man cannot deal with others unselfishly. Meekness is confused with weakness by the one who is not cleansed of the spirit of pride and self-elevation.

In Christian terminology, then, meekness is an essential Christian virtue and an evidence of the Spirit-filled and Spirit-directed life. It demonstrates the confidence and resiliency which result from unreserved trust in and an unconditional obedience to God in Christ Jesus.

See SEVEN CARDINAL VIRTUES, HUMILITY, CHRISTLIKENESS, MIND OF CHRIST, GENTLENESS.

For Further Reading: Kittel, 6:645-51; *Nave's Topical Bible*, 830-32. GORDON WETMORE

MELCHIZEDEK. Melchizedek, "righteousness is my king," or "king of righteousness," is mentioned in Gen. 14:18-20; Ps. 110:4; and in Heb. 5:6-11; 6:20—7:28.

In Gen. 14:18-20 Abram, returning from the

defeat of the four kings, is met by Melchizedek, "king of Salem" and "priest of God Most High" (NIV). Melchizedek brought out bread and wine, presumably to refresh Abram. Then he blessed Abram by God Most High, blessed God Most High for giving Abram the victory, and, although a foreigner, received tithes from Abram. Salem is usually thought to be Jerusalem (Ps. 76:2), and Melchizedek, a Canaanite king. "God Most High" was a title for God among Canaanites and Phoenicians. Nevertheless, the Bible identifies the God of Abraham with the God of Melchizedek.

In Ps. 110:4 the Lord, with an oath, proclaims the Davidic king a "priest for ever after the order of Melchizedek." Jesus applied Ps. 110:1 to himself (Mark 12:35 ff), and in this He was followed by much of the NT. Only in Hebrews is Ps. 110:4 applied to Jesus.

In Heb. 6:20—7:28, Gen. 14:18-20 is used to aid in the application of Ps. 110:4 to Christ. Melchizedek is superior to Levi, as proven by the fact that Levi's father Abraham paid tithes to Melchizedek and also by the fact that Melchizedek "lives" (Heb. 7:1-10). Therefore Jesus, the "priest . . . after the order of Melchisedec," the priest "after the power of an endless life," replaces the merely typical Aaronic/Levitical priesthood (vv. 11-25). This new Priest is able to save completely (v. 25).

Most interpreters understand v. 3 to mean that Melchizedek's lack of genealogy made him a symbol of the eternal priesthood of Christ. A few interpreters have held that the verse describes Melchizedek as an eternal being, a preincarnate manifestation of Christ or a theophany similar to the appearances of the Angel of the Lord in other parts of Genesis. The sudden appearance and disappearance of Melchizedek in Genesis 14 is not altogether uncongenial to this interpretation.

Philo allegorized Melchizedek as "divine reason" in man. Josephus refers to him as the first priest, the founder of the Temple at Jerusalem. The rabbis sometimes identified him with Shem, to avoid Abram's giving tithes to a foreigner. The Dead Sea Scroll 11QMelch depicts Melchizedek as the angel who in the last days will deliver God's chosen people and bring judgment on the wicked. This scroll has little apparent relationship to Hebrews 7.

See ABRAHAM, HIGH PRIESTHOOD OF CHRIST.

For Further Reading: Waltke, *ZPEB*, 4:177-78; Horton, *The Melchizedek Tradition;* Demarest, *The Evangelical Quarterly* (July, 1977), 141-62.

GARETH LEE COCKERILL

MEMORIAL THEORY. See HOLY COMMUNION.

MERCY. In the deepest sense, mercy is an attribute of God given to His creation. For this reason we find the verb "to be merciful" attributed to God and man in both the OT and NT. Although the word may be translated "have compassion," there is a significant theological difference carried by the term "mercy," especially when referring to God's mercy to man.

The OT's main word for "mercy" denotes a combination of righteousness and love. Many Bible scholars are inclined to translate the word as "steadfast love," implying that God has entered into a covenant with His people. The result of this relationship is a readiness on God's part to relieve the oppressed and pardon the guilty. It is in the context of relief and pardon that God's righteous love becomes mercy. Mercy is compassion in action. Although guilty and deserving no mitigation, God's mercy is extended to man; and when accepted, it results in pardon. Only as man accepts the steadfast love of God revealed in the Cross can he receive mercy and experience pardon from sin.

See SUPPLICATION, JUSTICE, GRACE.

For Further Reading: *HDB*, 644: *IDB*, 3:352-54.

W. STEPHEN GUNTER

MERCY SEAT. From the biblical languages this means "propitiation" or "place or means of atonement." It was an important object of the Tabernacle preempted and fulfilled by Jesus, Lord and Savior.

In the Pentateuch the mercy seat was a base of fine gold, about four feet long and two and one-half feet wide (Exod. 25:17; 37:6), with a cherub at each end. The cherubim faced each other with outstretched wings, touching each other at the midpoint above (25:18-20; 37:7-9). It fit on top of the ark of the covenant, which was placed beyond the veil inside the holy of holies (Exod. 26:34; 30:6). Within the inner sanctum God spoke to Moses concerning His people Israel (Num. 7:89; cf. Exod. 25:21-22). To the mercy seat the high priest applied atoning blood on the annual Day of Atonement (Lev. 16:2, 13-15).

From archaeology it is known that the Israelites reflected their cultural setting in the use of cherubim. However, they rejected their cultural setting by prohibiting an image of their God, Yahweh, on the cherubim, in keeping with the second commandment. Further, the mercy seat, where God *abode* in His invisible presence, was sprinkled with atoning blood on the annual

Day of Atonement and therefore was the place and means whereby God in mercy forgave sin among the people of Israel.

In the NT the passing reference to "mercy seat" in the Epistle to the Hebrews (9:5) suggests that it and other older covenant features have been superseded and fulfilled in Jesus Christ.

See MOSAIC LAW, SACRIFICE, ARK OF THE COVENANT, DAY OF ATONEMENT, BLOOD, HOLY OF HOLIES, TEMPLE, VEIL.

For Further Reading: *IDB*, 1:354; Wright, *Biblical Archaeology*, 98-119, 136-40; *Wycliffe Bible Encyclopedia*, 1104, 1416.

HARVEY E. FINLEY

MERIT. See WORK (WORKS).

MESSIAH. The word "Messiah" is derived from the Hebrew word *meshiach* and means "anointed" or "the anointed"; its Greek form is *Christos*, and its English equivalent is "Christ." "On the early pages of the New Testament, 'Christos' occurs with the definite article, 'the Christ' (e.g., Matt. 16:16; 27:22; John 4:29; 1 John 2:22; 5:1). It was only later that 'Christ' came to function as a name rather than as a title" (*GMS*, 183).

In the OT, when applied to persons, the term indicates induction into a sacred office. It is "applied exceptionally to prophets, occasionally to the chief priests and most commonly to the king of Israel, 'the Messiah of Yahweh'" (Bruce, *New Testament History*, 122). For example, Saul is designated "the Meshiach of Yahweh," the anointed of the Lord (1 Sam. 24:6). In general usage kings, high priests, the Jewish people as a whole, even non-Jewish Cyrus, the king of Persia (since he was used by God to accomplish the divine purpose) were spoken of as "the anointed of the Lord" (Exod. 29:7; Isa. 45:1; 61:1; Psalms 2; 28:8).

In the centuries following the destruction of Judea (586 B.C.), the Jews found their hopes centering upon an early restoration of their independence and the reestablishing of the monarchy by a descendant of David, whose throne would be "forever" (2 Sam. 7:16; Ps. 89:29). Haggai and Zechariah saw this future king who would be Meshiach Yahweh (Zech. 3:8; 6:12-13; 9:9-16; 12:8; 14:3-4).

Beside this national hope or superimposed upon it was the slowly emerging vision of "the Day of the Lord," a time of moral and spiritual meaning, when sin would be punished, whether Israel's or others', and when universal righteousness and peace would reign over all men, with Jerusalem, "the joy of the whole earth," as the center of it all. This universal dimension in OT "messiahship," while sometimes obscured by nationalism, is consistent with Jewish monotheism. "It flashes through the darkness in Isaiah in the four Servant songs (42:1-7; 49:1-7; 50:4-11; 52:13—53:12), where is seen the Servant of Yahweh whose mission is the spread of the knowledge of the true God to the ends of the earth . . . not by imposing his will on others but by uncomplaining endurance of contempt, injustice, suffering and death" (Bruce, *New Testament History*, 128). But it comes to its true focal point and fulfillment in the words "the anointed Lord" (*Christos Kyrios*), used so significantly in the angelic annunciation to the shepherds in Bethlehem (Luke 2:11).

All Bible scholars recognize the duality, if not multiplicity, of Jewish "messiah" concepts at the time of Christ. Theologically liberal Jewish and Christian theologians are prone to emphasize the nationalistic concepts and to minimize or deny the universal and spiritual mission of Christ. This point of view is expressed by Rabbi Silver and M. S. Eslin in *ER*, 485 ff. An opposite, though much less serious, error is found in some conservative eschatology when historical substance is largely ignored or allegorized into prophetic interpretation.

Sound biblical exegesis exposes the unity of the Bible in progressive revelation, lays bare the realities of God's redemptive work with a wayward Israel, and then lets shine forth the glories of the kingdom of God through our Lord Jesus Christ, the Messiah.

See CHRIST, SON OF MAN, PROMISES (DAVIDIC), DAY OF THE LORD, PROGRESSIVE REVELATION.

For Further Reading: *GMS*, 183-93, 322-28.

JOHN E. RILEY

METAPHYSICS. The term *metaphysics* refers to that branch of philosophy which deals with the nature of what is called "ultimate reality" or Being as such. *Ontology* is sometimes used as a synonym for *metaphysics*. The term originated curiously from a reference to the place occupied on Aristotle's bookshelf by his volume on "first principles"—that is "after" (*meta*) the "physics" (*physica*)!

Metaphysics, as a subject of human thought, originated with the Greek thinkers of the sixth century B.C. who were concerned about the nature of the stuff out of which everything else is made: the *basic principle* of the universe. In the two and one-half millennia since then, scores, perhaps hundreds, of views have been formulated in answer to this question.

Metaphysics, through the centuries, has

played an important role in Christian theology by providing to theologians a ready-made vehicle for interpreting Christian thought to a non-Christian world—a world which already understands the particular metaphysical view selected.

The employment of metaphysical thought in this task has not been universally accepted by the church. During the patristic period there was opposition to all pagan thought in the writings of Tertullian, who asked, "What has Athens to do with Jerusalem?" Clement of Alexandria, however, considered philosophy to be an excellent preparation for the knowledge of God. In the writings of Augustine, bishop of Hippo, it is possible to see the influence of Plotinus, whose metaphysics asserted a single, all-inclusive deity.

During the early Middle Ages, a strong Platonic influence which stressed the role of eternal forms (Ideas) may be seen in the theology of Anselm of Canterbury. In the later Middle Ages, in the theology of Thomas Aquinas, we find great use of the metaphysics of Aristotle—a view which sees the entire universe as seeking to realize Pure Form, the First Cause, the completely transcendent God.

Since the Reformation, metaphysics has not played as dominant a role in Christian theology as before, although liberal Protestantism in the 19th and 20th centuries derived much help from idealistic metaphysics (primacy of "mind" as ultimate reality). The recent decline of metaphysics within philosophical circles has influenced much contemporary theology: the existentialism of Soren Kierkegaard and Paul Tillich, neoorthodoxy, and radical theology.

See NATURAL THEOLOGY, ONTOLOGICAL ARGUMENT, PERSONALISM, ONTOLOGY.

For Further Reading: Since most books on metaphysics contain the author's *particular* metaphysical view, the reader who desires to understand the field in a *general* way would be advised to consult a recent introduction to philosophy and to read the chapters or section which deal with the topic of metaphysics. One such popular book is Titus and Smith, *Living Issues in Philosophy*, 6th ed. (1974). Almost any other such text would do, however. ALVIN HAROLD KAUFFMAN

METEMPSYCHOSIS. See REINCARNATION.

METHODISM. John Wesley writes definitively of the people called Methodists. In November, 1729, four young men of Oxford—John Wesley, Charles Wesley, Mr. Morgan, and Mr. Kirkman—began to spend some evenings each week to read together, chiefly the Greek NT. Others joined them later. "The exact regularity of their lives, as well as studies, occasioned a young gentleman of Christ Church to say, 'Here is a new set of Methodists sprung up,' alluding to some ancient physicians who were so called (because they taught that almost all diseases might be cured by a specific *method* of diet and exercise). The name was new and quaint; so it took immediately, and the Methodists were known all over the University" (*Works,* 8:339, 348).

These four Methodists were zealous members of the Church of England and also carefully followed the university statutes, "but they observed neither these nor anything else any further than they conceived it was bound upon them by their one book, the Bible." It was their "one desire to be downright Bible-Christians, taking the Bible, as interpreted by the primitive Church and their own, for their whole and sole rule." The charge laid against Methodists was that they were too scrupulous, too strict in following the teachings of the church and the statutes of the university.

John Wesley's mother, Susanna, in a long letter to John explained that in rearing her children, all were "always put into a regular *method* of living, in such things as they were capable of, from their birth, as in dressing and undressing, changing their linen, etc."

So first of all Methodism relates to a methodical practice of piety, in prayer and Bible reading, in visiting the sick, in helping the poor, in regularly attending the sacraments and services of the church.

Methodism in the second place relates to various evangelistic methods in teaching and preaching Christ. In addition to evangelism by sermons, printed tracts, and books, John Wesley introduced itinerant evangelism. On foot and horseback Wesley took the gospel across England, Wales, Scotland, and into Ireland. Some heart-warmed laymen began to share their faith, and Wesley, following his mother's advice, refused to forbid them. In fact, had not John Wesley received and trained laymen to be itinerant soul winners, Methodism would not have captured England. But any method that honored Christ, John Wesley approved: street meetings, house-to-house meetings, field preaching, prison ministries, and others. Methodism is the gospel on the move.

In the third place, Methodism may be known by its synergistic theology. One may observe these types of soteriological theology: (1) that of liturgy and sacrament; (2) that of creed and confession; (3) that of universalism; and (4) that of the divine-human encounter and cooperation. Methodism belongs to the fourth class.

At issue are the mysteries of free will and of sovereign election. No one who reads the Bible will deny that man is responsible for his damnation, if he is lost, or that Christ alone is to be praised, if man is saved. To systematize a theology that accents one mystery at the expense of the other is neither necessary nor wise. Methodist theology includes both emphases, holding them as twin truths in tension, unwilling to reject one or the other, and willing to admit that the salvation of any one person is quite as mysterious, if not so unique, as the incarnation of God in Jesus Christ.

Methodistic doctrine and Methodistic evangelism go together. The "persuasive techniques" of Methodistic evangelism—so strongly condemned by strict Calvinists—are logically the extension of the Methodist doctrine of free will, meaning a freedom to accept or reject the overtures of the gospel. In this respect Methodism is Pauline (2 Cor. 5:11; Phil. 2:12-13). Yet Methodism, when true to its moorings, is not Pelagian, but Augustinian, in its view of sin and human depravity. The ability of the sinner to decide for or against Christ is not traced to natural ability but to prevenient grace, as a universal and unconditional benefit of the Atonement.

See WESLEYANISM, HOLINESS MOVEMENT (THE), ARMINIANISM, AUGUSTINIANISM.

For Further Reading: Wilcox, *Be Ye Holy;* Rose, *A Theology of Christian Experience;* Turner, *The Vision Which Transforms.* GEORGE E. FAILING

MIGHT. See POWER.

MILLENNIUM. The word (from the Latin *mille,* "a thousand") refers to the idea of a future reign of Christ with His saints on the earth for a period of 1,000 years. Those who embrace the idea are called millennarians or chiliasts (from the Greek *chilias,* "a thousand").

The idea is rooted in the Jewish expectation that the advent of the Messiah and the inauguration of the new age would bring about the final destruction of evil in the world order. God's chosen people would be restored to national integrity and righteousness and would live in holiness upon earth (cf. Daniel 7).

This hope was taken over into Jewish-Christian apocalyptic, with the Church being identified by many as the new Israel, the restored people of the Messianic kingdom. Jesus used the prophetic imagery of the Messianic banquet (Luke 22:16; cf. Isa. 25:6-8; Luke 14:15) and spoke of His apostles as reigning in that day (Matt. 19:28).

However, the most influential passage on millennial thought is Rev. 20:1-7, the only NT mention of a 1,000-year rule of Christ's resurrected saints. This passage is chiefly responsible for the belief that at the end of this age, but before the final bliss of heaven, there will be an intermediate period on earth (a millennial kingdom) in which Christ will reign with His saints.

One's view of the millennium will be determined largely by one's answer to two basic questions. First, what is the relation between the millennium and the second coming of Christ? Different answers to that question are represented by premillennialism, postmillennialism, and to some extent amillennialism. Second, how does one interpret apocalyptic literature in general, and Rev. 20:1-7 in particular, especially the words "a [or the] thousand years"?

In regard to the second question, some choose to interpret the words *literally,* expecting an earthly millennial kingdom of 1,000 years duration either following or preceding Christ's second coming. Others take the words *symbolically,* as expressing the believer's hope for the future and his faith in the ultimate triumph of God and His Christ, arguing that since apocalyptic literature is replete with symbolism, it is inconsistent to make an exception in the interpretation of Rev. 20:1-7.

See ESCHATOLOGY, AMILLENNIALISM, PREMILLENNIALISM, REVELATION (BOOK OF).

For Further Reading: Clouse, ed., *The Meaning of the Millennium;* Erickson, *Contemporary Options in Eschatology;* Lawson, *Comprehensive Handbook of Christian Doctrine,* 236-56; Lohse, "Chilias," Kittel, 9:466-71; Ludwigson, *A Survey of Bible Prophecy;* Ladd, *Crucial Questions About the Kingdom of God.* ROB L. STAPLES

MIND. In general current usage, *mind* or *intellect* refers to that part of a person that enables him to know, to think, to will, to act. It is regarded as being distinct from the body.

In the English Bible, "mind" is used to translate several Hebrew and Greek terms. While all of those terms differ somewhat in meaning, they all do include the idea of a person's capacity for rational thought.

Among the important Hebrew words translated "mind" is *lebh* —usually translated "heart." It refers to a person's inmost center of personality which determines his outward acts. It is used especially, it would seem, with reference to recollection (Isa. 65:17) or purpose (Jer. 19:5). *Nephesh*—usually translated "soul"—is also sometimes translated "mind" to designate the deepest part of man, the self, the personal center of feelings, desires, and inclination.

In the NT we are admonished to love God with all the "mind" (Mark 12:30). The Greek term here is *dianoia,* referring to a person's power of reason, perception, imagination—his creativity.

Paul declared, "I myself in my mind am a slave to God's law" (Rom. 7:25, NIV). The Greek word here is *nous,* the seat of a person's reflective consciousness. In a later passage the apostle, using the same term, urges his readers to "be transformed by the renewing of your mind" (12:2, NIV). He seeks thereby to show that the transformed mind is a new, a different mind. It will provide new thought patterns, give a new orientation to life. No longer conformed to the world, the Christian no longer thinks like the world. His viewpoint is changed.

In both of these passages Paul uses "mind" to mean a person's inner self which is able to reflect and purpose. It is the mind, as Paul uses the word, which enables a person to understand the revelation of God and respond to it. We see, then, that in the use of "mind" the apostle Paul stresses action rather than abstract thought.

Paul also speaks of the carnal, sinful mind being hostile toward God (Rom. 8:7). The Greek term for "mind" in this instance is *phronēma,* which refers to the habitual disposition of a person's intellectual faculty, his frame of mind, his bent. Literally it is the mind-set or bent toward the flesh.

We see in the various contexts a variety of inferences expressed by the word "mind." But there is so much overlapping and interpenetration in the meanings that one is brought to see that in spite of the various faculties suggested, the Bible indicates man to be a holistic being. In fact, in a very real sense "mind" is often used in the Bible to mean the whole person, practically the same as soul (Rom. 1:28; 2 Tim. 3:8).

See MAN, HUMAN NATURE, HEART, SOUL, SPIRIT.

For Further Reading: *IDB,* 3:383-84; Purkiser, ed., *Exploring Our Christian Faith,* 218-20; *GMS,* 257-62, 334.

ARMOR D. PEISKER

MIND OF CHRIST. This term is based on the KJV rendering of Phil. 2:5—"Let this mind be in you, which was also in Christ Jesus." Its significance is twofold: first, it demands an inquiry into the nature of Christ's mind; and second, it raises the problem of the possibility of that mind being in us, and the means by which this can occur.

It should be noted at the outset that this verse is one of a cluster of passages which stress Christlikeness as the objective of God's grace, and make this inner conformity the central essence of Christian character. Our predestination, declares Rom. 8:29, is to be "conformed to the image of His Son" (NASB). While this conformation must await the resurrection for its full consummation, its essence must and may be experienced now, by crisis and process (Rom. 12:1-2; 2 Cor. 3:18; 1 John 3:2-3). Another example of this cluster of related texts is Gal. 4:19—"My children, with whom I am again in labor until Christ is formed in you" (NASB). The birth pangs once experienced by the apostle in bringing forth these spiritual children are now being experienced the second time. The purpose of this apostolic travail is for Christ himself, in His very character, to be reproduced in them.

The Philippians verse carries a similar import. The exact meaning of the passage only partly turns on *phroneite,* "let this mind," or "be minded," but we must begin here. The verb *phroneō,* "to be minded," is in v. 2, also 3:16; 4:2; and elsewhere. The exact sense in v. 5 is best expressed by "to be in a certain frame of mind" (*Analytical Greek Lexicon*). Earle believes that Lightfoot most aptly renders the clause: "Reflect in your minds the mind of Christ Jesus" (*WMNT,* 5:33). The substitution of "attitude" for "mind" in NASB and NIV is not an improvement, for it is putting a weak word for a strong one. "Mind-set" would be better, as it would more nearly express the deeply rooted disposition which is intended.

Apart from the word *phroneite,* Paul makes perfectly clear in vv. 6-8 exactly what he means by the mind of Christ. It is a mind or disposition motivated by love for a lost world, a love demonstrated by emptying himself of His heavenly glory, and though truly God, becoming truly man; not only a man but a slave who is obedient unto death, even the death of the Cross. Such a mind is marked by humility, sacrifice, and total unselfishness.

The relevance of this mind to the Philippians is seen in the fact that this exhortation or command is the culmination of vv. 1-4. They will succeed in relating themselves to each other as indicated in those verses if they are governed by the same frame of mind which prompted the Second Person of the Trinity to become our Redeemer. The possibility of Christians actually possessing such a mind-set is a staggering conception. But its difficulty is due primarily to the presence of its opposite, the carnal mind, with its disposition toward pride, self-serving, and self-willfulness. The radical displacement of one mind by another cannot occur simply by resolving, but only by a profound work of divine grace.

See CARNAL MIND, KOINONIA, AGAPĒ, HOLINESS, KENOSIS, MEEKNESS.

For Further Reading: *GMS,* 464-66; Wesley, *Works,* 10:364.
RICHARD S. TAYLOR

MINISTER, MINISTRY. "Minister" comes from the same root as *minor,* "less," and etymologically means "servant." "Whosoever will be great among you, let him be your minister" (Matt. 20:26). The term has come to have a wide spread of usages from the humblest servant to the exalted official: ecclesiastical, such as clergy, pastor, or priest; social, such as officer or administrator; political, such as an official representative or executive of a sovereign state up to ambassador or prime minister. In its verb form "minister" may mean to serve, to supply, to provide, to do things helpful, or to adminster; each of these meanings may be found in the NT.

Vine provides an excellent NT study of terms for "minister": *diakonos,* a servant, attendant, deacon (Mark 10:43; Rom. 13:4; 1 Cor. 3:5; Eph. 6:21); *leitourgos,* a public servant (Heb. 8:2; 1:7; Rom. 13:6; 15:16; Phil. 2:25); *hupēretēs,* an under rower as distinguished from *nautēs,* a seaman (Luke 4:20; Acts 13:5; 26:16; 1 Cor. 4:1); *doulos,* a bondservant or slave. Vine says, "Speaking broadly, *diakonos* views a servant in relation to his work; *doulos,* in relation to his master; *hupēretēs,* in relation to his superior; *leitourgos,* in relation to his public service" (Vine's *ED,* 3:72).

The NT Church sets the parameters for the Christian ministry and describes the basic principles, though not the detailed structure, for church life and service.

Although for Protestantism there is a universal priesthood of believers, there were, in the NT, nevertheless, some persons who were called of God and set apart or ordained for special service or ministry. Mark 3:14 and Luke 6:13 tell how the Lord called, chose, and sent out 12 "apostles." Then Luke goes on in 10:1 to record how He ordained 70 and sent them out. In Eph. 4:11-12 Paul enumerates the classes of service in the Church as given by Jesus: "And he gave some, apostles; and some, prophets; and some, evangelists; and some, pastors and teachers . . . for the work of the ministry." Wiley believes that the bishops, elders, and deacons might perform any or all of these offices as needed and as appropriate. Furthermore, he distinguishes the first three as extraordinary and temporary, and the latter two as regular and permanent types of ministry. The elders and bishops are to be responsible for the spiritual care of the churches, while the deacons are to care for the management of its temporal affairs (Wiley, *CT,* 3:129 ff, cf. 118).

Since NT times, ecclesiastical structure and the forms of Christian ministry have been in constant change. There have been churches from the almost formless house groups (no membership or organization), through the small congregational type, to the huge superchurches, to the massive hierarchy of the Roman Catholics. And there has been "ministry" from the humblest teaching of a few believers to the colorful cathedral ritual and the corporation-type multiple staffs of the largest congregations.

In all the diversities of ministry there are a few fundamental principles to be kept in mind: the nature of the NT ministry; the command of our Lord to "go and make disciples of all nations" (Matt. 28:19, modern versions); the guidance and enablement of the Holy Spirit; the spiritual needs of humanity; and the building of the kingdom of God.

Purkiser offers an outline of the NT ministry by noting some of its figures of speech: messenger, voice, fisherman, shepherd, witness, vessel, servant, laborer, builder, steward, athlete, ambassador, playing coach, prisoner of Jesus Christ, pattern, soldier, husbandman. He then notes some of the broader terms: disciple, apostle, elder, bishop, minister, preacher, prophet, evangelist, man of God, priest (*New Testament Image of the Ministry,* 30 ff).

Perhaps the most significant note in all of this for all Christians, whether clergy or laity, is that each is to be a *doulos,* a love slave to Jesus the Lord.

See CLERGY, CHURCH GOVERNMENT, DISCIPLING, SERVANT, SERVICE.

For Further Reading: Wiley, *CT,* 3:118 ff, 129 ff; Kittel; *TWNT.*
JOHN E. RILEY

MIRACLE. A miracle is an event in which God acts to demonstrate His power to assist man in some beneficial way. There are many words in the OT and in the NT for "miracle." One term is *oth,* which is usually translated "sign" (Num. 14:22; Deut. 11:3, RSV). Another Hebrew word for "miracle" is *pala* (Judg. 6:13). It is often used of God's actions in the realm of nature. In the NT the words *sēmeios* (Luke 23:8; John 2:11, 23) and *terata,* "signs and wonders" (cf. RSV) are used to describe the acts of God in unusual ways.

The question of miracles versus natural law has been debated for centuries. Does God ever interrupt the natural process? If He does, what does this mean in our understanding of God in His relationship to man? Some have attempted to explain the unknown in life by holding that a miracle is a phenomenon produced by a natural law which we do not yet understand. This interpretation of "miracle" eliminates the direct action of God in His world.

Our Western view of nature and God is often at odds with biblical man's view. Biblical man saw God at work in the mundane and in the total structure of the universe. The rain and the heat were gifts of God. Thunder and lightning were evidences of His nearness. The processes of life—in the field, in the birth of cattle, and in the life of man—were in the direct will of the Lord. The Psalmist portrays a God who acts in the realm of nature: "When I consider thy heavens, the work of thy fingers, the moon and the stars, which thou hast ordained" (Ps. 8:3); and the prophet presents a God who is directing and sustaining the creation in a marvelous, miraculous manner: "[He] that bringeth out their host by number: he calleth them all by names by the greatness of his might" (Isa. 40:26). This speaks of God directly involved in the "miracle" not only of creation but of providence.

The OT and NT also portray God as One who enters into the lives of human beings in special ways. This may involve the revelation of God's will through prayer, vision, or divine voice. This experience of the divine can transform, shape, command a person's total outlook on life. This happens often, not only in the study of the Book, but by the direct involvement of God in the experience of man. It can occur when one is in worship or when one is at work in the field or in the town. Amos experienced the "miracle" of God's revelation while pasturing the flock; Isaiah in the context of Temple worship; Hosea in the experience that shaped his view of God at work in restoring broken Israel.

The Bible records instances of miracles of healing. This is particularly true in the case of the ministries of Elijah and Elisha, and of the ministry of Jesus. These miracles appear to be instantaneous and in most cases to result from the faith of the person in the power of God to act. The lame walk, the blind see, the paralyzed move, and in several cases the dead arise. Either these events are phenomena outside the processes of nature or in temporary suspension of nature. The biblical record is clear in its statement that these events did take place and at the express command of God.

What is essential for us to understand is the purpose of God in the sustaining care and nurture of His people in the midst of a well-ordered universe. Faith in a God who loves is essential in the comprehending of miracles. God's purposes were not always completely comprehended by those who experienced the miraculous; but their faith was strengthened and their allegiance confirmed.

See SUPERNATURAL (SUPERNATURALISM), HEAL (HEALING), CREDENTIALS OF SCRIPTURE, SIGN.

For Further Reading: *HDNT,* 2:186-89; Wiley, *CT,* 1:149-56.

FRED E. YOUNG

MISSION, MISSIONS, MISSIOLOGY. *The terms for mission.* The central meaning of all the biblical and theological terms for mission is "sending." It is the mission of God *(missio Dei),* who wants all people to be saved and to come to the knowledge of the truth (1 Tim. 2:4). He sends His Son into the world, the Son sends His disciples into the world, and both Father and Son send the Spirit to empower the Church in its mission of seeking the lost. Ideally, it may also be said that when the Church sends its workers, the Spirit is also sending them (Acts 13:1-4).

The term *mission* is the broadest theological term and includes all that is involved in the salvation activities of the Trinity and the Church in the extension of the kingdom of God on earth (Verkuyl). The term *missions* as a singular noun refers commonly to the world missionary enterprise, though it may also relate to the theology and theory of mission. As a count noun that may be pluralized, *mission/missions* denotes the organizations involved in mission. There is a tendency, especially among ecumenicals, to prefer the use of *mission* to *missions,* though both terms are used concurrently. *Missiology* is the scholarly discipline which studies and delineates the whole field of mission and missions from the biblical, theological, and historical perspectives with additional relevant input from the social sciences.

Mission in Scripture. The revelation of God as the Creator and Redeemer of all mankind first begins to come into clear focus in the covenant promise to Abraham that through him all the people on earth will be blessed (Gen. 12:3). Although this universal motif continues to be developed in the OT, particularly in the Psalms and prophetic books, Israel tended to understand its religion as an ethnic monopoly and failed to fulfill its God-intended mission of being a light to the nations (Isa. 42:6). So God had to create a New Israel, the universal society of the Church, which could serve as His missionary agent in the world. Christ initiated the mission first to the Jews through His own missional activity and in the sending of the Twelve and also the Seventy-two. Between His resurrection and ascension, Jesus made the mission explicitly universal in the terms of the Great Commission, which sent the whole Church to the whole world with the whole gospel. Acts and the Epistles record how the Early Church faithfully carried out their Lord's command and carried the gospel to the ends of the earth in their known world (Acts 1:8).

One of the mysteries of NT interpretation is that while there were obviously missionaries active in the Early Church, where is the NT term for *missionary*? A clue can be found in the usage of the Greek Church from the beginnings right up to the present in which the word *apostolos* or "apostle" has continually been used for the missionary ministry, including biblical references to James and companions of Paul (Gal. 1:19; Rom. 16:7; 2 Cor. 8:23; Phil. 2:25; Acts 14:4, 14). The Roman Catholic church has retained the term *apostolate* to designate the missionary ministry. Kirsopp Lake states flatly that there are two usages of *apostolos* in the NT, one limiting it to the Twelve in certain contexts, and another used in the sense of a Christian missionary (Jackson and Lake, *The Beginnings of Christianity,* 5:50-51). There is a growing consensus among scholars to consider that this wider usage of "apostle" is indeed the "missionary" of the NT (Hesselgrave).

The theological meaning of mission. The ultimate goal of missions is to glorify God in the fulfillment of His redemptive purposes for mankind through the extension of the kingdom of God. This evangelistic goal is delineated by the Great Commission as (1) making disciples and (2) incorporating them into churches. The evangelical commitment to biblical evangelism is not to be understood as excluding social concern, including the seeking of social justice for all, but rather as requiring it as a proper corollary to evangelism. The mission of the Church must be pioneered by specialists (missionaries, evangelists, church planters), but it is best completed by a universal commitment to witness by all believers through the use of their spiritual gifts in response to the need for and the call to ministry, whether among tribal peoples or in the inner city of the world's great metropolitan areas.

The only safeguard against the syncretism of the content of the gospel is the proper indigenization and contextualization of the forms of the gospel in responsible, self-sufficient churches. Sending missions must continue while the vast majority of people in the world are without the gospel and have no near neighbors who can share it with them. The base and field of mission must be seen as worldwide, not excluding or neglecting any who are without the gospel, whether across the street or across the world.

See EVANGELISM, GREAT COMMISSION, SOUL WINNING, CHURCH, GOSPEL, APOSTLE, MISSION OF CHRIST.

For Further Reading: Kane, *Understanding Christian Missions;* Verkuyl, *Contemporary Missiology;* Hesselgrave, "The Missionary of Tomorrow—Identity Crisis Extraordinary," *Missiology* (1975), 2:231 ff.

PAUL R. ORJALA

MISSION OF CHRIST. Mission derives from the Latin *missio,* "to send." It is a term of wide and varied use in the Christian Church, including what Webster titles its theological meaning: "The sending of the Son or the Holy Spirit by the Father, or of the Holy Spirit by the Son."

The mission of Christ is found in the protevangelium (Gen. 3:15), the Messianic prophecies of the OT, and in the numerous names, titles, and attributes ascribed to Him (Zech. 3:8; Isa. 7:14; 9:6; Hag. 2:7; Num. 24:17). The three major aspects of His office and work are prophet (Deut. 18:18; Isa. 61:1-3), priest (Ps. 110:4; Zech. 6:13), and king (Ps. 2:7; Isa. 11:1-5). Closely related to His priestly mission is the OT picture of the Suffering Servant, with the two strange paradoxes: king/suffering servant, priest/sacrificial lamb (Acts 8:32-35; Heb. 9:11-12).

In the NT, from the "Wist ye not that I must be about my Father's business?" of childhood (Luke 2:49) to the "It is finished" of the Cross (John 19:30) and the promise "I will come again" (14:3), Christ's own sense of mission sounded so clearly that it still rings out to us. In the synagogue at Nazareth, He said, "This day is this scripture fulfilled in your ears" (Luke 4:16-21). He affirmed both His purpose and authority in delivering His people from their sins (Mark 2:17; Matt. 9:13; Luke 5:32; Matt. 18:11; Luke 19:10; Mark 2:9; Luke 7:48). He clearly related His saving from sin to His future atoning death (Mark 10:45; Matt. 26:28; John 10:11-18; Acts 5:31).

The glorious redemptive purpose and work of Jesus in saving "his people from their sins" was to the end of bringing them to eternal life in the unending kingdom of God. "To this end was I born, and for this cause came I into the world," He said to Pilate (John 18:37). The glorious purpose of a holy, loving God, before time began, is to be brought to fulfilment in His resurrection from the dead, in the coming of the Holy Spirit, in the love and labors of the Spirit-filled Church, in His return to earth, and in the glorious consummation of all things. And then "every knee [shall] bow . . . and . . . every tongue [shall] confess that Jesus Christ is Lord, to the glory of God the Father" (Phil. 2:11).

The mission of Christ can never be fully understood without an appreciation of the nature of His personhood: very God of very God, very man of very man, the God-man.

See CHRIST, ESTATES OF CHRIST, REDEEMER (REDEMPTION), MISSION (MISSIONS, MISSIOLOGY), HOLINESS.

For Further Reading: *DCT,* 217; Wiley, *CT,* 2:143 ff; *Baker's DT,* 358; Dufour, *Dictionary of Biblical Theology,* 365.

JOHN E. RILEY

MISTAKES. Mistakes are unintentional errors in judgment or action which are a result of the infirmities of the flesh.

Mistakes are not sins, "properly so-called" (Wesley). Since a mistake is unintentional, it lacks the element of moral blameworthiness which is essential to sin. A mistake may be the result of ignorance, inexperience, or immaturity —handicaps which are not sinful in themselves. Also, mistakes are consistent with the doctrine of perfect love. Because a mistake is unintentional, the motivation behind a mistake may be compatible with love from a pure heart. The motivation of love could hardly be classified as sin.

While mistakes are not sin as properly defined, mistakes may indeed be unintentional violations of law, and hence require both correction and covering. Through Christ God overlooks our mistakes, just as He always is ready to forgive sin when confessed.

In a sermon on Christian perfection John Wesley concluded, "No one, then, is so perfect in this life, as to be free from ignorance. Nor, secondly, from mistakes" (*Works,* 6:3). Wiley concurs: "The depravity of his spiritual nature may be removed by the baptism with the Holy Spirit, but the infirmities of flesh will be removed only in the resurrection and glorification of the body" (*CT,* 2:140).

See SIN, FAILURE, INFIRMITIES.

For Further Reading: Wesley, *Plain Account of Christian Perfection;* Wiley, *CT,* 2:140, 506-9.

JAMES L. PORTER

MODALISM. See SABELLIANISM.

MODERATION. See TEMPERANCE.

MODERN REALISM. This is directly opposed to *idealism* (the modern philosophical term for the older realism). Modern realism's main contention is in opposition to any theory that would reduce the phenomenal world to a system of ideas. It shifts from *ontology* to *epistemology.* Its concern is with man's perception of individuals and particulars as he experiences his world of material things. It is a reaction from the belief that the ultimate "stuff" of our universe is essentially of the nature of mind (spirit) and is basically spiritual and dynamic. It contends (1) that not all entities are mental, conscious, or spiritual; and (2) that entities are knowable without being known. It is the epistemological position which asserts that the object of knowledge is distinct from and independent of the act of awareness. It contends that the object of awareness, when we are aware of it, is precisely what it would be if we were not aware of it.

Of course man, as a creature of time and space physically, develops a kind of *naive realism* (sometimes called *common sense realism*) which says that things are just as they are given in consciousness through immediate perception. But this makes no allowance for error in perception or hallucinations in perceiving things not actually present in sense but only in imagination.

Two schools of realism arrived on the scene of American philosophy in the early 20th century. The first was known as *neorealism.* It was sometimes called "presentational realism." It subscribed to epistemological monism and made no clear distinctions between seeming and being, insisting that things *are* just what they *seem.*

The second was known as *critical realism* and was referred to as "representative realism." It was epistemologically dualistic and made a distinction between the sense data directly present to the mind and the real external object. Thus ideas are representative of the external objects. For this sort of realism perception had two aspects: (1) the sensory and ideational content, and (2) the meaning and outer reference. Knowledge is the insight into the nature of the object that is made possible by the contents which reflect it in consciousness. Thus mental states exist as much as do physical objects. Such realism had preference for the correspondence theory of truth, and our ideas, if valid, must conform to the existential realm of physical nature. Yet there is the possibility of error and things may not be just what they seem.

Both types of American realism were inclined toward evolutionary naturalism, holding that the physical is but another term for being and existence. Thus most modern realists are evolutionary humanists. Mind therefore becomes only a tool of the organism and not the instrument of an ontological self.

Thus in their concern for epistemology they have not been able to escape ontology and the taking of some kind of a metaphysical stance.

See REALISM, SCOTTISH REALISM, REALISM AND NOMINALISM, REALISM IN THEOLOGY.

For Further Reading: Perry, *Philosophy of the Recent*

Past, 197-220; *Present Philosophical Tendencies,* 271-347; Stace, "The Refutation of Realism," *Mind,* 53 (1934).

ROSS E. PRICE

MODERNISM. See LIBERALISM.

MONARCHIANISM. This refers to certain unitarian views of God, originating in the second and third centuries A.D., according to which God is thought of as unified, as a monarch is. The truest, clearest form of Monarchianism was that of Modalism, the view that there is but one God, and that He has manifested himself successively in three modes: as Father, then as Son, then as the Holy Spirit.

See SABELLIANISM.

J. KENNETH GRIDER

MONASTICISM. Monasticism, a term derived from the Greek adjective *monos,* "alone," and the related verb *monadzein,* "to live alone," is used to describe a movement in the church which advocated renunciation of, and withdrawal from, the world as a means of attaining Christian perfection. Followers of this method of attaining perfection are known as *monks,* and their dwelling place is known as a *monastery.* Monks live an ordered life within their community, and the guidelines for living are called *rules.* Monastic rules are governed by three vows which every monk must make before being accepted in the *order* (the technical term for the monastic community). These are the vows of *poverty,* i.e., the monk vows never to have any personal possessions (in some cases, however, the monastery as a whole may own possessions); *chastity,* i.e., abstinence from carnal gratification; and *obedience,* i.e., humility expressed in following the commands of a superior without question.

Origin. Monasticism arose as a lay protest movement at the end of the third and the beginning of the fourth centuries in Egypt. The decline of belief in the immediacy of the Parousia meant that the church had to come to terms with her continued existence in the world. To this was added the increasing acceptance of Christianity as the official religion of the Roman Empire, with the result that the church became increasingly wealthy and worldly. Spiritual and political power were frequently merged, and being a Christian became a formality.

In this situation a young Christian orphan named Antony (c. A.D. 250-355—he lived to the age of 105!) heard the words of Jesus, "If thou wilt be perfect, go and sell that thou hast, and give to the poor" (Matt. 19:21); and, desiring no less than Christian perfection, he resolved to obey the instruction to the letter. He disposed of all his possessions and distributed them to the poor before withdrawing to the desert to commune with God in solitude. Antony's fame as a man of God spread, and so many there were who would be his disciples and follow his example, that he emerged from solitude in A.D. 305 to organize a community of hermits. Monasticism was born.

Types of Monasticism. The motivating force was the desire for personal sanctification through the renunciation of the world. This renunciation expressed itself in a variety of ways. The community of Antony was of the so-called *anchorite* type; that is to say, they lived individually as hermits or, if they lived in community, they practiced absolute silence. This type of discipline is practiced today in the Carthusian Order.

Contemporary with Antony was Pachomius, who also formed a monastic order. Here, however, normal community life was practiced. This is known as *coenobite,* or fellowship monasticism.

In the Middle Ages monastic life in the West was largely dominated by the *Mendicant Friars* who, unlike other monks, were forbidden to own any property either personally or in common, and lived either by working or begging. Also unlike other orders, the mendicants were not restricted to one monastery, but travelled around from town to town.

Monasticism was spread in the East by Basil the Great, and in the West by John Cassian.

Strengths and Weaknesses. The strength of the monastic movement lay in its attempt to keep the goal of personal sanctification before an increasingly worldly church. The words of Jesus which Antony heard, "If thou wilt be perfect," have been the pattern for virtually all monastic orders. Another strength lay in the fact that it was a lay movement. While many priests also became monks, the movement itself was lay in character. A monk aspired to no higher title than "Brother," while the priest was called "Father."

The weaknesses of the monastic movement were that, in the first place, it presented the Christian ideal as something impossible for everyday life and therefore attainable only by those who withdrew from the world. A double standard of Christianity was thereby introduced which divorced the demands of God from normal living. The second weakness of the movement was that in its ideal it was intensely individualistic. Frequently in the history of monasticism, warnings had to be given regarding the monastic rejection of the church and the sacraments. The monk was so concerned with his own salvation that community life was a matter of little importance to him. The monk proposed to himself no great or systematic work beyond that of saving his own soul. What he did more than this was the accident of the hour.

See CHRISTLIKENESS, SANCTIFICATION, CHURCH, KOINONIA.

For Further Reading: Workman, *The Evolution of the Monastic Ideal;* Chadwick, *John Cassian* (2d ed., 1968); Kirk, *The Vision of God.* THOMAS FINDLAY

MONERGISM. This is the view that salvation is solely and independently the work of God. Thus it is contrasted with *synergism,* which leaves some room for human action in the total saving or redeeming process. *Monergism* was expressed very forcefully by Augustine in his debate with Pelagius. Since then it has been embraced by schools of both Catholics (e.g., Jansenists) and Protestants (e.g., Calvinists). Its best exponents have been in the Reformed tradition. Both Luther and Calvin embraced monergism enthusiastically; the followers of Calvin have preserved it to the present; much contemporary theology has ignored or discarded the concept entirely. Wesley is generally recognized as opposed to monergism, but his position is extremely subtle in that his doctrine of prevenient grace attempted to preserve the stress on divine action in regeneration. It enabled him to assert that any human action related to regeneration was only possible because of prior divine action.

The support for monergism has been manifold. Proponents insist that it alone does justice to the following considerations. It exalts God by giving Him all the glory for man's salvation. It fully preserves justification by faith by ruling out any human cooperation or contribution to regeneration. It takes very seriously the radical corruption of human nature by stressing the complete inability of man to save himself. It makes sense of the experience of salvation by illuminating the resistance of the human will when confronted with the claims of the gospel. It preserves the biblical emphasis on divine initiative and constant divine action in salvation.

Monergism cannot be divorced from the wider set of doctrines in which it is embedded. Thus it finds its natural home in the classical Calvinistic scheme that begins with total depravity, and moves through unconditional election, limited atonement, and irresistible grace to the perseverance of the saints. All of these doctrines develop the implications of monergism by specifying the divine activity that alone results in any individual's salvation.

Two other themes that naturally deserve extended consideration in order to accommodate fully the implications of monergism are the nature of human freedom and the relation between divine action and human action. Of the two the first has received most attention. In this case either free will is rejected entirely (Luther), or it is so interpreted as to be compatible with complete divine determinism (Edwards). Recent work by Lucas has shed light on the relation between divine and human action in salvation.

As noted above, Wesleyan Arminianism is monergistic to the degree that all saving grace is acknowledged as coming from God, and that even man's free cooperation is made possible by prevenient grace. But Wesleyans object to radical monergism on the grounds that pure determinism makes God equally responsible (by default) for the damnation of those He chooses not to save; it reduces freedom to puppetry and holiness to a legal fiction; and it runs counter to the total tenor of Scripture, which assumes a real capacity in man either to cooperate with God or resist Him.

See SYNERGISM, FREEDOM, PELAGIANISM, SEMI-PELAGIANISM, DETERMINISM, CONTINGENT.

For Further Reading: Luther, *The Bondage of the Will;* Calvin, *Institutes of the Christian Religion,* vol. 3, chaps. 21—24; Lucas, *Freedom and Grace.*

WILLIAM J. ABRAHAM

MONEY. The Bible attaches great significance to money and its use. It is not only a form of wealth and a medium of exchange, but its use is an index to the character of those who possess it.

The sinful heart is prone to love money, first for what it can buy or do, but soon for its own sake. Such love is a root of all sorts of evil (1 Tim. 6:10, NASB). For the love of money is a form of covetousness, which, as Paul says, is idolatry (Col. 3:5). Its possession is seen by the carnal mind as the key to power, prestige, position, and pleasure—the four *p's* of the world's value system. When one is in the grip of this love, all more worthy loves are either tarnished by it or withered completely. Blinded by this unholy obsession, men and women have sacrificed family, friends, and health, to say nothing of honor and integrity. This lust is often the driving force behind prostitution, crime, and violence, on the dark side of society; but also injustice and oppression in business and industry.

Because of these evils spawned by an inordinate craving for money, the Bible is full of warnings. For one thing, money will not satisfy; its promise of happiness is an illusion (Eccles.

5:10). Equally delusive is its promise of security (Matt. 6:19-20). Its possession, moreover, is a constant peril to the soul (13:22; 19:21-23). It is no wonder that the Word says: "Those who want to get rich fall into temptation and a snare and many foolish and harmful desires which plunge men into ruin and destruction" (1 Tim. 6:9, NASB).

How can Christians avoid the pitfalls of handling money? Fundamentally, of course, their love of money must be thoroughly broken and displaced by an all-consuming love for Jesus Christ. This means that not only the interests and goals of a new kind of life must captivate them, but they must experience total deliverance from the old bondage, so that they are no longer touchy about "money talk," but free to enjoy the delights and blessings of the cheerful giver (2 Cor. 9:6-7). This requires nothing less than total sanctification of the inner affections. A revised and Christianized value system will follow naturally (cf. Phil. 4:10-14; 1 Tim. 6:6-8).

There are two evidences of such inner sanctification. One is the capacity to be happy without a lot of money. The other is the actual cheerful demonstration of day-by-day stewardship with what we have. For we will now see money from a new perspective, not as a means of gratifying self or as something to hoard, but as a means of serving God and doing good (Eph. 4:28; 2 Thess. 3:7-12).

Energetic and able people especially need to watch the single-mindedness of their devotion, and guard against the peril of the subtle allure of affluence. For in the nature of the case, industrious and capable people are apt to become more or less prosperous. Such prosperity is not sinful but dangerous, as many have found to their sorrow. Only great devotion and discipline will avoid the creeping incubus of returning materialism, and enable Christians to own money without being owned by it (1 Tim. 6:17-19; Heb. 13:5).

In OT times, material wealth was seen as a sign of divine blessing. Often it really was (Abraham, Isaac, Jacob, Job, etc.). But not always did this sign hold (Heb. 11:36-39).

In the NT one test of spiritual depth is seen as the willingness to divest oneself of wealth for the Kingdom's sake, if called upon to do so; or if not so required, at least to use one's wealth for the Kingdom. Money and things became the hinge of discipleship for the 12 disciples themselves, for the rich young ruler, Zacchaeus, Barnabas, Ananias, and Sapphira.

Jesus measured generosity not so much in terms of the amount given but by the amount left (Mark 12:42-44). He further laid down the principle that one's faithfulness in handling money would be the yardstick by which his trustworthiness in more important matters could be gauged (Luke 16:10-12). He urged such an investment of one's means in the Kingdom that they would when he died be to his eternal credit instead of to his eternal condemnation (v. 9). Yet one's stewardship is not to be showy and ostentatious, but quiet and modest (Matt. 6:2-4).

The legitimacy of money was never denied by Jesus, but dependence on it was. When the disciples were first sent out, they were to take no money with them, but trust themselves to the hospitality of the people (Mark 6:8). Yet elsewhere He concedes the inescapability of the material aspect of life, in the words "Your heavenly Father knows that you need all these things," and, "But seek first His kingdom . . . and all these things shall be added to you" (Matt. 6:32-33, NASB).

John Wesley advised his Methodists to make all they could, save all they could, and give all they could. The advice is still timely.

See STEWARDSHIP, CONSECRATE (CONSECRATION), COVETOUSNESS, MATERIALISM.

For Further Reading: Timothy L. Smith, ed., *The Promise of the Spirit* (Charles G. Finney on Christian Holiness), 94-105, 231-39. RICHARD S. TAYLOR

MONISM. *Monism,* a word derived from the Greek *monos* and coined by Christian von Wolff (A.D. 1679-1754), a German philosopher, is a world view or metaphysical system which emphasizes one ultimate form or substance of reality. This means either that reality is unchanging, i.e., permanent or motionless, or that reality cannot be differentiated into pieces or parts. Monism is thus to be contrasted with dualism, which holds that there are two basic powers or elements in the ultimately real, and with pluralism, which accepts common-sense experience, the dynamic and changing, and the need for free play as requiring a world of many initiating centers.

Monism emphasizes the need for a single explanatory principle to adequately satisfy rational demands; it may regard the real as the permanent and find change as illusory; it may give great consideration to the area of moral requirements in which standards must be established. Finally monism may develop the preceding into a concept of God with characteristics of perfection, absoluteness, and changelessness.

Absolute monism must be distinguished from ultimate monism in that in absolute monism every piece within reality is so dependent upon the single will/energy/power that it has little or no sense of difference from it. In ultimate monism all things could derive from the one origin and be significantly dependent upon it, and yet have some degree of significant independence of it.

One of the key and crucial problems in monism is the presence of evil. Can evil really appear in such a closed system? Why, if it does not, do we seem to have so much evil?

See IMMUTABILITY, COSMOLOGY, METAPHYSICS, PERSONALISM, EVIL, DUALISM.

For Further Reading: Urmson, *Concise Encyclopedia of Western Philosophy and Philosophers,* 273; Bradley, *Appearance and Reality;* Hartshorne, *The Logic of Perfection*.

R. DUANE THOMPSON

MONOPHYSITISM. *Monophysite* is a combination of two Greek words that mean "single nature." This is a name applied to a Christian group which took form about A.D. 453. The Council of Chalcedon (A.D. 451) took the position that Jesus in His divinity was consubstantial with the Godhead in His Godhood, and consubstantial with humanity in His manhood. The aim was to avoid a position which compromised either His full deity or His full humanity. Monophysitism was one of the reactionary modifications which arose in the East. The monophysite concept was that the two natures were so united that, although the one Christ was partly human and partly divine, His two natures became by their union only one nature. Christ's humanity was an "accident" of His divine nature. This was but a revival of Eutychianism.

The movement survives today in the Coptic, Jacobite, Ethiopian, and Armenian churches. In Lebanon they are known as Maronites.

The church has viewed monophysitism as a heresy (condemned A.D. 553). The orthodox view is that the human and divine natures of Christ remain distinct, but find their union in one Person. This is called the hypostatic union.

See HYPOSTATIC UNION, CHRISTOLOGY, CREED (CREEDS), EUTYCHIANISM, MONOTHELITISM.

For Further Reading: Heick, *A History of Christian Thought,* 1:183-86; Wiley, *CT,* 2:163.

MENDELL L. TAYLOR

MONOTHEISM. *Monotheism* is a term used to indicate belief in one, and only one, God. Monotheism is distinct from polytheism, the belief in many gods, and henotheism (sometimes referred to as monolatry), the worship of one god without denying the existence of other gods. Of the world's religions, Judaism, Christianity, and Islam (Mohammedanism) are monotheistic.

One school of thought contends that monotheism developed gradually throughout the history of Israel from earlier polytheistic ideas. In this view Israelite monotheism is thought to have its beginnings in the eighth-century prophets. Earlier texts are said to presuppose a situation recognizing the existence of gods other than the supreme god of Israel. Many others, however, reject such views, asserting that monotheism is present in the teachings of Moses and is either directly taught or implied throughout all stages of the biblical record. Indeed, many regard monotheism to be one of Judaism's great contributions to the religious thought of mankind.

Those holding the latter view regard the idea of monotheism as implied in the Ten Commandments: "I am the Lord your God . . . You shall have no other gods before me" (Exod. 20:2-3, RSV). Deut. 6:4 is also regarded as a classic expression of Israel's faith: "Hear, O Israel: The Lord our God is one Lord" (RSV). The clearest affirmations of monotheistic faith are found in Isaiah. "Thus says the Lord, the King of Israel and his Redeemer, the Lord of hosts: 'I am the first and I am the last: besides me there is no god'" (44:6, RSV; cf. 45:5 ff).

The monotheism of postexilic Judaism was such that the Jews reacted strongly against Jesus. His claim to be the Son of God was, in their minds, irreconcilable to the idea of the unity of God, stemming from their monotheistic thought. The NT writers, however, did not believe that the claims of Jesus regarding His divinity conflicted with OT monotheism. The Revelation to John affirms: " 'I am the Alpha and the Omega,' says the Lord God, who is and who was and who is to come, the Almighty" (1:8, RSV).

See THEISM, GOD, ATTRIBUTES (DIVINE), TRINITY (THE HOLY).

For Further Reading: von Rad, *Old Testament Theology,* 1:210-12; Rowley, *The Faith of Israel,* 71-73; Wright, "The Faith of Israel," *The Interpreter's Bible,* 1:357-62; Baab, *The Theology of the Old Testament,* 48-53.

DON W. DUNNINGTON

MONOTHELITISM. Monothelitism, a Christological theory which appeared about the middle of the seventh century, might be said to represent the final ancient phase of the long debate on the problem of the two natures in Christ, stretching across some 300 years. How could the eternal Son be truly man?

Monothelitism (the word comes from Greek roots signifying "a single will") attempted to reconcile the disputants by positing that in Christ, the unique theanthropic Person, there are not two wills or modes of operation, one divine and one human, but only one divine-human will. Otherwise, it did confess the two natures.

The concept, devised by Sergius of Constantinople, was promoted by the emperor, Heraclius, as a compromise attempt to persuade those who persisted in the monophysite position (the notion that the divine and human natures in Christ are blended into one nature in a "natural" union) to accept the Chalcedon Definition of A.D. 451. In this it failed.

Chalcedon had earlier defined the boundaries of the doctrine of the two natures, safeguarding the completeness and integrity of each. Beyond this human minds could hardly go. But because human logic and speech are inadequate in the face of this revealed mystery, controversy had persisted.

The Third Council of Constantinople (A.D. 681) condemned monothelistism and declared that in Christ there were two natural operations and two wills, with the human will always subject to the divine will. The monothelite heresy was seen as a threat to faith in the complete humanity of the God-man, a very precious and essential truth.

See CHRISTOLOGY, MONOPHYSITISM, HYPOSTATIC UNION.

For Further Reading: Bethune-Baker, *An Introduction to the Early History of Christian Doctrine;* Burkill, *The Evolution of Christian Thought;* Berkhof, *The History of Christian Doctrines.*

ARNOLD E. AIRHART

MONTANISM. This was a movement founded in the last half of the second century by a Phrygian named Montanus. He proclaimed the "Age of the Spirit" as the preparation for the end of all things. Montanism constituted a revivalistic reaction to the increasing worldliness of the church and the centralization of authority and charismatic gifts in the office of the bishop. In one or the other of its many factions it prevailed until the ninth century.

Charges of irregularity were brought against the self-proclaimed prophet Montanus and his female associates, Maximilla and Priscilla, not because of doctrinal deviation but because of their challenge to the growing institutional authority of the Catholic church of the time. Opposition arose largely in response to their claims to the right of personal revelation, personal prophesyings, and their radical moralism which required a much stricter code of discipline than was held to by the church in general. They were against remarriage for any reason, mandated strict asceticism, and invited martyrdom. The movement was greatly strengthened by the conversion of the famous Tertullian to its cause.

Similar tensions between irregular renewal movements and the contemporary established structures of the church have recurred throughout history. Reformers frequently have found comfort and support in early Montanism. John Wesley, among others, looked upon this "heresy" with more charity than did its Catholic contemporaries.

See REVIVALISM, FANATICISM.

For Further Reading: Lietzmann, *The Founding of the Church Universal,* 189-203; Baur, *Orthodoxy and Heresy in Earliest Christianity,* 132-46.

MELVIN EASTERDAY DIETER

MORAL ATTRIBUTES OF GOD. Biblically, there is only one moral attribute of God—holiness. Other moral attributes of God are derivatives of His holiness and fall into two seemingly contradictory categories, variously characterized as: God as a consuming fire/God as a transforming presence; the wrath of God/the love of God; the justice of God/the mercy of God; the righteousness of God/the forgiveness of God.

The apparent dichotomy of these moral attributes of God emerges from the interplay of God's holiness and His will for those beings whom He has created in His own image and likeness. God "spoke us forth" (a more dynamic rendering of the roots of the Greek *ek-legō* ["choose"] which reflects God's creative acts in Genesis 1: "God said . . . and it was so") in himself before "the foundation of the world, that we should be holy *[hagios]* and blameless before him in love" (Eph. 1:4, author's free translations in this paragraph); "this is the will of God, your sanctification *[hagiasmos]*" (1 Thess. 4:3); "for God has not called us for uncleanness but in sanctification *[hagiasmos]*" (1 Thess. 4:7). God's repeated call to His covenant people throughout the Bible is that they are to be a holy (LXX, *hagios*) nation (Exod. 19:6, et al.): "You shall be holy [LXX, *hagios*], for I the Lord your God am holy [LXX, *hagios*]" (Lev. 19:2, et al.; cf. 1 Pet. 2:9; 1:15-16); "Pursue . . . the holiness *[hagiasmos]* without which no one will see the Lord" (Heb. 12:14). Behind these sample statements of God's will and call is the implication (often expressly stated, Rom. 3:10, 23) that those addressed are not holy as God created them to be. The interaction of the holiness of God with the unholiness of humanity creates the seeming dichotomy of the moral attributes of God.

On the one hand, the holiness of God is a moral purity of being of such a total, absolute, infinite intensity that nothing unholy can endure or exist in His presence. The holiness of God "burns" against all that is unholy until it is completely consumed. The intensity of this antipathy to unholiness is often called the "wrath" of God. The uncompromising nature of this holiness is characterized as the "justice" of God. The unchanging quality of this holiness is termed the "righteousness" of God. These astringent attributes of God are manifestations of His holiness *against* the unholiness of humanity.

On the other hand, God's "holiness as the sum of His being must contain the creative love which slays but also makes alive again" (Kittel, 1:93). The "consuming fire" of God's holiness has at its heart the transforming purpose of God to make us holy. The "wrath" of God's holiness is but the love that abhors all that pollutes the beloved. The "justice" of God's holiness illumines His mercy which comes to us *in* our unholiness. The "righteousness" of God's holiness is magnified in His forgiving grace which delivers us from the bondage of our unholiness that He might make us holy. These regenerative attributes of God are manifestations of His holiness *for* the holiness of humanity.

Thus the basic dynamic of the moral attributes of God is encompassed in the fact that He is the holy God who kills, and makes alive; who wounds, and heals (cf. Deut. 32:39).

See ATTRIBUTES (DIVINE), GOD, HOLINESS, WRATH, JUSTICE, AGAPĒ.

For Further Reading: Anderson, "God, OT view of," *IDB*, 2:417-30; Mac Donald, "The Consuming Fire," *Creation in Christ*, 157-66; Moule, "God, NT," *IDB*, 2:430-36; Muilenburg, "Holiness," *IDB*, 2:616-25; Procksch, *"hagios,"* Kittel, 1:88-115.

M. ROBERT MULHOLLAND, JR.

MORAL INFLUENCE THEORY OF THE ATONEMENT. As important as was the life and ministry of Jesus, of primary significance was His death and subsequent resurrection. Throughout the history of the Church, attempts have been made to determine how it is that Christ's death on the Cross atones for man's sin. The many theories can usually be classified into three main categories: (1) Those which follow the thinking of Irenaeus and Origen. They held that Christ's death paid the ransom price due Satan for man. This theory is often called the classic or patristic theory. (2) Those which follow the thinking of Anselm or of Calvin. Anselm contended that Christ's death satisfied the honor of God; and Calvin, God's justice. (3) Those which follow the thinking of Abelard. It is this third category that commands the attention of this article.

Abelard (1079-1142) disagreed with Irenaeus and Anselm. He felt that Christ came to be the perfect example for man to follow. Christ died in order to show man how much God loves him. Salvation comes when man recognizes this ultimate example of love as a life-style that he desires to pursue. God's purpose in the Cross, then, was to make such a disclosure of His love that men would be won over by it to a forgivable state (Hughes, *The Atonement,* 203). Some of the proponents of this view down through the centuries have been Socinius, Schleiermacher, Ritschl, Bushnell, and Rashdall, to name a few. Although variations have been made on the theme, the major thrust has remained the same.

The theory is an obvious attempt to deal with some of the flaws in the penal satisfaction theories. Since moral influence advocates contend that there is nothing in the divine nature that demands justice or penalty for sin, the sole obstacle to forgiveness of sins is found in the sinner's unbelief and hardness of heart. When through education and exposure to God's love this obstacle is removed, forgiveness is the natural outcome.

Some shortcomings of this theory need to be noted. For one thing, it is atonement by mere example. The Incarnation becomes the atoning event rather than the Crucifixion. Scripture is clear that it was Christ's death that makes possible forgiveness and renewal of the relationship between man and God. Another fault lies in the fact that it is totally subjective in nature. There is no room in this theory for God to act in the salvific process. Forgiveness comes as the natural outcome of a spiritual law. With this theory nothing happens in the mind of God when a person seeks forgiveness. The emphasis is on the human obedience rather than the divine sacrifice. Still another weakness is that there seems to be little sense of the cost of redemption in this theory. Little mention is made of the great price paid on the Cross.

While it is true that the motive for the Atonement is found in the love of God (John 3:16; Rom. 5:8), its necessity is grounded in God's holiness. Christ's death was more than an example to observe, and more than a moral influence on society. His death was a vicarious sacrifice. Passages like John 11:50; Rom. 5:6-8; 2 Cor. 5:14; Eph. 5:2; 1 Tim. 2:6; and a multitude of others, compel us to look beyond the moral influence theory for the definition of the Atonement.

See ATONEMENT, GOVERNMENTAL THEORY OF THE ATONEMENT, PENAL SATISFACTION THEORY OF THE ATONEMENT, MYSTICAL THEORY OF THE ATONEMENT, MORAL ATTRIBUTES OF GOD.

For Further Reading: Abelard, *Commentary on Romans,* vol. 10; Bushnell, *The Vicarious Sacrifice;* Robert Culpepper, *Interpreting the Atonement,* 87-118; Purkiser, ed., *Exploring Our Christian Faith,* 243-68; Wiley, *CT,* 2:259-66, 271-76, 282-90. D. MARTIN BUTLER

MORALITY. Morality is the consistent practice of the mores (rules) of a culture. It is related to ethics as application is related to theory. The moralist may moralize, but only when theory is translated into conduct does the moralist become moral.

Christian morality differs from secular or other-religion morality in its basic assumption of a revealed divine standard of right and wrong, to be found in the Bible. From the standpoint of the Judeo-Christian ethic, any violation of the Decalogue is immoral. The Christian would refine this to specify the principles of the Decalogue as expanded and expounded in the NT, with love as the primary rubric.

In this respect Christian morality differs radically from process philosophy or any form of humanism, which eschews absolutes, and which is essentially relativistic and developmental. Harold B. Kuhn observes that Whitehead's philosophy, for instance, "has no place for either human redemption from outside man, nor for morality as obedience to a revealed will of a personal God" ("Philosophy of Religion," *Contemporary Evangelical Thought,* 228). Morality severed from supernatural revelation must in the nature of the case be a "soft" morality, pliable and changeable.

Yet Christian morality cannot justly be charged with being merely moralistic rule keeping. Christianity more than any other religion or philosophy drives straight to the heart and locates morality there. Rule keeping in the biblical view does not make a person moral unless the rules are kept for the right reason, in the right spirit, and with the active involvement of a personal moral sense. The substance of both the right reason and the right spirit is love, which seeks at once to please God and do right toward others. A loveless moralism falls far short of Christian morality. Many persons who are "moral" in the bare sense of rule keeping are immoral, in God's sight, in the secret springs of the life.

Christianity pushes moral persons toward moral maturity. This is vastly different from the so-called maturity of a licentious and permissive society, which glories in the abandon with which laws, divine or human, are thrust aside. It is rather the maturity of persons who learn to think ethically—"who by reason of use have their senses exercised to discern both good and evil" (Heb. 5:14). The revealed law of God will be such a person's base, but everyday life will be his sphere of application. He will see the moral issues and implications that are everywhere, in business methods (including his own), politics, taxation, affluence, pleasure, recreation, leisure, social class—all of the myriad and complex situations not covered specifically by law, but which need the application of law principles to a razor-honed degree, an application prompted by love and aided by the Holy Spirit.

However, while most decisions, proposals, and actions have at least indirect moral overtones, it is conceivable that some may be amoral. In thought at least, sharp distinction should be maintained between morality and expediency. A question of expediency may not necessarily be a moral question. Two courses of action may be equally legitimate but not equally wise.

See VIRTUE, CHRISTIAN ETHICS, PRINCIPLES, NEW MORALITY, EXPEDIENCY. RICHARD S. TAYLOR

MORTAL, MORTALITY. "Mortal" is the word that indicates that man is subject to death. "Mortality" is the condition of being mortal. The Greek word is *thnētos,* and according to Brunner (Kittel, 3:21) was used in Greek thought of "men in contrast to gods." Paul uses the term primarily in reference to man's physical body (Rom. 6:12; 8:11; 1 Cor. 15:53-54; 2 Cor. 4:11).

According to Wesley, mortality is more than subjection to death. Wesley (*Works,* 7:347) held that the soul is "hindered in its operations" because of mortality. Infirmities are not sins; they are a part of mortality.

Mortality per se is not sinful. Neither does mortality make sin necessary or inescapable. Wesley's teaching (*Works,* 6:277) must be emphasized—"a thousand infirmities will remain . . . sin need not remain." Paul confirms this as he writes, "Do not let sin reign in your mortal body" (Rom. 6:12, all NASB).

"Death" is a broader term than mortality, and in the Bible reference is made to both physical and spiritual death (Mark 10:33; Rev. 2:11). The ideas are related in that the cause of the broader is obviously the cause of the narrower.

Christian theologians have generally held that there is an inseparable relationship between sin and death. Early biblical evidence is found in Genesis: "In the day that you eat from it you shall surely die" (Gen. 2:17). Paul's discussion in Rom. 5:12-21 is incisive. He observes that sin leads to death, "and so death spread to all men" (v. 12). Where the word "death" is not qualified, it should be taken to include physical death. The whole race suffers the consequence of Adam's sin.

The biblical writers leave to conjecture what might have been had man not sinned.

"To dust you shall return" (Gen. 3:19) is an authentic word, but it is not the final word. Paul writes, "For . . . this mortal must put on immortality" (1 Cor. 15:53). On this text Grosheide (*New London Commentary,* 32:377) says, "The verb [put on] expresses identity along with a qualitative difference." It is *this* mortal body that becomes immortal. This is in keeping with the Wesleyan view that the body is not inherently evil. The final word to the Christian is not "to dust" but "Christ Jesus [has] brought life and immortality to light through the gospel" (2 Tim. 1:10).

See CONDITIONAL IMMORTALITY, IMMORTALITY, DEATH, RESURRECTION OF THE BODY, SOUL.

For Further Reading: Wright, "Death," *New Catholic Encyclopedia,* 4:687-95; Wesley, "The Fall of Man," *Works,* 6:215-24; "The Heavenly Treasure in Earthen Vessels," *Works,* 7:344-48. ALDEN AIKENS

MORTIFY, MORTIFICATION. This concept appears only in Paul's writings, Rom. 8:13 (*thanatoō,* "make to die") and Col. 3:5 (*nekroō,* "make dead"). Union with Christ calls for the "putting to death" of the "deeds of the body" (Rom. 8:13) and "your members which are upon the earth" (Col. 3:5, KJV) or "what is earthly in you" (RSV).

Across the centuries, some groups in the church have taken mortification to be an ascetic practice in which the body of the Christian is subjected to forms of discomfort in order that "the flesh and its lusts" may be subdued and eventually overcome. Fasting and abstention from other pleasurable activities are means of mortification, the end result of which is thought to be the purifying of the soul and the increase of holiness of life.

In the Wesleyan tradition, in particular, these Pauline passages have been taken to refer to the act of consecration, through the help of the Holy Spirit, whereby the believer is delivered not only of "evil actions, but evil desires, tempers, and thoughts," and as a result the life of faith becomes more abundant (J. Wesley). While experience of mortification is central, the idea of daily discipline is not denied.

See ASCETICISM, TEMPERANCE, DISCIPLINE, DEATH TO SELF, BODY. WILLARD H. TAYLOR

MOSAIC LAW. The Mosaic law refers to the revelation of God given to Moses at Mount Sinai. In the OT this consists of the Ten Commandments plus other statutes for the life of the covenant community of Israel. That it was a revelation from God and normative for Israel is clearly stated in the OT, and failure to obey the law is the primary factor in Israel's spiritual failure. Over the many centuries since the time of Moses there have been different assessments of the Mosaic law, including pronouncements and evaluations from the NT.

The original intention of Mosaic law is seen by examining the Hebrew word for law, *torah*. It has a broader and more personal meaning than its English translation, coming from a root which signifies "teaching, guidance, or instruction." In this light, its basic nature is better understood as revelation from God and constituting divine guidelines for Israel.

The form of the Ten Commandments, the heart of Mosaic law, is mostly apodictic law—strong negative statements which do not admit to any qualifications or exceptions. Those negative commandments begin with the Hebrew negative which means "never." (There is a different negative particle in Hebrew for temporary injunctions.) Much of the rest of law statement in the OT, such as the Book of the Covenant (Exod. 20:22—23:33), as well as law codes of the ancient Near East outside of Israel, are in the form of casuistic law, wherein specific cases are covered, using the formula, "If . . . , then . . ."

Moses is the mediator of the law, and the five books of law in the OT (Pentateuch) are traditionally attributed to him. This era of Moses has lasting theological importance for Israel. The giving of the law must be seen in connection with the Exodus from Egypt, a deliverance which provided a setting of mercy and grace for the law, and Israel's response in the acceptance of the law. God had delivered Israel from Egyptian bondage, and now they were His people, bound to Him by covenant law.

In the subsequent history of Israel the theological meaning and importance of the law of Moses changed, especially during and after the Babylonian exile. Judaism became ingrown and developed as a religion of the law, and obedience to its letter became paramount. Motivation for such obedience lay in the fact that it was a means of meriting justification, rather than in gratitude for gracious redemption. It was this legalistic understanding of the law that brought forth strong condemnation by Jesus and Paul.

Jesus summarized the significance of the law and prophets by calling attention to two things: (1) Israel's *Shema* (Deut. 6:4-5), which calls for loving God with one's total being; and (2) the command to love one's neighbor as oneself (Lev. 19:18). This emphasis on the moral inwardness of the Mosaic law stands in stark contrast to the literal legalism of Judaism. Paul's response to those who insisted that Gentile converts must keep the law in order to be justified is clearly stated in Gal. 2:15-16: "by the works of the law shall no flesh be justified." For Paul, the purpose of the Mosaic law is twofold: (1) to reveal the nature of sin (Rom. 3:20); and (2) by man's inability to keep the law, he is brought to a recognition of grace given through Christ (the pedagogue idea expressed in Gal. 3:24).

"Freedom from the law" does not mean license to violate the basic moral law, reaffirmed so vigorously in the NT, but annulment of the Mosaic law-system as a means of either (1) being reconciled to God or (2) becoming personally holy.

See LAW AND GRACE, FREEDOM, LICENSE, JUSTIFICATION, WORK (WORKS), MOSES, PENTATEUCH, TALMUD.

For Further Reading: Richardson, ed., *A Theological Word Book of the Bible*, 122-24; *IDB*, 3:77-89; *New Schaff-Herzog Encyclopedia of Religious Knowledge*, 6:425-27.

ALVIN S. LAWHEAD

MOSES. Moses was the great leader and lawgiver of ancient Israel. Of Israelite birth, he was at the same time an Egyptian. He resided in the court of Pharaoh from his very early days until his adult years (Exod. 2:1-10; Heb. 11:23-24). He also experienced the austere, frugal life of the desert as a member of the household of Jethro in the land of Midian (Exod. 3:1). Thus his roots reached deeply into the ancient cultural soil. He was a man *of* his time.

The faith of ancient Israel in its beliefs, worship, and ethics, much of which is both basic and antecedent to the Christian faith, was fashioned by Moses out of the revelation God gave to him at Sinai. As for beliefs, the Israelites were to believe in and be committed to the only God, Yahweh. There was to be no place for gods of other peoples, nor any image or likeness of Yahweh among them for any purpose whatsoever. This was in striking contrast to what prevailed in the ancient setting, and it had ramifying effect on all Israel's religious beliefs. As regards worship, Moses, under divine leadership, consecrated Aaron as high priest and established the sacrificial system as the means for atonement of the sins of the people (see Exodus 24—31). Concerning ethics, he made the Ten Commandments (Exod. 20:1-17) and specific case laws the code for the conduct of Israel. He thereby categorically indicated that many aspects of behavior acceptable to other religions were prohibited among God's people. This ethic, long the foundation for society in the Western world, is tragically crumbling under the impact of an encroaching pagan, non-Mosaic ethic.

The prophets, in their many references to Moses or Moses' law, show they were revivalists or reformers and not innovators, with respect to religious and ethical understanding. They called repeatedly for repentance and return to Mosaic faith on all major counts: belief in God, sacrifices, conduct.

The many references of the NT to Moses' deeds and words indicate there was concern with him not only as lawgiver and prophet, but with his life as an example for life under the new covenant. Especially is this so in the Epistle to the Hebrews.

See MOSAIC LAW, NEW COVENANT, LAW, LAW AND GRACE.

For Further Reading: Albright, *From the Stone Age to Christianity*, 179-96, 236-44; Bright, *History of Israel*, 122-26; *ZPEB*, M-P: 279-94. HARVEY E. FINLEY

MOTHER OF GOD. This is a phrase which Roman Catholics apply to Mary, the mother of Jesus. In the very early centuries, some theologians began to speak of her as Mary, bearer of God, because of her giving birth to Jesus, who was fully God as well as fully man. Then advancement was made from "Bearer of God" to "Mother of God." It is this "high" view of Mary which, later, figured in various advances in Catholic Mariology. It figured in such Roman Catholic doctrines as her being called Redemptrix and Co-Redeemer, perpetually a virgin, conceived without original sin in her mother's womb, assumed into heaven without physical death, and, in general, so significant in the total faith and life of the Roman Catholic church.

Most Protestants are pleased to honor Mary because of her office in giving birth to the God-man Jesus, but object to the designation as Mother of God. Not only does the term unjustifiably elevate Mary, but it implies that she was the mother to God the Father—since that is the member of the Trinity usually called God in the NT.

See MARIOLATRY. J. KENNETH GRIDER

MOTIF RESEARCH. Especially related to the theological methodology of the Swedish theologian Anders Nygren, motif research (m.r.) is the tool employed to distill from a theological system the one element which is absolutely foundational and which distinguishes it from all others. Instead of employing the insights gleaned from other systems of belief, as practiced in the history of religions school in vogue when Nygren first developed his methodology, m.r. seeks to establish the motif and its meaning from a careful reading of the data in the "natural context" within which it occurs. Applied to Christianity, Nygren identifies and defines *agapē* as the sine qua non.

Nygren begins his m.r. from the assumption that all religions are valid and distinct forms of experience which seek to answer the question, "How does man relate to the Eternal?" but that Christianity alone answers the question in a theocentric fashion. Even Judaism is essentially egocentric, with its foundational motif being *nomos* (law) or man's achievement.

Two major strengths can be seen in Nygren's m.r.: it seeks to identify unifying themes in a religious system, and it takes seriously the meaning in the natural context for precise definition of the motif. Two weaknesses may also be identified. First, because it seeks to identify the one basic motif in a rather complex religious system, on the one hand it risks reducing these complexities into a lowest common denominator so basic that its value and distinctiveness is lost; and, on the other hand, it risks forcing divergent concepts into one mould or even totally disregarding incompatible ideas. It may be questioned whether one can reduce Christianity to the one motif of love, however basic it may be, without doing an injustice to several other cardinal motifs. Similarly, the reduction of Judaism to the one motif of law, however carefully defined, leads to serious distortion of the spirit of Judaism.

Second, from a specifically Christian perspective, any attempt to subserve all the distinctive emphases of the biblical writers under one rubric can only lead to distortion. The recognition of the rich diversity of emphases in the Scriptures within unity is essential if one is to properly understand the dynamic character of God's revelation to man.

See AGAPĒ, LAW, BIBLICAL THEOLOGY, HERMENEUTICS.

For Further Reading: Nygren, *Agape and Eros;* Quanbeck, "Anders Nygren," *A Handbook of Christian Theologians;* Hall, *Anders Nygren.*

KENT BROWER

MOTIVES. Motives refer to the internal factors which produce human behavior. They speak to the question of *why* a person behaves as he or she does. Motives are anything which consciously or unconsciously moves a person to action, anything that impels or induces him or her to act in a certain way. They are internal to the human being.

Motives and *intentions* are sometimes used as if they were synonyms. Intentions, however, are prompted by motives. A minister *intends* to be a good pastor. The question is, *why* does he want to be a good pastor? That is the question of motivation. His motives may include a desire to be liked, a desire for professional success, or a desire for ecclesiastical recognition.

Are these wrong motives for *intending* to be a good pastor? Not necessarily, if they are secondary to one's primary motive to glorify God. The highest-placed motive is showing gratitude for the grace of God who, through the atoning work of Christ, has redeemed, cleansed, and called.

This implies that motives may be mixed, yet "pure." They are pure if kept subordinate to the will of God, and if they are free from malice, slander, bitterness, or any other motive contrary to love for God and His people (Eph. 4:31—5:2).

Motives may be better than performance or worse. A good deed may be done with a wrong motive; also, a serious blunder may be well motivated. The moral quality of the spirit of the doer is determined by the inner motive. Only God sees this without error. He will not record good deeds if done with poor motives, and He will not blame poor performance if the motive is love.

See INTENTION, HEART PURITY.

For Further Reading: *Baker's DCE,* 427 ff, 437 ff, 622.

LEBRON FAIRBANKS

MURDER. Narrowly defined, "murder" means "to kill a human being unlawfully and intentionally." Biblically defined, however, murder includes *thoughts* as well as acts, *failing* to maintain as well as deliberately taking persons' lives (Matt. 5:21-22; 1 John 3:15).

In Adam Clarke's view, the sixth commandment, "You shall not murder" (Exod. 20:13, NIV) clearly applies to a multiplicity of acts, including, he says: (1) whatever *"abridges"* the life of a person; (2) killing in unjust wars, such as those waged for land or wealth; (3) forming and enforcing laws which impose capital punishment for less than capital crimes; (4) "all bad dispositions" whereby one inwardly hates his neighbor; (5) failing to help the needy, for letting people die is the same as killing them; (6) all forms of intemperance which damage our own bodies and shorten our own lives (*Commentary,* 1:405 ff).

Thus, while we frequently label only "first degree murder" as murder, restricting our definition to legal terms, the Scripture will not allow us to evade murder's full significance. For, as Lord Acton said: "Murder may be done by legal means, by plausible and profitable war, by calumny, as well as by dose or dagger." To refrain from murder involves our heart's attitude and our social conscience as well as our personal behavior. In all aspects of our life we must choose life rather than death.

Sinful people, from Cain onwards, have tried to gain their ends through violence. Some have, with premeditation, slain individuals, as did the two killers in Truman Capote's dramatic case study, *In Cold Blood.* Others, like David eliminating Uriah, have used their authority to dispose of others by ordering them killed. On a larger scale, Joseph Stalin and Adolph Hitler have systematically slaughtered millions.

Despite its civilized facade, the 20th-century Western world has writhed with murderous activity. Violence on the streets and in the homes takes thousands of persons' lives each year. Unjust wars have liquidated millions. Over a million aborted, unborn children die each year in America. Vast numbers of hungry people starve to death each year—people who could have been spared were the world's wealth shared fairly.

From the perspective of the sixth commandment, the world abounds with murders and murderers. A few pay for their crimes. Most kill indirectly and are not tried for their victims' deaths. But from God's standpoint he who sheds innocent blood, whether directly or indirectly, stands guilty of murder.

See HATE (HATRED), CAPITAL PUNISHMENT, ABORTION, EUTHANASIA, LIFE.

For Further Reading: DeWolf, *Crime and Justice in America;* Shakespeare, *Macbeth;* Wolfgang, *Patterns in Criminal Homicide.*

GERARD REED

MYSTERY, MYSTERIES. It has long been thought that the NT use of the word family *mustērion* draws its technical signification from the pagan mystery cults. While it is certainly true that some NT writers, Paul in particular, used terms familiar to the mystery religions of the day, such use really found no parallel with the sacramental use of the word family identified with those religions (Bornkamm, Kittel, 4:802-28). In recent years, several scholars have suggested that later Judaism provides us with the best context and background for a proper understanding of how the NT writers used the *mustērion* family.

In later Judaism, "mystery" was a description of both Yahweh's will and the revelation of it within Israel (M. Barth, *Ephesians,* 1:19-21). According to the Qumran materials, the term "mysteries of Yahweh" shaped Yahweh's plans at three primary levels: (1) the order of the cosmos; (2) the history of His salvation; and (3) the history of His judgment on Belial's kingdom (i.e., of evil). The latter two especially—God's salvation and His judgment—were the very ground of Qumran's eschatology, for it was at the Day of the Lord when His redemptive will was to be made fully known.

The "mysteries of Yahweh" were disclosed to the prophets (or teachers) who then transmitted them to the faithful community. Indeed, mystery was understood only by the faithful; faith was revealed by comprehension. Thus, it was the privilege of the truly faithful community to know and to understand the "mysteries of Yahweh," which were hidden from all the others and which prepared them for the coming Day of the Lord. Their gnosis insured their salvation.

All of this has import for the student of the NT who locates these same emphases especially in the writings of Paul (cf. Ephesians and Colossians). However, we must hasten to suggest that Paul radicalizes the plural, "mysteries of Yahweh," into the singular, "mystery of Christ." For Paul, God's will and word were incarnated and revealed in the dying and rising of His Son, Jesus Christ. One mystery—the mystery of the Incarnation—was substituted for all the rest. Salvation and judgment, indeed the plan for the cosmos (Col. 1:15-17), were all revealed and represented in *Christological* terms by *Christ's* apostles to *Christ's* Body, the Church (Eph. 3:1-13).

Further, the mystery of God disclosed in the last days to that community which exists in Christ becomes for that community its new moral imperative. The mystery of Christ obligates the community in Christ to live a life which imitates Him (Eph. 4:1; 5:1-2). By so living, the community not only affirms the gift of life they have received by grace through faith, but they prepare for their day of redemption as well (Eph. 4:30).

See CHRIST, SALVATION, CHURCH.

For Further Reading: Kittel, 4:802-28; *BBC,* 9:154; Ladd, *A Theology of the New Testament,* 383 ff.

ROBERT W. WALL

MYSTICAL THEORY OF THE ATONEMENT. This term designates what is really a group of related theories within the general category of moral influence theories of the Atonement, i.e., the effect it has upon man, rather than upon God ("satisfaction theories") or Satan ("dramatic" or "classic" view). These theories suggest that the work of Christ so affects man as to draw him into participation with the life of Christ, a life characterized by love, obedience, and service to God and one's fellowmen. There is therefore a "mystical" identity between Christ and man: Christ identifies with man in His humanness and brokenness in the Incarnation, partaking of man's suffering, but in so doing sets a perfect example of sacrifice of self to God. Even more than this, Christ is seen as a kind of archetype of humanity, so that His perfect sacrifice is in some sense actually the sacrifice of all humankind. Such complete and perfect sacrifice establishes humanity on a "new plane" which individuals may share through repentance and faith, and living a Christlike life.

A basic assumption of the mystical theories—as of all moral influence theories—is that the only real impediment to forgiveness of sins is the sinner's own hardness of heart. Christ in himself overcomes this hardness of heart and in so doing moves the individual sinner to renounce *his* obstinacy and self-will and be reconciled to God. The stress here is on Christ's influence by example. Ideas of propitiation, satisfaction, and ransom are foreign.

Mystical theories of the Atonement may be traced all the way back to certain of the Early Church fathers and have been articulated in some form by such subsequent spokesmen as Abelard, Schleiermacher, F. D. Maurice, and notably in America by Horace Bushnell, the "Father of Modern American Liberalism."

See ATONEMENT, MORAL INFLUENCE THEORY OF THE ATONEMENT, GOVERNMENTAL THEORY OF THE ATONEMENT, PENAL SATISFACTION THEORY OF THE ATONEMENT, RANSOM, REDEEMER (REDEMPTION).

For Further Reading: Aulen, *Christus Victor,* 133-42; Bushnell, *The Vicarious Sacrifice;* Rashdall, *The Idea of Atonement in Christian Theology,* 435-64; Wiley, *CT,* 2:261-69.

HAROLD E. RASER

MYSTICISM. Because of its claims to the possibility of personal, experiential knowledge of God, the mystical element in religion is difficult to define. Mystical experiences are a part of both Christian and non-Christian faiths. Examples of the latter are the Sufiism of the Muslim tradition and the transrational states induced by meditation or other means among Hindus and Buddhists. Drugs have also been used to induce experiences that transcend those produced by the normal functions of the intellect, will, and emotions.

The popular conception of mysticism has been shaped frequently by the unusual phenomena which have been associated with it but are not of its essence. Visions, trances, prophecies, special spiritual gifts, occult knowledge are not the realities of mystical experience. John Gerson's definition of it as "the knowledge of God arrived at through the embrace of unifying love" expresses the essence of Christian mysticism as well as any other.

Mystical experience frequently arises in Christianity as a counterbalance to the formalizing tendencies of liturgical, institutionalized worship. It is essentially wedded to Christian faith by the "Christ in you" and "you in Christ" themes of the Pauline and Johannine literature. The theology of the Eastern church is basically mystical, rising out of the Christian-Platonism of Alexandria. In the Western church mystical theology found its home largely in monastic circles under the encouragement of Augustine and other Catholics in the Christian-Platonic tradition who followed him.

The Reformers and Wesley make strong disclaimers against the mysticism of their times. All, nevertheless, were strongly influenced by it—Luther by Thomas à Kempis and the *German Theology,* among others, and Wesley by William Law, Thomas à Kempis, Madame Guyon, and the Cambridge Platonists. In spite of Wesley's vigorous rejection of the passive nature of the mysticism of his day, mystical writers from Macarius to the Cambridge school are broadly represented in his *Christian Library.* His common concern with them for perfection in love as the ultimate end of biblical Christianity made a complete divorce impossible.

The personal, experiential nature of American revivalism has created a similar affinity with the mystical tradition in historic Christianity. Through Wesley and the writings of Thomas Upham, the American holiness movement, particularly, found historic witness to its experience of entire sanctification in such Catholic mystics as Catherine Adorna, Molinos, Fénelon, Francis de Sales, and Madame Guyon. In the nonrevivalist tradition in America, mysticism found parallel expression among the New England Transcendentalists.

See EXPERIENCE, IN CHRIST, UNITY, COMFORTER, FORMALISM, QUIETISM.

For Further Reading: Hoffman, *Luther and the Mystics;* Inge, *Mysticism in Religion;* Tuttle, *John Wesley,* 330-34; Underhill, *Mysticism.*

MELVIN EASTERDAY DIETER

MYTH. In working with OT materials, some critics have determined that the stories of creation, the Fall, the Deluge, and their counterparts in Mesopotamian and Canaanite religions are mythological. Also, NT statements concerning the Atonement, the Resurrection, Christ, miracles, and "last things" fall into this literary and historical category. Such critics find the basis for these mythological views in the dependence of biblical writers on religious ideas and ideologies current in their times. Syncretistic activity is considered to have been common, so that, for example, Gnosticism is believed to have had a profound influence on first-century Christianity.

While this method of studying the Bible became prevalent following the Enlightenment, it was popularized by Rudolph Bultmann through a publication in 1941. Essentially Bultmann and the post-Bultmannians have defined *myth* as that language which finite man uses to express infinite truth. It is the best he has available to him at any moment of attempted expression of his faith. As new information of his world opens up to him, man must "demythologize" or, better, "remythologize" what he knows about the infinite order. In the study of the Gospels, the issue of demythologization has become most crucial in the search for the so-called historical Jesus.

The presuppositions and methods in the use of the category of myth have varied from writer to writer. They have used existentialism as well as structuralism and evolution as presuppositions, sometimes identifying myth and symbol. It is quite obvious that the evangelical views of the inspiration of the Scriptures conflict with this method of interpretation.

However, one good result of this way of interpreting the *kērygma* has led to a renewed interest in the Scriptures and a revival of the study of hermeneutics. Some see all this as a conflict between religion and natural science (Miles, in loco).

The conservative and liberal scholars are quite apart in their methods and doctrinal beliefs that result from their study of the Holy Scriptures. The conservative scholar sees the narratives of the OT and the NT as the record of historical events and truths that are the gospel *(kērygma)* of Jesus Christ, the Savior of the world. They find very little myth as such, but do recognize parable, allegory, and symbol. The Scriptures are the full and final revelation of God through Jesus Christ, and He is the Source of our personal salvation.

See BIBLE, DEMYTHOLOGIZATION, BIBLICAL AUTHORITY, CRITICISM (OT, NT), INSPIRATION OF THE BIBLE, TYPE (TYPOLOGY), LIBERALISM, HERMENEUTICS.

For Further Reading: *IDB; HDB; ZPBD;* Gill, "Myth and Incarnation," *Christian Century,* 94 (December 21, 1977): 1190-94; Miles, "Burhoe, Barbour, Mythology, and Sociobiology," *Zygon,* 12 (March, 1977): 42-71; Neuleib, "Empty Face of Evil: Myth," *Christianity Today,* 19 (March 28, 1975): 14-16; Saliba, "Myth and Religious Man in Contemporary Anthropology," *Missiology,* 1 (July, 1973): 281-93.

ROBERT L. SAWYER, SR.

N

NATION. The Hebrew word *goy* is translated as "Gentile," "nation," and "heathen." The Hebrew *am* seems to reflect a group of individuals or persons with common blood ties. *Am* and *goy* seem almost antithetical after the Exodus. The Greek word *ethnos* is like *goy,* never a person, but "Gentile," "nation," or "heathen." The contrast between the nation of Israel and the surrounding nations is significant throughout the OT (Isa. 43:9).

There are at least 70 nations or ethnic groups mentioned in Genesis 10; and a great multitude from every nation, tribe, people, and tongue mentioned in Rev. 7:9.

The prophets of Israel were constantly calling the people to their responsibility to evangelize the nations (cf. Jonah). They were to receive the Revelation to share it with all the nations of the earth (Jer. 1:10; Ps. 66:7; Ezek. 5:6). But instead of fulfilling this mission, Israel became like the nations and succumbed to the same idolatry.

While the words do not show a relationship, it is reasonable to assume that the nation of Israel, God's chosen people, was the forerunner of the concept of the kingdom of God and/or heaven. Spiritual Israel inherits the theocratic promises of the OT prophets.

The NT concept is more spiritual than material, more of a reign than a realm. But John reminds us of the new heaven and new earth and the coronation of our King of Kings, Jesus the Christ. All the covenantal promises will be brought into fruition by the second coming of Christ.

"All nations will be brought into judgment" is the basic presupposition of the prophets.

See ISRAEL, CHURCH, MISSION (MISSIONS, MISSIOLOGY), KINGDOM OF GOD.

For Further Reading: *HDB; HBD; ZPBD.*

ROBERT L. SAWYER, SR.

NATURAL LAW. Natural law is that part of the eternal law which pertains to man's behavior, according to Aquinas. The eternal law he believed, is God's reason which sets and controls the integration of all things in the universe. A law is called natural because it is universally valid. Natural law, *lex naturalis,* in Christian theology "traditionally refers to the inherent and universal structures of human existence which can be discerned by the unaided reason and which form the basis for judgments of conscience . . . right is the rational" (Harvey, *A Handbook of Theological Terms,* 157).

Originating in early Greek philosophy, natural law became basic in the moral philosophy of Aquinas, and hence in subsequent Catholic theology. Protestant theologians, especially Luther and Calvin, argued that fallen man cannot have direct knowledge from God apart from revelation (the Ten Commandments and supernatural law in Christ). Liberal theologians, both Catholic and Protestant, warn against accepting unchanging precepts based on unchanging nature, holding that natural law is an existential concept, the insurgent authenticity (Macquarrie, *Principles of Christian Theology,* 506).

On the other hand there can be seen a synthesis of natural law and revealed law in the revelation of God's love through Jesus Christ. "Love is the natural law because it is the law of man's essential nature" (Stumpf in Halverson, *A Handbook of Christian Theology,* 248). While fallen nature distorts or denies love as the law of life, redemption through sanctification restores it.

See REVELATION (NATURAL), REVELATION (SPECIAL), NATURAL THEOLOGY.

For Further Reading: Harvey, *A Handbook of Theological Terms;* Macquarrie, *Principles of Christian Theology;* Halverson, *A Handbook of Christian Theology.*

MEL-THOMAS ROTHWELL

NATURAL MAN, THE. The term is used to designate the man who is unregenerate, and therefore insensitive to spiritual matters. The apostle Paul contrasts the natural *(psuchikos)* man with the spiritual *(pneumatikos)* man, depicting the natural man as unresponsive and ignorant of those things spiritually discernible (1 Cor. 2:14; cf. John 12:40; 2 Cor. 4:4; 1 John 2:11).

The *natural* man is not to be confused with the *carnal* man, who, while being a child of God, is not fully surrendered to Christ but lives under the domination of the flesh (*sarkinos,* 1 Cor. 3:1-3).

Wesley characterizes the state of the natural man to be one of sleep, where neither spiritual good nor evil is discerned. Because of his spiritual insensitivity, he is unaware of his true, precarious position and imagines himself to be wise, good, and free from "all vulgar errors, and from the prejudice of education; judging exactly right, and keeping clear of all extremes" (Sermon 9, "The Spirit of Bondage and Adoption").

The term "natural man" refers to that state in which man was found after the Fall. Though the divine image was marred, it was not totally lost, since he retained some degree of self-determination and a certain amount of intelligence in natural things. However, he was and is utterly incapable of understanding the things that have to do with obtaining God's grace and salvation without the aid of God's prevenient grace. In this condition and without the aid of the Holy Spirit, natural man cannot but regard the gospel, his only salvation, as foolishness (1 Cor. 2:14). Not only is the understanding darkened (Eph. 4:18; 5:8) but also the will is misguided (cf. Romans 7), and he is ruled by profound enmity toward God (Rom. 8:7).

See SPIRITUALITY, AWAKENING, REGENERATION, ORIGINAL SIN, FALL (THE), PREVENIENT GRACE.

For Further Reading: Wiley, *CT,* 2:32; Wesley, "The Spirit of Bondage and Adoption," *Works,* vol. 5.

FOREST T. BENNER

NATURAL REVELATION. See REVELATION, NATURAL.

NATURAL THEOLOGY. The term *natural theology* has historically signified the interaction between humans and the world about them, through which was derived some knowledge of God's existence and being. The process of derivation of such knowledge usually assumes that some reliable intimations of His "eternal power and Godhead" (Rom. 1:20) may be gained apart from any special revelation. As such, the information thus gained is inferential, acquired by process of observation and deduction. Its raw material is, of course, the world, which is available to every normally perceptive person.

The classic scriptural statement is found in Rom. 1:19-20. This passage was basic to the development of this phase of Christian teaching for the first 14 centuries. In the medieval era, natural theology was viewed as forming a basis for recognition and acceptance of revealed theology. It found its most complete expression in the *Summa Theologica* of Thomas Aquinas (1225-74) and especially in the five classical proofs for God's existence. The schoolmen of the Middle Ages were confident that natural theology could yield a good grade of certainty concerning God's existence, and some valid insight into His nature.

The Reformers, while valuing naturally derived intimations concerning God, made less of it than did, for example, Thomas Aquinas, for they felt more keenly the weakening of the human perceptive powers in the Fall. But both the Lutheran and the Calvinistic wings of the Reformation took seriously the biblical statements with respect to a degree of theological understanding derivable from a reverent study of nature.

The teaching has met with varying fortunes in more recent times. The Enlightenment, typically of the 18th century, exalted natural theology to a point at which it came to be regarded to be the chief source of religious knowledge. To reason was ascribed the ability to learn all that one needed to know concerning religion. Others in the same period (and down to our own day) held with Immanuel Kant that no knowledge of a personal God could be derived from impersonal nature.

In our century natural theology has again met with varying degrees of acceptance. The scientific world view has tended to merge "God" with the world. The process theologians see "deity" as a phase of the larger totality of the world process. Here the question resolves itself to the identification of the dynamic aspects of nature with "the divine."

The dialectical theology (commonly called neoorthodoxy) raised the question in the second quarter of our century. Karl Barth, eager to establish the uniqueness and adequacy of Scripture, sought to deny utterly the possibility of natural theology. His erstwhile colleague, Emil Brunner, took issue and tried to restate a modified view of man's ability to infer something vital concerning God from nature. This type of approach is generally accepted among evangelical Christians today.

See NATURAL LAW, REASON, RATIONALISM, REVELATION (NATURAL).

For Further Reading: *Baker's DT*, 372-73; *New Schaff-Herzog Encyclopedia of Religious Knowledge*, 8:85; Wiley, *CT*, 1:51 ff.

HAROLD B. KUHN

NATURALISM. This term may be defined most simply as a frame of reference which denies the possibility of any reality which transcends material existence. By definition, naturalism is opposed to every form of supernaturalism. In a modern world which derives virtually every category of meaning from natural sciences and technology, all of which operates empirically, naturalism is a pervasive world view.

It does not necessarily follow that such nonmaterial values as beauty, truth, goodness, etc., would be denied by a naturalist or that he would automatically be an atheist. These values and others are for the naturalist a reflection of what religious man terms God. They are a reflection of the highest forms of experience for natural man. It is essential for a consistent naturalist, however, to insist that all reality is temporal and spatial.

See GOD, CREATION, THEISM, MATERIALISM.

For Further Reading: Harvey, *A Handbook of Theological Terms;* Henry, *God, Revelation, and Authority*, 1:37 ff.

W. STEPHEN GUNTER

NATURE. This term designates the essential character or structure of being. A primary constituent, or the combination of those qualities which together give a thing or a being its true character, is said to be its nature. The Greek word *phusis* refers to "everything which . . . seems to be a given" (Koster, Kittel, 9:253).

Often the word "nature" refers to the sum total of the universe apart from the interference of man. As such, it is frequently personified, almost deified, by those who refuse to acknowledge that it is created and sustained by God. Creationists, in contrast, believe that through nature God gives a limited understanding of himself.

The crucial issues concerning the term "nature" are in anthropology and Christology. In Christ we have one Person or Being, existing in two natures, human and divine. In respect to man, the question is whether nature is to be identified with (1) generic manness, or humanness, with (2) the individual self as an ultimate core of reality which remains unchanged throughout changes in its qualities or states (Moustakes), or (3) the individual traits which characterize the self. The first two are fixed and inalienable. The third is malleable.

Hence, while the being of man, or human nature as endemic and essential, remains unchanged, the moral nature of any person may be changed by God's grace. Wesleyans have been optimistic about this possibility. Wesley (*Works*, 10:367) insists, "You are really changed; you are not only accounted, but actually 'made righteous.'"

The word "nature" is used in an accommodated sense by Wesleyans who speak of the sin nature as a propensity to evil, in contrast to acts of sin. This sin nature must be seen as an acquirement and not as an integral part of man's being.

Rom. 5:12 is a crucial text on this subject. Scholars generally agree that the use of the article with the singular noun *(hē hamartia)* introduced by Paul at this point in the Epistle means that from here on, the discussion majors on this kind of sin in such a way that the perversity being described can be called a nature. But it is "an inner moral tyranny that is alien to man's true nature" (*GMS,* 291).

Many attempts have been made by holiness writers to find a word or an expression that would adequately convey the notion of this "inner moral tyranny." Wesley (*Sermons,* 2:454) uses "proneness to evil" and "tendency to self-will." Delbert Rose (*The Word and the Doctrine,* 127) refers to the sin nature as "a principle," "an inherited corruption," "a disposition."

While Christians have generally held that this sin nature remains in the justified, believers are exhorted by Wesley (*Sermons,* 2:391) to press on to the "great salvation" through which God brings full deliverance from "all sin that still remains." This deliverance comes at the moment of decisive faith when one believes for entire sanctification. Various words and phrases such as "done away with" (Rom. 6:6) and "crucified" (Gal. 5:24) are used by the apostle Paul to express this deliverance.

Man's nature may be so deeply affected by God's grace that its renewal is profound—in place of the tendency to sin is love made perfect.

See MAN, HUMAN NATURE, ORIGINAL SIN, SELF, CARNAL MIND.

For Further Reading: Harris and Taylor, "The Dual Nature of Sin," *The Word and the Doctrine,* 89-117; *GMS,* 67-87, 251-302; Rose, "Sin in Believers: As a Principle," *The Word and the Doctrine,* 127-36; Wesley, *Sermons,* 2:360-97, 442-60.

ALDEN AIKENS

NAZARENE. As a designation for Jesus in the Gospels and Acts, this is understood to indicate that He came from Nazareth in Galilee. The one English term represents in fact two alternative Greek adjectives which are used as roughly equivalent. One of these, *Nazarēnos,* is the only form found in Mark, while it occurs twice in Luke but not at all in Matthew or John. The other term, *Nazōraios,* perhaps better translated into English as "Nazorean," is used exclusively by Matthew and John, and is found in Luke-Acts some eight times.

This variation in spelling is generally accounted for by one theory or another regarding the origin of the second term, *Nazōraios.* Such theories are coincidentally bound up with the interpretation of Matt. 2:23. There, the question which must be answered concerns the exact location of Matthew's citation of that which "was spoken by the prophets." Three alternatives have been proposed: (1) that the term is derived from the village name, Nazareth; (2) that it is derived from the OT word rendered Nazirite (specifically, Judg. 13:5, 7; 16:17 read in connection with Isa. 4:3); (3) that it originated from the Hebrew word root that means "branch" (cf. Isa. 11:1) and that may mean "watchman" (cf. Jer. 31:6-7).

R. E. Brown argues convincingly for the position that these three theories need not be mutually exclusive. On the one hand, to argue for only one view on the basis of strict rules of word derivation in the biblical languages is to ignore the reality that biblical etymologies more often are the result of analogical thinking than they are the consequence of consistently followed rules of phonology. And furthermore, a particular term applied to Jesus may have been attractive to the early Christians because of its wealth of possible allusions, rather than by its well-defined limitations (Brown, 209).

See CHRIST, CHRISTIAN.

For Further Reading: Albright and Mann, *The Anchor Bible: Matthew,* 20—23; Brown, *The Birth of the Messiah,* 209-13, 223-25.

HAL A. CAUTHRON

NECROMANCY. See SORCERY.

NEIGHBOR. The concept of "neighbor" was familiar to any Jew in Christ's day who knew the Hebrew Scriptures. That there was nevertheless some uncertainty concerning an exact definition might be indicated by the lawyer's question, "And who is my neighbor?" (Luke 10:29, NASB). The fact that the word had come to have in the Jewish mind an exclusive connotation can be understood when the various OT words, translated by "neighbor" in English, are noted. *Amith* means "equal, fellow." *Qarob* designates "near one." By far the most common word, *rea,* means "friend, companion." When *rea* is changed to *reuth,* it becomes "female friend, companion." *Shaken* means "dweller, inhabitant," generally nearby. Together these terms imply proximity and acquaintance. The Jews came to limit the meaning of neighbor to friends of the same race and class, with whom one was on intimate and congenial terms. They could thus say, "Thou shalt love thy neighbour, and hate thine enemy" (Matt. 5:43). By their definition an enemy was not a neighbor, therefore they were not under obligation to love him.

It was necessary therefore for Jesus to follow up His reminder that the second greatest commandment was, "Thou shalt love thy neighbour as thyself" (Matt. 22:39 and parallels), by rebuking their narrow and exclusive application of the term. This He did, not only by direct command in 5:44-48, but by the parable of the Good Samaritan. Then Jesus turned the tables on the quibbling lawyer by asking: "Which now of these three . . . was neighbour unto him that fell among the thieves?" (Luke 10:36). The point was so unmistakable that the lawyer could not avoid giving the obvious answer. Fulfilling this second great commandment cannot be done by restricting the sphere of obligation but by expanding the concept of neighbor to include any person in need of any aid one can give. Especially did Jesus by the parable demolish the barriers of race and class. Loving the neighbor demands neighborly love, which not only *feels* ("he had compassion"), but *acts*, daringly, sacrificially, and selflessly—and with follow-through. The second great commandment points beyond convention and convenience. It is more than the absence of hate. It is practical and dynamic.

See GREAT COMMANDMENTS, LOVE, AGAPĒ.

For Further Reading: *Baker's DCE;* Taylor, *Life in the Spirit,* 19-28; DeWolf, *Responsible Freedom,* 60 ff; Muelder, *Moral Law in Christian Social Ethics;* Wirt, *The Social Conscience of the Evangelical.*

RICHARD S. TAYLOR

NEOEVANGELICALISM. Evangelicalism reached a high point in the mid 19th century when it dominated American religion. After the Civil War, conflict between evangelicalism and liberalism led to decline and separation. By 1910 the theological battle had resulted in the fundamentalist movement, which insisted on belief in certain basic doctrines as a minimum for a Christian. These doctrines primarily were the virgin birth of Christ, His deity, His substitutionary atonement and bodily resurrection, His second coming, and the authority and inerrancy of the Bible (*NIDCC,* 396). This movement reached its peak in the 1920s.

After 1940 there came a resurgence of evangelical activity both intellectual and evangelistic, often called *neoevangelicalism.* Among many similar developments which could be cited, the founding of Fuller Theological Seminary, the Graham campaigns, and the launching of the periodical *Christianity Today* were especially influential. Neoevangelicalism agreed with the doctrines of the fundamentalists and the historic church confessions, but disagreed on matters of emphasis and strategy. The movement won an intellectual respectability with writers such as E. J. Carnell and Carl Henry (William Hordern, *A Layman's Guide to Protestant Theology,* 55; Bernard Ramm, *Handbook of Contemporary Theology,* 88). Also in the 1940s arose the National Association of Evangelicals.

In the 1960s the new evangelicalism took on a new mood that increased emphasis on the spiritual mission of the church. This "resurgence of evangelicalism" flowered in the 1970s by Intervarsity Missionary Conference (Urbana), Campus Crusade for Christ, Key 73, church growth emphasis, new publications, evangelical colleges and seminaries, the "This Is Life" movement, and a revitalization of the Christian Holiness Association and other Wesleyan advances (Donald G. Bloesch, *The Evangelical Renaissance,* 13-18).

See EVANGELICAL.

For Further Reading: Wells and Woodbridge, *The Evangelicals; Baker's DT,* 200; Quebedeaux, *The Young Evangelicals: Revolution in Orthodoxy;* and *Christianity Today.*

LEO G. COX

NEOORTHODOXY. *Neoorthodoxy,* a term that can be loosely applied to an influential theological movement of this century, is best understood as a reaction to the failure of religious liberalism to provide an adequate answer to the crisis of Western society in the early part of the century. World War I had brought into question many of the major beliefs of religious liberalism: the belief that progress in Western society was bringing the kingdom of God to fruition; the belief in the intrinsic goodness of man; the overemphasis on the immanence of God; and the reduction of Christianity to experience and ethics. This questioning burst as a bomb in the playground of Europe's theologians with the publication in 1919 of Karl Barth's *Commentary on Romans.* Barth strongly criticized theological liberalism as being unable to provide adequate answers to the questions he as a pastor in Safenwil, Switzerland, was being asked to answer. The "strange new world of the Bible," where God was God and not "man written large," which Barth sought to explore in his commentary, became known as "new" or "neoorthodoxy." This theological viewpoint, also known as *crisis* theology or *dialectical* theology, found varied expression in the writings of men such as Barth, Emil Brunner, Rudolph Bultmann, Paul Tillich, and Reinhold Niebuhr.

The varied expressions which range from the more "orthodox" Barth and Brunner to the more "neo" Bultmann, Tillich, and Niebuhr, still find some common principles and themes in their theologies. At least three basic principles undergird their thought. First is the influence of existentialism as espoused by Soren Kierkegaard (though Barth later sought to repudiate his reliance on S. K.). Second is the dialectic method (i.e., dialectical theology) which is not the progression of the Hegelian dialectic but rather sees religious truth as best expressed in *paradoxes.* Third is the acceptance of modern critical methods and modern views of science in the interpretation of the Bible.

Along with these three principles of interpretation, a number of common theological themes are found in neoorthodoxy. God is the Wholly Other, the one whose "infinite qualitative difference" from man makes it impossible for finite man to bridge the infinite gap between them. God transcends man as Creator and Redeemer, pointing to man's responsibility for his radical sinfulness and his inability to save himself. The infinite gulf between God and man can only be bridged when God speaks His Word, thereby revealing and disclosing himself to man. The Bible is the witness to this Word of God, though it is not the Word of God itself. This means the Bible is more than just great religious literature, it is inspired, but its inspiration is "hidden" in the words of men. It is thus historically conditioned and contains human error.

The Word of God is most fully expressed in Jesus Christ, in whom eternity breaks into time, the infinite becomes finite, and God becomes man. Jesus reveals both God's judgment on man's sin and His grace which alone can redeem man. The paradox of judgment-grace as revealed in the Word, Jesus, lays a claim on man, obligating him for responsible decision. Thrust into the knowledge of God's claim, man is faced with a "crisis," a decision which he cannot escape. The crisis, hence "crisis theology," is one of faith, where the "leap of faith," while not resolving, transcends in a divine-human encounter the paradox of judgment-grace. Man only truly knows himself and God in this divine-human encounter.

The theme of man's knowledge of himself as sinner is important in neoorthodoxy. The question of how man became a sinner is answered by saying we are all our own "Adam." We all rebel against our finitude and, wanting to be God, we all commit the Fall. Thus, the Fall is important in the explanation of the sinfulness of all mankind but not as a historical event. Concern for its historical facticity only leads to conflict with science, a conflict in which the Bible comes second best (according to neoorthodoxy).

The seriousness with which neoorthodoxy takes the sinfulness of man calls for a concomitant seriousness about the Atonement. Jesus, as the Word of God, was more than just a religious genius and martyr. It is in the Cross that victory over sin, death, and evil was realized because "God was in Christ, reconciling the world unto himself" (2 Cor. 5:19).

Man's radical sinfulness taints all his life, including society. This led neoorthodoxy to state that the structures of society are sinful also and in need of redemption. Therefore they concerned themselves with critiquing politics and unjust social structures, and commenting on controversial social issues, in hopes of bringing a Christian viewpoint to shine on them. But, there is no unanimity among these theologians on the answers to the perplexing social problems.

Though there is a variance of views on social issues, neoorthodoxy agrees that man's sinfulness makes it impossible to find more than a poor approximation of the kingdom of God within history. One result of this has been a renewed interest in the church as the unique bearer of God's purpose and grace within history. The other result is the renewal of interest in eschatology as the object of ultimate hope. While never being literalists in their view of eschatology, they did see the kingdom of God as being beyond historical analogy and man's ethical attainments. Eschatology is not so much about the end times as about the end of time.

Neoorthodoxy has provided a much-needed corrective for the theological liberalism of the early 20th century, in its emphasis on orthodox doctrines such as the transcendence of God, the sinfulness of man, and the efficacy of the Atonement for sins. But there are issues such as the relation of the Word of God to the word of man in Scripture, and the relation of religious symbolism to historical fact, along with others, that make neoorthodoxy less than satisfactory for most evangelical scholars.

See ORTHODOXY, EVANGELICAL, NEOEVANGELICALISM, FALL (THE), LIBERALISM.

For Further Reading: Kuhn, *Contemporary Evangelical Thought,* ed. Henry, 233-36; Porteous, *Prophetic Voices in Contemporary Theology;* Gundry and Johnson, *Tensions in Contemporary Theology;* Patterson, *Makers of the Modern Theological Mind;* Heron, *A Century of Protestant*

Theology; Nineham and Robertson, *Makers of Contemporary Theology;* MacKintosh, *Types of Modern Theology.*

MAXIE HARRIS III

NEO-PENTECOSTALISM. Sometimes referred to as the "Charismatic Revival," Neo-Pentecostalism is a movement active both in and out of organized churches that gives renewed attention to the work and ministry of the Holy Spirit and particularly to the spiritual gifts. Although it does not include some of the excesses and extravagances of the earlier and more revivalistic type of classical Pentecostalism, Neo-Pentecostalism is similar in affirming the distinctive teaching regarding the "baptism in the Spirit" as a spiritual experience for believers subsequent to their conversion. A more recent development within the movement seeks to give greater emphasis to tongues as a private prayer language than to public tongues speaking. Within Neo-Pentecostalism there is a much greater emphasis placed on experience than doctrine, allowing those involved to have a sense of unity that crosses many traditional doctrinal lines.

While often a divisive force within the established churches, Neo-Pentecostalism has contributed positively by necessitating a reexamination of the scriptural teachings regarding the work and ministry of the Holy Spirit, by bringing a renewed sense of emotion into many relatively "dead" religious groups, and by encouraging a more widespread involvement of the laity within the work and worship of the churches.

Most Wesleyans rejoice in whatever authentic renewal has occurred in Neo-Pentecostalism. They do, however, disavow the hermeneutical underpinnings of the movement, believing that the excessive emphasis on tongues speaking has insufficient biblical support.

See PENTECOST, PENTECOSTALISM, BAPTISM WITH THE HOLY SPIRIT, GIFTS OF THE SPIRIT, TONGUES (GIFT OF).

For Further Reading: Synan, ed., *Aspects of Pentecostal-Charismatic Origins;* O'Connor, *The Pentecostal Movement in the Catholic Church;* Quebedeaux, *The New Charismatics;* Hollenweger, *The Pentecostals.*

DON W. DUNNINGTON

NEOPLATONISM. This refers to a revival of Platonist teachings that began in the third century A.D. and largely ended by the sixth century. The most distinguished of the Neoplatonists were Plotinus (c. 205-70) and Proclus (411-85). Ammonius Saccas (c. 175-242), Plotinus' teacher, is often considered the founder. Porphyry (c. 232-303), a student of Plotinus, collected his teacher's writings into the many volumes of the *Enneads*. The Neoplatonists influenced Christian theology especially through Origen, Augustine, and Pseudo-Dionysius.

See PLATONISM.

J. KENNETH GRIDER

NEO-THOMISM. This has to do with the official revival of the teachings of Roman Catholic theologian Thomas Aquinas (1225-74). Through papal encyclicals of 1879 and 1907, Roman Catholic priests and priests-to-be were required to read Aquinas—partly, to ward off the encroachments of modernism. Theologians such as Etienne Gilson and Jacques Maritain, who adapt Aquinas' teachings to our 20th-century times, are called Neo-Thomists. Neo-Thomism is most respectful of Aristotle's views, and it makes wide use of natural as well as revealed sources for constructing Christian theology.

See THOMISM.

J. KENNETH GRIDER

NESTORIANISM. This is a Christological heresy. It represents the theology of Persian Christianity and the Christology of the Antiochian School. Named after Nestorius, patriarch of Constantinople (428-35), Nestorianism attempted to preserve the humanity of Christ, and held that in Christ there are two distinct substances (Godhead and manhood) with their separate characteristics (natures) complete and intact, though united in Christ. However, this concentration upon the humanity (in contrast to the Alexandrian focus upon the divinity of Christ), and the emphasis upon the separateness of substances and natures, implied in Christ a dual personality. The Incarnation becomes therefore merely a moral and voluntary union between the Logos and the man Jesus. "The man whom the Word assumed was a temple in which divinity dwelt through a voluntary union" (Gonzalez, *A History of Christian Thought,* 2:215). Since the Logos knew what the man Jesus would become, He entered into fellowship with His person in the womb of Mary. "As the man Jesus became morally stronger this intimate relationship became closer, climaxing into the resurrection and the ascension" (Heick, *A History of Christian Thought,* 1:175).

Restricted by this conceptuality with emphasis upon the humanity of Christ, it was natural therefore that Nestorius should object to the term *theotokos,* "mother of God," attributed to the Virgin Mary. It was this objection which brought Nestorius to a head-on clash with Cyril, patriarch of Alexandria (412-44), and Nestorian Christology was declared unorthodox in 431 at the Council at Ephesus. Nestorius was banished in 436, but he found a home in Persia, where the imperial ban could not harm him. Here his teaching became the official theology of Persian Christianity. Concern for the lost motivated this body of Christians who took the gospel as far as India.

Some scholars in recent years have sought to exonerate Nestorius from the charge of heresy. "He did not teach that in Christ two persons were mechanically joined together," declares Bethune-Baker. It was personal rather than doctrinal reasons which determined Nestorius' fate. "Nestorius was sacrificed to save the face of the Alexandrians. Nevertheless, the manhood of Christ was safeguarded, as distinct from the Godhead. . . . the union was left an ineffable mystery" (Bethune-Baker, 197-211).

See HUMANITY OF CHRIST, HYPOSTASIS.

For Further Reading: Bethune-Baker, *Nestorius and His Teaching, A Fresh Examination;* Cullmann, *The Christology of the New Testament;* Moule, *The Origin of Christology;* Pannenberg, *Jesus—God and Man.*

ISAAC BALDEO

NEW BEING. In contemporary theology this is a term used by Paul Tillich (1886-1965) to describe Jesus the Christ as the bearer and manifestation of the New Being. In His life, ministry, and death, He remained in complete union with the Ground of all Being. He sacrificed everything He could have gained for himself to conquer "estrangement" and maintain this unity. Hence He is the Man-from-above, the Christ, the Son of God, the Spirit, the Logos-who-became-flesh, the "New Being" (Tillich, *Systematic Theology,* 1:135-36; 2:97-180).

The term also describes the new life and even nature of the Christian whose life is radically transformed by the Holy Spirit. He is one who participates in Christ and as a result is a new creation (Tillich, *The Shaking of the Foundations,* 130-48; *Systematic Theology,* 3:138-72). Natural man belongs to the "old creation"—the "old state of things." In his "estrangement" (*Systematic Theology,* 2:29-78) he knows himself as the old being, flesh, the distortion of human nature, the abuse of his creativity (*Shaking of the Foundations,* 133). The new being is essential being under the conditions of existence, conquering the gap between essence and existence and united with the Ground of all Being. Christ brings in this new state of things, and Christianity is the message of the new creation (*The New Being,* 15-24).

The term New Being has its biblical basis in the Pauline terms "new creature" and "new creation." Salvation from the old state of things includes "participation" in the New Being (regeneration), "acceptance" of the New Being (justification), and "transformation" (sanctification) by the New Being. It is a complete "renewal" in terms of reconciliation, reunion, and resurrection (*Systematic Theology,* 3:221-43; *The New Being,* 20).

The theology of the "new being" is a theme central to the Law, Prophets, and Psalms. It is God who will make a *new covenant* with His people in which the law will be written in the heart. It is the gift of the *new heart* and a new spirit (Jer. 31:31-34; Ezek. 11:17-19; 18:31-32; Heb. 8:10-12). It is the creation of a new heart and the renewal of a right spirit resulting in love and obedience (Ps. 51:10; Jer. 9:23-26; Deut. 30:6).

In the NT Jesus is at once the Initiator and Fulfillment of the new covenant, as the only Mediator between God and man (Heb. 9:11-22; 12:24; Matt. 26:28; Mark 14:24; Luke 22:20; 1 Cor. 11:25; John 14:6; Acts 4:12). Through His life, death, and resurrection, all who belong to the old order of things (the first Adam) and therefore dead in trespasses and sins, can be created anew in Him (the Second Adam) by faith and have the witness of the Spirit that they are the children of God by redemption. Through Christ, God is doing a new thing (Romans 5—8; Ephesians 2; 2 Cor. 5:17; Gal. 6:15). Those made new in Christ no more live after the flesh (Rom. 6:6; Gal. 5:19-21), but live in the Spirit through faith as new creatures. They are born of the Spirit and made alive from the dead (John 3:1-7; Eph. 2:1-6). Their hearts may be made pure through faith in the blood of Jesus Christ and by the infilling of the Holy Spirit (1 John 1:1-9; Acts 15:8-9). They may be sanctified wholly by the Spirit (1 Thess. 5:23).

See NEW COVENANT, NEW BIRTH, REGENERATION, NEOORTHODOXY, SANCTIFICATION.

For Further Reading: Tillich, *Systematic Theology; The New Being; The Shaking of the Foundations;* Kerr, *Readings in Christian Thought;* McKelway, *The Systematic Theology of Paul Tillich.*

ISAAC BALDEO

NEW BIRTH. The term *new birth* refers to that work of grace wrought by God in the heart of a repentant sinner when he believes in Christ as his Savior and is given spiritual life. *New birth* is not found in the Bible but is based on statements found in John 1:12; 3:3, 5, 7; 1 John 3:1; etc.

The word "regeneration" is synonymous with *new birth.* It comes from the Latin word *regeneratus,* meaning "made over" or "born again." It appears twice in the NT: in Matt. 19:28 and in Titus 3:5. In the latter passage it refers to the personal spiritual birth of a believer; in the former, to the general renewal at the end of time when God will make all things new (cf. Isa. 11:6; 65:25; Rom. 8:18-23; 2 Pet. 3:13; Revelation 21—22).

The spiritual renewal that takes place in a believer is described in John 3:5-8; 10:28; 1 John 5:11-12; and 2 Pet. 1:4 as the communication of divine life to the soul. In 2 Cor. 5:17 and Eph. 2:10; 4:24 it is shown to be the impartation of a new nature.

Jesus, Peter, James, and John refer to spiritual regeneration as a birth (John 3:5, 7; 1 Pet. 1:3, 23; 2:2; Jas. 1:18; 1 John 3:9). Paul uses the term "adoption" to describe it (cf. Rom. 8:15; Gal. 4:5; Eph. 1:4-5). *New birth* underlines the reception of the nature of God (the Father) by the believer; "adoption" stresses the believer's change of family. Once he was a child of the devil (John 8:44; 1 John 3:10), but now he belongs to the family of God (Ephesians 1—2; 5:1).

Because regeneration sometimes is referred to in Scripture as a birth, some Calvinists hold that the new birth, like physical birth, is an experience in which the individual does not participate. That is, repentance and faith are said to come after regeneration, which is completely a sovereign act of God (cf., e.g., Berkhof, *Systematic Theology,* 465). But the Scriptures indicate that repentance and faith precede and are conditions for regeneration (Isa. 55:7; Luke 13:3, 5; John 3:16, 18; Acts 2:37-38; 3:19; 16:31; etc.). No scripture passage suggests that repentance and faith have their origin subsequent to regeneration. Some Calvinists press the analogy of birth farther than Jesus and the apostles intended.

Birth and adoption are among a number of analogies used in the NT, none of which excludes the others. Christ is called the Good Shepherd, and believers are called sheep. Christ is the Vine; believers are the branches. Christ is the King (Lord); believers are subjects (servants). Christ is the Master (Teacher); believers are called disciples. Christ is the Chief Cornerstone; believers are building stones. Christ is the Bridegroom, and believers are the Bride. Each analogy expresses an important truth; but none of them can safely be pressed beyond the point of scriptural support. To do so is to fall into error.

See REGENERATION, FIRST WORK OF GRACE, JUSTIFICATION, ADOPTION.

For Further Reading: Ralston, *Elements of Divinity,* 417-33; Berkhof, *Systematic Theology,* 465-79; Gamertsfelder, *Systematic Theology,* 503-13; Wakefield, *A Complete System of Christian Theology,* 424-32.

W. RALPH THOMPSON

NEW COMMANDMENT. Jesus' statement in John 13:34 immediately raises the question of how He could describe the love command as a "new" commandment. The injunction to love one's neighbor as oneself is found in the OT (Lev. 19:18), and the Synoptic Gospels recount Jesus' application of that commandment earlier in His ministry (Matt. 22:39; cf. Mark 12:31; Luke 10:27). The context of Jesus' words in the Gospel of John supplies three possible meanings for the newness of the commandment, any one or all of which may be applied with edifying results.

The command may be new in the degree of love it enjoins. The evangelist has already described the extent of Jesus' love for the disciples (13:1). Later in the discourses, Jesus himself will speak of demonstrating love by laying down one's life for one's friends (15:13). The newness of the command may be in terms of the motive for loving one another. Jesus does not ask them to do any more than He himself has done (cf. vv. 10-12). The disciples are to love to the degree which Jesus commands, because He has loved them to that same degree. There is the new motive. But the commandment may be understood as new because it is at the center of the new covenant. In John's Gospel, Jesus' words of command have the place that is filled in the Synoptics by His words instituting the Lord's Supper (cf. Luke 22:20). This new covenant of mutual love is the earthly counterpart of the relationship between the Father and the Son (cf. John 14:23; 17:23, 26).

See AGAPĒ, NEW COVENANT, GREAT COMMANDMENTS.

For Further Reading: Brown, *The Gospel According to John XIII-XXI,* 612-14; Ladd, *A Theology of the New Testament,* 278-80; Lindars, *The Gospel of John,* 463-64; Morris, *The Gospel According to John,* 632-33.

HAL A. CAUTHRON

NEW COVENANT. "Covenant," biblically and theologically speaking, is an agreement between God and man which becomes the basis of divine blessing and eternal salvation. Such an agreement or contract is initiated by God, and its terms specified by God. Man becomes a partner to the agreement voluntarily. In the covenant God undertakes certain obligations and promises certain divine blessings on clearly defined moral conditions. God will not violate His promises, though they may be annulled and hence forfeited by man's violation of the terms.

The entire Bible is a history of covenants entered into by God with man, first with Adam, then Noah, Abraham, and then with the children of Israel at Mount Sinai, through the mediatorial agency of Moses. The "new covenant" is the covenant of grace instituted by Christ Jesus, an agreement made available by God through His Son to all believers. That portion of the Bible called the New Testament is totally about the new covenant. It is "new" in relation to all previous covenants, now made old and obsolete. Especially is its newness in contrast to the Mosaic system.

The exposition of the new covenant is the very backbone of Paul's writings, even though the word "covenant" is not often used. His interest focuses on "two covenants" (Gal. 4:24), the Mosaic and the Christian, one providing justification by law, the other justification by faith. Paul's exposition of these two major contrasting systems are primarily in Romans and Galatians, though fundamental motifs of his covenant teaching run throughout his Epistles.

The Epistle most systematically devoted to an elucidation of the new covenant is Hebrews. In this Epistle the writer argues that the new covenant is better, because initiated by One greater than Moses, because based on better promises (content, not reliability), and ratified by better blood. The epitome of the new covenant is given twice, in 8:6-12 and 10:15-18. This epitome is a quotation from Jer. 31:31-34, the clearest OT promise of a new covenant.

The new covenant provides for three privileges distinctly superior to any previous covenant. (1) Reconciliation with God will not depend on repeated sacrifices, but will be complete forgiveness based on a once-for-all sacrifice of Christ's own blood (Heb. 10:1-18). (2) Knowledge of the Lord will not be secondhand but personal, individual, and experiential (8:11). One could be under the Mosaic covenant, even honestly endeavoring to observe it, without personally knowing the Lord. But under the new covenant, knowing the Lord belongs to its very essence. (3) Righteous behavior will not be achieved by law and its sanctions, by elaborate systems of ceremony and restraint, but by an inner transformation so profound that the nature is conformed to the demands of righteousness.

From being written on tablets of stone, the new covenant provides for the writing of God's moral law on the heart (8:10). The lack of such inward conformity was the one cause for the failure of all previous covenants. Yet this could not become experientially available until Christ and Pentecost had come (though individuals did at times leap ahead of their dispensation, e.g., Isaiah). Paul before his conversion exemplified that kind and measure of righteousness which was normative under the Mosaic system, but he testifies to its inadequacy and the great superiority of that righteousness made available in Christ (Phil. 3:4-9).

The old covenant was corporate first, then individual as a reflex of its corporate inclusiveness. That is to say, an Israelite was born into the covenant and received subvolitionally its mark, circumcision. He had no choice in being in the covenant, though he could be "cut off" from Israel by deliberate affront to the community. Physically or racially no one is born into the new covenant. Access is by the new birth and is personal and voluntary first, corporate only second, as the reflex of the personal.

An emphatic insistence in Hebrews is the radical obsolescence of the old covenant (8:13, NASB). With it goes the validity of any religion which depends on forms and ceremonies. Even the sacraments must not be allowed to become the absolutes that circumcision was.

See COVENANT THEOLOGY, BIBLE: THE TWO TESTAMENTS, LAW AND GRACE, HOLINESS, HOLY COMMUNION.

For Further Reading: Wesley, *Works*, 5:63-76; 10:238-42; *BBC*, 10:91-129; Taylor, *A Right Conception of Sin*, 91-101; Hughes, *A New Heaven and a New Earth*, *115-27*.

RICHARD S. TAYLOR

NEW HEAVENS AND NEW EARTH. This is a phrase used several times in the Bible to describe the ultimate destiny of the redeemed. The popular Christian idea of final salvation is that we die and go to heaven. This contains a truth, for indeed to be absent from the body is to be present with the Lord (2 Cor. 5:8). However, this refers to the intermediate state, not to final salvation. Redemption includes the redemption of the body in the resurrection, and it includes also the redemption of the earth. "Creation itself will be set free from its bondage to decay and obtain the glorious liberty of the children of God" (Rom. 8:21, RSV). In creation the earth was created to be man's dwelling place, and at the end the earth will be redeemed and transformed to be the dwelling place of the resurrected saints.

The new redeemed earth stands in both continuity and discontinuity with the present order. Sometimes in the OT the new order is pictured in very "this worldly" terms, as though the redeemed earth is nothing but this earth delivered from its bondage to decay and death. "The wolf shall dwell with the lamb, and the leopard shall lie down with the kid . . . The sucking child shall play over the hole of the asp . . . They shall not hurt or destroy in all my holy mountain; for the earth shall be full of the knowledge of the Lord as the waters cover the sea" (Isa. 11:6, 8-9, RSV). This concept of a renewed earth appears with great variety of detail in the prophets. Later in Isaiah we have a different picture where the element of discontinuity is prominent. "'For behold, I create new heavens and a new earth; and the former things shall not be remembered or come into mind'" (65:17, RSV; see also 66:22).

The element of discontinuity is most strongly emphasized in 2 Pet. 3:12 f. In the day of God "the heavens will be kindled and dissolved, and the elements will melt with fire! But according to his promise we wait for new heavens and a new earth in which righteousness dwells" (RSV).

This is the picture given us in the Book of Revelation, but with considerable detail. "Then I saw a new heaven and a new earth; for the first heaven and the first earth had passed away, and the sea was no more" (21:1, RSV). The center of the new earth was the new Jerusalem, the holy city, which John saw coming down out of heaven, prepared as a bride adorned for her bridegroom (v. 2). The city is pictured in highly symbolic terms. It seems to be the shape of a cube 1,500 miles high, 1,500 miles long, and 1,500 miles wide. Such a city is nearly impossible to visualize in this-worldly terms; it relates to the vastness and the perfect symmetry of the city. It is surrounded by a wall 225 feet high—obviously out of proportion to the dimensions of the city. But why does the heavenly city need a wall? Only the redeemed have access to the city. The answer again is simple: ancient cities had walls, and John is trying to describe the ineffable by the familiar. Through the middle of the street of the city flowed the river of life. On either side of the river was the tree of life, whose leaves were for the healing of the nations. Taken as stark prose, this presents an impossible picture, for we must then ask, In which street was the river? Obviously, this is the wrong question.

The great reality of the new earth and the heavenly city is that "there shall no more be anything accursed, but the throne of God and of the Lamb shall be in it, and his servants shall worship him: *they shall see his face*" (22:3-4, RSV, italics added). In these words the whole of redemption is embodied.

See HEAVEN, RESURRECTION OF THE BODY, ESCHATOLOGY.

For Further Reading: Biederwolf, *The Millennium Bible,* 708-26; Smith, *The Biblical Doctrine of Heaven,* 223-36; Hughes, *A New Heaven and a New Earth.*

GEORGE ELDON LADD

NEW HERMENEUTIC. The root meaning of *hermeneia,* from which *hermeneutic* is derived, is "translation" or "interpretation." It includes exegesis (what *did* the text mean?), interpretation (what does it *now* mean?), and the transition from one to the other. Linguistically, *hermeneia* includes language translation and clarification or articulation of the obscure or mystical (commentary), particularly by priests in reference to numinous or revelatory events.

The *new hermeneutic* focuses specifically on the reinterpretation of the ancient text (Bible) for contemporary (20th century) proclamation by attempting to transfer the meaning of the past into present reality and by emphasizing the interrelatedness of language, faith, history, and understanding. Three basic areas are addressed: the credibility of the Bible for the modern age; the normative nature of the past for the present; the validity of historical knowledge.

The roots of the new hermeneutic are found in Schleiermacher, Dilthey, and Heidegger; its chief recent proponents are Bultmann, Fuchs, and Ebeling. Against the fragmented results of the historico-critical method and the presuppositional approaches of philosophical theology, the new hermeneutic questions the unchanging structure of reality, and advocates existential involvement with the text through both historical awareness of prior interpretations and openness to new expressions and forms.

God's "word-event" of Scripture discloses the truth and reality of the human situation; this "essential word" (Heidegger) must be renewed in each situation as new reality is uncovered. The text is independent but also interrelates with the listener (interpreter). The more that is known, the greater is the possibility of asking the right questions of the text in an I-Thou relationship. The text is interpreted; the interpreter is in turn interpreted by the text (the hermeneutical circle).

The process of "demythologization" seeks to reaffirm language as communication, rather than information; the text interprets, challenges, and affirms human existence in the decision of faith as authentic, interrelated, united, and freeing, or inauthentic, fragmented, enslaving, and corrupting. God himself is the *word-event* of biblical language. Man is not *creative* of language but responsible toward it. Language reflects what is taking place within a given culture but also expedites our authentic self-understanding.

The response of faith is thus a way of life to be rearticulated further as God confronts us in the *word-event* of the biblical language, the sermonic proclamation and its challenge, and the hearer's response of authentic existence within the changing cultural context.

See HERMENEUTICS, BIBLICAL AUTHORITY, EXEGESIS, BIBLE: THE TWO TESTAMENTS, KERYGMA, BIBLICAL THEOLOGY, CRITICISM (OT, NT), PROGRESSIVE REVELATION.

For Further Reading: Achtemeier, *An Introduction to the New Hermeneutic;* Robinson and Cobb, Jr., *The New Hermeneutic* (*New Frontiers in Theology,* vol. 2); Ridderbos, *Studies in Scripture and Its Authority.*

JOHN S. LOWN

NEW MORALITY. Popularly, this refers to the recent "playboy" philosophy which advocates new moral views that have maximum sexual pleasure as their goal.

Theologically, the *new morality* refers particularly to the views of Joseph Fletcher, advocated in his *Situation Ethics* and elsewhere. This new kind of ethical theory advocates acting, in each life situation, according to what is the most loving thing to do at the time. Fletcher, an Episcopalian seminary professor, said his view is not antinomian because it does advocate obedience to one law—the law of love. Also, Fletcher wanted people to be informed by the stored-up Christian wisdom of the centuries as they make the decision about what is the most loving thing to do.

Yet the view has many inadequacies. One is in its advocating that there is only one principle: love. For example, the most just thing might be to put a mass murderer to death. Justice and other interests, as well as love, surely, are proper bases for our actions. Another inadequacy of the view is that the individual is the one who decides what to do, instead of God (by His revealed will). Still another inadequacy is that it advocates deciding "in the situation"; and that might be a poor time to do this deciding. On the basis that there are rights and wrongs, a person can decide ahead of time what course he would follow on, say, sexual relations—before he or she is thrown into a situation when sexual desire might well prejudice the situation. Still another inadequacy is that what seems the most loving thing to do might not take into account future guilt and guilt feelings, or other future undesirable results, of doing what seems to be the most loving thing at the time.

Perhaps the most serious defect in Fletcher's thesis is its assumption that man is able to know what is the most loving thing to do and able to do it. This presupposes inherent goodness and wisdom, and ignores the sinful proclivity toward selfishness and moral obtuseness which is universally observable. The underlying optimism in the so-called new morality, which in effect denies man's sinfulness and need of regenerating grace, is not supportable by either Scripture or the facts of life.

See ETHICAL RELATIVISM, ETHICS, CHRISTIAN ETHICS, MORALITY.

For Further Reading: Henry, *Answers for the Now Generation,* 89; DeWolf, *Responsible Freedom,* 25-39; Geisler, *Ethics: Alternatives and Issues,* 60-77.

J. KENNETH GRIDER

NEW TESTAMENT. See BIBLE: THE TWO TESTAMENTS.

NICENE CREED. The Nicene Creed is one of the so-called ecumenical creeds of the Christian church, i.e., those statements of belief adopted by "ecumenical" councils of clergy as definitive of the church's theological understanding and teaching prior to the permanent split between Eastern and Western Christians in A.D. 1054.

The creed takes its name from the Council of Nicea called by the Emperor Constantine in June, A.D. 325, to settle a dispute over the teachings of Arius and his supporters, and thereby to bring about much-needed unity in the church and the empire as a whole. Constantine's goal was not realized, however, for while the council did agree on an anti-Arian statement of belief, it did not bring to an end debate in the church, which swirled on for over a century. In fact, the version of the Nicene Creed most widely accepted and used in later times did not reach its final form until the Council of Constantinople set it down in A.D. 381 after a tumultuous period in which, totally contrary to the creed, the Arian position had actually managed to become the "official" one in the church for a time and various pro- and anti-Nicene leaders had been alternately banished and reinstated. The Council of Chalcedon in A.D. 451 was still wrestling with some of the same issues, in somewhat altered form, raised by Nicea.

The main issue addressed by the Nicene Creed is the full deity of the Second Person of the Trinity; this it affirms. Arius, by contrast, taught that the Son was a being created in time, qualitatively different from God the Father, by no means immutable or coeternal with God, "alien from and utterly dissimilar to the Father's essence and individual being" (Kelly, *Early Christian Doctrines,* 228). Arius believed that the Son was "God," but only in a derivative sense, yet held that He is worthy of worship.

Arius' opponents, led by Alexander and Athanasius, saw this as practical polytheism and held that the Scriptures affirm that God is One, the Son being eternal, uncreated, and in essence the same as the Father. They also saw the Christian doctrine of redemption in Christ assaulted by Arius' position, for, only if the Redeemer were truly divine, they argued, could fellowship with God be reestablished by Him. Their position was adopted by the clergy at Nicea and reaffirmed at Constantinople with the essential identity of Father and Son being enshrined in the creed in the Greek phrase *homoousian*—i.e., Christ as the Son is of "the *same* essence or substance" as the Father, and thereby is himself God. This has remained the teaching of the Christian church through the centuries.

See APOSTLES' CREED, ATHANASIAN CREED, CREED (CREEDS), CHRISTOLOGY, HYPOSTASIS, ARIANISM.

For Further Reading: Kelly, *Early Christian Creeds,* 205-62; *Early Christian Doctrines,* 223-51; Pelikan, *The Emergence of the Catholic Tradition,* 191-225; Schaff, *The Creeds of Christendom,* 1:24-29. HAROLD E. RASER

NOMINALISM. See REALISM AND NOMINALISM.

NON-CHRISTIAN RELIGIONS. In order to be properly understood and evaluated, the non-Christian religions need to be examined in the light of some general observations.

1. *The Bible's own explanation of their appearance.* This is to be found in Rom. 1:18-32 and 2:14-18. Romans 1 states that, at the beginning, all men knew God but did not want to retain Him in their knowledge because of their sin; therefore they invented gods of their own which did all of the wicked things they committed. The polytheism of Greek and Roman religion is a particularly clear example of this. However, though man rejected the true God, he still retained the "work of the law" in his heart (2:14-18).

These two facts are clearly illustrated in all of the primitive religions. They have certain moral standards corresponding to the principles stated in the Ten Commandments, though in perverted forms. And they do retain, in their folklore and religious practices, days when they commune and worship the "High God" or "Sky God." Because He is entirely kind and good, they generally worship Him only one day in the year. In contrast they worship the other deities often in order to protect themselves from their evil powers.

2. *The appearance of biblical concepts and customs among the primitives.* Don Richardson, as a missionary of the Christian and Missionary Alliance in Indonesia, discovered and used the concept of a "peace child" in some cannibalistic tribes, and deciphered other biblically related phenomena (cf. his *Lords of the Earth* and *Eternity in Their Hearts*).

3. *The existence of certain highly rational monotheistic concepts.* These may be found in Zoroastrianism with its Ahura Mazda, and in Muhammadanism (Islam) with its Allah. However, only the Christian, with the aid of the Scriptures, can develop monotheism in a fully logically satisfactory manner. The monotheism developed by Zoroaster and Muhammad, as well as that of modern Unitarianism, is self-destructive.

A study of Aristotle's view of God illustrates this. When he developed his idea logically, he ran into serious difficulties. If God, who has existed as a personal being from eternity past, were to create a physical universe, then He would add an I-it or subject-object relationship between himself and the universe; and if He made man, an I-thou relationship between himself and man; and He would experience, for the first time, a we-you, or social relationship, as He saw Adam and Eve bring forth and nurture their first child. This would be impossible, Aristotle argued, since it would mean that God was not eternally fully developed within himself, or, as he put it, *actus purus.* Further, we can add He would need the universe, man, woman, and child, to be equal to man.

The Christian revelation alone handles this problem. God has always been *actus purus.* All of His personal potentialities have been fully developed within himself since eternity past. The explanation for this is in the doctrine of the Holy Trinity.

Reason without revelation has always led to error in all man's unitarian views of God. From this we can make a further observation.

4. *Revelation and reason belong together.* Revelation, so-called, which conflicts with reason cannot enable men to reach a sound view of God. Aristotle's struggle with the problem of the need for a monotheistic view of God proves that reason alone is insufficient. Muhammad's writings in the Koran prove equally that a mystical revelation which is not rationally self-authenticating also fails.

5. The Bible addresses itself *to the entire spectrum of man's existential problems* and yet distinguishes man's primary need (guilt and sin and the need of salvation) from his lesser problems (cf. Mark 8:36). The non-Christian religions address themselves only to certain secondary and often tangential needs.

Specific non-Christian religions should be examined with these background observations in mind. They may be summarily classified as follows.

Primitive religions. Primitive religions are polytheistic, and yet they retain, in the form of myths, a worship of the true God.

Greek and Roman religions. These were polytheistic and illustrated Paul's description of paganism very clearly. They included the "mystery" religions, so expressive of both spiritual darkness and spiritual hunger.

Eastern mysticism. This starts off with the concept of monism, with everything existing as Being or God, and called the One, in which—as a logical consequence—no dualities, such as subject and object, good and evil, and time and space, exist. Being becomes active and creative through a polar dialectic which develops between Yang and Yin, male and female principles. The universe and man come into being through this dialectic. Eastern mysticism stresses the total difference between existence in God and physical existence, which it calls *Maya* or illusion. Man passes through thousands of reincarnations —as man, animal, insect, or plant—before returning to *Being*.

The problem addressed by Eastern mysticism is that posed by inequalities due to birth and race, to health, and to personal fortune and misfortune. The *law of karma,* or cause and effect of man's deeds, determines man's particular existences both as to class and kind. Because of the successive cycles of existence Lord Krishna returns, from time to time, to repeat revelation. Salvation consists in attaining to reunion with Being or the All through enlightenment and meditation. At this point the soul enters *Nirvana,* which is timeless and spaceless and beyond good and evil (no dualities), and becomes totally impersonal.

Eastern mysticism lacks a truly personal God. He materializes himself in the physical universe and comes to self-consciousness in man. Man is therefore greater than God, on the one hand, and needed by God, on the other. Eastern mysticism uses evil to make God creative, and it leaves man to struggle with this evil in his existence. It presents the most extended religion of works, on the one hand, and the most hopeless plan of salvation on the other. In its own way it builds in all of the polytheism found in the later Greek and Roman religions. It confines itself to one problem and ignores the rest. And it finally consigns man to the oblivion of Nirvana.

Humanism. This needs to be studied separately since it is essentially atheistic. Confucius was the first great humanist. He worked out a religion of social ethics. Humanism emerged as a distinct system of religion in the Western world with the appearance of *Humanist Manifesto* No. 1 in 1933 and No. 2 in 1973. It deceptively describes itself as "religious humanism," though it is totally atheistic. It defines religion as love and concern for man and his needs alone. It is the main cause of the failure of modern education.

Monotheistic religions. These fall into two classes. First, there is the rationalistic monotheism of Zoroastrianism and of Muhammadanism (Islam). Second, there is the revealed monotheism of Judaism and Christianity. The two examples given of rationalistic monotheism are based upon reason plus mystical experience. In contrast, revealed monotheism rests upon revelation and logical reason—it clears with reason. This is most clearly seen in Christianity where the doctrine of the Triune God presents the only absolutely holy, yet fully personal God.

In the OT, which alone is accepted by the Jews, all of the manifest qualities of a fully personal, self-sufficient God appear, though in such a form that they have never been grasped without the acceptance of the NT. The blindness of the Jews to the revelation of the Triune God in the OT is paralleled by their blindness to the prophecies of the Messiah, concerning His first coming and His substitutionary atonement on the Cross, as revealed in Isaiah 53.

See HUMANISM, ZOROASTRIANISM, CULTS, ISLAM, HARE KRISHNA, JUDAISM, GNOSTICISM, CHRISTIANITY, UNIFICATION CHURCH, TRANSCENDENTAL MEDITATION, TRINITY (THE HOLY), COMPARATIVE RELIGION.

For Further Reading: Perry, *The Gospel in Dispute;* Anderson, ed., *The Theology of the Christian Mission,* 135-228; Parrinder, *A Dictionary of Non-Christian Religions;* Noss, *Man's Religions*. R. ALLAN KILLEN

NONCONFORMITY. In the general sense of the term Webster defines nonconformity as "absence of agreement or correspondence in any matter." Thus each snowflake or grain of sand is nonconformist in that it differs from others.

Usually the term has social, cultural, or religious relevance. It is "a relative term which supposes some previously existing system of observances, established either by political authority or general consent, and denotes a practical secession or non-communion, on grounds conceived by the parties to require or justify it" (McClintock and Strong, *Cyclopedia,* 7:161).

"Nonconformist" with a capital *N* is "used generally to describe the position of those who do not conform to the doctrine and practices of an established church," more particularly to "those who left the Church of England rather than submit to the Act of Uniformity (1662)" (Douglas, *NIDCC*, 714). "Dissenters," "Nonconformists," "Free Churchmen" were and are terms used to describe Quakers, Methodists, Baptists, Presbyterians, Congregationalists, and others. The intensity of the feelings and rigors of the ecclesiastical and political tensions across three centuries would be difficult to exaggerate.

However, with the erosion of the dominance of established or state churches and the fluid relativism of church life in general, nonconformity has tended to become so common as to be the conformity of our day.

Biblical Christians are not to conform to secular worldliness, and yet as the salt of the earth they must identify with society in order to exert their saving influence. It is reasonable to suppose that one should balance a respect for the opinions of one's social and religious groups with a commitment to one's own choice and conscience.

See WORLD (WORLDLINESS), OBEDIENCE, CONFORMITY, SURRENDER.

For Further Reading: *Baker's DT,* 380; Qualben, *A History of the Christian Church,* 326; Taylor, *A Return to Christian Culture,* 62-77.

JOHN E. RILEY

NONDIRECTIVE COUNSELING. See ROGERIAN COUNSELING.

NUMINOUS, THE. *The numinous* is a term for the mystery and majesty of God, who is "wholly other," beyond sensory perception, logical definition, or even the beautiful or good. He does, however, make us aware of His presence and His holiness. A study of the holiness of God so perceived attracts those who stress holiness in Christian experience.

The root meaning of the holiness of God is what Rudolf Otto seeks among primitive people, reporting that they sense His power, not His purity. In *The Idea of the Holy,* Otto analyzes this concept: overwhelming might, yet fascination for men, even bliss in God's fellowship. These make up what Otto calls the *numinous.*

Evangelical believers appreciate Otto's motive: to establish intuitive knowledge of God, transcending rationalistic objection. Men cannot comprehend God but they can contact Him.

Some holiness theologians accept the concept of the numinous, for purity without mystery and awe could lead to ethical standards without power. God, however, is not wholly "wholly other," for He can redeem and sanctify men through Christ, and is pleased to indwell through the Holy Spirit. And while Jesus taught reverence ("Hallowed be thy name"), He also taught us to pray, "Our Father" (Matt. 6:9; Luke 11:2).

See GOD, ATTRIBUTES (DIVINE), TRANSCENDENCE.

For Further Reading: Otto, *The Idea of the Holy;* Purkiser, ed., *Exploring Our Christian Faith,* 324-27; Barker, *Who's Who in Church History,* 213.

LOUIS A. BOUCK

NURTURE. See DISCIPLING.

O

OBEDIENCE. Obedience is compliance with external commands or requirements. The authority to be obeyed may be statutory law, of God or man, or it may be an authority person such as parent, employer, policeman, or commanding officer. Obedience may be external and formal only, perhaps even grudging, or it may be willing, prompted by an inward acknowledgment of the other's rightful authority. There seems to be, therefore, two clearly defined uses of the term, one objective and practical, and the other ethical and psychological. The first refers more to conduct, and the second to belief and one's mental attitude toward the object of obedience.

In the OT God revealed His plans and purposes to Israel by the use of His "word" or His "voice" through His messengers. Thus the idea of obedience is intimately connected with the Hebrew word *shama,* "to hear." So closely intertwined is "hearing" and "obeying" that translators are often pressed to know when to translate *shama* "hear" or "obey." In Hebrew religion to truly hear is to obey. Failure to obey would indicate that a person had not really heard.

In Scripture the matter of hearing and obeying is often used in human relationships, as between parents and children, slaves and masters, kings and subjects, etc. But it is man's obedience to God that is of paramount importance. It is plain that God expected obedience from man from the very beginning. Obedience then is the supreme test of one's faith in God and one's love for God. In the OT it is the one important relationship that must not be broken. Man's relationship to God at this point is best expressed by the prophet Samuel, "To obey is better than sacrifice, and to hearken than the fat of rams" (1 Sam. 15:22).

In the OT the future blessedness and prosperity of the chosen people were conditioned upon their obedience to the covenant God made with them at Sinai (Isa. 1:19; Exod. 19:5; 23:22). Unfortunately, Israel's history has been one of persistent refusal to follow God's plan and program. All the nation's troubles can be traced to her failure to obey God's commands.

The NT follows the OT idea of obedience. The usual Greek term is *hupakoē*, "to hear." Jesus was following the OT usage when He said to the multitudes, "He that hath an ear, let him hear." He clearly meant that He not only wanted them to hear from a physical standpoint, but to respond in faith to the precepts that He had laid down, that is, obey His injunctions. In this way their hearing would become obedience. This is precisely the kind of action that the prophets of the OT had hoped to get from their hearers. Again Jesus said, "Every one who hears these words of Mine, and acts upon them, may be compared to a wise man, who built his house upon the rock" (Matt. 7:24, NASB). Thus "to hear" meant that the hearers believed and acted. The evidence that people had "heard" (obeyed) was that they repented and believed the gospel and went forth to live different lives.

In the Wesleyan movement the idea of obedience is intimately bound up with the doctrine of entire sanctification or Christian holiness. For most people who seek to enter into this relationship with God the matter of genuine obedience is the sticking point. It is at the same time the most difficult and the most important prerequisite for entering into this experience. Thus wholehearted obedience lays the groundwork for real faith—in fact, it is real faith. We can now see that the terms "complete consecration," "utter abandonment," or "absolute surrender" mean nothing more or less than complete obedience to all the known will of God; and further, that there is no such thing as *saving* faith apart from obedience.

See FAITH, CHRISTIAN, UNBELIEF, REPENTANCE.

For Further Reading: Clippinger, "Obedience," *ISBE;* Kittel, 1:216; Knight, "Philippians," *BBC;* Stoger, *Sacramentum Verbi,* vol. 2.

C. PAUL GRAY

OBEDIENCE OF CHRIST. The obedience of Christ is inextricably bound up with God's plan for redeeming the human race. Sometime, somewhere, the Godhead had to make a decision if the race was to be saved. We do not know all the details of this decision. But we do know from Scripture that a sacrifice had to be provided as an atonement for man's sin. We know still further that Christ gave himself to be the Propitiation for the sins of the whole world (Rom. 3:25; 1 John 2:2; 4:10; Gal. 1:4; Eph. 5:2; 1 Tim. 2:6).

But for the plan to work, the Second Person of the Triune Godhead had to become man; the Creator must become the creature. What condescension! It is at this point that the program of obedience began. Finding himself a man, Christ the Son humbled himself and became obedient to death—even death on a cross (Phil. 2:8).

While here on earth, although He knew himself to be the Son of God, He was definitely, and sometimes painfully, human. Since He had emptied himself of His heavenly prerogatives, He must live and learn, work, suffer, and die as a man. "Although He was a Son, He learned obedience from the things which He suffered; and having been made perfect, He became to all those who obey Him the source of eternal salvation" (Heb. 5:8-9, NASB). His obedience to the Father's plan led Him straight to the Cross. And His death on the Cross marked the fulfillment of His perfect obedience.

Many have raised the question, If Jesus was really the Son of God, why was it necessary to *learn* obedience? How and why should the perfect be *made* perfect? The answer seems to be that since He, the Son of God, emptied himself of His heavenly powers to become true flesh-and-blood man, it was necessary for His humanity to pass through all the stages of human life in order to complete His Saviorhood. Only then could He be truly the God-man. He must learn as men learn, He must obey as men must obey, for His Saviorhood to be complete.

Let us see what His obedience accomplished. First, He was the perfect exemplar of obedience: He was subject to His parents; was careful to keep the moral law; had a proper attitude toward authority; and was always ready to obey the Father. The old pattern so characteristic of Israel's disobedience was broken by the perfect obedience of Christ.

Second, His obedience qualified Him to be our Savior. A failure would have been fatal—the salvation of the race was at stake. But since He passed through all the vicissitudes of human existence, and was obedient in everything, no finger of scorn can be pointed at Him, but with the redeemed hosts of the Book of Revelation we cry in exultation, "Worthy is the Lamb" (Rev. 5:12).

Third, His obedience was the means by which He procured eternal salvation for men. The first Adam failed to obey God and brought death and destruction upon the human race. The Second Adam, although under the fiercest kind of temptation, rendered perfect obedience to the Father. His obedience, reversing what happened at the Fall, now makes it possible for man "to have a life that laughs at death, overleaps the grave, and swings outward and sweeps upward forever."

See OBEDIENCE, KENOSIS, CHRIST, ESTATES OF CHRIST, GETHSEMANE.

For Further Reading: Crannell, "Obedience of Jesus," *ISBE;* Knight, "Philippians," *BBC;* Wiley, *CT,* 2:143-216.

C. PAUL GRAY

OBJECTIVITY. Objectivity, usually contrasted with subjectivity, refers to the attitude of being unbiased in the process of knowing. Objectivity is usually considered, certainly by the scientific community, as a highly desirable goal, since it implies the absence of all distractions, all intervening or distorting (subjective) elements in the process of knowing an object. Since this goal is extremely difficult to achieve, *pure* objectivity is rarely if ever claimed. Many would say that such a state of pure receptivity is psychologically impossible.

In recent theological discussion, however, the traditional dichotomy between subject and object has, to some extent, given way to an "I-Thou" vs. an "I-It" distinction. In this context, subjectivity and objectivity are both viewed in their relation to the eternal. Truth, in the thought of Emil Brunner, for example, is seen as "encounter" rather than "truths" objectively revealed to man through the Bible and the Church. Revelation thus is not knowledge *about* God; rather, it is God *giving himself.* For this reason, natural theology and metaphysics cannot ever provide adequate knowledge of God; they see God as an *"It"* rather than as a *"Thou",* whom to know in the latter fashion is to be shaken to the depths and remade.

A more conservative approach sees revelation as both divine, personal self-disclosure *and* authentic teaching of timeless truths about God.

See I-THOU, PROPOSITIONAL THEOLOGY.

For Further Reading: Brunner, *Man in Revolt;* Hordern, *A Layman's Guide to Protestant Theology* (rev. ed.).

ALVIN HAROLD KAUFFMAN

OBLATION. See OFFER, OFFERING.

OCCULT, OCCULTISM. *Occult,* from the Latin *occultus,* means "secret" or "mysterious." The term has come to refer to knowledge beyond the range of ordinary understanding; knowledge of a supernatural kind, not bounded by modern scientific law. A fortune-teller, for example, claims knowledge of the occult because he says he can explain things which people generally cannot know.

Occultism is the belief in hidden, mysterious, supernatural agencies and the possibility of subjecting them to human control. Through alleged occult sciences, such as astrology, fortune-telling, magic, spiritism, and sorcery, occultists, usually insecure persons, seek to bend the will of God, as it were, and to hold their own against men whom they think oppose them. They try thereby to gain the upper hand in life's power struggle.

During ancient times there was wide belief in the occult, and the OT abounds with references to it. But both in Mosaic and prophetic times all types of occult practices were condemned. Examples are: Lev. 19:26; Deut. 18:9-13; Isa. 8:19. In the NT Jesus and His followers also met and opposed various forms of the occult. The apostle Paul, for example, faced up to the occult in Philippi (Acts 16:16-18). In Gal. 5:20 witchcraft, a form of the occult, is listed among the grossest of sins.

Writing of the theological place of the occult in the Bible, Kurt Koch suggests that in the OT occult phenomena are rooted in heathen magic; whereas in the NT activities are understood as symptoms of the conflict between the kingdom of the devil and the kingdom of God. Because of their implications in this conflict, all forms of occultism come under divine judgment and end in chaos (*Christian Counselling and Occultism,* 274).

The fact that in the last half of the 20th century the occult has mushroomed to epidemic proportions, much of it with clear marks of demon power, could very well be a sign of the times. When people reject Christ, their unbelief often becomes credulity. Not receiving a love of the truth, they are easy prey for satanic deception (2 Thess. 2:1-12).

See UNIFICATION CHURCH, TRANSCENDENTAL MEDITATION, HARE KRISHNA, SWEDENBORGIANISM, SATAN, DEMONS (DEMON POSSESSION).

For Further Reading: Unger, *Biblical Demonology;* Koch, *Christian Counselling and Occultism;* Tenney, "Worship of the Occult," *New Testament Survey.*

ARMOR D. PEISKER

OFFER, OFFERING. To offer, in religious context, is to present a sacrifice or gift as an act of worship. That which is presented or given is called an *offering* or *oblation.* The latter term derives from the Latin *oblatus* (offered up, devoted, dedicated), used as a past participle of the verb, to offer.

In the OT, these terms are especially prominent in Leviticus and Numbers (where there are more than 500 occurrences). Several kinds of offerings are prescribed within the Mosaic sacrificial system: (1) Sin offerings, for acts of unconscious transgression, mistakes, or other inadvertencies; (2) Trespass offerings, for guilt incurred by specific offenses; (3) Burnt offerings, symbolizing entire surrender to God; (4) Peace offerings, in renewal of right spiritual relations; (5) Meal and drink offerings, from the fruits of God's blessings upon the earth; (6) Heave and wave offerings (so called from the ceremony for their presentation), regarded as special gifts unto God.

The prophets and Psalmists repudiate the efficacy of multiplying offerings (Amos 5:21-23; Isa. 1:11-14; Mic. 6:6-9; Ps. 40:6-8). The protest was not so much against the sacrificial system itself as its abuse. Offerings and oblations alone cannot atone for sin. The presenting to God of a gift implies the personal surrender of the giver in living obedience to God's will.

Several fundamental ideas underlie the biblical conception of offerings: (1) God desires communion with His people; (2) Sin must be punished and/or expiated (atoned for); (3) Without the substitutionary sacrifice of life (shedding of blood), there is no forgiveness of sin.

The NT, especially Hebrews, points to the fulfillment of the old sacrificial system in Jesus Christ. The former repeated sacrifices were ineffectual to cleanse the conscience of the worshipper. But now Christ's sinless self-offering has effected once for all a perfect and eternal redemption.

The NT also exhorts us, as Christians, to present certain offerings to God: (1) The dedication of our bodies and minds (Rom. 12:1-2); (2) Deeds of love and fellowship (Heb. 13:16); (3) Material gifts and offerings (Phil. 4:18); (4) Praises and prayers (Heb. 13:15). Such are well-pleasing to Him.

See SACRIFICE, CONSECRATE (CONSECRATION), STEWARDSHIP, MOSAIC LAW, EXPIATION.

For Further Reading: Richardson, *Theology of the New Testament,* 297-301; *Unger's Bible Dictionary,* 942-52; Behm, *TDNT,* 3:180-90.

WAYNE G. MCCOWN

OFFICES, ECCLESIASTICAL. The simple distinction, well established by the early third century if not before, between *clergy,* as signifying those Christians set apart as ministers by consecration or ordination (cf. Acts 6:6; 13:3; etc.), and *laity* (from the Gr. *laos,* "people"), as signifying the remainder of the Christian community, through the centuries grew into a more complex situation involving distinctions between several offices within the Christian ministry itself.

In fact, some differentiation in ministerial function is discernible already in the NT, though there can be no certainty as to exactly what the titles there signify or how they differ from one another. Among the various names for those who were involved in the instruction and care of the churches are "elders" (Gr. *presbyteroi,* Acts 15:2; 20:17; 1 Tim. 5:17; Titus 1:5; Jas. 5:14); "those having charge over you" (1 Thess. 5:12); "overseers" or "bishops" (Gr. *episkopoi,* Acts 20:28; Phil. 1:1; 1 Tim. 3:2); "deacons" (Phil. 1:1; 1 Tim. 3:8, 12); "pastors" (Eph. 4:11); "apostles," "prophets," "evangelists," and "teachers" (Eph. 4:11; 1 Cor. 12:28). Paul, writing to the Corinthians, places some order on this array of ministerial offices in declaring that apostles, followed by prophets, and then teachers, head up a kind of "hierarchy" in which helpers and administrators of various sorts occupy lesser roles (1 Cor. 12:28 ff).

By the time of Ignatius of Antioch (d. A.D. 115) the "apostles," "prophets," and "teachers" of the first missionary generation had given way to "bishops," "presbyters," and "deacons" as the chief offices of ministry. The process of change is obscure, but it would appear that as local congregations consolidated, travelling missionaries came to be eclipsed by permanent resident ministers who could more adequately and consistently oversee the needs of the Church in each area. In this way a transition occurred from an itinerant ministry to a local and pastoral ministry. The "bishops," "presbyters," and "deacons" were the primary practitioners of the developing pastoral ministry.

Numerous writings of the second century indicate that at first the offices of bishop and presbyter were the same, with deacons making up a second, somewhat lesser office. Liturgical functions apparently set them apart with the presbyter-bishop presiding over the celebration of the Eucharist while the deacon assisted. Deacons were also administrators of church property and charitable relief. The latter role was shared by "deaconesses" who had special responsibilities for women.

In time, as certain presbyter-bishops arose to positions of preeminence, they assumed exclusively the title "bishop," while their ministerial brethren continued as "presbyters." These bishops claimed the power to ordain and to correspond on a church's behalf with other churches. Both offices came to be assisted not only by deacons but also a host of lesser offices, including those of "reader," "exorcist," "sub-deacon," and "acolyte."

See CLERGY, EPISCOPACY, CHURCH GOVERNMENT, CHAIN OF COMMAND, MINISTER (MINISTRY).

For Further Reading: Chadwick, *The Early Church,* 41-53; Dowley, ed., *Eerdman's Handbook to the History of Christianity,* 117-19, 187-95, 239-40; Walker, *A History of the Christian Church,* 39-42, 81-84, 150-52, 189-90.

HAROLD E. RASER

OFFICES OF CHRIST. See ESTATES OF CHRIST.

OLD MAN. Although it occurs only three times in the NT (Rom. 6:6; Eph. 4:22; Col. 3:10), the expression "old man" (KJV) is a central concept in the Wesleyan interpretation of Christian holiness. However, within this tradition differences exist as to the exact relation of the term to the preconversion life-style and to the sinful nature in the unsanctified believer. Because Rom. 6:6 appears in a more detailed and extended setting than the other two references, it provides the primary meaning of the term and may perhaps provide the clue to approaching this interpretive problem in the Wesleyan tradition. With this as our point of departure, we may proceed through three intersecting areas of concern:

Grammatically, a common environment for all three passages is the contrasting moods of the indicative (statements of fact) and the imperative (commands) involving the status and treatment of the "old man." (See *BBC,* 9:218-21, 414-15; Howard, *Newness of Life,* 102-3, 134-48.) This raises the questions, *When* were or are these indicative facts accomplished, and *What,* then, are the foci of the imperative commands?

The answer to these queries are contextually discovered. The indicative statement about the "old man" in Rom. 6:6 is related to sin as an inner, dynamic force rather than to sin as an act (vv. 1-11). The means for dealing with this sinful principle is death (vv. 2-4, 7); for the "old man" it is crucifixion. Because the instrument of death *of* and *to* indwelling sin is the cross of Christ (vv. 3-5, 9), the "old man" which is crucified is thereby identified with the sinful nature.

Since the "old man" is identified with the sin principle and the purpose of its crucifixion is the destruction of the "body of sin" (v. 6), the latter expression cannot be the sinful nature, otherwise a tautology is created. In light of the subsequent imperatives of vv. 12-19 being related to the body as representative of the total person, we may say that the "body of sin" is the human personality when it is the vehicle of the sinful nature (cf. Howard, 104). By this purposive function of the destruction of the "body of sin," the indicative mood in which the crucifixion of the "old man" is expressed is thereby so related to the imperatives for liberation from inbred sin as to indicate that the "old man" refers to the principle of sin rather than to the preconversion life-style.

Lexically, by recognizing the close identification of the "old man" with the term "flesh" (Barclay, *The Mind of St. Paul,* 199-200) and by understanding the "old man" as a likely rephrasing of "in Adam" (Rom. 5:12-21), it is possible to state that the "old man" is an inner, moral condition "carried over" from the preregenerate state into the justified relationship, rather than the complex of preconversion deeds.

Although this approach does not solve all interpretive difficulties, we may, by employing the above framework, relate the three references to the "old man" in this way: The "old man" is closely related to the past life of sin (Col. 3:10), but is not necessarily identical with it (Eph. 4:22). Rather, it is a morally dynamic "carry-over" from the unregenerate state (Rom. 6:6) which may be resolved subsequent to conversion through a personal, subjective, and decisive identification with the death and resurrection of Christ (cf. Purkiser, *Sanctification and Its Synonyms,* 89, fn. 14).

See CARNAL MIND, CARNAL CHRISTIANS, CLEANSING.

For Further Reading: Agnew, *Transformed Christians,* 99-111; Chapman, *The Terminology of Holiness,* 108; Corlett, *Lord of All,* 37-38; *GMS,* 406, 502.

JOHN G. MERRITT

OLD TESTAMENT. See BIBLE: THE TWO TESTAMENTS.

OMNIPOTENCE. Omnipotence as an attribute of God is "that perfection of God by virtue of which He is able to do all that He pleases to do" (Wiley, *CT,* 1:349). God is "almighty" (Rev. 1:8). He has all power and is the ultimate Source of all the power and authority which exists.

Omnipotence is necessarily consistent with the attributes of self-existence, infinity, unity, and sovereignty. There is but one God, hence, there is no other who limits Him. In order to be sovereign, God must be free to do whatever He wills, at any time, anywhere, and in every detail (Ps. 115:3).

Divine omnipotence is consistent with moral impossibilities, i.e., whatever is contrary to God's nature and will; e.g., the fact that God cannot lie, do unjustly, or love sin. It also implies the power of self-limitation, since it does not exclude human freedom. It is consistent with delegated creaturely powers. Whatever God entrusts remains His and returns to Him again (Rom. 13:1).

God's power is inferred as absolute from the incomprehensible work of creation (Ps. 33:8-9; Jer. 10:12-13; 32:17, 27; Rev. 4:11). It is evident in nature (Rom. 1:20). It is the source of nature's orderliness (Heb. 1:3). The so-called laws of nature are "the paths God's power and wisdom take through creation" (Tozer, *The Knowledge of the Holy,* 72).

Modern positivistic philosophies which allow for no knowledge beyond scientific description deny such power inasmuch as they deny causality in the usual sense. A few theistic thinkers, wrestling with the problem of natural evil, have been impelled either to deny God's goodness or limit His power, and have usually opted for the latter. Such answers merely push the problem further back and create greater problems with the resulting dualisms. Such are contrary to Scripture.

Practically, the revealed truth of the divine omnipotence has given faith, hope, courage, and strength to the inner life of believers under testing (Gen. 17:1; Isaiah 40; Matt. 19:26; John 10:29; Eph. 3:20-21).

See EVIL, ATTRIBUTES (DIVINE), DIVINE SOVEREIGNTY.

For Further Reading: Tozer, *The Knowledge of the Holy;* McConnell, *The Christian God;* Clarke, *The Christian Doctrine of God.*

ARNOLD E. AIRHART

OMNIPRESENCE. This is a term that signifies that God is everywhere present at the same time. He is present with all that exists; He is absent from nothing that exists, thus we can speak of God's immanence. Daniel Steele held that God exists everywhere, not by an extension of His parts, but by His essential being. That God is repletively in space is not to be understood as God being diffused or extended like matter. Extension as a property of matter is subject to division and fragmentation. Hence, omnipresence does not presage, or betoken, pantheism, a view which holds that all things and beings of nature and existence are merely modes, attributes, or perhaps appearances of a single reality, as Spinoza believed. Christian theologians reject pantheism since it fails to make a distinction between the Creator and His creation; such failure portends fateful theological consequences. The nature god of pantheism is without personality.

Omnipresence indicates divine essence, not simply knowledge and power. God could not be omniscient unless omnipresent; His perfection is preconditioned by all-presence, all-knowledge, and all-power. God is not habituated or restricted by space in His power and acting; the full force of His omnipotence can be brought to bear anywhere, any time. For instance, God is not obligated to move from place to place in case of emergency—He's already there. To challenge this thesis is to impugn His very existence as God, for He could not be a real and living God, sufficient for His universal responsibilities, apart from all-inclusive, boundless presence.

God acts equally diverse and detailed wherever crises arise, whether redeemingly, lovingly, creatively, knowingly, or illuminatingly. God in total potential and full actuality can respond in infinite fashion to aggregate claims and needs. Contemporary theologians argue that omnipresence does not refer to an imprecise, extended space any more than eternity implies only unlimited time. These theologians disallow metaphysical significance for the divine attributes and claim that omnipresence is the ability of divine love to maintain itself unimpaired by the discrepancies of space (cf. 1 Kings 8:27; 2 Chron. 2:6; Isa. 66:1; Acts 17:28; Eph. 1:23).

See ATTRIBUTES (DIVINE), OMNIPOTENCE.

For Further Reading: Clarke, *An Outline of Christian Theology,* 3rd ed.; Hills, *Fundamental Christian Theology;* Chafer, *Systematic Theology,* vol. 7.

MEL-THOMAS ROTHWELL

OMNISCIENCE. See ATTRIBUTES, DIVINE.

ONENESS. See UNITY.

ONLY BEGOTTEN. The word *monogenēs* occurs nine times in the NT, referring to Isaac (Heb. 11:17), the widow's son (Luke 7:12), Jairus' daughter (8:42), the demoniac boy (9:38), and Jesus Christ (John 1:14, 18; 3:16, 18; 1 John 4:9).

In the first four references the word simply means "one child" born to a father. In a culture where children were considered to be a "heritage of the Lord" (Ps. 127:3), it is quite natural to expect that the greater the number of children, the greater the heritage. In an "only child" family the heritage was therefore precariously restricted to a single offspring. And where this was the case, the quality of relationships within the family structure was marked by a peculiar concern.

In the Johannine writings the use of *monogenēs* in describing Jesus Christ goes beyond a mere exercise in numbering. It is used in the sense of a title which God ascribes to His Son. It is meant to convey an honor which is unparalleled and incomparable. The idea of "one of a kind" is projected. The singularity of Jesus Christ being the only One who can mediate salvation and life is stressed. Thus the emphasis of the Apostles' Creed is upon God's "only Son."

Consistent with the whole thrust of Scripture is this emphasis upon the fact that Jesus Christ alone is the Savior of the world: "Neither is there salvation in any other: for there is none other name under heaven . . . whereby we must be saved" (Acts 4:12).

The significant fact is preserved that there is not a variety of salvations; there is only one Door into the sheepfold (John 10); there is "one God, and one mediator between God and men, the man Christ Jesus" (1 Tim. 2:5).

See ETERNAL GENERATION, FIRSTBORN, CHRIST.

For Further Reading: Kittel, 4:739-41; Westcott, *The Epistles of St. John,* 169-72; Vos, *The Self-disclosure of Jesus,* 213-26. ROBERT A. MATTKE

ONTOLOGICAL ARGUMENT. The ontological argument infers the being of God from the nature of thought. (Other traditional arguments infer God from design, purpose, and values.) For the ontological argument God alone exists in a way thought is powerless to deny.

In the 11th century Anselm of Canterbury developed this line of reasoning, the validity of which has been debated ever since. "God is that than which a greater cannot be conceived. Whoever understands this correctly at least understands that he exists in such a way that even for thought he *cannot not* exist. Therefore, whoever understands that God is so cannot even conceive that he is not" (Proslogian, cited in *The Many-faced Argument,* ed. Hick and McGill, 8, italics added).

Anselm began his reasoning from the posture of prayer: "O Lord, . . . give me to understand that you are just as we believe, and that you are what we believe" (ibid., 4).

The devotional approach, *faith seeking to understand,* epitomized medieval philosophy. Dogmatism eroded and distorted that value. Under Descartes, Leibniz, and Hegel, the argument supported the autonomy of reason.

To move from a logical necessity (God as idea in the mind) to an ontological necessity (God as really "here" or "there") lacks logical force for many persons as it did for Gaunilo who debated Anselm. Some reject this proof for devotional reasons—God cannot be reached by inference, but by faith alone. Others do this for humanistic reasons. God cannot be verified, hence stands with other value terms as a human construct.

The wars of this century diminished confidence in the autonomy of reason and once again theologians examined ontology, both as a means of reassessing faith (Paul Tillich) and as a way of understanding God (Karl Barth).

Barth reasoned that Anselm's "proof" breaks out of the circle of human thought by acknowledging the falsity of a god who exists in the thought alone and by confirming the God who, uniquely, reveals himself. "We can interpret his Proof only when, *along with* Anselm, in Anselm's own sense, we share the presupposition of his inquiry—that the object of the inquiry stands over against him who inquires . . . as the unmediated 'thou' of the Lord" (*Many-faced Argument,* 153).

Eugene Fairweather properly acknowledges that Anselm is parent to a mode of thought which "recognizes in faith the ultimate key to reality . . . working from principles accessible to reason" (*Library of Christian Classics,* 10:53).

See THEISM, THEISTIC PROOFS.

For Further Reading: Hick and McGill, eds., *The Many-faced Argument;* or Anselm, *Library of Christian Classics,* vol. 10. ARTHUR O. ROBERTS

ONTOLOGY. The word *ontology* is a combination of two Greek terms, the participle of the verb "to be," *ontos,* "being," and *logos,* the term for "discourse, science or doctrine of." Hence we may define it simply as "the science of being, or the theory of being as such." Some distinctions that need to be kept in mind are in order here.

When we speak of "isness," we have the concept of *existence,* which is simply the assertion *that* a thing *is.* When we refer to "whichness," we have the concept of *being* in the simple assertion of "that which is," or "that which acts." When we declare "what a thing is," we have the concept of its "whatness," its makeup or its *essence.*

In the field of philosophy *ontology* may be identified with that branch of philosophical thought called metaphysics. Aristotle referred to this under the heading of "first principles."

The word *ontology* was first introduced into philosophy by Christian F. von Wolff. He divided metaphysics into four parts: Ontology, Psychology, Rational Cosmology, and Theology. The modern philosophical theologian, Paul Tillich, defines God as "BEING in and of itself." This relates closely to the sacred Hebrew name for God,

Yahweh; a term which specifies God as "He who has absolute Being and who causes to be whatever comes into being and has existence."

Thus in ontology we are concerned with a study of the fundamental stuff of existence. We grapple with the problem of reality itself. Ontology is a quest for a reasoned understanding of what comprises reality. Is it mind or is it matter? Is it one or many? Is it dynamic or is it static? Is it personal or impersonal? Is it experience or does it take its stance in a subway below experience? Is it knowable or unknowable?

It is Tillich's contention that: "God is the answer to the question implied in being"; for "the ontological question is: What is being itself?" (*Systematic Theology,* 1:163).

We Christians affirm that "God is a Spirit" (John 4:24), and that "in him we live, and move, and have our being" (Acts 17:28). H. Orton Wiley defines God under the three categories of: "Absolute Reality," "Infinite Efficiency," and "Perfect Personality" (cf. *CT,* 1, chaps. 11—13).

What one thinks about God, the Source of all Being, largely determines what one thinks about reality as a whole. And Being is given not so much in the *conclusions* of one's philosophic thinking as in its *basic premises.*

See METAPHYSICS, PLATONISM, PHILOSOPHY, THOMISM.

For Further Reading: *ER,* 548 ff; Brightman, *Person and Reality;* Harvey, "Being," *Handbook of Theological Terms,* 39-41; Hutchinson, "Being," *A Handbook of Christian Theology,* Halverson, ed., 31-35; "Ontology," *Encyclopedia Americana* (1947 ed.), 20:696; Tillich, *Systematic Theology,* vol. 1, part 2, chap. 1; Wiley, *CT,* 1:255-78.

ROSS E. PRICE

ORDAIN, ORDINATION. In the NT we have a record of the ordination of man to several types of ministry. The procedure was that of "laying on of hands." Thus, the word has come to imply the setting aside of persons to holy office in the church by the laying on of hands.

In the Roman Catholic and Anglican confessions ordination is deemed to be a sacrament of the church and is performed only by bishops. This highlights the concept of "apostolic succession" which is accepted by these groups. This, of course, is not seen as the passing on of grace but rather of apostolic authority. Other religious bodies follow to a lesser degree in this tradition. Some make ordination a matter of authority, and others make it a function of a local church when a man in inducted to a first pastorate.

In each case it is admission to the official ministry of the visible church, and there is no ordination apart from the church. The word for appoint *(cheirotonein)* means "lay on hands." The practice is derived from the Jews—Jewish rabbis were appointed by the laying on of hands. Paul's practice was to appoint "elders" in every city (Acts 14:23; Titus 1:5).

The role of the appointee in the NT included that of pastor, steward, or ruler in the local church; and to this end the ordained was to be duly consecrated. In the Protestant confession ordination is viewed as a symbolic act of setting aside to special ministry.

See LAYING ON OF HANDS, CLERGY, MINISTER (MINISTRY), OFFICES (ECCLESIASTICAL).

For Further Reading: *HDNT,* 4:114-18; Wiley, *CT,* 3:135.

HUGH RAE

ORDINANCES. The Bible term "ordinances" is translated from various word meanings. In the OT, the main Hebrew words used are: *choq* (or *chuqqah*) (cf. Exod. 18:20; Job 38:33), meaning "statute, decree"; *mishpat* (cf. 2 Kings 17:34, 37; Ps. 119:91; Isa. 58:2), meaning a "judgment"; *mitsvah* (Neh. 10:32), meaning a "command, charge, precept."

In the NT, the Greek words commonly used are: *dikaiōma* (Luke 1:6; Heb. 9:1, 10), meaning a "judicial appointment"; *paradosis* (1 Cor. 11:2), is a "binding tradition," or "apostolic rule"; *dogma* (Eph. 2:15; Col. 2:14), meaning a "determination, decree"; *dogmatizō* (Col. 2:20), "to be under a decree."

It is clear that the Church very early developed customs and rules regulating conduct in public worship, dress, ordination procedures, and such matters as social welfare.

Wesley required members of his societies to attend all the ordinances of God. These were "the public worship of God; the ministry of the word, either read or expounded; the supper of the Lord; family and private prayer; searching the Scriptures; and fasting, or abstinence" (*Works,* 8:271).

Christians ignore much of the Jewish legal system, but problems of the law and legalism remain. It is inevitable that church groups should develop a legal framework for their common life. But regulations should foster unity, not disunity. The fellowship of the Spirit should be the supreme objective.

See CHURCH, CHURCH GOVERNMENT, CANON LAW.

For Further Reading: *HDNT,* 4:114; *ISBE,* 4:2201.

IVAN A. BEALS

ORDINATION OF WOMEN. This controversial issue has brought some churches almost to schism, with both sides appealing to different scriptures.

contradict itself, the problem is to understand the meaning of texts which on surface may appear contradictory.

Churches which refuse to ordain women appeal to such passages as 1 Cor. 11:2-16; 1 Tim. 2:9-15; and Eph. 5:22-24. Those which ordain women stress Gal. 3:28, as well as Jesus' own treatment of women, noting especially that the first tidings of His resurrection were imparted to women, who were charged to announce it to His (male) disciples (Mark 16:6-7).

Some dispose of the apostle Paul's strictures on women as just a residue of unchristianized rabbinic prejudices, but this does violence to the belief that the Scriptures are inspired throughout and were written under the guidance of the Holy Spirit. Much more convincing is the argument that (as in the case of human slavery) the passages in question, and others in both Testaments, were intended to ameliorate the condition of women caught in societies dominated by unregenerate males, both the patriarchal society of OT times and the NT world in which Greek and Roman women were often "liberated" to standards and conduct contradictory to Christianity and disruptive of the Church. Some strict discipline of church members in Corinth, both male and female, was apparently necessary in Paul's day. But just as the application of standards of Christian love to all men led to the abolition of slavery, though by an evolutionary rather than a revolutionary process, so the recognition that in Christ there is "no male and female" removes all barriers to the participation by women in ministries to which the Lord calls them.

Some writers stress the fact that headship or sequential order, shown in the creation of Adam before Eve and in the place of man as the head of the family, does not prove inequality or inferiority of women, even though male chauvinists may so interpret. Scriptures teach and otherwise imply the equality of women; the "battle of the sexes" is a result of the Fall, through which mutual loving support and recognition have often been turned to jealous striving. The standard of holy discipleship, rather than the prejudices of unregenerate humanity, should set the standard for this and all other relationships.

See WOMAN, CHAIN OF COMMAND, FAMILY.

For Further Reading: Jewett, *Man as Male and Female*; *Baker's DCE*, 712.

PHILIP S. CLAPP

ORIGINAL RIGHTEOUSNESS. See DIVINE IMAGE.

ORIGINAL SIN. *Original sin* in the exact sense is man's first transgression of God's law. In a more general sense, original sin is often defined as "the universal and hereditary sinfulness of man since the fall of Adam" (*A Handbook of Theological Terms*, 221). Original sin has also been described as "the human self corrupted, diseased, fevered, or warped—a condition brought about by alienation from God" (*GMS*, 86).

Survey of basic issues. A leading issue in any consideration of original sin is whether or not the biblical account of the Fall has any basis in history, or whether it is mythical, i.e., a timeless but nonhistorical truth about man's existence. Those who hold to a mythical view of the Fall move in the direction of Pelagianism or existentialism. Pelagius rejected the doctrine of original sin. The existentialists hold that all men "fall" at some point in their psychological development. In either case, the result is to damage the key doctrines of the Atonement and redemption.

Wiley and Culbertson conclude: "The account of the probation and fall of man found in Genesis 3:1-24 is an inspired record of historical fact bound up with a deep and rich symbolism" (*Introduction to Christian Theology*, 160-61).

Some hold that pride is the essence of sin; others would see this essence as selfishness or self-sovereignty. Perhaps no single quality is sufficiently comprehensive. Whatever the conclusion, "the most characteristic feature of sin in all its aspects is that it is directed against God" (*NBD*, 1189). Paul speaks of the carnal mind as "enmity against God" (Rom. 8:7); hence it is more than a weakness, it is a deeply rooted dispositional hostility or resistance to God's authority. But whatever its inner essence, most Christians would concur with Reinhold Niebuhr's assertion: "The view that men are 'sinful' is one of the best attested and empirically verified facts of human existence" (*A Handbook of Christian Theology*, 349).

Development. Like other Christian doctrines, the doctrine of original sin developed gradually. The raw materials were present in the Bible, but the church soon found it imperative to clarify its teaching. This historical development included the fifth-century debate between Pelagius and Augustine. While Pelagius rejected the concept of original sin, Augustine made it a cornerstone of his theology. In later centuries, Roman Catholic theologians developed a view known as semi-Pelagianism, that original sin is a weakness rather than an inability. In post-Reformation times Calvinists stressed the effectual calling of the elect as God's means of breaking the barrier of original sin, whereas Arminians emphasized the power and availability of grace for all. Despite erosion of the doctrine of original sin among theological liberals, it seems to be robust today (See *Christian Theology: An Ecumenical Approach,* 159).

Biblical data. The early chapters of Genesis describe the Fall and its racial consequences. Created superior in talent, with capacity for fellowship (1:26-28), man sought self-exaltation (3:1-6). The result was humiliation (vv. 7-10), alienation (vv. 12-13), suffering (vv. 16-19), and a morally twisted nature, described as an "imagination" which "was only evil continually" (6:5; cf. 8:21). The word "imagination" may be rendered "inclination" or "propensity." Abel's blood sacrifice suggests that he too was aware of personal sinfulness, even though it did not erupt in violence as did the sin of Cain. Accelerating universal depravity resulted in the Flood. But the virulence persisted, and soon evil was again rampant, requiring the dispersal of the people (11:1-9).

David confesses, "I was shapen in iniquity; and in sin did my mother conceive me" (Ps. 51:5). This is not normally understood as a confession of illegitimacy or as an indictment of the procreative act per se, but as a clear tracing of his evil acts to an original or transmitted moral defect (cf. 58:3). Between the Testaments, the Apocrypha clearly teaches the idea of original sin (2 Esdras 3:21-22; 4:30-31).

In the NT, the concept of racial sinfulness is equally pervasive. Jesus teaches that man's moral woes spring from the depravity of his heart (Matt. 15:18), and Paul's contrast of the two Adams in Rom. 5:12-21 and 1 Cor. 15:22, 45-47 clearly requires the development of a doctrine of original sin. His most vivid and powerful exposé of human sinfulness, as a subvolitional propensity which overcomes both reason and resolution, is Rom. 7:7-25 (cf. Eph. 2:3).

Wesleyanism. John Wesley considered the doctrine of original sin a cornerstone of biblical religion. Without it, he says, "the Christian system falls at once" (*Works,* 9:194). According to traditional Wesleyanism, original sin is cleansed in the divine work of entire sanctification (cf. Wiley, *CT,* 2:470, et al.).

Wesleyans have differed concerning the relation of original sin to the guilt of Adam's representative disobedience. Wesley himself was thoroughly Augustinian in ascribing to Adam's posterity an element of guilt, but insisted that such guilt was removed as one of the universal and unconditional benefits of the Atonement.

See SIN, FALL (THE), AUGUSTINIANISM, PELAGIANISM, ARMINIANISM, CARNAL MIND.

For Further Reading: *NBD,* 1189-93; *GMS,* 79-87, 268-302; Wiley, *CT,* 2:96-140.

A. ELWOOD SANNER

ORTHODOXY. *Orthodoxy,* derived from two Greek words (*orthos* and *doxa*), can be translated "right thought" or "correct belief," and is related to *orthopraxy,* which means "correct conduct." Orthodoxy is most easily understood in contrast with the *un*orthodox, defined first as *heterodoxy* (a divergent mode of belief), and then as *heresy* (a condemned choice of belief).

It was from the Trinitarian, Christological, and Gnostic controversies of the first five centuries that an orthodox and universally acceptable understanding of Christianity emerged. Orthodoxy eventually encompassed that which the "faithful" believed was "right" and that which they were convinced God would ultimately vindicate as right. The roots of orthodoxy, though not its terminology, are to be found in the Bible and the gospel itself (cf. 1 Tim. 6:3 and 2 Tim. 1:13 for an "orthodox" reaction to the implications of wrong belief, and Gal. 1:6-9; 1 Cor. 15:1-13; 1 John 4:1-3; and 2 John 7-11 for the ramifications of right belief in doctrine, preaching, and practice).

The earliest community's belief in "sound doctrine" implied the normative nature of the Christian revelation, encapsulated in the canon as a "fundamentally orthodox collection of books" (Turner). This somewhat tautologous position vis-à-vis Scripture was basic to the evolution of Christian orthodoxy and crucial to its polemic and apologetic. Appeal and argument was made to Scripture, to tradition, and to reason—to consolidate and protect the purity of the received gospel from distortions of Scripture, denial of common tradition, and assimilation to secular philosophical movements. These remain today the primary concerns of orthodoxy.

Historically orthodoxy was constituted in the "rule of faith" *(regula fidei)* with considerable fluidity during the first three Christian centuries. Only in the next two centuries was an attempt made, in response to heterodox movements and groups, to render traditional beliefs into definitive terminology through the major church councils (Nicea, 325; Ephesus, 431; Chalcedon, 451). Arianism, Apollinarianism, and Nestorianism were all refuted and condemned, as the Apostles', Nicene, and Athanasian creeds affirmed orthodox statements concerning Christology, the Trinity, and the work of the Holy Spirit.

Development of these dogmata in the Western church led to the dictum: "Outside the church there is no salvation" *(Extra ecclesiam nulla salvatio est),* thus tying together ecclesiology and soteriology in orthodoxy. Eastern orthodoxy maintained a less definitively dogmatic and differentiated view of the mystical unity (Sobornost) of belief, practice, and liturgy, and recognized only seven great councils, ending with Nicea II in A.D. 787 and the reaffirmation of iconism. The Catholic West recognized 21 councils (including Trent, 1545-63, and Vatican II, 1965), and continued to promulgate individual dogmata for orthodoxy into the 20th century (e.g., Assumption of the Blessed Virgin Mary, 1950).

The rise of Reformation scholarship and historical criticism led to reexamination of the dogmatic approach to orthodoxy, affirmed the revelatory nature of immutable reality, and reopened the question of changing conceptual frameworks in which orthodoxy might be articulated *(sola fidei, sola gratia, sola scriptura).* Creeds were not replaced but reformulated for contemporary classification in the various denominational confessions. The core of orthodoxy is therefore still affirmed in Protestantism by adherence to the historical, revelatory character of biblical faith; the doctrines of the Incarnation, the Atonement, and the Trinity; and the sacraments of baptism and the Eucharist. These are the fundamentals of the faith.

See CHRISTIANITY, APOSTLES' CREED, CHURCH COUNCILS, HERESY.

For Further Reading: Turner, *The Pattern of Christian Truth,* 241-498; Webber and Bloesch, eds., *The Orthodox Evangelicals,* 43-67; Chesterton, *Orthodoxy.*

JOHN S. LOWN

OVERSEER. See BISHOP.

P

PACIFISM. Based on the word "peacemakers" (Matt. 5:9), pacifism is the belief that war is contrary to the scriptural way of peace, and therefore Christians are not to participate in it. Some authorities have used the word *nonresistance* to identify a conservative, nonpolitical, biblical rejection of war, and have related the word *pacifism* to a more liberal and pragmatic rejection of war.

The high points in the history of pacifism have been the first centuries of the Christian church (to Constantine, A.D. 313), the emergence of the historic peace churches (Mennonites, Friends, and Brethren—16th to 18th centuries), the rise of modern liberal pacifism (19th century), and the contemporary wrestling over the use of nuclear weapons. Opposition to war has been based on the life and teachings of Jesus Christ and on the NT love ethic. Also there are humanitarian considerations, the demonic character and destructiveness of war, the power of nonviolence, and the possible annihilation of mankind. Often these bases of objection have been combined.

Biblical pacifists deal with the OT endorsement of war by suggesting that the fullness of the revelation or the revelation for today came in the NT. Thus, the NT is determinative. Furthermore, they believe their position to be essentially Christological.

Those who are born again know God's love overcomes evil because when they were alienated from God, Christ's love overcame their hostility (Rom. 5:10). In sanctification perfect love becomes a heart reality, and sin is no more a necessity for the saint. The Lordship of Christ means that all of life, including governmental responsibilities, is lived in obedience to Christ. Unconditional loyalty can be given only to Jesus Christ. Christ's Lordship includes His Headship of the Church. That Body is international, and for Christians to be fighting other Christians is to deny Christ's Headship. His Lordship also calls for obedience to the Great Commission. Christians killing non-Christians is to deny those killed the opportunity to accept Christ.

The repeated teachings of the NT that Christians are to love their enemies in the loving, self-sacrificing manner of the crucified Christ, must be taken, according to the biblical pacifists, with all seriousness. Both the deity of Christ and the authority of Scripture are involved. Jesus Christ is the Model of love and holiness. Christian perfection involves a loving that seeks the highest good even for the most wicked, and a holiness that will have no part of evil. To take life is inherently an evil act.

The cross and resurrection of Christ are therefore central to the biblical pacifists. As Christ died in loving Servanthood, so must His disciples be faithful unto death (Mark 8:31-35). Christ's resurrection is the sign that Christ has conquered death and the devil. It is tangible evidence that the way of the Cross is the power of the resurrected Lord bringing in the new age.

Those who reject pacifism on biblical grounds use some of the following arguments. (1) God commanded war in the OT, and there is no explicit teaching against war in the NT. (2) Romans 13 and similar scriptures call upon Christians to obey government. (3) The heart of perfect love can be maintained in war. (4) Since God at times works His will through the state, a Christian in fighting can be doing God's will. (5) The Western nations have at times through war kept the world open for missionary work, as well as for democratic freedoms.

See WAR, CITIZENSHIP, CIVIL DISOBEDIENCE.

For Further Reading: Hostetler, ed., *Perfect Love and War;* Bainton, *Christian Attitudes Toward War and Peace;* Myra, *Should a Christian Go to War?* Yoder, *Nevertheless.*

MARTIN H. SCHRAG

PAGANISM. This is any life-style, value system, and complex of beliefs not based on and shaped by Christ and the Bible. As a term it is equivalent to heathenism. It was into a thoroughly pagan Roman Empire that the fledgling Church was thrust on the Day of Pentecost. But Christians so outthought, outlived, and out-died the pagans, that paganism was subdued, though of course never eradicated. Today paganism is again on the rise, in the avowed humanism, scientism, ethical relativism, materialism, and raw hedonism which threatens to engulf and suffocate the Church. Western nations are once again more pagan than Christian. The expression *post-Christian* has its validity in the fact that cultures which once openly claimed ties with the Judeo-Christian ethic have now openly severed all such ties. The Church that does not challenge the surrounding paganism will succumb to it. And paganism will either purify the Church or permeate it.

See CHRISTIANITY, EVANGELISM, MISSION (MISSIONS, MISSIOLOGY).

For Further Reading: Anderson, ed., *The Theology of the Christian Mission.* RICHARD S. TAYLOR

PAIN. See SUFFER, SUFFERING.

PANENTHEISM. Whereas *pantheism* means "all is God," *panentheism* means "all in God." It is a term peculiar to process theology, especially to the thought of Charles Hartshorne. *Surrelativism* and *dipolar theism* are terms used interchangeably by Hartshorne for panentheism.

Panentheism differs from traditional theism by stressing the dependence and interrelatedness of God upon the world as a condition for His own being. Alan Gragg explains: "Panentheism entails that there never could have been God without a world" (*Charles Hartshorne,* 95 ff). In theism God relates himself voluntarily to the world, through providence and omnipresence, but in His essential being is transcendent, which means separate and independent. But in panentheism the world is in God and God in the world, in what Hartshorne prefers to explain as a mind-body relationship.

Panentheism differs from pantheism by denying the flat equivalency of God and the world, and predicating a degree of independent thought and action to both. The freedom of the cosmic side of this dipolar reality is sufficient to make evil possible; the union is sufficient to impinge on God's consciousness and make the suffering His own.

The theology and cosmology of panentheism, with their endless evolution of both God and man, is far from biblical Christianity.

See THEISM, PANTHEISM, ATTRIBUTES (DIVINE), TRINITY (THE HOLY).

For Further Reading: Gragg, *Charles Hartshorne.*

RICHARD S. TAYLOR

PANTHEISM. *Pantheism* is that religious or philosophic theory which postulates the identity of God and the universe. The theory has taken two forms. If the assumption is from a scientific conception of the world as a unity, God as a person is lost in the cosmos, and pantheism becomes the equivalent to naturalism and may be called *pancosmism.* If, on the other hand, the assumption begins in a religious or philosophical position that God is infinite and eternal reality, then the finite and temporal world is so eclipsed by God as to result in *acosmism* (i.e., the world is illusion and God alone is reality). The first approach becomes, in fact, a form of atheism, while the latter becomes a form of belief in which a dynamic personal God is only indirectly involved (if indeed at all) in a temporal universe.

As Charles Hartshorne points out *(ER),* pantheism leaves many questions unanswered. Is this pantheistic god a person? Is it conscious? Is it immutable or in flux? What is the relation of the parts to the whole? In what sense are the parts free—if at all?

The statement that "God is everything" can mean (1) that everything (i.e., all actual being) is completely bound by God as well as God being completely bound by everything. Then God is without distinct individual being and without personality. If, on the other hand, the statement means (2) that God includes everything but yet is more than the aggregate of the material universe, then the way is left open to conceive of God in personal terms. But this is hardly pure pantheism, and Hartshorne suggests it might better be called *panentheism.*

Pantheism as a religious concept was present in Greek and Roman thought, and is basic to all of the Hindu religions, and from time to time has appeared in Western thought (e.g., Christian Science). It is not possible to reconcile pantheism with Christianity, for the Bible teaches that God is personal, transcendent as well as immanent, eternal in contrast to the world's temporality, and is both the universe's Creator and its Ruler.

See PANENTHEISM, THEISM, TRANSCENDENCE, CREATION.

For Further Reading: *ERE,* 9:609-17; *ER,* 557; *Lutheran Cyclopedia,* 599. FOREST T. BENNER

PAPACY. See CATHOLICISM, ROMAN.

PAPAL INFALLIBILITY. The doctrine of papal infallibility is the claim that the pope of the Roman Catholic church can and does speak without error and with divine authority when he speaks according to certain stipulations. These stipulations are three: (1) The pope must be addressing the entire Christian church. Papal decisions concerning the problems of a particular parish, for example, could not be considered infallible on the basis of the dogma. (2) The pope speaks infallibly only when he addresses the issues of faith and morals. Although the pope may direct his considerable influence to the solution of international tensions, the dogma of infallibility will not buttress papal enunciations concerning purely secular issues. (3) The enunciation must be made *ex cathedra;* i.e., it must be a formal and official pronouncement in harmony with (1) and (2), and by virtue of his office.

The dogma was established on July 18, 1870, by a vote of a Vatican Council called by Pope Pius IX. The pope had flexed his muscles earlier by raising to the status of dogma the doctrine of the immaculate conception of Mary without the consent of a council. Liberal Catholics, who at first believed that the council called by Pius IX would provide them with an opportunity to assert the authority of council decisions, soon discovered that, in fact, the intent was just the opposite. A quasi-official publication of the Holy See anticipated the council with the words, "All genuine Catholics believe that the Council will be quite short. . . . They will receive with joy the proclamation of the dogmatic infallibility of the sovereign pontiff." In spite of a few abstainers and only two negative votes, the dogma was promulgated. Authority passed clearly from council to pope.

Since the establishment of the dogma only one decree has borne the character of infallibility (the doctrine of the bodily assumption of Mary into heaven). However, the elasticity of the stipulations governing infallibility makes it difficult to discern exactly when the pope is speaking infallibly.

See CATHOLICISM (ROMAN), PROTESTANTISM.

For Further Reading: Heick, *A History of Christian Thought,* 2:312 ff. DANIEL N. BERG

PARABLES. A parable is a story meant to teach a religious truth, "an earthly story with a heavenly meaning." Usually it is fictitious.

The word "parable" comes from the Hebrew *mashal* and the Greek *parabolē,* meaning "a comparison."

A parable is similar to an allegory with an important exception. While the parable is meant to convey but one truth, all parts of the allegory are meaningful. A fable also emphasizes but one truth; but it differs from the parable and the allegory in that it puts words in the mouths of fanciful characters (animals, trees, etc.). Jesus never used fables, but some of His stories blended elements of allegory and parable.

Various people spoke parables in the OT (2 Sam. 12:1-7; 14:5-11; 2 Kings 14:9; Isa. 5:1-7), but only Jesus used them in the NT. Because scholars do not agree on a standard definition for parables, the number of them spoken by Jesus has been variously estimated from 33 to 79. Most authorities agree on about 50.

Jesus began to use parables after the leaders of the Jews blasphemously charged Him with deriving His power from Satan. When His disciples enquired why He spoke in parables, His reply seems to imply that His purpose was to conceal spiritual truth from those who obstinately rejected it (Mark 4:10-12). A careful exegesis on the parable passage in Matt. 13:10-15 indicates the opposite intention. Jesus speaks ironically, implying that while the parables are intended to illuminate the truth, they unfortunately have the opposite effect due to the hardness of the hearts of the hearers. The result was much like that which Isaiah experienced centuries earlier. But, Jesus said, parables are vehicles of truth to receptive hearts (Matt. 13:11, 16-18). Because one's *attitude* toward truth is so critical, Jesus cried, "He who has ears, let him hear" (Matt. 13:9, 43, NASB, NIV, RSV; cf. 11:15; Mark 4:9, 23; 7:16; Luke 8:8; 14:35; Rev. 2:7, 11, 17, 29; 3:6, 13, 22).

Jesus drew His parables from nature and from the domestic, social, and political life of the times—things with which the people were familiar.

See HERMENEUTICS, ALLEGORY.

For Further Reading: Hunter, *Interpreting the Parables;* Buttrick, *The Parables of Jesus;* Armstrong, *The Gospel Parables;* Dodd, *The Parables of the Kingdom.*

W. RALPH THOMPSON

PARACLETE. This is a transliteration of the Greek *paraklētos,* variously translated as "Comforter" (KJV), "Strengthener," "Instructor," or "Encourager" (Wesley), "Counselor" (RSV), "Helper" (Moffatt), "Spokesman" (Danish), "another to befriend you" (Knox), "Someone else to stand by you" (Phillips), and "Advocate" (NEB; Weymouth). Literally the word means "One called alongside to help."

Paraclete appears only four times in John's Gospel (14:16, 26; 15:26; 16:7), and once in 1 John 2:1 in reference to Christ himself. Elsewhere Christ consistently uses the Greek word *pneuma* (breath, wind, or spirit) for the Holy Spirit. Outside the NT usage Paraclete conveyed the sense of "one who speaks in favor of another (an intercessor, or helper) in an active sense—corresponding to Manahem, the name given the Messiah" (Souter, *A Pocket Lexicon of the New Testament,* 190; so Arndt and Gingrich, 623).

Advocate has a strong forensic significance—one who pleads in favor of, defends, vindicates, or espouses the cause of another. Thus Christ delegates to *another* (Gr. *allon; not different, heteron*), the Holy Spirit, His own authority as Revealer, Teacher, Guide, and as Prosecutor of sin and Satan (John 16:7-11). Christ himself is the believer's Advocate before the Father (1 John 2:1-2). The idea of advocacy had strong OT roots (esp. Job 1:6-12; 2:1-10; 5:1; 9:33; 16:19-22; 19:25; cf. Zech. 3:1-10).

Thus, following Christ's ascension, the Paraclete was God's permanent Gift to all believers (John 7:38-39), from whom all other divine gifts issue. This included (1) representing the Father to the believer (Rom. 8:11-16), as Christ represents their cause before the Father in heaven (1 John 2:1-2); (2) instructing the believer concerning the person, work, and teachings of Christ (John 14:25-26; cf. 1 John 2:20-27); (3) witnessing to Christ in the lives of believers, and through them to the unconverted world (John 15:26-27); (4) acting in the world as the divine Witness *against* sin, *to* the righteousness of Christ, and *of* God's final judgment upon Satan (John 16:7-11). To the Christian the Paraclete is One "who has, reveals, testifies, and defends the truth as it is in Jesus" (Wesley, *Notes*). Adam Clarke admirably sums up Christ's teaching concerning the function of the Paraclete as follows:

> The Holy Spirit is thus called [*Paraklētos*=Advocate or Helper] because He *transacts* the cause of God and Christ with us, *explains* to us the nature and importance of the great atonement, *shows the necessity of it, counsels* us to receive it, *instructs* us how to lay hold on it, *vindicates* our claim to it, and makes *intercessions* in us with unutterable groanings. As Christ acted with His disciples while He sojourned with them, so the Holy Ghost acts with those who believe in His name (1:623).

See COMFORTER (THE), HOLY SPIRIT, ADVOCATE.

For Further Reading: Carter, *The Person and Ministry of the Holy Spirit,* 126-43, 324-31; *CC,* 1:623; Kittel, 5:800-814; Agnew, *Transformed Christians,* 42-52; Wesley, *Notes,* 364-73.

CHARLES W. CARTER

PARADISE. The word "paradise" has its roots in the Persian word *pardes,* meaning a garden or wooded park. It describes the pleasure gardens of Persian kings and nobles.

In the OT the word means an orchard, a garden, and a forest (Eccles. 2:5; Neh. 2:8; Song of Sol. 4:13). The original paradise was the Garden of Eden at the beginning of human history. Here, God walked with the first humans in their innocence; here the tree of life and the tree of knowledge stood in the midst of the garden, and the animals were friendly and harmless (Genesis 2—3; cf. Danielou, *The Theology of Jewish Christianity,* 297-98). As a consequence of their disobedience and sin, the first pair were driven out of the garden and forbidden to return.

In the NT paradise refers to the "intermediate state." It is the abode of the righteous dead, in the presence of Christ and awaiting their resurrection, judgment, and final reward and future life (Luke 23:43; 16:22-31). Paul speaks of paradise as the "third heaven" (2 Cor. 12:1-4).

Finally, paradise describes the final abode of the righteous after their resurrection. It is a new creation restoring the original beauty and blessedness. The righteous live in the presence of God; they partake of the tree of life and participate in the blessedness of paradise (Rev. 2:7; 21—22). The unjust and the unrighteous are without and shall not share in the blessings (22:11, 15).

Originally, paradise was a creation of God and a gift to man in his innocence. It was lost to him because of disobedience. It is restored to the righteous through the life, death, and resurrection of the Second Adam, the Lamb of God (Matt. 4:1-11; Mark 1:12-13; Luke 4:1-13; Rom. 5:12-21). Those who are washed in the blood of the Lamb are made holy and righteous and have the right to participate in the tree of life that is in the midst of the paradise of God (Rev. 2:7; 21:1-7; 22:14).

See SHEOL, INTERMEDIATE STATE, HEAVEN.

For Further Reading: Danielou, *The Theology of Jewish Christianity;* Wiley, *CT,* 3:224-40, 375-86.

ISAAC BALDEO

PARADOX. Literally, *paradox* meant what was "contrary to expectations." It is commonly used in contemporary theology to refer to the phenomenon of making two apparently contradictory statements about a single subject. But the contradiction is only apparent in a true paradox, since both statements are necessary to explain the nature of the subject, which reconciles the paradox within its own nature. The more complex the subject is, the more needful it is to employ paradoxical language. As long as it is possible to completely comprehend the essence of the subject, the two truths may be explained. For example, when Jesus declares that "whosoever will save his life shall lose it" (Matt. 16:25 and parallels), we understand that the "saving" and "losing" are referred to the subject "life" in different ways, and that "life" is such a complex subject that it can be rationally referred to as being "saved" and "lost" without involving a contradiction.

However, in the case of God it is different, because God cannot be known in His essence. He is known only to himself (Wiley, *CT,* 1:218). Consequently we may experience the manifestation of God in such a way as to require us to both assert and deny the same quality to Him; and this must forever remain a mystery.

Augustine expresses this irreducible mystery in his classic passage: "What, then, art Thou, O my God . . . stable, yet contained of none; unchangeable, yet changing all things; never new, never old. . . . Always working, yet ever at rest; gathering, yet needing nothing; . . . seeking, and yet possessing all things" (*Confessions,* bk. 1, chap. 4).

The supreme paradox of the Christian faith is the Incarnation in which we affirm Jesus to be both fully God and fully man.

See TRUTH, REASON, RATIONALISM, NEOORTHODOXY, EXISTENTIALISM.

For Further Reading: Gilkey, *Maker of Heaven and Earth;* Hepburn, *Christianity and Paradox.*

H. RAY DUNNING

PARDON. See FORGIVENESS.

PARENTS AND CHILDREN. Parenthood is both privilege and responsibility. Children are a gift from God, but they still belong to Him. Parenthood is one form of Christian stewardship, and the Bible clearly indicates the duties of parents.

Parents are to be loving and accepting. Human fatherhood is derived from the fatherhood of God (Eph. 3:15). Parents must treat their children as God treats His sons and daughters. From the child's perceptions of his parent's esteem, he develops his self-concept. In a warm and loving home environment, he is more likely to be able to develop love for God and others.

Parents are the primary agents of moral and religious education. In His covenant with Israel, God clearly commanded parents to teach their children His laws, first by obeying and making them part of their own lives, and then orally, visually, and continually, impressing them on their children that they may fear the Lord (Deut. 6:1-9).

Parents are to give guidance and discipline, meted out with understanding and encouragement. The writer to the Hebrews asserts that love and discipline are inseparable and a proof of sonship even when the discipline brings pain (Heb. 12:5-11). But Paul warns against the kind of harsh treatment that frustrates and discourages the child (Eph. 6:4; Col. 3:21). Fathers are not "to excite the bad passions of their children by severity, injustice, partiality, or unreasonable exercise of authority" (Charles Hodge, *Epistle to the Ephesians,* 359).

Children also have duties. The Christian ethic is one of mutual obligation (Barclay, *The Daily Study Bible,* 10:193). As parents are responsible for training and discipline, children are responsible to respect and obey their parents (Eph. 6:1-2; Col. 3:20).

Among the theological implications of the parent-child relationship are these. Because of Adam's sin, the child begins life with a tendency toward sin, an inherent selfishness. Moral behavior is not natural but learned. Learning will not take place without resistance. On the positive side, the prevenient grace of God is at work in the child's total personality, awakening to need and gently drawing his soul toward God. The

Holy Spirit will give discernment and wisdom to parents who seek His aid.

Although the influence of parents is the most determinative factor in developing a child's character, parental power is not absolute (*Family Love in All Dimensions,* 119-20). The child is a free moral agent. Through grace and his own personal faith, he can experience true repentance, genuine conversion, and a life-changing relationship with Jesus Christ. So although parental influence is an important element in what a child will become, the final product is the result of the child's own choices in the midst of positive and negative forces.

See FAMILY, FATHERS, CHILD (CHILDREN), OBEDIENCE, CHRISTIAN EDUCATION.

For Further Reading: Dobson, *Dare to Discipline,* 222 ff; *GMS,* 553 ff; Wiley, *CT,* 3:92-95; Taylor, "Growth by Design," Nielson, ed., *Family Love in All Dimensions,* 115-33; Sanner, Harper, eds., *Exploring Christian Education,* 148 ff.

MAUREEN H. BOX

PAROUSIA. *Parousia* is a term that has been brought over from the Greek (transliterated) into the common language by the theologians. It originally meant "presence" but eventually came to mean "coming" or "arrival." It appears 24 times in the NT, 17 of which (Matt. 24:3, 27, 37, 39; 1 Cor. 15:23; 1 Thess. 2:19; 3:13; 4:15; 5:23; 2 Thess. 2:1, 8; Jas. 5:7-8; 2 Pet. 1:16; 3:4, 12; 1 John 2:28) refer to the eschatological coming of Jesus Christ in glory (Second Coming) at the end of the age. It is an integral part of the "doctrine of expectation" so characteristic of both Testaments. And the NT is quite emphatic that all history is moving toward this climactic event.

Modern theologians have sought to interpret the above scriptures to mean that only Christ's spiritual presence is intended, but evangelical Christians have always insisted that the passages can only mean that there will be a personal, visible return of our Lord.

The idea of Christ's return appears many times throughout the NT, and other terms are used along with *parousia* in regard to Christ's coming. From *apokalupsis* we get our word *apocalypse,* which means an "uncovering," "disclosure," or "revelation." When used with *parousia,* it indicates that Christ's coming will be an "unveiling" or "disclosure." In the light of His presence many things will become clear. *Epiphaneia* (from which we get our word *epiphany*) carries the meaning of a visible manifestation of some important personage or deity. Its use in 2 Thess. 2:8; 1 Tim. 6:14; 2 Tim. 4:1, 8; Titus 2:13, strongly supports the idea of a personal, visible appearance of our Lord.

Christ indicated that His coming would be sudden and unexpected (Matt. 24:42-44; 1 Thess. 5:2; 2 Pet. 3:10). Only the Father knows the time of His coming (Matt. 24:36; Acts 1:7); therefore, believers should be ready and watching (Matt. 24:44; Luke 12:40; Phil. 3:18-21; Jas. 5:9). However, men need not be caught unawares (Matt. 24:14; 2 Thess. 2:1-2; 1 Tim. 4:1-3).

Why will He come? From Christ's own words we can discern a threefold answer. (1) He comes to judge men. There is so much in this world that is unfair, unjust, and wrong that He will come to set things right. The righteous will be rewarded and the wicked will be punished (Matt. 25:31-34, 41-46; 13:41-43, 49-50). (2) He will bring about a final consummation of this present world order (Rev. 10:5-6). And (3) He will usher in the reign of God (Rev. 11:15; 19:6).

The *parousia* holds such an important place in the NT that it is viewed as the climax of the earth's history.

See SECOND COMING OF CHRIST, RAPTURE.

For Further Reading: Oepke, Kittel, 5:858 ff; Purkiser, ed., *Exploring the Christian Faith,* 538-59; Wiley, *CT,* 3:246-62.

C. PAUL GRAY

PASCHAL CONTROVERSY. The Paschal Controversy was the disagreement in the Early Church concerning the date for the celebration of Easter. The controversy began in the second century and ended in the eighth century.

The churches in Asia Minor followed the custom of observing Easter on the traditional day of the Jewish Passover, the 14th day of the month of Nisan. This practice meant that Easter might be observed on any day of the week.

The Western churches, led by Rome, developed a tradition of observing Easter on Sunday, the first day of the week. For a period the Western church celebrated Easter on a fixed date in March. In 325 the Council of Nicea attempted to present a uniform date by declaring that Easter should be observed on the first Sunday following the final full moon after the spring (vernal) equinox. Because various calendars were used in different areas of the church, the date set by the Council of Nicea was not universally accepted.

Even today the time celebration of Easter in the Eastern and Western churches may vary as much as five weeks.

See PASSOVER, CHRISTIAN YEAR.

For Further Reading: *New Schaff-Herzog Encyclopedia of Religious Knowledge,* 4:43-47; *ODCC,* 1020 ff.

DONALD S. METZ

PASSION OF CHRIST. See DEATH OF CHRIST.

PASSOVER. The name "Passover" is taken from Exod. 12:23, which tells how the destroying angel did "pass over" the houses of Israel when the last of the plagues took the lives of the Egyptian firstborn. In the Bible the Passover celebration is called the Feast of Unleavened Bread.

The word "Passover" denotes the paschal lamb, the sacrifice offered on the eve of the celebration. The nature of this ceremony is described in detail in Exodus 12. At the time of the full moon in the first month of spring every Jewish family slaughtered a lamb at twilight (the "lamb" could be a kid, v. 5). Then, in the middle of the night, the family hastily ate the roasted lamb, along with unleavened bread and bitter herbs. In addition, as soon as the animal was killed, a bunch of hyssop was dipped into the sacrifice's blood, and a few drops sprinkled on the doorposts of each house.

The Passover Festival began on the 15th of Nisan (March-April), the first month of the Jewish religious year. The feast lasted seven days. The Passover was celebrated as an agricultural feast also, a kind of Thanksgiving Day. It marked the beginning of the barley harvest in Palestine. In harmony with Lev. 23:9-12 a sheaf of barley (omer) was presented as a wave offering to the Lord.

The primary meaning of the Passover comes from the special historical event it celebrates—the Exodus from Egypt. The Passover commemorated the great deliverance—the deliverance which transformed a horde of slaves into the people of God. It was Israel's birthday. Passover is the festival of freedom. The freedom of Israel was the freedom to serve God voluntarily. Passover leads to Sinai. Sinai points to Israel's voluntary acceptance of its special distinction and mission.

See BLOOD, LAMB (SACRIFICIAL), LAMB OF GOD, PASCHAL CONTROVERSY, SACRIFICE, EXODUS, ATONEMENT.

For Further Reading: Gaster, *Festivals of the Jewish Year,* 31-58; Segal, *The Hebrew Passover,* 189-230; Golden, *A Treasury of Jewish Holidays,* 128-85.

DONALD S. METZ

PASTOR. Addressing the elders of the church of Ephesus, Paul speaks of two functions of ministry that belong to the office of elder. He writes: "Take heed therefore unto yourselves, and to all the flock, over the which the Holy Ghost hath made you overseers, to feed the church of God, which he hath purchased with his own blood" (Acts 20:28). The first function is that of overseer (Latin, "supervisor," sometimes translated "bishop," Phil. 1:1; 1 Tim. 3:2; Titus 1:7; 1 Pet. 2:25). A second function is that of pastor or shepherd. Inasmuch as feeding the flock is of primary concern to the shepherd, the pastoral concept is dominant. Implied also is the expected capacity of the elder to give wise counsel and demonstrate his wisdom, as a man of God.

The pastor is one called of God to minister, especially to the spiritual needs of God's people, with concern to present every man mature in Christ (Col. 1:28). His concern also for all sorts and conditions of men is shown by his interest in those peoples who are without the light of the gospel: "I am debtor both to the Greeks, and to the Barbarians; both to the wise, and to the unwise" (Rom. 1:14).

In his personal life the pastor seeks to live above reproach and "provide things honest in the sight of all men" (12:17). In our world of competitive values with its emphasis upon "becoming" rather than on "being," the pastor's watch-care over himself is inseparable from his pastoral concern for others. In the pulpit he speaks the things that become sound doctrine (Titus 2:1). In problem confrontation with individuals or groups, he seeks solutions in the light of God's Word. He must manage his own household well, keeping his children submissive and respectful (1 Tim. 3:4). In his Epistles Paul, speaking of the spirit of the pastor, cites among others these qualifications: not partial, not violent, not quarrelsome, not arrogant, no lover of money; but upright, dignified, hospitable, gentle, master of himself.

As administrator, the modern pastor is responsible for the total well-being of the church, including such areas as church budget, Christian education, music, church witness, church growth, missions, and recreation. Confronted with involvement in these tasks, the pastor usually requires help from qualified laymen, either by election or by appointment.

See CLERGY, ELDER, CHURCH GOVERNMENT, PASTORAL COUNSELING.

For Further Reading: Jones, *The Pastor: The Man and His Ministry; NBD,* 1175-76; Schaller, *The Pastor and the People.*

JAMES D. ROBERTSON

PASTORAL COUNSELING. Pastoral counseling is the effort of a Christian minister (or a trained lay counselor) to help people through personal mutual discussion of difficult life situations. It combines a knowledge of the Christian religion, a basic understanding of the human psyche, and interviewing skills. Its most immediate purposes are (1) to lead troubled people to a better understanding of their problems, and (2) to enable them to make self-chosen decisions that are right from Christian and personal points of view.

Pastoral counseling differs from the broader term *pastoral care* inasmuch as the latter refers to all of the minister's personal and group efforts to help parishioners grow. Pastoral counseling differs from many of the professional therapies inasmuch as it rarely gives attention to the areas of the unconscious, dreams, and psychotic processes. Pastoral counselors deal primarily with many of the less "psychologically difficult" life problems such as normal grief, marriage, physical illness, guilt over wrongdoing, and matters of religious and theological concern. The pastor normally carries on a shorter series of interviews than many therapists, perhaps not more than 10 or 12 and usually fewer. He has brief series for two reasons: (1) active pastors cannot spend all of their counseling time with only a few persons in their parishes, and (2) they have not been trained to deal with highly complex life problems that often arise in extended counseling.

There are three primary values in pastoral counseling: (1) it provides support to troubled parishioners, (2) it helps them to make wise solutions of problems, and (3) with deeply troubled persons, it leads to the pastor's referral to professional therapies.

Counseling is related to other aspects of an active pastor's work. His sermons on difficult human problems are an indirect invitation for needy people to confer with him. His pastoral calling is a favorable context for people to mention inner needs. His pastoral concern for his parishioners often provides him with an opportunity to take the initiative and, as in precounseling, to mention personal needs that are not clearly recognized by anxious and frustrated parishioners.

Pastoral counseling, as a practice based on an organized body of knowledge, developed in the 20th century. In 1925, Anton Boison began clinical training and supervision of pastors' "counseling" in mental hospitals. In 1936 Richard Cabot, a physician in Massachusetts General Hospital, and Russell L. Dicks, a Christian minister, began teaching pastors certain principles of ministering to the sick in hospitals. That practice spread rapidly, and today there are many hospitals, as well as other institutions, where ministers learn pastoral counseling by actual practice along with academic study (commonly called CPE—Clinical Pastoral Education). Many of the Protestant theological seminaries have structured clinical opportunities for many of their students.

The competence of pastoral counselors depends upon a number of basic personal factors: (1) good personal adjustment, (2) a personal sensitivity to and concern about the problems of troubled persons, (3) the ability to empathize with needy persons, (4) an ability to listen to others, and (5) nonjudgmental attitudes.

In addition to local church settings, pastoral counseling is increasingly being carried on by chaplains in hospitals and prisons and by ministers who set up counseling offices that are associated with professional therapists.

See PASTOR, ROGERIAN COUNSELING, REALITY THERAPY.

For Further Reading: Clinebell, *Basic Types of Pastoral Counseling;* Adams, *The Christian Counselor's Manual;* Howe, *The Miracle of Dialogue;* Hiltner, *Pastoral Counseling.*

W. CURRY MAVIS

PASTORAL THEOLOGY. See PRACTICAL THEOLOGY.

PATRIPASSIANISM. See MONARCHIANISM.

PEACE. Peace is a state of tranquility and harmony. In an organism it is produced by homeostasis, a tendency toward balance among the organism's interacting and interdependent systems. Between nations peace is not only the absence of either "hot" or "cold" war but open relations with freedom of movement and exchange. Seldom is such peace absolute, for generally while nations may technically be at peace, they are usually struggling with some tensions and disputes. In interpersonal relationships peace is, minimally, freedom from quarreling and bitterness, and, maximally, a mutual sense of ease and pleasure.

However, the peace most universally coveted and sought is inward—peace of mind or heart. This is freedom from guilt, hostility, and anxiety; positively it is a deep sense of personal well-being. Such peace Jesus promised His followers (John 14:27) and such peace is actually experienced by Spirit-controlled believers (Gal. 5:22).

The peace which is available is spiritual, not necessarily environmental. It is not freedom from tribulation (John 16:33). Its prerequisites are not freedom from economic necessity or physical pain; nor do they include the possession of ideally happy relations with people (Phil. 4:10-13; 2 Cor. 12:7-10; Rom. 12:18; Gal. 2:11). The Christian may possess a profound rest of soul in the midst of outward tumult or even at times his own emotional agitation.

The one absolute requisite for peace of mind is rightness with God (Rom. 5:1). Any so-called peace not thus based is illusory. It is but the inertia and stupefaction of a seared conscience (1 Tim. 4:2). While peace with God becomes possible through faith in the atoning work of the Lord Jesus Christ, certain moral concomitants belong to such faith. One is repentance; clinging to sin will make authentic peace impossible. Another is obedience, including adjustment with one's estranged fellows (Matt. 5:23-24; Heb. 12:14). Unchristian disruption with those around one (i.e., disruption not morally required, or demanded by conscience) disrupts peace with God.

Such moral concomitants of peace are reminders that peace with God is much more than a personal feeling, or the absence of a sense of condemnation; it is true rightness with God, involving the forgiveness of our sins, and an inner knowledge that we are reconciled to God and God is reconciled to us. Peace with God is therefore inseparable from fellowship with God. Many gain relief from guilt feelings through tears, confession, or counsel of men, and mistake this for peace with God, when the ethical dimension has been deficient, or the faith has not rested solely in Christ and His cross as the basis of the reconciliation.

Requirements for the maintenance of peace are faith, obedience, and meekness. It is only through unwavering faith in God that poise and tranquility can endure in the face of puzzling providences and crushing events. It is only through obedience that fellowship can be sustained. But perhaps the most difficult requisite is meekness. Pride, self-willfulness, self-importance, and ego touchiness are all destroyers of peace. For this the word is: "Take my yoke upon you, and learn of me; for I am meek and lowly in heart: and ye shall find rest unto your souls" (Matt. 11:29).

Yet the meekness which is essential to personal peace must never be interpreted as capitulation to evil. Peace cannot be kept without also keeping a clear conscience; and a good conscience demands the prosecution of the war against sin and evil. In the name of peace Christians must never compromise with the devil or any of his representatives. Whether thinking of the nation, the church, the family, or self, "peace at any cost" is a slogan never on the lips of those sharing the nature of a holy God. Holiness may demand the abandonment of peace on one level in order to preserve it on a deeper level. For peace can be costly, as "the blood of his cross" demonstrates (Col. 1:20).

See RECONCILIATION, REST (REST OF FAITH), FRUIT OF THE SPIRIT, PACIFISM.

For Further Reading: Wesley, *Works,* 5:80, 216, 283; 6:34, 79, 399, 486; 7:433. RICHARD S. TAYLOR

PELAGIANISM. Pelagianism is a system of moral and doctrinal concepts originating with Pelagius, a British monk who visited Rome in the fifth century. Pelagianism expresses the rationalistic tendency in early Christianity (Wiley, *CT,* 2:415). The doctrines had three great leaders: Pelagius himself; then Julian of Eclanum, who served as the architect of the teaching; and Celestius, who popularized the dogma (Pelikan, *The Christian Tradition,* 1:373).

Spiritual and ethical neutrality of Adam. Pelagius taught that Adam was born spiritually neutral. Adam was endowed with freedom and placed under the law of righteousness. Adam, and all men, had the capacity of achieving sinless perfection in this life. The presentation of a commandment by God implied the ability of Adam to obey.

Denial of original sin. The denial of primitive holiness in favor of initial spiritual neutrality carried with it a denial of the Adamic fall and the subsequent depravity of the human race. Adam's sin injured only himself, not his descendents. Pelagius placed extreme emphasis on the self-determination of the individual to good or evil. Man is born capable of either good or evil. Each individual enters life without either virtue or vice. There is no inherited depravity. The doctrine of original sin is rejected. Because of the denial of original sin and death as the result of sin, Pelagianism was formally condemned as a heresy by the General Council of Ephesus in A.D. 431.

The innocent state of all newborn infants. Newborn infants are in the same condition as Adam before the Fall. Every descendent of Adam is born morally neutral. Sin is the result of the free choice of every man. Wiley quotes a statement describing the state of each person: "At birth, each man's voluntary faculty, like Adam's, is undetermined either to sin or holiness. Being thus characterless, with a will undecided for either good or evil, and not in the least affected by Adam's apostasy, each individual man, after birth commences his voluntariness, originates his own character, and decides his own destiny by the choice of either right or wrong" (*CT,* 1:44). Personal sin is entirely a matter of wrong choices.

Personal holiness is possible by means of right choices.

A humanistic view of salvation. The change effected in regeneration results from an act of the human will. Regeneration is not a renewal of the personality by the operation of the Holy Spirit. Regeneration comes when God's grace illuminates the intellect by the truth. The individual hears of God's grace, learns of God's commandments, accepts the truth, makes a decision to obey, and by self-discipline follows divine commands by his natural power.

The mortality of the human race. Man was destined to die even if Adam had not sinned. The human race neither dies on account of Adam's sin nor rises on account of Christ's resurrection.

The central principle of Pelagianism is a belief in man's ability to do by his own power all that God's righteousness demands.

See AUGUSTINIANISM, ORIGINAL SIN, FREEDOM, PREVENIENT GRACE, ABILITY.

For Further Reading: Wiley, *CT,* 2:102-3, 348, 415; Pelikan, *The Christian Tradition,* 1:313-31; Warfield, *Studies in Tertullian and Augustine,* 291-92.

DONALD S. METZ

PENAL SATISFACTION THEORY OF THE ATONEMENT. Among the Christian interpretations of Christ's atoning work, the penal satisfaction theory has been dominant, especially among orthodox voices of the church. Based on the language of Isa. 53:4-5, 10 (see 1 Pet. 2:24), and on the legal interpretation of Christ's death which was congenial to Roman Christianity, the theory stressed the requirements of divine justice. Sin is a violation of the divine will, which declares that the sinner must pay the penalty of death (Gen. 2:17 and Ezek. 33:14-16). Nevertheless, the principle of substitution permitted the penalty to be borne by another. Thus the penalty, while not removed, could be diverted. The substitute's acceptance of the penalty satisfied the justice of the divine demand and freed the sinner.

This theory is found in Origen of Alexandria (A.D. 185-254) and is developed by Anselm of Canterbury (A.D. 1033-1109).

Anselm's thought lacks the "penal" aspect. His concept is sometimes denoted a "commercial" theory because of its emphasis on debt and payment. Anselm does not develop the substitution motif in his doctrine of the Atonement. In his famous work *Cur Deus Homo* (Why God Became Man), he stresses the necessity of the Incarnation. If Christ is to pay mankind's debt, He must become one with us. His life and death is a full compensation for the dishonor man has done toward God.

Penal satisfaction receives its full explication in Reformed theology. Sin must be fully punished or God's justice is abrogated. As the Reformed position matured, it incorporated the concept of substitution, including substituted punishment and substituted obedience. Sin requires punishment. This is satisfied by the substitutionary death of Christ. In Reformed thought substituted obedience must be added. Since human obedience can never satisfy, Christ's obedience is necessary. Jesus bears both penalty and the demand of obedience for those who are among the elect.

See ATONEMENT, MYSTICAL THEORY OF THE ATONEMENT, GOVERNMENTAL THEORY OF THE ATONEMENT, MORAL INFLUENCE THEORY OF THE ATONEMENT, SACRIFICE, PROPITIATION, SATISFACTION.

For Further Reading: Miley, *The Atonement in Christ,* 135-43; Wiley, *CT,* 2:241-51. LEON O. HYNSON

PENANCE. This is one of the seven sacraments of the Roman Catholic church. It originated, in part, because Jerome's Vulgate version of the Bible translated the various NT imperatives "Repent ye" *(metanoeite)* as "Do penance." Thus Roman Catholics, instead of understanding that we are to change our minds about sin and become obedient to God, have supposed that we are to do this or that good work.

The sacrament arose also through incorrect interpretations of Heb. 6:4-6 and 10:26. Those passages were interpreted as suggesting that a person who has known Christ, and falls away, cannot be forgiven. So they worked out a system of good works for reinstatement. These good works were made into a sacrament in medieval times—the sacrament of penance. It is such doctrines as those on which penance is based that Luther and Protestants in general were reacting to when they began to teach that salvation is by grace alone, through faith alone.

See REPENTANCE, PENITENCE.

J. KENNETH GRIDER

PENITENCE. This describes the penitent's disposition or state of being. It is associated with an experience of remorse or a feeling of sorrow. In NT times a clear distinction was made between *penitence* and *repentance.* The latter described a change of heart which led to changes in attitude and actions. Even though the former word was used less frequently, it referred to a change in the emotions so as to express feelings of regret or contrition. This result comes not so much because of a fear of punishment but because a just and holy God is offended.

There seems to be in the NT a stress on keeping the rational acts of the will independent of passing moods and feelings. In actual life, however, the distinctions are less obvious. One complements the other. A good example is Paul's statement: "For godly sorrow worketh repentance to salvation not to be repented of: but the sorrow of the world worketh death" (2 Cor. 7:10).

Judaism's appreciation for penitence is evident in its liturgical forms. The following psalms were labeled Penitential Psalms: 6; 32; 38; 51; 102; 130; and 143. And in the writings of Isaiah there is an interesting emphasis upon the "contrite heart" (57:15; 66:2).

In Roman Catholic theology the fourth of the seven sacraments is called the sacrament of penance. In order to stress the element of godly sorrow, this sacrament has at times been referred to as a second baptism in terms of a "baptism of tears."

See REPENTANCE, PENANCE.

For Further Reading: Kittel, 4:626-29; *IDB*, 4:33-34.

ROBERT A. MATTKE

PENTATEUCH. Pentateuch is the Greek name for the first five books of the OT, forming the first division of the Hebrew canon of Scripture, also known as the Torah. The name means "the five scrolls" and was used by Alexandrian Jews as early as the first Christian century to correspond to the Hebrew description of Torah as the five-fifths of the law.

The material of the Pentateuch has always been of supreme importance for the theology of Judaism, much more so than the Prophets and the Writings of the Hebrew Scriptures. This fact is reflected in the attitude of the Samaritans and Sadducees who accepted only the Pentateuch as being divinely inspired. The NT clarifies the proper place of the Pentateuch in Christian theology and records the conflict which distinguished Christianity from Judaism on this basis.

The problematic question of authorship of the Pentateuch is one of the most persistent in biblical studies. The traditional view is that Moses wrote the Pentateuch, based on the internal evidence of the text where specific passages state that Moses wrote the law (Exod. 24:4; 34:27; Deut. 31:9). Later historical books such as Chronicles, Ezra, and Nehemiah reflect this well-established tradition. The conservative date for the composition of these books indicate that this tradition of Mosaic authorship was well settled by the fifth century B.C. This was not the *beginning* of such a tradition; it merely perpetuated an established tradition from earlier centuries. Later witnesses from the intertestamental period assert that Moses authored all of the Pentateuch. In the NT the Pentateuch was regarded as the work of Moses (Mark 12:26; Luke 24:27, 44; John 5:45-47).

A serious challenge to the tradition of Mosaic authorship of the Pentateuch was mounted in the 16th century A.D., climaxing with the wave of higher criticism which centered in Germany during the 19th century. Ingenious attempts were made to explain the composition of the Pentateuch from various sources and different hands across the centuries. A bewildering plethora of theories and modifications resulted. At present, there is little agreement among critical scholars on this question, and the more specific one becomes, the more disagreement is evident.

The dominant element in the Pentateuch is the direction or guidance contained therein. God's purpose in revealing the law was to provide direction and guidance for the worship and life of His covenant people. At such, it was never intended to be a penal burden to be borne, but an expression of divine grace and caring.

During His ministry Jesus recognized the authority of both the law (Matt. 5:17) and its official interpreters (23:2-3). Paul also recognized the basic worth of the law in the purpose of God (Gal. 3:24). But the NT is equally clear that Christ is the end of the law (Rom. 10:4); it was never an end in itself. The NT writers saw clearly that the law was only temporary until the time had fully come when God sent forth His Son to redeem those who were under the law (Gal. 4:4).

Distinction must be made between the moral law contained in the Pentateuch and the ceremonial law concerned with sacrifices and the rituals of worship as a means of justification. The former, such as the Ten Commandments, is binding upon NT believers, while the latter is superseded by Christ. A careful reading of the Epistle to the Hebrews is enlightening as Christ is presented as a *better* revelation, sacrifice, high priest, etc., so that the old is done away with because of the actualization of the new.

See TALMUD, MOSAIC LAW, LAW, LAW AND GRACE, LAW OF LIBERTY, FREEDOM, ANTINOMIANISM.

For Further Reading: *The Interpreter's Bible*, 1:185-200; Harrison, *Introduction to the Old Testament*, 495-541; *ISBE*, 3:711-27. ALVIN S. LAWHEAD

PENTECOST. "Pentecost" is a term which comes from the Greek word *pentecostē*, meaning "50." Being Greek, it does not appear in the OT. It was a Jewish feast which fell 50 days after the Passover. The Jews called it "The Feast of Weeks" (Exod. 34:22; Deut. 16:9-11); "The Feast of Harvest" (Exod. 23:16); and "The Day of the Firstfruits" (Num. 28:26).

The day was established for the celebration of the firstfruits of the wheat harvest. After the Romans destroyed the Temple and its sacrificial system (A.D. 70), the day was remembered as the anniversary of the giving of the law to Moses.

All adult males were required to go to the sanctuary to celebrate this feast (Exod. 23:14, 16). The worshipper brought a sheaf of wheat to the priest who waved it before the Lord in recognition that the harvest comes from God. A lamb and a cereal offering likewise were brought (Lev. 23:11 ff; cf. v. 18). A portion of the sheaf was placed on the altar as a burnt offering. The rest was given to the priests for food. Two loaves of bread made from new wheat were waved by the priest for all the people. Then the priests, eating the loaves and sacrificial animals, concluded the feast with a communal meal to which the poor, the Levites, and strangers were invited.

It was fitting that God should choose the Day of Pentecost on which to give the fullness of the Spirit to the Church (cf. Acts 1 and 2). As Pentecost was 50 days after the Passover, so the gift of the Spirit came 50 days after Calvary when "Christ our passover" was "sacrificed for us" (1 Cor. 5:7). As on Pentecost the firstfruits of the harvest were given, so the Holy Spirit is the Firstfruit of the abundant blessings which God has in store for His people (Eph. 2:7; 1 Cor. 2:9). And as God gave the law 50 days after delivering Israel from bondage to Pharaoh, so, having delivered believers from bondage to Satan, God, through the gift of the Spirit, writes the law on their hearts (cf. Jer. 31:33; Ezek. 11:19; 36:25-28; 37:1-4; Acts 15:8-9; Heb. 8:10).

Because the Holy Spirit in His fullness was given to the Church on the Day of Pentecost, the word "Pentecost" is used symbolically by some to signify the fullness of the Spirit of God which was promised to believers (Luke 3:16; 24:49; John 14:15-18; Acts 1:4, 8; etc.). Others who use the term confuse the gifts of the Spirit with His fullness, identifying phenomena which attended the original outpouring of the Spirit with the fullness of the Spirit. Yet the same Spirit gives a variety of gifts to His people as He himself chooses (1 Cor. 12:4-11). Therefore, no particular gift is proof of His fullness, nor even of His presence (Matt. 7:22-23).

See FEASTS, BAPTISM WITH THE HOLY SPIRIT, DISPENSATION OF THE SPIRIT, NEW COVENANT.

For Further Reading: Carter, *The Person and Ministry of the Holy Spirit;* Schauss, *The Jewish Festivals from Their Beginning,* trans. Jaffe Samuel.

W. RALPH THOMPSON

PENTECOSTALISM. The cluster of religious ideas and practices now called "Pentecostal" and, in their modern extension, "charismatic" are chiefly a 20th-century phenomenon. Their roots, however, lie deep in the evangelical past. The three great spiritual movements of the 18th century—the Wesleyan, the revivalistic Calvinist, and the German Pietist—all sought explicitly to revive as much as possible the primitive Christianity of the Early Church. Central to their evangelism was the declaration that the saving power of the Holy Spirit, given at Pentecost to all who would repent, believe, and be baptized, was available in all times and places.

The leaders of each of these three movements, and especially John Wesley, made a sharp distinction between the "extraordinary" and the "ordinary" gifts of the Spirit at Pentecost; the latter, which they specified as the gift of His "sanctifying graces," was the one they thought was permanently available. They declared that the "extraordinary" gifts of languages, healing, or other miraculous powers were largely, if not wholly, confined to the apostolic generation. During the remainder of the 18th and throughout the 19th century, the doctrine of the new birth, in which the Holy Spirit freed repentant sinners from both the guilt and the power of evil (as Jesus had promised and Paul, in the Epistle to the Romans, had described), steadily triumphed in Protestant consciousness in America, Great Britain, Scandinavia, and Germany.

Meanwhile, however, a tiny minority insisted upon the more radical notion that the extraordinary gifts of the Spirit would be widespread in the "last days," as the apostle Peter's quotation from the prophet Joel at Pentecost seemed to declare. Joseph Smith's Church of Jesus Christ of Latter-Day Saints, popularly known as Mormons, affirmed this view; and a few who claimed power to heal or to speak in "unknown" tongues, known technically as *glossolalia,* appeared among them. The same thing happened in London, in the congregation of radical believers in the Second Coming gathered around Edward Irving, who was briefly influential among a segment of England's high society. Although the phenomenon of tongues disappeared almost entirely, interest in divine healing grew in several evangelical communities, and with it the hope of multiplying miracles in the "last days."

The leaders of the Wesleyan holiness movement in America and, at least until 1903, the Keswick movement in England resisted all of this and excluded from their platforms emphasis upon either divine healing or doctrines of the Second Coming. Moreover, the ancient and apostolic custom that the elders of the church should, on request, anoint and pray for the sick in faith for their healing continued in many denominations. On the other hand, both movements encouraged the use of Pentecostal language to describe the experience of a second work of sanctifying grace. Following John Wesley's beloved theologian, John Fletcher, they called it the "baptism of the Holy Spirit."

On the fringes of the popular revival movements which spread through America, Wales, and, to a much smaller degree, Scandinavia, however, were independent evangelists, Bible schools, city missions, and healing ministries insisting on a more radical restoration of primitive Christianity. This included the miraculous gifts and gift of tongues. The spark that set fire to this conviction and created the Pentecostal movement, however, was the experience of speaking in what the faithful believed was a language they had not learned. A small group of women attending an obscure Bible school in Topeka, Kans., first experienced this on December 31, 1900, under the promptings of Charles F. Parham, an eccentric holiness evangelist who had no formal tie to any organized religious body. Local newspaper reporters appeared in a few days, and a University of Kansas professor established that the young women were not speaking Chinese, as they had originally thought. Soon, they and Parham decided that the "unknown tongues" were usually languages of heaven, unknown on earth. But the movement never formally abandoned the belief that human languages might be miraculously granted also, as at Pentecost, to sustain foreign missions.

Pentecostalism spread but little until 1906, when Charles Seymour, a black man who had attended a tiny Bible school that Parham conducted in Houston, appeared at an interracial holiness mission on Azusa Street, in Los Angeles, and began to proclaim the promise of the gift of tongues. A revival broke out, amidst torrents of emotion and numerous cases of tongues-speaking. These gained almost instant nationwide attention. Within months a Scandinavian mission worker, T. K. Barrett, spread the movement to Sweden, Norway, and Denmark. Others carried the news to England and Germany, and set Christians to seeking similar experiences there.

The identifying mark of the Pentecostal movement has been from the outset, therefore, speaking in tongues. Its theological corollary emerged very soon, namely, that this experience was the indispensable "sign" that one had received the baptism of the Holy Spirit, whether or not the "sign" was extended in a continuing "gift" of praying or speaking in glossolalia. Pentecostal groups whose backgrounds were Wesleyan sharply distinguished the experience of being baptized or filled with the Spirit from the second work of grace. They continued to call the latter "entire sanctification," and to define it as Wesley did—a work of the Spirit that cleanses believers' hearts from inbred sin. Those whose backgrounds were Calvinist, Disciples of Christ, or Southern Baptist made the Pentecostal experience simply a variant of the Keswick understanding of the second work of grace, namely, a baptism of the Spirit that brought power to triumph over all temptation (including that stemming from the remains of inbred sin) and to witness effectively.

The largest denomination to emerge among non-Wesleyan Pentecostals was the Assemblies of God. Its founders minimized the doctrine of sanctification and eventually embraced that of the "finished work" of Christ on the Cross, teaching that His righteousness was imputed rather than imparted. From this wing of the movement emerged also the United Pentecostal church. The preoccupation of Pentecostals with the name of Jesus and the NT's strong identification of the Holy Spirit with the risen Lord prompted its leaders to develop a unitarian doctrine of God, popularly called "Jesus only." More typical was Aimee Semple McPherson, who in the mid-1920s taught a large following at her Angelus Temple in Los Angeles to honor Christ as Savior, Healer, Baptizer (with the Holy Spirit), and Soon-Coming King. The result was the International Church of the Foursquare Gospel.

Virtually all Pentecostals believed in the premillennial return of Jesus, preceded by the outpouring of the Holy Spirit in the "latter rain" Joel had prophesied. Their doctrine of the Church varied greatly, though the tradition of independency, stemming from the Anabaptist and radical Puritan movements, was the most pervasive one.

Notable has been the appeal of Pentecostal foreign missionaries in Central and South America, among Spanish- and Portuguese-speaking populations. The reasons are complex but seem to include the mental habits nurtured by the Latin Mass, in which spiritual experience took place as the priest spoke in a language no one understood, and the neglect of the poor by the Catholic governing elite.

While modern Wesleyans acknowledge that new spiritual vitality, together with a fresh discovery of the ministry of the Spirit, has broken into hitherto formalistic settings, they nevertheless have misgivings concerning the Pentecostal movement as a whole. The central issue is whether or not the claims and emphases of modern Pentecostalism are supportable by a sound exegesis of Scripture. Many careful scholars are convinced that there are disparities between Pentecostal practices and biblical teachings, particularly on the question whether the "tongues" spoken at Pentecost were "unknown" or well-known languages. Others believe they see a stress on miraculous and emotional experiences that sometimes outweighs ethical commitment.

See NEO-PENTECOSTALISM, PENTECOST, BAPTISM WITH THE HOLY SPIRIT, TONGUES (GIFT OF), WESLEYANISM, HOLINESS MOVEMENT, GIFTS OF THE SPIRIT.

For Further Reading: Synan, *The Pentecostal-Holiness Movement in the United States;* Carter, *The Person and Ministry of the Holy Spirit,* 191-219, 261-89; Agnew, *The Holy Spirit: Friend and Counselor,* 47-117.

TIMOTHY L. SMITH

PERDITION, SON OF PERDITION. The word is derived from the Latin *perdere,* "to destroy," and is used in the English Bible to translate the Greek word *apōleia,* "destruction." Generally speaking, the term is used to express the fate which awaits the unrepentant, and his loss of eternal salvation. Frequently a contrast is drawn between the state of the believer and the unbeliever by contrasting salvation with destruction (e.g., Phil. 1:28; Heb. 10:39; Rev. 17:8).

There are two references in the NT to the "son of perdition": John 17:12, where it is used of Judas; and 2 Thess. 2:3, where it describes the Antichrist.

A problem arises with its use in John 17:12 as applied to Judas. Here we read that the son of perdition is lost "that the scripture might be fulfilled." The implication of the passage seems to be that Judas was predestined to betray Jesus and therefore could do no other. On this two points should be made: First, there is a play on the words "lost" and "perdition" (in Greek the word for "lost" is *apōleto,* and for "perdition," *apōleia*). Now, it was customary for the Jews at the time to coin a name which expressed the character of an individual: Barnabas, e.g., means "son of consolation"; Barsabas (Acts 15:22), "son of the Sabbath." Jesus, with this play on words, here coins a name for Judas which characterizes his condition ("lost") and his end which results from it ("destruction").

The second point to be made is that predictive prophecy (Ps. 41:9 is very likely the passage in mind) is in no way deterministic. There is built into the prophetic message a moral condition, which, if it produces repentance, annuls the predicted doom (e.g., Jonah and Nineveh). Judas chose to betray Jesus and in so doing sealed his own fate.

Still, as of old
Man by himself is priced.
For thirty pieces Judas sold
Himself, not Christ.

The comment of John Calvin on this verse is apposite: "It would be wrong for anyone to infer from this that Judas' fall should be imputed to God rather than to himself, in that necessity was laid on him by the prophecy."

See CONTINGENT, PROPHET (PROPHECY), PREDESTINATION, DETERMINISM, FREEDOM.

THOMAS FINDLAY

PERFECT, PERFECTION. The word "perfect" as normally used in English means "having all the properties belonging to it; complete; sound, flawless." It "further implies the soundness, the proportionateness, and excellence of every part, every element, or every quality" *(Webster's New Collegiate Dictionary).*

To get at the biblical meaning, one must observe the original words used in the Bible. *Tamim,* the Hebrew word most used, is applied to God (Ps. 18:30), to the law (19:7), and to persons (Job 1:8; 2:3). The other Hebrew word, *shalem,* is used with only one exception to describe persons, such as "perfect heart," or wholly devoted to God (1 Kings 8:61; etc.). The NT word *teleios* means "brought to its end" or "finished." It also indicates "wanting nothing necessary to completeness" or "full-grown, adult, of full age, mature" (Thayer, *Greek-English Lexicon of the New Testament,* 618).

The use of the word "perfect," both in modern English usage, and in understanding the biblical words, cannot be precise. Some want it to mean only the absolute perfection of God, and deny its use for man or things. To do this rejects the common usage of the terms as they should be understood.

Most careful students of the Bible recognize the latitude in the application of these words. When applied to God or His law, there is preciseness and absoluteness about them; but when applied to man, the terms become relative. There is then both absolute perfection and relative perfection.

God's perfection becomes the standard of all other perfections. There is a kind of "perfection . . . ascribed to God's works," and "it is also either ascribed to men or required of them. By this is meant complete conformity to those requirements as to character and conduct which God has appointed. . . . But fidelity to the Scriptures requires us to believe that, in some important sense, Christians may be perfect even in this life, though they still must wait for perfection in a larger sense in the life which is to come" (*Unger's Bible Dictionary,* 843). Such relative perfection is recognized by other writers (see *ZPBD,* 636; and *HBD,* 538).

We believe it is biblical to hold that there is a perfection attainable in this life (Matt. 5:48; 1 John 1:7-9; Eph. 4:12; Phil. 3:15). Since to be perfect means to attain the goal God intends, then, when one reaches that goal, he is perfect in this one sense. One can hardly believe God requires a person to be perfect in an area he cannot because of human weakness. God knows man is weak and will be so while in this life. Yet He requires a perfection of love and character that is compatible with human failure.

Thus a Christian may be perfect in his heart while imperfect in his performance. He always aims for a greater maturity in his actions. Only in the resurrection will he attain all the perfection he lost when sin came into the world. Never in this life or the next can man be as perfect as God is in the absolute sense.

See CHRISTIAN PERFECTION, PERFECT LOVE, PERFECTIONISM, HOLINESS, FAILURE.

For Further Reading: Wesley, *A Plain Account of Christian Perfection;* Cox, *John Wesley's Concept of Perfection;* Wiley, *CT,* 2:496-517; *GMS,* 479-83; Wood, *Purity and Maturity.*

LEO G. COX

PERFECT LOVE. Perfect love is the experienced reality of a relationship with God in which the believer loves God with all the heart, soul, mind, and strength, and the neighbor as oneself. It is the actualizing of God's purpose that we should be holy (inner holiness) and blameless (outer holiness) before Him *in love* (Eph. 1:4).

In the OT, love for God is at the heart of the Decalogue (Exod. 20:6) and is consistently enjoined upon God's people throughout their history. It finds its quintessential expression in the extended form of the Shema (Deut. 6:4-5) which, by NT times, had become the foundational creed of all Jewish worship. Jesus employed this extended form of the Shema as the first of all commandments (Mark 12:29-30). Love for neighbor, while implied in the Decalogue (Exod. 20:12-17) and specifically enjoined in Lev. 19:18, did not have that integral correlation with love for God which Jesus gave it when He quoted Lev. 19:18 as the commandment second only to love for God (Mark 12:31). Instead, in the OT, love for God (inner holiness) is linked with keeping His commandments (Exod. 20:6; Deut. 7:9; 11:1; et al.) and walking in His ways (10:12; 19:9; et al.) (outer holiness).

At the early stages of the OT perception of loving God and keeping His commandments, the condition of the human heart became a focal element. Moses exhorted the people to circumcise their hearts in order to love God and serve Him (Deut. 10:12-16), and then recognized that God would have to perform this act so that they *could* love Him with all their heart (30:6). In Ezekiel, after exhorting His people to get "a new heart and a new spirit" (18:31), God promised He would give His people a new heart and a new spirit—that He would put His Spirit within them, thus enabling them to walk in His statutes and observe His ordinances (36:25-27). Thus the OT recognized (1) that keeping God's commandments and walking in His ways is a consequence of loving God with all the heart, soul, mind, and strength; and (2) that God must do a transforming work in the human heart to enable persons to love in this manner.

Jesus clearly epitomizes the Decalogue (the base of all other commandments, ordinances, and statutes of the OT) in the commandments to love God (quoting Deut. 6:4-5) and to love the neighbor (quoting Lev. 19:18). His radically new emphasis is that love for neighbor (outer holiness) is the inherent and inseparable corollary of love for God (inner holiness); so much so that even when the neighbor becomes an enemy, love is still the rule if we are to be perfect *(teleios)* as our Heavenly Father (Matt. 5:43-48): *perfect in love.* While Jesus retains the OT affirmation that love for God results in obedience (John 14:15, 21, 23; 15:10), it should be noted that these statements are bracketed by the commandment to love one another (13:34-35; 15:12, 17). Thus the essential obedience of love for God (inner holiness) is love for others (outer holiness).

The NT writers repeatedly highlight this reality (Rom. 13:8-10; Gal. 5:14; Jas. 2:8; 1 John 4:20-21; 5:2-3), further affirming: the love of God is perfected *(teleioō)* in whoever keeps God's Word (2:5—John immediately follows this statement with an exposition of the commandment to love in vv. 7-11); if we love one another, love of God is perfected *(teleioō)* in us (4:12); the bond of perfection *(teleiotēs)* is love (Col. 3:14); and the goal (or "perfection," *telos*) of the Christian exhortation is love from a clean heart (1 Tim. 1:5).

The experience of perfect love is the work of the Holy Spirit in the believer's heart which has been cleansed by faith (Acts 15:9; cf. Matt. 5:8; 1 Tim. 1:5; 2 Tim. 2:22; 1 Pet. 1:22 [var.]). The love of God poured into our hearts through the Holy Spirit (Rom. 5:5) is the decisive reality of Christian existence (Kittel, 1:49). This love (Gal. 5:22) is the perfect way (*teleios*—1 Cor. 13:10) which supercedes the gifts of the Spirit (1 Corinthians 12) and is greater even than faith and hope (1 Corinthians 13). First John brings all these together when, with his repeated injunctions to love one another (2:7-10; 3:11, 14, 23; 4:7, 11, 21), he notes that love is from God (3:1; 4:7, 9-10, 19); that those who love remain in God and God in them (3:24; 4:7, 12, 16); that this dwelling in God and God's indwelling has the witness of the Spirit (3:24; 4:13); and that those who so yield themselves to loving obedience are perfected in love (2:3-5; 4:12, 17).

See ENTIRE SANCTIFICATION, HOLINESS, PERFECT (PERFECTION), CHRISTIAN PERFECTION, LOVE.

For Further Reading: Wesley, *Plain Account of Christian Perfection;* "The Scripture Way of Salvation," *Works,* 6:43; Quell and Stauffer, "agapaō," Kittel, 1:21-55, esp. 27-35 and 44-55; Wood, *Perfect Love;* Taylor, *Life in the Spirit.*

M. ROBERT MULHOLLAND, JR.

PERFECTIONISM. The term *perfectionism* specifies the view that moral or spiritual perfection is the Christian ideal and is realizable in this life. It also designates a multifaceted movement of great power and interest in 19th-century American church life.

Prior to the Reformation, perfectionism appeared mostly in ascetic, Pelagian, or mystical forms. The Reformers were generally hostile to these forms of perfectionism, but their opposition paved the way for a more genuinely biblical orientation. Christian perfectionism entered the mainstream of Western Protestantism through the Wesleyan revival and received definitive formulation in the writings of John Wesley and John Fletcher.

In America, the merging streams of Wesleyan theology and Scottish common sense philosophy brought into dynamic conjunction the twin themes of free will and free grace. Lit by the fires of Finney revivalism, these conceptual explosives released into the mid-19th century church a perfectionistic energy which was to affect every vital nerve center of national life. Educational, social, economic, ecclesiastical, political, physiological, moral, and spiritual aspects of life all came under intense scrutiny as zealous Christians pursued the goal of universal reform.

The movement included various types. Most prominent among them were the community enterprises at Oneida, N.Y., and Oberlin, Ohio. At Oneida, John Humphrey Noyes advocated in the name of Christian perfection a style of living whose biblical underpinnings were suspect and whose ethical principles were scandalous. In his view, a Christian could rise above all need for external light and external authority and could actually become incapable of sinning. Central to the Oneida ethos was the practice of "open marriage," a concept which Noyes somehow derived from the principle of universal benevolence. The term *perfectionism* as such was probably most closely associated in the 19th-century mind with John Humphrey Noyes and Oneida.

In terms of biblical orthodoxy, moral consistency, and widespread influence, however, early Oberlin College stands without peer as the institutional embodiment of American perfectionism. Perfectionistic concern at Oberlin began with the sanctification of individuals. Here it was proclaimed that the new covenant in Christ promised a work of the Holy Spirit which could bring the human heart into perfect conformity with the moral law.

Individual sanctification, however, had social ramifications. Oberlin's president, Asa Mahan, maintained that the Christian Church is a universal reform society. The duty of Christians is to fight sin and wrong wherever it exists and to bring all of life under the sway of biblical principles through the powerful gospel of Christ. For Oberlinites and perfectionists generally, this meant such things as immediate emancipation of slaves, equal educational opportunities for women, temperance in eating and drinking, union among churches, and peace among nations. Benevolent societies were spawned to assist the needy, and moral suasion was brought fearlessly and effectively to bear upon the powerful. Motivating all was the vision of an approaching millennium which would consist primarily in the sanctification of the church.

See CHRISTIAN PERFECTION, PERFECT (PERFECTION), SOCIAL HOLINESS, SOCIAL ETHICS.

For Further Reading: Dayton, *Discovering an Evangelical Heritage;* Handy, *A Christian America: Protestant Hopes and Historical Realities;* Smith, *Revivalism and Social Reform.*

JAMES E. HAMILTON

PERISH. See LOST, LOST SOUL.

PERMISSIVE WILL. See PROVIDENCE.

PERMISSIVENESS. This is a neutral word denoting an attitude of allowance, permission, or enablement, such as *permissive legislation.* It receives negative or positive value from its context.

In the 20th century, permissiveness has acquired a distinctly pejorative connotation, particularly in Christian circles. The term conveys images of antinomianism, indiscipline, and immorality. As such, it is said to be an attitude which pervades society as a whole—a spirit of lawlessness and excessive tolerance (2 Tim. 3:1-5). It affects child-rearing practices, where sentimentality may replace loving correction; adolescent relationships, where self-gratification is called "love"; and adult life, where white-collar crime, infidelity, tax evasion, and lowering of ethical standards are all symptoms of permissiveness. A permissive society is one based upon the hedonistic philosophy of "Do your own thing."

Theologically, permissiveness has been equated with antinomianism, a problem in some Early Church circles (cf. 1 John), and a label sometimes attached to Paul's doctrines of grace and freedom from the law. But the equation is inaccurate; Paul was neither an antinomian nor a legalist. For Paul, all of life was to be viewed from the dual perspectives of being "in Christ" and being part of the "body of Christ." Within this context Paul's freedom was remarkable, but his freedom would never extend to practices which were not helpful or uplifting (1 Cor. 10:23).

Jesus' ethical teaching was in a similar vein: He was the fulfilment to the law. In Matthew, He proclaims the higher meaning of the law, summarizing His own teaching in the two commandments: to love God and to love one's neighbor. To lift Jesus' doctrine of love out of its biblical context of responsible action under God and use it as the slogan to justify the hedonism of "the permissive society" is a perversion of the first magnitude.

See FREEDOM, DISCIPLINE, LAW AND GRACE, ANTINOMIANISM, LICENSE.

KENT BROWER

PERPETUAL VIRGINITY. This refers to the Roman Catholic teaching that Jesus' mother, Mary, remained a virgin, even after she had become married to Joseph. Protestants understand, on various bases, that Joseph and Mary had normal marital relations. It is implied where we read, "But he [Joseph] had no union with her until she gave birth to a son" (Matt. 1:25, NIV). It is also implied where we read of Jesus' "brothers" and "sisters," all children of "the carpenter" and "Mary" (13:55-56, NIV). Actually, Protestants, who do not believe that marriage is a less spiritual state than celibacy, have no interest in trying to show that Jesus' mother was a perpetual virgin.

See MARIOLATRY, MOTHER OF GOD.

J. KENNETH GRIDER

PERSECUTION. See TRIBULATION.

PERSEVERANCE. As a theological term, *perseverance* relates to the persistence of the regenerate believer in running the Christian race (Heb. 12:1), and the certainty of the final outcome. Calvinists understand the concept differently than Arminians. Calvinists believe that the certainty of successful perseverance is inherent in the new birth. Arminians believe that perseverance is contingent. This is to say that the believer bears an obligation to choose continuously to maintain his relationship to God, and that there is real danger that he may fail to do so.

In the Calvinistic schema the doctrine of the perseverance of the saints is a correlative of (1) a concept of divine sovereignty which absolutizes the will of God in determining individual destiny, and (2) a view of the Atonement which sees it as a totally objective transaction, assuring unfailingly the salvation of the elect.

Unquestionably grace for perseverance is the constantly available gift of the Holy Spirit (2 Cor. 9:8). However, the Scriptures clearly warn against the danger of apostatizing. Paul speaks of his own concern: "Lest . . . I myself should be a castaway" (1 Cor. 9:27). The writer of Hebrews reflects this same concern for the Body of Christ when he states: "We want each of you to show this same diligence to the very end, in order to make your hope sure" (6:11, NIV; cf. vv. 4-6). Christ himself warns of the danger of not abiding in Him and of being cast into the fire (John 15:4-6). It is, therefore, perfectly clear that a man as a free moral agent must cooperate with God's grace, and himself persevere. See Col. 1:21-23; 1 Tim. 1:18-20; 6:12; Heb. 3:12; 5:9; 10:26 ff; 12:1-17; Rev. 2:5.

See ETERNAL SECURITY, FREEDOM, CONTINGENT, MONERGISM, SYNERGISM.

For Further Reading: *The New Schaff-Herzog Encyclopedia of Religious Knowledge,* 8:469-70; *The Catholic Encyclopedia,* 11:447 ff; *Baker's DT,* 403 ff.

FOREST T. BENNER

PERSON, PERSONALITY. A person is a human or suprahuman self, characterized in its normal state by self-consciousness, self-decision, and uniqueness. A person is essentially unitary, not multiple, though he may possess conflicting or variant natures. The "Dr. Jekyll and Mr. Hyde" phenomenon reflects two natures, not two persons or individuals. Personality is the sum total of qualities which comprise individual personhood. A fetus is a true person in an embryonic stage of development, therefore without full legal rights as a person. God is the perfect prototype personality, after which all other levels of personhood are patterned. The divine image in man lies supremely in the fact that both God and man are personal beings.

Anthropology, sociology, psychology, and theology all have great concern for the person both individually and corporately. Cultural anthropology seeks to understand both the impact of cultural determinants upon the individual and the impact of the individual upon culture. Sociology considers social structures, power and organizational structures, service and maintenance structures, economic and technological forces as they all affect societal or community matrices. Psychology seeks to understand the individual as a total person.

Theories of personality attempt to understand, depict, and predict the structure of the personality, the development of personality, and the dynamics of personality. Personality, for the psychologist, is more than the connotation afforded by the street phrase "She has a vivacious personality" or "He has no personality at all."

There are several theories of personality. At the risk of semantic distortion or oversimplification we can say that these theories include a mechanistic view of man (behavioristic, Skinner), a genetic or physiological (Sheldon), a psychic determinism (Freud), a teleological or goal oriented (Allport), an environmentally determined (Lewin), or various combinations of source positions. No theory of personality has yet found universal acceptance among scholars in the field. The science is still rather new and imprecise both from the theoretical perspective and from the total validity, reliability, and interactive precision of instruments or designs for empirical research.

Theologically and biblically, the study of man is rather limited, also. OT terms for man include *basar, ruach,* and *nephesh. Basar,* "flesh," may denote all living creatures, man as a created being by the will of his Creator, or as a frail, powerless being in God's sight. *Basar* deals far less with the essences of man than with his power.

Ruach is the life-giving power of the breath or Spirit of God that makes man a living soul. *Ruach* is not a substance but a power that is both creative and purposive. It brings wholeness, will, courage, direction, and resource to man as the sign and principle of God's Spirit at work in and upon man.

Nephesh is the life principle or life force which is often viewed as the soul when the context refers to loss or preservation of life. It is the seat of the senses, affections, and emotions of man, seldom referring to the wills and purposes of man. It is the *nephesh* which exhibits the power that the *ruach* provides. The Hebrew sees always the indivisible unity (both biological and psychic life) of the individual and sees him as incomplete apart from his corporate dimension and without meaning apart from the vitalizing power of God. The Hebrew mind deals with the intellective, affective, and behavioral dimensions of man and metaphorically refers to various organs as the seat of the will, the desire, the emotions, etc., of man. But it always sees man-in-relation-to-God as the whole person.

The NT use of two and sometimes three words to encompass the totality of the person has given rise to a theological debate that has renewed itself periodically throughout the history of the Church, viz., whether man is essentially dual (dichotomous—body and soul/spirit) or threefold (trichotomous—body, soul, and spirit). Today many scholars believe that the intent of such biblical delineations of man is to encapsulate every aspect and vestige of man into one wholistic totality of the corporate man in Christ.

Again, whether man is viewed as *sarx* (akin to the Hebrew *basar*), flesh; *sōma,* biological body; *psuchē* (often translating *nephesh*), the free soul of man; or *pneuma* (translating *ruach*), spirit, he is seen as having no power apart from God's inward redemptive activity. Even his value as a person is linked to his salvability in Christ. Without Christ personhood atrophies and becomes distorted. Personhood finds its normalcy and development through the sanctifying of the Spirit upon and in the life of the believer.

The person, therefore, is a personality involving the dynamics of genetics, life forces, environment, and individual choice, in interaction with the grace of God. He is both unique and corporate, finding his completion only by and in Christ and His Body.

See MAN, DICHOTOMY, TRICHOTOMY, DEVELOPMENT (THEORIES OF), SOUL, SPIRIT, HUMAN NATURE, NATURE,

HUMANISM, PERSONALISM, DIVINE IMAGE, PERSONALITY OF GOD.

For Further Reading: Tournier, *The Whole Person in a Broken World;* Adcock, *Fundamentals of Psychology;* Mavis, *The Psychology of Christian Experience;* Arndt, *Theories of Personality;* Hall and Lindzey, *Theories of Personality.* CHESTER O. GALLOWAY

PERSONALISM. The philosophy of personalism holds personality to be the key to understanding our world. The concept comes primarily from metaphysics and philosophy of religion.

The term is relatively new in the history of thought, although personalism is largely "a new name for some old ways of thinking." The word has been used for about 200 years, and its roots are found in both Europe and America. Borden Parker Bowne, professor of philosophy at Boston University 1876-1910, was its most systematic and influential exponent.

All who think seriously about Christian theology must have a special interest in the philosophy of personalism. The Bible teaches that a personal God created man in His own image; He created the physical world as a home for man; He loved even sinning persons so much that He sent His Son to redeem them and to provide eternal life for them. The philosophy of personalism offers a reasoned support for these truths.

Personalism is, therefore, usually a theistic world view, though some who use the term have denied the existence of a personal God. Others have been pantheistic. For them God is not a self-conscious spirit. Rather, all conscious persons are parts of Him. Typical personalism, however, supports a scriptural theism.

Personalism affirms the absoluteness of God. It holds the creation of the world to be a free act of the divine will, thus affirming the sacred Record. "In the beginning God created the heaven and the earth" (Gen. 1:1). But nature has no independent reality. It is continuously produced by an intelligently directed power outside of itself.

The reality of the human spirit is the fundamental presupposition of personalism. All personalists hold that the self has a unique character. This human personality includes four fundamental elements: (1) individuality, including unity and identity; (2) self-consciousness—persons know and feel; (3) freedom to choose; and (4) dignity with worth. This high view of human personality owes its origin to Christian influence.

Albert Knudson writes, "The personality of God and the sacredness of human personality express the true genius of the Christian religion . . . and . . . these beliefs have received their completest philosophical justification in modern personalistic metaphysics. . . . Personalism is *par excellence* the Christian philosophy of our day" (*The Philosophy of Personalism,* 80).

See PERSONALITY OF GOD, PERSON (PERSONALITY), METAPHYSICS.

For Further Reading: Knudson, *The Philosophy of Personalism;* Ferre, *A Theology of Christian Education,* chap. 6; Sanner and Harper, eds., *Exploring Christian Education.* A. F. HARPER

PERSONALITY OF GOD. A person is a conscious, unique, individual entity; identical through the passage of time; permanent amidst change; a unifying agent experiencing itself in privacy; possessing the power of creativity through rationality, imagination, and the anticipation of the future; and an active, free agent, the only carrier of intrinsic value.

H. Rashdall in his analysis of personality singles out five elements: consciousness, permanence, a self-distinguishing identity, individuality, and most important of all, activity. J. W. Buckham finds four: self-consciousness, unity, freedom, and worth. In these respects Christian theism maintains that God is a person, and it is His personality that constitutes His reality. God is a conscious, unified, and individual entity. He is separate from material things; in fact, God is the Creator and Sustainer of matter. He is noumenal while everything else, except other persons, is phenomenal. God is an active, unifying agent and, along with other persons, is a carrier of ultimate, metaphysical value and intrinsic worth.

God, through His personality, is a thinking, feeling, and acting being. He loves, hates, reasons with, warns, communes with, entreats, judges, condemns, rewards, and punishes. All of these activities can be verified by many scriptural references.

See GOD, ATTRIBUTES (DIVINE), PERSONALISM.

For Further Reading: Buckham, *Personality and Psychology;* DeLong, *The Concept of Personality in the Philosophy of Ralph Barton Perry* (Ph.D. diss.); Knudson, *The Philosophy of Personalism.* RUSSELL V. DELONG

PERSONALITY OF THE HOLY SPIRIT. The collective faith of the Christian Church gives witness to the personality of the Spirit. In the NT, the Spirit is revealed in such personal concepts as "Counselor" or *Paraclete* (John 14:26; 15:26; 16:7). He possesses the attribute of intelligence ("mind" as in Rom. 8:27). He makes intercession for us and helps us in our weakness (v. 26).

Again, the Spirit as a person may be grieved (Eph. 4:30).

While many have no problem in thinking of the Father and the Son as personal, the Spirit seems more difficult to describe. He seems like the personification of divine motion, not a truly personal member of the divine Trinity. Yet, Scripture attributes the powers of personhood to Him consistently. Thus for Paul the Father elects, the Son redeems, and the Spirit seals in the economy of grace (Eph. 1:4-14).

Full recognition of the Spirit's personhood emerged gradually during the first four Christian centuries. Christian theologians wrestled with the intellectual conflict between monotheism and Trinitarian thought. The Jewish religion was uncompromising in its belief in one God. The Council of Nicea (A.D. 325) defined the godhood of Christ, while Constantinople (A.D. 381) emphasized the personality of the Spirit.

The Early Church described Father, Son, and Spirit as a triunity of persons (Latin, *personae*). The concept "person" connoted the reality of each divine manifestation. In interpreting the Trinity, modalists like Sabellius erred in asserting a unity with an *apparent,* not a real, trinity. Orthodox theology insists that the three *personae* are the fullness of God, whose unity is a triunity, not a diversity of gods or a tritheism. Orthodox Trinitarianism never allows, as does tritheism, that Father, Son, and Spirit exist or function in separateness. There is *one* God, whose fullness is triune.

When we describe the Holy Spirit as personal, we mean that He is possessed of all the attributes known to be in God. There is no *essential* difference. Personhood for the Holy Spirit includes power of choice, self-consciousness, intelligence, and sensibility, even as for Father and Son, and, indeed, for human persons created in His image.

See ESSENTIAL TRINITY, HYPOSTASIS, TRINITY (THE HOLY), SABELLIANISM, PERSON (PERSONALITY), HOLY SPIRIT.

For Further Reading: Berkhof, *The Doctrine of the Holy Spirit;* Thomas, *The Holy Spirit of God;* Carter, *The Person and Ministry of the Holy Spirit.*

LEON O. HYNSON

PHARISAISM. The term is derived from the sect of Pharisees who were one of the three main parties of the Jews at the time of Christ. Though at first this party was strong in religious character and some of its members were some of the best Jews, later generations deteriorated. Jesus was compelled to characterize them as "hypocrites." Of course not all were hypocrites: Paul before his conversion, Gamaliel, and Nicodemus were examples of the better Pharisees. This sect, more than any other, preserved Judaism and the law.

It was love of display and strict but empty legalism that earned for the Pharisees as a class the epithet "hypocrites." In NT times this term meant "playacting." Such acting led to the concept of *pharisaism,* which is rigid observance of external rules of religious conduct without any genuine piety. The term has come to be applied to all religions that make conformity to the law primary, and promise God's grace only to those who are doers of this law. Rather than religion being a disposition of heart, it becomes the performing of outward acts. Often called legalism, pharisaism bases salvation upon observance of external regulations and neglects the more important aspect of love and mercy.

See LEGALISM, LOVE, PERFECT LOVE, PHARISEES.

For Further Reading: *HBD,* 544 ff; *New Westminster Dictionary of the Bible,* 741 ff; *NBD,* 981 ff.

LEO G. COX

PHARISEES. A religious party or sect of Judaism originating in the times of the Maccabees and surviving after A.D. 70 as the dominant Jewish faction. Their new Jewish center at Jamnia provided the foundation for modern rabbinic Judaism.

The Pharisees probably grew out of the *hasidim* or Hasidaeons, the "godly people" who, after the return from exile, gave concerned leadership to practicing the sacred law and opposing Hellenization. Two great Jewish parties emerged in this period, the Sadducees from the priestly class, and the Pharisees from the scribes or students of the law. The name Pharisees, which means "the separated ones," first appears in the record of the king John Hyrcanus (134-104 B.C.) whose policies the Pharisees opposed. They came to favor and great influence in the time of Queen Alexandra (76-67 B.C.), a prestige which continued through the time of Jesus. Josephus estimated their number in Jesus' day at about 6,000. Because of popularity with the people many were chosen to the Sanhedrin. They were generally middle class.

The Pharisees were the orthodox core of Judaism. They held to the whole body of Jewish Scripture. They were the supernaturalists, believing, for example, in the resurrection of the righteous and in angels. In politics and moral philosophy they held mediating views: Most submitted to foreign domination as an expression of God's providence, at the same time holding to free will and the right of resistance to interference with their practice of God's revealed will. Various schools of Pharisaism developed, such as those founded by Hillel and Shammai.

They passionately believed the written law of Moses, but equally the oral "tradition of the elders" which encased the law. They tried to apply the written law, in terms of the oral law, to every situation with meticulous, sometimes ludicrous, detail. Law keeping, often merely ceremonial, was to them meritorious, the only way to righteousness. They separated themselves from all other Jews, the "sinners," who failed to follow their practices.

Although Jesus maintained friendship with a few Pharisees, in general He clashed with their practices. They, in turn, harassed Him and plotted His death.

At the heart of Jesus' difference with the Pharisees lay His emphasis on love as the inner meaning and implementation of the law's requirements (Matt. 22:34-40). He taught a righteousness surpassing that of the Pharisees (5:20). They tended to see the law as a code sufficient within itself.

Jesus warned against the Pharisees' self-righteousness; their attention to outward ceremonies to the neglect of inward truth and purity; their inclination to trifling questions while neglecting "weightier matters" of judgment, mercy, and faith; their stress on the external "letter of the law" while overlooking the law's higher principle and intent; their pride and ostentation in performance of prayers, fasting, and alms; their imposition of burdens which they themselves could not carry; their censorious, exclusive spirit in place of loving concern. Because of this He called them hypocrites and blind guides (Matthew 23).

See PHARISAISM, LEGALISM, SADDUCEES, MORALISM, LOVE.

For Further Reading: Bruce, *New Testament History;* Barclay, ed., *The Bible and History;* Tenney, *New Testament Times.* ARNOLD E. AIRHART

PHILANTHROPY. See LIBERALITY.

PHILIA. See BROTHERLY LOVE.

PHILOSOPHY. Philosophy, as the meaning of its Greek original may be interpreted, is the quest for or love of wisdom. The philosopher does not know so much as he seeks to know.

Thus philosophy is basically an attitude or spirit, a method of attaining knowledge, and the knowledge thus attained. As such, philosophy is a spirit of questioning which leaves no "sacred cows" untouched. Authority, convention, and common sense are the constant victims of its interrogations. As individual sciences become absolute, philosophy helps in breaking the myth.

The areas of philosophy's concerns are *epistemology, ontology* or metaphysics, and *axiology. Epistemology* is an attempt to resolve the question of how we know (q.v. Knowledge). It is a study of the sources of knowledge: sensory experience and perception, intuition, tradition, logic and rational processes (q.v. Reason). It is a search for the test or criterion of truth: Can truth be found in sense perception, intuition, tradition, reason, scientific method, pragmatic method, or elsewhere? It is the function of philosophy to set up the method to determine which evidence is acceptable in progressing to understanding and truth.

Ontology is the attempt to use the methods determined in epistemology in order to know the nature of reality, being, or the ultimate. But since neither epistemology nor ontology can be independent of the other, it is a genuine problem as to which is prior to the other. Metaphysical systems are *idealism* (the ultimately real is of the nature of ideas, persons, or values), *materialism* (the ultimately real is of the nature of material particles, objects, or energy), and *realism* (the real is a many comprising mind, matter, values, etc.; or the real is that which is independent of mind).

Axiology is the study of the worthwhile or the valuable. It is concerned with what men do desire as well as what they ought to desire. This area is subdivided into Ethics, Aesthetics, and Philosophy of Religion. Ethics attempts to deal with such problems as the origin, nature, and truthfulness of conscience; the possibility of freedom and responsibility; as well as specific moral problems: capital punishment, sexual morality, racial relations, war and peace, genetic engineering, experiment on human beings. Aesthetics is primarily concerned with beauty in nature and human productions, principally called the fine arts. It examines the possibility of aesthetic standards, aesthetic truth, and aesthetic greatness. Aesthetics, ethics, and the philosophy of religion look together at the relationship between aesthetic experience, spiritual development, and maturity; and together they examine the problem of censorship. The philosophy of religion deals with proofs or evidence of God's existence, the nature of God, the manner of divine self-disclosure, the problem of evil, and the possibility of an afterlife.

Some ask whether there can truly be a Christian philosophy. Some say that a revelational system excludes all questioning; and if the philosophy-theology relation be regarded as a question-answer relation, then philosophy has no real role. Others hold that while Christianity is much more than a theoretical system, it is at least this much. Therefore, since philosophy provides the methodology and impetus toward system building, there can certainly be a Christian philosophy: a Christian world view is a Christian philosophy.

The only use of the term "philosophy" in the NT is in Col. 2:8. This passage could refer to philosophy in general or to some particular type of philosophy, or it could refer to the setting aside of faith for some heretical philosophic stance. It is too brief and too unclear to be used as the basis for a wholesale rejection of philosophy. Nevertheless, both philosophy and theology may fear the other due to the possible threat that one may be limited by the other. Philosophy does not wish its questions to be merely secondary to theology's answers and thus return to its subservient status as *ancilla theologiae* (handmaid of theology). Nor is theology willing to accept the severe unsettling of questions which may lead to a rejection of its dogmas (or settled opinions from which it must not deviate). These concerns are common both to Roman Catholics and to Protestants. To these concerns it has been well said that both philosophy and theology are "modes of service of a truth which is always greater than what can be said of it in philosophical or theological propositions" *(Sacramentum Mundi).*

See THEOLOGY, METAPHYSICS, TRUTH, REVELATION (SPECIAL), EPISTEMOLOGY, VALUES, POSITIVISM, AESTHETICS, ETHICS, KNOWLEDGE, AXIOLOGY, REALISM IN THEOLOGY.

For Further Reading: *Sacramentum Mundi,* 5:1-20; *Concise Encyclopedia of Western Philosophy and Philosophers;* Merleau-Ponty, *In Praise of Philosophy;* Wheelwright, *The Way of Philosophy.*

R. DUANE THOMPSON

PIETISM. In the narrow sense, Pietism signifies a movement of spiritual renewal within the Lutheran and Reformed churches in continental Europe in the 17th and 18th centuries, though some beginnings were already discernible in the late 16th century. It is associated with such names as Johann Arndt, Philip Spener, August Hermann Francke, Willem Teelinck, Gerhard Tersteegen, Count Nicolaus Ludwig von Zinzendorf, and Johann Albrecht Bengel. In the broader sense it includes these kindred movements of spiritual purification: Puritanism, Methodism, and later evangelical revivalism (which should probably be called neo-Pietism). It also has an affinity to Jansenism and Quietism in the Roman Catholic church, both of which emphasized the religion of the heart.

Pietism is noted for its stress on heart religion *(Herzensreligion).* The heart in this context signifies the center of the personality. True religion must be inward, existential, total, and experiential. Yet the Pietists insisted that our experience is not the source of faith (only the Word of God is that) but the medium of our faith. In this perspective, faith that results in salvation is not just outward or intellectual: it must affect the very center of human being, the "inner man."

Another salient theme in Pietism was the new birth *(Wiedergeburt).* While Luther and orthodox Lutheranism placed the accent on forensic, extrinsic justification, the Pietists, perhaps under a Calvinist influence, underlined the need for regeneration as well. It was not any particular experience of the new birth but the fact of the new birth that was deemed of crucial importance. Neither Spener nor Zinzendorf claimed a special, datable experience of conversion, though in the later Pietism of August Francke increasing significance was attached to a specific or patterned experience of conversion.

The concern for the imitation of Christ *(Nachfolge Christi)* was still another earmark of Pietism. While the Reformation was preoccupied with right doctrine, the Pietists focused upon right life. Attention was given not only to the saving work of Christ but also to His teachings. In their emphasis on a reformation in life they saw themselves as fulfilling the Reformation. At the same time, they regarded Christian practice or discipleship under the Cross not as the basis of our justification but as its cardinal fruit and evidence.

Reacting against the Reformation stress on the total helplessness of man, they insisted that the Christian could make real progress toward perfection in holiness through the grace of God. According to Spener, we cannot fulfill the law, but as Christians we can keep the law.

Whereas both Lutheran and Reformed orthodoxy were fascinated with the Cartesian model of clear and distinct ideas, the Pietists remained closer to the original Reformation in their candid recognition of the limitations of reason. God cannot be comprehended by the mind but can only be felt in experience (Zinzendorf). They did not deny the natural knowledge of God but generally regarded it as sufficient to condemn, not save us. Spener attacked the dependence of theology on the "heathen philosophy" of Aristotle.

The idea of the preparation of the heart was also present in Pietism as in Puritanism. Although Spener held that faith is usually given instantaneously through the hearing of the Word, he did believe that sometimes the Spirit of God by a prior work of grace prepares people for a more ready acceptance of the Word. Francke was convinced that the law sets the stage for the gospel and that before there can be real faith, there must be a struggle toward repentance *(Busskampf)*.

The moral dualism of the Pietists reveals their affinity with the Reformers and their distance from the tradition of mysticism (which was inclined toward monism). Even though the Pietists encouraged the reading of the mystics for personal devotions, they saw the principal cleavage as being not between time and eternity (as with the radical mystics) but between faith and unbelief, salvation and sin, the kingdom of God and the demonic kingdom of darkness.

Pietists have often been accused of subjectivism, and it is true that they emphasized the spirit over the letter of the Bible. They occasionally differentiated between the form and content, the kernel and husk, of Scripture. Yet their concern was not to find a Word beyond the Bible but to discover the treasure of the gospel within the Bible. Above all, the Bible was to be read in a spirit of devotion rather than with academic curiosity. Though acknowledging the possibility of special revelations, they held that these private illuminations must be conformable to Holy Scripture and not conflict with the light that has already been given in Jesus Christ.

Pietism is also noted for the fact that it gave tangible expression to the Reformation doctrine of the priesthood of all believers. Spener advocated the formation of conventicles, private gatherings which usually met on Sunday evenings for Bible readings, prayer, and discussion of the sermon. These meetings came to include hymn singing, meditations, and even sermons, which were given as a supplement to the morning homily. These fellowships became known as the *collegia pietatis,* from which the Pietist movement derives its name.

A final distinguishing feature of Pietism is its emphasis on the urgency of mission. Zinzendorf declared: "My joy until I die: to win souls for the Lamb!" Indeed, Protestant missions can be said to have begun with Pietism. The great missionary societies within Protestantism in the 18th and 19th centuries as well as the Inner Mission of the 19th and 20th centuries have their roots in Pietism. The Reformation generally saw the two practical marks of the true Church as the preaching of the Word and the right administration of the sacraments; to these the Pietists in effect added the fellowship of love *(koinonia)* and a zeal for missions.

The Pietists remind us that Christianity has to do with life as well as doctrine, ethical action and spiritual devotion as well as theology. We need to heed their warning that justification cannot stand by itself but must be fulfilled in sanctification. Even though the righteousness of Christ entitles us to heaven, we are not qualified to enter heaven apart from personal holiness.

We can learn from Pietism that Christian practice is the field in which our sanctification is carried forward. The Pietists sought to hold the practical and mystical dimensions of the faith in balance, though Pietism was more aggressive than contemplative, more practical than theological (John F. Hurst).

Out of the awakenings associated with Pietism came a concern for the oppressed and destitute in society. Besides founding orphanages, homes for unwed mothers, homes for epileptics, and deaconess hospitals, the Pietists and later evangelicals pioneered in the area of social justice. Their efforts played a major role in the abolition of slavery, prison reform, and legislation against child labor abuse, animal cruelty, and prostitution.

A constant danger in Pietism is that its inclination to elevate life and experience over doctrine often promotes doctrinal indifferentism and latitudinarianism. It is an open fact that the University of Halle, founded by the early Pietists, became within two generations a bastion of rationalism.

Subjectivism is another temptation within Pietism. Even though the early Pietists had a high view of the sacraments and preaching,their stress on the immediacy of the Word tended to obscure the mediate role of the Church and the sacraments. The radical Pietists became sectarian and individualistic.

Pietism was also inclined to neglect the doctrine of creation by focusing so intently on personal salvation. We need to remember that redemption does not annul creation but only the sin that distorts creation.

At its best, Pietism sought to penetrate and transform society with the leaven of the gospel. At its worst, Pietism became defensive, cultivating a fortress mentality that regarded the world as totally under the sway of the powers of darkness; the strategy then became that of building citadels of light in a dark world.

See PIETY, EVANGELICAL, PURITAN (PURITANISM), METHODISM, SYNERGISM, PREVENIENT GRACE, WESLEYANISM, HOLINESS MOVEMENT, DEVOTE (DEVOTION), SOCIAL ETHICS, PIETISM (ENGLISH EVANGELICAL).

For Further Reading: Brown, *Understanding Pietism;* Stoeffler, *German Pietism During the Eighteenth Century;*

The Rise of Evangelical Pietism; Continental Pietism and Early American Christianity; Bloesch, "The Legacy of Pietism," *The Evangelical Renaissance,* 101-55.

DONALD G. BLOESCH

PIETISM, ENGLISH EVANGELICAL. Few religious movements have been so misunderstood and unjustly maligned as Pietism. Until recently the role of English Pietism has gone unchronicled. Springing from the Geneva-Rhineland tradition of Martin Bucer and antedating continental Pietism (Spener), the movement was to profoundly influence Anglicanism, producing the Puritan sector of the British and American church, and creating the ethical and spiritual concerns that were to mark Methodism and the later American holiness movement. Many Wesleyan scholars now recognize the roots of Wesley as being more entwined in English Pietism than in Continental sources.

Following the Bucerian emphasis on "living doctrine," Pietism's interest lay in practical, everyday living rather than doctrine. The Bible, rather than the creeds, became the authority. Christianity is to be lived as well as confessed. In following the rules of biblical interpretation as set down by Thomas Greenham, the movement adopted the principle that not only is sin forbidden but its occasion as well. Thus, the contemporary evangelical's antagonism to the theatre, the dance, and the saloon is rooted in English Pietism. The terms characteristic of this tradition, such as *experiential, inward,* or *personal,* reflect a concept of the essence of Christianity as being a personally meaningful new-birth relationship to God. Henry Smith's statement that "an almost Christian is no Christian" discovers the pietistic drive to a Christian perfection which prepared England for Wesley's position. The pietistic insistence on an experiential "I-Thou" relationship, resulting in an inner personal knowledge of divine approbation, was closely related to Wesley's doctrine of assurance. England's 17th-century pietistic conventicle anticipated the Methodist society, the holiness prayer meeting, and the contemporary home Bible study group.

See PIETISM, PURITAN (PURITANISM), WESLEYANISM.

For Further Reading: Stouffler, *The Rise of Evangelical Pietism.*

FOREST T. BENNER

PIETY. *Piety* refers to the attitudes and practices which God demands, requests, and expects of those who place faith in His person and His work. Today, in some circles, the term has bad connotations, being associated with pretensions and spiritual pride (see Paul's "form of godliness" [2 Tim. 3:5]).

The noun used in the NT is *eusebeia,* mentioned 14 times in the Pastoral and General Epistles, and is usually translated "godliness." Godliness is associated with holy living, as well as performing acts of spiritual worship (1 Tim. 2:2; 5:4; 6:3; 2 Pet. 1:3, 6). Piety is synonymous with "holy and godly lives"—the fruit of faith and hope in the second coming of Christ (Jas. 1:26; 2 Pet. 3:11-12).

Piety is synonymous with the OT "fear of the Lord." Among OT saints a holy and godly life was grounded in reverence, submission, and obedience to God.

Piety is a response to God's revelation of himself and His will. It is equated with holiness (1 Pet. 1:15; 2 Cor. 7:1; 1 Thess. 4:3) and includes separation from the world, overcoming temptations, mortification of sin, and the cultivation of faith, hope, and love.

See PIETISM, GODLINESS.

For Further Reading: Kepler, ed., *The Fellowship of Saints;* Law, *A Serious Call to a Devout and Holy Life;* Sangster, *The Pure in Heart,* 95-182.

BERT H. HALL

PIGEON. See DOVE.

PILGRIM. A pilgrim is one visiting a sacred place for worship, as the Jews coming to Jerusalem on feast days. Also, a pilgrim is a traveler, dwelling temporarily as a stranger and an alien, but moving toward a specific destination. The term will be considered in the latter sense.

The people of the old covenant were considered strangers and pilgrims. They were on a pilgrimage toward the Promised Land and beyond (Gen. 15:13; Exod. 22:21; Lev. 25:23; 1 Chron. 29:15). This journey was both physical and spiritual, a pilgrimage of revelation plus destination.

Peter describes the people of the new covenant as strangers away from home, and admonishes them to abstain from fleshly lusts which war against the soul. As aliens, strangers, and pilgrims on earth, their real citizenship is in heaven (1 Pet. 1:1, 17; 2:10-11; Phil. 3:20; 1 Pet. 1:4).

The classic passage which describes the concept of the pilgrimage of the people of God throughout history is Heb. 11:8-16. The patriarchs and those who followed were considered strangers and pilgrims on earth. They were moving towards their permanent home with the Lord God Almighty and the Lamb (Rev. 21:22-26).

This call to the life of a pilgrim, not unlike that of Abraham, is the same for all believers. We are called from what we are to what we can become in Christ Jesus. We look forward to the eschatological kingdom of God coming in all its glory (1 John 3:1-3).

The Christian is a pilgrim of eternity; a traveller on the way, never wearily giving up the journey, but living in hope and dying in expectation. For this reason alone God is not ashamed to be called his God. He lives as one who is looking beyond the visible and tangible, and through the eye of faith, sees the coming kingdom of God.

Living in the world as a stranger and pilgrim does not mean that the Christian despises the world. Being a member of any community implies responsibility. However, the Christian keeps himself unspotted from the world by nonconformity to its standards. A pilgrim lives by the law of the kingdom of God (Rom. 12:1-2; John 17:12). The world is his stage towards his permanent home, not his goal.

See LIFE-STYLE, WORLD (WORLDLINESS), HEAVEN, VALUES, HOPE.

For Further Reading: Barclay, *New Testament Words*, 142-50; *BBC*, 10:142-46; Wiley, *The Epistle to the Hebrews*, 366-70.

ISAAC BALDEO

PITY, PITIFUL. See COMPASSION.

PLATONISM. This refers to the kind of philosophy taught by the great Athenian thinker, Plato, who lived 427-347 B.C.

Unlike the Greek philosophers from Thales onwards, who had been materialists of various sorts, Plato was the first distinguished idealist. The earlier men had believed that such material elements as water, or earth, or air, or fire, or combinations of them, are what ultimate reality is composed of. In distinction from them, Plato taught that materialities of that sort have only shadowy and not-really-real existence. What is real, metaphysically real, for Plato, is ideas, or concepts—the most significant of these concepts being the true, the beautiful, and the good (with the "good" as the very highest).

It is this kind of metaphysics that was in vogue when Christianity was being birthed. Actually, it was in vogue for many centuries in the East and in the West, but much more especially in the East.

Some early Christians such as Justin Martyr, who flourished at around the middle of the second century of the Christian era, had been professional philosophers, of the Platonic sort, before becoming Christians—and they carried that kind of understanding over into their theologizing as Christians. This was not altogether unfortunate, for metaphysical idealism is much more congenial to Christian faith than metaphysical materialism is—for materialism does not even admit the existence of God.

However, Platonism was so extreme that it tended to deprecate materiality in a wide-scoped way. Insofar as materiality has any existence at all, it was conceived of as evil per se, and not as the creation of God.

This extreme antiphysicalism tended, therefore, to depreciate the biblical doctrine that God created the world—some, Gnostic-inclined as well as Platonic, saying that an evil God, the Demiurge, had created matter. The human body was also deprecated because it partakes of materiality—as Origen (185-254) and others taught. If Platonism was not in agreement with the plain teaching of Scripture (as it is not, on the body, and on sexuality expressed in marriage), the Platonic Christians such as Origen viewed Scripture as having a hidden, allegorical meaning; and they taught that that meaning is in agreement with Platonism's idealism.

While it was customary for OT prophets (such as Isaiah, Hosea, and Ezekiel) to be married, and while NT figures such as the apostle Peter were, it was Platonism, with its deprecating of physicality, that occasioned the refraining from marriage in the hermits—and later among the monks, nuns, and priests of Catholicism.

Biblical teaching, with its doctrine of creation, of incarnation, of the sacraments (with their material elements), of marriage, and of the resurrection of the body (Platonism had taught that only the soul will survive death), locates somewhere between the materialism of the pre-Platonic philosophers, and Platonism.

See METAPHYSICS, THOMISM, REALISM AND NOMINALISM, REALISM, REALISM IN THEOLOGY, NEOPLATONISM.

For Further Reading: Copleston, *A History of Philosophy*; Goeghegan, *Platonism in Recent Religious Thought*; Merlan, *From Platonism to Neo-platonism*.

J. KENNETH GRIDER

PLEASURE. We feel pleasure when physical, mental, or spiritual experiences satisfy us. Certain pleasures accompany the easing of pain, e.g., we feel good when a blanket chases away the cold. Other pleasures accompany the realization of our personal potential, e.g., we feel satisfied after building something or scoring well on an exam. Perhaps "the greatest of all pleasures," as Thomas Aquinas thought, "consists in the contemplation of truth."

So pleasures vary widely. Men and women, young people and aged people, illiterate and erudite people, all have different criteria for pleasure. Individually, some things please us more at one time in our lives than they do at other times. Thus it is difficult to define pleasure clearly, though all of us prefer pleasure to pain.

Pleasures may ultimately be good or bad. One of life's great pleasures, eating tasty food, becomes gluttony if undisciplined. The healthy pleasure of sex may be perverted into promiscuity and infidelity. The normal pleasure of rest and sleep may slip into sloth and shiftlessness. The positive pleasure of pursuing and finding truth easily leads to intellectual arrogance and pride. The spiritual pleasure of sins' forgiveness can be perverted into a pharisaical pride in one's sinlessness. Good pleasures become bad when pursued or attained contrary to what is Good.

Some thinkers have argued we should seek pleasure itself as life's *summum bonum.* In ancient Greece, Epicurus suggested we should avoid pain and enjoy the peaceful pleasures of home and garden. His Roman interpreter, Lucretius, further advises us to consider good only what physically pleases us. Later English thinkers (Hobbes, Locke, Hume) decided that pleasure gives measurable guidance in ethics, and 19th-century utilitarians such as Jeremy Bentham even sought to devise a "calculus of pleasures" to determine what we ought to do. Sigmund Freud's psychoanalysis rests largely upon his notion that we are happiest when indulging in sensual pleasure. Rather like the ancient preacher of Ecclesiastes, we are told: "A man hath no better thing under the sun, than to eat, and to drink, and to be merry" (8:15).

In contrast, other thinkers have admonished us to resist the pleasure impulse. Ancient Stoics urged us to deny fleshly appetites in order to live the life of reason. Baruch Spinoza counsels us to sacrifice physical for intellectual goods.

Though the ascetic impulse certainly helps cultivate self-discipline and creates vigorous cultural institutions, excessive denial of the goodness of God-given pleasures may lead to psychological frustrations and social cruelties, such as those evident in certain rigorous 17th-century Puritans.

As is true in so much of life, pleasures should be balanced, moderate, and temperate. God's gifts may be properly enjoyed (1 Tim. 6:17); but they also may be improperly enjoyed. The intent with which we seek pleasure, the impact our enjoyment has on us and others, and the ultimate contribution the pleasure makes on our development as disciples of Christ all help determine the moral worth of a given pleasure.

In the final analysis pleasure must be kept subordinate to holiness, as exemplified in Moses, who chose "rather to suffer affliction with the people of God, than to enjoy the pleasures of sin for a season" (Heb. 11:25). Being "lovers of pleasures more than lovers of God" is a mark of the last days (2 Tim. 3:4). The biblical standard for Christians is to favor spiritual pleasures over purely natural ones, not by denouncing the natural as sinful, but by disciplining them to keep their place in a Christian hierarchy of values. The supremacy of Christ in one's life makes pleasing Him the supreme pleasure.

See AXIOLOGY, VALUES, HAPPINESS, HOLINESS, LIFESTYLE.

For Further Reading: Festigiere, *Epicurus and His Gods;* Lewis, *The Problem of Pain;* Freud, *Beyond the Pleasure Principle.*

GERARD REED

PLENARY. This word means "full"; and, in theology, it is used especially of the conservative view of the inspiration of Scripture—that all of Scripture is inspired, and that God helped the Scripture writers so "fully" that what they wrote is altogether trustworthy. It is not a theory of the mode of inspiration, but the view that all of Scripture is inspired. Only conservatives would advocate plenary inspiration—not liberals. Some conservatives who advocate it are verbal inspiration theorists, who understand that each word of Scripture was inspired. Others are dynamic plenary-inspiration theorists, who believe that the Scripture writers were inspired with certain thoughts, but that the choice of words was their own. Some combine both views, affirming that inspiration extended to the words as far as necessary to achieve accuracy, but not in such a way as to constitute dictation, or hamper a writer's own natural style.

See INSPIRATION OF THE BIBLE.

J. KENNETH GRIDER

PLURALISM. This usually has to do with a rare kind of metaphysics taught by Harvard's William James, at around our century's turn, in *A Pluralistic Universe.* James taught that ultimate reality is not one, nor two (a good and a bad ultimate being), but many. He says that ultimate reality exists distributively, as numerous qualitatively different ultimate "eaches," only one of which is God.

Pluralism is sometimes a term used to describe a tolerant attitude in which varying views are acceptable within a given group, such as a church denomination.

See MONISM, DUALISM, REALISM.

J. KENNETH GRIDER

POLYGAMY. It is generally assumed in Christian theology that polygamy runs counter to the concept of godly living. Surprisingly, though, there is little written against the practice of polygamy in the Bible. Kings were warned not to "multiply wives" lest they be led to turn away from God (Deut. 17:17), and bishops and deacons were to be "the husband of one wife" (1 Tim. 3:2, cf. 12), but there is no explicit commandment forbidding polygamy. In fact, there was a law to protect the children of the least favored wife when a man had more than one wife (Deut. 21:15-17).

However, the basic presumption of the Bible is that each man will have only one wife. In the creation account, God provided Adam with one helper (Gen. 2:18-24); the Torah seems to assume monogamy in its legal pronouncements (Lev. 18:8; 21:13-14; Deut. 22:22; etc.); the portrait of the good wife in Prov. 31:10-31 suggests only one wife; and the advice Paul gave the Corinthians concerning marriage implies a monogamous relationship (1 Corinthians 7). The indication from the Bible is that the common people generally practiced monogamy, though this may be more reflective of their economic status than their spirituality.

Perhaps it is significant that the first mention of polygamy in the Bible occurs in connection with one of the descendants of Cain (Gen. 4:19), the implication being that the departure from the monogamous standard set in creation occurred in the lineage of one who had gone away from the presence of the Lord.

It is of unquestionable significance that the monogamous relationship of the "two" becoming "one flesh" is utilized by Paul as an analogue of the relationship between Christ and the Church (Eph. 5:31-32). The spiritual dimensions of the analogy absolutizes the Christian conviction that monogamy is God's will for those whom He created in His image.

See MARRIAGE, FAMILY, SEX (SEXUALITY).

For Further Reading: Westermarck, *The History of Marriage,* 2:1-222; Mace, *Hebrew Marriage,* 121-41; Parrinder, *The Bible and Polygamy.*

WILLIAM B. COKER

POLYTHEISM. Polytheism literally means "many gods." It refers to the belief in and worship of more than one god.

Concerning the origin of polytheism, there is a difference of opinion. Theological liberals tend to believe that it is a stage in the development of belief towards one supreme God. The conservative view is that it is a corruption of the original revelation of God to man.

The Genesis account teaches that originally man was fully aware of his Creator and worshipped Him only. The Bible is confirmed by scholars such as N. Schmidt who insist that there is historical evidence that polytheism is a corruption of the belief in one God. On Rom. 1:22-23, C. H. Dodd comments: "There is a surprising amount of evidence that among very many peoples . . . a belief in some kind of Creator Spirit subsists along with a more or less obscure sense that this belief belongs to a superior, or a more ancient order" *(Epistle to the Romans).*

Polytheism differs from animism, which is the attribution of living soul to inanimate objects and natural phenomena. It is a higher state of belief than polydaemonism. The gods of polytheism are of a higher order and are more clearly defined. Among the ancients some of the gods were tribal or national heroes, adulated in their lifetime and deified after death.

The Bible roundly condemns polytheism and its close attendant, idolatry. In polytheism man makes "gods" in his own depraved image. He attributes to them not only the virtues which he admires but also unlimited freedom to practice the vices he craves to indulge. This in turn gives him a license to sin. Furthermore, polytheism divides the human race into partisans of different deities instead of uniting it under one Father.

In the realm of science, monotheism is essential for the belief in a *uni*verse, bearing the imprint of one Mind and sustained by one Almighty Power.

See GOD, RELIGION, MONOTHEISM, IDOL (IDOLATRY).

For Further Reading: *ERE,* 10:112-14; Pope, *A Compendium of Christian Theology,* 1:252, 373-81; *Baker's DT,* 248-52.

JACK FORD

POPE. See CATHOLICISM, ROMAN.

POSITIONAL HOLINESS. As a biblical concept, the term *positional holiness* derives from the truth that because of their spiritual *position* of being *in Christ,* all believers are holy. A NT example of this objective and inclusive use of holiness is the carnal Corinthian Christians whom Paul said were "sanctified" because they were "in Christ" (1 Cor. 3:1-3; 1:2).

As a theological expression, positional holiness occupies a more central place and is used with greater frequency in the Keswick movement than in Wesleyan-Arminian circles. This fact may be rooted in some underlying presuppositions which constitute more than semantic and/or apparent differences between these theological systems. For careful analysis reveals that the Keswickian understanding of positional holiness is grounded in the realistic and the federal or immediate imputation theories of the transmission of original sin.

With the realistic theory constituting the context for the federal or immediate imputation theory, the two are fused in Keswickian assumptions and form a nonethical concept of solidarity with Adam. That is, all men are condemned for that which they did not *personally and willfully* do, viz., the committal of Adam's transgression. This concept of nonethical solidarity at the presuppositional level in Keswickian theology carries over into its understanding of sanctification. For when the realistic theory is logically extended to the foundation for holiness in Keswickian thinking, it is necessary to posit that all believers *really* or actually participated in the death and resurrection of Christ, even as all men *really* participated in the sin of Adam. Consequently (and consistently), even as *all men* sinned because of a realistic relationship to Adam, so *all believers* were perfectly sanctified because of their realistic relationship to Christ.

Taking a somewhat different approach, the federal theory centers in the *legal imputation* of Adam's sin to the race. If the antithesis between Adam and Christ in Rom. 5:12-21 is interpreted in terms of this theory, then Christ as the Federal Head of the new humanity legally imputes the benefits of His redemptive deed (which includes holiness) to believers. And if men are regarded as sinners by virtue of their connection with Adam, their federal head, then it logically follows that all believers are to be considered perfectly holy by virtue of their relationship to or "position" in Christ.

Because these theories of original sin, separately and unitedly, make men sinners without ethical response, they set the stage for making believers holy without ethical response. Consequently, *positional holiness* as a general objective term descriptive of all believers is so radically changed that it displaces subjective, experiential sanctification as the central focus of NT holiness, making it an optional (albeit important) rather than an essential component in the process of salvation.

See IMPUTED RIGHTEOUSNESS, HOLINESS, ORIGINAL SIN, IN CHRIST, IN ADAM.

For Further Reading: Brockett, *Scriptural Freedom from Sin,* 152-55; Chafer, *He That Is Spiritual;* Howard, *Newness of Life,* 96, 203-4; Purkiser, *Conflicting Concepts of Holiness,* 9-21.

JOHN G. MERRITT

POSITIVISM. Positivism is the modern and rather widespread belief that the only knowledge which is possible comes to us through the data provided by sense experience. Real knowledge is said to be limited to scientific description, i.e., to sense objects and the experimental and observable relations between them. Such knowledge is said to be "positive" as over against the claim to knowledge from any other source. Coming from the empiricist tradition, the view represents a dogmatic faith in the assured results of the scientific method.

The French philosopher Auguste Comte (1798-1857) taught that civilized human thought has advanced through three stages: (1) the theological, (2) the metaphysical, and (3) the positive. The latter, the present stage, repudiates all appeal to supernatural or other-than-physical agencies or abstractions which characterized the earlier stages.

Logical positivism is the 20th-century school of thought which sees the task of philosophy as the verification or falsification of truth claims by means of the analysis of language, based on the appeal to experience.

Positivism, professing humility as regards knowledge, is, in relation to knowledge, skeptical, and in relation to religion, agnostic or atheistic. It brushes aside all questions as to ontology or ultimate reality, including a "world view," as meaningless, professing interest only in phenomena, "the given" or sense experience. It affirms that reality is without purpose, and denies the supernatural, divine revelation, and the afterlife.

See PHILOSOPHY, METAPHYSICS, EPISTEMOLOGY, REVELATION (NATURAL), REVELATION (SPECIAL).

For Further Reading: Ferm, ed., *A History of Philosophical Systems;* Hutchison, *Living Options in World Philosophy;* Titus, *Living Issues in Philosophy.*

ARNOLD E. AIRHART

POSTMILLENNIALISM. Postmillennialism is the view that Christ will come supernaturally to this earth to establish His kingdom *following* the period of 1,000 years of peace, prosperity, blessing, and grace known as the millennium or the golden era. It stands opposed to premillennialism, which teaches that Christ must come back in glory and power to establish His kingdom in this world, as a political entity, for 1,000 years (Rev. 20:1-7).

Historically, the postmillennial thinker held that the Church is to rule on the earth for 1,000 years. It is a period in the Holy Spirit age when the Church shall be renewed and so conscious of its spiritual strength that it shall triumph over the powers of evil. This will come about through the conversion of the heathen, the revivals in the culture, the obtaining control of society by Christians, and the transformation of societal forms by believers.

According to some postmillennialists, the period of 1,000 years is figurative, like most figures in Revelation. The era was introduced by Jesus' victory over Satan on Calvary in which the strong man was bound. He can no longer deceive the nations as he did previous to Calvary. He is limited in his activity so that Christian conversions of individuals, transformation of social institutions, and improvement of social, political, and economic conditions will grow apace. Charles G. Finney was a postmillennialist who believed that revivals would ultimately cease because so many people would be converted that the millennium would come. It was to be introduced by the increase of Christians, their assuming places of leadership and power as reigning with Christ, and their preparation for His advent.

A more modern form of postmillennialism is the popular view of naturalistic evolution. By this the upward development of people toward a utopia is inevitable. The golden era will be gained by purposeful development of human effort. History demonstrates this process.

Biblically, the second coming of Christ will usher in the resurrection of and the judgment of all men, the external Kingdom, and the new creation.

Many Christians find postmillennialism difficult to harmonize with the Scriptures.

See REVELATION (BOOK OF), PREMILLENNIALISM, AMILLENNIALISM.

For Further Reading: Ludwigson, *A Survey of Bible Prophecy,* 94-103; Hills, *Fundamental Christian Theology,* 2:339-60.

HAROLD J. OCKENGA

POVERTY. Poverty may be defined as a state of material deprivation, wherein the necessities of life are either inadequate or uncertain. Obviously such a definition permits a large spread of opinion as to the level of need to be labelled the poverty level. That which is so labelled in prosperous Western nations would seem like affluence in the eyes of millions elsewhere.

Concern for the poor is deeply pervasive in the Bible. It runs through the Law, the Wisdom literature, the Prophets, and certainly the NT. Poverty can be said to be a touchstone of character, both of those not poor and of those who are.

Those not poor are commanded to assist the poor and are promised blessings for so doing. Among the Israelites loans were to be made without interest. If lands had to be sold, they were to be returned in the year of jubilee. Inherited property rights were not to be violated. Crops were to be partially left in the vineyards and fields for the gleaning of the poor. The rights of the poor were to be scrupulously guarded in the courts.

Yet the Bible outlines no foolproof social structure or system guaranteed to prevent poverty. The universal counsels are love and hard work. On the one hand communities are to exercise loving care for those in need (1 Tim. 6:17-19; 1 John 3:17-18), and on the other hand everyone is to find some useful and if possible gainful occupation, in order that he might cease being a receiver and become a giver (Titus 3:14).

The Bible is not very optimistic about the prospect of completely eliminating poverty in this era (Deut. 15:11; Matt. 26:11). This is because the causes of poverty are complex, and there are no simple solutions. Sin, of course, is the root cause, for sin prompts the selfishness, greed, callousness, injustice, and oppression which perpetuates poverty. But sin also must be blamed for much of the indolence, mismanagement, and dissipation often found among the poor themselves, which aggravates their plight. But beyond this are the factors of poor health, unequal intelligence and abilities, and unequal access to resources, factors for which the poor cannot be blamed and which cannot always be changed. In spite of their best efforts some human beings will in the nature of things be dependent. They are entitled by virtue of our common humanity to the love and care which they need. Throughout history care has gladly been given by both devout Jews and true Christians (cf. Gal. 2:10). It was from the Church that society learned how to care.

But poverty is a touchstone of character for the poor as well as others. For in the Bible is also a vein of philosophy which refuses to exaggerate the calamity of poverty. It can be a blessing as well as a curse. It need not be—if the poverty is only moderate—an impediment to a high standard of living (properly defined). For Jesus had no place to lay His head, and when He died He left behind only the clothes He had on. Yet who could have lived a fuller life or in the process made others richer—"that ye through his poverty might be rich" (2 Cor. 8:9).

Furthermore, poverty can be a test of stewardship. Paul was elated to tell of the churches in Macedonia, "how that in a great trial of affliction the abundance of their joy and their deep poverty abounded unto the riches of their liberality" (v. 2; cf. Mark 12:44).

Not only can poverty be a test of stewardship but of one's sense of values. While there are proper ways to improve one's lot in life, an excessive scrambling to get ahead can be spiritually fatal (1 Tim. 6:6-10). Churches also can fall into the snare of chasing after the rich to the neglect of the poor; even in this way poverty is a touchstone of character. But James has some pointed things to say about such churches (Jas. 2:1-9).

See MONEY, HUMILITY, STEWARDSHIP, LABOR.

For Further Reading: *Baker's DCE,* 515 f, 518 f; Wirt, *The Social Conscience of the Evangelical;* DeWolf, *Responsible Freedom,* 257-76. RICHARD S. TAYLOR

POWER. Paul Lehmann's simple dictum claims that "power is the energy and the authority by which whatever happens in the world occurs" (*A Handbook of Christian Theology,* 269).

Runes's *Dictionary of Philosophy* lists at least 10 definitions and uses of *power.* In psychology, for instance, *power* and *faculty* are usually coequal. In ontology, especially Aristotelian, *power* stands for potency. In natural philosophy, *power* is the force which overcomes resistance; whereas in optics, *power* is the measured degree an instrument magnifies.

In living contrast to these natural and measurable *powers* is the spiritual dynamism of God, a Holy Being force motivated and directed by love. Metz says: "The God of the Christian faith is not a metaphysical abstraction, but a God who is personal; who acts, speaks, and becomes involved in man's life" (*Studies in Biblical Holiness,* 24). God's omnipotence consists of an overwhelming adequacy of power. Macquarrie puts it tersely: "God's omnipotence means that he himself, not any factical situation, is the source and also the horizon of all possibilities, and only those are excluded that are inconsistent with the structure and dynamics of God himself" (*PCT,* 189). Conflicts between God's attributes are resolved in the fundamental unity of the whole through holy love. God as Free Being can exercise self-limitation on any, and all, of His natural and moral attributes. On that account, no confrontation need arise between, say, power and goodness or holiness or justice.

"Power," in Christian theology, also relates importantly to an adequacy—especially for witnessing—given to believers when they receive the baptism with the Holy Spirit. Thus we read, "But you will receive power when the Holy Spirit comes on you" (Acts 1:8, NIV).

See GRACE, VICTORY (VICTORIOUS LIVING), ANOINTING, TESTIMONY (WITNESS), OMNIPOTENCE, DIVINE SOVEREIGNTY, ATTRIBUTES (DIVINE).

For Further Reading: Metz, *Studies in Biblical Holiness;* Runes, *Dictionary of Philosophy;* Macquarrie, *Principles of Christian Theology.*

MEL-THOMAS ROTHWELL

POWERS. See PRINCIPALITIES AND POWERS.

PRACTICAL THEOLOGY. Practical theology is that department of study which seeks to apply the truths of the gospel to the hearts and lives of men in daily living. It is theology because it has to do with the things of God and His Word; it is practical because it seeks to apply truth to the various facets of human existence. It is action and performance as opposed to mere ideas, theories, and speculations.

Practical theology includes a vast array of disciplines. Building on exegetical theology, historical theology, and systematic theology, it includes the composition of sermons (homiletics) and their delivery (preaching). It involves all phases of evangelism, counseling, and the administration of the church. It includes the caring for people (shepherding), the rites of the church and the altar (priestly functions), guiding God's people in worship and stewardship, as well as training them for life and service (Christian education). One should be aware that the methods of applying the truths of the gospel to the hearts and lives of men are constantly changing.

So vital is this area of theology that no person, however learned in other branches of knowledge he may be, can be considered well-fitted for the ministry until he is trained in the rules and the art of bringing the gospel in a practical fashion to the homes and hearts of men.

See EVANGELISM, PASTOR, PASTORAL COUNSELING, TEACH (TEACHING, TEACHER), PREACHING, CHRISTIAN EDUCATION, MISSION (MISSIONS, MISSIOLOGY).

For Further Reading: *ERE,* 12; Turnbull, ed., *Baker's Dictionary of Practical Theology.* C. PAUL GRAY

PRAGMATISM. This is a system of belief especially associated with the names of C. S. Pierce (1839-1914), William James (1842-1910), John Dewey (1859-1952), and others. As the name implies, the pragmatists sought to apply a practical test to the main problems connected with ascertaining the truth of things.

They insisted that definitions should be tested by applying them in various contexts to the things which they were intended to define. Insofar as they proved useful and intelligible, they were valid.

A similar test was applied to truth. On the assumption that "all truths are useful," a statement was considered verified by its practical consequences.

The pragmatists also recognized the place of psychology in the quest of truth. William James emphasized "the will to believe" as an important element in arriving at the truth.

The words of Christ in John 7:17 indicate how important is the will in the quest of truth. And the Bible also applies a pragmatic test to religion: "Faith apart from works is dead" (Jas. 2:26, RSV).

But in applying the test of what is practical and valuable, the pragmatists have tended to rely on contemporary educated opinion, which is equivalent to humanism.

See TRUTH, PHILOSOPHY, POSITIVISM, FAITH, REVELATION (NATURAL), REVELATION (SPECIAL).

For Further Reading: Wiley, *CT,* 1:277, 283; *DCT,* 261; *The New Schaff-Herzog Encyclopedia of Religious Knowledge,* 9:152; *Dictionary of Ecclesiastical Terms,* 151.

JACK FORD

PRAISE. Praise is an act of devotion and adoration offered to God by His creatures for His being and attributes. Thanksgiving is an expression of indebtedness to God for His mercies. Praise is magnifying the person of God; thanksgiving is gratitude for His gifts. Yet the two ideas overlap in the Bible. One of the main root words in Hebrew, *yadah,* is translated almost as many times "thank" as "praise."

Praise rises from every part of the Bible (cf. Psalms 148; 34:1; Isa. 43:21). Yet praise is not mere duty. It is the joyful response of a heart enjoying communion with his God. It is commanded, not merely because it is the right of Deity to receive it, but because praise opens the soul to receive more of that life. The Westminster Catechism states that "man's chief end is to glorify God and enjoy Him forever." C. S. Lewis comments: "In commanding us to glorify Him, God is inviting us to enjoy Him" (*The Joyful Christian,* 120).

How are we to praise? The Psalmist calls us to come into God's house with thanksgiving (Ps. 100:4), to praise Him in song and on musical instruments (149:1-3; 150). Our petitions should always be accompanied by thanksgiving (Phil. 4:6). We should also praise the Lord with our testimony (Psalm 145). Under the Levitical system, when a worshiper offered an animal, he called his family and friends together to eat the sacrifice with him. At that time he told them all the wonderful things God had done for him (Roland de Vaux, *Ancient Israel: Its Life and Institutions,* 417). Jesus made animal sacrifices unnecessary, but we are to offer continually "a sacrifice of praise—the fruit of lips that confess his name" (Heb. 13:15, NIV). Such a sacrifice glorifies God (Ps. 50:23).

Paul began his letters with praise to God, and thankfulness was often his theme. He prayed that believers would live a life pleasing to the Lord, characterized by "joyfully giving thanks to the Father" (Col. 1:10-12, NIV; cf. 3:15-17). He was talking about praise as a way of life. This is more than gratitude when things go well. In spite of bleeding backs and frustrated plans, Paul and Silas in the Philippian jail proved it was possible to "give thanks whatever happens" (1 Thess. 5:18, NEB).

Praise then is not an indicator of our feelings nor a response to our circumstances. It is a commitment of the will. In the midst of personal deprivation, Habakkuk willed to rejoice (Hab. 3:17-19). In the same way God's people declare His praises. For this they were called out and made holy (1 Pet. 2:9).

Vocal praise, to be acceptable, must be supported by a life of righteousness. Augustine wrote, "*You* are His praise, if you live righteously."

No one expressed the importance of praise more concisely than John Wesley: Praying without ceasing, he asserted, "is the fruit of always rejoicing in the Lord." Giving thanks "in everything" is the fruit of both the rejoicing and the praying. "This is Christian perfection. Farther than this we cannot go; and we need not stop short of it" (*Notes,* 1 Thess. 5:16-18).

See TESTIMONY (WITNESS), WORSHIP, REVERENCE.

For Further Reading: Klopfenstein, *WBC,* 5:540; Wallace, *NBD,* 1018-19; Wesley, *Notes,* "1 Thessalonians."

MAUREEN H. BOX

PRAYER. Prayer is a conscious turning of a man to God for communication or to seek divine help in time of need. Man may be impelled in his reach for God by inner longings or by the emergencies of life, or by his own daily inadequacies or inability to cope with difficult situations. Hunger and/or danger may also drive him to his knees. Prayer can be a sigh, a moan, or an inarticulate cry.

Man's view of prayer is colored by his view of God. In the Hebraic-Christian approach to prayer God is more than a tradition or even a discovery; He is a Christlike Heavenly Father, who pays attention to the cry of His children, and who is always taking the initiative on their behalf—but on moral terms. Surrendering to God in prayer is one aspect of meeting those moral terms. Prayer, therefore, must be confessional. The desire for God may be smudged by man's own sins that cause him to dodge the real issues in his dialogue with God. This squirming makes for unreality in prayer.

Jesus himself is our clearest Teacher on prayer. His inner circle asked for guidance in this area of life. He gave them a model prayer that we call the Lord's Prayer (Matt. 6:9-13). His own greatest prayers include John 17:1-26 and the agonizing of Gethsemane (Luke 22:39-46); in these prayers He is our Example. Fénelon's advice is apropos: "To pray . . . is to desire; but it is to desire what God would have us desire. He who desires not from the bottom of his heart, offers a deceitful prayer."

Jesus probed His followers when He instructed them in prayer. He insisted on sincerity, transparency before God, even secrecy—always free from bitterness or censoriousness—in prayer. He actually made prayer a Person to Person call. It was one of Dante's angels *(Divine Comedy)* who pointed out, "In His will is our peace." This is the climax of prayer.

Prayer, therefore, is the Christian's primary mode of access both to the divine Person and the divine power. The theology of prayer affords some difficulties as well as challenges. But at the very least, we can say that prayer brings us into the sphere of the divine activity, so that we become real participants in the great drama of redemption.

See INTERCESSION, INTERCESSION (PROBLEM OF), PRAISE.

For Further Reading: Buttrick, *The Power of Prayer Today;* Chambers, *If ye shall ask . . . ;* Harkness, *Prayer and the Common Life;* Torrey, *The Power of Prayer;* White, *They Teach Us to Pray.*

SAMUEL YOUNG

PRAYERS FOR THE DEAD. Public prayer for the dead in the Christian Church made its appearance only after the Apostolic Fathers. The earliest literature, if we exclude inscriptions in the catacombs, is from Tertullian (third century), who admitted that the practice had no direct biblical sanction. Other literary references include Origen, Cyprian, Cyril of Jerusalem, Eusebius, Chrysostom, and Augustine.

The earlier use of such prayers was not necessarily related to the idea of purgatory, nor to any doctrine of the intermediate state, but rather to the assumption of progress in holiness after death. However, the advocacy of the purgatory concept by leaders such as Augustine produced, by the fifth century, celebration of the Eucharist as a sacrifice for both the living and dead, as well as the use of memorial Eucharists on anniversaries. Augustine implies that the custom, although then universal, was debated. Some held that it was profitless and that it encouraged a sinful life.

The practice was for neither the very good nor the very bad, inasmuch as it usually excluded the heathen and those who died in wilful sin, as well as the saintly dead, such as martyrs, who were thought to be already with Christ. The main issue, it seems, was postbaptismal sin. Petitions included forgiveness of sins, escape from purgatory, and the felicitude of heaven.

Luther did not oppose the practice. The Church of England ritual of 1549 included prayers for the dead, but these were removed from public services in the revision of 1552. Contemporary Anglicans have in their ritual an optional prayer for the dead. The Westminster Confession condemned the practice. Protestants generally are opposed on the grounds that Scripture teaches that death ends moral probation and seals personal spiritual destiny.

See PROBATION, DESTINY (ETERNAL), BAPTISM FOR THE DEAD.

For Further Reading: *NIDCC; ERE; BBC,* 8:465.

ARNOLD E. AIRHART

PREACHING. Preaching is the oral communication of divine truth through man to men with the purpose of persuasion. Two of the major Hebrew words used in the OT are *basar,* meaning "to bear tidings," and *qara,* meaning "to call, proclaim, read." In the NT, the Greek word most characteristic in references to preaching is *kērussō,* meaning "to proclaim, to herald."

Preaching as a method of presenting divine truth from God to man is as old as the Book of Genesis. Noah is referred to as "a preacher of righteousness" (2 Pet. 2:5). Abraham commanded his household to keep the commandments of the Lord (Gen. 18:19). When the house of Jacob lapsed into idolatry, he exhorted them at Bethel to put away strange gods and repent (35:2). In some powerful and eloquent orations, Moses pled with Israel to keep the covenant (Deuteronomy).

Public preaching does not appear to have been a necessary part of the priesthood. We have many instances of discourses delivered in religious assemblies by men who were not Levites (Ps. 68:11). Joshua, an Ephraimite, gathered the tribes to Shechem and preached to the people of God (Joshua 24). Both Solomon, a prince of the house of Judah, and Amos, a herdsman of Tekoa, were preachers.

Samuel opened a school of the prophets in

Ramah. Here the people went on the Sabbath to receive public lessons (1 Sam. 19:18-20). Later schools flourished at Bethel, Jericho, and Gilgal (2 Kings 2:2, 5; 4:38). The prophets preached in camps, courts, streets, schools, cities, often with visible symbols, such as yokes of slavery, to illustrate their messages.

When the Jews were carried captive into Babylon, the prophets who were with them taught the principles of pure religion and set up standards against idolatry. The success of their preaching was so overwhelming that the Jewish nation has never again lapsed into overt idolatry. The synagogues arose during the captivity and were continued after the return so that the people could come on the Sabbath and at special festivals for the reading and expounding of the Scriptures.

The most celebrated preacher before the appearance of Jesus was John the Baptist. He came in the spirit of Elijah and was much like that prophet in his vehement style, his use of bold images, his solemn deportment, his eager actions, and his strict morals.

Jesus was certainly the Master Preacher. Who can but admire the simplicity and majesty of His style, the beauty of His parables, the alternate gentleness and severity of His address.

The apostles copied their Master. They traveled about proclaiming what Jesus had done and said (cf. Acts 14:1).

The church of Rome had some great preachers. Among them were Francis of Assisi, who moved the multitudes to repent, and Savonarola, who preached like an OT prophet and, due to reproving the pope, was martyred.

The Reformation produced the day of the preacher. Martin Luther lit the lamp of justification by faith and called upon the people to become personally acquainted with Christ. Other preachers committed to doctrinal emphasis followed, among them Zwingli, Calvin, Knox, and, two centuries later, Wesley.

Since the Reformers there have been many preachers who have brought honor to God. All have done so by setting forth the demands of Bible doctrine. The history of revivals shows that doctrinal preaching, not ethical preaching alone, has brought reform. Among the British pulpit giants of the 18th and 19th centuries were, in addition to Wesley, George Whitefield, John Fletcher, Adam Clarke, Robert Hall, Thomas Chalmers, R. W. Dale, Joseph Parker, and, of course, the illustrious Charles Haddon Spurgeon. Great preachers in America have included Jonathan Edwards, Charles G. Finney, Henry Ward Beecher, Phillips Brooks, and Dwight L. Moody, plus a host of Methodist and Wesleyan masters such as John Inskip and Bishop Matthew Simpson. These were men who magnified their calling by the total devotion of their giant intellects and personal talents to the task of effectively and powerfully proclaiming the gospel. They were not triflers or dilettantes.

Preaching differs from public speaking. Preaching is communicating divine truth given through the power of the Holy Spirit. The minister has experienced, believes, and feels what he preaches. Yet preaching involves more than personal conviction. It is obedience to a divine commission to proclaim a revealed message. The preacher stands as a major source of communication between God and man.

Not only is the content of the message preached foolishness to the natural man (1 Cor. 1:18, 21), but preaching itself as a means of communication is an affront. For this reason many shrink from this role, even as pastors; it seems to them unseemly and authoritarian for one fallible man to stand before a congregation and presume to "tell them what to do." This mood reflects a loss of confidence in the divine authority of the Scriptures, a vitiated faith in the validity of the gospel itself, and a misconception of the nature of their divine calling. Needed is a recovery of a sense of God's authority and the awesome wonder and responsibility of being chosen, not by ourselves, but by God himself to be His spokesman. Needed also is a renewed conviction that God has ordained preaching as a method and is pleased to flow through it into the hearts of listeners. Great preaching cannot be matched as an effective agent of change; God sees to it that this is true. A God-called and -anointed man in the pulpit has authority, but it is not authoritarianism.

While all Christians are to be witnesses, and many will occasionally have the gift of prophecy in the sense of delivering a message from the Lord, the vocation of preaching is not to be self-chosen but is to be undertaken only upon a profound, inescapable conviction that this is the call of God. A preacher needs to be able to say with Paul, "Woe is unto me, if I preach not the gospel!" (1 Cor. 9:16).

See EVANGELISM, KERYGMA, TEACH (TEACHER, TEACHING).

For Further Reading: Burns, *Revivals: Their Laws and Leaders;* Miller, *The Way to Biblical Preaching;* Pattison, *The History of Christian Preaching.*

LEON CHAMBERS

PREDESTINATION. The word for "predestinate" occurs six times in the Greek NT: Acts 4:28; Rom.

8:29-30; 1 Cor. 2:7; Eph. 1:5, 11. It is a combination of two words, *pro,* meaning "before," and *horizō,* meaning "to mark out definitely," thus conveying the idea of limiting in advance or marking out beforehand. All six references set forth various facets of the divine scheme of redemption and its unfolding. The *EGT* favors "foreordain" as the best translation (3:251). In the KJV it is translated "predestinate" in four verses: Rom. 8:29-30 and Eph. 1:5, 11.

These verses have primary significance since they relate to God's redemptive plan for those who are "in Christ," that is, believers. Thus, predestination is primarily a doctrine for the saints, not for sinners. As Hermann Cremer points out, the question "is not *who* are the objects of this predestination, but *what* they are predestinated to" (*Biblico-Theological Lexicon of New Testament Greek,* 462).

This is precisely the import of the verses in Romans and Ephesians, where, first of all, we observe that God has predestinated believers "to be his sons" (Eph. 1:5, RSV). He has also determined that those "in Christ" should be "conformed to the image of his Son" (Rom. 8:29)—Christlike in character. In addition, the successive steps leading to glorification are divinely assured to those who, in steadfast faith, entrust themselves to God (v. 30). Finally, with their destiny in focus, God has "predestinated" His Christlike children to obtain an inheritance "at the coming of the climax of the ages" (Eph. 1:10, Williams). The "crown" awaits those who are ready in the last time (cf. 1 Pet. 1:3-5; 5:1, 4; 2 Tim. 4:8). Thus, the divine plan, marked out beforehand, is a glorious provision and prospect for those who are "in Christ."

Much controversy has arisen in church history over this term, particularly in Calvinist and Arminian circles. Calvinists have strongly emphasized the absolute sovereignty of God, His predeterminate counsels, the divine decrees, and double predestination God's decrees, including predestination, are the eternal purpose of His will concerning everything that is to be and is to occur. Predestination is the eternal counsel of God whereby He has determined the eternal destiny of every individual. For a biblical basis, Calvinists cite such scriptures as Eph. 1:4-5; 2 Tim. 1:9; Rom. 8:28-30; 9:11-13, 15.

For Arminians, predestination is based on the divine foreknowledge (Rom. 8:29), with emphasis on universal grace and conditional election; i.e., salvation is contingent on human response to the divine call to repentance and faith (Acts 20:21; John 3:14-17; 5:40; 2 Cor. 5:14-15; Gal. 1:4; 1 Tim. 2:4, 6; 1 John 2:2; 4:14; Heb. 2:9; etc.). Salvation is divinely initiated, as in Calvinism; but the human will, awakened by prevenient grace and the continuing ministry of the Holy Spirit, must cooperate with divine grace and receive by faith the gift of God. God has sovereignly predetermined the conditions upon which He will save us eternally. The *power* to believe is of God; the *act* of believing necessarily belongs to man.

See FOREKNOWLEDGE, DIVINE SOVEREIGNTY, DETERMINISM, MONERGISM, SYNERGISM, CONTINGENT, DIVINE DECREES, CALVINISM.

For Further Reading: Boettner, *The Reformed Doctrine of Predestination; GMS,* 424-35; "The Debate over Divine Election," *Christianity Today,* Oct. 12, 1959; Wiley, *CT,* 2:335-57.

WILLIAM M. ARNETT

PREEMINENCE. This is the quality of being supreme, of paramount importance, of superlative rank. The Scriptures apply the term to Jesus Christ in light of His Headship in creation and in the Church (Col. 1:18).

In relation to the universe, Jesus Christ is the "firstborn" (*prōtotokos,* a term indicating paramount rank rather than procession). He is the Creator who antedated all things and who sustains all things now existing (v. 17). Such activity gives Him superlative importance among celestial beings. He is "Lord of Creation."

In relation to the Church, Jesus Christ is the Head of the Body, the Beginning (originator of the believers), and the first to be raised from the dead (v. 18). Such activity gives Him supreme dignity among spiritual Saviors. Indeed, all the fullness of the Godhead dwells in Him, making Him the Savior of Saviors. His preeminence places Him far above the angelic beings worshipped by the Colossian heretics.

Preeminence is a quality sometimes usurped by man. Diotrephes was one "who loveth to have the preeminence" (3 John 9), and consequently rejected the admonitions of the apostle John. This carnal expression of pride is the antithesis of Jesus' words, "And whoever would be *first* among you must be your slave; even as the Son of man came not to be served but to serve" (Matt. 20:27-28, RSV, italics added). When man exalts self above God and Christ, he falls into the most deceptive form of idolatry.

The Christian's goal is to make Jesus Christ preeminent in thought, life, and conduct. As John the Baptist said, "He must increase, but I must decrease" (John 3:30). Jesus Christ is Lord; I am His love-slave (servant).

See CHRIST, FIRSTBORN, EXALTATION OF CHRIST, PRIDE.

For Further Reading: Liddon, *The Divinity of Our Lord.*
BERT H. HALL

PREEXISTENCE OF CHRIST. By the preexistence of Christ is meant that before He was born of His mother, Mary, He already existed, not as a created being, or as an ideal, impersonal principle, but as the Eternal Son, one of the infinite Persons of the Triune Godhead.

The doctrine is explicit in the Nicene Creed (A.D. 325): "I believe in . . . one Lord Jesus Christ . . . begotten of His Father before all worlds . . . by whom all things were made; who for us men and our salvation came down from heaven, and was incarnate by the Holy Ghost of the Virgin Mary."

Jesus' own claims to preexistence are clear (e.g., John 8:58; 17:5; 3:13). Whether or not Jesus inferred His preexistence in His repeated use of the title "Son of man" is less clear. The term probably connoted for contemporary Jews a preexistent heavenly being who would appear on earth. For Jesus' followers His preexistence could only come into clear focus after the Resurrection and Ascension.

For the apostolic writers this truth was foundational to a true doctrine of the Incarnation and thus to their concepts of divine condescending love, revelation, creation, and redemption and atonement.

In Paul the most explicit statement is Phil. 2:5-11 (cf. Gal. 4:4; Col. 1:15 ff; and 2 Cor. 8:9). The writer to the Hebrews sees Jesus as the preexistent, glorious Son, Creator of all, and Revealer of God (1:1-14). In John, Jesus is the Eternal Word, the Creator, the Source of life and light, who became a man (John 1:1-15).

See ARIANISM, CHRISTOLOGY, TRINITY (THE HOLY).

For Further Reading: Lehman, *Biblical Theology,* vol. 2; *GMS,* 303-56; Wiley, *CT,* 2:169-75.
ARNOLD E. AIRHART

PREEXISTENCE OF SOULS. This term refers to the belief that every soul had a career prior to its present incarnation in the body with which it is now united. It is of ancient and obscure origin, and is found in various lands. The Buddhists, the Hindus, ancient Egyptians, the Pythagorean philosophers, and many primitive animistic religions taught it in conjunction with another doctrine known as transmigration of souls. The doctrine appears frequently in the Jewish Talmud.

The philosopher Plato thought of the soul as part of the ideal world which existed previously and independently as an unembodied spirit. Among early Christian theologians, Origen, in the third century, embraced this doctrine as he attempted to account for human depravity as the result of sin in a previous state. Origen's position was immediately rejected by the Early Church as heretical.

Since then, in modern times, certain other philosophers and theologians have embraced it, arguing that inborn depravity can be explained only by a self-determined act in a previous state of being. Plato argued for it on the basis of man's possession of innate ideas. These he thought remained in the soul and mind of man as reminiscences of a prior learning and a previous existence.

Among the religions of the 20th century the Mormons are the chief exponents of the theory of preexistence of souls. There is no scriptural basis for a belief in the preexistence of souls. The Scriptures teach that souls depart this life either to be with God or to eternal retribution, and not to either a higher or lower animal reincarnation.

See THEOSOPHY, TRADUCIANISM, CREATIONISM, REINCARNATION.

For Further Reading: DeWolf, "Pre-existence," *ER,* 604-5; Harvey, *Handbook of Theological Terms,* 189; Stanton, "Pre-existence of Souls," *Baker's DT,* 148; Wiley, *CT,* 2:26 ff.
ROSS E. PRICE

PREJUDICE. The term is usually associated with *partiality.* Derived from the Latin *prejudicare, prejudice* means prejudgment without sufficient evidence either for or against people, places, or things. Discussing Christianity as theological science, Karl Barth calls for freedom from prejudice of any type. Gordon H. Clark cautions that if prejudice be misunderstood as presupposition, neither science nor theology can accept such a restriction (*Karl Barth's Theological Method,* 66). There is a proper discrimination in making value judgments.

John Wesley notes how partiality beset early Christians, in his sermon "The Mystery of Iniquity" (*Works,* 6:257). Those who made distribution had respect of persons, supplying those of their own nation, while the other widows, who were not Hebrews, "were being overlooked in the daily distribution of food" (Acts 6:1, NIV).

Elsewhere the Scripture decries partiality. God declares, "'So I have caused you to be despised and humiliated . . . because you have not followed my ways but have shown partiality in matters of the law'" (Mal. 2:9, NIV). James forbids favoritism, asking, "Have you not discriminated among yourselves and become judges with evil thoughts?" (2:4, NIV).

We are all equal before God, "for God does not show favoritism" (Rom. 2:11, NIV; cf. Col. 3:25; Eph. 6:9). The Lord clearly discerns between those who are sincere and those who do wrong (cf. Jas. 3:16-17).

William Barclay says *diekrithēte,* translated "discriminated" in Jas. 2:4 (NIV), can have two meanings. (1) "You are wavering, vacillating, hesitating in your judgments. . . . If you pay special honour to the rich, you are torn between the standards of the world and the standards of God." (2) "You are guilty of setting up distinctions between man and man which in the Christian fellowship should not exist" (*Daily Study Bible,* 77). This breaks Jesus' commandment: "Do not judge lest you be judged yourselves" (Matt. 7:1, NASB).

See DISCRIMINATION, RACISM, JUDGE (JUDGMENT), DISCERNMENT, AESTHETICS.

For Further Reading: Wiley, *CT,* 3:51-79; Purkiser, ed., *Exploring Our Christian Faith,* 462-80.

IVAN A. BEALS

PREMILLENNIALISM. The English term was coined from three Latin terms *(prae, mille, annus)*, meaning, "before the thousand years." Premillennialism has also been called chiliasm and millenarianism. It identifies a type of Christian eschatology notably distinguished by an emphasis upon the personal return of Christ to earth before the millennium (mentioned only in Rev. 20:1-10), i.e., a 1,000-year interim reign of Christ and certain of His saints, itself preceding the final consummation.

It exists in two basic forms, each with characteristic theological and hermeneutical assumptions and conclusions: historic, and dispensational premillennialism. Great differences in detail appear within as well as between the two forms.

Historic premillennialism is historic in two senses: (1) Some early (pre- and/or post-Christian) noncanonical, Jewish apocalyptic literature predicted an interim, sometimes Messianic Kingdom (cf. 1 Enoch 91:12-17; 93:1-14; 2 Enoch 32:3—33:1; Sibylline Oracles 3, 652-60; 2 Esdras 5:2—7:29; 2 Baruch 29:3; 30:1-5, 39-40). A variety of beliefs in some form of literal millennium is also attested in certain early Christian writers (Letter of Barnabas 15:3-9; Papias, cf. Irenaeus, *Against Heresies,* 5:32-36; Justin, *Dialogue with Trypho,* 81; anonymous Christian interpolations in the Testament of Isaac 8:11, 19-20; 10:11-12; Tertullian, during his Montanist period, *Against Marcion* 3, 24; 4, 31; and the Gnostic Cerinthus, cf. Eusebius, *Ecclesiastical History* 3, 28). Significantly, however, modern adherents often reach their conclusions apart from these predecessors. (2) Advocates characteristically reach their conclusions on the basis of the so-called historical interpretation of the Book of Revelation. George Eldon Ladd (in numerous publications, including *Theology of the New Testament,* 624-32) is the most articulate recent proponent of historic premillennialism.

Dispensational premillennialism arose in the early 19th century largely through the influence of J. N. Darby and the Plymouth Brethren. It forms the substance and structure of the *Scofield Reference Bible* (1909), whose subtle but powerful influence is largely responsible for its popularization in evangelical circles. Distinctive of the view is: (1) the division of history into dispensations or eras (usually seven); (2) the division of the Second Coming into two events, the secret Rapture and the public revelation, normally separated by seven years, during which time the earth experiences the Great Tribulation and raptured saints celebrate the marriage supper of the Lamb in heaven; (3) the division of the elect into two bodies: the (Gentile) Church, saved by faith, and Jews, saved during the millennium by divine fiat; and (4) a literalistic interpretation of prophecy.

See MILLENNIUM, DISPENSATIONALISM, RAPTURE.

For Further Reading: Boettner, *The Millennium,* 139-384; Clouse, ed., *The Meaning of the Millennium: Four Views;* Hoekema, *The Bible and the Future,* 173-238 (an amillennial critique); Ladd, *Theology of the New Testament,* 624-32; *GMS,* 642-48; Sandeen, *The Roots of Fundamentalism: British and American Millenarianism* (a history); Wiley, *CT,* 3:243-319.

GEORGE LYONS

PRESBYTER. See ELDER.

PRESENCE, DIVINE. In the Bible, God's presence is revealed to persons ("face" is a common term); He is made known in particular places (Temple, Tabernacle, etc.); and He is communicated to the race (the Jews, humanity).

Face. A personal communication, the "face" of God connotes His presence in both blessing and judgment. Moses saw God "face to face" (Exod. 33:11); the righteous shall "behold [his] face" (Ps. 11:7, NASB); He hides His face (13:1; 27:9; 51:9); the Lord's face "is against those who do evil" (1 Pet. 3:12, NASB).

Place. God graces places with His presence; thus, Shechem (Gen. 12:6-7), Beersheba (21:33), Bethel (28:10 ff), and Peniel (32:24 ff) were worship cities. Horeb and Sinai were sacred places, too (note hills and mountains as representations of presence—e.g., Psalm 48). The ark, Tabernacle, and Temple became presence places; in the NT the believer's heart becomes God's temple (1 Cor. 3:16). In the history of the church consecrated sanctuaries are also God's dwellings. In the Lord's Supper He is present (see references below for interpretations).

Race. God's presence is revealed to the Jews (e.g., Ps. 22:3). He also promises His presence to go with the Jews (Exod. 33:14; 40:34-38; Isa. 63:9). The NT reveals that God came to the whole human race—Jesus is "God with us" (Emmanuel—Isa. 7:14; Matt. 1:23; John 1:14). The Holy Spirit is Christ's continuing presence (Matt. 28:20; John 14:16). Heaven, the place of God's unclouded presence, is His goal for the race (Rev. 21:3).

See PAROUSIA, IMMANENCE, GLORY, PARACLETE, HOLY COMMUNION, TRANSUBSTANTIATION, CONSUBSTANTIATION.

For Further Reading: Brockington, "Presence," *A Theological Word Book of the Bible,* 172 ff; For views on Christ's presence in the Lord's Supper: Berkhof, *Manual of Christian Doctrine,* 325 ff; A mystical conception: Julian of Norwich, *Showings.* DONALD E. DEMARAY

PRESUMPTION. When this word is descriptive of sin, it means sin that is open, defiant, and deliberate. Such sin in the OT theocracy merited radical, even capital, punishment (Exod. 21:14; Num. 15:30; Deut. 17:12). The Psalmist prayed earnestly to be kept from such sins (Ps. 19:13).

The word also describes the bold arrogance of the religious charlatan. This person brashly intrudes himself where he does not belong, presumes liberties which are not his and knowledge which he does not possess. Of such persons Peter says that they "walk after the flesh . . . despise government. . . . selfwilled, they are not afraid to speak evil of dignities" (2 Pet. 2:10). This is the egomaniac.

However, good people may also be presumptuous, in less culpable ways. Mary and Joseph exhibited this kind of presumption; they, "supposing him [Jesus] to have been in the company, went a day's journey" (Luke 2:44). This is the presumption of carelessness—of taking for granted things which ought not to be taken for granted. This is a common fault of parents and administrators. Such carelessness may spell disaster in one's personal spiritual life also, when one presumes on divine grace to compensate for prayerlessness, or assumes spiritual well-being without honest self-examination.

When related to Christian work, presumption is akin to fanaticism, one definition of which is to expect results without giving due attention to adequate means. A preacher is being presumptuous when he habitually enters the pulpit without careful preparation, under the guise of relying on the Spirit. This is a self-deceptive, affected, and misguided piety.

Similar is the distinction between presumption and faith. An action may be taken in true faith; the same action at another time or by another person may be presumptuous. The difference is the difference between obedience and self-will. For the Israelites to have entered Canaan at Kadesh when exhorted to would have been a demonstration of faith which God would have honored. When they self-willfully attempted the conquest two days later, it was presumption, and they fell before their enemies. Faith is responding to divine order; presumption is plunging ahead on one's own. Often ambitious Christians assay to imitate the exploits for God of others, supposing that whatever others have done they can do too; but this is presumption.

This kind of presumption reflects an inordinate confidence in one's own judgment and abilities. Such error may occasionally slip up on truly devout persons. Joshua and his associates were guilty of such presumption when, in respect to the Gibeonites, they "took of their victuals, and asked not counsel at the mouth of the Lord" (Josh. 9:14). It is to be feared that many church building or other projects are prime examples of this kind of presumption.

See FANATICISM, GUIDE (GUIDANCE), OBEDIENCE, FAITH. RICHARD S. TAYLOR

PREVENIENT GRACE. This has to do with the many ways in which God favors us prior to our conversion. It means that God takes the initiative in the matter of our conversion, inclining us to turn to Him, wooing us, breaking down the barriers to our repenting and believing. It includes also, as taught by Arminius, Wesley, Wiley, and others, the alleviation of guilt for Adam's sin (but not, of course, of the depravity stemming from Adam). It is different from the common grace as taught by Calvinists, which consists of restraining the wickedness of the nonelect.

Due to original sin, which resulted from Adam's bad representation of the whole human race, we are born with a condition that inclines us toward a life of sin acts. Scripture thus speaks of our being enslaved to sin (Rom. 6:16-17). It shows that in ourselves we are incapable of doing what we know we ought to do (7:15, 18). Jesus says, "You brood of vipers, how can you who are evil say anything good?" (Matt. 12:34,

NIV). He also said that "a bad tree cannot bear good fruit" (7:18, NIV); also, that "apart from me you can do nothing" (John 15:5, NIV). All these passages of scripture suggest fallen man's inability to do any good thing unless he receives God's special help—i.e., prevenient grace.

Yet Scripture also shows us that God, in His graciousness, strikes out after us, to help us towards himself. "We love because he first loved us" (1 John 4:19, NIV), it reads. Also, "No one can come to me unless the Father who sent me draws him" (John 6:44, NIV). This is why it was said of Cornelius and his household that "God granted repentance unto life" (Acts 11:18, ASV)—where the word for "granted" (used also in KJV, RSV, NEB, NIV) is from the usual Greek word for "to give, bestow, present." The rebel must respond to God's offer of salvation; but still, his repentance is called a gift that is bestowed upon him. This, because he cannot repent unless he is aided by prevenient grace.

In the OT, also, it is clear that God initiates our salvation. While some passages, there, simply urge people to turn to God, as in Ezek. 18:32: "Turn yourselves, and live" (ASV); others make it clear that we must be helped, if we do turn. Thus we read in Ps. 80:3, "Turn us again, O God . . . and we shall be saved" (ASV). And in Ps. 85:4 we read, "Turn us, O God of our salvation" (ASV). The most vivid OT passage, on this need for prevenient grace to help us to turn, is in Jer. 31:18-19: "Turn thou me, and I shall be turned; for thou art Jehovah my God. Surely after that I was turned, I repented" (ASV).

While both Pelagians and the semi-Pelagians denied prevenient grace, the need of it has usually been recognized. It was a particular emphasis of both James Arminius and John Wesley. Arminius said that "the free will of man towards the true good is . . . maimed, . . . destroyed, and lost" (*Works,* 1:526-27). Wesley said, "We [he and John Fletcher] both steadily assert that the will of fallen man is by nature free only to evil" (Burtner and Chiles, *Compend of Wesley's Theology,* 132-33).

Christian hymn writers have often extolled prevenient grace. One of them, Lewis Hartsough, has us singing:

I hear Thy welcome voice,
That calls me, Lord, to Thee.

Charles Wesley has us singing:

Saviour, Prince of Israel's race, . . .
Give me sweet, relenting grace.

Charlotte Elliott's great invitation hymn also points up the place of prevenient grace:

Just as I am! Thy love unknown
Hath broken every barrier down.

One thing this doctrine means is that God does not meet us halfway, but instead comes all the way to where we are and initiates in us the first desires to be saved. Thus the importance of intercessory prayer for unsaved persons.

See GRACE, MONERGISM, SYNERGISM, FREEDOM, CALVINISM, ARMINIANISM, WESLEYANISM, FEDERAL THEOLOGY.

For Further Reading: Grider, *Repentance unto Life;* Chamberlain, *The Meaning of Repentance;* Wiley, "Prevenient Grace," *CT,* 2:344-57.

J. KENNETH GRIDER

PRIDE. Synonyms of pride are *ostentation, haughtiness, swaggering, imposture, bragging, vaunting, vain boasting,* "puffed up." The word "pride" is from the word meaning "smoke or cloud" (Westcott; see Jas. 4:16; Rom. 1:30; 2 Tim. 3:2; 1 Cor. 13:4).

Jesus includes pride in His list of heinous sins (Mark 7:22). It comes from within a person, expressed or not. It is a spirit of self-sufficiency and superiority (see Dan. 4:25; 5:20-22).

John makes pride one of three marks of worldliness (1 John 2:16). It relates not so much to life as existence, as to the manner of living. A pride-filled person trusts his own resources, lives according to this present world system (see Gen. 3:6; Col. 2:8).

Good pride is boasting wholly in the Lord (1 Cor. 1:31; Phil. 3:3). Paul boasts about some Christians (2 Cor. 9:2; see also Phil. 2:6).

Evil pride glories in praise to self. It yearns for applause from man instead of from God (but see Acts 14:27). It reveals itself when earthly advantages make one feel superior to him who lacks these things. The proud forget that all is of God. Pride may be expressed in at least two ways: (1) in speech—vain boastings (Jas. 4:6, 16); and (2) in thought—arrogance, independence, repression (1 Pet. 5:5; Jas. 4:6; 1 Cor. 4:6; 8:1).

Pride is the root sin. It consists of enmity against the rule of God in the soul. It is a disease in human nature which only grace can cure. It is idolatry. Pride seeks the recognition of men rather than of God alone.

Pride may exist even in the heart of the believer (Rom. 12:3; 1 Cor. 4:6).

It tends to backsliding, even from the grace of entire sanctification. Pride goes before failure (Prov. 11:2; 13:10; 16:18; 1 Tim. 3:6). One of Wesley's warnings to the sanctified was, "Beware of pride" *(Plain Account).*

It is opposed to the Christian grace of love for

God and all men, which is pride's only remedy (1 Cor. 13:4).

See HUMILITY, SEVEN DEADLY SINS.

For Further Reading: *HDNT;* Murray, *Humility.*

JOHN B. NIELSON

PRIEST, PRIESTHOOD. "Priest" in Hebrew is *kohen;* in Greek, *hierus.* It is a term applying to a person set aside to serve as a mediator between the worshiper and his God. "Priesthood" applies to the order of hierarchy of persons who serve as priests and to the rituals or ceremonies priests conduct in their mediating role.

Priest, a Theological Necessity. The Bible presents "priest" and "priesthood" and all related redemptive aspects from the perspective of special revelation. Man, although a creature in the image of God, has sinned; and therefore, as unholy and estranged from God, is unable of himself to come effectively before God, who is holy, for forgiveness and reconciliation. The priest became a gracious divine provision who in his holy office served as mediator between God and man to the end that man might know forgiveness, cleansing, and reconciliation with God. Thus "priest" may be understood as both a theological necessity and a merciful provision.

Priesthood of the Believer in Full Cycle. The "priesthood of the believer" emphasis, important for Protestants (from the Reformation), went full cycle across the span of biblical times. In very early and patriarchal times, persons offering blood sacrifices to God acted without a mediating priest. Individual worshipers were apparently exercising their individual priesthood. (Melchisedek, a one-time officiant for Abraham, was later considered a type for the "forever" priesthood of Jesus—Gen. 14:18; cf. Ps. 110:4; Heb. 5:6, 10).

The OT priesthood hierarchy from Moses consisted in the high priest, ordinary priests, and Levites. The high priest, of the greatest importance, officiated as the mediator between God and those who offered sacrifices for sin. The priesthood of the OT, while emphasizing essentials of salvation, nevertheless precluded the individual priesthood of the worshiper. In the NT, especially in Hebrews, Jesus is presented as Founder of the new covenant from the standpoint of being the High Priest who supersedes the earlier Aaronic priesthood as the Mediator and Intercessor on behalf of the sinner before God the Father, and of being the Sacrifice who died on the Cross and whose atoning blood is a once-for-all atonement for sin (Heb. 8:6—10:25). It was from this standpoint that early Christians readily understood that the older priesthood and sacrifices were no longer necessary; they could come without the assistance of priest and sacrifice through Christ, to God the Father. Thus the priesthood of the believer had come around full cycle.

See MEDIATOR, PRIESTHOOD OF BELIEVERS.

For Further Reading: *IDB,* K-G:711-27, 877-91; *The New Schaff-Herzog Encyclopedia of Religious Knowledge,* 248-54.

HARVEY E. FINLEY

PRIESTHOOD OF BELIEVERS. The biblical doctrine of the priesthood of believers is an expression of the ministry of the community of believers to the world through its immediacy to God in Christ.

The OT roots are found in Exod. 19:4-6. At Sinai God promised, "And you shall be to Me a kingdom of priests and a holy nation" (v. 6, NASB). The primary meaning is that Israel should be the representative of God to the outside world (cf. Isa. 61:6).

The whole NT reflects the influence of these ideas. In 1 Pet. 2:5 the community of believers is called a "spiritual house for a holy priesthood, to offer up spiritual sacrifices acceptable to God through Jesus Christ" (NASB). In verse 9 a chain of OT references is applied to the new Israel: "a chosen race, a royal priesthood, a holy nation, a people for God's own possession" (NASB). Again the primary purpose is to witness "the excellencies of Him who has called you."

In Revelation (1:6; 5:10; 20:6) the members of the Kingdom are designated as priests of God. The emphasis here lies on the ministry of individuals to God as a form of priestly service.

The whole NT is replete with sacrificial language. Technical terms for service such as "presenting an offering," "firstfruits," and "sacrificial" are used regularly. In Rom. 12:1-2 believers are exhorted to offer themselves as living sacrifices, which is designated as a rational priestly service.

The priesthood of believers is not a special caste of ministry, but involves every member of the Body of Christ both in individual and corporate responsibility. Each person is indeed his own priest through immediate access to God through Christ, but each man shares as well in the mediation of Christ to the world.

See PRIEST (PRIESTHOOD), MEDIATOR, PROTESTANTISM.

For Further Reading: Richardson, *An Introduction to the Theology of the New Testament,* 301 ff.

MORRIS A. WEIGELT

PRIMAL HISTORY. Some OT scholars prefer to designate Genesis 1—11 as primal history, because they believe the contents of these chapters have no historical validity. This creates a contradiction, for if Genesis 1—11 contains no history, why use the term in the title? Nevertheless, it is a common phrase.

This position holds that the creation of the world, the great Flood, and the tower of Babel never happened as told. Nor were there such individuals as Adam and Eve, Cain and Abel, or Noah and his family. Instead, the materials in the first 11 chapters of the Bible are understood to be based on ancient Near Eastern creation and flood stories. Various writers in the 10th, 9th, and 6th centuries B.C. reworked the non-Israelite stories and gave them distinctly Israelitish understandings about creation, God, man, sin, and judgment. Emphasis is placed on the themes which permeate these chapters. The stories are often relabeled as myths, sagas, and legends.

Conservative scholars have recognized Genesis 1—11 as containing accounts of events that really happened and people who really lived. These accounts are not based on pagan myths, but constitute a God-given and God-preserved revelation—which either existed in writing before Moses' time or was put into writing by him.

The analysis that conservatives make of the themes and doctrines found in these chapters does not differ greatly from that made by liberal scholars. Their estimates of the historical reliability of the material, however, are diametrically opposed to each other.

Traditionally, the material has been understood as historical.

See INSPIRATION OF THE BIBLE, BIBLICAL INERRANCY, HEILSGESCHICHTE.

For Further Reading: Harrelson, *Interpreting the Old Testament,* 45-58; Fohrer, *History of Israelite History,* 176-84; Livingston, *The Pentateuch in Its Cultural Environment,* 137-50; Williams, *Understanding the Old Testament,* 74-84.

GEORGE HERBERT LIVINGSTON

PRIMITIVE HOLINESS. See DIVINE IMAGE.

PRINCIPALITIES AND POWERS. Five NT words refer to the hierarchy of angelic beings (both holy and fallen): *archai*—principalities; *exousiai*—powers; *dynameis*—powers; *kuriotētes*—dominions; and *thronoi*—thrones. These seem to be ranks of heavenly beings. The most common terms are "principalities and powers."

All were created by and for Christ (Col. 1:16). All must recognize His supreme Lordship (Eph. 1:20-22; Col. 2:10; Heb. 1:4-14; 1 Pet. 3:22). Fallen angels seem temporarily permitted to retain under Satan (Eph. 2:2; 2 Cor. 4:4) their former ranks. They are part of Satan's dark host (Luke 22:53). The Christian need not fear them (Rom. 8:38-39), for Christ has rescued us from their dominion (Acts 26:18; Col. 1:13). Christ defeated them on the Cross (2:15), disarming them, and making public a spectacle of them (John 12:31; Eph. 4:8). Col. 2:15 pictures a Roman emperor who conquers his foes, strips them of their armor, and compels them to march in chains behind his chariot in his triumphal procession.

Their doom is sure (John 12:31; Rev. 12:9), for hellfire is prepared for them (Matt. 25:41; Rev. 20:10).

The Christian wrestles with this host, including the demons, in his service and prayer (Eph. 6:12). They are hostile to God and man, and sometimes hinder Kingdom advance (1 Thess. 2:18). God limits their authority (Job 1:12; 2:6); the Christian through prayer has victory in Christ's name over them (Eph. 6:18). Hades' gates cannot prevail (Matt. 16:18). From Calvary's viewpoint they are weak and beggarly (Gal. 4:9). Demons know they are defeated and doomed (Matt. 8:29; Mark 1:24; Luke 4:34). We have no fear, for the Conqueror, Christ, is with us (2 Chron. 32:7-8), and His hosts far exceed Satan's (2 Kings 6:16; Rom. 8:31).

See SATAN, DEMONS, ANGELS.

For Further Reading: *HDNT,* 4:273.

WESLEY L. DUEWEL

PRINCIPLES. This term carries two meanings in theology. First, it denotes the underlying elements of a system, the primary ideas or postulates. (The first systematic theology, by Origen, was called *De Principiis,* "First Principles.") Second, principles are the standards and policies which govern action.

The first meaning is expressed in the NT by *stoicheion,* translated by "element" (Gal. 4:3, 9; 2 Pet. 3:10, 12); by "rudiment" (Col. 2:8, 20); and by "principle" (Heb. 5:12). The Galatians and Colossians passages warn against returning to the systems either of Moses or paganism. The Christians addressed in Hebrews are shamed for not having progressed beyond the "elementary principles of the oracles of God" (NASB). The idea is continued in 6:1 with the word *archē,* "beginning." Vine says the word is used "in its relative significance, of the beginning of the thing spoken of; here 'the first principles of Christ'" *(ED).*

The passage does not leave to guesswork the sort of truth which the writer classifies as fundamental principles: "repentance from dead works and of faith toward God" (NASB). These are among the ABCs of the Christian faith, which, while never outmoded or displaced, are not expected to mark the limits of spiritual knowledge and progress. The need for believers to go on to Christian perfection both in thought and experience, and to continue to grow thereafter, is itself a fundamental Christian principle.

Doctrinal principles need to be translated into personal norms of conduct—the second meaning of the term. In this sense, principles are needed to bring into life direction, system, and stability. To live by self-accepted moral standards is the opposite of impulse or random living. An unprincipled person has no moral guidelines, which means that he is ruthless, opportunistic, and capricious. He is without a trained conscience. In contrast the person who lives by principle is predictable. He strives to make everyday decisions compatible with his principles.

A principled person may have rules also, but principles differ from rules in that they lie back of rules as their reasons. Honesty may be with a person a basic life principle. The practice of honesty will therefore be his policy. To aid him in holding to his principle and practicing his policy, he may impose on himself certain rules, such as to pay bills on the first day of the month.

A mark of maturity is the ability to acquire and live by a set of clearly thought-out and biblically supportable principles.

See DOCTRINE, MORALITY, CHRISTIAN ETHICS, MATURITY.

For Further Reading: "Elements," "Principles," "Rudiments," Vine, *ED; Baker's DCE,* 530.

RICHARD S. TAYLOR

PRIORITY. See VALUES.

PRISCILLIANISM. This is a movement which arose in Spain at the end of the fourth century. Named for Priscillian, bishop of Avila, its supposed founder, it taught a kind of Sabellianism on the doctrine of the Trinity; a Manichaean dualism; and Docetic views.

See SABELLIANISM, DUALISM, DOCETISM.

J. KENNETH GRIDER

PROBABILISM. This is the ethical theory that, since it is all right to hold a probable opinion, it is also all right to do things that are only probably right. It was first taught by Bartolome Medina (1528-80), and was agreed to by many; but it was condemned by Pope Alexander VII (1667) and by Innocent XI (1679).

See ETHICS, MORALITY, EXPEDIENCY.

J. KENNETH GRIDER

PROBATION. Probation is a period or method of trial to determine one's fitness or unfitness for projected privileges. Not only is the element of testing present, but the element of training and preparation.

The fact that all of life is probation permeates the entire Bible. It begins with probation in the Garden of Eden (Gen. 2:15-17) and concludes in the last chapter of Revelation with the promise of rewards or punishment (Rev. 22:11-19).

Probation presupposes that man was highly created and endowed by God (Gen. 1:27; 2:7). Saints are not made by divine fiat, but through man's deliberate choices in the presence of the possibility of choosing contrary to divine law or requirements. As created, his inclinations were toward God and righteousness, for he was "created in righteousness and true holiness" (Eph. 4:24) with the added presence of the Holy Spirit. His love and loyalty to God must be tested, however, and temptation in some form was a necessity. Man fell into sin (Rom. 5:12), and all history has been under the terms and conditions of the Fall. The Scriptures teach, however, that men are free agents (e.g., John 7:17; 5:40; Luke 15:18, 20), with moral responsibility (Eccles. 12:13-14; Acts 17:30-31; Rom. 2:16; 14:12; 2 Cor. 5:10), while at the same time God is sovereign and works "all things after the counsel of his own will" (Eph. 1:11).

Is man's probation limited by death, or is the probation of some continued beyond the grave? Some believe that 1 Pet. 3:18-20 favors this possibility. Beyond this moot passage is the clear teaching of Scripture that this life is probationary (Matt. 7:24-29; Rom. 2:6-16) and is followed by divine judgment (Heb. 9:27; Rev. 20:12-13).

Probation is also used as a trial or test of suitability for church office or membership (1 Tim. 3:10; cf. 1 Cor. 16:3).

See TEMPTATION, FREEDOM, FREE WILL, ACCOUNTABILITY, FUTURE PROBATION, DESTINY (ETERNAL).

For Further Reading: *GMS,* 529-30, 627-28; Wiley, *CT,* 2:58.

WILLIAM M. ARNETT

PROCESS THEOLOGY. This is a theological movement primarily influenced by the process philosophies of Alfred N. Whitehead (1861-1947) and Charles Hartshorne (1897-). Largely Anglo-American and Protestant in background, process rather than timeless being is regarded as the ultimate metaphysical insight. As a form of philosophical theology this movement reinterprets the Christian faith in terms of a developing, changing, dynamic understanding of reality. This marks a return to speculative philosophy in a theological context and provides a new basis for natural theology in the 20th century. A list of process theologians would include John Cobb, Schubert Ogden, Daniel D. Williams, Norman Pittenger.

For Whitehead "the Church gave unto God the attributes which belonged exclusively to Caesar." God was fashioned in the image of an all-powerful oriental despot. God suffers not, is unaffected by time, and is absolute. Hartshorne calls this view classical theism: God is immutable, omnipotent, *a se,* impassible. For process theology classical theism fails to relate an unchanging God to a changing world. Therefore God's nature and relation to the world are reinterpreted through process categories. A dipolar view of God's primordial and consequent natures recognizes temporality in God's being, with His relation to the world now defined in terms of pan*en*theism.

During the 1970s process theologians systematically began to explore many traditional doctrinal themes, including Christology, theological anthropology, ecclesiology, the Trinity, and eschatology. With their roots in 19th-century liberalism, evolutionary thinking is emphasized, but without the old liberal identification of process with progress. Although individual differences exist between these theologians, they tend to be optimistic with respect to human existence, confident of love as the primary quality of God, and convinced of the illuminating power of the Whiteheadian vision of reality for Christian thinking.

Evangelical reception of this movement is mixed. On the one hand process theology suggests the inevitability of philosophical currents in theological work, fosters appreciation of the humanity of Jesus, overcomes the modern dualistic split between history and nature, and stresses the reality of freedom. On the other hand, evangelical criticism is forthright on the processive interpretation of theism, the denial of *creatio ex nihilo,* an apparent "finite God," a questionable basis for subjective immortality, and the tendency to adjust biblical theology to fit the Whiteheadian scheme of thought.

See PANENTHEISM, IMMUTABILITY, ATTRIBUTES (DIVINE), MORAL ATTRIBUTES OF GOD.

For Further Reading: Cobb and Griffin, *Process Theology: An Introductory Exposition;* Cousins, ed., *Process Theology: Basic Writings;* Mellert, *What Is Process Theology?* Williams, *The Spirit and the Forms of Love;* Kantzer and Gundry, eds., *Perspectives on Evangelical Theology,* 15-42; Peterson, "Orthodox Christianity, Wesleyanism, and Process Theology," *WTJ,* Fall, 1980, 45-58.

HERBERT L. PRINCE

PROCESSION OF THE SPIRIT. This term refers to the relationship of the Holy Spirit to the Father and the Son. In the early centuries of the church considerable energy was given to a clear and careful definition of the Trinity. God is one substance in three Persons; Christ's humanity and deity are kept in balance; and the personality and deity of the Holy Spirit are affirmed.

The attention of the church was directed next to a clarification of the relative place of each of the three Persons. God the Son was "begotten of the Father" (eternally begotten) and bore a filial relationship with the Father as the Second Person of the Trinity. The Holy Spirit as the Third Person of the Trinity was "breathed out" (spirated). The Nicene Creed (A.D. 325) referred to the Holy Spirit "which proceedeth from the Father." This wording seemed to support a "subordination" of God the Son. To counter any such thought and in keeping with the total context of the Scripture (John 14:26; 15:26; 16:7), the church moved from a "single procession" to a "double procession" of the Spirit. The phrase "and of the Son" (the *filioque*) was added to the Nicene Creed at the Council of Toledo (A.D. 589). The Council at Aix la Chapelle (Synod of Aachen, A.D. 809) officially sanctioned the *filioque.*

The church in the West early contended for the inclusion of the *filioque,* while the Eastern branch of Christendom vehemently opposed it. So significant was the issue that it became a contributing factor in the final break (A.D. 1054) which divided Christianity into Roman Catholic and Eastern Orthodox branches.

See HOLY SPIRIT, TRINITY (THE HOLY).

For Further Reading: Neve, *History of Christian Doctrine,* 1:121 ff, 177; Wiley, *CT,* 1:414-44.

RONALD E. WILSON

PROFANE, PROFANITY. This is the opposite of "holy" in Scripture. The profane person is one who is purely secular and evidences a disregard for things that are sacred. Profanity, popularly, relates to taking God's name in vain and to the use of words which only slightly miss, and are substitutes for, any of the names of Deity.

See SECULARISM. J. KENNETH GRIDER

PROGRESSIVE REVELATION. This term first appeared in liberal circles; it means something entirely different for evangelical Christians. The concept is crucial if one hopes to interpret Scripture correctly.

Evangelical Perspective. Progressive revelation means that God has spoken by word and sign over a large span of time, rooted in such solid historical events as the Exodus, conquest, kingdom, Exile and return, life-death-resurrection of Jesus, outpouring of the Holy Spirit, and the expansion of the Church (Packer, "An Evangelical View of Progressive Revelation," *Evangelical Roots,* 149). "Progressive" speaks of the steady advance that God's self-disclosure took from its first faint beginnings to its glorious completion in Jesus Christ. It recognizes that in the historical process one word, one event, one epoch followed another until the climax came (Heb. 1:1-2). It notes that God first revealed himself to select individuals, then progressively to a family, a tribe, a nation, and finally in "the fulness of the time" (Gal. 4:4) to the whole world in the Word made flesh and the Word written.

Progressive revelation suggests that God's disclosure in both Testaments is an organic whole. But in that whole there is progressive development of understanding as former revelation lays the foundation for later revelation; the law prepares the way for the prophets; "each promise fulfilled brings the sense of a larger promise" (Westcott, *Epistle to the Hebrews,* 482); finally the Jesus of history in the Gospels makes possible the Christ of faith in the Epistles until at last the whole of God's self-revelation is fully seen and understood. Evangelicals resist such views as C. H. Dodd's that all stages of the revelatory process except the last involved beliefs that were partly wrong (Dodd, *Authority of the Bible,* 255).

Liberal Views. All forms of liberalism adhere to belief in natural evolutionary development. When applied to "progressive" revelation, liberal views believe that the revelatory process was a natural religious development which slowly advanced by human insight and discovery into the true character of God and the moral nature of man. This evolutionary process applies to both the theological and literary development of Scripture.

The "history of religion" theory about the emergence of monotheism illustrates well the concept of *theological evolution.* Rather than monotheism being a God-given revelation from the outset of OT history, it is assumed that Israel began with a polytheistic religion like her ancient neighbors. Only gradually did she progress from a crude patriarchal polytheism to the ethical monotheism of the prophets and of Jesus of Nazareth.

Progressive revelation, according to liberal views, also involved *literary evolution.* One example is the Graf-Wellhausen documentary hypothesis which postulates a long and gradual development of the Pentateuch. Rather than Genesis through Deuteronomy being authentically the work of Moses as writer, they comprise instead many centuries of oral and literary evolution with various editors forming and shaping its theology as late as the Exile and placing it in the historical framework of the idealized past.

A similar literary evolution is seen in the Gospels. Form criticism, for example, suggests that Gospel materials first circulated orally in small, independent units of teaching. The Early Church developed and embellished the material during its many decades of oral transmission and usage. Some form critics (e.g., Dibelius and Bultmann) believe that many parables, miracle stories, and episodes attributed to Jesus are actually fictional literary creations by the Early Church as the meaning of her faith and the character of her Lord were being formulated.

These and other liberal views of progressive revelation supposedly account for the "faulty" and "wrong" conceptions of God, man, and the world in Scripture and for the "primitive" elements which embarrass the modern mind. All such concepts of progressive revelation err, however, since revelation concerns not what man *discovers* but what God *discloses.*

Implications for Scripture Interpretation. Progressive revelation, evangelically understood, implies that the Old and New Testaments are two parts of one continuum of revelation; in both parts it is God himself who is revealing His character and redemptive purposes by words and deeds. But progressive revelation acknowledges a distinction between the two Testaments: the OT records an incomplete progressive revelation, while the NT records God's revelation in its full and completed form. Each part of the OT is incomplete, though not incorrect, and looks forward to the time of fullness and fulfillment in Jesus Christ.

Furthermore, progressive revelation means that to interpret Scripture accurately, one must "interpret a passage in its revelatory progress. This means that we recognize the Old Testament as always pointing toward a more full Word which came in the New Testament" (Augsburger, *Principles of Biblical Interpretation,* 17). This is true both theologically and ethically. Theologically, for example, the sacrificial system of atonement in the OT was fulfilled in Jesus' once-for-all offering of himself for sin's atonement, thereby making obsolete the OT method (see Heb. 8:13—10:18). Ethically, certain OT practices such as polygamy proved to be sub-Christian. Although God through Moses instructed against polygamy (Deut. 17:17), the practice of it continued, undoubtedly because of the hardness of their hearts (cf. Matt. 19:8 on divorce). When the moral conduct and holiness required of God's people became the object of more and more precise revelations, the practice of polygamy disappeared, as in the NT.

Progressive revelation implies, therefore, that in Scripture interpretation, "the authority of certain portions of the Bible may not be, in detail or application, the same for us as it was for those to whom those portions were originally addressed" (Taylor, *Biblical Authority and Christian Faith,* 66). Consequently, the incomplete progressive revelation must be interpreted and applied always in the light of the fullness of God's revelation in His Son.

See REVELATION (SPECIAL), BIBLE, BIBLICAL AUTHORITY, COMPARATIVE RELIGION, HERMENEUTICS, BIBLE: THE TWO TESTAMENTS.

For Further Reading: Baker, *Two Testaments: One Bible,* 59-87; Pache, *The Inspiration and Authority of Scripture,* 102-10; Packer, "An Evangelical View of Progressive Revelation," *Evangelical Roots,* 143-58; Ramm, *Special Revelation and the Word of God;* Taylor, *Biblical Authority and Christian Faith,* 64-68, 81-83.

J. WESLEY ADAMS

PROGRESSIVE SANCTIFICATION. The use of the term *progressive* with reference to sanctification suggests that there is a process of time in which the instantaneous experience of entire sanctification is realized. This second work of grace, entire sanctification, comes in successive stages, each of which has a gradual approach and an instantaneous consummation. Three things should be noted in this respect.

First, sanctification, in its larger meaning, is both initial and entire. In conversion the repentant sinner is justified, regenerated, and adopted into the family of God. But, in addition, he is initially sanctified: cleansed from the acquired depravity which is a result of the sinner's actual sinning. But initial sanctification has not affected his inherited depravity. In a second crisis he is sanctified wholly: delivered from the presence of inbred sin or inherited depravity.

Second, sanctification is both gradual and instantaneous. Every act which brings God's grace to the being of man is the result of faith, and faith for entire sanctification must be preceded by a recognition of inner sin and a confession of that sin. This renunciation of sin is only possible by the convicting power of the Holy Spirit. This sense of awareness of inbred sin is progressive or gradual. But when this gradual aspect of entire sanctification brings the child of God, through the Holy Spirit, to a complete renunciation of inbred sin, simple faith in Jesus Christ will result in an instantaneous cleansing from inbred sin.

Third, sanctification is both instantaneous and continuous. It has already been stated that while there is a gradual approach to entire sanctification, the actual cleansing from inbred sin is done in an instant. While this cleansing from inbred sin is a definite act completed in a moment, the retention of the freedom from sin is the result of a continuous cleansing by the Holy Spirit. Thus the cleansing from inbred sin which was completed in an instant in answer to faith, is retained by the sanctified Christian only as he walks in the light and trusts the blood of Jesus Christ to keep him cleansed from all sin (1 John 1:7).

Sometimes "progressive sanctification" is used in reference to growth in Christlikeness and to the deepening of holy character after the crisis of entire sanctification. Great care must be exercised in such a use of the term, lest "progressive" be understood as a gradual cleansing from sin.

See SANCTIFICATION, ENTIRE SANCTIFICATION.

For Further Reading: Wiley, *CT,* 2:479-86; Curtis, *The Christian Faith,* 373-93; *GMS,* 268-302, 462-507.

NORMAN R. OKE

PROMISE. Although possessing certain factors in common, a *promise* (Gr. *epaggelma*) and a *covenant* (Heb. *berith;* Gr. *diathēkē)* possess certain essential differences. A promise is "a declaration that something will or will not be done, given by one" *(Random House Dictionary).* A covenant is "a compact or agreement between two [or more] parties binding them mutually to undertakings on each other's behalf" *(Baker's DT,* 142).

The assurance of the fulfillment of a promise rests exclusively upon the veracity of the promisor, whereas the fulfillment of the terms of a covenant rests upon the fidelity of each party to the agreement. Violation of those terms by either party abrogates the provisions of the covenant. God's redemptive promises are unconditional: "For when God made the promise to Abraham, since He could swear by no one greater, He swore by Himself" (Heb. 6:13, NASB; cf. 14-20; Gal. 3:10-18; Gen. 22:15-18; Luke 1:73-79).

God's covenants are many, and each is included, like a concentric circle, within the larger circle of His promises. God's great redemptive promises are three, and consist, first, of Christ the Redeemer, which appears first in Gen. 3:15 and continues progressively throughout both Testaments, including His virgin birth, death on the

Cross, resurrection, and ascension. The Father's promise of the Gift of the Holy Spirit constitutes the second great redemptive promise to man (Luke 24:49; Acts 1:4-5), which was fulfilled with the Spirit's effusion at Pentecost (2:1-4). The third is God's promise of Christ's second coming (Acts 1:11; 3:19-21; 1 Thess. 1:10; 4:13-18; Titus 2:13; see also John Fletcher, *Works*, 3:166-69).

See COVENANT, NEW COVENANT, PENTECOST, PROMISES (DAVIDIC).

For Further Reading: Walker, "Promise," *ISBE*, 4:2459; Smith, "Promise," *Baker's DT*, 422-23; Miner, "Promise," *IDB*, K-Q:893-96.

CHARLES W. CARTER

PROMISES, DAVIDIC. The promises made by God to King David, found in 2 Samuel 7, assure David that the throne of his offspring will be established forever. The occasion for these promises was David's intention to build a house in which the Lord would dwell (the Jerusalem Temple). God refuses David's offer and instead, employing a play on words, promises to build a house (dynasty) for David. This meant that for Judah there would be but one ruling dynasty in their national history of over 400 years. (Compare this with Northern Israel's nine dynasties in approximately 200 years.) The promises are regarded as a binding covenant (see the last words of David in 2 Sam. 23:1-7; also Jer. 33:20-21) and form an important aspect in Israel's covenant history.

Some scholars see a vital historical connection between the Abrahamic and Davidic promises. Promises made to Abraham (Gen. 12:1-3) of land and a great nation are seen as fulfilled in David. It is also noted that David began his reign in Hebron, the general area where Abraham had settled and where traditions surrounding the patriarch would be kept alive (see Clements, *Abraham and David*). This approach provides continuity in the covenantal purposes of God in the OT.

Based on the promises to David, Israel developed a royal theology which said that as long as a son (descendant) of David was enthroned, they were under the special favor and protection of God. This interpretation of the Davidic promises became the basis of hope in times of national adversity (Ps. 89:20-52; Isa. 37:35), but gave rise to a false sense of unconditional security. Closely coupled with this thought was the belief that God's choice of Zion as His dwelling place on earth insured the political and spiritual security of the nation. Typical prophetic reaction to this misunderstanding is seen in Jeremiah's Temple sermon (chap. 7).

With the passing of time the promises made to David were used to refer to Israel's future restoration under God, and the expectation of an ideal king took root. The following prophetic references indicate this: Amos 9:11-12; Hos. 3:5; Isa. 9:7; 16:5; Jer. 23:5-6; 33:15-16; Ezek. 34:23-24; 37:24. No human king ever fulfilled these hopes and aspirations, but the NT recognizes our Lord, the Son of David, as fulfillment of the ideal King.

See MESSIAH, SON OF MAN, PROPHET (PROPHECY).

For Further Reading: Clements, *Abraham and David;* Bright, *A History of Israel*, 203-7; Mowinckel, *He That Cometh*, 165-69.

ALVIN S. LAWHEAD

PROPERTY RIGHTS. There is no biblical "blueprint" for a Christian approach to property. There are, however, scriptural ethical principles relating to property and its use.

All property belongs to God. He created all things, and all things belong to Him. He alone has absolute ownership (Ps. 24:1; Isa. 66:2). Use of the land, air, water, and even of other living creatures have been freely given to man by God (Gen. 1:26-29), but the ultimate right is God's.

Ownership of property by man, then, is secondary, not absolute. As a gift from God, it is to be held in trust by man and used for human need (Job 31:16-34; Isa. 58:7-8). Man's response is not only one of gratitude and thanksgiving, but of stewardship (Matt. 20:1-16; Luke 19:11-27). Property is to be used in accordance with the will of the One who is sovereign over all. Ownership implies a duty as well as a privilege. Property rights are, therefore, to be subordinated to human need.

Within the framework of the absolute ownership by God alone, biblical faith assumes the necessity of some measure of individual ownership of property. The OT injunction "You shall not steal" presupposes the right of individual ownership. The communal sharing of goods by the Jerusalem church following Pentecost (Acts 2:44-45; 5:1-15) presupposes the freedom to place or not to place property at the disposal of the community.

George Thomas believes that "historical facts make it clear that the Church has usually recognized the right of property as *legitimate*, but has been keenly aware of the moral and social *dangers* of property and has imposed *limitations* upon it to protect the welfare of the less fortunate" (*Christian Ethics and Moral Philosophy*, 310). He does not believe that this justifies a person in claiming an unconditional right to acquire property and dispose of it without regard for the consequences to others (312).

From the standpoint of the Christian ethic, absolute equality of property distribution and ownership is not demanded. Individual differences between persons cannot be ignored. What is called for is "equality of consideration" or equality of opportunity, which means "that each person should be effectively taken into account in the distribution of social benefits and that each should be helped to develop his capacities and fulfill his needs to the greatest extent possible" (Gardner, *Biblical Faith and Social Ethics,* 291).

The apostle Paul provides some guiding principles for economic life. Christians are urged to earn their living by honest work (Eph. 4:28), not only to support themselves, but in order to have something to share with the needy. Christians are to share their possessions "with simplicity"; and to distribute to the necessity of the saints (Rom. 12:8, 13). Men of wealth are "not to be arrogant nor to put their hope in wealth, which is so uncertain, but to put their hope in God, who richly provides us with everything for our enjoyment" (1 Tim. 6:17, NIV). Paul personally has little concern for money (Phil. 4:11).

For the apostle, possessions, including property, "are to be acquired honestly, and restitution must be made when wrongly appropriated; and riches must always be under the rule of God—otherwise, they prove to be deceitful and dangerous" (Barnett, *Introducing Christian Ethics,* 147).

See STEWARDSHIP, COVETOUSNESS, CHRISTIAN SOCIALISM, RIGHTS, RICHES, LABOR, POVERTY.

For Further Reading: Thomas, *Christian Ethics and Moral Philosophy;* Gardner, *Biblical Faith and Social Ethics;* Barnett, *Introducing Christian Ethics.*

LEBRON FAIRBANKS

PROPHET, PROPHECY. A prophet (from Gr. *prophētēs,* to speak for or before) is one called to discern God's purpose and action in history and to proclaim the divine word of judgment and grace. The Hebrew term in the OT is applied to a broad range of persons including Abraham, Moses, Aaron, Deborah, Samuel, Nathan, and Elijah, as well as those whose writings are labeled major and minor prophets. In the NT, Jesus, John the Baptist, and Silas are among those thus designated, and Paul sees prophecy as an essential function continuing in the life of the Church. Broadly speaking, most biblical writings are prophetic in that they convey the divinely inspired interpretation of human history.

The heyday of prophecy, however, is the era of the Israelite kingdoms, particularly times of national crisis from the ninth to the mid-sixth centuries B.C. Although these crises were precipitated by the invasion of foreign powers, the classical prophets saw the deepest crisis of the people in their pervasive unfaithfulness to the covenant with Yahweh, upon whom their peace ultimately depended. Yahweh's spokesmen proclaimed that worship of the "other gods" of nature and state—evidenced by widespread social injustice, political and religious corruption—was the essence of their evil and reason for their doom.

The popular tendency to narrow prophecy to apocalypticism and prediction of the future should be checked by the biblical stress upon prophetic proclamation of "the word of the Lord" to the present. Moreover, the challenge to kings, priests, and people to radical obedience and faith gets its meaning and demand from the mighty acts of God in Israel's past—preeminently the deliverance from Egyptian bondage and establishment of the Mosaic Covenant at Sinai.

To be sure, this inspired "retelling" and "forthtelling" of God's purpose and action, in terse and graphic language, issues often in bold "forthtelling" of His future acts of judgment and redemption. Prophetic NT writers see in the whole pattern of OT history, as well as specific statements, God's promise of and preparation for His climactic saving revelation in the life, death, and resurrection of Jesus as the Christ. The spokesmen of the Lord in both Testaments are eschatological because, in the biblical story and the larger historical process, they discern telling signs of the ultimate goal and triumph of the kingdom of God.

The task of theology today, as in every age, involves a twofold interpretation: to understand the prophetic literature in its own terms and times, and to expound the meaning of prophetic faith in our terms and times. Sensitive theology thus respects the distance and appreciates the profound relevance of the prophets' words for the issues of life, death, and destiny today.

See HERMENEUTICS.

For Further Reading: *IDB,* 3:896-920; Richardson, ed., *A Theological Word Book of the Bible,* 178-82; Sanders, *Radical Voices in the Wilderness.*

WILFRED L. WINGET

PROPITIATION. The Greek word is *hilasterion.* To propitiate is to "appease and render favorable" or to "conciliate." Propitiation is "that which propitiates; atoning sacrifice." By this term Christ's death is viewed as appeasing divine justice and effecting reconciliation between God and man.

The word in the OT was applied to the mercy seat in the holy of holies. On the lid of the mercy seat was sprinkled blood once a year by the priest. This act made an atonement for Israel's sin and was viewed as the "propitiation" for sins.

Sin separates from God; man is estranged from God because of his rebellion. God is offended and man separated and guilty. To effect reconciliation the holy God must be satisfied in His justice, and man's guilt must be removed or "expiated." The original word has both the idea of propitiation and expiation, which latter term is used in translating 1 John 2:2 in the RSV. Actually, God's wrath is propitiated and man's guilt is expiated.

In order for God to justly forgive men, as the Bible teaches, a sacrifice for sin is essential. "Paradoxically, the God who is propitiated also lovingly provides the propitiation" (*NIDB,* 807). No man is able to appease God's wrath on his own. It is only through the death of Jesus that God's anger against sin can be set aside. The God who was angry is also the God who "so loved the world, that he gave" (John 3:16). He provided the propitiation that removed the barrier to the giving of His free mercy.

However, this objective provision for the reconciling of God to man was not enough; man must be reconciled to God. In that same act of atonement, God provided for the expiation of man's guilt and proclaims the forgiveness of his sins. Thus the act of propitiation is both Godward and manward (see 2 Cor. 5:18-20). "God's righteousness which makes sin a barrier to fellowship, and God's love, which would destroy the barrier, are revealed and satisfied in one and the same means, the gift of Christ to be the Mediator between Himself and men" *(HBD,* 586).

One must never look upon the death of Christ as an act of vengeance on God's part to enable Him to be merciful. Christ's death is God's love expressing itself in glad removal of the barrier to the showing of His mercy to guilty man. He wanted to show mercy but could not justly do so until divine justice was fully satisfied. This was done in the provision for the removal of guilt by Christ becoming the propitiation for man's sins.

Now man only needs to bring his broken and contrite spirit to the "mercy seat" and there plead for forgiveness on the basis of what Christ did on the Cross.

See ATONEMENT, SACRIFICE, EXPIATION, SATISFACTION.

For Further Reading: Crawford, *The Doctrine of the Atonement; ZPBD; ISBE;* Wiley, *CT,* 2:229 ff, 283-86.

LEO G. COX

PROPOSITIONAL THEOLOGY. Propositional theology is a form of theological reflection that begins with a conviction that revelation is essentially the divine communication of rationally comprehensible truths to humanity. Being rationally comprehensible, because they are revealed in language or in events which can be put into language, these truths are said to be propositional. In form, these truths are of the same kind as any other, though their aim may be quite different from the aim or objective of, say, mathematical truths or propositions. The method by which such truths come is, of course, very different. God sends revealed truths or propositions to us on His own initiative. We may intuit or rationally deduce mathematical truths.

Propositional theology takes these revealed propositions or truths, all of which are stated as information that can be intellectually grasped, and analyses, synthesizes, and deduces implications from them. While Christ is recognized as the ultimate revelation of truth, and as the Truth, the Bible is often referred to as "inscripturated revelation," i.e., revelation in written form. The purpose of the Bible, then, is to give us intellectual or cognitive information about God and about the nature of reality. The Bible is seen as essentially a collection of propositions or declarations about God, given by God himself.

A basic presupposition operating in propositional theology is confidence that Christian faith is essentially rational, resting on revealed facts and revealed propositions. Christ is the Foundation of Christian faith because He is the ultimate reason or rationality and the ultimate reality. He is the ultimate proposition. He is rationally comprehensible.

While propositional theology seeks to be thoroughly orthodox and claims to be the ancient faith of the Church, it is a recent offspring of the Reformed tradition. Its principal categories and chosen issues reflect a concern to counteract the more subjective views of revelation and of theology developed by classical liberalism, Barthianism, and existentialism. Thus, it is a very precisely aimed theology.

Classical liberalism reduced the idea of the divine revelation in Scripture to a notion of some sort of spiritual sensitivity on the part of a collection of very fallible people who were deeply immersed in their cultures as they wrote. Propositional theology wants to restore the idea that the Bible is God's very own thoughts, that human fallibility entered only at the point of reproducing God's words, and that cultural accretion in no way covers the essential point being made.

Barthianism and existentialism insist that God

reveals only himself, not knowledge about himself, and that this self-revelation can be believed only as we are personally confronted by it and decide to act upon it as true. Such belief, then, will radically change us. For Barthianism and existentialism, then, the Bible is not a book of propositions but a book meant to invoke an encounter between God and ourselves. Our intellects, with their demand for rationality, are believed to be either too self-serving and fallen (Barthianism) or too narrow and abstract (existentialism) to be recipient of saving revelation. Propositional theology agrees that the Bible invokes divine-human encounter. But propositional theology insists that this encounter, engendered by the Holy Spirit, is dependent for its outcome upon our consent to propositions that God has stated about himself and about us and our world. These propositions are objective and true regardless of our decision concerning them or the God who gives them.

Propositional theology views Barthianism and existentialism as having hung the truth and authority of Scripture on human decision in that both speak of the inspiration and authority of Scripture depending upon a response, positive or negative, by the hearer or reader. Propositional theology insists that such a procedure makes the human being the determiner of the truth and value of Scripture.

Conflict between propositional theology and other theologies has generally been primarily located at the point of the meaning and content of the Bible itself. But, of course, this implicates a number of other doctrines, issues, and concerns. So, the propositionalists have usually insisted on the correctness of the decision of the older fundamentalists concerning the absolutely nonnegotiable, unchanging, and essential character of Christian faith. To be Christian, one must hold to the "fundamentals": verbal inerrancy of Scripture, the deity of Jesus, the virgin birth of Jesus, substitutionary atonement, and the physical resurrection and bodily return of Christ. All of these are believed to be stated as propositions in Scripture, as propositions to be taken as literally as any scientific description. And denial of any one of them is finally seen as denial of all of them, for they are interdependent and biblical.

Theology for the propositionalist, then, is not simply reflection on the Christian faith. It is analysis, synthesis, and deduction of truth itself. Theology or dogmatic statement thus has an authority for the propositionalist that it does not have for most other sorts of contemporary theologians.

See REVELATION (SPECIAL), BIBLICAL AUTHORITY, BIBLICAL REALISM, TRUTH, DOCTRINE, DOGMA, FUNDAMENTALISM, FIDEISM.

For Further Reading: Henry, ed., *Revelation and the Bible;* Ridderbos, *Studies in Scripture and Its Authority;* Taylor, *Biblical Authority and Christian Faith,* 38-50.

PAUL M. BASSETT

PROSELYTE. The word "proselyte" is the equivalent of the Hebrew word *ger,* meaning a resident alien, "a stranger and sojourner" (Lev. 25:23; Deut. 14:21). The word later described a convert to Judaism and finally to Christianity (Matt. 23:15; Acts 2:5, 10; 6:5; 13:43).

The NT opens with Judaism making proselytes (Matt. 23:15; Luke 3:7-15). On the Day of Pentecost both Jews and proselytes were present in Jerusalem from every nation under heaven (Acts 2:5, 10). One of the chosen deacons was a Gentile and proselyte of Antioch (6:5). Paul and Barnabas found some "devout proselytes" at Antioch in Pisidia (13:43, 50). Paul addressed both Jews and Gentiles in the synagogue as "men of Israel, and ye that fear God" (vv. 16, 26, 43). These were Jews and religious proselytes. In Thessalonica and Athens, there were "devout Greeks" and "devout persons" in the synagogue (17:4, 17).

In summary: Proselytes were (1) non-Jews living among the covenant people and adopting their life-style partially and/or wholly; (2) Israelites born and living outside Palestine; and finally, (3) Gentiles converting to Judaism and to Christianity (13:26-52; 18:7-8; Matt. 23:15).

See PROSELYTISM.

ISAAC BALDEO

PROSELYTISM. Proselytism is the practice of making proselytes, a practice which is highly offensive in some circles. This offensiveness is at two levels: first, the attempt to make Christian converts from adherents of other religions is objectionable; second, even more objectionable is the attempt to make converts from other branches of Christendom, as for instance, missionaries working with populations claimed by the Greek Orthodox church.

Authority for seeking converts from other religions is rooted in the nature of the Christian religion itself, and in the specific command of Jesus (Matt. 28:19-20). Christianity declares the exclusiveness and solitariness of Christ as Savior (e.g., John 14:6; Acts 4:12; 1 Tim. 1:15; 2:5-6; 1 John 5:11-12; et al.).

Proselytism among different branches of Christendom is more delicate and complex. It is to be deplored that some workers, both in the home field and on foreign fields, become flagrant "sheep stealers," sometimes without any valid doctrinal basis, at other times without an adequate doctrinal basis. Minor differences in doctrine should not be pressed into major ones in order to enlarge one's own congregation, if basic spiritual needs are being met. On the other hand evangelicals who believe that the new birth is essential for salvation will have a guilty conscience if they ignore real spiritual needs. It cannot be denied that some branches of Christendom are so nominal or doctrinally derelict that their effectiveness in leading their own people to Christ is slight if not completely nonexistent. In a real sense, therefore, these people become a needy mission field, toward which a Spirit-filled missionary or pastor cannot but feel some sense of obligation.

See MISSION (MISSIONS, MISSIOLOGY), EVANGELISM, CHRISTIANITY, EVANGELICAL, PROSELYTE.

RICHARD S. TAYLOR

PROTESTANTISM. The term *Protestantism* is applied both to the sum of the ecclesiastical fellowships and bodies which emerged from the 16th-century Reformation movement, and to the principles which are held in common by such groups.

The term originated in 1529 when the German Reichstag met at Speier. The princes and cities loyal to Roman Catholicism were in the majority and voted for a virtual abolition of Lutheran territorial churches and the perpetuation of the ecclesiastical status quo. Those forces which had already joined in the movement to reform the church responded with a strong *Protestatio.* The document was not solely negative, but rather positive. For both in the derivation of the title and the intention of its authors, the word was not limited to the raising of an objection; but rather, it indicated the witness or confession of that which was believed. From the title of the document, its supporters were called Protestants; and eventually the movement by which they were the vanguard was called Protestantism.

In its proper sense, Protestantism depends upon certain characteristic views. Perhaps the most important one of these is the belief that the Bible is the only totally reliable Source of authority in religion; tradition is only an aid in understanding the Bible. Closely tied with this is the concept of the right of private judgment, that in the absolute sense the individual is responsible to God alone and not to the visible church. Justification is by faith alone, and good works are the result of salvation rather than contributors toward it. The church is found where there are believers united in Christ as their Head—it is an organism more than an organization. The ministry is not spiritually different from the laity but only functionally distinct; each person has direct access to God through Christ but can also fill a priestly role toward his brother. The sacraments are limited to those established by Christ in the Bible; they are two in number (baptism and the Lord's Supper) and are visible proclamations of the Word.

In its broader sense, Protestantism is sometimes applied to all Christians who are neither Roman Catholics nor members of one of the Eastern churches. The term can be applied in a limited sense to groups which antedate the Reformation but which came wholly or partially to accept Protestant views. But it cannot properly be applied to groups with marked differences from the views summarized above, including the modern cults. Furthermore, there are those who reject their inclusion within Protestantism, such as some Anglicans (especially the Anglo-Catholic or high church party), the spiritual heirs of the Anabaptists, some Baptists, and some modern Pentecostals.

See LUTHERANISM, CALVINISM, ARMINIANISM, ANGLO-CATHOLICISM.

For Further Reading: Cobb, *Varieties of Protestantism;* Marty, *Protestantism;* Van de Pol, *World Protestantism;* Ritter, "Protestantism," in *Twentieth Century Encyclopedia of Religious Knowledge,* 2:914-20; Steinmetz, "Protestantism," *NIDCC,* 808-9; Tillich, *The Protestant Era;* Whale, *The Protestant Tradition.*

LEE M. HAINES

PROVIDENCE. The doctrine of divine providence is eminently scriptural, even though the word *providence* does not appear in Scripture. Christian faith is opposed to pantheistic confusion of God *with* the world, to deistic separation of God *apart* from the world, to fatalistic resignation of an impersonal God *over* the world, and to naturalistic exclusion of God *from* the world.

Divine providence may be defined as that activity of God by which He conserves and preserves His creation and cares for and directs all things to their final destiny. This definition indicates that there are three elements in divine providence, namely conservation, preservation, and government.

Conservation. Conservation is God's sustaining providence in the realm of the physical universe, i.e., in inanimate, or lifeless, nature. While rejecting pantheism, deism, fatalism, and naturalism, Christian faith affirms the immediate presence and agency of God in the physical world. The Scriptures are explicit in claiming the immanent power of God in upholding all things with His word (Acts 17:25, 28; Col. 1:17; Rom. 11:36). A strong statement from John Wesley illustrates the general evangelical position regarding conservation: "God acts in heaven, in earth, and under the earth, throughout the whole compass of His creation; by sustaining all things, without which everything would in an instant sink into its primitive nothing; by governing all, every moment superintending everything that He has made" (*Works,* 7:240). Even the so-called laws of nature may be regarded as principles of the divine activity.

Preservation. Preservation relates to God's work of providence in the animate realm, i.e., in the area of living things. Admittedly there is a mystery of life from the lowest cell structure to the most complex of all living creatures, man. There is the additional problem of past and potential extinction of specific forms of life. Yet the overarching activity of God in living organisms remains a biblical and Christian belief. The Bible is emphatic at the point of God's involvement in the totality of life (Prov. 30:25; Jer. 8:7; Ps. 145:15-16; Matt. 5:45; Acts 17:28; Col. 1:17; Heb. 1:3). Without the preserving will of God, the world would fall into nothingness in a flash (Brunner, *The Christian Doctrine of Creation and Redemption,* 152).

Government. In passing from the existence and development of lower forms of life to man, a change in the activity of divine providence is noted. Here God's relationship is not causative, as in conservation and preservation. Rather, God's providential care and government is moral. Providence is exerted in the form of motive rather than compulsion.

Because God has given the power of freedom to man and permitted freedom's exercise, neither a sinful act nor its consequences may be said to be God's act. In exercising His providential care, God may permit certain acts (2 Chron. 32:31; Ps. 81:12-13; Hos. 4:17; Acts 14:16; Rom. 1:24, 28); He may restrain or prevent particular deeds (Hos. 2:6; Gen. 20:6; Ps. 19:13); He may overrule the acts of men (Gen. 50:20; Isa. 10:5; John 13:27; Acts 4:27-28); He may establish the extent or boundaries of sin (Job 1:12; Ps. 124:2; 2 Thess. 2:7; 1 Cor. 10:13).

On the positive side the root idea of divine providence is that God rules over all in love (Rom. 8:28). The notion that within the Christian dispensation the idea of God's sovereignty is replaced by His Fatherhood is not valid. God is truly Father. God is also Sovereign, the Eternal Ruler of the universe.

See DIVINE SOVEREIGNTY, GUIDANCE, EVIL, CHANCE, DEISM, PANTHEISM, FATALISM, CONTINGENCY.

For Further Reading: Brunner, *The Christian Doctrine of Creation and Redemption,* 148-85; Bruce, *The Providential Order,* 231-310; Berkouwer, *The Triumph of Grace in the Theology of Karl Barth,* 163-65; Wiley, *CT,* 1:477-87.

DONALD S. METZ

PRUDENCE. Prudence is caution, care, and wise foresight in the face of only partially seen contingencies. This quality of mature character needs to be exercised in delicate social tensions, in the care of one's health and that of those for whom one is responsible, and also in matters of finance and business. Paul practiced prudence several times in quietly going elsewhere when violence against him was threatened. It was prudent for Jesus to send Peter fishing to get the tax money, rather than stand their ground in refusing to pay. While Jesus was not intending to encourage dishonesty, He nevertheless commended the unjust steward for his prudence in looking ahead. Jesus himself fulfilled the prediction: "My servant shall deal prudently" (Isa. 52:13). And certainly prudence was highly praised in the Wisdom literature, especially in Proverbs and Ecclesiastes; as, for instance, Prov. 14:15—"A prudent man gives thought to his steps" (NIV).

But the question of prudence can create personal tension, even become a theological problem. Jesus seemed to unchristianize prudence in the Sermon on the Mount (esp. Matt. 6:25-34). After warning against anxiety, He concluded: "'Therefore do not worry about tomorrow, for tomorrow will worry about itself. Each day has enough trouble of its own'" (v. 34, NIV). Is it not very imprudent to give tomorrow no thought at all?

While the basic principle enunciated in v. 33 applies to all, the passage as a whole has special relevance to those called to full-time Christian work, who will often be compelled to make choice between a prudent and secure life-style, and daring, even risky, adventuring for God. There is an abandonment to the work of God in total consecration which places security on the altar and literally lives by faith. Yet faith does not require foolhardiness or presumptuous carelessness—only the sober, calculated risks inherent in utter obedience. Harmon Schmelzenbach subordinated prudence to the need of souls, when he responded to the vision and went into the malaria-infested lowlands of Swaziland. That obedience cost his life. But is it not greater and higher prudence to gather sheaves at any cost than to protect self at any cost? Some are prudent only for time; God's people must learn to be prudent for eternity. This is really Jesus' point concerning the unjust steward: "'I tell you, use worldly wealth to gain friends for yourselves, so that when it is gone, you will be welcomed into eternal dwellings'" (Luke 16:9, NIV).

See WISDOM, SERVICE, FAITH, CONSECRATION.

RICHARD S. TAYLOR

PSEUDEPIGRAPHA. This term refers to a group of books not included in the biblical canon or the Apocrypha and written under assumed names, e.g., Abraham, Enoch, Moses, Isaiah, Job. They are of the Jewish origin and are generally dated between 200 B.C. and A.D. 100. A few oriental Christian groups have included them either in the Bible or among special writings thought to have importance for an understanding of the roots of the faith. The pseudepigrapha, however, have not achieved an acceptance anything like the Apocrypha. Not all of these writings are pseudonymous, but since most of them can be so classified, it is appropriate to employ the term *pseudepigrapha.*

The books included in the pseudepigrapha are: *Testaments of the Twelve Patriarchs, Psalms of Solomon, Lives of the Prophets, Jubilees, Testament of Job, Enoch, Martyrdom of Isaiah, Paralipomena of Jeremiah, The Life of Adam and Eve, The Assumption of Moses, Syriac Apocalypse of Baruch, Apocalypse of Abraham, Letter of Aristeas, Sibylline Oracles 3-5, 3 and 4 Maccabees, Slavonic Enoch (2 Enoch), Greek Apocalypse of Baruch (3 Baruch).* At Qumran, the following books were found and should be included in the pseudepigrapha: *Apocryphon of Genesis, Pseudo-Jeremianic work, War Scroll, Description of the New Jerusalem, Liturgy of Three Tongues of Fire, Book of Mysteries, Hodayoth, Psalms of Joshua.* Besides these writings there are numerous manuscripts or fragments with commentaries on biblical books, works on liturgical and legal matters, and wisdom pieces.

Categorization of these books, most of which exist in fragmentary form, is extremely difficult. They can be grouped, somewhat superficially, into Hebrew-Aramaic Palestinian and Greek Alexandrian writings, with language being the basic determinant. However, literary genre provides a more helpful classification, such as apocalypses, legendary histories, testaments, liturgies, and wisdom works.

The value of these writings lies in the insight they provide into the thought life of the Jews during the intertestamental period, and in the light they shed on the Jewish background of the NT. With the discovery of the Dead Sea Scrolls, which are dated in the first and second centuries B.C., information concerning the period immediately preceding the Christian era has been radically increased.

See APOCRYPHA, HAGIOGRAPHA, CANON.

For Further Reading: Charles, *The Apocrypha and Pseudepigrapha of the Old Testament;* Fritsch, "Pseudepigrapha," *IDB,* vol. 3; Pfeiffer, *History of New Testament Times.*

WILLARD H. TAYLOR

PSEUDO-ISADORIAN DECRETALS. See FALSE DECRETALS.

PSYCHOANALYSIS. Strictly speaking, psychoanalysis involves an investigation of the nature, structure, and dynamics of the psychic dimension of personality. The best-known architect and proponent of psychoanalysis was Sigmund Freud, an early 20th-century Viennese neurologist.

Some of the basic assumptions for psychoanalysis are: (1) all behavior is determined; (2) all behavior is meaningful behavior; (3) there is an interpenetration of biological and psychological dimensions of personality at the conscious, subconscious, and unconscious levels; (4) psychic energies are either locked or cathected by need objects of the person through drives, desires, or defenses; (5) there is psychodynamic growth from infancy to maturity, but this growth may be hampered or halted at any stage. Therefore, analysis attempts to take into account all personal history including origins, antecedent-subsequent behaviors and relationships, and repetitions; (6) the role of the analyst includes: listening, associating, and interpreting as a participant-observer; and (7) the purpose of psychoanalysis is to discover, define, and interpret psychodynamic processes of growth (descriptively, organizationally, and analytically) in all their uniqueness in order to facilitate more personally and/or socially acceptable behavior.

As in other fields, the term *psychoanalysis* has been broadened to include variant basic assumptions and consequent systems and procedures. Freudian psychoanalysis was antithetical to evangelical Christian theology. Any psychoanalysis should be investigated to determine its theological presuppositions before Christians seek to engage in it either as patients or analysts.

See REALITY THERAPY, ROGERIAN COUNSELING, PASTORAL COUNSELING, DEVELOPMENT (THEORIES OF).

For Further Reading: Bromberg, *The Mind of Man: A History of Psychotherapy and Psychoanalysis;* Schneck, *History of Psychiatry,* vol. 6; Wolman, ed., *International*

Encyclopedia of Psychiatry, Psychology, Psychoanalysis, and Neurology. CHESTER O. GALLOWAY

PSYCHOLOGY. Psychology is a disciplined attempt to explain, evaluate, and control behavior.

To explain behavior is to relate it to motive; the "why" of personal conduct. It is important to understand motive, since problem behavior will not be changed until causative factors are identified. Those factors generally include a combination of heredity, environment, and experience. However, one should not expect a given set of factors to produce the same behavior in all instances. That would be the kind of determinism which holds that certain parents are likely to produce children with criminal tendencies, that some environments foster problem conduct, that many people act wrongly because they do not know better. The problem here is an abject surrender to extrinsic and uncontrollable factors, a surrender which makes redemption unlikely if not, in fact, unnecessary.

To evaluate behavior is to relate it to values; judgments must be made about the acceptability of conduct in a prescribed context. Obviously, a moral order depends upon a discernible system of absolutes. Similarly, an ordered society survives by the definition and communication of behavioral standards whereby membership and acceptance are achieved in that society. And each individual must achieve that level of conduct where he gains self-esteem. "Happy is he that condemneth not himself in that thing which he alloweth" (Rom. 14:22). This "triad of morality," so described by David Belgum (*Guilt, Where Psychology and Religion Meet,* 17-34) is jeopardized by psychology's eagerness to replace God's immutable values with society's transient ones. Karl Menninger perceived this tendency in asking, "Whatever became of sin?"

Rejecting the biblical concept of sin, sinners have denied the wrongness of their deeds. Emboldened by false security of numbers, they have next pronounced their behavior normative and have accepted new justificatory terms for their conduct. So sin has evolved into situationism and hierarchalism. The former refuses to pronounce any evaluative judgment upon behavior apart from the situation in which the act occurred. It is left to the individual to defend as "right" his response to the demands of the situation. Hierarchalism goes one step further by supposing situations in which a traditionally "right" act could actually be the wrong thing to do.

In either case, the absolutes of God have been replaced by the judgments of man. And so there is no way to know God's approval, society's approbation, or a positive self-acceptance. To control behavior is to change it, caused by the introduction of prophylactic or therapeutic procedures intended to produce acceptable behavior. Most of us have faced the need to change our behavior in order to function in society. Functionality is always relational; the way we live unavoidably involves people. And the need to function in all three of the worlds Belgum describes—cosmic, social, and personal—requires a right relationship with God as well as our fellowman.

This concept of mental health is, however, one of bilateral relationships. Any technique which proposes to control behavior unilaterally is dangerous and immoral. Manipulation of this sort is common in totalitarian states, e.g., exercises in brainwashing and even some attempts to propagandize.

The biblical teaching on behavioral control is well stated in Rom. 12:2 where the Christian's surrender of his will to that of God produces a reciprocal and inestimable benefit—a total transformation (change) in life-style.

Psychology can be constructive in helping us identify the many causes which contribute to our behavior. It is helpful in requiring qualitative measures of conduct. It is useful in demanding functionality. But to change all that psychology may reveal as needing to be changed is the special province of the grace of God (2 Cor. 5:17; Phil. 1:6).

See MAN, HUMAN NATURE, GRACE, COUNSELING, PSYCHOLOGY OF RELIGION, PSYCHOANALYSIS, PSYCHOTHERAPY.

For Further Reading: Belgum, *Guilt, Where Psychology and Religion Meet;* Lutzer, *The Morality Gap;* Menninger, *Whatever Became of Sin?* MERNE A. HARRIS

PSYCHOLOGY OF RELIGION. Any study of religion is larger than just the Christian religion. To understand religious behavior, special research into the religious experiences of men has been made. This research results in the psychology of religion.

Often these studies have resulted in humanizing religious ideas, and making the supernatural to be only secular statements of distinctly personal interpretations of religion. Harold Kuhn sees most of the writers on psychology of religion at the end of the 19th century and the early part of the 20th century to be philosophers rather than true psychologists; "their systems elaborate deeply embedded assumptions." In them the objective quality of miracles, faith, and incarnation evaporated. Some struck at the supernatural origin of conversion and the reality of the divine origin of Scripture. Regeneration became merely a human, natural change (*Contemporary Evangelical Thought,* 224-26).

Psychology in religion is the study of the behavior and experiences of religious people. It is used in the two major subdivisions of psychology, namely, experimental and applied. "Applied" becomes pastoral psychology, while "experimental" is psychology of religion. The values of psychology in recent years are more readily seen. Some of the hostility felt earlier is disappearing (*Baker's DT,* 427-30).

Wayne Oates sees psychology of religion as "a concerted effort to bring these sacred and secular definitions of human life into dialogue with each other and to speak of God in both a sacred and secular manner." He further writes, "As such, the Psychology of Religion is a combined effort to appreciate the idea of the holy in human life and to keep the experiences of religious consciousness down to earth" (*The Psychology of Religion,* 15).

Great strides have been made in understanding the human mind, the emotions, and the reactions of persons under stress and when in real religious experiences. If the psychologists can keep an open mind, be faithful to the empirical method without assuming preconceived positions, and give critical evaluation of evidences discovered, then helpful conditions do result in such studies.

It is well to remember that observations of outward behavior of a person may be studied, catalogued, and analyzed. But it may be impossible to determine whether that outward action is prompted by the supernatural or arises only from human nature. A true biblical view will hold that the Holy Spirit does have a special place in touching the human heart in a distinct way.

See PSYCHOLOGY, SIN, REDEMPTION, GOSPEL, PASTORAL COUNSELING.

For Further Reading: Kuhn, *Contemporary Evangelical Thought;* Oates, *The Psychology of Religion.*

LEO G. COX

PSYCHOTHERAPY. Semantically speaking, psychotherapy is any healing of the psychic dimension of personality. Psychotherapy as a specific art or science seems to have begun most significantly with Sigmund Freud early in the 20th century. Because of the contributions made by Freud and his disciples to the psychoanalytic field of study and practice, many still tend to equate psychotherapy with "healing" of the unconscious part of the person's personality.

The field of psychotherapy has expanded to include such approaches as rational or cognitive, existential, perceptual, social-learning, and behavior modification in addition to the earlier psychoanalytic approach. Despite the approach employed or the basic assumptions held by the practitioner, there seem to be certain common elements involved which help to identify psychotherapy. Some of these elements are: (1) therapist has had some medical and/or clinical training; (2) the patient or client seeks relief from real or perceived disorder through the assistance of a therapist via interpersonal communication; (3) the disorder involved is perceived to be psychic rather than physical in both source and presentation; (4) there is a series of specified and circumscribed contacts between the sufferer and therapist; (5) there is at least one goal which results in enduring modification of assumption or behavior agreed upon and sought by both therapist and patient or client; (6) all behavior is meaningful behavior; (7) there is an undeniable respect for persons.

There appears to be general agreement that psychotherapy is one dimension of, or one approach to, the broader field of counseling. Psychotherapy is not necessarily antithetical to the Christian faith. However, for the Christian therapist there must be harmony between the basic assumptions underlying his/her theory and practice of psychotherapy and his/her theology of Christian ministry.

See COUNSELING, PASTORAL COUNSELING, MAN, REALITY THERAPY, PSYCHOLOGY.

For Further Reading: Frank, *Persuasion and Healing: A Comparative Study of Psychotherapy;* Oden, *Contemporary Theology and Psychotherapy;* Outler, *Psychotherapy and the Christian Message;* Roberts, *Psychotherapy and a Christian View of Man.*

CHESTER O. GALLOWAY

PUBLIC PRAYER. At its lowest acceptable level public prayer is group recognition of divine authority. This religious exercise may be despoiled by such evil motives as vengeance, pride, or unholy ambition. A newspaper reporting on a part of a religious service, said: "It was the most eloquent prayer ever delivered to a Boston audience." If such was the intention of the one who prayed, his purpose was evidently achieved.

Public prayer is appropriate in a thousand places such as grace before meals, dedication of buildings, formal or informal ceremonies, official gatherings, or other solemn or sublime occasions, as the reverent recognition of Deity. Either clergy or laity may offer such prayer.

Public prayer achieves its highest and holiest purpose in the biblical sense as one redeemed soul, most often the pastor of a congregation of believers, in his priestly function speaks to God for and with the people. In those moments of *koinonia* the one voice, speaking for all, pleads the merciful favor of God, offers reverential praise, reaffirms the congregation's loving commitment, and rejoices in the blessed warmth of God's surrounding love and grace. Only when the pastor has thus spoken to God for the people may he speak effectively to the people for God.

The language of public prayer need not be restricted to the classic "Thee" and "Thou." However, it certainly will avoid the excessive familiarity of folksy colloquialisms. And it must always be remembered that it is directed to God and must never refer to God in the third person.

The communion of the soul with God may permeate all of life and express itself in sighs, songs, groans, cries of distress, whispers of adoration, or well-remembered phrases from the Scriptures. But when one prays to God in and for a group, whether large or small, one should reverently and sincerely seek so to speak as to bring the eternal God and those immortal souls together in high and holy fellowship.

See WORSHIP, PRAYER, CHURCH.

For Further Reading: *The Book of Common Prayer; Baker's Dictionary of Practical Theology,* 385 ff, 400, 406.

JOHN E. RILEY

PUNISHMENT. This term indicates a penalty imposed for transgression of law. It commonly specifies any ill suffered in consequence of wrongdoing. The verb refers to the act of inflicting pain or chastisement for crime or fault. In the strict sense of the term we may discern a definite expression of public indignation, whereby the offender suffers pain or loss of honor. He suffers because he has perpetrated a wrong against another person, or society as a whole. Punishment implies a forefeiture in some sense and degree of personal rights.

Punishment is usually one of three kinds: corporal, pecuniary, or capital. The first involves suffering to one's body, the second involves the paying of a fine, and the third, loss of one's life. In ancient times punishment was only twofold and took the nature of either retaliation or restitution, i.e., compensation to the injured party for the wrong done by the offender.

Retribution for sin is a cardinal point in the teaching of both Testaments of the Christian Scriptures. There the primary object of punishment is to maintain, or restore, righteousness in keeping with the will of both God and the social order. In an ultimate sense, God will see to the punishment of sins, taking vengeance upon the ungodly and rendering to every man according to his deeds (Rom. 2:5-11).

The removal of sin's punishment is brought about by repentance and confession of one's sin (1 John 1:9), and personal trust in and commitment to the saving work and atoning blood of Jesus Christ, as the only basis for one's forgiveness.

On the civil level three justifications may be set forth for punishment: (1) as a deterrent to wrongdoing; (2) as a means of inducing repentance and rehabilitating the wrongdoer; and (3) as a guarantee against the repetition of the crime (in the case of capital punishment or life imprisonment).

See ETERNAL PUNISHMENT, RETRIBUTION (RETRIBUTIVE JUSTICE).

For Further Reading: DeWolf, "Rewards and Punishments," *ER,* 661-62; Greenberg, "Crimes and Punishments," *IDB,* A-D:733-44; Kennedy and Roberts, "Crime and Punishments," *HDB* (rev.), 189-90; Munsey, *Eternal Retribution;* Orr, "Punishment, Everlasting," *ISBE,* 4:2501-4.

ROSS E. PRICE

PURGATORY. This term means literally "a place of, or means of, purification." In Roman Catholic theology, it designates an intermediate state between death and eternal bliss where souls are made fit for heaven by means of expiatory sufferings. It is reserved only for penitent souls who, after departing this life, are cleansed from venial sins and the temporal punishment due their remitted mortal sins. Contrary to popular thinking, it is not a period of probation, but rather a cleansing process for those who are already partakers of divine grace, yet who, by reason of imperfection, are not qualified to enter heaven directly. It is for that mass of partially sanctified Catholics who have died in fellowship with the church. These, though their time of probation is past, and they are assured of heaven eventually, are not sufficiently pure and holy to be in the presence of God.

Such souls may be aided in their intermediate penance and suffering by the prayers of their brothers and sisters on earth, both lay and priestly. Hence, there have arisen in that church purgatorial societies—confraternities which have for their main purpose the assistance in every possible way—through gifts, services rendered to the church, masses provided for, and prayers by members of the priesthood—of these poor souls in purgatory.

The doctrine of purgatory was taught by such Catholic divines as Gregory the Great, Bonaventura, and Aquinas. It was professed at the Council of Lyons (1274), the Union of Florence (1445), and reaffirmed against Protestant denials at the Council of Trent (1545-63).

Although Gregory contended that this purgatorial punishment consisted of both absence from God and burning by fire, it was the contention of St. Catherine of Genoa that the fire of purgatory was nothing other than God's love, burning away whatever in us had not been cleansed away prior to death.

Protestant thinkers have raised four strong objections to the doctrine of purgatory: (1) It is without true scriptural basis, since 2 Macc. 12:39-45 is not accepted as inspired; (2) if Christ's gospel promises full forgiveness, then there is no need for purgatory; (3) moreover, the doctrine retains the necessity of punishment after forgiveness; and (4) it implies that the atoning death of Christ was not sufficient to purchase man's full justification and cleansing from sin. To these, the Wesleyan theologian would add a fifth objection on the basis of his belief in instantaneous sanctification by faith following regeneration and occurring during the believer's lifetime.

See HEAVEN, HOLINESS, PROBATION, CATHOLICISM (ROMAN).

For Further Reading: Bigham, "Purgatory," *ER*, 628; Boettner, "Purgatory," *Baker's DT*, 430; Harvey, *Handbook of Theological Terms*, 200; Wiley, *CT*, 3:230.

ROSS E. PRICE

PURIFICATION, CEREMONIAL. Basic to this fundamental religious concept is the belief that man must rid himself of any defilement which hinders his fellowship with God. It is necessary to determine the sources of defilement and the proper means of purification. In the OT this is largely a ceremonial consideration, but in the NT it becomes moral and personal.

In the OT any contact with that which is unclean results in defilement and requires purification. The following are sources of defilement: (1) unclean animals; (2) dead bodies; (3) leprosy; (4) bodily secretions associated with reproduction, and (5) idol worship in all of its forms.

The need for purification preceded the giving of Mosaic law (Gen. 35:2; Exod. 19:14); but a strong emphasis on ceremonial purification began with the establishment of Israel as the covenant people of God. The covenant ceremonial law provided for purification, including the idea of expiation for certain sins. This ceremonial law sets the standard for purification in the OT. While some religions regarded purification as being completely ceremonial and nonethical in character, for Israel purification had both ceremonial and ethical significance. These two considerations grew side by side in the OT. It is true that in the Psalms, Prophets, and Wisdom literature of the OT there is a tendency to emphasize moral purity; but the ceremonial aspect is not denied.

However, it is not until after the Exile that the Jews developed an elaborate system of rules for ceremonial purification deduced from those stated in the OT. Significantly, the largest of the six sections of the *Mishnah* deals with purification. Such a ballooning of ceremonial purification led Jesus to declare, "'You have a fine way of rejecting the commandment of God, in order to keep your tradition!'" (Mark 7:9, RSV).

An important principle of biblical theological thought is that God's people should reflect His character. This includes personal moral purity in response to the holiness of God (Lev. 19:2; 1 Pet. 1:15). The NT emphasizes moral and spiritual purification with little interest in ceremonial considerations. Likewise in the NT, impurity does not come from external sources, but is moral and from within. Purity then begins in the heart of man and extends outward to encompass the entire life. This moral purification is part of the redeeming work of Christ (1 John 1:7). Jesus' teachings on moral purification are well summarized in Matt. 5:8, where purity of heart is a prerequisite to seeing God.

In the NT, purification is thus personal and evangelical, completing the development of the concept begun in the prophetic and devotional writings of the OT. The external and ceremonial emphasis recedes into the background, and purification becomes the work of God in human hearts, so that man becomes partaker of the divine nature (2 Pet. 1:4). To deny the objective reality and impartation of this nature of holiness in favor of a mere imputation of holiness as our standing or position in Christ is to deny NT purification and to return to the OT concept of external ceremonial purification.

See TALMUD, CLEANSING, HOLINESS, IMPARTED RIGHTEOUSNESS, ERADICATION, HEART PURITY, PROGRESSIVE REVELATION.

For Further Reading: *IDB*, 1:641-48; *The New Schaff-*

Herzog Encyclopedia of Religious Knowledge, 3:386-90; *Encyclopedia Judaica,* 8:1406-14.

ALVIN S. LAWHEAD

PURIFICATION FROM SIN. See HEART PURITY.

PURITAN, PURITANISM. Under Queen Elizabeth I the place of the Church of England was established and clarified politically through the power of the English throne and doctrinally by the famous 39 Articles of Faith. However, the Church of England was still threatened from two sides. On the one hand was the faction that looked toward Rome, and on the other were the earnest Reformers who wished to go further in purifying the church from its Catholic overtones and leanings. By 1564 these were popularly nicknamed Puritans.

Many who had been exiled under Queen Mary had come under the influence of Swiss Protestantism and had returned filled with admiration for its thoroughgoing commitments. They were men with deep religious earnestness upon whom Elizabeth had to depend in her conflict with Rome. However, they drove hard to purge from the worship services what they believed to be remnants of the Roman church. In particular, the Puritans objected to the prescribed clerical dress, to kneeling at the reception of the Lord's Supper, the use of the ring in marriage as continuing the view of matrimony as a sacrament; and they strongly disliked using the sign of the Cross in baptism, believing it to be superstitious. Doctrinally, the Puritans were (for the most part) Calvinistic and insisted on the primacy of the Bible as the basis of authority.

Furthermore, the Puritans saw in the NT a definite pattern of church government quite unlike the Church of England. They came to believe in effective discipline maintained by elders. And they wanted ministers in office with the consent of the congregation.

By the end of Queen Elizabeth's reign all of the Separatists, or radical Puritans, had been driven underground or had gone into exile in places like Leyden in Holland, from which the Pilgrims sailed to the New World.

See PROTESTANTISM, WESLEYANISM, PIETISM (ENGLISH EVANGELICAL), WORSHIP, METHODISM, CHURCH GOVERNMENT.

For Further Reading: Sweet, *Religion in Colonial America;* Faughan, ed., *The Puritan Tradition in America;* Walker, *A History of the Christian Church.*

LESLIE PARROTT

PURITY AND MATURITY. The distinction between purity and maturity has been a basic postulate of the holiness movement. Failure to make this distinction, says Wiley, "lies at the base of practically every objection to entire sanctification" (*CT,* 2:506).

Purity is a matter of the heart, of present soundness, integrity, and rectitude; maturity is a matter of growth and development, in knowledge, strength, and skill. Purity is a condition of freedom from sin, of singleness of mind, of entire devotement to God. As soon as a believer becomes convicted of his remaining double-mindedness, the correction of the condition is both his privilege and obligation. His self-cleansing should be immediate (2 Cor. 7:1; Heb. 12:1, 12-15; 1 John 3:3), and his appropriation of the inner cleansing of the Spirit must be, and can only be, by faith (Acts 15:8-9; 26:18; Gal. 3:2-3). Time is not the purifying agent. But maturity and growth are correlates, both dependent upon time and process. Maturity is an advanced degree of understanding and establishment in spiritual things.

"No Christian is *cleansed* into *maturity,* nor do any *grow into purity,*" writes J. A. Wood (*Perfect Love,* 85). Wood is typical of the leading authorities of the last century, who carefully insisted on the preservation of the distinction between purity and maturity.

Some ambiguity appears in the writings of Wesley, who often seemed to associate Christian perfection with spiritual adulthood. However, this is a relative stage of attainment, which, while beyond spiritual infancy, is only the threshold of what shall be. When tracing the stages of spiritual progress, he reaches entire sanctification with the words, "in another instant, the heart is cleansed from all sin, and filled with pure love for God and man." Then immediately he adds: "But even that love increases more and more . . . till we attain 'the measure of the stature of the fulness of Christ'" (*Works,* 6:509). In his sermon "On a Single Eye" he declares that those with a single eye, who walk in all the light they have, "cannot but 'grow in grace.'" Such persons will "continually advance in all holiness, and in the whole image of God" (*Works,* 7:299).

Even more serious confusion is introduced by the substitution of "mature" for "perfect" as the translation of *teleios* by modern versions (e.g., NIV has "mature" at 1 Cor. 2:6; Eph. 4:13; Phil. 3:15; Col. 4:12; and Heb. 6:1 [*teleiotēs*]). Since *teleios* is more qualitative than quantitative in import, such substitution is at least questionable. Doubtless it is justified in Eph. 4:13 since maturity is the obvious goal. It is less certain in the other passages, especially Phil. 3:15, where it is more likely Paul is saying, "Let us therefore as many as are complete in our devotion to God be thus minded," rather than "Let all of us who have reached a level of advancement called maturity." Who is likely to step forward and assert, "I am among the mature"? The context describes the normal attitude of a Spirit-filled person, no matter how inexperienced and immature.

To confuse purity with maturity is to confuse things which are qualitatively different. To expect a young, inexperienced Christian, clearly sanctified wholly, to demonstrate full maturity, is to lay the groundwork for his frustration, discouragement, and perhaps defeat.

See HOLINESS, MATURITY, GROWTH, HEART PURITY.

For Further Reading: Rose, *A Theology of Christian Experience,* 230-35; Jessup, *Foundations of Doctrine,* 130-34; Wood, *Purity and Maturity.*

RICHARD S. TAYLOR

Q, R

QUIETISM. Historically Quietism has been an understanding of Christian perfection which emphasizes union with God not by asceticism and aggressive personal devotion but by passive surrender of the senses, intellect, and will to the divine. As a result God, not oneself, is responsible for one's life and actions. Avid espousal of this theory often led to both an antinomianism which disclaimed moral responsibility and an interior kind of holiness which separated one from concern for sin in any social sense.

Specifically the term may be applied to a school of Catholic mystics in France and Italy in the late 17th century. Miguel de Molinos emphasized passivity of the soul to such an extent that his enemies had his doctrines condemned by the church. The same fate fell on the French Quietist, Madame Guyon, whose emphasis was more on "surrender" than "passivity." Later Catholic scholars have largely exonerated the Quietists of any major doctrinal error.

Although their influence upon Roman Catholicism has not been great, the Quietists have had an enduring influence upon revivalism and Wesleyanism in particular. Molinos and Guyon together with other Catholic mystics have become strong witnesses to the experience of perfection in love in the American holiness tradition, especially through the writings of Thomas C. Upham.

See MYSTICISM, PERFECT (PERFECTION), PERFECT LOVE, PERFECTIONISM.

For Further Reading: Daniel-Rops, *The Church in the 17th Century,* 367-93; Upham, *Life of Madame de la Mothe Guyon;* Dieter, *The Holiness Revival of the 19th Century,* 53-56.

MELVIN EASTERDAY DIETER

RABBINIC THEOLOGY. Basically, rabbinic theology is the orthodox system of doctrine which Jewish people of pious nature have held from ancient times. The Maccabean revolt of 160 B.C. was led by priests known as Hasidim, "pious ones," who rejected Greek culture. In NT times, the proponents of keeping the ancient laws and customs were the Pharisees. Their spiritual heirs were the Rabbinites of the 8th—10th centuries A.D. and the Hasidim of the 18th century.

All these groups held to doctrines that were based on the OT and elaborated in the Talmud. Yet, rabbinic theology was more than doctrine; it was also a way of life. It was more than doctrine believed in by individuals, for doctrine and life were tied to national customs that were retained even during the dispersal of Jewish people around the world.

The basic doctrine of rabbinic theology is the existence of God as the Creator of the universe and all its creatures. All things were created out of nothing as an act of God's will. God is also the Ruler of the world and of the history of mankind. Extending from this doctrine is the belief in God as eternal and spiritual, omnipresent and omniscient. He is one God, and besides Him is none other. His resolutions are unchangeable, and His will is constant.

This theology also holds that God's will includes His intent both to punish the wicked and to provide merciful forgiveness for those who repent of their sins. He also wills to hear and answer the prayers of the penitent.

A second basic doctrine is the genuineness of the revelation of God through the Torah, i.e., the first five books of the Bible, known as the Pentateuch. The Torah was given to Moses at Mount Sinai and has been preserved intact. It is to be obeyed by applying its regulations to every aspect of life. Man must obey the law in freedom of choice and with wholehearted commitment.

After death, man continues to exist and will know punishment or reward for his deeds. A belief in the resurrection is common.

Rabbinic theology also believes that the Jewish people are the Chosen People and will be restored to their land by a Messiah who will come when the people are ready for him.

See JUDAISM, JUDAISTIC CONTROVERSY.

For Further Reading: Cohen, *Judaism: A Way of Life;* Markowitz, *Jewish Religion, History, Ethics, and Culture;* Heschel, *God in Search for Man;* "Theology," *The Jewish Encyclopedia,* 128-37.

GEORGE HERBERT LIVINGSTON

RACIAL SIN. See ORIGINAL SIN.

RACISM. This is the belief that some races are inherently superior to others, and the attitudes, policies, and practices which express this belief. Hitlerism with its doctrine of the Aryan superrace is a glaring modern example. The belief in the inferiority of the black races is an equally odious form of racism.

Yet not all adverse value judgments can be labeled racism. Distinctions can be made between advanced or primitive cultures which acknowledge a sociological retardation without the implication that the backwardness is due to inherent racial inferiority.

While racism has been a sociological phenomenon throughout human history, it has been encouraged by Darwinism, with its doctrine of the survival of the fittest. It has also provided a rationale for war. Arlie J. Hoover says: "Racism asserts that struggle, not cooperation, is the normal, yea even the desirable, state of race relations and that competition proves some races superior to others in intelligence, creativity, and cultural capacity."

Racism is not biblical. Over and over God reminds the Israelites that His choice of them was not due to any superiority in them, but that all nations might be blessed through them. The destruction of the Canaanites was not on racist principles but on moral grounds: their decimation was a divine judgment on them for their sins. While separatism was demanded, the purpose was not to safeguard them from inferior peoples but to prevent their religious corruption.

However, the Jews did tend to become infected with a racist mentality, contrary to God's intention. An example might be Peter's reluctance to eat with Cornelius. However, on the other hand, perhaps a purely ceremonial connotation should be seen in his "common or unclean" (Acts 10:14), rather than racism as such. At least Peter sincerely, though mistakenly, believed such social separation from the Gentiles to be a divine requirement; so his reluctance was prompted by a desire to obey God, not necessarily by a belief in his personal superiority.

According to the NT, the gospel levels all men, assuming for all races equal need and equal access to all the benefits of the Atonement, including the fullness of the Holy Spirit (Matt. 25:31-46; 28:19; John 1:9; Acts 2:17; 10:28, 34-35; Rom. 3:9-30; 11:16-23; 1 Cor. 1:24; Gal. 3:28; Eph. 2:11-17; 1 Tim. 2:1-6; Rev. 7:9-10).

Christian love alone is the antidote for the disease of racism. Love acknowledges all men as human beings created by God, all as the subjects of God's love and the objects of redemption. Yet love does not extinguish cultural differences, nor does love condemn them. While love creates a kindred feeling, and prompts equal respect to all regardless of race, it does not demand external uniformity. Furthermore, a very natural preference for one's own kind on a social plane is not in itself proof of either prejudice or racism; though love will gladly transcend this preference in the interests of community or evangelism.

See JUDAISM, MISSION (MISSIONS, MISSIOLOGY), MAN, GOSPEL, REDEMPTION.

For Further Reading: Hoover, *Fallacies of Evolution,* 70-72; Henry, *Christian Personal Ethics,* 397; Geiger, ed., *The Word and the Doctrine,* 413-18; DeWolf, *Responsible Freedom,* 203-8.

RICHARD S. TAYLOR

RANSOM. To ransom (verb) is to set free from captivity, slavery, or sin. The price paid or means of release is the ransom (noun). In the OT, ransom describes (1) payment to free a slave (Lev. 25:47-48; (2) restitution for injury or damages (Exod. 22:10-12); (3) redemption (buying back) of family property (Lev. 25:24-28); (4) assessments substituted for a man's life (Exod. 21:30); (5) God's deliverance of Israel from Egyptian bondage (Deut. 7:8; Isa. 51:11).

NT usage reflects a centering of focus on Jesus' death. The key text is Mark 10:45 (cf. Matt. 20:28). Here Jesus describes the offering of His life as "a ransom [*lutron*] for many" (similarly, 1 Tim. 2:6 and Titus 2:14). Word for word, this description echoes Isa. 53:10-11. A substitution is implied: God's Servant gave himself (as a guilt offering), He died for us (as sinners), in our place.

Through His death, we have been brought back to God, set free from servitude to sin.

To whom did Christ pay the ransom for our redemption? The Early Church fathers (especially the Greeks) were much exercised over this question. They interpreted the Cross as a stratagem by which God hoodwinked Satan in bargaining for the souls of men. Some theologians today (e.g., Kittel) argue the opposite conclusion: God was the recipient of the ransom. Most scholars dismiss the question as unbiblical. Certainly there is no hint that Christ's life was paid to Satan. We are reminded, however, that our ransom was costly (1 Cor. 6:20; 7:23; cf. Acts 20:28). The biblical emphasis is on the deliverance itself, from the thraldom of sin, not on a "deal" or transaction with a third party.

See REDEEMER (REDEMPTION), ATONEMENT.

For Further Reading: Jeremias, *NT Theology,* 1:292-94; Richardson, *Theology of NT,* 218-23; Kittel, 4:340-56.

WAYNE G. MCCOWN

RAPTURE. The term *Rapture* is used to refer to Paul's teaching concerning what shall happen to living believers at the second coming of Christ. In 1 Thess. 4:14-17, he explains that, in addition to the resurrection of the righteous dead, "we who are still alive and remain on the earth will be caught up with them in the clouds to meet the Lord in the air" (TLB). The Vulgate (Latin version) rendered the word translated "caught up" as *rapio,* hence *Rapture.* Two other passages are directly related to this idea, since they describe the change which will take place in believers at the Second Coming (Parousia): 1 Cor. 15:51-53 and Phil. 3:20-21. According to 1 Cor. 15:51 the Rapture is a mystery—that is, a divine truth which has previously been hidden but is now made known. Since OT writers did not envision a *second* coming, they spoke only of a resurrection of the dead. The fate of the living did not come within their purview.

In recent times, dispensationalist theology has developed the idea of a "secret Rapture." This relates to their view that there will be a definable seven-year period of intense persecution of the Jews, called "the time of Jacob's trouble" (Jer. 30:7). In order for this to occur, the Church must be removed from the earthly scene; consequently dispensationalists structure their eschatology to include a "pretribulation Rapture" which is secret in nature and separated, by the "Tribulation," from the Parousia. That this is a presupposition not explicitly taught in Scripture, honest dispensationalists freely admit.

All that one can legitimately affirm from Scripture itself is that the righteous, both living and dead, will be transformed at Jesus' parousia; and as a result of the transformation, they will be caught up to meet the Lord in the air and so be ever with Him.

See SECOND COMING OF CHRIST, TRIBULATION, DISPENSATIONALISM, PREMILLENNIALISM.

For Further Reading: Ladd, *The Blessed Hope;* Erickson, *Contemporary Options in Eschatology.*

H. RAY DUNNING

RATIONALISM. Rationalism holds to the supremacy of reason (*ratio* = "reason"). This means human reason is sufficient to solve solvable problems. Rationalistic attempts at discovering truth are often associated with the philosophies of such thinkers as Descartes, Leibnitz, and Spinoza. The common base from which all rationalists operate is just this: the self-sufficiency of reason; in other words, that reason is the source of all knowledge.

The school of empirical rationalism leans on sensory data for knowledge, and men like Francis Bacon, John Locke, John Stuart Mill, to name but three pioneers, built the foundation for what today we know as the scientific method. Without that method modern technology would be impossible. The scientist's laboratory is the most obvious symbol in our society of the empirical methodology used in the verification of truth.

Theological rationalism means dependence on what man's natural abilities teach him. Revelation is an impossibility; that is, no outside source can inform us. Naturalism, humanism, and liberalism share this with rationalism: man's native abilities constitute the one single instrument for arriving at truth and the structure of belief. We are here dealing with the doctrine of the full competence of human reason. The province for gathering data, then, is exclusively that of ordinary or so-called verifiable experience.

This leaves little place for any such otherworldly phenomenon as mysticism, not to speak of miracles or anything at all connected with the Bible's supernatural religion. Rationalism explains biblical religion developmentally; indeed, all religious experience is seen to grow from primordial beginnings to maturation, from superstition and animism to a sane and balanced grasp of reality.

Great men and movements in the history of the church have challenged naturalistically oriented authority. The 18th-century evangelical revival was one such thrust. Our own day is another such period: the advent of the Billy Graham movement; before that, the theology of

Barth and Brunner (their mission: to show the validity of revelation); the current dissatisfaction of man with his own ability to solve his problems; and the accompanying move toward biblical religion.

See REASON, REVELATION (NATURAL AND SPECIAL), HUMANISM, SUPERNATURAL (SUPERNATURALISM), RATIONALITY.

For Further Reading: James, *The Varieties of Religious Experience,* 73-74, 428; Lewis, *A Philosophy of the Christian Revelation,* see "Rationalism" in Index; Loomer, "Reason," *A Handbook of Christian Theology,* 293 ff.

DONALD E. DEMARAY

RATIONALITY. Man, like God, is a rational being (cf. Gen. 1:26). Rationality is the ability to reason, to know and communicate logically organized truth through the higher cognitive powers of the mind.

It is important to distinguish between rationalism and rationality. Rationalism regards human reason as the ultimate judge and only reliable means of ascertaining truth. It places reason above Scripture. Evangelicals believe biblical revelation must necessarily precede and supercede human reason. Since the Fall affected the mind (as all other faculties), man cannot know God rightly by the "unaided exercise of reason" (cf. 1 Cor. 2:4-16; 3:20).

We affirm rationality while rejecting rationalism. Man should love God with all the vigor of a redeemed mind. He should train the mind and be reasonable in all things. He should endeavor to interpret Scripture accurately, while refusing to permit reason to sit in judgment on Scripture as a higher authority.

Human rationality is limited: "I know in part" (1 Cor. 13:12). Some mysteries of life remain (Rom. 11:33) and await the unfolding of life yet future when we "shall know fully" (1 Cor. 13:12). The complexity of truth may appear self-contradictory to finite rationality (e.g., paradox). We must avoid being "wise in our own eyes" (cf. Prov. 3:7), and heed the command to bring "into captivity every thought to the obedience of Christ" (2 Cor. 10:5).

See REASON, RELIGIOUS KNOWLEDGE, FAITH, RATIONALISM.

For Further Reading: *Baker's DT,* 435-36; *ERE,* 7:370-73; Trueblood, *Philosophy of Religion,* 17-32.

J. WESLEY ADAMS

REAL PRESENCE. There are in general three doctrinal views concerning the Lord's Supper. The Roman Catholic view is known as transubstantiation, the view that the substance of the bread and wine are literally transformed into the body and blood of Christ. Luther's view is that of consubstantiation, viz., that the elements when consecrated remain substantially unchanged, but that the real body and blood of Christ are *present in, with,* and *under* the consecrated bread and wine. The unbelievers who take the elements are taking into their mouths Christ, but unto their condemnation, not their consolation. Thus, it is in the use of the elements by faith, and not in the elements per se, that Christ is present.

The view held most commonly among Protestants is that Christ is present in the Lord's Supper spiritually through the Holy Spirit, not in any sense physically. The elements of bread and wine are symbolic and the ritual is memorial in purpose and nature. This does no injustice to the confidence that the observance, when sincere and contrite, is also a means of grace.

See LORD'S SUPPER, SACRAMENTS, SACRAMENTARIANISM, MEANS OF GRACE.

For Further Reading: *Baker's DT,* "Lord's Supper," 330-32; Burtner and Chiles, *A Compend of Wesley's Theology,* 262-68; Wiley, *CT,* 3:189-208; *ZPEB,* 3:978-86; *Augsburg Confession; Formula of Concord.*

CHARLES W. CARTER

REALISM. Realism denotes the doctrine that *universals* (general concepts) have an existence which is in some sense independent of the *particular* things (individuals) that appear to the senses. The term has its origin in philosophical speculation but takes on technical meanings in such areas as politics, law, morality, education, and theology. The question whether universals have real and transcendent existence is especially important for the two main fields of philosophy known as *ontology* (the study of being and existence), and *epistemology* (the study of thought and knowledge). In philosophy, metaphysics and epistemology are logically interdependent.

Realism had early beginnings in Hindu thought many centuries before its appearance in the Platonic Academy and the Aristotelian Lyceum in Athens. The idea of Brahman as the neuter world soul, a monistic world view, and a pantheistic conclusion are its main features.

Greek speculation came under the influence of this thinking and with modifications found statement in the writings of Plato and his student, Aristotle. Plato's doctrine of real transcendent universals stems from the Socratic view that only through the concept, or universal idea, is it possible to obtain real knowledge. Thus *Platonic realism* is the doctrine that universals have in some sense an independent existence to their particular individuations which appear to us in sense perception. These universals are the *real forms,* and appearances are merely imperfect, transitory, and inadequate representations.

Aristotle, on the other hand, contended that these universal forms found their reality only in the case of concrete individuals and partook of no real substantial being apart from them. The objects of nature are but loci of determinate potentialities that become actualized through the activity of these forms. In short, the concept of "horseness" in general can only become real in the individual horse, such as "Old Dobbin" or "Old Paint."

Until medieval times the position of Plato, and more especially Neoplatonism as set forth by Plotinus, was the influential philosophy for Christianity through the writings of Augustine and others. But with the rediscovery of Aristotle's complete works and their influence upon the thinking of Thomas Aquinas, Aristotelianism became primary in Christian teaching. Not without considerable debate, however. For the speculations passed from transcendent ontology into dialectics and theology, touching off a grand controversy during the Scholastic period over the essential character of *genera* and *species,* as to whether they are corporeal or incorporeal, and whether they are separable from particulars or existent only in perception. This argument concerning the nature of *universals* divided thinkers into hostile camps and led to passionate controversies, throwing all society into intellectual and religious turmoil.

At this juncture most of us wish to raise the question, So what? But we must remember that these metaphysical *(ontological)* stances have marked implications for such theological problems as creation, God, man, faith, reason, the Trinity, the Incarnation, original sin, redemption, and Christian holiness. Space limitations do not allow explanations of its implication for each. The apostle Paul seemed to believe that the *unseen* behind things transient and visible is what partakes of eternal reality (2 Cor. 4:18).

So: *Realism* is the belief that a general idea in the human mind refers to something beyond the mind as real as things individual. It is the contention that the realm of *essence* (possible universals) is every bit as real as the realm of *existence* (actualities); and that the former is prior to the latter (versus modern existentialism).

See PLATONISM, THOMISM, REALISM AND NOMINALISM, MODERN REALISM, REALISM IN THEOLOGY, REPRESENTATIVE THEORY.

For Further Reading: "Hinduism," *ER,* 337 ff; Brightman, *An Introduction to Philosophy* (rev.), 271-88; *Person and Reality,* 190-98; Cornford, *Plato's Theory of Knowledge.*

ROSS E. PRICE

REALISM AND NOMINALISM. These terms represent an apparently endless debate going back to Plato (realism) and Aristotle (nominalism) over principles of theological discourse generally, and specifically over the nature of *universals*—by which are meant general ideas or class terms, the opposite of *particulars.* Only the context of the debate changes.

Medieval or classical realism was akin to modern metaphysical idealism, while nominalism corresponds to modern realism.

For theology, these terms became prominent in medieval Scholasticism, roughly A.D. 1000-1350, among scholars and schools struggling with concepts of faith and reason (or knowledge), seeking to interpret all of life in terms of theology. The presuppositions of Platonic realism (universal forms or ideas) had largely dominated theology, including Augustine's, until the revival of Aristotle in the 12th century, a fact which led in turn to the revival of nominalism in the church.

Realism held that universals, which transcend space and time, have real existence apart from all particulars—which are mere transient things expressing the universal form. Indeed, universals are the foundation of individual existence. They are *ante rem:* before the particulars; e.g., humanity subsists as an essence quite apart from individual persons.

Nominalism stated that universals are merely names or symbols describing individuals. They are *post rem:* after the particulars. Only particulars are real; e.g., humanity does not exist, but only individual persons.

There was a moderate realism; e.g., humanity exists as a structure embodied in particular human beings, but not independently. It is *in re:* in the particulars.

In connection with realism the contributions of John Scotus Erigina (c. 810-77) and Anselm of Canterbury (1033-1109), both in the Platonic tradition, were important. Roscellinus (1070-1125) was a thorough nominalist, while William of Ockham (1300-1350), 200 years later, espoused nominalism in connection with valid claims to knowledge on empirical grounds. Peter Abelard (1079-1142), Thomas Aquinas (1225-74) who attempted to synthesize Aristotle with Christian faith, and Duns Scotus (1265-1308) each represent different forms of moderate realism.

Certain tendencies or trends may be observed. Realism, inasmuch as reality transcends space-time experience, was congenial to the idea that "faith leads to understanding," rather than the opposite view. In doctrine, the idea of humanity as a single reality with each individual within the universal essence, made possible certain views of the origin of souls and of original sin in Adam. On the other hand, nominalism questioned the view of a universal church deriving its reality from the hierarchy, and opposed transubstantiation (that the real body and blood of Christ are present in the Eucharist) among other controversies. Nominalism stressed individual development rather than community or collectives. The emphasis on the data of sense experience gave impetus to the scientific method. Starting from particulars to solve problems tended to a loss of absolutes and to humanistic answers. In Ockham there was a separation of "valid" knowledge from matters of faith.

The extreme forms of either position tend to be destructive of rational thought and thus call for some mediating position.

See PHILOSOPHY, THEOLOGY, THOMISM, PLATONISM, REALISM IN THEOLOGY.

For Further Reading: Burkill, *The Evolution of Christian Thought;* Tillich, *A History of Christian Thought;* Gonzales, *A History of Christian Thought,* vol. 2.

ARNOLD E. AIRHART

REALISM IN THEOLOGY. As related to theology, the exponents of realism may be separated into three classifications.

Extreme Realism. Hinduism's speculation as to the nature of reality suggested that it is one single generic nature, partaking throughout of one common life-principle. With its idea of Brahman as the neuter world soul, it set forth a monistic world view and resulted in a sort of dynamic pantheism in both philosophy and theology. Brahman is the life principle and source whence all things proceed, by which all things are sustained, and to which all things return. Material existence in nature and man (individuals in matter) is a movement away from true reality. Concrete existence is therefore evil and illusory.

Salvation was deemed possible through knowledge of the identity of the finite self with the self of the universe. To this must be added knowledge of the total unreality of material existence. All is sheer illusion.

This salvation through acquired understanding called for a process of highly disciplined meditation under the most favorable physical conditions possible. Thus one might achieve the highest religious state when all desire for existence is gone and the finite soul is reabsorbed into the absolute real being of the infinite world soul. Later, Buddhism would refer to this reabsorption as *Nirvana,* using the Sanskrit term indicating "a blowing out, or extinction."

Holding as it does to a single generic nature in which individuals have no real (only illusory) separate existence, and are mere modes or manifestations of the one neutral world substance, extreme realism amounts to pantheism. Therefore it can have no place in *Christian* theology, and most Christian theologians dismiss its consideration with but a sentence or two. Yet we must acknowledge it as one of the three forms of theological realism. Shades of such realism reappear in the Scholastic period in the teachings of Amalric and John Scotus, who suggest that as the world of phenomena has come from God, so it will return to Him and abide in Him as one unchangeable individual eventually. We might surmise that neorealism's conception of *neutral entities* may be borrowed from Hinduism and its neutral world soul.

The Christian theologian will argue that substance is more than that which takes its stance in a subway below experience in the form or classification of neutral entities. Substance is "experienced efficient cause." It is what endures and what acts; it is not a blind abstraction; it has potentiality, and though it may be either simple or complex, it is dynamic reality. This is its basic essence.

Moderate, or Higher Realism. One of the chief exponents of this type of realism is the Calvinistic theologian William G. T. Shedd. He holds that species are individualized by propagation but partake of one unitary generic nature. He would allow that nominalism is true for nonpropagatable entities such as inkstands, which, though making up a general concept, have no common nature. Species, he contends, have a specific nature, an invisible dynamic principle, which is a real entity, not a mere concept.

It is the belief of this type of realism that the species has inlaid (inherent) in it all that evolves from it. It contains all the individuals that may come from it by propagation. Its specific nature has a real, not nominal, existence. When a specific vital substance is in view, then realism is true. When a nonspecific (inorganic substance) is in view, then nominalism is correct. Inkstands are not propagated from a common nature. The concept is but a general term partaking of no transcendent reality. Its only reality is in some particular model.

On the other hand a species contains a primitive, invisible, and propagatable substance. It is created as a single nature and exists as such prior to its distribution by means of propagation.

The chief concerns of theological realism are to explain: (1) the racial nature of mankind; (2) the racial nature of human depravity; (3) the racial nature of death as sin's penalty; and (4) the racial nature of mankind's redemption through Christ.

1. *Human nature is racial.* Man is the manifestation of the general principle of humanity in union with a given corporeal organization. Human nature as a general principle existed antecedently (chronologically and logically) to individual men. It is a *res,* an essence, a substance, with a real objective existence in time and space. John and Mary are the revelation and individualizations of this general substance which is the species or genus. Each is only a subsequent *modus existendi,* human nature being the essence of each.

What God created was not an individual man, but the species *homo,* generic humanity—an intelligent, rational, and voluntary essence. As such it manifests itself in a multitude of individuals. Thus each human is an individualized portion of the race. The species as a single nature was created and existed prior to its distribution by means of propagation.

2. *Human sin is corporate.* The sin of Adam and his generic complement, Eve, was the sin of this generic substance which thus became the subject and bearer of guilt and depravity. Numerically it was the same substance which constitutes each of us individual men and women.

Thus all men have sinned in Adam. "In Adam's fall, we sinned all." God contemplates all men as actually one with Adam in his sin. And since the whole race was involved in Adam's sin, the whole race is punished for that disobedience so that all must die. Furthermore, hereditary depravity in each human is truly and properly sin, involving guilt as well as pollution. These are passed on to successive generations through propagation. Shedd affirms that the soul is originated by psychical propagation even as the body is by physical propagation. So each man "received and inherited the corruption that was now in human nature, and subsequently acted it out in individual transgressions" (*Dogmatic Theology,* 2:89). "The individual man derives and inherits his sinful disposition from his immediate ancestors but originated it in his first ancestors" (94).

With the exception of C. A. Strong, not many theologians have subscribed to this higher realism.

Lower Realism. According to this theory individualizations always characterize seminal and germinal essences of their species, as they exist in aggregate in their progenitors. They have their germinal existence in a racial progenitor. So the contention is that the human race had its germinal existence in Adam. It therefore identifies Adam's posterity with himself in the one original (first act of) sin. This rudimentary existence of all men in Adam included the soul as well as the body.

The aim of lower realism is the same as that of higher realism, i.e., so to identify the offspring of Adam in a real oneness with him in the primitive transgression that they may be justifiably charged with a guilty participation in that sin. Thus the common guilt is charged to the account of seminal existence in Adam when he committed the first sin.

This lower realism is open to the doctrine of seminal guilt, guilt for all ancestral sins; and the denial of any share in Adam's personal repentance on the part of his offspring.

Whether the *souls* of all his offspring so existed in Adam is open to question by many theologians. Augustine was in serious doubt of it. Calvin rejected it, and in his rejection was followed by most of the Reformed thinkers. If in the nature of Adam there existed such an aggregate of individuals, then he must have lacked the unitary essence of a single personality. It must also be remembered that sin can be predicated only of persons.

The common reaction to this realistic involvement of all of Adam's descendants in his personal guilt is twofold: (1) No one believes that he acted thousands of years before he was born. To act before one exists is impossible. So unless one adopts the theory of multiple incarnations and the transmigration of souls, and the *karma* of one or many previous existences, he wants to reject guilt for Adam's transgression. (2) One wishes to ask why the descendants of Adam are responsible for, and guilty because of, his first act of sin and not for his subsequent sins. Shedd's answer is that his postlapsarian sins were mere violations of the moral law, not of the human race's probationary law (2:88).

Against theological realism it may be argued that the human race has no such cohesion in entity. Mankind is not to be regarded as a racial *thing.* It has no actual coalescence like that of a body of water where the individual drop is swallowed out of meaning and existence. This is not to deny that the race originated in one human pair, and carries a common human nature in all of its individuals. Nor is it to deny the basic fact of racial nexus and the disordered state of man's moral nature. Nor is it to deny the dictim of John Donne: "No man is an island."

The critics of theological realism contend there are better and more valid ways to explain: (1) the racial nature of mankind; (2) the racial fact of human depravity; (3) the racial meaning of death; (4) the racial work of Christ's redemption; and (5) the realization of the new race of those born from above by grace through faith.

See REALISM, REPRESENTATIVE THEORY, REALISM AND NOMINALISM, ORIGINAL SIN, TOTAL DEPRAVITY, BUDDHISM, TRANSCENDENTAL MEDITATION, NON-CHRISTIAN RELIGIONS, IN ADAM, MAN, NATURE, PLATONISM.

For Further Reading: Miley, *Systematic Theology,* 2:474-92; Shedd, *Dogmatic Theology,* 2:64-94; Tennant, *Philosophical Theology,* 1:219-56; Wiley, *CT,* 2:109-14.

ROSS E. PRICE

REALITY THERAPY. Reality therapy is a counseling theory which emphasizes responsible behavior. The leading exponent of the theory is William Glasser. In his book *Reality Therapy* he assumes that it is impossible to maintain self-esteem if one is living irresponsibly. He declares, "Morals, standards, values, or right or wrong behavior are all intimately related to the fulfilment of our needs for self-worth" (11). Thus he aims at teaching counselees to maintain a satisfactory standard of behavior, to correct themselves when they do wrong, and to credit themselves when they do right. Self-respect comes through self-discipline and loving closeness to others.

Glasser maintains that persons have only two essential personality needs—to love and to be loved, and to feel that one is worthwhile to oneself and to others. This may be reduced to a single indispensable need—to experience authentic love in a dependable relationship.

Responsibility is defined by Glasser as the ability to fulfill one's needs, and to do so in a way that does not deprive others of the ability to fulfill their needs (xv).

While there is much about reality therapy which may be useful to the Christian minister, the redemptive dimension is missing. Fallen man is not able to merit salvation apart from the grace of God (Rom. 3:10-18, 23; Eph. 2:8). The danger of this counseling technique is that, in its emphasis on the humanistic, to love one's neighbor as oneself, the vertical dimension may be neglected, to love God with all one's heart, soul, strength, and mind (Luke 10:27).

See INTEGRITY THERAPY, COUNSELING, TRANSACTIONAL ANALYSIS.

For Further Reading: Clinebell, *Basic Types of Pastoral Counseling;* Glasser, *Reality Therapy;* Hamilton, *The Ministry of Pastoral Counseling.*

NORMAN N. BONNER

REALIZED ESCHATOLOGY. This designates the approach to interpreting Jesus' proclamation of the kingdom of God which was proposed by the British scholar C. H. Dodd in his book *Parables of the Kingdom.* This interpretation of the kingdom of God in the ministry of Jesus sees the reign of God as fully present, i.e., realized in the person and work of Jesus. Dodd formulated his approach in reaction to the earlier position of the German scholar Albert Schweitzer, which was known as *consistent* or *thoroughgoing* eschatology. Schweitzer had argued that Jesus was a Jewish apocalyptic prophet, who announced that the kingdom of God was about to break into history in a climactic way. But history did not come to an end with the cataclysm which Jesus expected. Jesus had been mistaken.

Dodd sought to deemphasize any futuristic expectation in the teaching of Jesus. He was convinced that the eschatological dimension of Jesus' preaching consisted in the affirmation that all for which the prophets had hoped had now been fulfilled in history by Jesus' appearing. Dodd was strongly criticized for minimizing the futuristic aspect of the kingdom of God, and that criticism led him to modify his position. It is now the general consensus of NT scholarship that for the ministry of Jesus, the kingdom of God is in a real sense both present and future. The eschatology of Jesus is to be thought of as an eschatology in process of realization.

See ESCHATOLOGY.

For Further Reading: Bruce, "Eschatology," *Baker's DT,* 187-93; Evans, "Kingdom of God," *IDB,* 3:17-26; Hunter, *The Work and Words of Jesus,* 90-100, 122-30; Ladd, *A Theology of the New Testament,* 57-69; Perrin, *The Kingdom of God in the Teaching of Jesus,* 58-78.

HAL A. CAUTHRON

REASON. Reason is the power of the person to experience order in the universe and to bring order into his own thoughts and actions. When something is meaningful or makes sense, it is because it is appropriately ordered by reason. Thus the various forms of reason (e.g., logic) do not exhaust or reduce reason to themselves.

Often the term *reason* is used to refer to the human power to have knowledge by mediation, in which we infer that one thing is true because something else is true. By a series of necessary relationships we arrive at a conclusion. Immediate knowledge would be contrasted with mediation (not necessarily with reason, as defined above); immediate knowledge would be gained from sense experience, memory, and intuitions. Yet reason need not be reduced to mediation and eliminated from the immediate.

Reasoning is often contrasted with free association. The necessary relationship is opposed to the mere drifting from idea to idea.

Rationalism is the utilization of certain modes of reasoning as the only insight into truth. Empiricism (gaining knowledge through the senses) is usually contrasted with rationalism; in this relationship empiricism is rejected as confused or distorted knowing (cf. Plato). Attempts to employ all dimensions of the human capacity for knowing would regard either rationalism or empiricism as one-sided approaches to reality and truth (cf. Hegel).

The critique of reason by romanticism, mysticism, authoritarianism, existentialism, and biblical literalism reveals both the many-sided character of reason as well as the numerous problems which it poses to man's quest for truth.

Some people contrast faith and reason as if there is no basis upon which they can exist simultaneously in the same mind. Others think of faith as primary with reason included or of reason as primary with faith included. The problem of the relation between philosophy and theology is comparable to this, for philosophy employs reason and theology is based upon faith. If one observes the broader meaning of reason along with an equally intelligible meaning of faith, then to say that faith and reason require each other is very intelligible. It means that nonsense and absurdity cannot be believed; only that can be believed which makes some kind of sense or has some meaning.

Christianity calls for all a person's ransomed powers to be employed in the service of eternity; and certainly this includes man's reason.

See RATIONALISM, FAITH, HUMANISM, REVELATION, RATIONALITY.

For Further Reading: *Concise Encyclopedia of Western Philosophy and Philosophers*, 339-40; Harris, "The Power of Reason," *The Review of Metaphysics*, June, 1969.

R. DUANE THOMPSON

REBAPTISM. Rebaptism is the practice of baptizing adults who have already been baptized as infants. It was the practice of the Anabaptists in Europe during the period of the Reformation and has since been a mark of such groups as the Mennonites and Baptists. Rebaptism is in effect a protest against infant baptism or christening, and a denial of its validity. The underlying belief is that the sacrament of baptism was in NT times administered only in the case of adults becoming believers, and was intended to serve as an expression of a personal and voluntary commitment to Christ. A corollary is that baptism is unique to the NT and not the counterpart of circumcision, a rite administered to Jewish infants at eight days of age.

Basic to the believer baptism posture is the belief that repentance and faith (the new birth) are prerequisites of and are symbolized by baptism. Baptism is the sign that one has heard God's convicting and saving Word, that one's life has been buried with Christ, that one has arisen with Christ to new life (Rom. 6:1-11), has experienced the forgiveness of sins (Acts 2:37-39), and has become a part of the new community.

See BAPTISM, INFANT BAPTISM (PRO AND CON), SACRAMENTS, SACRAMENTARIANISM.

For Further Reading: Cullmann, *Baptism in the New Testament*; Jewett, *Infant Baptism and the Covenant of Grace*; Barth, *The Teaching of the Church Regarding Baptism.*

MARTIN H. SCHRAG

RECEIVING THE HOLY SPIRIT. While there is a unique reception of the Holy Spirit in the life of the believer subsequent to the new birth, it is the same Spirit whom we receive at conversion. Devotionally speaking, there is no difference between Christ and the Holy Spirit, for the Spirit is the exalted Christ (Acts 2:33; 2 Cor. 3:18). Theologically speaking, there is a real differentiation among the Father, Son, and Holy Spirit, but it is a differentiation in unity. This triunity of God's being means that whatever unique function one of the divine Persons has, the other divine Persons also share in the same activity. The concept of the Trinity does not mean three independent centers of consciousness within the divine life. Nor do the progressive stages of Christian experience lend itself to the notion that one can have the Son without the Spirit, as if the Christian life were made up of disjointed events.

Terminologically, we can speak of the deeper Christian life as the fullness of the Spirit without depreciating the reception of Christ in conversion, even as we can speak of the unique coming of the Spirit on the Day of Pentecost as a deeper revelation of God without depreciating the person of Jesus Christ in His earthly ministry. The Spirit of Pentecost is the continuation of the earthly Jesus. Even as there were stages in salvation in which God was progressively known as Father, Son, and Holy Spirit, so there may be stages in one's personal history of salvation in which one may know God successively as Father,

Son, and Holy Spirit. Yet it is the one and same God who is known. The dispensation of the Spirit signifies that the fullness of the Triune God has been revealed and that this fullness is given to the believer.

See DISPENSATION OF THE HOLY SPIRIT, BAPTISM WITH THE HOLY SPIRIT.

For Further Reading: Wood, *Pentecostal Grace;* Bultmann, *Theology of the New Testament,* 155; *GMS,* 484-88.

LAURENCE W. WOOD

RECONCILIATION. The Christian doctrine of reconciliation is derived primarily from four major statements on the subject in Paul's letters: Rom. 5:10-11; 2 Cor. 5:18-19; Eph. 2:16; and Col. 1:20-22. The term presumes on the one hand a previous enmity and on the other a subsequent friendship. Both of these need to be thoughtfully held in view if one is to appreciate the richness of biblical reconciliation.

The enmity is represented by Scripture to be in the mind and heart of man. Cain, the Pharaoh of the Exodus, and Ahab and Jezebel are notable examples of those who apparently maintained their enmity to the end. Yet to all of these, God extended gracious overtures of friendship.

When the references in Paul's letters are consulted, it will be seen that without exception reconciliation is linked to the atoning death of Christ. There is propitiation in the Atonement—the appeasing of the wrath of offended Deity whose just laws have been violated; but Christ's death was not necessary to initiate God's love, for the propitiation was God's own action. God's infinite love is never seen in Scripture to have ever wavered at man's sin, no matter how selfishly, cruelly, and inhumanely expressed. Rather, in the fullness of time, God sent forth His Son, whose sacrificial death redeems us from the guilt and wretchedness of sin's bondage.

Theology defines various aspects of the salvation experience and sometimes the order of events. We may differ in the way these are realized, but there is certainly justification and the forgiveness of sins. The rebel who once hated God because of His moral demands surrenders and exercises simple faith in the fact of Christ and His meritorious death. Reconciliation flows naturally and immediately. The new believer may not realize it, but by faith he has been adopted into the family of God. Glimpses of divine reality and glory follow, and love grows as God is revealed in the heart by the Holy Spirit. Friendship of the closest order now prevails, for the soul is "in Christ."

See JUSTIFICATION, REPENTANCE, ATONEMENT, IN CHRIST.

For Further Reading: Wiley, *CT,* 2:229-32; Banks, ed., *Reconciliation and Hope,* 104-24; *GMS,* 403-5.

MYRON D. GOLDSMITH

REDEEMER, REDEMPTION. Salvation is the end result of redemption; redemption itself is the means. The NT word (usually *lutron* and its family) refers to "ransom," payment for deliverance from some evil, "the price of release."

Love is the grand motivation for redemption, and it focuses in Jesus Christ the Redeemer, though God as Redeemer worked toward His salvation goal throughout the OT. "God so loved the world, that he gave" (John 3:16) is the cornerstone of the house called redemption. This cannot surprise us, for God's very nature is love (1 John 4:7-8; 2 Cor. 13:11). His love is universal, not confined to the Jews (John 3:16). That verse also lets us know His love is sacrificial; so does 1 John 4:9-10; Gal. 2:20; Eph. 5:2; and Rev. 1:5. The amazing truth is that He loves us though unworthy, and even when we are His enemies (Rom. 5:8; 1 John 4:10). The NT teaching is that His love is merciful (Eph. 2:4-5). More, the love that made redemption's plan complete saves and sanctifies us (2 Thess. 2:13).

An important personage in OT society was the *Go'el,* "redeemer," the nearest of kin charged with the responsibility of buying back an inheritance which had been alienated from the family line to which it properly belonged. Boaz, by redeeming Elimelech's property, and with it obtaining Ruth, prevented the line of Elimelech from terminating with the death of the two sons Chilion and Mahlon. In this respect also Jesus fulfills the type. Hs is our *Go'el,* our Redeemer, in restoring us to our proper owner and lineage.

The payment of the *lutron* was common in OT times and applied to anything that released a man from an obligation or debt of his own. But of special significance was the ceremony of the firstborn, traced to sparing sons on Passover night in Egypt. Customarily, the firstborn were given to the Lord and could be bought back for five shekels (Num. 18:16; cf. Barclay, *New Testament Words,* 190). It is worth noting in passing that *lutron* may also refer to buying a slave's freedom (sinners are slaves capable of being freed).

Mark 10:45 and Matt. 20:28 tell us Jesus is our *lutron,* our ransom to free us. Man, caught in the grip of sin and quite incapable of releasing himself, is rescued. (Thus one definition of salvation is "rescue.") Sometimes the figure implies or indicates rescue in and from a battle (sin and righteousness are at war).

Redemption is through the blood of Christ (Eph. 1:7), and one OT meaning of this term is "blood money." This redemption means the forgiveness of sins (Col. 1:14).

Redemption also means a new interpersonal relationship with God (Rom. 3:24). This new relationship means transformation and adoption into the family of God (Gal. 4:5). The old life is forgotten, the new life is present reality, and the future filled with possibilities. Note carefully: The plain NT view is that redemption is due entirely to Jesus Christ, His life in God, His works and teachings, His death and resurrection—the entire person and work of the Redeemer. The *lutron* He paid cost His entire life; we do well to remember this enormously significant fact.

Redemption carries provision for the future life too. True, the new life it enables begins now, but continues throughout eternity.

See RANSOM, SACRIFICE, ATONEMENT, PROPITIATION, EXPIATION, PASSOVER, RESURRECTION.

For Further Reading: Barclay, *New Testament Words* (*agapē* and *lutron*); Burtner and Chiles, *A Compend of Wesley's Theology,* 64 ff; "Redeemer, Redemption," *NBD.*

DONALD E. DEMARAY

REFORMATION. See PROTESTANT REFORMATION.

REGENERATION. Regeneration is the inward quickening of the repentant and believing sinner from spiritual death to spiritual life which occurs in Christian conversion. As such it is simultaneous with the other aspects of this religious experience, viz., justification, adoption, and initial sanctification.

The Greek equivalent of regeneration, *palingenesia,* "new birth," or being "born again," is used only once in reference to conversion (Titus 3:5); however, the idea is expressed frequently by other equally precise terms (Eph. 2:1, 5; Jas. 1:18; 1 Pet. 1:23).

The most incisive declaration of the necessity of being "reborn" is our Lord's well-known dialogue with Nicodemus (John 3:1-8). In this conversation Jesus laid down the major elements involved in what the Christian faith intends by the terms "regeneration," the "new birth," and "born again." In reply to questions concerning the kingdom of God, Jesus shifted the discussion drastically. "I say unto thee, Except a man be born again, he cannot see the kingdom of God." Clearly Nicodemus was being led to see that moral goodness, zeal for religious observance, and the performance of exact legal duties were insufficient to qualify him for the Kingdom.

Jesus' idea of the inner transformation which regeneration implies was not new in Scripture. Ezekiel, as God's spokesman, declared, "A new heart also will I give you, and a new spirit will I put within you: and I will take away the stony heart out of your flesh, and I will give you an heart of flesh" (Ezek. 36:26). The language is figurative; and Nicodemus' perplexed response to the words of the Lord in John 3:4, 9 suggests that our Lord's insistent words could only be understood in this way.

The NT unfolding of the meaning of regeneration begins with the assumption that man, by the Fall, has been placed in a state of sin—a state so negatively profound that he cannot lift himself from his predicament. The reply of grace to this is, that the Holy Spirit offers a change in human nature so decisive that the dominion of sin which is natural to man is broken, so that repentant and believing persons may serve God freely and walk in His ways.

The effective agent of regeneration is the divine Spirit, who moves quietly into the penitent and believing heart (which has been justified), to bring the inner life into conformity with the new relationship as child, as heir of God, and joint heir with Christ (see Rom. 8:16-17). Clearly this has elements of the mysterious about it; our Lord put this in words as He said: "The wind bloweth where it listeth, and thou hearest the sound thereof, but canst not tell whence it cometh, and whither it goeth: so is every one that is born of the Spirit" (John 3:8).

More formally, regeneration means literally "to be again" and involves the replacement of the old individual with "a new creature" (2 Cor. 5:17). This indicates at least an initial—though partial—restoration to the moral image of God which was lost in the Fall, plus the reestablishment of a relation of devotion and obedience to God. The "new man" is, in regeneration, made alive, given new patterns of incentive and motivation, and enabled to walk in "newness of life" (Rom. 6:4). The felt reality of this produces the response of the human spirit which is a confirming counterpart of the witness of the Spirit.

See NEW BIRTH, CONVERSION, FIRST WORK OF GRACE, JUSTIFICATION.

For Further Reading: "Conversion," *Baker's DCE;* "Regeneration," *ZPEB;* Wiley, *CT,* 2:402-39.

HAROLD B. KUHN

REINCARNATION. This is the reinhabitation of a personal spirit, released by death from its former house, in another bodily form. The spirit of a human may return as another human or as an animal. Whether the reincarnation is an improvement or a downgrading depends on Karma, or just fate. The doctrine is variously called Metempsychosis, Transmigration, or Rebirth. It is congenial to Platonism, which supposes an extreme dichotomy between spirit (or soul) and body; but in origin it is more Eastern than Western. It underlines the incubus of animal reverence in Hinduism, since the animal might be an ancestor. The teaching was first systematically taught in the Upanishads, a collection of sacred writings in Hinduism, most of which antedated Plato. The supposed purpose of reincarnation is the gradual purification of the soul, as it passes through higher and higher forms, until it reaches Nirvana. The doctrine is thoroughly pagan and non-Christian. The Bible teaches that "it is appointed for men to die once, and after this comes judgment" (Heb. 9:27, NASB). The creation of man was unique, constituting him a unitary body-soul being which cannot be compounded with lower forms of being. This life is man's sole probation. His redemption is not by Karma but by the blood of Christ.

See NON-CHRISTIAN RELIGIONS, DUALISM, THEOSOPHY, FATALISM.

For Further Reading: Stilson, *Leading Religions of the World;* Parrinder, *A Dictionary of Non-Christian Religions.*

RICHARD S. TAYLOR

REJOICE. See JOY.

RELATIONAL THEOLOGY. This is sometimes referred to as a "theology of relationships." The category of relationship is seen as the locus of religious reality. The concept is that of persons in interaction with each other. Sin is wrong interaction; holiness is right interaction. Christian holiness therefore consists of right relationships with God, other persons, and with oneself; some would insist on the necessity of right relationship with one's environment also (the ecological dimension). Love is seen as the central note of Christianity, since love is the attitude which makes right relationships possible.

This is a dynamic approach to Christian holiness, which moves away from the Calvinistic imputed righteousness, which is a legal rightness through an objective atonement, but which falls short of personal relationships which are truly holy. The approach also moves away from the kind of Wesleyanism which defines holiness as a subjective state of the nature, wrought by a work of grace, and which may also fall short of expressing itself in terms of relationships. Relational theology would insist that the focus of reality is not in a subjective experience but in the degree to which the experience affects the relationships.

This emphasis on the relational nature of biblical holiness is essential to the preservation of a true moral sense; i.e., that holiness must be moral to the core, and that any understanding of holiness which obscures the moral dimension is false. By "moral holiness" is meant a relationship with God in which the person is never a mere pawn, but is actively and intensely committed to Christ in loving obedience and trust. Every nerve is stretched in the quest for God's best (cf. Phil. 3:13-14, NASB). By implication, this insistence on preserving the moral nature of holiness constitutes a repudiation of any mechanical system of security, which severs sonship from fellowship, legal relationship from loving relationship, and acceptance from obedience.

Relational theology becomes aberrant when its advocates impress upon it the categories and concepts of process theology. This results in a failure to see that the effecting of right relationships, and their maintenance, can only be accomplished by real subjective changes in the nature of the relator. For the human relator is sinful by nature and by choice, and is hence incapable of right relationships with either God, man, or himself. It is his sinfulness which is the moral impediment to harmonious relationships. If the relationalist replies that disharmonious relationships do not result from sinfulness but constitute the sinfulness, it becomes necessary to remind him that deeply rooted in orthodox Wesleyanism is the doctrine of original sin, the need for a real change called regeneration, and a deeper real change called sanctification—and that these changes become not only the means by which right relationships are effected but the conditions for those relationships.

A concept of either holiness or sinfulness which is exclusively relational cannot claim Wesley for support. In his classic debate with the Unitarian John Taylor, speaking of original sin as an inbred proclivity of the nature, he exclaimed, "Believe this, and you are so far a Christian. Deny it, and you are a heathen still." To Taylor's premise that "righteousness is right action," Wesley replied, "Indeed it is not. Here . . . is your fundamental mistake. It is a right state of mind; which differs from right action, as the cause does from the effect" (*Works,* 9:342).

Right relationships then are the goal of grace, and the touchstone of religious validity. But they presuppose the atonement of Christ, as the necessary moral ground for reconciliation with God; and they also presuppose real, substantive changes in the human relators.

That Jesus himself made process dependent upon state and becoming dependent upon being, instead of the other way around, is clear from such passages as: "You will know them by their fruits. Grapes are not gathered from thorn bushes, nor figs from thistles, are they? Even so, every good tree bears good fruit; but the rotten tree bears bad fruit. A good tree cannot produce bad fruit, nor can a rotten tree produce good fruit" (Matt. 7:16-18, NASB; cf. 12:33-35). The state of goodness does not exclude process but controls it. A good tree can keep on growing and producing, but it will not thereby be becoming a good tree; the production will only express what it already is. No amount of growth or fruit bearing will turn a bad tree into a good one. Likewise, no amount of growth or time will transform a sinful heart into a pure heart. Relationships are objective states which depend upon subjective conditions.

See SANCTIFICATION, NATURE, HUMAN NATURE, SUBSTANCE (SUBSTANTIVE), NEW COVENANT, PROCESS THEOLOGY, WESLEYAN SYNTHESIS.

For Further Reading: Wood, *Pentecostal Grace;* Wynkoop, *A Theology of Love;* Wiley, *CT,* 2:440-96; Turner, *Christian Holiness,* 98 ff; Purkiser, *Sanctification and Its Synonyms;* Chapman, *The Terminology of Holiness;* Grider, *Entire Sanctification,* 20-24; Wesley, *Works,* 9:192-465; Henry, *Christian Faith and Modern Theology,* 92.

RICHARD S. TAYLOR

RELIGION. There is no universally accepted definition of the term "religion." Even the origin of the Latin word *religio* is disputed. Cicero connected it with *religere* as meaning attention to divine things. Lactantius and Augustine saw it as derived from *religare* with the meaning "to bind back," thus representing religion as the ground of obligation. The term "religion" came into English usage from the Vulgate, where *religio* is used to translate the Greek word *thrēskeia* in Acts 26:5 and Jas. 1:26-27. In these passages *thrēskeia* refers to external religious devotion, while a fourth occurrence in Col. 2:18 is translated "worship."

Contemporary Usage. In modern times religion is approached from a bewildering variety of viewpoints. It means one thing to the anthropologist, another to the sociologist, another to the psychologist, another to the Marxist, another to the mystic, another to the Buddhist, and yet another to the Jew or the Christian. For the humanist, a definition of religion relates to the logical development of some aspect of human culture which becomes an object of intensive investigation, and "God" is reduced to an idea which occurs within the total complex. For the religious person, a definition of religion involves a description of the individual's particular religious creed.

Definitions and Characteristic Features. Among the philosophical comprehensive definitions of religion, the following few are representative. Schleiermacher believed the essence of religion was "the feeling of an absolute dependence"; Huxley, "those things, events, and ideas which arouse the feeling of sacredness"; Kant, "the observance of moral law as a divine institution"; J. G. Frazer, "a propitiation or conciliation of powers superior to man which are believed to direct and control the course of Nature and of human life"; Tillich, the dimension of depth in all of man's life functions, being "ultimately concerned" about the ultimate.

However, the *Encyclopedia of Philosophy* regards all such definitions inadequate. It offers instead the following list of "religion-making characteristics" as criteria for defining religion.

1. Belief in supernatural beings (gods).
2. A distinction between sacred and profane objects.
3. Ritual acts focused on sacred objects.
4. A moral code believed to be sanctioned by the gods.
5. Characteristically religious feelings (awe, sense of mystery, . . . guilt, adoration) . . . which are connected in idea with the gods.
6. Prayer and other forms of communication with gods.
7. A world view, or a general picture of the world as a whole and the place of the individual therein. . . .
8. A more or less total organization of one's life based on the world view.
9. A social group bound together by the above (Alston, "Religion," *Encyclopedia of Philosophy,* 7:141-42).

A religion need not embody all these features, but when enough of them "are present to a sufficient degree, we have a religion" (ibid., 142).

Conclusions. First, the universal inclination to religion among all nations and in all conditions suggests that man is religious by nature. Since human nature is marred by sin, however, the religion of unregenerated humanity is one of form without authentic divine content. Second, human religion represents man's attempt to enter into communion with God on man's own terms (Karl Barth). Thus religion is not good in itself; it bears the marks of the Fall. Religion crucified

Christ, even good religion as far as religion goes. Third, although true knowledge of God is inaccessible in human religion because of man's finitude and sinfulness, God has revealed himself to man by word and deed over a long span of history, climaxed by the incarnation of the eternal *Logos.* The total revelation is carefully preserved for humankind in the Bible. Fourth, the reason the term "religion" seldom occurs in the Bible is due to the nature of humanistic, nonrevelatory religion which "is itself alien to the core of biblical thought" (Gealey, "Religion," *IDB*).

See CHRISTIANITY, NON-CHRISTIAN RELIGIONS.

For Further Reading: Alston, "Religion," *Encyclopedia of Philosophy,* 7:140-45; Beckwith, "Religion," *The New Schaff-Herzog Encyclopedia of Religious Knowledge,* 9:453-57; Gealey, "Religion," *IDB;* Hick, *Philosophy of Religion,* esp. 81-90. J. WESLEY ADAMS

RELIGIOUS EDUCATION. See CHRISTIAN EDUCATION.

RELIGIOUS KNOWLEDGE. Since 1918, the most important debate in theology has been whether theological language can have as its base a philosophical metaphysical system (as both Aquinas and Whitehead argued) or whether "it must derive entirely from faith in relation to revelation, and so be formed from the biblical Word," as the neoorthodox and some neoevangelicals and Wesleyans have insisted. (It is, of course, dependent upon how "biblical Word" is interpreted.)

The question is important epistemologically when the question is asked, "How do I know the *truth* of religious belief—by faith or by metaphysical speculation?" It is important to the evangelical to understand how he can transcend the confinements of a secular world view which can exclude him from a valid knowledge of God.

The initial consideration is that knowledge unaided by a special help from God is limited. This limitation is never overcome. The consequences of man's limitations in knowledge are recognized by every serious philosophy and theology. That limitation, according to both Catholic and Protestant thinkers, is grounded not only in lack of time and opportunity, but in the nature of man's powers clouded by sin. Thus revelation is necessary as an aid to knowledge. We are incompetent in ourselves but dependent upon the definitive Word who is revealed through Christ in the Scriptures as a loving and concerned Heavenly Father.

Man is free by grace to ignore or respond to those revelatory acts—to "recognize or fail to recognize His presence." God always leaves room in that "fateful freedom" to respond in faith. Thus faith, as a gift of God's grace, is a correlate of freedom. While the validity of religious knowledge attained by faith may not be demonstrable to the empiricist, its certainty is assured by the inner witness of the Holy Spirit.

See KNOWLEDGE, THEOLOGICAL LANGUAGE.

For Further Reading: Clark, "Apologetics," *Contemporary Evangelical Thought,* ed. Henry, 137-61; Ramsey, *Religious Language;* Gilkey, *Naming the Whirlwind: The Renewal of God-Language.* OSCAR F. REED

REMARRIAGE. See DIVORCE.

REMISSION OF SINS. See FORGIVENESS.

REMNANT. From the Hebrew root *shr,* meaning "what is left behind after a process of elimination," there are derived two nouns, *shear* and *sheerith,* that can be translated as "remnant," "posterity," "rest," and "residue." Sometimes they are used in the OT to designate material things that are left behind: a city (1 Chron. 11:8), money (2 Chron. 24:14), trees (Isa. 10:19), timber (44:17), etc. In a number of passages these two nouns refer to a "remnant" of people remaining after a disaster; e.g., giants of Bashan (Josh. 12:4), Amorites (2 Sam. 21:2), Amalekites (1 Chron. 4:43), Syrians (Isa. 17:3), and Israelites (Neh. 10:28).

A more distinctive understanding of "remnant" began with the ministry of Isaiah, with *shear* and *sheerith* being used as technical terms for Israelites who survive a national disaster. From this understanding of a residue remaining after a calamity, there emerged what might be termed the "remnant doctrine." Very significantly Isaiah named his son Shear-jashub, meaning "a remnant shall return" (Isa. 7:3). This testimonial name was a prophetic witness to Judah that although the nation's sin would eventually result in exile as a divine judgment, yet, in the mercy of God, a remnant would return. This remnant is the "holy seed" (Isa. 6:13; cf. Ezek. 9:8), and the hope of its survival continued throughout the Exile and into postexilic times.

Jeremiah and Ezekiel saw the hope of Israel in this minority (e.g., Jer. 24:4-7; Ezek. 6:7 ff). God's love for His people was such that this remnant would be gathered from the nations, cleansed from their sinful ways, and formed into the nucleus of a new Israel (e.g., Isa. 4:2-6; Amos 9:8-15; Mic. 2:12; 4:6-8; 5:7-8; Ezek. 36:24-32; Zech. 8:12; 13:9; Hag. 1:12, 14). The remnant hope persisted through the intertestamental period (see, e.g., Enoch 83:8; 2 Esd. 12:34; 13:48; 2 Bar. 40:2), and there are echoes of it in the Gospels (e.g., Matt. 3:9; 22:14; Luke 12:32; John 1:11).

From many passages in his letters, it is difficult to escape the conclusion that Paul saw the Church fulfilling the function of the promised faithful remnant (Rom. 9:24-33; 11:1-12; Gal. 3:7-14; 6:16). In Jas. 1:1, the scattered Christian Church is identified as the true Israel, and Peter describes the Church as "God's own people" (1 Pet. 2:9). Thus the "remnant doctrine" of the OT finds its ultimate fulfillment in the Church of Christ, i.e., in all those, Jews and Gentiles, who, by grace, are in "the household of God" (Eph. 2:18-22).

See PROMISES (DAVIDIC), RESTORATION OF ISRAEL, CHURCH.

For Further Reading: Campbell, "God's People and the Remnant," *Scottish Journal of Theology* 111 (1950), 78-85; Heaton, "The Root SH'R and the Doctrine of the Remnant," *Journal of Theological Studies* (1952), 27-39.

HERBERT MCGONIGLE

REMONSTRANTS. This referred initially to the 42 followers of James Arminius, led by John Uitenbogaert, who signed the *Remonstrance* that was presented to the governing body of the United Netherlands at the Hague in 1610. This document, the Remonstrance, "remonstrated" against the Calvinistic teachings on total depravity, unconditional election, limited atonement, irresistible grace, and the perseverance of believers. It also sought the privilege of continuing to teach Arminianism in Holland. The term later came to be a kind of synonym for the Arminians, and it is in the name of a still-existing denomination, in Holland, which dates back to the time of the first Remonstrants: The Remonstrant Brotherhood.

See ARMINIANISM, CALVINISM, TOLERANCE.

J. KENNETH GRIDER

REMORSE. See REPENTANCE.

REPENTANCE. The word *metanoia,* "repentance," means a change of mind. The Bible acknowledges repentance in God as well as man. God's repentance means sorrow or regret followed (usually) by positive action (Gen. 6:6; Exod. 32:14; Deut. 32:36; Jer. 18:8). This does not contradict the doctrine of the divine immutability. God's unchanging law is that His mercy is toward them that love and obey Him, and His judgments toward them that disobey Him. Which of these attitudes God assumes at a given moment depends on man (cf. Rom. 11:20-23). When a person, as e.g., King Saul, disappoints God, God is sorry and alters both attitude and action in relation to that person (1 Sam. 15:11, 23).

In respect to man's repentance, it can be said to be evangelical if it has in it three elements.

The first is intellectual. By it the sinner comes unto "the knowledge of sin" (Rom. 3:20) and its consequences.

The second element is emotional. It is a genuine sorrow for sin. It must be deeper than sorrow at being caught ("worldly sorrow"). It must be "godly sorrow," sorrow because one has sinned against God (2 Cor. 7:9-10).

The third element in evangelical repentance is volitional, a change of the will and purpose. It is a turning from sin unto God, the heart crying out for pardon and cleansing (Ps. 51:7, 10).

The importance of repentance is underlined by John the Baptist. In his ministry, which was to prepare the way for the Lord, he made repentance the theme. Jesus himself said, "Except ye repent, ye shall all likewise perish" (Luke 13:3, 5).

Although evangelical repentance is basically an act of man, it is impossible apart from the work of the Holy Spirit (Acts 5:31; 11:18; Rom. 2:4; 2 Tim. 2:25; Heb. 12:17).

Repentance is antecedent to and a preparation for salvation. It is necessary if God is to forgive (Acts 2:37-38; 11:18; 20:21). It involves confession and restitution (Exod. 22:1-4; Luke 19:8-9; 1 John 1:9).

See SALVATION, FAITH, WORKS, RESTITUTION.

For Further Reading: Purkiser, ed., *Exploring Our Christian Faith,* 280-83; Turner, "Repentance," *ZPEB,* 62-64.

W. RALPH THOMPSON

REPRESENTATIVE THEORY. This is one of the views about the so-called transmission of original sin from Adam to the rest of us humans. It views Adam as the federal head of the race, and therefore as chosen by God as our representative. When he sinned, we suffered a detriment because he was representing us; and he represented us badly by willfully disobeying God. This is the view held by such theologians as James Arminius and John Wesley. It is contrasted with the realistic mode view of Augustine and others, that we are now in original sin because we actually and realistically participated in Adam's sin, by being racially "in his loins" at the time. Both theories are in great part attempts to interpret what Paul means in Rom. 5:12-21. The realistic mode view suits the view of unconditional predestination because, then, God, in predestinating some individuals to eternal hell before they were born, would be decreeing in that way, based on their actual guilt for participating realistically in Adam's transgression.

The representative theory suits Arminianism's viewing predestination as conditioned on each person's accepting or rejecting Christ during his sojourn upon the earth. It admits that a certain guilt accrued to all of us because of Adam's sin, but states on the basis of Rom. 5:15-19 that God removed this guilt in a blanket way because of Christ. According to this passage, this is the "free gift" which passes upon everyone. This is why Wesley, Wiley, and others have taught that original sin inclines us to acts of sin, but that, without the acts, original sin alone would not occasion anyone's entering into eternal hell.

See ORIGINAL SIN, PREVENIENT GRACE, REALISM IN THEOLOGY, IN ADAM.

For Further Reading: Wiley, *CT*, 2:107-18.

J. KENNETH GRIDER

REPROBATION. Reprobation is the ultimate state of one who has been controlled completely by a reprobate mind. Such a person has so thoroughly and willfully rejected the overtures of a seeking God in Christ Jesus as to have placed himself purposefully outside the grasp of salvation. His mind is so twisted and distorted by the saturation of sin as to be unable to perceive anything but evil (Rom. 1:28).

The word "reprobate" is used in Jer. 6:30 and Heb. 6:8 in reference to a testing, as in determining the purity of metal, coins, or soil. If the testing indicated the sample was valueless, it was reprobate, i.e., rejected. The apostle Paul uses the idea of testing and proving as regards the message he preached (2 Cor. 13:5-7). He also said that he exercised discipline over his body to avoid becoming a castaway (reprobate, 1 Cor. 9:27).

The harsh usage of the term (Rom. 1:28; 2 Tim. 3:8; Titus 1:16) implies a deliberate rejection and distortion of truth. Falsehood is not only entertained but promoted. The mind of the reprobate is perverted to the point that the normal and beautiful are twisted into that which is depraved, abnormal, and ugly. This condition is the final dreadful result of continual evil choices.

See SIN, UNBELIEF, UNPARDONABLE SIN.

For Further Reading: *HDNT*, 3:318.

RONALD E. WILSON

RESENTMENT. See HARDNESS OF HEART.

RESPECT. Respect is the honor, deference, and courtesy we show to persons, places, customs, traditions, institutions, or offices. It may also be a subjective perception of worth. We may (and should) act respectfully even though we do not admire the person or object. We may respect a spouse, a minister, or an officer of the law, out of deference to his or her relationship to us, or their office, even when we cannot inwardly respect them as persons.

The habit of showing respect is an indispensable ingredient of civility. This is universally and intuitively recognized in all societies. Respectful conduct fosters harmonious and pleasant relationships, and softens the harsh and difficult facets of life. So much has this virtue been prized that many cultures have built up elaborate protocol specifying exact forms for the expression of respect. Tipping the hat, bowing (in Oriental countries), and standing when the national anthem is sung are typical of the countless ways civilized peoples have of showing respect.

The Bible is adamant in its insistence that Christians show respect in all proper situations and forms, and to all persons. Respect is to be shown to parents (Eph. 6:1-2), to spouses (4:33; 1 Pet. 3:7), to kings and all who are in authority (Rom. 13:7), to ministers and church leaders (1 Thess. 5:12-13), to the aged (Lev. 19:32), to all persons irrespective of sex, color, nationality, creed, or class (1 Pet. 2:17-18)—or even present degradation (John 4:7-9, 18).

We are to respect our bodies (1 Cor. 6:19-20); the property of others (Eph. 4:28); their good name (Lev. 19:16); their opinions (Acts 21:18-26); their civil rights (Lam. 3:35; Amos 5:12); and we are to respect the house of God (Eccles. 5:1; Matt. 21:13); and the Word of God (Prov. 13:13).

The ultimate basis for respecting persons is the sanctity of human beings as having been created by God in His image and for His glory and service. To fail to respect persons is to show disrespect to God their Creator. It is noteworthy that whenever society becomes irreligious, the bonds of courtesy and honor among men begin to loosen. Forms of courtesy become hypocritical because motivated solely by self-interest. The smile and deferential manner is sustained by the prospect of the tip or other forms of personal gain. Christians are to guard rigorously against superficial and insincere graciousness. They avoid hypocrisy, however, not by deliberate rudeness, or by being blatantly unconventional, but by inwardly cultivating the Christian virtue of respect.

Respect (or disrespect) is shown in many subtle ways—not only by what we say, but by tone of voice, facial expression, bodily posture, choice of words, including names and colloquialisms. Many Christians are slow in perceiving the relation of humor to proper respect. Some things or persons or concepts are not suitable subjects for joking. We should not joke, for instance, about sacred things or handicapped people. Christians also fail, too often, to understand that we show respect or disrespect by our dress. To be excessively casual in social situations is to say to others that we do not consider them important. This is doubly significant in the house of God. Our manner of dress when attending church is an indicator of our real respect for the place and for the Person we have gone there to worship. Or, if our inner respect is deeper than our dress shows, our carelessness is at least an indicator of our ignorance.

See CULTURE, HONOR, LOVE, REVERENCE, SANCTUARY, SECULARISM, DISCRIMINATION.

RICHARD S. TAYLOR

RESPECT OF PERSONS. See PREJUDICE.

RESPONSIBILITY. See ACCOUNTABILITY.

REST, REST OF FAITH. The Epistle to the Hebrews uses the theme of rest to appeal for faithfulness in a congregation that is discouraged and disillusioned. Heb. 4:1-13 is the conclusion of an exposition of Ps. 95:7-11 which the author began in Heb. 3:7. That OT passage recounts the story of Moses' failure to lead the generation of Israelites who came out of Egypt into the land of Canaan. The reason for the failure was their rebellion against God and their putting God to the test (cf. Exod. 17:1-7; Num. 20:1-13). They were unable to enter because of unbelief and disobedience (Heb. 3:19; 4:6). But even the next generation did not find God's rest, as is evident from the fact that David long afterward wrote of God's continuing promise (Ps. 95:7; Heb. 3:7, 15; 4:1, 6-7). "So then, there remains a sabbath rest for the people of God" (4:9, RSV). This promise is now proclaimed as the Christian gospel, and entering God's rest is accomplished by believing (vv. 2-3).

What then is this rest? It is akin to the sabbath rest of God, when He rested from all His works of creation (Gen. 2:2; Heb. 4:10). God rested on the seventh day, when His purpose of creation had been fulfilled. By analogy, entering into the promised rest would be to participate in the full realization of God's redeeming purpose. Rest represents for the writer to the Hebrews the completeness of God's redemptive provision and the fullness of man's experience of salvation. This latter fact has prompted some Wesleyans to understand "rest of faith" as a synonym for entire sanctification. The analogy of rest expresses something very beautiful and meaningful regarding Christian perfection. However, the expression as found in its NT context could be understood better as including the fullness of salvation experience in this life as well as the ultimate participation in God's rest which will come only in the presence of God.

See FULL SALVATION, REDEMPTION, HEAVEN.

For Further Reading: Bruce, *The Epistle to the Hebrews,* 60-83; Wiley, *Epistle to the Hebrews,* 134-55.

HAL A. CAUTHRON

RESTITUTION. Restitution is making wrongs right. It may consist of the correction of a falsehood, or the restoration of stolen or damaged property. The Mosaic directives for the restitution of things stolen, damaged, or lost, ranged from simple indemnity to a fourfold restoration (Exod. 22:1-6; Lev. 6:5; Num. 5:7; cf. Exod. 21:22-36).

While the principle of restitution for wrongs committed is not specifically emphasized in the NT, it is within the spirit of its teachings. Restitution is a logical component of repentance. When salvation came to Zacchaeus, love, replacing selfishness, impelled him to give half of his goods to the poor. He thereby did what he could to correct the imbalance which his greed had helped create in his socioeconomic world. From the money which remained he imposed the strongest demands of the law upon himself, restoring fourfold anything which he had taken by false means (Luke 19:1-10).

See REPENTANCE, BACKSLIDING.

For Further Reading: Marchant, "Restitution," *Baker's DT;* Archer, "Crimes and Punishments," *ZPBD.*

W. RALPH THOMPSON

RESTORATION OF ISRAEL. The concern of this article is: "What does the NT teach about the restoration of Israel?" There are two ways of studying prophecy. One makes the OT the primary source for the outline of the last things and fits the NT with it so far as it is possible; the other, recognizing progressive revelation, takes the NT as the primary source for the doctrine of the last things. We are concerned in this article only with what the NT teaches. Jesus was rejected by His generation of Jews, and so it is clear that they forfeited the Kingdom He proclaimed. The owner of His vineyard (God) would come and destroy the tenants (the Jews) and give the vineyard to others (the Church, Mark 12:9). However, He hinted rather darkly that in the future Israel will be saved. "Jerusalem [i.e., Israel] will be trodden down by the Gentiles, until the times of the Gentiles are fulfilled" (Luke 21:24, RSV).

Paul devotes three chapters of Romans (9—11) to this question. He first points out that physical descent from Abraham does not make one a true Jew. Not all who are physically descendants from Abraham are the sons of Abraham (9:6). Earlier he had written, "He is not a real Jew who is one outwardly, nor is true circumcision something external and physical. He is a Jew who is one inwardly, and real circumcision is a matter of the heart" (2:28 f, RSV). As the sovereign Creator God and the Lord of history, He can do as He pleases with His creatures. There can be no criticism of God's actions.

Now Paul does something which is of utmost significance. He takes two quotations from Hosea which in their OT setting apply to Israel (Hos. 2:23; 1:10) and applies them to the Church, which consists of more Gentiles than Jews. As he says in Philippians, "For we [Christians] are the true circumcision" (Phil. 3:3, RSV; cf. Col. 2:12). Israel was lost because she rejected the way of righteousness by faith and substituted for it the righteousness of good works (Rom. 9:31).

Paul illustrates this by the figure of an olive tree which represents the people of God. God has broken off natural branches (Israel) and grafted in alien branches *contrary to nature* (11:24); but this is a gracious work of God in which the Gentiles cannot boast. However, Israel is still a holy people (v. 16), i.e., a people who belong to God. The reason for their unbelief and fall was not an arbitrary work of God. Israel stumbled and fell so that salvation has come to the Gentiles. There is in fact among the Jews a remnant of true Jews, chosen by grace (v. 5); and if the rest of the Jews do not remain in unbelief, they will be grafted again into the people of God (v. 23). Then Paul utters a dark saying. "Through their trespass salvation has come to the Gentiles, so as to make Israel jealous" (v. 11, RSV). Paul gives no hint as to how the salvation of the Gentiles will provoke Israel to jealousy and so turn them to faith. However, there is yet to be a great salvation of Israel.

In fact, Paul says, "And so all Israel will be saved" (v. 26, RSV). From the context of this verse, where Paul is speaking of the Jewish people and the Gentiles, it is difficult to do what some scholars do at this place, interpret Israel as spiritual Israel. Of course all spiritual Israel will be saved; to present that fact is tautology. How or by what means and order ethnic Israel will be saved Paul does not say. One thing is clear: They must be saved by the exercise of faith. They are still in some sense a holy people and are destined to be included in the people of God and take their proper place in the redeemed company.

See JUDAISM, DISPENSATIONALISM, TRIBULATION, PROPHET (PROPHECY), REMNANT, ISRAEL, ESCHATOLOGY.

For Further Reading: Ladd, *The Last Things.*

GEORGE ELDON LADD

RESTORATIONISM. This is the belief, almost universally held by modernists, that ultimately all will repent and be saved; those who refuse to do so in this life will in the next, as they see reality from the standpoint of eternity and as they are prodded by the pangs of hell. Restorationism does not deny the reality of hell, but denies its finality; it is disciplinary only. The belief is thus a form of Universalism.

While the doctrine is sentimentally appealing, it cannot be supported biblically. The passage which declares God's unwillingness for anyone to perish (2 Pet. 3:1-9) shows clearly that the very interface of God's unwillingness is the reality of the possibility. For God's unwillingness is given as the explanation for His delay in terminating earthly probation. If death does not terminate probation, why the delay? Such a passage is reminiscent of Jesus' solemn warning of the closed door (Luke 13:25; cf. Matt. 7:22-23; 12:32; 25:1-13, 46; Mark. 9:47-49; Luke 16:26; 2 Thess. 1:9; Rom. 2:1-12; Revelation 20—22).

See FUTURE PROBATION, ETERNAL PUNISHMENT, UNIVERSALISM.

For Further Reading: Wiley, *CT,* 3:358-63.

RICHARD S. TAYLOR

RESTORE, RESTORATION. See BACKSLIDING.

RESURRECTION OF CHRIST. This is a central item in the NT *kerygma,* the proclamation of the Good News. The apostle Paul declares it to be a crucial truth without which faith is worthless and sin is without remedy (1 Cor. 15:12-19).

Against all efforts to "spiritualize" or "demythologize" the Resurrection, the NT clearly indicates that the body of the crucified Lord was raised from the dead and ascended into heaven, leaving behind an empty tomb and a believing Church.

The resurrection of Christ is proclaimed as the first instance of true *anastasis* ("standing or rising up"), the NT term translated "resurrection" (38 times). "In fact Christ has been raised from the dead, the first fruits of those who have fallen asleep" (1 Cor. 15:20, RSV). All prior instances of restoration of life to the dead were instances of revivification rather than resurrection as such.

Christ's resurrection is the prototype and guarantee of ours (John 14:19; 1 Cor. 15:21-26), and His resurrected and glorified body is our best clue as to the nature of the eternal state of the redeemed (1 Cor. 15:49-54; Phil. 3:20-21; 1 John 3:1-3).

For these reasons, the resurrection of Christ is evidenced in Scripture as few other facts are. Ten evidences of the Resurrection have been given:

1. The certainty of Christ's death is clearly established in the certification of the Roman officer (Mark 15:44) and John's observation of the water and blood from the spear wound in Jesus' side (John 19:34-35). The "swoon theory" of a natural resuscitation is thereby explicitly denied.

2. The burial of the body was not by avowed disciples in a secret place but by members of the Sanhedrin (Joseph and Nicodemus, John 19:38-39) in a new tomb in a private garden, the location known to enemies as well as friends.

3. No living person expected to see Jesus again. The caution of the Sanhedrin leaders was not based on expectation of resurrection but on fear of deception by the disciples (Matt. 27:63-64). It was quite impossible for the psychologically defeated disciples either to contrive the removal of the body or to invent the story of the Resurrection.

4. The first testimony to the Resurrection came from Christ's enemies, not from His friends. The soldier guards reported not to Pilate but to the Sanhedrin, and were bribed to tell a story that on the surface involved contradiction ("While we slept, His disciples stole Him away" [see Matt. 28:11-14], when if they slept they could not know who came or what happened).

5. There is the incidental reference to the graveclothes, wrappings lying in the form of the body which had passed through them. The napkin that had been about the Savior's head was folded and laid to one side. The stone had been rolled away, not to let Jesus out but to let the disciples see what had happened.

6. Ten separate appearances of the risen Redeemer to more than 518 persons under a wide variety of circumstances are recorded (Matt. 28:9-10, 16-20; Mark 16:9-19; Luke 24:9-53; John 20:11-31; 21:1-25; Acts 1:3-9; 1 Cor. 15:5-8).

7. Only total conviction that Christ was physically alive could account for the revolution in the attitude of the disciples: from deepest gloom to highest joy. The apostolic preaching of the Resurrection was never challenged by the authorities; the disciples were simply ordered to stop. What the disciples became is as convincing an evidence for the Resurrection as what they said.

8. There was no effort to preserve the tomb, the location of which is uncertain to the present time. The Resurrection alone could account for such an unnatural development. The opposition in that time had only to produce the body of Jesus to completely destroy the Christian witness. This was never done.

9. The change in the day of worship from Saturday to the Lord's day is indirect evidence of the Church's conviction that Christ rose early on the first day of the week (Mark 16:9). The day is often not mentioned; when it is, it is always "the first day of the week."

10. "The power of his resurrection" (Phil. 3:10) in the ongoing life of the Church is witness to the reality of the Resurrection. No movement based on deceit or error could have the morally constructive power manifest in normative Christianity across the ages.

Theologically, the Resurrection is central to Christology as well as soteriology or doctrine of salvation. Without the Resurrection, Jesus was a martyr; with it, He is "declared with power to be the Son of God" (Rom. 1:4, NIV). The Resurrection was the Father's seal on both Christ's life and teachings, and His atoning death (Acts 17:31).

See SOTERIOLOGY, CHRISTOLOGY, REDEEMER (REDEMPTION), DEATH OF CHRIST.

For Further Reading: Barth, *Church Dogmatics,* 3:2; Clark, *Interpreting the Resurrection;* Thomas, "The Resurrection of Jesus Christ," *ISBE,* 4:2565-69; King, *The Forty Days;* Wiley, *CT,* 2:204-8. W. T. PURKISER

RESURRECTION OF THE BODY. The Apostles' Creed declares, "I believe . . . in the resurrection of the body." Other Early Church creeds echo and amplify the teaching of Scripture that the bodies of the dead shall be raised. Jesus declared, "I am the resurrection and the life" (John 11:25). Because of the empty tomb, believers have been assured of final victory over death (1 Cor. 15:57). The apostle gave words of reassurance to believers that loved ones who had died in the faith would not be left out at the coming of Christ. "The dead in Christ shall rise first" (1 Thess. 4:16), promptly to be followed by believers living and remaining. Before Felix the governor, Paul testified that "there shall be a resurrection of the dead, both of the just and unjust" (Acts 24:15).

The Scriptures go beyond the Greek concept of "the immortality of the soul," to declare a reunion of soul and body. Instead of nonmaterial, ghostlike phantoms, recognizable bodies of loved ones who have died would come forth from the graves. The resurrected body will assure a preservation of personal identity, without being identical atomically and biologically. Rather the resurrected body will be changed, and made "like unto his glorious body" (Phil. 3:21).

While the OT assumed the resurrection of the body in teaching and example (e.g., Ps. 49:15; Dan. 12:2; Ezek. 37:1-14), its highest expression is found in the NT. The apostle Paul outlined the truth in most significant detail in 1 Corinthians 15. He directed his writing in answer to those who questioned the fact and significance of the resurrection (v. 12). Paul declared that failure to affirm this truth would be a denial of Christ's own resurrection and its meaning (vv. 13, 16). The validity of one's testimony and the facts of faith together with the power of preaching would be at stake by such denial (vv. 14-15). But Christ's resurrection clearly opened the way for the resurrection of the dead (vv. 20-22).

Paul next addresses the questions: "How are the dead raised up? and with what body do they come?" (v. 35). Our resurrected bodies shall be gloriously fitted for eternal fellowship with our risen Lord. Our earthly bodies are sown in "corruption," "dishonour," and "weakness." They will be raised in "incorruption," "glory," and "power" (vv. 42-43). Our earthly bodies are created after the "first man"; our resurrected bodies will "bear the image of the heavenly" (vv. 47, 49). The old "flesh and blood" body (v. 50) will give way to the incorruptible body especially created for "immortality" (vv. 52-54). This final resurrection of the body will declare the ultimate triumph, "O death, where is thy sting? O grave, where is thy victory?" (v. 55).

See RESURRECTION OF CHRIST, BODY, ESCHATOLOGY.

For Further Reading: Wiley, *CT,* 3:320-28; *GMS,* 652-58; Ladd, *A Theology of the New Testament,* 464 ff.

RONALD E. WILSON

RETALIATION. See REVENGE.

RETRIBUTION, RETRIBUTIVE JUSTICE. This is the rendering of condign punishments according to the deserts of an individual. Retribution might be the receiving of rewards as well as punishments, but the term is used generally in connection with punishments. Retribution is the exacting of a penalty for wrongdoing. Hebrew law was grounded on this principle.

Retribution is to be distinguished from remedial punishment, or punishment inflicted for the good of the offender. The death of a murderer is not for the good of the murderer. Sin is to be punished irrespective of the effect upon others. It is punished because the wrongdoer deserves to be punished. The state must requite the sinner or be held responsible for participating in the sin.

Capital punishment for murder is retribution. The state executes justice and punishes the offender, else it is held as participating in the crime. The people must cleanse the land by the execution of the murderer (Num. 35:34).

In theft, restitution is not sufficient. The law has been violated and punishment is demanded (Num. 35:33-34; Lev. 6:2-7). This principle reaches its fulfillment in the Atonement, in which Christ's death satisfied divine justice in place of the death of the sinner. To reject retributive justice is to reject the biblical doctrine of the Atonement.

See CAPITAL PUNISHMENT, ETERNAL PUNISHMENT, ATONEMENT, PROPITIATION.

For Further Reading: Berkhof, *Systematic Theology,* 74-76; Wiley, *CT,* 1:387 ff; 3:356 ff.

HAROLD J. OCKENGA

REVELATION, BOOK OF. There are four traditional methods of interpreting this last book of the Bible. First, the *Preterist* approaches it as history and literature and limits its message to the troublous times in which it was written. Second, the *Historical* interpreter treats it as a series of prophecies of progressive world history in a religious context. Third, the *Futurist* interprets this book as prophecy pertaining to the end time of history, with strong emphasis upon the millennium as a literal period of 1,000 years. In postmillennialism Christ will return at the end of a 1,000-year utopian world order. In premillennialism Christ will return to set up His kingdom of 1,000 years. In dispensational premillennialism a resurrected Jewish state will be the focal point of Christ's millennial reign on earth. This brief review illustrates the time and place orientation of these approaches which tend to minimize the ageless message of the Revelation—which message it shares with the rest of the NT.

The fourth is the *Idealist,* essentially a spiritualizing approach which tends to perpetuate the allegorical method of Bible interpretation, which in turn seeks to find moral and spiritual lessons in details apart from the central message.

These approaches offer contributions to the understanding of the Revelation, but they are weakened by their primary presuppositions. As with other books of the Bible, the presuppositional norm must be that the author wrote for his own day in a manner understandable to his readers. On this basis one proceeds quite naturally, first, to a study of the historical situation which gave rise to the writing; second, to an analysis of the language—while recognizing its literary forms—in order to understand what the author meant to say; and third, to a formulation of the message for preaching, teaching, and living.

The second step encounters the greatest problems because the book is unique in the NT. The author calls it a prophecy (1:3). Chapters 2 and 3 are epistolary. The remainder is apocalyptic, a literary form which makes abundant use of revelations, visions, symbolism, and figures of speech. The author presents a dramatic picture of the great conflict being waged between the kingdoms of good and evil, between God and Satan, from both the heavenly and the earthly points of view (cf. 4:1; 17:1 ff). The events John saw taking place on earth were manifestations of extraterrestrial activity. He viewed them in relation to the end (Gr. *eschaton*) which refers to *kairos* time (event, happening) rather than *chronos* time (historical sequence). The focus is upon God's redemptive activity in establishing His kingdom among men rather than upon the succession of these acts in history.

This kingdom, prophetically manifest in the OT people of God and actualized in Christ and His Church, now awaits its consummation in the last great eschaton. John apprehends this panorama in midstream and assures his readers that God will ultimately triumph through Jesus Christ. In emulation of John, our hearts must supplement our minds if we would interpret this book aright.

See PROPHET (PROPHECY), RAPTURE, APOCALYPTIC, MILLENNIUM.

For Further Reading: "Revelation," *BBC;* "Revelation," *WBC;* Swete, *The Apocalypse of St. John;* Bowman, *The Revelation to John.* HARVEY J. S. BLANEY

REVELATION, NATURAL. This term, known also as *general* revelation, describes the knowledge of God made known through nature, history, and the nature of man. It stands in contrast to *special* revelation, which refers to the truths of God found only in the Bible.

Scripture teaches that the creation testifies to God's existence as the Creator. His fingerprints are all over the things which He has made. Ps. 19:1-6 says the creation testifies day and night to people of every land and language about the glory of God. Thus the Hebrew poets and prophets ridiculed the heathen practice of idol worship (Psalm 135; Isaiah 40). Such a vast, beautiful creation required a Creator of wisdom and might, qualities no idol could possess. In Rom. 1:18-23 Paul says everyone who does not worship God is without an excuse, for God's existence is clearly revealed by the things He has created. In preaching to the Gentiles, the apostles began with the revelation of God through nature and proceeded to proclaim the perfect revelation of God in Jesus Christ (Acts 14:8-18; 17:16-34).

The Bible portrays history as evidence of God's activity. He rules over the affairs of men (Ps. 22:28), rewarding righteousness and judging wickedness (1 Kings 8:32; Ps. 34:15-22; Prov. 14:34). He sets boundaries of time and space to nations (Acts 17:26), raising up rulers and putting them down (Dan. 4:17, 25, 32; Luke 1:51-52). God prophesies His intentions and history records their fulfillment. History is God-fashioned and moves toward the end which He has determined.

Man's own nature reveals God. Sin could not erase the fact that man was made for fellowship with God. The religious practices of the world's peoples reflect their groping for that fellowship. God's law is written on man's heart and works through his conscience to approve well doing and condemn wrongdoing (Rom. 2:14-16).

Natural revelation, however, has serious limitations resulting from man's fall into sin. Creation was subjected to futility and can no longer reveal God perfectly (Rom. 8:19-23). Man's abilities, corrupted by sin, can no longer perceive clearly God's revelation in nature (2 Cor. 4:4). At best, nature speaks only of God the Creator; it is silent about God the Savior. Thus special revelation, as found in the Bible, is absolutely necessary for us to know about redemption from sin provided through Jesus Christ, in order that we might be restored to fellowship with God (1 Cor. 1:21).

See NATURAL THEOLOGY, NATURAL LAW, REVELATION (SPECIAL).

For Further Reading: Berkouwer, *General Revelation;* Wiley, *CT,* 1:51-52, 126-34. LUKE L. KEEFER, JR.

REVELATION, SPECIAL. This term distinguishes God's immediate and unique self-disclosure to and through individuals, from general revelation, or His oblique self-disclosure through nature. *General* revelation is necessarily implicit in creation and God's providential care of the world, while *special* revelation is special in two respects: The *means* and *channels* are special (selective), and the *purpose* is special: redemption.

Three avenues have been used by God in the special revelation of himself to the human race. (1) He has manifested himself directly to individuals. (2) He has revealed himself through the inspired writings of prophets and apostles. And (3) He has revealed himself in the person of Jesus Christ.

There are many accounts of God's revelation of himself in special ways to individuals. He appeared to Abraham once in a smoking firepot and a flaming torch (Gen. 15:17), and again in the form of a man (18:1-33). He appeared to Moses in a flame of fire out of the midst of a bush (Exod. 3:2—4:17). Thunders and lightnings, a consuming fire, an earthquake, and the sound of a trumpet were the media through which He manifested himself to Israel at Sinai (19:16 ff). Sometimes He revealed himself to men in dreams (e.g., 1 Sam. 3:4-14). David experienced His presence in "the sound of marching in the tops of balsam trees" (2 Sam. 5:24, RSV). Often God spoke through prophets (e.g., 12:1-14; 1 Kings 21:17-24; Ezek. 6:1 ff). At times a voice was His means of revelation (Gen. 4:6-15; 1 Sam. 3:4-14). Isaiah experienced Him in a vision in the Temple (Isaiah 6). Saul of Tarsus became aware of Him in a blinding light and a voice (Acts 9:1-9). God sent His angel to Peter (12:6-11). Miracles sometimes have been God's medium of revelation. John beheld Him in glory in the Apocalypse.

In view of the time span covered between Adam and John, it is apparent that God's special, personal revelations of himself have been relatively infrequent. Furthermore, their occurrences have been governed by the will of God rather than by dint of human effort. In another sense, however, God specially awakens and calls sinners everywhere and reveals himself to all who draw near to Him (Isa. 55:1; Jas. 4:8).

The Scriptures are a special revelation of God to man, made necessary because of the Fall. For sin not only brought guilt and separation from God; it darkened man's intellect, plunging him ever deeper into moral degradation (Rom. 1:18-32). In such a state he was unable to see God in general revelation.

The Scriptures reveal those divine acts by which God has made himself known unto the race. They reveal His deep concern for the race. They display His deep concern for every man, motivated by love—love so profound that He sacrificed His only begotten Son that rebellious man might have eternal life. The OT reveals God's preparation of a chosen people through whom to give salvation to the world. The NT describes the Savior's coming and the gift of the Holy Spirit. It sets forth those principles by which the new life in Christ can be brought to perfection. The Scriptures reveal things about God which otherwise would be totally hidden from man. Among them is the trinity of divine Persons within one essence. Another is the equality of the divine Persons within a functional hierarchy. Still another is the extent of His concern for man.

Because they were inspired, the human writers of the Scriptures sometimes recorded truths so profound that they themselves did not comprehend them (1 Pet. 1:10-11). They spoke better than they knew.

But God's greatest and best means of self-revelation was the incarnation of the eternal Son of God. "And the Word became flesh and dwelt among us, and we beheld His glory, the glory as of the only begotten of the Father, full of grace and truth" (John 1:14, NKJB). When one of the Eleven asked Jesus to show them the Father, Jesus' response was, "'Have I been with you so long, and yet you have not known Me, Philip? He who has seen Me has seen the Father'" (14:8-9, NKJB). To see and hear and touch Jesus was to observe God's love, His compassion, His power, His detestation of hypocrisy: the perfections of God's character.

When the Son had finished His mission, He returned to the Father and sent the Holy Spirit to abide in believers forever. In fact, a careful reading of John 14:18-23 makes clear that with the Holy Spirit comes the entire Trinity to make of obedient believers their dwelling place.

But the end is not yet. At best, we still see "in a mirror, dimly" (1 Cor. 13:12, NKJB). After a while we shall see Him as He is (1 John 3:2). That will be special revelation indeed!

See REVELATION (NATURAL), BIBLE, CHRIST, NATURAL THEOLOGY, THEOPHANY, INSPIRATION (OF THE BIBLE).

For Further Reading: Pinnock, *Biblical Revelation;* Ramm, *Special Revelation and the Word of God;* Wiley, *CT,* 1:134-41.

W. RALPH THOMPSON

REVENGE. This refers, in a technical sense, to a practice among Semitic people whereby a person avenges any hurt or breach of honor. In the case of murder, the next of kin must take vengeance. This was a basic part of the primitive form of justice practiced at a time when there was no recourse to public courts of law. The Hebrew word for revenge or vengeance is *nagam,* which represents an ethical demand and connotes justice. It refers to restoration, a balancing of honor, and is something "taken" by the offended party. It does not necessarily carry the derogatory overtones of our English term "revenge." Thus we must read of its OT occurrences in this context.

An indication of the human nature of Israel's practice of vengeance is seen in its application to manslaughter. If a man unwittingly killed another, he could flee to one of the six cities of refuge designated for this purpose, where he would be safe from the avenging kinsman. Here he must remain until the death of the current high priest, at which time he could return to his home (Joshua 20).

A further restraint placed upon the expression of revenge is set forth in the familiar words of the law of retaliation found in Lev. 24:19-20: "When a man causes a disfigurement in his neighbor, as he has done it shall be done to him, fracture for fracture, eye for eye, tooth for tooth; as he has disfigured a man, he shall be disfigured" (RSV; see also Exod. 21:24 and Deut. 19:21). This restraint is unique in Israel, indicating that the punishment or revenge must fit the crime and stands in contrast to other ancient law statements outside Israel where revenge usually exceeded the crime.

The NT standard of Christian love completely excludes the taking of personal revenge (Matt. 5:38-42; Rom. 12:19-21).

See LOVE, FORGIVENESS, JUSTICE.

For Further Reading: Pederson, *Israel,* 2:378-92; de Vaux, *Ancient Israel,* 1:160-64.

ALVIN S. LAWHEAD

REVERENCE. This is the attitude toward a person or object which expresses respect, awe, affection, and veneration.

In the KJV the verb "reverence" occurs seven times in the OT and six times in the NT. In each instance it is a command or call to pay respect to or to venerate a person or an object, as in Lev. 19:30: "Ye shall keep my sabbaths, and reverence my sanctuary: I am the Lord."

Wiley defines the noun "reverence" as a "profound respect mingled with fear and affection," or "a strong sentiment of respect and esteem, sometimes with traces of fear" (*CT,* 3:38). Coleridge, the great poet and philosopher, defined it as a "synthesis of love and fear." Reverence therefore may be said to be fear tempered by love.

Reverence extends to all things that are considered as divine; in the Judean and the Christian contexts, it relates primarily to God. It is also used in reference to the Word of God and His ordinances, name, day, house in which we worship, and people. In the NT it has reference to the names of God the Father, Christ the Son, and the Holy Spirit.

In Eastern tradition, reverence was given to the aged, to superiors, and to parents. Reverence is conceived of as respect and deference due to the aged, especially to parents (Eph. 6:1; Heb. 12:9).

Reverence for, and the worship of, Christ was the distinguishing peculiarity of the NT saints. His followers gave Him such worship as could not be given to any other being but God. Many texts show that He received such supreme worship as could not be given to any but God without idolatry. Jesus claimed it and received it, and God honored it and blessed those who rendered it (Luke 24:52; Acts 7:59; 1 Thess. 3:11-13).

Christ is to be worshipped by every creature in the universe (Phil. 2:10).

See WORSHIP, RESPECT, FEAR, LOVE.

For Further Reading: *IDB,* 4:71; Miley, *Systematic Theology,* 1:254; Vine, *ED,* 3:293; Wiley, *CT,* 3:38, 94.

DONALD R. PETERMAN

REVIVAL. This may be defined as a religious awakening, prompted by the Holy Spirit, that (1) restores in the church a vivid awareness of God's holiness and love, and (2) revitalizes its comprehension of what love for and obedience to God actually mean. Through the Holy Spirit's activity the church in revival is brought to intense reflection on the central themes of its faith, to repentance and renewal, and to expanded realization of the dimensions of discipleship.

Although the social, political, ecclesiastical, and individual factors that form the context in which revival occurs are important and cannot be ignored, they do not finally account for its occurrence. The factors that accompany revivals in the church are diverse and cannot be reduced to a formula. Additionally, since only the Holy Spirit adequately understands the church, the world, and the mind of the Father, no formula can ever circumscribe His activity. But this does not exclude the church's responsibility to seek and prepare for revival. Appropriate preparation for revival gives serious attention to prayer, is sensitive to the state of the church and the community at large, learns from the history of revivals, and seeks biblical guidance.

Revivals normally result in renewed evangelism, a revitalized missionary impulse, and in expanded circulation of religious literature. They often result in the formation of educational institutions, and reform of existing social, political, and economic institutions. In sum, they open all aspects of life to the power and meaning of the gospel.

Among the great revivals in the Christian church may be listed the Cluniac Reform in the 10th century; the Protestant Reformation in the 16th century; the Pietist movement in the 17th and 18th centuries; the Evangelical Revival in the 18th century; and the First and Second Great Awakenings in 18th- and 19th-century America.

See REVIVALISM, EVANGELISM.

For Further Reading: Autrey, *Revivals of the Old Testament;* Orr, *The Flaming Tongue;* Wood, *The Inextinguishable Blaze.* ALBERT L. TRUESDALE, JR.

REVIVALISM. The theory and practice of seeking religious conversions in large numbers amidst awakened understanding and excited group emotions is called revivalism. Insofar as a plan of gathering crowds, preaching the gospel, and training converts is evident in the earliest Christian communities in Jerusalem, Samaria, Damascus, Corinth, and Ephesus, the Book of the Acts and the Epistles of Paul indicate that revivalism was pervasive in the Early Church.

Occasional religious awakenings, guided by human agents, took place during the long centuries following the establishment of the papacy and the Eastern patriarchate, especially in the conversion of the Slavs, in the founding of the Cistercian and Franciscan monastic orders, in the preaching that inspired the Crusades to wrest Jerusalem from the Turkish Empire, and in the popular preaching of Savonarola in Renaissance Florence. During the Reformation, the Anabaptists used both revivalism and evangelism in small groups to spread their intensely spiritual version of the gospel. The more radical preachers of the Puritan revolution in 17th-century England and the Quakers that emerged in succeeding decades, followed studied practices of preaching and witness intended to bring about large-scale awakenings. So did the Presbyterian ministers who accompanied the first Scottish settlers in northern Ireland.

The origins of modern Protestant revivalism, however, lie more clearly in the evangelical awakening that George Whitefield and John and Charles Wesley led in England and America during the 18th century, and which Pietists meanwhile promoted in Germany and among the German-speaking settlers of America. The major elements of those revivals have remained central to this day: preaching which affirmed the work of the Holy Spirit in regeneration and sanctification, as at Pentecost; reliance upon the authority and inspiration of Scripture to communicate unerringly all the truth necessary for Christian faith and ethical conduct; and a call to fulfill the Great Commission of evangelizing all peoples. Modern missions and revivalism have, accordingly, gone hand in hand, from the times of the Wesleys and of William Carey and Adoniram Judson, right down to the present moment of mass awakenings in Korea, Indonesia, and central Africa, and the mixed African and Indian population of northeastern Brazil.

During the 19th century—the great century of Christian expansion—the theory and practice of revivalism was greatly enriched. In North America, Charles G. Finney and many Arminianized Presbyterians and Congregationalists joined Methodists and Baptists in measures that they believed were scriptural to promote revivals. Among these were camp meetings, which early in the century became as important to eastern and urban congregations in the United States as to the religious life of the midwestern frontier; interchurch concerts of prayer; protracted meetings; calling of repentant persons forward to a "mourner's bench" or the Communion rail, thereafter called the "altar"; encouraging exhortation by women; and, later, city-wide campaigns such as Dwight L. Moody made famous on both sides of the Atlantic. In the decades preceding the Civil War, Finney, the Methodists, and a growing number of Congregational, Baptist, and Presbyterian revivalists in both America and England made devotion to such social reforms as antislavery, temperance, and justice to the poor and oppressed to be indispensable marks of biblical conversion.

A considerable reaction set in, however, when conservative Calvinists charged that reliance upon such allegedly human measures demeaned God's sovereign and electing grace. That resistance became especially strong in the American South before the Civil War, and among antimission Baptists in the Mississippi Valley. It fortified the growing opposition to efforts to eliminate social evils, especially slavery. And it generated a contrary theory of revivals that allowed only "spiritual" efforts, namely, prayer, the preaching of the Word, the administration of the sacraments, and the renewal of discipline within the believing community. These would prepare human hearts to receive the salvation that must come by divine initiative and election. The doctrine of the "spiritual" church, set out by James H. Thornwell and other Southern Presbyterians, maintained that whatever efforts revivals might have in eliminating social injustice or oppression were incidental to the purification of the church, and not properly the concern of the ministry.

Little known until recently was the rebirth of

revivalism among Roman Catholics in the 19th century, first in Germany and elsewhere on the Continent, then, through the work of the Redemptorist Fathers and other immigrant priests, in the parish missions of Catholic congregations in America. Following closely prescribed formats, traveling evangelists preached with as much passion as possible the model sermons provided for them, and helped to win many of the wandering immigrants back to the church. The sermons moved step by step from warnings of future damnation to descriptions of the loving heart of the Crucified Lord and the Blessed Virgin. The aim was to bring people back to the confession and to regular participation in the Mass.

Among Protestant evangelicals, preoccupation with the restoration of the power of primitive Christianity to convict and convert the masses and so to sanctify a culture increased steadily in both the Old World and the New, despite the arguments against preaching social reform. Millenarian doctrines, stressing the imminence of the Second Coming and emphasizing the promise of an outpouring of the Spirit in the last days, won a following on three continents, especially in the Niagara Bible conferences that Plymouth Brethren sponsored. The use of Pentecostal language, passed down from John Fletcher, to describe and define the Wesleyan doctrine of entire sanctification as the "baptism of the Holy Ghost" spread widely during the last decades of the 19th century, especially in the Keswick conferences in England and the National Holiness Association in America. And, in the early years of the 20th century, the Pentecostal movement was born in what were at first tiny revivals where Christians believed they had received the baptism of the Holy Spirit attested by the experience of speaking in an "unknown" language.

In the 20th century, therefore, revivalism has remained a dominant note in Protestant Christianity and a significant one in the Catholic religion as well. All the major evangelical movements, save the most conservative of the Calvinists, affirm a theory and practice of revivalism suited to their theological traditions and forms of ecclesiastical organization. All tend to support, most of them heartily, the continuing tradition of city-wide revival campaigns, represented by the names of Billy Sunday in the first part, and Billy Graham in the last part of the century. And all, however much they may reject the politics of social reform or the confrontation of particular social evils, affirm the power of religious awakenings to reorder a society's social and political priorities, renew devotion to the law of the Lord, and place a revitalized Christian faith at the center of cultural life.

See REVIVAL, EVANGELISM, MISSION (MISSIONS, MISSIOLOGY), SOUL WINNING, SOCIAL ETHICS.

For Further Reading: Sweet, *Revivalism in America;* Townsend, *The Supernatural Factor in Revivals;* Mallalieu, *The Why, When, and How of Revivals;* Finney, *Revival Lectures;* Wood, *The Burning Heart;* Orr, *The Light of the Nations.*

TIMOTHY L. SMITH

REWARDS. A reward is generally thought of as a boon, recognition, or prize given because of a specific achievement or good deed. It may also be a consequence, such as an inner feeling of well-being or an assurance of divine approval. The term usually denotes pleasing consequences, but may also be used as a synonym for punishment, as "the reward of unrighteousness" (2 Pet. 2:13; cf. Matt. 16:27; 2 Tim. 4:14; Rev. 18:6; 22:12).

There can be no doubt that both Jesus and the apostles held out the prospect of rewards as an incentive to works of righteousness (Matt. 5:12; 6:4, 6, 18; 10:41-42; 1 Cor. 3:14; 1 Tim. 5:18; 2 John 8). This fact creates two theological problems. One is the question of motive. Moral philosophy says we are to do well not for the sake of reward but to please God, or at least simply because it is right. How can any concern whatsoever for rewards be reconciled with pure love, which sings, "I will serve Thee because I love Thee"? How can the promise of rewards escape the odium of bribery?

This objection loses its weight when we remember that love itself desires appropriate response, and the Christian views rewards, not materialistically, certainly not as bribes, but as the self-giving of God himself in His own special forms of approval and blessing. What greater reward could a child of God have than to hear the Master say, "Well done, thou good and faithful servant: . . . enter thou into the joy of thy lord" (Matt. 25:21)? In his struggle on earth he is sustained by the joy of receiving what God desires to give him. Many of these recompensing blessings he will enjoy now (cf. 6:6); others are incentives from the other side. The power of incentives cannot be scorned when God himself provides them; and perhaps in providing them, God displays a truer view of human nature and of virtue itself than the moral philosopher.

The other theological problem suggested by the concept of rewards is the lurking implication of salvation by works. But nowhere is eternal life held out as a reward for good deeds; rewards are additional blessings promised to those whose salvation is by grace through faith. Paul affirms the principle: "Now to him that worketh is the reward not reckoned of grace, but of debt" (Rom. 4:4). The basis of reward is merit; the basis of salvation is entirely different—it is grace alone. Therefore, while "the wages of sin is death," eternal life is "the gift of God . . . through Jesus Christ our Lord" (6:23).

Divine rewards in this life are analogous to reaping (Gal. 6:7-8). They are the blessings of consequences—a clear conscience, a sense of God's smile, a sense of achievement, souls won, prayers answered. As to the nature of rewards at the Judgment and in heaven we can only speculate. The distinct impression gathered from the Scripture is that sacrificial service in this life, beyond the call of duty, will have some bearing on the privileges and responsibilities bestowed upon us in the next. At any rate, the conclusion of Dawson Walker is appropriate: "The idea of reward accompanies, almost of necessity, belief in a personal God. Viewed as the apostolic writers were taught by our Lord to view it, it is the loftiest and most potent incentive to holiness of life" *(HDNT).*

See SOWING AND REAPING, WORK (WORKS).

For Further Reading: *HDNT,* 3:368; Smith, *The Biblical Doctrine of Heaven,* 171-89.

RICHARD S. TAYLOR

RICHES. See MONEY.

RIGHT, RIGHTEOUSNESS. To be right is to be fair, just, straight, or equal. The word carries the concept of correct judgment or righteous acts. The word "righteousness" is applied to one who is right in character and action.

God is righteous, and thus possesses righteousness. He "is the fountain of justice so everything that He does may be relied upon as just" (*Baker's DT,* 461; cf. Gen. 18:25; Rom. 9:14). God is under obligation to do right, whether that means He saves or punishes (Isa. 42:6; 10:20-21).

Since God is righteous, He will deal with man in accordance to His character. For that reason sin must be punished. However, God has provided a way by which man may be forgiven, declared righteous, and made right in God's eyes. This is the meaning and purpose of Christ's death for all men—the righteous One dying to make righteous the sinner.

This must not be seen as a transfer on legal terms of God's righteousness to the sinner. The sinner is no longer reckoned a sinner because he has placed his faith in Christ, who is God's righteousness, and has accepted the obligation entailed in such faith to act righteously. His faith is counted for righteousness (Rom. 4:5-8), because it is a turning from self-righteousness (which is always an illusion) to Christ's death as the only adequate basis for pardon and source of moral power (*Exploring Our Christian Faith,* 290-92).

Thus it can be said that a forgiven man is a righteous man in relation to God and His law, but this man "is under moral obligation to proceed from that point to be righteous in heart and life (cf. Rom. 6:12-16)." He has not been given a "non-forfeitable legal title of a standing of innocence on the basis of an objective transaction in his behalf, the benefits of which are imputed to him unconditionally" (*GMS,* 457).

Man's righteousness, then, is his conforming through grace to the image of God in childlike innocence and simplicity. It is a positive inclination to goodness which is more than just outward, although inward righteousness manifests itself outwardly.

See JUSTIFICATION, IMPUTED RIGHTEOUSNESS, HOLINESS.

For Further Reading: *ISBE,* 4:2591-93; *The New Schaff-Herzog Encyclopedia of Religious Knowledge,* 10:37-38; *The New Westminster Dictionary of the Bible,* 805.

LEO G. COX

RIGHT HAND. This is one word in Greek, *dexios.* It means "right hand" or "right side." It indicates the place of honor. In the NT it is used for the exaltation of Jesus at the right hand of God. The "right hand" of the Father is more than the place of honor; it is delegated power and authority (Acts 2:33).

Psalm 110 is probably the OT chapter most frequently quoted in the NT. The first verse reads (NIV):

> The LORD says to my Lord:
> "Sit at my right hand
> until I make your enemies
> a footstool for your feet."

In the first line "LORD" repersts the Hebrew *Yahweh,* while "Lord" represents *adon.* We interpret this as meaning here: "The Father said to the Son."

Jesus quoted this passage and applied it to the Messiah, who was both David's Son and David's Lord (Matt. 22:44; Mark 12:36; Luke 20:42). On the Day of Pentecost Peter quoted it as proof that Jesus was the Messiah (Acts 2:34-36). The writer of Hebrews does the same (Heb. 1:13). Jesus also asserted His Messiahship before the Sanhedrin by saying: "'But from now on, the Son of Man will be seated at the right hand of the mighty

God'" (Luke 22:69, NIV). And that is where He is today (Eph. 1:20; Col. 3:1; 1 Pet. 3:22).

See EXALTATION OF CHRIST, ASCENSION (THE), ADVOCATE, MEDIATION (MEDIATOR).

For Further Reading: Vine, *ED*, 3:296.

RALPH EARLE

RIGHTEOUSNESS OF GOD. See ATTRIBUTES, DIVINE.

RIGHTS. In and of itself, the word *right* refers to that which is correct, legal, and equitable. A derivative meaning is *a* right, i.e., a privilege which may properly be claimed. The question of "rights" thus becomes the question of personal privileges and legal claims.The question covers civil rights, property rights, domestic rights, and other categories. Problems arise from three sources: (1) a failure to understand the philosophical basis for determining a right; (2) the apparent conflict of rights; and (3) the tendency of people to claim rights which do not exist.

Problems arising from (2) and (3) can be more readily resolved if the basis for determining a right is clearly understood. The *democratic* principle is the assumption that rights are defined from below, by the people. The *constitutional* principle saves the democratic principle from anarchy by adopting a common law, in the form of a constitution and its expanding and supporting legislation, as the ground for determining individual rights—a constitution adopted by the people themselves. The *statist* principle assumes that rights are determined not from below but from above. This may be the *monarchial* form ("the divine right of kings"); the *party* form (communism); the *dictatorship* form (fascism); or the *power* form which supposes that the ability to enforce a claimed right validates the right itself (e.g., the neighborhood bully).

It is easy for theorists to declare the prior claim of the utilitarian principle, viz., that personal rights are to be determined by the highest good and happiness of the largest number of people. But this is an abstract principle which always tends to get lost in the concrete systems of power actually operating. The basic selfishness of sinful man is such that in the practical situation special interest groups as well as individuals always tend to define rights in terms of what is in their favor. This keeps the whole question of rights ambiguous, and private notions of "my rights" almost invariably warped. The results are claims—often loud and vehement—to "rights" which are purely imaginary.

The fault lies in failing to see that God is the Source of human rights, and that God's law is the sole basis for defining them. The fundamental rights presupposed by the American constitution, for example— the "unalienable Rights [to] Life, Liberty, and the pursuit of Happiness"—were ascribed in the Declaration of Independence directly to God the Creator. History shows that the rights themselves have tended to be lost when God has been forgotten as their Source and Basis.

However, the Christian is bound to penetrate to the very core of the entire question by perceiving that only God's rights are absolute. All human rights are subordinate to His. More specifically, the central claim of fallen human nature—"my right to myself"—is itself the grand delusion. As Millard Reed says, the very essence of the carnal mind is the delusion of self-sovereignty. When one has enthroned himself as lord, he will be touchy about his rights and forever fighting for them. On the other hand, when once the Lordship of Christ is established, the question of personal rights falls back to proper size and perspective. From then on the question of rights is handled, not from the perspective of "my rights," but of their relationship to the advancement of the Kingdom.

The apostle Paul is the perfect example of what the Christian attitude toward rights should be. He was inwardly free either to use his rights or to forego them. Luke records three times that he exercised his civil rights as a Roman citizen (Acts 16:37; 22:25-29; 25:10-11). But other rights he chose not to claim in order that he "might win the more" (1 Cor. 9:1-19, NASB).

The Spirit-filled, self-crucified believer can more readily resolve the problems created by the seeming conflict of rights. Two principles will be operative here: Lesser rights will be set aside in order to realize higher rights; and personal rights will be secondary to the rights of others. At the same time the Spirit-filled Christian will more readily recognize phony "right" claims. He may at times refuse what another claims as a right because he sees it is a false claim, and harm rather than good would result from conceding it.

The distorted, often upside-down perception of rights common in today's society is a serious sickness. An exaggerated emphasis on individual and minority rights has resulted in the crippling abridgement of proprietary rights. Pupils claim not only the rights of students, but the rights of teachers and administrators. Employees claim not only the rights of employees but the rights of ownership and management. Examples could be multiplied. And in the confusion one seldom hears a reminder that all rights carry corresponding responsibilities. Christians, at least, should endeavor to think clearly in this vexed and complex area of human life.

See CITIZENSHIP, MONEY, STEWARDSHIP, PROPERTY RIGHTS, CIVIL RIGHTS.

For Further Reading: Wiley, *CT*, 3:68-100.

RICHARD S. TAYLOR

RITSCHLIANISM. This is a form of theological modernism as taught by Albrecht Benjamin Ritschl (1822-99). It denied Christ's deity, as all modernists have done. It denied the doctrine of original sin. Ritschl said, for one thing, on original sin that it cannot be a correct teaching, for it would have meant that all humans would have been sinful to the same degree.

After publications such as Charles Darwin's *Origin of Species* (1859) had caused many people to think that science was going to destroy the Christian faith, Ritschl tried to divorce factual and historical matters from what is "important" in Christianity, so that science could not hurt Christianity—and to affirm Christianity's importance in the realm of values and the moral life. But Christianity is rooted in the very soil of history and facticity, and orthodox Christians feel that Ritschl's divorcement of facticity matters from values, and affirming only the values, was far too much of a sacrifice.

Karl Barth (1886-1968), who emphasized such facticity matters as Christ's virgin birth and His bodily resurrection, led out in a theological movement which pretty well succeeded in discounting Ritschlianism.

See LIBERALISM, DEMYTHOLOGIZATION, DARWINISM.

For Further Reading: Barth, *Protestant Theology in the 19th Century;* Fletcher, *The Moderns.*

J. KENNETH GRIDER

RITUAL. This is the conscious effort to remind ourselves of, and to exhibit to others in accurate form, the substance of our Christian faith. It seems that usually, the more simple ritual is, the more authentically it fulfills its function of symbolizing realities of our faith.

Both the OT and the NT reject ceremonialism as a substitute for a right heart relationship with God. The Lord delights not in sacrifices, but in a contrite and obedient heart (Ps. 40:6-8; 51:16-17; 1 Sam. 15:22). Outward ceremonies do not effect salvation (Acts 15:1, 24; 1 Cor. 1:14-17). Pure religion is not ritual, but participation in the grace of God (Rom 14:17). Ordinances, rites, and holy days are no substitute for a heart and life altogether devoted to God (1 Cor. 7:19; Gal. 5:2, 6; Col. 2:16-17).

However, when the prophets condemned ritualism, they were not rejecting Temple worship with its sacrifices and offerings. They meant that when these are performed without a heart and life that corresponds with the religious profession, they are vain (Isa. 1:13-14; 1 Sam. 15:22). Rituals are not magical formulae to atone for sin.

The purpose of rituals, then, is to seek to embody and convey in a form other than words the true attitude and condition of the heart toward God. The performance is designed to strengthen the resolve (Acts 2:38, 41; Luke 22:19).

The NT allows few rituals: baptism and the Lord's Supper, and perhaps ordination. Circumcision was substituted by the Early Church with the rite of baptism as the NT sign of the people of God.

Jesus taught that ceremonialism is not Christianity. The forms of religion, with their rules and regulations outlined in the oral traditions of His day, are neither an excuse nor a cure for breaking the commandments of God (Mark 7:7-9). With Jesus' full approval, His followers did not observe the oral traditions, which many times violated the direct commands of God (vv. 9-13).

However, ritualistic ceremonies may manifest a righteous heart. They help fulfill all righteousness, as in the case of Jesus in Matt. 3:15. They are fitting for us, also, not as payment for our salvation, but as a testimony to it and as an aid in reverent worship.

See LITURGY (LITURGICS), WORSHIP, SACRAMENTARIANISM, REBAPTISM.

For Further Reading: "Sacraments," *DCT;* Wiley, *CT,* 3:147-52, 185; *GMS,* 99 ff, 179, 415 ff.

JOHN B. NIELSON

ROGERIAN COUNSELING. Carl R. Rogers is one of the best-known therapists and teachers of counseling of our day. Part of the existential school of psychology, he, along with Rollo May, Abraham Maslow, and others, believes a person's constant flow of choices, big and little, add up to a kind of life's cumulative grade point average, determining the kind of person one becomes. Rogers and the existentialists focus on one's efforts at finding fulfillment, personal identity, and meaning, all of which are interlocked.

Client-centered therapy, primarily associated with Carl Rogers, tends not to hold clients responsible for their problems. But Rogers is criticized because he provides no clear guidance for dealing with difficulties. Clearly there is a happy medium between the directive counseling of Jay Adams and the nondirective approach of Carl Rogers.

Part of the problem with Rogerian counseling is theological. Rogers believes man is inherently good. Why, then, does one suffer corruption? The answer lies in the influence of others. Believing that, patients will, of course, engage both in self-pity and hostility. It is difficult to imagine Carl Rogers raising Karl Menninger's question, "Whatever became of sin?"

Rogers believes personality maladjustments result from failure to integrate all experiences into one's self-image. Acceptance of experiences good and bad is healthy; denial of experiences creates feelings and perceptions not consistent with one's self-image. Denial also makes "inconsistent" experiences threatening and divorces one from reality. These false (dishonest) perceptions persisted in, cause the building of defenses against reality (truth) and result in mounting tensions. Healthy personalities adjust to reality as it comes and therefore tend to perceive accurately.

Rogers' experience taught him therapy comes in a three-step process: (1) The patient begins to accept himself as he is with his feelings, sexuality, understandings, perceptions, etc.; (2) he begins to get insight about the dynamics (reasons) underlying his behavior; (3) he gets handles for a more constructive life-style—i.e., he accepts himself as he is and learns to live out that self, to be himself. That true self expressed, Rogers believes, will behave in socially acceptable ways. The Christian theologian is not so sure; regeneration and continuing works of grace have capabilities of saving people from egocentric action associated with sin.

See PERSON (PERSONALITY), PASTORAL COUNSELING, INTEGRITY THERAPY, ACCOUNTABILITY, PELAGIANISM, MATURITY.

For Further Reading: Kagan and Havemann, *Psychology: An Introduction;* Rogers, *On Becoming a Person;* Tweedie, *The Christian and the Couch,* 119-20, 151.

DONALD E. DEMARAY

ROMAN CATHOLICISM. See CATHOLICISM, ROMAN.

RULE, RULER. See KINGDOM OF GOD.

RULE OF FAITH. There are two aspects to the rule of faith (Latin, *regula fidei*): the Bible itself and summaries of its main doctrines—i.e., creeds and articles of faith.

Among Protestants, there is a general agreement that the Bible is the sole and supreme Rule of faith and conduct (2 Tim. 3:14-17). As such, the Bible marks out the territory of essential belief. Anything outside its limits cannot be imposed as an essential article of faith. Anything which contradicts it, rightly interpreted, is unorthodox and, if persisted in, is heretical.

Creeds, or confessions, are derived from the Bible. They constitute the rule of faith in a secondary sense.

Some people seize on certain expressions of Holy Writ and wrest them into a system which is contrary to the teaching of the Bible as a whole. This can be prevented or corrected by drawing up confessions of faith which summarize essential and orthodox belief as revealed in the Scriptures. For the Protestant, they derive their authority from the Bible, and are only valid as they are true expositions of its message.

We can see the beginnings of this process of forming creeds in reference to the apostles' teaching (Acts 2:42), and in such passages of Scripture as 1 Cor. 15:1-4; Eph. 4:4-6; Phil. 2:5-11; 1 Tim. 2:3-6; Titus 2:11-14; etc.

Though it cannot be historically traced back to the apostles, what is known as the Apostles' Creed is a summary of biblical doctrine. As such, it is accepted by many denominations. For theologians, the creeds of Nicea (325) and Chalcedon (451), the beginning and end of a process defining the deity and humanity of Christ and the unity of both in One Person, are a valid definition of biblical truth and, as such, a test of orthodoxy.

Although the Bible is such a vast depository of truth, there is a remarkable agreement on the basic doctrines among those churches which give it the supreme place as *the* Rule of faith.

See HERMENEUTICS, BIBLE, BIBLICAL AUTHORITY, CANON.

For Further Reading: Wiley, *CT,* 1:185-214, esp. 201-14; Pope, *A Compendium of Christian Theology,* 1:33-230.

JACK FORD

S

SABBATARIANISM. This refers to the Christian observance of the seventh day in conformity with the fourth commandment, or the transference of Sabbath observances to Sunday.

Seventh-Day Sabbatarianism. Palestinian Jewish Christians probably continued to observe the customary Sabbath to avoid unnecessary offence and as an occasion for evangelism. But during the first two centuries the church as a whole abandoned the Sabbath in favor of worship on the Lord's Day. Following the precedent of Col. 2:16 ff and Heb. 3:7—4:11, patristic writers understood the Sabbath rest not as bodily inactivity but as spiritual and perpetual abstinence from *evil* works for devotion to worship and/or as the awaited eschatological Sabbath.

During the third and fourth centuries the Sabbath was kept by many Christians as a memorial of creation. Significantly, however, this Christian observance was *not* marked by not working. After the fifth century the practice once again disappeared—only to be revived in modern times by Seventh-Day Adventists and others.

Sunday Sabbatarianism. The disappearance of seventh-day Sabbatarianism was perhaps a consequence of Constantine's decree (A.D. 321) making Sunday the official Roman day of rest and the resulting tendency to regard it as "the Christian Sabbath." Until Constantine it was not possible for many Christians, because of their low socioeconomic status, to treat Sunday as a day of rest, had they desired to do so. Subsequently the unexpectedly successful state church, newly responsible for the moral life of the entire empire, reacted to the abuses of Sunday idleness by applying the fourth commandment to Sunday. Sabbatarianism was an important feature of medieval Catholic theory, if not practice, against which many early Reformers protested.

The most striking development of Sabbatarianism occurred in late 16th-century English Puritanism, originally as a reaction more to the drunkenness and sordid amusements which Sunday holidays occasioned among the lower and middle classes, than to Sunday labor. Eventually nearly all the OT Sabbath regulations were applied to Sunday. This is the background of American expressions of Sabbatarianism, such as the so-called blue laws.

Implications. It is a fact that of the Ten Commandments only the 4th, "Remember the sabbath day, to keep it holy" (Exod. 20:8; cf. Deut. 5:12), is not repeated in the NT. In view of the occasional nature of much of the NT literature, its omission may be entirely coincidental however (cf. Rom. 13:9 which specifically cites the last five commandments and "any other commandment").

Despite Jesus' clear rejection of Pharisaic casuistry as applied to the Sabbath, He customarily participated in the weekly synagogue worship assembly (cf. Luke 4:16-27) and used the traditional cessation of ordinary labors afforded, not for inactivity but to act mercifully in behalf of needy men (Mark 1:29-31; 3:1-6; Luke 13:10-17; 14:1-6; John 5:2-18; 9:1-41).

Paul specifically rejects the Judaizing observance of the sabbath (Gal. 4:9-11; Col. 2:16-17), for every day for the Christian is the Lord's although one day may be observed in preference to the others (Rom. 14:5-6). The widely shared view that Christianity fulfilled Judaism by no means led early Christians to diminish the importance of regular community worship (cf. Heb. 10:19-25, esp. 25) or the sanctity of the Lord's day, but instead led them to sanctify every day.

This offers no support for legalistic or rigidly scrupulous expressions of Christian Sabbatarianism, but neither does it endorse the all-too-easy modern disregard for regular worship in favor of self-indulging leisure. At issue in the modern setting is not only the respect due the Lord's day, but the proper utilization of the increasing hours of leisure which are also the Lord's. On these issues Paul advises, "Let every one be fully convinced in his own mind," and, "Happy is he who has no reason to judge himself for what he approves" (Rom. 14:5, 22, RSV).

See LORD'S DAY, REST (REST OF FAITH), LAW.

For Further Reading: Breward, "Sabbatarianism," *NIDCC,* 869 f; Corlett, *The Christian Sabbath;* Knappen, *Tudor Puritanism,* 442-50; *IDB,* 3:151 ff; Rordorf, *Sunday: The History of the Day of Rest and Worship in the Earliest*

Centuries of the Christian Church; Beckwith and Scott, *This Is the Day;* Wiley, *CT,* 3:143-50; *GMS,* 542.
GEORGE LYONS

SABBATH. See LORD'S DAY.

SABELLIANISM. This is the anti-Trinitarian teaching of the ancient Sabellius, that the Father, Son, and Spirit do not exist at the same time as three Persons in one nature (as in Trinitarianism), but as three successive ways in which the unipersonal God has manifested himself historically: first as Father, then as the Son, then as the Holy Spirit. The view is called Modalism because the three are not persons, but three successive modes or fashions in which the uni-personal God has manifested himself. It is called Monarchianism when the stress is upon the oneness in God which this antithreeness view of God makes possible.

See UNITARIANISM, TRINITY (THE HOLY), ECONOMIC TRINITY.

For Further Reading: Tertullian, *Against Praxeas;* Lowry, *The Trinity and Christian Devotion;* Augustine, *On Christian Doctrine.* J. KENNETH GRIDER

SACRAMENTARIANISM. This is the attachment of exaggerated importance to the sacraments. It is the tendency to link personal salvation too rigidly to the correct performance of approved sacramental rituals. The sacraments in general are seen as the primary if not sole means by which grace is mediated and received. An accentuation of the sacramentarian viewpoint can be seen in the inflexible insistence of some groups that there can be no salvation apart from immersion in water; a variation is the observance of the Lord's Supper in every worship service, or at least on every Lord's day. Some Lutherans rely on the Lord's Supper as the periodic absolution from sin; to withhold the Lord's Supper is to withhold forgiveness. In these and other ways the sacraments are thus elevated to the level of spiritual mechanics, and become a revival of Judaism within a Christian context.

See SACRAMENTS, BAPTISM, HOLY COMMUNION, BAPTISMAL REGENERATION.

For Further Reading: Wiley, *CT,* 2:413 ff; 3:157; Curtis, *The Christian Faith,* 425-33. RICHARD S. TAYLOR

SACRAMENTS. Our word *sacrament* comes from the Latin *sacramentum,* originally applied to money deposited in a sacred place by parties involved in court proceedings. It was regarded as a pledge that the participants considered their cause good and just. It came also to signify the Roman soldier's oath of fidelity. Early Latin church fathers used the term to translate the Greek *musterion,* "mystery": something eminently and especially sacred. So it is the word has come to signify a sacred ordinance or rite in which the Christian believer receives blessing from God and deliberately binds himself in covenant to Him. Theologically, the term "signifies an outward and visible sign of an inward and spiritual grace given unto us, ordained by Christ himself, as a means whereby we receive the same, and a pledge to assure us thereof" (Wiley, *CT,* 3:155).

The Roman and Greek Catholic churches observe seven sacraments: baptism, the Lord's Supper, confirmation, penance, extreme unction, ordination, and matrimony. These sacraments, it is held, actually contain the grace they signify, and when properly administered by the priest convey grace to the soul of every person who, without mortal sin, receives them.

At the opposite pole from this belief in the inherent virtue of the sacraments themselves is the Socinian view that the sacraments do not differ from any other religious rite or ceremony. Their only use, it is said, is to incite pious sentiments and give the believer an opportunity to testify to his faith.

Protestant doctrine generally recognizes two sacraments: baptism and the Lord's Supper. Only these are observed because only they were instituted by Christ (Matt. 28:19; 26:26-27). Also, it is believed by some that these two have their origins in the OT rites of circumcision and the Passover. The first, a sacrament of the covenant of grace symbolizing the cutting away of sin, was replaced in the NT by baptism. The latter, symbolizing the deliverance of God's people, was replaced by the Lord's Supper.

Saving grace does not come through observing the sacraments. That is received only through personal faith in Jesus Christ; but the sacraments are a source of divine blessing. "To everyone who receives the sign a seal and pledge of the invisible grace is also given; and everyone who draws near with a true heart and with full assurance of faith does, in his own person, enter into God's covenant" (Wakefield, *Christian Theology,* 556).

Some Protestant groups do not participate in either of the sacraments. The Quakers, or Friends, and the Salvation Army are examples. The Quakers in particular hold that the visible rites and symbols distract from what the Spirit of God really wants to do for the believer.

See SACRAMENTS (QUAKER AND S.A. VIEWS), SACRAMENTARIANISM, BAPTISM, HOLY COMMUNION.

For Further Reading: Wiley, *CT,* 3:155-74; Purkiser, ed., *Exploring Our Christian Faith,* 409-15; Demaray, *Basic Beliefs,* 113-30. ARMOR D. PEISKER

SACRAMENTS: QUAKER AND SALVATION ARMY VIEWS. The Religious Society of Friends (Quakers) and The Salvation Army are unique in Christendom because of their outward nonobservance of the sacraments of baptism and the Lord's Supper.

At the ideological level, the sacramental understanding of Quakers and Salvationists is largely structured by four factors: First, the philosophical framework of the Quaker and Salvationist interpretation is a sacramental world view. Because they "take so seriously the idea that ours is a sacramental universe . . . they cannot limit the notion to a particular ceremony" (Trueblood, *The People Called Quakers,* 138; cf. *The Sacraments: the Salvationist's Viewpoint,* 78).

Second, inseparable from this sacramental world view is the theological focus that since Jesus came to replace shadow with substance, as the writer to the Hebrews emphasizes, why would He then institute two more ceremonies which point to spiritual reality?

These two factors are crucial, for without an awareness of them the Quaker and Salvationist viewpoints are incomprehensible.

Third, the philosophical framework and theological focus interact within a biblical perspective called "the prophetic tradition." In contrast to the "priestly" emphasis on ritual in the worship of God, the prophets insisted "that an inward life of conformity to the mind of God was the only condition on which His will could find expression in the outward life" (*The Sacraments: the Salvationist's Viewpoint,* 74). This tradition, however, does not necessarily negate ceremonies. Rather, it provides a corrective to at least two dangers inherent in ceremonial: "To think that unless the sign is there, God's Spirit will not be there . . . [and] to think that *if* the sign is there *my* spirit need not be there" (William Metcalf, *The Salvationist and the Sacraments,* 30). Thus, as those who identify themselves with the prophetic tradition, both Quakers and Salvationists confess that God's grace may be received apart from as well as in conjunction with the sacraments. Hence, they do not criticize those who meaningfully observe the sacraments.

Fourth, Quakers and Salvationists believe that the effect of the three preceding factors makes room for a valid hermeneutical approach which enables them adequately to account for and interpret the obvious presence of baptism and the Lord's Supper in many of the NT documents. This approach involves the concept of progressive revelation: Not only is there in the NT itself a development away from and beyond the ceremonial emphasis in the OT, there is within the NT itself an apparent movement away from and beyond sacramental emphases. This may be seen in the increasing silence concerning baptism and Communion in the chronologically later writings of the NT. When baptism and the Lord's Supper are viewed within the broader, progressively revelatory context of Scripture, Quakers and Salvationists believe that we cannot say that they are necessary for salvation and/or a maturing Christian experience, nor can we substantiate that Jesus instituted them as binding and perpetual observances in the Church.

As a result of this understanding of the sacraments, Quakers and Salvationists affirm that their attitude toward baptism and the Lord's Supper is positive rather than negative. This is because both movements witness to the fact that apart from the outward observance of the sacraments we may experience the realities to which they point: the baptism with the Holy Spirit and continual communion with the indwelling Christ. In this way they seek to observe the sacraments existentially, at their deepest level, rather than ceremonially.

See SACRAMENTS, SACRAMENTARIANISM.

For Further Reading: Booth, *Echoes and Memories,* 201-10; Brown, *Sacraments: A Quaker View;* McKinley, "Quaker Influence on the Early Salvation Army: An Essay in Practical Theology," *Heritage of Holiness,* 47-55; Trueblood, *Robert Barclay,* 215-30.

JOHN G. MERRITT

SACRIFICE. "Sacrifice" is a translation of a Hebrew noun *(zebah)* meaning literally "slaughter" and referring to the killing of a domestic animal as an offering to the Deity. A sacrifice may function in two ways: as a gift to God or as an atonement in overcoming estrangement between man and God. Since the OT gives no rationale for sacrifice as atonement, one must decide how it functions on the basis of theological analysis. There are two options: (1) propitiation, in which the sacrifice appeases the Deity and changes His attitude toward man; (2) expiation, in which the offerer's sin is removed so that he is "qualified" to stand in God's presence.

Pagan sacrifices are merely propitiatory in nature and thus do not necessarily call for an ethical response on the part of the worshipper. By contrast, the preexilic prophets constantly rebuke Israel for a lack of ethical responsibility. In fact, they condemn the sacrificial system so severely, even in some instances seeming to question its place in the divine order (cf. Amos 5:21-25; Jer. 7:21 ff), that many scholars have felt that they were against sacrifices per se. However, a more adequate interpretation suggests that they were actually condemning its misuse, that is, practicing it as propitiation as defined above rather than as expiation.

Since the term "propitiation" has traditionally been included in atonement vocabulary, most Wesleyan theologians retain it by redefining it so as to include expiation as still the primary element. This is done in terms of the holiness of God which is seen as love's opposition to sin and experienced by the sinner as wrath. His holiness stands as a barrier to a divine-human relationship, since love cannot abide the presence of sin. When the sin of man is removed, he then finds acceptance by God and, in his experience of being reconciled to God, senses that God is reconciled to Him. The removal of sin "satisfied" the holiness of God in this sense, and to that "satisfaction" the term "propitiation" is applied; but its meaning is radically altered from the pagan concept of changing God's mind by an offering. As H. Orton Wiley states it, quoting W. B. Pope, "Strictly speaking the atoning sacrifice declares a propitiation already in the divine heart" (Wiley, *CT,* 2:287).

The NT applies the symbol of sacrifice to the death of Christ. Hebrews stresses the inadequacy of the OT system to "really take away sins" (10:4, TLB), that is, to change the worshipper. It provided for a justification in which the worshipper is forensically declared righteous (a relative change) but not for sanctification (a real change). In contrast, the sacrifice of Christ "made perfect forever those who are being made holy" (v. 14, NIV). The death of Christ was not a sacrifice which appeased God or changed His attitude toward man; rather, it was the act of God in Christ reconciling the world to himself.

See GOD, ATONEMENT, OFFER (OFFERING), SATISFACTION, DAY OF ATONEMENT, EXPIATION, PROPITIATION, SIN OFFERING.

For Further Reading: Gray, *Sacrifice in the Old Testament;* "Sacrifice," *Theological Word Book of the Bible,* ed. Richardson.

H. RAY DUNNING

SACRIFICIAL LAMB. See LAMB, SACRIFICIAL.

SADDUCEES. This group of Jews constituted one of the three leading religious sects of Palestine preceding and during the life of Christ. Their name may have been derived from Zadok, the progenitor of the high-priestly line under King Solomon (1 Kings 1:32, 34, 38, 45). Ezekiel refers to the chief priests as "sons of Zakok" (Ezek. 40:46; 44:15 ff). On the other hand, their name may be a Hebraization of the Greek word *syndikoi* ("syndics"—"members of the council"), a term which may go back to the Hasmonaeans, of which the Sadducees were councilors. However, the Sadducees gave the impression that their title derives from the Hebrew *saddiqim,* which means "righteous ones."

During the postexilic period, these men, who came from the upper levels of society, controlled the life of the Jews through religious sanctions.

The views of the Sadducees may be summarized as follows: (1) They accepted only the written law, the Torah, and rejected the oral tradition which grew up around it and which was accepted by the Pharisees. They were very literal in their interpretation of the Torah. (2) They were antisupernaturalists to the extent of denying the existence of angels and the doctrine of the resurrection of the dead. (3) They insisted on a very formal style of worship, a natural consequence of their control of the Temple.

History has not been too kind to the Sadducees, in that it has perpetuated the idea that they were very this-worldly and were materialistic in their outlook. Being the ruling party in their time in a small country whose existence, at the best, was tenuous, they tended to act according to expediency with respect to matters of culture and politics. They have been accused of capitulating easily to the Romans and to the Greek culture, much to the dismay of the rank and file Jews. The attitude of the Qumran community toward the Temple practices and the priesthood in Jerusalem is a clear witness to this fact. The Pharisees constituted the part of the people and for that reason were constantly at odds with the Sadducees.

With the fall of Jerusalem in A.D. 70 the Sadducees disappeared from the life of the Jews.

See PHARISEES.

For Further Reading: Bruce, *New Testament History,* 69-81; Lohse, *The New Testament Environment,* 74-77; Jeremias, *Jerusalem in the Time of Jesus,* 222-32.

WILLARD H. TAYLOR

SAINT, SAINTLINESS. A saint (Latin *sanctus*) is a holy and eminently godly person. However, believers are customarily called "saints" *(hagioi)* in the NT (some 55 times), even when yet carnal (1 Cor. 6:2; 14:33; 16:1, 15). Such positional sanctity is expected to become true saintliness in life and character (1:2, NIV).

Beyond this religious and/or biblical use there is the formal, official practice of the Roman Catholic church of the beatification and canonization of specially chosen people. More than 100 days of the year are dedicated to some saint. There is also the diverse, rather loose, usage of the term *saint* in naming people, places, events, or even birds and beasts.

One net result of all of this is the obscuring of the true biblical meaning and the avoidance of its serious use lest one be regarded as spiritually proud.

Nevertheless, biblical basics remain. (1) Man is hopelessly lost and away from God, sinful in act and disposition. (2) God, by His redeeming grace in Christ and the presence and power of the Holy Spirit, can deliver man from all sin and make him a saint fit for heaven. "This sainthood is not an attainment, it is a state into which God in grace calls men" (Vine, *ED,* 2:226; cf. Eph. 5:25-27).

The order of salvation by which God makes saints is conviction (convincing people of their sinfulness), conversion (initial sanctification), progressive sanctification, entire sanctification (the baptism with the Holy Spirit), further progressive sanctification, glorification. In this saint-making process there are both continuity and crisis, both human and divine elements; but the origin and adequacy are all of God.

See HOLINESS, CHRISTIAN PERFECTION, CHRISTLIKENESS, SANCTIFICATION.

For Further Reading: Wiley, *CT,* 3:7-67; *GMS,* 462-507; Sangster, *The Pure in Heart.*

JOHN E. RILEY

SALT. Crystallized rock salt was valued as a seasoning and food preservative by all ancient people. In earliest times the Hebrews obtained salt from the Salt Sea (Gen. 14:3), and particularly from the hill of salt at the southwestern corner, an area associated with the fate of Lot's wife, who, looking back at Sodom, turned into a pillar of salt (19:26).

Highly valued, salt became a symbol of fidelity and constancy, and was used in salt agreements —covenants between man and man and between God and man (Num. 18:19; 2 Chron. 13:5). In the Levitical cereal (grain) offering salt was the key preservative, symbolizing God's faithfulness and man's constancy (Lev. 2:13).

While usually a symbol for that which was held in esteem, occasionally salt suggested the result of destruction, the wasteland, the desert (Deut. 29:23; Job 39:6; Jer. 17:6). Abimelech sprinkled salt on Shechem after his destruction of the city, thereby symbolizing its perpetual desolation (Judg. 9:45).

Jesus spoke of His disciples as "the salt of the earth," referring to their seasoning and preserving qualities (Matt. 5:13). He did note that when they lose those spiritual qualities, they become insipid and worthless (Luke 14:34-35).

Paul urged that the Christian's speech be "seasoned with salt," a metaphor meaning gracious wholesomeness (Col. 4:6). Salt is also a symbol of Christian peace and unity (Mark 9:50).

See LIGHT, LEAVEN.

For Further Reading: *NBD,* 1125. BERT H. HALL

SALVATION. Deeply embedded in the record of the OT is the Exodus from Egypt. The vocabulary of salvation harks back to this birthday of the nation of Israel. Israel saw itself as having been saved from bondage to foreigners and given civil and religious freedom to worship Yahweh their God, and henceforth attributed their deliverance to their miracle-working Deity. Gradually this concept acquired a more spiritual and personal meaning of deliverance from sin and/or sickness. This is especially evident in Psalms and Isaiah. Most of the occurrences of the term "salvation" occur in these two OT books. The concept came into prominence during the Exile when once again God was asked to save them from their Assyrian and Babylonian captors and restore them to their homeland. Accordingly the connotation given the term "salvation" is best determined by its immediate context.

The idea of salvation is often presented under different terminology. Thus, in Ezekiel the sinner will "live" if he repents (chap. 18). In the Psalms the trend is from the national and corporate to the personal and individual. The deliverance sought in the Psalms is from enemies (7:1), from disease (6:2-4), from bloodguiltiness (51:14), and from sin (38:8; 79:9).

It is in the Epistles that the concept of salvation acquires its most specific Christian expression. As stated in Romans, all have sinned, whether Jew or Gentile, and hence all need salvation from sin (1:18—3:18). Mankind is "dead in trespasses and sin" (Eph. 2:1) and therefore is powerless to save itself by good works or attempts to keep the Mosaic law. The law itself is not the means of salvation; it simply exposes the sin; hence the need for salvation only through Christ.

Salvation comes only through Jesus Christ who offers His own sinless life as a substitute for the guilty. He died that believers may live eternally. This idea of a sinner, treated as though he had never sinned because his guilt is borne by the Son of God himself, is the central and most distinctive feature of the Christian religion.

Thus salvation from personal sin involves the removal of guilt and also the sentence of death. Positively it bestows the new status of adoption or sonship, and hence of "joint-heirs with Christ" (Rom. 8:17; cf. 1 Pet. 3:7). It may be experienced immediately when one believes. It is also a continuing process as one grows in grace and in the knowledge of Christ (2 Pet. 1:3-11). Finally, salvation occurs when one receives the commendation following the Last Judgment, "Well done, thou good and faithful servant; . . . enter thou into the joy of thy lord" (Matt. 25:21). The climax of the salvation theme, and of the Bible itself, is found in Rev. 21:3—"Behold, the dwelling of God is with men. He will dwell with them, and they shall be his people, and God himself will be with them" (RSV); God and man in at-one-ment.

During the intertestamental period the idea of a future judgment became increasingly prominent as the doctrine of a general resurrection was stressed by the Pharisees. Such was the situation when John the Baptist began to call people to repentance to escape the "wrath to come," the "day of wrath"—not as catastrophe to the nation, as in the prophets (Zeph. 1:14-16), but rather a day of general judgment on all mankind to determine their destiny (cf. Matt. 3:6-12; 12:41-42). Salvation of the individual and of the nation was linked with increasing emphasis on the individual (cf. 12:36; 25:31-46). Repentance, as the condition for salvation, stressed first in the prophets (Amos 4:11-12; Isa. 1:16-18), addressed to the nation, became more personal in the exilic and postexilic periods (Ezek. 18:5-24), and received its most emphatic expression in John the Baptist.

In the period of Jesus' ministry, salvation of the lost was focused on such villages as Capernaum and Chorazin (Matt. 11:20-24). They failed to receive Jesus' message and repent. By contrast the Samaritans did receive the gospel (John 4:39-42) with great joy (Acts 8:5, 8, 25).

Increasingly the emphasis was on individual repentance, faith, and salvation from sin in this life. In the Fourth Gospel salvation is equated with eternal life, a spiritual life, given by God, and experienced now, and not limited to an extension of this life in heaven. Salvation here is a quality of life, not simply an extension of life (John 5:21-29).

In addition to the salvation of the soul is the resurrection of the body into a new level of personal existence (1 Cor. 15:21-28). Paul speaks of the "redemption of our body" in connection with "adoption" as sons (Rom. 8:23).

Salvation also involves all of creation in a manner not specifically indicated—"the creation itself will be liberated from its bondage to decay" (v. 21, NIV) and ultimately there will be "new heavens and a new earth in which righteousness dwells" (2 Pet. 3:13, RSV). Accordingly, "every knee [shall] bow . . . and . . . every tongue . . . confess that Jesus Christ is Lord, to the glory of God the Father" (Phil. 2:10-11).

See REDEEMER (REDEMPTION), CONVERSION, SANCTIFICATION, RESURRECTION OF THE BODY.

For Further Reading: Stevens, *The Christian Doctrine of Salvation;* Denney, *The Death of Christ;* Cullmann, *Salvation in History.* GEORGE ALLEN TURNER

SANCTIFICATION. This is the English translation of the Greek *hagiasmos* (10 times in the NT; noun form of *hagiazō,* "sanctify," 29 times; adjective *hagios,* "holy," 229 times). The OT equivalent, *qadosh* (830 times in various grammatical forms), is often translated "holiness."

The English terms "sanctification" and "holiness" mean the same in derivation and translate the same Hebrew and Greek terms ("sanctification" from the Latin root *sanctus,* "holy"; "holiness," from the Anglo-Saxon root *halig,* "holy"); but sanctification is popularly used to describe the act or process whereby a state of holiness is realized.

The OT *qadosh* includes ideas of radiance, separation, and purity. The NT *hagiazō* is characteristically defined as separated, consecrated and/or purified, made free from sin.

Biblical theologians characteristically note two basic elements in sanctification in both OT and NT but related in different proportions.

In the OT, the idea of separation or consecration is predominant. Sanctification is separation from the profane and unholy and devotement to God, and thus may be used of things—days, mountains, altars, cities, priestly vestments, the priesthood, the nation, an army. But even in the OT, when used of persons, the idea of cleansing or purity is present and becomes increasingly so in the prophetic writings. The nature of God is seen to be reflected in what human beings ought to be who are separated or consecrated to Him (Isa. 6:1-8; Lev. 19:2; cf. 1 Pet. 1:15-16).

In the NT, the idea of moral purity is predominant, although concepts of ritual purity and consecration are not absent (cf. Matt. 23:17-19; 1 Cor. 7:14).

Theologically, sanctification "means to make clean or holy in the ethical sense, though the idea of consecration is not necessarily lacking" (Rall, *ISBE,* 4:2683, II, 3). It is the total act or process by which inner renewal takes place in the justified. Justification may be said to be "Christ *for* us *with* the Father"; sanctification is "Christ *in* us *by* the Spirit."

As such, technically speaking, sanctification begins in regeneration which may properly be called initial sanctification.

The Wesleyan concept of entire sanctification (1 Thess. 5:23-24) is especially related to the doctrine of the Holy Spirit (Rom. 15:16; 2 Thess. 2:13; 1 Pet. 1:2). While the Holy Spirit is vitally active at every stage of the believer's experience, there is frequent reference to an infilling of the Spirit after conversion (John 14:15-17; Acts 2:1-4; 8:4-8, 14-17; 15:8-9; Eph. 5:18; Gal. 3:14); and Acts frequently distinguishes believers as "filled with the Spirit" from those who as yet lack this full grace (Acts 4:8; 6:2-6; 13:9; etc.).

The essential condition for entire sanctification is faith (Acts 15:8-9; 26:18), but a faith the prerequisite of which is an act of consecration or self-surrender such as only a Christian can make (Rom. 6:13, 19; 12:1-2; 1 Thess. 4:3-8). The NT stresses the requirement that what was potential in the Atonement become actual in the believer (Rom. 6:1-14; 8:1-11; Heb. 12:14-17; 13:11-14).

In the Epistles, entire sanctification as a subsequent work of grace shows up most explicitly in 1 Thessalonians (3:9—4:8; 5:22-24 in relation to 1:2—2:20). It must be remembered that the NT Epistles were written within the context of faith, as *didachē* or instruction for believers and are not addressed to unconverted persons as such. Their frequent exhortations to sanctify must therefore be applied to believers primarily.

A succinct modern formulation of the doctrine of entire sanctification is found in Article 10, "Articles of Faith," *Constitution* of the Church of the Nazarene:

> We believe that entire sanctification is that act of God, subsequent to regeneration, by which believers are made free from original sin, or depravity, and brought into a state of entire devotement to God, and the holy obedience of love made perfect.
>
> It is wrought by the baptism with the Holy Spirit, and comprehends in one experience the cleansing of the heart from sin and the abiding indwelling presence of the Holy Spirit, empowering the believer for life and service.
>
> Entire sanctification is provided by the blood of Jesus, is wrought instantaneously by faith, preceded by entire consecration; and to this work and state of grace the Holy Spirit bears witness.
>
> This experience is also known by various terms representing its different phases, such as "Christian perfection," "perfect love," "heart purity," "the baptism with the Holy Spirit," "the fullness of the blessing," and "Christian holiness."

See ENTIRE SANCTIFICATION, SECOND WORK OF GRACE, HOLINESS, PROGRESSIVE SANCTIFICATION, PURITY AND MATURITY, SERVICE, MORAL ATTRIBUTES OF GOD.

For Further Reading: Lindstrom, *Wesley and Sanctification;* Purkiser, *Sanctification and Its Synonyms;* Steele, *The Gospel of the Comforter;* Taylor, *Life in the Spirit;* Turner, *The Vision Which Transforms;* Wesley, *A Plain Account of Christian Perfection.* W. T. PURKISER

SANCTIFICATION, PROGRESSIVE. See PROGRESSIVE SANCTIFICATION.

SANCTITY OF THE BODY. There have been two major attitudes toward the body on the part of the human race: embarrassment, because it is viewed as evil or shameful; or idolatrous, because it is viewed as the ultimate good or reality. The latter, in the various forms of the body-cult, is the contemporary mood. The body becomes, not an instrument for serving God, but an end in itself. The perspective of 1 Tim. 4:8 is lost.

Frank G. Carver wrote: "There are several ways a person may regard his body. He may pamper and idolize it. He may regard it with disgust or shame. He may use it like a machine to produce work. He may use it as a weapon to gain power. He may dedicate it to carnal pleasures and use it as an instrument of vice. Or with Paul, he may look upon it as a temple" (*BBC,* 8:369). The apostle Paul shows (in 1 Cor. 6:15 ff) that the believer's body is sacred in a way even more special than for the rest of mankind, because it is the means by which his mystical union with Christ is evidenced.

The Judeo-Christian view is not that the body is an evil enemy, to be put off as soon as possible, but a holy constituent of man as divinely created. The dualism of body and spirit is also a unity, to be reestablished by the resurrection. As Wiley put it, "Christianity regards the body not as a prison house of the soul, but as a temple of the Holy Spirit" (*CT,* 3:47).

According to Wiley, the Christian care of the body includes exercise, rest, and recreation; the subjugation of the appetites to man's higher intellectual and spiritual interests; proper clothing, not only for protection and comfort but for propriety and decency. Above all, the body must be preserved holy, as an instrument of the Holy Spirit rather than an instrument of sin. "Holiness destroys nothing that is essential to man, either physically or spiritually. The appetites and passions remain, but they are freed from the incubus of sin" (ibid., 49). And Richard Taylor adds:

"Christian discipline never despises earthly blessings but consecrates them to spiritual ends" (*The Disciplined Life,* 42).

The sanctity of the body is a matter of holy conviction with the Spirit-filled Christian. A wholesome and healthy body is as much a part of his or her divine calling as devotional exercise. He or she will follow Paul in ruling the body rather than in being ruled by it (1 Cor. 9:27). The Christian will not permit it to become an instrument of pride or incitation to lust, but will keep it consecrated always to God as a living sacrifice (Rom. 12:1).

See BODY, CONSECRATION, STEWARDSHIP.

For Further Reading: Wiley, *CT,* 3:47-51; Taylor, *The Disciplined Life.*

NEIL E. HIGHTOWER

SARX. See FLESH.

SATAN. The term "Satan" comes from *Satanas* and is used over 50 times in the Bible. It identifies the one who is man's chief adversary, accuser, and deceiver, which is the meaning of the term. Satan is also the source of slander and the destroyer of peace, which is why he is called the devil (Diabolus), the one who hurls himself against God and man in defiance and prideful rebellion.

Because Satan is the devil, he is also cited in Scripture as being Belial, low and unworthy (2 Cor. 6:15), Beelzebub, the prince of demons (Matt. 12:24), Apollyon, the destroyer (Rev. 9:11), the serpent and dragon (12:7-17), the wicked one (Matt. 13:9), and the enemy of God and man (vv. 25, 28).

That the devil is a personal being is supported by three lines of evidence: First, the Bible describes Satan as having personal attributes (2 Cor. 2:11; Matt. 25:41). Second, the theological teaching about sin is that it began as personal revolt against God, an attempt to set up an autonomous existence (John 8:44; 1 Tim. 3:6). And third, God's people are often keenly and painfully aware of personal opposition in doing God's service (1 Thess. 2:18).

Because Satan's power is large (Matt. 4:8-9; Luke 13:11, 16; Rev. 2:10), albeit limited (Luke 22:31; Jas. 4:7; Jude 9), he is referred to by Christ as being "the prince of this world" (John 12:31; 14:30; 16:11). These references, along with others, provide insight as to Satan's purposes. He seeks to dominate (Isa. 14:12-14), to deceive (Matt. 4:5, 7), to incite disobedience against God (Eph. 2:2), and to destroy God's people and God's kingdom (Eph. 6:10-18).

In attempting to accomplish his purposes as world ruler, Satan seeks to blind the eyes of the unsaved to the gospel (2 Cor. 4:3-4), to snatch the work of God from people's hearts before it can take root (Matt. 13:19), to encourage disobedience (Eph. 2:2), and to make people subservient to his power (1 John 5:19).

To be victorious in the war against Satan, it is important to realize the nature and methods of Satan's attacks. The Christian must be sober, vigilant (1 Pet. 5:8), humble (Jas. 4:6-7), strong in the Lord (Eph. 6:10), prepared for hard trials (1 Cor. 10:13), and aware of Satan's methods (2 Cor. 2:11).

The judgment of Satan has already begun, and his final punishment is certain. Christ came to destroy Satan's work (1 John 3:8). He began by exposing the devil's lies (John 8:44; Matt. 4:1-11). He continued by expelling Satan's dominion (John 12:31; 14:30; 16:11). The climax of Satan's defeat will come when he and his angels are cast into the lake of fire (Matt. 25:41; Rev. 20:2, 10). Thus the Christian is assured of victory over all the power of Satan (Luke 10:19).

See SATAN WORSHIP, DEMONS (DEMON POSSESSION), EXORCISM, SPIRITUAL WARFARE.

For Further Reading: Wiley, *CT,* 2:74-81; Herbert Lockyer, *All the Doctrines of the Bible,* 132-39.

ELDON R. FUHRMAN

SATAN WORSHIP. The biblical terms "devil" or "Satan" describe the source of the evil which entraps humanity. The name "Satan" came from postexilic Hebrew history, but the concept appeared earlier, e.g., as the Genesis serpent (cf. Babylonian "leviathan" and Native American "trickster"—usually a coyote or a bear).

Satan appears in the OT as accuser and adversary who disrupts the divine-human covenant (see Job and Zechariah). Possessing power, Satan nonetheless is subject to God.

In the NT Satan's kingdom of evil contrasts with Christ's kingdom of light. The triumph of Christ over Satan is a central theme of the Revelation.

Satan worship utilizes all modes of knowing, thus depraving sense, reason, and intuition. It is overtly present in ritual and covertly present in idolatry.

Ritualization occurs in the Church of Satan, founded by its high priest, Anton La Vey, who also wrote the Satanic Bible (1969). Rituals may include sexual exploitation and human sacrifice. Occult practices are extracted from ancient religions such as Druidism.

Idolatry occurs more subtly, within the powers which shape human society. As indicated by

Jesus' wilderness experience, satanic temptation to turn commerce, governance, and religion into ends rather than means lies at the root of false worship. Satan's messengers masquerade as angels of light (see 2 Cor. 11:13-15). "Culture religion" is a term used to describe modern idolatry.

The Church overcomes evil by the blood of Christ and the word of testimony (Rev. 12:11). Christian holiness affirms this triumph.

See SATAN, DEMONS (DEMON POSSESSION), SIN (ORIGIN OF).

For Further Reading: Eliade, *Occultism, Witchcraft, and Cultural Fashions; HDNT,* 2:569 ff.

ARTHUR O. ROBERTS

SATISFACTION. This word appears in only two places in the KJV and translates the Hebrew *kopher* which means "a price paid as compensation" (Num. 35:31-32). Other versions employ the word "ransom" in these verses, but even so the concept of atonement is incipient in these instances. The term "satisfaction" is not used in the NT, but the idea surfaces in passages which speak of Christ's death as satisfying some divine and human necessities (cf. Rom. 6:23; 2 Cor. 5:14-15, 21; Gal. 3:13; Titus 2:14; 1 Pet 2:24).

In the history of the Christian church "satisfaction" became a significant theological term expressing some of the deep meanings of the work of Christ. Until the Middle Ages the term was related to repentance. Tertullian in the second century wrote that God as Judge demands justice of His creatures, and this demand can only be met by repentance. The practice of repentance in subsequent centuries became formalized in penance as a sacrament and in expected religious deeds, which fulfilled the satisfaction due to God.

It was Anselm of Canterbury (1033-1109) who tied the word to soteriology, especially the doctrine of the Atonement. He published his classic study *Cur Deus Homo,* in which he rejected the long-held ransom theory and set forth the view that the death of Christ was a satisfaction rendered to God's justice and honor. This was the first scientific statement of atonement ideas implicit in teachings of the church fathers. Wiley summarizes Anselm's theory as follows: "Sin violates the divine honor, and deserves infinite punishment since God is infinite. Sin is guilt or a debt, and under the government of God, this debt must be paid. This necessity is grounded in the infinite perfections of God. . . . Man cannot pay this debt, for he is not only finite, but morally bankrupt through sin. Adequate satisfaction being impossible from a being so inferior to God as man is, the Son of God became man in order to pay the debt for us. Being divine, He could pay the infinite debt; and being both human and sinless, could properly represent man. But as sinless He was not obligated to die, and owing no debt on His own account, He received as a reward of His merit, the forgiveness of our sins" (Wiley, *CT,* 2:235-36).

Anselm's theory was amplified by Aquinas (1225-74) and became normative for Catholic theology and influential in Protestant thought. However, the major change occurred in Protestant atonement theory when the Reformers invested the idea of satisfaction with the meaning of substitution instead of merit. The satisfaction of the divine justice was effected by Christ bearing the punishment due mankind. This penal satisfaction theory has held the field in the Reformed tradition. Its major weakness rests in the doubtful assertion that Christ who is sinless can really bear our penalty.

Hugo Grotius (1583-1645) advanced the governmental theory which acknowledges the need for satisfaction but limited it to the maintenance of the government of God throughout the universe. The sufferings of Christ are substituted for our rightful punishment, and God's acceptance of them is the point of satisfaction. As a result, the dignity of the divine government is effectively upheld and vindicated just as if we had received the punishment deserved.

Liberal views of the Atonement, such as Abelard's moral influence theory, give little attention to the issue of satisfaction and substitution and focus on the saving impact of the demonstration of divine love in the death of Christ.

Finally, the satisfaction aspect of atonement theory takes seriously the exploration of the meaning of the NT's consistent declaration that Christ died for us.

See ATONEMENT, ATONEMENT (THEORIES OF), PROPITIATION, VICARIOUS.

For Further Reading: Anselm, *Cur Deus Homo;* Bromiley, *Historical Theology; An Introduction,* 177-80; Wiley, *CT,* 2:270-302.

WILLARD H. TAYLOR

SAVIOR. The One who saves from sin and who is the Source of salvation. Salvation implies the existence of a Savior.

God is a God of salvation; this is the message of both Jewish and Christian faith. He has saved His people and will save them. In the Bible, Savior is both a historical and eschatological reality. God is often called "Savior" (e.g., RSV), which is hence a name for God in the Bible.

The OT allows no other savior than Yahweh.

"I, I am Yahweh, and besides me there is no savior" (cf. Isa. 44:11, RSV). Though appearing as a shadowy form at times, His role as the Deliverer and Savior of the Jewish people is never in question. Repeatedly in the OT the Jewish people are in need of deliverance from adversity, oppression, death, and captivity.

In the NT, the word *sōtēr* occurs 24 times and is translated "Savior" on each occasion. There is a sense in which Christ became the Savior by His incarnation, that is, His taking of human flesh. In a much fuller sense, He became Savior when He died on the Cross. However, the uniqueness of Christ's power to save does not reside in His life or teachings, or even in His person, but primarily in His atoning death and triumphant resurrection. As A. M. Hills says, "No other one ever put his own life and blood into the efficiency of his religion. No other is or can be such a Savior as Christ" (Hills, *Fundamental Christian Theology,* 304-5).

There are many lesser saviors— political, military, medical—but only one Savior from man's three great perils—sin, death, and hell. But the NT assurance is that "he is able also to save them to the uttermost that come unto God by him, seeing he ever liveth to make intercession for them" (Heb. 7:25). He saves from sin now, from death in the resurrection, and from hell in the Judgment. His power to save from all sin now is the assurance of His ability to save from death and hell.

See CHRIST, SOTERIOLOGY, CROSS, ATONEMENT, SALVATION.

For Further Reading: Richardson, ed., *A Theological Word Book of the Bible,* 20; *GMS,* 303-57; Hills, *Fundamental Christian Theology,* 2:104-10.

DONALD R. PETERMAN

SCANDAL. This English term derives from the Greek *skandalon,* which means "that which causes sin" or "gives occasion for sin," or "that which causes stumbling," or "trouble, obstacle." It can also carry the idea of offense or that which offends.

Theologically, "scandal" relates to the exclusiveness of biblical religion. Gerhard Kittel once coined the phrase *das Ärgernes der Einmaligkeit,* "the scandal or offence of particularity." Why did God elect to mediate His salvation through a small, Near Eastern nation like Israel? Why did He choose a Roman cross as the means of propitiation and reconciliation of mankind to himself? These ideas are scandalous and offensive to the sin-bound reason of man. The apostle Paul speaks of his people as having "stumbled over the stumbling stone" (Rom. 9:32, RSV). A crucified Messiah was a stumbling block or scandal to the Jews and folly to the Gentiles (1 Cor. 1:23; Gal. 5:11). But these are facts or truths with which mankind must come to terms. Those who commit themselves to God in faith do not stumble, are not offended, do not sin (1 John 2:7-11; Luke 7:23). Failure to accept God's way of salvation through Christ and the Cross is to remain in sin. Indeed, rejection causes the Stone of Stumbling to become the Rock of Judgment.

See CHRISTIANITY, NON-CHRISTIAN RELIGIONS, COMPARATIVE RELIGION, HEATHEN (FATE OF).

WILLARD H. TAYLOR

SCHISM. The term comes from the Greek *schisma,* literally meaning "a split" or "a tear." In the NT it is usually translated "division" or "dissension," and in 1 Cor. 1:10 and 11:18 refers to factions and parties in the Corinthian congregation.

In the Early Church it describes groups which broke away and formed rival churches. At first it referred to divisions not based on basic doctrine and so not necessarily heretical. According to Calvin (*Institutes,* 4:2-5), Augustine emphasizes this distinction. After the time of Irenaeus (second century), as emphasis on the institutional unity of the church increased, gradually all disruptions were considered schismatic and even sinful.

In Roman Catholic canon law, schism is any break with the unity of the church, whether based on difference in basic doctrine or simple refusal of church authority (*New Catholic Encyclopedia,* 12:1131).

The most serious schism in the Christian church before the Reformation was the East-West division in 1054 in which the church was divided into the Eastern Orthodox and the Roman Catholic churches. This schism was never healed, though certain overtures were made to the Eastern church in 1965.

See HERESY, DIVISION, SEPARATION.

For Further Reading: *Encyclopaedia Britannica Micropaedia,* 5:960; *ERE,* 7:232-35.

M. ESTES HANEY

SCHOLASTICISM. This has to do particularly with the kind of Christian theology that was in vogue during the 9th to the 14th centuries. It made little use of Scripture and much use of ancient pagans such as Plato and Aristotle. It discoursed about God on the basis of reason or dialectics, and on the basis of nature, with its observable phenomena.

See THOMISM, NATURAL THEOLOGY, NATURAL LAW, REALISM AND NOMINALISM.

For Further Reading: Pieper, *Scholasticism: Personalities and Problems of Medieval Philosophy.*

J. KENNETH GRIDER

SCOTTISH REALISM. This term refers to the philosophical movement which was articulated by Thomas Reid during the 18th-century Scottish Enlightenment and which permeated American thought from the Revolution through the Civil War.

Reid sought to apply Newtonian inductive methodology to the study of the human mind, and to combat the skeptical tendencies of Descartes, Locke, Berkeley, and Hume through appeal to "common sense" (common convictions as revealed in practical behavior and common language traits) and "consciousness." One happy outcome was a continuity between the philosophizing of the man in the street and that of the professional, on the one hand, and between professional philosophy and Christian orthodoxy on the other.

Because of Scottish Realism, philosophy in 19th-century America was considered to be the handmaid of biblical revelation. It provided support for the theistic doctrines of Deists, Unitarians, and Transcendentalists, as well as for Calvinistic thinkers such as John Witherspoon, Charles Hodge, and James McCosh at Princeton. However, it also supported a free will position and thus was warmly embraced by such Methodists as Asa Shinn, Nathan Bangs, Wilbur Fiske, and Daniel Whedon, and by such Arminianized Calvinists as Timothy Dwight, Albert Barnes, and Charles G. Finney. It led to a spate of books purporting to refute Edwardian determinism.

Probably Scottish Realism received its finest expression in America in the philosophical writings of Christian holiness authors Asa Mahan and Thomas Upham. Upham gave definitive articulation to a "faculty psychology" which distinguished between intellect, emotion, and volition on the basis of conscious experience. His formulations became the context for understanding human nature in terms of which American evangelical Christianity yet today interprets spiritual experience.

See REALISM AND NOMINALISM, REALISM, EPISTEMOLOGY, HUMAN NATURE.

For Further Reading: Grave, "The Scottish Philosophy of Common Sense," *The Asbury Seminarian,* October, 1977; *The Monist,* April, 1978; Hamilton, articles in *WTJ,* 1974, 1975, and 1978 issues.

JAMES E. HAMILTON

SCRIPTURE. See BIBLE.

SEALING OF THE SPIRIT. Three times in the NT, reference is made to believers being sealed by or with the Holy Spirit (2 Cor. 1:22; Eph. 1:13; 4:30). As John Owen has so succinctly interpreted these statements, "God's sealing of believers then is his gracious communication of the Holy Spirit unto them, so to act his divine power in them, as to enable them unto all the duties of their holy calling, evidencing them to be accepted with him, both for themselves and others and asserting their preservation unto eternal life" (*The Holy Spirit,* 347).

In sealing, the mark can only be made upon the seal by the possessor of the signet, and the seal can only reflect the image of the signet which marks it. The sealing with the Holy Spirit denotes God's ownership of the one sealed, and the life of holiness reflects the presence of the Holy Spirit who seals.

Calvinists understand the sealing with the Spirit as the guaranteed eternal security of the Christian. As Paul indicates in Ephesians, believers are "sealed for the day of redemption" (4:30, RSV), and this sealing is "the guarantee of our inheritance until we acquire possession of it" (1:14, RSV). Arminians have no difficulty accepting the idea of security, but they reject the teaching of an unconditional security effected monergistically by the sealing with the Spirit. When Paul exhorted his readers not to "grieve the Holy Spirit of God, in whom you were sealed for the day of redemption," he did so because they were not being unconditionally preserved for eternal life.

The sealing with the Holy Spirit is not to be identified with conversion. It is distinct from regeneration and subsequent to it (2 Cor. 1:22; Eph. 1:13). It is the work of the Holy Spirit in a believer's heart in sanctifying grace, the witness of a pure heart and the evidence of Christ enthroned.

See HOLY SPIRIT, BAPTISM WITH THE HOLY SPIRIT.

For Further Reading: Carter, *The Person and Ministry of the Holy Spirit,* 302-5; Marsh, *Emblems of the Holy Spirit,* 26-37; Gordon, *The Ministry of the Spirit,* 75-89.

WILLIAM B. COKER

SECOND BLESSING. See SECOND WORK OF GRACE.

SECOND CHANCE. See FUTURE PROBATION.

SECOND COMING OF CHRIST. The revelation of eschatology (end-time events) in the Bible clearly sets Christianity apart from, and above, all non-Christian religions. An adequate view of God is the basic foundation of Christianity. And such a view provides an order of events from creation to the closing events of time. The second coming of Christ is central to this understanding of end-time events, or eschatology.

Among the many passages which form the basis for our belief in the Second Coming are: "Hereafter shall ye see the Son of man sitting on the right hand of power, and coming in the clouds of heaven" (Matt. 26:64), and Jesus' promise, "I go to prepare a place for you. And if I go and prepare a place for you, I will come again, and receive you unto myself; that where I am, there ye may be also" (John 14:2-3). The very last words recorded in Scripture, given some 60 years or more after Christ's ascension, were spoken to John on the Island of Patmos and are recorded in Rev. 22:20, "Surely I come quickly." To these words John responded, "Even so, come, Lord Jesus."

Signs of His coming include great tribulation, false prophets and "christs," social disturbances, and worldwide evangelization (Matthew 24; 2 Thess. 2:1-12; 1 Tim. 4:1-3; 2 Tim. 3:1-5).

Another sign of His coming will be apostasy among Christians and a falling away. Within the Church there will be a cooling off spiritually: "Because iniquity shall abound, the love of many shall wax cold" (Matt. 24:12).

As to the manner of Christ's coming, the NT indicates suddenness and surprise. "For as the lightning cometh out of the east, and shineth even unto the west; so shall also the coming of the Son of man be" (Matt. 24:27; cf. 36-41; 1 Cor. 15:51-53; 1 Thess. 4:14-18). Because Christ's second coming is sudden and unannounced, there must be maintained a perpetual readiness on the part of each believer. "Take ye heed, watch and pray: for ye know not when the time is" (Mark 13:33).

Some believe that the Second Coming will inaugurate a 1,000-year visible and literal reign of Christ on earth; others believe that Christ's appearance will signal the destruction of the earth, its remaking, and the Final Judgment (cf. 2 Pet. 3:10-13). Christ will judge the wicked, for when He comes, He shall "bring to light the things now hidden in darkness" (1 Cor. 4:5, RSV).

See ESCHATOLOGY, RAPTURE, TRIBULATION, MILLENNIUM, JUDGE (JUDGMENT), PAROUJIA.

For Further Reading: *GMS*, 624-48; Wiley, *CT*, 3:243-62.

NORMAN R. OKE

SECOND DEATH. See DEATH.

SECOND WORK OF GRACE. This is the teaching that, besides conversion, there is a second special crisis in Christian experience. Such is taught, in a sense, by Roman Catholics, who teach that after the time of one's initiation into salvation at baptism, one receives the Holy Spirit at his confirmation.

In general, also, Pentecostals (the older Pentecostals and the Neo-Pentecostals) teach that, after the time of one's conversion, he should be baptized with the Holy Spirit as a second work of grace. This is a time, for Pentecostals, when a believer speaks in tongues—either as an initial evidence of being Spirit-baptized, or as the beginning of what will be a gift that is exercised thereafter.

The holiness people, or Wesleyans, are the ones who most emphasize a second work of grace as such. For them, it is a synonym of entire sanctification, and it is their most distinctive doctrinal emphasis.

Holiness people understand that several things occur at the first work of grace, often called conversion—when a sinner repents and believes. At that time he is justified (Rom. 5:1); regenerated (John 3:5-8); initially sanctified (Titus 3:5); reconciled (2 Cor. 5:18-21); and adopted as God's child (John 1:12; Rom. 8:15-16).

They also find, in Scripture, that a second crisis in Christian experience is sometimes told about and at other times is urged. It is often told about in Acts, where persons who are evidently already believers receive or are filled with or are baptized with the Holy Spirit (see Acts 1:5-8; 2:4; 8:1 ff, 10-11; 19:1-7). Besides, it seems to be described as already having happened in such passages as Rom. 6:1-6; 8:1-9; and Phil. 3:15.

There are other times, in Scripture, when persons who are already believers are urged to receive another special grace. It is most clear that the Thessalonians are Christians (see 1 Thess. 1:3-4, 6, 8, 10). Yet Paul says he would like to see them in order to "supply what is lacking" in their faith (3:10, NIV). Then he tells them that it is God's will that they be sanctified (4:3); and he virtually prays: "May God himself, the God of peace, sanctify you through and through" (5:23, NIV).

The basic reason why Scripture describes Christian experience as received through a first and a second work of grace is because there are two kinds of sin: acts of sin; and the state of original sin which characterizes the whole human race because the first Adam, as the representative of the race, sinned against God (cf. Genesis 3; Rom. 5:12-21; 1 Cor. 15:21 ff). The acts of sin are forgiven in the first work of grace; and the state of original sin is cleansed away in the second work of grace (see Rom. 8:1-2).

See SIN, ORIGINAL SIN, FIRST WORK OF GRACE, ENTIRE SANCTIFICATION.

For Further Reading: Jones, *Perfectionist Persuasion: The Holiness Movement and American Methodism;* Knight, *The Holiness Pilgrimage;* Ruth, *The Second Crisis in Christian Experience;* Turner, *The Vision Which Transforms;* Grider, *Entire Sanctification.*

J. KENNETH GRIDER

SECT. See CHURCH.

SECULARISM. Secularism (Latin *saecula,* "age" or "period") refers to an ideology which turns man's attention away from the supernatural and worlds beyond toward this world and the present age. Harvey Cox *(The Secular City)* attempts to distinguish between secularism as a closed world view which functions much like a new religion and secularization which he views as an irreversible historical process liberating society from closed world views. It seems, however, that the move toward secularization in theology is an accommodation of unbelief or a capitulation to unbelief rather than the confrontation of unbelief by the biblical faith.

Secularism puts everything in man's hands. It denies absolutes and idealizes pluralism and relativity. It makes man responsible for developing his own morality and ethics with reference to himself alone. It is a religious response to the supposedly religionless modern scientific and technological man. In one breath its advocates say that secularization is necessary to reach man in his religionless condition, and in the next breath they say that secularization is necessary to free man from the tyranny of his religious concepts.

Coming from opposite directions, however, the secularist and the biblical Christian meet in agreement on one point. The compartmentalization of life into sacred versus secular is wrong. To the secularist, we must secularize all of life. The Bible, however, views all of life as sacred, even the mundane, and therefore the attempts to secularize it are wrong. The Christian shares Paul's view of life when he says, "Whether, then, you eat or drink or whatever you do, do all to the glory of God" (1 Cor. 10:31, NASB; cf. Col. 3:17).

See WORLD (WORLDLINESS), PROFANE (PROFANITY), SANCTIFICATION, HUMANISM.

For Further Reading: Cox, *The Secular City;* Ellul, *The New Demons,* 1-47; Schaeffer, *Death in the City.*

GLENN R. BORING

SELF. "Self" is a relatively new term as it is used in theology today. It is a creation of the modern science of psychology. A theological treatment of man today—in his relationships with himself, other persons, and God—is veritably impossible without an extensive use of the term. In the theological context "self" refers to one's *inner* identity —that which makes him an individual and/or a person as distinct from others. There are many factors that relate to the formulation of that self, which in turn also determine its "health" or pathology. It is the self that remains constant through all of the various conditions that either develop or destroy it.

How is this modern term "self" related to Scripture? Significantly, there is no term for self, per se, in the NT. Some modern versions translate *anthrōpos* (man) as "self" in Rom. 6:6 (NASB, NIV, RSV); 7:22 (RSV, NEB); Eph. 4:22, 24 and Col. 3:9-10 (NASB, NIV). But the diversified translations of *anthrōpos* in these same verses reflect the lack of any clear concept—"man" (Rom. 7:22, NASB); "nature" (Eph. 4:22, 24 and Col. 3:9-10, RSV, NEB); and even "being" (Rom. 7:22, NIV).

Most often "self" is part of the compound words "myself," "yourself," "himself," etc., which are translations of reflexive pronouns (*heautous* et al.) or the reflexive use of the pronoun (*autos* et al.). The *self* is that which one is able to objectify as *himself.* However, in contrast to modern psychology where the self is exclusively inward, in the NT the objectified self is the whole or total person, both inner and outer.

Very close to the meaning of "self" is the dramatic use of the first person singular ("I"), especially when it is reinforced by the personal pronoun *ego* (cf. Gal. 2:19-20). In his dramatic introspection (Rom. 7:14-25) Paul described the conflict between his mind and flesh and equated the mind with his inner self (*anthrōpos,* v. 22), and the flesh with his "members," obviously outward (v. 23). Significantly, *both* the mind and the flesh were identified as "I" or "me" (cf. vv. 18, 25). Paul exhorted the Romans to present *(paristēmi)* "yourselves to God . . . and your members" (Rom. 6:13, NASB); and the identical "presentation" terminology in v. 19 and 12:1 makes it clear that such a presentation included their members or body.

Yet a word of caution is needed. When Paul wrote, "I have been crucified with Christ; and it is no longer I [*ego*] who live" (Gal. 2:20, NASB), he does not mean that the self (as understood today) actually dies! If that were so, the *person* would cease to exist. In the strictest sense the "I" that is crucified with Christ, dies in a theological sense—meaning that we participate by faith in the Cross death of Christ. The essential self does not die or cease to exist, nor can we crucify ourselves. Thus the expression "self-crucifixion" is a misnomer. "Dying with Christ" is a metaphor and is best understood as dying *to* self.

See MAN, HUMAN NATURE, DEATH TO SELF, CROSS (CROSS-BEARING).

For Further Reading: Howard, *Newness of Life;* Adcock, *Fundamentals of Psychology;* Tournier, *The Whole Person in a Broken World.* RICHARD E. HOWARD

SELF-CONTROL. See DISCIPLINE.

SELF-CRUCIFIXION. See DEATH TO SELF.

SELF-EXAMINATION. The biblical basis for the Christian discipline of self-examination is most explicit in such passages as 1 Cor. 11:28-32 (where it refers to preparation for receiving the Lord's Supper), Gal. 6:4 (where the reference is to conduct as evidence of grace), and 2 Cor. 13:5. In the latter, it is the recommended antidote for judging others, and its purpose is to discover whether one is truly Christian, i.e., shares the life of Christ.

Historically at the extremes, classical ascetic theology (mostly Roman Catholic) contrasts with monergistic views of salvation by grace which see such self-discipline as self-righteousness. Overemphasis on the practice has been rightly criticized as unhealthy subjectivism, or morbid preoccupation with self.

Proper self-examination, however, is on firm ground theologically. Only man, made in God's image, is endowed with the power to pass judgment upon himself in the lonely privacy of his personhood. He alone can differentiate between what he is and what he ought to be, an endowment reflected in conscience. He cannot permanently escape this responsibility. One's "inwardness," in spirit and intention, is the supreme test of Christian faith. To face God is also to face self, since God looks on the heart. To be afraid of silence and one's true self is the revelation of inner poverty.

William Law, in his chapter on evening prayer, laid stress on the deliberate, step-by-step recollection of the actions of the day, along with confession, not of a general sort, but of each particular failure, as a means to reformation and blessing. Law warned of the ease with which we excuse human frailty, without sorrow, and thus without amendment. Searching self-knowledge of one's natural temperament, chief weaknesses, prevalent temptations, as well as providential opportunities, through the Spirit's ministry, becomes an important means of grace.

The older writers on this theme recommend the earnest contemplation of death as a means to the illumination of life. The Scheme of Self-examination used by the first Methodists at Oxford gave attention, in a series of self-addressed questions,to the practicality of the expression of neighbor love in the daily round.

See CONSCIENCE, CHRISTIAN PERFECTION, SELF, GROW (GROWTH).

For Further Reading: Lewis, *The Practice of the Christian Life;* Law, *A Serious Call to a Devout and Holy Life;* Taylor, *The Rules and Exercises of Holy Living.*
ARNOLD E. AIRHART

SELF-IMAGE. The idea or concept one has of oneself is one's self-image. Such an image is possible because self-consciousness is a part of the image of God in man (Gen. 1:26-27). O. A. Curtis describes self-grasp and self-estimate as capabilities of a person which allows one to say, "I am not this or that, I am myself" (*The Christian Faith,* 20-22).

Lewis Sherrell identifies "self-transcendence" as the quality which makes it possible to ask, "What does the self 'see' when it thinks of itself?" (*The Gift of Power,* 9, 35).

The self-image may be an idealized conception of oneself, or an intelligent and honest insight into reality. Paul warned of the peril of thinking of oneself "more highly than he ought to think" (Rom. 12:3).

If the self-image corresponds to reality, self-understanding and self-knowledge result in a healthy personality. If not, this becomes the basis for anxiety and certain mental and emotional illnesses. The key to a healthy self-image is loving God with the whole self, a loving made possible and natural by being sanctified wholly (Luke 10:27; 1 Thess. 5:23).

See SELF, DEATH TO SELF, HUMILITY, LIFE-STYLE.

For Further Reading: Shoemaker, *Self-knowledge and Self-identity;* Wolman, *Dictionary of Behavioral Science,* 342.
J. OTTIS SAYES

SEMI-PELAGIANISM. Semi-Pelagianism is a name which was introduced during the Scholastic period to describe a system of doctrine that was formulated quite simultaneously in the fifth century in southern France and North Africa, as an attempt to find and maintain a middle ground between the extreme views of Pelagianism and Augustinianism (Philip Schaff, *History of the Christian Church,* 3:857-58; 4:537-39).

After the Synod of Carthage in 412 and just

prior to the Council of Ephesus in 431, both of which condemned Pelagius and his doctrines, John Cassianus founded, expounded, and defended the views which became known as Semi-Pelagian. Other earnest men, such as Vincent of Lerins and Faustus, bishop of Rhegium, fearing the demoralizing, fatalistic, and deterministic effects of Augustine's doctrines of irresistible grace, predestination, and perseverance, carried the system forward until it was condemned by the Synods of Orange and Valence in 529 (Latourette, *Christianity Through the Ages,* 59-61).

Primary emphases of Semi-Pelagianism included the views that original sin and free will are not mutually exclusive, that the divine and human wills cooperate and are coefficient factors in regeneration, that regeneration is the divine blessing on human volition, and that guilt comes, not from original sin, but only by an individual act willingly committed.

Wesleyan-Arminian theologians reject the idea of human merit and other tendencies toward naturalism and humanism of Semi-Pelagianism, by placing the weight of the synergistic system on the side of God and His prevenient grace.

See PELAGIANISM, AUGUSTINIANISM, SYNERGISM, MONERGISM, ARMINIANISM.

For Further Reading: Ayer, *A Source Book for Ancient Church History,* 466-69; Bruce, *The Spreading Flame,* 311, 335-36, 359, 370; Latourette, *A History of Christianity,* 179-82; Wiley, *CT,* 1:69; 2:27, 39-40, 43-44, 348, 351, 415; 3:184.

WAYNE E. CALDWELL

SEPARATION. A key doctrine of both Old and New Testaments, separation, as it relates to Christian experience, indicates the Christian's distinction from sin and sinners and his being set apart to God. Israel was called out from heathen people and pagan practices. So Christians are urged to come out from among the unclean and to be separate (2 Cor. 6:17). Fellowship with the Lord is possible only to those who, like Him, are holy, harmless, undefiled, separate from sinners (Heb. 7:26).

Separation is illustrated by the wedding vow. Israel in Scripture is considered married to Yahweh. The NT Church is the Bride of Christ, and friendship with the world is branded as adultery (Jas. 4:4). The "world" may designate the people who do not serve God, and/or their culture.

Conservative Christians believe that to be saved, men must separate from all evil by thorough repentance. Holiness theologians stress also—perhaps more than other conservatives—a further separation. The converted must renounce self and yield all ambitions and affections into the hands of God. This act Paul calls a crucifixion. He says, "The world is crucified unto me, and I unto the world" (Gal. 6:14).

Separation is not the same as either regeneration or entire sanctification, but both a precondition and a result. Needed divine grace is freely given, both to cease the committing of sin, in repentance, and to see and renounce its inner nature in consecration.

See REPENTANCE, CONSECRATE (CONSECRATION), WORLD (WORLDLINESS).

For Further Reading: Steele, *Love Enthroned,* 134 ff; Will, *Commentary on Matthew,* 68-69.

LOUIS A. BOUCK

SERAPH, SERAPHIM. See ANGEL.

SERVANT. The Hebrew word for servant, *ebed,* initially referred to bond relationships within tribal society. It became an important term within covenant theology, defining God's redemptive mode through the Messiah and His faithful followers.

The OT shows servants managing possessions, looking after family affairs, giving counsel, and carrying messages—much like service professions in today's technical society. But servanthood meant more than that. The patriarch Job, King David, and the prophet Isaiah are all called "servants of God." So was Israel; indeed, prophetic writings contain frequent calls to its faithful servanthood.

Nowhere is the paradox of leadership through service more forcefully expressed than in Isaiah (esp. chaps. 42; 52—54: The stricken one who "hath borne our griefs" will be exalted). Jewish theologians draw from these passages the messianic character of Israel, despite dispersions and holocausts. Christians acknowledge Christ as the One through whom the Abrahamic covenant becomes the "light to the nations." The Church proclaims this Good News.

Jesus consciously accepted the servant role as prophesied by Isaiah, teaching it in respect to himself and to His followers (see Mark 10:42-45; Matt. 20:27; Col. 2:5-11; 2 Cor. 4:5). He rebuked His disciples for seeking preferment and privilege, admonishing them repeatedly to find greatness in service. Christ is Pioneer of the new humanity which regains righteous mastery of the earth (Hebrews 2).

Jesus washed dusty feet, served tables, touched untouchables, ate with outcasts, and healed the sick. That His example has been followed, in part at least, by the Church can be evidenced by a long history of compassionate service activities and agencies. The Protestant principle of the universal priesthood of believers arises from servant theology, both in worship and in work, whereby each becomes a channel of God's grace to another.

See DEACON, MINISTER (MINISTRY), SERVICE, SERVANT OF JEHOVAH.

For Further Reading: Greenleaf, *Servant Leadership;* Yoder, *The Politics of Jesus.* ARTHUR O. ROBERTS

SERVANT OF JEHOVAH. One who is voluntarily committed to the redemptive mission of God in the world after the pattern of and in the likeness of Jesus Christ.

OT meanings are rooted in the divinely anointed obedient persons (patriarchs, Moses, Job, Elijah, Isaiah, etc.) who gave their complete obedience to God as Master. This allegiance and the relationship grew to a sacred bond, reaching its culmination in the description of the Suffering Servant of Jehovah (or Yahweh) in Isa. 42:1-4; 49:1-6; 50:4-9; 52:13—53:12.

The models of and the concept of servanthood in the old covenant find their completeness in the new covenant in the person of Jesus Christ. He saw himself as servant of God (Mark 9:12; 10:45; 14:14) and presented himself as the Model to His disciples for all time.

A contemporary servant of God is one who is totally offered to the will of God the Father even as was Christ (Matt. 23:11; Mark 10:45; Luke 22:26; John 13:16).

The most frequently used words in the NT for servant are "child" and "slave." A servant of God, then, in the likeness of Christ, is adopted by grace into the household of God and achieves fulfillment by joyous abandon to do the Father's will. Other biblical words that are translated as "servant" suggest meanings of "attendant," "table waiter," "domestic servant," "public servant," and "menial slave."

Historically, the meaning of being a servant of Yahweh began to take shape in the mission of the covenant people Israel as typified in their leaders (i.e., Moses), came to its personal embodiment in Jesus Christ, and has since been finding its application in the lives of followers of Christ who are anointed by the Spirit of God. At the center of the mission of the Church is the continuation of the servant role (Phil. 2:5-11).

Christian servanthood should not be seen as cringing servility or joyless subjection to bondage. Rather, it may be seen, as Christ understood it, as the highest form of selfless dedication to the redeeming purpose of God the Father. A servant of Yahweh is a divinely honored ambassador, a minister, a commissioned and empowered colleague with Christ (1 Cor. 4:1-2).

The doctrine of the Church as the Body of Christ in the world has direct relationship to the scriptural teaching that living Christians are the enfleshment of the servant Christ. Contemporary servants of Yahweh share corporately the same mandate and joy as did Jesus.

See SERVANT, CONSECRATE (CONSECRATION), SERVICE, STEWARDSHIP.

For Further Reading: Schultz, *Portraits of a Servant;* Mudge, *Scottish Journal of Theology,* 12:113-28; Kittel, 2:81-93, 261-80; 5:654-717. GORDON WETMORE

SERVICE. This has to do with working for another as he directs. Service to God is doing His bidding, laboring in His will.

The word is applied in the OT largely to priests of the sanctuary. Their consecration by blood and by oil suggests the need in Christian service for the blood of Christ and the oil of the Spirit.

To serve the Lord is both our privilege and our choice. "Choose you this day whom ye will serve" (Josh. 24:15). It is Christ or Belial, God or mammon (money), but not both, for no man can serve two masters (Matt. 6:24).

To serve Christ is to follow Him through death to self, and a resulting fruitfulness (John 12:24-26). Like Him we must bear the cross, for the servant is not above his Lord (Matt. 10:24).

To everyone, Christian service brings responsibility to fulfill the Great Commission. This may involve suffering: "Serving the Lord with all humility of mind, and with many tears, and temptations" (Acts 20:19); but it brings blessing: "There stood by me this night the angel of God, whose I am, and whom I serve" (27:23).

Service to God should be grateful and joyful (Deut. 28:47). An example is the OT love-slave. Bankrupt, he served six years, going free in the seventh. If, however, he renounced freedom, saying, "I love my master," he became a servant forever, entering into a new and closer relationship to his master.

Like the Hebrew servant, Christians at some point face a choice. Either we go back to our "freedom" and failure, or forward, declaring, "I am, O Lord, wholly and forever Thine." Our reasonable, or spiritual, service is to present our all to God, receiving a divine transformation, and proving in personal experience what is that good, and acceptable, and perfect will of God (Rom. 12:1-2).

See CONSECRATE (CONSECRATION), OBEDIENCE, SERVANT, MINISTRY, PRUDENCE.

For Further Reading: Wood, *Perfect Love,* 227-31; Taylor, *Life in the Spirit,* 109-24; Geiger, *The Word and the Doctrine,* 271-429. LOUIS A. BOUCK

SERVITUDE. See BONDAGE.

SEVEN CARDINAL VIRTUES. The seven cardinal virtues stem from the field of Christian ethics; they are sometimes related to the seven gifts of the Spirit (cf. Isa. 11:2). These virtues were named by the medieval church as the basal elements of character. The seven attitudes include faith, hope, love, justice, prudence, temperance, and fortitude.

They are called *cardinal* because all other Christian virtues are said to hinge on one or the other of these seven. The first three are often called theological virtues because they are firmly rooted in the NT (cf. 1 Cor. 13:13). The last four are known as natural, or moral, virtues because they are rooted chiefly in Greek philosophy: Plato's *Republic* stressed the virtues of wisdom, courage, temperance, and justice.

Though these four natural virtues were prominent in ancient philosophy, the churchmen found ample support for them in Scripture. Justice was a hallmark of the prophets; inspired wisdom came from Hebrew teachers; temperance was commended by Peter (2 Pet. 1:6) and by Paul (1 Cor. 9:25; Gal. 5:23; Titus 1:8). In the Scriptures "courage" is akin to the parallel Greek "virtue," but the source of biblical courage almost always derives from one's confidence in the promises and the power of God.

The churchmen of the Middle Ages thus saw the best ethical thinking of the Greeks corroborating God's revelation in Scripture. A. B. D. Alexander writes: "Under the influence of Ambrose and Augustine, the cardinal virtues henceforth form a generally accepted scheme for the Christian treatment of systematic ethics" (*ERE,* 11:431). This has been true especially for Roman Catholic theology.

Protestant ethics has given less attention to the cardinal virtues. But both Catholics and Protestants agree that it is man's relationship to God which gives cohesion and unity to his moral life. The NT attitudes of faith, hope, and love toward God are the primary elements for coordinating Christian character.

See CHARACTER, GROW (GROWTH), HOLINESS, SEVEN DEADLY SINS, TEMPERANCE, VIRTUE.

For Further Reading: *ERE,* 11:430-32; Stalker, *The Seven Cardinal Virtues.* A. F. HARPER

SEVEN DEADLY SINS. The concept of the seven deadly sins, related to the field of Christian ethics, comes from the medieval church. The original classification, however, may go as far back as the monastic period. The concept today is discussed chiefly by Roman Catholic theologians.

The idea arises from the religionist's concern to discover the relative importance of moral values —or disvalues (cf. the question of the NT lawyer, "Master, which is the great commandment in the law?" [Matt. 22:36]).

The seven sins at the top of this list were pride, covetousness, lust, envy, gluttony, anger, and sloth. Of these, lust and covetousness are named in the Ten Commandments. Jesus warned against pride (Mark 7:22) and sloth (Matt. 25:26). The Epistles speak specifically of envy (Jas. 4:5) and anger (Eph. 4:26), while the wise man of the OT warns against gluttony (Prov. 23:21).

These sins head the list because they represent the primary human urges that are most likely to give rise to sin. They are thus highly subversive of the law of God and of the church.

Such sins are *deadly* or *mortal* because they wilfully violate the divine law, destroy friendship with God, and cause the death of the soul. The Roman church contrasts these *deadly* sins with the sins that are only *venial.* Even these lesser sins tend to injure the spiritual life, but they do not of themselves bring eternal death (cf. 1 John 5:16-17).

Some theologians note that the seven are *root* sins—most likely to be sources for other sins. They are "deadly" in their fatal effects on both character and salvation. They are not deadly in the sense of being unforgivable or beyond the curative and delivering power of God.

See SIN, CHARACTER, HOLINESS, SEVEN CARDINAL VIRTUES.

For Further Reading: Alexander, *ERE;* Stalker, *The Seven Deadly Sins.* A. F. HARPER

SEX, SEXUALITY. The Scriptures of the OT and NT are clear that human sexuality is a matter of sacred concern for God. Man's sexuality finds its origin in His creative design. His most holy purposes for man are inextricably linked with its proper expression. His best gifts of human joy and fulfillment are most commonly related to its proper use. It is part of a great and sacred mystery (Eph. 5:32).

Human sexual activity is the occasion for the begetting of human life. In this, man exercises the power that is God-given and godlike. Two people give existence and destiny to another without that person's request or consent. This power, granted to man in his freedom, is his to use or abuse. It is one of God's most serious gifts to man. Failure to use this power responsibly brings judgment. Correct use brings blessing.

Sex can become the means for the expression of the most sacred form of human love. Greater than the love of friend for friend, or that of parent and child, the love of spouse for spouse within a biblical marriage covenant can assume a quality without equal in any other human relationship. Love within that covenant when exclusive (monogamous) and enduring, can produce a level of mutual giving and receiving, a life of exchange, that is uniquely fulfilling. The union then of one life with another produces a unity which the Scriptures call "one flesh" (Gen. 2:24). The beauty and sacredness of this is in striking contrast to the products which result when man expresses his sexuality outside this God-intended context.

This should not be surprising when one notes the biblical context in which man's sexuality is introduced. In Gen. 1:27 and 5:1-2, we are told that God made man in His own image, male and female. The purpose here is not to suggest sexuality in God. Rather, it is to indicate the nature of man which enables him to share in a life that is like that which God knows, a life in love. It is clear that God intended human sexual differentiation and that to be a human person is to be either male or female. No one is both. Thus the concept of man transcends maleness or femaleness because it is inclusive of both. In this sense neither male nor female in himself or herself is fully man. The minimal unit of humanity that is fully man must be inclusive of both. Every human individual is thus incomplete, and his or her sexuality is the sign of that incompleteness. The individual person finds fulfillment in another whose difference makes that fulfillment possible. In the union of those differences human love at its best is obtainable. Only in the union of those differences is reproduction and the future of mankind possible.

The fact that human sexuality biblically is related to the making of man in God's image has led some theologians to see in the expression of man's sexuality within marriage that is exclusive and enduring a limited, finite analogy at the human level of the inner nature of the Triune God. There three Persons, none of which exhausts in himself the Godhead, and each of which is to be differentiated from the others, coinhere in a life of mutual giving and receiving of which man's "one flesh" is supposed to be a creaturely analogy. See the remarks of Jesus in the Gospel of John on the relationship of the Father, the Son, and the Spirit to each other.

The above makes marriage a viable analogy for illustrating the relationship of Christ to the Church (Eph. 5:21-33). It must be kept in mind, though, that the relationship of Christ and the Church is the prior one. Logically the plan of God for a bride for His Son was before His plan for a bride for man. Thus the relationship of Christ and the Church should not be seen as like that of husband and wife but vice versa. In this man has an eternal and an unchanging pattern for the use of his sexuality. Man's sexuality is both analogy and parable. It is to illustrate and to teach an eternal purpose. No man's fulfillment is in himself. His true life is found in another. The human marriage relationship is biblically defined. Man's true fulfillment in love is in God.

This should make obvious why the Scripture attaches the highest penalty to the nonbiblical use of man's sexuality. When engaged in with the person to whom one is not married, sex brings God's judgment instead of His blessing. Sexual relations with a person of the same sex or with an animal are perversions and abominations biblically. See Leviticus 18. One's sexuality is a sacred gift to be used for sacred purposes. What one does with his sexuality is indicative of what he does with the God who gave it to him.

See MAN, WOMAN, DIVINE IMAGE, FAMILY, ADULTERY, POLYGAMY.

For Further Reading: Barth, *Church Dogmatics,* 3, 1:206 ff; Piper, *A Christian Interpretation of Sex;* Thielicke, *Theological Ethics,* vol. 3: Sex.

DENNIS F. KINLAW

SHAME. This may be objective or subjective, or both. If objective, it is a situation in which one is bearing disgrace and reproach. Shame is the loss of the public image of respectability and good character. The shame or disgrace may be deserved or it may be undeserved; if undeserved, no actual sin is involved, but rumor, misunderstanding, or slander.

If the shame is subjective, it is an emotion of acute embarrassment and humiliation. It may be a superficial issue, yet socially painful (Luke 14:9). Unfortunately, the perversity of the sinful heart is such that people frequently are ashamed of things of which they ought to be proud, and proud of those things of which they ought to be ashamed (Phil. 3:19).

Jesus was put to an open shame (Heb. 6:6) by the ignominious death on the Cross; this was shame in the objective sense. But He refused to allow the shame to become subjective; He despised it (12:2).

Inability to blush is not a mark of maturity but decadence. Christians should have a capacity for shame in the presence of evil. They should be ashamed to expose themselves indecently (Jer. 13:26). They should be ashamed of doing less than their best in the Lord's service (2 Tim. 2:15). They should avoid embarrassing their brethren or the poor (Ps. 14:6; 1 Cor. 11:22).

Shame is at the very heart of true repentance. This is not an embarrassment for having been caught, or regret because of consequences (called the "sorrow of the world" [2 Cor. 7:10]), but a painful and profound grief for having done the wrong.

A sense of shame is generally associated with a low self-image. If the self-depreciation is over superficial matters, such as worry about good looks or talents, it may accompany the usual insecurity of immaturity; or it may be a sign of neurotic pride and self-preoccupation. In either case efforts to remove the false shame are legitimate. But in many instances a low self-image is caused by a secret awareness of real guilt. People do not like themselves because they know themselves. Only a bungler will try to trump up a better self-image in such cases. Let the person face that which causes shame, and make it right both with God and man, and he will stand tall without psychological hocus-pocus.

It will come as a surprise to many to learn that there are far more frequent references in the Bible to shame than to guilt. Fear of being shamed is seen as a powerful incentive to good behavior.

See REPENTANCE, GUILT, SELF-IMAGE, REALITY THERAPY.

For Further Reading: Noble, "Shame Versus Guilt," *WTJ*, Spring, 1971. RICHARD S. TAYLOR

SHEKINAH. This is a term for the visible manifestation of the presence of God, as in the pillar of cloud and fire which led Israel through the wilderness (Exod. 13:21). Though in our Bible the word does not occur, it was used in Jewish paraphrases as a synonym for God or for His glory. In the OT the Shekinah pointed forward to Christ, the brightness of God's glory (Heb. 1:3).

The Shekinah was seen as a fire enfolded in a cloud. Usually only the cloud was visible, but at times the fire appeared, as on Mount Sinai when the law was given (Exod. 19:18). The Shekinah of the Lord dwelt among His people, especially in the Tabernacle, where God spoke to Moses face-to-face (33:11). Christ is the Word made flesh, who tabernacled among us (John 1:14, NASB marg.).

Identified by some with the Holy Spirit, the Shekinah (meaning "to dwell") suggests the companionship, purity, and radiance of the Comforter abiding in the sanctified heart.

See HOLY OF HOLIES, GLORY, PRESENCE (DIVINE).

For Further Reading: *NBD*, 1174; *ZPBD*, 782.

LOUIS A. BOUCK

SHEOL. The location and nature of Sheol (Heb. *sheol*) are described in a number of OT passages. Synonyms for Sheol in the OT are: pit, region dark and deep, Abaddon, land of forgetfulness (Ps. 88:12), place of no return (Job 3:13-19; Isa. 14:9-23), hell, death (Prov. 5:5), sleep (Nah. 3:18).

Man goes down to Sheol (Gen. 37:35, RSV). His body returns to the dust from which it was quickened (2:7); his spirit (breath) returns to God who gave it (Eccles. 12:7); and a "shade" of the self goes to Sheol. Darkness (Job 10:21-22), slumber (Nah. 3:18), weakness (Isa. 14:10), and forgetfulness (Ps. 88:12)—such symbols of death are the opposites of life, light, and activity. Job 3:13-19 states that silence reigns in Sheol, while Isa. 26:14 says that the inhabitants of Sheol are unremembered.

Biblical man never prayed to go to Sheol, neither did he fear going to Sheol. What he didn't want was to enter Sheol before he had enjoyed the fullness of life. A number of prayers in the Psalms were to insure long life, not to avoid Sheol.

Isa. 14:15; Ezek. 32:23, 25, 28-30 appear to some to suggest that the Pit is a special place in Sheol for special enemies. Ezek. 32:17-32 seems to indicate some separation in Sheol. The circumcised are separated from the uncircumcised, those slain in battle from those who were properly buried, and some nations were separated from other nations.

The deliverance of Enoch (Gen. 5:24) and Elijah (2 Kings 2:11) from death and passages such as Isa. 26:19 and Dan. 12:2 indicate belief in life beyond the temporary abode of Sheol. Luke 16:23 suggests the partitioning of Sheol into Gehenna and Paradise. The resurrection of Jesus insures the final abolition of sin and death (Sheol).

See HADES, RESURRECTION OF THE BODY, IMMORTALITY, INTERMEDIATE STATE.

For Further Reading: Baillie, *And the Life Everlasting*, 142-58; Pache, *The Future Life*, 279-325; Shaw, *Life After Death*, 10 ff. FRED E. YOUNG

SIGN. In the scope of scriptural usage, a sign can be a physical mark (Gen. 4:15), a warning (Num. 16:38), a monument (Josh. 4:6), an ensign (Ps. 74:4), a reminder (Deut. 6:8), a portent (Isa. 20:3), a signature (2 Thess. 3:17), or a miracle (John 4:54). Underlying all of these, however, is the idea that a sign is something visible which points beyond itself for its real meaning. In its predominant religious sense it indicates God's presence and activity which demand a human response of faith and obedience.

In respect to the past, signs are reminders of God's covenants (the rainbow [Gen. 9:12-13] and circumcision [17:11]), and His redemptive acts (the signs and wonders of the Exodus [Exod. 10:1-2]; the Passover festival [13:9]; and the 12 stones from the Jordan [Josh. 4:6]). In the present they signify His presence in healing (John 6:2), in revealing His Son (Acts 2:22), and in confirming the word of His servants (Rom. 15:18-19; Heb. 2:4). In references to the future they confirm the word of prophecy (1 Sam. 2:34; Isa. 7:11, 14) and indicate the advent of eschatological events (Matt. 24:3).

Signs are not exclusive grounds for faith. Magicians can produce them (Exod. 7:11, 22; Acts 8:9-11) as well as false prophets working under satanic power (Mark 13:22; 2 Thess. 2:9; Rev. 13:13-14). Some in Jesus' day were characterized as sign-seekers (John 2:18; 6:30; 1 Cor. 1:22), but He refused to satisfy their demand for signs (Matt. 12:38-42). Notwithstanding this reserve, miracles did have evidential value, and they were recorded as a means to faith, at least for that generation (Heb. 2:3-4). John 20:30-31 reflects the apostolic outlook: These signs are "written that you may believe that Jesus is the Christ, the Son of God, and that believing you may have life in his name" (RSV).

See MIRACLE, CREDENTIALS OF SCRIPTURE, FALSE CHRISTS.

For Further Reading: Richardson, ed., *A Theological Word Book of the Bible,* 152-55; Kittel, 4:200-269.

LUKE L. KEEFER, JR.

SIMPLICITY OF MORAL ACTION. This term signifies a doctrine maintaining the impossibility of a divided heart in moral matters. The doctrine came into prominence and received precise definition in connection with the Oberlin theology of Charles G. Finney and Asa Mahan.

Following Kant and Cousin, the Oberlin men held that the moral character of actions is determined exclusively by the ultimate or controlling intention. An intention is a conscious choice of the will. A choice is "ultimate" when two conditions are fulfilled. First , it must control all other choices and be subordinate to none. Second, its exclusive basis must be the intrinsic character of its object. All states of mind or of feeling, as well as all outward actions, derive moral character only from one's ultimate intention. On this view, such incompatible elements as right and wrong, obedience and disobedience, or sin and holiness cannot coexist in a single moral act.

This doctrine affected Oberlin teaching concerning both conversion and entire sanctification. First, together with the biblical doctrine of repentance this concept made it possible to argue that there is a sense in which moral perfection, perfect love, and entire consecration are essential elements of the new birth. Second, Mahan and Finney both spoke of entire sanctification as vastly more mature, confirmed, and settled state of Christian experience, wrought by the Holy Spirit's renovation of the feelings. Finney referred especially to the relative permanence of this state.

James H. Fairchild, however, argued that entire sanctification as an experience distinct from conversion belongs only to a theology maintaining mixed moral action. This Finney implicitly conceded in his self-correcting lectures on entire sanctification delivered at Oberlin in late 1838 and printed in the *Oberlin Evangelist,* and only recently made currently available by Timothy L. Smith.

See SIN, MOTIVES, INTENTION, HEART PURITY, HOLINESS, BAPTISM WITH THE HOLY SPIRIT.

For Further Reading: *The Asbury Seminarian,* October, 1977, 20-35; *WTJ,* Spring, 1978, 51-64; Finney, *Lectures on Systematic Theology,* 95-114; *The Promise of the Spirit,* comp. and ed. Smith, 117-216, 262.

JAMES E. HAMILTON

SIN. That branch of theology which deals with the doctrine of sin is called *hamartiology.* It claims a very large share of careful attention, since sin is man's basic problem. It is sin which necessitates salvation, indeed, the entire plan of redemption, including the Incarnation, the death and resurrection of Christ, and the gift of the Holy Spirit. The peril of eternal damnation is due solely to sin. In addition, the earthly dislocations and conflicts of humanity are either expressions of sin or traceable to it. One's doctrine of sin reveals his concept of God, of the nature of man, of the Atonement, and of the principles and possibilities of grace.

There are many Hebrew and Greek words that are rendered "sin" in English translations of the Bible. The words appearing most frequently are the Hebrew word *chattath* and the Greek word *hamartia.* The idea expressed by these words is "missing the mark" or "failing." However, they have several shades of meaning. *Hamartia* is used as the basic generic term for sin in the NT.

In respect to the etymological sense of a marksman missing a target, interpreters commonly assume that the target is missed because of fallen man's inability to attain the perfect standard which God demands and for which man strives. But man, in his fallen condition, misses the mark primarily because of a wrong aim (aiming at the wrong target). The picture is not that of the sinner desiring to be holy and falling short. Sinful man, until awakened by the Holy Spirit, does not want to be holy. He wants fulfilment, but he misses it because he seeks it through selfish pursuits rather than through submitting to the will of God where it is found. He is in rebellion against God (Rom. 8:7). Because he shoots at the wrong target, he misses the fulfilment which he desires.

Other Hebrew and Greek words which are translated "sin" reveal its varied nature. The main Hebrew nouns are *resha,* "wickedness, confusion"; *avon,* "iniquity, perversion, guilt"; *pesha,* "transgression, rebellion"; *aven,* "wrongness, trouble, vanity"; *sheqer,* "lying, deceit"; *ra,* "evil," usually in its judicial or natural effects; *maal,* "trespass, breach of trust"; *asham,* "error, negligence, guilt"; and *awel,* "injustice." Hebrew verbs for "sin" include *sarar,* "to disobey"; and *abar,* "to transgress."

Greek words for sin besides *hamartia* include *adikia,* "unrighteousness"; *anomia,* "lawlessness"; *asebeia,* "impiety"; *parabasis,* "transgression"; *paraptōma,* "a fall" from a right relationship with God; *ponēria,* "depravity"; *epithumia,* "desire, lust"; and *apeitheia,* meaning "disobedience." In one sense, "Sin is the want of conformity to the divine law or standard of excellence" (Hodge, *Systematic Theology,* 2:187). In another sense, it is the wilful transgression of a known law of God (cf. Romans 6—8; 1 John 3). This was John Wesley's definition of sin "properly so-called."

There are two general kinds of sin. Sin is that quality of man's fallen nature which inclines him to commit acts of sin. On the other hand, sin is a specific event of rebellion, transgression, or omission, in thought or practice.

Every individual inherits the sinful nature from Adam (Gen. 5:3; Rom. 5:12, 18). The Church has called this nature by such terms as "inbred sin," "inherited sin," "moral depravity," "the carnal mind," "the old man," and most commonly, "original sin." That the sinful nature leads to acts of sin is stated by the apostle Paul in Rom. 7:7-9. There Paul testifies that he was spiritually alive as an innocent child, but when the years of accountability arrived, his sinful nature impelled him to transgress. This brought guilt and death.

Acts of sin must be confessed, forsaken, and forgiven (Isa. 55:7; Luke 13:3, 5; Acts 17:30; 1 John 1:9). The sinful nature must be confessed, deplored, and cleansed. Cleansing happened to the first Christian disciples, to the Samaritan believers, and to the house of Cornelius when they were filled with the Holy Spirit (Acts 15:8-9). In many ways the Thessalonian Christians were exemplary when Paul wrote his first Epistle to them (1 Thess. 1:5-10). Yet he desired that they have complete cleansing from sin (5:23). Peter shows that holiness must extend to every activity of the believer's life (1 Pet. 1:14-16).

Christ came to save from acts of sin and to destroy the sinful disposition (Matt. 1:21; Rom. 6:6; 12:1-4). He died that His people might be sanctified (Eph. 5:25; Heb. 13:12). Holiness is necessary if any person would see the Lord (12:14). Those who truly desire to be filled with God's righteousness are assured of its complete availability (Matt. 5:6).

See LEGAL SIN (ETHICAL SIN), ORIGINAL SIN, FALL (THE), FAILURE, SINNING RELIGION, INIQUITY, LIABILITY TO SIN, INFIRMITY, MISTAKES, SINLESS PERFECTION.

For Further Reading: Purkiser, ed., *Exploring Our Christian Faith;* Dubarle, *The Biblical Doctrine of Original Sin;* Taylor, *A Right Conception of Sin; GMS,* 268-302; Wiley, *CT,* 2:51-140; Metz, *Studies in Biblical Holiness,* 52-85; Geiger, *The Word and the Doctrine,* 47-136.

W. RALPH THOMPSON

SIN, ORIGIN OF. Our world, with all of its suffering, grief, and tragedy, is a very different world from the "very good" world described in Genesis 1—2. The further biblical records in chap. 3 and throughout the Bible accounts for this evil as the result of man's disobedience to a known and clearly understood command of God. Therefore, although God is the Creator and Sovereign Ruler of all things, He is not thereby the author of sin.

Genesis describes the divine-human relationship as unique, compared with the other forms of life. Into man was breathed the "breath of life," by which he became a creature in God's own image, able to have fellowship with God and to hold dominion over all other living creatures. While according to our best knowledge the animals obey God by instinct, a part of man's having the divine image was the gift of personality with all thereby connoted about free choice and responsibility. Life at its highest is not instinctive or robotlike. It involves a free and loving relationship, maintained by active choice.

As personal creatures in a perfect world, it was the place and privilege of Adam and Eve to glorify the Creator by free and loving service. This would have been impossible without probation —some test by which they might demonstrate their love and glorification of God. Therefore the one forbidden tree stood in their midst, and the warning that in the day they ate of it, they would die.

It is often asked how holy beings such as Adam and Eve could have fallen into sin. This has been well spoken to as follows: "A will determined to do good with an omnipotent energy is not subject to change, but a will determined to do good with a finite and limited force is so subject" (Wiley, *CT,* 2:58). The finite will of a holy being can change or be induced to change, a profound and provocative fact for every entirely sanctified soul to consider.

The temptation and fall of man as described in Genesis 3 succinctly and adequately accounts for sin in human experience. Under the experience of deception and a solicitation to be more than the Creator had made them, the first pair allowed doubt to be stirred in their hearts, lingered in the presence of the tempter, and did that which was forbidden. Realizing something of their loss and guilt, they now dreaded to meet their glorious Creator.

In the reference to the serpent, it is necessary to realize the presence of the satanic. Without the person of Satan on the scene, deceiving the pair by an illusion and thus slandering the Creator, holy beings would never have fallen.

For the ultimate origin of sin, therefore, Christian theology is dependent upon what the Scriptures teach about the devil. A spiritual order of creation exists, angels from which order an unrevealed number did not keep their first estate, but fell (2 Pet. 2:4). Jesus declared, "I beheld Satan as lightning fall from heaven" (Luke 10:18). It appears that Satan was the leader of the rebellion in heaven, and that within his personality as a holy and spirit creature of God, sin first originated. While Scripture speaks with great reserve on this subject, some see evidence that pride of his high rank in creation and the desire for greater glory was the cause of the original act of sin. From personality and freedom comes the power to glorify God forever or to rebel against Him and experience spiritual ruin.

See SIN, FALL (THE), SATAN, PROBATION, TEMPTATION.

For Further Reading: *GMS,* 79-83; Stevens, *Doctrines of the Christian Religion,* 154-55; Wiley, *CT,* 2:52-78.

MYRON D. GOLDSMITH

SIN OFFERING. Among the several kinds of sacrifices referred to in the OT, there is one category for dealing specifically with sin. Peculiar to Israel in this category is the sin offering, related to the word for sin which means "to miss the mark or fall short." The ritual to be used at the time of this offering is found in Lev. 4:1—5:13.

The sin offering was first of all to atone for sins of ignorance, which might come to light later. This is clearly reflected in the words of the RSV translation of the ritual mentioned above, "If any one sins unwittingly." Some willful sins could also be atoned for, such as deception and stealing, provided that, in addition to the animal sacrifice, full restitution be made (Lev. 6:1-7). But in either case, animal sacrifices were typical and anticipatory of the blood of Christ (Heb. 10:4).

A second significant point concerning the sin offering in the OT relates to a feature in the ritual accompanying the offering. It was required that the worshipper lay his hands upon the sacrifice, thereby identifying himself with the sacrifice which becomes his substitute. In like fashion, Christ, our Sin Offering, completely identified himself with us and became our Substitute on the Cross. It is in this light that we are to understand the words of Paul in 2 Cor. 5:21, "God made him who had no sin to be sin [fn., *a sin offering*] for us, so that in him we might become the righteousness of God" (NIV).

See ATONEMENT, SACRIFICE, OFFER (OFFERING).

For Further Reading: Gray, *Sacrifice in the Old Testament;* Oehler, *Theology of the Old Testament;* Oesterley, *Sacrifice in Ancient Israel.*

ALVIN S. LAWHEAD

SINCERITY. The words "sincere" and "sincerity" are found in the KJV in the following NT passages: 1 Cor. 5:8; 2 Cor. 1:12; 2:17; 8:8; Eph. 6:24; Phil. 1:10, 16; Titus 2:7; and 1 Pet. 2:2. In these passages six different Greek words are being translated. The closest to our understanding of "sincerity" is *gnēsios,* "true, genuine." Paul reminded the Corinthians that their promptness and faithfulness in fulfilling their previous pledge toward the offering for the poor in Jerusalem would prove the "sincerity" of their love. Love that is all promise and no performance is insincere. Thus sincerity is measured by action, by follow-through, by willingness to sacrifice.

In sincerity there is a correspondence between beliefs and faith, between words and feelings. To believe certain doctrines sincerely is to be committed to them without secret equivocation. To love another sincerely is to love him or her exactly as one says he does (Rom. 12:9). To be sincere in one's commitment to Jesus Christ is to be obedient when it is costly.

Furthermore, sincerity is to be gauged by one's attitude toward the truth. To say that sincerity is all that matters is to demonstrate insincerity. Genuineness of commitment always attaches itself to the truth. The masses will be deceived by the Antichrist because they "did not receive the love of the truth" (2 Thess. 2:10, NASB)—which is to say, they were insincere in their professed interest in spiritual realities.

See TRUTH, CHARACTER, INTEGRITY, HONESTY.

RICHARD S. TAYLOR

SINLESS PERFECTION. Wesleyanism has never taught "sinless perfection" in the form its critics have imputed to it. W. T. Purkiser observes that "one special whipping boy has been the phrase 'sinless perfection.' Few, if any, advocates of scriptural holiness use the term, but it is commonly used by opponents of the doctrine" (*Sanctification and Its Synonyms,* 69).

John Wesley said: "Absolute or infallible perfection I never contended for. Sinless perfection I do not contend for seeing it is not scriptural" (*Works,* 12:257). One reason is Wesleyanism's *definition of perfection.* It is the believer's heart that is made perfect in love; it is not a perfection of head or hand, and therefore not a perfection beyond the need of the atoning merits of Christ's blood.

A second reason for not using the term "sinless perfection" is Wesleyanism's definition of *sin.* Sin, "properly so-called"—a phrase popularized by John Wesley—is a voluntary transgression of a known law of God. Wesley refused to call involuntary transgressions sin, because he believed the intention or motivation of an act determined its moral quality. However, he knew that many Christians used the broader definition, and that, indeed, there was such a twofold use reflected in Scripture. The term "sinless perfection" is usually interpreted as implying sinlessness in the broader sense as well as the narrower.

A third liability in the term "sinless perfection" is that it seems to imply the impossibility of *temptation.* Wesleyans have never taught that any work or state of grace places the entirely sanctified beyond moral testing or trial. Temptation is not, however, sin.

Thomas Cook's comment is appropriate: "Some assert that the doctrine of entire extirpation of sin from the heart puts the soul beyond real temptation. 'There can be no real temptation,' they say, 'to a soul which has nothing in its nature responsive to solicitations to sin.' But such an assumption is much too broad. It renders angels in probation, Adam and Eve, and our Lord Himself, incapable of real temptation. But the fact that some angels fell, that Adam sinned, and that Jesus Christ 'was in all points tempted as we are,' should be sufficient proof that holy souls are capable of temptation" (*New Testament Holiness,* 16).

See CHRISTIAN PERFECTION, SIN, INFIRMITIES, TEMPTATION.

For Further Reading: Purkiser, *Sanctification and Its Synonyms;* Flew, *The Idea of Perfection in Christian Theology;* Cook, *New Testament Holiness.*

NEIL E. HIGHTOWER

SINLESSNESS OF CHRIST. This term refers to the condition or state of moral purity in the Son of God before, during, and after His 33 years on earth. He was without either original or committed sin.

There was no original sin in Christ. The Jews believed that inherited depravity was transmitted from Adam through the male; but Christ was conceived of the Holy Spirit and was born without that sinful bias that belongs to all other members of the human race. The birth of the infant Christ was not a birth out of sinful human nature, but a conjoining of the human nature from Mary with the divine nature of the Holy Spirit. In a sense, Christ was sanctified by this conception. Because of this, Christ was perfect in His relation to His Heavenly Father from His birth, and absolutely free from the sinful bias which is characteristic of every other son of Adam.

Christ was also free from committed sin: "Who did no sin, neither was guile found in his mouth" (1 Pet. 2:22). As a child, He was obedient: "He went down with them, and came to Nazareth, and was subject unto them" (Luke 2:51). As a youth, He was respectful and upright: "And Jesus increased in wisdom and stature, and in favour with God and man" (v. 52). As a man, He was "holy, harmless, undefiled, separate from sinners, and made higher than the heavens" (Heb. 7:26).

The question is often asked in reference to the temptation of Christ (Matt. 4:1-11), "Could Christ have sinned?" The technical terms around which the debate has raged have been *peccability,* "capable of sinning," and *impeccability,* "incapable of sinning." As a man with a free will Jesus could have sinned. The temptation was not a charade, but very real. As Second Adam He was exposed to the power and peril of real options. Yet His unity with the Father was such that disobedience was a moral impossibility. While He may have felt the force of Satan's appeals, there was in Him no wavering, but instant and total loyalty to His Father.

Christ not only loved righteousness, He hated sin. He was always strong in applauding right, and equally strong in denouncing evil. The holiness of Christ was full-orbed as well as spotless. A full manifestation of holiness does not consist merely in doing nothing wrong, but in doing all that is right. Christ exemplified all of that in His own life.

It was the sinlessness of Christ which qualified Him to give His life as an atoning sacrifice for others.

See TEMPTATION OF CHRIST, CHRISTOLOGY, HUMANITY OF CHRIST.

For Further Reading: Miley, *Systematic Theology,* 2:246; Newell, *Hebrews Verse by Verse,* 147-50; *GMS,* 350; Westcott, *Epistle to the Hebrews,* 107; Wiley, *Epistle to the Hebrews,* 163-64. DONALD R. PETERMAN

SINNING RELIGION. The term really should be in quotes—"sinning religion"—for it is meaningless excepting as a colloquial symbol of a common doctrine of sin. The belief is that Christians cannot avoid sin, that in fact, every Christian sins "in thought, word, and deed" every day. This pessimism concerning the possibilities of the Christian life is very pervasive and widespread, among Lutherans, Reformed, and even some Arminians. Not all would express themselves as crassly or extremely, but they share one thing in common—a doubt concerning the adequacy of grace to save from sinning in the practical wear and tear of everyday life.

Whether this produces the chronic grief of chronic defeat, or dull indifference to what is a habitual way of life, or even elation and buoyancy in the belief that the sinning doesn't really matter anyway, depends upon the soteriological foundations on which the sinning religion is based. An antinomianism which understands grace to mean deliverance from obligation to the moral law will of course foster a high-handed libertarianism of life-style, all within the framework of Christian profession and religious activity. Generally in the theological background is some form of "finished salvation" and "imputed righteousness" which makes salvation depend entirely on the objective validity of the Atonement, the benefits of which are unconditionally the nonforfeitable possession of the elect. In this scheme the sins are already forgiven anyway, therefore need be no cause for serious concern.

Some few are sufficiently spiritually sensitive to know that holiness is the biblical standard, and that sinning should be avoided, certainly not taken lightly; but they experience no power by which they are enabled to avoid sinning, and in their doctrinal system they know of none. Their system postulates a failure in the scheme of divine redemption, which provides salvation from guilt now and sin's power and presence in the next life, but offers no promise of complete victory over sin now.

The "sinning religion" complex is rooted not only in an inadequate doctrine of grace, and a radically erroneous doctrine of the Atonement, but also in a faulty doctrine of sin. That man out of grace is a mass of corruption is undeniable, but that he remains such as a Christian makes mockery of the saving power of Christ, and insults the sanctifying efficacy of the Holy Spirit's influences. But this affront to the power of grace is due in part to (1) the hangover of Augustinianism's attachment of sinfulness to the physical body, and (2) the notion that sin is to be defined by the letter of the law rather than by the spirit. Those who cannot see the moral difference between sins and mistakes, or between the disease of sin and its scars, or between a carnal disposition and human infirmities, will of course have no place for any true freedom from sin.

But if "love is the fulfilling of the law" (Rom. 13:10), then the nonfulfillment of the law—i.e., sin—should be defined in terms of love. Love is a matter of heart—of motives, intentions, affections, priorities; not a matter of hair-splitting details of external performance. Sin cannot properly be ascribed to an attitude of true love or a deed truly done in love, even though the deed itself may be mistaken or even wrong. Of course the doer must be open to light respecting the rightness or wrongness of the deed; if he is not amenable, the deed becomes sin; but in such a case the defect is a defect of love. Since love "worketh no ill to his neighbour," it will naturally desire to know what may or may not be harmful to the neighbor—which is to say, love always listens, is "easy to be intreated" (the true wisdom, Jas. 3:17), therefore always sensitive, teachable, improving. And these are the focal points of blameworthiness or blamelessness, which means the focal points of sin. Any other view of sin destroys its moral content and reduces it to an accident or a misfortune, not a misdeed.

The indictments which can be leveled against a "sinning religion" philosophy of Christianity are grave. (1) It inevitably breeds either chronic spiritual depression or presumptuous carelessness. If one expects to sin daily, he doubtless will; indeed, he will not be likely to struggle very hard to avoid doing so. (2) The attitude of impotence impresses itself upon the church, resulting in either an incubus of nominalism or a frenzy of churchly activities to cover up the spiritual poverty. (3) It gives the lie to commands and promises in the Bible. For instance, the doctrine of a sinning religion is totally irreconcilable with 1 John 3:1-10. But the NT is teeming with passages of similar import (cf. Matt. 1:21; John 17:15; Rom. 6:1-2, 11-22; 8:1-4; 2 Cor. 7:1; 1 John 2:1; et al.). Christians are commanded to "make not provision for the flesh, to fulfil the lusts thereof" (Rom. 13:14). Our doctrine of sin should allow for successful obedience to this command. If it does not, we had better change it.

Perhaps the fourth indictment is the most sobering of all. (4) The doctrine of a sinning religion imprints on the entire redemptive scheme the stamp of abysmal failure. The Savior is unable to save from the *one* enemy—sin—*where* we most need salvation—on earth—*when* we most need it—now. Satan remains stronger than Christ, sin stronger than grace, and the believer's death must be appended to the Cross to make the Blood adequately effective in its sanctifying efficacy.

While Wesley refused to use the term "sinless perfection," and Wesleyans generally disavow it, there is a sense in which sinless perfection is the only kind Wesleyans do believe in. The term is objectionable because of its unintended connotations. But if it is proper for Wesleyans to profess belief in "perfect love," and if sin is defined in terms of love, then, while "faultless perfection" would miss the mark, "sinless perfection" does not really merit the reproach generally heaped upon it.

Notwithstanding that digressing consideration, the conclusion is that for Christians to talk about continual or even frequent sinning is no credit to them, and certainly a dishonor to their Lord. Only one biblical advice is to be given to sinners: Stop it!

See SIN, HOLINESS, SINLESS PERFECTION, INTENTION, PERFECT LOVE, MISTAKES, INFIRMITIES, LIABILITY TO SIN, CALVINISM.

For Further Reading: Purkiser, *Conflicting Concepts of Holiness;* Brockett, *Scriptural Freedom from Sin;* Sweeten, *Sinning Saints;* Taylor, *A Right Conception of Sin;* Fletcher, *Checks to Antinomianism.* RICHARD S. TAYLOR

SINS AGAINST THE SPIRIT. Sins against the Holy Spirit may be listed as (1) grieving Him (Eph. 4:30); (2) quenching the Spirit (1 Thess. 5:19); (3) resisting the Spirit (Acts 7:51); (4) attempting to commercialize the power of the Spirit (8:19-20); (5) trifling with the Spirit (Heb. 6:4-6); (6) despising the Spirit (10:29); and (7) blaspheming the Spirit (Matt. 12:31-32).

When the above scriptures are examined in context, it becomes clear that warnings against grieving, quenching, trifling, and despising are directed to Christians. These sins represent progressively grave stages in apostatizing. To grieve the Spirit is to make Him sad because of conduct unbecoming to a Christian which dishonors Christ (Eph. 4:25-32). Furthermore, to grieve the Spirit by careless insensitivity to His rebuke and guidance is to deprive ourselves of that degree of His power so much needed and which He desires to give. A grieved Holy Spirit is forced to stand on the sidelines of life.

Quenching the Spirit is putting out the fire. The promised baptism with the Spirit included "and fire" (Matt. 3:11); and when He came at Pentecost, it was to the accompaniment of symbolic "tongues as of fire" (Acts 2:3, NASB). Some people want the Spirit, but not His fire, and as a consequence they become cold and powerless. Where the Spirit is honored, there will be intensity, fervency, emotion, joy. Both the prayers and the preaching will be "hot," animated not with the wildfire of fanaticism but the energizing, purifying, controlled fire of the Spirit.

Trifling and despising are related both in meaning and in biblical context. To experience the awakening and regenerating ministration of the Spirit, then turn away is to trifle with divine grace and expose oneself to final apostasy (Heb. 6:4-6). The language of 10:28-29 is even stronger. To turn from Christ back to Moses is to insult the "Spirit of grace" who was the Agent in the Virgin Birth, in the anointing and enabling of Christ in His earthly ministry, and through whom Christ "offered Himself without blemish to God" for our redemption (Heb. 9:14, NASB).

Only the blasphemy against the Holy Spirit is specifically designated unforgivable. However, all sins against the Spirit are fatal if persisted in. This is true because in the "economic" roles of the members of the Trinity it is the Spirit with whom the human race is in immediate contact. It is through the Spirit that awakening, repentance, and faith are possible; it is by means of the Spirit that we reach the Son and the Father. To cut ourselves off from the Spirit is to cut ourselves off from God.

Some maintain that even though we do grieve the Spirit, the "seal" remains unbroken; the Spirit will never leave the heart in which He has taken up residence. If so, the above warnings are without meaning. Sins against the Spirit are sins, and like all other sins bring eternal condemnation unless forsaken and forgiven. As Robert Shank says, "The Holy Comforter cannot continue to dwell in men who close their hearts against His loving ministry" (*Life in the Son,* 118).

See SIN, HOLY SPIRIT, ECONOMIC TRINITY, PERSONALITY OF THE HOLY SPIRIT, UNPARDONABLE SIN, SEAL.

For Further Reading: Shank, *Life in the Son,* 103-18; Stauffer, *"When He Is Come,"* 170-76; Steele, *The Gospel of the Comforter,* 232-45, 267-71.

RICHARD S. TAYLOR

SITUATION ETHICS. See NEW MORALITY.

SKEPTICISM. Skepticism is an attitude of doubt and wariness toward dogma. In its milder form it is a safeguard against credulity, but in its more radical forms it denies the possibility of certain knowledge. As a philosophical stance skepticism has its roots in Greek thought; perhaps its most famous modern exponent was David Hume (1711-76).

Skepticism gained prominence in the 17th century as a reaction against the well-meaning Scholasticism which sought to "remove doubt wherever possible" from religion by depending upon reason rather than revelation (Rowen, *A History of Early Modern Europe,* 600). In this attempt the stress was shifted from the faith element in Christianity to reason; but reason was inadequate to prove miracles and other supernatural aspects of biblical revelation. As a result the pendulum swung to skepticism. Thus the effort to protect religion from doubt by substituting reason for revelation became counterproductive.

While devout Christians may by temperament or on principle be skeptical in scientific and other secondary areas of knowledge, they cannot advertise themselves as skeptics in relation to the core of biblical claims. As an epistemological position skepticism is irreconcilable with Christian theology, which postulates historical veracity for the claims of biblical revelation and demands complete and open intellectual commitment.

See UNBELIEF, DOUBT, EPISTEMOLOGY, TRUTH, FAITH.

For Further Reading: Beecher, *Lecture on Scepticism;* Rowen, *History of Early Modern Europe;* McDowell, *Evidence That Demands a Verdict.* MERNE A. HARRIS

SLAVE, SLAVERY. The most common NT word for slave is *doulos* and designates one who is in subjection to a master, whether the master be a person or a passion or influence. Both John and Paul refer to those who are slaves to sin or to righteousness (John 8:34; Rom. 6:16). The writers of the Epistles refer to themselves as *christou doulos,* Christ's slave (cf. Gal. 1:10; 2 Pet. 1:1; Jude 1).

Slavery as an institution has existed from antiquity. Men were usually enslaved as punishment for misbehavior, as captives in war, or to fill the need for laborers. Aristotle saw all barbarians (non-Greeks) as slaves by nature rather than by circumstance. Plato's ideal state was dependent upon a large slave class.

The NT does not condemn slavery directly. Rather it accepts slavery as a contemporary social fact but deals with master-slave relationships so as to render slavery meaningless if not unjustifiable. Slaves and masters are brothers. In Christ all are one, there is no bond or free (Gal. 3:28; Eph. 6:9; Philemon).

The Apostolic Church looked upon slaves as brothers and equals. The post-Apostolic Church admitted slaves to all rights of the Church, some becoming priests and even bishops. Church collections were often used to purchase freedom for slaves, and the freeing of slaves was considered praiseworthy (Harnack, *The Mission and Expansion of Christianity,* 168-70).

See SOCIAL ETHICS, MAN, BROTHERHOOD.

For Further Reading: Westermann, *The Slave Systems of Greek and Roman Antiquity,* 327-51; Maclaren, "Peter," *Expositions of Holy Scripture,* 215-24.

M. ESTES HANEY

SOCIAL ETHICS. The Christian is always concerned with the question, What does God require of me? But he is also confronted with the problem of what society requires. How he reacts to such social requirements in harmony with God's will constitutes the field of social ethics.

Man is by nature a social creature. Everything he does affects others; that is, all his actions have social consequences. And what is right or wrong morally is usually influenced by community standards. Thus man usually acts as a group member and behaves according to what his group approves or disapproves. And when he acts, he is faced with concern for his person-to-person relationships, his relationship to society, and his own personal responsibility in his social behavior.

Christianity is both personal and social. It is impossible to be saintly in isolation. And this personal/social matrix in which we are born and nurtured exhibits several problems which confront the believer. First of all, there is the tension which exists between the interests of the individual versus the demands of society or the state. The Christian must decide whether in obeying God he is also right in obeying man, that is, the state. He must render unto Caesar, it is true, but what is Caesar's? God commands us to obey the ordinances of man. Is there any place to draw the line between conformity and nonconformity? This the Christian must face.

A second area of problems concerns man's relationship to others, the problem of group decisions. Sometimes one must go along with group opinion which is different from his own; sometimes one must stick by his own decision when it is contrary to that of his group. Both human wisdom and the leadership of the Holy Spirit are essential.

A third problem area concerns the relations of group to group. The familiar church and state relationship is a good example of this problem. The ecumenical movement to unite denominations into one group is another.

A fourth area of problems lies in the plural nature of society. In the Middle Ages the unity of society was effected by the overwhelming influence of the church. Today, religious diversity, ethnic heterogeneity, cultural variety, and the other cultural varieties unloosed by the Renaissance and the Reformation have made social pluralism the character of Western civilization.

All these complexities tend to make social ethics a most difficult area for Christians. Fortunately, such need not be the case. The Bible, and particularly the NT, contains teachings which apply to every social situation. The example and teachings of Jesus, the attitude of always considering the good of others, the importance of holy motives for all personal conduct, plus simple faith that one is trying to obey God will make every social decision a moral one. In these conditions one can always be right ethically even when judgment is immature or even mistaken.

See CHRISTIAN ETHICS, ETHICS, DUTY, WORK (WORKS), SOCIAL HOLINESS, NONCONFORMITY, WORLD (WORLDLINESS), LIFE-STYLE.

For Further Reading: DeWolf, *Responsible Freedom;* Wirt, *The Social Conscience of the Evangelical;* Muelder, *Moral Law in Christian Social Ethics;* Smith, *Revivalism and Social Reform.*

OTHO JENNINGS

SOCIAL HOLINESS. This is holiness in its interpersonal and societal relationships. When John Wesley said that he knew of no holiness but social holiness, he was repudiating the monastic premise that holiness was possible only in isolation, with complete concentration being given to the relation of the soul with its God. This, in Wesley's view, was a perversion of Christianity, for it completely missed the social emphasis of the Bible. Holiness was possible in the midst of everyday life, including the home, the marketplace, and the factory; in fact, holiness which was not practiced in the normal affairs of life was illusory.

Social holiness perceives that Christian love is more than minimal legal righteousness but a practical concern with the total person, and with the social structures which affect the person. Wesley raised money for the poor, found jobs for the unemployed, provided medicine for the sick, started schools for the unlearned, and arranged loans for the destitute. But he also opposed evil systems, such as the institution of slavery.

However, while traditionally holiness people have not minimized the importance of the political process, their major energies have been expended in evangelism. This reflects their realistic view of human sinfulness, which provides no basis for trust in social reform alone, apart from the sanctifying influences of the gospel.

See SOCIAL ETHICS, HOLINESS, SIN.

For Further Reading: Hopkins, *The Rise of the Social Gospel in American Protestantism from 1865-1915;* Mouw, *Political Evangelism;* Thompson, *John Wesley as a Social Reformer.*

MERNE A. HARRIS

SOCIAL WELFARE. The term *social welfare* is synonymous with the term *social work* when the reference is to functions of federal, state, and local governments. In private and/or religious programs, terms like *charity* and *benevolence* are commonly used. So far as publicly supported programs are concerned, there were few examples before the New Deal programs of the 1930s and afterward. But the concept of charity among Christians is as old or older than Christianity itself.

Traditionally, Christians have been taught to love and care for their families, neighbors, and even strangers. The words of Jesus, "Inasmuch as ye have done it unto one of the least of these my brethren, ye have done it unto me" (Matt. 25:40), are often cited as a principle of charitable consideration.

The welfare movement of today has its roots in the Christian concept of charity. The early colonists had strong religious influences. Theoretically there should have been affluence enough to care for all the needy. However, the sinful complications of the day plus the growing number of different sects, together with the weaknesses of the religious organizations, soon made their efforts at charity inadequate.

The result was that the colonies tried various adaptations of the Elizabethan Poor Laws which they had known in England. These programs were administered by the colonial officials in one way or another, and thus became the first examples of public responsibility for social welfare.

Not all social work, however, is accounted for by public funds and agencies. Numerous church auxiliaries, plus parachurch groups, such as World Vision and World Human Fund, dispense money, goods, and services on a huge, worldwide scale. The Salvation Army is famous for its effective social service. Among the nonchurch movements the best known is United Way, sponsored by community businesses for the support of local charitable agencies.

Since social work/welfare has been defined theoretically as the art of applying professional skill to help people to learn how to help themselves solve their problems, there is good reason to think that social work at its best should be a Christian service of love to mankind. For this reason there exists an organization known as the National Association of Christians in Social Work. The members are professionals who have dedicated themselves to applying Christian principles in connection with their work in social welfare.

See SOCIAL HOLINESS, SOCIAL ETHICS, LABOR.

For Further Reading: Geisler, *Ethics: Alternatives and Issues,* 178-95.

OTHO JENNINGS

SOCINIANISM. This is the name given to the Unitarian teachings of Faustus Socinus (1539-1604) and later persons who taught similarly. The Racovian Catechism (1605), based on his writings, outlines his Unitarian and generally liberal teachings. His Arian-like denial of the deity of Christ and the Holy Spirit contributed to the Latitudinarian liberalism within the Church of England in the 17th and 18th centuries.

See LATITUDINARIANISM, LIBERALISM, UNITARIANISM.

J. KENNETH GRIDER

SOCIOLOGY. In its primary sense, sociology is the analysis of social structures, orders, and styles, in contrast to the personal or individual. Sociology describes the interaction of persons in community; racial characteristics; aberrant behavior such as delinquency or criminal activity; marriage and family; the statistical evaluation of group activity and population trends; and it develops "labels" or "types" which describe various groups having similar interests.

Sociology assesses religious groups and behavior. Sociology of religion is one approach to the study of religion. It considers denominational patterns, theological commitments, regional religious differences, and religious attitudes. Describing an area of the United States as the Bible Belt is a sociological label. The sociologist of religion *describes* religious values but does not *as sociologist* make value judgments about religious attitudes. While theology is a normative science which sets forth standards of value for life and behavior, sociology is a descriptive science which systematically describes theological viewpoints, groupings, etc. The discipline of sociology has no competency to judge the worth of a theological concept like "revelation."

One of the most valuable results of sociology is the way it classifies religious diversity. As the botanist classifies plant life for purposes of study, the sociologist classifies religious patterns, orders, and opinions. H. Richard Niebuhr's *Christ and Culture* is a classic example of the sociology of religion. Niebuhr proposes types of interaction between the church and the world. The "Christ Against Culture" type describes those Christians who oppose the world's structures—for example, politics—seeking to avoid contact with its evil influences. Descriptions of the various types of Christianity—liberal, conservative, fundamentalist, evangelical, holiness, or Pentecostal—are as often sociological types as they are descriptions of theological differences. Charles Jones's *Perfectionist Persuasion* is a fine sociological study of the holiness movement in America.

Andrew Greeley's *Denominational Society* is an example of the sociological study which assesses structural, organizational, and religious differences. Studies like these offer insight through statistics, graphs, and surveys. Jones is particularly helpful.

See SOCIAL HOLINESS, SOCIAL ETHICS, SOCIAL WELFARE.

For Further Reading: *Journal for the Scientific Study of Religion;* Moberg, *Inasmuch;* Wach, *Types of Religious Experience;* Niebuhr, *Christ and Culture.*

LEON O. HYNSON

SON OF GOD. This term is used in Scripture primarily to signify the unique relation of God's only begotten Son to the Father and the spiritual relationship made possible for all men to God through the atoning work of that Son.

To understand the term in any particular passage, one needs to be familiar with its usage throughout the Scriptures. It seldom occurs in the OT. It is more frequently found in the Synoptics. It is almost ever present by implication in

John. It is commonplace in Paul and the rest of the NT.

Three expressions are found in the OT which are translatable by "son[s] of God": *ben elohim, ben elim, bar Elahin.* The last occurs in Dan. 3:25 and refers to the supernatural presence that the three Hebrews found accompanying them in the fiery furnace. The second occurs in Ps. 29:1 and 89:7. Here the term seems to indicate supernatural beings, but not divine, who are part of the divine court. The first term occurs in Gen. 6:2, 4, and Job 1:6; 2:1; 38:7. The references in Job are clearly to supernatural beings who appear before God. It is sometimes translated "angel." The references in Genesis are debatable. It is this writer's conviction that it refers to some in the lineage of Seth who were characterized by a spiritual relationship to God not common among the sons of Cain. This anticipates the second usage of this term in the NT. The line between the Creator and the creature is so sharply drawn in the OT that the thought of a procreative relationship between Yahweh and any of His creatures is completely alien. The preservation of that distinction is basic to a clear understanding of the use of the Fatherhood of God and the Sonship of Jesus in the NT.

In the Synoptic Gospels Jesus is identified as the "Son of God." Mark does this in the title line of his Gospel (1:1). The angel who announces to Mary that she is to have a child informs her that he is to be called "the Son of God" (Luke 1:35). The voice from heaven at the Baptism calls Him "my beloved Son" (Mark 1:11). The same voice on the Mountain of Transfiguration repeats that identification (9:7). Demons whom Jesus exorcises recognize in Him the divine Son (5:7). Satan in the Temptation demands that He prove that He really is (Matt. 4:3, 6). Peter affirms this at Caesarea Philippi (16:16). The priests put His claim to Sonship at the heart of their argument for His crucifixion (26:63). The centurion at the Crucifixion bears the same witness as that with which Mark begins his Gospel (Mark 15:39; cf. 1:1).

Jesus, however, rarely used the designation of himself. He preferred the term "Son of man" or simply "Son." He did not deny His divine Sonship. He acts in the Gospels as if this were a saving secret which He will wait for men through faith and illumination to discover, rather than simply repeat a proposition in which they have been indoctrinated. It is in moments of intimacy in the Synoptics when He acknowledges His identity (Matt. 11:25-26) or else in ambiguous parable when He tests men (21:33-46; 22:1-14). So the centurion sees (Mark 15:39) what Israel's leaders had no hearts to understand (14:60-65).

John's usage is another story. The Father-Son relationship is almost omnipresent in John as Jesus' view of His relationship to God. Usually, though, He uses just "Son" without qualification or the term "Son of man." Only three times does one find the expression "Son of God" used by Christ of himself (5:25; 10:36; 11:4). There is no question, though, for His hearers as to what He meant. Nathanael (1:49), Martha (11:27), and the apostle himself identify Him (1:18; 20:31). More dramatically, the religious leadership is ready to destroy Him because He claimed equality with God (5:18; 19:7). They understood His claim to a unique and generative relationship with God. To help us understand this, John uses the expression "only begotten" (1:14, 18; 3:16, 18).

John not only establishes the unique and divine Sonship which Jesus enjoys with the Father, but he introduces the kind of sonship which others may enjoy with the Father (1:12). He develops this further in his First Epistle (3:1-2). This sonship is spiritual and imparts new life but is not a generative relationship. It comes as a gift to those who discover the nature of the unique relationship of Jesus Christ to the Father and believe in the only begotten One (John 20:31).

Paul now is free to use the term "Son of God" of Jesus Christ to indicate His deity and is able to use the same term "son of God" of the believer to reflect his relationship by faith through grace into the spiritual family of God. Christ's Sonship speaks of essential and eternal nature. Our sonship is a divine gift of adoptive relationship and spiritual regeneration which does not alter our nature as creatures. This twofold usage of the term occurs consistently throughout the rest of the NT writings.

See CHRISTOLOGY, ETERNALLY BEGOTTEN, ETERNAL GENERATION, SON OF MAN, ADOPTION, REGENERATION.

For Further Reading: Nineham, *The Gospel of St. Mark; Baker's DT,* 117-23; Kittel, 8:359-97; Botterweck and Ringgren, eds., *Theological Dictionary of the Old Testament,* 2:157-59; *GMS,* 303-20.

DENNIS F. KINLAW

SON OF MAN. In the OT, this phrase is characteristically a poetic synonym for "man" as a weak creature before God and yet possessing great dignity compared to the rest of creation (cf. Num. 23:19; Ps. 8:4; 144:3; 146:3; Isa. 51:12; 56:2; Jer. 49:18; 50:40; 51:43). Likewise the plural refers to "humankind" (e.g., Ps. 4:2; 33:13; Prov. 8:4, 31; Eccles. 3:18 f; Isa. 52:14; Dan. 5:21; 10:16; Joel

1:12; Mic. 5:7). "Son of man" occurs over 90 times in Ezekiel (e.g., 2:1, 3, 6, 8) as Yahweh's designation of the prophet. Daniel is similarly identified in Dan. 8:17 (cf. 10:11, 19). Although "the son of man" in Ps. 80:17 is used synonymously with "man," in its context it appears as a collective symbol for the nation of Israel.

In the important apocalyptic vision of Daniel 7, after four beastlike kings are stripped of their rule, "one like a son of man" is given everlasting dominion (vv. 13 ff, RSV) by the Ancient of Days. In the subsequent interpretation this one is identified with "[the people of] the saints of the Most High" (vv. 18, 22, 25, 27, RSV), i.e., Israel. The pre-Christian date and influence of the non-canonical developments of Daniel 7's Son of man figure have been vigorously disputed (cf. the *Similitudes of Enoch; 4 Ezra* 1 and 13; and the *Jewish Sibylline Oracles* 5). A resemblance exists with pre-Christian Oriental myths of the Primal Man and Adam speculations.

The rather inelegant Greek expression *ho huios tou anthrōpou,* "the Son of man," is a very literal translation of the Hebrew *ben ad-am* and Aramaic *bar nas-ha/nash/enosh.* The expression occurs 81 or 82 times in the Gospels; of these 69 are in the Synoptics. There are no real exceptions to its exclusive use by Jesus (cf. Luke 24:7; John 12:34). The four other NT instances (Acts 7:56 [cf. Luke 12:8]; Heb. 2:6-8; Rev. 1:13; 14:14) refer to Jesus, employing OT quotations.

In Jesus' time "Son of man" was sometimes used idiomatically to avoid the pronoun "I," but it apparently was not a current messianic title. Its titular use in the Gospels is therefore unique (cf. e.g., Mark 8:27 = Matt. 16:13; Mark 8:31 = Matt. 16:21). The evangelists never find it necessary to explain the enigmatic expression, and no one is ever reported to have found Jesus' self-reference difficult (but cf. John 12:34).

Three groups of Synoptic Son of Man sayings have been distinguished: (1) Apocalyptic sayings which refer to His future coming (e.g., Mark 8:38; Matt. 24:27, 37, 39; Luke 12:8 ff; 11:30; 17:30); (2) Present sayings which refer to Jesus' earthly activity (e.g., Mark 2:10, 28; Matt. 8:20; 11:18 ff); and (3) Suffering sayings which predict Jesus' passion and resurrection (e.g., Mark 8:31; 9:31; 10:33 ff; 14:21, 41).

John employs "Son of man" as one of many essentially equivalent Christological titles. Paul's "Second Adam" doctrine (cf. Rom. 5:12-21; 1 Cor. 15:21 ff, 45-49; Phil. 2:6-11) is perhaps an attempt to reconstruct the "Son of Man" concept for a non-Jewish milieu. In later Hellenistic Christianity "Son of Man" comes to be contrasted with the title "Son of God" to indicate Jesus' humanity (cf. Epistle of Barnabas 12:10; Ignatius' *Letter to the Ephesians* 20:2).

See CHRIST, SON OF GOD, CHRISTOLOGY, MESSIAH.

For Further Reading: Borsch, *The Son of Man in Myth and History;* Colpe, *"ho huios tou anthrōpou,"* Kittel, 8:400-477; Cullmann, *The Christology of the New Testament,* 137-92; Fuller, *The Foundation of New Testament Christology;* Johnson, "Son of Man," *IDB,* 4:413-20; Ladd, *The Presence of the Future;* Longenecker, *The Christology of Early Jewish Christianity; GMS,* 306-12.

GEORGE LYONS

SON OF PERDITION. See PERDITION, SON OF PERDITION.

SORCERY. According to the biblical view, sorcery is an attempt to use spirit-world powers to influence either people or events and is regarded as a grave sin in the same category with idolatry.

Sorcery is a complex topic, and a comprehensive overview will lead to a survey of magic and witchcraft as well. Sorcery may be associated with divination, which is soothsaying in its broadest sense, i.e., the revelation of secrets from the past, present, and future. Sorcery used in this way is associated with the supernatural, though no attempt may be made to influence events by supernatural means. In biblical times the sorcerer may have used demonic powers to deceive an inquirer or impress him with his own mystical powers.

Sorcery is especially attractive to primitive peoples where there is an ignorance of natural law. However, the view that world affairs are governed by the unseen and irrational is also found among civilized people.

Sorcery is noted in the OT in such references as Exod. 22:18; Lev. 20:6; and Deut. 18:10-14. A survey of these verses strongly impresses the reader that sorcery is associated with idolatry and is always condemned even to the point of the death penalty. Not only is this condemnation found in the Torah, but the prophets also note that the wrath of God comes upon Israel because of openness to magic (Isa. 47:9).

The significant fact for the believer and the curious is that there is no doubt about the spiritual reality behind occult powers. These powers can only be resisted and defeated through the power and blood of Christ.

See SATAN, SATAN WORSHIP, DEMONS (DEMON POSSESSION), OCCULT (OCCULTISM), SPIRITUALISM (SPIRITISM).

For Further Reading: Hauck, "Sorcery and Soothsaying," *The New Schaff-Herzog Encyclopedia of Religious*

Knowledge, 2:6-9; Kitchen, "Magic and Sorcery," *NBD,* 766-71; Kittel, 4:356-59. LARRY FINE

SORROW. See SUFFER, SUFFERING.

SOTERIOLOGY. Soteriology (*soteria* = salvation + *logos* = word) is that branch of Christian theology which treats the doctrines of salvation, including (1) atonement for sin—the provision of salvation through Christ; and (2) salvation from sin—the application of salvation by the Spirit

Christ's death on the Cross atones for man's sin as a conditional substitute for the penalty due the sinner. Thus the Atonement is vicarious, substitutionary, and sufficient for all. It is foreshadowed in OT sacrifice and prophetic prediction and is motivated by God's love. Atonement is termed propitiation (1 John 2:2; Rom. 3:25), redemption (v. 24; 1 Cor. 6:20; Gal. 3:13), ransom (Matt. 20:28; 1 Tim. 2:6); and reconciliation (Rom. 5:10-11; Col. 1:20-22).

Atonement has been provided for all (2 Cor. 5:14-15; Heb. 2:9; 1 John 2:2). Its unconditional benefits include the continued existence of our race, man's restoration to salvability, God's prevenient grace leading man to repentance, the salvation of infants, and continued intercession by Christ. The conditional benefits of the Atonement are all God's saving ministries to the soul.

The Holy Spirit administers the plan and provision of redemption. Through the Spirit and the Word God's gracious call is available to mankind (Rev. 22:17). God's prevenient grace provides mercy (Rom. 2:4), the Spirit convicts of sin (John 16:8), draws (6:44), and works with man's free will in every step the soul takes toward God.

Repentance for sin is essential to salvation (Luke 13:2-5; Acts 3:19; 17:30), along with saving faith (Rom. 1:16; 10:10; Eph. 2:8). Repentance is proved by godly sorrow for sin (2 Cor. 7:9-10) and forsaking sin (Matt. 3:8). This turning from sin to God is called conversion (18:3; Jas. 5:19-20).

Justification is the gracious, judicial act of God declaring the repentant sinner forgiven, released from the penalty of his sins, and accepted as righteous. It is received by grace (not by man's works) through faith (Rom. 3:24-25; 5:1; Eph. 2:8) and through Christ's shed blood (Heb. 9:12).

Regeneration is the mighty change produced by the Holy Spirit by which man is born of God (John 1:12-13), is born of the Spirit (3:5-6), passes from death to life (5:24), is made alive (Col. 2:13), is made a new creation (2 Cor. 5:17), becomes a child of God (John 1:12), and receives a new nature (2 Pet. 1:4). The evidences of regeneration are the witness of the Spirit with the believer's spirit (i.e., a twofold witness) (Rom. 8:16; 1 John 5:6, 10), victory over sin (3:9; 5:4, 18), God's overflowing love (Rom. 5:5), love for God's Word (1 John 5:2-3), love for the unsaved (2 Cor. 5:14); love for other Christians (1 John 4:19—5:1), spiritual joy (Rom. 5:2, 11; 14:17), and peace with God (5:1; 14:17).

Adoption is God's declaratory act receiving us into His family and giving us the privilege of sonship, filial confidence, and eternal inheritance with Christ (Rom. 8:15-17; 1 Pet. 1:4).

Initial sanctification occurs at regeneration. Entire sanctification (the infilling of the Spirit) occurs at that moment subsequent to regeneration when the believer totally surrenders in consecration (Rom. 12:1-2) and faith (Acts 26:18). Its instantaneous nature is indicated by the aorist tense used in the verses referring to this experience of grace. The Spirit cleanses (Acts 15:9; 2 Cor. 7:1; Titus 2:14) and fills with God's holy love (Rom. 5:5; 1 Pet. 1:22). Progressive sanctification is growth in spiritual maturity, aided by the Spirit (2 Cor. 3:17-18; Eph. 4:13).

See ATONEMENT, SALVATION, SANCTIFICATION.

For Further Reading: Wiley, *CT,* 1:24; 2:217-517; Ralston, *Elements of Divinity,* 193-472; Harvey, *A Handbook of Theological Terms,* 224. WESLEY L. DUEWEL

SOUL. The soul is the personal self. Generally the term is used in distinction, even in contrast, to the physical body; at other times it represents the entire person, including the body.

The term "soul" is found 494 times in the KJV. All but two cases are translations of the Hebrew *nephesh* in the OT and its Greek equivalent, *psuchē,* in the NT. Purkiser points out that *nephesh* is used 756 times in the OT but is translated "soul" in only 428 instances. Other meanings are "life," "self," "person," "desire," "appetite," "emotion," and "passion" (*GMS,* 71). Both *nephesh* and *psuchē* are bewilderingly flexible, and move from simple animal life to the immortal spirit of man.

Two problems especially plague any discussion of "soul." One is the relation of soul to spirit, while the other is the propriety of speaking of the soul as immortal. In respect to the first problem it can be said that most scholars, from Augustine down to Laidlaw, Delitzsch, and James Orr, have tended to see soul as the life of a personal spirit inhabiting a physical body. It is thus the connecting link between matter and pure spirit. In the vivid phrase of Augustine soul is "the watchtower whence the spirit looks forth." Biblically this distinction between soul and spirit is sometimes stressed (e.g., Heb. 4:12), but at other times spirit and soul are used interchangeably (e.g., Luke 1:46-47). On the whole, however, in the NT especially, spirit is that aspect of the soul which can be said to be Godward in its nature, while soul is that aspect of the spirit which is outward and manward.

This distinction is implied by Paul's contrast between the "natural man" and the "spiritual" person in 1 Cor. 2:13-15. The natural person—obviously the unregenerate—is the *psuchikos* or "soulish" person. He is alive in soul but not in spirit. His horizontal life is intact, but the vertical dimension of his nature is dead (or dormant). The person's spirit must be quickened by the Holy Spirit in regeneration.

The question of the soul's immortality has been befogged by the intrusion into Christian tradition of the Platonic doctrine of the soul. This identifies the soul as the preexistent and indestructible personal being which temporarily is subjected to the prison house of an evil body, a body to be escaped as soon as possible. Biblically the body is not evil, and God's design for human beings is that they shall in the resurrection resume their normal spirit-body unity. But in the meanwhile the spirit returns to God, to await the resurrection (Eccles. 12:7; Luke 23:46; Acts 7:59; 1 Cor. 5:5; Heb. 12:23; cf. Phil. 1:22-24; 2 Pet. 1:13-14). Therefore, to speak of the immortality of the soul is a popular way of speaking which is not technically accurate, excepting as soul and spirit may be used interchangeably.

That there is an essence of the person which survives death is implied also in the OT teaching on *sheol* and the NT equivalent of *hadēs.* Even Alan Richardson, who plays down Platonic dualism, is forced to concede that the Hebrew concept of man includes a possible separation of soul (spirit) from the body "in the unreal and shadowy world existence of Sheol, the underworld of departed spirits" (*A Dictionary of Christian Theology,* 316). And Delitzsch says: "It is thus a contradiction against Scripture, to make man a being, so to speak, of one casting. Neither is the body the precipitate of spirit, not the spirit the sublimate of matter. Both views derange the limits of creation drawn by Scripture" (*Biblical Psychology,* 106).

The position of Oscar Cullmann that the prospect of life in the future belongs to the order of redemption, not to the order of creation, can be misleading. If there is no created immortality in human nature, in any sense, then how can death be said to be the consequence of sin? It would rather belong to the order of nature. Furthermore, on what basis could Christian theology postulate future existence for the wicked? Resurrection, according to both Daniel and Jesus, is shared equally by the righteous and the evil: "And many of those who sleep in the dust of the ground will awake, these to everlasting life, but the others to disgrace and everlasting contempt" (Dan. 12:2, NASB; cf. John 5:28-29; Matt. 25:46; Heb. 9:27; Rev. 20:11-15). What kind of "redemption" would it be to be brought back to life out of nonexistence, only to be sent to hell?

"The sting of death is sin" (1 Cor. 15:56)—not the peril of nothingness, but the peril of knowing that sin creates postdeath consequences. Those who believe that death ends all do not necessarily fear it; to them it is often seen as welcome escape. Those who suffer the "fear of death . . . all their lives" (Heb. 2:15, NASB) are apprehensive, not of nonexistence, but of sensing that death ends probation and brings judgment. It is from this fear, and from this judgment, that redemption is needed. True, a resurrection unto eternal life belongs to the order of redemption, but not postdeath existence itself. It is the certainty of postdeath existence, made sure by creation and made terrible by sin, that constitutes the awful need for redemption, and makes redemption so glorious.

See MAN, DIVINE IMAGE, HUMAN NATURE, SPIRIT, BODY, DUALISM, DICHOTOMY, TRICHOTOMY, IMMORTALITY, RESURRECTION OF THE BODY, PERSON (PERSONALITY).

For Further Reading: Delitzsch, *Biblical Psychology;* Orr, *Christian View of God and the World,* 137-39; Cullmann, *Immortality of the Soul or Resurrection of the Body?* Purkiser, ed., *Exploring Our Christian Faith,* 215-20, 362-65; *GMS,* 69-76, 257-59, 262 ff, 649-58.

RICHARD S. TAYLOR

SOUL SLEEP. Does man remain in the grave until the day of resurrection, or does man go immediately into the presence of the Lord at the moment of death? The answer to this question revolves around one's view of the nature of man. Is man made up of body, spirit, and soul; of body and soul; or of body-soul? Is man tripartite, bipartite, or a unity? If man is tripartite, or bipartite, one might claim that the body goes back to earth and the soul (and/or spirit) goes immediately into the presence of the Lord. This view further claims that the body is raised on resurrection day to rejoin the soul in a new soul-body form which becomes everlasting and lives in this form forever in the presence of the Lord.

If man is a unity, the question of soul sleep arises. Where does the soul go at death? Some claim that man sleeps in the grave awaiting the day of resurrection. On the day of resurrection, it is held that the body-soul is raised, is transformed in the twinkling of an eye, and lives ever after in the presence of the Lord. What does the Scripture say?

From the idea of man's being quickened from the dust of the earth and in light of his return to the dust came the image of death as "sleeping in the dust of the earth." Sleep as an image for death is used by Jeremiah (51:39, 57) to describe the unending death of the Babylonian conquerors of Judah; by Jesus (John 11:11) to indicate the death of Lazarus; by Luke (Acts 7:60) to tell of the death of Stephen; and by Paul (1 Thess. 5:10) to note the death of believers in Christ.

The OT intimates that sleeping in the dust of the earth was not the ultimate fate for mankind. Dan. 12:2 states that the dead rest in their graves until aroused at the resurrection (cf. Matt. 22:29 ff).

However, the NT does not permit us to rest in an ambiguous position in this matter. The Scriptures clearly imply that upon death the believer is immediately in the presence of the Lord (2 Cor. 5:6-8; Phil. 1:23). Whether the story of Dives is interpreted as parable or event, the teaching is unmistakable that both Lazarus and the rich man were in full possession of their mental faculties; yet their state was preresurrection.

And Paul writes two seemingly disparate ideas in seeking to comfort the church at Thessalonica. When Jesus returns, "God will bring with Jesus those who have fallen asleep in him" (4:14, NIV), yet also "the dead in Christ will rise first" (v. 16, NIV). Admittedly v. 14 is capable of a different interpretation. But if Paul intends what he seems to be implying, he is saying that the spirits of the departed are already with Jesus and will share in His second advent, but that in that event they will be reunited with their bodies—now glorified—thus recovering their wholeness. There is therefore a conscious bliss now (thus ruling out "soul sleep"), but the state is incomplete until the resurrection occurs. While saying no to soul sleep, therefore, we must concede a transitional state marked by an attenuated form of being. The body-soul unity marks man on earth, therefore, and will also mark him in a postresurrection heaven; but the earthly body is a temporary mode of being and does not belong to the *esse* (2 Cor. 4:16-18).

See INTERMEDIATE STATE, IMMORTALITY, RESURRECTION OF THE BODY.

For Further Reading: Bonnell, *I Believe in Immortality;* Shaw, *Life After Death: The Christian View of the Future Life.*

FRED E. YOUNG

SOUL WINNING. This is a term that has come into prominence in the Church in recent decades. Although Christianity has always emphasized sharing the Good News, recent times have seen a rise in interest in this area. The decline of mainline denominations has caused them to look toward evangelicals to observe their reason for growth—which is due, in great part, to various soul-winning efforts.

Briefly defined, soul winning is the act of bringing people to a place of personal acceptance of Jesus Christ as Lord and Savior. It is the larger term of which *witnessing* is a part. Witnessing is the sharing of one's faith or Christian experience with another. Soul winning goes one step further by asking the person shared with to do something about what they have heard—to act by repenting and inviting Jesus Christ into his or her life.

The term *soul winning* is often used synonymously with evangelism. In mass or public evangelism a group of people are presented the challenge of the gospel and then invited to act by praying at an altar, or in a prayer room, or in their seats. In personal or private evangelism, the plan of salvation is presented on a one-to-one basis. The same invitation is given to respond to the gospel call.

Actually, the term *soul winning* is a figure of speech. It is not man who wins people to Christ. The changing of a heart and life is an activity of God through the Holy Spirit. It is the Spirit who burdens the evangelist with the desire to share his faith; who interprets the words of the speaker to the listener; who convicts of sin, grants forgiveness, and bestows newness of life. The Book of Acts alone has some 41 references to the work of the Spirit in the lives of men.

The theological basis for soul winning stems from the very nature of God himself. He has always sought the fellowship of His human creation. Man was designed to worship Him, but the relationship was severed by sin. It is God who has initiated the means by which that relationship can be reestablished. He chose to send His Son to earth and to Calvary's cross on man's behalf. He sent the Holy Spirit to be the Paraclete to the Church. From first to last, salvation has its rootage in the initiative of God.

Having said that, however, it is important to realize that God has ordained that Christianity be a spoken religion (Matt. 28:18-20; Rom. 10:14). People are reached by others sharing their faith (Matt. 4:19). Philip is pictured in the NT as sharing his newfound faith with Nathanael, and later the other Philip (the deacon) shared with the Ethiopian eunuch. NT personages are vitally involved with bringing others to Christ. The soul winner shares Christ in the power of the Spirit, but he leaves the results with God (1 Cor. 3:6). Man cannot be praised for his part in the activity nor held responsible if the person rejects the gospel message.

The deepest motivation for soul winning comes from the soul winner's love for God. It must be love for God, even more than concern for the lost, that impels him. There are many organizations and agencies that care about people. The tragedy of the People's Temple cult in 1979 will ever underscore the fact that caring for people is not enough. Caring is certainly an incentive for soul winning as are church growth and other legitimate concerns; but they are not the deepest motivating force. That motivating force must be a love for God so deep and sound that the soul winner desires to help others to find that relationship, apart from whatever other incentives there may be.

The methodology for soul winning has created considerable discussion in the Church. Scores of procedures have been developed by those who wish to share their faith with others. These range from intricate evangelism plans containing memorized Scripture and illustrations to simple one-line statements that are designed to elicit thinking in the direction of spiritual matters. The discussion has centered around whether or not these programs are manipulative and, therefore, lead to shallow commitment. The key issue to remember is that Christ was the first soul winner—"'The Son of man came to seek and to save the lost'" (Luke 19:10, RSV). If the soul winner would be Christ's envoy, he must study the Master's characteristics and His spirit until those characteristics and that spirit are reproduced in him; remembering always that only the Holy Spirit can use methods in the awakening of sinners.

See EVANGELISM, MISSION (MISSIONS, MISSIOLOGY), TESTIMONY (WITNESS).

For Further Reading: Coleman, *The Master Plan of Evangelism;* Olford, *The Secret of Soul Winning;* Wood, *Evangelism: Its Theology and Practice,* 9-48.

D. MARTIN BUTLER

SOVEREIGNTY. See DIVINE SOVEREIGNTY.

SOWING AND REAPING. This phrase is a reminder of a fundamental law of life, viz., we reap what we sow. The biblical declaration of this law is Gal. 6:7—"Whatsoever a man soweth, that shall he also reap." The law is threefold: reaping follows sowing, what is reaped is determined by what is sowed, and reaping is certain. It may be called the law of consequences.

What is explicitly being affirmed is that there is a moral order as well as a natural order, and that a fundamental principle of both is that effects are the products of causes. In the natural order the farmer who sows wheat can expect to reap wheat, not corn. It is a simple but predictable and inviolable "mechanism" of action and reaction, cause and effect—i.e., sowing and reaping. The same mechanism operates in the spiritual and moral sphere, and is equally predictable and inviolable.

We witness daily the operation of this law. Here is a teenager who has found a job, but he lacks transportation, because he can't get a driver's license, because he failed his driver training course in high school, because he fooled around and, as a consequence of not studying, failed his exam. Here is a chain reaction, beginning with carelessness and ending (yet not ending—for the effects flow on) with embarrassment. This is a tiny sample of real life throughout the world around us.

The Scripture relates this law to God, who established it. "Be not deceived; God is not mocked." Wesley says that "to think to reap otherwise" than we sow is to mock God *(Notes),* for such thinking supposes we can outwit God and His law. But God stands back of the order which He has ordained. Both in the natural world and in the moral sphere the law is an expression of God's own holiness. The immutability of God's character makes His reactions and operations predictable and sure. Nowhere is this declared more precisely than in Rom. 11:22—"Behold therefore the goodness and severity of God: on them which fell, severity; but toward thee, goodness, if thou continue in his goodness: otherwise thou also shalt be cut off."

The particular biblical expressions of this law—those cases which demonstrate and exemplify the law at its ultimate level of gravity—are the two fundamental life options: sowing to the flesh or sowing to the Spirit. We experience the law of consequences in many ways which are not ultimate, such as eating unwisely and producing stomach discomfort. But if we choose a life-style which pampers the self, which is marked by indulgence and appetite and impulse, we can expect to reap decay of body, soul, and mind, and ultimate damnation. If we choose to seek the things of the Spirit, to subordinate the physical to the spiritual, to set our "affection on things above" (Col. 3:2), and do it day after day as a consistent commitment and way of life, we may be equally sure of "life everlasting" (Gal. 6:8), plus greater richness of life now.

The biblical concept of sowing and reaping presupposes true freedom of choice, but not freedom of consequences. The contrasting life-styles are not predetermined by heredity or environment, certainly not by divine decree. They are true options. But the end result is not optional.

Yet the biblical concept of sowing and reaping must not be confused with either fate or Karma. Fate by definition is outside of personal control or cause. The term relates to what is *destined* to occur by unknown forces or causes; as such it is essentially pagan. Those who ascribe everything to fate live in pessimistic fear and helplessness.

Karma, a doctrine deeply imbedded in Hinduism, Buddhism, and Jainism, recognizes the basic law of action and its fruit. But it falls short of the biblical doctrine in at least two respects. First, it presupposes that much that occurs in this life is the fruit of a previous life; and that this life determines the happiness or unhappiness of the next. While this latter is similar to the Christian doctrine, it is salvation by works apart from the intervention of a living Savior. The Christian doctrine is not that "life everlasting" is the product of sowing to the spirit (one's own) but to the Spirit. The acknowledgment that Paul is speaking of the Holy Spirit is the dividing line between a pagan works-salvation and the way of redemption through Christ.

Second, Karma lacks the Christian mode of escape. By repentance one can cease sowing to the flesh and begin sowing to the Spirit. While he may still suffer some consequences of the old life, much will be softened by the power of God, and the ultimate outcome changed. The Atonement is man's sole hope of breaking the merciless chain.

See MORTAL (MORTALITY), WORK (WORKS), FORGIVENESS, NON-CHRISTIAN RELIGIONS, PROVIDENCE.

For Further Reading: *CC,* 6:415 ff; *BBC,* 9:117 ff; *WBC,* 5:360 ff.

RICHARD S. TAYLOR

SPEAKING IN TONGUES. See TONGUES, GIFT OF.

SPIRIT. In man spirit describes that vital life force which, even though it is invisible in its essence, nevertheless energizes and directs all that constitutes the sphere of his human existence. The spirit is the seat of man's self-consciousness, emotions, and will.

In reference to God, spirit describes what He is in His essence: "'God is spirit; and those who worship Him must worship in spirit and truth'" (John 4:24, NASB). It is this fact that both God and man are spiritual beings which enables them to enjoy a personal relationship. Though Jesus has ascended to the Father, His Spirit is mediated to human hearts by the indwelling presence of the Holy Spirit of God.

The Bible also recognizes the presence and power of demonic spirits, able to tempt, possess, and subjugate the human spirit. Satan, however, has more than met his match in Jesus, who came to destroy the works of the devil.

In the NT the "spirit concept" is not to be understood in a Platonic sense as in contrast to the body or to nature. Rather, the Spirit is the supernatural power of God that stands in contrast to all that is human. That which belongs to the sphere of human existence is bounded by time, limited by finitude, and is always already passing away. So the one who lives "according to the flesh" (Rom. 8:4, NASB), i.e., centers his affections upon the human and natural order, is under the sentence of death.

That which is of the Spirit, however, is unbounded, unlimited, and eternal. So the one who lives "according to the Spirit" (Rom. 8:4, NASB), i.e., fixes his heart upon God and that which is spiritual, in harmony with the tutelage of the Holy Spirit, is the one who knows true life and peace.

To live in the Spirit does not mean a disembodied existence, nor does it imply a denigration of that which constitutes the full range of human existence—body, mind, and soul. It does mean, however, that God's Spirit possesses, controls, and directs man's spirit in such a way that his energies are focused upon God, others, and eternal values.

See GOD, ATTRIBUTES (DIVINE), MAN, SOUL, HOLY SPIRIT.

For Further Reading: *GMS,* 257-60, 484-507; Wiley, *CT,* 1:313-15; 2:303-33; Taylor, *Life in the Spirit,* 109-48.

C. S. COWLES

SPIRIT, HOLY. See HOLY SPIRIT.

SPIRITS IN PRISON. See DESCENT INTO HELL.

SPIRITUAL DEATH. See DEATH.

SPIRITUAL GIFTS. See GIFTS OF THE SPIRIT.

SPIRITUAL WARFARE. The modern pulpit accent is on comfort, affirmation, celebration, encouragement, peace, and personal happiness. Very little is said about the fact that Christians are in a real warfare with a real enemy. Less still is being offered to teach believers how to wage a spiritual war. But the Christian life is not intended to be a picnic or a dress parade; nor are Christians promised exemption from hand-to-hand conflicts with the enemy. There is a "gory" side to the Christian life for which most are ill prepared.

The war is being waged on three fronts, the personal, corporate, and cosmic. On the personal front the biblical counsel is to "resist the devil" (Jas. 4:7) and to give no "place to the devil" (Eph. 4:27). In the matter of disciplining the offending church member at Corinth, Paul was anxious that the forgiveness be as prompt and ready as the discipline had been, "lest Satan should get an advantage of us" (2 Cor. 2:11). He follows with the statement "for we are not ignorant of his devices." But the tragedy is, most of us are. No more profitable effort could be made than to study in depth these and other biblical references, that we might acquire an understanding of the subtle and devious ways Satan, through demonic suggestion, influence, and maneuvering, presses his attack on the individual Christian. The mind, body, possessions, feelings, and interpersonal relations, are all the objects of vicious assault. Declaration of our faith in public testimony, combined with a reliance on the power and merit of the blood of Christ, are two means of overcoming (Rev. 12:11). To valiant fighters the promise is: "He that overcometh shall inherit all things; and I will be his God, and he shall be my son" (21:7).

The warfare on the corporate front is the battle for souls, first in evangelism and Christian missions, and second, in the discipling of converts, that they may not be lost. In contemporary concern about church growth always lurks grave danger of monumental naivete. It is easy to forget that the church will not succeed by adopting Satan's weapons and failing to utilize those God has provided (2 Cor. 10:4). Timothy was urged by Paul to "war a good warfare" (1 Tim. 1:18). He was to do it by remembering and adhering to "the prophecies once made about you" (NIV) and by "holding on to faith and a good conscience" (v. 19, NIV). Sadly some have tried to substitute fleshly methods for spiritual, even abandoning a good conscience; but in the end they have "shipwrecked their faith" (NIV) and that of others.

To speak of the cosmic front of the war is to be reminded that the forces of Satan are locked in deadly combat with the forces of the kingdom of God. The history and causes of this conflict cannot here be discussed. This conflict was utterly real to Jesus and to His apostles, including Paul, who declared: "For our struggle is not against flesh and blood, but against the rulers, against the authorities, against the powers of this dark world and against the spiritual forces of evil in the heavenly realms" (Eph. 6:12, NIV; cf. 1 John 5:19, NASB). The vastness and violence of the conflict is portrayed vividly and dramatically in the Book of Revelation.

Christ is "Christus Victor" and has actually won the war, though for the present Satan is permitted to continue a rearguard action. Oscar Cullmann made famous the concept of "D day"—the decisive turning point, which assured the final outcome.

Christians therefore should be wary, and avoid presumption, yet be bold and confident, knowing that "greater is he that is in you, than he that is in the world" (1 John 4:4).

See SATAN, KINGDOM OF GOD, TEMPTATION, PAGANISM, NEW COVENANT, ESCHATOLOGY, PRINCIPALITIES AND POWERS.

For Further Reading: Bunyan, *The Holy War;* Jessop, *The Ministry of Prevailing Prayer;* Lewis, *Screwtape Letters;* Aulén, *Christus Victor;* Cullmann, *Christ and Time;* Smith, ed., *The Tozer Pulpit,* 4:119-31; Booth, "It's Cowardly Service vs. the Real Warfare," *Popular Christianity.*

RICHARD S. TAYLOR

SPIRITUALISM, SPIRITISM. Spiritualism is a religion which maintains that communication with the dead is possible, and such communication is the center of the religion. It maintains that after the death of the body the spirit lives on in the spirit world. A medium, a person on earth supposedly sensitive to vibrations from the spirit world, holds meetings called séances to seek messages from the spirits.

Although this belief is an ancient one, the modern spiritualist movement in America began in 1848 in Hydesville, N.Y., when the Fox sisters heard strange knockings and interpreted them as sounds coming from spirits of the other world. Interest in spiritualism peaked in the early 20th century, then declined, but interest in the occult has recently been renewed. Spiritualists consider themselves Christians and have churches, ministers, and doctrine. Christ, however, is not considered to be God, but the "great medium." Worship services are much like Protestant worship services, with the addition of messages from spirits of the dead.

A biblical example of communicating with the dead is the episode of Saul talking to Samuel in the house of the witch of Endor (1 Samuel 28). Asking a medium to do such a thing was specifically prohibited, and this act itself was part of the reason for Saul's death (Deut. 18:9-14; 1 Chron. 10:13-14). The conversation on the Mount of Transfiguration between Christ and Moses and Elijah (Matt. 17:1-8) cannot be classed as an example of spiritism, for it was a unique action of God in His revelation of Christ as Son and Savior.

Although it may be possible, God has forbidden any attempt on our part to communicate with the dead through mediums (Lev. 19:31; 20:6; 1 Tim. 4:1; et al.). Spiritualism itself says little or nothing about communication with God because its interest is in man, not God.

See SORCERY, SATAN, DEMONS (DEMON POSSESSION), OCCULT (OCCULTISM).

For Further Reading: "Spiritism" and "Spiritualists," *New Catholic Encyclopedia,* 13:576-77, 593-94; Wright, *Christianity and the Occult,* 105-60; Martin, *The Christian and the Cults.*

RONALD L. KOTESKEY

SPIRITUALITY. Spirituality may be most simply defined as the character or quality of spiritual-mindedness as opposed to worldliness and sensuality. In NT context an infusion of the Holy Spirit is always presupposed for a person to be considered spiritual. Paul affirms that to be spiritual is to be totally controlled by the Spirit (Rom. 8:1-17).

Although there is a difference in the Spirit's activity between the Old and New Testaments, it is helpful to look at two OT models of spirituality, especially since these are confirmed by NT writers. The first is the "friend of God" concept which was modeled by Abraham (Isa. 41:8; 2 Chron. 20:7). Several factors immediately present themselves as one thinks of Abraham. The first is suggested by James, "Abraham believed God" (2:23). Abraham is not remembered because he dressed differently or acted in a peculiar fashion or was a bit "spooky." His image is embedded in biblical memory because he believed God despite humanly insurmountable obstacles.

The picture received is not one of a superhuman personality who never made mistakes, but of a man who believed through all delays and all apparent modifications of what he believed God's will to be. Here is a man, very much a man, with all of the desires of a man, one in every way representative of the human race, who was able to demonstrate a faith in the veracity of God that could not be shaken. God had given him a staggering promise which could not possibly have been fulfilled in his lifetime, but he "staggered not . . . through unbelief" (Rom. 4:20)—even when God asked him to sacrifice the child of the promise (Gen. 22:1-11). As a friend of God, Abraham demonstrated constant trust, instant obedience, unwavering loyalty, costly magnanimity, and consistent service. An intense study of the choices of his life reveals a coherence and consistency compatible with the quality of life which can properly be designated as "spiritual."

A second OT concept helpful in understanding the term *spirituality* is "A man after God's own heart" as applied to David (1 Sam. 13:14; Acts 13:22). This could be said of him because of the intensity of his devotion to God. With the exception of his sin with Bathsheba his life was marked by a spontaneous turning to God for guidance, deliverance, and strength, in every situation. God could say of him, "a man . . . which shall fulfil all my will" (Acts 13:22). And in respect to his grievous sin, there was profound sorrow and repentance. His prayers are models of humility, remorse, and contrition. Such qualities as a forgiving spirit, a nonretaliatory attitude toward undeserved wrongs, and a quickness to confess errors and sins make him in the biblical sense a consistent example of a truly spiritual person.

As one turns to the NT, the apostle Paul appears as a model of spirituality. He assures us that he speaks words taught of the Holy Spirit, "comparing spiritual things with spiritual" (1 Cor. 2:13-14). The qualities of spirit observed in Abraham and David—obedience, and a spirit malleable in the hand of God—begin to flow together as one studies the life of Paul and considers the sharp contrast he makes between the spiritual and the worldly (Rom. 8:1-17).

It has been suggested by some that the possession of spiritual gifts is a mark of spirituality. Paul, who has more to say about spiritual gifts than any other biblical writer, emphatically declares that it is love, not gifts, that marks the spiritual person. This is the full intent of 1 Corinthians 13. In actual experience some naturally gifted persons tend to exercise their gifts for other than purely spiritual purposes while claiming solely spiritual aims for themselves. A natural credulity in human nature makes the "gift test" a persuasive measure for spirituality, while in reality it becomes a deceptive type of logic leading to erroneous conclusions. It was not the gifts that the apostle possessed which made him a spiritual person, but it was his courage in the face of grave physical suffering and danger, and his tenacious persistency in fulfilling the calling of God in his life (Acts 20:18-35).

Not all Christians are spiritual. "Ye which are spiritual," Paul writes to the Galatians (6:1), implying that some among them are not. The same differentiation is made in writing to the Corinthians (1 Cor. 2:6-15). The primary hindrance to spirituality is carnality (3:1-4). The possession of gifts did not prove the Corinthians spiritual nor make them such.

See HOLINESS, DEVOTE (DEVOTION), PRAYER, OBEDIENCE, FAITH, SECOND WORK OF GRACE.

For Further Reading: DeWolf, *Responsible Freedom,* 144-78; Lovelace, *Dynamics of Spiritual Life,* 61-80; Wiley, *CT,* 3:65-70. FLOYD J. PERKINS

STANDING AND STATE. In general "standing" and "state" may be distinguished as follows: "state" is one's real moral and spiritual condition; "standing" is one's relationship of acceptance or rejection, or position in the mind of others. With the Christian, a good state is dependent on the work of Christ *in* him; a good standing (with God) is dependent on being justified through faith in the work of Christ *for* him.

The so-called "standing and state" theory implies that one's standing and state do not need to match; that one may have a good standing with God without a righteous state. This theory has its roots in the post-Reformation conception of justification as developed in the theological streams originating in the thought of Martin Luther and John Calvin. To Luther, justification was not a change in the nature or character (state) of man, nor was it an overcoming in him of sin; it was a change in his relation to divine justice. Through justification the righteousness of Christ was imputed to man as his own righteousness. The expression of this concept is similar in Calvinism. Man's sin is removed by imputation to Christ.

Thus, the "standing and state theory" joins "hand in hand with the doctrine of imputed righteousness" (Taylor, *A Right Conception of Sin,* 40). The practical consequence of this doctrine is to remove anxiety for sinful acts or deep concern for one's sinful state. Believers are reckoned as righteous or holy by their "standing" in Christ. God does not take notice of their actual "state" because "he sees them only through Christ" (Wiley, *CT,* 2:459). The believer's sin is not actually removed as in a change of "state" but remains in the believer to be covered over by Christ's imputed holiness. Thus "holiness and righteousness are only imputed, never imparted" (Wiley). The responsibility of the believer, according to this theory, is to recognize what has already been accomplished in Christ.

Proponents of this view note 1 Cor. 1:2-9 as a reference to "standing" and v. 11 and 3:1-4 as a reference to "state" (Chafer, *Systematic Theology,* 7:293). That the Corinthians illustrate the possibility of a temporary partial disparity between standing and state is obvious; but it must be denied that this disparity is normative, or that its continuance will have no ultimate fatal effect on the standing.

The concept of changing one's standing by the imputation of Christ's righteousness without a corresponding change in one's state or moral nature is essentially to deny the possibility and necessity of personal holiness. John Wesley expressed concern about the doctrine of imputed holiness in his sermon "A Blow at the Root." Wesley comments as follows: "Wherever this doctrine is cordially received, it leaves open no place for holiness. It demolishes it from top to bottom, it destroys both root and branch. It effectually tears up all desire of it, all endeavor after it" (*Works,* 10:366).

The concepts of standing and state are sometimes advanced under the rubric of "declarative grace" (standing), and "operative grace" (state). God's declarative grace in justification is followed by operative grace in sanctification; but according to some interpreters, the fixedness of the declarative grace is unrelated to the success or failure of operative grace.

See IMPUTED RIGHTEOUSNESS, IMPARTED RIGHTEOUSNESS, GRACE, HOLINESS, ETERNAL SECURITY, OBEDIENCE, PERSEVERANCE.

For Further Reading: Chafer, *Systematic Theology,* 7:295; Taylor, *A Right Conception of Sin,* 26-42; Wesley, *Works,* 10:364-69. LARRY FINE

STATE, THE. That the state is ordained of God is clear from the general testimony of the biblical record and is made explicit by Paul in Rom. 13:1, as it was implicit in Christ's teaching (Mark 12:17). However, H. Orton Wiley correctly suggests that "the sovereignty of the civil authority lies in the state itself, and not in any king or ruler whatsoever. This is established by the fact that the state exists before all rulers, and by the additional fact, that rulers are at the most, but its instruments" (*CT,* 3:96). Thus the state, and not wicked Nero, was ordained of God when Paul wrote Romans 13. Without the state, whatever form it may take, society would destroy itself in anarchy.

Two conflicting views of state exist. One holds that the state was instituted by God after and because of the Fall, and without the entry of sin the state would have been unnecessary. However, the other view, known as the naturalistic, regards the state as based upon the law of God operative over Adam before the Fall, both permissively and prohibitively. When Adam sinned, he violated the law of God's previously existing governmental law. This view sees the state as inherent in the very nature of man and society by reason of the fact that man bears God's personal image, marred and perverted by the Fall, but never annihilated.

Further, in support of this view is the fact that the family which was instituted before the Fall was organizationally constituted with Adam as its head. The family is the basic God-ordained unit of society, upon which every form of the state ultimately rests. In the biblical view the entire human race is the God-ordained "extended family" from creation (Acts 17:26).

While certain fundamental principles are laid down by Christ and Paul, no political theory as such is given. Though recognizing and approving the state in His famous command in Mark 12:17, Christ makes only occasional and incidental references to the state or political orders. H. D. A. Major states that "Jesus lays down the fundamental principles which must guide His disciples in the future crises in which human authority and divine authority make conflicting claims" (*The Mission and Message of Jesus,* 148).

Paul sees the purpose and function of the state as limited to the maintenance of order, the execution of justice, the prevention and punishment of crime, the promotion of peace, and the general advancement of the welfare of its citizens. The state in the biblical view is always subservient to God's sovereignty (Acts 5:29; cf. 4:19).

See CITIZENSHIP, CITY, CIVIL DISOBEDIENCE, CIVIL RELIGION, CIVIL RIGHTS.

For Further Reading: *ZPEB,* 2:790-98; *IDB,* E-J:457-62; *Baker's DT,* 501-2; Wiley, *CT,* 3:96-98.

CHARLES W. CARTER

STEWARDSHIP. Stewardship is an open acknowledgment that man is a creature who is the chief object of divine beneficence, both in creation and through redemption. From the beginning, man received dominion over God's creation both as a gift and a task, and thereby a close personal relationship was established between God and man. Man was given a wide range of freedom, but not without guidance of law. Man from the outset was amenable and responsible. In its historic meaning, stewardship is always personal.

"Stewardship" is the English word used to translate the NT word *oikonomia.* The Greek word is a compound of *oikos,* meaning "house," and *nomos,* meaning "law." It thus refers to the management of a house or household affairs.

Through Jesus himself we discover what God the Father is like and learn His benevolent attitude toward all mankind. The apostle Paul, however, seems to be our special teacher in the NT concerning the practical theology of stewardship. The real issues of stewardship do not come before us clearly until we learn the message of redemption in the gift of God's own Son, our Savior. Paul summarizes this truth in a word picture which makes the entire universe as a landscape: "Through him [Jesus] God chose to reconcile the whole universe to himself, making peace through the shedding of his blood upon the cross—to reconcile all things, whether on earth or in heaven, through him alone" (Col. 1:20, NEB).

When Jesus came as Redeemer, He came as a man, "born of a woman." He appeared on the arena of man's defeat to provide for man's salvation. In what could be the most daring venture of redemption, Jesus committed to His disciples (on the eve of His departure) the agency of redemption. To be sure, the superintendency and power were afforded by the personal indwelling Holy Spirit. On the issue of transfer of power Jesus said, "As my Father hath sent me, even so send I you" (John 20:21). This becomes the assignment of each succeeding generation of Christians.

Paul was careful to ground his gospel message and mission on God himself. He witnessed with clarity to one of the young churches he founded, "But just as we have been approved by God to be entrusted with the gospel, so we speak, not to please men, but to please God who tests our hearts" (1 Thess. 2:4, RSV).

But God requires stewardship of all men, everywhere, no exceptions. "God is Lord, but he is not a landlord who can be cheated, cajoled, and treated shabbily" (Kantonen, *Stewardship* 73, 51). Jesus himself told the parable of the talents. The man who begged off had been given but one talent for investment and service. He buried his talent and then returned it without increase on the day of reckoning. He moaned, "Lord, I knew thee that thou art an hard man, reaping where thou hast not sown, and gathering where thou hast not strawed" (Matt. 25:24). The man said he was afraid and therefore hid his talent in the earth. His lord, however, identified the trusted man as, "You lazy rascal!" (NEB). John Wesley in his *Notes* on the passage addresses an apostrophe to the faithless servant: "No. Thou knowest Him not. He never knew God who thinks Him a hard master."

The basic issues of stewardship cover every area of our lives—not the religious only. The familiar trilogy is simple and far reaching: (1) Time; (2) Talent; (3) Treasure. Someone observed (tongue in cheek?), "The Terrible Trilogy." We would agree, but amend to read, "terribly" important and practical. Stewardship affords an edge to the Christian's witness and bears fruit both here and hereafter. It was Augustine who concluded: "The reward of God is God himself."

See TITHE (THE), SERVICE, CONSECRATE (CONSECRATION), MONEY, REWARDS, INTEGRITY.

For Further Reading: Kantonen, *A Theology for Christian Stewardship: Stewardship* 73; Young, *Giving and Living.*

SAMUEL YOUNG

STIGMATA. In Christian history, the bodily marks of Christ's wounds upon the hands, feet, side, head, or back of certain persons. Sometimes bleeding occurred. The term can refer to the pain only, without the wounds. Several hundred cases have been catalogued. The earliest well-known instance was that of Francis of Assisi. In 1224 his friends reported seeing the stigmata on his hands, feet, and side. Some modern examples have been attested by medical examination.

Stigmata were associated with the medieval stress upon participation in and indentification with Christ's sufferings. When spontaneous rather than deliberate, the wounds appeared during an emotional state of ecstasy or in connection with some mystical revelation.

Among Catholics, popular opinion ascribed stigmata to divine miracle, but officially the church has refrained from this view. There seems to be no reason not to attribute the phenomena themselves to natural but abnormal organic functions, given the conditions of intensive mental absorption, hysteria, and suggestibility. Similar phenomena have been observed outside the sphere of Christian faith.

See MYSTICISM.

For Further Reading: *NIDCC; The New Catholic Encyclopedia; ERE.*

ARNOLD E. AIRHART

STOICISM. Stoicism was an ancient philosophical perspective launched by Zeno of Citium, who began teaching in Athens 300 B.C. He lectured on the Painted Porch *(Stoa Poikele),* which gave the word *Stoic* to his school.

Following Zeno, many Hellenistic thinkers expanded his teachings into a rather comprehensive world view. Roman philosophers such as Cicero (106-43 B.C.), Seneca (4 B.C.-A.D. 65), Epictetus (60-138 A.D.), and Marcus Aurelius (121-80 A.D.) absorbed and articulated Stoic philosophy.

In Greco-Roman society, Stoics advocated a metaphysical *monism.* Some thought only matter to be real; others advocated pantheism; all believed reality is one. Thus Stoics said much about Nature, a vast, organic, purposeful system of which men and women and other creatures are but parts. Those with religious sensitivity (and many were deeply religious) thought God was the thoroughly immanent "rational spirit" who structures and guides all things and is inseparable from them.

In ethics, Stoics admonished people to live wisely and righteously. They sensed an orderliness and benevolence in Nature and thought human beings should follow her instruction and example. The "natural law" could be discerned and followed. Virtues such as prudence, courage, justice, and temperance make one good. Stoics frequently warned against the deceptive allure of riches and pleasures, teaching that simplicity and moderation, and indifference to pleasure or pain, help one live the good life.

Much about Stoicism attracted Christians in the Early Church. The Stoic ethic, based upon the natural law, fused easily with the Scripture's call for righteous living. Early thinkers such as Tertullian clearly used Stoic ideas as a framework for Christian theology. In political philosophy, the "idea of human rights," says L. Harold DeWolf, "or 'the rights of man' has come down to us from Stoics through the long tradition of natural law" (*Responsible Freedom,* 313).

Stoicism further refers to a general attitude toward life. Those who "keep a stiff upper lip," those who believe in rigid self-discipline, those who resign themselves to "fate" mediated through natural events, all reflect a stoical approach to life. While not conscious of historic Stoicism, such people nevertheless live according to some of its tenets.

Much that is true in Stoicism can be ascribed to the Holy Spirit, "the only fountain of truth" (Calvin). Yet while a philosophy of life, it is not a way of salvation. For that men must turn from noble resignation to simple trusting, in the Christ whose cross was foolishness to the Greeks and an offense to the Jews (1 Cor. 1:23); but to those who believe, the true "wisdom from God—that is, our righteousness, holiness and redemption" (v. 30, NIV).

See VIRTUE, SEVEN CARDINAL VIRTUES, CHARACTER, SUFFER (SUFFERING), PLEASURE, ETHICS, CHRISTIAN ETHICS, SOWING AND REAPING.

For Further Reading: Copleston, *A History of Philosophy;* Zeller, *The Stoics, Epicureans, and Sceptics;* Epictetus, *The Discourses of Epictetus;* Aurelius, *The Meditations of*

Marcus Aurelius; Cave, *The Christian Way,* 107-17; DeWolf, *Responsible Freedom,* 21, 122-24, 313.

GERARD REED

SUBLAPSARIANISM. See INFRALAPSARIANISM.

SUBMISSION. See OBEDIENCE.

SUBSTANCE, SUBSTANTIVE. The English word *substance* comes from the Latin *sub,* "under," and *sto* or *stans,* "to stand." It is thus that which stands under, or behind, mere appearance (the phenomenal). In Greek the word is expressed by *ousia* which means that which truly is: essence or reality. A long line of thinkers, including such giants as Philoponus of Alexandria, John Scotus, Descartes, Aquinas, Locke, Kant, and Berkeley, have struggled with the concept of substance since Aristotle wrote his *Categories* and his *Metaphysics.* Conclusions expressed by these writers as to what is basic in the universe vary from a fundamental natural entity to a mere mental thought more hypothetical in nature than factual.

In the face of all practical and observational evidence that change prevails in life, Aristotle declared that there must be some "ground" that is inalterable, and that ground he called substance. Personalistic philosophies have found this changeless substance in personhood. At least a convincing demonstration, close at hand, of an essence which survives change is individual identity or personal being, which remains the same through continuous earthly change in appearance, personality, external relations, and even character. The ego or self which is the identifying essence of a particular child is the same self which identifies the old man or old woman as the same person.

In the absolute sense, substance can be ascribed only to God, for according to Christian theology only God is absolute being, underived, uncreated, unconditioned, and essentially unchanging (cf. Mal. 3:6; Exod. 3:6; Heb. 13:8). As such God is the Ground of all lesser or secondary substances.

The term *substance* was also made the key in Early Church history to the doctrine of the Trinity. The formula was *tres personae, una substantia,* "three persons, one substance." The three Persons shared the same nature or essence; the Godhead was one. Thus the substance of God comprised the unity and at the same time was the ground of the threeness.

Confusion arises from the fact that in practical usage substance has gone full circle, from the immaterial reality of the Greek philosophers to concrete, material reality. Cotton, wood, gold, et cetera, may be the substance of an object, determining its qualities though not altogether its form. An understanding of the nature of sin is befogged by this confusion. Sin as a nature is neither an immaterial entity in itself (the Greek concept of substance) nor a lumpish, materialistic entity.

In respect to the Greek concept, sin is the perversion of being, not being itself. All true being apart from God is derived from or created by God and as such essentially good. But one form of true, and essentially good, being is a free moral agent, either angelic or human. Such an agent has the power to pervert God's gifts to selfish ends; even to pervert his own nature to sinfulness of inclination. But this is a condition, not an entity.

But in respect to the popular meaning of substance, sin is not a physical thing. Wood says: "It is a confusion of categories to think that Wesley believed that sin was a physical-like substance which was extracted through the circumcision of the heart. . . . Wesley was simply using the metaphorical language of Paul when he described in a concrete-functional way that the *being* of sin was cleansed in entire sanctification" (*Pentecostal Grace,* 168). Sin can be said to be substantive only in the sense that it (whether actual or original) is a real factor in human life rather than imaginary.

See BEING, ONTOLOGY, REALISM, SIN, RELATIONAL THEOLOGY.

For Further Reading: O'Connor, "Substance and Attributes," *Encyclopedia of Philosophy,* 8:36-40; Wood, *Pentecostal Grace,* 161-68.

FLOYD J. PERKINS

SUBSTITUTION. See VICARIOUS.

SUFFER, SUFFERING. All theology recognizes that people undergo experiences *(pathos)* which distress, afflict, injure, chasten, and bring on pain and death. Suffering may be physical, mental, or spiritual. The Bible relates this fact of human suffering to the Fall, to man's sin against God (Gen. 3:14-19; Rom. 8:18-25).

The burden of suffering has often fallen upon God's people (Exod. 1:11; Ps. 90:9-10). This occasions several problems, since God's people believe that He is in charge of all human life. It is relatively easy to conclude that sin will result in suffering. But why do the righteous suffer? Why does God permit His people to undergo afflictions?

One problem—that of the origin of pain and suffering—is expressed in the ancient dilemma: either God is good but powerless to prevent suffering and evil, or He is all-powerful but malevolent—not wishing to rid the world of it. Christian theodicy has wrestled with this problem from early times.

While naturalism has often used this dilemma as a justification for its agnosticism, the Bible does suggest that God controls and regulates suffering (Job 1:12). He has a plan and purpose in life for every person. That plan may include prosperity for the wicked and suffering for the righteous.

Since God chose a cross, a means of suffering, by which to redeem mankind, it may well be that He will permit the righteous to suffer for redemptive reasons. This is the meaning of "taking up the cross" for Christians (Matt. 16:24).

The plan and purposes of God includes several explanations of why people suffer. Some suffering is caused by Satan and his cohorts—but Satan is limited by God's sovereign will (Job 1:12; 2:6). Some suffering is disciplinary; God uses afflictions to educate those who will learn (Job 35:11; 36:10 ff). Some suffering can only be resolved in the mystery of the Infinite. God, who knows all, does not explain to people all of His workings (Job 38—39; John 9:4).

Another problem is the nature of sin and suffering. While idealisms and non-Christian religions deny the real nature of suffering, equating it with man's finiteness, Christian theology sometimes relates suffering to sin. Suffering is real because man lives in rebellion against God. Man creates many suffering situations because he refuses to take God's way of life. Although not all suffering is caused by sin (John 9:1-4), Christian theology always takes seriously the doctrine of divine punishment upon sin (Lev. 26:14 ff; Ezek. 18:4). Some suffering is a punishment for sin.

The greatest problem faced by a theology of suffering is its elimination. Here non-Christian philosophies have no real solution, while the Bible offers the plan of a Redeemer God who has wrestled with the problem of sin and finally eliminates all suffering for those who trust Him (Rev. 21:4).

The Christian gospel reveals a God who knows the fact and the meaning of suffering. The Cross of Calvary is the sublime and majestic picture of a Redeemer who bears our griefs and carries our sorrows (Isa. 53:4), in order to reconcile people to God. The fact of human suffering can be borne by the hope of its ultimate banishment (1 Cor. 15:25-26). God's plan for the banishment of suffering and sin centers in the triumphal return of the Son of God to defeat the powers of sin and Satan and restore God's creation to its created harmony (Rev. 22:1-4).

See EVIL, PROVIDENCE, CHANCE.

For Further Reading: Hopkins, *The Mystery of Suffering;* Lewis, *The Problem of Pain;* Jones, *Christ and Human Suffering;* Lewis, *The Creator and the Adversary;* Weatherhead, *Why Do Men Suffer?* Hick, *God and Evil.*

BERT H. HALL

SUICIDE. Suicide is death which is voluntarily self-inflicted. Factors contributing to suicide are anxiety, envy, suffering, and depression. Alienation and guilt are emotions frequently mentioned with hopelessness and doubt (Farberow and Shneidman, *The Cry for Help,* 290-302). Suicide occurs when there appears to be no available path that will lead to a tolerable existence. Demonic suggestion and oppression doubtless are significant factors in some cases. Secular students of suicide would of course take no account of this possibility.

Some religions (Hinduism and Buddhism) condone suicide as a cog in the wheels of Karma and reincarnation. A depressed predestinarian may justify his actions and lay his misfortune at the feet of Providence. Stoics and Epicureans see suicide as an honorable exit out of life.

In the OT five cases of suicide are recorded: Samson (Judg. 16:30); King Saul and his armor bearer (1 Sam. 31:1-6); Zimri, another king of Israel (1 Kings 16:15-19); and Ahithophel, advisor to Absalom (2 Sam. 17:23). In the NT there is the single case of Judas, who also died by hanging after he failed to right the wrong in betraying Jesus (Matt. 27:3-5; Acts 1:18). The cases cited have behind them stories of greed, hate, and loss of faith in God (revenge in the case of Samson).

The Bible has no direct injunction against suicide. The word is not even mentioned in Scripture. However, the sixth commandment would imply its prohibition, and both Judaism and Christianity have opposed the practice. From Deut. 20:1, 6-9, the rabbis and fathers have argued that it is unlawful for anyone to take his own life. The act shows lack of faith in God and betrays an absence of a proper sense of responsibility and stewardship, both toward God and toward others.

Judgment upon the suicide must be left entirely with God. He alone sees the motivation and intentions. He alone sees the degree of sanity possessed at the time of the action, therefore the moral responsibility.

See MAN, DIVINE IMAGE, STEWARDSHIP, LIFE, PASTORAL COUNSELING.

For Further Reading: Lum, *Responding to Suicidal Crisis: For Church and Community;* Farber, *Theory of Suicide;* Farberow and Shneidman, *The Cry for Help.*

ISAAC BALDEO

SUNDAY. Since the days of the primitive Church, Sunday has been the specifically Christian day for worship. The word comes from *dies solis* (*helios* day), second of the seven-day planetary week. The day corresponds with the Jewish first day.

Evidence indicates that Sunday as the specific day of worship began in the primitive Gentile church. But Eusebius says that the early Jewish Christians "celebrated rites like ours [the Jewish] in commemoration of the Savior's resurrection"—probably on Sunday and in addition to their Jewish Sabbath.

Until the end of the first century, the Eucharist was celebrated weekly on Sunday evening. But at the beginning of the second century, probably due to an imperial ban against night assembly, the Sunday evening service was terminated; and celebration of the Lord's Supper was incorporated into an already existing predawn service that consisted of prayers and hymns. The predawn hour made it possible for the Christians to get to their places of employment on time for what was a common day of labor in the Roman Empire. Two specifically Christian names were given to the day by Christians: "The Lord's Day" (cf. Rev. 1:10), and "the eighth day" (the latter was probably associated with the day on which baptisms occurred).

Not until after Constantine designated Sunday as a day of rest throughout the empire (in A.D. 321) did the Christian day of worship also become a day of rest.

See LORD'S DAY, SABBATARIANISM, PURITAN (PURITANISM).

For Further Reading: Rordorf, *Sunday;* Cowan, *The Sabbath in Scripture and History.*

ALBERT L. TRUESDALE, JR.

SUPEREROGATION. This is a concept of Roman Catholic theology describing virtuous acts surpassing that required by duty or obligation. The doctrine first appeared toward the close of the 12th century and was modified and enlarged by Thomas Aquinas in the 13th century. It is based on the doctrine of salvation by grace and works rather than by grace alone. It also depends on a distinction made between the precepts and the counsels of the church. Precepts refer to works commanded; and counsels, to works only advised (Matt. 19:21)—especially the monastic counsels of poverty, chastity, and obedience.

The total merits of Christ exceeded what was necessary for man's salvation. In addition, the saints did and suffered more than was required for their own salvation. These superabundant merits go into a treasury of merit and are at the disposal of the Roman Catholic church. At the discretion of the pope, these merits may be dispensed to those who lack sufficient merit for salvation. This led to the system of indulgences so pointedly rejected by Luther.

The treasury of merit is also based on a concept of the community of grace. Protestantism rejected any form of salvation by works, holding salvation to be by grace alone. It also rejected the community of grace, contending that grace is individually bestowed and not transferable, and rejected the concept of works of supererogation (*New Schaff-Herzog Encyclopedia of Religious Knowledge,* 11:165-66).

See MERIT, WORK (WORKS), JUSTIFICATION, CATHOLICISM (ROMAN), INDULGENCES.

For Further Reading: *New Catholic Encyclopedia,* 13:810; Heick, *A History of Christian Thought,* 1:289.

M. ESTES HANEY

SUPERNATURAL, SUPERNATURALISM. Christian theology has always emphasized that there are many experiences, events, and manifestations that cannot be ascribed to natural causes. To describe these phenomena, Christians have used the word *supernatural.* These events or experiences must be explained by reference to something beyond the natural realm or sense experience. The word *supernatural* is not specifically used in Scripture, but it has an important function in defining scriptural emphases. When God speaks to men and women, when Jesus Christ descends to human level in the Incarnation, when Jesus is raised from the dead, these may properly be designated supernatural events, since they are totally inexplicable by human sources of understanding. Such events express God's immediate and special action within the sphere of nature, but not according to nature's usual order.

Religious naturalism rejects the idea of transcendence, or the God who is above and beyond us. "God" is whatever saves a person from evil, but "God" cannot be defined as a supernatural person. To the naturalist, to talk about God in heaven doesn't make sense, since this God cannot be weighed or subjected to empirical methods. Thus "God" is reduced to something temporal, present in the world, never external to the natural order. "God" becomes the projection of human wishes and hopes. In an extreme naturalism "God" is an aspect of the total reality called nature. Supernaturalism, on the other hand, insists that God is above man and free to act upon and within nature however He pleases.

It is of course necessary to protest a supernaturalism which pushes God and man so far apart that no means of communication exist. Jesus did come from heaven to reconcile God and man. Supernaturalism does not contradict this reconciliation, but in fact presents a God who is great enough to bring the supernatural and the natural into interaction.

One expression of 20th-century theology has spoken of God as so remote that no point of contact between God and man could be expected. Another theological school in its radical forms stresses that God is so near as to be virtually identified with nature. Both views are extreme and are out of touch with biblical faith. Christian faith insists upon the realm existing above nature, but places equal insistence upon the ways in which God is present through Jesus Christ and the Holy Spirit in the realm where humanity dwells.

See MIRACLE, PROVIDENCE, DIVINE SOVEREIGNTY, ATTRIBUTES (DIVINE), IMMANENCE, THEISM, RATIONALISM.

For Further Reading: Cauthen, *The Impact of American Religious Liberalism;* Carnell, *The Case for Orthodox Theology.* LEON O. HYNSON

SUPERSTITION. Superstition is an unwarranted and irrational regard for rituals, signs, and omens. Primitive folklore is full of beliefs in the portent of certain events, such as a black cat crossing one's path, or in the power of a good-luck charm. Superstition may also take the form of blind trust in the performance of certain rituals apart from sound biblical authority or compliance with ethical conditions. When the Israelites pinned their faith in their Temple worship and sacrificial system as a sure security against misfortune, their religion had become a superstition. Divinely prescribed rituals are not designed as forms of magic, by which the supernatural can be manipulated for our protection or our advantage.

Even the Christian sacraments can become superstitions when participants rest in the efficacy of the ceremony without regard to its doctrinal meaning or its inherent ethical demands. The Bible itself can be used as a talisman and certain verses as charms. Soldiers have sometimes believed they would be protected from harm by having a Testament in their pocket. In such forms of superstition the symbol has been accepted as a substitute for reality, scientific cause-and-effect principles have been disregarded, and credulity has been mistaken for faith. The antidote to superstition is a growing relationship with Christ himself, a life of holiness and obedience, and an intelligent approach to biblical and theological principles.

See FAITH, PRESUMPTION. RICHARD S. TAYLOR

SUPPLICATION. This is prayer as petition, as entreaty, as earnest request, on behalf of oneself or on behalf of others. See Acts 1:14; Eph. 6:18; Phil. 4:6; Heb. 5:7.

See PRAYER, INTERCESSION, PRAISE.

J. KENNETH GRIDER

SUPPRESSION. The theory of suppression teaches that the believer's sin nature is never cleansed away. Constant warfare with the carnal self ("old man") is normal. The Spirit's power enables suppression of carnality but no deliverence.

Many NT words express suppression: *krateō*—to be master of (Matt. 18:28); *pnigō*—to choke (v. 28); *deō*—to bind (Mark 3:27); *katapauō*—to restrain (Acts 14:18); *katechō*—to hold down (Rom. 1:18); *hypōpiazō*—to hit beneath the eyes (1 Cor. 9:27); *doulagōgeō*—to enslave (v. 27); *sunechō*—to constrain (2 Cor. 5:14); and *sugkleiō*—to shut up (Gal. 3:22). However, none of these are used in reference to carnality. Rather, the Spirit used *katargeō*—to destroy (Rom. 6:6); *sustauroō*—to crucify with (v. 6); *eleutheroō*—to free (8:2); *ekkathairō*—to cleanse thoroughly (1 Cor. 5:7; 2 Tim. 2:21); *apotithēmi*—to put off (Eph. 4:22); *katharizō*—to cleanse (5:26); and *apekdusis*—the putting off (Col. 2:11).

Scripture teaches cleansing from all sin (Ezek. 36:25-27; Eph. 5:25-27), crucifixion of "the old man" (Gal. 2:20), and the sanctifying infilling of the Spirit in a crisis moment of total consecration and faith (John 17:17-20; Acts 2:38-39; 19:2; Rom. 12:1-2; 1 Thess. 5:23-24). The Greek aorist tense of the verbs teaches this (John 17:17; Acts 15:9; Rom. 12:1; 1 Cor. 1:21-22; Gal. 5:24; Eph. 1:13; 1 Thess. 5:23; Heb. 13:12; 1 John 1:9), as do Bible commands and promises for purity in this life (Luke 1:73-75).

The believer aided by the Spirit should discipline body, mind, emotions, and will to (1) obey God's Word, (2) overcome temptation, (3) maintain self-control, and (4) control and sanctify legitimate bodily appetites, aspirations, imaginations, passions, instincts, drives, temperament, strengths, and weaknesses. This is the role for biblical self-control or suppression (Gal. 5:23; Acts 24:25; 1 Cor. 7:9; 9:25-27; 2 Tim. 1:7; Titus 1:8; 2:5; 1 Pet. 1:13; 4:7; 5:8; 2 Pet. 1:6).

See CLEANSING, ERADICATION, DISCIPLINE, TEMPERANCE.

For Further Reading: Taylor, *Holiness the Finished Foundation*, 65-81; Carter, *The Person and Ministry of the Holy Spirit*, 168-72; Grider, *Entire Sanctification*, 20-24.

WESLEY L. DUEWEL

SUPRALAPSARIANISM. See INFRALAPSARIANISM.

SURRENDER. When used in a militaristic connotation of forced subjection, "surrender" is an unacceptable idea for expressing Christian experience. Yet the Scriptures abound in words like commitment, yielding, submission, obedience, and servanthood, which do not imply the loss of free moral agency, but precisely its exercise. If surrender is used in the sense of a free self-conscious decision, then it agrees with the essence of these biblical expressions. It thus becomes a synonym of consecration, as in the song "I Surrender All."

As a spiritual act of self-giving, surrender can nevertheless be ambiguous. Surrender may be distorted because of self-interest, as in the instance of Ananias and Sapphira (Acts 5:1-6). It may be a manipulative device whereby the weak gains an advantage over the strong, as in the case of passive resistance. Surrender to a morally questionable person or cause may not only be useless, but destructive as well. The Scriptures recognize the possibility of surrender to sin, Satan, and the flesh (cf. Rom. 6:12 ff).

God as He has revealed himself in Christ Jesus is not only the only unambiguous object of self-surrender, but the ultimate Example as well. "For God so loved the world that he gave [up] his only Son" (John 3:16, RSV; cf. Phil. 2:5-11; Rom. 5:8). Self-surrender to God does not cancel human freedom but exercises it in its ultimate expression; it does not destroy the self but releases it from bondage to inordinate self-love and sin.

See CONSECRATE (CONSECRATION), OBEDIENCE, DEATH TO SELF.

For Further Reading: Wiley, *CT*, 2:471-87; Ellul, *The Ethics of Freedom*, 112-32, 236-69.

C. S. COWLES

SWEDENBORGIANISM. This cult is also called New Church or Church of the New Jerusalem. The first society was begun (1783) in London by Robert Hindmarsh, a Methodist, after reading the writings of Emanuel Swedenborg (1688-1772). Swedenborg, the son of the Lutheran bishop of Skara, Sweden, and a brilliant scientist, wrote extensively on scientific, philosophic, and theological subjects. His theological writings are based on reputed mental travels in the spirit world. These began with "a violent fever in 1743" (Wesley, *Works*, 13:62, 426). To Swedenborgians, he is God's seer through whom God is ushering in His New Church, and whose writings are either inspired interpretations of the Word or *The Word*.

God, the spiritual world (heaven and hell), and the physical world all have correspondence. The Word (most of the OT and only the part of the NT not including the Epistles and Acts) has an exact correspondence with the spiritual world and God. Perfect understanding of this correspondence is gained through symbolic interpretation, revealed by Swedenborg from his mental travels. He differs from orthodoxy in the following: God is the Grand Man, and thus all existence, as well as man, is in God's image. Angels and demons were formerly men. The Trinity exists only as manifestation. Jesus is the same as God the Father and is to be worshipped as such. Heaven and hell are extensions of this physical life including social structure, and are chosen according to one's desires: either concern for others, or self-satisfaction including sexual. The separation in the afterlife occurs as each increases in the direction of his dominant desire. Salvation is by good works. "Faith alone" is strongly opposed.

See CULTS, ORTHODOXY, WESLEYANISM.

For Further Reading: Block, *The New Church in the New World*; DeBeaumont, "Swedenborg," *ERE*, 11:129-32; Van Dusen, *The Presence of Other Worlds*; Wesley, *Works*, 13:62, 425-48.

DAVID L. CUBIE

SYMBOLIC ESCHATOLOGY. See ESCHATOLOGY.

SYMBOLICS. See CREED, CREEDS.

SYMBOLISM. The concepts *sign* and *symbol* have an extremely wide range of application even within a purely religious context. Consider the following very incomplete list: A red face is a sign of anger; immorality is a sign of the times; the road is not clearly sign-posted; this fire is a sign that someone has camped here; the Cross is a symbol of Christianity; the house was a symbol of prison in your dream; the hero symbolizes goodness. Common to most uses of the concept is the idea of a symbol as something which by convention stands in place of or suggests something else. Some writers have, however, suggested that one can draw a distinction between conventional and intrinsic symbols. The conventional symbol has no connection with what it symbolizes other than the fact that by arbitrary convention it has been agreed to allow it to represent a particular symbolizandum. On the other hand, the intrinsic symbol has an inherent relationship to what it symbolizes: in Paul Tillich's language it participates in that which it symbolizes.

The English word *symbol* derives originally from the Greek *symbolon,* which meant a sign or token which authenticated one's identity, as in a soldier's *symbolon.* This term was appropriated by Christian theology to mean creed or summary of faith, something which established one's allegiance. Thus Christian theology is often divided into *philosophical* theology, which deals with the philosophical presuppositions of the faith; *symbolic* theology, which treats the key assertions and doctrines of Christianity in a systematic fashion; and *applied* theology, which addresses itself to the practical implications of symbolic theology for the ecclesiastical community.

The problem of the use of symbols in theology is today most often connected with the problem of religious language, that is, the question of how the predicates (love, goodness, wisdom, power, etc.) used in connection with God function in theological assertions such as "God is love" or "God is infinitely wise." Traditionally, Christian theologians have argued that such predicates are cognitive in the sense of conveying meanings about God which are either true or false. Several contemporary theologians have argued, however, that religious predicates are in fact noncognitive, in that they are not to be construed as true or false. Instead, religious language is symbolic.

The leading exponent of this theory is Paul Tillich, who distinguishes between a sign and a symbol. Both point to something beyond themselves, but a sign does so because of a convention while a symbol "participates in that to which it points" (*Dynamics of Faith,* 42). A flag, to use Tillich's example, which, it should be noted, is certainly not without its problems, is a symbol because it is not conventionally instituted and participates in that which it symbolizes. Tillich's conception of religious symbols is not clear, but he seems to suggest that: (1) religious symbols have a twofold purpose in that *(a)* they "open up levels of reality which otherwise are closed to us," and *(b)* "unlock dimensions and elements of our soul" (ibid.); and (2) religious faith is a state of being ultimately concerned and thus can only express itself symbolically. There is only one nonsymbolic statement that can be made about God, that He is Being itself.

While Tillich's doctrine of religious symbols is perhaps the best-known modern attempt to understand the role of symbols in Christian theism, it is certainly not a carefully elaborated idea which is free from difficulties. Many Christian thinkers, for instance, would feel extremely uneasy about construing all religious language as noncognitive, particularly as this seems to suggest that theological propositions are ultimately nonmeaningful.

See TRUTH, REVELATION (SPECIAL), CREED (CREEDS), PROPOSITIONAL THEOLOGY, HISTORICAL THEOLOGY, RELIGIOUS KNOWLEDGE.

For Further Reading: Bevan, *Symbolism and Belief;* Ramsey, *Models and Mystery;* Tillich, *Dynamics of Faith.*

JOHN C. LUIK

SYNCRETISM. Syncretism refers to the reconciliation or union of conflicting religious beliefs. The syncretist believes that every religion offers a legitimate way to God, so he attempts to harmonize Christianity with non-Christian religions. Syncretists attack the "parochialism" of Christianity, its claim of exclusive redemption. They say the way should be left open for other religions to develop their own formulae for redemption.

Of course, interaction with members of other religions can be helpful and stimulating. We can learn from those who disagree with us, but we cannot agree that they have their own way of salvation apart from the death and resurrection of Christ.

Syncretism has been attempted since ancient times. Even though Moses pointed out that there was none other beside God, at times Baal was worshipped in the Temple in Jerusalem even to the extent of sacred prostitution (Deut. 4:35-40; 2 Kings 23:4-14). The apostle Peter made it clear that Jesus is the only Way to salvation (Acts 4:12), and the apostle Paul pointed out that Jesus Christ was the only Foundation (1 Cor. 3:11). While respect for the views of others is expected of Christians, it should not be permitted to lead to an undermining of the truth that Jesus Christ is the only Way to God (John 14:6).

See HEATHEN (FATE OF), SALVATION, NON-CHRISTIAN RELIGIONS, CHRISTIANITY.

For Further Reading: Anderson, *Christianity and Comparative Religion;* Newbigin, *The Finality of Christ;* Visser 't Hooft, *No Other Name;* Anderson, ed., *The Theology of the Christian Mission,* 179-228.

RONALD L. KOTESKEY

SYNERGISM. This term is a compound of the two Greek words: *syn,* meaning "together" or "with," and *ergein,* meaning "to work." Theologically it has reference to the cooperation of the divine and human for the salvation and character building of man. It sets forth the doctrine of the cooperation of the human will with divine grace, and views faith as a personal response to a prior act of divine solicitation to salvation by God—the invitation being extended to whoever will respond. Such passages as Rev. 22:17; Rom. 10:13; Isa. 1:18; 55:3; Matt. 11:28; Rev. 3:20; Joel 2:32 (cf. Acts 2:21); Isa. 55:6-7; Ezek. 33:11; 2 Pet. 3:9; John 1:12; Mark 1:15; 1 John 1:9; etc., presuppose the ability of man to respond to and cooperate with God's grace working in him both to will and to do God's pleasure (Phil. 2:12-13).

Salvation, as a divine-human covenant, presupposes a mutual cooperation between man and his God. Hence it is both of divine grace and of human choice. The act of believing unto salvation is always man's own. But man is not saved by his own efforts apart from the grace of God working in him. Yet synergists do contend that the human will is a *causa concurrens* to one's personal salvation.

The term *synergism* became definitely fixed as a theological concept in the 16th century. It was applied to the more mature views of Philip Melanchthon and his followers, who contended that the human will can cooperate with the grace of God for man's regeneration. They referred to the human will when aided by divine grace as a *vera cause regenerationis,* though not as a primary cause.

The Lutheran position was stated as follows: "There are three concurrent causes of good actions, the Word of God, the Holy Spirit, and human will assenting to and not resisting the Word of God." And the Augsburg Confession declares: "Although God does not justify men through their merits, nevertheless the merciful God does not act on man as a block but draws him so that his will co-operates, provided he has come to years of discretion" (Art. 20).

In this position Melanchthon seemed to recall some of Augustine's strong statements in the treatise entitled *The Spirit and the Letter.* One of them reads: "To yield our consent, indeed, to God's summons, or to withhold it, is (as I have said) the function of our own will. And this not only does not invalidate what is said, 'For what hast thou that thou didst not receive?' (1 Cor. 4:7) but it really confirms it. For the soul cannot receive and possess these gifts, which are here referred to, except by yielding its consent. And thus whatever it possesses, and whatever it receives, is from God; and yet the act of receiving and having belongs, of course, to the receiver and possessor."

In the 17th century James Arminius stated the operations of grace to be upon the whole man, not merely his will, when he declared: "It is an infusion both into the human understanding and into the will and affections" (*Works,* 1:253, Declaration of Sentiments). Moreover he called it "preventing [preceding] and exciting, following and cooperating grace." Nor does he look upon God's grace as "a certain irresistible force," for he says, "I believe, according to the Scriptures, that many persons resist the Holy Spirit and reject the grace that is offered." In his refutation of William Perkins he insists: that "the free will of man is the subject of grace. Hence it is necessary that the free will should concur with the grace, which is bestowed, to its preservation, yet assisted by subsequent grace, and it always remains in the power of the free will to reject the grace bestowed, and to refuse subsequent grace; because grace is not the omnipotent action of God, which can not be resisted by the free will of man" (*Works,* 3:509).

In the 18th century, Wesleyans talked and wrote about the prevenient grace of God operating upon all men to move them, if they will cooperate with it, unto saving faith and personal salvation. Their contention being that:

It is the continuous cooperation of the human will with the originating grace of the Holy Spirit that merges prevenient grace directly into saving grace. Arminians hold that through the prevenient (preparatory) grace of the Spirit, unconditionally bestowed upon all men, the power and responsibility of free agency exists from the first dawn of the moral life. This unconditional benefit of Christ's atonement came unto all men as a "free gift" (see Rom. 5:18; and more fully vv. 15-19). Furthermore, they hold that man, by cooperating through faith with prevenient grace, fulfills the conditions for saving grace (cf. John 1:12-13). This, of course, is contrary to true Calvinism, which insists that "common grace" never merges into "saving grace," nor is the universal call or summons to salvation to be identified with "effectual calling," wherein "irresistible grace" regenerates the elect to actual personal salvation.

We may affirm, then, that conviction of sin and the divine summons to salvation are involuntary but not therefore compulsory. For, as Brightman declares: "All the rest of the Universe cannot compel a free act" (*Person and Reality,* 185).

Synergism arose as an ethical protest against religious fatalism which threatened to submerge the conscience of man and disarm the Church in her fight against moral corruption, license, and anarchy. That attitude which sings: "The Lord our God in His *own good time* shall lead to the light at last, all who are predestined and unconditionally elected to eternal life" serves to create the philosophy of irresponsible, unrepentant, and unregenerate living. The practical result of monergistic determinism is to paralyze the quest for morality and righteous living. It also makes God the author of sin.

Synergists do contend that the help of the Holy Spirit is necessary to enable man to accept and act upon the gospel. Thus human cooperation becomes a *causa subordinata* in regeneration. No man can truthfully say that he is compelled to sin by fate, or what is worse, by divine decree. The unconverted man still has the power because of prevenient grace, of either obeying or resisting God's call to salvation through the Holy Bible illuminated by the Holy Spirit and impressed upon him by the faithful and anointed preaching thereof. But to reject God's grace is an act of the human will and not a withholding of saving grace by an arbitrary divine decree or omission.

See MONERGISM, PREVENIENT GRACE.

For Further Reading: Arminius, *Works,* 3:281-525; Augustine, *Basic Writings of Augustine,* 2 vols.; Brightman, *Person and Reality;* Mackenzie, "Synergism," *ERE,* 12:158-64; Miley, *Systematic Theology,* 2:334-37; Pope, "Prevenient Grace and the Conditions of Salvation," *A Higher Catechism of Theology,* 207-21.

ROSS E. PRICE

SYSTEMATIC THEOLOGY. Systematic theology is the attempt by the church to describe the faith relationship with God in Christ in an ordered, structured, reasonable way. Human minds cannot be satisfied with less than the attempt to understand revealed truth and Christian experience in an integrated, interrelated fashion. This is justified. God is One, and within His words and works are both unity and harmony. As a good map orients the traveler to the larger area and the connectedness of its parts, systematic theology aims at both overview and coherent detail respecting God, man, and the redemptive relationship between them.

Essential to the task are clarity of expression within the contemporary idiom, and dynamic interaction with the contemporary culture. The discipline itself facilitates the testing and correcting of the church's understanding as well as true communication of the faith. Because theologians are but creatures thinking about the Creator, the goal can be only approximated. The term *systematic theology* (German and Dutch scholars seem to prefer *dogmatics*) is not meant to imply that other forms of theological study are without an orderly system.

Systematic theology relies upon the work of biblical theology, which deals expressly with the Word of God to which the church must conform, as well as upon the work of historical theology, which traces the insights and movements within the church's teaching to the present time. In turn, systematic theology provides guidance for the work of pastoral theology.

Some organizing principle will become the key, consciously or not, to the systematic theologian's method. The starting point may determine it: God, or man, or the redemptive relationship. Any list of methodologies would include the Christological, Trinitarian, anthropological, covenantal, confessional, analytic, or synthetic.

See THEOLOGY, BIBLICAL THEOLOGY, HISTORICAL THEOLOGY.

For Further Reading: Wiley, *CT,* 1:13-98.

ARNOLD E. AIRHART

T

TABERNACLE. See TEMPLE.

TALMUD. The Talmud, a word deriving from the Hebrew word *lamad* meaning "to study," is an encyclopedia of Jewish tradition arising out of and supplementing the OT. The Talmud developed over a period of centuries through an oral process and was eventually preserved in writing. For the Jews the Torah was the central, authoritative document of their faith. It contained the revealed will of God for them. With the loss of the Temple as the focal point of their worship, and the fall of Jerusalem in 586 B.C., the Jews began to rethink and reorder their lives in keeping with the law of Moses. Out of this strong impetus came the Talmud which records the interpretations and applications of scriptural laws to the changing social situations in which the people found themselves across the centuries.

The Talmud developed in two layers, the first being the Mishnah, and the second, the Gemara. The Mishnah (derived from the Hebrew meaning "repeat" or "study") contains the Oral Torah. It is composed of six main divisions and 63 tractates which give case law on numerous matters relating to agriculture, feasts, the role of women, cultic practices, etc. The Torah gives the statute, while the Mishnah applies the statute to a particular situation in life.

The second layer or phase of the Talmud is the Gemara, the comments of the rabbis (the Amoraim, literally "speakers") on the Mishnah. These interpretations come from the period A.D. 200 to 500. Apparently the brevity and specific nature of the mishnaic laws, in due time, required further interpretation and new application. Essentially, the Gemara was a supplement to the Mishnah, and the two constitute the Talmud.

During the course of Jewish history two Talmuds were assembled, the Palestinian or Jerusalem Talmud and the Babylonian Talmud. The latter Talmud is more copious and elaborate in its notes and for that reason has become the more prized one. Both Talmuds were concluded about the fifth century A.D. It is to be understood, however, that much of the material contained in them reaches well back into pre-Christian times.

See PENTATEUCH, MOSES, MOSAIC LAW, JUDAISM.

For Further Reading: Neusner, *Invitation to the Talmud;* Steinsaltz, *The Essential Talmud;* Strack, *Introduction to the Talmud and Midrash;* Trattner, *Understanding the Talmud.*

WILLARD H. TAYLOR

TARGUM. An Aramaic translation, paraphrase, or interpretative note of an OT passage is called a targum. When Aramaic, a northwest Semitic language, became the *lingua franca* of nearly all of southwestern Asia, it became necessary for translations to be made from the Hebrew to the Aramaic in order for the Hebrews to understand the old Scriptures. Thus, as suggested by Neh. 8:8, public reading of the Scripture included a verse-by-verse rendering of the text into Aramaic. Oftentimes this process became an exposition; in other words, someone "gave the sense" of what had been read. In time, these Aramaic translations and expositions were written down. The two most famous targums date from the fifth century A.D. One is a translation of the Pentateuch, the Targum Onkelos, and the other a free rendition of the prophets, the Targum Jonathan. There are extant targums for all of the OT with the exception of Daniel, Ezra, and Nehemiah. Interestingly, parts of Daniel and Ezra, as found in the Hebrew text, are written in Aramaic.

See BIBLE.

For Further Reading: Bruce, *The Books and the Parchments.*

WILLARD H. TAYLOR

TEACH, TEACHING, TEACHER. The practice of teaching is probably as old as higher forms of animal life. It can be observed as mother birds or animals teach their offspring to forage, to defend, to socialize. With man it appears to be as old as history itself. Teaching is necessary to perpetuate and to propagate custom, code, culture, or skill. Where teaching takes place, by definition one or more teachers are involved in the teaching activity.

Teaching is recognized as both an art and a science. Persons who have the art or the gift of teaching may be creative and highly individualistic in their approach to the teaching-learning encounter. Likewise, those who have studied human growth and development, learning theories, and educational psychology may become skilled to an admirable degree. In fact, the science of teaching has become so proficient that man's behavior and choices can be subtly determined by subliminal instruction. Conscious and subconscious influences can be so effective that even personality change can be induced by electrochemical cortical stimulation or by "brainwashing" teaching techniques. The power of teaching and teachers cannot be overestimated for positive or negative impact upon man individually or corporately.

Teaching may be formal or informal, accidental, incidental, experiential, or systematized. *Teaching* may refer to the acts of instruction, the methods employed, the content of instruction, or the "body of truth" by which a group perpetuates itself as a distinct subculture.

The Bible is replete with references to teaching and teachers. Teaching and teachers in the OT were highly respected if not revered. The historical narrative, the Torah, and the wisdom literature alike stress the importance of both the role and the content of teaching. It was integral to the concept of a covenant people. The role and responsibility were imposed upon parents, priests, prophets, leaders, and scribes. The term "Rabbi," loosely translated "Master," was reserved as title of address to a noteworthy teacher.

The NT terminology is rich in nuances of meaning. The verb *didaskō* perhaps has the broadest connotation of any word used. It may mean to perform, execute, demonstrate, or show; to apprise of or to prove; to instruct or teach. It is used to denote the passing on of information or knowledge, to teach a skill, or to clinch a point. It presupposes expertise in the teacher. It often depicts the teaching by God or the Holy Spirit to denote revelation or inspiration. It also defines relationship between teacher and pupil.

The verb *katēcheō,* "to sound from above," was more restrictive to recounting, narrating, informing, or instructing. It carried the didactic connotation. It is from this authoritative understanding that the Church developed and perpetuated the *catechisms* and the *catechetical* approach to teaching creeds, doctrine, and practice.

The term *paideuō* denoted upbringing, disciplining, directing character formation of the pupils (usually for children or youth). It came to mean a way of education, a cultivation, and a goal to be attained.

Another term, the noun *paradosis,* related to the transmission and reception of tradition. It often denoted exhortatory moral instruction.

Although preaching and teaching in biblical and Early Church records were generally separated in act and understanding, they were meant to be complementary offices and practices for propagating the gospel and nurturing the body individually and corporately. These offices and functions demand the best the Body of Christ can provide. Likewise, they demand the utmost in character, competence, and commitment that the teacher can achieve to deserve the privilege and responsibility as teacher in the Body and to the Body of Christ.

See CLERGY, ELDER, DISCIPLING, CHRISTIAN EDUCATION, PERSON (PERSONALITY), PREACHING.

For Further Reading: Harper and Sanner, eds., *Exploring Christian Education;* Leypoldt, *Learning Is Change;* Augustine, "Concerning the Teacher"; Kittel, 2:135.

CHESTER O. GALLOWAY

TELEOLOGICAL ESCHATOLOGY. See ESCHATOLOGY.

TELEOLOGY. See THEISTIC PROOFS.

TEMPERANCE. The Greek NT term most often translated "temperance" is *egkrateia,* and it means self-control or continence. In 1 Cor. 7:9 it refers to control of sexual desire. In Gal. 5:23 it applies to all the "flesh-works" listed in vv. 19-21 (*Interpreter's Bible,* 10:569). In 1 Cor. 9:25 it refers to the discipline of the athlete who controls even the lawful and good desires for the sake of a higher goal, and so he "is temperate in all things."

Temperance or self-control was one of the four cardinal virtues of classical Greek thought. Aristotle uses the word to describe a man in whom reason prevails over passion, one in whom passions and instincts, though not extirpated, have become servants rather than masters. Temperance is the ideal of perfecting the self into a harmonious whole (*IDB,* 5:268). The motive for self-control was to demonstrate that reason and self-will are sovereign.

In Pauline thought self-control is not an end in itself but a means to the glory of God and a normal expression of the Spirit-filled life (Gal. 5:16-24). "The evil things of the old self are dead with Christ and the lovely things of the Spirit are manifest" (Barclay, *Daily Bible Study Series,* Gal. 5:23).

A more limited and technical use of the term confines it to a movement to eliminate the use of alcoholic beverages. After the first temperance society was formed in 1789 at Litchfield, Conn., the word "temperance" came to stand for total abstinence in the use of intoxicating beverages and rigid control of the production and sale of these beverages. Under the advocacy of such organizations as the Women's Christian Temperance Union, total prohibition was the goal for the American society.

While the legal prohibition was not retained, and the 18th Amendment was repealed, the conviction against the use of alcoholic beverages has become deeply rooted among evangelicals. This position is based more on the application of biblical principles than numerous proof texts. In this a parallel can be seen with the gradual quickening of a conscience against slavery. Modern alternatives as beverages, a gargantuan liquor and wine industry devoting billions to increase consumption, the high social cost of alcoholism, the technological demands on modern society, the proven tendency of alcohol to enslave, our advanced knowledge concerning its physical effects—all point to a vast difference between biblical times and ours, and constitute overwhelming arguments for total abstinence.

See SEVEN DEADLY SINS, DRUNKENNESS, SEVEN CARDINAL VIRTUES.

For Further Reading: Maclaren, *Exposition of the Holy Scriptures,* Gal. 5:22-23. M. ESTES HANEY

TEMPLE. The Temple of Jerusalem was the center of worship for the Jewish people. The Temple was the only place a sacrifice could be offered, and it was the dwelling place of God on earth.

The Jerusalem Temple was patterned after the Tabernacle which was used in the wilderness and through the early history of Israel. David had the vision for a permanent place of worship, but it was Solomon who had the Temple built and dedicated. As in the Tabernacle, the Temple was built to specifications providing for an outer court, an inner court, the holy place, and the holy of holies. The furniture of the Temple was the same as the Tabernacle's: the altar, table for shewbread, candlestick, the altar of incense, a veil, and the ark of the covenant.

Symbols of Things to Come. Each part of the Temple and every piece of furniture for the Temple held symbolic significance. The Book of Hebrews identified these as "patterns of things in the heavens" (9:23). "For Christ is not entered into the holy places made with hands, which are the figures of the true" (v. 24). The candlestick and the shewbread point to Christ, the Light of the World, and to Christ, the Bread of Life. Christ is symbolized in the altar of incense as the continual Intercessor to God. As Jesus died upon the Cross, the veil of the Temple was rent in two (Mark 15:38), thus indicating that the division between the holy place and the holy of holies was removed, giving all mankind direct access to God. Christ became the High Priest who offered the sacrifice for sin once and for all.

The Body. The Bible also speaks of our bodies as temples. Paul asked, "What? know ye not that your body is the temple of the Holy Ghost which is in you, which ye have of God, and ye are not your own?" (1 Cor. 6:19). In the Book of Hebrews the body is referred to as the temple not made with hands (Heb. 9:11).

The Church. The true meaning and purpose of the Temple finds its fulfillment in the Church of Jesus Christ (Eph. 2:21; cf. 1 Pet. 2:5-6). The designation is also applied to a local body of believers (1 Cor. 3:16-17; 2 Cor. 6:16). Paul warns the Corinthians: "If any man defile the temple of God, him shall God destroy; for the temple of God is holy, which temple ye are" (1 Cor. 3:17). A. T. Robertson comments: "The church-wrecker God will wreck" (*Word Pictures,* 4:99).

See CHURCH, TYPE (TYPOLOGY).

For Further Reading: *NBD,* 1242-49.

JAMES L. PORTER

TEMPTATION. The idea of temptation is expressed in the Hebrew by the noun *massah,* usually translated "temptation," and the verbs *nasah* ("tempt") and *bachan,* usually translated "try" or "prove." The corresponding Greek terms are the noun *peirasmos* and the verbs *peirazō* and *dokimazō.* The biblical concept of temptation is not primarily the notion of enticement to sin as the English word suggests, but more basically the idea of "testing" or "proving." The intention is "to prove the quality of a person." Improvement of one's life may be the purpose by exposing latent defects in one's character.

Numerous scriptures depict God as "testing" people, that is, leading them into situations in which their faith or lack of it is exposed. A most familiar example is Abraham's "sacrifice" of Isaac (Genesis 22). These times of trials have purifying (1 Pet. 1:6-9), patience-inducing (Jas. 1:2-4), and assuring effects in the life of the believer (Rom. 5:3-5). Satan is the eternal foe of believers, and he seeks to destroy their faith in devious ways. The classic examples in the OT are Adam and Eve (Genesis 3) and Job (Job 1:12; 2:6). In His earthly life Jesus was confronted by the tempter (Matt. 4:3; cf. 1 Thess. 3:5). Paul refers to his "thorn in the flesh" as a "messenger of Satan, to harass me, to keep me from being too elated" (2 Cor. 12:7, RSV, here and subsequently).

1. God is not the provocateur of temptation, but He may permit it to come into a believer's life as in the case of Job. James cautions, "Let no one say when he is tempted, 'I am tempted by God'; for God cannot be tempted with evil and he himself tempts no one" (1:13). The petition in the Lord's Prayer, "And lead us not into temptation" (Matt. 6:13; Luke 11:4), is a request not to be put to the test. It recognizes the need to preserve one's freedom, but at the same time it acknowledges that situations can develop which may cause one to "enter into temptation."

2. Human desire accommodated by the will leads to sin. James clarifies this point: "Each person is tempted when he is lured and enticed by his own desire. Then desire when it has conceived gives birth to sin" (1:14-15).

3. God's intention is to provide "the way of escape" for His people whenever they are tempted in order that they may endure it (1 Cor. 10:13).

4. The fact that Christ was tempted "in every respect" *(ta panta)* "as we are, yet without sin" (Heb. 4:15) would support the fact that temptation is not sin. Yielding to the enticement offered is the point of sinning.

Watching that one "not enter into temptation" is the exhortation for the Christian (Matt. 26:41).

Also no opportunity should be given to the tempter to gain a foothold in one's life (Eph. 4:27). The devil, the adversary, "prowls around like a roaring lion, seeking some one to devour"; and for that reason the Christian must resist him with a passion but with a consciousness that "the God of all grace" will strengthen him after a little while of suffering (1 Pet. 5:8-10).

See TRIBULATION, VICTORY (VICTORIOUS LIVING), SIN, FORGIVENESS, BACKSLIDING, TEMPTATION OF CHRIST, SPIRITUAL WARFARE, SUPPRESSION.

For Further Reading: Bonhoeffer, *Temptation;* Packer, "Temptation," *NBD;* Seesemann, "peira," "peiraō," et al., Kittel, vol. 6; Taylor, *Life in the Spirit,* chap. 12.

WILLARD H. TAYLOR

TEMPTATION OF CHRIST. We think of the temptation of Christ only in terms of Matt. 4:1-11 and Luke 4:1-13, where the Savior, after fasting for 40 days in the wilderness, was "tempted of the devil." This was obviously a personal encounter with Satan. But Christ was also tempted by many different means during His earthly life and ministry. The Jewish leaders tempted Him often, enticing Him to work miracles simply for exhibition. The "contradiction of sinners" was a real test to the purity of the Son of God (Heb. 12:3). The absence of faith on the part of His followers must also have been a great temptation to Christ. These, with many more, became the repetitive temptations that would try the spirit of any man, and certainly became a test to the Son of God. Was it this that Jesus referred to in Luke 22:28—"Ye are they which have continued with me in my temptations"?

Temptation is the devil's chosen work. He is the tempter, *ho peirazōn.* Satan tempts either by inflaming the evil lusts which lurk within, or by external enticement.

In the cases of Adam and of our Lord the temptations were of the latter kind, because there was no evil lust in Adam before the Fall, and certainly none in Christ during His earthly life. Therefore, when the devil tempted Christ, he had nothing in Him (John 14:30).

There is an interesting parallel in the temptations of Adam and of Christ when studied in the light of 1 John 2:16: "For all that is in the world, the lust of the flesh, and the lust of the eyes, and the pride of life, is not of the Father, but is of the world." The three identifying qualities of temptation confronted both the first Adam and the Second Adam (Christ) in their temptations.

First Adam (Gen. 3:6)—

a. "The lust of the flesh"—"Tree was good for food."

b. "The lust of the eyes"—"pleasant to the eyes."

c. "The pride of life"—"desired to make one wise."

Second Adam, Christ (Luke 4:1-13)—

a. "The lust of the flesh"—"If thou be the Son of God, command this stone that it be made bread."

b. "The lust of the eyes"—"And the devil, taking him up into an high mountain, shewed unto him all the kingdoms of the world in a moment of time. . . . All this power will I give thee, and the glory of them."

c. "The pride of life"—"If thou be the Son of God, cast thyself down from hence: for it is written, he shall give his angels charge over thee, to keep thee."

Sin and death came from the first Adam's yielding to temptation. Righteousness and life came from the Second Adam's rejecting temptation. The first Adam was tempted and fell. The Second Adam was tempted and conquered.

Adam became the victim because he failed to heed the Word of God. Christ became the Victor because He used the Word of God as a defense against Satan.

Some have suggested that the temptation of Christ is mythological and allegorical and was not a real struggle. If we accept the Bible as the Word of God, then we must lay aside such untenable hypotheses, accepting the Matt. 4:1-11 record as a historical narrative of the life of Christ.

As the incarnate Son of God, was it possible for Him to have yielded to the temptation and sinned? Was Christ impeccable? At least two affirmations are true: (1) His temptation was real. There is no question about the reality of His temptation; (2) He could not have sinned and remained the Savior.

The strength with which the Master resisted temptation is available now to His people who are made partakers of His divine nature (Matt. 6:13; 1 Cor. 10:13; Heb. 4:15-16; 7:25; 1 Pet. 4:1-2).

See SINLESSNESS OF CHRIST, TEMPTATION.

For Further Reading: Abbott, *A Dictionary of Religious Knowledge,* 928; Benton, *Church Cyclopedia,* 724; Blunt, *Dictionary of Doctrinal and Historical Theology,* 734 ff; *Baker's DT,* 514 ff.

DONALD R. PETERMAN

TEN COMMANDMENTS. See DECALOGUE.

TESTIMONY, WITNESS. Testimony is an open declaration or profession of faith or agreement and an evidence given primarily to the actions and revelations of God.

In the OT, to give a testimony is to repeat or to affirm, to reprove or admonish in reference to the pronouncements or covenants of God. The Hebrew root form is to bear witness (Ruth 4:7). To testify to God's action called for decision and action on the part of His people (Josh. 24:15, 22).

The ark of the covenant is called the ark of the testimony (Exod. 25:22; Josh. 4:16) because it contained two tables of stone upon which God wrote the Ten Commandments (Exod. 25:16). This became God's witness against Israel's sin (Deut. 31:26).

Some testimonies were tangible memorials or ceremonies to mark transaction and agreements. Jacob raised a heap of stones as a boundary between him and Laban (Gen. 31:44-55).

Two witnesses were required to establish a charge against a person (Num. 35:30). Anyone committing a grave crime had to be denounced by witnesses (1 Kings 21:13). A sin which the prophets denounced was witnesses who could be bought for money (Amos 5:10-13; Isa. 5:23).

In the NT, testimony takes on a wider meaning of a proclamation in word, deed, or suffering. Our word "martyr" focuses on the affirmation of one's belief in the gospel by personal suffering. Stephen was stoned to death as a result of his testimony and is usually considered the first Christian martyr (Acts 6:8—7:60). Jesus is said to have been a faithful and good witness unto death (Rev. 1:5).

During the past three centuries, testimony became a way of telling how one came to be saved. It was a particular part of Methodist class meetings and has been continued by many of their conservative followers to the present time.

"Witness" has sometimes been distinguished from "testimony" as telling of God's deliverance or action in one's life in the presence of those who are unconverted. As such, testimony is confined to affirmation of such action among those who are already Christians.

Witnessing is at the heart of the Great Commission, for the Church advances by a kind of proclamation that is linked with personal testimony. Twice in Acts Paul tells of his conversion (in addition to Luke's narrative in chap. 9). In fact, the promised power of the Holy Spirit had effective witnessing as its primary objective and manifestation (Luke 24:45-49; Acts 1:8).

See GREAT COMMISSION, EVANGELISM, MISSION (MISSIONS, MISSIOLOGY), PREACHING, SOUL WINNING.

For Further Reading: *IDB*, 4:1864; Harmon, ed., *Encyclopedia of World Methodism*, 2:2327; Lawlor, *Wake Up and Witness*; *HDB*, 743, 820-21.

J. OTTIS SAYES

TEXTUAL CRITICISM. This discipline studies the manuscripts of a work whose original (autograph) is not available, seeking to determine the wording of the original. Textual criticism of the Scriptures is entirely consistent with a belief in their divine inspiration, truthfulness, and providential preservation. It is necessary, because God's providential care has not prevented the occurrence of various differences in the manuscripts.

Before the appearance of the Greek NT in print, differences in texts were little noted. The first printed Greek New Testaments were therefore produced from whatever manuscripts were readily available. The so-called Textus Receptus was of this sort; it owed its preeminence to its being first on the scene rather than to the intrinsic quality of its text.

Textual criticism began when manuscript differences were studied carefully. For unintentional variations (from errors of sight, hearing, memory, or judgment), a careful comparison of manuscripts yielded clues as to the original wording. Intentional changes, made by copyists or editors, were made in order to provide explanations, solve difficulties, eliminate apparent discrepancies, or correct supposed errors. This often produced additions to the text which were passed on to other manuscripts. The textual critic, seeking the original wording, therefore looks favorably on (1) the shorter reading, (2) the apparently more difficult reading, or (3) the reading which is more characteristic of a given author. Across the years textual criticism has developed into a highly technical science.

The process of textual criticism has yielded a very dependable text, undoubtedly close to the original. At the same time it gives remarkable testimony to God's providential preservation of His Word through the centuries; the Church has never been without a dependable witness to the message of salvation, whatever form of Scripture it possessed at that time.

See BIBLE, BIBLICAL INERRANCY, CRITICISM (NT), CRITICISM (OT), EXEGESIS, HERMENEUTICS.

For Further Reading: Greenlee, *Introduction to New Testament Textual Criticism*; Metzger, *The Text of the New Testament: Its Transmission, Corruption, and Restoration.*

PHILIP S. CLAPP

THANKSGIVING. See PRAISE.

THEISM. Christian theism is the belief in one personal God, Creator and Preserver of everything, who is both immanent and transcendent. Classical arguments for God (Aristotle and Thomas Aquinas pioneered the arguments) do not hold the same cogency as in earlier days because modern science, working with verifiable sensory data, has captured the mind of technological man.

Theism is seen in contrast to deism, the belief that God is there but not here, not involved in His world. Deism overextends God's otherness (separateness) and denies revelation (God breaking into history).

Theism, likewise, contrasts with pantheism, which overextends God's hereness (immanence). Pantheism believes that God not only is *in* His creation (in the sense of putting His creative stamp on it), but that He *is* the creation. Pantheism robs God of His objective personhood.

Theism stands in direct opposition to atheism, the belief that there is no God (atheism: *a* = against; *theos* = God). In our century the late Bertrand Russell, the British mathematician and philosopher, was an intellectual leader of atheism.

Christian theism differs, too, from polytheism, the belief in many gods, as in Hinduism, the religion of countless divinities.

Theism also separates itself from agnosticism, the belief that one cannot really know if there is a God (agnosticism: *a* = against; *gnosis* = knowledge).

The most powerful proponents of theism in our time, by virtue of their appeal to the modern mind, do not work with historic theistic proofs (as noted above) so much as with inferential materials and contemporary images. This is seen in the writings of Francis Schaeffer, C. S. Lewis, Sheldon Vanauken, et al. Such authors are read widely not merely because of their "popularity"; in point of fact, their works are characterized by depth of insight and a remarkable breadth of knowledge. That very depth and breadth, cogently expressed, make their apologetic literature challenging and prove that one vast segment of modern man is seriously concerned to find the truth about God. One cannot read C. S. Lewis' *Problem of Pain* or *Mere Christianity,* for example, without careful attention.

Couple these apologetic works with the testimonial and devotional literature coming off the presses, and one begins to understand the mindset of contemporary man. The sensory and technological, whether understood in depth or on the surface, spills over into Christian literature. Actually, contemporary Western man does not so much ask, Does God exist?—he often assume that—as he asks, What kind of a God exists? And how can He help me live a meaningful and coherent life?

Christianity teaches that God is Spirit (John 4:24)—self-aware, free, and not made of parts as something material. He is omnipresent—that is, everywhere. He is unchangeable and unchanging; He is not passive but active; He is dynamic: He can create and move and do and achieve. Practically, this all means the God who is there is also here, involved in His world and ever ready actually to help His children.

See GOD, TRINITY (THE HOLY), SPIRIT, PERSONALITY OF GOD, DEISM, PANTHEISM.

For Further Reading: "Theism," *The Harper Dictionary of Modern Thought,* 631 ff.; Lewis, *Mere Christianity;* Wiley, *CT,* 1:217-440; Lockyer, *All the Doctrines of the Bible,* 11-36; *GMS,* 48-66, 207-50.

DONALD E. DEMARAY

THEISTIC EVOLUTION. Theistic evolution is the view that God created by means of the evolutionary process. It is thus a combination of theism and evolution. But the view poses contradiction, because the idea of creation is directly opposed to the concept of evolution. There is no revelation in the Bible that would indicate that evolution had a part in God's creation method. Creation was an act of Deity in bringing this world and its inhabitants into existence.

Theistic evolution is quite plainly in radical opposition to all the fundamental teaching of biblical Christianity. God did not use evolution to finish a good work; He did not surrender the creative process to the chance and randomness postulated by evolution.

Evolution is essentially development from innate processes out of prior materials that appeared by chance and random variations, through natural selection, not under God's direction.

From the very beginning the hypothesis of evolution has failed. In 1859 Charles Darwin published *The Origin of Species,* which overturned the world of thought, shifted the whole attitude of science, and caused upheaval to the very foundation of religion and morality for his followers. He wrote that life had not been created in distinct kinds, but had developed in all its variations, including man, from a single cell.

He was in error in the big three issues. In the first place he wrote that natural selection could improve indefinitely. Geneticists now agree that once selection within a species has reached homozygosity (a pure state), then selection has no further influence. Secondly, Darwin thought that life had been spontaneously generated. Many scientists have tried to generate life without success. Life comes from preexisting life which was created as it is revealed in the Bible.

Darwin missed it in the third big one by stating that acquired characteristics were inherited. This issue has been proven false many times and is perhaps the greatest blow to Darwin and evolutionists today. If acquired characteristics were inheritable, then evolutionists would have at least one working basis for organic evolution. They are now leaning heavily on mutations and chromosomal aberrations as the answer for evolution, which do bring changes within species, but harmful in most cases.

God did not use such a failure as organic evolution as a method of bringing into existence His world. As evolution fails, so theistic evolution fails. The failure of evolution as an alternative for origins strengthens our faith in Him as Creator. "In the beginning God created" (Gen. 1:1). The existing universe and the different kinds of plants, animals, and man did indeed arise through separate acts of special creation by God; so theistic evolution has no place in truth. The Christian ideal hopes for a concentration on nature that leads not away from but toward God.

See DARWINISM, EVOLUTION, CREATION, CREATIONISM, MAN.

For Further Reading: Smith, *Man's Origin, Man's Destiny,* 167-84; Hoover, *The Fallacies of Evolution;* Clark, *Darwin: Before and After.* DWIGHT J. STRICKLER

THEISTIC PROOFS. Historically the human attempt to know God has given rise to four main ways of reasoning about the ultimate reality. In philosophical (or natural) theology, these are known as "theistic proofs" or "arguments for God's existence."

1. The *ontological* argument (from the Greek *ontos,* "of being") is a statement of the basic assumption of the rationality of existence. This mode of argument was first clearly stated by Anselm (1033-1109) and was characteristic of the great medieval system of Christian philosophy known as Scholasticism. It was later restated by Descartes (1596-1650), one of the formative thinkers of 17th-century rationalism.

For Anselm, the name God stands for the most real being there is. By definition God is the Being than which a more real one cannot be conceived. Therefore, to understand the name correctly is to understand that God does in fact exist, for what we think of as *most* real, we must think of as *really* real. The human mind can conceive of a perfect being, and a necessary part of this perfection is that this perfect being should exist. The idea of perfection includes the idea of existence. A *perfect* being cannot not be. That which does not exist is less than perfect. Since therefore we can have the idea of a perfect being, that being must exist.

Descartes argued similarly, pointing out that to think of a right-angled triangle is to think of it as having a hypotenuse; you cannot think of a right-angled triangle as not having one. Likewise, you cannot grasp what "God" means unless you grasp the fact that He cannot not exist.

Some have suspected this argument of being a kind of verbal trick. Others have denied that it has logical force, regarding it simply as an assertion that God *ought* to be thought of in a certain way. But many Christian thinkers have seen that there is something at stake in this pattern of reasoning, for it gives logical expression to the *radical inescapability* of God. It expresses the fact that thinking cannot rid itself of a relation to reality. Whatever names might be substituted for God, there is always a final reality whose nonexistence is unimaginable.

2. The *cosmological* argument (from *cosmos,* "world") attempts to answer the question "Where did the world come from?" It can be stated as follows: "Everything that exists must have an adequate cause. The world exists. Therefore the world must have an adequate cause." The name for this adequate cause is God. The cosmological way of reasoning holds that we cannot doubt the ultimate foundation of the cosmos. We can, of course, doubt any particular version of it, but this very doubting presupposes the foundation itself. Here cosmological reasoning overlaps ontological reasoning. The difference is this: The ontological argument says that if we think of an ultimate foundation of everything, we must think of it as real. Cosmological reasoning declares that the cosmos constrains us to think of an ultimate foundation and points us in that direction. The Bible contains expressions of such an argument (e.g., Ps. 19:1-4; 94:9; Acts 14:17; Rom. 1:19-20). It was given most notable philosophical form by Thomas Aquinas (1225-74).

3. The *teleological* argument stresses something still more specific about the ultimate reality. It derives its name from the Greek *telos,* the "goal," "end," or "aim" of a process. It argues for God's existence from the appearance of design or purpose in the universe, because a sense of rational purpose in the development of the natural world speaks of an origin in an intelligent mind. Thus God is seen not merely as the ultimate

cause of all things, but also as giving directional order (goal-orientation) to the cosmic whole.

4. The *moral* argument is associated with the teaching of Immanuel Kant (1724-1804). Kant questioned the validity of the traditional Scholastic arguments. He held that *pure reason* cannot prove the existence of God. Instead, he rested the case for God's existence upon the "moral ought," stressing the universal fact of moral awareness. This way of reasoning finds God not in the "top of the mind" but in the "bottom of the heart." It is argued that there is within the heart of man a majestic voice which tells him he ought to do what he knows to be right (although one's perception of what in fact *is* right will vary, depending on background, experience, tradition, etc.). Since this moral ought is universal, it must have an ultimate source or Author. God is thus one of the three postulates of the *practical reason* (freedom and immortality being the other two).

These are the four major historical ways of reasoning about God. Theology recognizes that everyone cannot be *argued into* believing in God; belief is more likely to precede rather than follow an understanding of these arguments. Yet these ways of reasoning, with their varying degrees of cogency for different individuals, do help to clarify the meaning of God for the thinking mind. Though they cannot compel belief, they can clarify what is involved in believing and thus make one's belief (or even unbelief) more authentic.

See GOD, ATTRIBUTES (DIVINE), APOLOGETICS, THEISM, EPISTEMOLOGY.

For Further Reading: Barth, *Anselm: Fides quaerens Intellectum;* Burrell, ed., *The Cosmological Arguments; A Spectrum of Opinion;* Hartshorne, *Anselm's Discovery: A Re-examination of the Ontological Proof for God's Existence;* Hick, *Arguments for the Existence of God;* Hick and McGill, eds., *The Many-faced Arguments;* Kung, *Does God Exist?: An Answer for Today.* ROB L. STAPLES

THEOCRACY. A theocracy is a government in which God is the supreme Ruler and His laws serve as the basis for all civil, social, and political relationships. Though the word itself is not found in the Bible, the idea is fundamental to both Testaments. It is inherent in the emphasis on God's sovereignty in the creation; it is explicit in John's vision of the great white throne in the Book of Revelation.

Israel's unique relationship to God as His chosen people essentially formed the foundation for the development of OT thought: "You shall be my own possession among all peoples . . . and you shall be to me a kingdom of priests and a holy nation" (Exod. 19:5-6, RSV). Yahweh, as king, would "reign for ever and ever" (15:18). Even though the theocracy was later governed by an earthly king, his reign was mediatorial, for he served as the Lord's anointed. Ultimately, on "the day of the Lord" all rule will yield to God's sovereign reign, "and the Lord will become king over all the earth" (Zech. 14:9, RSV).

The kingdom of God in the NT reveals the development of the concept of theocracy. The Messiah is of the house of David, and He has brought near the reign of God. He has established a kingdom that is not of this world (John 18:36), and of which there will be no end (Luke 1:33). Though He has ascended to the Father until the fullness of times, He will one day come in His kingdom (23:42), and the earth will recognize that He is "the blessed and only Sovereign, the King of kings and Lord of lords" (1 Tim. 6:15, RSV).

Theocracy allows no place for secularism. All regulations of society are essentially theological. All human accountability is ultimately to God. History itself is moving inexorably toward His appointed conclusion.

See DIVINE SOVEREIGNTY, STATE (THE), KINGDOM OF GOD.

For Further Reading: Bright, *The Kingdom of God;* Gray, "The Hebrew Conception of the Kingship of God: Its Origin and Development," *Vetus Testamentum,* 6:268-85; Vriezen, *An Outline of Old Testament Theology,* English ed. (1958), 227-31. WILLIAM B. COKER

THEODICY. See EVIL.

THEOLOGICAL LANGUAGE. In Christian theology language possesses a significance beyond its ordinary function in communication. In the theology of the gospel, John described Jesus as the "Word" (Gr. *logos*), meaning the bridge by which God communicates himself to mankind. *Theology* is a compound word, combining *theos,* "God," with *logos,* "word," describing those things which comprise the entire field of study about God and His revelation.

Theological language requires great precision. Language is a complex phenomenon. A word may be given a univocal meaning, or it may be interpreted equivocally. This means it may have one meaning, or it may have several meanings depending on the intention of the speaker or the interpretation of the hearer. Language is formed from images, concepts, signs, and sounds.

Theological language participates in all the characteristics of language. It is not divine or angelic speech. Nevertheless, it is distinctive because it speaks about God. It is sometimes referred to as "God talk" by philosophers. Language which speaks of or describes empirical objects is not adequate to speak about God. There is a visual and verbal correspondence between the word *table* and the physical object, at least on the level of common sense. Such a correspondence does not exist between the word "God" and the Reality who created the world. Therefore, theological language is particularly conceptual and symbolic. Theological language seeks analogies or comparative pictures with which to describe the supernatural realm. A parable may be defined as an "extended analogy" which pictures some aspect of God or spiritual insight. For example, in the parable of the prodigal (Luke 15), the father represents the love of God the Father. An analogy may be defined as "a word made flesh." When ideas are clothed in persons, the ideas become understandable. By looking at Jesus, "the image of the invisible God" (Col. 1:15), we see God in a veiled expression—God incarnate.

From the beginning of the Church's history, and especially in the era of the church fathers (up to the sixth century), theological language has possessed crucial significance. Using philosophical language drawn from the Greeks, the fathers reconstructed and redefined this language to convey to their age the meaning of Christian faith. The important concepts of God as "person," the Trinity, the divinity and humanity of Jesus Christ, and many more received their major theological formulation. Tertullian was the first to use the word *Trinity.* The term *person (persona)* originally meant "face" or "mask," but it became an analogy of the personhood of Father, Son, and Holy Spirit, signifying unity in trinity, not diversity in trinity.

Some persons are so convinced of the inadequacy of theology to express divine truths that they fall back on a mystical union with God, while an extreme form of linguistic analysis (logical positivism) rejects theological language as nonsense. Either of these leaves the Church in virtual, if not complete, silence about the faith. This is an abdication of responsibility and in opposition to the Church's mandate to be a witnessing community in the world.

See POSITIVISM, EPISTEMOLOGY, METAPHYSICS, THEOLOGY, COMMUNICATE (COMMUNICATION), TESTIMONY (WITNESS).

For Further Reading: Kelly, *Early Christian Doctrines;* Michalson, *Worldly Theology,* chap. 3.

LEON O. HYNSON

THEOLOGICAL METHODOLOGY. See SYSTEMATIC THEOLOGY.

THEOLOGY. Theology may be defined as a systematic explanation of the contents of a religious faith. Such a general definition can apply equally to Jewish, Muslim, Christian, or a number of other theologies. Theology aims at a comprehensive and coherent exposition of the various doctrines that are essential to the particular religion in question. It seeks to give linguistic structure and conceptual wholeness to what can be known about God and His relationship to the world.

Christian theology is the methodical explanation of the contents of the Christian faith and is primarily a function of the Christian Church. It results from participation in and orderly reflection upon God's self-disclosure in Jesus of Nazareth; it is Christian faith brought to a particular kind of expression. Christian theologians work within this community and are responsible to it.

But Christian theology is not simply a restatement of what the Church has believed in the past. Because the Church bears witness to Christ in the contemporary world, and because it too lives in the world, theology must remain a dynamic enterprise. Through theology the Church repeatedly answers the question—for itself and for the world—"What does it mean to confess that Jesus is the Christ?"

Christian theology is not primarily reflection on Christian faith as such but on the God who became redemptively incarnate in Jesus of Nazareth and who by the Holy Spirit creates faith in the Church.

Christian theology may be arranged into at least five classifications, normally called theological disciplines. They are: (1) *Biblical theology;* (2) *Historical theology,* which concentrates on the history of Christian thought, its thematic organization, and its continuing instruction for the Church; (3) *Systematic theology,* which is heavily influenced by biblical and historical theology, but whose assignment is to systematically state the contents of the Christian faith with reference to the general milieu of the time in which the theologian is working; (4) *Moral theology,* or Christian ethics, which aims at a systematic understanding of how the Church, and the individual Christian within the life of the Church, can bear witness to the new reality established by Christ; and (5) *Practical or applied theology,* which includes pastoral theology, missiology, and Christian education.

See BIBLICAL THEOLOGY, HISTORICAL THEOLOGY, SYSTEMATIC THEOLOGY, PRACTICAL THEOLOGY.

For Further Reading: Wiley, *CT,* 1:13-99; MacQuarrie,

Principles of Christian Theology, 1-36; Brunner, *The Christian Doctrine of God: Dogmatics,* 1:3-85.

ALBERT L. TRUESDALE, JR.

THEOLOGY, NATURAL. See NATURAL THEOLOGY.

THEOLOGY OF MISSIONS. See MISSION, MISSIONS, MISSIOLOGY.

THEOPHANY. A theophany is a mode of revelation, an appearance of God to human beings in a visible or audible form.

The OT records several such appearances: angelic visitors came to Abraham's tent, one of whom spoke as the Lord (Gen. 18:2-22); Jacob wrestled with a man whom he called God (32:22-32); Moses talked with "the angel of the Lord" at the burning bush (Exod. 3:2) and spoke with God face-to-face at Mount Sinai (19:20 ff); Gideon talked with the angel of the Lord (Judg. 6:11-24); Manoah received instruction from a personage whose name was Secret (Wonderful, RSV) (13:1-20); a dream theophany came to Solomon (1 Kings 3:5-15); Elijah heard "the still small voice" of God speaking to him while in a cave at Horeb (19:9-18); even Ezekiel saw "the likeness as it were of a human form" while on the banks of Chebar (Ezek. 1:26-28, RSV).

The NT records that God spoke to Jesus at His baptism (Matt. 3:17); that three disciples heard a voice out of the cloud at the Transfiguration (17:1-13); that Paul saw the risen Christ on the Damascus Road (Acts 9:1-9); and that John had a vision of the exalted Christ on the Isle of Patmos (Rev. 1:12-20).

In general, theophanies were brief and temporary, but the appearance of God in a pillar of cloud and smoke accompanying His people during the Exodus, and the Shekinah Presence in the Tabernacle and Temple were lasting phenomena.

The key theophany of "the angel [messenger] of the Lord" may be interpreted as a preincarnate appearance of the Messiah. Often the heavenly messenger is identified with the Hebrew name *Adonai* (Ps. 110:1; Mal. 3:1), a name which the author of Hebrews ascribed to the Son-Creator (Heb. 1:10-12; Ps. 102:25-27).

Since a theophany is a revelation of God's person and proclamation, it cannot be bounded by the laws of human psychology, although God undoubtedly used the sum and substance of human nature in making himself known. God is His own messenger as He reveals His person and will to man.

See REVELATION (SPECIAL), HEILSGESCHICHTE.

For Further Reading: *Baker's DT,* 520.

BERT H. HALL

THEOSOPHY. Theosophy is a highly complex religio-philosophical system that claims to give systematic expression to an "ancient wisdom" derived from many cultures and religions. The "ancient wisdom" has been held in trust and communicated by a complex of suprahuman masters. Theosophy purports to introduce its communicants to ecstatic and expanding forms of consciousness that ascend hierarchically into the cosmic levels of reality that supposedly lie behind the visible world. All elements of reality are parts of an ultimate harmony and are themselves expressions of intricate chains of consciousness. Entrance by the communicant into these transcendent realities is achieved primarily by interiorized myth and doctrine rather than through ritual or social interaction.

Theosophy teaches that the solar system emanated from the ONE, an eternal, unknowable, boundless, and immutable principle. The emanation occurred in a series of major cycles of divine activity and rest, of which the evolution of man through several worlds and races is a part.

In addition to a hierarchy of divine beings who are subordinate to the ONE, there is an earthly plane which is constituted and energized by seven rays or lines of activity that govern all aspects of terrestrial life, each of which is headed by a master.

Theosophy was founded in 1875 by Madame (Helena Petrovna) Blavatsky (1831-91), and Col. Henry Steel Olcott. Others who were significant in its formation were Annie Besant, C. W. Leadbeater, and W. Q. Judge.

See CULTS, OCCULT (OCCULTISM), NON-CHRISTIAN RELIGIONS, TRUTH, SALVATION, GNOSTICISM, PRE-EXISTENCE OF SOULS.

For Further Reading: Ellwood, *Religious and Spiritual Groups in America;* Judah, *The History and Philosophy of the Metaphysical Movements in America.*

ALBERT L. TRUESDALE, JR.

THEOTHANATOLOGY. See DEATH OF GOD DOCTRINE.

THOMISM. The most general description of Thomism is that it is a theological/philosophical movement originating in the 13th century with Thomas Aquinas and continuing with great force into the 20th century. Thomism places primary emphasis upon attempting to understand and explain each generation's problems and needs in a systematic way with Aquinas' spirit, insights, principles, methods, and conclusions as the key to understanding.

Thomas Aquinas (A.D. 1225-74), variously known as the "great dumb ox of Sicily" and the "Angelic Doctor," was the most outstanding philosopher and theologian of the medieval church. He was born in Italy, became a Dominican in 1244, studied under Albertus Magnus, and was a teacher at Paris.

Several of his teachings were almost immediately condemned as heresy, but this decision was later reversed. And in 1323 he was canonized by Pope John XXII; in 1567 he was declared by Pius V the "Fifth Doctor of the Church"; in 1879 Leo XIII gave Thomism "official" (though not exclusive) place in the Roman Catholic church; and in 1918 Thomas became an institution in the church with his being mentioned in the Code of Canon Law—this is the only name in the code—with the strong position urged that his system should be the basis of all theological instruction.

Thomism is the complex melding of Aristotle (no superficial baptism), Augustine, and general Catholic Christianity into a massive whole. It stands in opposition to a Neoplatonic projection of a world of reality beyond this (the medieval form of realism), with the world of human experience and action as a mere appearance or shadow of the truly real world beyond. In harmony with Aristotle he focused on the significance of the empirical and gave a Christian interpretation as focusing on knowledge of this world as infused with divine reality rather than separated from it.

In opposition to a world of pure process (cf. Heraclitus: all is flux) as well as to total rigidity (cf. Parmenides: reality is immobile), Aquinas took the middle road of accepting both being and becoming, both substance and process. God has no potentiality: He is *actus purus* or pure actuality. God does not change or become; however, all other beings change. And the point is that for Aquinas, both God and the world are real.

In opposition to extreme positions on the evils of human nature and culture, Aquinas held that man himself, his reason, appetites, and achievements are significant and positive. He attached positive values to the state, law, art, philosophy, and culture in general. This would be substantiated by his celebrated five ways (proofs of the existence of God) as well as his development of natural theology.

While Aquinas may have held that there are two orders of truth corresponding to the natural and supernatural dimension of reality, he also maintained that these two levels do not stand in opposition. Rather, all realms of truth are held together and are harmonious with each other through coming from the one God who brings unity to all dimensions of His creation.

Aquinas' vast philosophic synthesis stands with those of Aristotle and Hegel as encyclopedic monuments to human rational effort.

See HISTORICAL THEOLOGY, REASON, REALISM AND NOMINALISM, SCHOLASTICISM, PLATONISM, RATIONALISM, PROCESS THEOLOGY, NEO-THOMISM, SUBSTANCE (SUBSTANTIVE).

For Further Reading: *New Catholic Encyclopedia,* 14:126-38; *Sacramentum Mundi,* 6:249-55; *NIDCC,* 60-61; Schaeffer, *Escape from Reason;* Barrett, *A Christian Perspective of Knowing,* 60-86, 91.

R. DUANE THOMPSON

THOUGHT. See REASON.

TIME. Time and history are crucial concepts to Christianity, for time makes possible creation, the whole range of salvation history, the Incarnation, human freedom, and the movement of this age toward a significant goal. Without time such action would be neither possible nor meaningful. All would be locked up in a motionless system with no experiencer to contemplate it, enjoy it, or act upon it.

Thus time, in the most basic theological and philosophical sense, must not be conceived of as aligning with views of time held by science and technology. It must be thought of as the passage or duration comprehended within the matrix of the experiencing person. And while *chronos* may refer to the simple passage of such time or to time as measured by clocks and calendars, *kairos* refers to the importance of proper timing and fulfillment: "The time is fulfilled, and the kingdom of God is at hand" (Mark 1:15).

Time or the temporal may be seen as providing the potential for birth, life, growth, creativity, and perfection; on the other hand, it may be seen as a power enslaving man to wear and tear, fatigue, old age, and death.

The temporal is often contrasted with the eternal and thus takes on the character of the secular or this-worldly. It may also mean in some theological systems the order of change or process (the material world) as opposed to the timelessness of the eternal.

Time has a past, present, and a future; various types of mind tend to emphasize or exaggerate one or the other. Overemphasis on the past will produce traditionalism and authoritarianism. Overemphasis on the present may be tied in with a barren empiricism or hedonism (pleasure is the highest good). Overemphasis on the future may create utopianism or a violent form of revolution.

A Christian can observe a significant coming together of past, present, and future in accepting creation, Incarnation, and inscripturation from the past within a present context which sees history as moving in a genuine direction toward a divinely projected goal. In his life and thought these all come together in his cooperation with God in the fulfillment of the divine goals.

See IMMUTABILITY, CHRONOS, PROCESS THEOLOGY, ETERNITY, LEISURE, ATTRIBUTES (DIVINE).

For Further Reading: *Sacramentum Mundi,* 6:257-62; Wood, "Space-Time and a Trinitarian Concept of Grace," *Pentecostal Grace,* 101-36; Cullmann, *Christ and Time.* R. DUANE THOMPSON

TITHE, THE. In simplest terms the tithe is 1/10 (or 10 percent) of our wages or salary, or net gain (profits) from our own business or investments, or any combination of these.

In ancient days Abraham was the first recorded example of paying tithes, when he so honored the priest of God, Melchizedek (Gen. 14:20). Also, Jacob, his grandson, volunteered to give a 10th of all that God gave him. It was more than a trader's bargain, however, for he did it in gratitude for God's promise of food and clothing, protection and guidance (Gen. 28:13-22).

Under the Mosaic covenant God taught His people to tithe the increase. Even the priestly tribe (Levi), who lived on one of the tithes, was taught to tithe the tithe (Num. 18:26; Neh. 10:38). In general the teaching was, "The tithe . . . is the Lord's" (Lev. 27:30). Malachi even accuses tithe withholders of robbing God (3:8).

Some have thought that on the advent of the new covenant all tithes were done away. But Jesus was careful to teach, "'Think not that I have come to abolish the law and the prophets; I have not come to abolish them but to fulfill them'" (Matt. 5:17, RSV). And to the Pharisees He said: "'But woe to you Pharisees! for you tithe mint and rue and every herb, and neglect justice and the love of God; these you ought to have done, without neglecting the others'" (Luke 11:42, RSV). Thus He endorsed the tithe, even while putting it in perspective.

But Jesus never encouraged a legalistic spirit which would tithe carefully, then be just as careful to go no farther. Actually He underscored "Plus Giving." A classical illustration is the scene where He called attention to the widow who put in two copper coins while the rich put in their much larger gifts. Jesus said: "'I tell you . . . this poor widow has given more than any of them; for those others who have given had more than enough, but she, with less than enough, has given all she had to live on'" (Luke 21:3-4, NEB). And Paul quotes the positive insight of Jesus, "It is more blessed to give than to receive" (Acts 20:35).

Paul taught the Corinthians some basic principles in Christian giving. (1) Let everyone engage in giving (1 Cor. 16:2); (2) Give regularly (weekly); (3) Give proportionately "according as he hath been prospered" (v. 3, Wesley); (4) Give cheerfully (2 Cor. 9:7).

Proportionate, cheerful giving would imply the tithe as a minimum, never the maximum. It would be unthinkable for the Christian under grace, prompted by love, to give less than the Israelite was required by law.

Roy L. Smith observes wisely: "The value of the system [tithing] is not in the funds that it produces but in the spiritual integration that results" *(Stewardship Studies).*

See STEWARDSHIP, MONEY.

For Further Reading: Young, *The Tithe Is the Lord's; ISBE,* 5:2987. SAMUEL YOUNG

TOLERANCE. This has special reference to one of James Arminius' teachings, which urged that his own view of conditional predestination be permitted in the Dutch churches—along with the unconditional view. It also refers to the view held by many who are liberal in doctrine and practices, that the promoting of varying views should be permitted within given denominations. There is a great difference, however, between divergent views which are essentially evangelical being tolerated by the government in a state church, and the toleration of evangelical and nonevangelical views within an autonomous, confessional denomination. There is a tolerance which is Christian, and there is also a tolerance which is betrayal—as the apostle Paul would agree (cf. Galatians).

See LATITUDINARIANISM. J. KENNETH GRIDER

TONGUES, GIFT OF. This gift refers to a 17th-century English word used to translate the Hebrew *lashon* and the Greek *glossais,* "language/languages" in KJV and subsequent translations; now, by wide usage, applied to the practice of glossolalia, speechlike sounds unintelligible both to speaker and hearer unless interpreted.

Languages or tongues as a phenomenon of the Holy Spirit are mentioned in two NT books, Acts (2:4-13; 10:44-46; 19:6) and 1 Corinthians (12:10, 30; and possibly 14:2-39).

Interpretations of the biblical phenomena differ widely:

1. Some hold that 1 Corinthians 14, interpreted as relating to ecstatic or unintelligible speech, is the normative NT gift of languages, and that Acts is to be understood in harmony with 1 Corinthians.

2. Others hold that Acts 2:4-13 represents the normative NT language gifts and that 1 Corinthians is to be understood as related to intelligible (although not locally understood) languages.

3. Others hold that the Acts and Corinthian phenomena are different: Acts reporting the use of intelligible languages, and 1 Corinthians relating to an esoteric language or languages used in prayer and praise but otherwise unintelligible unless accompanied by a parallel gift of interpretation.

Modern "Pentecostal" denominations regard glossolalia as the biblical evidence of the baptism with or "in" the Holy Spirit. Some nondenominational charismatics deemphasize glossolalia as an evidence of the Spirit's fullness, but regard its practice as a gift to be expected normally by those filled with the Spirit.

The languages of Acts 2 seem clearly to have been foreign languages understood without interpretation. Luke goes beyond the necessity of simple narration to insist three times on the intelligibility of the tongues (vv. 6, 8, 11). Intelligibility is also implied of the speaking at Caesarea and Ephesus (Acts 10:46; 19:6). Each instance represents a breaking out of the gospel beyond previous limits—to Gentile proselytes, and to converts directly out of paganism.

That Luke wrote Acts nine years after Paul wrote 1 Corinthians, and that Luke had firsthand knowledge of the situation at Corinth (e.g., 2 Cor. 8:18 as a possible reference to Luke), makes Luke's insistence on intelligibility a matter of crucial importance as indicating what NT language gifts really are.

First Corinthians 14 is the major biblical basis for the modern practice of glossolalia. Three chief interpretations have been offered:

1. First Corinthians 14 represents a practice introduced into Christian worship from the Corinthian background of pagan mystery religions.

2. First Corinthians 14 reports the practice of glossolalia understood as a genuine gift of the Spirit for use in devotion.

3. First Corinthians 14 relates to the polyglot background of Corinthian society in which the introduction of foreign languages locally unintelligible and untranslated resulted in confusion in Christian worship.

Even a casual reading of the chapter shows Paul's grudging permissiveness in regard to the Corinthian practices.

Isbell (cf. "For Further Reading") makes a good case for the theory that common English translations have misinterpreted Paul in 1 Cor. 14:39, which should read, "So, my brothers, earnestly desire to prophesy, and do not impede prophesying with glossolalia."

See GIFTS OF THE SPIRIT, BAPTISM WITH THE HOLY SPIRIT, SIGN.

For Further Reference: Robert H. Gundry, "'Ecstatic Utterance' NEB?", *Journal of Theological Studies,* October, 1966, Charles D. Isbell, "Glossolalia and Propheteialalia: A Study of 1 Corinthians 14," *WTJ,* Spring, 1976, 15-24; Kildahl, *The Psychology of Speaking in Tongues;* Purkiser, *The Gifts of the Spirit;* Synan, *The Holiness-Pentecostal Movement in the United States;* Taylor, *Tongues: Their Purpose and Meaning.*

W. T. PURKISER

TORAH. See MOSAIC LAW.

TOTAL DEPRAVITY. Certain distinctions should be made among the terms *original sin, inherited depravity,* and *total depravity.* Strictly speaking, *original sin* refers to man's first sin, the disobedience of Adam and Eve, resulting in the Fall. *Inherited depravity* has reference to the fact that the sinfulness of man is passed on from one generation to the next. *Total depravity* describes the extent to which each person is affected by this racial corruption.

The concept of total depravity is often misunderstood. It "does not mean that man is totally bad; rather it means there is nothing in man that has not been infected by the power of sin" (*Handbook of Theological Terms,* 68). The mind is darkened, the will enslaved, the emotions alienated. "The whole head is sick, and the whole heart faint" (Isa. 1:5).

Theologians in the Reformed tradition often misunderstand and therefore misinterpret the Wesleyan view (e.g., *Baker's DT,* 164). Three questions emerge: (1) the meaning of natural inability in spiritual matters, (2) in what sense guilt attaches to original sin, and (3) the extent of *total* depravity.

Wesleyans take sin as seriously as the Scriptures do. They insist that sin is "exceeding sinful" (Rom. 7:13), that mankind is "dead in trespasses and sins" (see Eph. 2:1-3; 4:17-24), that apart from grace man is totally unable in spiritual things. "We believe that . . . through the fall of Adam he became depraved so that he cannot now turn and prepare himself by his own natural strength and works to faith and calling upon God" (*Manual,* Church of the Nazarene).

It is helpful to make a distinction between guilt as *culpability,* or personal blameworthiness; and guilt as *liability* for consequences. The former was Adam's guilt alone, the latter belongs potentially to the race, if the remedy in Christ is rejected. It is remarkable that Louis Berkhof (Calvinist) and H. Orton Wiley (Wesleyan) use almost identical language on these subjects (see "For Further Reading"). Moreover, no responsible evangelical advocates total depravity in the *intensive* sense (that man is totally evil), only in the *extensive* sense: that the corruption of sin extends to the whole of man's being.

It is the testimony of both the OT and the NT that the image of God in man has been seriously marred (not destroyed) by the Fall. Man lost the moral image (holiness), while retaining the natural image (personality). The divine warning against disobedience had come to pass: "Thou shalt surely die" (Gen. 2:17).

The OT sees the sinfulness of man in such terms as "perversity," "crookedness," "stubbornness." "The heart is deceitful above all things, and desperately wicked" (Jer. 17:9). Isaiah's vision in the Temple (Isa. 6:5), the Psalmist's prayer of confession and plea for cleansing (Psalm 51), and Ezekiel's vision of the need for the new covenant (Ezek. 36:25-27) are further examples of man's moral plight (Turner, *The Vision Which Transforms,* 24-31).

NT references are likewise numerous, but Rom. 5:12-21 brings the issue into focus—by one man (Adam) sin penetrated the race. Because all men have sinned, some in ignorance, others willfully, death and condemnation have passed to all men. Between Rom. 5:12 and 8:10, the phrase "the sin" appears 28 times. Paul sees this force as a "principle of revolt . . . against the divine will." It is an "inner moral tyranny . . . alien to man's true nature" (*GMS,* 291). That is, though it marks man's fallen nature, it does not belong to true human nature, as created. From this corruption proceed all the evils that trouble and harass mankind (Mark 7:20-23). Contravening all this darkness is the "gift of righteousness" available to all men through the Last Adam, Christ (Rom. 5:17).

See SIN, ORIGINAL SIN, PREVENIENT GRACE, DIVINE IMAGE, FALL (THE).

For Further Reading: Berkhof, *Systematic Theology,* 244-54; *GMS,* 285-302; Wiley, *CT,* 2:119-30.

A. ELWOOD SANNER

TRACTARIANISM. This is the popular name for the Oxford Movement. This movement, headed up by J. H. Newman of Oxford, published *Tracts for the Times* between 1833 and 1840—and thus was designated Tractarianism. The movement emphasized the authority of ecclesiastics such as bishops, based importantly on the apostolic succession doctrine, and purity of doctrine generally (based on the church's received creeds). The movement suffered decline when its leader, Newman, left Anglicanism and became a Roman Catholic—a rather natural development, based on his interests.

See APOSTOLIC SUCCESSION, ANGLO-CATHOLICISM.

J. KENNETH GRIDER

TRADITION. Tradition is the beliefs, values, and customs transmitted from one generation to the next, assuring the continuity of the culture or the institution and providing each emerging generation with the stabilizing influence of its heritage. It provides an understanding of the foundations of the community and of the relationship between the individual and the larger fellowship in which he participates.

The idea of tradition is negative in much of modern Protestantism. This is partly due to the general tenor of the recent humanistic period which tends to equate antiquity with obsolescence. It is also partly due to the tension between the Reformation doctrine of *sola scriptura* and the pronouncements of Roman Catholicism.

Evangelicals are particularly wary because Scripture speaks negatively of human traditions. Jesus told the Pharisees that they had nullified the Word of God through their traditions (Mark 7:13); Paul warned the Colossians against the traditions of men (Col. 2:8); and Peter reminded his readers that they were not redeemed by the futile traditions handed down from their fathers, but through the blood of Christ (1 Pet. 1:18-19).

Modern Bible scholars approach the Bible as the repository of traditions which developed in Israel and the Early Church. These traditions grew out of various situations in the community and came to be accepted as authoritative for the community. This obviously denies the divine inspiration of the Bible and negates any ultimate authority for the Bible.

Tradition plays an important role in the Church and should not be disregarded. The creeds, which formulate the essentials of Christian faith, the interpretation of Scripture, and the theological statements of historic orthodoxy, are traditions, even though they are rooted in Scripture. They reflect the Holy Spirit's ministry of illumination and have a subordinate authority. All traditions are subject to the Word of God.

See INSPIRATION OF THE BIBLE, HERMENEUTICS, PROTESTANTISM, BIBLICAL AUTHORITY.

For Further Reading: Harrison, *Introduction to the Old Testament,* 19-82; Barrett, *Jesus and the Gospel Tradition;* Cullmann, *The Early Church,* 53-99; Stott, *Christ the Controversialist,* 65-89.

WILLIAM B. COKER

TRADUCIANISM. This is the belief that the soul is procreated by parental conception along with and in the body. Natural generation thus includes both the spiritual, immaterial faculties of human personality as well as those purely physical organs which can be observed and verified scientifically. This is most in harmony with the Hebrew concept of man as a body-mind unity, and also most congenial to the biblical concept of inherited sinfulness. The alternatives to traducianism are (1) *preexistence,* i.e., that souls or spirits exist before conception either in the ideal world or in a previous incarnation, and are infused into the embryo or fetus at some point before or at birth; or (2) *creationism,* i.e., that God creates a personal soul for each conception. Since the creation of a sinful spirit by God is inconceivable, creationism implies that inbred sin is solely physical.

See SOUL, GENETICISM, CREATIONISM, ORIGINAL SIN, PREEXISTENCE OF SOULS.

For Further Reading: Wiley, *CT,* 2:26-29, 104; Berkhof, *Systematic Theology,* 196-201.

RICHARD S. TAYLOR

TRANSACTIONAL ANALYSIS. Transactional Analysis (TA) is an approach to interpreting reactions and relationships which has gained widespread acceptance in its practical applications to counselling. As a method of analyzing interpersonal behavior it is widely used in marriage counselling.

Developed as a model by Eric Berne, Transactional Analysis is based on the hypothesis that at any given time we are functioning at either the parent (P), adult (A), or child (C) ego state level. The "parent" level is viewed as the nurturing, correcting aspect of human response. The "child" level represents the carefree, irresponsible, uninhibited level. The "adult" ego state corresponds with the responsible, rational, reasonable level of response.

Using these concepts, any conversation or social interaction can be identified in terms of these three levels. The P-A-C formula is used not only to analyze and interpret communications, but to explain crossed communications which produce misunderstandings and conflict. Communications may be "complementary" or "crossed," "simple" or "ulterior" transactions. Complementary transactions produce agreement and understanding. Crossed transactions usually occur when the participants are operating from different ego states. Simple transactions are communications at the verbal, conscious level. Ulterior transactions are those where the verbal communications have other motivational implications.

The P-A-C formula is also used to identify the unconscious elements and influences from the past on present responses—i.e., to identify irrational elements such as prejudice, internalized parental expectations, and childhood ways of responding. These unconscious elements are described as the "archaic" child or parent, and are seen as "contaminating" or complicating responses to present events and relationships. The archaic parent is made up of attitudes received as a child, primarily of a controlling, manipulative nature. The archaic child is dependent and immature.

The P-A-C formula is an easily understood concept. It can be used to compare the neurotic, psychotic, and sociopathic syndromes in terms easily grasped by the layman.

The concepts are used not only to enable diagnosis and recognition of problem responses, but also in therapy. A growing body of literature traces its practical applications. Though originating in a Freudian psychological approach, it is not necessarily antithetical to the Christian understanding of human nature, in that it sees man rooted in a basic "not O.K." feeling and in need of "okayness."

It is exactly at this point, however, that the sub-Christian, and therefore dangerous, nature of TA is seen. For the "okayness" sought and provided is entirely humanistic and horizontal. There are no conceptual structures for handling sin and guilt or even for their recognition. The real root of dislocated interpersonal relationships is not misunderstanding (as important as that is), but sin. There can be no true "okayness" which ignores God, His forgiveness, and the vertical dimension. To foster an illusion of "okayness" when the spiritual need is not only untouched but ignored, is to perpetrate a deceptive panacea and imperil eternal destiny.

See HUMANISM, HOLINESS, GUILT, GROW (GROWTH), CARNALITY AND HUMANITY, SIN.

For Further Reading: Berne, *Games People Play;* Harris, *I'm O.K., You're O.K.;* Reuter, *Who Says I'm O.K.?*

JAMES M. RIDGWAY

TRANSGRESSION. See SIN.

TRANSCENDENCE. Transcendence is affirmed of God by theists. It is God's primacy over, but also

His wholly otherness from, the universe which He has created. The transcendence of God rules out any form of pantheism, but may be viewed as complementary to immanence.

To be unsure about the transcendence of God is to be unsure about the character of God. With no absolute basis of judgment, human behavior is beyond condemnation, a notion clearly perceived by Ralph Waldo Emerson who developed a philosophy of religion which saw man as essentially good. The divine transcendence means that above man and all earthly affairs is an independent Creator, Preserver, Observer, Law-giver, and Judge. Man is dependent on this God for his very being, and every action is subject to God's scrutiny and evaluation. Because God is transcendent He is free to act upon and within His creation without being assimilated by it or subjugated to it.

The transcendence of God is thus positively related to existence and character. For it is the majesty of His power which moves us to declare as did the Psalmist: "The heavens declare the glory of God; and the firmament sheweth his handywork. Day unto day uttereth speech, and night unto night sheweth knowledge" (Ps. 19:1-2).

See THEISM, IMMANENCE, ATTRIBUTES (DIVINE).

For Further Reading: Berkhof, *Systematic Theology,* 61; DeWolf, *A Theology of the Living Church,* 117-23; Wiley, *CT,* 1:223, 279, 284-89. MERNE A. HARRIS

TRANSCENDENTAL MEDITATION. Transcendental Meditation (TM), also known as the Science of Creative Intelligence (SCI), is a movement founded by Maharishi Mahesh Yogi, whose claim is that TM brings relaxation and creative thinking. While claiming to be neither a religion nor a philosophy, but a science, it is root and branch a part of Hinduism. Its founder was born Mahesh Brasad Warma in 1918 in India. Upon completing his B.A. in physics at Allabad University, he became a disciple of His Divinity Swami Brahamanda Saraswati, popularly known as Guru Dev (Divine Leader), who commissioned him to find a simplified form of meditation and spread his master's teaching to the West.

In 1959 he arrived in California with his meditative technique, founded the Spiritual Regeneration Movement, and gained followers in the entertainment world. When in the late 60s the movement declined, a secular image was developed. Now coordinated under the World Plan Executive Council (WPEC), it presents a scientific image through such peer groups as Student International Meditation Society (SIMS), American Foundation for the Science of Creative Intelligence (AFSCI) for those in business, and International Meditation Society (IMS) for the general public.

While TM's appeal is that it is a science for increasing relaxation and mental productivity, it actually is an expression of Vedantic Hinduism. The meditator is inducted into this TM with a prayer in Sanskrit to the various Hindu gods, including a succession of grand masters, now elevated to deity, by the presentation of offerings of fresh flowers, fresh fruit, and a clean white handkerchief, and by the bestowment of a *mantra.* This supposedly neutral sound, repeated as the vehicle of meditation, is frequently the name of a Hindu god.

See CULTS, OCCULT (OCCULTISM), ORTHODOXY, MEDITATION.

For Further Reading: Boa, *Cults, World Religions, and You,* 156-66; Ellwood, *Religious and Spiritual Groups in Modern North America,* 231-35; Means, *The Mystical Maze,* 133-46; Maharishi Mahesh Yogi, *Transcendental Meditation,* formerly titled: *The Science of Being and the Art of Living;* Lewis, *What Everyone Should Know About Transcendental Meditation.* DAVID L. CUBIE

TRANSFIGURATION. All three of the Synoptics record the "transfiguration" of Jesus on a mountain and in the presence of Peter, James, and John (Matt. 17:2; Mark 9:2; Luke 9:28-36). There He "took on the form of his heavenly glory" (Arndt, Gingrich).

The early tradition of the Church identified Mount Tabor as the Mount of Transfiguration, but many scholars today consider Mount Hermon, much higher and nearer to where Jesus was at that time according to the account, to be a more likely possibility. Luke tells us that Jesus took the three disciples there to pray. In the presence of His disciples, the body of Jesus was changed into the splendor of His preexistent glory, with His clothing and even His face (cf. Matthew) taking on a brightness far surpassing any earthly glow (see Mark 9:3, NASB). Then Moses and Elijah (Mark reverses this order) appeared and talked with Jesus, which Luke explains was a discussion concerning His soon-coming exodus.

Moses and Elijah are usually viewed as simply representing the law and the prophets of the OT. Yet their presence appears to be more an "attendance" on Jesus, and some have even suggested they had come to salute their successor. A further reason for their coming could be that Elijah was identified as the "forerunner" prophet (cf. Mal. 4:5) and was thus making an eschatological appearance.

As on so many occasions, Peter totally misunderstood the significance of what was happening. His suggestion that "tabernacles" be built for Jesus and His two guests suggests a *finality* of mission rather than the *preparation* that it was. Then a cloud overshadowed them, concealing from the disciples the three who were conversing. But the cloud, often seen in the OT as the tabernacle of God, proved to be a vehicle of divine self-revelation as well as self-veiling (cf. Cranfield, *The Gospel According to St. Mark*). From it God spoke: "This is My beloved Son, listen to Him!" (Mark 9:7, NASB). Here is the same basic language given to Jesus (Luke and Mark) and to those in attendance (Matthew) at His baptism.

As might be expected, the three disciples were terrified, but the touch of Jesus (Matthew) brought them assurance. He then instructed them to keep secret what they had experienced.

The event is similar to the language of theophany in the OT. Matthew clearly identifies their experience as a vision (17:9, the Greek term being *horama*). Mark's statement that "all at once they looked around . . ." (9:8, NASB) suggests the actions of people recovering from a vision.

Of greatest importance is the significance of the event. For whose benefit did it occur? Was it only for the disciples? Although we shall see that this was undoubtedly the primary purpose, it also ministered to Jesus. Shortly before, He had received human confirmation of His messianic mission at Caesarea Philippi. Could it not be that, at least in part, the mission of Moses and Elijah was to bring to Jesus assurance from another world as He faced the Cross? They did discuss His exodus! Jesus was human, and the Cross was a terrifying and ugly prospect.

The context is important for understanding the message of the Transfiguration. In all three accounts, the experience follows closely the Great Confession. Jesus' first prediction of His passion on that occasion brought a scandalous response from Peter. Significantly, Jesus warned that whoever is "ashamed of me and of my words" (Mark 8:38; Luke 9:26; cf. Matt. 16:27) would one day face Him as an eschatological judge. But He had encouraging words for those who listened to His words. "And He was saying to them, 'Truly I say to you, there are some of those who are standing here who shall not taste of death until they see the kingdom of God after it has come with power'" (Mark 9:1, NASB).

In the days of the Early Church, this most difficult promise of Jesus was seen fulfilled in the Transfiguration. Peter, James, and John were "some of those . . . standing here," and what they experienced could well be understood as seeing the kingdom of God. This is a choice example of "proleptic revelation." In the Transfiguration the disciples *saw* (although they did not then understand) in anticipation, or prefigurement, the coming Resurrection. Even further, the Resurrection would be seen as a preview of the Parousia. Thus Cranfield says that "both the Resurrection and the Parousia may be said to have been proleptically present in the Transfiguration" (288).

Such an interpretation gives the fullest possible significance to the Father's words: "Listen to Him!" They sound a solemn warning to those who reject or ignore the message of Jesus, while at the same time they bring the strongest assurance to those who believe. As Jesus faced the climax of His humiliation, for a brief moment the veil was drawn and we see Him in all His glory—transfigured.

See CHRIST, THEOPHANY, KINGDOM OF GOD.

For Further Reading: Lane, "Mark," *New International Commentary;* Cranfield, "Mark," *The Cambridge Greek Testament Commentary;* Tasker, "Matthew," *Tyndale Bible Commentary;* Ramsay, *The Glory of God and the Transfiguration of Christ.* RICHARD E. HOWARD

TRANSIGNIFICATION. This is the view that in the Eucharist there is a transformation in what the bread and wine signify—so that they come to signify the body and blood of Christ. It is a recent variation in the Roman Catholic theory of transubstantiation. Pope Paul VI officially opposed the variant view and disallowed its being taught by Roman Catholic scholars. It was only to be expected that the pope would oppose the teaching, because it was a basic divergence from their official view: that the substance of the elements is transformed into the actual body and blood of Christ.

See TRANSUBSTANTIATION, IMPANATION, CONSUBSTANTIATION. J. KENNETH GRIDER

TRANSMIGRATION OF SOULS. See REINCARNATION.

TRANSUBSTANTIATION. Transubstantiation is the Roman Catholic doctrine that the bread and wine of the Eucharist become the actual body of Christ when they are blessed by the words of the priest: "This is my body and my blood." This teaching leans heavily on Aristotelian and medieval scholastic conceptions and would be impossible to state in terms of any modern metaphysics.

The word *transubstantiation* is a compound of two Latin particles (*trans* = "across" and *substan-*

tia = "substance") and suggests that the invisible substance or essence of the bread becomes the essence of the body of Christ and the substance of the juice or wine becomes the essence of Christ's blood. The "essential substance," not visible to the eye, is to be contrasted to the unchanged "accidental properties," visible to the five senses, such as color, taste, and smell. Although the "accidents" remain the same, the miracle of this transference takes place at the moment of blessing by the priest.

The Protestant church has never accepted this teaching. Indeed the chief divisions of the 16th century were over the interpretation of the Lord's Supper.

There are three dominant views among Protestants regarding the Lord's Supper. Martin Luther, closest to the Roman position, taught "consubstantiation" (*con* meaning "with"), the reality of Christ's body and blood is in the elements "like light is in your eye." John Calvin taught a spiritual presence which was received or known only by the elect. Ulrich Zwingli, the Swiss Reformer, taught a symbolic presence in which the sacrament is barely more than a mental remembrance, a picturesque way of recalling Calvary.

Most Wesleyan theologians have held to a position closer to Calvin, with the stipulation that the spiritual blessing is not reserved for only a few.

See CONSUBSTANTIATION, SACRAMENTS, SACRAMENTARIANISM, HOLY COMMUNION, EUCHARIST, REALISM IN THEOLOGY.

For Further Reading: Parris, *John Wesley's Doctrine of the Sacraments,* 62-96; Wiley, *CT,* 3:138-210; Lawson, *Comprehensive Handbook of Christian Doctrine,* 179-81.

JOHN A. KNIGHT

TRIBULATION. The concept of tribulation is a prominent doctrine in the NT and in some quarters today. It practically becomes a test for one's orthodoxy. The word for "tribulation" occurs no less than 19 times.

According to the NT, the Christian can hope for nothing in this world except tribulation. Indeed, the basic summons of Jesus to follow Him means to take up one's cross in discipleship (Mark 8:34; 10:21). This is often interpreted as carrying burdens, but a cross is not burden; it was an instrument of death. When a man follows Jesus, he can expect nothing but tribulation which leads to death. When the seed of the kingdom of God is sown in the ground, tribulation may come upon hearers who have received the word only superficially. This is the message of the seeds falling among thorns. Weeds spring up and choke the word (Matt. 13:21). In John Jesus said, "'In the world you have tribulation; but be of good cheer, I have overcome the world'" (John 16:33, RSV). Luke wrote Paul's reminder that "through many tribulations we must enter the kingdom of God" (Acts 14:22, RSV).

Paul constantly suffered tribulations, but he gloried in them because only by experiencing them could he complete his apostolic mission (2 Cor. 7:4; Eph. 3:13). Addressing the seven churches in Asia, John speaks of himself: "Your brother, and companion in tribulation" (Rev. 1:9). Believers are to react in such a way that they glory in tribulation (Rom. 5:3), and therefore they can be patient in tribulation (12:12).

The NT teaches that at the end of the age there will occur a time of great tribulation. "For then there will be great tribulation, such as has not been from the beginning of the world until now, no, and never will be. And if those days had not been shortened, no human being would be saved; but for the sake of the elect those days will be shortened" (Matt. 24:21-22, RSV). In other words, the persecution which will come at the end of the age in the Great Tribulation will be qualitatively no different from what the Church has to expect from the world throughout her history. The only difference will be the intensity of the tribulation, not its method.

This is spelled out in the Revelation. The beast (Antichrist) will be "allowed to make war on the saints and to conquer them" (Rev. 13:7, RSV). But in a later vision, John sees a victorious Church standing before the throne of God. We are told that these are the people who had conquered the beast and its image. Here is a superficial contradiction: The beast conquers the saints, but the saints conquer the beast. What can this mean? The point is that the martyrdom of the saints is their victory. The beast tries to compel them to worship him. When they refuse, they are martyred. But their martyrdom is proof of their loyalty to Christ. Luke records a similar saying of Jesus: "Some of you they will put to death . . . But not a hair of your head will perish" (Luke 21:16, 18; cf. Rev. 14:9-13).

The revelation above shows us that the time of Great Tribulation will also be a time of the outpouring of God's wrath. But at the threshold of that time, John sees 144,000 who are sealed in their foreheads that they may not suffer the wrath of God. These afflictions are not human, but the outpouring of the wrath of God upon the beast and his worshippers (16:2). The Church will not suffer the wrath of God.

See RAPTURE, SECOND COMING OF CHRIST, REVELATION (BOOK OF).

For Further Reading: Smith, *Prophecy—What Lies Ahead?* 27-31; Ludwigson, *A Survey of Bible Prophecy,* 184-87. GEORGE ELDON LADD

TRICHOTOMY. This, defined as division into three parts, contrasts with dichotomy, division into two parts, as a theory of the correct analysis of the human being. Each considers man to consist of a material part, the body, and an immaterial part or parts. Both accept the reality of soul or spirit. The essential question between them is whether soul and spirit are one or two, identical or different.

Trichotomy is most often based on "spirit and soul and body," as used in 1 Thess. 5:23. Dichotomists question whether that verse is an analytical statement of man's being, or whether it is not rather a descriptive statement meaning the whole human being, like Mark 12:30, which names four parts without requiring a fourfold division of man. Verses mentioning only a twofold division include Gen. 2:7; Eccles. 12:7; Matt. 10:28; and 1 Cor. 7:34. Trichotomists, differentiating between soul and spirit, have the problem of deciding which of these is the locus of mind, or consciousness.

Both trichotomy and dichotomy are to be contrasted with those materialistic, naturalistic theories which claim that all mental life, spirit, soul, and similar concepts are but names for phenomena inherent in the highly developed matter of complex human brain cells, and have no existence apart from matter.

See MAN, HUMAN NATURE, DICHOTOMY.

For Further Reading: Cross, *An Introduction to Psychology: An Evangelical Approach,* 15; Symposium, *What, Then, Is Man?* 319. PHILIP S. CLAPP

TRINITY, THE HOLY. This is the audacious Christian understanding that God consists of three Persons, Father, Son, and Holy Spirit, who share a common nature or essence. It is the understanding that God is tripersonal, but, at the same time, one in substance or nature or kind of being. There are three *Hims,* but the three are one in a most fundamental, elemental way.

This means that while we are talking about three Persons, three Thous, we are not talking about three Gods (Tritheism)—but only one. In fact, it might be that, since the three are one, there is an intensification of the oneness, the unity, that would not obtain if there were not three who make the one. This is not the three of arithmetic, where you have three of, perhaps, the same kind. It is the kind of oneness that obtains in an organism—when one organism is characterized by three systems (and more): respiration, circulation, and reproduction.

The deistic Thomas Jefferson deprecated the doctrine of the Trinity as an "incomprehensible jargon." Matthew Arnold referred to it as "the fairytale of the three Lord Shaftesburys." It has been called "an intellectual elixir." Nonetheless, this is our confidence as Christians: that God is three-in-one, one-in-three.

The doctrine is a revealed mystery and cannot be comprehended merely with our natural capacities. In part, the fact that we could not figure it out with our natural faculties is because we have no analogies of it in the natural world. No three human persons are structurally one so that there is a full interpenetration of the three. And, while an individual person is three in the matters of intellect, feeling, and will, such an individual is not three at the level of personhood. Further, while there are a few "rough" analogies in nature, such as water, which exists in three states (liquid, steam, and ice), the analogy does not apply very aptly. Likewise, the analogy of the family does not. A father, a son, and a mother (= the Holy Spirit) are not one in the structural way that the three Persons of the Trinity are.

Of course, Scripture does not in any one passage describe God as three Persons in one nature or substance. First John 5:7 pretty nearly does this, but that passage, found almost exclusively in the KJV, is not in any of the older Greek NT manuscripts. Scripture clearly teaches that there is only one God, and also, it teaches that the Father, the Son, and the Holy Spirit are all Deity.

On the oneness, we read, "The Lord our God, the Lord is one" (Deut. 6:4, NIV). Jesus, addressing the Father in prayer, calls Him "the only true God" (John 17:3). Paul, having referred to the "so-called gods," adds that "yet for us there is but one God, the Father, from whom all things came and for whom we live; and there is but one Lord, Jesus Christ, through whom all things came and through whom we live" (1 Cor. 8:5-6, NIV). Paul also says that there is "one Lord, one faith, one baptism; one God and Father of all, who is over all and through all and in all" (Eph. 4:5-6, NIV).

While the last three passages quoted are the special supports given against the Trinitarian view by Unitarianism's Recovian Catechism, we Christians believe them all, heartily, for we, too, stress that God is one and that the Father is the first-numbered Person of the Trinity. But we incorporate into such passages as those the ones that indicate the threeness of God. One such is in

Matt. 28:19, where we are to baptize "'in the name of the Father and of the Son and of the Holy Spirit'" (NIV). Another is where Paul closes 2 Corinthians with what we often use as a benediction: "May the grace of the Lord Jesus Christ, and the love of God, and the fellowship of the Holy Spirit be with you all" (13:14, NIV). Besides, the three are spoken of at Christ's baptism (e.g., Mark 1), and in John 14—16; Eph. 2:18; 1 Pet. 1:21-22; etc. And the Son is called God in John 1:1 where we read, "In the beginning was the Word, and the Word was with God, and the Word was God." And there is Thomas' post-Resurrection declaration addressed to Jesus, who had appeared to him, "My Lord and my God" (20:28). Christ also seems to be called God in 1 Tim. 3:16 and Heb. 1:8. That the Holy Spirit is God is implied in Heb. 9:14; 1 Pet. 3:18; and 2 Pet. 1:21.

While some have so stressed the deity of Christ as to teach what almost amounts to a "unitarianism of the Son," the Church has always taught that the Father holds a place of priority in the Trinity. All three are of equal eternity, all are fully divine, and all have infinite attributes. Yet, eternally, the Son has been generated from the Father's nature (as light comes from the sun), and not from His will. This is suggested by the *monogenēs* passages as in John 1:18 where Christ is said to be the "only begotten" or the "only born" one. The world was made, created, out of nothing; but the Son was eternally begotten, from the Father's nature.

Somewhat similarly, the Holy Spirit has eternally proceeded. In Eastern Orthodoxy it is understood that the Holy Spirit proceeded eternally only from the Father. They feel that this is supported in John 15:26 where we read, "But when the Comforter is come, whom I will send unto you from the Father, even the Spirit of truth, which proceedeth from the Father."

In the Roman Catholic and Anglican and Protestant West, however, we have followed the Athanasian Creed, which declares, "The Holy Ghost is of the Father and of the Son; neither made, nor created, nor begotten; but proceeding." This double procession of the Holy Spirit (from both the Father and the Son) is probably the teaching of certain NT passages. One is Rom. 8:9, where we read of both "the Spirit of God" and "the Spirit of Christ"—which probably means "who proceeds from God," and "who proceeds from Christ." The Western view is also suggested in 1 Pet. 1:10-11, where "the Spirit of Christ," that is, who proceeds from Christ, is quite evidently a reference to the Holy Spirit and not to Christ, because through the prophets He "testified beforehand the sufferings of Christ."

Opposers of the doctrine of the Trinity have appeared, as the centuries have passed. Sabellius, of the early third century, taught that the three are successive ways in which the unipersonal God has revealed himself. The fourth-century Arius taught that Christ is neither divine nor human (instead of both of these); and that the Holy Spirit is still farther from deity than Christ is. Faustus Socinus (1539-1604) was of course anti-Trinitarian and fathered the Unitarians—who, now amalgamated with the Universalists, are among the impugners of this doctrine. Protestant modernists in general have denied the Trinity as not suiting their rationalism, opposing the deity of Christ and the personality of the Holy Spirit. One of the rather recent oppositions to the Trinity came from Union (N.Y.) Seminary's Cyril Richardson, who preferred to say that the three are "symbols" and not persons (see his *Doctrine of the Trinity,* 14-15, 98, 111).

This doctrine, taught clearly by implication in Scripture, and spelled out in so many Christian creeds and confessions, which means that God is not an eternal solitary but an Eternal Society, might be the one most basic of all the Christian beliefs. Charles Lowry calls it "at once the ultimate and the supreme glory of the Christian faith" (*The Trinity and Christian Devotion,* xl).

See GOD, CHRIST, HOLY SPIRIT, ECONOMIC TRINITY, ESSENTIAL TRINITY, ETERNAL GENERATION, ETERNALLY BEGOTTEN, SABELLIANISM, UNITARIANISM.

For Further Reading: Grider, "The Trinity," *Basic Christian Doctrines,* ed. Henry; Lowry, *The Trinity and Christian Devotion;* Wiley, *CT,* 1:394-440.

J. KENNETH GRIDER

TRITHEISM. See TRINITY, THE HOLY.

TRUST. See FAITH.

TRUTH. The primary meaning of the Greek word *alētheia* (truth) is openness. It thus refers to what is not concealed. In Hebrew the primary idea is that which sustains. Truth implies steadfastness. It is that which does not fail or disappoint one's expectations.

Truth or "the true" is therefore (1) what is real as opposed to what is fictitious or imaginary; (2) what completely comes up to its idea or what it purports to be; (3) what in reality corresponds to the manifestation; (4) what can be depended upon, which does not fail or change or disappoint (Hodge, *Systematic Theology,* 1:436).

The quest for truth is universal. Philosophy,

science, and religion are all committed to the search. Philosophy seeks the truth about being, science the truth about phenomena, religion the truth about God and ultimate meanings. Each science brings to the quest its own methods and tools.

The truth of discrete parts is partial; to be complete it must be seen in relation to every other part. Science, therefore, without philosophy and religion, can never arrive at truth, for science alone can never get beyond facts.

Furthermore, truth of necessity must be harmonious. The truths in one branch of knowledge cannot be in ultimate contradiction to the truths in other branches of knowledge.

This is the case because absolute truth is God, and truth apprehended is the knowledge of God. He is both the Key and the Core of truth, and all lesser truths relate to Him and flow from Him. In scriptural terms Christ is the Revelation of the truth in God (John 14:6-9). Jesus Christ, being God incarnate, is not only the true Way to God but also the true Representative, Image, character, and quality of God. Likewise the Holy Spirit is the Spirit of truth, who communicates truth, who maintains the truth in believers, who guides believers in the truth, and who hates and punishes lies and falsehoods. This plainly implies that in God there is no fallacy, deception, or perverseness (John 16:12-13).

Since man is the creation of God, all valid knowledge of truth and right must come from Him. Whether knowledge comes from God immediately or ultimately is of secondary importance (Burrows, *An Outline of Biblical Theology,* 40-42).

Truth as one of the moral attributes of God may be resolved into veracity and fidelity. Thus the truth of God refers also to His perfect and undeviating truthfulness in all His communications to mankind, whether in words or in deeds or mode. His communications are in exact accord with the real nature of things (John 17:17). There is utmost sincerity in all His declarations. Fidelity in God especially respects His promises and is the guarantee of their fulfillment.

Since God is the Source of all truth, it follows that He is true in His revelation and true in His promises. He keeps His promises and is ever faithful to His covenant people. God has made available to finite minds such truth about himself as is needed for redemption, although finite minds approach the truth and the perfections of God only by degrees. Man's incomplete systems of thought, thus, can never pass beyond probabilities.

God is perfect truth because His nature is pure love and forms the character of God. Men become true as their character becomes good, for truth in the heart is a quality of personal character which coincides with the law of love (Carnell, *A Philosophy of the Christian Religion,* 450-53).

See GOD, METAPHYSICS, PROPOSITIONAL THEOLOGY, HEART PURITY, REALITY THERAPY, THEISTIC PROOFS, FIDELITY, INTEGRITY.

For Further Reading: Carnell, *The Case for Orthodox Theology,* 27, 87-88; Henry, *Basic Christian Doctrines,* 31; Purkiser, ed., *Exploring Our Christian Faith,* 34-36; Wiley and Culbertson, *Introduction to Christian Theology,* 108.

WAYNE E. CALDWELL

TYPE, TYPOLOGY. A type is a person, event, or institution in the OT which foreshadows a corresponding person, event, or institution in the NT. Typology is the hermeneutical principle which recognizes the presence of types and antitypes in the Bible and establishes guidelines for identifying them and for understanding the relationship of the type in its original historical context to its more complete fulfillment in the development of God's eternal purposes.

The use of typology in the study of the Bible assumes the unity of the Old and New Testaments which makes typology possible: viz., that "the New is in the Old concealed; the Old is in the New revealed." It likewise assumes the presence of predictive prophecy in Scripture and the progression of revelation. This necessitates a linear view of history and a supernaturalism which allows for divine irruptions into the historical order of human experience.

Typology differs from allegory in that allegory attempts to exegete a spiritual meaning from a historical account, often without due regard for historical meaning or even historicity. Typology finds in the historical account that which prefigures a later historical development. The relationship between type and antitype is that of pattern and reality, promise and fulfillment, anticipation and completion.

There are certain restrictions to the use of typology. Some scholars would go as far as to disallow any typology other than that which is indicated in the NT. While this establishes safeguards against abuse, it wrongly insists that the NT has exhausted all correspondences between the Testaments. Types should be restricted to those instances where there is historical correspondence or, as Bernard Ramm insists, there is "a genuine resemblance in form or idea" (*Protestant Biblical Interpretation,* 228). Furthermore, the use of typology should be limited to historical analogies and not extended to matters of minute detail. As in the case of the parable, the central truth must be grasped without expecting each detail to bear spiritual fruit.

There are several dangers in the use of typological interpretation. First, the history of the church verifies the problem of unrestrained imagination. Doctrinal heresies and aberrant theories have resulted from "supposed" OT types. Second, the OT may cease to be valued as the objective revelation which God gave to Israel and be spiritualized into a religious book of signs and symbols. Even though the OT is incomplete in itself, it remains as the historical record of God's progressive preparation of His people for the fullness of times when the Word would become flesh. Third, the historicity of scriptural accounts is undercut when there is little concern for the historical context as though that were secondary or unimportant. Bultmann's demythologization of the NT exemplifies such an unconcern for history.

The value of a typological interpretation of the OT is that it recognizes the historical continuity of revelation and God's redemptive program. It immeasurably enriches and vivifies our understanding of basic biblical motifs. It takes seriously Jesus' declaration that the OT bears witness to Him (John 5:39) and finds an embryonic Christology in the Hebrew Scriptures that anticipates the birth of the Babe of Bethlehem.

See ALLEGORY, ALLEGORICAL INTERPRETATION, HERMENEUTICS, PARABLES, PROGRESSIVE REVELATION, BIBLE: OLD AND NEW TESTAMENTS.

For Further Reading: Fairbairn, *The Typology of Scripture;* Westermann, ed., *Essays on Old Testament Hermeneutics;* Harrison, *Introduction to the Old Testament,* 443-61; Ramm, *Protestant Biblical Interpretation,* 215-40; Laurin, "Typological Interpretations of the Old Testament," *Hermeneutics,* Ramm et al., 118-29; Wood, *Pentecostal Grace.*

WILLIAM B. COKER

U

ULTIMATE CONCERN. Ultimate concern is one of the central concepts in the theological system of the Protestant theologian Paul Tillich. It forms an important link in a series of words the meaning of which constitute the highly integrated fabric of his theology. Because of the tight integration of his system one can choose any of his major terms as an introduction to his thought.

As is true of most of his key concepts, Tillich gives *ultimate concern* differing but consistent shades of meaning, depending on whether he is speaking specifically to the Christian community for whom the word "God" already has a markedly Christological content, or whether he is speaking as a Christian apologist to those of other religions, or to a secular philosophy or political ideology for which the term "God" may not play a significant role.

Man is finite, contingent, and he is deeply aware of this. He is concerned about his finitude and expresses this concern by his efforts to guarantee his finitude against the threats to it that appear in many forms, death being the ultimate threat. Man's natural efforts to keep from losing himself to these threats result in the creation of and participation in political, national, cultural, domestic, moral, and personal forms. But all of these are preliminary concerns, for they are also finite. They too are subject to erosion.

It is precisely the preliminary nature of these concerns which shows that they cannot finally be of ultimate significance to man. Man's principal error, which Tillich calls sin, is that he tends to treat preliminary concerns as though they were ultimate, unconditional, nonfinite. He tends to elevate them to a place of ultimacy. But time and the events of history have a way of "shaking these foundations" and exposing them for what they are. Shaken, man is driven beyond preliminary concerns to what concerns him ultimately, to the truly Unconditioned. As preliminary concerns reveal their finitude, he is driven toward the God who is not one thing among others, but the Creator God, the Giver of all life. God is Being itself. He does not exist as things exist; rather, *He is.*

Tillich believed that Jesus' summary of the law in Matt. 22:37-39 is the principal biblical statement of the central meaning of ultimate concern. He believed that Heb. 12:25-29 accurately describes the way we are led to the unshakable foundation (Christ) as preliminary concerns reveal their finitude.

Tillich believes that all people are concerned

about that which concerns them ultimately, even though they may not recognize God as the Object and Fulfillment of that quest. He believed this to be the sure testimony in all people. The reality of God cannot finally be denied by anyone. Tillich used this concept as an apologetic device for reaching moderns for whom the term "God" has lost its meaning.

All people give some form of expression to the belief that reality is ultimately meaningful, that finite being is anchored in some ultimate, noncontingent reality. This state of being ultimately concerned, Tillich says, is faith, the fulfillment of which is faith in God's Christ, the bringer of the New Reality.

See RELIGION, RELIGIOUS KNOWLEDGE, FAITH, IDOL (IDOLATRY), COSMOLOGY, CHRISTIANITY.

For Further Reading: Magee, *Religion and Modern Man*, 22 ff, 25-26; Hughes, ed., *Creative Minds in Contemporary Theology*, 451-79; McKelway, *The Systematic Theology of Paul Tillich*.

ALBERT L. TRUESDALE, JR.

UNBELIEF. This is the moral resistance to, and lack of confidence in, the commands and promises of God, which arises from an evil heart (Heb. 3:12). It is a refusal to trust that God's commands are valid and that what He has promised He is able to perform. So unbelief is beyond mere doubt and questioning as to the *how* and *why* of divine ordinances. The refusal to believe or trust renders one culpable in the eyes of biblical writers.

Unbelief is thus both an intellectual and moral attitude toward God, truth, and reality. It is a refusal of the volitional action which faith calls for.

In the NT the two common terms for *unbelief* are *apeitheia*, "disobedience, and unpersuadedness" (Rom. 11:30, 32; Heb. 4:6, 11), and *apistia*, "distrust, or absence of faith." The noun, *apeitheia*, really indicates "obstinate opposition to the divine will." The verb, *apeitheō*, specifies "the refusal or withholding of belief" (John 3:36; Heb. 3:18; 1 Pet. 2:7-8; 4:17). The adjective, *apeitheis*, describes one who is "unpersuasible, uncompliant, and contumacious" (Rom. 1:30; 2 Tim. 3:2; Titus 3:3). The verb, *apisteō*, means "to betray a trust, to entertain no belief" (Rom. 3:3; Luke 24:11, 41; Mark 16:11, 16; 2 Tim. 2:13). Its noun, *apistia*, means the "lack of faith and trust" (Mark 6:6; Rom. 4:20; 11:20, 23; Heb. 3:19). And its adjective, *apistos*, describes one who is "without faith or trust in God, and is thus unbelieving and incredulous" (Matt. 17:17; [cf. Mark 9:19; Luke 9:41]; Luke 12:46; John 20:27; 1 Cor. 6:6; 7:12-14; 2 Cor. 4:4; Rev. 21:8).

Since *unbelief* is an absence of the will to believe, it exerts a determinative influence on conduct. He who refuses the implications of faith likewise denies the contents of faith. To trust or put confidence in a person or a proposition involves and calls for a commitment thereto. This the unbeliever is unwilling to do. Hence unbelief is the attitude of the irreligious person.

It was William James who contended for man's right to adopt a believing attitude in religious matters in spite of the fact that his merely logical intellect may not have been compelled. He defended to his students the lawfulness of voluntarily adopted faith. He insisted that "the question of having moral beliefs at all or not having them is decided by our will." He said, "If your heart does not *want* a world of moral reality, your head will assuredly never make you believe in one." Furthermore, he declares, "We have the right to believe at our own risk any hypothesis that is live enough to tempt our will." In the final analysis he is sure that "belief is measured by action," hence the one who believes is unlike the person he would be in unbelief.

It has been rightly said: A man has the right to believe as he *must* in order to live as he *ought*. Hence faith is a proper and scriptural attitude toward God, and *unbelief* is its opposite.

See FAITH, BELIEF, OBEDIENCE, SKEPTICISM.

For Further Reading: Burton, "Word Study XVI," *Pistis* and *Pisteuō*, *Commentary on Galatians* (ICC); James, "The Will to Believe," *Essays in Pragmatism*, 88-109.

ROSS E. PRICE

UNBLAMABLE. See BLAME, BLAMELESS.

UNCONDITIONAL ELECTION. See ELECT, ELECTION.

UNCTION. See ANOINTING.

UNDERSTANDING. See WISDOM.

UNIFICATION CHURCH. The Unification Church or United Family is a cult composed of some 2 million members worldwide, including 1 million in South Korea, 50,000 in Japan, and 10,000 in the United States, whose goal is the reconstitution of the human race by way of the third Adam, who by implication is Sun Myung Moon, the founder. Moon was born on January 6, 1920, in what is now North Korea, to Presbyterian parents. He claims that at 16 he had a vision in which Jesus commanded him to finish the work of redemption. He studied electrical engineering in Japan. Between 1944 and 1948 he evangelized in North and South Korea and was excommunicated by the Presbyterians. He was imprisoned by the Communists, but escaped in 1950. In 1954, he founded the Holy Spirit Association for World Christianity and was divorced by his wife of 10 years. In 1958, he established the Divine Principle and in 1960 married Hak Ja Hon.

Moon's ideas combine the Korean-Chinese philosophy of Ying and Yang, Korean shamanism (spiritualism), with Christian eschatology and spiritual gifts. God, instead of being Trinity, is both male and female. Jesus is not God, but the Second Adam who failed His mission because He did not marry and have children. Christians are Jesus' spiritual offspring by way of the Holy Spirit, His heavenly Bride. Redemption must be completed physically through marriage because the first sins were sexual; Lucifer's spiritual seduction of Eve and Eve's physical seduction of Adam.

According to Moon, on the day he married Hak Ja Hon "the Heavenly Son came to the earth, restored the base, and welcomed the first Bride of heaven." As a result Moon is greater than Jesus, having restored "the spiritual as well as the physical" ("The Significance of July 1st, 1973," *Master Speaks*, 381, 7-1-73, 3).

See CHRIST, CHRISTIANITY, CULTS, FALSE CHRISTS.

For Further Reading: Boa, *Cults, World Religions, and You*, 164-77; Ellwood, *Religious and Spiritual Groups in Modern America*, 291-96; Sparks, *The Mind Benders: A Look at Current Cults*, 121-53; Kim, *Unification Theology and Christian Thought*. DAVID L. CUBIE

UNION WITH GOD. See MYSTICISM.

UNITARIANISM. This is self-described as "a free faith for the modern mind"; "a faith that will help you develop the religion that is within you . . . [not] . . . the ready-made 'religion of a church.'" While committed to "staunch noncreedalism," its core concept is of a God with single rather than Trinitarian personality or being. Clustering about this concept are certain key emphases: a nondogmatic approach to religion so that the personal beliefs of its clergy and laity run the gamut of liberalism; a commitment to humanism with a theistic tinge—"salvation by character"; tolerance toward other religions; exaltation of reason; advocacy of religious and civil liberty; eager, uncritical acceptance of science.

They differ sharply whether they should be characterized as Christian. Example: "All of us in the liberal church are basically Christian"; but "Christianity is a religion whose adherents subscribe to an essential core of doctrine which no Unitarian Universalist . . . would accept." Their denials include belief in the Trinity, Jesus as divine, original sin, eternal damnation, virgin birth of Christ, infallibility of the Bible, miracles, and vicarious atonement. They possess no binding statement of belief. Private judgment in matters of faith and morals is supreme.

Unitarians are found in various Protestant pulpits and pews. Those openly committed are to be found mostly in the 1961 merger of Unitarians and Universalists in the Unitarian Universalist Association.

See SOCINIANISM, CHRISTIANITY, TRINITY (THE HOLY), ORTHODOXY, HERESY, UNIVERSALISM.

For Further Reading: Mead, *Handbook of Denominations* (4th ed.), 208-12. LLOYD H. KNOX

UNITY. Unity is to be distinguished from oneness, since oneness may be a fact of experience, while unity is a spiritual and intangible quality of harmony which should inhere in the oneness. While unity is hard to define, its absence in any social unit is easily recognized. The parts of an engine may all be present and share in a common oneness in the sense that they all belong to the same engine; yet if unity is lacking, we say the engine is not performing properly. So in marital relationship, cohabitation creates oneness but does not guarantee unity (Matt. 19:5; 1 Cor. 6:16). Similarly, Christians are one in Christ—they are actually members of the one body—yet they may be emotionally divided.

Therefore unity is a virtue to which Christians are exhorted (Eph. 4:3, 13; Phil. 1:27; 2:2). The prayer of Christ for the unity of believers (John 17:20-22) has been misconstrued by ecumenists to provide authority for calling for a single church and for branding all denominational separateness as sin. But the unity for which Jesus prayed was spiritual, a true oneness with each other based on a true oneness with the Triune God. The context shows that such a oneness finds its reality not in external uniformity or conformity but in personal sanctification. It is holiness which unites; carnality divides (1 Cor. 3:1-3). Changing denominational labels does not change hearts.

The achievement and preservation of unity requires humility, unselfishness, and fervent love. But these are the constituent elements of biblical holiness.

See IMITATION OF CHRIST, SEVEN CARDINAL VIRTUES, MIND OF CHRIST. RICHARD S. TAYLOR

UNIVERSALISM. Universalism claims that no person is excluded finally from God's redemption. Through freedom God will bring all human or heavenly persons into conformity to His will. A third-century scholar, Origen, wrote: "God will 'show the riches of his grace in kindness' (Eph. 2:7): When the greatest sinner . . . will, I know not how, be under treatment from beginning to end in the ensuing age" ("On Prayer," *Library of Christian Classics,* 2:304). The Church considered Origen had speculated beyond scriptural warrant.

In the 16th century Socinus laid the foundation for the doctrine's revival. Against Calvinist doctrines of election and atonement, Socinus argued for God's universal forgiveness because of Jesus' death and resurrection.

Universalism became an organized movement in America about 1800. A leader, Hosea Ballou, asserted that Christ's death conveyed moral, not legal, force over sin. A general conference was established by 1866. Adherents numbered under 100,000 at most. Under various rationalistic influences (and because of inner inconsistencies, its critics charged) the movement lost its Socinian foundation. The movement merged with the Unitarians in 1961 and no longer claims to be a Christian denomination.

"Universalism" should not be confused with "universal salvation," which signifies that Christ died for *all*—that is, every person of every kind in every nation—although any may reject Him. The Quaker, Robert Barclay, used the phrase "the universal and saving light," whereas the Arminian, John Wesley, used the term "prevenient grace" to describe the universal character of salvation. The divine witness antecedent to, or even independent of, outward hearing of the gospel, they asserted, is more than a condemnation for sin. For the faithful it is Christ's saving light.

Scholars such as C. S. Lewis and Charles Williams, while acknowledging God's respect for human freedom (including eternal punishment), urge Christians to yearn for the salvation of all, and warn against limiting the freedom of God who is unwilling that any should perish. Yet God in the Scriptures declares the moral bases of salvation and gives no indication that these will ever be set aside to accommodate the impenitent. The fundamental tenet of universalism, viz., that every heavenly or human person must in the end be saved, is expressly repudiated in the Scriptures.

See UNITARIANISM, SOCINIANISM, PROBATION, ETERNAL PUNISHMENT, IMPENITENCE, FREEDOM.

For Further Reading: Corpus *Dictionary of Western Churches,* 1970; Lewis, *The Great Divorce.*

ARTHUR O. ROBERTS

UNIVERSALS. This has to do with the degree to which concepts are real. Realists, in medieval times, were people who believed that concepts, such as man, or cow, are real—and that individual humans and cows are not actually real. Erigena and Anselm and others taught in this way. At the opposite extreme were the nominalists, such as Roscellinus, who believed that only particulars are real, and that concepts are no more than names that describe look-alike particulars. Two views, on universals, mediated between the extremes of realism and nominalism. One of them is conceptualism, espoused by Peter Abelard. Here, a concept exists, but not prior to particulars, only afterwards. Another of them is moderate realism, held by Thomas Aquinas, who eclectically taught that both concepts and particulars are actually real.

Probably no question was as significant to the Scholastics of the 9th to the 14th centuries as the degree to which universals are real. Interest in the matter waned after Aristotle was received into Christian orthodoxy in the 12th and 13th centuries, during which times such theologians as Albertus Magnus and Thomas Aquinas engaged themselves most especially with amalgamating Aristotle with orthodoxy. But while interest in universals waned at that time, universals still is, and always will be, an important matter for theologians and philosophers to consider.

See REALISM, REALISM AND NOMINALISM, REALISM IN THEOLOGY.

For Further Reading: Suarez, *On Formal and Universal Unity;* Landesman, *The Problem of Universals.*

J. KENNETH GRIDER

UNLIMITED ATONEMENT. See ATONEMENT.

UNPARDONABLE SIN. Much misunderstanding has surrounded the so-called unpardonable sin. The misunderstanding has grown up in part through incorrect interpretations of a few isolated passages of Scripture; in part, too, no doubt, due to an excessive zeal to secure an immediate response to the gospel in evangelistic services.

This sin no doubt consists of a repeated and willful attributing to demons the work of the Holy Spirit. This is what Mark 3:28-30 suggests, where we read, "'All the sins and blasphemies of men will be forgiven them. But whoever blasphemes against the Holy Spirit will never be forgiven; he is guilty of an eternal sin.' He said this because they were saying, 'He has an evil spirit'" (NIV). This sin, of saying an "evil spirit" accomplishes what one knows full well was accomplished by the Holy Spirit, is blasphemy (cf. Matt. 12:31). And it is unpardonable because the person himself sets himself into this kind of stance and will not let God transform his mind and forgive him. It is therefore unpardonable more from man's standpoint than from God's—for we read elsewhere in Scripture that God will graciously forgive anyone at all who asks for pardon (see Hos. 14:4; Eph. 4:32; Luke 7:21; Rom. 8:32; Col. 2:13; Heb. 10:17; Luke 15:11-32).

Some people use Isa. 63:10 to teach that God will refuse to forgive some people, where we read: "Yet they rebelled and grieved his Holy Spirit. So he turned and became their enemy and he himself fought against them" (NIV). Adam Clarke is no doubt correct when he suggests that this turning to become their enemy, on God's part, is a reference to the Last Judgment—when probation is past.

Some people feel that 1 John 5:16 refers to the "unpardonable sin," where we read, "There is a sin that leads to death. I am not saying that he should pray about that" (NIV). This more likely refers to a sin which carries the death penalty in civil law. We are not necessarily to pray that the civil law's penalty will be alleviated, although God might, of course, forgive a person of such.

Since a repeated and knowing attributing to demons what the Holy Spirit does is unpardonable only from man's standpoint instead of God's, the most important thing to remember about the unpardonable sin is that anyone who fears that he has committed it, and is concerned about the matter, hasn't.

See SIN, REPENTANCE, FORGIVENESS, APOSTASY.

For Further Reading: Carter, *The Person and Ministry of the Holy Spirit,* 108-12; Fitch, *The Ministry of the Holy Spirit,* 230-33. J. KENNETH GRIDER

UNRIGHTEOUSNESS. See INIQUITY.

UPRIGHT, UPRIGHTNESS. See RIGHT, RIGHTEOUSNESS.

V

VALUES. These are the established ideals of life, the standards people live by. The study of values—their nature, type, criteria, and status—is referred to as axiology.

One's system of values determines the choices he makes, the things he appreciates and strives for. It guides a person's course of action, and so it determines one's general pattern of behavior.

While it is an empirical fact that all people live by values, there is considerable difference of opinion as to what the basic values for living are. For the Christian, values are not individualistic and subjective. For him the rule or standard for making value judgments is God himself, the highest of all values. The key, therefore, for developing a Christian system of values is found in Jesus' words: "Seek ye first the kingdom of God, and his righteousness" (Matt. 6:33).

This reference to the Gospel suggests that the Bible provides the basis for a doctrine of Christian values. In the OT the Book of Proverbs, for example, gives guidance for discriminating among values. It points out that the way of wisdom in every area of life is found in the fear of the Lord. A NT principle is that persons are always of much greater value than things (Luke 12:6-7; Matt. 6:25-26; 16:26; Mark 8:36-37).

The frequent use of the Greek term *axios* in the NT further suggests a basis for establishing a standard of values. It is usually translated "worthy," "counted worthy," or "worthily." In such passages as Phil. 1:27 and 2 Thess. 1:11, for instance, Paul indicates concern that his readers may in God's sight be living worthy of the gospel to which they have been called. Another passage of this type is Matt. 10:37-38.

Some of the fundamental human values about which the Bible speaks are: bodily health and care, recreation, home and family, education, work, and the trilogy: the beautiful, the good, and the true.

In the light of what the Bible teaches, the Christian assigns value to anything, abstract and concrete, in relation and in proportion to its worth in bringing glory to God and in advancing His kingdom among men. Anything which does not have potential for glorifying God is not to be considered valuable and should, in fact, be disvalued.

Even with this criterion, every Christian may

not have the same arrangement of priorities, for individuals and their circumstances differ. Even an individual's circumstances may vary from time to time, and there may need to be a comparable rearrangement of values. But Christian discipline and stewardship demand that every Christian arrange his priorities in the fear of God. To arrange values in proper relation to each other and to the ultimate Good is difficult. To do it well is a mark of Christian maturity. All through the Christian pilgrimage one should, then, be learning better how to order life's values.

See AXIOLOGY, TRUTH, MATURITY, DISCIPLINE, DISCIPLESHIP, VALUES CLARIFICATION.

For Further Reading: Brightman, *Religious Values;* Purkiser, ed., *Exploring Our Christian Faith,* 461-76.

ARMOR D. PEISKER

VALUES CLARIFICATION. Values clarification is a term used to identify a particular systematic educational approach aimed at developing skills in choosing values and making decisions based upon one's values. The approach was formulated by Louis Raths (1966) and is concerned with the *process* of valuing rather than the *content* of values.

The values clarification approach utilizes strategies designed to help the student learn to: (1) choose his values freely; (2) choose his values from alternatives; (3) choose his values after consideration of the consequences of the alternatives; (4) prize and cherish his values; (5) publicly affirm his values; (6) act upon his values; and (7) act upon his values consistently. Many strategies have been developed, utilizing interviews designed to draw out values, values games, hypothetical values dilemmas, creative writing on personal values, personal goals inventories, ordering various lists according to priorities, etc.

While many of the suggested strategies can be useful in helping individuals to become aware of their values as well as alternatives, the weakness of the system is found in its root of humanism. While purporting to be not concerned with the content of values, the system itself is a statement of humanistic values and can be a subtle tool in promoting those values. The system begins with man and relativity and rises no further. Values clarification encourages children (who have the least amount of experience upon which to base their judgments) to choose their values without any reference to values and attitudes that have stood the test of time, let alone to God and revealed truth. The values clarification approach presupposes that man himself (even the juvenile) is capable not only of choosing his values, but that it is proper to create one's values strictly with reference to oneself.

See VALUES, AXIOLOGY, HUMANISM, STEWARDSHIP.

For Further Reading: Simon, Howe, and Kirschenbaum, *Values Clarification;* Simpson, *Becoming Aware of Values;* Simon and Clark, *Beginning Values Clarification;* Raths, Harmin, and Simon, *Values and Teaching.*

GLENN R. BORING

VEIL. This term is frequently used in the Bible as a reference to an article of clothing used to wrap, cover, or disguise an individual (Gen. 24:65; 38:14; Exod. 34:33). More significantly, a veil, or curtain, was used in the Tabernacle and later in the Temple to "separate . . . the holy place from the most holy" (26:33, RSV). This sacred veil, made according to divine instructions of blue, purple, and scarlet linen, screened from view the ark of the testimony and the mercy seat contained in the most holy place (vv. 31-36). The glory of God was so awesome and holy that the veil was necessary because men could not stand before His unveiled presence and live (33:20).

The holy of holies, behind the veil, was entered only once each year by the high priest who presented an offering of blood for his own sin and for the sins of the people. The veil was also used to wrap the ark of testimony when the Tabernacle was in transit (Num. 4:5).

Matthew and Mark report that at the time of Jesus' death this veil in the Temple was "torn in two, from top to bottom" (Matt. 27:51, RSV; cf. Mark 15:38-39). The writer of Hebrews sees the veil as a symbol of Christ's "flesh," the rending of which opened the way for all believers into the holiest—the immediate presence and grace of God (Heb. 6:19-20; 10:19-20).

In 2 Cor. 3:12-18 the apostle Paul uses "veil" as a symbol for that which prevents a thing from being clearly understood. Referring to the veil Moses wore following his encounter with God on Mount Sinai (Exod. 34:29-35), he declares that when the Israelites read the old covenant "that same veil remains unlifted, because only through Christ is it taken away" (v. 14, RSV). It is in turning to Christ that the veil is lifted; then, with "unveiled face" we are enabled to behold the glory of the Lord and to be "changed into his likeness" (v. 18, RSV).

It is quite possible to speak of God's presence during the OT time period as somewhat "veiled." The inner sanctuary of the Temple was covered by the veil. However, in the NT the veil is rent, and we see the glory or self-revelation of God in the person of Christ.

See HOLY OF HOLIES, DAY OF ATONEMENT.

DON W. DUNNINGTON

VENGEANCE. See REVENGE.

VERBAL INSPIRATION. See INSPIRATION OF THE BIBLE.

VICARIOUS. This is a theological term. While the term is not in the Bible, the concept is biblical. It is especially appropriate as descriptive of Christ's death. *Vicarious* defines an act as performed, received, or suffered on behalf of another person, so that the benefits of the act accrue to that person. In biblical theology, it is most often used in reference to Christ's death, as being for us, on our behalf, or in our stead.

More than two dozen specific biblical texts support this understanding of Calvary. In John 10:11 Jesus himself declared to His disciples, "'I am the good shepherd. The good shepherd lays down his life for the sheep'" (NIV). That is to say, He gives His life for the sake of theirs. Later, at the Last Supper, Jesus described His blood as "shed for many" (Mark 14:24) and His body as "given for you" (Luke 22:19). Also, 1 Pet. 3:18 depicts Christ's death for sins as "the righteous for the unrighteous" (NIV); and 1 Tim. 2:6 declares His self-sacrifice "a ransom for all men" (NIV).

In spite of the fact that substitution is inherent in the concept of vicarious, many contemporary interpreters resist the designation of Christ's death as substitutionary. But a careful study of the Greek preposition *huper* (translated by "for" in the texts cited above) supports the traditional view. A. T. Robertson affirms: *huper* commonly means "in behalf of," "for one's benefit"; but often it further conveys the notion "instead" as a resultant idea, "and only violence to the context can get rid of it" (*Grammar,* 631).

Christ died not only in our behalf, but in our stead. He became accursed in our stead (Gal. 3:13); He died in our place (Rom. 5:6-8). That is to say, His death is vicarious. It holds crucial significance and meaning for us.

See ATONEMENT, SIN OFFERING, CROSS, CRUCIFIXION, GOVERNMENTAL THEORY OF THE ATONEMENT.

For Further Reading: Ladd, *Theology of NT,* 426-28; Robertson, *Grammar of the Greek NT,* 630-32.

WAYNE G. MCCOWN

VICE. Vice is the term applied to those immoral or evil habits which degrade both individuals and society. Vice is *the opposite* of virtue, as wrong is of right and darkness is of light.

While the KJV does not employ the word "vice," some recent versions do (e.g., Rom. 13:13 and Eph. 4:19, NEB; 1 Cor. 5:8, NBV, Williams' NTLP). In NT times the Graeco-Roman world was vice-ridden, especially with sex sins. Premarital and extramarital sex, homosexuality, and incest were practiced without shame. Prostitution was connected with and sanctioned by the rituals of heathen temples.

Medieval theologians set forth seven vices—called "capital" or "deadly" sins— as the root cause of all of humanity's moral and spiritual ills: pride, covetousness, lust, envy, gluttony, anger, and sloth.

In today's society paganism's ancient immoralities are again flourishing—often glamorized. There is widespread fear that illicit sex, abortion, divorce, drug addiction, alcoholism, nicotine addiction, pornography, gambling, cheating, thievery, demoralizing recreations, and the like are propelling our civilization toward destruction.

Biblical Christianity (Eph. 2:8-10) is the perfect antidote to humanity's vices (Rom. 1:29-32; 1 Cor. 5:1; 6:13-20; 1 Thess. 4:3-8).

See VIRTUE, SEVEN DEADLY SINS, SIN.

For Further Reading: *GMS,* 120-28, 268-84, 527-47.

DELBERT R. ROSE

VICTORY, VICTORIOUS LIVING. In the Scriptures, words such as "triumph," "conquer," and "overcome" express the various facets of victory. The victory is always the Lord's and is credited to others only as He is willing to make it His gift, or with whom He graciously and gratuitously shares it (Deut. 20:4; Ps. 18:50; 44:1-8; Judg. 5:11; 2 Sam. 22:51; et al.).

In the OT "victory" is synonymous with the manifested supremacy and complete preeminence of Jehovah, perhaps even with His attributes of glory. Creation (Ps. 92:4) and redemption (Exod. 15:1, 21) alike demonstrate His victory and triumph.

The victory of God indicates also the ultimate and universal vindication of God's will and purpose, the full accomplishment of His intentions and activities (1 Chron. 29:10-13; Isa. 25:8-9; et al.). The thought of the moral and spiritual triumph of His people is also included (Dan. 11:32, RSV).

Nor must we forget that the concept of victory also includes and expresses the praise and joy of those who share the victory of God, for the ideas of public acclaim and personal jubilation are embraced (Exod. 15:1-2; Judg. 5:1-32; Josh. 10:24;

cf. Rom. 16:19-20). The "God of peace" is that God of efficient action and all-triumph.

In the NT all of these elements are in the Christian concept of "victory." The divine victory is achieved in the Lord Jesus Christ. Although His life was one of unrelieved conflict, it was one long trail of triumph of faith, obedience, and discipline, coming to final unequivocal triumph in His death and resurrection, in which He was the Victim-Victor (1 Cor. 15:54; Rom. 4:25). The Cross is the raw material of the Crown; the victim's scaffold is the victor's chariot (Col. 2:13-15).

The victory is and ever will be the Lord's (Rev. 11:15-18). But He shares it now and in the future with all who trust Him and keep His commandments. "The victory is our's, thank God!" (1 Cor. 15:54, Moffatt). In Paul's world the "triumph," strictly speaking, was a festival *celebrating* the victory. This too is part of victory in the NT (2 Cor. 2:14) and means a whole "fount of blessing" to the believing heart: triumph in trouble (Rom. 5:3-5, RSV, cf. Moffatt), inward assurance (8:37), the possibility of triumphant faith (1 John 5:5).

These logically lead to and postulate a victorious life-style. Life is built from the inside; victorious Christian living depends on yieldedness and submission to the triumphant Spirit of Christ. "Greater is he that is in you, than he that is in the world" (1 John 4:4). And, it is the great positive that determines the matter of victory in Christian life: "Let God re-make you so that your whole attitude of mind is changed. Thus you will prove in practice that the will of God's good, acceptable to him, and perfect" (Rom. 12:1-2, Phillips). Paul exults, "I can do all things in him who strengthens me" (Phil. 4:13, RSV). Triumphant Christian life-style in a hostile and aggressive age demands not only that we put on "the whole armor of God" (Eph. 6:11-18, RSV), but first of all that the man in the armor be "strong in the Lord and in the strength of his might" (v. 10, RSV).

See IN CHRIST, GROW (GROWTH), HOLINESS, HIGHER LIFE, LIFE-STYLE.

For Further Reading: Cattell, *The Spirit of Holiness;* Redpath, *Victorious Christian Living.*

T. CRICHTON MITCHELL

VIRGIN BIRTH. Virgin birth is a specific term. There has never been but one, that of Jesus Christ. The conception and birth took place without sexual union between the mother and any man. The preexistent Son of God took to himself human nature and "came" as a man among men. The Word was made flesh (John 1:1-14). Technically, it was only the conception that was unique. Once the babe was "conceived of the Holy Ghost" (Matt. 1:20), the natural processes seem to have carried through to birth. The Son of God became also the Son of Man and the Seed of the woman.

The Virgin Birth can only be explained as an act of God. God had created Adam with no parent, Eve with no mother, and others with both parents. Now He brought His Son into the world (Heb. 1:6) by a fourth method. God supplied what was lacking in the ovum of Mary and implanted the Son of God in human flesh in the womb of the virgin. This new thing that God did brought excitement in heaven and good tidings to earth (Luke 2:9-14). However else God could have done it, He did bring salvation through the virgin-born Messiah. To make a myth of it would dilute and call in question the whole plan of salvation.

Nor does the Virgin Birth furnish scriptural or logical grounds for the myth of the "perpetual virginity" of Mary. She remained a virgin until after the birth of her "firstborn son" (Matt. 1:25). Then she apparently surrendered her virginity in the God-ordained way. The fruit of love and marriage is evident in sons and daughters, half brothers and half sisters of Jesus (Matt. 13:54-56). Her virginity had accomplished its purpose. It was not standardized as the ideal adult state.

The Virgin Birth is reasonable, though neither proved nor disproved. It is not a problem but a solution. It is a unique fact that explains how the Incarnation took place.

On what authority, then, does the Virgin Birth stand? The Word of God. Whether or not the Greek and Hebrew words *(parthenos* and *almah)* always retain the usual meaning of unmarried and pure virgin (Matt. 1:23 and Isa. 7:14), there is no question in the NT context. The case does not rest on linguistics. The angel made factual affirmation of the Virgin Birth to both Mary and Joseph (Luke 1:26-38 and Matt. 1:18-25). Although these details of God's act are not fully repeated elsewhere in the Scriptures, the announced facts are the key to the mysteries of both prophecy and fulfillment in the plan of redemption. This is how Jesus "came," "was sent," "was made flesh," etc. Nothing contradicts these facts. Everything leans on them. As Machen says, "The virgin birth is an integral part of the New Testament witness about Christ" (*The Virgin Birth of Christ,* 396).

The announcements of the Virgin Birth are addressed to faith—as are the existence of God and the truth of God's Word. It may not have been best to share the facts immediately with the skeptical public. One wonders at what point

Mary's knowledge spread to the family and to the community of believers. Certainly it was known by the time of the earliest written Gospels. And it is in the earliest creeds, baptismal formulae, and even in exorcism. Accepting God's explanation of the coming of the Savior seemed to be a test of faith. In the Early Church one had to profess belief in the Virgin Birth to be baptized. Historically, the doctrine has always been considered to be one of the fundamentals of the Christian faith.

See CHRIST, INCARNATION, CHRISTOLOGY.

For Further Reading: Machen, *The Virgin Birth of Christ;* Edwards, *The Virgin Birth in History and Faith;* Orr, *The Virgin Birth of Christ;* Boslooper, *The Virgin Birth; GMS,* 353-56.

WILBER T. DAYTON

VIRTUE. This is a word rarely used in the Scriptures. All four OT references describe women: "A virtuous woman is a crown to her husband" (Prov. 12:4; cf. Ruth 3:11; Prov. 31:10, 29). In this context, virtue is synonymous with moral uprightness, chastity, and goodness.

Virtue is ascribed to God once in the NT (1 Pet. 2:9, where it is translated "praises" in KJV), and to men four times. In each instance, virtue is better translated as "Moral excellence." It represents a positive quality of personal character derived from the character of God himself: "His divine power has granted to us everything pertaining to life and godliness, through the true knowledge of Him who called us by His own glory and *excellence"* (2 Pet. 1:3, NASB, italics added). It is an attribute, however, that must be actively cultivated: "Applying all diligence, in your faith supply moral excellence [virtue], and in your moral excellence, knowledge" (v. 5, NASB).

The Greek philosophers distilled four virtues —self-control, courage, justice, and wisdom— which represent the epitome of human moral achievement. And for that very reason, virtue, in the classical sense, proved to be only marginally useful to NT writers. Moral excellence is not the result of man's efforts but of God's grace, appropriated by faith: "For we are His workmanship, created in Christ Jesus for good works" (Eph. 2:10, NASB).

See SEVEN CARDINAL VIRTUES, CHARACTER, GROW (GROWTH).

For Further Reading: Wynkoop, *A Theology of Love,* 165-83; Ferm, *Encyclopedia of Morals,* 11-38.

C. S. COWLES

VISION. A popular use of the word "vision" is based on a misunderstanding of Prov. 29:18 inculcated by the poor rendering of it in the KJV. "Vision" is not merely a hunch of something that should and must be done, and the challenge to rise up and do it. Vision is one means by which God reveals His will and gives guidance. The idea of "oracle" or oracular is also involved and has reference to the Word of God by which all things are to be tested (Acts 7:38; Rom. 3:2; etc.).

"Vision" is an ecstatic experience in which new knowledge is revealed through something seen. Usually the recipient of the vision (not always a "visionary" in the usual sense of the word) is assigned to do something, say something, or go somewhere; he is commissioned to communicate the new knowledge to others. Hence vision, prophecy, and oracle are closely connected. OT prophets, NT prophets, and apostles are alike in this respect: They have God's Word in trust for transmission.

Prov. 29:18 (RSV) insists that unless some persons had received special communications, and passed them on to others together with their meaning, anarchy and chaos would have and still would overtake mankind. Disregard for the vision and the Word still breeds anarchy and terrorism. The revelation of God's will was made by means of visions (Ps. 89:19, NASB). Nathan the prophet exemplifies the receiving of a vision, the communication of the word of the vision, and the challenge to obey that word (1 Chron. 17:3-15).

The NT apostles and prophets likewise were granted visions prompting the communicating of divine truth (Acts 2:17; 10:1-8; 16:9; Rev. 1:9-20). Paul relates visions and revelations in 2 Cor. 12:1-5, but it seems clear that to him visions are subject to higher laws, especially the law of perfect love (1 Cor. 13:1-3; 14:32-33).

Paul received both "visions" and "revelations"; the former suggests seeing, the latter suggests hearing; the former will be subject to the latter, and both will be held within the control of perfect love. We must note also that the Pauline formula "in Christ" overarches all, and that the visions and revelations are "of the Lord," received in the context of spiritual discipline through physical suffering (2 Cor. 12:7-10). Even the moderating element "a thorn in the flesh" was a "gift" from God—in spite of its designation as "a messenger of Satan."

The element of challenge should not be overlooked, however. The vision is the call, and it is inspired guidance to follow the call. Without it we lose our way, get out of touch with God, and yield to the vagaries of human reasoning; and so, in the words of the wise man, we "run wild" but are not free.

See TRUTH, REVELATION (SPECIAL), HOLY SPIRIT, GUIDE (GUIDANCE), VOCATION, PROPHET (PROPHECY), PREACHING.

For Further Reading: *NBD,* 1312; *ISBE,* 5:3057.

T. CRICHTON MITCHELL

VOCATION. In Christian theology, "calling" (Lat. *vocatio*) means *both* God's summons (election) to saving faith and fellowship in the covenant community, *and* divine assignment to serve the neighbor through one's daily work. Biblical thought gives a central place to the former and a sound basis for the latter, more fully developed in Protestantism.

God calls the Hebrews out of slavery into covenant community, names them as His own, and claims them for His service. He also calls individuals such as Moses and the prophets for particular tasks. In the NT God calls a new people into being in Christ. Gentiles are invited to share the fellowship, inherit the promises, and bear the ministry of reconciliation. All are "called to be saints" (holy ones, Rom. 1:7) and servants, to belong to God and become like Christ in all of life (cf. Eph. 4:2). Within this universal or general calling, some are specially assigned to perform particular functions within the Body of Christ for the effectiveness of its ministry.

Building upon this base, Luther and Calvin gave Christian vocation a distinctive meaning by uniting the biblical themes of divine vocation and daily work. In opposition to the double standard of medieval Christianity which limited vocation to the religious life of priests and monks, the Reformers stressed that every Christian is called into God's service in and through the daily occupation. One's common work is assigned by the Lord, to be done in faith and disciplined obedience, for ministry to the neighbor. Herein are the priesthood of all believers and the equality of all before God—profoundly biblical ideas with revolutionary social consequences. The transition to modern secular, technological society, however, has brought with it serious obstacles to this understanding of vocation as stewardship and service in the common life.

See CALL (CALLED, CALLING), STEWARDSHIP, WORK (WORKS), LABOR, LEISURE.

For Further Reading: Brown, *The Spirit of Protestantism,* chaps. 7—9; Gardner, *Biblical Faith and Social Ethics,* 297-303; Nelson, ed., *Work and Vocation: A Christian Discussion;* Scheef, "Vocation," *IDB.*

WILFRED L. WINGET

VOLUNTARISM. See INTELLECTUALISM.

VOWS. A vow is a solemn promise. It may be legally binding, supported by documents and signatures; or it may be verbal only. A vow differs from an oath in that a vow relates to future action or performance, while an oath is a commitment to the truth, usually accompanied by invoking Deity or some sacred object. However, vows in the OT were usually confirmed by an oath.

The biblical view of vows is that they must be voluntary in order to be binding (Deut. 23:22), and that they are subject to the approval of those who may have authority over one (Num. 30:10-15). But once made and validated, they are to be sacredly kept. A mark of one who will abide in the Lord's tabernacle is the kind of fidelity that "sweareth" to one's "own hurt, and changeth not" (Ps. 15:4). The Preacher bitingly prods: "When thou vowest a vow unto God, defer not to pay it; for he hath no pleasure in fools" (Eccles. 5:4). Clearly the biblical viewpoint is that there is no more accurate index to character than the carefulness with which one fulfills one's vows.

Most of the vows in biblical times were religious. The first instance was Jacob's promise at Bethel to serve God and pay tithes. Two NT cases are Acts 18:18; 21:23, both involving Paul. The vows (whatever they were) required certain formalities and religious rites.

Human relationships today are bound together by vows also, in spite of the fact that the contemporary mood is to deny them. The most basic to society are civil vows, commercial vows, and marital vows (most under attack). In church circles there are also membership vows and ordination vows.

Even a utilitarian philosophy of social contract should prompt fidelity to vows; for when vows are despised and disregarded, the fabric of society disintegrates. How much more conscientiously should Christians keep their vows, who are prompted by Christian love, undergirded with a sense of integrity. Church members who flagrantly violate their church vows, and clergy who forget their ordination vows, bring dishonor to Christ and His Church.

The most concerted attack in modern society is on marriage vows, not only by the increasingly easy divorce, but by the trend to live together without benefit of legal contract. But marital vows serve a dual purpose. First, they acknowledge the stake which society has in the marriage. The community which must "pick up the pieces" if the marriage fails, is inescapably implicated because property rights, personal protection of wife and children, and such matters all depend on the network of law. Young people who conform to state requirements and exchange vows publicly, signing official documents, are acknowledging these inherent rights of the community and accepting responsibility in conformity to them.

But even more importantly, vows if taken in the name of God, or especially within a religious context, are the public acknowledgment of the claims of God upon the union: that marriage is instituted of God, to be governed by His laws, and ultimately to be judged by God. These rights of God prevail whether they are acknowledged or not. The exchange of vows is a public acknowledgment of an awareness of these divine rights.

It must not be forgotten, however, that while marriage vows are indirectly to God and to the community, they are primarily made by the principals in the marriage to each other. A man and a woman are solemnly promising fidelity to the most sacred union possible to men on earth, as long as both shall live. In Malachi the Lord declares His hatred of divorce (2:14-16) and in Hebrews promises judgment upon "whoremongers and adulterers" (13:4).

The question whether it is ever right to break vows is an acute one. A rule of thumb might be that an evil promise had better be broken than kept. Such a case would surely have been Jephthah, whose foolish vow, followed by his stubbornness in keeping it, cost the life of his daughter (Judges 11).

See FIDELITY, INTEGRITY, DISCIPLINE, CHARACTER, CHURCH, MARRIAGE.

For Further Reading: *ISBE*, 5:3058.

RICHARD S. TAYLOR

W

WALK. See LIFE-STYLE.

WAR. War is the resort of nations to settle issues by force of arms. Wars are always the product of human sinfulness, in either immediate instigation or indirect occasion.

While civilized nations should pursue a policy of peace, it is unlikely that what ought to be done will always be. Jesus understood the hard fact of human sinfulness when He predicted wars and rumors of wars throughout the age (Matt. 24:4-8). Universal peace will be established only by the personal presence and reign of the Prince of Peace.

However, Jesus' prediction is no excuse for failing to work for peace. The advent of the nuclear age has compelled nations to reassess the perils of war and weigh the risk of a nuclear holocaust against the possible gains of military action. Christians also have been prompted to examine anew what is their duty.

Christ undoubtedly established among men a new kind of kingdom, to be extended by spiritual means, not carnal. The only sword in its arsenal is the Sword of the Spirit, which is the Word of God. This Kingdom transcends earthly kingdoms and is compromised when any attempt is made to amalgamate with them. Its objective is the salvation of men for time and eternity; its enemies are sin and Satan; and its methods are prayer, preaching, witnessing, teaching, and if need be, dying.

The problem confronting the believer whose allegiance is committed to the heavenly Kingdom is how to relate now to the old kingdoms, those of earthly political sovereignties.

Radical separatists see only bifurcation between the two kinds of kingdoms with no possibility of the Christian functioning in both, excepting in the minimal sense of living within the law and being a good neighbor. The state is seen as demonic and politics as so thoroughly corrupt that Christians can remain uncontaminated only by remaining strictly aloof. According to this view the world should be left to run its own affairs. This approach rules out not only participation in war but in legal and police activities. These activities by their very nature require the use of force, which is forbidden, the radical separatists believe.

A more moderate group of pacifists recognize the divine ordering of the state as a necessary means of protecting and controlling sinful men, and they perceive the legitimacy of law enforcement functions. There is some ambivalence concerning how far Christians can engage in this necessary activity; this ambivalence extends to the degree in which Christians should involve themselves in the political process, especially in seeking office and playing a part in the formulation of the laws and the system. But even those who see the possibility of combining active citizenship in both kingdoms feel that the higher principles governing the kingdom of Christ prohibit them from any function which might involve them in the taking of life; this of course would include war.

A third group of Christians believes that there is no such sharp conflict between their two levels of citizenship. Their reasons include the biblical position that government is ordained of God, and in bearing the sword, law enforcement is God's minister (Rom. 13:1-7). It is a kind of work made necessary by the mass of sinful people yet in the old kingdom; and because mandated by God, it is righteous, and if righteous, as equally appropriate for the child of God as for the child of the devil. Indeed it would be done better if all judges, enforcement officers, and lawmakers were Christians. They believe further that no activity within this secular frame of reference depends on hate or is incompatible with love; on the contrary those ruled by love will do it better. Love itself demands action against evil.

This group further believes that the Bible recognizes the necessity of at times taking human life, and provides no basis whatsoever for labeling all killing as murder; the entire OT and to a lesser degree the NT assume the contrary. While the NT identifies hate as murder, it does not imply that the minister of God who bears the sword is a murderer.

Again, this group further believes that the legitimate duties of the state include not only protecting citizens from each other but protecting them from international predators. Whether this function is carried out by means of so-called police action through the United Nations, by other alliances, or unilaterally, in any case if the action is to be effective, the possibility of killing, and of even mild action erupting into war, is always present. There are in every generation Hitlers who must be restrained and disarmed. The alternative is capitulation. If capitulation is not acceptable, then nations—including the Christians in them—must bear the burden of deciding what is worth dying for, and acting accordingly. To deny that the cause of freedom, justice, and righteousness have at times been defended or advanced by war is to be blind to the facts of history. Furthermore, it is to forget that God utilizes military action as a means of punishing wicked nations and disciplining His own people, as well as bringing about the political changes He sovereignly wills (Deut. 9:4; 28:49-52; 1 Kings 11:14, 23; et al.).

See PACIFISM, MURDER, WRATH, RETRIBUTION (RETRIBUTIVE JUSTICE), PROGRESSIVE REVELATION.

For Further Reading: DeWolf, *Responsible Freedom*, 330-58; Hostetler, *Perfect Love and War.*

RICHARD S. TAYLOR

WARFARE, SPIRITUAL. See SPIRITUAL WARFARE.

WATER. References to water are abundant in the Bible, not only because it was so essential to the welfare of God's people—indeed of humanity everywhere—but because it spoke of life, refreshing, cleansing, verdure, health, and abundance. The symbolism of water is especially pronounced in the Gospel of John. Without too much strain it is possible to see the miracle at Cana (John 2) as a promise of transformed life, the promise to the woman at the well of living water (John 4) as eternal life, and the "rivers of living water" (John 7) as the promise of the fullness of life through the infilling of the Spirit.

The chief theological problem concerns the meaning of water in John 3:5—"Except a man be born of water and of the Spirit, he cannot enter into the kingdom of God." The water here has been variously interpreted as the water of natural birth, the water of John's baptism of repentance, the water of the baptismal sacrament, the water as a symbol of the Word of God, and the phrase as a figure of speech called a hendiadys, wherein water is intended to serve as a parallel or equivalent of Spirit. Only the last two carry through the thread of typology in the Gospel, and they alone harmonize with the spiritual nature of the gospel.

The first would imply that the Kingdom is restricted to human beings. The second could be acceptable if the emphasis was on repentance instead of water. The third is an extreme sacramentarianism as rigid as Judaistic circumcision, totally incompatible with the free, untrammeled activity of the Spirit in regeneration. Water as the Word has real support, since water as a cleansing agent is sometimes linked with the Word (John 13:10 with 15:3; Eph. 5:26; the spurious 1 John 5:7 placed between vv. 6 and 8 proves that someone in the past associated water with Christ as the Word). The requirement therefore is understandable if Jesus is saying that except a person be quickened into spiritual life both by the word of the gospel and the inner action of the Spirit, he or she cannot enter the Kingdom. Does the

Spirit ever regenerate apart from the truth about Christ?

Water also is a type of cleansing. It is important to see that the heart may be purified at two levels, the water level and the fire level. The water level is the level of expiation or forgiveness—hence John's baptism, and hence the figurative language of Acts 22:16; 1 Cor. 6:11; and Titus 3:5. But water cannot reach the inner nature as can fire; hence the cleansing accompanying the baptism with the Holy Spirit is linked not with water but with fire (Mal. 3:1-3; Matt. 3:11 and parallels; Acts 2:3). This is why the word *katharizō,* "to cleanse, make free from admixture," is the most appropriate word for Acts 15:9.

See NEW BIRTH, EMBLEMS OF THE HOLY SPIRIT, CLEANSING, ETERNAL LIFE.

For Further Reading: Marsh, *Emblems of the Spirit,* 220 ff; *HDNT,* 2:814; *CC,* 5:530 ff; Thomas, *The Holy Spirit of God,* 62 ff. RICHARD S. TAYLOR

WEALTH. See MONEY.

WEDDING GARMENT. The parable concerning the guest who came to a wedding feast with inappropriate attire is found in Matt. 22:1-14. A question is raised as to which party was responsible for providing the wedding garment. Was the guest to obtain the garment for himself, or was the appropriate garment to be supplied by the host? The biblical account appears to avoid the question in order to address a more crucial issue.

The significant theological question is, What did Jesus have in mind when He suggested that a guest had come to a wedding feast without a wedding garment and was therefore to be expelled? The theological discussion centers on whether the wedding garment symbolizes the righteousness of Christ which is imputed to the individual, or if it indicates that man must obtain something for himself in order to stand in the presence of a holy God.

It appears that the wedding garment denotes an element in moral character. Paul has a parallel admonition when he suggests that the Christian is to "put on Christ" (Rom. 13:14; cf. Gal. 3:27). To "put on Christ" is to choose to be in a definite relationship with Christ, which produces personal holiness of character. Likewise, the wedding garment would be neither good works nor the imputation of a cleanness that does not belong to an individual. Rather the availability of the wedding garment suggests the possibility of a holiness of character available to all. If this quality of character is chosen by the moral agent, he will be enabled to stand in the presence of a holy God. Thus the symbolism of the parable would appear to indicate that while grace is available to all, personal holiness must be personally chosen and "worn."

In his sermon entitled "The Wedding Garment" John Wesley noted that "holiness becometh his house forever! This is the wedding garment of all that are called to 'the marriage of the Lamb.' Clothed in this they will not be found naked: 'They have washed their robes and made them white in the blood of the Lamb.'"

See HOLINESS, HEAVEN, SALVATION, IMPUTED RIGHTEOUSNESS, IMPARTED RIGHTEOUSNESS.

For Further Reading: Jeremias, *The Parables of Jesus,* 65 ff and 187 ff; Trench, *Notes on the Parables of Our Lord,* 75-83; Wesley, *Works,* 7:311-17. LARRY FINE

WESLEYAN SYNTHESIS. At the very heart of holiness doctrine are four sets of categories which, when kept together as congenial complements, prevent lopsidedness, but when allowed to polarize into antithetical and competing concepts, result in fragmentation and serious distortion. These are *process* and *crisis, grace* and *freedom, state* and *becoming,* and as subheads under that, *being* and *relation.* Other terms which become involved are *substance, dynamic,* and *nature.*

Take the first set of terms, *process* and *crisis.* At its best, holiness theology has preserved a fine balance, seeing experiential salvation as being an overall process involving many minor but two major crises, the major crises being the new birth and entire sanctification, and the process including all the influences of prevenient grace and all the growing between the major crises and thereafter. Wise Wesleyans pay equal respect to works of grace and the walk of grace.

A similar biblical synthesis is maintained—or should be—between *grace* and *freedom.* Grace is seen as the redemptive action of God, freedom is seen as the capacity of man to cooperate with grace or frustrate it. One of the watershed issues of theology is the relation of divine action to human action. An authentic Wesleyanism sees grace as prior and primal, but always as restoring and enabling freedom, never as overpowering it.

Likewise does a biblical holiness doctrine refuse to allow *state* to become the contradictory of *becoming,* or the idea of becoming to constitute an antithesis to the concept of state. Rather there is possible a state of holiness, knowable and definite; but this state, if genuine, is never static. It is a state which in its very nature is essentially dynamic.

In like manner we must refuse to pit *being* and *relation* against each other. Being is not only existence but *what* a person or thing is in itself—its internal nature; relation is the connection which beings sustain to each other. The state of being will determine the quality of relationships, and equally, poor relationships will alter the quality of being. But the two are not totally identical. We cannot simply define *being* as the sum total of relationships. There is an entity which is independent of relationships. Yet in the concrete order of things all entities are in relation to all other entities, in such a way that being/relation becomes both causal and reciprocal. Those who think largely in *relational* terms prefer dynamic and relational kinds of language, while those who emphasize *being* use substantive kinds of language.

See RELATIONAL THEOLOGY, ARMINIANISM, WESLEYANISM, SYNERGISM, COMPLEMENTARIANISM, CALVINISM.

RICHARD S. TAYLOR

WESLEYANISM. The term Wesleyanism has a broad application, being in some cases used as a synonym for Methodism. In this usage, the connotation of institutional range and of denominational organization is prominent. In a more specific sense, however, Wesleyanism as a term is employed to indicate a theological pattern, based upon the ministries of John and Charles Wesley (1703-91 and 1707-88 respectively). Out of the literary heritage left by the Wesleys and their contemporaries, their successors have produced a theological system which has been normative for those acknowledging themselves to be the heirs of historic Wesleyanism.

John Wesley's own thinking was shaped by the orthodox standard of Anglicanism. This is suggested by his adaptation of the Thirty-nine Articles of the Anglican church to a body of Twenty-five Articles of Methodism, long normative for major Methodist bodies. Basic to Wesley's theological stance was his acceptance of the following tenets: the sovereignty of God, the full authority of Holy Scripture, the full deity and Saviorhood of Jesus Christ, the fall and consequent depravity of man, and mankind's need for supernatural deliverance from sin. He reinterpreted significantly the Reformed understandings of the depravity of man, of grace, of atonement, and of sanctification.

Wesleyanism has traditionally rejected the Genevan interpretations of election and reprobation, of irresistible grace, of unconditional perseverance, and of merely forensic sanctification. On the positive side, there has been an insistence upon personal salvation, and as a particular emphasis, entire sanctification as an instantaneous crisis experience by which the "remains of sin" which survive regeneration are eliminated from the heart.

In the decades following the lives of the Wesleys, this last emphasis was developed, by making explicit that which was implicit in John Wesley's sermons and Charles Wesley's hymns. That is to say, there came to be a frank identification of entire sanctification with the baptism of the Holy Spirit. Continued in this elaboration were Wesley's terms for the state of grace to which the sanctifying crisis led, namely, Perfect Love and Full Salvation. Continued also was Wesley's disavowal of flawless perfection in favor of "perfection in love" and of evangelical perfection.

Wesley's solution to man's total depravity, and hence moral inability, was his doctrine of prevenient grace, as a universal and unconditional benefit of the Atonement. While all therefore were born sinful, they were also born in grace. This not only assured salvation for the infant but constituted an influence toward God, and a restoration of sufficient moral ability to turn to God in repentance and faith. This ability was not a residue of the Fall, but a first provision of redemption. Yet it was an influence and an enablement, not a coercive or determinative power.

From the viewpoint of church government, the Wesleys basically followed the pattern of Anglicanism, but were ultimately forced into a free-church mode of organization—but retaining the episcopacy and a connectional system. This model was followed by major Methodistic bodies. In response to special conditions and needs, religious bodies which were Wesleyan in doctrine appeared during the 19th century. Such were the Free Methodist church, the Salvation Army, the Wesleyan Methodist church (now united with the Pilgrim Holiness church to form the Wesleyan church) and the numerically larger Church of the Nazarene.

While the doctrine of Christian perfection became part of standard Wesleyanism, there came a gradual resistance to it upon the part of mainline Methodism, which gathered momentum in the last quarter of the 19th century. From being suspect in many circles, perfectionism came to be regarded officially as unacceptable, the crisis coming in 1893-94. The emphasis upon this aspect of Christian doctrine was maintained by elements within mainline Methodism, who continued to sponsor camp meetings, and when possible, to foster protracted evangelistic meetings within their local churches. There had already (in 1867) been organized the National

Association for the Promotion of Holiness, whose leaders were largely ministers in the Methodist church, and who found means by which the historic emphasis upon Wesleyanism in general, and of Christian perfection teaching in particular, could be implemented within the constituency of general Wesleyanism.

Through the interdenominational outreach of Wesleyanism, a number of other denominations not definitely known as Wesleyan, have been greatly influenced by this form of theology. Among these are the Christian and Missionary Alliance, and Evangelical Friends (Ohio, Kansas, Oregon, and Rocky Mountain yearly meetings).

Wesleyanism today is maintained as an emphasis by both denominational and interdenominational agencies. It is the basic theological stance of at least four graduate theological seminaries, and of several score of liberal arts and Bible colleges. It is also the predominant theological emphasis in the missionary arms of the denominations mentioned above, and in a number of "faith" missionary societies, notably the World Gospel Mission and the Oriental Missionary Society, International.

See CHRISTIAN PERFECTION, HOLINESS, HOLINESS MOVEMENT (THE), PERFECT LOVE, PERFECT (PERFECTION), PERFECTIONISM, WESLEYAN SYNTHESIS.

For Further Reading: Wesley, *A Plain Account of Christian Perfection;* Wesley, *Standard Sermons* (selections); Wiley, *CT,* 2:217-517; Cox, *John Wesley's Concept of Perfection;* Turner, *The Vision Which Transforms;* Geiger, ed., *The Word and the Doctrine;* Wood, *John Wesley: The Burning Heart.*

HAROLD B. KUHN

WHITSUNDAY. See CHRISTIAN YEAR.

WHOLE, WHOLENESS. This has to do with our becoming redeemed, through grace, and thereby becoming whole in the sense of healed of sin and made adequate for life—physically to some extent, psychologically, and spiritually. It sees a tie-up between our receiving holiness and our being given a "wholeness." The person made holy through grace, then, is the truly well person.

An exaggerated stress on wholeness fails to preserve the sharp distinction between body and soul, hence has no basis for distinguishing between physical health and spiritual health. That there can be sick saints and robust sinners is patently obvious, both in Bible and contemporary times.

See HOLINESS.

J. KENNETH GRIDER

WHOLLY OTHER. This refers to God's being entirely different from us humans. It is the view that God is infinitely different from us, qualitatively. The emphasis was that of Soren Kierkegaard (1813-55), who was reacting to the pantheistic view of Friedrich Hegel in which God and man are thought of as akin to each other. Karl Barth (1886-1968) says that he was helped in a basic way by Kierkegaard, to view God as wholly other than us—in our sinfulness. The view is salutary in that it speaks against pantheistic understandings. But it is so extreme that it hesitates to admit that we are like God in any way—as in our being persons, and as in our being holy (through grace).

See TRANSCENDENCE, GOD, ATTRIBUTES (DIVINE), IMMANENCE.

For Further Reading: Otto, *The Idea of the Holy;* Hitchcock, *The Rediscovery of the Sacred;* Kraft, *The Search for the Holy.*

J. KENNETH GRIDER

WICKED, WICKEDNESS. See SIN.

WILL. See FREEDOM.

WILL OF GOD. See GUIDE, GUIDANCE.

WINE. See TEMPERANCE.

WISDOM. Wisdom literature in the OT distills the insight and experience of the Hebrew people as they reflected upon God's ordered creation and man's position within it. Wisdom is more than knowledge or intelligence. It is the capacity of the mind to understand and the heart to rejoice in the inner meaning, coherence, beauty, and enduring principles upon which existence is established. Wisdom is the God-given ability to deal with life's varied experiences intelligently and with the result of bringing true blessedness to the lives of all who are involved.

Proverbs embodies wisdom's optimism arising from Israel's golden age. Its theme is expressed in the memorable refrain, "The fear of the Lord is the beginning of wisdom" (9:10; Ps. 111:10). The wise man knows and obeys God's laws and thus enjoys a long and blessed life. The fool disregards God's order and brings swift destruction upon his head.

Ecclesiastes, however, underscores the futility of a life that has been lived in outward conformity to wisdom's dictates, but has remained self-centered and self-serving. A wisdom devoid of a dynamic relationship to God leads inevitably to despair.

Wisdom literature in the OT achieves its greatest profundity in Job. Here is the saga of a righteous man who lives according to the dictates of Proverbian wisdom and still is overwhelmed by catastrophe. The presence of the demonic, the principle of irrationality, and the problem of evil in human existence are faced. Yet, in the midst of inexplicable suffering, Job's faith rises to affirm, "I know that my Redeemer lives, and at the last He will take His stand on the earth" (Job 19:25-26, NASB).

Surprisingly, OT wisdom literature is never directly quoted or referred to in the NT. This is not because the collective wisdom of the Hebrew people is false, but likely because it is a result of the saving knowledge of God rather than a medium of that knowledge.

In contrast to the sacred wisdom of the OT, man's human, secularistic wisdom is of no value in acquiring a true knowledge of God (1 Cor. 1:21). Human wisdom can no more obtain a knowledge of God than works of righteousness can merit His favor.

There is, however, a "wisdom . . . taught by the Spirit, combining spiritual thoughts with spiritual words" (1 Cor. 2:13, NASB). The wisdom greatly to be desired is not that derived by human reflection but by divine revelation. This wisdom is incarnate in Jesus Christ, "in whom are hidden all the treasures of wisdom and knowledge" (Col. 2:3, NASB). In His followers, the marks of wisdom are humility, holiness, and Christlikeness (Jas. 3:13-18).

See DISCERNMENT, FOOL (FOOLISHNESS, FOLLY), PRUDENCE.

For Further Reading: *GMS,* 107-9, 152-53, 332-33; *Eerdman's Handbook to the Bible,* 317-18, 463.

C. S. COWLES

WITCHCRAFT. See SORCERY.

WITNESS. See TESTIMONY, WITNESS.

WITNESS OF THE SPIRIT. The witness of the Spirit, as understood by Wesleyans, is the direct, inward communication to the believer of the fact of his acceptance with God. It is not just an emotional release or a special enablement to act or speak in a certain way. It is not the same thing as the Spirit's witness to the truthfulness of Scripture (as in Ramm, *The Witness of the Spirit,* 65, etc.) or the confidence (claimed by many Calvinist and neoorthodox believers) that one is of the elect. It is a direct witness to a conscious relationship with God.

In Rom. 8:15-16, there are two distinct witnesses. One's own spirit is aware of the new life from God and of the fruit of the Spirit. (First John enumerates evidences by which one can take inventory and arrive at the certain knowledge reflected in 5:13.) To the human witness is added the divine. The Holy Spirit testifies that one is a child of God. As in home owning, to the conscious blessings of possession is added the clear title of a warranty deed. Certainty is of inestimable value in the matter of destiny.

In practical matters the witness of the Spirit cannot be separated from the fruit of the Spirit. Wesley says, "Let none ever presume to rest in any supposed testimony of the Spirit which is separate from the fruit of it," and "let none rest in any supposed fruit of the Spirit without the witness" (*Works,* 5:133). Otherwise, one might exalt human experience above the Word of God. The twofold witness assures that the human experience is shaped by the Word and the work of God.

Sanctification is attested by a similar witness "both as clear and as steady" as of justification, and this witness is "necessary in the highest degree" (*Works,* 11:420). In both instances, variations are admitted as to the clarity of the witness. Wesley says, "I know that I am accepted: And yet that knowledge is sometimes shaken, though not destroyed, by doubt or fear. If that knowledge were destroyed, or wholly withdrawn, I could not then say I had a Christian faith" (*Works,* 12:468). This agrees with the understanding that both salvation (in any degree) and its witness can be threatened or lost by sin or by preoccupation with the world. Likewise, these may be recovered upon repentance and faith.

See EXPERIENCE, JUSTIFICATION, ADOPTION, DOUBT, FRUIT OF THE SPIRIT.

For Further Reading: Wesley, Sermons 10-12 on the "Witness of the Spirit" and "Witness of Our Own Spirit"; also *Works,* 5:111-44; *GMS,* 459-61; Ralston, *Elements of Divinity,* 435-43; Wiley, *CT,* 2:431-39.

WILBER T. DAYTON

WOMAN. Scripture portrays woman as man's equal companion in all areas. Both creation accounts stress the unity of the human race. Gen. 1:27 reads, "God created man in His own image, in the image of God He created him; male and female He created them" (NASB). Together they were given the tasks of being fruitful, multiplying, and having dominion over the earth and its creatures (vv. 26, 28). Genesis shows God's creation of woman to be a companion corresponding to man in all ways, "bone of my bone and flesh of my flesh" (2:23), that the two might be "one flesh" (v. 24).

Their harmony, however, with one another and with nature was broken by sin. Together in the garden (3:6), both ate of the forbidden tree. While the man tried to blame the woman and

God for his disobedience (v. 12) and the woman blamed the serpent (v. 13), God punished all by driving them from the garden. The consequences of their sin are toil and pain in childbearing and food production. While the woman yearns for the lost oneness, the man in sin becomes dominant (3:16).

In Christ unity is renewed (Gal. 3:28). The Bible presupposes basic biological functional differences but stresses mutuality of responsibility. Both parents are responsible for their children, and both are to be honored (Exod. 20:12). Both women and men are to display the fruits of the Spirit (Gal. 5:22-23) and to be strong in the faith, ready to defend it. All Christians are to submit to each other as Christ modeled for us in His life and death (John 13:14-16; Rom. 12:10; Phil. 2:3-4; 1 Thess. 5:15; 1 Pet. 5:5). In marriage Paul teaches mutual submission and mutual nurture toward wholeness (1 Cor. 7:3-4; Eph. 5:21-33).

Jesus, contrary to the customs of His culture, taught, touched, and healed women. Many followed as His disciples (Luke 8:1-3) and were last at His cross and first at the tomb. To women was entrusted the message of the Resurrection.

Peter, quoting the prophet Joel, saw the Holy Spirit's empowering of women for ministry as a sign of the Kingdom's arrival (Acts 2:17-18). Women like Priscilla taught in the Early Church (18:26); Phoebe was a deacon (Rom. 16:1-2); many others are listed as Paul's co-workers. While Paul recognized women's right to pray and prophesy (1 Cor. 11:5), he warned against disorder, idle chatter, and interruptive questioning in services (1 Corinthians 14). The ban in 1 Timothy against women teaching at that time could have been prompted by the danger of false teaching by uneducated women. The added concern that a woman not "usurp authority" does not prohibit a woman's exercising legitimate authority given her by the Church through normal processes of leadership designation, for in this same Epistle we read of women deacons (3:11) and possibly women elders (5:1-22).

When seen in contrast to the cultures from which it sprang and in which it has taken root through the centuries, Christianity has been a source of woman's elevation. While the equality displayed in creation and redemption has rarely been actualized in society, woman's role has been steadily expanded under the gospel's encouragement.

See ORDINATION OF WOMEN, WOMEN'S LIBERATION, MARRIAGE, FAMILY, FATHERS, PARENTS AND CHILDREN, CHAIN OF COMMAND.

For Further Reading: Jewett, *Man as Male and Female;* Mollenkott, *Women, Men, and the Bible;* Scanzoni and Hardesty, *All We're Meant to Be: A Biblical Approach to Women's Liberation.* NANCY A. HARDESTY

WOMEN, ORDINATION OF. See ORDINATION OF WOMEN.

WOMEN'S LIBERATION. The movement of the 1960s and 1970s is but a reflowering of the 19th-century call for "woman's rights."

As women became active in temperance and abolition, their rights to organize, speak out, and engage in public political activity were challenged on the basis of traditional scriptural interpretations. From evangelical circles surrounding revivalist Charles G. Finney and from Wesleyan/holiness groups came a series of defenses, first of woman's right to work for reform and eventually for her right to preach the gospel in its fullness. Finneyites Sarah Grimké (*Letters on the Equality of the Sexes,* 1838) and Antoinette Brown Blackwell ("Exegesis of 1 Corinthians, xiv., 34, 35 and 1 Timothy, ii, 12," *Oberlin Quarterly Review,* 1849) declared that whatever was morally right for man to do was morally right for woman. Methodists Luther Lee (*Woman's Right to Preach the Gospel,* 1853), Phoebe Palmer (*Promise of the Father,* 1859), Catherine Booth (*Female Ministry,* 1859), Frances Willard (*Woman in the Pulpit,* 1888), and B. T. Roberts (*Ordaining Women,* 1891) all argued that John Wesley allowed women to preach and the Bible not only permits but encourages women's service to the church and the world. Thus many holiness and Pentecostal denominations do ordain women.

After the 19th Amendment gave women the right to vote in 1920, women's rights as an organized movement went into decline, only to be reborn as an adjunct to a renewed concern for civil rights. Goals of the women's movement have been equal pay for equal work, equal recognition under the law, and individual fulfillment unfettered by restrictive cultural sex roles.

Within the church, women began to be fully ordained in a number of mainline denominations in the mid-1950s. During the 1970s biblical feminists sought to recover the liberating exegesis of Scripture used by their grandparents; to foster the use of inclusive language in Bible translations and worship materials; to achieve mutual submission and responsibility in home, church, and society; and to realize the full giftedness of every person in Christ, in whom there is neither male nor female (Gal. 3:28).

See WOMAN, ORDINATION OF WOMEN.

For Further Reading: Dayton, *Discovering an Evangelical Heritage;* Gundry, *Woman Be Free;* Scanzoni and Hardesty, *All We're Meant to Be: A Biblical Approach to Women's Liberation.* NANCY A. HARDESTY

WORD OF GOD. This term may refer to: (1) an isolated message from God; (2) the Holy Bible, commonly called the "Word of God written"; or to (3) Christ as the living Word, the divine Logos.

There are many references in the OT to isolated messages, which God usually gave to prophets (e.g., 1 Sam. 3:11-14; 1 Kings 12:22-24; Jer. 1:4-5; 51:33; Ezek. 7:1 ff).

The written Word of God as the aggregate of His recorded messages is the theme of Psalm 119 (though only a part of the Scriptures had been written at that time). In the NT the sacred writings are called "scriptures" (Matt. 21:42; Mark 14:49; Luke 24:27; John 5:39; et al.). The Bible as a whole can properly be called the Word of God even though it contains words which are not God's, as for instance the words of Satan or of evil men. Such are inspired in the sense that God directed the human writers to include them for a divine purpose.

But it is through the Living Word, Christ, who was from the beginning (John 1:1 ff), that God has revealed himself most clearly to man (14:9).

The above categories of the Word of God are so closely associated that they blend into each other. If, for example, Jesus is the Truth (John 14:6), and God's words, whether spoken or written, are true (2 Sam. 7:28; Ps. 19:9), then the Word of God in all categories possesses the quality of truth. A dramatic example of the coalescing of their meaning is seen in Heb. 4:12. There, what seems at first to be a statement about the qualities of the spoken and written Word quickly becomes expressed in personal terms and is "a discerner of the thoughts and intents of the heart." All things are "manifest in his sight" (v. 13).

To take another example, the Word of God, spoken, written, and personal is "a lamp unto [our] feet" (Ps. 119:105; John 8:12) and the Inspirer of faith (Rom. 10:17; 2 Pet. 1:4; Heb. 12:2). But the Living Word alone is the source of salvation (Acts 16:31; 4:12).

See CHRIST, LOGOS, BIBLE, INSPIRATION OF THE BIBLE.

For Further Reading: Walls, "Word," *Baker's DT;* Wiley and Culbertson, *Introduction to Christian Theology, 185-238.* W. RALPH THOMPSON

WORK, WORKS. This is the English translation of several Hebrew (e.g., *maaseh, melakah, poal, yagia*) and Greek words (*ergon, poiēma, pragma, koriaō, energeia,* etc.) whose generalized meaning is purposeful activity. Work or works may be variously classified according to the agent (God or man), sphere (sacred or secular), variety (physical or intellectual), evaluation (positive or negative, good or bad), purpose (contextually defined), and/or the distinctive uses of specific biblical authors.

Scripture presents God himself as the Model of positively evaluated work, primarily in creation and redemption (cf. Gen. 1:1—2:3; Isaiah 43—45; Ps. 8:3; 19:1). Of His healings Jesus said, "My Father is always at his work to this very day, and I, too, am working" (John 5:17, NIV; cf. v. 36; 9:3-4; 17:4; Matt. 11:2-6).

Work, both physical (Gen. 1:28; 2:15; Ps. 104:14, 23) and intellectual (Gen. 2:19-20; 1:26, 28), intended to create, conserve, control, and classify, was part of God's original purpose for man, not a consequence of the Fall. Sin distorted the character of man, and since work is a fundamental act of human existence, it was directly affected by that sin. Work became wearisome toil, aggravated by an uncertain relationship between exertion and achievement (cf. Gen. 3:17-19; 5:29; 8:21; Eccles. 2:4-11, 18-23; 4:4-8; 6:7), and an occasion for sins of avarice (cf. Luke 12:13-21; Prov. 23:4) and exploitation (cf. Exod. 1:11-14; Jer. 22:13-17; Jas. 5:1-6). Idleness and sloth are considered vices (cf. Prov. 6:6-15; 10:2-5; 13:4; 14:23; Eph. 4:28; 1 Thess. 4:11-12; 2 Thess. 3:6-13). The apostolic ultimatum is: "If any one will not work, let him not eat" (2 Thess. 3:10, RSV). But through God's work of redemption even everyday secular tasks become sacred when performed in obedience to the divine will, "as to the Lord" (cf. Eph. 6:5-9; Deut. 2:7; 14:28-29; Job 1:10).

When we move from "work" to "works," we find ourselves at once grappling with an age-old theological problem. There developed in late Judaism the notion that the fulfillment of God's law was a holy work which established a man's righteousness or a treasury of merit before God. This accounts for Paul's negative appraisal of "works," i.e., doing what the law requires as a means of achieving or securing salvation (Rom. 3:20, 28; 9:30—10:4; cf. Matt. 20:1-15; Luke 17:7-10). He argues that salvation is by grace alone, God's work. Even the human response of faith and the subsequent performance of good works are not meritorious, but a ceasing from vain efforts to secure self-salvation (Eph. 2:1-10; Rom. 3:21—4:25; 7:7-25; Gal. 2:15-21; 3:21-22; cf. Heb. 4:9-11).

The obedience of faith (Rom. 1:5; 15:18) working through love (Gal. 5:6) will keep God's commandments (1 Cor. 7:19) and thereby fulfil the law's intent (Rom. 8:1-4; 13:8-10; 1 Cor. 15:58; Gal. 5:13-14; Eph. 4:10; Phil. 1:27; Col. 1:10). James's reminder that "faith by itself, if it has no works, is dead" (Jas. 2:17, RSV; cf. vv. 14-26) only apparently contradicts Paul. Paul was writing against legalistic piety, while James's concern was dead orthodoxy which did not issue in a transformed life.

See MERIT, FIDEISM, VOCATION, JUSTIFICATION, LAW AND GRACE, MOSAIC LAW.

For Further Reading: Bertram, *"ergon,* etc.," Kittel, 2:635-55; Braun, *"poieō,* etc.," Kittel, 6:458-84; Hahn and Thiele, "Work, Do, Accomplish," *NIDNTT,* 3:1147-59; Maurer, *"prassō,* etc.," Kittel, 6:632-44; *GMS,* 38-39, 107-19, 527-59; Richardson, *The Biblical Doctrine of Work.* GEORGE LYONS

WORK ETHIC. See LABOR.

WORLD, WORLDLINESS. The principal word in the Hebrew is *tebel,* which means "the earth, the globe, its inhabitants." The term is often parallel to and synonymous with "earth." In the Greek the most common word is *kosmos,* meaning "orderly arrangement or ordered world."

The Hebrew had no concept of the world as it is known today. To his mind the physical world was not the whole. Beyond were the heavens where God's throne was located with all His heavenly host. He did not think of the universe but rather thought in terms of the abode of God (heaven). God was the Author of both, and the orderly movements of the heavenly bodies and the seasons were testimony of His creating and keeping power. When man sinned, a curse fell upon all creation (Ps. 104:29).

A striking fact is the way in which the NT uses "world" as something evil. Man is divided between the followers of Christ and the followers of the world: "If ye were of the world, the world would love his own" (John 15:19); "They are not of the world, even as I am not of the world" (17:16).

Worldliness is not a scriptural term, but it is a biblical concept. The life that is ordered by a love for earthly things which separate from God is worldly. The Christian is opposed by all the elements of the present world and opposed by the spiritual powers of this world: "The whole world lieth in wickedness" (1 John 5:19). The person who loves this system is not of Christ (Jas. 4:4). Worldliness is to be in harmony with the spirit of this age as opposed to Christ. Satan directs the course of the world that now is: "We wrestle not against flesh and blood, but against principalities, against powers, against the rulers of the darkness of this world" (Eph. 6:12).

Love is the motive that sets priorities, determines and gives direction. Love helps one to select and limit. Love directs itself toward pleasure, not suffering, hurt, and privation. Because of this guiding factor in life, the Bible teaches: "Love not the world, neither the things that are in the world. If any man love the world, the love of the Father is not in him" (1 John 2:15). To love the world is to accept the aims of the visible world, its plans, customs, and values. The worldly person is caught up in the spirit of the age. Worldliness is not an act, not *things,* but a *spirit,* by which one is engrossed with the now, the physical, as opposed to the eternal and the spiritual.

See SEPARATION, SPIRITUALITY, PIETISM, LIFE-STYLE, TEMPTATION.

For Further Reading: Chafer, *Systematic Theology,* 6:179-82; Trench, *Synonyms of the New Testament,* 200-205. LEON CHAMBERS

WORLD VIEW. See COSMOLOGY.

WORSHIP. Worship is the acknowledgment of the "worth-ship" (Anglo-Saxon, *weorthscipe*) of God. It is the human response to the divine nature. "When thou saidst, Seek ye my face; my heart said unto thee, Thy face, Lord, will I seek" (Ps. 27:8). Man's response is itself divinely inspired. "No man can come to me, except the Father which hath sent me draw him" (John 6:44). If the Holy Spirit is the divine Agent who motivates our worship, it is Christ who by His finished work on Calvary makes that motivation possible.

Worship can only rightly be offered to God himself. He alone is worthy! The heart of Christian worship is adoration, the most self-abnegating devotion of which man is capable. It is part of the mission of the Church to recognize the need of cultivating in its members the spirit of reverence and awe that leads to adoration. Here is the vital spark of heavenly flame that is to inspire, promote, and sustain the life of the soul. The worship service is a tryst with God. "And there I will meet with thee, and I will commune with thee" (Exod. 25:22).

Worship involves the whole man. It cannot be divorced from moral and ethical content. The qualification for fellowship with God is fitness for it. "Who shall ascend into the hill of the Lord? or who shall stand in his holy place? He that hath clean hands, and a pure heart" (Ps. 24:3-4). Worship also embraces obedience and service (Luke 6:46). In Scripture there is no difference between the two. The Hebrew verb "to serve" *(abhaah),* when used in reference to God, includes every form of service, whether offered in Temple worship or in daily life. In the NT the noun *leitourgia* (from which our word *liturgy* is derived) is used without distinction between worship and service. The revelation of God to man is never one of presence only; it involves also God's purpose. "There can be no apprehension of the divine Presence that is not at the same time a summons to a divinely-appointed task" (Baillie, *The Sense of the Presence of God,* 206).

From the human side Christian worship implies both offering and receiving. The subjective element (man's receiving) is essential to all true worship: "Strength and beauty are in his sanctuary" (Ps. 96:6). Attendance at worship is intended in part for the therapeutic values that the Christian faith offers. Keeping a balance between the objective and the subjective aspects of Christian worship is not always easy. Our theology of God conditions our worship perspective. For some, God may be almost exclusively transcendent; for others, He is altogether immanent. Man's nature calls for a sense of both the ultimate and the intimate. But when one is magnified at the expense of the other, religious experience is in danger of becoming either cold and legalistic or overfamiliar and sentimental. The worship of God is a blend of both awe and love.

See REVERENCE, CHURCH, CHURCH MUSIC, BLESS (BLESSED, BLESSING), PRESENCE (DIVINE), LITURGY, PRAYER, PUBLIC PRAYER.

For Further Reading: *NIDCC,* 1062-63; *ER,* 830-31; *DCT,* 361 ff. JAMES D. ROBERTSON

WRATH. The Bible speaks both of the wrath of man and the wrath of God. As to man, he is exhorted against any uncontrolled rage or passionate anger (Gen. 49:5-7; Matt. 5:9, 21-22; Rom. 12:19; Gal. 5:19-20; Eph. 4:26-31; Col. 3:8; Jas. 1:19-20). The NT view of grace carries with it the possibilities of enjoying a sanctified spirit from which any violent anger has been removed. In the OT, in particular, men were often called upon to carry out certain responsibilities related to the wrath of God (cf. Josh. 9:20). In cases of this type of behavior, the person functioned under the Spirit of God, and the initiation of God was made known to men.

As to God, the Bible speaks clearly about the wrath of God. The apostle Paul, for example, uses such phrases as "the wrath to come" (1 Thess. 1:10); "children of wrath" (Eph. 2:3); "the day of wrath" (Rom. 2:5); "vessels of wrath" (9:22); and other similar phrases. Obviously, the concept of wrath as it relates to God plays a significant part in Paul's theological understanding. In the Book of Romans, after introducing the theme of the Epistle in 1:16-17, he proceeds to deal with the issue of sin in the history of mankind. "The wrath of God is being revealed from heaven against all the godlessness and wickedness of men who suppress the truth by their wickedness" (v. 18, NIV). Needless to say, these declarations make it abundantly clear that "a principle of retribution" is at work in this moral universe.

Is the wrath of God personal or impersonal? Many scholars find offensive the suggestion that God's wrath is personal. They see His wrath as "an impersonal system of cause and effect in the moral realm." For example, Brunner speaks of the wrath of God as "the headwind against which every sinner walks." This position rests upon a fear that God's wrath may be understood in psychological terms, that is to say, it is some type of emotional rage, much like what we witness among humans. Therefore, God's wrath cannot be personal.

On the other hand, God's wrath may be considered personal in the sense that it is His steady, holy displeasure at sin. As Purkiser writes, the wrath of God is His "unfailing and unceasing antagonism to sin, which must be so long as God is God." Moreover, His wrath is His judicial attack on evil. The end result of the divine wrath is twofold: (1) to maintain the created order; (2) to punish justly those who rebel against His providences and redemption and who persist in acting wickedly.

Three facts must be kept in mind with respect to this issue of the personal or impersonal character of God's wrath. First, the moral law, under which all of us live, originates in the nature of God, not His will. This means that the wrath of God is not "an unbridled and normless exercise of vengeance" but an indignant response to sin based upon His own holy nature. Second, since the moral law arises out of His being which is unchangeable, it too is changeless. This removes any capriciousness from God's wrath. Third, wrath and love are not opposites. Hate is the opposite of love. "Wrath is the unfailing opposition of God's holy love to all that is evil," writes Purkiser.

See GOD, ATTRIBUTES (DIVINE), RETRIBUTION (RETRIBUTIVE JUSTICE), ETERNAL PUNISHMENT, ANGER, LOVE.

For Further Reading: Purkiser, "Second Thoughts on

'The Wrath,'" *The Seminary Tower,* Fall, 1958; Stahlin, "orgē," Kittel, 5:419-47; W. White, Jr., "Wrath", *ZPEB,* 5.
WILLARD H. TAYLOR

WRITE, WRITING, WRITTEN. Writing is the recording and communicating of visual and verbal symbols objectively (White, "Writing," *ZPEB,* 5:995). While oral tradition merely restates horizontal communication, writing transmits data across time spans beyond the life of the individual or his social group. Documents have been found in western Asia dating back to 3000 B.C. From them still earlier beginnings may be inferred. Long before Moses it was not necessary to depend on oral transmission to preserve a tradition. In Abraham's day, five distinct and complete writing systems were in common use around him (ibid., 1014).

Though memory was highly cultivated in the ancient East, important matters have long been put in writing. Laws, court records, decrees, and contracts are kept for accurate reference. Throughout the Bible, writing is an important mark of revelation. One is forbidden to tamper with it (Rev. 22:18-19).

The word for *a writing* or *writings (graphē)* is used 51 times in the NT, referring exclusively to the Holy Scriptures. To say, "It is written," is tantamount to quoting God himself (e.g., John 7:38; Rom. 9:17; 10:11). Since Scripture is God-breathed, it is of unique value to the people of God (2 Tim. 3:16-17). Once God has gone on record, His decree *stands written.* And His Word is Truth (John 17:17).

See BIBLE, BIBLICAL AUTHORITY, TRADITION, INSPIRATION OF THE BIBLE.

For Further Reading: *ZPEB,* 5:302-13, 995-1015; Brown and Mayer, "Scripture, Writing," *Dictionary of New Testament Theology,* 3:482-97; Schrenk, "Graphō, etc.," Kittel, 1:742-73.
WILBER T. DAYTON

Y, Z

YAHWEH. See JEHOVAH, YAHWEH.

YOKE. The yoke as noted in the Bible was a bar which connects two animals, usually two of a kind. The construction of the yoke varied as to material. Often the construction was that of a piece of wood made to curve near each end, and connected to this bar were two other pieces of bowed wood which were to be placed around the necks of oxen.

In biblical times the yoke was also used on human beings when they were taken captive from their homeland (Jer. 28:10). Slaves, too, were sometimes held captive by the use of a yoke.

Figuratively, any burden imposed on another or any means of subjection would be viewed as a yoke. It is for these reasons the yoke became the object of one of the metaphors of Jesus' teaching. The metaphor would be well understood when used as a symbol of slavery to the law or slavery to sin.

Theologically, the most significant aspect of the yoke as a teaching metaphor is the concept of slavery. The slavery noted by use of this metaphor is spiritual rather than physical.

Jesus and Paul both used the yoke to allude to those who had become slaves to the law. The law applied in an extremely legalistic way became a yoke of burden (Acts 15:10). Gal. 5:1 is a direct reference to such servitude with regard to the law. By comparison, servitude to Christ was easy (Matt. 11:29). When comparing Christ's yoke with the yoke of the law, "the contrast is not between 'yoke' and 'no yoke' but between my teaching (light yoke) and the current scribal teaching (heavy yoke)" (*ISBE,* 5:3127).

The yoke of Jesus is to do the will of the Father (John 8:29). When an individual comes to Christ, he is coming to one whose use of the law does not produce a legalistic bondage.

See SERVANT, SERVICE, OBEDIENCE, DISCIPLESHIP.

For Further Reading: Waetjer, *Baker's DCE,* 563; Brown, ed., *NIDNTT,* 3:1160-65; Wolf, *IDB,* 4:924-25.
LARRY FINE

ZEAL. This word translates the Hebrew *ganna* and the Greek *zēlos.* The Hebrew noun occurs 43 times in the OT, while *zēlos* occurs 16 times in the NT. In both of the Testaments, whether zeal has a positive or negative meaning is dependent on the context. It may be used in a good sense as "zeal, ardor, jealousy for" (cf. Ps. 69:9; 2 Cor. 7:7). In its negative sense it is considered as "envy or jealousy of" (Num. 5:14; Acts 5:17). Zeal may be misdirected even when sincere (cf. Rom. 10:2; Phil. 3:6). Once Paul qualifies the term with the adjective "godly" (2 Cor. 11:2).

"Zeal" in its original Greek usage had various

meanings such as (1) the capacity or state of passionate committal to a person or cause; (2) orientation to a worthy goal; (3) envy or jealousy. Sometimes it means jealousy in the married life (Prov. 6:34; Song of Sol. 8:6). When used of God or of man in relation to God, it usually has religious significance. Often in the LXX it is used to denote a specific intensity in the divine action and is sometimes listed with *orgē* (Deut. 29:20) and *thumos* (Num. 25:11; Ezek. 34:14; Deut. 4:24; 6:15), where God is described as a "jealous God." God is jealous for Israel as a husband is jealous for his wife; Israel is peculiarly His own according to the covenant made with her. His jealousy is as much a part of His character as righteousness, holiness, and love. In the NT it is not God, but rather His Son (John 2:17) and His spiritual sons (2 Cor. 7:11; 11:2) who express this "divine zeal" in behalf of God's holiness and kingdom. A basic mark of God's purified people is that they are "zealous of good works" (Titus 2:14).

See DEVOTE (DEVOTION), JEALOUSY.

For Further Reading: Kittel, 2:877-88; "Zeal," *IDB;* Arndt and Gingrich. JERRY W. MCCANT

ZEALOTS. This militant party of Jewish patriots came into existence during the early years of the first century A.D. in Palestine. In A.D. 6, Quirinius, the Roman legate of Syria, ordered a census to be taken of the newly created Roman province of Judea. The census was to provide the basis for the taxation of the Jews. In retaliation, Judas of Galilee, along with some of his Jewish compatriots, organized a revolt (cf. Acts 5:37).

Josephus is not too kind in his assessment of these people. He depicts them as fanatics who engaged in rash deeds which finally hindered rather than advanced their cause. Furthermore, he attributes the fall of Jerusalem in A.D. 70 to their nationalistic spirit. Some of the Zealots fled to Herod's fortress-palace, Masada, and held out there against the Romans until A.D. 73.

This party functioned with strong theocratic sensitivities, being firmly committed to the principle that acceptance of a Gentile as sovereign was unlawful for the Jews. They shared the theological beliefs of the Pharisees except with respect to the Jewish political situation under the Roman rule. While the Pharisees pled for patience in the matter of release from the bondage, the Zealots felt they were religiously required to take the initiative in breaking the Roman yoke, in much the same way as the Maccabeans had done in their time.

One of the disciples of Jesus was named Simon the Zealot (Luke 6:15; Acts 1:13). We are not to assume from this reference that Jesus' activities and preaching were associated with the political messianism of the Zealots.

See PHARISEES.

For Further Reading: Bruce, *New Testament History,* 93 ff; Josephus, *Wars of the Jews,* 4. 3. 9, 12-14; Lohse, *The New Testament Environment,* 83-84.

WILLARD H. TAYLOR

ZIONISM. The term *Zionism,* from "Zion," an early OT synonym for Jerusalem, was first coined by a European Jew, Nathan Birnbaum, in April, 1890. It designated a Jewish nationalist movement which aimed to establish a Jewish homeland in Palestine. Increasingly in the 19th century there were movements among the numerous European Jews towards a return to Palestine, then part of the Ottoman Empire. Influential Jews such as Mordecai Noah (in 1818) and Moses Hess (in 1862) had proclaimed *Eretz Israel* ("the land of Israel") as the Jews' rightful possession; and the growing movement of *Choveve Zion* ("Lovers of Zion") protested against any permanent assimilation of Jews into Gentile lands and culture.

The true founder of Zionism was Theodor Herzl (1860-1904), a Jewish Viennese journalist whose concern about growing anti-Semitism in Europe was climaxed by the proceedings of the famous Dreyfus case in France in 1895. In 1896 Herzl wrote a short but very influential pamphlet entitled *Judenstaat* ("The Jewish State"). He argued that such was the menace of anti-Semitism that the Jewish people could only survive if gathered together and concentrated in one geographical area. Herzl convened the first Zionist Congress in Basel in 1897 which agreed on a Zionist Charter: "Zionism aims at establishing for the Jewish people a publicly and legally assured home in Palestine." Thousands of Jews all over the world supported the Zionist cause, including many wealthy American Jews and European Jews such as Chaim Weizmann (1874-1952), an internationally recognized scientist and later to be elected the first president of the state of Israel in 1949.

See JUDAISM, ISRAEL, RESTORATION OF ISRAEL.

For Further Reading: Cohen, *The Zionist Movement;* Halpern, *The Idea of a Jewish State.*

HERBERT MCGONIGLE

ZOROASTRIANISM. The dualistic religion founded by the Persian prophet Zarathustra (c. 630-583 B.C.) and important because it stands as one of man's earliest attempts to explain the origin of sin (Wiley, *CT,* 2:71). In reaction to Persian polytheism, Zoroaster (Greek form of Persian name) taught the existence of one supreme God, Ahura Mazda or Ohrmuzd, author of all good, who sought only the good of man. Angra Mainyu or Ahriman, the source of all evil, was coeval in origin with Ahura, yet not truly eternal because ultimately he would be annihilated. Man's soul is the battlefield where the conflict between good and evil is fought. Zoroaster stressed man's freedom to ally himself with Ahura Mazda and thus share his ultimate triumph through eternity.

See NON-CHRISTIAN RELIGIONS.

For Further Reading: Parrinder, *A Dictionary of Non-Christian Religions,* 83-84, 316-17; Archer, "Zoroastrianism" in *Twentieth Century Encyclopedia of Religious Knowledge,* 15:1203-4. MAUREEN H. BOX

Bibliography

Dictionaries, Lexicons, and Word Studies

Abbott, Lyman. *A Dictionary of Religious Knowledge.* New York: Harper and Bros., 1885.

Barclay, William. *New Testament Words.* Philadelphia: Westminster Press, 1964, 1974.

Bauer, Walter. *A Greek-English Lexicon of the New Testament and Other Early Christian Literature.* Translated and edited by William F. Arndt and F. Wilbur Gingrich. Chicago: University of Chicago Press, 1957.

Blunt, John Henry. *Dictionary of Doctrinal and Historical Theology.* London: Rivertons, 1972.

Brown, Colin, ed. *The New International Dictionary of New Testament Theology.* Grand Rapids: Zondervan Publishing House, 1975, 1978.

Buck, Charles, ed. *A Theological Dictionary.* London: James Duncan, 1833.

Buttrick, George Arthur, ed. *The Interpreter's Dictionary of the Bible.* New York: Abingdon Press, 1962, 1976.

Cremer, Hermann, ed. *Biblico-Theological Lexicon of New-Testament Greek.* Edinburgh: T. and T. Clark, 1980.

Cross, F. L., ed. *Oxford Dictionary of the Christian Church.* London: Oxford University Press, 1957, 1958, 1974.

Cully, Kendig Brubaker. *The Westminster Dictionary of Christian Education.* Philadelphia: Westminster Press, 1963.

Douglas, J. D., ed. *The New Bible Dictionary.* Grand Rapids: William B. Eerdmans Publishing Co., 1962, 1971.

———, ed. *The New International Dictionary of the Christian Church.* Grand Rapids: Zondervan Publishing House, 1974.

Ernst, Cornelius, ed.; trans. Richard Strachan. *Theological Dictionary.* New York: Herder and Herder, 1968.

Ferm, Vergilius, ed. *A Protestant Dictionary.* New York: The Philosophical Library, 1951.

Harrison, Everett F., ed. *Baker's Dictionary of Theology.* Grand Rapids: Baker Book House, 1960, 1973.

Hastings, James. *A Dictionary of the Bible.* New York: Charles Scribner's Sons, 1900.

———. *A Dictionary of Christ and the Gospels.* New York: Charles Scribner's Sons, 1908.

———. *Dictionary of the New Testament.* Reprint. Grand Rapids: Baker Book House, 1973.

Henry, Carl F. H., ed. *Baker's Dictionary of Christian Ethics.* Grand Rapids: Baker Book House, 1973.

Hill, David. *Greek Words and Hebrew Meanings.* London: Cambridge University Press, 1967.

Kittel, Gerhard, ed.; trans. Geoffrey W. Bromiley. *Theological Dictionary of the New Testament.* Grand Rapids: William B. Eerdmans Publishing Co., 1964, 1965, 1967.

Liddell, H. G., and Scott, Robert, comps. *A Greek-English Lexicon.* Oxford: Clarendon Press, 1943. Revised by H. S. Jones, 1958.

Macquarrie, John, ed. *Westminster Dictionary of Christian Ethics.* Philadelphia: Westminster Press, 1967.

McKenzie, John L., ed. *Dictionary of the Bible.* New York: Macmillan Co., 1965.

Miller, Madeline, and Lane, J., eds. *Harper's Bible Dictionary.* New York: Harper and Row, 1952, 1973.

Richardson, Alan, ed. *A Dictionary of Christian Theology.* Philadelphia: Westminster Press, 1969.

———, ed. *A Theological Word Book of the Bible.* New York: Macmillan Co., 1951, 1962, 1964, 1967.

Roberti, Francesco, comp.; trans. Henry J. Yannone. *Dictionary of Moral Theology.* Westminster, Md.: Newman Press, 1957, 1962.

Robertson, A. T. *Word Pictures in the New Testament.* New York: R. R. Smith, 1930.

Runes, Dagobert D., ed. *Dictionary of Philosophy.* New York: Philosophical Library, 1959.

Souter, Alexander. *A Pocket Lexicon of the Greek New Testament.* Reprint. Oxford: Clarendon Press, 1966.

Tenney, Merrill C., ed. *The Zondervan Pictorial Bible Dictionary.* Grand Rapids: Zondervan Publishing House, 1963.

Unger, Merrill F. *Unger's Bible Dictionary.* Chicago: Moody Press, 1964.

Vincent, Marvin R., ed. *Word Studies in the New Testament.* Grand Rapids: William B. Eerdmans Publishing Co., 1957.

Vine, W. E., ed. *An Expository Dictionary of New Testament Words.* Old Tappan, N.J.: Fleming H. Revell Co., 1966.

Wiener, Claude, ed. *Dictionary of Biblical Theology.* New York: Seabury Press, 1973.

Wolman, Benjamin B., ed. *Dictionary of Behavioral Science.* New York: Van Nostrand, Reinhold Co., 1973.

Wuest, Kenneth S., ed. *Wuest's Word Studies.* Grand Rapids: William B. Eerdmans Publishing Co., 1966.

Encyclopedias

Adler, Cyrus, et al., eds. *The Jewish Encyclopedia.* New York: Funk and Wagnalls, 1901-6.

Alexander, David and Pat, eds. *Eerdmans' Handbook to the Bible.* Grand Rapids: Wm. B. Eerdmans Publishing Co., 1973.

Baver, Johannes, ed. *Encyclopedia of Biblical Theology.* 3 vols. London: Sheed and Ward, n.d.

Benton, A. A. *Church Cyclopedia.* New York: M. H. Mallory and Co., 1883.

Denham, J. F., ed. *The Popular and Critical Bible Encyclopedia.* Chicago: Howard Severance Co., 1911.

Edwards, Paul, ed. *Encyclopedia of Philosophy.* New York: Macmillan Co., 1967.

Fallows, Samuel, et al., eds. *Bible Encyclopedia and Scriptural Dictionary.* Chicago: Howard Severance Co., 1910.

Ferm, Vergilius, ed. *Encyclopedia of Morals.* New York: Philosophical Library, 1956.

———, ed. *An Encyclopedia of Religion.* New York: Philosophical Library, 1945.

Hastings, James. *Encyclopedia of Religion and Ethics.* New York: Charles Scribner's Sons, 1951.

Jackson, Samuel M., et al., eds. *Schaff-Herzog Encyclopedia of Religious Knowledge.* New York: Funk and Wagnalls, 1909. Revised as *The New Schaff-Herzog Encyclopedia of Religious Knowledge.* 13 vols. 1909. Grand Rapids: Baker Book House, 1949-50.

Loetscher, Lefferts A., ed. *Twentieth Century Encyclopedia of Religious Knowledge* (an extension of the original *Schaff-Herzog Encyclopedia*). Grand Rapids: Baker Book House, 1955.

M'Clintock, John, and Strong, James, eds. *Cyclopedia of Biblical, Theological, and Ecclesiastical Literature.* New York: Harper and Bros., 1891. Reprint. Grand Rapids: Baker Book House, 1970.

Meagher, Paul Kevin, et al., eds. *Encyclopedia Dictionary of Religion.* Washington, D.C.: Corpus Publishers, 1979.

The Mennonite Encyclopedia. Scottdale, Pa.: Mennonite Publishing House, 1956.

New Catholic Encyclopedia. New York: McGraw-Hill Book Co., 1967-69.

Orr, James, ed. *International Standard Bible Encyclopedia.* Grand Rapids: Wm. B. Eerdmans Publishing Co., 1943, 1959.

Pfeiffer, Charles F.; Vos, Howard F.; and Rea, John; eds. *Wycliffe Bible Encyclopedia.* Chicago: Moody Press, 1975.

Rahner, Karl A., et al., eds. *Encyclopedia of Theology.* New York: Seabury Press, 1975.

Rahner, Karl A.; Ernst, Cornelius; and Smyth, Kevin; eds. *Sacramentum Mundi: An Encyclopedia of Theology.* New York: Herder and Herder, 1968-70.

Seligman, Edwin R. A., and Johnson, Alvin, eds. *Encyclopedia of the Social Sciences.* New York: Macmillan Co. and Free Press, 1963. (International edition, ed. David L. Silla, published in 1968.)

Tenney, Merrill C., ed. *The Zondervan Pictorial Encyclopedia of the Bible.* Grand Rapids: Zondervan Publishing House, 1975, 1977.

Urmson, J. O., ed. *The Concise Encyclopedia of Western Philosophy and Philosophers.* New York: Hawthorn Books, 1960.

Wolman, Benjamin, ed. *International Encyclopedia of Psychiatry, Psychology, Psychoanalysis, and Neurology.* New York: Aesculapius Publishers, Inc., 1977.

Major Works and Theologies

Arminius, James. *Works.* Translated by Nichols and Bagnall. Buffalo, N.Y.: Derby, Miller, Orton, and Mulligan, 1853.

Barth, Karl. *Church Dogmatics.* Edited by G. W. Bromiley and T. F. Torrance. Edinburgh: T. & T. Clark, 1936—.

Chafer, Lewis Sperry. *Systematic Theology.* 8 vols. Dallas: Dallas Seminary Press, 1947-48.

Fletcher, John. *The Works of the Rev. John Fletcher.* New York: B. Waugh and T. Mason, 1833. Reprint. Salem, Ohio: Schmul Publishers, 1974.

Hills, A. M. *Fundamental Christian Theology.* 2 vols. Pasadena, Calif.: Pasadena College, 1931. Abridged ed., C. J. Kinne, 1932.

Marty, Martin E., and Peerman, Dean G., eds. *New Theology.* 2 vols. New York: MacMillan Co., 1964-65.

Miley, John. *Systematic Theology.* 2 vols. New York: Hunt and Eaton, 1892-94.

Souter, A., ed. *The Ante-Nicene Fathers.* New York: Macmillan Co., 1920.

Wesley, John. *Standard Sermons.* Edited by Edward H. Sugden. London: Epworth Press, 1968.

———. *The Works of the Rev. John Wesley.* London: Wesleyan Methodist Book Room, 1872 reprint. Kansas City: Beacon Hill Press of Kansas City, n.d.; also Baker Book House.

Wiley, H. Orton. *Christian Theology.* 3 vols. Kansas City: Nazarene Publishing House, 1940.

Commentaries

Barclay, William. *The Daily Study Bible.* Philadelphia: Westminster Press, 1956-58.

Broadman Bible Commentary. Nashville: Broadman Press, 1970.

Bruce, F. F., ed. *The New International Commentary on the New Testament.* Grand Rapids: Wm. B. Eerdmans Publishing Co., 1954, 1959.

Calvin, John. *Calvin's New Testament Commentaries.*

Grand Rapids: Wm. B. Eerdmans Publishing Co., 1961.

Carter, Charles W., ed. *The Wesleyan Bible Commentary.* 7 vols. Grand Rapids: Wm. B. Eerdmans Publishing Co., 1964-66.

Clarke, Adam. *The New Testament of Our Lord and Savior Jesus Christ.* 6 vols. New York: Abingdon Press, n.d.

Cranfield, C. E. B. *The International Critical Commentary.* 2 vols. Edinburgh: T. & T. Clark, 1962, 1975-79.

Greathouse, Wm. M., and Taylor, Willard H., eds. *Beacon Bible Expositions.* 12 vols. Kansas City: Beacon Hill Press of Kansas City, 1974—.

Grosheide, F. W. *New London Commentary.* London: Marshall, Morgan, and Scott, 1953.

Harper, A. F., ed. *Beacon Bible Commentary.* 10 vols. Kansas City: Beacon Hill Press of Kansas City, 1964-69.

Keil, C. F., and Delitzsch, F. *Biblical Commentary on the Old Testament.* 25 vols. Reprint. Grand Rapids: Wm. B. Eerdmans Publishing Co., n.d.

Morris, Leon, ed. *Tyndale New Testament Commentaries.* Grand Rapids: Wm. B. Eerdmans Publishing Co., 1957.

Whedon, D. D. *Commentary on the New Testament.* Reprint. Salem, Ohio: Schmul Publishing Co., n.d.

Will, Harold E., ed. *Commentary on the New Testament.* Traverse City, Mich.: OCI Missionary Publications, 1975.